on Meech as well. So the national mood was good as it slowly made its way through the House of Commons and the provincial legislatures. On July 7, 1988 Newfoundland and Labrador became the 8th province to do so.

In 1989 Clyde Wells was elected Premier of Nfld and on Oct 18 wrote me a 10 page letter in opposition to Meech. As Constitutional law expert and U of T law school dean Patrick Monahan wrote: "Reading the letter, one is struck by the one sided nature of his analysis[24] ... one searches in vain for any sense of balance or proportion"

Memoirs

Memoirs

1939–1993

BRIAN MULRONEY

McCLELLAND & STEWART

Library and Archives Canada Cataloguing in Publication

Mulroney, Brian, 1939–
Memoirs : 1939–1993 / Brian Mulroney.

Includes index.
ISBN 978-0-7710-6536-1

1. Mulroney, Brian, 1939– 2. Canada – Politics and government – 1984–1993. 3. Prime ministers – Canada – Biography. 4. Progressive Conservative Party of Canada – Biography. I. Title.

FC631.M84A3 2007 971.064'7092 C2007-901813-0

We acknowledge the financial support of the Government of Canada through the Book Publishing Industry Development Program and that of the Government of Ontario through the Ontario Media Development Corporation's Ontario Book Initiative. We further acknowledge the support of the Canada Council for the Arts and the Ontario Arts Council for our publishing program.

Typeset in Fairfield by M&S, Toronto
Printed and bound in Canada

A Douglas Gibson Book
This book is printed on acid-free paper that is 100% recycled, ancient-forest friendly (100% post-consumer recycled).

McClelland & Stewart Ltd.
75 Sherbourne Street
Toronto, Ontario
M5A 2P9
www.mcclelland.com

1 2 3 4 5 11 10 09 08 07

To Mila

CONTENTS

Prologue: September 4, 1984

It was rainy and cold in Baie-Comeau when Mila and I left the victory celebration at about one o'clock in the morning and returned to our hotel suite in what I had grown up calling "the Mill Manager's House."

Earlier, at eight o'clock, the CBC decision desk had announced that "Brian Mulroney has led the Progressive Conservative Party to a majority government and will become Canada's eighteenth prime minister." I stood before the TV set with Mila, surrounded by cheering friends, as the beauty of the moment washed over me. I turned to my old pal Sam Wakim and joked, "I always said the CBC was an intelligent network."

As promising returns had come in from Newfoundland, I had asked Fred Doucet, my long-time friend and chief of staff, to call into Madawaska for a poll – any poll – result. French-speaking northern New Brunswick had been Liberal territory forever, but a promising young candidate, Bernard Valcourt, was running for us there, and Mila and I had campaigned tirelessly with him, trying for a breakthrough. I knew that if we were ahead in a rural poll there, we were in for a big night. When I saw the grin on Doucet's face as he concluded the call, I realized that we were looking at a landslide. Valcourt was rolling to victory, and so were we.

My own constituency was vast and remote. Owing to reporting difficulties, for some hours the returns from Manicouagan were limited to one large Indian reserve that had overwhelmingly voted Liberal, conveying the impression to the watching nation that, while we were winning everywhere else, I was in serious danger of losing my own seat. This began to be reported almost as fact. Watching at Stornoway, our Ottawa home, ten-year-old Caroline was deeply dismayed. "I'm outta here!" she announced. She gathered her brothers silently and went upstairs to bed, awakening the next morning to the refreshing news that her father had indeed made it back to the House of Commons.

Toward the end of the evening, when the dimensions of the PC sweep looked historic, I got a call from Prime Minister John Turner, conceding the election. I'm sure it was a very painful moment for him – once the golden boy of Canadian politics, now defeated after barely two months in office. He was extremely gracious, congratulating me on a strong campaign, promising a smooth transition and wishing me well. I congratulated him on winning Vancouver Quadra, and we both chuckled over the tremendous effort his sister Brenda had put into the fight, just as my sister Olive and brother Gary had won Manicouagan for me. We agreed to an Ottawa meeting to finalize the transition.

Immediately after John's call, I changed from the old pair of slacks and green V-neck sweater I had worn all evening to a blue business suit, so that Mila and I could speak to our supporters (by now in varying degrees of lubrication) gathered in the local arena. The atmosphere was electric when we arrived, as the band belted out our campaign song and thousands of Baie-Comeauites – including hundreds of childhood friends who had encouraged me all my life – chanted "Brian! Brian! Brian!" just as countless supporters had done across Canada. When we ascended the stage, the cheering was almost intoxicating, so joyful was the mood, with people surging forward in waves. I could sense the great pride this hard-working crowd took in watching one of their own achieve the highest office in Canada. It was like a réveillon, St. Patrick's Day, and Pierrette Arsenault's wedding all rolled into one. I could hardly believe what I was seeing, and what I knew really was happening.

For a few days I had worked on a victory speech. Although a little too long, it was well received by the enthusiastic crowd. After the speech we returned to our suite in the Annex, the former manager's house, where Mila and I changed into sweaters and slacks before joining friends and the travelling staff for a party at Le Manoir Comeau, a hotel I had worked at as a waiter and bellboy when I was young, and was now entering as prime minister-designate.

When the partying was over, back at the Annex I accepted congratulatory calls (everybody loves a winner), spoke to my mother, Mila's parents, Conservative premiers from across Canada, our key organizers, and Robert Bourassa. Finally, at about five in the morning, we headed up to bed. Mila, exhausted from an almost nonstop eighteen-month campaign (beginning in March 1983 for the PC leadership), was soon sound asleep. I went to an adjacent room to change. Not wanting to disturb Mila but too charged to sleep, I lay down on the room's small bed and turned on the radio, which was carrying regular reports on our election success. Eventually I dozed off, only to be awakened, at three minutes to seven, by the mill whistle calling the men to work. That sound had shaped my childhood, because it governed my father's life, telling him when to get up and go to work, when to leave and go home.

As the whistle pierced the grey of a drab September morning, and the rain beat down on the copper roof, I thought of my dad. I thought of his struggles and of the great courage that had allowed him, an electrician who held down two jobs most of his life, to support a wife and six children in an isolated community like Baie-Comeau. As I got up to look out the window at our home at 79 Champlain Street – the only house my dad ever owned – I wondered what he'd think and what he'd say today, although I already knew the answer. He'd look at me, smile proudly, hug my mom, sit down, and beam – just the way he always did when I was little and pleased him with my school marks, minor jobs, or athletic achievements. My father was my hero, and I knew that this moment would never have occurred without him. I was overwhelmed by emotion as I reflected on his death, nineteen years earlier, in that small mill home on Champlain Street not five hundred yards from my hotel room.

The sound of the whistle seemed to hang in the air.

PART I

The Early Years

1939–1960

1. Champlain Street

CHAMPLAIN STREET WAS central to my life. It was like a sanctuary, a reliable place where I knew everybody, and in the mind of a child they were all kind, good people. The Halls lived next door to the Dumonts; the Dawsons next door to the Beaulieus; the Andersons across the street from the Mineaus. It was a remarkable atmosphere where the children spoke English and French interchangeably, irrespective of their origins or religion. In the 1940s and 1950s, Baie-Comeau was idyllic, and Champlain was the Elm Street of every kid's dreams. It was one of the first streets built in Baie-Comeau after the mill construction was completed, and its small, tidy homes – rented by employees from the company for a modest amount – wound around the crest of the bay, giving residents an unsurpassed view of the opening to the St. Lawrence River.

In winter, however, we paid for the majesty of the view as icy winds swept across the river's frozen surface, month after month, and made grown men and their families weep for the brief, delightful summers. From my earliest recollections, the Mulroneys had always lived on Champlain Street, at numbers 132, 99, and 79, leaving only after the death of my dad on a snowy February day in 1965.

As a young university student, I once tried to sum up my part of Canada, calling the North Shore the "Unknown North." "When a Canadian refers to the North, there are many reactions," I wrote in my youthful scrawl. "Pierre Berton reflects wistfully on the Yukon. Alvin Hamilton points excitedly to a map, his finger tracing the route of the proposed Great Slave Lake Railway into northern Alberta. The legends which surround the opening of the . . . Noranda gold mines are told by one; vivid accounts of Mackenzie's first voyage down the raging Fraser River by another. But there is another North, containing fifty thousand residents of Quebec's St. Lawrence North Shore. More colourful than Berton's; more prosperous than Hamilton's; more steeped in legend and drama than a dozen Frasers. Theirs is the Unknown North."

My dad was born in Ste-Catherine-de-Portneuf, a tiny Irish enclave about twenty-five miles west of Quebec City, on October 9, 1903. The Mulroneys – a modestly successful innkeeping family in Ireland – had joined the tragic Irish exodus of the 1830s, in search of a better life across the sea. They left Leighlinbridge, a beautiful village in County Carlow in the southeast, in exchange for government-sponsored land on the banks of the Jacques Cartier River.

Hundreds of immigrant Irish settled there – in the very heart of a French-speaking area – and were warmly welcomed as hardscrabble farmers and tradespeople by the local community. They quickly learned that the streets of the New World were not paved with gold. As Catholics, they attended the local French schools and churches, which explains why my father – named Benedict by his parents – was designated as "Benoît" on his official birth certificate.

Although many Catholic Irish immigrants were fully assimilated into Quebec's French-speaking community – hence all the Ryans, Flynns, Johnsons, Blackburns, and so on whose mother tongue became French – the Irish settlers in that area were numerous enough to provide marriage partners for each other and to maintain the use of English, though most if not all of them (including my father) became fluently bilingual.

My father was the second youngest of fourteen children and grew up in a happy, boisterous home, doted upon by his six sisters and seven brothers. His parents, Jeremiah Mulroney and Margaret Ann Donovan, were neither well educated nor prosperous, but they provided for their children, encouraging them to get a better education than many at that time.

My aunts Jenny (Keenan), Vera (Perego), and Ena (Lacombe, the family's youngest) all became executive secretaries with leading companies in Quebec and Montreal; another aunt became a saleslady, and there was one who was a teacher. The older sons migrated to the United States, finding work in the pulp and paper mills of Maine and New Hampshire. My Uncle George even wound up in faraway Texas.

Dora, one of my dad's older sisters, married Hugh Kane, who worked for the Quebec government. On extremely limited resources, the Kanes managed to send five of their children to engineering schools and universities, and they all went on to successful careers. Such academic ambitions were unusual at that time, certainly among Irish Catholics in that area, and my dad admired his older sister for her strength of character and her insistence on education. But his greatest display of admiration for Dora occurred earlier, on a Friday night in the middle of the Depression. Dora, my dad, and his favourite brother, Mike (who bore a strong resemblance to Spencer Tracy) had been peddling charcoal all week from a cart through the wealthy districts of Quebec City, and they were now headed home to Ste-Catherine in Mike's Model T for a family celebration that weekend. At an intersection in Lower Town, Mike ran a stop sign and immediately attracted police attention. As the police vehicle approached, Dora burst out of the back seat of the Model T. Clutching three quarts of whisky for the party securely to her chest, she went, as my dad said later, "like a bat out of hell," paying no attention to yells and screams from the cops or the passersby she left in her wake. She was determined to save the crown jewels for the party, and she did – to the delight and everlasting gratitude of all her celebrating brothers and sisters.

My father attended local schools, leaving after grade 9 to look for work, which he found as an electrician's helper at a paper mill in nearby Donnacona, on the St. Lawrence. He quickly developed a natural talent for the trade and enrolled in correspondence courses that he studied carefully for years. Our family still has reference letters from his employers. "The bearer, Ben Mulroney, was employed by this company for several years as an electrician on both construction and maintenance work," a representative of the Donnacona Paper Company wrote in November of 1932. "He is familiar with all kinds of conduit and wiring work, control wiring in connection with sub-station and other remote control apparatus, high and low tension bus work, meter wiring for power boards and other miscellaneous equipment."

The letter goes on to illustrate what the Great Depression was doing to families across Canada. "We have always found him a very capable workman and are glad to recommend him to anyone desiring the services of a first-class electrician. He left Donnacona Company when it became necessary to lay off all single men who had no dependents."

In my library today, I have some of the books my father used to learn his trade. Eventually he became a skilled electrician, rising to the post of general foreman at Baie-Comeau's Quebec North Shore Paper Company in the mid 1950s and early 1960s. But things were still tough when he returned to Ste-Catherine and met my mother.

My dad first met my mom, Irene O'Shea, outside the church one Sunday. According to my Uncle Jimmy, he promptly went home and told his family that he'd met the girl he was going to marry. That afternoon, to the surprise of my O'Shea grandparents, my dad brought his brother, along with his brother's wife and children (to provide a cover of respectability) to visit. It's easy to imagine them all sitting in the parlour, balancing their teacups and making polite conversation, while the eyes of the young couple met.

Certainly, Ben and Irene fell deeply in love and, after a whirlwind courtship, they were married in Ste-Catherine on October 29, 1934. Grandpa Mulroney stood up for dad and her father gave the bride away. As was the custom, the reception was held at the O'Shea home, and it must have been quite an occasion: Irene O'Shea had married into a famously merry family that knew how to enjoy a party.

She was the beautiful daughter of Edmund and Mary O'Shea, who farmed in Shannon, on the opposite bank of the river, upstream from the Mulroney farm. The O'Sheas had emigrated, in 1825, from Kearny Bay, County Kilkenny. The eldest of four children and educated through grade 6 at local schools, my mother was eleven years younger than the dashing and persistent thirty-one-year-old Ben Mulroney, but her parents were pleased with her choice because he was a handsome, ambitious young man from a good local family. Soon after the wedding, they were headed for High Falls, in southwestern Quebec, close to Ottawa, where my dad had been given a job at the MacLaren Company power plant.

By all accounts my parents soon settled down into happy domesticity. They had a nice, tiny house close to the plant, some good friends, and great dreams for their future and the futures of their children. Their neighbours and close friends included the parents of Marion Dewar, who went on to become mayor of Ottawa and a respected NDP member of Parliament. It was here that their first child – my older brother – was born, only to die within hours. His short life generated a family mystery that I have been unable to solve for sixty years. We know that, late in her pregnancy, my mother developed toxemia and began to lose blood. When the baby, baptized John, was born, he was gravely ill and he died later that day. My mother went into a postpartum depression so worrisome that her mother moved to High Falls to help her through this difficult period. "A baby boy born two months premature," my mother wrote in her diary for June 8, 1935, "died [and] same day buried at Buckingham. I was seriously ill for some time."

My mother, of course, saw the baby immediately after he was born and was promptly informed of his death. My father, the priest, and her doctor were with her and the baby at the time. Yet during a period when Catholic

Church documents recorded every moment of importance in a family's existence, there is no record of the life and death of John Mulroney, who at the time of this writing would be seventy-two.

My father died without telling anyone in our family where John was buried. None of the children knew enough to question my mother, and in later years her recollection was vague. One day, after Mila and I had hosted a dinner party in her honour in our home at 47 Forden Crescent, we gathered in the living room to linger over coffee and chat. I asked my mother directly, with my sisters Olive and Peggy joining in the conversation, what had happened. She may already have been affected by the dementia that became so evident a few years later and eventually caused her death, but I can't be sure. In any case, she looked at me and said, "I just don't know what happened. I was very sick and never inquired when I recovered. I don't know where the baby is buried – and I remember him as such a beautiful child – because I assumed all that had been looked after by your dad and the priest." This was a worrying and strangely incurious answer from a mother who loved her children fiercely, and devoted her life to their well-being.

This small but important family mystery has troubled my siblings and me for decades. We have tried to reconstruct events, to interview people who might shed light, and to search the entire area for records – all without success. We wanted John to know that he had never been forgotten, that we loved the brother we never knew. We do know that somewhere in Buckingham, Quebec, in June of 1935, John Mulroney was buried, with neither a trace nor a memory. I have often reflected on the sadness of his story and on my complete powerlessness, even in the highest office in the land, to make it right in any way.

A year later, in 1936, Olive was born in Buckingham. She was a happy child who would often tease Peggy and me with the observation that her "royal" roots were in Buckingham Palace, while ours were in far humbler surroundings. This interest in royalty was not confined to my sister. After my mother's death in 2001, we found a file of clippings from the famous Royal Tour of Canada of 1939 that my mom had kept all those years. She may have been Irish to the core, but she couldn't resist the allure of the British monarchy and greatly admired the Royal Family.

This is a good point for me to slip in an excerpt from the personal journal that I kept over the years, jotting down my reactions to the day's events between 1984 and 1993. I quote from the journal from time to time in this book.

—

PERSONAL JOURNAL: APRIL 1, 1989

Mila and I were invited to the palace for a private luncheon with Her Majesty. We both enjoy and admire her a great deal. She is intelligent and pleasant and, in my view, a woman without the slightest intention of stepping down in favour of anyone. She appears to deeply understand the nuances of the monarchy and her personal value to it. On that she is entirely right, because I believe that she should remain at the helm for the foreseeable future. During our frank and open chats, she points out scenes in the palace gardens and I quite calmly comment – never, however, entirely overcoming my own sense of awe and quiet reverence for the office and the setting, which have dominated so much history for so long. I'm not sure that either Mila or I, in our youth, ever contemplated private luncheons with the Queen at Buckingham Palace. In any case it could not have been more enjoyable – as usual, because neither of us recalls an unpleasant moment in her company.

—

My sister Peggy was born in 1937 and my dad seized an opportunity to join the construction crews headed to Baie-Comeau, where a new paper mill and townsite were being built to service the requirements of the *Chicago Tribune* and its owner, the legendary Colonel Robert R. McCormick.

"Arrived at Comeau Bay by plane," my father wrote on January 3, 1938 in a personal diary he kept intermittently during the lonely winter he spent away from his wife and daughters as the construction of Baie-Comeau continued. While apart from my mother, Dad sent most of his pay back home. He recorded his pay slips and they remain in our possession today. On January 18, 1938, for example, he was paid $42.57. My mother was sent $30. Two weeks later he was paid $60.75, with $45 going to my mother. And so it went, as the long winter continued.

The construction of Baie-Comeau from scratch was a task of massive proportions. A writer named Carl Wiegman later wrote a book about it, *Trees to News: A Chronology of the Ontario Paper Company's Origin and Development*, and I have Dad's copy in my own library. According to this official history, 140,000 tonnes of supplies had to be unloaded at the newly constructed wharf that first year alone. Wiegman wrote:

> The first task was to build dormitories, dining halls, a water supply, and sanitary facilities for the thousand workers expected during the first year of construction. After the machine shop came the paper-storage building, 568 feet long and 168 feet wide. This huge structure was to be used as a storehouse for materials arriving in the following spring and eventually it would be a place for storing 50,000 tonnes of newsprint. The office building, mill stores, and finishing room were also completed in the first year. . . . A portable saw mill was erected on the English River to begin turning out lumber. Caches were built in preparation for the start of timber cutting to supply the mill with pulpwood. The woods department also had the task of building six large dams and seven smaller ones to provide a permanent water supply for the mill and water for conveying wood in the flumes. The most urgent of the woods department's jobs was the building of the main highway from Baie-Comeau to Outardes Falls, a distance of 14 miles through muskeg swamps that had to be drained and granite hills that had to be blasted with dynamite.

The work was dangerous and injuries were not uncommon. "Line man hurt at Outardes Falls," Dad wrote on March 13, 1938. "Came in contact with 66,000 volts and fell 20 feet off ladder at 11:15 a.m. Snowing outside, can't get plane out. Waiting for more news as to his chances for life. Name is Connie Imhoff. Going back to work at 9 p.m. for the start up."

Meanwhile, the girls and my mother moved to Quebec City, where they shared an apartment with my father's sisters, Vera and Jenny, until construction was completed and Baie-Comeau was able to welcome families in 1938.

My dad had originally planned to work construction in Baie-Comeau only long enough to earn money to re-establish the family near Quebec City. It was, however, the tail end of the Depression, and well-paying construction jobs were still rare and prized. The attraction of permanent employment, not to mention a small house in a new townsite that came with schools and an equipped hospital, proved irresistible. He signed on as a permanent employee on August 26, 1937.

The work hours were long, and the town, 250 miles northeast of Quebec City on the North Shore of the St. Lawrence, was completely isolated and inaccessible except by water, and by sporadic flights in the company plane. The summers were fleeting, and the winters long and bitterly cold. But it was all brand new, and life was promising for the young parents of two, just emerging from the hopelessness of the Depression and the indescribable pain of losing a child. And so my mother moved the family to Baie-Comeau to join her husband.

"Left Quebec on the 17th [May] on the SS *New Northland* with Olive and Pats [Peggy] for Comeau Bay," she confided in her diary. "Had a lovely trip down, the weather was perfect. Ben met us at the wharf and we were quite happy to be together again. We have a very nice little home [on Laval Street, at first], with room for improvement but it's 'home' for us and that's everything."

"We are quite happy in our new home, trying to get it fixed up," Mom added two days after she arrived in Baie-Comeau. "Olive is having a grand time. Her Daddy bought her a pup. We call her 'Topsey' but to Olive she is just 'Toffey.'"

Soon, she began to witness the seemingly endless hours of work her husband was putting in. "Ben is tired," she wrote on May 25, 1938. "He works practically every evening. Hope he will soon get a rest."

Outside of the Mulroney family home, Baie-Comeau was preparing for the official opening of the mill on June 11. Even Quebec's premier, Maurice Duplessis, was scheduled to attend the ceremonies. "My, my, what a busy little town preparing for the big event," Mom wrote on the evening of June 8, "the official opening of the mill."

"The Big Day in Baie-Comeau and the weather is perfect," she continued on June 11. "The guests arrived at eleven sharp. This afternoon the ladies are invited to a tea on the SS *New Northland*. Ben is very busy and unable to come home for dinner."

Premier Duplessis spoke at the opening. "I am glad to express the pride of the province in this achievement and in the example of cooperation that it affords to the rest of Canada," he said, according to Carl Wiegman's book. "Here Catholics and Protestants, representatives of government and of industry, labour and capital, have worked side by side to create this new community."

It was in Baie-Comeau, on March 20, 1939, that I was born at the Boisvert Hospital and was baptized Martin Brian. My mother chronicled my birth and early days in her faithful diary: "Baby Brian arrived on Monday evening March 20th at 10:17. Both baby and mother are fine. The baby weighed 8 lbs., 6 ounces at birth."

"The baby is very sick and has what Dr. Thurber calls a kink in the stomach," she wrote on March 22. Later that week: "Baby worse, he was baptized this evening by Father Gagné . . . Still recovering, a temperature – very weak."

More than a week after I was born, my mother and I remained in the hospital.

"Baby is improving but he has lost a lot of weight," she wrote on March 31.

Within a few days, my mother was very sick.

"Took a bad chill this morning," she wrote on April 5, "and sent for Dr. Thurber, temperature 104."

Soon she had to return to hospital. "Had two operations . . . very, very sick and weak. Spent four days in hospital last week," she managed to write.

After she recovered, my mother had little time for her diary, and it trails off.

When Dr. Donald Thurber, the doctor who assisted at my birth, turned ninety, I sent him greetings as Prime Minister of Canada. He responded by writing, "I feel at a loss for words to fully express my gratitude in your sending congratulations on my Ninetieth Birthday in the form of a personal letter praising me for my work in Baie-Comeau, where I had the privilege of being your parents' family physician. I consider their confidence a great honour. Little did I know that one of my duties would be to assist a future Prime Minister in his entry into the world. I seem to recall that your response to being rudely treated on your arrival was prompt and vociferous."

Some things, my critics might point out, have never changed.

2. Growing Up in Baie-Comeau

My mother, father, sisters Olive and Peggy, and I, and our beloved dog, Waggy, lived in a semi-detached mill-owned house at 132 Champlain Street; the other half was occupied by Bob and Hilda Hall and their five children. The Halls were Protestants and the Mulroneys were Catholics, but we lived in friendship, cheek by jowl, for almost thirty years. Later the two families shared a somewhat larger semi-detached at 99/97 Champlain; and when my family moved to 79 Champlain, the Halls lived across the street. Number 79 was the first house my parents ever owned, purchased for $10,000 in 1960.

Bob Hall and my dad worked together in the paper mill and often when they worked the night shift, we kids would tap out messages on the common wall that separated the houses. As a teenager, I tried my hand at the exercise again, attempting elegantly to signal my availability to Valerie, the oldest Hall daughter and a real beauty. She responded kindly, and my hopes soared, but soon the tapping lifeline went silent. In time, Valerie became engaged to Don Anderson, and my youthful dream of sharing a home with a Hall daughter, thereby extending a long tradition, went out the window.

I was enrolled in the Académie Ste-Amélie, a primary school within easy walking distance that was run by the sisters of the Holy Cross, a teaching order from Montreal. I attended English-speaking classes that were taught within a larger French-speaking unit, and I quickly learned French in the corridors, schoolyard, and hockey arena, as well as in class.

The sisters, led by Sister Rosarita, were kind and loving, though strict and exacting in matters of scholarship, manners, and religion. I must have sensed this reality quite early because I promptly became a polite honour student who served as an altar boy at the neighbouring church, proving, if nothing else, my adaptability and my unquestioning acceptance of rules of conduct and values if they gained me approval and advancement. (Still, I had my moments. Peggy remembers the day I was ordered to scrub graffiti off the church with two other friends. "And you, Brian," Sister said to me, "you may have the face of an angel, but you're no angel.") I remember helping prepare a large box of food, fruits, and sweets every Christmas. The girls and I would drag it through the snow to the convent, to be welcomed warmly by the grateful Sisters. My dad said they did so much and requested so little that we had to share whatever we had with them.

—

PERSONAL JOURNAL: FEBRUARY 24, 1987

The Vatican was impressive and the Pope warm and sympathetic. He looked well and strong and was looking forward to his September visit to the U.S. We spoke French throughout and touched on questions ranging from native rights in Canada to our vigorous role in the Commonwealth vis-à-vis South Africa. For someone of conservative Catholic upbringing, it was quite a moving experience to be in private conversation at the Vatican with the successor to Saint Peter. In my mind's eye I can see the Académie Ste-Amélie in Baie-Comeau with the good Sisters of the Holy Cross in about grade 3 or 4, teaching us about Rome and the role of His Holiness. I wonder what they'd think now and what it would be like for one of them to witness and participate in such an event. After my meeting, Mila entered for a private chat, followed by the staff. My thoughts were of how difficult it will be for anyone to fill the shoes of this brilliant and charismatic leader. The Church has been blessed by his presence.

—

Growing up, I was known as a good kid from a good family. My childhood friends like Jacques Provencher, Peter Dawson, Jules Guy, Gilles Lachance, Pierre Rocque, Jimmy Greene, and Pierre Arsenault all came from similar stock. We played hockey on freezing days after school on a rink at Danny Scott's house which was lovingly maintained by his father, Winston, also an electrician at the Quebec North Shore Paper Company. As time went on, we played hockey regularly at the indoor rink at the Baie-Comeau Community Association, and my dad became quite a good curler at an adjacent rink in the same building.

At the age of ten, I was sent to the Académie St-Viateur, which was run by a teaching order of priests and brothers of that name. The school was on Laval Street, much farther from home but still within walking distance. We all walked every day, rain or snow, because after September there was little "shine." I continued to do well in school, motivated partly by the fact that our marks were published for all the town to see. During the first month of grade 5, though, I achieved a mark of only 67.2 per cent. The following month, I had upped this to 81.2 per cent. Marks aside, I was also a very enthusiastic but fairly unimpressive hockey player. In 1952, I stunned our small community – and myself – by winning the Baie-Comeau junior tennis championship. My elation was only slightly diminished by Olive's taunt that my victory had been made possible by the untimely illness that had felled both Gaston Provencher and Danny Scott, the previous winners. To the dismay of my horrified mother, Olive joked that I had poisoned their corn flakes; otherwise my name would never have been emblazoned on the trophy that sat proudly for a year on the gramophone in our living room.

Five years after my birth, my sister Doreen was born, followed in short order by Gary and, a few years later, Barbara. They were all beautiful, happy children who filled our home at 99 Champlain with laughter and joy. But the financial demands grew and so my father started a small electrical contracting business, Saguenay Électrique Enregistrée, and my mother decided to take in boarders.

My father worked six days a week in a hot paper mill, a schedule that included sixteen hours on Sunday. At the time, mills were prevented from operating on Sundays, so all repairs were scheduled for that day, leading to a startup time of one minute past midnight on Mondays. This was hard, demanding work, but my father never complained. "It's pretty good, Brian," he once said when I asked if he was too tired, "on Sundays they pay me time and a half." In later years when I was in college and working similar hours during summers in the mill as a labourer, I would come home with my dad in the early hours of Monday morning and listen as he opened a cold beer, reclined in his La-Z-Boy chair in the living room, and said, "Well, Brian, we're almost over the hump. Just a few more years and everything will be okay." We both knew he was being unrealistic, but I always cheerfully endorsed his optimistic view of our family finances and future.

I can still see my dad coming home after a full day's work – trim, not tall, with a full head of silver hair – having a quick hot meal, a cigarette, and a coffee while chatting with my mom out of earshot of the six kids, and then heading out into the coldest northern Quebec winter nights to fix someone's oil burner or wire someone's new home. He would return several hours later, having made a few extra dollars. Then he would fall asleep and get up before six. An hour later, roused by the sound of the whistle, he would head for the paper mill and another workday.

I loved my dad and admired him enormously. I learned from him a sense of responsibility, commitment to family, and the importance of hard work. "We are 'sort of poor,'" he used to say, "but so is everyone else in Baie-Comeau." He was right: egalitarianism prevailed. Everyone, except the mill manager, our indispensable family doctor, and Gilles Rouleau, the town's only lawyer, was paid essentially the same wage, resided in nearly identical homes, and lived remarkably similar lives. As a consequence, we all felt we were doing quite well.

One year, when I was about sixteen, money was especially short. During a Sunday night conversation, I raised with my dad the thought that perhaps I would enter the excellent new apprenticeship program at the mill for a few years, to assist the family financially. My father looked straight at me and said, "I appreciate the offer, Brian, and we *do* need the help. But the only way out of a paper mill town is through a university door. That's what I want you to do."

The local managers and the company executives he had come to know, like Arthur Schmon and Terry Flahiff, were all university educated, and he was aware this had opened doors for them and their families. For a period he served on the executive committee of the union and was known as a strong union man and a tough bargainer. During his sessions with management, he came away with good settlements for the workers, but also with a growing appreciation of the knowledge and professional skills that characterized the Quebec North Shore mill management team at the time. He associated these with higher education and was determined that, if at all possible, his children should have a similar opportunity.

Payday at the Quebec North Shore mill was on Thursdays at three in the afternoon. Coincidentally, it was always the first – sometimes the only – day of the week we got to eat meat for dinner. Because the workers could not punch out till four o'clock, I would go to the mill with my mother. While she waited outside, I went in and met my dad, who would give me his pay envelope to deliver to my mom. Then we went on to the Hudson's Bay Company, the town's only store, for our weekly shopping. In those days, the mill workers were paid in cash, and I can remember my mother carefully examining the pay stub and counting the week's pay, mentally calculating how much she could spend on food and how much she had to allocate to pay the flood of bills – the dentist, clothes, piano lessons – occasioned by a family of six growing children.

We kids often responded to my father's wishes out of respect and a little fear. When tired out from work and discouraged by ongoing financial worries, he had a short fuse. Sometimes, after I had done something wrong, he would chase me around the house with his belt, scoring a few hits but missing most of the time, due to a combination of my agility and his reluctance to succeed in his endeavour.

In my mother's case it was different – she was the centre of our family's existence, and we kids obeyed her because we adored her. One of the earliest memories I have is of my mother, in the tiny living room at 132 Champlain on a typically freezing late afternoon in winter, ironing the family's clothes while Olive, Peggy, and I sat on the sofa, listening to her sing soft and sorrowful Irish ballads. She was a beautiful young woman – with auburn hair and laughing Irish eyes – and her children and husband were the focus of her life. Kind and gentle, she was nevertheless ambitious for her children and as devoted to the idea of education as my father.

To this end, and with no training, she assumed responsibility for the administrative side of Saguenay Électrique. She ordered materials, juggled the bills, and paid the helpers, sometimes staying awake all night trying to deal with those unfamiliar requirements from our kitchen table.

Her diary continued in 1946, again describing the difficulties and challenges she, a young mother in an isolated part of Canada, faced in those times.

"I am so tired all the time and so much to do with five small children," she wrote one day.

"Getting awfully tired of carrying meals upstairs," she wrote another time, when all of us were sick. "Was never cut out to be a nurse."

The entries continued over the years as she confided her private thoughts to her journal, which we children had no idea she was keeping.

"Ben is working tonight and I am all alone," she wrote on April 7, 1946.

"I am all alone and find it very hard," she confessed a few days later.

Over the years, the O'Shea grandparents helped out by sending along surprises from their farm. "Received a pig from home," my mother wrote in another entry. "Weight 155 pounds." It was put to good use.

My mother was omnipresent in our lives and we, understanding her goodness and her values, did everything we could to please her. We got good marks, worked at jobs after school, attended church regularly, respected our elders, and treated our friends well, because to have done otherwise would have disappointed her enormously. My mother and I talked constantly, about everything. She was always encouraging me at school, congratulating me on some small achievement, consoling me over a broken teenage heart. Until my late teens, I would never return from a night out without entering my parents' room for a chat before going to bed. My father fortunately slept through most of these rambling conversations, but my mom was always immediately awake, wanting to know everything (or almost everything) that had happened.

She was a devout, practising Catholic who attended mass regularly, never ate meat on Friday, and observed the Ten Commandments faithfully. My dad – perhaps because he worked every Sunday – was considerably less devoted to the Church, but he shared her enthusiasm for inculcating the principles of her own deeply held values in all her children. As time went by, some were affected more deeply than others: Peggy joined the Sisters of the Holy Cross, where she performed exemplary service until she withdrew to re-enter secular life some years later.

I remember attending a war coupon bingo in the basement of Ste-Amélie with my mother, during the last years of the war. To our astonishment and great joy we won a turkey and four pounds of butter, which we proudly carried home. My father viewed the day as a richly deserved payback to my mother for a lifetime of unbroken fidelity to the Catholic Church.

As I grew a little older and the road to Quebec City got a little better, most summers my parents would drive us to "the country," as we called it, so that we could spend a little time with our relatives.

Years later, in 1981 I returned to my hometown for a speech and relived with my audience those harrowing drives out of Baie-Comeau. "My father was inclined to think of himself as a Gilles Villeneuve," I said without exaggeration. "He would begin our fourteen-hour odyssey in his 1938 Pontiac at four in the morning – my parents, the six children, the dog, fourteen sandwiches, and a six-pack. It was a mad race over unpaved roads to catch the ferry at Bersimis, followed by a heroic gallop to catch the ferry at Baie Ste-Catherine, followed by a leisurely ride at seventy miles an hour to Quebec

City; the children were crying, the dog barking, my father grinding his teeth, and my mother saying her beads for the third time that day. . . . There was an imposing billboard situated at the entrance to the village of Sacré-Coeur with a picture of the Lord with the caption, 'Why do you use the name of the Lord in vain?' During my entire childhood, I always thought that the message was directed exclusively at my father."

Once the harrowing drive was over, I spent some part of those early summers with my grandparents O'Shea and my mother's brother Jimmy. But most of our time was spent at the Mulroney family home on the Fourth Range, a rambling white house overlooking the river that served as the focal point of return for all Mulroney family members. The homestead was maintained by my uncle Mike, a handsome, taciturn man whose wife, Lou, had died at thirty-six, when her three beautiful daughters, Bernice, Patricia, and Ena, were still children. Over time the three girls somehow learned – with guidance from Aunt Jenny, my godmother, who lived close by – to look after their father and act as hostesses to the family members who regularly arrived for indeterminate stays. To this day, Ena, Mike's youngest daughter, receives visitors in the very same house. Now the visitors are the children and grandchildren of my father's generation, and she remains the resident authority on the Mulroney family's roots and peregrinations.

When it became clear that even my father's two jobs would not suffice to support the family, my mother decided to take in a boarder. We had four bedrooms, one for the boarder, one for my parents, and two for the children. For a while, it felt as if we were stacked up like cordwood in those little rooms, but the arrangement soon became part of our lives and we readily made do.

Our first boarder was a tall, handsome young man from Winnipeg named Bill Becher, who was assigned to Baie-Comeau as a trainee for the Hudson's Bay Company. Within months, his stunning fiancée Betty arrived, and they were soon married in St. George's, the local Anglican church, with the wedding reception in our living room. What we lacked in elegance we made up for in enthusiasm that day, with Hedley Dawson, my friend Peter's father, leading us in song as my sister Olive and Helen Dawson spelled each other on the piano.

As part of a school project, I kept a daily diary that year, and my entries reflect the excitement that gripped our household at the time of the Becher wedding.

"Bill Becher, a man who lives at our house, is getting married," I wrote on October 15, 1947. "His wife is coming from Winnipeg and will be here at 2:15. I imagine she'll be nice too."

"Bill's girlfriend and her sister arrived yesterday and will be married today," I continued the next day. "They are very nice. Betty gave my sister Doreen a little plastic carriage and a little doll [and her sister] gave her a box of Chiclets."

"And you?" my teacher asked me in writing on my diary page.

"I never got nothing," I replied.

Still, this didn't dampen my enthusiasm, as my diary entry from October 17 shows.

"Yesterday was a big one," I wrote. "Bill Becher got married. We had to go down to the greenhouse and get flowers and when we came back Bill and Betty were almost married. So then they went to church to get married. When they came back all the guests had arrived. They threw confetti at them. Then they came out and after awhile they had their picture taken and then they cut the cake."

A few years later the Bechers moved to California, and after Bill's early death Betty moved with her two children to Arizona. My mother and Betty remained especially good friends and on September 17, 1984, Betty and her family joined us for the swearing-in of my new government. As I was hugging my mother after the ceremony at Government House, I remember that she whispered, "We did it, Brian. We really did it." And with a tear rolling down her cheek, she turned, took Betty by the arm, and swept off to the governor general's magnificent champagne reception.

Bill Becher got me my first job when I was about ten or eleven. He could see how tight the budget was at home, and so when an opening arose for a helper at the food store, I was hired to wash fruits and vegetables and help keep the store stocked. This was weekend and after-school work, and I was happy to have the job. All proceeds went right home to my mom, our central banker.

Through Bill, I got another Hudson's Bay Company job that I performed on Wednesday nights. Because Thursday was payday, the Hudson's Bay Company advertised its goods the night before. There was no daily newspaper in town, so flyers were distributed by hand to every household in town. I was given the contract for our part of town, and every Wednesday night at about six, after dinner and homework, I would happily take off and go to every house. I began this work in the summer, and I could not understand why I was being paid four dollars a week for the privilege of chatting with friends and neighbours up and down Champlain and Laurier streets while I strolled around, distributing flyers.

Then winter came, and four dollars appeared pretty paltry. Snowstorms in Baie-Comeau back then would regularly leave drifts that were six feet high, making streets almost impassable. After struggling nightly for two successive winter weeks up unshovelled pathways and streets – strolling up and down the town in summer now nothing but a faint and embarrassing memory – I told my dad I was going to quit. He firmly told me never to quit anything constructive in life, no matter the difficulties or criticisms. So, in a stroke of genius, I conscripted Olive and Peggy, who dutifully set out with me every Wednesday night that winter. Our trio worked productively together, the only sour note happening when Peggy berated me one night for leaving some flyers on a snowbank because I was too tired and cold to go to the porch of a house. "If we girls can do it, so can you," yelled Peggy, adding as an afterthought, "After all, it was you who got us into this mess in the first place." I was about twelve, and I think that was my first encounter with feminism.

My next gainful employment consisted of washing glasses at the bar of the Hotel Le Manoir Comeau down the street and acting as a bellboy when special company guests arrived. One memorable day Colonel McCormick arrived from Chicago with Jack Dempsey, for a tour of the mill followed by some salmon fishing. I was bowled over at the sight of Dempsey, the world heavyweight champ, and Irish to boot. As I was on bellboy duty, I got to carry his bags and secure an autograph that I kept for decades. The next night, Hedley Dawson called to say that at the big gala company dinner (to be held in the commissary that night), Colonel McCormick was hoping that someone could be rounded up to sing "Dearie," his new wife's favourite song. They had earlier scoured the town unsuccessfully and, by any chance, could I help? Somehow, having listened to my mother sing it over the years, I remembered the song, and Olive was pressed into service as my accompanist.

I recall standing on a table in the commissary as the Colonel and his few hundred guests cheered the official debut of my professional singing career. Colonel McCormick congratulated me warmly and placed a crisp American fifty-dollar bill in my hand, which I promptly ran home to give to my mother. (After I became prime minister, I told the New York Economics

Club this story and added the words, "In that way the Mulroney family became the first direct beneficiaries of American foreign aid." The audience roared with laughter, but Canada's dour economic nationalists failed as usual to see the humour, and denounced the incident as another appalling example of Canadian "subordination" to the wicked Americans.)

Though derided today by many as some sort of twentieth-century Republican robber baron, Colonel McCormick was in fact a larger-than-life figure who dreamed the great dreams necessary to carve a thriving community out of bedrock and forest on the North Shore, while building a newspaper empire in the United States. What's more, I like to think he was a shrewd judge of stage talent. Shortly after I became Progressive Conservative leader in 1983, Terry Flahiff, a company executive I greatly respected, wrote to me about my stage debut. He said he happened to be sitting next to Colonel McCormick as I performed.

"When you sang . . . that evening the Colonel leaned over to me and asked your name again," he wrote. "I told him that you were Ben's son and the Colonel said, 'That young fellow has a lot going for him. I'd like to see him in about twenty years from now.'"

Colonel McCormick influenced every part of Baie-Comeau life. Our parish, Église Ste-Amélie, named after his late wife, was decorated at his expense with frescoes by Guido Nincheri that take my breath away, even today. He built recreation facilities that communities half our size could only dream of – including a rink where he brought the NHL's Chicago Blackhawks to play a game for our enjoyment. You can imagine the impression that made on all of us. One of the community institutions he insisted upon was destined to mark my own life forever – the public library. By 1950, our town's population stood at 4,000 people and 1,400 were registered users of the library. More than 15,000 books circulated annually, and I took full advantage of the opportunity.

Throughout all my years growing up, money was tight. When I was away at school and then at university, each summer I would return to Baie-Comeau to work (briefly) as a truck driver, wagon driver, or labourer. At Christmas I got a job as a temporary sorter in the post office. I financed university and law school with the proceeds, borrowing second-semester expenses from the bank, paying the loan off the following summer, and so on.

One of my earliest paying jobs was that of a hard-bitten scribe writing a column – "A Matter of Opinion" – in the Baie-Comeau newspaper during the summer of 1958. For nine weeks of columns I was paid the grand total of twenty-five dollars. "Glass Houses," I headlined one column:

> During the last weeks the actions of some members of the Hauterive Town Council have been subjected to considerable comment, favourable and otherwise. There has been violent bickering among members about such items as "La Société de Développement," so much so that verbal pyrotechnics have become the rule rather than the exception. Recently Hauterive's new town engineer, Ed Gauthier, was assailed by a few of the councillors who decried his "dictatorial methods" in dealing with another town employee. Be that as it may. It does, however, seem very inconsistent that these same gentlemen, very concerned with vituperation and invective, show a like amount of indifference when the time comes to tend to their primary obligations. We refer to the shack town which has sprung up along Route 15 between Hauterive and Manic. This unsightly mess is a discredit to the town of Hauterive and one that should be rectified immediately. A suggestion to the Hauterive councillors: People who live in glass houses should not throw stones.

I simply can't remember if the town fathers of Hauterive took up my suggestion.

My social conscience was also developing. Under the headline "And Let the Sun Shine In" I wrote:

> Recently a young Baie-Comeau couple did something which we feel is very worthy of your attention. They adopted a child through Foster Parents Plan. The child is a six-year-old Vietnamese girl named Nguyen Thi Cay. The FPP is a non-sectarian, non-propaganda, independent, government-approved relief organization which, according to its bylaws, provides for the care, maintenance, education, training, and well-being of children orphaned and distressed and otherwise made destitute. Becoming a Foster Parent is a wonderful gesture, tangible proof of the humanitarianism ingrained in us, as Christians. The need of these children is real. And it is urgent. C'mon Mr. and Mrs. Baie-Comeau, open up your hearts and let the sun shine in.

The toughest summer job I ever had was with Cargill Grain at its elevator at the port of Baie-Comeau. It was after my first year of law school at Laval, and I reported for work in less than top physical shape. For four months, I went through my ten-hour working day like an automaton, punching in each morning at three minutes to seven, going to the elevator, shovelling the overflow grain from the belts into hundred-pound bags, sealing the bags, putting them on my shoulder, and carrying them through the film of a dust-ridden building to a secure area, where they could be loaded onto an incoming vessel for shipment overseas. These and other very demanding physical tasks left me covered in dust and sweat every night, with barely enough strength to get home, shower, sit down to the heavy dinner my mom cooked, and head down to the basement to sleep. (After we took in the boarder, another bedroom was fashioned in the basement next to the oil burner for my younger brother, Gary, and me.) I don't think I went out at all that entire summer, so exhausted was I at week's end. I returned to law school that fall with a heightened respect for manual labour and those who perform it – and with an equally firm determination to avoid the experience ever again, if at all possible.

Years later, Mila and I spent a few days as the guests of our good friends Gerry Schwartz and Heather Reisman aboard their chartered yacht, the *Carmac*, in the Caribbean. One day Gerry told me the yacht owners were the MacMillan family, the principal shareholders of Cargill, Inc. As I gazed around the elegantly appointed stateroom adorned with expensive paintings and tasteful furniture, I chuckled at the thought that my low-paid efforts in the summer of 1962 might have helped the family to purchase that magnificent yacht.

Most people have a childhood memory of intense personal embarrassment. My sister Peggy was at the heart of mine. The single bathroom at 99 Champlain was the only room in the house that could be locked, guaranteeing privacy. I would often use it to read or write, with the clothes hamper as a makeshift desk.

One day when I was about thirteen, I repaired to the bathroom to refine my list of "sins" for my monthly visit to the confessional at Église Ste-Amélie. My original and accurate list was unimpressive, I thought, and certainly not one that I could raise with any pride during the regular discussions among classmates that were held following church. And so I sat down, pulled the hamper close, and began a process of embellishing my list.

The results said much more about my imagination than about any real masculine prowess.

When satisfied that I had a list of peccadilloes and achievements that would impress my classmates, I left the bathroom, which was soon occupied by Peggy. Unfortunately, I had forgotten to bring the document with me and it was discovered by my sister, who, secure behind a locked door, gleefully began to read the document in a loud voice to my bewildered parents and siblings, who looked at me with a mixture of incredulity and concern.

In spite of entreaties from my mother, Peggy refused to unlock the door or to stop reading – editorializing on each "sin" as she went along – until my father placed a ladder on the back of the house, entered the second-floor bathroom through a small window, snatched the list from her, and opened the door. His intervention produced undying gratitude from me but visible disappointment among my siblings, who had not had as much fun since my father came home with a second-hand 1938 Pontiac and took us all for our first automobile ride.

And it was on Champlain Street, when I was about six years old, that I knew sadness for the first time. Our neighbours diagonally across the street were the Prévost family. Dulcine Prévost, a beautiful little girl almost exactly my age, was tobogganing down Blanchard's Hill late one afternoon, when the sky was dark grey. In the poor light she went over the snowbank onto the street, where she was killed by a car right in front of her home. It was my first encounter with death, and the sadness of that black and unforgiving day comes back to me each time I encounter a Prévost family member, or think of my early Baie-Comeau days.

When he was ten years old, my close friend Peter Dawson was struck by a car, also on Champlain Street, sustaining serious head injuries that caused him to be airlifted to Montreal. There, at the famed Montreal Neurological Institute, the brilliant team of Dr. Wilder Penfield and Dr. William Cone operated at least a dozen times on Peter, saving his life and eventually sending him back to Baie-Comeau wearing a large football helmet. Every child on the street was admonished never to jostle or hit Peter in any way, which gave him total protection when he provoked the rest of us for years with absolute impunity. I was the best man at Peter's wedding, after which he went on to become a successful ophthalmologist in Houston, Texas. I visited him there during the G-7 Heads of Government Summit held in 1990, and it was just like old times. The years fell away as Peter and I (now in our early fifties) chatted for hours about old friends and the impact

Baie-Comeau had had on our lives. To this day, while driving to my office in Montreal, I frequently take Doctor Penfield Avenue and always reflect with gratitude on the brilliant neurosurgeon who decades earlier had saved the life of my close childhood friend.

I continued to do well in the local grade and high school, coming first in almost every monthly report card, but when I was fourteen, my parents decided it was time for me to attend St. Thomas College in Chatham, New Brunswick.

Why New Brunswick? It was a long way away, clear across the Gulf of St. Lawrence, but there were links between the Atlantic province and the North Shore. In Baie-Comeau, we listened to CJBR radio (from Rimouski) in French and CFNB (from Campbellton, N.B.) in English. We shared a cultural affinity with New Brunswickers, and many Baie-Comeau citizens had originated from there, before coming to our new town in search of work.

I was uncertain about this move, and secretly afraid. But I used to lie awake at night and listen to the CBC and stations in New York and Philadelphia. I would think of those faraway places, their energy and promise, and doze off as the voices painted exciting pictures for me. I was thrilled to think that one day, in some slight way, I might be part of such a glamorous world.

And so in early September 1953, I left Baie-Comeau on the M. V. *Jean Brilliant* for Rimouski, where I was to catch the midnight train, arriving in Newcastle, N.B. the following morning, a brief bus ride away from Chatham. I can still see my mother and siblings on the dock as I mounted the small gangplank with my checkered cardboard suitcase, turned, and waved goodbye.

Although there was another Baie-Comeauite, Andy Morrow, at St. Thomas, initially I was very lonesome and homesick. It reached the point that, a few days after arriving in Chatham, I used the school's only pay phone at the main hall entrance to call home collect. I sobbed through the entire conversation, pleading to be allowed to come home. My parents lovingly yet firmly explained that I had to stay and get a good education that would eventually lead to a university degree; in any case, they explained, there was no coming home.

St. Thomas was not for the children of privilege or wealth. The cost for room, board, and tuition was $405 a year, which made it possible for my parents, with some sacrifice, to send me there. After I got over my loneliness,

I came to greatly enjoy the school. I was proud to be off on my own for the first time, solely responsible for my own well-being and advancement. I did well academically, eventually winning the graduation prize in Latin and emerging as the school's debating leader.

I also enjoyed the town of Chatham and fell under the spell of Dixie Lea, a smashing young student at nearby St. Michael's Academy. Dixie was the daughter of the town's only RCMP constable and they lived in a comfortable home on Wellington Street. The Leas frequently invited me for a hot meal or a holiday dinner and introduced me to the O'Reillys, O'Donnells, and Jardines. These families made me feel welcome, and I came to genuinely enjoy the Miramichi region and its people.

One day Lord Beaverbrook, a friend of the school's president, Father McFadden, decided to visit our school. All the students were lined up to shake hands with Beaverbrook – who had grown up as Max Aitken in the manse at Newcastle – and I remember the sense of awe that enveloped our student body as the great newspaper tycoon came by and politely greeted us one by one. I could not believe that a man of such modest beginnings just down the road had risen to a position of such wealth and influence in the world. I was strongly moved by the moment.

As graduation loomed in the spring of 1955, I was looking forward to the prom, for which I had acquired my first charcoal-grey suit and tie, along with a pink shirt – "a magnificent combination" said my school friend Danny Mills when he sold it to me at Jacobson's men's store in Chatham. "Dixie will be impressed," he said knowledgeably. At that time I was still both short (about five-foot-six) and thin (about 110 pounds). Unfortunately, my new suit could not alter either of those realities.

Because Dixie was taller than I was, we set off for the dance with her walking on the street and me (at her gentle suggestion) standing tall on the sidewalk. Sadly, the new suit and pink shirt provoked neither spasms of passion from my date nor expressions of envy from other partygoers. I was not surprised when soon thereafter Danny Mills abandoned his career as a clothing salesman and entered the seminary to become a Catholic priest.

When I went off to St. Francis Xavier University in Nova Scotia the next fall, Dixie entered nursing school; she eventually married an RCMP constable and lived a happy life in New Brunswick. When I was nominated as the PC candidate to stand in the Central Nova by-election after becoming party leader in 1983, Dixie was in the crowd, having organized a busload of supporters from Chatham to be present at the official launch of my parliamentary career.

Some forty-five years later, St. Thomas College had moved its campus to the University of New Brunswick, in Fredericton. On a glorious August day in 2003, they dedicated a splendid new building as "Brian Mulroney Hall." At the ceremony, I relived many powerful boyhood memories with teachers, classmates, and friends from the Miramichi. While I'm usually able to keep my composure in public, it simply wasn't possible that day. The sacrifices my parents made to help me on the journey that took me to my dreams were on my mind. Choking up, I spoke of them, and particularly of my father. Then I looked to the future, epitomized in the young faces of the many students who had gathered for the ceremony. "A man may be a great scientist, technician, or doctor," I told them, "and yet not be educated. The reason is that education, true education, is something that concerns the understanding heart, that concerns the spirit, that concerns the human soul. St. Thomas has given us the education we need. To the young people and students here today and to those who will frequent Mulroney Hall in the future, I say simply: May your standard of life be your gift to your nation. And may your idealism and principle be your legacy to the world."

Fine words. But I'm sure my young audience that day was much more impressed by my tears of gratitude to my parents.

3. StFX

MANY PEOPLE EXPERIENCE an event in their lives that changes everything. We often don't realize it at the time, but as we look back, that particular event becomes transformational. This happened to me in the autumn of 1955 when I entered St. Francis Xavier University in Antigonish, Nova Scotia, and settled into a four-year experience that set me on a course for a career in law, business, and politics.

Founded in 1852, by farmers, fishermen, and miners in eastern Nova Scotia and Cape Breton who wanted an institute of advanced learning for their children, St. Francis Xavier was not Harvard, but it had become a respected Canadian university. I had heard of StFX often while at St. Thomas College, since a number of graduates went there every year, and when I found out I was accepted as a student I was thrilled. Following my hard summer as a labourer in the mill back home, I eagerly looked forward to a new life there.

The campus on the hill above downtown Antigonish was large (to me) and attractive, with hundreds of students from across Canada, the United States, and around the world. This was an entirely new experience, and I revelled in the sights and sounds of a booming coeducational campus. I enrolled in the bachelor of arts degree course with honours in political science, determined to take full advantage of a brilliant faculty, and equally determined to make the most of complementary extracurricular opportunities and facilities. I knew that StFX had great sports teams and marvellous extracurricular opportunities. But as a freshman I was dazzled to find that there were debating and theatre clubs, campus political parties, a weekly paper, and groupings of what seemed to me to be every student interest under the sun.

I was assigned a room with two others in Aquinas Hall, close to the very centre of campus activity. I can still remember the excitement of that first

September and the pleasure of meeting the various student leaders. The student union president was Bobby Higgins, an impressive senior from Saint John who would go on to lead the Liberal Opposition in New Brunswick, eventually becoming a judge on the Supreme Court of New Brunswick. He was courteous, well spoken, and handsome, representing in my eyes the epitome of what an accomplished young leader should look like and be. Pat MacAdam, later to be senior assistant to me as prime minister, always entertaining and able, was editor of the *Xaverian*, the university weekly; Lowell Murray, who would sit in the federal cabinet and Senate, was both president of the Student Cooperative Society and leader of the campus Progressive Conservative Party; Rick Cashin, an eloquent Newfoundlander, who would later become a Liberal MP, president of the Newfoundland Fishermen's Union, and a member of the Privy Council, led a number of causes and parties. Gerry Doucet, from a poor fishing family in Grand Étang, rose to become the youngest cabinet minister in Nova Scotia history and the first Acadian minister of education in the provincial government; and Robert ("Mel") Shea, from Boston, the campus's best entrepreneur and most promising business graduate, went on to a very successful career in the States.

These were the upperclassmen who held most of the leadership posts on campus. Among my classmates I quickly made friends with Sam Wakim from Saint John; Jim Nasso, Ottawa; Terry "Ace" McCann, Pembroke; Myles Mills, Edmundston; Myles Pelletier, Madawaska, in Maine; and Bertrand Lavoie, Bagotville. They were a delightful and disparate group who made life at StFX challenging and rewarding, and with whom I maintain valued friendships today, forty-five years later.

In the flurry of activity that first autumn, I was approached by Lowell Murray to join the Progressive Conservative Party. I had little interest in politics at the time, knowing only vaguely of my parents' support for the Liberal Party; we seldom discussed the subject at home. The other kids were too young and my parents too preoccupied with daily responsibilities for them to have more than a peripheral interest in questions of public policy. But I was flattered to be asked, and attracted not so much by the PC ideology – although I found it compatible with my own views – but by the challenges that membership would represent. At that time, the federal Liberals had been in power for twenty consecutive years, and in Nova Scotia their provincial counterparts had governed for even longer. I had always considered myself a bit of an underdog and was impressed by Lowell's spiel about the tremendous opportunities we would enjoy together when our party defeated the Grits both in Halifax and Ottawa.

Well, that day came swiftly in Nova Scotia. A year later, in 1956, Premier Henry Hicks called an election for October 30. I immediately rushed down and signed up as a volunteer for the PC candidate in Antigonish, Bill MacKinnon, the lead announcer at local radio station CJFX and a member of one of the region's most distinguished families.

Hicks had been selected about a year earlier at a controversial convention called to elect a successor to the much beloved and admired Angus L. Macdonald, a StFX graduate who had served as premier for sixteen years. His tenure was interrupted by the war, when "Angus L." represented his province in the war cabinet of Mackenzie King as minister of national defence for naval services. He returned to the premiership for nine more years before his death in 1954. Upon Macdonald's death, Harold Connolly, a charming cabinet minister of Irish heritage, was chosen to become premier.

Connolly – the father of Sharon Carstairs, subsequently the Manitoba Liberal leader and senator – did run for the leadership and was narrowly defeated by Hicks. Many Catholics felt betrayed by the result – with no good reason that I could see – and were quickly embraced by the Conservatives, who were led by an unobtrusive, low-key lawyer from Truro called Robert L. Stanfield. Given this background, Antigonish proved to be exceptionally fertile ground, and when Stanfield swept to power on October 30, 1956, Bill MacKinnon was elected in Antigonish – the first PC in forty years – along with so many others that Stanfield formed a majority government.

I admired Bob Stanfield from the start and was greatly taken by the political know-how he demonstrated. "With skill and determination, the affable, soft-spoken politician began his campaign to reconstruct the party of Tupper," I wrote in an article published in a "Young PC" newsletter. "From Yarmouth to North Sydney, from Sutherland's River to Shubenacadie, he stumped the province tirelessly, recruiting party workers, promulgating Conservative policy, and soliciting support for a program designed to 'Remake Nova Scotia.' . . . Vigour was the fare of the day as Conservative members and organizers worked strenuously in every constituency . . . When Mr. Hicks decided to go to the people in 1956, the Conservatives were ready."

Vigour was the fare of the day at StFX, too. Our ranks had begun to swell at the university even before Stanfield's victory, and Lowell Murray had been elected Prime Minister of the Model Parliament. No skullduggery had been involved, but suspicions arose when it was reported that Lowell and the party were being supported by one Oonagh Macdonald, an accomplished student and the daughter of the beloved Angus L. himself. I had no difficulty in assuring reluctant voters in that election that, given the pulchritudinous evidence, it was clear that the election of a Progressive Conservative campus government was something that even the deceased Angus L. supported.

When the Model Parliament convened at Mount Saint Bernard – the principal female campus and educational building – I was seated as minister of fisheries, an appointment I reluctantly accepted, and only after the prime minister assured me I would not be embarrassed if I didn't know the difference between a halibut and a flounder.

People used to say of Winston Churchill and other great speakers that they made speech making look easy. What audiences don't see, however, are the hours and hours of preparation that go into any good speech. As a high school debater I learned early on about the value and necessity of preparing for a public address, although no one would have guessed at the amount of effort that went into my first speech to the Model Parliament at seventeen years of age. I was not going to leave anything to chance and I laboured for hours on my remarks. I even began them in French – not a common thing in 1950s Nova Scotia.

When I rose to make my parliamentary debut, speaking from handwritten notes, I took some time to congratulate the Honourable Speaker, then went on, in fine style: "When asked by the Prime Minister if I would second the address in reply to the Speech from the Throne, I, of course, immediately accepted the honour, but with some humility. However, I became proud indeed because I realized that the honour was not for me primarily, but for the people of my riding, Three Rivers, whom I have the honour to represent. But, may I add that this is an honour that is long overdue my constituency! For nigh on endless years, my people have been catching the largest fish, raising the biggest potatoes – and children – apart from providing the local liquor commission with the highest revenue for any constituency of its size in the Dominion. Now, as you will readily admit, this in itself is a tremendous feat worthy of the highest recognition, and therefore I deem my people quite worthy of this great honour bestowed on me today." After some well-merited insults for the Opposition, I dealt with issues great and small, standing against "the admission of Communist China into the

United Nations," and emphatically for "proposed legislation on offering scholarships to worthy Canadian students."

In spite of my preparation and my well-rehearsed attempts at humour, I have no recollection of either thunderous applause or waves of well-wishers rushing to congratulate me. Instead, there was embarrassment at my mispronouncing a word in my maiden speech. The word I had used to describe the Liberal lust for power was "insatiable," which I mispronounced as "insat-eye-able." To this day, I cringe in embarrassment as I reflect upon the gentle public correction by Governor General Bob Higgins and the look of undisguised dismay on the face of Prime Minister Murray.

When I started my university career, I was so rake-thin that my nickname around campus was "Bones." But I was a determined and ambitious young man, focused on self-improvement, advancement, and success. Among the things I did was write down every unfamiliar word, look it up in the dictionary, and write out the meaning for future use. I loved reading and the sound of language beautifully spoken and was determined to build a vocabulary that was both extensive and impressive. "Impressive" to me in those days meant the longer the word, the better the effect.

Any debater, even in a student parliament, encounters embarrassing moments. I suffered another moment of discomfiture late the following year when James Sinclair – Margaret Trudeau's father, and Prime Minister St. Laurent's fisheries minister – came to StFX in support of the federal Liberal Party, then preparing for the 1957 general election. After speaking to an overflow appreciative audience, Mr. Sinclair took questions. After a while I, in my full splendour as secretary of the campus Conservatives, rose and asked him a question that was certain to devastate his thesis and to impress the audience. Sinclair simply dispatched the question with a quip and me with a smile, to the hilarity of the audience and the distress of my PC followers, who had come to see me polish off a federal minister.

Less than a decade later I witnessed an event in the House of Commons that showed that StFX graduates were bipartisan in their masochistic approach to questioning established public figures. I and my good friend Dick Holden, an engaging lawyer from Montreal and an aggressive Conservative supporter, were in the House of Commons gallery during debate of the Munsinger Affair, a delicious sex-and-spies scandal that had captured the nation's attention. John Diefenbaker was again Opposition leader, a responsibility he exercised with lethal effectiveness against the Pearson government, and Holden and I were greatly enjoying his frontal attack. Midway during his speech, he was interrupted (an extremely rare event in the House) by a voice that yelled from the rear of the chamber, "Would the right honourable gentleman entertain a question?" I immediately recognized the voice as that of Liberal MP Rick Cashin, my friend and debating partner from StFX, who was clearly trying to derail the Chief. When Diefenbaker continued his verbal assault unabated, Cashin, in a display of raw courage rarely seen in Parliament, yelled again, "Would the right honourable gentleman entertain a question?"

Diefenbaker stopped abruptly, electrifying the House. He snapped off his glasses to glare at Cashin with undisguised contempt, paused for effect, and then snorted, "A big game hunter is never diverted by rabbit tracks." As waves of laughter pealed across the House, I knew that my old friend would be scarlet with embarrassment, precisely my colour the night Jimmy Sinclair slit my throat, with a chuckle, years earlier in Antigonish. No one has ever accused our generation of StFX graduates of self-effacement, nor have we ever learned the entirely sensible proposition that it is inadvisable for novices to tangle with the pros.

But over time we learned from our mistakes, and for a number of years beginning in the mid 1980s, three of the four officers of Parliament – the Prime Minister, the Leader of the Government in the Senate (Lowell Murray), and the Leader of the Opposition in the Senate (Allan MacEachen) – were StFX graduates, an event unreplicated by any other Canadian university of its size in recent history.

StFX was clearly left wing in its political orientation, an unsurprising fact given its roots. Dr. Moses Coady, founder of the Antigonish Movement, was largely responsible for this, although his philosophy was essentially non-political; rather, it was based squarely on the moral obligation we all had to assist the poor, here and abroad, and on his steely resolve that something practical be done to implement the vision. The Antigonish Movement grew out of a social philosophy based on adult education and the cooperative movement, which held the view that by working together selflessly, better and more prosperous lives could be achieved for all. Dr. Coady drove that great idea to brilliant success among the poorest and most needy throughout eastern Nova Scotia, and its success over decades led to the creation of the Coady International Institute. This was an organization at StFX whose objective was to train leaders from poor and developing countries to replicate the Coady experience at home. It always struck me as the very essence of charity and goodness that at a time of great need StFX would commit some of its very limited financial resources to funding the Coady Institute because others needed it more. That simple generosity explained the eventual fabulous success of Coady International and demonstrated the principles upon which StFX would rise to pre-eminent status in Canada, frequently ranking first in the nation among undergraduate universities.

That influence stayed with me. In late September 1984, Prime Minister Edward Seaga of Jamaica became the first foreign head of government to visit me in Ottawa. While Dr. Coady was long dead by this time, I know for sure that his spirit was in the room as the Prime Minister of Canada and the Prime Minister of Jamaica – men destined to work in partnership to rid South Africa of apartheid – held their talks. During most meetings between foreign leaders, each side is allowed to have a silent note-taker present. The Canadian report filed after Prime Minister Seaga and I met on Sept. 29, noted: "Prime Minister Mulroney responded by welcoming Mr. Seaga. He said that he was going to Toronto shortly and would later be going on to St. Francis Xavier University in Nova Scotia for the Silver Jubilee celebrations of his graduating class. He mentioned the contribution that university has made to the Third World, particularly through the Coady Institute, and noted that some of the experience gained by the university could be applied to the Canadian International Development Agency (CIDA)."

For the next nine years, the government I led placed Dr. Coady and his principles at the forefront of government policy and decision-making, from our quick response to the famine crisis in Ethiopia, to the forgiveness of African debt, to the fight against apartheid, and so much more.

In the late 1970s, I was able, in small part, to help repay StFX for all I owed it. Rolling up my sleeves, I agreed to chair a fundraising campaign for my alma mater. With an overall target of $7 million, we were able to report that we had been able to raise over $11 million, a campaign unique in the university's history. When officials at StFX wrote to thank me for my efforts, I proudly responded that all of the school's graduates were thankful for their time there. "Raising money for StFX was for me, in the best sense of the expression, a 'labour of love,'" I told Monsignor Malcolm MacLellan in an October 1980 letter.

For its growing influence in the earlier years, StFX could thank professors like Dr. Walter Kontak, a gifted American Oxford graduate who loved political science and taught it brilliantly; Father Rod McSween, as able and stimulating an English literature professor as was to be found anywhere;

John Sears, a skilled business professor with vast practical experience; Dr. Donald J. ("Rocks") MacNeil, the head of the geology department, whose penalty for his teaching talent was having to endure students like me avoiding chemistry or physics in the quest for the necessary "science" credits required for an honours arts degree; and Sister (we called her "Mother" out of respect) Veronica, whose knowledge of Canadian history was as deep as her love of the land itself (and who happened to be the sister of Angus L. Macdonald).

One year, while trying to get close to Judy Laidlaw, an attractive Mount St. Bernard secretarial student, I signed up for the typing class she took, figuring that propinquity would be at least half the battle. As it turned out, Judy, while impressed by my determination, soon thereafter married fellow student Roy Hines. With singular generosity, she invited me to propose the toast to the bride at the reception. My typing prowess enabled me to prepare an excellent toast, which I then flubbed by drinking one too many beers prior to the ceremony. I was sober enough, however, to overhear one of Judy's relatives remark later on in the evening, "Judy must have heard Brian speak before, and she promptly decided to marry Roy." Roy Hines went into the federal public service and I subsequently appointed him as a member of the International Trade Commission.

After my first year at StFX, I returned home in the summer of 1956 and found a job in the giant construction project for Canadian British Aluminium on a new site (St-Georges) somewhat removed from the original Baie-Comeau townsite. I began as a straight labourer, cleaning debris, carrying cases of supplies, and so on, until one day I was pleased to be assigned to driver status. My principal responsibility was to drive a large company station wagon to pick up project directors, deliver them to various sites at the break of day, shuttle them about as required during the shift, and return them home at night. During the day, I would occasionally spell drivers on the larger tonnage trucks – a real challenge – and I spent a full four months working hard and learning a lot about construction work, its burdens, trials, skills, and rewards.

That summer I took up with a smashing girl with whom I had gone to elementary school a dozen years earlier. Mary McGrath had blossomed during her years of secretarial training in Montreal, and I was only one of many young swains who hovered about any time she appeared in public. Somehow I prevailed, and Mary and I became an item. No one ever was prouder to squire such a striking and intelligent young woman around town, and I returned to StFX determined to do well and return home at Christmas to an appreciative girlfriend. After the holidays, however, I think Mary simply decided the wait would be too long – three more years of university and four of law school. Eventually she went off to Denver, Colorado, where she married a university hockey star from Saskatchewan, who later developed a prosperous construction company in Halifax.

I was then seventeen – becoming progressively convinced that any hopes of obtaining heartthrob status were doomed. I was getting taller but not heavier, still bearing the nickname "Bones," yet still enjoying life at StFX, developing great friendships on campus, and acquiring a deep and growing interest in public policy and politics. By the autumn of 1956, I was secretary of the campus PC Club, just as the national party was gearing up to convene a leadership convention to choose a successor to George Drew, who had resigned because of ill health. The candidates were John Diefenbaker, Donald Fleming, and E. Davie Fulton, and each campus club was eligible to send two delegates to the December convention in Ottawa. We met and I was elected as one of our representatives.

Soon the campaigning began, and one day the president of the National Youth for Diefenbaker Committee descended upon little Antigonish. His name was Ted Rogers, and he was a dynamic law student at the University of Toronto. We could see at once that Ted was a true force of nature. He later became one of Canada's most successful entrepreneurs, building a vast communications empire in the process. Having witnessed his skills first-hand years earlier, I was not surprised. So enthusiastic was Ted about Diefenbaker and so captivating was his presentation that I signed up on the spot, and Ted promptly named me vice-chairman, Atlantic Region. I took this tribute to my organizing skill and talent with the requisite aplomb; I did not flinch publicly upon learning later that my principal qualification for the job was the complete unavailability of anyone else.

In early December 1956, Paul Creaghan and I took the thirty-six-hour train ride from Antigonish to Montreal (where we stayed overnight with Paul's relatives). Then it was on to Ottawa, where we were billeted with the wonderful McDonald family, on Echo Drive. Joe McDonald, a friend from StFX, had kindly arranged our stay (for free, of course, our travel stipend being next to nothing and our wallets almost empty). His parents were warm and kind and friendly. They were also prominent Liberals, whose home overlooking the canal briefly sheltered two ambitious Conservatives.

It was my first time in Ottawa, and at first I wandered about the nation's capital in a dream, taking in the sights. But soon convention duty called. Any doubt about what career I would eventually choose was eliminated at that convention, although Ted Rogers and his tall, imposing deputy, Hal Jackman, were hard taskmasters. My dreams of glory collapsed when Ted informed me that my area of responsibility was posters. "What happens when I get all the Diefenbaker posters up?" I asked Ted, who replied, "You put up more. I want this town swamped in Diefenbaker posters, morning, noon, and night." And so, from early morning to late at night, my little team and I vigorously executed this command, though it was cold and occasionally snowing in Ottawa that December.

The excitement of the convention hall itself was intoxicating, and to my delight I discovered that any delegate could wander at will anywhere throughout the event. It was as a result of this exercise in democracy that I awoke one morning to hear Mrs. McDonald yell, "Brian, get up right away, you're on the front page of the *Journal* with [Ottawa Mayor] Charlotte Whitton!" And indeed I was. Over breakfast I snuck glances at the picture, not wanting others to notice how starstruck I was. I knew it was all right to enjoy such fame but not all right to make others uneasy by blowing it out of proportion. Still, to be on the front page of the paper – and at a national Tory convention!

Later that day, along with members of his youth executive committee, I met Mr. Diefenbaker. I was thunderstruck when he referred to me as "Brian" and thanked me for my "great help." Only when he referred to the importance of posters to a successful campaign did I see the fine hand of Ted Rogers in the compliment, which I nonetheless accepted with enthusiasm. Ted and I have remained fast friends for almost fifty years. While he built a media empire, he and his wife, Loretta, also nurtured a wonderful family. Years later Ted declined my offer of a Senate appointment, but his deputy at the 1956 convention, Hal Jackman, also a good friend, accepted the appointment as lieutenant governor of Ontario, and served admirably from 1991 to 1997.

I was there for the speeches and for the abrupt departure of the Quebec delegation after John Diefenbaker won. Convinced that Diefenbaker was somehow anti-Quebec and anti-French, the entire delegation, led by Quebec MP Léon Balcer, simply got up and left. It was my first experience with the self-destructive instinct of the PC Party, and I remember it troubled and embarrassed me greatly. How could we be providing our opponents with such ammunition? I was learning the importance of leadership in uniting and guiding a minority party to government, and realized that this kind of conduct must be avoided at all costs.

I left the convention exhilarated and I made a note in the Daytimer I then carried: "Voted today at convention. Diefenbaker elected on first ballot. Leave for Montreal tomorrow. Prediction for summer's election: Conservatives 93 seats."

(In the same Daytimer I also took time out to comment on that fall's Grey Cup game. The Edmonton Eskimos had gone on to victory over the Montreal Alouettes, and I noted the stellar play of a quarterback I later worked with in national politics, particularly on the Meech Lake Accord. "Grey Cup game day in Toronto," I wrote. "Als played poorly . . . Don Getty playing a great game, making excellent use of a superb ground attack.")

Boarding the train I headed home for Christmas, thrilled by the whole Ottawa experience. I was confident the entire country would soon share my enthusiasm for this towering figure and passionate orator from Saskatchewan whose social policies and empathy for "ordinary Canadians" seemed to me to replicate the teachings of Dr. Coady and the Antigonish Movement so many years ago.

4. The Making of a Young Tory

By June 1957, I had been elected vice-president of the Progressive Conservative Student Federation (PCSF). My admiration for John Diefenbaker was soon obvious in both campus and national PC youth circles. I was later to jokingly receive the "George Nowlan – A. Davidson Dunton CBC Award," at a party meeting. It was, ostensibly, awarded to the "ordinary citizen in the four Atlantic provinces who has seen every television appearance of John Diefenbaker." And indeed I had.

In his own memoirs, *One Canada*, Mr. Diefenbaker wrote that he had to drag our party "kicking and screaming into the 20th century." Many have forgotten that one of the ways he did just that was by making history and appointing the first woman ever, Ellen Fairclough, to cabinet. Inspired by Dief's progressiveness, I made a special appeal to the women of StFX during campus elections that fall and invoked the Chief's name in a pamphlet sent to all female voters on campus:

> Much has been said of women and their role in the political affairs of this country. I think the Liberal Party was the first to go on record commending the women for their interest and fine work in politics. If this is so, the Liberal Party is to be congratulated. But the Liberals did not go far enough, because from 1935 to 1957, the years they were in power, they left their praises hanging in mid-air. The Conservative Party has always held that the Canadian woman is needed in political life, that the Canadian woman [should] be encouraged to play an ever-increasing role in the governing of this country. The Conservative Party saw the combination of man and woman going forward together and making civilization more worthy of the name. It was this confidence in the women of Canada that prompted Mr. Diefenbaker to appoint Mrs. Ellen Fairclough, MP, to the cabinet last June. This was the highest political honour ever

> to have been bestowed on a Canadian woman. Now, as the Secretary of State for Canada, the Honourable Mrs. Fairclough is performing parliamentary and cabinet duties which the Liberals chose to reserve exclusively for men.

In the spirit of that 1957 pamphlet, when I became prime minister, I continued the Diefenbaker tradition of support for women in politics. On election night in 1984, I made the following pledge to the women of Canada: "From now on, the advancement of women's rights will be one of the major concerns of the Government of Canada. Injustices that women have suffered – belatedly recognized as such by many of us – will no longer be tolerated in this country, and our government will attempt to remedy the most glaring of problems and will vigorously address the difficulties that remain."

I spent the next nine years delivering on that pledge, by appointing more female ministers, deputy ministers, senators, and judges than any other prime minister up to that time. I also initiated anti-stalking legislation, and implemented many other measures to support women.

Another StFX political pamphlet featured a picture of me and a serious-looking portrait of Mr. Diefenbaker, and included this text: "Canadian Students Need: 1) A truly Canadian flag. 2) An Ambassador to the Vatican. 3) A New Ministry of Engineering. 4) Official Government Recognition of NFCUS as the Voice of Students. 5) Increased Student Income Tax Exemptions. 6) A Spanking New Student Scholarship Plan. Vote Progressive Conservative! Progressive Conservative – The Vision to Create – The Courage to Retain."

Again inspired by Mr. Diefenbaker's performance in Ottawa, I was improving at a rhetorical sport he had himself perfected during the decades before he became prime minister, Grit bashing: "The StFX Liberal Party is a fine example of political listlessness, indifference, and indolence," I thundered in one campus election manifesto, along with lots more.

Despite this youthful partisanship, I was already developing a profound respect for everyone who held elected office in this country. During the 1958 campaign I was honoured to be given the opportunity to sit down for a coffee with Lester B. Pearson, who took time to visit with students at StFX. Later as prime minister, I was to play a role in honouring both Mr. Pearson and Mr. Diefenbaker. At the unveiling of the Pearson statue in September of 1990, I said, "When I first visited Parliament Hill as a young Conservative, little did I think that one day I would have the privilege of dedicating statues to [both prime ministers]. Those were the days of epic parliamentary battles between those two outstanding leaders. The Chief, of course, was the Conservative leader, a gladiator of a thousand combats. But I had more than a sneaking admiration for the smiling man in the crisp bow tie, known affectionately to Canadians as 'Mike.' I wonder what the old Chief is thinking today as he glances over his shoulder here on the hill and sees Mike Pearson – on higher ground staring at him from behind!"

—

PERSONAL JOURNAL: SEPTEMBER 3, 1989

> *On the 17th I will have been prime minister for five years – longer than Pearson and closing in on Dief. A fact that would, I suspect, provoke indifference in Pearson and regret in the Chief.*

—

I was back working as a labourer in Baie-Comeau for the summer of 1957 – news of my glorious political achievements had clearly not yet reached Quebec's North Shore – when I celebrated Dief's victory with the small crowd gathered to support the local PC candidate in another losing campaign. That situation was to change within a year, when Dr. Perreault LaRue, the local dentist and our neighbour, won the riding handily in the 1958 sweep, when the PCs wound up with fifty seats in Quebec.

After I returned to StFX in the fall, Professor Kontak and a few of his prominent political science students began planning a Maritime Universities Student Parliament to be held in Antigonish during the federal election that most observers predicted would come early in 1958. Elections would be held on as many campuses as possible, and the winning party would form a "government" in Antigonish. In the euphoria surrounding the surprise PC win in the June federal election, PC campus clubs easily formed the student parliament. Having succeeded Paul Creaghan as leader of StFX's PC youth party, I was chosen to serve as Prime Minister. Daniel Hurley (a Liberal) was Leader of the Opposition, and Leo Nimsick, son of a CCF member of Parliament in British Columbia, led that party.

Allister Grosart, the Toronto ad executive who had managed Diefenbaker's successful leadership campaign, paid close attention to student and youth politics across Canada, and I had come to know and admire him greatly. Allister was a student of Shakespeare, and an extremely well-read and articulate national director. He encouraged me to communicate with him and, sometimes, directly with Prime Minister Diefenbaker.

Both the PM and Allister supported our student parliament; they helped the secretariat with some funding and dispatched Gordon Churchill, minister of trade and commerce, to be a senior minister in the student government. The Liberals responded by sending the illustrious Paul Martin Sr. to assist his party, and the CCF dispatched their brilliant new star, Douglas Fisher, who in June had defeated the legendary C.D. Howe in the riding of Port Arthur, in Northern Ontario.

The student parliament took place in the middle of the federal campaign and attracted enormous public attention, almost all favourable, which pleased me and the other student participants. There were vigorous and entertaining speeches from all sides, but the highlight came when the eloquent Paul Martin made a flattering remark about "Churchill." I immediately sprang to my feet and thanked Martin for his "kind and appropriate reference" to my Minister of Industry, whereupon Martin elegantly responded, "But no, no, Prime Minister – I meant the *other* great Churchill!" leaving the House in stitches and me with my head down, pretending to be hard at work on my papers.

After this momentary setback, I came back with a temerity that shocks me to this day. I stood and faced Paul Martin Sr. and told him that he and his party would be wiped out by Diefenbaker and my party come the March 31 election. I asked Martin – who had, of course, played a key role in the design and development of many of the social programs that Canadians hold dear to this day – whether unemployment insurance would cover him and all the Liberal ministers who would be permanently out of work once Canada had a Tory majority government.

Never one to be outquipped, Martin told the crowd that if I were a real prime minister, I would soon find out. He added that if Prime Minister Mulroney were on television, he'd turn me off!

I waited for the crowd to settle and then, as Prime Minister, got the final word: "We're going to turn *you* off," I said to shouts of approval from the Antigonish crowd. "We're going to shut you fellows down for good."

And so we did: at both our model parliament and at the ensuing 1958 general election.

In the course of his visit, Paul Martin Sr. also spoke to me privately, wondering aloud what "a good Catholic boy" was doing with the Tories. Years later Senator Lowell Murray ran into Prime Minister Paul Martin at an airport and the two joked about the question the prime minister's father had left with a StFX student in the 1950s. "The question still stands," the Prime Minister told Lowell with a grin.

After the great Diefenbaker sweep on March 31, 1958, I intensified my commitment to the PCSF, rising to the national post of executive vice-president. At one annual PC convention, which took place at the Eastview Motel in Ottawa in 1959–60, I gave the Chief a rousing introduction that had the delegates laughing, chanting, and calling for him to speak. My mom later wrote to me about a letter Dad had received from Prime Minister Diefenbaker, which read: "Having heard your son, Brian, address the annual banquet of the Progressive Conservative Student Federation on Saturday night I feel that you will consider it appropriate on my part to tell you of the outstanding speech he delivered. If you had heard him you would have been justifiably proud." We found that letter in my father's wallet, still neatly folded, the day he died.

My mother wrote, "First I must tell you the big news. On Saturday Dad got a personal letter from John Diefenbaker congratulating him on the speech you gave at the PC banquet. Honestly, you should have seen Dad, he didn't know what to do with himself and he was dying to show it to someone so away he went to CBA to Gillis and of course they were all excited. Then he got home, read it over again, and sent it over to Percy Neil, then over to Nick. Yesterday he took it to the mill and showed it to everyone that came his way and then he went out of his way to show it to the rest. He got a great kick out of that and today we went to get the mail and we looked up Mr. Corbière and Dad told him and he said, 'You know it was nice of him to take the time to write to me, he is a busy man.'"

Mom, Irish to the core, then went on to more important things. St. Patrick's Day, after all, was approaching fast. "Now before I forget, I want you to go to a music store," she requested. "I think there is a big one there because I bought records from there some years ago but can't remember the name. Ask them for the record by Bridie Gallagher. One of the songs she sings on the particular record is Molly Brown and Dad wants it . . . I would like to get it for March 17." She got it.

Along with a heavy academic workload I was extremely active on the debating team, partnering over time with Rick Cashin, Charlie Keating (who subsequently became a cable TV magnate in the Halifax area), and Ace McCann (later mayor of Pembroke, Ontario) against other Canadian universities. During those years our team was undefeated, and many participants went on to successful careers in law, politics, and business.

I was also working hard on a thesis for my honours degree. I chose "The Politics of Quebec, 1935 to 1958" as my theme, realizing only later the paucity of writing on the subject – this was pre-Quiet Revolution – available at the StFX and other Maritime university libraries.

In November of 1958 I attended – along with a young Jim Coutts from the University of Alberta, Brian Smith of UBC, Judith Bell of Dalhousie, Stephen Clarkson of the U of T, and Mort Zuckerman of McGill, to name just a few – the McGill Council on World Affairs. The brilliant scholar Mason Wade of the University of Rochester, author of the seminal book *The French Canadians*, gave a wonderful presentation. I buttonholed him afterwards to ask whom I should contact for information that might be helpful to my research. Professor Wade was more than helpful, and I soon fired off letters to everyone he had suggested. One was a professor from the Université de Montréal who soon replied in his own hand:

> Congratulations on the subject you chose for your thesis as a political science student. It is a difficult one, since there has not been much research in that or any period of Quebec politics. Here are a few suggestions you may find useful. Background: The best source, of course, is the Quebec newspapers. But as a good shortcut I would recommend: Mason Wade, *The French Canadians 1760–1945*, Robert Rumilly, *Historie de la Province de Québec*. Also, Professor Michael Oliver of McGill University has done a Ph.D. thesis on the social thinking of French Canadians during the period you wish to cover . . . P.E. Trudeau, ed., *The Asbestos Strike* (Montreal 1956). See my introductory chapter on the development of Quebec during the first half of the century. As to more specific material, I would refer you to certain issues of *Cité libre* which deal with politics, especially issue no. 6. Finally, you might find it useful to look at a recent issue of the *Toronto Quarterly* which had an article on Quebec politics, as well as an official issue, last year, of the *McGill Daily* (March 10, 1958). There was also an article of

> mine in last August's issue of the *Canadian Journal of Economics and Political Science* entitled "Some obstacles to democracy in Quebec." I hope these suggestions will be useful to you. And I would be very interested in reading your thesis when it is done. Best of luck to you.

The letter was signed "Pierre Elliott Trudeau."

Others on my list included Blair Fraser of *Maclean's*; Arthur Blakeley and Wilbur Atkinson of the *Gazette*; Premier Maurice Duplessis; the editor in chief of the Montreal *Daily Star*; Grattan O'Leary of the *Ottawa Journal*; Bruce Hutchison; Allister Grosart; J.J. Connolly, national director of the Liberal Party; and the deans of political science at Laval, Montréal, and McGill. I sent them all an identical letter:

> I am entering my final year as a Political Science student at Saint Francis Xavier University in Antigonish, Nova Scotia. One of the requisites for a degree is that I compile a thesis on a topic of my choice, providing it is within the realm of my major subject. As a native of Baie-Comeau, and one with more than a passing interest in politics, I have selected for my thesis title: Quebec Politics: 1933–1958. I realize that a sizable amount of reading will have to be done on the topic to ensure that the thesis is worthwhile. Thus far, my reading has been concentrated along historical lines so that I might have a general understanding of past and contemporary Quebec political problems. As my finances are very limited, I would appreciate greatly your affording me with any books, speeches, or other information that you feel would be helpful in the writing of the paper.

Even Duplessis, whom I had criticized repeatedly during my debating speeches on campus, responded, mailing to me his government's submissions to various Dominion-Provincial conferences.

While I had obviously been influenced by the fact that I grew up in a largely French-speaking milieu in Baie-Comeau, researching "The Politics of Quebec" gave me an intellectual grounding in the approach to Canadian federalism I was to take with me to the Prime Minister's Office in Ottawa. Looking back at my thesis today, I see that the seeds of the Meech Lake Accord are evident: "It is not generally understood among English

Canadians that Confederation is not, in the minds of French Canadians, simply a federal union of the British North American provinces, in which the will of the majority should prevail. To the French, it is a pact or treaty between French and English, which guarantees each group an equal right to its own faith, language, laws, and customs. Sir John A. Macdonald did not regard the BNA Act as any panacea – he was much too astute for that. Rather, he saw it as a treaty through which minority rights of both English and French would be assured. The French Canadian's insistence upon 'autonomy' and his violent opposition to the centralization of power in Ottawa then, is not just a weak and flimsy cry. It is based on the clearly enunciated interpretation of Macdonald."

I delved into the history of the French Canadians after the Conquest and spent hour upon hour reading, writing, and contemplating their situation. Sadly, some of the stereotyping I discovered in my research persists today: "The cultured propaganda of tourist bureaus, and the Quebec myth as pontificated by some French-Canadian spokesmen, do not give an accurate picture of the province. It is not a quaint, rural area of softly winding hills and smiling *paysans*, whose faces dotted the pages of *Maria Chapdelaine*. And it is not an enigmatic land, unapproachable to Anglophiles and known only to the Tremblays, the Arsenaults, the Thériaults, and the Comeaus – good, solid, French-Canadian Catholics. It is a strange month indeed when Quebec is not visited by an outlander, equipped, as Leslie Roberts says, 'with a portable typewriter and the grim determination never to understand French-speaking Canada.'"

Then, as today, however, I have never given up believing that a united Canada – with a vibrant and distinct Quebec at its heart – is in the best interests of all who inhabit this land. "The myth has been current since long before Confederation that no English-speaking person is supposed to comprehend what people of Norman origin have on their minds. This premise is utterly ridiculous. Quebec and its inhabitants, as we shall see, are quite different from the rest of Canada. But not irreconcilably so."

That is what I wrote in my thesis in 1959. I wouldn't change a word today.

Canada, Quebec, and federalism aside, my research allowed me to delve into the secrets of successful political leadership as illustrated by the lives of two influential Canadians who were both Quebecers: Sir Wilfrid Laurier and Maurice Duplessis. I read everything I could on both men.

Laurier was Canada's most eloquent and elegant prime minister, and the first French Canadian to head the government in Ottawa. The Laurier years were filled with triumph and tragedy (as I was to see first-hand when dealing with the Manitoba Language Question as leader of the opposition in 1983–84) for both French and English Canadians. "Laurier was a magnetic leader," I wrote as a student. "Endowed with striking personal appearance, he became a master of oratory and was equally eloquent in the French and English language. He was a skilled parliamentarian and a genial leader whose gentleness at times belied his strength of purpose. Most important of all was the fact that he was a worker whose main goal was the consolidation of Canada."

My research also led me closer to the very complex man that was Duplessis. As has been said of Lyndon Johnson, Maurice Duplessis of Trois-Rivières was indeed a man "reeking of human juices." While I opposed him politically – my father was a union man, after all – I was fascinated by Duplessis as I sat in my dorm at StFX and read everything I could about him, recalling that my mother had taken me to hear him speak near Baie-Comeau when I was a little boy. In my thesis, I wrote:

> Contrary to general opinion, Duplessis was not born with a silver spoon in his mouth, although it is said that his glibness of tongue and terse, witty comments – sparkling attributes for an aspiring politician – were widely recognized characteristics at an early age. [I little knew that similar things would be written about me someday.] He came from the small-town petit bourgeoisie, the son of a French-Canadian father and a Scots-Irish mother. He led a fairly circumscribed childhood, and, acquiescing to the call of the day, either to *le séminaire* or *le barreau*, Duplessis entered the law faculty of Laval, from which university he took an undistinguished degree in 1922. After this he was set in the groove from which he has never veered . . . M. Duplessis is a colourful personality. He does not play the part of a grand seigneur like his predecessor, Alexandre Taschereau. He was able, at the outset of his victories, to fashion for himself an unaffected language and a personality which not only tolerated but invited a certain affectionate familiarity: "Maurice," people call him. . . . In 1960, it will be a septuagenarian Duplessis who will face the electorate. But it will be a Duplessis nonetheless realistic and compelling. His speeches may

> be shorter than those he delivered over a quarter-century ago; but his phrases will still be cutting, his mind will still be alert; his eye just as quick; and his voice just as convincing. According to him, "Quebec is on the march. It has a rendezvous with destiny."

Never, I should have added, does it bode well for a politician to underestimate his or her opponent. The career of Maurice Duplessis is littered with now forgotten opponents who did just that. I resolved never to make the same mistake – although I later did, to my regret.

During my senior year I shared a room in MacNeil House with Sam Wakim. I had known Sam, a Lebanese kid from east Saint John, over the early years at university, but as roommates we became close friends, and we have retained that relationship to this day. Sam is tough, loyal, brusque, and honest – and the best street-smart politician in Canada. He married a StFX girl from Saint John, Martin, had six impressive children, and became counsel to the Ontario Securities Commission, a member of Parliament, and a successful attorney. He played a crucial role in all of my campaigns, and I remain deeply grateful for his unswerving friendship.

—

PERSONAL JOURNAL: SEPTEMBER 3, 1989

Just had a chat with Sam Wakim. Few people played a more important role in our victory in 1983 than Sam. He single-handedly put together the Ontario organization when nobody else would, and he has received very little in return. Sam is simply a decent, loyal, and devoted friend of mine who played a major role in my success in winning and retaining the prime ministership.

—

Back in 1959, however, Sam and I focused on eating the superb Lebanese food his mother and eight sisters regularly sent, going out to see movies (there was no TV in our room), and drinking beer while discussing our futures well into the night.

When graduation finally came in May 1959, it was a glorious event for both our families. I was the first Mulroney ever to graduate from university, and my parents, making their first-ever visit to a campus, were beyond elation. The same sentiments were held by the Wakim clan, and a memorable and delightful weekend unfolded as we said goodbye to StFX. I will never forget the look of sheer joy on my parents' faces, as they drank in every second of the colourful ceremonies. I always thought they – not I – should have been honoured that day, and years later I made it my business to establish scholarships in their names at StFX, St. Thomas, and Concordia. Without their love, encouragement, and support, I would recently have acquired pensioner status at the Quebec North Shore Paper Company at Baie-Comeau, Quebec, after a lengthy and no doubt productive career in the mill.

I am happy to report that the rest of the Mulroney family went on to lead productive lives. About the time of my graduation, Olive, my eldest sibling, got married. She had gone to secretarial school in Montreal and returned to work for a mill executive, helping out the family with an added salary, until she married Dick Elliott from Saskatchewan. Dick had come to Baie-Comeau as a young civil engineer on a major construction project and as a star player, he quickly dominated the local hockey league. They have had an extremely successful marriage for almost fifty years, with four children and twelve grandchildren. Olive and Dick have lived and worked on projects from the Caribbean to Iran, South Africa, and northern Canada. Olive and I have been very close all our lives, and Olive and Dick's generosity over many years did much to help the family financially and every other way.

Olive has claims to be the family orator. In the 1949 public-speaking contest sponsored by the Rotary Club and La Chambre de Commerce, Olive placed first with a rousing speech entitled "Welcome, Newfoundland!" in honour of Canada's newest province joining Confederation. Only recently we located Olive's speaking notes from that contest so long ago: "Ladies and gentlemen, let us join together to greet this new province, this land of rich prospects and high ideals with a hearty 'Welcome, Newfoundland!' trusting that she will be as proud to join us as we are to unite with her."

Forty years later, in the sad aftermath of the decision to cancel the vote on the Meech Lake Accord in the Newfoundland legislature, my heartbroken sister said, "I still believe all those nice things I said that day about Newfoundland – but I didn't know Clyde Wells!"

My sister Peggy was with the Sisters of the Holy Cross for years until she emerged and married Joe Fitzpatrick of New Jersey, with whom she had an extremely happy life, winding up with three lovely adopted children.

Doreen married a young doctor she met while studying nursing at St. Mary's hospital in Montreal. After two young sons were born, they divorced and she returned from Baltimore to Montreal where she took a master's degree and remained in the nursing profession.

Barbara married and moved to Toronto, where she was a highly specialized nurse at the Clarke Institute, which cares for patients with mental illnesses. But the marriage fell apart, and today Barbara divides her time between nursing assignments in Montreal and India.

Gary devoted himself to a successful teaching career, taking an extensive leave of absence in my first mandate to act as my constituency representative, a responsibility he fulfilled very effectively. He has now retired and lives in the Eastern Townships and in Florida.

As for me, I left StFX with a bachelor of arts degree, honours, in political science. My intention was to attend law school at Université Laval in Quebec City and return to Baie-Comeau to practise law. But I soon had second thoughts when I learned that I was in the running for an entrance scholarship to Dalhousie University Law School in Halifax.

Dalhousie is a great university, and upon reflection I decided that I wanted to try it. I had already spent six years studying in the Maritimes and thought that – as a "Maritimer by the baptism of desire" – this might be the right thing to do. Classmates from StFX were enrolling at Dalhousie and encouraged me to follow them. Moreover, a lovely StFX girl I had been seeing had enrolled at Mount St. Vincent University, also in Halifax. So all told, it seemed like a pretty compelling case. Dalhousie it was.

I arrived in Halifax and found a room at the Walter Leach family residence on South Street, close to the campus, on September 7, 1959 – the day Premier Maurice Duplessis died in Schefferville, Quebec, at the guesthouse of the Iron Ore Company of Canada. I was to get to know that historic house well, after I became president of that company some nineteen years later.

The Leach residence soon filled with people I knew – among them, Bill Kelly and Joe Khattar – and I at once found myself enjoying campus life. I secured a part-time job working in the law school library and made new friendships with locals like Ted Wickwire, Brian Flemming (who became my debating partner), David Matheson, and Stewart McInnes, scion of a prominent Halifax family who would later join my government as minister of public works. Stewart also joined a very exclusive club in Canada by twice declining an appointment to the Senate (in order to return to Halifax with his wife Shirley and their very young children). Normally a prime minister is lobbied nearly to death by Senate aspirants; after an appointment is made, he usually succeeds in creating, as Sir John A. remarked, "ten enemies and one ingrate."

Like every prime minister since Sir John A., I was to learn that the prospect of a vacancy in the Red Chamber brings out interesting attitudes in some people. In December of 1989 my appointments director, Marjory LeBreton, received a note from Pat Carney, a former minister in my government who had not run for re-election in the 1988 campaign. "I just read in the *Globe* on board the bus that B.C. Senator Mary Bell has died," Pat wrote. "For the record, of course I would be interested in taking her place, in case anyone asks you!"

Until that letter arrived in the Prime Minister's Office, I had never truly believed the story of Macdonald being lobbied for a Senate seat – at the funeral of a senator! "Sir John, I would like to take that man's place," the applicant whispered to Canada's first prime minister, motioning toward the coffin.

"I'm afraid it's too late," Sir John A. replied. "The coffin lid is nailed shut!"

The Senate, of course, was far from my mind while I was at Dalhousie. I had more immediate decisions to make after spending Christmas with friends and family in Baie-Comeau in 1960. I realized over the holidays that my future lay back at home in Quebec, but that with a common law degree from Dalhousie – as opposed to the degree in civil law required in Quebec – I could never be admitted to practice there. So I resolved to complete the year at Dalhousie as best I could and then head to Laval. It was far from my most successful academic year, but I made it to Quebec City and Laval in September 1960.

I spent a significant part of the preceding summer in Halifax working with Dalton Camp, Norm Atkins, and Finlay MacDonald on the Stanfield re-election campaign. I was chosen to do all the radio commercials out of CJCH, Finlay's radio station, becoming locally known as "the voice" of the PC Party, and learning something about the techniques for speaking effectively on radio.

Finlay was an attractive Haligonian who had secured a broadcasting licence during the time of the Diefenbaker government. Trim and dashing, he was a well-known man about town in Halifax, and a close friend of Premier Robert Stanfield. As a fellow StFX graduate, I had taken a liking to him some time earlier and we developed a good friendship in the course of the campaign.

Dalton Camp was a novel presence in Canadian politics, with skills that were both poetic and mercantile. A native of New Brunswick, with degrees from UNB, Columbia, and the London School of Economics, he ran a Toronto-based advertising agency and possessed strong talents for political analysis and elegant writing. He was reflective, thoughtful, and entertaining; he enjoyed both good liquor and good humour, which were in ready abundance in Canada's political salons during the Sixties.

Dalton's strategic skills were impressive. After he had been involved in a few Conservative victories, his reputation grew in provincial circles. When a provincial election was called, he would move into, say, Manitoba, Nova Scotia, or New Brunswick, ensconce himself in the largest suite in the best hotel in the capital city, and turn out excellent advertising copy and speech modules for the party and its leadership. After a victorious campaign, Dalton K. Camp and Associates would lay claim to the government advertising account, and the caravan would move on. Dalton and his brother-in-law Norm Atkins, made a great deal of money in this way, hitting the jackpot when I won federally; and the Government of Canada gave them the advertising contract that enabled them, some time later, to sell the company at a handsome multiple.

In addition to my radio commercials assignment, I also cheerfully took on many others handed out by Dalton and Finlay, as my modest contribution to the victorious Stanfield campaign. I'm still proud of some of the speeches I wrote in order to assist PC candidates in the province that year.

> You may have noticed that the Liberals don't even whisper about highways these days [I wrote for a candidate to use at his nomination meeting] and, believe me, Mr. Chairman, there's good reason not to! From 1957–1960, the PC government's Highways Department, under our tremendously capable guest speaker, G.I. Smith, made more progress than any other government in the history of Nova Scotia. In three years, the Conservatives paved 1,126.4 miles of highway compared with 636.7 miles in 1953–56 under the Grits . . . and they [the Stanfield government] built 232 bridges in three years when the Liberals under Mr. Hicks in a like period of time, could only build 127 bridges with over a 10-foot span. Ladies and gentlemen, you know Bob Stanfield and you know his record. [And

so on, ending with a flourish, a call to vote for] a man who has proved himself worthy of our trust – Premier Robert L. Stanfield!

Stanfield and his team also allowed me to play a small role in helping him reach out to Nova Scotia's tiny – but important – French-speaking community. I was called in to prepare some of his remarks in French. "We are always in need of your encouragement and we have worked for three and a half years to merit this encouragement," I wrote for the premier, including some relevant briefing material. "I would hope that you will express your support of the government on June 7 by saying, 'Il a gagné ses épaulettes' ["he has earned his stripes" – a French-Canadian expression said of someone who has accomplished something worthwhile and is deserving of continued support] and by voting for Progressive Conservative candidates."

Some twenty-five years later I elevated Finlay MacDonald to the Senate following a personal request from Stanfield (the only one he made of me during my premiership); Norm Atkins, by now my campaign chairman, to the Senate following a campaign he initiated (some say the best he ever ran); and Dalton Camp to the position of senior advisor to the prime minister, to purge him of the stain of "disloyalty" unfairly placed on him by Diefenbaker diehards following the 1965–66 crusade for the concept of leadership review in the PC Party. All in all, not bad for four men who, as much younger political activists, hung around Camp's suite in the Lord Nelson Hotel in Halifax in the summer of 1960, drinking whisky late into the night and dreaming of days when all of us, we were sure, would be called upon to play important roles in government.

—

PERSONAL JOURNAL: MAY 20, 1993

(Written en route to the airport after visiting Dalton Camp at the Ottawa Heart Institute, following his heart transplant)

As soon as I said hello and shook his hand, he said, "I owe you a tremendous apology. I knew I was sick when I took the job but pride kept me from telling you or anyone else. I never performed up to par – I couldn't even finish a draft or walk a flight of stairs without gasping for breath. Something was terribly wrong with me and I never delivered for you. I have always wanted to apologize for letting you down. You were always kind and thoughtful to me and my family and my response was always inadequate. You have achieved some marvellous things with your life and as PM.

"The morning after I entered the hospital, Premier McKenna called to wish me well and as I thanked him, he simply said, 'Dalton, it's my "Brian Mulroney" call.' Your legacy of friendship and civility will always be remembered by those of us who benefited from it."

I told Dalton he would outlast us all now with a nineteen-year-old heart. He said, "Provided I do what you've done and treat it with care." He looked relaxed and free from the brooding instincts that had come to dominate his personality in later years – induced, as we now know, by the defective heart that, according to Dr. Wilbert Keon, would not have lasted any more than a few days.

PART II

A Life in Quebec

1960–1975

1. Université Laval

Every person enjoys a period in his life that he later thinks of as "the golden years." The period from 1960–64, while I was studying law at Laval, was mine.

The timing was perfect. The Quiet Revolution was just beginning, initiated by Jean Lesage's stunning victory three months earlier. Quebec City was awash in the excitement of historic change as the government brought changes to every facet of life – education, health care, pensions, hydro development, and international affairs – under the arresting and dramatic slogan "Maîtres Chez Nous."

—

personal journal: September 1987

(Written after the Francophonie Summit in Quebec City)

When I lived at 71 rue St-Louis, the role of Quebec and Canada – and the possible role of Quebec in an emerging and highly sympathetic Francophonie – was much debated by my fellow students. The Laval Congress on Canadian Affairs dealt with these same questions. It was therefore with some emotion that I returned to Quebec City some 27 years later, as prime minister of Canada, having reached a constitutional agreement with Quebec and having devised a formula that allowed Quebec to play an appropriate role in the Sommet de la Francophonie. The years of bitterness and recrimination were over as Lucien Bouchard, Bernard Roy, and I walked to the Garrison Club for a luncheon meeting with Bourassa. We were within 1000 feet of 71 rue St-Louis. I could see my old boarding house from the corner. All the memories rushed back. Jean Lesage – so kind to me in the summer of 1963. Daniel Johnson saying, "Meet me at the Château for a Scotch"

> *– while he was in opposition; the violence associated with the Queen's visit; the referendum, the discussion, the bitterness; the 1983 leadership which began for me with a meeting in the Garrison Club; the 1984 election, the Meech Lake Accord, and now the Sommet de la Francophonie with 41 heads of government attending. Later that day at the official ceremonies I saw how deeply effective our policy of reconciliation had been. When at Laval, Clément Richard and Pierre de Bané had become close friends – I think they became law partners as well. De Bané entered federal politics and became a Liberal cabinet minister and later, a senator. Richard became a PQ cabinet minister and their friendship foundered, as I recall, quite acrimoniously, during the referendum debate and its aftermath. Friends had become enemies. I had always liked them both and had continued to enjoy their company over all these 27 years since law school. As Mila and I were saying goodbye to the Francophonie leaders following the official welcoming ceremonies, and just before we left the cordoned-off area, I looked across the square at two men who were waving at me and enthusiastically cheering on the official participants. I looked back and signalled my personal regards. It was Pierre de Bané and Clément Richard together. Enemies had become friends again.*

Université Laval had moved to a vast modern campus in Ste-Foy, but the law school was where it had always been, deep in the heart of the Quartier Latin, within easy walking distance of the Palais de Justice and the Assemblée Nationale. On most days, because of the way our courses were structured, we could attend lectures, walk over to observe the latest explosive trial or royal commission at the Palais, then head up to the Assemblée for question period or a major debate, with lots of time left to congregate for beer and pizza at La Page Blanche or La Chapelle in the Clarendon Hotel, where often we debated developments well into the night. I was young, healthy, and had grown and filled out – in good shape to withstand the rigours of our exciting student lifestyle. They were wonderful days.

The Salvas Royal Commission investigating corruption under the previous provincial government was a big draw for our group, as was the Brossard Commission set up to inquire into the circumstances of the arrest, prosecution, and hanging of Wilbert Coffin from the Gaspé for the murders of three visiting Americans. Jacques Hébert, the Montreal writer and publisher, had written a polemic entitled "J'accuse les assassins de Coffin" and was called upon to defend himself before the commission. His close friend and advocate Pierre Elliott Trudeau appeared sporadically before the inquiry, and it was in the corridors of the Palais de Justice that I first made his acquaintance. Although well known as a law professor, Trudeau had little courtroom experience and did not appear to know much of court procedures, which resulted in not infrequent remonstrations and stern rebukes from the commissioner. As the hearings continued, the atmosphere was electric, and we felt that we were at the nerve centre of the greatest show to hit Canadian politics in decades.

Our professors were exceptional, and to accommodate those who were practising lawyers, classes were held between eight and ten in the morning and four to six in the afternoon. They included three who went on to serve as justices of the Supreme Court of Canada – Louis-Philippe Pigeon, Julien Chouinard, and Yves Pratte. Although I was not yet eligible to enrol in the senior course he taught, I did from time to time encounter former prime minister Louis St. Laurent, a great and good man, in the law school corridors, and I sometimes engaged him in brief chats. (In fact, over my career to date, I have known, and talked with, no fewer than ten Canadian prime ministers.)

It is an indication of the talent of these remarkable professors that, while teaching constitutional law, Louis-Philippe Pigeon served as chief legal advisor to Premier Jean Lesage, whose government was then engaged in major constitutional initiatives. It was exciting to listen to Pigeon in the morning and then watch Lesage respond during the afternoon question period in the Assemblée as to how he planned, for example, to negotiate a new opting-out arrangement on old age pensions with the Pearson government, thereby bringing that vital program under the responsibility of the newly created Caisse de dépôt et placement. Watching the translation of complex constitutional law themes into practical benefits for citizens was a fascinating advantage for young and impressionable law students. Not surprisingly, it was during this period that I developed a keen interest in constitutional law. I followed and studied developments in this area very carefully for two decades before entering politics in 1983.

Jean Lesage was a brilliant leader. I believe his government was probably the most effective in modern Quebec history. Because of my friendly relationship with his son, Jules, a fellow law student, and his daughter, Marie, I met the premier, Mme Corinne Lesage, and their family quite often, including at several dinners at their summer residence at Lac-Beauport. In private,

Lesage was very different from the imperious leader described in the media. He was gracious and considerate, completely devoted to his family and his job. When my dad died, Premier Lesage stopped by the funeral home to pay his respects. After he left politics, he and I served on the same corporate board and enjoyed long dinners together in Paris with Corinne and Mila while in France for meetings. As a tribute to his memory, I called Mme Lesage in 1993 to advise her of my government's decision to rename the Quebec City International Airport in honour of Jean Lesage. She was deeply moved by the gesture, and our conversation that day brought back fond memories of their many earlier kindnesses to me.

During those glorious Laval years I also knew Daniel Johnson, both as Opposition leader and as premier. He was unquestionably the warmest and most charming public figure I have known. From about 1961, when he became Union Nationale leader, to 1966 when he stunned Canada by defeating the Lesage government and becoming premier, he was vilified constantly in the Quebec media, famously depicted by cartoonists as "Danny Boy," an unethical Tammany Hall-type political boss. He endured this abuse and much more with quiet good humour and unfailing resolve, determined to win election as premier, a wildly improbable scenario to any observer in the early 1960s. But his persistence paid off and he engineered a huge upset in 1966, sneaking by an astonished Lesage to form a majority government. He was a happy warrior and once explained to me his complete lack of vindictiveness or malice, in spite of years of unremitting personal denigration, by saying, "Ah! Brian, if you're going to be successful in political life, you must learn how to turn the page. There's no future in politics looking backward."

Daniel Johnson died suddenly while visiting a Hydro-Québec generating station, Manic 5, after only two years in office. He was greatly loved at the time of his death, a tribute to the enormously positive impact he had upon people, once the caricature was removed and the real person understood. He was a fine man, and I missed him a lot. When I won the federal election in 1984 I was presented with the set of pens his friends had given Johnson on his election, which Mme Johnson had returned to them on his death. They adorned my desk in the study at 24 Sussex until his son Pierre Marc became premier of Quebec, when I had the set reinscribed and delivered to him, as I am sure his father would have wished. Some years later, Pierre Marc's brother, Daniel, Jr., also became premier of Quebec, a family accomplishment without precedent in Canadian history. The three men all led different parties but had in common a warmth and civility unmatched in public life.

My Laval classmates made up an unusually talented and ambitious group. There was no separatist movement at the time, the Liberals were in power provincially, the Tories federally, and the mix of events and challenges was explosive. Our class was not noted for its reticence or modesty. Its members led parties on campus, edited the paper, led debates on the great issues, and participated in demonstrations.

In 1964 I definitely landed myself in the soup after I, with little prompting, agreed to serve as the spokesperson for Laval students in one such demonstration. In our wisdom we had decided to protest the decision to invite Queen Elizabeth to Quebec City that year. My quoted remarks landed, with a thud, in newspapers across Canada. Here is how the Canadian Press covered our protest:

> "We know that this protest will lead nowhere but it is a symbolic gesture that we found necessary under the circumstances," Brian Mulroney, . . . president of the law students at the French-language university said in an interview Thursday. The big complaint, he said, is money. Many students were broke while some $1 million was expected to be spent on the visit of the Queen and Prince Philip to Charlottetown and Quebec City. Mr. Mulroney, who proposed the protest resolution at a student meeting earlier this week, said that while students are in need, considerable sums are to be spent to assure "all possible comfort for Her Majesty." The money, he said, could be put to more useful purposes, such as 2,000 scholarships. Of the 6,000 students at Laval, there were at least 3,500 who were not getting any bursary or scholarship at the present time.

When the newspapers were published the next day, I was secretly pleased to see my name and comments featured so prominently. I had a bit of an extra bounce to my step as I walked through the old city that day.

Then came the reaction. "There seem to be too many bumptious, asinine people enrolled in universities," one angry monarchist from Toronto wrote to me at Laval. "Being an undergraduate seems to send a lot of them off the deep end. And we pay to keep up universities! Go and work your way through university the way I and countless others have done. Too many of your traitorous friends want all for nothing. People like you make universities 'stink.'"

"I noticed your remarks concerning the visit of Her Majesty the Queen to this country next fall," said another. "I think you ought to be ashamed of yourself for making such remarks. I would judge that you are a young, learned individual; you have a long way to go to improve yourself."

Then came the kicker. "Many of us earn our way through university. Why the hell can't you? Of all the childish exhibitions, your publicity stunt takes the cake. Grow up!"

I was not in fact anti-royalist, and I later came to greatly admire and enjoy Her Majesty and to appreciate her marvellous contributions to the Commonwealth and country. This episode quickly taught me the cost of any perceived disrespect to the sovereign. It was never to happen again.

More than twenty years later, I was honoured to host Her Majesty the Queen at a dinner at the Château Frontenac in Quebec City. It was the first time she had been there since her 1964 visit, and this trip had been tremendously successful. As I sat next to the Queen at dinner, I was proud to inform her that my father, an electrician, had wired the very room we were sitting in, decades earlier. Her Majesty was politely impressed.

I did not get around to mentioning my inhospitable actions of 1964 to the Queen, and she never brought them up. Perhaps she wasn't aware of the role her future Canadian first minister had played. Perhaps not. But as anyone who has advised her knows full well, Her Majesty is always well briefed. Very well briefed.

Debates and demonstrations took up only part of our time as law students. We saved a proper amount of time and energy to enjoy the beauty of Quebec City and its inhabitants, with Laval at its heart. Laval is now 350 years old – the second oldest university in North America after Harvard – and the class I was privileged to join is widely regarded as one of its most accomplished. There were sixty-five students in my class, which over time produced four senators, eight judges, five cabinet ministers, one ambassador, one premier, two chiefs of staff to the prime minister, and one prime minister of Canada.

The class was also unique for another reason. Over the decades an occasional English-speaking student, either ahead of his time or simply wishing to learn French, enrolled there. Prime Minister Arthur Meighen's son, Ted, graduated from Laval in 1929, with a silver medal, before beginning a successful career at the Bar in Montreal. But 1960 was the year of the anglophone "great invasion." Perhaps because of the huge changes taking place all over Quebec, a fairly large number of McGill graduates and a sprinkling of other English speakers enrolled at Laval that year. Some, like Peter White and Michael Meighen (Arthur's grandson), were already fluent in French, others much less so. Having been in the Maritimes for several years, I was somewhere in between. I had a lot of work to do.

We were a diverse and cosmopolitan group who enjoyed each other's company, helped each other with studies, and played together in the *boîtes à chansons* at night. It may seem hard to believe of such an active, energetic group, but I have no recollection of an untoward incident or major disagreement of any kind involving any of our classmates.

We all lived in rooming houses within the walled city. I lived at 71 rue St-Louis, with René Gagnon, Gilles Lever, André Tremblay, and Ghyslain Levasseur. The residence was owned and managed by Mlle Anne-Marie Fortin, who loved us all but despaired for the salvation of our souls.

Peter White, who became a very close friend, lived in a small motel room at 51½ rue St-Louis, a stone's throw away, and regularly astonished us all by beating the record for cutting the most classes while concurrently leading the Dean's List. Peter was widely acknowledged to be the smartest student in class, closely followed by Michel Cogger and Yvon Marcoux. Peter was also famous for his dramatic entrances. Having missed classes for a week or so – he owned a newspaper in the Eastern Townships and had to put it out himself until he hired a younger student named Conrad Black to do it for him – Peter would enter the class late, carrying a coffee and an egg salad sandwich, sit down in the front row and, after a quick bite and sip of the coffee, begin to loudly interrogate the startled professor regarding a divergence of opinion that Peter would shamelessly articulate. We all admired his nerve, and I noticed that quite a few of his colleagues liked to sit very close to Peter during written exams.

Not that there was ever any cheating. We were a pretty ethical group, if only because the *appariteur*, Robert Godbout, best known for selling homemade sandwiches to students (the favourite was called 'un OPO' – oeufs, pas d'onions), had intercepted a radio transmission the previous year from the toilet to the classroom, thereby solving the mystery of how the class dunce had continued to score highest on final exams throughout the year. The scene of Godbout forcibly hauling the point man, who had been comfortably ensconced in the toilet, out of the john, pants down to his ankles, walkie-talkie in hand, into the *salle des pas perdus* – where everyone saw his humiliation and shame – is engraved in the memories of all who witnessed it. It was a real "pensez-y bien" warning!

Struck by the tremendous enthusiasm sweeping the province for the reforms initiated by the Lesage government and the reaction elsewhere in Canada, Peter White decided that a national symposium on Canada's future was the tonic the country required. With typical industry and flair, Peter – assisted by Michel Cogger, Nicole Sénécal, and myself as vice-chairs – assembled a remarkable cast in the fall of 1961 to debate the issue "The Canadian Experiment: Success or Failure?" held under the patronage of Governor General Georges Vanier, the prime minister, and the ten provincial premiers. (When the Governor General's assent was slow in coming, inquiries to Michael Pitfield, his secretary, revealed that the hesitancy was due to a concern that the Governor General might be in an embarrassing situation if a "Congress on Canadian Affairs," as we named it, held under his patronage, decided that the Canadian experiment was indeed a failure!)

After solving Michael Pitfield's bureaucratic dodging, Peter and I briefed the prime minister on our little conference. I spoke to Mr. Diefenbaker on the phone about it one afternoon in October. I later followed up with a telegram, which may be worth repeating in detail, in light of later events in Quebec and Canada as a whole. I must concede that it is not the sort of letter a prime minister expects to receive from a young law student:

> With regard to our telephone conversation of yesterday afternoon I respectfully send you the following information: The first Congress on Canadian Affairs will be held at Laval University in Quebec City from November 15 to 18 . . . We have selected this theme (the Canadian Experiment: Success or Failure?) because we feel that as Canada approaches her centenary it is well that the abiding fundamentals of Canadian unity be re-examined and re-emphasized in the face of serious attacks from the separatist movements. It is authoritatively estimated that the three separatist movements now comprise 5,000 dues-paying members. Their sympathizers total many times this figure. Two recent books, *J'ai choisi l'indépendance* by Raymond Barbeau and *Why I Am a Separatist* by Marcel Chaput, are runaway bestsellers. A motion endorsing the principle

> of auto-determination was passed by the last Union Nationale convention. A more extreme version of the resolution was adopted last Sunday by the Quebec District of the Société St. Jean Baptiste at its annual meeting at which a Conservative MP openly espoused separatism. The widespread favourable reaction to these events is causing deep concern to nonseparatists.

I went on to speak personally:

> I feel that the above facts are indicative of a situation which could result in a real threat to Confederation. Quebec has had separatist movements before. They have appeared in the past especially during times of economic or political crisis. What makes this current resurgence so dangerous, however, is that in a period of relative prosperity the movement for an independent Quebec is succeeding in building a province-wide grassroots organization awaiting only the "opportune moment" to swing into political action. It is significant that separatism has also enjoyed a commensurate increase in respectability during this period. In this connection one of French Canada's leaders, André Laurendeau, yesterday wrote, "The religion of Confederation is no longer considered sacrosanct. If the leaders of the Canadian state are sensitive to events they will no doubt realize the importance of this."
>
> The current popularity of separatism is largely due to a new sense of freedom in the province and it is concomitant with the Lesage government's policies of grandeur and exaltation of the French-Canadian state. The basic cause of separatism is that nearly every French Canadian is made to feel a second-class citizen in his day-to-day dealings with business and government. French Canadians are also concerned with their language, their culture, and their religion, hence the vital importance to them of bilingualism among English as well as French Canadians; and complete provincial control of education and of provincial rights in general. The separatists, although they believe that French Canadians are probably the best-treated minority group in the world, wish to be a minority no longer. Indeed, the very fact of being a minority group makes this second-class citizenship inevitable, therefore they say

> the only solution is to form a separate self-governing state in which they will be the majority.

Finally, I proposed specific actions to Mr. Diefenbaker:

> It is unfortunately true that French Canadians often suffer discriminatory treatment in Canada. The basic fallacy of the whole separatist argument is the assumption that the only way to remedy this situation is by secession from Confederation. This is not so. On the contrary we strongly believe that there are several things the Canadian government could – and should – do to improve matters. Such measures would *ipso facto* serve to destroy much of the basics of the separatist cause. The surprise announcement of one of these measures in Quebec City next month would deal a heavy blow to the separatist cause. The measures which I would advocate are on a level less material than emotional, but the appeal of the separatist movement itself is largely emotional. These suggestions are not new, but recent events have shown that we can ill afford to neglect them much longer. They are as follows: 1) A declaration that bilingualism will be progressively established in all branches of the federal civil service and Crown corporations. 2) An announcement of the adoption of "O Canada" as our country's national anthem. 3) [A diplomat appointed to] the Vatican. A nominee of no less than ambassadorial status would be in the tradition of President Roosevelt and such a gesture would be extremely well received in Quebec. 4) Conditional grants to educational institutions specifically for the teaching of French. 5) A distinctive Canadian flag. I hope that these suggestions will not be considered presumptuous. I honestly feel that a statement from you on this topic would be of the utmost importance in the present situation.

As always, it seemed, when it came to French Canada, Mr. Diefenbaker took little action. He said nothing in reply. Lester Pearson and the Liberals would be the ones to advance bilingualism and to establish our own flag – although the Diefenbaker government did introduce simultaneous translation into Parliament, which had a major beneficial impact.

As luck would have it, during the few days of our congress, news elsewhere appeared to go completely flat, allowing the informative, entertaining, and sometimes explosive comments of the participants to dominate the headlines of Canadian newspapers.

Delegates were greeted with a lively edition of Laval's student newspaper, *Le Carabin*, that was filled with provocative essays designed to stir debate. Student journalist Lucien Bouchard did his part. "Many nights ago," he wrote, "well-meaning men dreamt of a Canadian nation. They prophesied with enthusiasm the blissful union of two national groups living in unity and aiming at common goals, in a land of milk and honey. One must admit that it was a beautiful dream. But, alas, the trouble with dreams is that they seldom come true . . . The only thing we know about the other group is that it represents a nation absolutely distinct from ours. History shows that no dialogue has ever been established between nations: We can't cheat history. So let's call a spade a spade. We form two nations. In these perspectives, the question is not 'Can we save the unity of the Canadian nation?' but 'Is it possible for our two nations to continue to live together?' We do not need any more dreams. Everybody longs for constitutional structures in which his nation is not doomed to extinction or Americanization. Perhaps the Confederation must be abrogated or modified for that. The answer belongs to the delegates."

Premier Lesage opened with a strong speech on "What does Quebec want?"; Justice Minister Davie Fulton spoke on the Fulton–Favreau formula; René Lévesque stirred the crowds with a powerful lament about Quebec's past and its future needs. Douglas Fisher responded with a brutal but entertaining remark about Quebec's culture being epitomized by Maurice Richard and Lili St. Cyr. With each passing session the headlines grew more dramatic as an excited press gallery saw a major story in each confrontation, attack, or promise.

I found myself accidentally at the centre of the most dramatic moment of the deliberations. Peter White had asked me to chair a panel on federalism that featured Dr. Marcel Chaput and McGill's Michael Oliver. Chaput, a research chemist with the federal government, had begun to attract media attention because of his involvement with the Rassemblement pour l'indépendance nationale, then an embryonic political movement dedicated to the promotion of Québec independence. A courtly, polite man of about forty, Chaput was keenly aware of the conflicted nature of his situation: a respected federal employee was actively promoting the separation of a province. His appearance at the congress caused all kinds of anticipation; the tiny independence movement saw in him an attractive and compelling spokesman for the cause, while the overwhelming majority of Canadians viewed him as a traitor.

His employer, the Ministry of National Defence, debated at length what to do, before denying him permission to attend. I lobbied Diefenbaker personally in a telegram asking that Chaput be allowed to present his views before us. I received the following reply from the prime minister: "Brian: Upon receipt of your telegram . . . regarding Dr. Chaput, it was brought immediately to the attention of the Minister directly concerned," he wrote. "The decision made was an administrative and departmental one. I would appreciate having a personal report on the Conference and the frank views of yourself and your colleagues."

In the end, they fired Chaput by a telegram that I read aloud to the huge crowd gathered for the panel discussion, thereby thrilling congress organizers and exciting the assembled media but, I suspect, greatly dismaying Dr. Chaput and his family.

Politics has its own special cruelties and ironies. René Lévesque attended the congress as a Liberal cabinet minister, and today highways, buildings, and schools in Quebec bear his name and mark his role as the first separatist premier. Marcel Chaput attended as a separatist and paid a huge personal price. Today he is largely unknown or forgotten by the people he daringly sought to lead. Six years later (in 1967) in the same city, Lévesque stormed out of the Quebec Liberal Party and formed the political vehicle that propelled the province to a separatist government a decade later. Chaput was nowhere to be seen; he played no significant role and received no honours from the separatist governments that gained power in Quebec during his lifetime. In politics, timing is indeed everything.

The conference helped to reveal the fragile state of French–English relations. I spoke about one experience I had in the aftermath with a Toronto journalist. "Mulroney," Robert McKenzie wrote, "also cites an example of the reaction to the Laval congress. 'I went into a store and the girl behind the counter, who was English speaking, had heard I was on the same platform as René Lévesque.' She asked me, 'Why didn't you speak up for your own?'"

Prime Minister Diefenbaker had told me both on the telephone and by letter that he wanted a full report on the conference. I did just that, making arguments I would soon grow weary of repeating as his government disintegrated. On December 3, 1961, I sent the Chief my very frank report, fearing that my career prospects as a young Conservative were by now in danger of being severely limited.

> You will have noted from the press reports that a salient feature of the Congress was the conviction with which Quebec spokesmen argued either (a) that Confederation has been a complete flop as far as French Canada is concerned and that secession is imperative (Dr. Marcel Chaput); or (b) that Confederation has been a relatively bad bargain for French Canada to date and that corrective measures must be tried forthwith. These measures are, of course, short of secession (Premier Lesage, René Lévesque, Jean-Jacques Bertrand, etc.). These opinions and, indeed, all others expressed during the Congress, throw little light on what seemed to me the most distressing characteristic of the Congress (and here I speak as a Conservative and not as an officer of the Congress): the general antipathy of French Canadians, students, newspapermen, intellectuals, representative businessmen, etc., toward the federal government.
>
> This hostility was less evident during the actual business session of the Congress than during the informal get-togethers every evening but it was, nevertheless, present at all times. Briefly, the French Canadians believe that Ottawa delights in treating Quebec as "just another province" when in fact it is supposed to be an "equal partner" with English Canada (the nine other provinces) in Confederation. They contend that Ottawa has denied the de facto existence of a French-Canadian "nation" and that French Canada does not get anything near a "partner's treatment" when federal appointments (for example, Royal Commissions) are made. French Canadians are angry because their language has been relegated to second-class status within the civil service and that no one in authority has declared that henceforth it will be scrupulously respected. They also deplore the absence of French-Canadian administrators from high positions in the civil service. They are offended because French-Canadian representation in the federal cabinet is not up to par generally and they wonder why the Prime Minister has not designated someone from Quebec as his chief lieutenant. They say that if "better Quebec wood is needed to build

> a better cabinet," it is available and that, as in the personal case of Mr. St. Laurent following Mr. Lapointe's death, it should be sought out. They ask how the Prime Minister can really "understand" Quebec when he has not a top-flight French Canadian in his office as an advisor.
>
> The items above acquire real significance when one considers that, in its ferment, French Canada is now convinced that it is going places under its own steam. The province has become completely self-confident and, as a consequence, its disenchantment with the federal government is beginning to harden. Unless swift action is taken to allay fears that Ottawa is indifferent to the aspirations of French Canada and insensitive to its demands, every Conservative candidate in this province will feel the effects in the next general election.

What surprises me today is that I sent such a letter to Canada's prime minister. I ended it more diplomatically, by reminding my hero what had first attracted me to him: "Although I am only a law student and, therefore, perhaps more prone than others to push panic buttons, I deeply believe that the foregoing is an accurate statement of fact. As I attend a French-Canadian university and live in an entirely French milieu, I think I have some idea of what is really going on in this province, and what is happening does not bode well for the Conservative Party. At the 1956 convention I served on the Youth for Diefenbaker Committee because I felt that you were the only man who could lead our party back to public favour. I am equally convinced that you will now act to hold the Province of Quebec."

There was no response from Ottawa. Nevertheless, I continued my interest in Conservative politics. I was among the leaders of the PCSF and was developing a very friendly relationship with Justice Minister Davie Fulton, whom I later supported for leader of the party at the 1967 convention. I had recommended to Allister Grosart that he appoint my old friend Pat MacAdam as secretary for youth activities, and in due course Pat and his family moved from Nova Scotia to join Allister, his secretary Flora MacDonald, and a few others at national headquarters. These were housed in an elegant former bordello, at 141 Laurier Avenue West. There, Allister supplied the erudition, Flora the energy, and Pat the good humour in a congenial ship that helped to create a contented party in the early years of the Diefenbaker government. I had also, as a one-man StFX placement agency, recommended Lowell Murray to Davie Fulton, and he was now ensconced in the ministerial suite as executive assistant. We were all moving up in the world.

2. Ottawa Interlude

One remarkable individual that I remember fondly and well from the early 1960s was Roy Faibish, then a senior advisor in Ottawa to Minister of Agriculture Alvin Hamilton. Roy was a small, wiry, dynamic Jewish guy from Saskatchewan who had developed a profound admiration for Diefenbaker, and a respect and affection for Hamilton that were boundless. They were like brothers together, Alvin the garrulous doer and Roy the committed idealist. The words *intellectual* and *brilliant* have been trivialized by overuse, but Roy Faibish was both, and an insatiable reader with the most catholic tastes. With a personal library in excess of eight thousand volumes, he was as at home with Aristotle as he was with the implications of change in the Soviet politburo; as knowledgeable of Daniel Johnson's skill as Quebec opposition leader as of the intricacies of the decision-making process in the papacy of Pope Pius XII. And here was his true genius – a wicked wit. Once, at an official 1983 London reception for High Commissioner Don Jamieson (whom he did not like), Roy greeted him loudly with the words, "I hear your clapped-out friend Joey Smallwood is being made ambassador to Panama, because we have no extradition treaty with them!" During the early 1960s, however, he was busy issuing brilliant policy ideas and profane directives throughout the department (and party), helping to make Alvin Hamilton one of the most influential policy-makers in town, and arguably the most powerful agriculture minister in recent history.

I had come to know Roy through my party activism, and I shared frankly with him my fears that Canada's Progressive Conservatives were out of touch with both my generation and the one rising in French Quebec. In early January of 1962, I put on paper, for Roy's benefit and at his request, my fears and how we as a party and government might counter and overcome them.

> As you suggested in our telephone conversation of last evening, I am sending along a few suggestions which might help to enhance

> the prestige of the federal government vis-à-vis the province of Quebec. 1) Invite Mayor Jean Drapeau of Montreal into the federal cabinet. 2) Appoint a top-flight French Canadian as chief counsel or special assistant to the prime minister. The current Quebec image of the prime minister as being anti-French Canadian is not, I think, the result of any one major event. It is, rather, attributable to a series of minor, sometimes insignificant items which assumed sensational proportions simply because there was no one around to nip them in the bud. 3) Acknowledge the validity of the "partnership theory" of Confederation in such things as federal nominations and appointments to royal commissions. One reads daily of such things as the O'Leary, MacPherson, Bladen, Glassco, and Hall commissions, but where are the Lapointe, Tremblay, Boisvert, and Lachance commissions? 4) Offer bonuses to those civil servants who are bilingual and to those who are willing to study to become bilingual. Let it be known that henceforth bilingualism will be considered as a requisite for advancement into the higher reaches of the civil service. 5) Spend less time avoiding charges of "collusion" between the Conservatives and the Union Nationale and infinitely more time in an attempt to bring about a rapprochement between the federal government and the present provincial government. . . . 6) Concentrate forthwith on building a strong Quebec political organization. At the moment, our party headquarters for the Eastern District (27 ridings) is manned by only one person – a girl who answers the phone. We have no organizers, no public relations men, no press liaison people – in short, nothing. This is in sorry contrast to the Liberals who are hellbent for elections already.

Looking back on these comments, I'm pleased to note that they precede by some years those of the Laurendeau-Dunton Royal Commission, which alarmed the nation with its findings about Quebec's place in Canada. Roy must have agreed with them: he contacted me in the spring of 1962, advising that the prime minister would soon be calling an election and that he had been conscripted as a Diefenbaker speechwriter and policy advisor for the campaign. Perhaps seeking an ally on staff, he asked me to drop everything and join Alvin's office to act as his private secretary and to travel with him throughout the campaign. I jumped at the chance and joined the

Department of Agriculture, following my second-year law school exams, in early May 1962. Lowell Murray invited me to share his digs on Cartier Street for the summer and, after briefings from Roy and Alvin's superb Deputy Minister, Gordon Robertson, I joined the minister in his suite of offices in the old Confederation Building, just off Parliament Hill.

Alvin was an extremely likeable, smart, determined politician who had endured a long Saskatchewan PC drought before finally winning election to the House in 1957. As minister of Northern Affairs and Natural Resources, he soon emerged as one of the stars of the first Diefenbaker administration, developing an idea a minute, including important dimensions of the Northern Vision and Roads to Resources policies that the prime minister powerfully articulated in the 1958 campaign, some six months later. He went about his work with a sense of humour rarely seen, before or since, among privy councillors in Ottawa. As minister, for example, Alvin grew concerned about bears harming visitors to Canada's national parks. Bears that had committed such offences were hastily dispatched to areas hundreds of miles from the place where they had encountered humans. There was always a chance, however, that they'd find their way back. Ever practical, Alvin figured out a way to distinguish bears that had previously come into troublesome contact with humans. As only a Tory would, Alvin ordered that the rears of these recalcitrant bears be painted Liberal red, to mark them until their dying day.

Earlier in 1962, Alvin had been felled by an attack of Bell's palsy that paralyzed part of his face and required him to secure his lip by using an apparatus hooked to his ear during periods of repose. But this illness affected neither his enthusiasm nor, surprisingly, his prolixity, as I quickly learned when we began the campaign at his home base, the Drake Hotel in Regina.

Alvin was much in demand across the country but especially in the West as PC candidates everywhere sensed great impending difficulties. Diefenbaker had been crippled by high expectations, a recession, and some policy mistakes, and he was under close surveillance by a press gallery hostile to his ambition for a third term. The most famous illustration of this hostility was the statement by Val Sears of the *Toronto Star*, who exhorted the travelling press on to another day of objective journalistic duty with the memorable cry, "To work, gentlemen, we have a government to overthrow!"

Soon after arriving in Saskatchewan, on my first trip to western Canada, we met with Alvin's organizers and supporters in his suite at the hotel. Roy had said to me, "You'll enjoy Alvin's key supporters. Some of them are bigots, but they're *our* bigots." I could quickly tell that some of them were less than enchanted with Alvin's new travelling private secretary – "a French-Irish Catholic from Quebec!" as one described me, with concern written all over his face. But in the genuinely smoke-filled rooms of the Drake – led, of course, by Alvin, who constantly puffed on good cigars – I began to understand and admire the individualism and integrity of westerners whose heroes were of recent vintage and whose successes were highly personal and hard won. I had grown up in Quebec, been educated in the Maritimes, and now I was experiencing a province that had been established within living memory.

That first evening, when I stepped out of the hotel I was struck by the endlessness of the prairies, the magnificent uncluttered sky and the sense that, in this vast land, achievement was fully dependent on personal initiative and sacrifice and not on international connections or government assistance. I was thousands of miles away from the North Shore, but I could feel the bond of common values and hopes between the peoples of these rural regions that defined the very nature of Canada.

I felt that sentiment even more strongly early one Sunday morning when Alvin and I flew on a small plane from British Columbia to Grande Prairie, Alberta. It was a sunny morning in May, and after we had crossed the Rockies and hundreds of miles of bush, I was overwhelmed by the stunning beauty of this vast expanse of rich farmland, grain elevators, and rivers sitting serenely on a far northern corner of this country. A few moments later another small plane arrived and, to my surprise, out popped another young Québécois, François Aquin, an active member of the Liberal Party. He was there as an officer of the Young Liberal Federation and was campaigning for his party's candidates throughout the West. We chatted briefly at the airport, reflecting on the majestic beauty of the Peace River country and how fortunate we both were to live in Canada. Aquin was an attractive and impressive lawyer who was soon thereafter elected to Quebec's National Assembly as a Liberal. I recalled that conversation in northern Alberta with some sadness when six years later he crossed the floor to become the first provincial member ever to sit as a separatist.

Alvin was a great campaigner and I enjoyed our travels enormously. One morning in Regina, while Alvin was recording commercials at leading radio station CKRM, I asked the general manager if he would mind my sending in reports to the station on Alvin's meetings from across the country. To my surprise, my offer, made half in jest, was accepted. As a result, Saskatchewan listeners were treated throughout the campaign to twice-daily reports about their minister's activities. From Orillia, Ontario to Bathurst, New Brunswick, my reports invariably began with the words: "Speaking before a large and enthusiastic crowd today in Sudbury, Ontario, Agriculture Minister Alvin Hamilton said" and ended with me saying, "This is Brian Mulroney, reporting to CKRM, Regina."

By today's standards, the dubious ethics of this journalistic activity would immediately be evident, and the consequences lethal. But when I returned with Alvin to Regina just before voting day, I was widely complimented on the streets for my "objective" coverage (no doubt my street encounters were only with Conservatives), and I was delighted when the station general manager offered me a permanent job as a morning man, "if this law business doesn't work out."

Prior to the campaign, Finance Minister Donald Fleming had announced the devaluation of the Canadian dollar to 92.5 cents. While Alvin lauded this decision as a boon to Canadian exporters, the Liberals derided it as the "Diefenbuck" and "a 92-and-a-half-cent Canada." In Vancouver, Alvin inadvisably told a reporter that some ministers had wanted a much lower dollar, while others preferred to keep it high. This suggested that the decision was basically a political one, unrelated to the realities of the Bank of Canada and exchange flows.

All hell broke loose. Within minutes Fleming was on the phone telling Alvin to "mind his own goddamned business" and never discuss the currency issue again. As I fielded dozens of calls from ministers and MPs in Alvin's hotel suite – all of them angry, many profane – the minister retired for a hot bath and a big Cuban cigar, growling at me not "to sweat the small stuff." It was the best demonstration of coolness under fire that I had ever seen; nevertheless, it was days before the incident blew over, leaving significant political damage in its wake.

Election night on June 18, 1962 was a disaster, especially when compared with the sweep of 1958. We lost 92 seats, plummeting from 208 to 116 and minority status in the Commons. Our strength held well in the West, and as we listened to the results, Alvin expressed delight every time an MP whose riding we had visited was elected. He was amazingly equable during the evening, which included some calls from Roy Faibish, who was with the prime minister in Prince Albert. Diefenbaker, we gathered, was not pleased.

Our group in Regina had gathered at what should have been a gloomy version of an Irish wake, but someone clearly had forgotten to tell Alvin, who maintained his good nature and high spirits throughout the night's events.

Until early the following morning, that is. I had been instructed to arrange for Secretary of State for External Affairs Howard Green, who was flying from B.C. the next day, to stop in Regina and pick us up for a return flight to Ottawa on a government aircraft. Green declined to do so, saying that important matters on the international agenda required his presence post-haste in Ottawa. When I advised Alvin, he erupted. "You get on the phone and tell those bastards that if they had won as many seats in B.C. as we did on the prairies we wouldn't be in this goddamn mess!" he shouted. When I shared this statement with Green's executive assistant, a phlegmatic young public servant with a slight British accent who had been seconded from the department, his reply was, "We will pick up your minister wherever and whenever it is convenient." In any event, we flew to Winnipeg where we had informal conversations with the prime minister and his travelling party on the tarmac in the sun while our planes refuelled. I spoke briefly with Diefenbaker – a press photo captured the moment – who was jovial, at least for the cameras, and courteous to all. I was amazed at his capacity to endure so much personal abuse and vilification, and the loss of a historic number of seats, without apparent bitterness. But that was soon to come.

During the campaign, Dief in full flight – and he was something to behold in full flight – would often highlight an achievement by saying, "They said it couldn't be done. We did it." When our aircraft touched down later that day I was met by Lowell Murray, who with characteristic impish humour intoned, "They said it couldn't be done. We did it. We fucked it up!"

Alvin sent me back into the field in the Stormont constituency, where the election had been deferred due to the death of one of the candidates in mid-campaign. Stormont was in eastern Ontario, near Cornwall. This was new territory for me. I was familiar by now with Quebec, New Brunswick, Nova Scotia, and, thanks to Alvin, Saskatchewan and the West. The chance to spend some time in Ontario was very valuable for me. We lost in Stormont, however, and the election result spoke to the clouds forming on the Tory horizon. I unloaded in a memo to my minister:

> I have just returned from Cornwall where I spent a few days working in the deferred election. Roy was also down for election

> day. I pass along to you the following observations. 1) The prime minister's name and personality were kept entirely out of the campaign. We were told during our canvasses that the prime minister was not a very popular man in that area, and apparently this was the reason the organizers ran a strictly Grant Campbell campaign. As a matter of fact, the name Progressive Conservative was not even used in the official party propaganda. Campbell was instead designated as the Government candidate. 2) There seems to be a lot of evidence to support the thought that old party "pros" give up much too quickly in fights of this nature. We were told here in Ottawa over and over again by most of our top people that Campbell hadn't the chance of a snowball in hell. When we got down there, however, we found that there was a real fight going on in every sense of the word . . . 4) Perhaps in future elections, party headquarters might interest itself a little more in choosing candidates who are representative of the people in the area, although it may be unfair to both Grant and voters of Stormont to say this. I can't help but feel that a constituency which is 60 per cent French Canadian and 80 per cent Catholic is not the most ideal place for a Scottish Presbyterian to be running. You certainly will have noted that the Liberals once again selected their candidate much more carefully than we did.

With the government now in a precarious minority status, the smell of impending doom affected all of the political discussions that raged everywhere in the capital throughout that summer. The prime minister shuffled the cabinet following the shellacking. Alvin was retained in Agriculture, but Davie Fulton was demoted from Justice (a portfolio he loved) to Public Works, a humiliation he endured with public good humour and private rage. Lowell Murray joked that after being surrounded by Mounties in red serge, Davie would now have to get used to being saluted every morning by the Department of Public Works elevator operators in dazzling blue.

Clearly, the wounds of the 1956 convention had never healed. Diefenbaker had never really taken his opponents and their chief supporters into his confidence or his inner circle. According to Alvin and Roy, who saw Dief quite regularly, the prime minister was starting to see strains of disloyalty and antagonism among people who wanted nothing more than to be sought out, flattered, thanked, or encouraged. The small kindnesses that motivate caucus members and inspire their families – an evening call just to chat, flowers and a personal note on the illness, death, or marriage of a close relative, a spontaneous invitation to drop by 24 Sussex for a drink after work – all of these encouraging courtesies evaporated in the recriminations and Monday-morning quarterbacking that dominated postelection discussions in the Prime Minister's Office. I carefully noted this change and saw the degree of erosion that sets in, at first subtly and then irretrievably, in the leader's base support in caucus and party when personal gestures by the leader and his wife cease. At the very moment he should have stepped up these contacts Diefenbaker withdrew, and the consequences soon became fatal. For me, another important leadership lesson learned.

—

PERSONAL JOURNAL: MARCH 14, 1992

I am deeply grateful for the tremendous support the caucus has always given me and I have a great feeling of respect for them. The PC caucus will always be a family for me. As I watch them on Wednesday mornings, I am struck by their differences and their commonality of interests; their healthy ambition and their selflessness; their vigorous defence of the provincial interest subordinated into a powerful statement of the national interest. They have done great things and sometimes do not appreciate the significance of their individual contributions. I feel a genuine affection for them all and have been proud to serve with each and every one, especially when I think of their loyalty and support, coming as it does from people who supported other leadership candidates; from people I hardly knew and others I knew less than well; from people I had disappointed by not being able to bring them into cabinet or give them another appointment.

—

Parliament was not yet in session, so Alvin Hamilton and his small team, headed by Roy Faibish and guided by his efficient secretary and close friend, Audrey Trotter, hunkered down in the department to work on the backlog of problems and preparations for the upcoming Throne Speech and recall of the House.

Thrilled as I was to be in a job at the centre of Canadian politics – and a job that was a lot more enjoyable than slugging it out at the mill in Baie-Comeau – Ottawa, too, in those days was a small, somnolent company town. Little government money had been spent on civic enhancement and beautification, and the city and region cried out for both. It is doubtful that, outside the Iron Curtain's Eastern Bloc, there existed a less inspiring and less attractive capital city of a large successful nation. The social agenda was no less dreary. The town visibly sagged by ten at night, just in time for residents seeking relief from the stifling boredom to cross the bridge to Hull, Quebec, where nightclubs, dance halls, bars, and a few great restaurants provided sanctuary and stimulation. Lowell and I frequently hit these spots after closing up the bar at the Château Laurier, along with friends and acquaintances like Louise and Paschal Hayes, private secretary to Postmaster General Bill Hamilton; Peter Jennings, already at twenty-two embarked on a brilliant career in broadcast journalism; Pat MacAdam; and other young executive assistants from the Hill.

Paschal Hayes was to run as a Tory candidate in Montreal in the disastrous 1963 election. His chances of victory in Notre-Dame-de-Grâce became rather remote when (aided by a fair infusion of gin, I suspect) he hauled off and punched the female Greek owner of a pool hall the day before voters went to the polls! The constituents he had hoped to represent in the House of Commons saw his picture – in the custody of the police – on the front page of the paper the next morning, and delivered the expected verdict on his candidacy.

Our group spent many evenings at a cottage near Kingsmere, in the Gatineaus on the Quebec side of the Ottawa River. Paschal had acquired it for the incredible price of three hundred dollars for the whole summer and fall. I remember passing by Mackenzie King's former home at Kingsmere on many early morning expeditions that year. Our trips were so frequent we even sang a special song as we came up to the former Liberal prime minister's home:

Hark, the herald angels sing,
Piss on you, Mackenzie King.

My future respect for all former prime ministers of Canada, which grew especially after 1993, was obviously not yet quite developed in 1962.

A few years earlier, while being interviewed for *Maclean's* magazine I had met Peter C. Newman, then a promising young journalist making his way in the Parliamentary Press Gallery. In 1963, he was to publish *Renegade in Power*, a new genre of reportage and probably the finest political book ever written in Canada. Peter – disciplined, focused, and considerate – and his extremely attractive and talented second wife, Christina, frequently had us to dinner or out on their boat on the Rideau Canal, where we would swim, sunbathe, and enjoy an excellent lunch and bottle of wine, whiling away the hours in funny, stimulating, and gossipy political discussions.

Over the years Peter and I became friends – eventually very close and trusting friends – and I even served as best man at his third wedding. I intended for him to become my literary executor and authorized biographer. (Little did I suspect the surprise he had in mind for me some forty years later.) I soon became one of Peter's many sources, helping him later with his grand sequel to *Renegade in Power*, entitled *The Distemper of Our Times*. On April 11, 1966, for example, I sent Peter a memo after attending a meeting at the home of former justice minister Davie Fulton at the height of the so-called Munsinger Affair (described by the Canadian Encyclopedia as "Canada's first major parliamentary sex scandal," it was based on the revelation that Pierre Sevigny, Diefenbaker's associate minister of national defence, was alleged to have had an affair with Gerda Munsinger, a German immigrant, a prostitute, and a possible security threat). Lowell Murray, Peter White, and Ed Houston were also at the meeting. The memo read as follows:

> We decided first of all that Fulton should not go on national TV; that Diefenbaker could go on if he wished, but that Davie should avoid swinging wildly at the [Royal] Commission [to Inquire into the Case Involving One Gerda Munsinger] at this juncture. I held the minority view that the proceedings of the commission were basically illegal and that some type of writ of prohibition should be sought to prevent its further operation. This point was roundly debated, and it was decided that Fulton would follow the advice of his Toronto counsel, Mr. Carson, who believed that such a move accompanied with public denunciation of the commission would only serve to muddy the waters and embitter the commissioner. It

> was therefore decided that he would appear with Carson at the next hearing but reserving the right to pull out should it appear that he was being railroaded. Around 8 p.m., we had a few drinks of Scotch and the meeting was conducted in a much lighter vein, with Murray making funny remarks. At about 9 p.m., we went to a private dining room in the Rideau Club for dinner and shortly after 10 p.m., White and I drove back to Montreal, arriving here around midnight. Murray, Fulton, and Houston remained there until about 11 p.m.

And to think I was destined later to lecture my ministers and caucus about the need for secrecy!

During that summer I worked hard in the department learning the rudiments of agricultural policy and the realities of Ottawa. To someone with my Quebec background, it was glaringly obvious that the ministry was overwhelmingly unilingual English. I was shocked by the paltry role accorded French Canadians, all the more so given the great importance of agriculture to the Quebec economy.

I outlined my concerns to Alvin in a lengthy memo in August:

> I am informed that agriculture, in terms of dollars and cents, is still the mainstay of the Quebec economy. Agriculture is also of considerable importance in New Brunswick, whose population is 50 per cent French speaking, as well as in areas such as eastern and northern Ontario where the French language predominates. It seems to me, therefore, that it is vitally important that this Department in particular be closely attuned to both the thinking and the happenings in the agricultural areas of French Canada. I ask whether we are accomplishing this in view of the following facts: 1) In the Minister's office and on the Minister's personal staff there is not, to my knowledge, anyone qualified to keep the Minister fully informed of goings-on in French Canada. French is not spoken in this office at all. Indeed, it would seem that over the years it has fallen into complete disuse. 2) In the Department of Agriculture there are 46 high-ranking officers from the deputy ministerial level down, all but one of whom are English-speaking Canadians. 3) It would seem that we are also losing at an impressive rate some of our very best French Canadians who apparently find the climate in the Department

anything but friendly and the atmosphere anything but one in which the French language is either respected or accepted. In 1959, at the time of the departmental reorganization, I am told that there were some two hundred promotions; not one French Canadian, however, was promoted either at that time or since.

What can be done: 1) For the above reasons, it is imperative that you appoint as soon as possible a top-notch French Canadian either as your Executive Assistant, or as personal advisor to the Minister on French Canadian agriculture. 2) French Canadians were not in the past entirely without blame for their failure to accede to high administrative posts in the Department. One reason for this was their system of education, with its tiny agricultural schools which did not always turn out graduates of the highest calibre. This situation appears to have been very substantially corrected with the transfer to Laval University in Quebec City of the Faculty of Agriculture which formerly was located at Ste-Anne-de-la-Pocatière. Now, for the first time, there is on a university campus a cohesive agricultural institute replete with every modern facility, staffed by professors of the highest ability, and designed specifically to turn out excellent graduates. It is, therefore, of great importance that this Department establish immediately a very close liaison with this Faculty of Agriculture. It might even be worthwhile to appoint a departmental liaison officer whose responsibility it would be to solicit ideas from faculty members there to find out and report on new developments and to court, in some measure, their best students as a means of inducing these same people to enter the department upon graduation. 3) There ought to be established at the earliest moment a new and intensive method of recruitment of French Canadians for this Department. It is a well-known fact that French Canadians frequently are reticent to leave Quebec and so these same people must be assured of good salaries and positions and must also be made aware of the fact that their language will in no way preclude them from consideration for regular promotion. 4) The reasons for the absence of French Canadians in this department, as well as the manner in which those French Canadians presently with us are being treated, will, I am afraid, cause you no little embarrassment one day in the House of Commons. You might, therefore, consider the possibility of setting up a departmental

> committee whose responsibility it would be to look into the matter as it presently stands and to make recommendations upon which the Minister could act to correct the situation. 5) You might also consider writing a ministerial directive to all high members of the Department inviting them to write to the Minister and his staff in French if they wish and assuring them that such a practice would be appreciated and not disdained.

What Alvin didn't know was that I felt so strongly about this issue that I was making similar arguments in memos to others throughout the government. I lobbied minister Davie Fulton and the prime minister's special assistant, John Fisher, among others, warning them that we were sowing the seeds of our own political destruction in French Canada.

While Fulton and others were sympathetic, John Diefenbaker apparently wasn't. Yet I continued my efforts within the Department of Agriculture. On September 11, Alvin gathered his deputy minister and other senior bureaucrats, his parliamentary secretary, Roy, Paschal, and myself for a full and frank discussion on the place the French language and French Canadians held in the department. I remember that Assistant Deputy Minister S.C. Chagnon admitted there had been a certain amount of discrimination against French Canadians when it came to hiring in the past. He also, fairly, pointed out that Quebec's educational system traditionally did not place a great emphasis on agricultural studies, leading to a dearth of qualified candidates for the position. In very clear terms, Alvin said he wanted an intense recruitment program aimed at French Canadians to be put in place and that the department had to develop a close liaison with the new faculty of agriculture at Laval. Alvin then ended the meeting by telling the bureaucrats they'd soon be hearing from him on the subject as he had other ideas.

The department didn't have to wait long. Only two days later, on September 13, Alvin sent an official communication to his deputy minister, announcing his plans to promote Chagnon to the newly created role of associate deputy minister of agriculture, to appoint as soon as possible a full-time liaison officer responsible for recruiting French-speaking Canadians into the Department of Agriculture, and other similar changes. As he summarized it, "I wish to make quite clear that the use of French in the department is to be encouraged."

Le Soleil discussed these reforms in an article published on September 15, 1962:

> The forceful move made by the Minister of Agriculture is no doubt inspired both by a spirit of "fair play" and by the hope of political gains, but all minds who are the least bit independent will recognize the merit. . . . These reforms will occur after the publication of the Royal Commission of the Glassco Enquiry that notably advocated a more authentic bilingualism in the federal public service. But the green light had been given by Mr. Hamilton well before the report was made public.
>
> One of the persons who initiated this affair was Mr. Brian Mulroney, a law student at Laval University who was the private secretary to Mr. Hamilton during the vacation period, replacing Mr. R. Faibish, who was loaned to Prime Minister Diefenbaker during the election campaign. Mr. Mulroney was purportedly stupefied to see how the French language was treated at the Ministry of Agriculture. Informed of this situation, Mr. Hamilton supposedly demanded an enquiry in order to obtain more complete information. The enquiry demonstrated that often in the past farmers from the province of Quebec had not made use of all of the advantages that the federal Ministry of Agriculture put at their disposition.

And so Alvin promoted bilingualism in the federal public service long before the *Official Languages Act*. I have no doubt that Pierre Elliott Trudeau – who had worked in the Privy Council Office a few years earlier – was inspired to introduce that act because he must have noted the same appalling language deficiencies in other federal departments.

Two vivid memories capture the informal style of Ottawa in those days. I remember standing outside Centre Block one steamy afternoon when Prime Minister Diefenbaker emerged, on crutches. Along with senators Bill Brunt and Davey Walker, he stepped carefully into a Blue Line cab and headed off to 24 Sussex for lunch. No security, no limo.

(While Ottawa was indeed to change in the years ahead, Senator Davey Walker never did. On October 28, 1987 – twenty-five years after that summer's day in 1962 – I had our caucus in stitches by summing up why we all loved Davey so. "There was a fire alarm yesterday that produced a new definition of class," I told them. "The television showed all the parliamentarians outside the building having had their lunches interrupted by the alarm. One of those outside was Davey – who left the Parliamentary Dining Room *with his glass of wine in hand*.")

I also recall a brief reception at 24 Sussex in the summer of '62 in which I was included. Entering the gates at the imposing residence on a promontory overlooking the Ottawa River that has been home to every Canadian prime minister since Louis St. Laurent left me greatly impressed. Soon, however, Pat MacAdam, Dick Bell, and I found ourselves sneaking through the house looking unsuccessfully for a cold beer. Not for a moment did I pause, awestruck, to imagine the day when I might live there. I was after a beer.

In early September 1962, I said goodbye to Ottawa and returned to Quebec City for my third and final year in law. My time in the capital had been an illuminating and enriching experience – in fact my only government experience until I was sworn in as prime minister, exactly twenty-two years later!

3. Legal Hurdles

Back in Quebec City I continued my political involvement as an active Progressive Conservative. At one party meeting at the Château Frontenac, I was even able to consider casting my ballot for a young man from Queen's University who was running for the position of executive vice-president of the Progressive Conservative Student Federation under the slogan, "We come here with determination, with a purpose, and with faith. We are determined to leave with that purpose and that faith fulfilled." The candidate's name was Derek Burney. Our paths were to cross again.

I also continued as a low-level advisor to Diefenbaker. During one conversation with some Laval classmates I suggested it might be very effective if we could get the prime minister to the law school to speak. Naturally, this suggestion was hooted down in derision by my skeptical classmates. All of them treated me with new respect, however, when I marched in on the scheduled day with the prime minister in tow! Dief was a great hit, and I basked in the reflected warmth of his visit for as long as I could. Even then, Conservatives didn't get much respect in Quebec, and it was good to enjoy it while I could.

In typical style, I sent off a personal thank-you note to the prime minister, not forgetting to compliment the great man on the success of his appearance: "I wish to thank you sincerely for having agreed to take time from a busy schedule to visit Laval Law School last weekend. The students, many of whom had not met you before, were delighted with your down-to-earth, 'lawyer to lawyer' talk and with your friendliness. Today the law school hummed with favourable comments on your visit and I notice that the popularity of our Conservative Club took an appreciable jump because we signed up thirteen new members between classes today."

Later, when I was prime minister, I was to nod approvingly as I read the letter that StFX student Alex Burney, son of Derek Burney, sent to me in 1992. "It is clear to me that one needs a mentor to emulate," he wrote, under the StFX PC Club's letterhead. "I believe there could be no better candidate than yourself, thus, I have become the second Xaverian student to proudly choose a Conservative Prime Minister as a mentor. I respectfully intend to repeat history in another area as well; in 1960 a young Laval law student was able to convince the Prime Minister of the day to visit his campus. That visit was a great personal triumph for the student as it dramatically raised his profile. It is then my task to convince you to return to your alma mater for a brief visit at your convenience."

While I wasn't able to visit Alex at StFX that time, I'm proud to say that my daughter, Caroline, was one of Alex Burney's most enthusiastic canvassers during the 1990 Ontario provincial election when he put his name forward as a Progressive Conservative candidate.

Also while I was prime minister, Mila was privileged to be given a tour of the Diefenbaker Canada Centre at the University of Saskatchewan. Archivists there had unearthed some of my youthful correspondence to the prime minister for her to read. When Mila arrived back in Ottawa, she told me she had seen some of my letters to the Chief. When I asked her what they were like, she said, "They were nice, but a little bit sucky."

I was more direct when I met Mr. Diefenbaker in the prime minister's parliamentary office to discuss some of the recommendations I had made to correct the growing perception that his government was insensitive to Quebec. After listening to me politely for some considerable time, Diefenbaker brusquely said, "Brian, I was defending French Canadians long before you were born." With that he summoned trusty Gilbert Champagne, who promptly reappeared with a 1922 Law Report that contained a Saskatchewan case, *Boutin* v. *Mackie*, that Diefenbaker defended and won on behalf of a local French Canadian. "When they criticize me, read them that," Diefenbaker barked at me, before escorting me out a few minutes later and saying a warm goodbye in the little office then occupied by Bunny Pound and a very young stenographer by the name of Marjory LeBreton, who in the decades ahead was to play a progressively influential leadership role in the party and government.

At Laval in the 1960s, we law students continued to hang out in delightful spots. The bar at the Château Frontenac, where we chatted easily with politicians of all stripes, La Chapelle at the Clarendon Hotel, the Café Buade, and the Cercle des étudiants (where I watched a young Gilles Vigneault hang up posters announcing his Quebec City concert). We frequented La Page

Blanche on rue St-Jean, listening to Les Jérolas and Les Compagnons de la Chanson. I especially remember the Théâtre Capitol where one magical evening I saw Yves Montand for the first time, performing his one-man show. As he sang and danced his way through a two-hour *tour de chant* I – a frustrated saloon singer – knew I was watching the world's greatest entertainer. I was a faithful fan of Sinatra and Crosby, but that night I learned the magnificent dimension of French entertainment – unknown to most English-speaking Canadians. To this day, I have Montand's CDs playing in my home and car along with those of Jean Lapointe, Charles Aznavour, Gilles Vigneault, Félix Leclerc, Robert Charlebois, and other great talents I came to know and love at Laval and since.

At Laval I met and fell in love with a very beautiful and captivating French-Canadian nursing student, Johanne Ross. Her mother had died when Johanne was a child, and her dad worked in Montreal while she was raised by her grandmother and aunt in a second-storey flat at 333 boulevard Ste-Cyrille in Quebec City. I saw her striding on rue Couillard toward Hôtel-Dieu Hospital late one afternoon in 1960. It was an immediate *coup de foudre* and, after getting her name and telephone number, I pursued her with an ardour that was intense and all-consuming. We developed a wonderful relationship that went on – and sometimes off, because we had some tumultuous times – for five years. Her presence, kindness, and charm brightened every day and provided laughter and excitement during my Quebec City years.

My cousin, Elmar Kane, and his partner, Jack Dinan, owned a restaurant called (of all things) Le Sweden at the foot of Côte-de-la-Fabrique, close to the Cercle des étudiants. Peter White and I would frequently have lunch or dinner there – at a generous discount – with my godmother and aunt, Jenny Keenan. My father's elder sister was a wonderful, matronly figure who was childless and took a special interest in me and my cousins Ena and Patricia Mulroney, her brother Mike's children in Ste-Catherine. She worked in Elmar's business office above the restaurant. She was especially proud of the fact that I, her godson, was the first Mulroney to graduate from college and was en route to becoming the family's first lawyer as well. She thoroughly enjoyed being brought up to date on campus developments, studies, gossip, social highlights, and political debates.

One day in late November while she and I were finishing lunch, a waitress named Mrs. Fitzpatrick rushed over and said, "President Kennedy has just been shot." Aunt Jenny and I were both stunned and almost paralyzed with shock. Together we tearfully said goodbye to an American president neither of us knew but whom we deeply admired and loved. I remembered hearing President Kennedy on the radio during his unsuccessful vice-presidential campaign in 1956 and I had excitedly followed his career through to his inauguration in 1961. Maybe it was the Irish thing. Maybe it was the vicarious pride a young Irish Catholic felt as he watched another achieve for the first time in history the pinnacle of world political success, the presidency of the United States of America.

Once, inspired by one of his speeches, I had even lobbied John Diefenbaker's office, through Dief's special assistant, John Fisher. I wrote on August 1, 1962 to suggest that the government emulate JFK's approach to the creation of the European Common Market. It was twenty-five years before my own government successfully negotiated a comprehensive free trade deal with the United States.

It would be misleading for me to suggest that this memo had any impact on Mr. Diefenbaker. In any case, on a personal level he and President Kennedy did not enjoy one another's company.

On that bleak November day in Quebec City I understood the poignancy of Mary McGrory's remark that "if you're Irish you know the world is going to break your heart one day." My student friends, transfixed by grief, gathered in boarding houses in small groups throughout the Quartier Latin, watching as flickering black-and-white TVs took us through the majesty and the sorrow of the Kennedy funeral.

Thirty years later, in November 1994, Senator Ted Kennedy and his wife, Vicki, with whom Mila and I had developed a genuine friendship, invited Mila, Caroline, Nicolas, and me to join them at the Cape Cod Kennedy family residence for a long weekend. Ted graciously insisted that Mila and I occupy the room that President Kennedy had used for most of his life. The beautiful wood-frame home – weather-beaten by a thousand storms and captured by a million cameras – was warm and inviting, filled with dozens of black-and-white photos of the family together and at play over the years. We walked for hours in the crisp November air as Ted regaled us with family anecdotes and fascinated us as he revealed the burdens and joys of belonging to America's most celebrated family. At dinner on Saturday evening, Ted got up and delivered a touching and sincere tribute to me and my accomplishments, at which Nicolas, then nine years old, leaned over to Mila and whispered, "*Psst*, Mom! Does Senator Kennedy know Dad's a Conservative?"

Later that evening as Mila and I were chatting, waiting to fall asleep, I reflected on that shocking moment with my aunt Jenny in Quebec City almost precisely thirty-one years earlier when the dashing young president was murdered. And I was deeply saddened by the thought that, had President Kennedy not been struck down, he would have been seventy-six years old and perhaps preparing to sleep in his own bed again.

In 1964, I graduated and was awarded a bachelor of laws degree from Laval. In those days, a fourth year was required (a combination of class work and time in a law firm) before taking the Bar exam, which was widely known as a test of one's capacity to memorize the entire Civil Code and regurgitate it word for word for examiners. This feat bore no resemblance to requirements for a successful law practice and has since been completely altered, but that's the way it was in Quebec in the 1960s.

Many of our classmates, including most of my close friends, went to Montreal to article with firms there and to take their final year at either the Université de Montréal or McGill. Among those who chose to stay in Quebec City were Jean Bazin, who became president of the students' union, the Association générale des étudiants de Laval. Jean was a dear friend who was to play a key role in my political career. Another was Lucien Bouchard, a pleasant and talented student from Lac-Saint-Jean, whom I had known casually during our first three years but to whom I was to become extremely close as the bonds of friendship between us tightened in our final year at Laval.

In his memoirs, *On the Record*, Bouchard accurately described those far-off days of our early friendship. "We came to know each other well," Bouchard wrote, "talking and walking in the old town, he improving his French while I obstinately refused to speak English because I was paralyzed with shame because of my ignorance. I can still see him in the park next to the law school, poring over a bronze plaque, reading with proper oratorical intonations the words of George-Étienne Cartier, 'In a country such as ours, all rights must be safeguarded, all convictions must be respected.' I later discovered in Donald Creighton's book on the life of Sir John A. Macdonald that the episcopal building, the site of the Quebec Conference and the signing of the confederal pact of 1864, had stood on this very spot."

I had been elected president of the law faculty and had responsibilities there, one of which was to sit on the Conseil général de l'AGEL, where all major student union decisions were made. Jean Bazin was the president and skilfully handled the vigorous and often caustic debate that surrounded all major issues, from proposed tuition increases to the already noted turbulence surrounding the royal visit by Her Majesty the Queen to Quebec City in 1964.

Bazin, an orphan, had been raised by his uncle, Mark Robert Drouin, a prominent lawyer who was appointed Speaker of the Senate by Mr. Diefenbaker. He was a strong federalist, and I can remember his expressions of displeasure when he returned to council after meeting with student leaders in Montreal – Bernard Landry, Pierre Marois, and others – who already were displaying increasingly strong anti-Canadian attitudes and vocabulary. Bazin was particularly incensed that at one student meeting in Montreal only Quebec flags were on display; any symbol of Canada had been banished to the back room. It was 1964 and such actions were a harbinger of what was to come.

I discussed this event and most other political developments with Bouchard. We frequently met for lunch or dinner and developed a warm friendship that deepened over the years as I came to trust him implicitly and to treat him with the affection and respect of a brother. Bouchard was smart and well read but not in any way an intellectual. He was a practical man – focused, disciplined, and hard-working – who came to love the law and who, like me, saw Laval as an opportunity to get ahead in life and to leave behind the harsh realities of working-class life. He had a biting and delicious sense of humour, regaling me and others with his take on the day's events. His vocabulary was strongly laced with profanity – to which I was no stranger, as Canadians would later discover – so we whiled away many hours that year with hilarious, uncensored discussions that fortunately have gone unrecorded. (My mother always expressed strong disapproval of my use of profanity, saying, "All it demonstrates, Brian, is a weak vocabulary." Despite a few attempts, I never succeeded in purging myself fully of this habit, a fact I regret deeply to this very day.)

In those days Bouchard was a Liberal who strongly supported the Lesage and Pearson governments. He also toyed with the idea of supporting the NDP, but later emerged as a Parti Québécois supporter in 1970, having supported Trudeau in 1968. By 1984, he was supporting the Conservatives – only to leave to form the Bloc Québécois in 1990. Then, he joined the PQ as premier in 1995, only to resign bitterly five years later to return to private life, where he remains. This lack of an enduring commitment to a cause was a trait we all recognized in Bouchard but failed to take seriously at the time.

We saw it as an almost charming display of political irreverence, which indeed it was, as we all dawdled at the time on the periphery of political authority. It was only much later when we were deeply involved in the governance of a great nation that the full impact of his chameleon-like loyalty – and the damage and anguish it would cause to Canada and to me – became clear.

I remember an incident that required a few of us AGEL leaders to meet with Premier Lesage's chief advisors, Claude Morin and Jacques Parizeau, prior to a large demonstration outside the Assemblée Nationale. Bouchard spoke that day to the crowd, demonstrating some of the powerful oratorical skills he was to unleash with such telling effect against Prime Minister Chrétien in the 1995 referendum. That afternoon as I watched Bouchard speaking in public for the first time at Laval I knew he had impressive gifts that would open up possibilities of an interesting political future.

For the moment, however, that particular future was non-existent. He was engaged to Jocelyne, his high school sweetheart, and every weekend he drove home to Jonquière to see her and prepare for marriage and his new career with Fradette & Associés, a leading law firm in Chicoutimi.

As for me, I was actually proceeding along a similar path that year. I had agreed to return to Baie-Comeau after the Bar exams and to enter into partnership with Sarto Cloutier, a sole practitioner who had developed a good practice and reputation. Johanne and I had discussed marrying after I was settled in the law practice there, but no final decisions had been made.

Toward the end of the 1964 school year, however, I received a completely unexpected call from John Kirkpatrick, Q.C., and Thomas Montgomery, Q.C., senior partners in Howard, Cate, Ogilvy in Montreal, Quebec's largest and most respected law firm (it would later become Ogilvy Renault). They had heard of me, they said mysteriously, and wondered if I could come to Montreal to interview with them. I was bowled over, but told them that it was my intention to return soon to Baie-Comeau. They politely repeated their invitation, which I accepted, landing a few days later in the impressive suite of offices that occupied two full floors of Place Ville-Marie, then Canada's most attractive skyscraper, in the heart of downtown Montreal. The face-to-face meetings went well, and I was soon given an offer to join the firm after passing the Bar exams. I was somewhat stunned by this unanticipated and unsolicited development, but highly flattered to be asked to join one of Canada's most prestigious firms.

Lucien Bouchard expressed his approval in one of the rare letters he wrote to me in English: "I see you have not stopped improving your French language achievements. For instance, I took notice, in your last threatening letter of [this fact]. This . . . proved [for] me that you carry on your ascetic search for bilingual perfection. In all events, Montreal is great for you. This town as well as Howard, Cate law firm are susceptible to provide you with everything necessary to quench your humble ambitions."

Johanne was very supportive, but I hesitated to accept until I had a discussion with my dad. I knew he had his heart set on me returning to Baie-Comeau as a lawyer, and not as a mill worker. But he listened carefully and then said, "Son, you can always come home, but you may never again get this kind of an opportunity. I'd do it."

Toward the end of April I began to focus on the dreaded Bar exams, which constituted an endurance test of memorization. Books, notes, or guides were not allowed in the exam, so students had to sit down and essentially memorize the entire Civil Code – all 2,615 articles, not to mention the Code of Civil Procedure and many other related texts. The questions did not deal with the manner in which you could translate theory or jurisprudence into practical solutions to a given problem. They dealt with the specifics of one's recollection of, say, article 1321 of the Civil Code, and what it said in its entirety.

During the first three years leading to the bachelor's degree in law, I had become friendly with a fellow student from Quebec City named Bernard Roy. He lived with his mother, a widow, in a small and tidy house on rue Ste-Amable in the shadow of the Parliament buildings and within shouting distance of the Quartier Latin and the law school. Bernard was a diligent student and superb athlete, a star of the varsity hockey team. He was strong willed, friendly, and fluently bilingual, a skill that he perfected as a tourist guide every summer in Quebec City. He and I agreed to work together on our Bar exam preparation, and to this end we moved for some six weeks to Lac St-Joseph where his family had a summer cottage.

We laboured in silence for week after week, committing as much as we could to memory. Every evening we would emerge for a walk and challenge each other, saying, "Okay, give me the eleven articles of the Civil Code beginning with 1204." When either of us faltered, the air was blue with frustration and profanity as we struggled to recollect the third paragraph of an obscure article of the Civil Code that, we were fairly certain, neither would ever use in his law practice or indeed ever hear of again in our lives.

The only respite from this monastic existence – we resembled the Odd Couple, with Bernard cooking and me cleaning up and washing the dishes – was a dash to Quebec City in Bernard's Volkswagen on Saturday nights to see our girlfriends, only to return in time to take up our studies at noon Sunday.

Finally, we travelled to Montreal, found the Sir Arthur Currie Gym at McGill University, and endured three days of exams there. Some weeks later the results were posted. I had sailed through all the exams with flying colours but had failed Civil Procedure. I was genuinely flummoxed. How could I have passed all the tough ones but flunked what most regarded as the easiest, inasmuch as it dealt with the most practical aspects of the law? To my surprise, Tommy Montgomery called from Howard Cate and said this happened to good students all the time, and when was I ready to report for work?

Bernard had passed all the exams and was a full-fledged lawyer signed up at O'Brien Home Hall, so he and I agreed to share an apartment in Montreal that September. Since I wanted to begin work immediately that June, I accepted the invitation of my Uncle Larry and Aunt Ena Lacombe to sleep in the basement of their duplex at 3030 Sherbrooke Street East, in the far east end of the city, across from de Maisonneuve Shopping Centre.

Every day that summer I boarded the Number 4 bus – jam-packed and terribly hot, as this was well before air conditioning in public transportation – in the new seersucker suit I had purchased at Eaton's, and began the trip to McGill College Avenue, where, incidentally, my office is located today. There I disembarked, walked down to Place Ville-Marie and entered the elegant reception area of Howard Cate as its latest recruit, with as much dignity as I could summon in my by now sweat-drenched shirt and suit.

As the latest recruit, I was warmly welcomed by everyone including Kirkpatrick and Montgomery, who spoke supportively and glowingly about my long-term future at the firm, displaying infinitely more confidence in me than I had in myself. Initially, I felt somewhat sheepish when the other young lawyers hired that summer reported for duty as full-fledged members of the Bar, but I quickly lost that feeling as we were plunged into the vortex of activity at a major law firm, dealing with the demanding research assignments and plain hard work that are the common denominators for all young professionals starting out in law.

In the evenings, we would sometimes gather in Le Carrefour, a large boisterous bar in the basement of Place Ville-Marie that eventually became the "in" place for many of the young up-and-comers in Montreal's exploding business scene. It was there I first met people like Peter Brown, on his way to becoming one of Canada's great business success stories, and baseball's Rusty Staub and hockey's Gordie Howe. Expo 67 was just a few years off, so major construction sites were everywhere and the city was booming. Those Montreal summer months were exciting and stimulating for someone fresh from a small town and experiencing the delights of big city life for the first time. There was even a heartwarming touch of home: no matter how late I returned to my aunt's basement apartment, she prepared a delicious hot meal for me.

In September Bernard and I snagged a first-floor apartment on Claremont Avenue in Notre-Dame-de-Grâce. It was a two-bedroom flat where Bernard's sleep was constantly interrupted by the superintendent shovelling coal just below his bedroom window or whistling loudly for his errant dog, Blackie. If that weren't enough, my old friend Pat MacAdam had secured employment at Expo 67 and asked if we could put him up for a few days, which we did by placing a cot in our already tiny and crowded living room. Pat worked late and sometimes arrived home much later after a fairly liquid dinner, stumbling over furniture in the darkened apartment and further irritating Bernard, who finally put his foot down when Pat's "few days" began to look like a "few years," in the finest tradition of Cape Breton hospitality. Bernard's relief was palpable when Pat found his own lodgings.

My social life was fairly limited at the time, for three reasons. There were the tremendous demands of work at the firm, which I thoroughly enjoyed. There was the fact that Johanne was still in Quebec City. And there was the fact that I was being paid $5,200 that year along with a $120 bonus at Christmas. Still, I was happily enjoying the challenges of a new job, a new life in Montreal, and the frequent weekend commutes to Quebec City to visit with Johanne, who at this point had graduated and begun her nursing career at Hôtel-Dieu. Everything was going well.

4. A Death in Baie-Comeau

IT WAS DURING THE Christmas holidays with Johanne in 1964 that I got the first news about my dad. It came like a bolt out of the blue. On New Year's Eve he had entered Boisvert Hospital in Baie-Comeau because of sudden pain, and within hours we heard the devastating news: cancer that had spread throughout his body. I broke down in tears. I knew the sorrow and helplessness that would soon engulf all the members of our family.

I rushed to Baie-Comeau and visited my father in the hospital where I was born. I was shocked to see that he was already beginning to lose weight. In the darkened room, lit only by late afternoon sunlight, his strong facial features and muscular torso seemed yellowish, almost waxen. Neither of us referred to the finality of his situation, which had already been conveyed to me (and no doubt to him) by his old friends Dr. Don Thurber and Dr. Norm Poole. Instead, he smiled at me and told me how happy he was to see me and how proud he was of my work in Montreal and of the progress I had made, slowly but steadily over the years, in spite of the fact that, as he said, "You had to start with very little."

I had rewritten the Civil Procedure exam and failed it again, and had decided to shield my parents from the disappointing news. Now, from his hospital bed, my dad unexpectedly and softly asked me how I had made out in my exam. I told him the truth. I could see the disappointment in his eyes, even though I quickly assured him it was only a hiccup, and that I'd get it the next time.

To this day, I wish I had given him another answer – either that I didn't know, or that the exams weren't marked yet, or that I'd be hearing soon. But I told him the truth because that is what he would have done, and because that is what he drummed into us daily. Dad was a pillar of uncompromising truthfulness, as were all of his hard-working, honest paper mill colleagues. But in responding as I did, I felt that I had failed him at the moment of his greatest need for reassurance and hope. My dad had held me up all my life and I was now letting him down at the end of his.

I left the hospital and walked into the biting January weather, struggling with tears and weighed down by the despondency that accompanies impending tragedy. I knew that with Dad's death imminent, my mother and my two younger siblings, Gary and Barbara, would not have the financial resources necessary to go it alone. As the eldest son, I would have to step in and somehow keep the family together and ensure our solvency until better days could come again. As I plodded home through freshly fallen snow on the old back path on the shoulder of the mountain, Baie-Comeau could not have been more bleak.

I was twenty-five years old.

I began to commute as frequently as possible to Baie-Comeau, where a death watch enveloped our home. When I had to remain in Montreal, Olive kept me updated on Dad's condition by mail. "Gertie just phoned me to say that Dad is home," she wrote in late January. "Yesterday they put him to sleep and he had a rectal examination, which failed to disclose cancer and Dr. Poole told Mother that he had no idea where the primary cancer was. Then when Dad awakened he was sick to his stomach, and he slept the rest of the evening. Mother of course didn't even come home for supper and stayed at the hospital until after nine. I was up to see Dad on Tuesday afternoon and his condition is the same. He seems tired and listless, for instance, he gave up his television set, and I thought his complexion looked yellow, though I didn't say anything to Mom. He asked the doctor how much time he had and Dr. Thurber told him. Mother and I haven't talked much about it but apparently Dad talks to her a lot about the future. In any case I'm glad he's home as it won't be lonely for both of them, and Mom has been walking to the hospital in this cold weather."

Dad's colleague, mill manager Gordon Cooper, also wrote to me. "I just returned home from a trip to the hospital, specifically to see your father," he said. "I saw Dr. Poole at the door. He told me that your dad had asked him the direct question if he had cancer of the liver. Dr. Poole had told him this was the case. As a result, he said your dad was naturally upset. Your mother was with him when I talked to Dr. Poole."

I did my part as well, keeping members of the extended family informed as Dad's condition worsened. One letter went to my Uncle Jimmy O'Shea. "As agreed during our telephone conversation, I was to call you upon my return from Baie-Comeau next week to apprise you of developments there,"

I wrote. "Last night, however, I called Dick, who told me that there has been a very pronounced change for the worse in Dad's condition. Dick was, I understand, informed by the doctors that any estimate of time left which exceeds two months would be optimistic. I pass this information along to you because I know that you will want to see him before time runs out."

As it turned out, my father only had five days left to live.

I returned home as often as I could, but home was different now. Where once I could hear peals of laughter and music bouncing off the walls, now there was only sorrow and grief and hushed voices as my mother struggled to make Dad's decline as gentle as possible, and my visiting sisters baked and cleaned to ensure that the sights, sounds, and smells of his surroundings remained unchanged from those of his fondest memories.

He and I chatted softly upstairs in the small bedroom he shared with my mom. He liked to reminisce about his life, the early days in Baie-Comeau, how well the children were all doing, and how promising he thought our futures were. Throughout, he never displayed the slightest trace of bitterness at what was happening. One day he said, "Brian, it's up to you now. I want you to look after your mother and the kids, just the way I would." I did not respond. He knew my answer. He spoke softly, his eyes slightly averted from mine, as if he knew how hard it would be for both of us, especially me, to reply. To do so would mean acknowledging that his death was at hand, that soon I'd never again hug him, or tell him I loved him and appreciated so much everything he had done.

In the evenings I would take him in my arms like a child – he was losing weight very quickly – and carry him downstairs to the living room so he could watch TV for a while and tune into the CBC nightly news. In those days the lead announcer was Earl Cameron, who always concluded his newscast with the words, "This is Earl Cameron saying good night from Toronto" and my dad unfailingly replied with a smile, "Goodnight, Earl." He continued to do this right to the end, which came on February 16, 1965. He was sixty-one years old.

That morning, as if to reaffirm the inexorable majesty of the cycle of life, his newest grandchild, Maureen Elliott, was christened. She was the daughter of my oldest sister, Olive, and her husband, Dick Elliott. Their older children, Rick and Tim, had brought a special joy to my father's final years. If Dad was a man who loved his children – and he was – it was a marvel to watch him dote on his grandchildren. He would leave the mill at noon, rush home for a quick lunch, drive to Pharmacie Ethier, pick up ice cream cones for the kids, drive over to Olive's home in St-Georges, play with Rick and Tim for a minute or two and then rush to the mill, where work resumed at one o'clock.

Just prior to his death my dad, in asking me to assume the leadership of the family, alluded to his funeral and said with a smile, "Whatever you do, don't pay any attention to what my sisters say. I love them dearly but you should make the decisions."

The Quebec North Shore Paper Company executive aircraft was coming to Baie-Comeau, and Terry Flahiff kindly arranged to have two of Dad's sisters, Vera and Ena, fly down for the funeral. When they reached Baie-Comeau, it was clear that they had already enjoyed the generous beverage service on the flight, and after learning of my plans for burying my father in a new part of the Ste-Catherine cemetery, they loudly declared that their brother Ben absolutely had to be buried in the Mulroney family plot. I had no knowledge of such a plot, but they stated their demand with such energy and pride that I had visions of a piece of hallowed ground dedicated to the greats, not unlike the Roosevelt or Kennedy ceremonial resting places. So I agreed.

After the funeral at Église Ste-Amélie in Baie-Comeau we drove through a snowstorm to Quebec City for a wake, prior to burial. My Aunt Jenny and I sat in the kitchen of her tiny bachelor apartment on the corner of boulevard St-Cyrille and wrote my dad's obituary, which I dispatched to the local papers. I wanted the life and works of this good man to be recorded for his family and posterity. "Funeral services took place today in Église Ste-Amélie, Baie-Comeau for Benedict Martin Mulroney, formerly of Ste-Catherine, Quebec, who died Tuesday, February 16 at Baie-Comeau at the age of 61," it read in part. "A resident of Baie-Comeau since the founding of the city thirty years ago, he was general foreman of the electrical department, Quebec North Shore Paper Company. He was a member of the Baie-Comeau School Commission and president of the Quebec North Shore Paper Quarter Century Club."

After the wake and mass, my dad was laid to rest in the famous Mulroney family plot in Ste-Catherine-de-Portneuf. After arranging my mother's return to Baie-Comeau with the kids, I returned urgently to Montreal to tackle a huge backlog of work at Howard Cate. I was actually pleased to be so overworked, because it allowed me to focus on something other than the sad events of the previous months, while trying to think through how I would handle looking after my mom and the children.

Friends reached out to me, and to my family, at this difficult time. Peter White sent a letter that I shared with my mother, and that she in turn kept in her most treasured papers until her own death, decades later. "I had only met Ben Mulroney once – before and at the third-year ball," he wrote. "I have known ever since that he was a fine rare man. He had a twinkling humour and lots of solidity. It was obvious from Aunt Jenny and the rest of the family how much they loved and valued him. He must have been a wonderful father. I wish I had known him better. I know you owed him a lot. In a sense, we all do, because it was men like him that really built Canada and Quebec. He was adventuresome – being a Baie-Comeau pioneer proves that. He was a master of his craft – the best electrician in the company. He was reliable and resourceful on the machines. His family must be the envy of the town. His hospitality and friendship were legendary."

Mom also treasured a letter I received from (former justice minister) Davie Fulton. "I have just learned from Lowell Murray the sad news of your father's death, and sent a telegram to you at Baie-Comeau," he wrote. "This letter is to bring you a fuller personal message to the same effect. I had heard that your father was not well but I know that, whatever the circumstances and however long the illness, the actual parting comes as a terrific wrench – especially when a family have been as close as you and your father were . . . Both Pat and I do want you and your family to know that we pray for the repose of your Father's soul, and pray also that God will stretch out the hand of comfort to your mother, yourself, and all your family."

About ten days after Dad's burial, I got a telephone call at the office from the parish priest in Ste-Catherine, who advised me that a parishioner had just died and would be buried within a few days. When I inquired politely why he thought this would involve me, he replied, "Well, because your dad is buried in his plot."

When I exclaimed, "No, no, my dad is buried in the Mulroney family plot," he quietly told me no such thing existed and that I would have to make a quick decision. (Only much later did I learn that the original family plot had long since been filled with deceased family members.) I asked René Dionne, a friendly lawyer in Quebec City who was married to Claire Lemay, a childhood friend from Baie-Comeau, to seek a writ of exhumation before the Superior Court. Accordingly, within the next few days my brother, Gary and I returned to the cemetery, witnessed the exhumation of my father's coffin, and its reburial in the new part of the cemetery we had originally chosen. As I left the graveyard that brutally cold February day and began the drive back to Montreal, I began to smile and then chuckle in spite of the overpowering sadness of the occasion. I could see my dad smiling down on me and saying, "Brian, I hope you now understand why I asked you not to pay any attention to my sisters!"

My main concern was how to go about keeping my promise to Dad to look after my mother and the two youngest in the family. After discussions with my mother, I arranged to rent a quite large second-storey flat on the corner of Addington and Notre-Dame-de-Grâce avenues in an attractive middle-class suburb of Montreal. Busy as usual, I concluded the deal after work one day and was especially pleased with the view from the spacious balcony from which that evening I could glimpse some of the downtown lights, and the South Shore, across the river. When I returned during working hours to arrange for formal occupancy, I understood why there had been so little competition for the apartment: nearby Decarie Boulevard, the main north-south artery through Montreal, was being expanded to accommodate visitors for Expo 67, and all day and into the early evening, dust billowed up across our balcony as the grinding sound of huge trucks and drilling equipment kept sleepers up and enthusiasm down. In any event, it was home – a place where I and my mother, Gary, and Barbara could reside, regroup, and rebuild lives now achingly affected by my dad's absence. In the few years that followed, I learned how to care for my mother, be a father to the kids, and keep the family unit together as best I could until the children completed their education – Gary as a teacher and Barbara as a nurse – and I had enough money to secure an apartment for my mother, and to resume, eventually, my own bachelor life in Montreal.

Prior to the move, I returned to Baie-Comeau to arrange for the sale of the house, my father's only asset. It went for $14,000. That was his total estate for my mother. There was no company pension for widows, and when I sat down to do his final income tax return, I discovered that his total income slightly exceeded $10,000 that year, for the first time ever.

All my father had ever wanted was to see his beloved Canadiens play at the Forum in Montreal. He never did, because he had neither the time nor the money. As we packed up and left Baie-Comeau for the last time that spring, I reflected proudly on my dad's life and achievements. Those recollections are now tinged with great sadness as I think of how easy it would have been for me in later years to indulge his interests and whims.

He was right when he used to say to me on Sunday nights as he relaxed in his La-Z-Boy chair, "Brian, we're almost over the hump." In truth, we were – although at that moment the state of our family fortunes would not have inspired great confidence that his forecast was accurate.

5. Labour Lawyer

As soon as I got my family established in Montreal, I began studying again (this time with Jean Bazin) for the Civil Procedure exam. Yves and Carol Fortier generously offered us the use of their cottage in St-Sauveur, north of Montreal in the Laurentians. An analysis of Bar exams over a period of years would show that many of the same questions recur. Successful students paid particular attention to this fact, and did correspondingly well. Neither Bazin nor I had paid much attention to this important reality. Tommy Montgomery at Howard Cate kindly volunteered to help by interrogating us on questions that, in his judgment, were likely to be raised by the examiners. When Tommy was certain we had all the necessary information, he left to go back to Montreal, but I will always remember his stinging remark, delivered affectionately whenever, through lack of preparation, we gave the wrong answer to one of his questions: "What a stupid bunch of bastards you are!"

He was right. Bazin and I passed easily, but I can remember the humiliation of our oversight to this very day. Jean went on to become a distinguished lawyer, a director of major corporations, a successful president of the Canadian Bar Association, and an effective member of the Senate of Canada, and I became prime minister. But I learned from that experience: preparation, thoroughness, tenacity, and completion are the essential ingredients of proper responsibility. In law school, I had been seduced by the excitement of politics, to the detriment of my principal obligation to my studies. Despite "a fever in the blood," as a love of politics is sometimes defined, I tried to avoid this serious mistake in all of my future endeavours, always carefully fulfilling my obligations, and only then devoting time to other matters.

After the Civil Procedure exam, I reimmersed myself in The Factory, as Howard Cate was known in legal circles. I was assigned as a junior to

Tommy Montgomery. I researched many of his cases and carried the document-stuffed briefcases to the courts where he was appearing, while he dispensed gruff pearls of wisdom like, "That story was flat as piss on a plate," or "That case was as easy as shit through a goose." We always repaired after work to the Club Car, his favourite bar at Place Ville-Marie, while I listened to stories about the firm, its foibles, and players from the man universally regarded as "the glue who holds The Factory together." Many years later, when he and his wife, Peggy, came to 24 Sussex for dinner, Tommy delighted the other guests with a vivid description of my role in a celebrated case of alienation of affection reported, as he said, "in the Dominion Law Reports by the names of the principals, *O'Hair* v. *Latouche*!", at which he burst into laughter, with everyone else joining in.

After a few years of general litigation practice and some limited experience before the criminal courts I was assigned to Paul F. Renault, Q.C., the partner charged with building a practice in the developing field of labour law. (And develop it he did. In 1966 I became the third member of our group. Today Ogilvy Renault, the successor firm, has over eighty lawyers in that area of practice alone.) Paul was from St-Georges-de-Beauce and was former prime minister St. Laurent's nephew. With that background he was obviously a strong Liberal supporter, but Paul spent little time on politics. He focused on building what soon was clearly Canada's most successful labour law practice. After giving me some training, Paul simply threw me into the water to see if I could swim, and I took to it immediately. By 1967, I was representing the Shipping Federation of Canada before the Picard Royal Commission, which was charged by Parliament with a mandate designed to restore order, productivity, and profitability to Canada's seven eastern ports. This was a complex brief, and it soon led to representation before the Waterfront Arbitration Commission chaired by Chief Justice Alan B. Gold, whose integrity and interpersonal skills were the only things that prevented Canada's waterfronts from exploding into repeated acts of violence and criminality.

In his memoir *Waterfront Blues*, Alex Pathy, a leading Canadian shipping executive, gave a very generous account of my work before the commission:

> From the start, it was clear that Mulroney was well suited for his new responsibilities. He was bilingual, had the "gift of the gab," and was a formidable debater whose skills were put to the test in the

> courtroom setting of the commission's hearing – a perfect training for a career in politics. Proving a formidable opponent of Phil Cutler, Mulroney succeeded to a remarkable degree in keeping the ILA [International Longshoremen's Association] counsel under control, thwarting most of his efforts to browbeat and dictate to [Commissioner] Picard. Young and inexperienced he may have been but he had all the right stuff to battle a seasoned labour lawyer to a draw. He also won a great deal of admiration for his dogged perseverance in keeping the hearings on track, ever mindful of the need for the commission to conclude its work in time for Picard to write his report and deliver it before the end of 1967.
>
> And there was still more to his contribution. Though he began with no knowledge of the shipping industry, and relied initially on facts and arguments given him by the Federation, he allowed himself to be a quick study, mastering the essentials of the business from scratch and displaying an immediate recognition of the importance of unity on the employers' side. In subsequent negotiations, Mulroney's increasing talents in the art of mediation would become apparent, and in the early days of the Maritime Employers Association, when the fledgling body was suffering from serious teething troubles, he would be a tower of strength both to me and to Arnie Masters, the association's president. There can be little doubt that Mulroney's work for the employers on the Montreal waterfront caught the eye of Premier Robert Bourassa, who in 1974 appointed him to the Cliche Commission . . . another stepping stone in his successful ascent to the office of Prime Minister.

As a young lawyer with a mother and siblings to support, I worked very hard in those years, and I am pleased to recall that I became known as one of the firm's good producers at a very young age, with billable hours significantly above the median, and accounts to clients far in excess of what the firm expected. This was heady stuff for a kid from Baie-Comeau.

By the early 1970s I had become the lead counsel for the entire shipping industry and, with board approval, incorporated the Maritime Employers Association and became its first president. This was on a pro tem basis, pending the arrival of Arnie Masters, whom I recruited to serve as our first permanent president and CEO. Arnie had been Minister of Labour Bryce Mackasey's executive assistant and served effectively for fifteen years in the job of overseeing the modernization of one of Canada's most vital economic generators, in the days before air freight rivalled shipping by sea.

During my early years I was involved in some fascinating and challenging cases, and one of them took my life full circle. In 1967, a wildcat strike shut down the entire Canadian British Aluminium operation in Baie-Comeau, and I was dispatched by Paul Renault as the first lawyer on the scene. By the mid 1960s Baie-Comeau's population depended for its livelihood on two major industries. The aluminium industry was represented by Canadian British Aluminium Inc., a subsidiary of British Aluminium Inc., of England, and the forestry industry by Quebec & Ontario Paper Company, whose parent company had its head office in Chicago. These two companies had given me summer jobs, and they also provided employment for the local population and for the surrounding municipalities, particularly Hauterive, which served as a bedroom community to Baie-Comeau, as well as containing its airport. The labour forces of both companies were highly unionized and the blue-collar employees, who constituted the vast majority of the work force, were represented by the CNTU (CSN) [Confederation of National Trade Unions (Confédération des syndicats nationaux)], which had a virtual monopoly on the North Shore.

As a result of some difficult bargaining over the renewal of the collective agreement, along with strained labour-management relations, the employees were induced by their local and regional union leadership into declaring an illegal strike. There was no forewarning of this wildcat strike. Relations were so bad that violence or threatened violence prevented plant supervisors from moving in to organize an orderly shutdown of the aluminium furnaces. As a result, much of the molten ore in the furnace froze, causing the loss not only of the product in process but, disastrously, of the furnaces themselves. It was many weeks before production could resume, initially with those furnaces that had been spared and subsequently with the addition of furnaces that could be salvaged. In the end, damages resulting from the illegal strike were estimated to be well over $6 million, in 1966 dollars.

I was responsible for conducting the sensitive negotiations that brought about a return to work and set in train an arbitration system headed by Judge René Lippé. In the end, the matter was resolved only years later before the Superior Court by my partners William Tyndale and Casper Bloom, where the essence of the decisions we made that summer of 1967 were sustained, and $6 million in damages was awarded to our clients at Canadian British Aluminium.

I also saw the difference in rewards that seniority brings. Early one Sunday morning, while returning in a small private plane from one of my many trips to Baie-Comeau and exhausted from another bruising week on the CBA file, I looked down to enjoy the view of the majestic St. Lawrence. As we flew low over an oncoming cargo ship, I noticed a distinctive white Cadillac secured to the deck. It was headed to Italy and it belonged to my boss, Paul Renault, who was taking his family to Europe for a summer vacation. I clearly had a long way to go, but was encouraged to see what the rewards of success actually looked like.

Although I invariably represented management in labour matters, it is fair to say that I acquired a reputation with union counsel and union leaders as someone whose word could be trusted and who would never take unfair advantage of the other side. I was raised in a unionized mill worker's home and I had a genuine appreciation of the important role good trade unions have played in improving the lives of countless Canadians. To me, fairness meant fairness for everyone. I think this attitude, which generated respect throughout the arcane world of sensitive labour conflicts, was also instrumental in my later political success. For example, when I first ran for the leadership of the Progressive Conservative Party in 1976, leaders of Quebec's biggest unions and their counsel, led by Louis Laberge and Phil Cutler, openly supported my candidacy, calling me "an honest man who was always fair and true to his word." André Dalcourt of the CNTU was another labour leader who spoke up for me. "He could have crushed us – we had no bargaining power – but he didn't," Dalcourt said in an interview unrelated to the leadership. My dad would have been pleased to see that I was making my way without turning my back in any way on our working-class roots.

At the end of 1969 I was approached by Terry Copp, a friend and history professor at Loyola College in Montreal, about a faculty purge at the college in which twenty-nine professors, associate professors, and teaching assistants were arbitrarily terminated. This caused an explosion in university circles and became a *cause célèbre*, involving as it did questions of academic freedom, due process, and basic justice. After reviewing all the facts, I concluded the firings were a major violation of the teachers' basic rights. Following meetings with Terry and with Donald Savage, who later served as president of the Canadian Association of University Teachers, I agreed to take on the case of "the Loyola 29."

(The professors who hired me were unaware that I had long known about the prickly attitudes that Loyola's administrators displayed on occasion. As far back as 1958, I had learned that activists – especially of the Progressive Conservative kind – were not always welcomed with open arms at Loyola. Pierre Panneton of the school's embryonic PC club had written to me at StFX in October that year. "Dear Brian: I am having some difficulty with the Jesuits in organizing a Conservative Club in Loyola," he wrote. "Could you send me word concerning your activities in Saint Francis Xavier? What are you allowed to do, what cooperation do you get from university authorities, if meetings are held on the campus or outside, if you are allowed to advertise meetings and distribute pamphlets, etc. Such precedents would be very useful: I am to meet the Superior of Loyola College soon and would be very grateful if I could get this information before then." Despite this forewarning, I did what I could to help out at Loyola.)

The administration at Loyola College in Montreal was led by its strong-willed president, Father Malone, and advised by Timothy Slattery, Q.C., a distinguished lawyer and the biographer of Thomas D'Arcy McGee. The administration was close to the leadership of the Royal Bank of Canada, our biggest client, and I was aware of questions raised about the propriety of my acting "for the unions." But no one at Howard Cate put pressure on me, and I met with the government and secured the appointment of a special inquiry headed by Professor Percy Meyer, who was empowered to take evidence and render binding judgment in the matter.

Professor Savage eventually published an analysis of these later events and my role in them, in which he wrote:

> Mr. Mulroney persuaded us not to advance the argument of a conspiracy or political purge which was difficult to prove in law although almost everyone believed they had existed. He then suggested the terms of reference should be to test through binding arbitration the reasons offered by the President to the media, namely financial exigency and the question of merit, which could be dealt with as matters of fact. The administration was trapped in its own rhetoric. When it seemed the administration would not agree, Mr. Mulroney threatened to leave the inquiry, inform the

Quebec government, and call a public meeting on the Loyola campus. The college agreed, and Professor Meyer was invested with the required powers. Mr. Mulroney had outmanoeuvred both the President, and his advisors and allies.

By this time, in my judgment, the issue for Mr. Mulroney had grown from being a favour to a friend [Terry Copp] to a growing anger that the administration of a Catholic college was not only operating in an unjust way but was victimizing young members of the staff simply because others were protected by tenure. It is true that the more radical members of ALP found Mr. Mulroney less than totally sympathetic . . . Mr. Mulroney wanted to save the college from itself so that it could continue to be a viable and useful Catholic institution. It was never his view that the college should be transformed politically – only that there should be due process, constitutional procedures, and justice to the December 15 victims. It should be remembered that Mr. Mulroney had inquired into a confrontation in the Federation of English Catholic Charities in Montreal with much the same ends in mind. Mr. Mulroney also found that the college could put pressure on Ogilvy, Cope, Porteous of a kind that is not hard to imagine. Fortunately, both the firm and Mr. Mulroney ignored these pressures.

The hearings went on for weeks. Professor Copp was the principal organizer on the side of the ALP. Mr. Mulroney made periodic appearances at the inquiry as promised, consulted on strategy, and made a devastating summation at the end . . . The victory party with Mr. Mulroney at the faculty club was one of the more memorable events of that remarkable academic year . . . As is often the way, the administration tried to weasel out of the award by writing new and objectionable contracts for those who had been restored. Mr. Mulroney saw to it that the contracts were revised and offered properly. [Almost all of the professors were rehired.] . . . The events of 1969–70 not only showed Mr. Mulroney to be a skilled negotiator but also someone willing to defend academic freedom and due process.

It was 1967, Expo year, and Montreal was alive with glamour and excitement. I remember how glorious the weather was that summer and how delightful and stimulating life was for me and all of my young friends. I had never seen anything so splendid – the music, sights, and sounds at La Ronde, and the sparkling islands in the river with their World's Fair pavilions. I recall the drama and headlines as Lionel Chevrier, Expo's courtly host, greeted one international leader or celebrity after another; one day it was General Charles de Gaulle, the next the Queen, the next President Lyndon Johnson. Although we young lawyers had punishing work schedules that summer, we still managed to gather frequently at Le Carrefour for a few Scotches before heading off to La Ronde for the evening, followed by a night of revelry at any one of an unlimited number of bars and singalong joints that had sprung up to accommodate the bursting, happy crowds of people that dominated every waking hour in Montreal. I don't know how I managed to show up for work every morning that summer with even a modicum of coherence in my thoughts and words. Only the resilience of youth could explain the miracle of an early rise after another night of celebration in that memorable summer of 1967.

6. Politics and Strikes

During my early law career in Montreal I also stayed actively involved in the affairs of the Progressive Conservative Party of Canada. But my misgivings about Mr. Diefenbaker, who was increasingly alienating both young voters and French Canadians, continued to grow. As far back as 1963 a sense of frustration at the situation – why couldn't a man who had energized and inspired a nation only a few years before see how Canada was changing? – had gripped me as I attended a meeting of Quebec's young Tories. I went public with my frustration, and proposed the following motion:

> Whereas the main problem facing Canada today concerns the continuing existence of Canada as a whole; Whereas this existence depends for the most part on a close collaboration between Canadians of French expression and Canadians of English expression; Whereas such harmony does not exist today because of the obstacles preventing the full development of the French "nation"; Whereas the leaders of the PC Party have been making declarations which can only harm relations between French and English speaking Canadians; Be it Hereby Resolved: 1) that the Party Leaders cease making statements on this matter; 2) that the research department of the PC Party develop a long-term policy on this matter; 3) that is to be presented for approval at the annual general meeting in February 1964 and then become an integral part of our party platform.

The motion passed. Joe Clark, then head of the Progressive Conservative Student Federation, was the most outspoken in his support of the initiative that Dalton Camp would soon launch (incurring in the process Diefenbaker's undying contempt), but the rest of us all rallied around. Later, in February of 1965, Joe bravely took to his feet at a meeting of the party's executive and said that Mr. Diefenbaker should resign and a leadership convention should be called.

"I have been following the events of the last few days quite closely," I wrote to him, "and was especially interested, not only in your Ottawa statement, but the manner in which you made it. I share the opinion of a lot of people who feel that your statement was a thoughtful one and, as usual, you were articulate in making it (this must come, at least in part, from the long nights of debating up in the Gatineaus with Paschal and Louise!). I spoke with Lowell a few days ago and it seems that we may have the opportunity of getting together in the near future. I do hope you will give me a call when next you are within striking distance of Montreal."

Later that year, in September 1965, Prime Minister Pearson called a general election for November 8. We all had to put our differences aside and do what comes naturally to any good Tory: Unite to fight the Grits. Davie Fulton, for example, returned and came back inside the tent to run under Mr. Diefenbaker's banner, and there were other rebels who joined up again for the fight. Early on in the campaign, I was there as George Hees agreed to return to the party fold and run again as a candidate. One day I found myself at lunch at the Laurentian Hotel in Montreal with Alvin Hamilton, Roy Faibish, the philosopher George Grant (author of *Lament for a Nation*), and others as we discussed Hees's return. After the campaign, I filled my friend Peter Newman in on the event with a memo, passing along an anecdote that shows why we all loved George Hees as we did. "Upon his return to [his riding of] Northumberland," I told Peter, "[Liberal] Pauline Jewett referred to him as 'nothing more than an aging Errol Flynn.' When asked to comment on her remarks, Hees replied, 'Well, if I'm aging, she'll certainly be the last to know about it.'"

The party's efforts in Quebec, however, where I was concentrating my own efforts, were no laughing matter. While Mr. Diefenbaker brilliantly waged war on the Grits across the Prairies and through small-town Canada – he ran a whistle-stop campaign in the manner of Harry Truman in 1948 – his efforts in Quebec were perfunctory at best.

I was angry and disappointed. My feelings spilled over after the former prime minister appeared in Montreal early in the campaign. "1) The welcome organized for Mr. Diefenbaker at Central Station last night was an absolute disgrace," I told Tom Van Dusen in a memo I also sent to campaign director Eddie Goodman the next day. "It had the further unfortunate effect of detracting from the success of his earlier foray into the Eastern

Townships. With a turnout of less than one hundred in a city of more than two million people, it is clear that no one in our Quebec organization made the slightest effort to arrange a suitable welcome. 2) Mr. Diefenbaker's future appearances in Quebec during the campaign must be skilfully organized well in advance so as to avoid repeat performances of last night. Strict orders should be given to Quebec organizers in this regard immediately. 3) Should Mr. Diefenbaker plan a Montreal rally within the next few weeks, and if our organizers are too preoccupied with other things to guarantee its total success, may I, on behalf of a group of young people here, offer to help: we will guarantee a dandy."

Despite the troubles in the Diefenbaker campaign, our dwindling band of Quebec Tories soldiered on. Montreal Liberal MP John Turner, whom I knew and respected through our contacts in Montreal legal circles, was already on the rise in the Liberal ranks and was sought after as a speaker in ridings outside the city and province. I read one account of one of his meetings and couldn't help responding – whatever my private doubts about my party's leader – in a letter to the editor that was published in the *Montreal Star*. I wrote, "Speaking at a Liberal nominating convention in Toronto last Thursday, Mr. John N. Turner, MP, is reported to have said: 'If Mr. Diefenbaker were to become Prime Minister again it would mean one-man government, palace revolutions, economic jingoism, anti-Americanism, and a new wave of French separatism.' It's unfortunate that Mr. Turner ran out of breath when things were just getting exciting. As his hindsight is, no doubt, just as well developed as his great capacity for prophecy, I am sure he would have wanted to tell his fellow Grits just how Mr. Diefenbaker stabbed Julius Caesar, started the War of 1812, and caused the Irish Potato Famine."

(John, it must be said, returned the favour years later when he accused me, in effect, of planning to visit all sorts of plagues upon our country through the Free Trade Agreement. I guess we were even.)

On election day in 1965, the PCs were once again losers. Although Mr. Diefenbaker had held the Grits to minority status, nothing could change the fact we were still out of power. While our leader dug in for the long haul, many party members were angry and believed there was only one solution: The leader had to go.

Mr. Diefenbaker didn't help his cause in the least when he fired one of the most popular and loyal workers party headquarters was ever destined to see, Flora MacDonald. For many thousands of party volunteers Flora, a hard-working woman who had made her own way from small-town Cape Breton, was the face of the party in Ottawa. She worked long hours in the interests of the party and was able and effective. Like most rank-and-file members, I was furious when she was fired. "Am shocked by this unspeakable example of ingratitude," I told her by telegram. "Be assured of my support. Please call me."

Twenty-three years later MP Flora MacDonald was defeated in the free trade election of 1988. At the first subsequent cabinet meeting, I said, "I met Flora thirty years ago. I know something about fighting the odds, but no one in public life fought longer odds to succeed than Flora. Any book or reference to the PC Party over the last three and a half decades has a place of honour for Flora. She and I sat together in backrooms and in the House of Commons. Her life has been a story of remarkable achievement. There would be few, if any, parallels to rival the impact Flora has made on this party, this country."

In 1966 the dam burst and Dalton Camp launched an all-out campaign for a leadership review. The idea was a good one, based on an obvious fact that is universally accepted today: that the leader governs the party only with its consent and that periodically, especially following electoral defeats, this consent should be reviewed.

When Quebec's Tories gathered in early October of 1966, I had no choice but to once again speak out in support of the principle Camp was fighting for, painful as that was for me. John Diefenbaker had been the first politician to inspire me, and I took no pleasure in addressing my fellow delegates. With sadness more than anything else, I later summed up my feelings in a letter to Terry Flahiff at my dad's old company, who had heard of my remarks and sent along his congratulations. "My remarks to the convention were quite brief," I wrote.

> I merely pointed out that everyone, humble or great, is called upon regularly to render a regular account of himself and/or his actions to his wife, to his family, to his associates, to his clients – and in some cases – to his bank manager. I said no one thrust the leadership on Mr. Diefenbaker. On the contrary, he very actively sought same and, once leader, he assumed, in my view, all the obligations of an ordinary trustee, chief among which is the obligation to render an account of the manner in which he has discharged his

> responsibility. I stated that I could see nothing dishonourable or demeaning in asking the leader of a major political party in a democracy to return to the source of his authority and seek a renewal of his mandate from ordinary party members in an atmosphere devoid of emotion, an atmosphere which would allow delegates to vote on the matter as they saw fit without fear of reprisal.
>
> I concluded with the observation that an unfortunate tendency seemed to be developing of late in some quarters of the Conservative Party, namely the confusion of dissent with disloyalty. It is a basic right of a party member to voice a dissenting opinion – especially in support of a democratic principle – and it is an equally basic right that such an opinion be respected by the leadership, however much the leader might think that he has long since acquired squatter's rights on the job.

Mr. Diefenbaker interpreted the overall initiative as an indirect and cowardly assault on his own leadership, and soon the battle was joined. The focal point was to be the election of the new president of the Progressive Conservative Association of Canada. Camp stood as the candidate in favour of a leadership review and my friend Arthur Maloney, a colourful and skilled Toronto criminal lawyer, represented the status quo. As Maloney said in one of his eloquent defences of the leader, "When John Diefenbaker enters a room, Arthur Maloney stands up!"

Emotions ran high, and bitter personal attacks dominated debate as we gathered in Ottawa in November 1966 for the annual meeting that was to resolve the matter. It was an especially difficult time for me because, while I supported Camp's motion and therefore his candidacy, I was a personal friend of Maloney. I decided to face the issue directly and spoke with Maloney and also wrote to him to express my feelings. "Although we have just spoken over the phone," I said, "I do want to tell you of the very real dilemma your candidacy poses for me: on the one hand, I have publicly committed myself to support the principle on which Dalton has been conducting his campaign and on the other, my deep affection and high regard for you as an individual and a friend. There are few things I would rather do than have the privilege of publicly supporting you for any office you chose to seek. Because of a month-earlier commitment [to Dalton Camp], however, this privilege is now denied me, and I do hope you will understand the real sense of regret and disappointment I feel at this time."

It was heartbreaking to see the bitterness at that convention – fistfights in the lobby of the Château Laurier, brutal insults hurled between the Diefenbaker loyalists and the so-called "Camp followers." Russell Keays, an otherwise amiable MP from the Gaspé, even took a swing at me one night as I entered Maloney's suite in the Château, in the mistaken belief that I was there to cause trouble. He inflicted only a small cut near my nose and was soon restrained.

Diefenbaker made a powerful speech, with a visibly uncomfortable Dalton sitting slightly behind him on the same stage. But it was not enough to carry the day, and Dalton – together with his resolution calling for a leadership convention, which also passed – retained the presidency of the party by a margin of sixty-two votes, 564 to 502. But that was the last joyful moment Dalton was to have in the party for many years. After the convention, he was pilloried as the architect of the regicide. Diefenbaker, until the day he died, made sure that his arch-enemy was unwelcome in the PC Party. And so Dalton – who had introduced this noteworthy reform into Canadian politics – became a pariah, playing a progressively marginal role in his own party until, wounded and embittered by the attacks and loss of influence, he retired to the New Brunswick countryside to write (which he did brilliantly), and to commentate (which he did entertainingly).

I had always thought this *fin de carrière* was deeply unfair to Dalton and it was largely with the view of rehabilitating his reputation – by now he was characterized only as "the man who got rid of Diefenbaker" – that I appointed him in 1986 to the position of senior advisor to the prime minister.

This ousting of Diefenbaker and the close vote deeply divided the party for the next twenty years. In retrospect, I think we made a serious mistake. Dalton Camp and his supporters should have introduced the accountability motion, but stated that it would apply only to future leaders. Because Diefenbaker rightly assumed that the initiative was designed to drive him from office, he fought it tooth and nail.

—

PERSONAL JOURNAL: JULY 23, 1987

My principal duty is to the country and then to my party and those who support it. I have long felt that an important reason for a lack of success came from the fact that some previous leaders failed to recognize that their personal interest and aspirations were subordinate to those of the general well-being of the party. The leadership of the party then became a symbol of hostility to many when it should have represented unity and openness to most. Simply put, while leader of this party, I am also its servant; its welfare takes precedence over my own ambitions. If I conclude that I have been – unfairly or otherwise – hobbled and no longer am a demonstrable asset to my party, I shall unhesitatingly submit my resignation and ask the party to choose a new leader.

—

At the time, Diefenbaker had been party leader for less than ten years, had won three consecutive elections, and had given the party almost six years of power, the longest such run since Sir Robert Borden. I believe now that he was entitled to choose his moment of retirement, although few trusted his comment to the effect that "if they will only stop pushing, I'll go under my own steam," believing that he wanted to win one more election, as a vindication. His removal from office by members of a party he had led to victory was more than he could endure, and the resulting disunity impaired our chances of success for years. The Ottawa media, especially the up-and-coming young Peter Newman, painted a very dark portrait of Diefenbaker and we were all foolish enough to believe it.

Diefenbaker had his flaws and failings, but he possessed many admirable traits as well. These tended to be blotted out by negative coverage that left Canadians with an unattractive, one-dimensional view of Mr. Diefenbaker. My generation had not yet learned that the media are relentless in their assault upon Conservative leaders who win, thereby depriving "the natural governing party," the Liberals, of time in office, which the Grits (and too many others in Ottawa) take as their rightful due. Joe Clark and I would one day find this out for ourselves.

—

PERSONAL JOURNAL: JULY 23, 1987

It is always difficult for politicians to realize that they have become an important part of the problem. They can cry unfairness and injustice for weeks, but such conduct and lamentation will change nothing. For my part, if I am satisfied that I am indeed part of the problem and that I am incapable of correcting the matter within the time frame remaining, I hope I shall have the decency and the courage to remember and to reflect upon my higher obligation to the democratic well-being of the general membership of my party, and through them, my ultimate duty to my country. Politics has a harsh and unforgiving dimension. I knew that when I entered without complaint but I shall leave at an appropriate time and manner without regret.

—

At the time of Expo 67, Daniel Johnson was Quebec premier, having led the Union Nationale to an absolutely stunning victory in June 1966 over the seemingly invincible and highly accomplished Lesage government. Johnson's stay in office was brief, as this engaging and talented leader, whom I had come to know well at many late-night sessions in Quebec City, was struck down by a heart attack in 1968. He was succeeded by Jean-Jacques Bertrand, a pleasant and unassuming lawyer from Cowansville, who would prove no match for the vaunted Liberal machine with its new leader, Robert Bourassa, two years later.

I knew both Johnson and Bertrand quite well, and assisted Bertrand in fending off a leadership challenge by Jean-Guy Cardinal. English-speaking supporters were few and far between in the party, so I was approached to become a member of the Montreal Catholic School Board, an important post that paid quite a handsome stipend in those days. Because I was unmarried, it seemed wrong to accept the appointment, and I declined it. I also declined the opportunity to acquire a Loto Québec franchise offered to me by Mario Beaulieu and party treasurer Marcel Faribault, because I thought others were more deserving, and that it would appear inappropriate for me to be so rewarded. While this decision might have had some merit from the standpoint of selflessness, it was in fact a significant misjudgment, as that franchise would have provided the financial security that I needed even then to look after my mother and my siblings, who had not yet graduated from college. I was progressing well in the firm, but I still needed every nickel to get by. I could have changed that by accepting the lottery franchise, which later made millionaires of other concession holders. My refusal to accept would surely surprise those critics who would later seek to paint me as avaricious and money-grubbing, among other elegant qualities.

In the wake of Camp's victory, the party had called a national leadership convention for September 1967 in Toronto. For some years I had been quietly raising money and organizing for Davie Fulton. "Please advise if you have any objections to my 'campaigning' (very discreetly, I assure you) on your behalf," I had written to him from Halifax way back in the winter of 1960, adding the names of certain student leaders he might think of contacting.

Davie soon responded, advising me to cool my enthusiasm. "I appreciate the campaigning you have been doing on my behalf," he wrote. "It is a very real encouragement to know that I have such good friends, but while I highly prize your friendship and support, I do not think that a campaign in the plain and ordinary sense of the word should be carried on or encouraged by me at the present time; all in good time."

Little did I know that I would be penning similar letters to overly enthusiastic friends and supporters during the Clark years. I do note today, however, that Davie, ever the politician, mentioned in that March 1960 letter that he had indeed sent letters of introduction to the Halifax student leaders I'd told him about. All in good time.

When Davie entered the 1967 race to replace Diefenbaker, I introduced him to future Power Corporation chairman and CEO Paul Desmarais over lunch at the Forest and Stream Club on the West Island. Paul made a major contribution to his campaign, but lunch was cut short because he and I had to attend a closing downtown; it was the day he bought *La Presse*.

During the campaign Davie had a good team. Lowell Murray served as his campaign manager and Joe Clark acted ably as one of his assistants. We did all right, but our thunder was surprisingly stolen by the low-key Bob Stanfield, whom we all supported when Davie withdrew after the fourth ballot.

Once again, Diefenbaker provided the drama. He had declared his candidacy at the last moment, and he made a riveting and memorable address to the convention, warning of the dangers of adopting the "two nations" theory being espoused by Marcel Faribault and others. It was heart-rending. There was Diefenbaker, whom I had supported eleven years earlier, surrounded by his loyal coterie of Tom Van Dusen, Greg Guthrie, Jim Johnson, and broadcaster Joel Alfred. Now he was seventy-two years old and fighting passionately for vindication and to prevent the "termites" (as he called everyone associated with Camp) from seizing central control of the party.

Once the smoke had cleared, and after the publication of his book *The Chief*, I summed up my feelings about this chapter in our party's history in a letter to Tom Van Dusen. "I was particularly impressed by the degree of impartiality you showed in judging the actions of others (the anti-Diefenbaker group, if you will) particularly when those of us who were members of that group often failed to exercise a commensurate degree of restraint," I told Tom. "My recollection is that the group, of which I was a member, did not oppose Mr. Diefenbaker merely for the pleasure of opposing him. I would like to think that we all honestly felt that he was no longer in touch with our generation, the mood of urban Canada, and the aspirations of Quebec. Whether we were right or wrong is an open question. I can only say that in my case, and I am sure in that of many others, the vote in favour of a motion requesting a review of leadership (which of course was a vote against Mr. Diefenbaker) was one cast more in sorrow than anger."

Tom, who later brought his skills, energy, and unparalleled knowledge of Tory and Canadian history to my own political offices as a senior and valued assistant, answered my letter. His reply showed that he, the ultimate Diefenbaker loyalist, knew the unity of the country was more important than any single politician's ambitions. It was time to move forward.

"Where do we go from here?" Tom wrote. "I personally believe the central issue is the relationship between French and English Canada; and I believe a line must be drawn between a province, Quebec, and French Canada, which is larger than Quebec. I am not so ready as Mr. Lévesque to sacrifice the one million French Canadians outside Quebec; nor can I see any prospect of realizing his vision of continuing conjugal relations after the divorce. It isn't done. I think we will have to ensure equality of language and educational rights from coast to coast if we want French Canada to stay within Confederation, in order to relieve the pressure in Quebec. I have no assurance that giving to French Canadians the right to be Canadian and remain French will hold Canada together; but if we do not go that far, at least, as far as the Fathers went within the territories then populated by French Canadians, then we cannot complain about what happens."

John Diefenbaker, however, had no intention of looking forward. After his defeat on the leadership review the previous year he addressed his troops, many in shock and in tears, in the Château Laurier lobby and quoted lines from a ballad about the fifteenth-century Scottish privateer, Sir Andrew Barton:

I am hurt but I am not slain
I'le lay me down and bleed a-while
And then I'le rise and fight again.

And fight he did. Unfortunately it was mostly with Tories, as Diefenbaker implacably settled scores over the years with anyone not fully on his side. He had to wait patiently for nine years, but at the 1976 leadership convention it was my turn to feel the pain of a Diefenbaker attack. It proved to be lethal.

I often reflected later on Diefenbaker's indifference to the party and caucus, which cost him dearly. Even more self-destructive, however, was his view that anyone who opposed him at the 1956 convention and over the years was an irreconcilable adversary, to be tolerated, perhaps, but never to be trusted. That lack of trust (and of any generous outreach) would eventually contribute to a serious erosion of his support within caucus, cabinet, and the national executive. This lesson became powerfully clear to me at an early age: caucus solidarity is indispensable for long-term success and only the leader can bring that about, provided he works at it relentlessly. I came away from this tumultuous period in the party with an enhanced appreciation of the role of caucus members and a conviction that any leader would be foolish not to ensure their paramountcy in any of his plans. I was frankly surprised to see that both Stanfield and Clark, for all their fine qualities, failed to give their caucuses the care, attention, and respect that would ensure unshakable loyalty and devotion. I knew how vital a priority caucus unity was and I was resolved to enshrine it in fact when I assumed the party leadership, many years later.

We soared in the polls in the early months of Stanfield's leadership but trouble was brewing. In the same way as I had (with little success) sent advice to Diefenbaker, I immediately advised the new leader, through Dalton Camp, to better acquaint himself with Quebec. A week after Stanfield had been elected leader, I sent him a memo with some suggestions regarding my home province. I proposed that he needed an adept and experienced French-Canadian assistant in his office, and regular contact with Quebec opinion leaders, and also suggested that he work to improve his French-language skills.

"I realize that Mr. Stanfield is going to be quite busy during the interim, but I would strongly suggest that he find time to take the Berlitz Total

Immersion Course at 50 Place Crémazie, Montreal," I wrote Dalton. "Davie Fulton took this course last May with outstanding results and I believe that now would be a good time for Mr. Stanfield to set aside a week for this type of activity . . . I believe it important that the leader undertake at some convenient time a regular series of dinner meetings with French Canadians from all walks of life. Let's say that Mr. Stanfield, once installed in Stornoway, decided to set aside one Sunday evening a month for dinner with people from Quebec. The guests at this first dinner could be people like [newspaper editor] Claude Ryan, poet Gilles Vigneault, Paul Desmarais . . . and [Father] Gérard Dion, dean of Industrial Relations at Laval University. After a half-dozen such encounters, I dare say that Mr. Stanfield would be as well attuned to the mainstream of Quebec thought as anyone else in the province."

Mr. Stanfield did indeed do his best to improve our party's and his own understanding of Quebec. One day, shortly after he became leader, I went to visit with him at the Berlitz school, off the Metropolitan Boulevard in northeastern Montreal. I had been instructed to get his signature on a sheaf of documents, after which we had a coffee and chatted in French. I was impressed: here was a successful premier from a very privileged background, almost fifty-four years of age, sitting in a hot little room learning conversational French. Language has always been the great equalizer in Canadian politics and I was touched by the sight of this equable and talented man struggling to learn a language he now desperately needed in order to campaign and eventually to govern. I feared, however, that he might be too late, because we discussed that day the rumours of Prime Minister Pearson's imminent retirement, and the possibility of the Tories facing a fresh and younger challenger. Justice Minister Pierre Elliott Trudeau had made a very favourable impression at a recent federal-provincial conference, and we were aware that many Liberals were speaking admiringly of his electoral appeal. If that happened, Stanfield and I agreed that we would be fighting a different election from the one we had confidently anticipated just a few short months ago.

In my personal life, it was soon clear that my impecunious state, aggravated by unanticipated family responsibilities, meant that Johanne and I could not proceed as we had planned. It would have been deeply unfair to ask her to wait any longer in Quebec City when my financial situation was so precarious, and my family commitments of such uncertain duration. And so we agreed to part. As I drove back to Montreal after our tearful meeting in Quebec City I felt an enormous sense of loss. Johanne was my first great love, a marvellous young woman, and I already missed her enormously. Some time later, I learned that she had met a well-regarded doctor, whom she eventually married and with whom she had a large, successful family.

My colleague Frank Common and his wife, Kay, frequently held dinner parties at their home on Edgehill Road in Westmount. These were fabulous events loaded with good food, great wines, and some of the most impressive people in town. Frank also was a great piano player who knew, I swear, almost every popular song ever written. After every dinner he would play and we would all sing the night away. The Commons frequently included unattached lawyers in their parties whenever they needed an extra man or someone to occupy a chair, and I was very happy to fill the role.

One night at a buffet dinner I wound up at a table where I was introduced to a young couple named Paul and Jackie Desmarais. It was 1965 and Paul was just beginning the series of daring initiatives that would make him one of the most successful and admired businessmen in Canadian history. He was tall and lean and he and his glamorous young wife made a striking couple. They were effortlessly bilingual, well informed, and intellectually curious, and we spent the entire evening discussing world events, the upcoming Expo 67, and local gossip. Until, that is, Frank sat down to play – and I discovered that Jackie was also a talented singer with a sultry voice who, like me, needed no second invitation to join in or perform solo.

That night sparked a wonderful friendship that has grown and endured for more than forty years. Outside of my immediate family, no one has been closer or kinder to me and Mila than Jackie and Paul, and no one has benefited more than I from their good judgment and support – given generously and loyally at every crucial moment of my career – both in victory and defeat, in good times and bad.

At work, I was graduating to even more challenging files. After a lengthy and explosive lockout had shut down his paper, *La Presse*, for eight months, Paul Desmarais approached me, hoping that I'd take over the stalled negotiations on behalf of management. I was reluctant at first. There didn't seem any way to find a winner in the *La Presse* situation. There was not one but eleven different unions involved, from two different umbrella groups, the Quebec Federation of Labour and the Confederation of National Trade Unions. The dispute was over management's plan to modernize the newspaper's printing process with the introduction of computers. Quebec's powerful unions weren't ready for this shift in 1971–72. Workers in all areas of *La Presse*'s production had been locked out, and the newspaper's journalists were to be next on the street. Reporters were now demanding a say in the editorial direction of the paper, and the right to choose their own editors. There were mass demonstrations, boycotts, even violence, and the situation became a *cause célèbre* that was taken up by the province's union movement.

In the end I replied, "Paul, it has to be clearly understood that I'm in charge, carte blanche, otherwise I don't get involved."

Paul agreed and I took over the file. I was very ably assisted throughout by a young John Rae, Paul's executive assistant. Rae was a delight to work with – well informed, hard-working, and entertaining – and, in spite of our political differences (Rae is a prominent Liberal), we have maintained an excellent relationship over the years.

Things were going so badly in the *La Presse* negotiations that the two sides had stopped talking. I knew we had to change the pattern. So I picked up the telephone and called Louis Laberge, president of the QFL and Marcel Pepin, from the CNTU, directly. Like me, they had taken over from their local reps and knew that it was time all three of us rolled up our sleeves and got everybody back to work.

After some initial skirmishing, the three of us wound up in a suite at the Queen Elizabeth Hotel. I produced a basic rule: nobody went home until we had hammered out a deal. We negotiated for seven straight days and nights. Throughout our negotiations, the suite was dark with the haze of cigarette smoke – all three of us smoked – and stocked with a generous supply of Scotch (for me), cognac (for Pepin), and Labatt's (for Laberge, who told me with a big smile, at about 4:00 a.m. during a break, "I get away with drinking so much Labatt's because they're unionized!"). Eventually, we emerged with an agreement that was acceptable to all sides, and the newspaper was soon back into production and profitable once again.

Though I had once again represented management, I was pleased that the unions respected my sense of fair play. "He defused a very tense situation," Claude Beauchamp, who headed the journalists' union at the newspaper, later said in an interview. "He came in, talked to everybody, sized up the situation and then, I suppose, talked to Desmarais. You've got to assume that Mulroney brought him around to a more realistic appraisal of the facts. Within three or four days, negotiations had resumed and we were on our way to a settlement."

This had been such a public and explosive strike that my role in ending it did wonders for my public profile. I was also retained to negotiate the first collective agreement at *Le Journal de Montréal* at the request of another brilliant young entrepreneur, Pierre Péladeau, who was on his way to creating Quebecor Inc., a new international media giant, and with whom I remained on close terms until his death, a quarter of a century later.

Quebec was changing dramatically. The Quiet Revolution had produced many shifts, none more dramatic than the nationalization of electricity and the creation of Hydro-Québec and of the Caisse de dépôt et placement with the vast economic might it would throw behind Quebec's rising entrepreneurial class. The political and economic self-confidence that ensued made for an exciting period. For the first time, French Canadians began to reach for leadership in business and finance, as they had for decades in politics, medicine, and the law. The province was a swirling centre of real power and real money and, as a thirty-year-old lawyer, I was being drawn into its vortex. Over time I acted for, and became friendly with, many of the most influential leaders in the province who would later play a key role in my rise to power.

Quebec is in many ways a tribal society. Although I was of Irish background, my Baie-Comeau roots and my French-language fluency made me part of the tribe. My working-class background gave me an easy rapport with union leaders across the province. My professional life brought me into familiar contact with many of Montreal's economic elite, and my political activity – especially on behalf of the unthreatening Tories – made me a bit of a player on the Montreal scene. I enjoyed it all tremendously.

One night I remember reading the bulldog edition of *The Gazette* while having a lean smoked meat sandwich at Ben's Delicatessen, and seeing my name in a Montreal paper for the first time, in a report on a strike I had just settled. I was starry-eyed and couldn't take my gaze off the story. All the way home on the bus, I marvelled about the opportunities and delights of Montreal, and how thrilled I was to be there at this special point in my life. I was a kid from a small town trying to make it in the city – the stuff of a million stories and as many dreams – but when I got back to the apartment in NDG that night and showed *The Gazette* to my proud mother I actually felt I was on my way. Needless to say, I had no idea of the challenges and defeats I would encounter on the journey, but that night I felt I could go anywhere.

7. Trudeau's October

In 1968 Pierre Elliott Trudeau was chosen by the Liberal Party to succeed Lester B. Pearson as leader. Only a few years earlier Trudeau had been an NDP activist unleashing bitter personal attacks on Pearson, whom he described as "the defrocked prince of peace" and on the Liberal Party, "the garbage pail of Montreal." I remember being shocked by his vitriolic personal attacks, but I agreed with most others that this was usual fare for a "frustrated socialist."

Trudeau had earned that description in early 1963, when he and a few others had travelled to Quebec City to persuade Robert Cliche, a charismatic, spellbinding speaker, to leave the Liberals and become the provincial leader of the NDP, which was led federally by Tommy Douglas. Cliche accepted and moved to Montreal to begin his herculean task – just in time to see Trudeau jump to the hated Liberals and seek election in Canada's safest Liberal seat, the largely English-speaking riding of Mount Royal.

When Trudeau promptly called for an election, the Conservative campaign in Quebec was run by Jean Bruneau, a tough-minded Montreal lawyer best known as Premier Bertrand's *homme de confiance*. I was one of his assistants and was present when a *poteau* (an uncompetitive candidate) was chosen by the PCs to run in Duvernay, given some "walking around" money, and told politely not to bother campaigning in the riding. This tactic was based on the theory that one less Liberal seat anywhere benefited the PCs, who were the only national alternative. Our strategy was to try and help Cliche win Duvernay for the NDP by encouraging our supporters to vote for him. Cliche, who was to have a major influence on my life six years later, had been one of my professors at Laval. Now he was campaigning brilliantly, with a real chance of winning. He had worked his heart out in the seat for over a year when, at the last moment, the Liberals parachuted the popular Eric Kierans into the constituency. On the last weekend of the campaign,

Trudeau, then at the height of his popularity, made a special helicopter trip into Duvernay in an attempt to knock off his old friend, which he did.

It was pretty clear to me why: the last thing Pierre Trudeau wanted facing him in the House of Commons was a dashing, eloquent, French-Canadian Second World War veteran. Cliche was a brilliant and successful lawyer who could have taken him on successfully, while articulating a compelling and competing vision of Canada. Thanks to Cliche's defeat and the PCs' failure to elect strong candidates from Quebec, Trudeau would have the floor to himself.

In spite of the defeat, the summer had gone delightfully for me personally, as I had met Mimi Morrow, the enchanting daughter of my law partner, Bob Morrow. Much of the late summer was spent in the pool of their beautiful home in St-Bruno, just off the twelfth tee of the Mount Bruno Golf Club. The limitations on my powers of persuasion became obvious, however, when Mimi and some of her friends announced they could not support Stanfield, and wound up as cheerleaders for Trudeau at a giant Place Ville-Marie rally, attended, if press reports are to be believed, by forty-five thousand people.

It wasn't only Liberal supporters and star-struck young women who were among the thousands on hand that day to watch Trudeau's appearance. On the edge of the crowd I was joined by Claude Ryan, the craggy, austere intellectual who edited *Le Devoir*. Claude, whose brother, Yves, was running for us in that election, had endorsed Robert Stanfield for prime minister in an editorial published during the campaign. He and I quickly agreed that the situation, as laid out so obviously before us that day in the screaming enthusiastic response of the crowd, was indeed deplorable. We immediately quit the rally in favour of a long and depressing lunch.

The next day, the Saturday before the election, in his editorial Claude mournfully predicted a Trudeau sweep. I was later to write about Campaign '68 in an opinion piece for a Montreal newspaper, where I attempted to keep my best Tory face looking forward. "Anyone who participated in the 1968 election will have his own special memory of [that time]," I told the readers of the *Montreal Star*.

> Mine came late in the campaign while watching the national news with a fellow worker. The lead item showed Trudeau executing perfect double-gainers at a swimming pool in Burlington, Ont. After a few minutes watching the display in silence, my friend,

> weary from a full day of meeting with importuning candidates, planning itineraries, and scratching for money, leaned over to me and grunted, "God dammit, there goes another 100,000 votes."
>
> Often we [Quebec federal Tories] are queried as to Bob Stanfield's chances here in the next election. I think he will do well. I know he is not much of a skin-diver, or Alpine skier. But, as T.C. Douglas stated last week, he is "a man of undoubted integrity and genuine interest and concern for people." Should Canadians decide they have had enough of rising separatist strength, unemployment, inflation, and the like, they may be inclined to take a good hard look at Bob Stanfield and what he is trying to accomplish. As Mr. Douglas noted, he is "the kind of person who, in times of stress, people will tend to look to." A lot of people in Quebec say, "Sure he's a decent guy who makes sense – but he just can't win." Isn't that what they said about Daniel Johnson in 1966?

During this period I was introduced to Jim Peterson and his wife, Heather, from London, Ontario. Jim, whose brother David would go on to become premier of Ontario, was studying for a master's degree in taxation at McGill. We saw each other regularly, watched the election debates at their apartment on Côte-des-Neiges, and when Jim decided to leave Montreal I gave the going-away party for him at my apartment at 331 Clarke Avenue in lower Westmount. As usual, that night we had a tremendous time with friends from all walks of life and all parts of the political spectrum. In those days, partisanship did not bite deeply among us. ("While I cannot remember [for obvious reasons] the precise basis of our wager, I make the necessary assumption that I was wrong!" I wrote, for example, to John Rae and Paul Martin Jr. after losing a bet to these Grit friends one day in the 1970s. "God bless Mackenzie King. Accordingly, please find my cheque in the amount of $5 made payable to your order – provided that said funds never find their way into a Liberal candidate's pocket.") And so that night Jim Coutts, Paul Martin, David Peterson, John Rae, Bernard Roy, and I – to name but a few – celebrated Jim and his achievements in my totally green (I had inherited the furniture from the previous occupant) apartment. Late in the evening Paul Martin Jr., whom I had come to know and like, along with his delightful wife, Sheila, told me of his intention to leave Power Corporation and move on, through a Maurice Strong connection, to a position at some United Nations agency. Paul had always spoken of doing this some day, but I told him of a luncheon I had had earlier that week with Paul Desmarais, who had just acquired control of Power Corporation. I told him that Desmarais had spoken very supportively of him, so that my strong advice would be to stay put and see what happened. Paul did so, eventually becoming the owner of Canada Steamship Lines – a transaction engineered with Desmarais's consent and generous assistance – which provided him with the personal fortune for a successful political career, which he began in 1988, running against Free Trade for John Turner's Liberals!

—

PERSONAL JOURNAL: APRIL 17, 1989

Paul [Martin Jr.] has not done well in his brief time here, in large measure I believe because expectations were so unrealistically high about him. He is a nice, quite gentle individual who may turn out to be a wonderful neighbour but an unsuccessful politician. Perhaps his parliamentary performance will improve and for his sake, I hope so. And I have sent messages to him via Brian Gallery to loosen up in the House; avoid mixing it up with people like Crosbie, who will kill him; and remember that, if he is seeking the Liberal leadership, his enemies are in the Liberal caucus, not the Conservatives with whose members he should, during this period, seek a détente so as to enhance his own performance without a fiery counterattack by any cabinet minister resolved to cut him down to size.

—

For his part, our honouree that night in Montreal, Jim Peterson, moved to Toronto, where in 1980 he was elected to the House of Commons as a Liberal MP, only to be ousted in the Tory sweep of 1984. Following his defeat I called Jim from Harrington Lake and offered to appoint him ambassador to Ireland, where he and Heather would have done a splendid job. He declined because his love was politics. He was re-elected in 1988 and served with distinction in the Chrétien and Martin cabinets. Jim Peterson is a rare specimen in the Liberal Party and indeed in federal politics: a truly happy warrior who supports his party without denigrating his opponents, and who doesn't have an ounce of malice or vindictiveness in his soul.

While my friendships with so many Liberals didn't prevent me from continuing to help carry the Progressive Conservative flag in Quebec, I too was able to keep my partisanship in check when appropriate. While I had many disagreements with the new Trudeau government, I felt the new prime minister deserved praise in certain areas. In a 1969 speech to the B'nai Brith Heritage Lodge, I said:

> I believe that Mr. Trudeau's main accomplishment so far is that he has brought French Canadians into the mainstream of the decision-making process in Ottawa. This was long overdue and is a far cry from the days when not one major portfolio was held by a French Canadian and the only French Canadians on the prime minister's staff were a male secretary, a female stenographer, and a confidential messenger . . . It seems to me that university recruitment, hiring practices generally, promotions within corporations, portfolio investments, and so on should be geared at least in part toward a greater degree of integration of French Canadians into positions of active command in the business community. Apart from the obvious reasons of justice and decency which militate in favour of this course of action, it is important for every man to remember that the sharing of economic power also precludes the possibility of forcing French Canadians to live apart and to work apart simply because they have been stymied on the way in.

My law practice continued to grow, and I was frequently at the centre of highly publicized labour confrontations in Montreal and throughout eastern Canada. My firm prospered and my financial situation improved considerably. I bought a beautiful second-hand Pontiac Parisienne convertible from my pal Peter N. Thomson, which came in handy in 1969 when the Montreal Expos baseball franchise came to town and friends like Richard Holden, David Angus, John Lynch-Staunton, and I became regulars at Jarry Park, using my new convertible to get there.

One night after a double-header we were invited by Expos' owner Charles Bronfman to the Director's Lounge, where we all downed a few Scotches that had been preceded by a number of beers with hot dogs at the game. By the time we staggered from the lounge, Jarry Park was deserted and my car was parked in a locked-up private lot across the street, attached to the Deaf and Dumb Institute. None of the residents could hear our shouts, of course, but we somehow managed to clamber over a quite high wire fence and tumble into the lot, where my convertible was the only car left. We all piled in and drove around the institute to the front gate, which was locked. Lynch-Staunton rang the doorbell, trying unsuccessfully to rouse someone. Dick Holden then came up with the brilliant idea – at least it sounded brilliant at two in the morning – that I should drive around the building at top speed with the radio blaring full blast, and the four of us singing *Happy Days Are Here Again* at the top of our lungs. I had never heard of anything more stupid in my life, but necessity is the mother of invention, so round and round we went until – surprise! – the lights went on inside, the gate magically opened, and we sped off into the Montreal night.

In April 1970, thirty-six-year-old Quebec Liberal Robert Bourassa swept to power in a provincial election that also brought separatists to the National Assembly for the first time. The Parti Québécois leader, René Lévesque, was defeated in Laurier riding, however, which meant that the opposition leadership fell to my friend and labour adversary, Robert Burns. I had met Bourassa briefly when he served as secretary of the Bélanger Royal Commission in the early Sixties and was impressed by the daring he displayed in capturing the Liberal leadership upon Lesage's resignation. I was equally impressed by the subsequent boldness of his successful campaign.

Quebec politics had always been exciting, even passionate, but the game had always been played within civilized rules. Six months later, in October 1970, that exciting but peaceful world was shattered, perhaps forever, by the kidnappings of British diplomat James Cross and provincial cabinet minister Pierre Laporte. Overnight our world changed. The Front de libération du Québec brought horror into our lives.

The senselessness of this group's terrorist activity was revealed by their murder of Pierre Laporte, a respected *Le Devoir* journalist, an able parliamentarian, and a much-loved father and husband. Laporte was known throughout Quebec as an incorruptible politician. I knew him a little and I liked him. The horrible reality of Laporte being abducted and strangled by fellow French Canadians in the name of "liberation" was more than most Quebecers could bear.

Bernard Roy and I had rented a small ski house near St-Sauveur that fall, and I can remember every detail of that Saturday night when *Radio-Canada* interrupted programming to announce Laporte's murder and to show photos of the trunk of the car in which his lifeless body was found. I

Family portrait about 1949. My mother and father with Peggy and Olive (rear), Barbara on her mother's lap, and Doreen, Gary, and me. Inset: My parents outside our home on Champlain Street in 1948

At home in Baie-Comeau in the snow

"But you're no angel." At school (standing) with my sisters Peggy (left) and Olive (centre, at back)

Dressed for my first Communion

Standing (right, at back) with my Baie-Comeau classmates

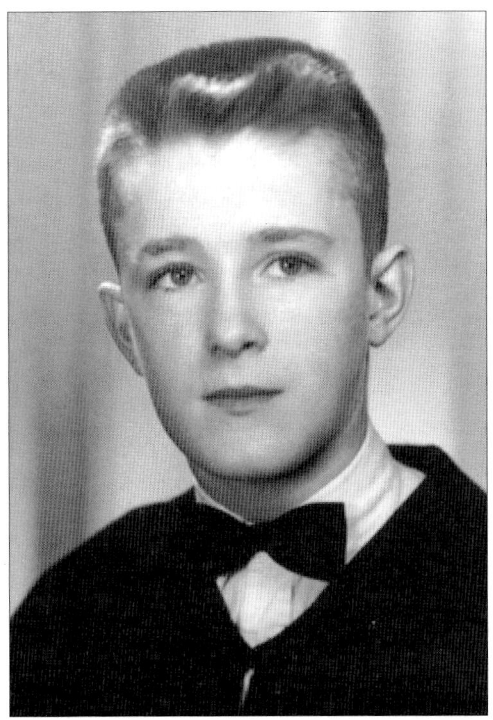

At boarding school at
St. Thomas, New Brunswick

The young student at work

The young student politician at work

The guys (including Rick Cashin, Paul Creaghan, Gerry Doucet, Sam Wakim, and me) making a presentation to Professor Walter Kontak

Celebrating an early victory in the world of student politics at StFX

A visit from Robert Stanfield

Preparing my dad
for a big event

With my parents
at my graduation
from StFX

Making a point at a Laval Law School student parliament

At the Laval Congress on Canadian Affairs, announcing that Marcel Chaput – sitting next to me – has been fired by the federal government

Checking in with my Ottawa mentor, Alvin Hamilton

Graduating from Laval Law School

can recall as well the genuine sense of fear we felt, knowing that the terrorists were really home-grown murderers, and that no one was safe.

Based on the information provided by Prime Minister Pierre Trudeau and Justice Minister John Turner, I supported the imposition of the *War Measures Act* and, when called, advised Bob Stanfield to do so as well – a decision he would later regret. Within hours, Quebec was flooded with armoured vehicles and armed military men in the streets. I was startled to learn that one immediate consequence was the overnight arrest of some 450 people, including such unthreatening souls as *Gazette* columnist Nick Auf der Maur and the poet Gérald Godin. Only later did we find that much of the information that the police were acting on was gravely flawed.

And only later still did we learn from Peter C. Newman in his autobiography that Trudeau himself, his chief of staff, Marc Lalonde, and Gérard Pelletier provided him with the shocking and false information that Claude Ryan was trying to take advantage of the seeming impotence of the Bourassa government to install a parallel government in Quebec. As it happens, Claude Ryan was in touch with me during this period because I was vice-chairman of the PC Quebec campaign committee established for the upcoming federal campaign, and he wanted to make sure that Bob Stanfield was privy to his innermost views. He and others sought to be helpful, if possible, in the tumult that followed the Laporte murder. It was a massive slander for Trudeau to tell Newman such a fabrication and urge him to print it, which Peter did, although in a measured way. Such are the instruments of federal Liberals: in the pursuit and preservation of power, *tous les moyens sont bons* against enemies real or perceived, even at the height of a monumental crisis. I was much later to learn personally just how vindictive a Liberal government could be in seeking to destroy a political opponent.

Since those days I've often reflected on Pierre Trudeau's disingenuous use of the *War Measures Act*. Mackenzie King's government had misused its provisions to intern thousands of Japanese Canadians during the Second World War – an event that stained all Canadians. The two events seemed to me to be linked. So, on June 29, 1984, when Pierre Trudeau entered the chamber of the House of Commons for the last time as prime minister of Canada, I, as leader of the opposition, gave him the opportunity to ease the pain of thousands of Canadians of Japanese origin.

"On this," I said, "his final day, would the Prime Minister grasp the moment to right a historic wrong that has been inflicted? Will the Prime Minister, on this special day, take the time to convey, either on behalf of the government or on behalf of the Parliament of Canada, a formal apology to Canadian citizens whose rights were so trampled upon in the war years? I think it would be a gesture that would sit well with all Canadians who believe so fundamentally in the sanctity of minority rights."

I then took my seat to await the prime minister's answer. Sadly, what we then saw was Pierre Trudeau at his worst. Instead of taking the chance to soothe the quiet pain of thousands of our fellow citizens, he lashed out, employing his customary cold logic. "Why does he not apologize for what happened to Riel?" Trudeau snarled at me. "Why does he not apologize for what happened during the Second World War to mothers and fathers of people sitting in this House who went to concentration camps? I know some of them, Mr. Speaker. They were not Japanese Canadians. They were Canadians of Italian or German origin, or some old French Canadians who went to jail, who went to concentration camps during the Second World War. Why do we not apologize to them? I do not follow the Leader of the Opposition who talks about my political partisanship. Why suddenly only the Japanese, Mr. Speaker? Is it because there are no votes in it? . . . Yes, come on. Is it because there are no votes in Manitoba for his party? Is it because there are no votes in all the other groups . . . I do not think it is the purpose of a government to right the past. It cannot rewrite history."

I have to admit I felt no anger against Trudeau that day – only a great deal of sadness. To heal, to build a better nation involves passion, not sterile, unfeeling reason.

Later, as prime minister, I presented a formal parliamentary apology to Japanese Canadians and established a restitution fund. This gesture did not right the wrongs of the past, but it did reveal the path toward healing. I took a similar action regarding those Italian Canadians whom the government of the 1940s had also failed. I saw it as my duty, and as Canada's duty, though too long overdue. As for the *War Measures Act*, in due course my government was to remove from our laws this piece of legislation that had harmed so many, and replace it with the *Emergencies Act* (1988). That too was our duty.

Some years after I had left office, I travelled to Chicago on business. At O'Hare International Airport, I was stopped by a young Quebecer who identified himself as Pierre Laporte's son and thanked me for the reappointment of his mother to the Citizenship Court, and for the kindness I had shown her with telephone calls and messages of support over the years. I in turn thanked him, wished him well, and turned into the crowds of the world's busiest airport. As I did, I was struck by the terrible contrast between Pierre Laporte – dead and buried for thirty-five years, deprived of the joy of seeing his son grow to manhood – and Laporte's murderer, Paul Rose, freed in 1982, courtesy of Canada's parole system, and no doubt enjoying the *boîtes à chansons* and coffee houses of Montreal.

8. Mila

PERSONAL JOURNAL: AUGUST 16, 1992

Mila is a remarkable person. She is not perfect and has failings but, as human beings go, she is about as close to perfection as you're going to find. She is an intelligent woman of very good judgment, strong loyalties, durable values, and an understanding of how and where it all fits together – perspective – a quality priceless in any partner, advisor, associate, or friend. Her ambition for her children is not for wealth or social standing but for them to be good people who care about truth and fairness and other people.

—

BY 1972 LIFE WAS great. I was thirty-three years old and had already made partner in the biggest law firm in town. I was handling exciting and challenging cases for major clients, and beginning to travel to Europe and throughout the United States in defence of their interests. I was living the happy bachelor's life, ensconced in a Clarke Avenue apartment where regular parties were held for friends and where attractive female company abounded. I had established my mother in a very nice flat not far away (I encouraged her always to phone before she dropped by my place), and both Gary and Barbara had graduated from college and were gainfully employed. I was having a wonderful time.

In the early summer Michel Cogger and I went to France and Spain on a long-planned holiday. In Monte Carlo I was called by Arnie Masters with the news that the ILA (International Longshoremen's Association) had just unleashed another wildcat strike, paralyzing the St. Lawrence River ports. My presence was required in Montreal urgently. I caught the next flight and plunged into nonstop activity upon returning, succeeding in about a month in getting the matter resolved and the parties back to work. Completely exhausted, I decided not to return to Europe then but to wait until September, when I would join Team Canada in Moscow for the eagerly awaited Russia–Canada hockey series. Meanwhile, I would relax and get fit at the Mount Royal Tennis Club, which had accepted my application for membership while I was away.

The club was nearly deserted on the late Monday morning in July when I showed up by the pool with my book and the *New York Times* to begin a week of swimming and tennis before returning to the law firm. I was sitting alone next to the pool about an hour later when I spotted a stunning young woman in a blue and white bikini strolling by, heading for the soft drink counter. I was, let's say, struck by her style and demeanour, and asked the manager, Charlie, for an introduction. He gave an interesting response, saying, "Well, Mr. Mulroney, why don't you wait until Thursday?" When I asked why, he answered, "Thursday July 13 is her birthday and then she'll be nineteen!" I thanked him for his cautionary advice but, through an acquaintance, managed my own introduction later that day.

Her name was Mila Pivnicki, and she was an engineering student at Sir George Williams University. She was tall, slim, and beautiful with striking Slavic features, and as soon as we began to chat I knew she was the girl I was going to marry.

I learned that she was the daughter of Dr. Dimitri Pivnicki and his wife, Bogdanka, refugees from Tito's Yugoslavia who had uprooted themselves and started building a new life in Canada in 1958 when he was forty. Dimitri, a genuine scholar and intellectual, was the well-educated son of a successful Novi Bečej lawyer and had followed his father into the legal profession before becoming a psychiatrist. A deeply religious Serbian Orthodox Church member, he despised the anti-religious bias of the Yugoslav communist regime and jumped at an opportunity to take up an internship in psychiatry in Montreal at the Allan Memorial Institute, although it had meant leaving Bogdanka, Mila, and baby John behind for a year. Then Bogdanka, a nurse whose father was also a doctor, pulled strings and they were given exit visas for Canada. After travelling twenty-nine days on a steamer via Portugal and New York, they arrived in Montreal by bus. Mila was five years old, starting life in a new country and speaking neither English nor French. But the family did well, building a successful life here. After some reticence, given my age, Dimitri and Boba welcomed me into their lives.

Although only eighteen at the time we met, Mila was uncommonly mature, thoughtful, and poised, and I was swept off my feet. Within hours I had driven her home and made plans to see her the next day. Within four months we were engaged, and within six more we were married.

As I write, that was over thirty-four years, four children, three grandchildren, two leadership campaigns, three constituency elections, and two general election campaigns ago – and I can honestly say that none of what I have been able to do in life could have been achieved without the support of an intelligent, strong, loving, and supportive wife who helped me climb the highest mountains, and consoled and encouraged me in the times of sorrow and anguish I experienced in the deep valleys of political life. Life with Mila has been exciting and fun. With her sunny disposition, good nature, and easy smile somehow everything always seemed possible.

I was delighted to find that Mila's politics were sound. She had been involved with the Progressive Conservative Party before we met, supporting Michael Meighen's exciting bid for election to the House of Commons in 1972. I was involved in that year's election fight as vice-chairman of the Quebec campaign, along with Claude Nolin under the leadership of Claude Dupras. Dupras was a successful engineer, and a booster who was tough and demanding as we struggled to shape an embryonic organization into a party that could win seats in Quebec. In the event, we failed, electing only two MPs as Trudeau and Réal Caouette swept Quebec, proving just how tribal Quebec politics can be. When a Quebecer is at the head of the ticket in a general election, the results are not going to be pretty for the other side. And they were not for us that year.

It was strength in Quebec and the French-speaking areas of New Brunswick and eastern Ontario that enabled Trudeau to cling to power on October 30, 1972, in spite of a massive repudiation of him and his government throughout English Canada as he campaigned under the slogan "The Land is Strong." It was a watershed moment for me. As I was to remind Tories repeatedly in the 1983 leadership campaign, thinking of that night, Pierre Trudeau would always beat us if the party handed him a gift of the hundred or so federal seats with large francophone populations that we lost time after time. And that's what happened – until 1984.

For the 1972 election campaign we had recruited Claude Wagner – the former Liberal provincial attorney general and unsuccessful leadership candidate against Bourassa in 1970 – from the bench. We did so in the belief, sustained by our private polling, that, as Quebec Leader, he could galvanize enough support to ensure a national victory. In the polls he showed great strength as a candidate, but we had neglected to ask if such appeal would continue if he ran as a Conservative. Quite an oversight, as things turned out. We had gone to great lengths to secure his approval and I had personally visited with him, very discreetly, on a number of occasions to ascertain his interest in making the move.

He told me that he could be persuaded to resign from the bench if the party would ensure some security for his family – a proposition that didn't offend me at all, because he would be giving up a judge's income and pension. I communicated with Finlay MacDonald, Stanfield's closest confidant and fixer, and Finlay and Stanfield made the decision to instruct Eddie Goodman, a charming and skilled Toronto lawyer and party operator, to visit with Wagner and close the deal.

I picked Eddie up at the airport and drove him to Wagner's home in Montreal, where I introduced him to the judge. Then I had coffee upstairs with Claude's wife, Gisèle, while Eddie and he retired to a downstairs den to talk business. I drove Eddie to the airport an hour or so later, the deal having been concluded. Although I was never privy to the details, I was familiar with the general parameters of the arrangement Eddie worked out. It was a perfectly ethical and legal arrangement.

A few weeks later, however, when Claude announced his candidacy at a press conference he denied the existence of any such arrangement. Claude Dupras and I got the news at the Queen Elizabeth Hotel and we were thunderstruck. "This," said Dupras, "will come back to haunt us big time." And it did.

"'The secret fund matter' – and especially the evasive and very unclear way Mr. Wagner has dealt with it – have greatly tarnished his credibility," Claude Ryan wrote in *Le Devoir* in 1976, when news of the arrangement became widely known. The story damaged Wagner's credibility and diminished the lustre we hoped he would bring to the campaign, which was meant to help us to elect other members. On election night in 1972 he was lucky to win his own seat in St-Hyacinthe. The only other victor in Quebec was Heward Grafftey in Brome-Missisquoi, who was extremely critical of the overture to Wagner in the first place and was re-elected on his own merits, with no credit due to anyone else.

It is worth adding a note here about how the Liberal machine operated. Claude Dupras had built an impressive Quebec organization – at least on paper – and attracted a number of new, talented professionals, business people, and labour officials to the party. One of those was a civil engineer called Floriant Toutant, a partner in a major Montreal engineering firm who was in charge of all major events during the campaign in Quebec. To encourage the view that we were indeed well organized and had the wind at our backs, Claude authorized the publication of our campaign organizational chart, complete with names.

The very next morning Toutant told us that he would have to leave. The publicity had provoked calls from Trudeau's principal secretary Marc Lalonde (who ran as a candidate in 1972) and cabinet minister Jean Marchand's offices to his partners, threatening economic reprisals if he didn't quit the PC campaign.

The single-minded malice of the federal Liberals was something to behold. Here was a French Canadian trying to help a weak federalist party get some traction in Quebec – a move that should have been applauded by all political parties – and the response was immediate and lethal: if you help the Conservatives you will never get another contract from Ottawa. Given the stranglehold the Liberals had over the Ottawa machinery, this meant severe damage, if not certain death, for the company involved.

Dupras, who was fearless in dealing with the federal government, had conveniently arranged to do most of his engineering business with the provincial government, Crown agencies, and municipalities, safely out of the vindictive reach of the Ottawa Liberal machine. But he knew what could happen, and knew that the threats to Toutant were serious. He didn't want to lose Toutant, who was very valuable to us, so he accepted his resignation – and a few days later Floriant Toutant re-emerged at party headquarters bearing the new surname of "Joseph," which Dupras had secretly bestowed upon him, thereby getting him through the election undamaged by the Liberals!

As prime minister, I was later to speak about the 1972 campaign with my caucus. It was October 30, 1985. "The Class of 1972," I said, "are outstanding people, including Joe Clark (who was first elected to the Commons that year). I always remember the campaign with sadness because we came so close. A little more and Robert L. Stanfield would have become prime minister. I often wonder what Canada would be like today had we defeated Trudeau after four years."

After the historically close election I went off to Freeport, Bahamas, with my friends Peter Thomson and Maurice Mayer and hung around the beach for a few days with Claude and Gisèle Wagner, who were also there for a post-election holiday. Although the talk was all about the election and our rising prospects in an extremely tight minority parliament, my own thoughts and priorities had switched completely to Mila and the future.

We married on May 26, 1973 in the Ascension of Our Lord Church in Westmount. Bernard Roy, my best man, caused consternation by arriving at the last possible second – he had been out getting a suntan! – and Michel Cogger, Yves Fortier, and Lowell Murray were among the ushers. Following a reception at the Faculty Club at McGill University, Mila and I took off for a wonderful honeymoon through Paris, Dubrovnik, Belgrade, London, Scotland, and Ireland before returning to Montreal a month later, thoroughly happy and solidly broke. As I responded to a congratulatory note from Brian Gallery, "Married life is great although much more expensive than I thought."

During that summer the PBS television channel replayed the Watergate hearings in the evenings. We watched them faithfully. One night I was struck by the reproach that Senator Sam Ervin addressed to a young John Dean, a Nixon aide who acknowledged he had spent $4,000 on his recent honeymoon. Lying in bed watching the performance I vicariously felt the sting of the senator's disapproval myself although, judging from the joy the trip had brought us both, I consoled myself with the thought that it was money well spent.

Some months later, acting upon the advice of my friend and law partner, Arthur Campeau, Mila and I decided to purchase a small semi-detached home on the corner of Devon and Upper Belmont in Westmount. Mila had had a miscarriage while accompanying me on a business trip to St. John, N.B., but as we both – and especially Mila – wanted a family, I concluded that a family home would be a good investment.

There was only one problem: I didn't have any money and would have to borrow almost the entire amount – purchase price $45,000 plus $17,000 for renovations – because of my ongoing financial responsibilities to look after my mother. This was a huge sum for me at the time, even though I had already made partner at the firm. I can remember having trouble getting to sleep, wondering how I was ever going to pay for all of this, in spite of the reassuring murmurs from friends and bankers who confidently predicted a financial future for me far rosier than anything I anticipated.

It was an attractive neighbourhood – our home fronted Devon Park and Upper Belmont – and we had great neighbours, including Shirley and

Harvey Corn, on the other side of the semi-detached house, and Jon and Diane Deitcher, who became very close and supportive friends, and remain so today, with John still acting as my financial advisor. It turned out to be an ideal time in our lives and a perfect home for us, especially when Caroline was born a year later. By then Mila had transformed the house into a lovely, gracious home, and we spent our first years there with Caroline, as delightful and wonderful a child as anyone could imagine.

—

PERSONAL JOURNAL: FEBRUARY 24, 1990

I've just finished dinner with Mila and the children, all except Caroline who, would I believe it, is out on a date! And she's not yet 16! Like all fathers I can't get used to the idea of my little baby out for dinner with a beau, though it is at moments like this that I am especially gratified by the presence of her RCMP detail.

9. Tricksters, Crooks, and Scum: The Cliche Commission

In April 1974 I was working hard at my labour law practice and Mila and I were enjoying life as newlyweds in Montreal when I got an urgent call from Jean Cournoyer and Réal Mireault, respectively minister and deputy minister of labour in the Quebec government.

Six weeks earlier, on March 21, 1974, a man called Yvon Duhamel had boarded a D-8 bulldozer and driven it unerringly into the electric generators at the heart of the James Bay construction site. Within moments, he had secured for himself an inglorious footnote in Quebec history: his deliberate and criminal action resulted in the evacuation of the largest construction job site in the history of Quebec, paralyzed Premier Bourassa's "Project of the Century," and caused direct costs to the consumers of Quebec of $35 million. For his dubious role in this bizarre event, Mr. Duhamel got ten years in a federal penitentiary.

Violence at the James Bay hydroelectric construction site had spiralled out of control. The vast project on which the province's future energy requirements depended was being destroyed by warring gangs dominated by criminals who had captured control of rival trade unions at the site. There were arson, and fights and beatings galore. It was a struggle to the death for control of the entire project and the headlines and photos of such insane destruction scandalized the province.

By the late Sixties the Quiet Revolution had paused for breath and certain things had become unfashionable in Quebec. It was unfashionable, for example, to proclaim any belief in the federal concept of government; it was unfashionable to acknowledge any possible benefits from our free enterprise system because no venture was considered of value unless Big Government was involved; it was unfashionable to stand firm on any moral issue because, in the minds of many, anti-clericalism and its attendant gospel of moral relativism were the wave of the future; and, most of all, it was unfashionable to contemplate anything but a totally unionized society because, we were told, politicized trade unionism would be our collective salvation. I remember well the alacrity with which some members of the Quebec media responded to these challenges: each night they showcased Louis Laberge, or Marcel Pepin, or Yvon Charbonneau in living colour on the national news, with their three-minute homilies. These invariably involved vitriolic denunciations of elected governments, business, social standards, each other – and anything else that happened to be lying around that day. Seldom has Canada seen such consistent and misplaced glorification of individuals and their causes.

I believe strongly in the value of vigorous trade unionism. The benefits of this kind of collective action are there for all to see. But trade unions and management associations are precisely what they are called, and are not there to represent the public. Political parties and elected governments are quite another thing.

In Quebec, as elsewhere, we tried to follow the basic rules of the game. During the late Sixties, however, thoughtful observers began asking whether highly vocal interest groups were exercising real and effective power, rather than the duly elected government. On March 24, 1971, this became a very serious question. That day, a parliamentary commission of the Quebec National Assembly was meeting in a formal session, in the process of analyzing a piece of legislation. Suddenly, led by André (Dédé) Desjardins, the director of the Quebec Federation of Labour construction wing, thirty weapon-wielding thugs invaded the National Assembly, disrupted proceedings, intimidated MNAs, assaulted other trade unionists, damaged four automobiles, then left Quebec City and laughed all the way home. No charges were ever laid, even though the witnesses – indeed, the victims – were duly elected members of the National Assembly. (After a starring role as a thug and crooked union boss at the Cliche Commission hearings, Desjardins was murdered years later in an organized crime hit.)

Little wonder, then, that Yvon Duhamel decided to destroy James Bay. He never expected to be punished for his actions – after all, if you can assault the Quebec National Assembly with impunity, what's wrong with a little friendly violence on a construction site in the far North? Such thinking, I believe, was the legacy of a decade of permissiveness, governmental inaction, and neglect in Quebec, particularly in the construction industry. But now the thugs had gone too far.

The premier and government decided to name a three-man commission of inquiry into these awful events, and Chief Judge Robert Cliche and Guy

Chevrette, vice-president of the Centrale des enseignants du Québec, had been chosen by the Quebec cabinet. The third man chosen, the minister of labour told me, was Brian Mulroney. Would I serve? I answered yes, and thus began a year unlike any other I had known, and one that would catapult me into the headlines, and eventually into high political office.

The first meeting of the three commissioners took place in Chief Judge Cliche's office in the old Palais de Justice, diagonally across from the Château Frontenac in Quebec City. Cliche and I knew each other well, of course, from law school days, and we were pleased to meet Guy Chevrette, a teacher from Joliette. He was a small, wiry union activist, an excellent athlete with an easy manner and a great sense of humour. He turned out to be a superb colleague, tough, loyal, and responsible. After the commission he too went into politics, was elected to the National Assembly for the Parti Québécois, and served for many years in senior positions in various PQ cabinets.

Our first order of business was administrative. We had to hire lawyers, investigators, and staff and get down to business as quickly as possible. The provincial government had named the secretary, who attended to all housekeeping matters, so over a few drinks in Cliche's office, followed by an animated and well-lubricated dinner around the corner at Le Continental, we made some decisions.

Cliche strongly recommended that we hire as chief counsel a lawyer and crown prosecutor from Ste-Marie-de-Beauce by the name of Jean Dutil. We agreed and he turned out to be a real find. Dutil was a bulldog, absolutely fearless in attack, and ready to work around the clock to ensure the commission's success. He was a natural leader who subsequently went to the Bench and himself chaired a royal commission into organized crime.

As assistant counsels, I suggested Paul-Arthur Gendreau from Rimouski and Lucien Bouchard from Jonquière, both classmates of mine. I made the case that most Montreal counsel would be conflicted in some way, so it would be better for us to hire "uncontaminated" provincial counsel, and that these were men of competence and skill. Cliche and Chevrette decided to rely on my judgment and asked me to communicate with them. Gendreau and Bouchard were well aware of the explosive nature of such an inquiry and were thrilled to accept the challenging assignment.

Gendreau, who has since served with great distinction for many years on the Quebec Court of Appeal, was a highly intelligent, thoughtful, and methodical lawyer who brought patience, thoroughness, and efficiency to our turbulent proceedings. As for Bouchard, he and I had stayed on very close terms after graduation, and I had been dismayed to learn that, after publicly supporting the PQ in the 1970 campaign, he had been asked to leave his law firm, Fradette et Associés. I felt this was extremely unfair. He opened a one-man firm in Jonquière and, as an excellent lawyer and hard worker, did well in his small-town practice. When I called, he jumped at the opportunity I was offering to join us on this great adventure soon to unfold in Montreal. Some lawyers from the huge Montreal firms tend to exhibit a degree of superiority when dealing with their confrères from the smaller towns of Quebec. This feeling is naturally resented by all non-Montreal lawyers, so I was certain that Bouchard would perform brilliantly, if for no other reason than to prove that his impressive skills were comparable to any in Montreal. As I told him in our conversations, "Lucien, this is your opportunity to play in the NHL. I know you're going to be a great success." And he was.

The Cliche Commission was really about uncovering a massive abuse of power. Trade unions had been infiltrated by criminals – many just out of jail – who sought to use otherwise legitimate unions to exercise control over Quebec's construction sites. Once in control, they could extort, punish, vandalize, maim, or destroy any individual or company that stood in their way and, in the process, become both wealthy and powerful in the industry.

The big losers were ordinary, hard-working construction industry employees whose rights were disregarded and, in many cases, destroyed as they became pawns in a much larger game. The construction companies were also losers, as they were frequently held to ransom and threatened with illegal work stoppages if they didn't give in to the extortion. It became clear to the commission, and to the public, that the provincial government had lost effective control of this vital sector of economic activity. The construction industry was, by far, the single most important in Quebec; the $6 billion expended annually in the field, the 150,000 people it employed, the multiplier effect it had on all sectors of economic growth, made it vital to the province.

We were sworn in on May 3, 1974, with the mandate to analyze the conduct of all those associated directly or indirectly with the construction industry and to ensure that basic union freedoms would be maintained in the future. We worked out of the Justice Department and Court House on Parthenais Street in the east end of Montreal. Our team, which now included Gilles Guèvremont, an able young lawyer, André Escogido, a friend of Cliche's who worked effectively on the drafting, Christian Van Houtte, and a group of crack investigators headed by Inspector Denis Viau, worked tirelessly to prepare for the public hearings that we felt were necessary to inform the province of what was really happening and why reforms were necessary.

The hearings began in September, and the Cliche Commission rapidly became the most heavily publicized and celebrated inquiry in memory. Every night it dominated the French-language networks, as a parade of witnesses told sordid tales of violence and corruption that ordinary citizens found appalling and riveting. One witness even told us that he'd rather be a perjurer on the stand, who lived, than someone who told the truth and was killed as a result.

In this atmosphere, skilful preparation was essential. When a witness denied a fact, we were frequently able to confront him with a secret recording of an earlier conversation when he could be heard coldly planning an act of violence or other equally illegal activity. When confronted with such obvious perjury, Cliche would look with theatrical disgust at the offending witness, shake his long mane of curly hair, and say to the chief counsel, "Très bien, nous allons écouter la musique!" (Very well, we'll listen to the music!)

Time and time again, those words signalled the slow disintegration of the witness, as he was forced to listen to his own voice contradict his perjurious testimony. The commission held public hearings for eighty days during which time 279 witnesses were heard, from all walks of life. During the course of these hearings, almost a thousand exhibits were filed and analyzed by the commission. The courtroom in which we sat was the hottest ticket in town, and the media delighted in the visuals and substance of the three Davids taking on the Goliath that was the Quebec construction industry.

Anyone who had eyes to see and ears to hear now knows full well that the corruption and violence that existed in the construction industry in Quebec were entirely without parallel in the history of labour relations in Canada. Our hearings revealed clearly, as we dug deeper, that a relatively small group of men had succeeded in erecting a new set of social standards in Quebec. The hallmarks of this new way of doing business were lawlessness and violence. Illegality was the key to success. Union monopoly of strategic services and industries was to be the end result. To achieve this domination, the laws were breached regularly, enthusiastically, and with impunity. Anarchy is not too strong a term to describe the Quebec construction industry during those years. Among the stories that emerged were those of workers being forced to join a union at gunpoint. Worst of all was the story, which curled my hair, of a union thug going to the home of a rival, a man who opposed the union's efforts to establish a reign of terror. When the man was not at home, the thug chose to beat up his fourteen-year-old son, who ended up in hospital; as a final touch, the family dog was strangled. The gangsters were in control. It was, as I said at the time, "a cancer that had to be excised."

Our team would often gather late in the evenings in Cliche's suite at the Queen Elizabeth Hotel for dinner as we analyzed the effectiveness of the day's testimony and scrutinized the growing impact of the media coverage that was dramatic, powerful, and almost universally supportive of our work. "It was the best show in town," one story in the *Financial Post* began in March of 1975. "The Cliche Royal Commission hearings, which ended last week, amused, titillated, and shocked the province of Quebec with a flow of headline-grabbing revelations that has not stopped since public hearings began eight months ago. In fact, it was even better than the US Watergate hearings – and may be more significant in the long run. Mr. Justice Robert Cliche vivisected a whole society and laid it out for all to see."

The commission functioned extremely well and the staff worked closely together. When Jean Dutil retired early in 1975 to become president of the Commission of Inquiry on Organized Crime, we elevated Lucien Bouchard to the position of chief counsel, where he performed effectively.

The only period of tension occurred when, following the appearance by Justice Minister Jérôme Choquette, Bouchard recommended to the commissioners that Premier Bourassa be called to testify. Cliche and Chevrette were open to the suggestion, but I was dead set against it. I thought this would have the needless consequence of politicizing the commission and undermining the credibility we had built up over the months – credibility the commission would surely need when our recommendations went to the government for enactment into law. When Bouchard pressed on, I told my fellow commissioners, "This will happen over my dead body. Absolutely not. It exceeds our mandate and will damage us in the eyes of the public. We've already exposed the real criminals' workings of a corrupt system and have great ideas how to correct it. If we overplay our hand by calling the premier, which he will properly resist, we'll do our cause much more harm than good."

Cliche and Chevrette sided with me and the crisis subsided. The commission proceeded to a conclusion with 257 recommendations, most of which were promptly enacted into law. We didn't mince words in our report. "We pledged to make haste, and we have kept our promise," we wrote in the introduction.

> Only 364 days have passed between our taking the oath and the submission of this report. Time has not been lost – only our illusions. At the outset, we had anticipated dealing with men whose strengths and weaknesses would reflect the dignity of common humanity. We were mistaken. It is true that we came across many honest and hard-working citizens, toiling in the hope of a better tomorrow. From such we derived both guidance and inspiration. All too often, however, our hearings offered a daily fare composed of tricksters, crooks, and scum.
>
> Despite this, we never gave up hope. We believe that, in a newfound climate of serenity, construction workers, business leaders, and public officials concerned with construction can find within themselves fresh motivation for working together. What they now must develop is the will to achieve this. The construction industry is vital to the Quebec economy . . . At present, this industry is sick and, to some extent, corrupt . . . And our wish now is for a new beginning. Let everyone forget past quarrels and bygone rivalry. Sordid pages should be turned forever. Today, a fresh new sheet lies unsullied before us.

In the early 1960s, when asked about his government's attitude regarding collective bargaining in the public service, Premier Lesage had replied, "La Reine ne négocie pas avec ses sujets" (The Queen does not negotiate with her subjects). How delightfully quaint that statement sounds now! Not only did the Queen negotiate with her subjects in the 1970s, she was required to do so in an atmosphere of hostility and rancour which would make even the bitterest political opponents in Canada look like a bunch of choirboys. I believe that the harmful politicization really got under way in 1971, when Bill 46 set out the bargaining structure in the health and education sectors and provided for government participation on the management team as well as allowing province-wide bargaining in these areas. By insisting upon a general salary policy for the entire public sector and a common bargaining posture regarding hospitals and schools, the government, unwittingly, I suspect, forced the unions into a common front for collective bargaining purposes. This new grouping representing some 250,000 people soon became a political instrument of unquestioned strength. Because they sat on opposite sides of the table to the government on bread-and-butter matters, they quickly took opposite sides in political matters, too – like an official opposition in everything except elected status.

The bitterness quickly accelerated. Defiance of a court injunction in 1972 sent Laberge, Pepin, and Charbonneau to jail. The *La Presse* strike was used as a symbol of worker oppression. In due course the unions threw themselves into an aggressive campaign against the government in the 1973 election. Positions – and people – became irreconcilable.

In this fight there were two quasi-winners: the government and the union establishment. There were two sure losers: the public and the worker – the forgotten guy who pays his dues, pays his taxes, respects the law, and does an honest day's work. He became the tragic victim of politicization; his interests were subordinated to the political aspirations of the leadership. Equally tragic was the fact that when his leaders later presented legitimate demands on his behalf, they were perceived by the government as the self-serving incursions of political adversaries, and were dealt with accordingly.

My role on the commission taught me a core truth about government: good laws are of little value unless they are enforced. Non-enforcement is an insidious thing, because it breeds a progressive suspicion in the minds of the governed that a statute need not apply at all, that exceptions can be made, that demonstrations can supplant debate, that Parliament is in fact somewhat less than supreme. This is not to say that, in drafting legislation, government should ignore voices or reason from any quarter. Only an exceptionally foolish and vain group of men and women would do that. But when our duly elected parliaments have spoken, there can be no turning back, no exceptions and, in the face of resistance, no compromise.

I realize that politics is still the art of the possible, that our society is highly complex, and that running a government is not an easy thing. But in regard to Parliament itself, its members are merely custodians of its supremacy. Anything that diminishes its magnificence, impairs its effectiveness, or erodes its authority in any way is a grievous act.

As commissioners, we were dismayed to hear a minister of the Crown, in sworn testimony before us, say that he was "powerless" to enforce legislation. And we were shocked to hear a deputy minister say, "When the unions have a gun to your head, what do you do? You cave in." And cave in they did, on a regular, ongoing basis.

After Quebec Labour Minister Jean Cournoyer testified that government was "helpless" and "powerless" to enforce the law, Cliche responded by saying, "It is you and your government which is responsible for having our laws respected. If those elected can't make the legislative system work, then what hope is there for the ordinary citizen?"

In our report, we fine-tuned Judge Cliche's words and bluntly laid down the rules that all governments have to follow. "The work that this commission has done," we wrote, "will matter little even if the undesirables are purged from the positions they hold, even if the laws governing the construction sector are improved, if those who make the laws do not have the will to apply them and see that they are respected. When a big house cleaning is required, strong people must wield the broom."

We made our key point in our concluding paragraph, "Men pass, structures change or disappear, the fortunes of government wax and wane. In the end, the State alone endures – and we, all of us, are the State."

In an editorial published shortly after our report was tabled in the National Assembly, the Montreal *Gazette* took our report and recommendations and issued the following challenge to the government, "The hour before the dawn is the darkest," says the commission encouragingly, "and we can only hope that the government will show what the Cliche commission cannot give it – courage. Courage to replace the spinelessness of recent years before a brutal union tyranny with which much of management in the construction industry colluded."

La Presse also weighed in:

> Brian Mulroney was right to criticize severely the inaction of the government in the presentation that he made in front of the Montreal Construction Association. As long as the employment problem is not tackled and investments in this sector are not planned, it will be impossible to guarantee work and a minimum wage to construction "professionals." And that is what counts above all if we want to see peace return to construction sites. The violence

> that we have deplored for years has generally been that of wage-earners who are trying to defend at any cost their livelihood. . . . The Cliche report specified that all of these conditions had to be met in order to make possible negotiations over a guaranteed income plan. Guaranteed income is one of the best suggestions put forward by the commission enquirers. Workers are surely having trouble, just as Mr. Mulroney is, in understanding why the government is not in more of a hurry to set up the necessary mechanisms for its realization. Will they have to wait much longer?

Following our report the Bourassa government did move swiftly to enact most of our recommendations, and there has not been a peep out of the Quebec construction unions – other than legitimate collective bargaining demands – for thirty years.

After concluding our work in May 1975, I was very happy to step out of the limelight and return to Mila, Caroline, and Ogilvy, Renault. And the death threats stopped. Few people are aware that the mobsters the commission was tackling were so ruthless that our home and family needed to be protected around the clock by armed guards. They and police drivers were assigned to the three commissioners after anonymous death threats came in directed at all three of us and our families. Once, after receiving death threats, I called home to check on Mila and Caroline, who I thought were scheduled to be there for the day. Getting no answer after repeated calls I rushed out of the office with my police escort and raced home to find it empty. Thoughts of kidnapping flashed through my mind until I called Mila's mother to find that Caroline was with her while Mila attended engineering classes at the university. I had forgotten it was a school day.

This police protection did give rise to at least one bizarre event. A young Torontonian named John Thompson, who was a rising star at IBM, had been transferred to Montreal, but before completing the move he thought it sensible to check out the neighbourhood in which he proposed to live. Early one morning as he strolled around taking photos, he stopped in front of our residence and innocently began to shoot a few frames of the area, only to be tackled, wrestled to the ground, and hauled off to our garage by two armed guards who thought he was getting ready to attack the Mulroney residence. He was eventually released after earnest protestations of innocence, and moved into the neighbourhood, despite the surprise attack.

A few years later Mila and I were guests at dinner at the St. Andrews Club in Florida. A distinguished-looking elderly lady began entertaining her dinner partners with a story of how a young Torontonian was attacked, arrested, and held in a Montreal garage as he innocently strolled through a residential neighbourhood early one morning. She wondered aloud how this could happen in a civilized country like Canada. Our hostess, it became apparent, was John Thompson's aunt. Neither Mila nor I said a word.

PART III

The Clark Years

1976–1983

1. "Politics Ain't Beanbag": The 1976 Leadership Campaign
2. Life at the Iron Ore Company of Canada
3. No Discipline, No Power
4. Winnipeg and Schefferville
5. The 1983 Leadership Campaign
6. Showdown in Ottawa
7. Picking Up the Reins

1. "Politics Ain't Beanbag": The 1976 Leadership Campaign

PERSONAL JOURNAL: FEBRUARY 18, 1993

Joe Clark has just left my office after an hour-long meeting. As usual it was cordial and indeed friendly. I've often regretted that the circumstances of our 1976 leadership bids and aftermath effectively precluded an especially warm relationship between us. He is an easy guy to like and has been, as I've often mentioned and written, a good, effective, and loyal member of the government. We both sought the leadership over 17 years ago, both too young, too inexperienced, and too ambitious and, unfortunately for him, he won.

—

IN THE SUMMER OF 1975, I was fresh from my work on the Cliche Commission, and my thoughts were far from Ottawa and very far from contesting the leadership of the Progressive Conservative Party. When it became clear that Bob Stanfield was thinking of resigning, I urged him to give it one more try, only one more election. We both knew, I argued, that Trudeau's campaign in 1974, highlighted by his pledge not to introduce wage and price controls, was particularly dishonest. I felt sure that Trudeau – whose economic stewardship of Canada was one of his greatest failings – would eventually collapse and impose the very wage and price controls he had campaigned against. As a result, Stanfield's credibility would soar, and the party would win behind him. (I still have no doubt Stanfield would have defeated Pierre Trudeau, perhaps more convincingly than Clark later did, in 1979, had he remained our leader.)

"No, Brian, I've had it," Stanfield told me. "I've had three runs at this. I'm going to stand down."

The race was on.

Having spent a busy year as a royal commissioner, away from involvement in all aspects of the Progressive Conservative Party both in Quebec and nationally, I still saw myself as simply an observer, although admittedly an interested one. Then one summer's day in 1975, Mila and I drove to visit our friends, Michel and Erica Cogger, at their farmhouse in the Eastern Townships. Michel Cogger, one of the most brilliant members of our law class at Laval, was a voice I respected. With degrees in philosophy, literature, and law, he had a political résumé unique among French-Canadian Tories of his day. After Stanfield's victory in 1967, I and others had prevailed upon the new leader to appoint him the party's associate national director. He did so and Cogger went on to Ottawa, acquiring an unparalleled knowledge of the national Progressive Conservative Party and of the country. He served later as one of the leader's press secretaries during the 1972 election.

While Erica and Mila played with the children and chatted, Michel and I went for a walk. Conversation turned to the leadership race. Michel described the candidate he was hoping for. He said the new leader should be young, attractive, and forward-looking. He had to be fluently bilingual and must instinctively understand Quebec, since it was imperative that the new leader eventually achieve a Conservative breakthrough in our province.

As Cogger spoke, it dawned on me who he had in mind: Michael Meighen, our classmate from Laval. The more I thought about it, the more realistic Michael's prospects seemed. He fitted Cogger's specifications and offered even more. Michael Meighen, grandson of former prime minister Arthur Meighen, had run for office in the 1972 and 1974 elections, and had just been elected national president of the party. I was enthusiastic about the idea.

Cogger shook his head. He said there was another person I should consider. His name? Brian Mulroney.

I was shocked. Until that time no one had ever said to me, with any degree of seriousness, that I should run for the party leadership. Yet having known Cogger for more than fifteen years, I was certain he had given the idea a great deal of thought, and was proposing it to me very seriously.

Our conversation weighed on my mind as Mila and I drove back to Montreal that night. We discussed the idea and my prospects, as the city grew closer. Mila said she'd support me in whatever path I chose. I began to consider a run.

Another friend from Laval, Jean Bazin, presented me with a strategy memo outlining a possible Mulroney campaign. I read it in a different light than I would have only weeks earlier. "The theme you have to focus on is that you are, above all else, serious," Bazin wrote, adding that my youth would be self-evident. "It *is* serious! Starting with this theme, you can then develop a whole strategy to reassure the delegates of all ages, and reaffirm all the elements that have worked in the party for the last number of years and are central to it."

Bazin also outlined what I already knew: I had quite a task ahead of me. I had to become known to the wider public, while at the same time convincing skeptical delegates that I was not just a relative youngster with ambition. The fact that I was not a member of Parliament and had never run for electoral office would, of course, be a major handicap. But I consulted widely, and by the fall of 1975, I was leaning toward entering the already crowded race, late as it was.

Today, I sometimes liken our efforts in 1975–76 to a children's crusade. I started with friends from high school, then my college and law school friends became involved, and finally the circle widened to include professional associates I'd come to know along the way. The media's idea that this was a band of wealthy Montrealers somehow intent on "buying" the leadership of the Progressive Conservative Party is preposterous. In hindsight, what we were was an often ragtag band of youngsters from the middle and working classes who came together because of the exciting prospect that one of their own was ready to stand for election as leader of a Canadian political party.

The very first campaign donation that arrived wasn't even solicited. From Pembroke, Ontario, Terry (Ace) McCann sent along five hundred dollars. A lifelong Liberal, Ace was ready to support me because we had been close friends and debating partners at StFX in the 1950s. My old Laval friend Peter White, who was destined to play a major role in all my campaigns, also came aboard, as did Charley McMillan, a brilliant university economics professor and author whose quick wit and irrepressible humour kept us focused in times of uncertainty and concern. Because of my work with Alvin Hamilton and family links in Rosetown, Saskatchewan, I had friends out west, and they too joined in, with Roy Faibish also sending contacts my way.

Lucien Bouchard was another who sent along his support. "Please find enclosed a very modest token of my friendship and of the pleasure that I would have to see you realize an ambition that is completely justified by your talent and your abilities," he wrote. "Jocelyne joins me in wishing you the best of luck next February."

And so the campaign began to snowball. Although we had little idea of what we'd encounter, the crusade was under way.

Michel Cogger was the natural choice for campaign chairman, while my friend David Angus, a successful young lawyer who specialized in maritime law, agreed to assume responsibility for finances. In Toronto my closest friend, Sam Wakim, had just finished a stint as senior counsel of the Ontario Securities Commission. Sam knew a lot of people in a city largely unfamiliar to me back then, and he immediately offered to help. Thanks to Sam's labours, in mid-October, I travelled to Toronto to make a speech to the Empire Club about the Cliche Commission and our report. My role on the commission had brought me to the public's attention, and audiences like the blue-chip Empire Club members were interested to learn more about it.

My speech was well received. While this was gratifying, something else that occurred that day had a greater impact. By good luck I sat next to Scott Young, a respected columnist at the *Globe and Mail*, who was there as a guest of the Empire Club. Four days later, Young's paper published his impressions on this young man from Montreal. The account was glowing. "Yeah, I was impressed by Brian Mulroney (pronounced Mullrooney)," Young wrote. "It isn't all that difficult to imagine him as leader of the Progressive Conservative Party of Canada. It might even be, barring some amazing upset, Brian Mulroney is a little before his time shooting for the leadership; but he is precisely in his prime if he chooses to try for the leadership."

Besides giving me a needed boost, that column shed new light on the mysterious workings of the media. In those days long before the Internet, fax machines, and the twenty-four-hour news cycle, politicians acted as their own spin doctors, busily clipping and copying any positive press stories that came their way. Once on the road, they would distribute them in press kits and sit back and await the results. To the surprise of my team, we watched as reporters took great interest in what had already been written about this Mulroney fellow, and that became the established opinion few dared to contradict. We had discovered the reality of pack journalism, and for now, at least, it was working in my favour. The change would come soon enough.

The reigning king of Canadian journalism back then was Allan Fotheringham. He owned the back-page column in *Maclean's*, a choice piece of real estate for a writer, and wrote another column for the *Vancouver Sun*. In true pack fashion, without having met me, he announced to his surprised readers – Mila and me included – that one Brian Mulroney, "the candidate from Whimsy," would be the next Tory leader.

I called him up.

"When did you decide to run?" he asked.

"The second time I read it in your column," I replied.

Then came the *Edmonton Journal*: "His eyes are Paul Newman blue, his hair has the swoop of the Robert Redford style, and his voice the resonance of a Lorne Greene school of broadcasting grad. The jaw is by Gibraltar." Such was the verdict of the writer, a man whose skills of observation seem obvious, even today. Nearly thirty years later, I remain haunted by those words. No matter how hard I try, the face looking back at me from the mirror has never remotely lived up to the standard set in type so long ago in Edmonton. But the flattering portrait was helpful at the time.

As the campaign progressed, my team and I grasped the powerful role that neighbours were playing in our early success. While we had started dead last in a twelve-person race in November, it was only a matter of time before things started to click. We had made a point of using television in all my early campaign appearances, because at that point not all the delegates had been selected. Television allowed me to reach those I couldn't see in person the first time out. In later sweeps, I planned to meet personally with as many delegates as possible in one-on-one situations. For now, though, and thanks to television, we discovered that practising Tories weren't the only ones following the leadership race. Delegates began telling us they were hearing about my candidacy from their neighbours.

Throughout the country the message from next door was the same: "Give this guy Mulroney a look," neighbours said. "Compared with the others, he'll energize your party and add the pizzazz you Tories need. I just might vote for him – but you'll have to elect him leader first."

Many delegates found themselves caught in these neighbourly pincers. As we heard this story again and again, the parallel campaign was born. One – the wider, more general one – was designed to impress the neighbours; the other was aimed at persuading delegates.

Our founding meeting had taken place on a Saturday in late October at the Bristol Place Hotel near the airport in Toronto. It turned out to be less confidential than we hoped when we discovered that, by a stranger-than-fiction twist, Joe Clark's equally embryonic organization committee was meeting in the room next to us in the same hotel! Clark and I were never close – perhaps we saw each other as competitors, who knows – but we had remained in touch over the years, and I had raised money and contributed to his successful campaigns for the House of Commons in 1972 and 1974.

A letter that Joe had sent to me years earlier hinted humorously at the unspoken tension that hung between us in those days. "I gather from something Mike said that I offended your Gallic sensitivities by not looking you up in Quebec," Joe wrote in November 1962. "Out west the onus of graciousness is on the host. Lacking your ability to adapt so passionately to the customs of places just visited, I have only western practice as guide. Someday we will conquer the diversity of this Canada. I trust some intermediary will bring us together when we next are both in Ottawa."

By 1975 Joe was a diligent and effective young MP, but neither he nor I was viewed as a major leadership candidate by the pundits, which probably explained the camaraderie and good humour that highlighted the encounters between the two groups in the hotel corridors and in the bar that day.

Stephen Leopold, an energetic and affable young Montrealer, signed on as my executive assistant, and soon we were off across the country, working from morning till night, meeting delegates, giving speeches, doing media events, and generally trying to persuade PCs to support me. It was a learning experience for both of us. One day we flew into Detroit en route to a scheduled meeting across the river in Windsor. Stephen awoke from a deep sleep, gazed out the window at the Detroit skyline, and exclaimed, "This campaign is really good for me. I had no idea Windsor was so big!"

On a trip to the West, Stephen and I were joined by David Angus and John Lynch-Staunton, who sought to raise money as we focused on delegates. On a late-evening phone-in TV show in Edmonton, I began to receive a flood of complimentary calls that typically began, "I'm thrilled to see you in Edmonton and must say you sound very much like a prime minister should." I was delighted to be receiving such great local support, and was into my third answer before it dawned on me that the callers' voices belonged to my travelling partners, back in their hotel rooms!

On the way to a meeting in Fort Frances in northern Ontario, Stephen and I disembarked from a chartered plane in a blinding snowstorm at the closest airport, located in International Falls, Minnesota. We were thrilled to be greeted by a fairly large crowd, whom I promptly thanked, only to be asked, "Who are you?"

"I'm Brian Mulroney."

"Well," said the spokesman, "it's good to see you, but we're waiting for Senator Hubert Humphrey!"

By November, a slew of prominent MPs had signalled their intentions to run; it was going to be a crowded and talented field. John Fraser, Jack Horner, Sinclair Stevens, Heward Grafftey, Flora MacDonald, Joe Clark, Paul Hellyer, and Claude Wagner were certain starters. They all held seats in the House of Commons and they signalled their resentment that I, the only significant candidate who was not a member, had not "paid my dues" – as if a lifetime of devotion to the party were a trivial and inconsequential thing.

I could understand their shared concern about perhaps being upstaged by an "outsider" – thereby debasing the currency of membership in the House of Commons – and had realized from the outset that it constituted a formidable obstacle to my candidacy. But, having toured the country and picked up a surprising and growing degree of support, I decided to try anyway.

—

PERSONAL JOURNAL: JUNE 13, 1993

(Written at Harrington Lake)

In March, I told Charest that he could be a has-been, a might-have-been, or a winner – but that if he didn't run against Kim Campbell it would be one of the first two; that he couldn't lose by running. 1) You run and win, you win. 2) You run and lose and Kim wins, you become deputy prime minister, you win. 3) You run and lose and Kim wins and wins the election, you become dauphin, and you win. 4) You run and lose and Kim wins and then loses the election, you win. 5) The only way you lose and become very ordinary is by not running. After about an hour and a half of this, he decided he was leaning toward entering the race. I told him to consult his wife, Michèle, and that if she said run, he should run. Otherwise not.

—

At *Le Devoir*, Claude Ryan assessed the effect my entry might have on the race. "If it were not only because of his excellent mastery of the two official languages, his solid and indisputable roots in Quebec, and his lengthy service in the Progressive Conservative Party, Mr. Mulroney, even if he is not an MP, would have an excellent chance of mobilizing a considerable proportion of Quebec votes at the leadership convention," he wrote. "But it also happens that, even though he is a member of the same party as Mr. Wagner, the Montreal lawyer offers in many ways a startling contrast with him. With his bubbling good humour, his gift of making easy contacts in every milieu (including intellectual circles which Mr. Wagner has always shunned like the plague), his ease in communicating with others and working as part of a team, his natural taste for give and take and for strong, direct confrontation, Mr. Mulroney is almost the living antithesis of the member for St. Hyacinthe."

I officially announced my candidacy in Montreal on November 13, 1975 and immediately issued my challenge. Did Tories want to be winners again, I asked?

"I am in this race to win," I said in my opening statement. "My purpose is to lead the party to victory. Canada has become a one-party state. The Liberal Party has acquired a stranglehold on the Government of Canada and we have a monopoly on the official opposition. By the next election in 1978, the Liberals will have been in power for fifteen unbroken years. In the last four decades, the Liberals exercised power for almost thirty-five years, the Conservatives for less than six. Entire generations of Canadians – of Conservative persuasion – have been denied the opportunity of serving in government, of influencing her policies, of charting her future. This situation is both unnatural and unhealthy. Democracy is best served by challenge and change; politicians become true public servants only when they understand the limitations of power and acquire the humility that accompanies defeat. I now ask Conservatives to reverse this trend. We must in the months ahead look not only for a party leader in 1976 but a prime minister in 1978."

It was a message and theme I hammered away at in speeches, over and over, until the most important speech – at the convention itself.

When I entered the race, I knew full well that Claude Wagner, the party's Quebec leader since 1972, would have a hammerlock on much of the province's support. That only made sense. He had many supporters both within and outside of caucus, for good reason; he was attractive, perfectly bilingual, had a nice manner, and could be thoughtful and pleasant. But although I had played a role in attracting him to the party, I was not the only one disappointed by his performance since he had become an MP. I knew

Wagner was looking to the leadership. Why else would he have left the bench and gone to Ottawa in the first place? He wanted to be prime minister, and there was nothing wrong with that. We all did. Wagner was building an organization and, as Stanfield's Quebec lieutenant, he controlled whatever resources the party had back then in Quebec. We knew he'd be a formidable opponent on the ground. The fight for delegates was tough in Quebec and elsewhere – as it always was in those days. What I was now encountering was a real foretaste of what was to come in the race against Joe Clark in 1983.

There wasn't, however, anything sinister or mysterious at play in how we all competed for delegates. Though it offended the virginal instincts of some of Ottawa's finest commentators, we all bussed in supporters and helped delegates financially as best we could. The object of the exercise was simple: each candidate tried to sign up as many delegates as they could and then get them to the convention. That's what Claude Wagner did. That's what our team tried to do, and that's what Clark and the others did.

"Politics," as they say, "ain't beanbag."

At the riding level in Quebec, there was one major difference from the rest of the national party, in both 1976 and 1983. In the first race there were only two sitting Quebec Tory MPs, Wagner and Heward Grafftey. This left seventy-three seats without Tory MPs – unlike in Ontario or the West, where members were in place. So there was a vast majority of untouched ridings in the province. While this was bad news on election night, it was good news if you were running for the leadership, because you didn't have to deal with members of Parliament who could direct or influence their constituency delegates to support other candidates.

It also meant there had to be one hell of a fight for delegates in those Quebec ridings, and there was. With Wagner's lead, it was important that I, the late starter, demonstrate the breadth of the support I could still attract in my home province. Before the convention we did just that, assembling almost two thousand supporters one night in Montreal for a fundraiser and a show of strength. We gathered excited Tories from across the province, and they were joined by prominent and not so prominent New Democrats and Liberals who had crossed party lines to support me. Then there were friends from outside politics, people like Bobby Orr of the NHL, Channel 12's Martha Howlett, Louis Laberge of the Quebec Federation of Labour, Phil Cutler, who was Montreal's best-known labour lawyer, Pierre Péladeau, the dynamic founder of Quebecor, and many more.

"Following the success of Sunday evening, Mr. Mulroney now comes into view as one of the four or five main candidates in the race for Mr. Stanfield's succession," Claude Ryan wrote in *Le Devoir*. "When the time comes, during the convention, for progressive elements of the Conservative Party to close their ranks, they will probably do so around Flora MacDonald or Brian Mulroney."

Despite these successful moments, or perhaps because of them, I soon came under attack. As my profile rose, questions began to surface about who was backing me. In my files in Library and Archives Canada, historians will some day see a list of the donations I received from members of the business community. Until I began researching this book, I believed I had received only one large donation in 1976, $10,000 from Paul Desmarais's Power Corporation. I was wrong. There were two. Stephen Roman of Denison Mines also gave $10,000 to my campaign.

What's never left me are memories of small but touching donations, like the fifteen dollars my campaign received from Xaverian Ray McNeil, who was working in the office of Ontario Premier Bill Davis. There was ten bucks sent by Bill Mooney, Class of '56 at StFX, while Jean Martin of Ste-Foy, Quebec arranged for a fifty-dollar donation from his company. There was also a twenty mailed in from Pat O'Neill, another proud Xaverian. "Perhaps the Maritime University Student Parliament of 1958 was a prelude for the real thing," Pat wrote me. "Wish you the best of success and hope the enclosed will help a little." And help it did.

Still, the problems continued as we soldiered on against the rumour that our campaign had so much money that we were "trying to buy the convention." Our cause wasn't helped when my direct order to cancel singer Ginette Reno's $10,000 appearance at the convention was ignored. Years later, Michel Cogger summed up our predicament well, telling a journalist that people would have believed it if they'd heard the Mulroney campaign had purchased the Château Laurier itself.

The rumours were so destructive that even some of my own supporters turned on me. "I sent you a sizable donation for your campaign expenses but never dreamt you would involve yourself in all that raz-a-ma-taz," began one letter, written on voting day. "However, I won't cancel the cheque because you weren't elected, but you will see the folly of a very superficial publicity fiasco which did you more harm than good."

It seems almost laughable today to consider that I was pounded as a big spender when Paul Martin raised $12 million to wrest the Liberal leadership from Jean Chrétien's clinging hands in 2003. Or when you consider the millions Chrétien himself raised and spent in Calgary in 1990 after he did the same to John Turner. In comparison, our team seemed like poverty-stricken elves running around Ottawa in 1976. Still, lacking experience and without proper business controls in place, we did make the mistakes that allowed our opponents to paint us as shallow, opportunistic big spenders who had arrived in Ottawa to buy the leadership of the Progressive Conservative Party.

When you enter a political campaign and you win, you're a genius. When you lose, everything you've done is dumb and full of misjudgments. When you do things right in politics, you're lucky. And when you do things wrong, you're right out of luck.

By the time the convention opened in February of 1976 John Diefenbaker was eighty years old. Proud and defiant, he had by then developed a unique view of history and his own place in it. He occupied a world of a thousand triumphs and legions of enemies. While nobody could be certain what advice the Chief would give the Progressive Conservative leadership convention that year, I had a pretty good idea of what had to be raging through his mind: the battles of 1966, when he was rejected and, as he saw it, betrayed. It was some comfort to know that I wouldn't be the only candidate waiting with trepidation for his speech that night. I had indeed played a modest and sad role in the events that precipitated his removal as leader of the party. There were others in that arena who carried heavier baggage than I. Joe Clark, for one, had been publicly identified with the anti-Diefenbaker movement. Flora MacDonald had served as Dalton Camp's personal secretary during those early months of division and anger, when the battle for a leadership review had rapidly become personal. Only candidates like Jack Horner, who would follow Dief until the end, or like Claude Wagner and Paul Hellyer, who hadn't even been Conservatives in 1966, had little to fear from him a decade later.

As our former leader was introduced and made his way to the stage, I knew that his address would be memorable and influential. This was his party, after all, gathered in convention before him. Everyone was aware it was likely the final time he would ever hold the floor, his last hurrah. On his feet and facing thousands, John Diefenbaker had power once again. And he intended to use it.

One of the truly outstanding stump speakers in Canadian political history, the Chief didn't disappoint. I turned out to be his target and John

Diefenbaker didn't miss. He rarely did. The leadership of the party, the old Chief thundered, should never be entrusted to someone who has never sat in the House of Commons. I turned immediately to Mila and said quietly, "Honey, we're dead in the water."

Of all the major candidates, only I fell into the lonely category the Chief had singled out. He didn't use my name. He didn't have to. Everyone knew he was speaking about me. Just as seven years later I was to look out over a different convention and feel from the floor that I'd be the winner, I knew that night, at that moment, that I was going to lose.

Years later, writing in his memoirs entitled *Both My Houses*, Sean O'Sullivan (Diefenbaker's former executive assistant who went on to join the priesthood) discussed his role in influencing Diefenbaker's speech that night:

> Keith Martin had put various people up to convincing Dief to stop Mulroney but hadn't succeeded. Keith came to see me and said, "You've got to convince the Chief to stop Mulroney and he's got one chance to do it – his speech at the convention." I was reluctant, but I concluded that the end justified the means. Mulroney had momentum and had to be stopped. Only Dief could do that; only I could convince Dief he had to do it . . . I had lunch with Dief and wrote him a five-page letter on February 12 that was designed to promote Hellyer and denounce Mulroney . . . Dief's attention by now was well seized. I began the pitch: "Only Paul Hellyer has the capability of stopping this complete Camp-designed takeover." Then I began to pluck every string I knew would appeal to Dief by explaining that I supported Hellyer because he had the best chance of returning the party to the "Diefenbaker traditions" of placing more faith in people than in power brokers. "Against all these vested interests . . . you succeeded and opened the Conservative Party to Canadians from all walks of life. Privately, Mulroney tells delegates and media people of your long-standing and close friendship, leaving the clear impression that you are supporting him. Publicly, he quotes you in every speech . . . One might ask where Brian Mulroney was and whose side he was on when you spoke those words to us in 1966." . . . My plea worked. That Thursday speech was clearly aimed at skewering Mulroney.

As Diefenbaker's words resounded through the hall that first night, the mood of the convention began to swing away from me. I could sense it and I could see it. My supporters were sitting, hunched and disconsolate. My opponents were visibly relaxing. Above all else, there was nothing I could do to change it. That is the way it is with conventions. Each has its own dynamic, and once in its throes the candidates and their supporters experience the gamut of human emotions. Conventions can be joyous and inspiring or they can be mean and irrational. For those about to lose, they are never forgiving.

On the eve of the convention, I had received an uplifting note from another of Diefenbaker's former assistants, John Fisher, the roving radio journalist known to many as "Mr. Canada." "It is a long road from Baie-Comeau," he wrote. "You were a mere urchin when I first met you there. In my travels since then I have met thousands of kids whose faces and names now are lost in a great grey mass – but yours I remember. There was something different about you. That's why the next time I write you it will be directed to: 'Dear Mr. Prime Minister.'"

Fisher's old boss obviously didn't agree.

Before Dief's speech, our campaign had energized what had been a lacklustre race to determine Bob Stanfield's successor. Delegates, the media, and Canadians across the political spectrum had taken notice of this young Mulroney and his team. We had started well behind the pack for sure, but our surprising momentum only increased as we travelled across Canada. At first no one was paying any attention to me, so I was free to roam like a vagabond, looking for votes. I was always trying to leave the delegates I met thinking, "This guy *can* beat Pierre Trudeau."

But by doing better than anyone expected, we invited attack. As the party faithful gathered in Ottawa, people began to look at us uneasily. What had at first seemed energetic and attractive was now regarded as garish and grasping. Once an interesting contender, I had somehow become a slick parvenu – after twenty years of service I was now an interloper in my own party. Going into the convention, I could sense the hostile feelings of caucus for this outsider.

After the former PM's speech, a political gangup against Mulroney could proceed. For the other candidates, a seat in the Commons was their chief claim to fame, the supreme political achievement. There was no way they could surrender the leadership to a person who did not share their most vital credential. Could Joe Clark, John Fraser, Jim Gillies, Flora

MacDonald, Sinclair Stevens, or Claude Wagner, after fighting so hard to become members of Parliament in 1972, and putting up with so many indignities along the way, announce they would support a non-member for leader? They could not.

I had put my name forward in the race, knowing with my closest advisors that my candidacy would be a historic long shot. Still, I believed then, as I was destined to prove later, that Quebec is key to Conservative electoral fortunes in Canada. I offered the party a plan for victory and a path toward it that ran through my home province.

I was now on the defensive, and the delegates and commentators could see and hear it when I delivered my speech. After months of delivering a barnburner that helped carry me across the country and into contender status – earning from Arthur Maloney the accolade that "Brian Mulroney is the best stand-up speaker in Canada since John Diefenbaker" – the speech I gave to the convention was, in a word, lousy. The only person to have done worse in these circumstances was Howard Green; at the 1942 leadership convention, he passed out at the podium after a few words and had to be carried off on a stretcher.

My self-confidence was badly shaken by the Diefenbaker attack, and I knew the crowd was primed to view me with suspicion. As a result, fearing that I would be accused of shallowness, I gave the wrong speech. Instead of my usual fiery crowd-pleaser about fighting the Grits, I tried to play the statesman and spoke to the nation when I should have been a Tory politician speaking to the party.

After an effective introduction from Newfoundland Premier Frank Moores, it was my turn. "This afternoon at this great convention, history and opportunity meet," I intoned from the podium, like a speaker at a small-town Canadian Club meeting. "At a single time in a single place we meet to choose our next leader. We are here to reaffirm our party's unswerving faith in a Canada, free and indivisible. We come together as Canadians with a common dream, a common purpose. This nation was built in spite of alien voices prompting us to forsake our dream, a dream of a great Canadian nationality, diverse and unique, on the northern half of this continent. We are now a country of different communities, a people of many cultures. And so, this afternoon, I speak for the unity of our nation, the destiny of our democracy." And so on.

The reviews were devastating. "Brian Mulroney did not set the Conservative world on fire Saturday afternoon," one story in the *Ottawa Journal* began. "Visibly nervous close up, he delivered a low-key speech to the Tory leadership convention in what appeared to be a deliberate attempt to rebuff or cool criticism of his slick and expensive campaign methods . . . It was, in short, a speech that was long on style but short on substance and impact."

The one good moment I had at the convention came during the policy sessions. "In the final session he faced for the day," read a report in the *Ottawa Citizen*, "Mr. Mulroney was asked about his attitude to a French-language television station in Vancouver. The prospect of the French station has provoked widespread opposition in Vancouver, much of it led by local Conservatives. But Mr. Mulroney, born and raised in Quebec, ran smack against the general uneasiness in the Conservative party over bilingualism – and he was cheered for his efforts. If the 16,000 English-speaking people in Quebec City can have their own station, he told them bluntly, then the 60,000 French-speaking citizens of Vancouver ought to have their own station. The statement brought a moment's silence and then a loud burst of cheers and applause from the packed crowed. However, although the statement obviously pleased much of the crowd, not all applauded, and some of those who remained silent looked far from pleased by Mr. Mulroney."

I received 357 votes on the first ballot, placing second, behind Claude Wagner, who had 531, and ahead of Joe Clark, who had 277. But I was stalled. With only a handful of caucus members supporting my campaign, I knew no departing candidate would be bringing their support my way as the voting continued. I was alone.

The gangup (and I might use another, similar term) began right after the first ballot. Jim Gillies and his 87 votes walked over to Joe Clark. He was followed by Heward Grafftey. Then it was John Fraser's turn to move to Clark. Though he left his decision too late to have his name removed from the second ballot, the damage had been done, as he and his supporters moved to the Clark area, putting on yellow Clark scarves. Then came the kicker: Sinclair Stevens stood and began his march across the convention floor. At first it appeared he was heading my way. Instead, he went to Joe. As for Paul Hellyer, he went to Wagner.

On the second ballot I slipped to third place with 419 votes, behind Joe at 532 and Wagner, in first place again with 667. In the end, Clark was victorious, beating Wagner on the final ballot by 65 votes.

I was stupid not to have seen the inevitable gangup from the very outset. I didn't understand that if I pressed on, without having any parliamentary experience or a record in elected politics, my campaign would generate jealousy and resentment from the Ottawa insiders, instead of the freshness and excitement I had aimed for and achieved in the early days.

Commentator Douglas Fullerton, writing in the *Ottawa Citizen*, summed up afterwards what I had been facing from the PC caucus. His column was headlined "The Tory Outsider: 'Club Snubbed Mulroney.'" It went on to say:

> Brian Mulroney must have realized after the first ballot results were announced what an impossible task he had taken on in trying to become national leader of the Conservative party. As one by one the losing candidates declared for Joe Clark or Claude Wagner, it was clear that the two overriding considerations in their decisions were loyalties and friendships forged in the House of Commons, and the ideological division in the party between left and right. This may be the day of the charismatic man, and many Mulroney supporters were hoping that he would "pull a Trudeau" – sweep the convention by the force of his personality. What they forgot was that Trudeau had been elected to the Commons, and that he had a considerable block of support with him – including the real if undeclared backing of Lester Pearson. Mulroney, for all his years of service to the party, was an outsider and he appeared to have no strong ideological convictions which could serve as a rallying point for defectors from other candidates . . . The lesson remains that it is a long, long leap into the leadership of a major federal party for someone without a seat in the House – even for someone with good political credentials, substantial financial backing, and many visible assets. Conventions are becoming more open these days – the boys in the smoke-filled backrooms are becoming less important all the time. Still, as Brian Mulroney has learned, the door is open very much wider to those who hold that vital Commons club membership.

As the convention reached its climax, Mila and I sat there awaiting the final results, trying to summon as much dignity as we could. People from other camps hovered around, expressing sympathy for how we'd been mistreated. In response, we said nothing untoward and expressed no bitterness, anger, or hostility. We never said an ungracious word. When Joe Clark eclipsed Claude Wagner on the final ballot, we mounted the stage, congratulated the new leader, smiled and waved. We departed for Montreal the next day.

Home in Montreal, the contrast with Ottawa was striking. We soon discovered that the public at large saw us as winners. Mila and I were treated like homecoming heroes.

A fellow Montrealer, Prime Minister Trudeau, was an early caller. "We were having coffee this afternoon and Keith [Davey] and Jimmy [Coutts] and I were talking about the convention, and I wanted you to know that I thought you and Mila did extremely well," Trudeau said. "But I'm extremely pleased with the decision of the Conservative Party. Your election would not have been a pleasure for me."

Before the convention, Trudeau had told Roy Faibish what he thought of the Tory contenders. Peter Newman filled me in on that conversation shortly after my defeat. It eased the pain and I found myself – privately, mind you – agreeing with Pierre Trudeau.

"[Your potential] was probably best summed up for me by a conversation I had with Roy Faibish late Saturday night," Peter wrote to me the day after the convention. "He had spent the afternoon as a pallbearer at the funeral of Fernand Cadieux, a brilliant French Canadian who had killed himself a few days earlier. A fellow pallbearer was Pierre Trudeau. As they were driving away from the cemetery, Faibish asked Trudeau, 'Who are you most afraid of, among the Conservative candidates?' Trudeau didn't hesitate a second: 'Mulroney. But the Tories won't be smart enough to pick him.'"

Another Liberal who reached out to me was David Peterson, the brother of my old friend Jim. Years later, David and I would again put aside partisan differences and work toward a better Canada – he as premier of Ontario and me as prime minister – as we pieced together the Meech Lake Accord. "I am writing to tell you I know exactly how you feel," David wrote in March of 1976. "I know when you work your ass off, how difficult it is to lose. But I must say, as a Liberal, I'm glad you lost. However, the Liberals' gain was the Tories' loss and Canada's loss. I thought you handled yourself with class and composure and I am proud to know you."

I was also to receive praise from ordinary citizens. One man from Aylmer, Quebec took time to write a letter to the editor praising my decision to release my delegates to vote their consciences – most then went to Joe Clark, making him the winner – after I was eliminated. This engaged citizen wrote, "As a non-Conservative watching the party's leadership convention with great interest, I wish to make the following observation. Brian Mulroney, the man supposedly snubbed by the party for lack of parliamentary experience, was the only candidate who, after being dropped from the ballot, didn't rush over to jump on somebody else's bandwagon in the hope of gaining future favours. Mr. Mulroney, and he deserves to be called Mister Mulroney, was the only one with enough class and courage to free his delegates to vote as they wished. I say hats off to Brian Mulroney, a credit to Canada and his party."

Following the defeat, Mila and I began life anew in Montreal. She had been over eight months pregnant at the height of the tension in Ottawa and two weeks later she delivered our son, Ben, at St. Mary's Hospital. From birth Ben was a delight. I should have known he would later take up a television career, because the next day the *Vancouver Sun* carried a huge front-page picture of him, looking right into the camera and with his hair perfectly parted!

I was relieved Ben didn't share all of his father's physical characteristics. "'Luckily he doesn't have my jaw,' Brian Mulroney said after his wife Mila gave birth to their [first son], Tuesday night," the Canadian Press reported. "The birth of the child had been expected Feb. 22 – the day the PC convention chose Joe Clark leader of the party. Mulroney, one of the leadership contenders, said the boy will probably be named Ben, 'after my father.' He said he'd been thinking of John George but rejected it 'about two weeks ago.'"

In Toronto, my old friend Sam Wakim clipped the *Toronto Star*'s coverage of the birth and wrote directly to Ben, enclosing the article and sending our boy his first letter. He wrote, "Ben: Your grandfather would sure be annoyed with the *Toronto Star* for the place where they put the announcement of your arrival; however, he would have been pleased they had enough sense to give you a proper greeting. I am sure you must have had a lot of laughs while you were curled up in Mila's lap during the convention. If your Dad doesn't become PM I am sure that your grandfather Ben wouldn't have been offended because he would have figured that the first Mulroney prime minister should be Ben. Just to make sure you know you have your first worker in Toronto. Sam."

Bob Stanfield also reached out to me at this difficult time. A proud family man himself, our party's former leader sent me a reflective note after learning that Mila and I had become the parents of a little boy. His touching note had nothing to do with politics or the recent convention. "It will be fascinating for you to watch the development of your children," he wrote. "In my case, the son was much more difficult as a child than the girls; but my daughter Sarah has a boy and a girl, and Ben, the boy, is much easier to 'bring up' than Amy, the girl. It was always fascinating to me to see how much my children had in common and yet how different they were."

Despite my happiness with Ben's arrival, I have to admit that losing the leadership in the circumstances I did was not easy to bear. Because I was not a caucus member, there was no possibility of joining the other losing candidates (Paul Hellyer aside) on the floor of the House, participating in question period, or actively supporting the new leader and generally keeping busy. Such activity was probably therapeutic for most of the other losers, although still painful. No one enters such a race without believing deep down that he or she is the best candidate and thinking – for a while, at least – that, in spite of public utterances to the contrary, the best man (or woman) had not won.

Some time after Ben's birth, Mila and I went to Florida for a few days of private reflection and discussion. Mila was positive and supportive; she showed none of the frustration and rancour that I did. Her most sensible advice was that I should be proud of having done so well. At thirty-six, I had come third in a field of eleven experienced candidates. I had established myself as a major contender if I chose to run the next time. I had done well, she argued, and I should be pleased. I listened carefully to what she said and what she recommended, and I regret not following through on her advice to the letter.

It was a bad time. I had come so close. There was also a surprising lack of outreach from the new leader and his colleagues. I was largely left alone in Montreal to replay the mistakes of my campaign and to read the cutting commentary of the Ottawa media types, now busily engaged in celebrating the qualities of the winner while denigrating those of the loser, namely me. Some MPs, like George Hees, phoned to wish me well, but most quickly got on with their lives, while a few, like Heward Grafftey, found time to make disparaging comments about me and my campaign.

I also had to deal with the overspending by my campaign team that saddled me with $200,000 in debts. Almost every other week a small and dispirited band led by Guy Charbonneau and David Angus gathered in Guy's insurance brokerage offices to sort out bills, negotiate with creditors, and call on old friends to see if they could help this one last time. I later compounded the problem when I made the decision not to turn over my donation lists to the party. Had I done so, I would have received a much-needed $30,000 campaign subsidy that the party offered all candidates after the convention.

For me it was a point of principle. After the start of the race, the party had changed the rules, meaning that the names of those who donated to our respective campaigns would become public. My campaign team had raised funds with a completely different rule in place. Some of the donations to my campaign obviously came from members of the business community in Quebec. These were people who were well aware the Liberals were still in power, and they knew how vindictive the party of Marc Lalonde and Jean Chrétien could be. Once the donors' names appeared on a published list, their chances of ever receiving government contracts in the province were over. When I approached these supporters about turning their names over to the party, many expressed fears of Liberal retribution. Though I needed the $30,000 to help pay down my debt, I honoured my original commitment and kept the names secret.

Today, I wouldn't hesitate to make my list of donors public. While the list was entirely innocent, not revealing it harmed me and my supporters. It just fed the media crowd in Ottawa, so consumed by the politics of envy, who said and wrote that we had something to hide. In the end, Mila and I paid off the debt in the fall of 1976, with the proceeds from the sale of our Devon Street home and with the help of a personal bank loan and the assistance of friends. By late spring we had managed to pay off all outstanding bills, and I was finally released from an enormous personal burden.

That was a difficult period for me, and I did not handle it well. I began to drink quite heavily with friends over lunch and dinner, and these sessions frequently degenerated into baleful expressions of recrimination and regret. I profanely attacked some people who had let me down. On several occasions I thought it appropriate later to apologize – at least once in writing – to colleagues and friends for my unbecoming displays of bitterness and improper conduct.

How Mila tolerated me in that post-convention period I'll never know. But Caroline and Ben were daily treats, and by early summer the cloud that had troubled me began to lift – although it would be a few years before I was finally rid of the disappointment I felt after the convention. Only a saint would find such public failure a positive experience, and I was no saint.

2. Life at the Iron Ore Company of Canada

BY THE TIME THE convention was over, I had been away from my work at Ogilvy Renault for almost six months. The firm had always been good to me. As a partner, I felt I owed them a long-term commitment. At the same time, I was restless. Soon I entered into long discussions with my colleagues about the future. While law firms are great places to work, one acquires no equity. I was at that stage in my life when I thought it might be time to cross the street.

Over the years, I had considered offers from the corporate world. The first came from Standard Brands, whose chairman, Ross Johnson from Winnipeg, was a great friend and one of the country's most accomplished business leaders. Ross felt I had the skills to be the company's president, even though I had no significant business background. The second offer came from friends in franchise ownership positions who wanted me to be considered for the presidency of the National Hockey League – surely one of the dream jobs for any Canadian boy who has ever laced up skates.

The third offer came from a group with whom I had very friendly relations as a lawyer. It was delivered by a crusty and principled man named Bill Bennett. In a previous life, he had been the powerful executive assistant to one of the truly outstanding federal cabinet ministers of modern times, C.D. Howe. Dubbed the "Minister of Everything," Howe served in the cabinet of the most conservative postwar administration to guide Canada until my own, that of Louis St. Laurent. As Howe's executive assistant, Bill Bennett had emerged as a man of great influence in Ottawa. Now he was the successful president of the Iron Ore Company of Canada. Through Bill, I had met Robert Anderson, who was chairman of the Hanna Mining Company in Cleveland, Iron Ore Canada's largest shareholder. Before the leadership race, in the summer of 1975, at a dinner at Ruby Foo's in Montreal, they had both asked me about joining Iron Ore Canada as executive vice-president. The idea was that I would spend a year in intense work with them to determine if both sides were comfortable with the other. If so, I'd assume the presidency of Iron Ore Company of Canada at a future date, succeeding Bill Bennett.

Because I was on the point of entering the leadership race, I turned down the offer, though I had been much attracted by it. Why wouldn't I be? I was from the North Shore, and the Iron Ore Company had about 7,500 employees at large installations at Sept-Îles, Schefferville, and Labrador City. It also owned and operated the Quebec North Shore and Labrador Railway. It was an important Canadian corporation and a major employer in Quebec and Newfoundland, and in Labrador. Taking this important new job would also quadruple my income.

When the offer was again extended in the spring of 1976, after discussions with Mila, I accepted. Given what had happened to me at the convention, I thought a change would be better than a rest. And it was. As president of Iron Ore Canada I developed skills, talents, interests, and aptitudes hitherto unknown to me. They were extraordinarily beneficial, as it turns out, during the campaign for the leadership in 1983 and, more importantly, when I became prime minister.

While it took some time, I was eventually to see how my loss in 1976 – a seminal moment in my life – was the key to later victories. Had I not run unsuccessfully I might never have made the decision to take the big risk of leaving the security of my law firm. By striking out on an unknown path, I gained a new perspective on life. While I had been kicked around, often unfairly, and been badly bruised, many of the mistakes were mine. More important than the scars was the knowledge that Mila and I were not mortally wounded.

Over time I turned my life around in Montreal and used the experience to improve myself. Thoughts of a return to politics (perhaps another run for leader?) were well and truly banished from my mind as I settled into the rigorous schedule and exacting requirements of an executive at a major company. I was thirty-seven years old.

I began at IOC in July 1976, travelling to the plants and offices with Bill Bennett, learning the ropes as I went. Bill conducted lengthy, detailed, intense, and highly beneficial seminars on the industry for me, giving an overview of markets, prices, costs, taxation arrangements, and operating challenges.

The first call I received welcoming me aboard was from Richard "Dick" Geren, our executive vice-president, operations. We were to develop an excellent working relationship and fast friendship over the years. Simply put, Dick was one of the finest, most principled men I have ever known. From a certain angle, he bore a startling physical resemblance to my father. Born in Ohio, he migrated as a geologist to Canada's North and emerged over time as one of the most admired and respected leaders in Canada's mining industry. He and his wife, Grace, loved Canada and had spent most of their lives in the North, They welcomed Mila and me – much younger and inexperienced in the industry – with open arms.

Dick had already assembled – along with Bob Anderson and Bill Bennett – an especially competent group of executives: Jack Galligan, in industrial relations; Walter Miller and Avit Ouellet, in finance; L.C Van Hoven in treasury; Mike Monahan, in operations; and Jean-Pierre Maltais in corporate and community relations. They were a superb group of operators and Bob Anderson was a gruff, demanding but highly ethical chairman of the board. When I became president a year later – after a tough year of travel and on-the-job training – I was ready to help lead the turnaround of IOC.

From StFX my former professor John Sears, now the university's dean of arts and sciences, congratulated me on my appointment. "And just think," he wrote, "you could have been in the position today where you would be worried about pipelines, the RCMP, bilingualism, Arab boycotts, and so on." I chuckled and responded, "Although I did not think so sixteen months ago, I am now quite happy to let Joe Clark worry about some of the problems you raise in your letter!"

After assuming the presidency in 1977, I set about solving our worst problem. In the decade prior to my arrival, the company had been hit with three major strikes and fifty-two separate work stoppages ranging in duration from an hour to three weeks. As a result, with over seven thousand employees and $1 billion in assets, the company had failed to pay a dividend for eight straight years. Our principal challenge clearly was in labour relations. They were very bad, exacerbated by a damaging attitudinal problem between labour and management. "It was so bad," Len Leyte, president of USW local 5795 in Labrador City, said in an interview, "that people were going to work in the morning not knowing whether they'd work that day or not."

In the same interview, Leyte described the situation that he and his fellow unionized workers faced from the shop floor. It was a throwback to a different age of industrial relations. "The people running the company set the supervisors up on a pedestal and told them, 'You're not going to associate with the hourly paid people. You're a supervisor and you're different.' That bred contempt from the top of the company to the bottom," he said. "They were dictators rather than leaders."

I convened the executive management committee I chaired and announced that, sadly, I had to agree with the union's assessment. And I announced that the situation – and with it the very culture of Iron Ore Canada – would be changing. Period. "People don't work *for* you any more," I said. "They either work *with* you, or they don't work at all."

I pointed out to my management team that both our workers and shareholders had been deprived over the previous decade, and I reminded them that we were being paid to provide leadership and that meant change. The team initially expressed some misgivings because the problems were on both sides: labour unions in Labrador had become very militant, and in Quebec some of the destructive practices and attitudes I had encountered during the Cliche Commission's investigations of the construction industry had migrated to the iron ore fields, plants, and railways. It was a time of hostility and mistrust that saw a great industry being crippled on an ongoing basis.

I hearkened back to my own family's experience in a company town in Baie-Comeau. Just like my dad, Ben Mulroney, I told the group, our workers would respond when they could feel and see that they were being treated with dignity and appreciation by their employers. It was our job, I said, always to show our good faith. Providing job security in a safe and productive workplace, and returning profits to our shareholders, did not have to be goals that the two sides approached differently. While it was self-evident to me, I had to remind my team, many of whom had risen through the ranks, absorbing a management culture I was now rejecting, that the situation would be better for everyone if we were all singing from the same hymn book.

After a protracted and frequently emotional debate, our management group developed a consensus on new corporate goals. Among them: to eliminate work stoppages, to reduce on-the-job accidents to below industry levels, to develop meaningful and direct relationships with both unions and employees, to improve the quality of our product, and to earn 10 per cent on assets ($100 million a year) by 1981.

We took a good look at ourselves as managers and we didn't like what we saw. So, for the first time, we introduced a corporate planning group, a human relations directorate, a productivity enhancement group, a management development program, and the most intense and comprehensive employee communications program the industry had ever seen.

In a major analysis of our efforts, in 1982 *Canadian Business* magazine editor Sandy Ross wrote:

> The crucial area, however, was labour relations. The company devised a formal communications program – thank-you notes from supervisors, informational brochures, plant tours for employees' children, ads in local newspapers back-patting IOC employees for participating in community activities . . . But thank-you notes and glossy brochures would have been worthless if they hadn't been accompanied by substantive changes in policy and by changes in attitudes that Mulroney tried to install. "You name anything that any enlightened employer in North America has done or will do, and we've done it," says Mulroney. "That meant dealing with the men. That meant me being there on Christmas Eve; going around and seeing people at regular times during the year – not to talk business but to find out what the hell they thought. It meant all of us talking to the unions. It meant making sure that, on all the social occasions, there would be joint union management representation. We set up joint human relations committees, separate from our bargaining committees. We set up brown bag programs where the ordinary guys have lunch with the superintendents and managers on a regular basis."

I tried to deal directly with the accusations of "dictatorial management" by laying down the law as clearly as I could. "I will personally fire anyone in this company who thinks I'm impressed by booting the unions around or kicking people in the ass," I said. "*They're* going to be kicked out, not the unions. We want sensible, reasonable, enlightened management."

And I meant it.

Our special emphasis on industrial safety prompted the following statement by union president Len Leyte, who pointed out the changes in this area to *CB* editor Sandy Ross. "In 1974 we had three fatalities in nine days – all due to carelessness and lax procedures. But we haven't had a fatal accident since 1977 [five years]."

In the early 1980s, I was already developing concerns about worrying trends in the natural environment, concerns that I would carry with me later into the Prime Minister's Office and expand with my efforts to convince two American administrations of the need for joint Canada–U.S. action on acid rain.

—

PERSONAL JOURNAL: April 6, 1985

(Reflection on the Shamrock Summit)

Mila and I flew to Quebec late Saturday night. A late-night crisis emerged when I tried to secure tougher language on acid rain and provoked outrage with [National Security Advisor] Bud McFarlane and others in Washington. When Derek Burney reported this through Allan Gotlieb and asked for my instructions, I told him to tell McFarlane to "fuck off." McFarlane is a fine gentleman and a great friend of Canada, but he is not the president. I told Burney to tell Gotlieb not to worry about him or others. Reagan is the one who matters, not the others, and he makes the decisions and wants the summit to succeed. I like the Americans but I'm not impressed with their bureaucratic bluster. I hope Gotlieb conveyed my message exactly as transmitted – it will do wonders for McFarlane's indigestion.

—

In 1980, a federal government report said that Labrador City–Wabush was the area with the worst air and water pollution in Atlantic Canada. When I was contacted by the press for comment as Iron Ore's president, I reported that we had identified our role in the conditions and had budgeted $7 million to fix the problem, a year and a half earlier. This expenditure was made despite internal company data revealing that IOC operated below acceptable levels 85 per cent of the time.

To me that wasn't good enough. "Our commitment is to make sure that our plant in Labrador City is the healthiest and safest in Canada, and we will spend whatever money it takes to do that," I told the *Truro Daily News* in December 1980. "Anything that affects our employees in terms of health and safety is of the utmost importance to us. Our commitment is to eliminate the hazard [from sulphur dioxide levels that could lead to respiratory diseases]. We want to make that plant the best in the business, and we will spend whatever money necessary to deal with the problem."

Iron Ore also participated fruitfully in a tripartite commission consisting of myself, Len Leyte from the union, and the provincial labour minister, Jerome Dinn. We agreed to analyze the health of our workers and to proceed from those findings to seek improvements in occupational health.

Our progress was slow but sure in all areas, and our senior management team made remarkable efforts to implement fully and effectively our turnaround policy. We had to endure a last-gasp strike in 1978, but from that moment until my resignation in 1983 there was not a single work stoppage related to labour–management disagreement. Productivity increased, communications blossomed, safety conditions improved, and profitability was restored to the company.

My approach to labour–management relations is best demonstrated in a letter I wrote to Len Leyte after he was defeated as president in his union's local elections. Len reminded me of my father: he fought hard for his membership but he fought fair. While we didn't always agree, we negotiated in an atmosphere of civility and mutual respect. "I was both surprised and disappointed with the results of the vote in your local," I wrote.

> Because I have been on the other side of the table from you so often and have seen the determination and commitment that you brought to bear on every problem on behalf of your members, it, quite frankly, never occurred to me that they might decide to change leaders. Such, however, is an illustration of the important uncertainty of democracy, and I know that you will accept the judgment with the elegance that has characterized your presidency. Whether our respective principals fully appreciated it or not as it unfolded, it is now clear that during the last four or five years, a new and important dimension of human relations was introduced into this company's affairs. The degree of civility and leadership shown by both sides in an attempt to improve the situation for all concerned has, in my judgment, been an admirable accomplishment and will successfully withstand objective analysis or scrutiny.

By late 1982, earnings had increased so dramatically that IOC shareholders collected more dividends in five years than they had in the previous twenty.

In keeping with the new philosophy I was working so hard to instill at the senior levels of management, the year before I had convinced my board to make each and every employee feel part of our success. This included significant pay increases, improved job security provisions, and a Christmas bonus for each worker.

In many ways, the presidency of IOC was a dream job. It was a demanding but challenging opportunity that provided new occasions to learn, travel, and grow. In the course of trips to China, Japan, Brazil, and central and eastern Europe, for example, I was able to witness first-hand the rise of a new economic empire in the East, the decay and paralysis in communist systems and their command economies, and the remarkable stirrings of extraordinary trade possibilities in our own hemisphere. I participated frequently in think-tank sessions at home and abroad, and with time devoted to reading, study, and reflection, I was able to begin the process of thinking through some of Canada's problems and elaborating realistic proposals to deal with them.

I had lived in both urban and isolated areas of Quebec, and had spent much of my youth in the Maritimes, and now the presidency of IOC gave me the chance to grapple with the realities of regionalism in a broader context. Through my participation in the business world, I began to understand the damage the Liberal government had inflicted – and was continuing to inflict – upon the Canadian economy, particularly in western Canada. During this period I was elected a director of Renaissance Resources in Calgary, which meant that I really got to understand the Calgary-based Canadian oil and gas industry.

From Calgary, N.R. "Buck" Crump, the legendary retired chairman and CEO of Canadian Pacific, wrote to me in 1980. "I believe western alienation (not separation) is very real," he said. "Personally, I believe we should start the new country at the Lakehead! Marc Lalonde's vendetta [against the West] and socialism are going to make it rough in Alberta, and I see now that Lougheed can win. Ask that stout Liberal who preceded you why he didn't sell iron ore (a depleting natural resource) to the West at half world prices? Of course the West for a hundred years has paid world prices plus protective tariff on everything shipped from the East. Or why natural gas has an export tax but not electric energy – Quebec to New York?"

I sent Buck a lengthy response:

> The issue of western alienation is beginning to trouble many easterners. The first reaction was one of indifference: "Oh, don't worry about it; it's nothing more than a bunch of greedy westerners grumbling about money." A more serious reaction has now set in. There is a growing awareness here that so many people in western Canada cannot all be wrong. The voices raised in opposition to the recent budget and constitutional proposals from western Canada, have, I think, begun to persuade a large number of central Canadians that we should stop, examine the matter most carefully, and respond in a generous manner.
>
> Very few of us down here understand the jargon of oil and gas or energy in general. As a result, many of the intricacies of the arguments pro and con are lost upon us. Alberta's case has not gone down well in eastern Canada for the simple reason that it is not understood. It is my hope that beginning in early January Peter Lougheed and other western spokesmen will seek out audiences in this part of the country and explain both the buzzwords and the substance of their arguments. It is not widely known nor appreciated, for example, that Alberta has been subsidizing eastern industry in large measure for a period of years. This case can be made – indeed must be made – if central Canadians are to grasp the fundamentals of the argument and develop a sympathy for many of the positions being articulated by leaders in western Canada. I view Canadians as the most fortunate people in the world. My regret is that politicians have so obscured this fact that we are now ready to follow any leader willing to tell us that we are poorly off.

Five years after that exchange of letters, I, as prime minister, ended the National Energy Program that had ripped the economic guts out of western Canada, confiscating almost $100 billion directly from the Alberta treasury. My government was also later to assist Newfoundlanders on the path toward self-sufficiency when we negotiated the Atlantic Accord and opened the doors to the development of offshore oil at Hibernia.

It was at Iron Ore that I began to appreciate the economic possibilities belonging to Newfoundland and Labrador. "One only has to reflect for a moment on the history and culture of this province and its proponents to appreciate the opportunities that await you," I told graduates of Memorial

University in October of 1980 during a convocation address. "There is an industrial base here that one day soon will be the envy of many; hydro power, oil and gas, fisheries, mining, pulp and paper, tourism – you have it all. There is a vigorous outport feeling of self-reliance to be respected and a Labradorian sense of isolation to be harmonized with the provincial sense of purpose." I feel the same exciting sense of promise today.

I also took Newfoundland's side – in a speech given in Quebec – in the disagreement over the Lower Churchill hydroelectric deal. "The present contract between Quebec and Newfoundland for electric power from Churchill Falls does not reflect in any way the new economic and energy realities that have developed since the OPEC crisis," I said in Baie-Comeau in 1981. "The inequality and absence of fair play in the contract in question is obvious. Simple decency and the most elementary spirit of justice demand its immediate renegotiation."

On the negative side, I also learned that members of the small and sometimes insular Canadian business class at the time could play politics as hard as anyone on Parliament Hill. In 1982 word reached me that David Radler, an associate of Conrad Black in Sterling Newspapers (which had benefited from IOC's royalty arrangements with Labrador Mining, which Sterling controlled), was disparaging IOC, suggesting that the company was actually being run out of Cleveland. In defence of my management team and myself, I fired off a letter to Radler to set the record straight:

> This kind of grossly inaccurate statement is deeply offensive [to all of us at Iron Ore] who are principally charged with the responsibility of operating in a very real way the complex affairs of this corporation and ensuring its financial success . . . As you will know, record dividends have been remitted to shareholders in recent times. In fact, the formula for our success is very simple: hands-on management, the control of costs, dramatically improved labour relations, productivity enhancement, and lots of hard work on the site. This approach is difficult to execute if one is located thousands of miles away in the United States. None of the officers of this corporation is a shareholder, as you know. Our shares are all held by other companies. We do not, however, feel diminished in our virility as a result of this. Nor does it lessen our commitment as professional managers to continue to make the Iron Ore Company of Canada a particularly successful operation of benefit to all

involved. I think you will find that your views expressed from the vantage point of the Vancouver Club are not widely shared in Labrador City, Schefferville, or Sept-Îles.

After I joined Iron Ore Canada in 1976, I was visited by an old friend, Jimmy Coutts, then principal secretary to Prime Minister Pierre Trudeau. He came to my Montreal office in the Standard Life Building to tell me that Trudeau wanted to bring me into the federal cabinet and would open a seat for me in Montreal, if I were ready to join the Liberal Party. I told Jim that while I deeply appreciated the offer – it was a lot more generous than any I had received from my own party – I was still a committed Progressive Conservative, despite being outside the political arena for the time being, if not permanently. He went away, and that was that.

—

PERSONAL JOURNAL: JANUARY 1, 1986

Jimmy Coutts once told me that he served Mr. Trudeau and Mr. Pearson with total devotion and absolute discretion, because as a political activist he could think of no greater honour and privilege than contributing to lessening the burden on a prime minister of Canada. Anyone who knows anything about Coutts knows he did that with distinction. I can only hope and work to ensure that members of my staff adopt the same positive attitude, which would both do wonders for their own morale and reputations and be a great benefit to the government.

—

A few weeks later, on November 15, 1976, a political earthquake that ranked as 10 on the Richter scale hit Canada: the Parti Québécois elected a majority government in Quebec and René Lévesque became premier, notwithstanding Trudeau's airy assertion some months earlier that "separatism is dead." A referendum on Quebec's future inside Canada was inevitable, which I knew would unleash ugly passions throughout the province and across the country.

In spite of the political turbulence, life went on. Mila and I had settled into a stimulating and satisfying life that provided me with a bedrock of support. During the 1980 referendum campaign I became active as vice-chairman of the Pro-Canada Committee. I was active in causes like the United Way/Centraide, where I served as Montreal general chairman, and I proudly chaired the fundraising campaign for St. Francis Xavier University. I slowly joined the upper reaches of the Canadian business community by accepting directorships in the Canadian Imperial Bank of Commerce, Provigo Inc., Standard Broadcasting, Ritz-Carlton Hotels, TIW, and the Hanna Mining Company.

As IOC president I had access to a sleek, elegantly upholstered de Havilland jet that the company had purchased from sports team owner Nelson Skalbania of Vancouver. From time to time it would take us to New York, where a corporate apartment in the Carlton House hotel at the corner of Madison and 61st was available for business meetings and long weekends. The company also maintained attractive suites in hotels in the cities where we operated, and excellent salmon and trout fishing camps in Labrador and northern Quebec, which I visited regularly with friends and associates.

Despite these enjoyable perks, I tried never to forget where I came from. As a boy, I had listened to Habs games on my radio in Baie-Comeau and dreamed that dream shared by millions of Canadian youngsters of watching my hockey heroes in person as they played and beat the hated Leafs. Our corporate seats for Canadiens games at the Montreal Forum were used on more than one occasion to make dreams come true for kids from the towns in which Iron Ore operated. I treasure nothing more from those days at Iron Ore than a letter I received one day in 1982 from Scott Campbell of Sept-Îles. "Thank you so much for the hockey tickets you gave to my family to see the first Stanley Cup playoff game," he wrote. "I play hockey here in Sept-Îles, so it was a great thrill, and it was the first time I had gone to a pro game. I was glad that my team won."

Another personal thrill was getting to know fascinating people from around the world. People like Frank Borman, the commander of the Apollo 8 crew that made history at Christmas in 1968 by becoming the first human beings to leave Earth's orbit and circle the moon in all its mysterious splendour. Frank was gracious in supplying autographs and information about his historic mission that I later related to all my children.

Mila and I frequently enjoyed the legendary hospitality of Paul and Jackie Desmarais in La Malbaie, and I would often join Paul for a few days of salmon fishing on Anticosti Island. Paul Martin Jr. and I once spent a sunny day together there, fishing, chatting and speculating about the political future. Paul was then president of CSL and I was president of IOC, and both of us secretly wanted to become prime minister one day, but neither of us was straightforward enough to admit it. We knew our ambition would have strained credulity. That night, back at the main camp, we joined Prime Minister Trudeau, his two young sons Justin and Sacha, Jean Chrétien, Marc Lalonde, Simon Reisman, Paul Volker, Jim Burns, and John Rae for drinks, dinner, and high-level political gossip. I was operating in a world I never dreamed existed when I was growing up in Baie-Comeau.

After my government was returned by the Canadian people in the 1988 election, John Rae reached from the Liberal backrooms across the partisan divide and recalled those salmon fishing trips. "In reflecting on your success, I was reminded of a trip we all took together many years ago on the Jupiter River," he wrote in a kind letter.

> You had said that this was your first opportunity to catch salmon, and allowed as to how it didn't matter to you if you caught a fish or not, and that you would have been happy to see someone else catch one. I must confess that I never quite believed this generous attitude on your part, selfless as it was. This suspicion was confirmed. After you caught your first salmon it was impossible to separate your grip from the rod. You quickly forgot the business of limits, and after catching many salmon I believe that it was only night-time and hunger which got you back to the camp. When you entered politics it was clear to me as a Liberal that if you got power, the same determination exhibited on the river would be applied to your view of appropriate political tenure, and that it would be a very long time before we got our turn to fish again. Your tenacity and accomplishment are admirable. Phyllis and I wish you and your family all the very best for success and happiness in the challenging years ahead.

That gesture was typical of John and his brother Bob. While we were all proud partisans from different political parishes, our friendship rose – and continues to rise – above political loyalties. Like their distinguished father, Saul, the Rae brothers have contributed much to this country and Canada is better for their labours – even if they both chose the wrong party.

During my corporate days, letters constantly went back and forth between me, John Rae, Paul Martin Jr., and other members of the Liberal Party. The reason? Iron Ore Canada was a generous financial contributor to the Canadian democratic system. I helped or arranged campaign donations to Jim Peterson, David Smith, Lloyd Axworthy, and several other Liberals. Paul and John always reciprocated and helped PC candidates across the country, at my frequent request.

Mila, the children, and I enjoyed our life at our beautiful home at 68 Belvedere Road (near the top of Westmount Mountain), a house I had purchased with an interest-free loan from the company. We also had fun, thanks to my job. One day in Collingwood, Ontario in 1980, Mila was called into service to christen a tugboat that Iron Ore had bought from Paul Martin's Canada Steamship Lines. She needed two swings of the champagne bottle to accomplish her task, but did it with her usual grace and humour. Later on the bus ride back to Toronto, Paul provided other bottles of excellent champagne that encouraged a rousing singalong led, as it turned out, by two future prime ministers. With a good income, an annual bonus, a retirement allowance, an expense account, and a car and driver – the perks then available to top executives in Canada – I was leading the life of Riley. As the years rolled by, I became progressively more disinclined to listen to the voices of those who urged me to return to active politics.

It is time to talk about my drinking.

Alcohol had not played a significant role in my life during the years growing up in Baie-Comeau. While my father certainly enjoyed his beer, he was never a regular at La Taverne Aux Amis, the watering hole in the basement of the local theatre that provided sanctuary to generations of Baie-Comeau's mill workers. On the rare occasion of a big night out such as New Year's Eve, I remember that he enjoyed drinking rye whisky, and my mother would take a drink, too, as they celebrated with their friends the Prévosts, Touchies, Halls, and Molloys. I have no recollection of drinking excessively in high school or college, although I certainly imbibed at dances, beach parties, and other social occasions where young friends gathered.

During my time in law school at Laval, I do remember the beginnings of some regular – but not especially worrisome – drinking as we students congregated in bars or restaurants late at night in the Quartier Latin, gossiping with journalists, chatting with politicians of all stripes, and debating until the wee hours.

Things changed when I reached Montreal as a young lawyer. Social mores in that city from the mid 1960s through the 1980s seem, in retrospect, to have actually encouraged unhealthy living. Tobacco was extremely popular, and I became an inveterate smoker, exacerbating a bad habit I had picked up years earlier in Baie-Comeau. Drinking, too, was widespread and socially acceptable. When Montreal's business and professional leaders gathered for lunch at the Beaver Club in the Queen Elizabeth Hotel, many, if not most, would begin with a Beefeater martini of such generous proportions that it was fondly known as a "birdbath." Lunch was usually washed down with a carafe of wine and coffee often was served with a *pousse café* (layered shots of liquor). After lunch, everyone rolled back to their offices to complete an afternoon's work. And at night, there was the party circuit.

In the 1970s, I would guess that of, say, one hundred Beaver Club luncheon diners on any given day, eighty-five would enjoy such service while fifteen would stick with a Perrier or soda water. Ten years later those percentages would be reversed, as drinking and smoking became less and less acceptable, and Canadians woke up to the damage such activities had to their health and to their families' well-being.

In June 1980, I went on a business trip to Romania, accompanied by three friends: Jim Courtney, executive vice-president of Hanna Mining, who had remarkable knowledge of the world iron ore market; Bob Coates, the veteran Nova Scotia MP who was serving as president of the federal PC Party, and who had developed impressive contacts within the Romanian government; and Pat MacAdam, my talented and entertaining pal from StFX days, who now served as IOC's representative in Ottawa.

During our stay in Bucharest, where we were skilfully shepherded about by Canadian Ambassador Peter Roberts, we met with President Ceauşescu in his massive office in a Stalinist-style building. After listening carefully to our idea about initiating a Canada–Romania iron ore sales program, the president turned to me and said, "Some years ago, Richard Nixon was out of office and came to see me. I predicted then that he would one day become president, and I say today, Mr. Mulroney, that one day you will be prime minister of Canada."

We all agreed immediately after the meeting to keep this surprising third-party endorsement an absolute secret, until now. It would have been the kiss of death to any future political aspirations that I still held. Ceauşescu and his regime were evil incarnate and I was unhappy when, early in my first term as PM, I was obliged to host a luncheon for him and his equally vile wife when they came to Canada on an official visit, one that had been agreed upon some years earlier.

So offensive were the Ceauşescus that even members of the royal family were capable of stepping out of their nonpolitical roles to express their outrage. "Here, as promised, is the book about that poor, persecuted country, Romania, which we talked about at dinner in Palm Beach," Prince Charles wrote to Mila in 1989. "It will make your flesh creep and is, largely, I believe, true. I do hope you can persuade your husband to join the hands of those of us who feel that Ceauşescu is a total affront to European civilization and that every means should be used to embarrass him into altering his inhumane policies."

Mila responded: "It was such a pleasure seeing you in Palm Beach, last February. I was particularly fascinated by our discussion of Romania, and I am especially grateful for your gift, *Red Horizons*, which I have read with great interest. You are absolutely correct in saying that it would make my skin crawl. Brian is now in the process of reading it and, judging by his comments, he too will have a strong reaction to the regime and to its leaders."

But all that was in the future as I returned to the government guest house Ceauşescu had chosen for me during that 1980 visit to Romania. I had been given the accommodation as a "mark of respect," I was told. It was horrible: the room was tiny, hot, and not air-conditioned; the food perfectly inedible; the sanitary conditions dubious. I became violently ill from a virus that flattened me completely, and it was only through the assistance of my travelling companions that I made it back to Montreal. Mila promptly put me to bed and got me excellent medical assistance.

As I slowly recovered, I had some welcome free time to reflect on my life. That was when I realized I would have to come to grips with the fact that I had developed what could only be described as a serious drinking problem.

Over the years in Montreal, and in my frequent travels to isolated mining towns, what had begun as pleasure in a few drinks after work or before dinner was progressing rapidly toward a need to be fuelled frequently by some alcohol at lunch, dinner, and in the late evening. So far I had not gotten into any serious difficulties either at work or socially because of the drinking, but my conduct was becoming unpredictable and worrisome and I realized I had entered dangerous territory. I was forced to confront the fact that I couldn't maintain my present lifestyle and achieve my goals if I didn't take drastic and quick action.

Mila had spoken frankly to me about the growing problem on a number of occasions, and my trusted friends Paul Desmarais, Maurice Mayer, and Sam Wakim had bravely given me helpful advice and warned me about the consequences for my family and my career.

Excessive drinking affects people differently. It has little impact on some, but it can be severely damaging for others. As I recovered from my Romanian trip I realized that I was in the latter category. As I thought about the lives and the marriage I was increasingly placing in jeopardy, I felt weak and ashamed.

On June 24, 1980 – celebrated in Quebec as St-Jean-Baptiste Day – I quit drinking. To this day, more than twenty-seven years later, I have never had another drop. I have not missed the alcohol (I can't say the same about the cigarettes that I gave up four years later), although it was very hard to break the social habits of decades. At first I told no one of my decision, although Mila, of course, quickly noticed the change. I attended no self-help group meetings. I firmly resolved that day that I would never again place in peril the well-being of those who loved and supported me, especially my wife, children, and other family members. I also wanted my young children, then six, four, and one, to be proud of me when they grew older, and I knew that would not be the case unless I changed course immediately.

I suffered from a weakness, an illness, and a combination of time and willpower made me better. Not cured, just better. It also made me extremely sensitive to people with similar problems, and I have met many such in the private sector and during my time as prime minister. I hope that recounting my own battle to overcome the problem was of some assistance to them, just as I hope that this account will help others combat this tough disease.

While I was prime minister, I would occasionally receive letters from people who, like me, had faced up to their problems with alcohol. During the summer of 1990, a leading Canadian journalist took time to pen a letter that I still treasure, which read in part: "A progress report: Yesterday I got my one-year medallion. At our . . . group you were held up as an example of coolness under fire. Despite the most unfair attacks, you continue to be an inspiration to all who fight the battle day by day. God bless you – we're all rooting for you."

3. No Discipline, No Power

From the tireless campaign volunteers in small-town Saskatchewan to the financial backers in the grandest office towers of Toronto and Montreal – and everyone in between – all members of a political party must think big and think of victory. Before a party can earn the trust it needs to govern, first it has to win. This requires leadership, with the right leader in place. The position of leader is one that each and every member of a party should consider a legitimate goal. When a party member believes himself or herself possessed of the abilities – what Sir Wilfrid Laurier described as skills in the "supreme art of governing men" – it is that person's duty to step forward. Given the sort of ego required for a political career, it is natural that many conclude things would be better if only *we* were leading our chosen party. As a result, leadership contests are frequently brutal.

Unbridled, stubborn ambition is the currency of political leadership. South of the border, Ronald Reagan sought the Republican nomination for the presidency three times before succeeding. He first ran for president in 1968 and was knocked out of the race by Richard Nixon. In 1976 he took on a sitting Republican president, and nearly denied Gerald Ford the party nomination. In 1980 the prize was finally his and, two terms later, the rest was history.

In the United Kingdom, Margaret Thatcher, who had served in Edward Heath's government, led a movement that saw Heath toppled from the leadership of the Tory party. Later, Prime Minister Margaret Thatcher refused to appoint her predecessor – a highly experienced former prime minister – to her own Conservative cabinet. In another part of the Commonwealth, Paul Keating led a revolt against a sitting Australian prime minister that drove Bob Hawke, a hugely successful leader and prime minister, from office. In Israel, Shimon Peres and Yitzhak Rabin were political opponents and party allies as they fought for decades over the leadership of their Labour Party.

At home in Canada, Jean Chrétien worked hard to destabilize John Turner as leader of the Liberal Party, and Paul Martin succeeded in organizing a putsch – fuelled by unprecedented hostility between the two cabinet colleagues – that drove Chrétien from the Prime Minister's Office. In politics such bitter rivalry happens fairly regularly. A pair of activists who are approximately the same age and have the same ambitions come together in the same party. There is only one job at the top, and both fight for it. One wins and one loses.

In Canada, however, this process has taken on an extra dimension. To human ambition and the competitive instinct are added whispers of personal betrayal and all the makings of a conspiracy theory. Those who search for such manufactured conspiracies do not understand human nature, and they fail to acknowledge that the desire to lead is a healthy reality found in every political jurisdiction, Canada included.

In 1976 Joe Clark and I had contested the leadership of our party. He had won fair and square and I had lost. While there were moments in the convention's aftermath of deep bitterness on my part and statements I regret, Joe and I developed a good relationship as the years went by. Together, in 1978, we both pulled one on Prime Minister Trudeau and his Liberals. At the time there was a great deal of tension between Trudeau and the new Quebec Liberal leader, Claude Ryan. So it was with great fanfare that the federal Liberals had announced that Ryan would be travelling to Ottawa on May 4 to consult on Quebec affairs with the prime minister. Seizing an opportunity, I called upon my friendship with Ryan and arranged for Joe to have dinner with the Quebec Liberal leader at his home in Montreal the night before his meeting with Trudeau. I drove Joe to the dinner.

"When it was over they walked into the spring evening and the national newscasts, smiles, and handshakes all round," L. Ian MacDonald of the Montreal *Gazette* wrote in his book *Bourassa to Bourassa*. "It dissipated the impression the feds hoped to create of a common front between Trudeau and Ryan. And it reminded voters in Ontario that with Ryan now in place in Quebec, Trudeau was somewhat less indispensable for the national unity debate."

It was reported that Pierre Trudeau was furious.

On May 22, 1979 I was in Toronto serving as an election commentator for CBC Television, along with the eloquent Stephen Lewis. As the night wore on, I and millions of Canadian Progressive Conservatives began to experience something we hadn't felt since 1962: the thrill of victory. For seventeen years all we had known was the sting of defeat, over and over, again and again. Lester Pearson had defeated us twice, in 1963 and 1965, and Pierre Trudeau three times, in 1968, 1972, and 1974. It had been a long haul. So that night was very sweet indeed. After the cameras had been turned off and the lights in the studio dimmed, I returned through the streets of Toronto to my hotel. Alone in my room I watched Joe Clark take the stage in Spruce Grove, Alberta and address the nation in his moment of triumph.

—

PERSONAL JOURNAL: JULY 6–7, 1989

In late May, just prior to my departure for the Dakar Summit, I hosted a luncheon at 24 Sussex for Joe Clark and his cabinet – members and close advisors – to mark the tenth anniversary of his election as prime minister on May 22, 1979. It was a lovely day, and after drinks an elegant luncheon was served, and both Joe and I made brief but warm and appropriate remarks. I pointed out that although Canada has had 18 prime ministers to date, only 12 of them got the job by leading the party to victory – six Liberals and six Tories. Clark was one of those, so this was already a personal achievement of historic proportions.

—

I was pleased for Joe personally, and I also felt strangely liberated. The leadership convention of 1976 had finally closed. Whatever doubts I may have had about Joe's leadership in the past no longer mattered. Now we could both get on with our lives. As I travelled back home the day after the Conservative victory, I had to conclude that life was taking the turn it should. I looked forward to continued success in the private sector, while Joe's success appeared destined to be played out on the wider public stage. Good luck to him; I was free.

I was also happy that my closest friend, Sam Wakim, had been elected under Clark's banner and would enter the Commons when Parliament resumed. "Bones," the new Toronto-area MP wrote me when he took his seat that year, "my first note has to be to the one who is most responsible for me being here – many thanks. My only problem is that without you being around it doesn't seem like too much fun! Looking forward to getting some big fish, Sam."

As Joe went about putting his administration in place, life continued for us in Montreal. Our third child, Mark, had been born in April, and Mila and I were thrilled with the addition to the family. When it was time for Mark's christening that summer we invited the prime minister and his wife, Maureen McTeer, to join us for the celebration. In a letter to Joe, I joked that they were being invited to an Irish bar mitzvah in honour of the third and, I thought, final Mulroney child. That glorious day they spent a number of hours with our guests and charmed one and all. As I watched Joe I could see he was very happy, confident, and serene in facing the awesome responsibilities his new job entailed.

I saw him again later that summer when we all gathered in Ottawa to pay tribute to John Diefenbaker, who had died on August 16. Bob Stanfield and I met up inside the church that day, both of us feeling more than a little self-conscious at our situation as honorary pallbearers. As I looked around at those the Chief had gathered around him for his final sendoff, I couldn't resist leaning over to Stanfield and whispering: "Bob, what are we doing here?"

"Brian," he replied dryly, "I was counting on you to figure that out."

I spoke briefly with the prime minister before Dief's body was taken to the train to make the final journey home to the prairies and into history. Later, on television, I watched Clark deliver one of his finest speeches. His graveside tribute to Canada's thirteenth prime minister was both touching and accurate.

Busy with my job at Iron Ore, my family, and my travels, I paid little attention to political events in Ottawa as the fall of 1979 dawned. Joe Clark's government was comfortably ensconced, and I felt there was little to worry about. Robert Cliche interrupted this happy state with a call to my home one Saturday. When he phoned, Parliament was finally in session and Robert had a warning for the young minority government about the six Créditiste MPs that Quebecers had sent to Ottawa. He revealed that the Créditiste leader, Fabien Roy, a friend of Robert's from the Beauce region, had called him, quite concerned. According to Robert, Roy and his troops felt Prime Minister Clark had left them out in the cold, despite his minority situation, and Robert warned me that the Créditistes could cause a great deal of damage if they were not placated. Their demands were minimal, dealing with matters like office and research budgets – a perennial concern of opposition parties, as I was later to learn. I promised Robert I'd relay the message to Joe before I left on a trip to China.

Standing there in my kitchen, I immediately placed a call to Bill Neville to tell him of Robert's warning. Neville, a good man with a warm manner and great sense of humour, was Clark's chief of staff in the PMO. We spoke for a long time. As the conversation went on I could sense that Neville was burdened by too many duties. Not only was he the prime minister's top aide, with dozens of staffers reporting to him, he was his political advisor, speechwriter, and much more.

It was clear to me that Neville understood what I was saying and that he appreciated the gravity of Cliche's analysis. Without directly saying so, he implied there was little he could do; the prime minister had made his decision. Foolhardy as it was, Clark intended to govern as if he headed a majority government – an intention he'd announced in public as well. Neville said the PM wouldn't budge. His mind was firmly made up.

I reminded Neville of the infamous meeting Lester Pearson's emissaries held with a previous generation of Créditistes at the Windsor Hotel in Montreal in the 1960s. It was there that the Grits cooked up a sweetheart deal to ensure that the last Tory government before Joe's was defeated in the Commons. "Get your arms around these guys, and do it fast," was the message I left with Bill. While I didn't advocate that we go as far as the Liberals did in 1965, I told him that accommodating the Créditistes could very well mean the difference between the government's survival or defeat in the Commons.

The day the Clark government fell – December 13, 1979 – I happened to be in Ottawa for a board meeting. Mila had come with me, and she spent part of that afternoon at lunch in the Parliamentary Dining Room with Jane Crosbie and Margaret McGrath, the wives of Finance Minister John Crosbie and Fisheries Minister James McGrath. At the end of the day, Mila and I boarded the Iron Ore Company's jet for the trip to Toronto. "The government is going to be defeated tonight," Mila said matter-of-factly. I laughed at the suggestion and told my wife that she must have made a mistake.

"Perhaps," Mila said, "but that's what they're saying on Parliament Hill."

With all the confidence of a backroom boy, I assured my wife there was no way the first Tory government in sixteen years would allow itself to be defeated unnecessarily on the floor of the House of Commons. "Not a chance in hell," I predicted confidently. I explained to Mila that if the government saw that the vote was going to be close, the House would be adjourned until the new year. The government would then change a few minor items in its budget to ensure the necessary support was in place for safe passage, and Clark's reign would continue. To round out the picture I reminded Mila that the Liberals would be preoccupied with replacing the retiring Pierre Trudeau at a convention, and would in no way want an election before a new leader was in place. A defeat for Joe and his government? "No way," I stated emphatically.

After dinner in Toronto that night Mila and I returned to our suite at the Royal York Hotel and I turned on the television. CBC and CTV were both running news specials: the government had fallen on a vote of confidence in the Commons. Not for the first time, Mila's intelligence (in both senses) proved better than mine.

As prime minister I was to remind my majority caucus of the events of that night. Some of our members were getting lazy about attending votes in the chamber. I once, with Joe Clark present, said I thought it was high time our MPs received a lesson on the realities of parliamentary government. "On December 13, 1979," I said warningly, as I looked out over the caucus, "the first Conservative government in sixteen years was defeated after thirty-eight days in the House. It passed no major legislation, left no heritage, and Pierre Elliott Trudeau was returned to office."

That lecture did the trick, and attendance by our MPs improved markedly in the weeks that followed.

But on the night Joe's government fell, I simply couldn't believe my ears. I was flabbergasted, shocked, stunned into silence. My first thought after the news sunk in was that perhaps the PCs had deliberately contrived this situation. Were they perhaps emulating the Liberals, who had engineered the defeat of John Turner's budget in 1974 as a prelude to an election and their (planned successful) return as a majority government? If so, the party must have some fantastic polling data they were concealing. I told myself that the prime minister and his team must surely have numbers that showed we would wipe the Grits out when an election was called.

The next day, at a board meeting of Standard Broadcasting, with Conrad Black in the chair, I was passed a message that read, "The prime minister is calling for you." Joe Clark is always cool and graceful under pressure, as I was to witness often in the years ahead. Despite his government's defeat, on the phone he was calm and in no way mean-spirited toward those who had defeated him. He said he was looking forward to the campaign and was confident of victory. He then asked me to be a candidate in Quebec. I told him that I was in the midst of a five-year contract with Iron Ore that involved a very significant retirement allowance and bonuses that, by my standards, meant a lot of money and future security for my family. I assured him I would help the party in any way I could, short of running myself.

Our family spent Christmas of 1979 in Florida at the St. Andrews Club. Joe tracked me down there, calling me and pressing me once again to get off the dime and run. My reply was the same. He asked me to describe what I would lose if I left Iron Ore, and I held nothing back. At the end of the conversation, the prime minister agreed that the financial downside was heavy, and we said amicable goodbyes and hung up.

We weren't the only Montrealers in Florida for the holidays. Over the years Mila and I had become friendly with Maurice and Jeanne Sauvé, who were staying nearby. As the vacation came to a close, I invited the Sauvés to fly home with us and the children on the IOC plane, and they accepted. Since both Jeanne and Maurice had served as members of federal Liberal cabinets (Jeanne would later be appointed governor general), it was no surprise that politics was on the menu as we ate lunch on the plane. Jeanne told me frankly that in the run-up to the defeat of the Clark government she had hoped that Pierre Trudeau would return to private life, and that she supported John Turner as his replacement. I said that this sort of dissension in Liberal ranks was good news for Joe and our party. Jeanne, who was anything but a mean-spirited Grit partisan, didn't agree. "I think it is actually bad news for the Tories," she warned. "Our internal Liberal polls show there is a significant movement on out there to sweep Joe out and put Trudeau back in."

Absorbing her news in shocked silence, I knew that if she were correct, there would be horrendous repercussions within the PC Party.

Sure enough, on February 18, 1980, triumphant Pierre Trudeau greeted cheering Grits who gathered at the Château Laurier for his victory party with the words, "Welcome to the 1980s!" And we once again assumed the position federal Conservatives had grown used to during most of the twentieth century: once again we were losers.

Looking back now, I think the party had a right to expect that we would not be summarily dismissed from office after nine short months, having just spent sixteen years in opposition. Our defeat was a wasted opportunity for both Canada and the Progressive Conservative Party. Between 1980 and 1984, the pent-up feelings of frustration among Tories grew and compounded with each passing day. People felt that if only Joe Clark had prevented this from happening, we would have avoided the political resurrection of Pierre Trudeau, and with it the repatriation of the Constitution over Quebec's all-party objections. In particular, we wouldn't have had the National Energy Program that was devastating western Canada and draining off almost $100 billion from Alberta. And we wouldn't have had the anti-Americanism in our foreign policy that ran rampant in Trudeau's final term. Clearly, he had an agenda, and he was acting on it.

All of these developments were odious to most Conservatives, particularly to the members of the party's parliamentary caucus, who felt that these policies and practices would never have seen the light of day if Joe had been more careful in approaching that vote on December 13, 1979. Once the Tories realized that they were out for the duration, they became even more frustrated, but all they could do was watch Trudeau from the sidelines and simmer.

Under a clause that Joe and I had both fought to have included in the party's constitution, Joe would have to face a leadership vote in early 1981. Within weeks of our defeat, I began receiving letters from grassroots Tories asking about the position I'd be taking on the leadership question. "I really have no thoughts on the question of the leadership review," I wrote to a fellow Tory in March of 1980. "In a general way it seems to me that given the disappointing results of last February, some thought should be given to our future as a so-called national party. It is clear from the results, however, that we are anything but. I have not, however, had the time to more clearly articulate my own thinking."

In Quebec, federalists, whatever their party affiliation, were more concerned with the May 1980 referendum on sovereignty-association than with questions surrounding the leadership of a Canadian opposition party. I must say that I, for one, never feared that Canada would lose the referendum vote. Going into the campaign, I advised the chairman of my board in writing that I thought the vote was split 60/40, with Canada coming out the winner, and that that's where we would land on referendum night. In the end, this prediction turned out to be right.

In the spring of 1980 Quebec simply wasn't ready to separate. The Parti Québécois hadn't been in place long enough for this debate to acquire its later hard edge, which Canadians were to witness so clearly in 1995, when the country was nearly lost. During the first referendum campaign, there was little of the intensity that gripped Quebec during the FLQ Crisis of 1970, for example. Many Quebecers were satisfied that a separatist party had been elected to office and that it was delivering stable government with a nationalist face.

To his great personal credit, René Lévesque was also a calming influence on Quebecers. An honest man and politician, Lévesque was widely admired in the province. While clearly a separatist, he was, above all else, someone who believed in and observed all the niceties of democracy. He had no interest in winning a hollow prize.

Some have claimed that the referendum campaign was won by Pierre Trudeau's intervention. While Trudeau's speech on May 14, 1980 at the Paul Sauvé Arena was a strong one, I don't think it had a great effect on the overall outcome of the referendum. Claude Ryan, who led the No forces, did a terrific job in organizing the campaign, and deserves much of the credit for the success of the federalist forces, as does Jean Chrétien, then justice minister and the federal minister on the No committee. Both did the hard, grinding organizational work that brought victory, and neither was fully recognized for this achievement.

During the referendum campaign, I was on the B team. I made speeches, knocked on doors, appeared on television programs, and participated in debates to promote the federalist cause. I had been vice-chairman of the Council of Canadian Unity and played a modest role in the founding of the Pro-Canada Committee, and I drew on these experiences as I spoke out against sovereignty-association during the campaign. "Over 113 years, with all its imperfections – and God knows there are many – Canada has achieved a level of economic prosperity enjoyed by very few nations and its standard in human rights, decency, and tolerance is without parallel in the world," I said on one occasion. "Why proceed to amputate it? When the Parti Québécois white paper on sovereignty-association talks about seeking the exclusive right to raise taxes, it is talking about total, absolute separation because the only way you have that power is by governing. They can call it sovereignty association or whatever they want, but as the politician said, 'No matter how thin you slice it, it's still baloney.'"

I was delighted that Canada carried the day in the referendum, and pleased that despite Lévesque's pledge of "À la prochaine," tensions began to ease quickly as Quebecers and other Canadians got on with their lives.

Senator Richard Doyle recalled this evening in his 1989 memoirs, *Hurly-Burly*, where he wrote that "there was more concern for the future than the past in the phone call from Brian Mulroney. He was elated with the result. 'Haven't I told you, Dic, Quebec doesn't want out. What an opportunity we've got. What an opportunity!'"

It preyed on my mind that the PC Party had been almost completely shut out again in Quebec, where we'd elected only two lonely Tory MPs. To emphasize the importance of this sorry fact, I accepted an invitation to speak to the Canadian Institute of Chartered Accountants, who were meeting in September 1980 in Montreal. I didn't mince words, laying out what I believed to be the prescription to start the necessary Conservative renewal and march back to power. "With few exceptions," I said, "the Conservative Party has been consigned to the opposition benches for one reason alone – its failure to win seats in the French-speaking areas of the nation. From northern and eastern Ontario through Quebec and into northern New Brunswick, the electorate has rejected the Conservative Party with a consistency that is at once staggering and overwhelming."

I called for the establishment of a vigorous provincial Tory party in Quebec; issued a demand that our party proceed immediately to nominate twenty candidates a year in Quebec, in anticipation of the next election; and argued that these nominated candidates had to be supported financially by the national party. I said that to help provide the party and caucus with a Quebec perspective on issues and trends, nominated candidates should attend meetings of the national PC caucus and other national gatherings. I proposed the establishment of small policy conventions to be held on a regional basis throughout the province; I called on each riding association in Quebec to commit to attracting one hundred new members per year in the lead-up to the coming election; and I challenged the federal party to seek top Quebecers, francophone Ontarians, and Acadians for major leadership roles in the leader's office, in national headquarters, and in all the party's decision-making bodies.

On the day I delivered my speech, I sent a copy to Joe Clark in Ottawa. Throughout the 1960s, he had demonstrated exceptional abilities in mastering all aspects of organizing a modern and mature national political party. The Joe Clark I had known as a young Progressive Conservative would surely appreciate my message and understand my concerns, and, I hoped, begin to implement my proposals for the good of the party.

Instead what happened was that some people in the party and in the media accused me of stoking my own leadership ambitions and seeking to undermine Joe. The mythmakers had a great time. "Iron magnate Brian Mulroney denies he is out to knife Joe Clark," *Maclean's* thundered. "Yet there was unmistakably a lean and hungry look about the man . . . when he let fly his first public critique of the PC Party since finishing third in the 1976 leadership contest which Clark won, partly because he was the only finalist not from Quebec."

I soon discovered that my message had fallen on deaf ears. Party officials and the resources they controlled were dedicated solely to protecting and promoting Joe Clark's leadership. This left precious little opportunity for the type of rebuilding process and open debate I was calling for.

Publicly and privately I supported Joe. During an interview that December I reminded a journalist of Montreal's sporting history. "Joe won one and lost one . . . This is a baseball town and we don't put .500 hitters on waivers," I said. "I'm going to vote for Joe Clark."

In the fall of 1980, strange things began to happen. Out of the blue I found myself accused by James McGrath – one of a handful of Tory MPs who had rallied to my side in 1976 – of plotting to force him to resign so I could take over his seat in the Commons! "I learned over the weekend there was speculation in Toronto, which was subsequently confirmed by one of our mutual friends, that I would be resigning my seat to take a major government appointment and that you would running in a by-election in St. John's East," McGrath wrote. "I just wanted you to know that I find such speculation offensive to my pride and highly mischievous, to say the least, on the part of whoever is responsible . . . I have no intention of resigning my seat, and the suggestion that I would do so to make room for somebody else – albeit a good friend – at this stage of my career I find highly repugnant."

Despite these sideshows, Mila and I travelled to the PC convention in Ottawa in February 1981 and marked our ballots for Joe. When everything was said and done, he received the support of more than 66 per cent of the delegates. Considering the recent loss of the government on his watch, it was an impressive showing.

While the media again played up the supposed rivalry between Joe and me, they missed the real story. Scant weeks after the convention, Newfoundland's John Crosbie and his organizers (as John admits in his own memoirs, *No Holds Barred*) were busy planning a Crosbie campaign. By the summer of 1981, their campaign had computerized lists containing the names of twelve thousand supporters. "The campaign I had been clandestinely waging for nearly two years was ready to go public," John wrote in his 1997 memoirs. With his eye on the leadership, Crosbie took his show on the road and spoke at ninety-four different engagements across Canada between 1980 and 1982.

The Progressive Conservative member for St. John's West wasn't alone. Former Toronto mayor David Crombie (hard at work on his French) and former cabinet minister Michael Wilson were also quietly dipping their feet into leadership waters. At Queen's Park members of the Tories' Big Blue Machine, without the formal approval of Premier Bill Davis, were also positioning for their man to run. But these developments were ignored by the Ottawa media, who chose to cast the story as simply Clark versus Mulroney.

But the one Progressive Conservative who wasn't busy organizing for a leadership run was someone I knew intimately. His name? Brian Mulroney. With a major company to run and the joyous pressures of helping Mila in raising a young family, politics did not look to me like an attractive prospect.

In Ottawa IOC's Pat MacAdam kept me abreast of the leadership plots fermenting within the Tory caucus. He also worked as assistant to a Tory MP, and there was nothing he didn't know about the many internal rumblings over leadership. His memos filled my in-basket and I quietly wondered as I read them if we knew where we were heading. As a veteran of the battle against John Diefenbaker for the right of ordinary party members to hold their leaders accountable, I could foresee a bloodbath, and knew from experience that we'd all take some hits.

Throughout 1981 and into 1982, the jockeying in a race I had no interest in entering only intensified. Continuing what had been a lifelong practice, I raised money for the party whenever I could. Late in 1981, I got word that a major party fundraiser, slated to be held in Montreal and featuring Joe Clark, was in deep trouble. Fewer than one hundred tickets had been sold! I contacted my friend Finlay MacDonald, then PC Canada Fund chairman and a confidant of Joe Clark. I outlined the situation, warning that the PC party would damage itself greatly in Quebec if word got out that a former prime minister could attract only a hundred people to a major fundraising dinner. Finlay asked for my help, and I readily agreed.

Having recently served as chairman of the city's United Way campaign, I plunged right in, mining all my contacts in the Montreal business community. I reminded them that political parties in opposition also have to be supported, for both financial and political reasons, and noted that it would be a disaster for the party and for the political system if the dinner were a failure. I told the business leaders that I expected a big turnout. My friends didn't let me down and the dinner was a grand success, with well over one thousand attendees. Hundreds of thousands of dollars were deposited in party coffers. But most importantly, the party had saved face in Canada's second-largest province.

Later, conspiracy theorists came up with the idea that I had deliberately caused the slow ticket sales so that I could step in, save the dinner, and walk away as the hero. I may be many things, but a latter-day Mackenzie King isn't one of them. That's the problem with many political legends; while they make for entertaining stories when whispered by so-called insiders, they usually lack one essential ingredient: truth.

I found that I was also being asked by many Progressive Conservative riding associations to help them with their own local fundraising efforts. MPs and their riding executives invited me because I tended to draw big Conservative crowds. This success, too, worked against me. My speeches around the country at these events (which I attended by invitation) attracted a great deal of attention – and a lot of criticism. Lowell Murray, now a prominent Clark supporter who had been appointed to the Senate in the immediate aftermath of the successful 1979 election, aimed some public shots my way. And at one point Peter Trueman accused me, on Global television news, of skulking behind Joe Clark's back by making speeches in public! Joe's office promptly released a transcript of Trueman's broadside to the Parliamentary Press Gallery, which did not help.

Le Devoir also got into the act. "Brian Mulroney makes long speeches in the best social clubs of the country," reported one 1982 editorial. "One day he talks of the need for dramatic reform of the fiscal system; the next day he accuses, attacks, and counterattacks. Like the prose he uses in his function as president of Iron Ore, the method is direct but complex. Perhaps one day he may explain his strange behaviour in his memoirs, which could well be titled *Me The Candidate*. For that is his one role despite his sleights of hand and his denials."

To borrow a phrase from President John F. Kennedy, I was reading more but enjoying it less.

I headlined a fundraising dinner for John Bosley, a strong Clark supporter, in Don Valley West, and made sure I kept the leader informed of all such political activities. None of it seemed to matter. While Joe and I maintained a proper personal relationship, I think he started to believe that I was his enemy and political opponent. While he honoured Mila and me with his presence at Mark's christening in 1979, he made no private moves after that to strengthen the ties between us. In his seven years as leader, for example, Mila and I were never once invited to dinner at Stornoway or 24 Sussex. While Joe failed to confront those on his own front bench who were actively and openly organizing against him, he was persuaded by his advisors that he shouldn't make me a friend and ally. They obviously felt his interests would be better served if I was viewed as a threat, and treated as such.

One day in July of 1982 Senator Guy Charbonneau and I had lunch in Montreal, at his request. Guy was a war hero, a tireless Tory champion during the wilderness years in Quebec, an old friend, and an important person in my political life. Guy (who had been appointed to the Senate by Clark) told me bluntly that I had to fish or cut bait if I entertained any thoughts of ever running again for leader. "Look," he said, "you ran in 1976 and were defeated. You've now re-established yourself here in Montreal, and you have a job and lifestyle that most would kill for. I just want to know, for my own purposes, where it is you stand."

Guy laid out the situation for me. As a member of the Tory caucus in Ottawa, he knew that John Crosbie, David Crombie, Michael Wilson, and many others were seeking the leadership, whether I liked it or not. The people around Bill Davis, led by Senator Bill Kelly, were also positioning for a run for their man. "If there's going to be a leadership race," Guy added, "I want to be involved. I want you to be the candidate, but if you're not running, I need to know and I need to know now for my own reasons. The race is on – and you'd better get prepared if you want to even place."

That lunch with Guy was my wakeup call. Still, I was reluctant. The most I would do was authorize what I'd describe today as a leadership holding pattern, to be put in place to protect my political interests.

Friends like Peter White, Sam Wakim, and Frank Moores began to hold intermittent meetings with me in Montreal. At these gatherings they would report in with intelligence they had gathered from their contacts in Progressive Conservative circles across the land. Moores, as a former premier of Newfoundland, had attended some of his old schoolmate John Crosbie's leadership meetings, and he assured me that the former finance minister was serious. Peter was a great admirer of Michael Wilson, another former Clark cabinet minister, and he had attended Wilson's leadership meetings in Toronto. Wilson's plans, too, had moved far along.

The message I received around the table each time was the same: The leadership train had left the station and I was the only one not aboard. One day Peter White pulled me aside. "Brian," he said, "I know you don't want to do this. I know what you're going through, but you have to keep your options open." Peter recommended that we develop an embryonic leadership campaign. We wouldn't be as advanced as Crosbie, Wilson, and others, but something was better than nothing if I eventually decided to run.

Still, I hesitated. By 1982 it had been six years since I'd stepped forward and run for the leadership of my party. There was nothing particularly noble in my reluctance to do it again. I cherished my family's comfortable lifestyle and saw that it was quite possible that Joe Clark could win the next election and return as prime minister. The polls were looking good. As leader of the opposition, Joe had put up a marvellous fight in the House opposing Trudeau's constitutional plans – probably his finest moment as leader. Strangely, however, while he had rallied the parliamentary caucus to his side on the Constitution, he still lacked the personal support for his leadership from many in the same group.

That fall, Joe was again scheduled to be the star attraction at a Montreal fundraising dinner. I was asked to introduce him to the crowd and met to discuss my introduction with Claude Dupras. Claude had supported me in 1976 but now he worked for Joe. At the Mount Royal Club, I ran through the text of my introduction with my rough and gruff old friend.

"We've never blamed the leader for what happened," I had written. "The best proof of this is this magnificent dinner tonight in honour of our leader, the Right Honourable Joe Clark. As Quebec Conservatives we have known more than our share of defeats, but we have never equated them with dishonour, nor have we blamed or disowned our leaders as a result. This is why we welcome Mr. Clark amidst us tonight with warmth, pride, and affection. Of all the Conservative leaders I have known, no one has ever worked harder. No one has ever travelled further. No one has ever made proof of as much openness in spirit, and no one has ever identified with us more in Quebec than Joe Clark. Joe and I have known each other since we were twenty years old. We're now a little older but unchanged in our mutual respect and our desire to promote the interests of our party and the triumph of our ideals across the country."

Claude said my introduction wasn't good enough. He wanted a flat statement that I wouldn't run and that I would support Joe. Nothing else would do. Heated words were exchanged. I withdrew my offer angrily. I knew this was yet another sign of the paranoia about me that was gripping the Clark team. His forces in Quebec were, let's say, not very skilled in their handling of people. When you tried to help them, this sort of crap happened. I was growing weary of it all. There comes a point when you have to say enough is enough. (I shouldn't have been surprised to learn, when I moved to Stornoway, that Claude's student son had been occupying an apartment there, above the garage.)

As it turned out Joe Clark, the media, and the Canadian public were to learn that any leadership aspirations I might have had were about to be dealt a body blow. In October, it was my painful duty as president of Iron Ore to go to the board of directors and recommend that our company's operations in Schefferville be shut down. I knew instinctively that it wouldn't be good for the company that had treated me so well, nor for our employees and shareholders, if I were engaged in partisan politics during a shutdown. I cannot conceive of a worse situation in which to launch a leadership bid than shutting down a town on the eve of one's campaign. It was time for me to get out of the traffic.

By now Finlay MacDonald was serving as Clark's senior advisor. We met over lunch in Toronto in late November, and I accepted Finlay's request to endorse Joe publicly in advance of the party's January convention in Winnipeg. Joe was scheduled to be in Montreal on December 6, and I agreed to hold a joint press conference with him, where I'd make my position known. I gathered my closest friends at our home the day before the press conference to inform them of my decision. With Mila present I said, "I don't want anyone organizing against the leader in my name. This is a decision I've made with my wife, and we believe it's in the interests of our family, and our personal lives. Given what is coming with the Schefferville shutdown, it is not the right time for me. I'm standing down." My supporters were so furious that I started to fear I was letting them down.

"The cure is worse than the disease," Peter White scrawled on a piece of paper as I spoke.

Rodrigue Pageau, a key Clark supporter who had since concluded that the party would never win again with Joe as leader, looked me straight in the eye. "Thank you very much," he said. "I respect your opinion but I don't propose to follow it. I'm a free man and I'm going to do what I want." He and others then marched out of my house and met elsewhere, eventually deciding to continue their efforts to force the leadership issue in Winnipeg.

There was nothing I or anyone else could do to stop them. They would continue to organize for a leadership review whether I liked it or not.

Joe and I met privately at the Ritz-Carlton Hotel before the press conference. Once again, he was calm and asked me to assess the situation. I told him I thought that about a third of Quebec's delegates would never support him, no matter what he did. Still, I told the leader, that fact shouldn't stop him. "Joe, they're broken-hearted that, after sixteen years in opposition, you allowed us to be thrown out of office after just a few months," I said bluntly. "But if 66 per cent was good enough in 1981, it's goddamned well good enough today."

And I went out and, at the press conference, I pledged my support to Joe. I was out of the race.

Before heading to Winnipeg for the convention in January, Mila and I were in Toronto for the CIBC's annual general meeting. We were staying at Toronto's storied King Edward Hotel and there was a definite buzz in the air. In the pillared lobby and in the ornate Victoria's dining room, all sorts of people, from bank presidents to waiters, kept approaching me to tell me they hoped I'd run for Tory leader if the position came open. I was humbled by these expressions of support and discussed them with Mila the night before we left for Winnipeg. "Do you think I did the right thing?" I asked. Mila assured me I had. I then asked if she saw any chance of conditions forcing a change in my position.

"Brian," she said, "if there is a change, you'll know it when you see it."

4. Winnipeg and Schefferville

On the ground at the annual meeting in Winnipeg, one thing was quickly apparent: at every opportunity, the Clark forces were upping the ante. A classic illustration of this was Flora MacDonald telling a television interviewer she expected that Joe would receive the support of a vast majority of the delegates. I watched Flora's interview from my hotel room where I was packing my bag for the trip out of Winnipeg. Like all delegates, I was waiting for the final numbers to be reported.

"That's an extremely unwise thing to say," I muttered. Perhaps members of Joe's team were trying to intimidate the pro-review forces, but I'll never know. Regardless, I simply didn't understand the strategy. I could only assume Flora must have had inside information to make such an extraordinary statement when the stakes were so high.

Shortly afterwards, the results were announced: 66.9 per cent of delegates had voted against a leadership review. Clearly, Joe Clark's leadership was safe and intact. Two years of infighting, tension in the parliamentary caucus, and turmoil in my own life had come to an end. The anti-Clark forces, supposedly led by me, had proved so skilled in their treachery they'd moved Clark's numbers *up* slightly since 1981.

When Joe took the stage that night with his closest supporters lined up behind him, I knew precisely what I would have done in his place. I would have looked out at a hall crowded with Tories and thanked them for such a wonderful validation of my leadership. Pointing out that our party had received only 32.45 per cent of the vote in the last federal election, I would have said that a 66.9 per cent approval rating is not a bad thing at all. Then, it would have been my happy duty to announce that Mila and I were hosting a big party that very evening to celebrate. Each and every Progressive Conservative in the hall would have been on the invitation list, and I can assure you the party would have continued until dawn.

Joe didn't do any of that. Instead, he announced that 66.9 per cent wasn't good enough. He was resigning, and recommending that the party call a leadership convention, where he'd be a candidate to succeed himself.

I was flabbergasted. "This is goddamned lunacy," I said to Mila and others in our room. "It takes significantly less than 50 per cent of the vote to be elected Prime Minister of Canada, and he's throwing in the towel with 67 per cent? This can't be happening."

Pundits love to speculate on the brutal manner in which Joe Clark was "removed" from the leadership. Let's make one thing very clear. Joe Clark was not overthrown as PC leader. He surrendered his leadership in Winnipeg in spite of the fact that slightly over two-thirds of the delegates voted for him to continue. He voluntarily resigned to run in a leadership race that would eventually be won by a candidate with 53 per cent of the vote.

I believe that Joe Clark's decision as prime minister to proceed with a non-confidence vote in the House of Commons – when he knew his government would be defeated, and when he hadn't polled to determine the overall political situation outside the chamber – was one of the greatest errors in strategy and calculation in modern Canadian political history. But I also believe that his decision in Winnipeg ranks right up there on the same scale. Perhaps Joe's memoirs will one day offer a rationale for both of these historic and damaging decisions.

Maybe the first decision was prideful. Having announced a vote, the new prime minister resolved to go through with it come what may, to avoid being characterized as weak and indecisive. The subsequent decision in Winnipeg may have been driven by his awareness of the growing caucus divisions and tensions, with so many front-benchers openly plotting leadership campaigns. Perhaps he felt the only way to force everyone back into line and end the bickering once and for all was with a decisive leadership win. Clark is a very good man who, like all of us, sometimes makes very big mistakes. My own are well known to Canadians.

—

PERSONAL JOURNAL: MAY 14, 1991

I have put out many signals of my intentions to lead the party into a third general election. In fact, such action has been largely strategic, to confuse my opponents and prevent the system from freezing on me

– because I have determined I will step down after the unity question is dealt with, call for a leadership convention, and allow for a new person to accede to the prime ministership and a clear advantage in an election campaign that would take place soon after. It is too soon to predict who my successor will be – it may well be my predecessor! I moved Joe Clark from External to Constitutional Affairs because he was the best person for the job, but also because it would give him an opportunity to display to the nation the skills developed in international affairs. The cabinet shuffle in general and his appointment in particular has been well received. One of Joe's advantages is that having been in External Affairs for seven years he was largely absent from the bruising deliberations and the partisan battles we have waged over the Free Trade Agreement, deficit reduction, the GST. As a result, he is largely undamaged, and Canadians are seeing a new Joe Clark – many of them, because of their ages, for the first time – and they are favourably impressed. If he can maintain the approach and draw on his experience (he has become an excellent colleague and a surprisingly close confidant), he may indeed find himself given another chance to become prime minister and lead the party into the general election from that quite prestigious spot. My journalistic adversaries would have a fit if they realized what I am now contemplating and planning. Imagine me, Joe's campaign strategist, and even he doesn't know it!

—

On CBC's *The National* broadcast of February 6, anchorman Peter Mansbridge provided this cogent analysis of the Winnipeg convention:

> Registration records from the recent PC convention in Winnipeg show a large group of missing delegates – Conservative members of provincial legislatures from the seven Tory governments. They were each entitled to a vote at the convention. With them, Joe Clark might still be leading his party. Their absence throws into question just how supportive their governments were.
>
> When Clark arrived in Winnipeg, he was counting on the support of the seven Conservative premiers. After all, they had pledged their support. But when the voting took place, many of the ballots the premiers could have controlled weren't even cast.

> Each of their caucus members had the right to vote – a potential voting bloc of 341, but only eighty-five turned up. Some of the worst turnouts were from the provinces with the most prominent premiers. Brian Peckford could have delivered forty-four Newfoundland votes; only nineteen were in Winnipeg, though. Nova Scotia's John Buchanan leads a caucus of thirty-seven, but only seventeen voted. Jim Lee's Prince Edward Island delegation could have totalled twenty-two, but only five turned up. Richard Hatfield is a strong Clark loyalist, but only eight of his party's thirty-eight New Brunswick representatives voted.
>
> Ontario's Big Blue Machine of Bill Davis – out of seventy members, registration records show only seven were in Winnipeg. Queen's Park argues there were more, but no more than twenty-five. Grant Devine's caucus has fifty-five MLAs, but only twenty-one made the trip across the border from Saskatchewan. And Peter Lougheed was on holiday, but so, it appears, were many of his fellow Alberta Tories. Of seventy-five possible, only eight voted. For Joe Clark, the irony is biting. If the votes had been delivered and delivered for him, there would be no leadership convention now because those votes would have given him a 70 per cent approval – the acknowledged figure he needed to stay on the job.

It was, in fact, the Ontario operation that caused Clark the most damage. Big Blue Machine counsellor Eddie Goodman later confirmed this in his memoirs, *Life of the Party*. "It was not until months later that I found out that the plan to make Davis the prime minister of Canada had been prepared well before the Winnipeg annual meeting by [Bill] Kelly, [Norm] Atkins, and [Hugh] Segal, unknown to Davis," Eddie wrote. "Most of the delegates at large and many constituency ones had gone to Winnipeg in January 1983 prepared to vote for a leadership convention. That was why Clark's support in Ontario was only about 60 per cent. There had been only one piece missing to make the operation successful: Bill Davis's early consent to run."

In any case, with or without Bill Davis, the race was on, and I still didn't want to be a candidate. Quebec's parliamentary hearings on the Schefferville mine closure were approaching fast, and I'd be making a crucial appearance.

Mila and I headed south to Florida directly from Winnipeg, and I holed up in our cottage to prepare for my presentation in Schefferville, slated for February 10. I spent almost two weeks prepping myself. I went over studies, I was repeatedly briefed by company officials, and I reviewed the numbers and documents until I knew my case cold. No matter how we crunched the numbers, one thing never changed: Schefferville had been mined out.

Internally I'd already sold my board on giving our displaced workers as generous a severance package as possible. Apart from an extensive package of benefits, each would receive more than $16,000, plus assistance if they wished to relocate. They could also buy their company-owned homes for one dollar if they wanted to remain in Schefferville. As the son of a union man, I was pleased when a ranking member of the United Steel Workers told the press that the terms of our package made an example that governments might think of including in legislation to "civilize company shutdowns" in the future.

I arrived in Schefferville on February 9, ready to appear before the politically charged committee the next day. There was press everywhere, with both national and provincial reporters on hand to scrutinize every word the president of the Iron Ore Company of Canada might say. Having grown up in an isolated company town, I knew that the community would be listening to my every word. Many of the media arrived armed with comments from other leadership candidates that "this will be Mulroney's Armageddon." Everyone knew that if I failed to do well in Schefferville I was through as a viable candidate. The stakes were enormously high.

The parliamentary committee had allotted me only twenty minutes to make my presentation. When the chairman tried to cut me off, I simply ignored him and continued for another hour, and then took questions for two more. "The first day of extractive operations at any mining town hastens the arrival of the end," I told the committee and audience. "That is an immutable fact of life and there are no exceptions to this rule."

I hid nothing. I explained how iron markets were weak and that our largest customers, south of the border, were operating at only 40 per cent capacity. We were also being battered by a higher grade of iron coming out of Brazil.

The facts established, I looked to the future. Why couldn't a national park be established to help draw tourists to the region, especially Americans? I volunteered to put up all the money necessary from Iron Ore Canada to fund studies to explore further mining potential in the area. I had visited cabinet ministers in Ottawa and Quebec City to explore how the citizens of Schefferville might be assisted through federal-provincial cooperation. (Later as prime minister I did everything humanly possible for the region, and I have the political scars to prove it. This included establishing a federal penitentiary in Port-Cartier, which employs many people from Schefferville.)

At the end of my presentation, the crowd applauded. Stories in the press were very positive. The *Vancouver Sun* said that "there is no businessman in Canada who doesn't admire what Mr. Mulroney has done. To close a mining town and then receive compliments for the fair and equitable manner in which it was done – including from the unions – well, one asks what this same man might be able to accomplish in Ottawa . . . His presentation was a masterpiece. Clearly this is a man to be considered seriously for the leadership of the PC Party."

The *Calgary Herald* wrote, "It is difficult to imagine another businessman winning the confidence and respect of unions and workers as Brian Mulroney did over the last decade . . . What Mulroney did was offer Canadians an astonishing lesson on how TV works, something few Conservatives have learned to do."

The French media were equally kind. On February 11, 1983, *Le Soleil* reported, "Under the spotlights, in a high school auditorium transformed for the occasion into the Salon Rouge [of the National Assembly] the President of IOC gave a presentation worthy of the greatest moments of Canadian politics." *Le Devoir* was impressed, too. "Everybody agrees that the President of IOC, who had everything at stake in this challenging matter, emerged with the full honours of a war that never even took place," the paper said. "Not only did Mr. Mulroney steal the show, as the popular expression goes, but he wasn't even scratched by those who had promised a tough accountability session. For an ambitious man that everyone, except himself, says will be a candidate to succeed Joe Clark, his performance was absolutely remarkable and warrants being underlined."

Members of my board of directors were also impressed at how well I'd handled the issue. They had a lot to lose and were thrilled the hearings had gone so well. Ordinary members of the public also took note. "If this letter should penetrate the army of secretaries which I would expect exist to protect you from trivia, you might be amused to know that in the summer of 1981 I laid an even bet of $100 with a friend of mine in Newfoundland that you would be the next elected prime minister of Canada," Peter

Henderson wrote from Vancouver during this period. "It is true that we had both drunk a great deal of Irish whisky at the time, but I have held to that opinion ever since, and I now see every chance of collecting."

Even Judy Erola, Trudeau's minister of state for mines, contacted me shortly after I appeared before the committee, writing that, "I have noted with great interest your company's compensation and relocation program for the workers affected by the closure of your Schefferville operation. I think that your actions in this regard are commendable. Your proposals for a new industrial base for Schefferville appear to have good potential and are worth serious attention . . . I would like to assure you that your efforts in diversifying the economic base of Schefferville are of high interest to me and that Energy, Mines and Resources will do what it can to support your efforts."

After the hearings I was exhausted but exhilarated. I had beaten the odds: the media were very favourable and my personal role was the subject of highly complimentary public comment. It had been a huge challenge, but my frank approach, aided by countless hours of intense preparation, had transformed the parliamentary hearings from political graveyard to launch pad.

I departed Schefferville for Montreal, where I met Mila at our favourite restaurant, Ruby Foo's. When I sat down at our table, she praised my performance.

"What do you think?" I asked. She knew that I had the leadership race in mind.

She reminded me of our recent conversation at the King Eddy before we left for Winnipeg. "I told you then that you're going to know if there's a change in the situation when you see it," she said. "And I think that's now happened."

As only husband and wife can, we discussed the pain and financial difficulties we had experienced after my loss in 1976, and the new life we'd built together since then. "So, tell me again, in light of what we've been through, what do you think?" I asked her.

"Do I think that you could win this?" Mila replied, "Yes, I do. Would you be a great leader and prime minister if given the chance? I think you would. Do I think you will win it? I don't know. But I do know this: *If you don't run, for sure you won't win.*"

That night was the turning point. It was February 11, 1983.

Later that night, after Mila and I arrived home from dinner, I began a round of calls to gauge my support. First on my list was MP James McGrath, one of my original caucus supporters in 1976. If I had learned anything from my defeat seven years previously, it was that I needed strong support from the caucus to have even a small chance of succeeding.

Jim and I had remained good friends and fishing companions – with the odd misunderstanding, as you'll recall – after the 1976 convention, and we stayed in close contact. He had been very critical of Joe Clark after the government was defeated, since it meant Jim had to forfeit the seat at the cabinet table he'd coveted for years. He often called me and filled me in on his doubts, and described how poorly things were going for Joe in the caucus.

But now, after only a few minutes on the telephone, I knew something was wrong. Jim said Flora MacDonald had told him that Clark was poised to sweep Quebec. While I respected Flora a great deal, her knowledge of French Canada was limited at best. "Flora MacDonald wouldn't know a French Canadian, especially in Quebec, if she tripped over one," I snapped.

Jim then asked if I had discussed my candidacy with "good friends." When I asked whom he had in mind, he mentioned Finlay MacDonald. "Jim," I snorted, "for Christ's sake, he's supporting Joe Clark!" Finally, I cut McGrath off. "Are you trying to tell me something?"

To my surprise Jim McGrath, who had spent the last number of years disparaging Joe Clark at every opportunity, then told me that he didn't want to see me hurt by launching a campaign that was doomed to fall short. He said Joe was doing better recently and now deserved our support. I held my temper and suggested that if Jim could not support me, he should back his fellow Newfoundlander, John Crosbie. No one could argue with that.

"Crosbie would be the last sonofabitch on the face of this earth I would support," McGrath replied, with some emotion.

I then asked Jim what today's date was. When he said it was February 11, I wound up the call by saying coldly, "On June 11, when you are looking for the leader of the Progressive Conservative Party, you are going to have to ask for me. Good night, Mr. McGrath." Clearly, my campaign was not off to a great start.

Later, Jim backtracked. He wrote to me early in March to assure me that his support for Joe amounted only to a first-ballot commitment. He also said that his wife and daughters would be delegates and that they were supporting me. I loved Margaret and the McGrath kids, but by then I didn't need him.

On March 20 – my forty-fourth birthday – I flew to Sept-Îles and officially resigned as Iron Ore's president. I also resigned from all the boards I served on as a director. That evening I boarded Iron Ore's jet for the last time to fly to Ottawa, where I'd officially announce I was entering the race. Shortly after takeoff, I looked out the window of the darkened plane and saw the lights of Baie-Comeau twinkling below me. I thought of my father and what advice he might have had for his son this day. Alone in the plane, I chuckled out loud because I knew full well what he would have said after learning that his son had just resigned the presidency of a great company he loved and had chosen instead the risky and unforgiving world of politics: "Brian, I don't think I would have done that. I wish you would have spoken to me before, but if you want to do it, I'll support you 100 per cent."

In Ottawa I met Mila, Pat MacAdam, Janis Johnson and her date for the evening, the journalist Allan Fotheringham, at the Château Laurier for a small birthday celebration. Janis, who had been married to Frank Moores and knew politics well, asked about my itinerary after the announcement at the National Press Theatre on Wellington Street. I told her that Mila and I would be returning to Montreal to attend a kickoff event at Mulroney campaign headquarters. Then I was departing for British Columbia, while Mila would campaign in Quebec. Janis didn't like that scenario. "Brian," she said, "if you're going to win this, you must have Mila at your side at all times. I know a thing or two about campaigning, and I can tell you that she's your greatest asset."

This was the smartest piece of advice I received during the whole leadership campaign. Later, after we'd won the leadership and I became prime minister, I appointed Janis – a wise and experienced woman in the predominantly male world of politics – to the Senate. It was the least I could do, after the high-quality advice she gave me that night. In kitchens and living rooms from Vancouver Island to the Maritimes, in small-town Ontario and Quebec, and on the Prairies, thousands of Progressive Conservative delegates were about to witness the wisdom of Janis's words first-hand.

5. The 1983 Leadership Campaign

PERSUADING THE THREE thousand delegates to the Progressive Conservative leadership convention to vote for me was a time-consuming, one delegate at a time business. Sometimes the decisive factors were unexpected, as I learned from a breakfast meeting with Jackie Cotnam.

Jackie was a delegate from Renfrew-Nipissing-Pembroke in the upper Ottawa Valley, my old friend Ace McCann's fiddle and step-dancing stomping grounds. While I was in Pembroke, midway through the campaign, Ace said that one of his riding's delegates wanted to meet with me privately. Apparently, this delegate was still undecided, even though voting day was only weeks away. I knew that every single vote would count come June 11, so I agreed with Ace's suggestion that I meet Jackie for breakfast the next day at a Pembroke diner.

"She's a very policy-oriented young woman," Ace warned me beforehand, tipping me off that Jackie would pepper me with questions on my positions on innumerable topics. I was well prepared as we slid into a booth the next morning.

Jackie was a delightful young lady but her interrogation was relentless. In the middle of her intensive questioning, breakfast arrived; we had both ordered bacon and eggs. As we continued talking, Jackie picked up a bottle of ketchup and began to shake it over her plate. After a few seconds, it was apparent that the ketchup wasn't moving, and Jackie picked up her knife, put it into the bottle and withdrew it, spreading ketchup over her eggs. She then handed the bottle to me. So I did the same thing, placing my own knife into the ketchup bottle and then spreading ketchup onto my own eggs, as she continued with every question under the sun.

When breakfast came to an end, Jackie went off to work – without letting me know if she would support me – and I continued on the campaign trail. That night I received a message telling me that Ace had called from Pembroke. "I've got great news for you!" Ace said. "Jackie Cotnam has decided to vote for you, and she's going to be one of your biggest supporters around here from now on."

Still mentally drained from the grilling I had received along with my breakfast, I couldn't resist asking Ace if he had by chance discovered which one of my policies caused Jackie to now look favourably upon my candidacy. Was it my ideas for an industrial policy aimed specifically at eastern Ontario? Or was it my stand on the forestry, as the Ottawa Valley has been supplying timber since Canada's earliest days? "What was it?" I asked Ace.

He didn't hesitate.

"She loved the way you handled the ketchup."

That was the story of the leadership race of 1983. It was one-on-one politics as it is rarely practised in Canada today. South of the border the closest comparison would be the New Hampshire primaries that take place every four years, but with a crucial difference: rather than the campaign being concentrated in one small rural state, this race took place over the vast expanse of Canada, the second largest country in the world, as leadership hopefuls tried to line up a simple majority of the delegates selected by PC riding associations and campus clubs located in all ten provinces and two territories.

For the candidate it was definitely mano-a-mano, as John Turner (who was destined to go through his own successful leadership campaign exactly a year later) might say. It was, I believe, an important, formative experience for me and for any political leader.

—

PERSONAL JOURNAL: JUNE 13, 1993

(Written at Harrington Lake)

I would not, indeed could not, be anything but delighted with a victory by Kim [Campbell] later today if that is the outcome. But I bet that she and the party needed the testing that only comes from the exposure, tension, and the challenges of a leadership campaign. No one should ever be handed the leadership on a platter. They must fight for it and want it badly enough to endure the pain and brutality of such a test. Otherwise, they should not be in any way considered, because they lack some of the fundamental strengths one discerns only in the solitary nature of powerful struggles – namely that leadership requires the capacity to stand alone against the tide, to see possibilities others ignore, and to pursue your goal against all odds, earning the most overwhelming confidence as you go. In such experiences you and the country ascertain if you have the stamina and the steel necessary for the job of prime minister.

—

As I planned my 1983 leadership campaign, I had learned from my mistakes in 1976. I knew I would be unfairly scrutinized by the media and the other candidates when it came to campaign spending. So I and my team devised what became known as "the rusty-station-wagon campaign." There would be no private jets, and Mila and I and a single staffer would travel the country on our own, without a retinue of aides.

Above all else, we would stay away from the media. To win, we simply had to run an effective delegate-driven campaign, while letting the other candidates compete amongst themselves for headlines. In 1976 I had needed to increase my public profile, but that was all behind me now. From day one my campaign team believed that on June 11 I'd find myself in a showdown on the final ballot with Joe Clark, and that belief governed all our strategic thinking.

With that strategy in mind, I stepped out of Ottawa's Château Laurier Hotel on March 21, 1983, prepared to head over to the National Press Theatre to announce that I was entering the race. I was composed, my statement was ready, and I was fully prepared to answer the press's predictable questions. There was, however, a surprise waiting for me. As I came through the doors of the hotel, I saw the car the campaign had arranged for me to arrive at my press conference in, a massive stretch Cadillac that I soon dubbed the "Elvismobile." I knew the media's coverage of my announcement would be dominated by that car and nothing else; I could already see the headlines and imagine the breathless coverage on CBC Television.

Turning to my aide, Michael McSweeney, I gave the first order of the campaign: "Michael," I said sharply, "get rid of that goddamn thing."

The switch was made, and I arrived in a suitably nondescript Chrysler sedan, to begin my press conference. If I was going to lose, I was going to lose for the right reasons, after the party had been given the chance to reflect on my candidacy, carefully and thoughtfully. If in the end they decided they didn't want me, I had no problems with that; it's only when you lose for specious reasons and tactical mistakes, as I had in 1976, that a loss is hard to accept.

Because of the internal turmoil our party had experienced in recent years, I followed my instinct to treat the other candidates with friendship and respect. Before heading to the press conference, I telephoned Joe Clark and John Crosbie to wish them both well in their own campaigns. When I couldn't get Joe on the phone, I penned him a letter, to which he quickly replied, in his own hand, the same day.

"Dear Brian," he wrote. "Thank you for your kind note. I'm sorry I missed your call and appreciate your thoughtfulness in trying to reach me before the official announcement. While neither of us will wish the other success in all of this, I hope you find the campaign satisfying and look forward to working with you when it is over. Maureen joins in best wishes to Mila and the family."

One of Joe's key strategists, our mutual friend Finlay MacDonald, also sent me a letter that day: "Brian, Win, lose, or draw, go with God and good luck." Liberal MP André Maltais, whose riding included Baie-Comeau, wrote to say, "Independent of any partisanship, I must admit that I would be very proud to see a guy from Baie-Comeau become the leader of one of the great political parties of Canada. It goes without saying that I – as well as the entire Côte-Nord – would be delighted if the 'god of the ballot box' were to grant you the highest position in the Canadian state. No matter what happens, I wish you good luck."

At the press theatre, I immediately pre-empted my opponents by announcing that I had resigned the presidency of the Iron Ore Company of Canada and all my directorships and that I would be seeking a seat in the House of Commons at the first opportunity. Then, going over the heads of the media, I spoke directly to each and every Progressive Conservative who might be watching newscasts that night or reading the papers in the morning. I offered the party a winner.

"This party has long since established its ability to be somewhat unruly and difficult," I said. "This will only be cured by an extended stay in government . . . I am in this race . . . to break the bizarre stranglehold the Liberal Party has developed on our national government. In Canada, for example, there are 102 seats with a francophone component in excess of 10 per cent. In the 1980 election, we won two. In the seventy-five Quebec seats, our popular vote dropped to 12.6 per cent, our lowest in thirty-five years. Conservative candidates lost their deposits in 56 seats, ran third in 41, behind the NDP in 39, and behind the Rhinoceros Party in two . . . Someone must address this fundamental electoral problem on behalf of the Conservative Party. I propose to do just that and, in the process, bring French Canada into the fullness and magnificence of Canadian life . . . I am in this race because I believe I can do these and other things for my party and for Canada."

(In crafting my statement, I recalled Bob Stanfield's farewell speech to the 1976 convention, one that was largely ignored at the time. "It is very difficult to obtain a working majority if we concede the Liberals seventy-five or eighty safe seats in parts of our country and the NDP a dozen or so safe seats in parts of our society before the election even starts," Bob had said. "We must see whole our country and her people. That is the way to serve our country. That is the way to beat the Liberals.")

Since Joe and others were already feeding the media the line that only they could hold off the reactionary wing of the party that I supposedly led, I also used my opening statement to talk about the social responsibilities of any political party. I chose the phrase "a dimension of tenderness" – awkward as it was – because I knew that it would force people to look at what I was saying. I highlighted my working-class roots, trying to say to the media that I didn't need any lessons in social progressiveness from them or from Joe Clark or from anyone else.

"We Conservatives must show the Canadian people that we have about us, as well, a dimension of tenderness," I said.

> It is that vital responsibility of government to demonstrate compassion for the needy and assistance for the disadvantaged, the equalization of opportunity for all, and an elevated sense of social responsibility that must continue to find favour with every thoughtful Canadian. Of all the challenges of government none is more noble, no obligation more sacred. We shall be judged both as individuals and as a political party by the manner in which we care for those unable to care for themselves. My background and that of my family is solidly working class. I know what hard work and feeding a family and paying a mortgage is all about. It is not an understanding I got from books. It comes from the imperishable memory of my father, home from the mill after a full day's work, eating quickly so that he could leave to resume his second job that night, before returning to the mill for his shift the next morning.

Then, quite deliberately, mind you, after the press conference I boarded a commercial plane and dropped off the media's radar. The race was on.

From the start I saw the wisdom in Janis Johnson's advice that Mila should campaign at my side. When our schedules briefly kept us apart, shouts of "Where's Mila?" were aimed my way at each event. I could not have won the leadership without her. At the time, Mila was only twenty-nine, but she had already developed a genuine empathy for people that delegates and their families could sense. She was tall, elegant, beautiful, and had a style that attracts people. As I was to witness countless times in delegates' living rooms and Legion halls from coast to coast to coast, she wasn't hurried in her approach, taking more time than anyone I've ever seen to chat with the party's rank and file, and was always the last person to leave a room. On top of that, she is a great note writer and has the best memory for faces and names that I have ever seen in politics. Having observed him up close in Quebec City in the 1960s, I used to think that honour belonged to Quebec Premier Daniel Johnson – until I saw Mila on the hustings in 1983.

I already knew that she would serve as the most hard-nosed analyst in my campaign. In fact, it was Mila who kept our campaign on track on one occasion less than a month before voting day. Southam News and Global Television Network combined their resources and on May 16 published a devastating poll. I'll never forget reading the results in that day's Montreal *Gazette* as I sat in our living room. I was shattered as I saw the numbers. The poll had Joe at 35 per cent in terms of first-ballot support, while I was at 19 per cent with Crosbie close behind at 14 per cent. But when it came to second-ballot support, the poll said I was in trouble. Seven per cent of delegates gave Joe the second-ballet nod while I picked up 14 per cent. Meanwhile, 27 per cent said they would go to Crosbie when their candidates dropped off or were forced to withdraw. The brilliant and witty Newfoundlander, it appeared, had the wind at his back.

I was stunned by the poll, as I thought I was doing much better than it reported. I knew very well that a poll like that is the last thing a campaign needs. It affects the morale of the candidate and of the staff. It taints the press coverage you receive, and it makes fundraising even more difficult, as people are reluctant to donate to a candidate who is likely to lose.

This is where Mila came in. "Look," she said, "you've forgotten that this campaign ends on June 11 and we're still three weeks away. The only reason that you should be the leader of the party is that large numbers of Canadians will vote for you. If we're wrong in that assessment, then you're not going to be the leader. The only way we're going to find out is by getting out of here now and campaigning and keeping on doing what we're doing. There's no doubt at all in my mind that you're going to be in a showdown with Joe Clark on June 11. That's the only place you have to be. Why would you be discouraged at being second when you're running ahead of all these people who are members of the caucus? We're wasting time. Let's get out there and get some delegates."

Thanks to Mila, we put the poll results out of our minds, went out our door and headed west. She was absolutely key to my victory.

In addition to ordinary delegates, Mila brought some heavy-hitters to our cause. In 1976 New Brunswick had been a wasteland for me. Premier Richard Hatfield had the province locked up and he personally supported Flora MacDonald. This time out Richard, stung by the defeat of the Clark government after only a few months in power, was more open to my candidacy. He was also enchanted by Mila. In many ways a lonely man, Richard would often have lunch with her during his frequent trips to Montreal. When the leadership race happened in 1983, this friendship was key in his opening doors for us in New Brunswick.

Sadly, Richard was later defeated by Frank McKenna's Liberals in 1987, losing every single seat. Some time after that election, Mila, who rarely got involved in specific issues when I was prime minister, suggested to me over lunch that Richard could still make many fine contributions to public life in Canada. "Why don't you make him a senator?" she suggested.

I thought her idea was an excellent one, and Richard was summoned to the Red Chamber in September of 1990. He spent only a short time in Ottawa, however, before he developed a terminal illness. After visiting him at the Elisabeth Bruyère Health Centre one day in the company of her friend Nancy Southam, Mila told me bluntly that Richard had little time left. I was about to embark on a trip overseas, but Mila warned me that she doubted he'd be alive when I got back.

Heeding her advice to visit him, I went over for a final talk with my friend from New Brunswick, who was by now in palliative care. Alone together in his room, we reminisced and pondered the peaks and valleys of a life spent in politics. It was an emotional discussion.

Richard was a true champion of the arts in New Brunswick. Before his final illness, he had taken up the cause of the Beaverbrook Art Gallery in Fredericton and had lobbied my ministers for support. When he didn't get the answer he wanted, he went to the prime minister and continued his campaign. I had promised Richard that I would look into his request but, frankly, I hadn't followed up.

All too soon, Richard and I came to the end of what was to be our final conversation. I told him I was heading overseas, but that I would see him when I got back. We both knew, however, that wouldn't be the case. I left his room and was walking down the corridor when I heard Richard's voice for a final time. "Prime Minister, don't forget the Beaverbrook Art Gallery," he shouted, still fighting for his beloved New Brunswick until the very end. I made certain that the government honoured his request.

While Mila was my key asset in 1983, I also couldn't have won without Peter White and Sam Wakim. Ahead of everyone else in our party, Sam and Peter identified one group of voters who would play a crucial role in electing the new leader of Canada's Progressive Conservatives in 1983: youth delegates. Changes to the party's rules before the leadership race meant that fully one-third of delegates in Ottawa on June 11 would come from the youth wing of the party. Since I had been active in the party as a teenager and university student, I wholeheartedly supported this change. When almost 50 per cent of the 874 votes I was to receive on the first ballot were revealed to have come from our youth operation, I had reason to be grateful for it.

By the time the leadership race began, Sam and Peter had already reached out and built bridges to PC youth leaders, particularly those in Ontario. And they were a tough bunch to bring onside; they showed a maturity and a degree of sophistication that older Tories would have done well to emulate. At one point, young Greg Thomas of British Columbia contacted me and demanded a personal meeting over dinner in Montreal. He picked the restaurant – and my brain – during a meal we had at the Ritz-Carlton. Recalling my own calls, letters, and telegrams to John Diefenbaker many years earlier, I admired Greg's gumption, and was thrilled when he joined our team.

On another occasion, Ontario's Tom Long and his young colleague Nigel Wright kept Peter White cooling his heels in a hotel corridor while they debated just whom they should support. Here was the highly successful Peter White, a senior member of Conrad Black's management team and an emissary of mine, left to wait outside looking at the wallpaper while the young people's discussions continued. Finally, Tom opened the door and told Peter that his group would be supporting me. Peter, who had been at the heart of business deals worth millions of dollars, told me that he was never happier than when that door opened and this set of negotiations was over. Other PC youth who played key roles in my campaign included Marc Dorion, Michael McSweeney, Stewart Braddick, George Marsland, Randy Bocock, Jim Crossland, Ian Hamilton, Doug Reid, and Ken Zeise, to name just a few.

My opponents in 1976 had been able to pound me without mercy – and with a great deal of success – in the area of policy. I wasn't going to allow that to happen this time out. York University professor Charley McMillan, a happy-go-lucky and intelligent friend from P.E.I. who had worked on my campaign in 1976, served as the campaign's policy advisor, senior speechwriter, and polling analyst. Charley helped me produce a book containing my recent speeches on a variety of public policy issues. *Where I Stand* was released during the campaign and helped fill the perceived policy void in my candidacy. Publishing *Where I Stand* also proved to be an extremely helpful political move. I mailed one to each delegate, and as we travelled the country, Charley ensured that additional copies were always on hand. I signed the book for anyone who asked (I continue to do so today). The book was a terrific marketing tool and I'd advise future leadership candidates to consider publishing one when they embark on their own campaigns.

It was John Crosbie who fired the most important policy salvo of the whole campaign. When he announced that he was entering the race (on the same day I did), John came out in favour of free trade with the United States. For me, this move represented a significant dilemma. On the one hand, having spent the previous seven years as the president of a major company operating in Canada, I had my private doubts about our ability to compete if a comprehensive free trade agreement were in place. This was two years before the release of the Macdonald Commission's study into Canada's economic prospects, which was a seminal moment in the history of Canada–U.S. relations, because of its importance and thoroughness, and because it called for Canada and its government to take a leap of faith and begin to negotiate free trade with the Americans.

At the same time, my travels throughout the United States and meetings with American business leaders as Iron Ore's president had made me wonder whether Canada could ever negotiate any free trade agreement with the United States that included an effective dispute resolution mechanism. Americans frequently referred to this sort of proposal as a "surrender of our sovereignty," something they were not about to do. Ironically, a dispute resolution mechanism was the very last item we secured on the final day of my government's historic negotiations that culminated in Washington in October, 1987, in the U.S.–Canada Free Trade Agreement.

—

PERSONAL JOURNAL: APRIL 6, 1985

(Reflection on the Shamrock Summit)

We talked about trade, our upcoming agenda, and I received a commitment from Reagan that he would "go to bat for Canada," guaranteeing us secure access to the American market. This is absolutely vital as far as we're concerned. Unless I'm totally wrong I think we're going to need it, because the American Congress will soon be working itself into a giant lather about Japan, and I don't want us to get hurt in the process.

—

To understand the quandary Crosbie's position put me in, you have to be fully aware of the strategy my team and I had identified as our only chance of winning the leadership. It was best summed up by Charley McMillan in an extremely prescient memo to me on May 6, 1983, written after he analyzed polling data available privately to us from a Gallup sample of 250 delegates: "Key Finding: It is clearly a Clark–Mulroney fight; even with all second-ballot support of other camps, Crosbie can't win. The only combination [that can beat us] is Clark/Crosbie, with Clark going to Crosbie on the second or third ballot."

That was our whole campaign in a nutshell; on June 11 we had to be in the number two position behind Joe Clark. Thanks to Frank Moores, who openly attended Crosbie meetings as a former Newfoundland premier and someone friendly to both John and me, we also knew that two-thirds of Crosbie's delegates would eventually come our way in a straight Clark versus Mulroney final ballot.

Charley and I acknowledged that Crosbie's support for free trade was a powerful idea that distinguished him from everyone else and made him an attractive candidate in parts of the country where he needed to gain support. But we also realized that I could not endorse John's plan for a free trade deal with the United States at that time. Had I done so, because of my second-place status in the race I would have been the focus of attacks on the idea, and would have had to spend two months being defined by the free trade issue. All of the false and vexatious arguments that were to be made against free trade in the 1988 election would have been made against me during the leadership campaign. And when I tried to fight back I would not have had the benefits of the Macdonald Commission and of five years of negotiation and experience that I had when I signed the deal as prime minister in January of 1988.

During the heat and dust of a leadership race I had no choice but to attack Crosbie's stance and thereby cement my second-place standing. "Now there's a real honey – free trade with the Americans," I told the *Globe and Mail*. "Free trade with the United States is like sleeping with an elephant. It's terrific until the elephant twitches, and if the elephant rolls over, you are a dead man. I'll tell you when he's going to roll over. He's going to roll over in times of economic depression and they're going to crank up the plants in Georgia and North Carolina and Ohio, and they're going to be shutting them down here."

To balance this viewpoint, Charley and I decided that *Where I Stand* should include my opinions on international trade. In the essay that concluded my book, I wrote:

> For Canadians, with over 30 per cent of our GNP devoted to trade, increasing global protectionism is totally contrary to our economic well-being. As the rivalry mounts among the major trading blocks of the United States, Japan, and the European Economic Community, we must view with alarm the damaging consequences to ourselves and others of orchestrated restrictions to the flow of trade. Although we have to work in the world as it is and cannot afford the Boy Scout role, we nevertheless must energetically stand and press for the lowering of barriers to trade because trade is our lifeblood. In that direction lies our future prosperity. Government in Canada must see its role as creating with the private sector a greater and freer access to world markets and higher levels of trade . . . Access to trade is therefore a top priority for us. We must revitalize our efforts and sharply reverse the performance of recent years. Canada is part of a tougher, changing world, and it is time we began to understand and deal with that fact.

(Later, I also began to lay the groundwork during my address to convention delegates the night before they voted. "First, the new government must re-establish that special relationship of trust at all levels with our allies, including our greatest friend and ally, the United States of America," I said. "Secondly, we've got to send signals around the world that investment capital is welcome here and this is a good, an honourable, and a decent place to do business again. We have got to state clearly . . . that the private sector is the only motor whereby new wealth and new jobs and new opportunity can be created by Canadians.")

—

PERSONAL JOURNAL: JUNE 22, 1984

I read to Ronald Reagan the paragraph from my speech to the convention about restoring trust with the Americans, and he looked around and seemed genuinely moved. I got the feeling that American presidents aren't used to hearing nice things said about the U.S. I said that while our relationship was not untroubled or free from challenges, it was so important that it required our constant attention and nurturing.

—

Still, it was a less than honest position for me to take. Crosbie was more direct and forthcoming than I was at the time. Years later, Kim Campbell was derided for telling the press that an election campaign was no place for a serious discussion of the issues. She had it almost right. Had she said instead that leadership campaigns were no place for explosive new issues, I would have agreed completely. In a leadership race you should be talking about your general approach and where you'd like to go on the economy, on the Constitution, and on national unity, and you should mention any new ideas only in general terms. You cannot defend an entire detailed program if you want to be a serious contender for a party's leadership. If you try, you won't win.

And winning was exactly what I meant to do. Over the years Joe Clark has been unfairly saddled with the image of a wimp. Anyone who believes that never stood against him in a leadership race. Joe is as tough and competitive as they come. Consider, for example, the 1983 leadership battle on the ground in Quebec.

I had entered the race on March 21. By March 25 – the day delegates began to be selected – Joe's control of the party machinery in Quebec was already paying off. In the first two weeks his organizers, led by Marcel Danis (who was so good at his job that I later appointed him to my own cabinet), set more than twenty-four delegate selection meetings in Quebec's seventy-five ridings. Joe won most of them.

Our party's recent poor showing in Quebec was a blessing for Joe during the leadership race. Because of our failures in the 1980 election, we had only one sitting Quebec Tory MP in 1983 – and he was supporting Joe! With seventy-four ridings without a Conservative MP, party headquarters, which Joe also controlled, had free rein over ridings and resources. With seven years as leader under his belt, you could also be damn sure that Joe had visited every riding he could in the province. Anyone who had been leader for so long would have been a fool not to have his own people in place on the ground.

In fairness, it also must be said that, while he was leader, Joe had worked extremely hard in Quebec, and the fact he hadn't been successful in an electoral sense was certainly not due to any lack of effort. The positions he took – including the constitutional repatriation issue, in which he played a powerful and starring role – were often very favourable to the legitimate needs and aspirations of Quebecers, but this never translated into seats at election time. In the leadership race, however, he was known throughout the party in Quebec as a candidate who deserved to be in the race and who was worthy of support.

Quite properly, Joe made the best of the situation, and I did what I could. Quebec turned into a hell of a battle that left all the other candidates sitting on the sidelines. We fought riding by riding, in meeting after meeting. Some of my enthusiastic organizers even signed up down-and-out seniors and war veterans who lived in the Old Brewery Mission in Montreal. Then they made matters worse by allowing the CBC to film the whole thing. As you can imagine, the journalists' well-developed sense of morality was aroused by this strategy. Privately, my attitude was pretty simple: let them moralize from Ottawa while we're winning votes. Publicly, however, some of the other candidates, David Crombie and Michael Wilson specifically, played to this hue and cry in the media and asked the party to investigate delegate selection meetings. I had to respond, telling members of my campaign team at an event at McGill that I expected my team to conduct themselves "the way I do in my public and private life – with intelligence, probity, and honour."

Meanwhile in Newfoundland, Crosbie was signing up every high school, flying club, and, it seemed, every driving school, and turning them into PC youth clubs. By the end, there were more delegates coming off The Rock than anyone could shake a stick at. We were all doing what we could within the law to advance our respective causes, and we all took advantage of everything we had going for us. We also tried to undercut our opponents without being too personal in the process.

While I was eventually able to hold Joe to a draw in Quebec, he handed me quite an opportunity early on that helped me improve my position in Canada's largest province. On March 25, Joe took it upon himself to announce that he thought Ontario Premier William Davis would be a "regional candidate" if he entered the race. He offended many Ontarians with that statement. Ontarians are the only voters in Canada who always place their country, not their province, first when they consider public affairs and policy. They always take the national perspective, unlike Albertans, Quebecers, or Newfoundlanders. Telling Ontarians that their premier was a "regional candidate" unfit for national office was a major gaffe. That aside, Ontario Tories were also responding as enthusiastically as Conservatives in all parts of the country to my call for the election of a candidate who could make historic gains throughout Canada and, in the process, finally return our party to the position it held in the days of Macdonald and Cartier, when Canada's Tories were truly a pan-Canadian governing institution.

I pounced, pointing out publicly that if Premier Davis of Ontario, the economic engine of Confederation, ran, he would certainly be a national candidate, and one who would likely win the race. While I believed in what I was saying, the incident also boosted my potential support among people who were not predisposed to my candidacy, or who were hoping that Davis would in fact run. When Davis later announced he wasn't running, I believe that many of his supporters came to me.

While I don't know how Bill Davis marked his ballot on June 11, 1983 – although he remains a good friend to this day, I've never asked – I do know this: he was certainly not hostile toward my campaign in 1983. A year later, during the federal election campaign, he placed the full resources of his much-vaunted Big Blue Machine at my disposal, including its most important asset, himself, in the 1984 general election. The results spoke for themselves.

Joe handed me another opportunity when he announced that he was willing, if returned as party leader and later as prime minister, to give Quebec full compensation should the province and its separatist government opt out of new national shared cost programmes. While I had little trouble with the substance of his plan, it was his strategy that I couldn't understand. Here you had a separatist premier, René Lévesque, in power and the prospective leader of a national political party was revealing his negotiating hand before talks had even begun.

I went on the offensive. "To try and curry the favour of the Parti Québécois organization during a leadership campaign is dangerous to the candidate who does it, it's dangerous for the future of the party he seeks to lead, and it's dangerous to the future of the united country he seeks to govern," I said. I later most famously continued my attack with the words, "I'm not playing footsie with the PQ, another candidate is developing an elegant style in that regard." (Little did I know that I would later face the same charges.)

It was tough politics we played in 1983 but it wasn't cruel. Did I go too far? Perhaps. Was I inaccurate? I don't think so. Joe had revealed his negotiating position without securing anything from the PQ in Quebec City.

It's true that I was later to negotiate the Meech Lake Accord with all the provinces, including Quebec. And the accord did contain provisions for financial compensation for provincial governments that opted out of national programs in areas of provincial jurisdiction – but only if they set up their own programs that were compatible with national objectives. I negotiated that agreement with Quebec Premier Robert Bourassa, a Liberal federalist, but only after he agreed to sign on to Canada's existing constitutional documents and make Canada constitutionally whole again.

Another premier who played a significant role in the race was Alberta's Peter Lougheed, one of the most successful premiers in Canadian history. Peter had very close friends in Montreal from his time at Harvard; they included Roger and Andrée Beaulieu and Philippe de Gaspé Beaubien and his wife Nan-B., who were also friends with Mila and me. Through them, I would get feedback on Peter's position on the federal leadership question, and it was clear he was not unfavourable to my candidacy. Still, he had to be careful, as both Joe Clark and another candidate, Edmonton tycoon Peter

Pocklington, were fellow Albertans. Joe had put up a marvellous fight on the Constitution on behalf of the provinces, and he had received, quite properly, residual goodwill in provincial capitals like Edmonton as a result.

Peter, however, wanted a winner. By 1983 Trudeau's National Energy Program was well into its looting of Alberta's treasury, and the Foreign Investment Review Agency was driving away foreign investment from Alberta. Peter had also been promoting the concept of free trade with the Americans, and knew this would go nowhere as long as the federal Liberals remained in power.

(It was only years later, during a dinner at 24 Sussex Drive that included Peter Lougheed and his former assistant Lee Richardson, that I learned the premier's true feelings about Joe. We were discussing the challenges any first minister faces in forming a cabinet and how a good résumé doesn't always reflect a candidate's true skill or judgment. We also acknowledged that geography often dictates whether a member is summoned to the cabinet or not. Lee recalled that in 1971, when Lougheed was swept to power, he had named five ministers from Calgary. If Joe Clark, who ran provincially under Lougheed's banner that year, had been elected, Lee observed, Peter would have faced a difficult choice in the early days of his premiership. Lougheed chuckled and then disagreed. "Lee," he said, "I don't think Joe Clark would have wound up in my cabinet.")

This was the background (some of it unknown to me at the time) as I made my way to Edmonton to meet with "King Peter" and the panel from his caucus that he had set up to interview all the candidates. I was to find that Peter was like Margaret Thatcher in meetings of this sort, inasmuch as his preparation was complete and absolute. He always had an agenda in front of him, planned exactly what he wanted to cover, and knew those files completely. I came away from that meeting and others with the premier well satisfied that I had his goodwill. I was able to build up significant second-ballot support from my trips to Alberta, and will always be grateful to Peter.

—

PERSONAL JOURNAL: LABOUR DAY, 1987

Peter Lougheed is of the view that the Meech Lake Accord was made possible during the final conference on aboriginal rights when, in the face of intractable positions by western premiers, I resisted the impulse to vilify or humiliate them publicly, in living colour on television. Some months later, bridges having not been burned, I was able to bring them together to complete the work of the Fathers of Confederation. This would not have been possible in a climate of malice and betrayal, such as had followed earlier meetings. The fact is there can be no constitutional amendment favouring aboriginal rights until Quebec, strongly sympathetic to the proposition, rejoins the Constitution. Without Quebec's presence, the votes are not there. Justice for native people, which I have carefully sought and forcefully advocated, shall be the eventual result of a completed constitutional process. Had I ruined the atmosphere with a vitriolic denunciation à la Trudeau following the breakdown of the First Ministers' Meeting on Aboriginal Rights, there would have, most likely, been no Meech Lake, and justice for native people would have been – as it might still be, if the accord is rejected – delayed for a generation.

—

One place I had little difficulty in attracting significant support this time out was from the federal caucus. In large part, this was thanks to the efforts of Pat MacAdam, who vigorously promoted my cause from his Parliament Hill vantage point. As leader for seven years, it was no surprise that Joe would attract the large majority of caucus members to his side. As an outsider, though, I was still able to attract more than twenty members of caucus to my team.

According to the media buying the Clark spin, Joe's caucus supporters were from the so-called progressive wing of the party, while my caucus supporters were said to be from the reactionary wing. I ignored the labels, basing my caucus operation on a truism I had learned from my mother: "Brian, beggars can't be choosers." While some of the MPs who announced for me were indeed right wingers ("So what," I said, "this is supposed to be a right-of-centre party!"), it was a stretch to label the thoughtful, soft-spoken Presbyterian minister Walter McLean, or accomplished and considerate people like Jack Murta, Tom Siddon, Alvin Hamilton, and George Hees, as representing the far right. Still, my opponents tried.

Joe had not done a good job of giving veterans of the Diefenbaker era their proper due while they sat in his caucus. The week before I announced I was in the race, I travelled to Ottawa for meetings with the MPs who had said they would support me if I ran. My meeting with George Hees that week was brief. "Brian," he said, "let's cut the bullshit. You have my support. Now, is there anything else you wanted to see me about?"

That was vintage George, a man I had known since the early 1960s when he was a flamboyant star in the Diefenbaker government. Later in the leadership campaign, George shared an airplane ride with us from Calgary to Victoria. Mila and I were having Cokes and he expansively ordered a Scotch. "This thing is coming down as you anticipated," the veteran announced, "a showdown between you and Joe Clark."

"What do you think about that?"

"Well, I'll tell you something, Brian," George said, "Joe Clark is a fine man and all that, but when he walks into a room, I don't know whether to stand up and salute, or send him out for a fresh pack of Sweet Caps!"

I was later to make George minister of veterans affairs in my first cabinet, where he served with great distinction. He also never changed. Back during George's first run as a minister, Diefenbaker had insisted that his ministers greet him at the airport whenever he returned from representing Canada abroad. I never felt the need for such displays from my own ministers, but I was secretly pleased to see George standing proudly on the tarmac at Uplands as I returned from a trip during my first term in office. Stepping off the plane, I approached my greeting party and thanked George for taking time out of a busy schedule to welcome the prime minister home. I was truly touched by the gesture and thought that maybe Diefenbaker had had a point – until George spoke up.

"You're welcome, I guess, Prime Minister," he said, "but I'm only here to hitch a ride on your plane back home to Trenton."

As the leadership campaign continued, I hammered home my theme in every speech I made. "Progressive Conservatives point to western Canada as a stronghold and a solid wall of Tory Blue seats," I said in North Bay, Ontario, less than a month before voting day.

> It was not always this way. Prior to the Diefenbaker minority government of 1957 and the Chief's 1958 sweep of 208 seats, the West provided twin beds for the CCF, the Liberals (they now share a double bed), and the Social Credit Party. Mr. Diefenbaker was fond of saying the only protection a western Conservative had was the game laws. Alberta was once a monolith of Social Credit MPs until

> John Diefenbaker broke the stranglehold. Don't ever tell me that there is such an animal as a safe Conservative seat anywhere in Canada . . .
>
> A safe seat is a myth: A secure province is a transitory fiction. Our party is riding high in the popularity polls; we've never been higher to my knowledge. But, plot the Gallup poll over a couple of years and you will find what statisticians call a perfect bell curve. Soon, if history and experience are accurate indicators, we will start down the curve into a modest valley. What could be at the bottom of the slope? An improving economy which will boost Liberal fortunes in the public perception? A new Liberal leader? Canadians may not have Pierre Elliott Trudeau to kick around any more. Who, then? Eugene Whelan? Herb Gray? Are you kidding? The Liberals go with winners. They'll pick John Napier Turner because they feel he can win. That is the challenge of June 11. The question is not only who can win a convention. The question is also who can win an election.

My partisan crowds responded with cheers and ovations. You could still feel the anger over Clark's loss of government in 1980. I reminded Tories of it each and every day I campaigned.

That defeat still pained me, but it did present an advantage. While my lack of parliamentary experience had crippled my campaign in 1976, my opponents in 1983 – principally Joe and his finance minister, John Crosbie, on whose budget the government fell – couldn't make that one stick this time, though they tried.

I frankly admitted that I had no parliamentary experience. I pointed out that instead I had been out in the real world, making decisions and participating actively and effectively in the private sector, while the others had been lobbing questions at the Liberals in the House. Then came the punchline: "If parliamentary experience means that you lose the levers of government after only weeks in Parliament – and after our party had spent sixteen years in opposition – during a vote on the floor of the House of Commons, and then lose the ensuing election, I'll take my own experiences in the private sector, thank you very much."

During the first fifty-two days of the campaign Mila and I visited a total of seventy-four cities and towns, from Vancouver to Charlottetown, meeting delegates from two hundred and fourteen ridings – but we had fun. We still joke about spending our tenth wedding anniversary in Pembroke, Ontario. With our friends Ace and Mary McCann and Paul and Judy Dick, our anniversary dinner consisted of pizza ordered up from a local restaurant and served from our hotel room bed. "Remember, Mila," I said with a laugh, "when you married me I told you I'd take you travelling and show you the world – and I have!" While Pembroke is beautiful, I don't think the Ottawa Valley was where either one of us suspected we'd be marking our first ten years together. Despite the hectic campaign schedule, we still found time to host a birthday party for Mark and to attend Caroline's first communion.

One of our greatest campaign swings took place in New Brunswick. We decided to do a sweep from Fredericton all the way up the Saint John River Valley, through Edmundston, St. Leonard, over into Dalhousie, down to Bathurst, and on to Chatham, and Newcastle, before winding up in Moncton at a rally that featured Premier Hatfield and countless delegates. Generally, we stayed away from the big showy events that would attract national media. This was an extraordinary exercise in retail politics, and we loved every minute.

We travelled the province in a big van supplied and driven by an extremely wealthy and well-known New Brunswick lawyer-entrepreneur named Jim Ross. Mila and I were in the back of the vehicle and Sandy LeBlanc, an outstanding organizer, and Jim took turns driving. At every event my message was the same: "There are all kinds of reasons you should vote for me," I told New Brunswick Tories. "I am going to win this leadership, and I'm going to win the next election by bringing Acadians, Brayons, and French Canadians together into a great national party. We will be the next national government, and I'm going to be able to work with Richard Hatfield. Together we'll do great things for New Brunswick. But there's another reason you should vote for me: I'm the only candidate in the race who has a millionaire for a driver!"

It brought the house down every time.

After I won the leadership, people would ask me just how it was that we were able to accurately predict our first-ballot support. In April, I had forecast to Peter White that we would attract approximately 875 votes on the first ballot. We received 874. How did we do that? We counted. We totalled up every single delegate in far-flung places that most members of the national media couldn't even name.

Because of the CBC's superior resources, one reporter who did try to follow Mila and me across Canada was Jason Moscovitz. Toward the end of the campaign, our paths crossed at a small airport in eastern Ontario. We were flying on to an early evening event in London organized by Tom Long. Mila went into the small terminal building to make a call and left me alone to contemplate the sunny Ontario landscape.

Jason came out of the terminal and greeted me. As we looked out past the runways, both with thoughts of June 11, we had a brief and rather untypical exchange.

"You're going to win this thing, aren't you?" Jason said.

"Yes, Jason, I think I am," I replied.

"And nobody knows it," he continued.

"Now you do," I replied.

Though the campaign ran out of money (a group of friends signed a promissory note so we could continue on financially), convention week opened with a bang. Gallup had polled 250 delegates for us between May 30 and June 2. John Crosbie had been labelled "the Tory to watch" in a May 23 cover story in *Maclean's* magazine, but we now knew for sure that the media – not for the first time, of course – had missed the real story. Charley McMillan and I reviewed our data, which showed Clark was at 37 per cent, Crosbie had fallen four points to 17 per cent, and I'd risen to 28 per cent – a four-point increase – since the middle of May.

Thanks to *Maclean's* and the previous disappointing *Southam–Global* poll that had received such wide circulation, it was time to play hardball. I gave Charley permission to leak the new poll's results to the *Globe and Mail*. As a result, only four days before voting day, delegates in Ottawa were greeted by a headline that shouted, "Mulroney Gaining in Latest Poll."

The *Globe* also published a positive editorial about my economic platform – a platform that Charley and the industrious Sinclair Stevens were instrumental in preparing. "Just what effect would these and other policies proposed by Mr. Mulroney have on the cold, hard numbers of Canadian economic performance?" the newspaper asked. "Well, according to [a study by] Data Resources, Mulronomics would be a tonic for a national economy already on its way to restored help. The combination of improved productivity and other export-related policies would raise real export growth to 8.2 per cent over 1985–90 . . . As Data Resources acknowledges, the projections hinge on 'certain assumptions' about 'the effectiveness of some of the proposed policy measures.' They've covered themselves. At the same time, they have underlined the scope of the economic alternatives offered by the candidate who, oddly enough, is sometimes accused of dodging policy issues."

My campaign printed as many copies of the editorial as we could, making sure that each and every delegate had the opportunity to digest it. This vote of confidence from the *Globe*, combined with our improvements in our last poll and the ensuing press we received, meant we were entering the convention on the rise – the position any leadership candidate hopes for and works to achieve.

6. Showdown in Ottawa

As I WORKED ON my convention speech, I again decided to ignore the media, the wider country, and everybody else. I had matured since 1976, and I now planned to deliver an old-fashioned tub-thumping partisan speech to Canada's Tories, a speech that I suspect even old Sir John A. would have liked. I'd worry about attracting the nation's support later. With record-high interest rates, rising unemployment, and so much other bad economic news under Trudeau, the Liberals were doing much of our work for us. I could sense that Canadians were looking for a change. My job was to talk to Tories and Tories alone.

"Ladies and gentleman," I told the crowd gathered in the Ottawa Civic Centre, "the significance of June 11 has nothing to do with June 12. It has everything to do with all the June twelfths that follow. The issues before you are competence and leadership . . . Your response will affect this party and this country, not for a day, but for a generation."

Then, as best as I could from the podium, I tried to look every single delegate in the eye – the men and women from Corner Brook and Calgary, Kingston and Kelowna, and Sherbrooke and St. Stephen who had toiled for the party and had been led into the wilderness every time since, except for 1979 when their hopes were raised and then foolishly dashed.

> I first came here in 1956 as a youth delegate, to vote for John Diefenbaker, and I can tell you that, with modest exceptions, we, as a party, have excelled at winning conventions and losing elections. You've got to ask yourselves why? All of you, everyone in this room, is a winner in his private life, in his professional life, in his community life. In eight of the ten provinces, we have formed governments on a regular and sustained and ongoing basis. You are here today because you are winners and held in esteem by your communities.

> Why is it that when we put on our hats as federal Conservatives and go into another room, everyone in the country says we are a bunch of losers? Why is that? This has been confirmed on more election nights than we care to remember. What has happened to transform us, and you, from winners to losers? The answer is, nothing. We remain the winners we are, but the cause of our problem is spelled out in our history books, yours and mine. President Truman used to say that a page of history is worth a volume of logic. He must have been thinking of us. Our area of weakness – *mais c'est écrit dans nos volumes d'histoire* (but it's written for all of us to read) – our area of weakness is French Canada. Time after time, decade after decade, election after election, it has staggered this party and debilitated the nation. More importantly, it has deprived this country of talented Conservatives, such as yourselves, serving in government and influencing the course of our history.
>
> The facts are unassailable. Our losses in francophone seats from Nova Scotia to Manitoba impede us, election after election. And what about the challenge of new Canadians? A continuing concern must be to attract and hold the sympathy and the support of millions of the new Canadians who populate the major industrial cities of this country and who have stayed away from this party, notwithstanding generous efforts [to include them]. I tell you that bringing with affection and openness and open-mindedness French Canadians and new Canadians to join you and me together is the challenge of this generation for the Conservative party. I invite you to reach out tonight and take their hands of friendship and say, "Together we will build a new party."

In conclusion, I asked Canada's Tories to consider the legacy of the man I, as prime minister, was later to honour in June of 1991, on the one-hundredth anniversary of his death when I humbly stopped by a quiet grave in Kingston. "The party and this country want new leadership and new vision and a new expression of our national purpose," I told the delegates. "Sir John A. Macdonald told us that the only way, if you are a Conservative leader, that you can implement your policies is by recreating that grand alliance of West and East, English and French, together. He told us to proceed that way, and that if one of the elements is lacking, we are doomed to opposition. And I tell you, we have been in opposition too long. Now is the time, now is the time. Let us respond to [our founder's] challenge, let us accept his invitation, and let us recreate that grand alliance, and in the process, together we shall build a new Conservative party and we shall build a brand-new Canada."

The hall exploded with applause and I left the stage confident that I had done my best and that the party had received my message loud and clear. I could do no more.

Although I had pounded him repeatedly after he'd said he could speak adequately to French Canadians through a translator were he to become PM, I thoroughly enjoyed John Crosbie's speech. At one point, his campaign blimp floated free of its tether and began bumping blindly around the hall, which was hilarious and went well with his image of being a happy warrior in the Conservative cause. I was to witness Crosbie's good humour and sharp wit again and again when the Tories left the opposition benches and took hold of the levers of power.

I remember little of the content of Joe's speech, but I recall thinking that his people had made a bizarre strategic decision in the demonstration they chose to mount ahead of his speech. Where my team had tried to showcase newness and change, Joe chose the opposite approach. Joining him on the stage were Robert Stanfield, Davie Fulton, Heward Grafftey, Flora MacDonald, and other party stalwarts. They all shared a common denominator, I thought: they had led our party or their own campaigns to defeat, time after time. They were all good people who had made great contributions to party and country but, frankly, the Clark demonstration looked like an endorsement of the past and a repudiation of the future. By contrast, I was looking ahead to the future, and to victory.

Despite my being one of the principal actors in the drama that unfolded before millions of Canadians watching the action in the Ottawa Civic Centre on their televisions, I believe there are lessons political parties, my own in particular, could learn from that convention. We should go back to delegated leadership conventions, for so many reasons. As the Liberals discovered with Stéphane Dion's win in December 2006, a party can't afford to buy the television coverage that an exciting convention generates with its colour and pathos and drama. Viewers relish seeing the unfeigned, raw anguish and joy that they witness on the faces of the hard-working delegates and their chosen candidates. At one end of the hall, you have the victor and at the other end, the loser. In between, there is pure human emotion for all to see.

The democratic process is the beneficiary of the delegated convention. Ordinary Canadians pick their own candidates and develop their own likes and dislikes. The next day, at water coolers across the country, the conversation continues, "What did you think of that Mulroney's speech?" people will say. "Well, it was good but I think Clark is the better man." "No way," a third party might interject, "Crosbie had more style, while Wilson was quiet, but I admire his experience." And on it goes, as a national conversation is generated by this unique political event. Giving up the traditional convention system has been, I believe, an enormous loss for the Conservative Party and for Canadian democracy.

There were few surprises when the first-ballot results were announced:

Joe Clark 1091
Brian Mulroney 874
John Crosbie 639
Michael Wilson 144
David Crombie 116
Peter Pocklington 102
John Gamble 17
Neil Fraser 5

Crosbie had done better than we had thought, but my numbers were still on track. Throughout the campaign, I made sure that the lines of communication were kept open between our team and those in the Pocklington and Wilson camps. As I've already described, Peter White and David Angus played a special role in seeking out second-ballot support from Wilson. Quietly and without fanfare, Peter let me know that he felt confident Wilson would publicly endorse me once he made the decision to drop off the ballot.

As for Pocklington, he didn't have a seat in Parliament. Instead he had made a successful career in business that included the high-profile ownership of Wayne Gretzky's Edmonton Oilers. If I was an outsider to the elites who ran the party, Peter was the outsider's outsider. The denizens of the Albany Club and others like them viewed him as a Neanderthal who had ridden in from the West and the world of Amway to take over "their" party. While it is true I found some of his positions too far right for my own liking, he was a delightful, intelligent and straightforward guy. I felt that his views definitely deserved to be aired and that he had every right to contest the leadership.

In the months leading up to voting day, I made sure to pay Peter the respect I felt he deserved as a fellow candidate. I had breakfast with him in Toronto shortly before the convention opened, and we kept in constant touch by telephone. While he never came out directly and said it, I felt he would come to me when he was eliminated.

The night before the convention we met in person, in Peter's Ottawa hotel suite, along with two Toronto backroom operatives, Paul Godfrey and Ralph Lean, both friends of mine. I told Peter that I'd be in a very strong second-place position after the first ballot, with Crosbie well behind. "That's where you'll have to make your move," I told him. "And you won't have much time. I've been around these conventions long enough to know that you'll only have about ten minutes to make up your mind."

Peter replied that his mind was indeed made up and that he knew what he'd be doing. I didn't press him further, and left his suite feeling confident. There was no deal, however, despite the best attempts of the CBC, and others, to suggest that there were. Untrue then, untrue now.

After the results of the first ballot were made public I was reasonably assured that Pocklington and Wilson would soon begin their walk toward my section of the arena. And sure enough, they began to move at the same time, meeting on the main floor and starting their march together – *toward John Crosbie*! I was speechless. Montreal *Gazette* journalist L. Ian MacDonald later described my reaction as the scene unfolded in front of my widening eyes. "Brian Mulroney looked like someone who was witnessing a bank holdup or a shooting in the street," he wrote. "His face was frozen in helpless fascination. He was unable to stop it, unable to cry for help, unable to look but unable to look away."

Remembering the gangup against me in 1976, Mila broke into tears beside me. In that moment, all our work together – the thousands of miles she'd logged, the countless notes she'd written, the hands she'd shaken, and so much more – had apparently gone to waste. Crosbie would now gain the momentum he needed to eventually place him alone against Joe on the final ballot.

Later I learned that Michael and Peter had simply got lost in the hurly-burly of an exciting convention's crowded floor. Surrounded and blinded by a crush of delegates, journalists, and television cameras and lights, they didn't know which way to turn to come to my box. Finally, one of my supporters helped clear a path for the two candidates, and soon they were standing next to me, all of our arms raised in triumph.

Unbeknownst to me at the time, there was some behind-the-scenes drama going on among youth delegates. Perhaps smelling a winner, a large group of Clark youth delegates from Quebec announced to my convention strategists that they wanted to cross over to the Mulroney section right after the first ballot. Far from helping us, this could have been a disaster. If Clark's vote had eroded too quickly, it might have left Crosbie facing us in the final vote, and nobody on our team was sure how the Clark vote would split when he fell off the ballot. It was therefore quietly explained to the Quebec youth for Clark that they should stay where they were until only two names remained on the ballot: Mulroney and Clark.

I was now sure that I'd have what I wanted: the eventual showdown between Joe and me. The party would make its choice and finally clear the air. Thrilled to have Pocklington, Wilson, and their delegates at my side, I had forgotten about David Crombie. Toronto's former mayor had a surprise for us all: he was staying on for another ballot.

I was never sure where Crombie would attempt to take his delegates once he was eliminated. After an all-candidates debate at Toronto's Massey Hall during the campaign, the *Toronto Star* announced "Mulroney-Crombie win debate." That headline actually meant that Clark had lost the debate, and it also meant that the guy who was not a member of Parliament had defeated him. I had been happy to share the laurels with Crombie, because we were aware that for all his popularity as Toronto's former "Tiny Perfect Mayor," there was little possibility he would win the convention.

Michel Cogger had developed a friendship with MP Chris Speyer, a leading Crombie supporter. The pair had many friendly discussions between March and June about what Crombie might do when he was eliminated, and Cogger was positive about my prospects of picking up Crombie votes. Privately, I disagreed.

In the end, by staying in Crombie deprived Crosbie of any shot at carrying the convention. Had he made the walk to Crosbie right after the first ballot, he would have given him a boost that might have allowed John to move farther ahead. By waiting an additional ballot before making his move, Crombie had denied his eventual choice the momentum needed. Eventually, as Cogger later described it, he marched toward John with four hundred supporters holding their yellow umbrellas, but took only forty votes with him.

On the second ballot, Joe actually lost six votes, coming in at 1085. I had risen to 1021, Crosbie had increased his numbers to 781, while Crombie had slipped to 67 votes. Just when TV viewers thought the excitement and drama couldn't possibly get any more intense, Crosbie's team played their final card. Viewers were treated to the incredible sight of Joe Clark, a former prime minister and seven-year party leader, being asked to withdraw in favour of the third-place candidate, just to defeat me. Newfoundland Premier Brian Peckford was sent from the Crosbie team to persuade Joe to withdraw. In full view of the cameras, Joe's wife, Maureen McTeer, looked at him with disdain and uttered the memorable (and I still believe, highly justifiable) phrase "Fuck off." It simply wasn't going to happen.

Why would Joe Clark, who had fought to make the Progressive Conservative Party bilingual and accepted in French Canada, desert those honoured principles to support a unilingual candidate who was running against a bilingual Quebecer? Had he done so, it would have been like hanging Louis Riel once again, and decades would have passed before our party recovered in Quebec. I knew there was no chance that Joe would even consider such a preposterous scenario. Joe Clark, up to then and since, would never knowingly do anything that would harm the country or damage the party.

The numbers after the third ballot set the stage for the final act. We stood at Clark, 1,058; Mulroney, 1,036; and Crosbie, 858.

I made no attempts to lobby John to make the long walk to my box before the final ballot. In 1976, I had been in the same situation as he was now, and wanted to leave him his dignity at a time of deep hurt. He had fought an honourable campaign and, if he had been bilingual, he might very well have carried the day. Those feelings of empathy aside, the realist in me also knew that upwards of two-thirds of John's delegates were coming my way anyway.

The crowded Ottawa Civic Centre was a steam bath. Fortunately, each candidate had his own dressing room with telephones, a television, and a shower. Between ballots, I'd escape for brief moments of solitude, or for private discussions with Mila or senior members of my team. My old law school comrade Sonny Mass was manning the telephones in that room throughout the day. While we all anxiously awaited the results of the fourth and final ballot, I retreated to my dressing room and headed for the shower.

Any peace that I might have found under the jets was soon interrupted by Sonny's shouts. "Brian," he exclaimed, "Clark is heading your way!"

I didn't understand what he meant until I stuck my head out from the shower and glanced at the television. Sonny was right. There was Joe Clark, and he was heading for my section of the arena for a ceremonial handshake before the final results were known. It was a lovely gesture of party solidarity – especially since he probably knew, as I did, that his campaign was doomed. But Joe's people hadn't telephoned ahead to warn me, and there I was, buck-naked and dripping wet, watching this scene unfold. Mila had to inform a bemused Joe Clark where I was. "Tell him to dry off," Joe told her with a smile.

Some time later, Joe and I – in a gesture that was greeted by wild cheers from the thousands in the hall – were able to meet on the floor for our handshake. "I'll see you on the stage in a few minutes," Joe told me.

Bernard Roy, who was my chief scrutineer for the vote counts, gave me the advance news that I'd won. He walked out on the stage for the official announcement not wearing his glasses. That was the signal we'd privately arranged, and I now knew, only seconds before everyone else in the hall, that I would be the next leader of Canada's Progressive Conservative Party.

"Total votes cast: 2,928," came the words from the convention stage. "Spoiled ballots: 19. Number of votes needed to win: 1,455. Joe Clark: 1,325; 45.5 per cent. Brian Mulroney: 1,584; 54.5 per cent."

Mila jumped to her feet like a colt. She had been so shaken when Pocklington and Wilson had lost their way to our box earlier; now she was absolutely joyous, as pictures taken at the moment reflect. My mother was also right there, her arms around me. "Son, I can't believe it," she said. "Your dad would be so proud, so proud."

Mila and I began to make our way to the stage. I don't know if it was a combination of fatigue and emotion, but I had an out-of-body experience as we made that slow walk through the crowd. It was as if I were watching myself in a movie and I was thinking: "This is an interesting moment to watch, but it has nothing to do with me." The sensation was overwhelming. There was noise, applause, and people coming forward to greet me, and I was somehow impervious to it all as I allowed myself to be jostled, thumped on the back, and then helped onto the stage.

It was only when we got there and Mila grabbed my hand that I snapped back into the present, realizing with a start that this wasn't a movie.

It was really happening. After Joe and I had again shaken hands onstage, to wild rounds of applause from the delegates, Interim Leader Erik Nielsen cast a pall over the convention. Called upon to introduce the new leader, he chose to highlight division instead of solidarity at this crucial moment. "I want to make it clear that although Brian was not my first choice as leader, he will now have my full and undeviating support in the difficult challenge ahead," he said. I could feel the hall's collective gasp at his inappropriate remark. I decided to use my victory speech to extinguish the feelings of rejection and division Nielsen had chosen to reignite at my moment of victory.

Initially, however, I spoke about Joe. "First a word to Joe Clark, who has served this party with dignity, honour, and courage," I said. "I salute him as a friend, as a colleague in arms, and as a distinguished and most thoughtful Canadian. I assure Joe and Maureen, who have contributed so much to the party and to this country . . . I assure them of our deep respect, genuine admiration, and profound gratitude at all times. Joe and I met when I guess we were both seventeen or eighteen. Joe has played over all these years – and must continue to play – a major and prominent role in the leadership of the Conservative Party and of Canada."

I then turned and thanked the other candidates, who had also put themselves, their careers, and their families on the line because they believed they had something positive to offer their party and country. I also addressed their supporters. "I salute them for their magnificent contribution to the party, as I salute you for the wonderful support you gave all of them on behalf of the party and the country. I need their advice and I need their counsel, and I need your support and your advice and counsel. And I shall be seeking it often and actively, and I count on you giving it to me freely and regularly."

Then it was time to deal with Erik Nielsen. "I hadn't planned on making any announcements tonight, but Erik has given me no choice," I said. "He indicated that perhaps I wasn't his first choice for leader. I want you to know, he is my first choice for House Leader of this party." This brought the house down, and his infelicitous comment was soon forgotten.

I saved my most important words for last: "I mentioned the fact that I have family here and I'm honoured. But if you'll allow me a personal note, I want to thank one person very much – Mila, who has made such a contribution to my life and to the campaign. And now we go on with the business of building a country that is more generous, more tolerant, more equitable, and more just. That is our obligation to Canada: to provide the basis for an opposition which will command the respect . . . and the growing confidence of the Canadian people. We reach out to Canadians and together, *ensemble*, we're going to build a brand-new party and a brand-new country."

Exhilarated and exhausted, Mila and I left the stage and walked into the waiting arms of CBC's Peter Mansbridge and David Halton. Mansbridge said it was a very important day, and I quickly agreed, providing all his viewers except one with an answer they didn't expect. I told him that it was indeed an important day because today Caroline Mulroney turned nine. We found out later that Caroline, who was at home in Montreal, burst into tears upon receiving a birthday greeting from her father on television.

7. Picking Up the Reins

Finally, after twelve intense and sometimes bewildering hours, we were able to leave the Ottawa Civic Centre and head to the Château Laurier. There we were greeted by the cheers of hundreds who had gathered to welcome us in the storied hotel's lobby. After more handshakes and hugs of congratulations, Mila and I went up to our suite, which was well supplied with champagne and other beverages for the private party that followed. My veteran assistant, Ginette Pilotte, was there, as were Janis Johnson and Allan Fotheringham. André Desmarais, a rising star in the Montreal business community, and his lovely wife, France Chrétien, daughter of Jean Chrétien, spent a good part of the evening with us. (Interestingly, at our last formal event in Ottawa a decade later we hosted, with André and France as our special guests, a dinner at the National Gallery, for the Americas Society, in which André played a leading role. Quite the bookends.) It was close to four in the morning by the time Mila and I were alone with our dreams.

On June 12, I was up at dawn and already at work. I telephoned as many members of caucus as I could, concentrating mainly on those who had not supported me. Ray Hnatyshyn, who had stood with Joe, was woken up by his new leader. I told Ray what I later told all the losing candidates I made a point of seeing that first day: I need you, the party needs you, and above all else, the country needs you. I wanted every Conservative to feel welcome under the very large – and even broader – tent I was already beginning to construct.

Later that morning, I sat for my first full interview as Leader of the Progressive Conservative Party of Canada. "Exactly one week ago today, a young man sat in this very studio and predicted with utter confidence that he would be the next leader [of the PC Party]," Bruce Phillips, host of CTV's *Question Period*, told his viewers while introducing me, "and anybody who took him seriously and bet the family fortune on it would be smiling today, because he was absolutely right. At the same time he made another commitment that, if he won, as he was sure he would, he would reappear this week to speak about his plans as the new leader."

One of the first questions I was asked, not surprisingly, was about my lack of a seat in the Commons. I took this as an opportunity to give Prime Minister Trudeau a short history lesson.

"I remember when Mr. Stanfield was elected leader," I responded. "I remember that one of our caucus members stepped aside and that Mr. Pearson, who, of course, was somewhat more gracious than the present occupant, in some ways, of 24 Sussex, called a by-election very quickly. And indeed, in keeping with that strong Pearson tradition, he announced that Mr. Stanfield would go in uncontested as far as Mr. Pearson was concerned."

After the taping, I returned to the Château Laurier and met privately with each defeated leadership candidate, save Joe Clark. Our entire family also spent part of that day celebrating Caroline's birthday at a special brunch at the hotel. Life, after all, is about more than politics, and that was the happiest part of my day.

In the early evening, I had one more meeting to attend. I travelled to Stornoway to meet with Joe one on one. While I knew it wasn't an easy time for him and his family, I certainly owed him the courtesy of going to see him. Maureen, I remember, stayed upstairs as I spoke with her husband, and I could feel the sadness in the soft summer air inside the house. I told Joe that I had great admiration for him. We both now had run twice for the leadership of our party. He had won once and I had won once. I said that I hoped we could continue to work together and that I, and the party, needed his support and presence. Most importantly, I gave Joe my word that he would be treated with the greatest courtesy and respect by the new leader, and by the party as a whole. I also assured him that I would not be occupying either Stornoway or his former Parliament Hill office until I had won a seat in the Commons. I invited him to do whatever he wished until that time.

It was a brief conversation, and I tried to imagine how things would have been if the roles had been reversed. I did and said everything I could to make the transition as bearable as possible for him. While I knew nothing could take away from the hurt, I resolved that Joe, as a former prime minister and party leader, would be treated with the kind of courtesy he had earned and deserved. After that night, Joe and I were to spend a year in opposition and almost nine years in government together, and I kept my word. In recent years, both of us watched with bemusement as our old rivals in the Liberal Party, notably Paul Martin and Jean Chrétien, rejected the approach Joe and I followed – to their cost.

"Mr. Mulroney and I had been fierce opponents, in two tough leadership campaigns," Joe wrote in an opinion piece for the *Globe and Mail* in 2002, when he was once again in the role of leader of our party. "We agreed on fundamental issues about the country but, in personal terms, were probably more different from one another than Jean Chrétien is from Paul Martin. Yet, through [almost nine] contentious years in office, we put our differences aside, and worked together. It was more than my being a gracious loser; he was a gracious winner . . . To get things done you have to respect the positions of people who disagree with you. And they have to believe you respect them . . . As a result, Mr. Mulroney will [through his official portrait] be hanging in the corridor [of the Parliament Buildings] with a legacy intact, while Mr. Chrétien is hanging in the wind."

Joe was not the only member of his family who was gracious in the convention's aftermath. His brother Peter, a well-known Calgary lawyer and fierce supporter of Joe, took time out to write to me soon after June 11. While I was touched that he enclosed a cheque for $3,000 from his law firm to help my campaign pay off its debts, it was his words that mattered more. "Few families have had the opportunity to participate directly in the political process at what must be considered to be the ultimate level," Peter wrote in a letter I shared with my own family at the time.

> The Clarks have had the privilege of being so involved and are quite aware of the stress, the tension, and the emotional highs and lows that you and your family will experience. The elation of victory transcends the trials and tribulations of the position, and the proudest moment for the Clark family occurred when Joe was sworn in as Prime Minister of Canada. I have every confidence that the Mulroney family will have the opportunity of realizing and sharing the pride of that moment after the next election . . . You and your family will react with consternation to the vagaries of the polls, the constant public attention, the often less than flattering and unwarranted dissection by the national press, the vicious caricatures, and the public intrusion into your private lives. I have no doubt that the Mulroneys will be subjected to the same frustrations that the Clarks

> have felt over the years and I similarly have no doubt that your family will rise to the situation as occasion demands.

When I met with caucus for the first time, I began the fence-mending process that Joe would write about later. As a child of the Progressive Conservative Party, I was well aware that dissension in the caucus had severely damaged Clark, Stanfield, and Diefenbaker. I resolved that this wouldn't happen to me. I wrote out my notes for that first caucus beforehand, promising my new colleagues what I termed a new "unity of purpose and principle within our caucus and party."

Three sitting MPs – Chuck Cook, Gordon Towers, and Elmer MacKay – had offered me their seats. I immediately chose MacKay's Nova Scotia riding for my first run. The riding was a natural for me as I had gone to nearby StFX for four years and I knew the area well. Elmer was a great friend of mine, and his constituency was solidly Conservative.

Elmer resigned as MP for Central Nova, I announced my intentions to run there, and – nothing happened. While Pierre Trudeau was many things, he quickly proved he was no Lester Pearson. Exasperated that he wasn't calling the by-election, I placed a personal call to the prime minister. When his assistant told me that he was in a cabinet meeting, I asked that he leave the meeting to take the call, which he did.

"Look, Pierre, I'm going to contest Central Nova, and this by-election has to be called," I said. "I have three young children and I have to decide what I'm going to do about them for school in the autumn. I just want you to know that summer is over pretty fast and we both have to have our kids in school. I would appreciate it if you could focus on this matter right away."

Trudeau said he'd do just that. "I have ignored it a little bit, but I will do it right away, and I'll get right back to you," he said.

The prime minister kept his word, and by-elections in Central Nova and in Mission–Port Moody were called for August 29. While I had been going out on the hustings in federal campaigns since I was a teenager, this campaign would be different. For the first time, my name was on the ballot, and there was no way I was leaving anything to chance.

—

PERSONAL JOURNAL: JANUARY 2, 1991

Had Meech passed, as I told Paul Desmarais, I would have stepped down in September 1991 to allow for a change in leadership and allow for my return to Montreal. Mila has made no secret of her preference for private life, even though she has been remarkably successful in her many different and important roles, and I have been on the record since my interview with La Presse *in 1983 (during the Central Nova by-election) that two terms and out was the proper approach. I've long felt that hanging onto the leadership too long is fatal, Richard Hatfield's decision being the most recent example.*

—

Hundreds jammed a hall in Trenton, Nova Scotia, on the night of July 14, 1983 for my nomination meeting. Premier John Buchanan, Bob Stanfield, provincial MLAs, senators, and various MPs from across the country helped round out the crowd. Central Nova's Tories wanted a partisan, Grit-and-NDP-bashing tub-thumper of a speech, and I delivered:

> You remember Mr. Trudeau. A great quote – he comes out with them every once in a while – "I've wrestled inflation to the ground." Then he said, "Separatism is dead." And you know his one last year; he said that he was going to stay on as Liberal leader until such time as there was an economic recovery. People are down on their knees in churches across this country praying for an economic upturn. They are lighting candles as they pray, and I understand that John Turner's shoes are covered with wax. Ah, Pierre Trudeau, isn't he a beaut? As he said in 1974, he wouldn't touch wage-and-price controls with a ten-foot pole . . . I've got to tell you I first saw Pierre Trudeau twenty years ago in Montreal when he was a guest speaker at the NDP fundraising dinner. I saw him on TV, and he had a great line at the time. He said that the federal Liberal Party is so bad, it is so devoid of principle, that it will accept absolutely anybody in its ranks. And then he proved that in a real big way by joining himself.

> When I reflect upon fifteen, sixteen years of Pierre Trudeau, the person that I feel sorry for, apart from you and me and everyone else in the country, the guy that I feel sorry for is [NDP leader] Ed Broadbent. As my friend would say, *pauvre Broadbent*. All Broadbent ever wanted in his life was to work hard, be a good socialist, lead the party, become the first socialist prime minister of Canada. He did all that and walked into the House of Commons, and there's somebody sitting in his seat. It's his old pal from the fundraising dinner in Montreal. He knows that. But where I lost my affection for Mr. Broadbent, because I do have personal respect for many of them, as we ought to, was when his predecessor [David Lewis] and himself in 1972, they contracted a spurious organized marriage with the Liberal Party to keep Bob Stanfield from becoming prime minister and to keep their socialist pal, Pierre Trudeau, in office. That's what happened. And I've got a copy of the marriage contract and the articles of confirmation. We've all seen them, and they range from 1972 right through to the Constitution debate. We're going to take that marriage contract into every NDP constituency across this country and we are going to say, "When you vote for Broadbent, you get Trudeau every time. Now is the time to vote Conservative. You'll get a real Tory government."

The partisan crowd responded with rousing standing ovations.

Can you tell I was having a good time?

Stanfield's presence allowed me the opportunity to remind my riding association's members of my deep roots in the region and the party. "In the autumn of 1955, twenty-eight years ago, I first met and listened to an individual who would do so much for his beloved Nova Scotia and contribute so greatly to the development of a mature and thoughtful Canada," I said. "Bob Stanfield was then the leader of the opposition in Nova Scotia, and I was a sixteen-year-old student attending my first Conservative meeting. As we all know, the passage of time occasionally erodes memories, but I have a very clear recollection of that day and the meeting that took place just down the road from here so many years ago."

I praised Elmer MacKay and pledged I would work as hard as he had to represent Central Nova's interests in Ottawa. Beginning the next morning, I also placed my political future in Elmer's hands as the by-election campaign got under way. I kept his campaign manager and team in place and embarked on a journey, with Elmer at my side, into a constituency campaign run Nova Scotia–style.

It was entirely different than anything I'd ever seen. Elmer and I would set off very early each morning in his Oldsmobile, and we would visit Sheet Harbour, Trenton, Stellarton, and every community in-between. Elmer drove with me sitting beside him, smoking away. At each small community we would stop and see people, and I would make a short speech. I'd find groups of fifteen, twenty-five, sometimes fifty people. "Elmer," I said one day, "why don't we have big meetings for five hundred or six hundred people, rather than all these small meetings?"

He was shocked at my suggestion. "No, Brian," he said sternly, "that's not the way it's done. Everyone has to have their own meeting."

Properly chastised by an expert who had been winning elections in Nova Scotia for more than a decade, I continued on our campaign through the strawberry socials, the evening meetings where corn on the cob was served, and barbecue after barbecue as that glorious summer went on. The many evening events made for long days; I asked Elmer why we had to keep having such early morning meetings. I've never forgotten his reply: "Once you've earned a reputation in Central Nova for being up early, then you can afford to sleep in."

Mila, who turned thirty the day after my nomination meeting, joined me with the children for the summer in Central Nova. We moved into a cabin at the Pictou Lodge and, despite our busy schedule, we were able to spend more time with the kids than we had since the leadership campaign began in March. The weather was beautiful, and Caroline, Ben, and Mark had the time of their lives.

Four-year-old Mark injected himself into the Central Nova campaign with a stunt we still tease him about. It marked the beginning of his role – one that he continues today – as the Mulroney family jokester. At the nightly small meetings, Mark would often come with me and sit with Pat MacAdam as I spoke. Like all politicians, I only had so many one-liners in my repertoire, and tended to use those that got laughs again and again. Mark soon had them memorized. The CBC was filming the event for a special they were doing on me. Just as I would get to the punchlines of my road-tested one-liners, Mark would shout them out from his seat! As the crowd roared, I turned to MacAdam and said, "I want this man removed from my meeting." The cameras dutifully recorded Mark's ejection, and our family still laughs about it today.

Back at Pictou Lodge, Mila and our aide and family friend Michael McSweeney (valued for both his sound instincts and his knowledge of the party) took turns at cooking and performing most of the chores. I came in late one night to find Mila and Michael in the kitchen wearing rubber gloves as they furiously scrubbed and cleaned up after a lobster dinner. "Mila," Michael said, "Just think – I'm the envy of Canada!"

As I was to remind Prime Minister Trudeau during my inaugural remarks in the Commons after the by-election, the Liberals sent most of their cabinet – eleven all told – into the riding to campaign against me. In a portent of what was to come, I remember that it was Jean Chrétien who made the most partisan personal attack of them all during his visit.

We countered with NHL great Bobby Orr, a long-time friend of mine, who outdrew anyone the Grits could throw at us. Joe Clark also came and campaigned at my side – the two of us again demonstrating party unity in a manner that Chrétien and Paul Martin never even attempted. When they're in opposition, Liberals often talk a good game about the need to have a new party leader enter the House unopposed, but they rarely reciprocate. In fairness, however, Prime Minister Trudeau eventually confessed that this had been his plan, but the local Liberal association, as well as his party's national executive, had vetoed it. "My stepping in to stop them will cause me nothing but harm within the party, and I need them," he told me frankly, and I fully understood. The NDP were also pushing for a race – and I gave it to them.

I left Nova Scotia only once before voting day, flying to Mission–Port Moody just outside Vancouver to help our candidate, Gerry St. Germain, on his own road to victory. We had crowds in the thousands, and journalists wrote that I had developed the timing of a Las Vegas comic as I tore strips off the Liberals and NDP, while outlining a vision of life under a PC government.

Both Gerry (en route to a fine career as caucus chairman, cabinet minister, and senator) and I swept to victory on August 29, my Liberal rival Alvin Sinclair receiving only 7,858 votes to my 18,882. When I arrived at my New Glasgow committee room, I found an excited crowd of Scotsmen and women singing "When Irish Eyes Are Smiling."

"While I enjoyed that opening song," I quipped, "we Scots have our own preferences."

Mila and I knew we would miss the Pictou Lodge and our wonderful supporters, but we were eager to get to Ottawa. Though I had been visiting the House of Commons since I was a teenager, I was now about to take a seat on the floor of the chamber. My days as a tourist were over.

PART IV

Leading and Winning

1983–1984

1. Leader of the Opposition
2. Exit Trudeau, Enter Turner
3. A Summer Election
4. Transition to Power

1. Leader of the Opposition

THE OPPOSITION LEADER'S office on the fourth floor of Centre Block on Parliament Hill is located one floor directly above the Prime Minister's Office. So, when you're sitting in that office for the first time, you realize you've made some progress, geographically at least. All you have to do is walk down one flight of stairs and you've made it to the seat of power in Canada. The trick is to figure out how to get down those stairs.

When I arrived in Ottawa as the newly minted Leader of Her Majesty's Loyal Opposition in Canada, I realized those stairs would be fairly difficult to descend because the Liberals had pretty much owned them and protected them against intruders for most of the century. And before they surrendered the keys to that office and those for 24 Sussex Drive, they would put up a brutal fight. Mila and I decided that we would spend every ounce of strength we had to win that fight.

Once behind the desk, I found a memo to me written by Tory party veteran Tom Van Dusen. After observing the Commons for decades, he had some frank advice for his new leader. "The House is the cockpit where reputations are made and broken, governments upheld or defeated," the elder Van Dusen wrote.

> The Diefenbaker government was defeated in the House in February 1963 and the Clark government was defeated in the House . . . Lester Pearson lost his virginity as well as the image of international statesmanship when he came into the House, Nobel Prize aloft, and was reduced to a quivering mass of protoplasm by Diefenbaker in 1958. Tommy Douglas, a major force on the Prairies, was cut down to size by the House when he appeared as NDP leader. In essence, the House is the arena where performance is assessed. This is where you either skate, stickhandle, bodycheck,

> and score, or get benched. George Drew, a titanic figure in Ontario, managed to bore the House by repeating in the second part of his speeches everything he had said in the first part. It took the Pipeline Debate to show what he was made of. There is a tradition of House performance in the country which lingers among commentators and even a few media analysts which it would be unwise to disregard.

The first weekend after Labour Day I took Tom's memo with me when I met with the party's entire caucus at Mont Ste-Marie, Quebec, for three days of discussions and socializing. Behind closed doors, I spoke frankly with the elected members of my team. Right off the bat, I told them that they were the most important wing of the party. I promised them that there would be no access to caucus, without their agreement, by any unelected advisors. The caucus knew full well that I'd be on the road for much of the time during this pre-election session, so I also assured them that decisions made in my absence would be made by Erik Nielsen or other elected members – not by unelected advisors.

I continued the healing process Joe and I had started together in June, thanking all members of caucus, and especially Joe and Erik, for their efforts since the convention. I was pleased to see that John Crosbie, too, was rested and ready to go. If he retained any ill feelings from his loss, I would never have known it as we discussed the Liberals' proposed changes to medicare.

"The health care system is provincial," the irrepressible John told us that weekend. "I'm the father of medicare in Newfoundland. Why don't we shout that we're against user fees?" Soon we would do exactly as John advised, catching the Liberals off guard.

Waterloo MP Walter McLean also spoke that weekend, telling us all bluntly and eloquently that more women had to be brought into the party. The member from Joliette, Roch La Salle, who was a strong Clark supporter, suggested that a committee should be set up to ensure that our party had the best possible candidates in Quebec, where our riding associations remained weak.

I wasn't surprised that after sixteen years in opposition and only nine months in power many of our MPs were suspicious of the public service. Ottawa was a Liberal town, and that weekend I heard many calls for change and for the sacking of numerous bureaucrats when we came to power. I shared some of the feelings that were expressed that weekend but urged our troops to keep their powder dry and their comments guarded. "We want to build for the future," I reminded the group. "We don't want to convey that we're on a witch hunt." I was already thinking ahead to the days when we'd be relying on those same bureaucrats for nonpartisan advice when we were in the midst of transition to government. But we had to get there first.

With that, the first Mont Ste-Marie conference came to a close (there would be two more such gatherings there before our victory at the polls in September of 1984) with the federal Progressive Conservative caucus and its leader primed for what was to come. For the first time in decades, our caucus entered a new parliamentary session fully united, eager to wage political war, and, above all else, ready for power. I had read Jeffrey Simpson's book, *Discipline of Power,* describing the decline and fall of the Clark government. His title was apt. I was going to demand that even out of power our party must demonstrate a "discipline of power" such as it hadn't seen in years. Not to do so would have been to continue the culture of defeat we had perfected in the past.

I vividly remember setting the tone at one meeting that fall where I brought together members of a planning committee that included representatives of the party, the PC Canada Fund, senior staff, and some members from caucus. The meeting, held in the opulent boardroom the leader of the opposition enjoys, was scheduled to begin at four o'clock. I took my chair at exactly that moment and called it to order. "Close and lock the doors," I said.

About twenty minutes later, there was a knock at the door. Janis Johnson, whom I had appointed as the first woman ever to be the director of the party, was outside and obviously surprised to have encountered a door that wouldn't open. The people nearest the door were uncertain what to do and asked for direction.

"Keep it locked," I said.

I then delivered the message the locked door symbolized: "The Liberals think we're stupid. They think that because we're now installed in these lovely offices, and because a car and driver are at my disposal, along with a stately mansion called Stornoway, that you and I will think we've won. Well, we haven't won anything. They treat us this way because they have to, but I'm not happy with it, and neither should you be. The real prize is over there at 24 Sussex Drive, but we can't get there without discipline. So, with your help, we'll know we've really won when I'm able to go over there to Langevin Block, throw out all the furniture and the political people, replace them with ours, and then go for a swim in Trudeau's swimming pool. When I'm in that water, I'll know for sure that we've won – but not until then."

Then I relented and let Janis into the meeting. No one was ever late again. The message had been sent: it was time for us to focus on the prize.

A few months later I delivered the same message to the members of the party's shadow cabinet, when I met with the group in the basement of Centre Block. I took them through their reports, one by one, and without holding back, I informed some MPs that their work was, in a word, lousy. I told them that if our portfolio critics continued to submit sloppy proposals and reports that I would have rejected instantly in the private sector, I'd find new critics. I warned them that I would be conducting similar meetings in the future; if we weren't making progress, I would make good on my promise.

Pat Carney, the member from Vancouver Centre, was one of the targets, and she was furious. In a pattern that would become all too familiar to me when I became prime minister, she fired off a letter in anger. As is her style, she struck out instead of reflecting: "Brian, since you are the first person in my thirty years in the work force to express dissatisfaction with my work, and since you have stressed that members of caucus should treat each other with respect and courtesy, I respectfully submit that we should discuss your displeasure with my performance personally."

Ah, Pat Carney.

—

PERSONAL JOURNAL: JANUARY 1, 1988

At a meeting at Meech Lake in late August I constituted an executive cabinet committee on trade with myself in the chair. This had the practical, if less than evident, effect of removing Pat Carney from a position of influence or control in the free trade negotiations. Derek Burney became my personal representative in this area, and it was soon obvious to the ministers that I was going to personally call the shots from there on in. What had particularly troubled me – apart from the constant demands from Carney that Reisman be fired, and the growing petulance she exhibited in dealing with cabinet and officials – was the unnecessary enthusiasm for the prospects of an impossible conclusion to the negotiations. She had developed a theory that such a failure would propel Canada to a new position of leadership at the GATT, where we would emphasize multilateralism, etc.! I often pointed out to her that the two were not mutually exclusive and that our principal market was the U.S., that a FTA with the U.S. would, at this time in our development, be an act of uncommon vision and leadership that would benefit Canada for decades to come.

—

Others saw my reproach to the caucus for what it was: a call for excellence. We were playing in the political equivalent of the NHL, and I intended for us to take home the Stanley Cup. Saskatchewan's Ray Hnatyshyn told me he relished the challenge. "I really had to think whether I was in the same party," he said at the time, "because, in the past, we all kind of did what we thought was right, and did it on our own schedules. There was no sense of urgency, no sense of rigour in what we were doing. Above all else, our work didn't mesh together in a common plan."

And urgency, whether we liked it or not, was on the agenda that fall. I knew that Prime Minister Trudeau and his Liberals wouldn't give us any breathing room, although Trudeau and I began the session with some traditional gentle sparring after I was introduced as a rookie member of the Commons on September 12.

"The honourable member for Central Nova has come a long way from that log cabin in Pictou County," Trudeau said. "I see that he has put away his rumpled trousers and old sweaters, to be brought out again at the next election. In the meantime it is nice for us in this chamber to be able to bask in the glow, in the benign smile of a man who sent such shivers of pleasure down the spines of the matrons all the way from Oyster Pond to Mushaboom."

The House roared with laughter as he continued. "I can assure the leader of the opposition that we all wish him good luck, good health, and, as they say in show business, 'break a leg.'"

The NDP's Ed Broadbent followed the prime minister. He zeroed in on my long association with Robert Cliche, a former leader of the NDP in Quebec. "I look forward in the days ahead in this chamber, hopefully even today, when the member for Central Nova will be just a wee bit more specific on some of his policy orientations," Ed said. "No doubt because of the little publicity he has had in recent weeks we have not had a detailed provision of his policy positions, but when he does reveal them, I hope we will begin to note the impact on his life of Robert Cliche. I shall watch with interest. And once more, I would like to say, very sincerely, as they say in Baie-Comeau, *bienvenue, bonne chance*, but perhaps not too much of the latter."

Then it was my turn. I wouldn't be truthful if I didn't admit that I was more than a little nervous. Within minutes of taking my seat, I had realized that all my previous speech-making experience hadn't prepared me for this forum. What confused me right away were the sounds of the House. I struggled with my earpiece – one channel is for amplification and one for translation – and all I could hear were MPs yelling and screaming around me.

The House of Commons is the grandest stage in the nation, and I was about to face off against a prime minister who had been in the job for most of the past fifteen years. As for Broadbent, he'd been a member since 1968 and was an excellent parliamentary performer. With a quick look up toward Mila in the gallery for luck and support, I rose to my feet.

"The prime minister has always been a man of great accomplishment and distinction," I said. "I was honoured by the thoughtfulness and the generosity of his words today. I wait with bated breath for tomorrow! But I want particularly to welcome the prime minister back from Greece and the cabinet back from Central Nova. I want you to know, prime minister, that during the summer, while you were otherwise occupied, it was a very pleasant summer for me. There was one untoward incident, only one. The Liberal candidate in Central Nova persistently referred to a candidate from Quebec who lived in a million-dollar house rent-free, and I defended you, sir, regularly. I rose to your defence with an alacrity that surprised even me. I was also delighted and interested to read in the weekend press, Madam Speaker, the fact that the prime minister announced he is not a quitter. I want you to know, sir, that we are behind you all the way."

Trudeau laughed as hard as anyone, thoroughly enjoying the good humour of the event.

The President of St. Francis Xavier University, the Reverend Greg MacKinnon, was in the gallery that day, and I delighted in pointing out to the House three people with StFX degrees: Pierre Trudeau, myself, and former finance minister Allan MacEachen, who was now the secretary of state for external affairs, after a disastrous stint at Finance.

"On behalf of the prime minister and myself, we want to say we did not study economics at StFX under [MacEachen, who had taught there]," I said, to shouts and laughter from all sides of the House. "I only mention that because the prime minister asked me to."

Then it was time to turn the tables on Broadbent. "Indeed," I said, facing the NDP leader, "on many occasions Judge Robert Cliche, a truly great Canadian, spoke well and eloquently with regard to the qualities of the honourable member, and with good reason. Judgment, as Robert Cliche used to say, was always so important. I want you to know that we Nova Scotians appreciate your judgment, sir, in taking your caucus down to Nova Scotia. It did my heart good to see the socialists spending $90 and $95 a day. And then, prime minister, they have the temerity to say things are not going well!"

Afterwards, the Ottawa media rated me the winner. Allan Fotheringham weighed in with a column headlined "Mulroney Outbarbs PM during Commons Debut." "Mulroney a Big Hit in Commons Debut," read another report. "Mulroney was a quick study in theatrical terms," Tom Van Dusen later wrote. "It didn't take long for him to get the mood and the swing of the House, to realize it was much like hockey, a game he'd been good at. The trick was to keep hold of the puck. The same applied in the House, the puck being the issue at stake."

The day after I entered the Commons, I found out that the first puck Trudeau would fire at me was the language issue in Manitoba. Like others before me, I also discovered that Pierre Trudeau held his elbows high when he went into the corner.

On September 13, Manitoba Liberal MP Robert Bockstael stood and asked Trudeau a question. "The Government of Manitoba is proposing to amend Section 23 of the *Manitoba Act* of 1870, which will partly reinstate the status of the [French language] in Manitoba, and so provide certain provincial government services in the French language," he said in opening. "Given the controversy surrounding this proposal, and the extremism and hostility which have characterized much of the reaction exhibited by the official [PC] opposition in Manitoba in the past few weeks, does the federal government intend to reinforce its support for the amendment as introduced? And if so, in what manner?"

Before Bockstael had even finished his first sentence, I knew exactly what was going on. As the backbench Grit read out what clearly had been prepared for him, I could see Lloyd Axworthy smirking. After a lifetime of watching the Liberals, I knew instinctively they were laying a trap for me on my second day in the Commons.

"I am at a loss as of now as to what the best approach would be," Trudeau replied innocently. "I am thinking of perhaps proposing a resolution which could be sponsored jointly by the leader of the opposition and myself, or by the leader of the NDP, in which this House would enjoin the Legislature of Manitoba to rethink the opposition which is mounting against this very progressive and, I must say, very Canadian legislation. However, I have not yet raised it with the leader of the opposition. I probably will seek an appointment with him within a few days to see if there can be some progress in this regard."

I was up and on my feet facing the prime minister so quickly that an unnamed Tory MP later muttered, "I think he might have held off a bit" to a journalist. I could see Liberal MPs laughing and congratulating each other as I began my remarks. As the leader of Canada's Progressive Conservative Party, and as a Quebecer, I proudly told Trudeau that my office door was always open when it came to nonpartisan discussions concerning such a crucial issue.

"I would be delighted to prepare immediately for a meeting on a subject he would like to see handled with generosity and respect," I said, also adding that Broadbent should be included. "The question therefore is, when the prime minister would like to see us so that we can receive him in a manner appropriate to the circumstances."

Trudeau appeared to backtrack slightly, wondering aloud whether I would prefer a bilateral approach whereby I would speak with Manitoba's provincial Tories. I wasn't going to fall for that one and had already planned my next move.

"Do we have an appointment for tomorrow afternoon?" I asked. "If so, I will be delighted to attend, at his convenience."

There was no way I was going to allow the Liberals to split our party, hiving off sixteen Conservative MPs to stand on the wrong side of the official languages issue. This had happened under Stanfield, with even John Diefenbaker and Don Mazankowski voting against the *Official Languages Act* in 1969. If I allowed that split, I knew the Liberals could then campaign in the next election by making the case that if the new Tory leader couldn't even hold his own caucus together on the sensitive issue of language in Canada, how could he keep the country together? It was a tried and true Liberal tactic. There was only one problem: I wasn't going to be caught.

Trudeau saw the trap I had in turn begun to lay for him, and so continued to try to sow division between our party in Ottawa and its provincial cousins in Manitoba.

"Once again, if the leader of the opposition can get better results by talking to his friends in Manitoba, I am perfectly willing to withdraw the resolution," he said. "Perhaps the best thing would be for him to convince Mr. Sterling Lyon and others who are opposed to this measure to take a broader view and see the importance to Canada and its future of entrenching the agreement that was concluded several months ago."

Because this tactic had been so successful in the past, the Liberals were very pleased with themselves. With his habitual supercilious and erroneous interpretation of events, Roy MacLaren, a junior cabinet minister, wrote the following diary entry about me that night, which he later included in his memoirs. "All grins, mellifluous intonations and bluster, he made the error of asking the PM about language rights in Manitoba. With his left hand, Trudeau casually skewered Mulroney, merely inviting him in turn to co-sponsor a resolution setting forth their 'common position.' Mulroney flummoxed. Blurts out that he will meet the PM. Consternation behind him as the bigots from Manitoba begin to realize to what their new leader is committing their party."

The media followed that lead. John Gray of the *Globe and Mail* wrote that the Liberals had set a trap for me big enough to catch an elephant in. But I already knew – whatever the diarists, reporters, and columnists might write – that I wouldn't be taking the bait.

I assembled the caucus as quickly as possible. Behind closed doors, I told them bluntly what was going on. This Manitoba resolution, I explained, had absolutely nothing to do with the well-being of Franco-Manitobans. Trudeau had had many opportunities in the past, especially during the recent constitutional negotiations, to help them, and he didn't lift a finger. So, I asked the caucus, if his resolution isn't about Franco-Manitobans, what is it about?

I told them what I knew to be true: "It is based on the assumption that each and every one of you is stupid enough not to recognize what is going on, and that some of you will vote against this, thereby splitting the party and holding us up to the accusation that if we can't govern ourselves, we can't govern Canada. If we don't stand united in support of Franco-Manitobans, the next Liberal accusation will be that you won't stand up for Anglo-Quebecers and the French speakers of New Brunswick." I reminded them that we were all tired of losing and wanted to be winners.

As I looked out over the caucus, I could sense that my message was sinking in. Using the saltiest of language, I told my MPs to keep their mouths shut. The media, I warned them, were waiting outside to ambush each and every Tory MP. All it would take was one anti-French comment from any of them, just one, and eight-column headlines would trumpet the remark in newspapers from coast to coast the next day. They kept their mouths shut.

The next day, as planned, I met with Trudeau in the Prime Minister's Office. Afterwards, I made a note to file about the conversation:

> The PM said he was "relentless" in this area. He feels that [Manitoba NDP] Premier Pawley had backed away from his undertaking, and he wants to "steel him up." . . . His further concern is how this issue is being perceived in Quebec if Lévesque is allowed to say, well, hell, I can get away with anything on language, look what they are doing in Manitoba. I told him I stood where Stanfield and Clark stood on this issue . . . He is concerned about Quebec – concerned it may impact in favour of the PQ. I shared his concern . . . I said I believed that this issue is so delicate and sensitive it ought never to be politicized – certainly not for partisan gain. PM said he would not say anything to the press or in the House until he communicated with Pawley, Broadbent, and me. I referred to the fact he had chosen, presumably, not to go this route during the constitutional debate in regard to Section 133 of the Charter and Ontario. Why not, inasmuch as he now proposed to act in Manitoba? No answer.

After that first meeting with the prime minister, I knew what I had to do: lay down the law to caucus. The way to prevent division in my party and do right by the country was to support the resolution. Unanimously. And move on. Not all my MPs were happy. Manitoba's Dan McKenzie, one of our most fervent right wingers and a foe of bilingualism, came to see me in private. He had, I knew, voted for me at the convention. "I bring you bad news," he said. "Despite your remarks to caucus, Mr. Leader, we won't be unanimous. I know of one person at least who is going to vote against this."

I looked him straight in the eye as I gave him my response. "That's too bad," I said, "because that would break the unanimity we require at this time and on this issue, and might keep us from taking office. To ensure this won't happen, I will personally expel from caucus any of my members who propose to vote against the resolution."

The blood drained from Dan's face. "I'm going to go see that son of a bitch right now and deal with him," he said, before quickly departing. I suspect that Dan went home, looked in the mirror, and dealt with the MP in question.

I met again with Trudeau on September 23. Looking around the office, I noticed that he had two pictures prominently featured: one of his beautiful young children and the other a portrait of Sir Wilfrid Laurier. Perhaps recalling my research for my thesis in 1959, I couldn't resist commenting upon the irony of the situation. Laurier, the man Trudeau honoured in his private office, was in fact the Liberal prime minister who had sold out Franco-Manitobans in the 1890s during the schools issue. "Had Sir Wilfrid done what was right, prime minister," I said, "you, as today's leader of the Liberal Party, wouldn't be asking me, as the leader of the Progressive Conservative Party, to help you out on this matter."

Trudeau sat back, reflected on my words, and then produced a thoughtful review of the Manitoba language situation and his party's role in the past. I dictated a memo to file about our discussions as soon as I arrived back at my office. I wrote: "Trudeau indicated in unequivocal terms that 'it shall never be said of me, as it was of Laurier, that I left a language minority unprotected.' I referred him to my own record in this regard, and he readily acknowledged its excellence. He, in his analysis, did not spare the Liberal Party. He clearly holds the Liberals responsible for the betrayal of Franco-Manitobans. He went out of his way, for example. to indicate that Laurier and [nineteenth-century Manitoba premier Thomas] Greenway had long traditions with the Liberal Party and referred to [Clifford] Sifton as 'a Liberal who had opened the floodgates in western Canada to ensure the French minority would drown.'"

We met again on October 4. Ed Broadbent was also there. Faced with a reflective Pierre Trudeau that day, I sprang my own trap. While I recognized that he had some legitimate concerns – especially regarding the anger and hostility toward Franco-Manitobans that Sterling Lyon and his colleagues had used this issue to unleash – I told Trudeau that the manner in which he had thrust this issue upon the House had politicized it.

"If you want our support, here are some terms and conditions," I said.

I demanded that there be no recorded vote when the Manitoba resolution came before the House. Broadbent agreed with my approach. I would speak for my party and vote on behalf of all of them, and Broadbent and Trudeau would do the same. To his credit, after first trying to play partisan politics with the very unity of the country, Trudeau agreed with the plan. In my party, those Manitoba MPs facing political Armageddon in their ridings because of the issue wouldn't have to take a personal stand. They could remain quiet and save face. It would be up to me to help heal the wounds in their constituencies.

I again made a note to file: "I indicated that while I had no assurance of unanimity of support from my caucus, it was my sense that caucus would overwhelmingly support such a resolution, if it were satisfied that none of us was seeking to take political advantage of the situation."

Because Stornoway wasn't ready for the family, Speaker Jeanne Sauvé had graciously allowed us to stay at her official residence at Kingsmere, the former home of Mackenzie King, and where the wily Grit prime minister had died in 1950. While I never saw his ghost during the weeks we stayed there, I definitely felt his presence as I sat down to write, by hand, the speech on the Manitoba resolution I was to deliver on October 6. The irony again was striking: here was the leader of the PC Party – the successor to Arthur Meighen, R.B. Bennett, Robert Manion, John Bracken, and George Drew, all Tory leaders King had vanquished, thanks in large part to their inability to come to terms with the legitimate aspirations of French Canadians – sitting in King's own home preparing an address that could help reverse that chapter in Tory history. King, after all, regarded himself as the principal architect of Canadian unity, a role that he believed no Conservative could or should ever hold.

Writing the speech was not a difficult task, as the words came naturally. I walked into the office when I was happy with my notes and asked my assistant, Ginette, to type them up. I was ready for what I knew would be a major event in the House, and possibly a turning point in our history.

In the House, Prime Minister Trudeau spoke first, laying before the members and the country an impressive case for the passage of the resolution. Whatever was to come between us later, I have to say today that it was a remarkable parliamentary performance. "I should like to say, not without emotion, that it is perhaps the most important day of my life as a parliamentarian," Trudeau said. "For by the resolution which is before the House, we in this chamber are called upon to do two things: first, to ensure that the Constitution will be obeyed; second, to right a wrong."

Despite his earlier attempts to cast a partisan cloud over the issue, I was pleased that Trudeau quoted from Sir John A. Macdonald to make his case. Canada's first prime minister had spoken in the Commons in February of 1890 during the debate on a resolution calling for the abolition of the status of the French language in western Canada.

"'I have no accord with the desire expressed in some quarters that by any mode whatever there should be an attempt made to oppress the one language or to render it inferior to the other; I believe that it would be impossible if it were tried, and it would be foolish and wicked if it were possible.' So spake Sir John A. Macdonald," Trudeau said, to cheers from all sides of the Commons.

When the prime minister had concluded, I rose to my feet and addressed the silent House. Not a seat was empty, either on the floor or in the galleries above me. Like Trudeau, I could feel the presence of those who had gone before us and debated this issue – so fundamentally important to who and what we are as a people – in the historic chamber. While our speeches that day dealt with the past and the currents that run through Canadian history, I also looked to the future and sought to heal the present.

> I speak today on a resolution of consequence before this House. I do so with pride and in the genuine hope that our action will be helpful to our fellow Canadians in Manitoba as they search for an equitable solution to a problem that has troubled the soul of this nation for over one hundred years . . .
>
> This resolution compels us to remember our overriding commitments in this country of almost limitless space, overflowing with great opportunities for the future. These commitments comprise a respect for our linguistic and other minorities, a long-held desire to encourage their flowering, and the duty to protect the rights of our minorities – wherever they are . . .
>
> Thus we have today the occasion to state our position on this question here in the House of Commons. By this resolution before us, we are asked to make a gesture. The significance and the impact of this action relate first and foremost to profoundly human values, values which define to a large degree the kind of generosity of spirit typical of Canadian society. It is with pride today, I pledge, in the name of my colleagues in the Progressive Conservative Party, our unanimous support for the resolution which is before this House.
>
> Years ago this House approved the principle of official bilingualism for Canada. Simply put, it means that English and French Canadians shall have equal rights and equal opportunities across Canada. It is a noble principle, one which is capable of enriching the life of this nation. By our stand today we reaffirm our commitment

> and that of our party given earlier in the same House of Commons by outstanding and distinguished Canadians such as the Honourable Robert Stanfield and the Right Honourable Member for Yellowhead [Joe Clark] . . .
>
> The issue before us today is also one of simple justice. There is no painless way to proceed. There is no blame to be apportioned. There are no motives to be impugned. There is only the sanctity of minority rights. There is no obligation more compelling and no duty more irresistible in Canada than to ensure that our minorities, linguistic and otherwise, live at all times in conditions of fairness and justice.
>
> The Manitoba members of Parliament in our caucus, along with many Manitobans at home, have been deeply troubled by this issue. I have shared with them their moments of anguish, but they have responded with courage and with respect. In a great unifying gesture to all of Canada, they stand with me and our party today in a historic and unforgettable endorsement of a fundamental tenet of this nation.
>
> My friend Robert Cliche was a great humanist who sought, at all times, conciliation, the right approach, respect for the common man whose rights have been abused. He often quoted Félix-Antoine Savard who once wrote, "Happy are those men and those people who live together in unity." I believe, Madam Speaker, that with this resolution we have helped the process of reconciliation which must take place in Manitoba . . . This resolution is about fairness. It is about decency. It is an invitation for cooperation and understanding. It speaks to the finest qualities in this nation. I say to you on behalf of my entire party on this or any great issue that affects this nation that we stand before you, united in the sunlight, ready to work for a better Canada.

When I took my seat, I was mobbed as Tory MPs and those from other parties offered their congratulations. Ed Broadbent then spoke and he, too, rose to the occasion. "What we are doing today in unanimously supporting this resolution goes beyond support for the details of a particular bill in a single province on a given date," the NDP leader said. "We are now acting in the spirit of those who created Canada in 1867, who out of necessity and by imagination created our fundamental duality. We are supporting a spirit

With Mila on our honeymoon in Dubrovnik in 1973

Many years later, in 1986, with my father-in-law, Dr. Dimitrije Pivnicki, and a cheerful crowd of supporters

On the bench at the Commission alongside Robert Cliche

Mila, Ben, me, and Caroline

As president of the Iron Ore Company of Canada

At IOC I enjoyed the chance to travel to places like China . . .

. . . and to places like the IOC camps in the North, to fish with friends Sam Wakim and Ace McCann

Leading the St. Patrick's Day Parade in Montreal

On the leadership campaign trail with my mother and my sister Peggy in 1983

I always enjoyed campaigning

Among the crowds in Montreal

Mila and me campaigning

Leading the cheering at the convention

Speaking to the convention

Watching as the results are announced

Yes!

of tolerance and a respect for diversity which should always be the hallmark of Canada and Canadians. Never again should any Canadian say, 'I am a stranger in my own country.' And, with the collective leadership demonstrated by all Canada's national parties today, I am confident that in the future of our great land no Canadian ever again will have to say that."

The three party leaders met in the centre of the chamber for a handshake. Whatever our partisan backgrounds and regardless of the process that had brought us there, we were united, as Canadians, in a common cause: the building of a better Canada.

I left the Commons that day knowing that the party supported me completely, and knowing, absolutely, that we had done the right thing. As time went on, it became clear that my stand was increasingly seen as being about more than language. It was about leadership, and about how the country viewed a leader's handling of difficult national issues.

In caucus afterwards, I was treated like a conquering hero. There was a long ovation, and one of our MPs got up and announced to his colleagues, "We've just been to Politics 101 on Parliament Hill, and our leader has taken us over the mountain." The metaphor may have been mixed, but it was heady stuff for someone who had only been in the House a few weeks. Outside the caucus room, and in Quebec especially, Canadians were taking the measure of a new man, a new caucus, and a new party.

On October 30, Mila and I attended a Quebec City fundraiser that attracted more than a thousand people. Robert McKenzie of the *Toronto Star* covered the event. "Without ever actually naming Riel – the Métis leader hanged in 1885 despite the pleas of French-Canadian nationalists to the Conservative government of Sir John A. Macdonald – Mulroney made it clear he thinks a page had been turned for Conservatives in French Canada," McKenzie observed. "He compared the Manitoba bilingualism issue to a mortgage that had held down the Conservative Party for 100 years and told the audience, 'I am before you tonight here in the heart of French Canada to tell you that we have finally paid that debt and now we can get on with something else – the election of a Conservative government.'"

Having successfully avoided falling into the Liberal trap on the Manitoba language issue, I decided it was time our party returned the favour. I sensed we were faced with an increasingly tired government whose instincts were sometimes dulled by their lengthy period in office, and with an increasingly distracted prime minister. Despite their much-vaunted skills in achieving and holding power – and the presence of 74 MPs from Quebec in their caucus – the Grits were asleep at the switch when it came to Bill S-31, which came out of the Senate that fall.

In a nutshell, the bill was designed to prevent Quebec's massive pension fund, the Caisse de dépôt et placement du Québec, from buying more than a 10 per cent share in Canadian Pacific. The Caisse was an invention of Premier Jean Lesage in the 1960s and it is still one of the most popular creations of any Quebec government. It also stands as a powerful symbol of French-Canadian pride and promise. Not only does it fund the pensions relied on by millions of Quebecers, it also allows the province's entrepreneurial class to acquire the positions of ownership they had been denied for decades by the chartered banks. By contrast, Canadian Pacific, fairly or unfairly, was considered one of the last remaining symbols of the days when French Canadians were shut out of their own business community's decision-making apparatus and profits, and in some quarters was viewed as a reactionary symbol of the anti-French establishment.

How the Grits didn't see this shaping up as a public relations disaster I'll never understand. We knew they were vulnerable and that S-31 was a sleeper issue just waiting to be exploited. I sat down for a strategy session on the bill with Roch La Salle and Joe Clark (the only two other members of our caucus who could ask full questions in French). The government minister responsible for the file was Judy Erola, a unilingual anglophone from Sudbury.

Our caucus bided its time, and Trudeau himself helped to further our strategy when his office announced he'd be leaving the country to embark on a peace mission abroad, and would be away from the Commons in early November. The prime minister's absence meant that all we had to do was wait for a Thursday-afternoon question period. If we began our assault on a Thursday, toward the end of the parliamentary week, it would be almost a week before the Liberal caucus would assemble again – minus their leader. If things went the way I thought they might, it would prove to be quite a caucus, and the Liberals would be in terrible trouble with the public.

I fired the opening salvo against S-31 on November 18. While I directed my questions in French to Deputy Prime Minister Allan MacEachen (who spoke only English), Judy Erola ended up answering them.

"Could the acting prime minister today give millions of Quebecers whose pension funds are administered by the Caisse the assurance that this vital instrument will not be prevented from proceeding legitimately in investing the assets of our taxpayers in Canada?" I thundered.

Joe and Roch continued the assault, making it clear to the Quebec audience just what was at stake for them. The optics were terrific. Here were Tories asking questions of federal ministers in French while the Grits, who owned Quebec on the federal scene, were replying in English only. How the tables had turned! The French-speaking members of the Parliamentary Press Gallery quickly perked up. By that evening, the story began to dominate in the Quebec media. We were on a bit of a roll.

On November 21, Erola's parliamentary secretary, Montreal MP David Berger, was the one on his feet to answer our continued attack, although I had addressed the question to the minister. There was a rowdy atmosphere in the House that day as Berger tried his best to respond. I waited for the right moment. Then, in a voice dripping with sarcasm and scorn, I said, "I want to hear it from the organ grinder, not the monkey." The Liberals erupted with indignation and the rest of the House burst into open laughter.

Joe was superb as he went after the Liberals. I knew he was really scoring hits when I questioned Erola again on November 23. "I am terribly pleased," she said in response to one of my questions, "that we have the head organ grinder asking the question today." You know a parliamentarian is in trouble when she resorts to copying lines delivered by the opposition. As we suspected, the Liberal MPs were now in crisis. Their government was being pounded night after night on the news, and they were bleeding, badly, from the wounds we'd inflicted.

We knew this because before the S-31 assault began, Mila and I had toured several Quebec ridings in the Trois-Rivières area. In the 1980 election, our party had received less than 13 per cent of the vote in Quebec. I asked our people to poll these few ridings specifically during November, before and after we visited. Just as I expected, the party's defence of the Caisse, combined with Mila's and my visit, was bringing the numbers up. Four days after our S-31 plans had been launched, we were up to over 30 per cent, and we kept climbing.

Not surprisingly, the first demographic to respond were the owners of small and medium-sized businesses, *les petites et moyennes entreprises*. They depended on the Caisse for some of their financing. But more importantly, they clearly saw the Caisse as an instrument of pride for Quebecers, which the Liberals were seeking to diminish.

Soon after our visit to Quebec, the Liberals announced they would let the bill die on the order paper. The PCs had carried the day. Our S-31 campaign, combined with our stance on the Manitoba language issue, helped us plant the seeds of what was to be a historic crop of votes for our party in Quebec, and throughout French Canada, in 1984.

The Liberals, however, still weren't done with us that fall. Having failed to divide us on the Manitoba language issue in September and October, then after flubbing S-31 in November, they threw the medicare grenade into our midst in December. The reforms to medicare proposed by Health Minister Monique Bégin in the Canada Health Act included a ban on extra-billing by doctors.

Doctors, who are essentially small business owners, were traditionally among our party's strongest supporters. The Liberals figured that we'd revert to our old ways and implode on this issue, to find ourselves yet again on the wrong side of a key public issue. To be sure, extra-billing was a live grenade for us.

As I went into caucus to discuss the matter with my troops, I figured it was time to share with them a page of history. With Bégin and the Liberals wrapping themselves in the medicare flag and telling all and sundry that the Liberal Party had created Canada's most precious social program, the Tory caucus needed a good pep talk. I reminded them that we had passed the first Liberal "stupidity test" on Manitoba. Now, they thought we were stupid enough to vote against the Canada Health Act, with an election about to be called.

"Medicare is a Conservative creation," I told the caucus. "Prime Minister John Diefenbaker appointed a royal commission to study health insurance in Canada, and he appointed a great jurist from Saskatchewan to chair the commission, Mr. Justice Emmett Hall of the Supreme Court of Canada. The Hall Commission then laid out the scope and imperatives of what was to become medicare. This was done by two Conservatives from the West who were law partners."

I reminded my members, most of whom were viscerally in favour of a free market, of the tough position the party was in. "In the short time we have," I explained, "we can't propose amendments to this bill. We have to endorse it the way it is. Then, when we become the government and we want to change something, we will."

And so, in April of 1984, our caucus voted unanimously in favour of the bill. While that action surprised many commentators and even some members of my party, it was senior Liberals who were the most shocked. Their latest ploy had fizzled completely. Don Johnston, who at that time was Liberal minister of state for economic and regional expansion, later described that day in his 1986 memoirs, *Up the Hill*. "It was a historic moment," he wrote. "Conservative free market doctrine dictated that they support doctors in charging over and above the fee set by medicare. They had argued long and battled hard in committee against the bill. The Speaker called the House to order and the poll of members began. A strange scene unfolded. Not only were Liberals and, predictably, the NDP, voting yes but one by one every Tory in the House, including Brian Mulroney, the Leader of the Opposition, was voting yes too. Many of our members were incredulous . . . When the final vote was counted, not a single Tory had voted no." Another Liberal election weapon had been thrown on the scrap heap.

We Tories were far from perfect in opposition. While I quickly gained confidence in the ways and means of parliamentary debate, I had my share of slip-ups and mistakes. In September of 1983, for example, I went after Lloyd Axworthy, demanding that he ensure that Atlantic freight subsidies be maintained. Axworthy grinned delightedly and stated he had made that exact announcement in New Brunswick earlier in the day. I looked foolish and I could only blame myself. I resolved that an episode like this would never happen again.

As we headed into 1984 I had a personal matter to attend to: my smoking. While I'm loath to do this, I have to commend Marc Lalonde's role in my finally giving up the weed. While he was health minister in the 1970s, Lalonde and his department spearheaded the production of television commercials that showed Canadian viewers the health risks faced by those who continued to smoke. While I had ignored the ads and kept on smoking, my children were watching them.

I was addicted. In the same league as René Lévesque, I smoked like a Trojan; I couldn't even get through question period without disappearing behind the curtains for a puff. Outside the chamber, I was now in public view most of the time, and the habit wasn't helping my image. At official dinners I'd be seated at the head table, smoking away. Sometimes I said that I was expecting an important call but instead slipped into the leader of the opposition's car for a quick nicotine fix.

At home, Caroline, Ben, and Mark began to warn me that I was endangering my health and their futures. While I had ignored Lalonde, I couldn't ignore my kids. "Daddy," four-year-old Mark said to me one day, "you're going to die. What am I going to do then?"

One night in February, during a trip to Florida, Mila and I were having dinner with Charles Bronfman and his wife, Andy, at their home. It was a smoker's paradise as we sat at the table; Charles smoked a pipe, Andy and I smoked cigarettes, and even Mila, an infrequent social smoker, was partaking. There was smoke everywhere. When I got up the next morning, my chest hurt and I was nearly sick because I had smoked so much the night before.

Mila returned to Canada on her own because she had to deliver a speech in New Brunswick. Alone in the house, I threw out all my cigarettes, and got a supply of Nicorette gum to help curb my cravings. I didn't tell anybody that I was trying to quit smoking for fear that I wouldn't be successful. Soon, however, some of my staff noticed. One decided to leak the story to the papers that I was no longer smoking. Soon I was inundated with letters of support and congratulations from across Canada. Even a group of journalists from CBC Radio wrote to share their own experiences in quitting smoking and to applaud my move. I was now trapped. I couldn't light up again even if I wanted to – which I sure did, as any recovering smoker will tell you.

Later, as prime minister, I introduced one of the first and most comprehensive antismoking laws in western industrialized countries. Still, I retain sympathy for smokers as I watch attitudes harden against them. "Go easy on smokers," I blurted out to my caucus one day. "I'm just a single puff away from being one myself."

When Ed Broadbent's lovely wife, Lucille, was trying to rid herself of the habit, I arranged for a supply of Nicorette gum to be delivered to their Ottawa home. As you can see, battling cigarettes was becoming a unifying matter for Canadians of all parties. After the 1984 election I received many letters of congratulations. NDP strategist Gerald Caplan sent me a memorable one. A former smoker, he noted that the truly historic part of my party's winning 211 seats was the fact that the leader went through a whole campaign without starting to smoke again!

2. Exit Trudeau, Enter Turner

PIERRE TRUDEAU CHOSE the last day of February 1984 to announce that he was stepping down as prime minister and Liberal Party leader. The decision didn't surprise me. Mila and I had met him privately when we, along with Premier Bill Davis, his wife, Kathy, and others, attended a New Year's celebration at Paul Desmarais's splendid new home in Florida over the holidays. That night it was clear to me that he would soon depart. My party was soaring in the polls – Gallup had us at 56 per cent, with the Liberals trailing at 27 per cent in a poll published on December 1 – and I knew he wouldn't want to risk another election defeat. It was also clear to me that John Turner would be his successor, and that the PCs would be up against a new prime minister when the election was called.

I flew home from Florida the day after Trudeau's announcement. Ed Broadbent was on the same plane, also returning from the sun to face a changed political situation. When scrummed by reporters at Dorval Airport, I gave my response to the resignation, telling the press that Trudeau was an "extraordinary asset" for the Liberal Party. "He stands head and shoulders above anyone else in the Liberal Party . . . and clearly he's going to be missed," I said.

With Trudeau's resignation now announced, I and my closest advisors sat down and made an important strategic decision, the success of which became apparent once the 1984 federal election was under way. We knew that the big national media would quite understandably be preoccupied with the Liberal leadership race. With this reality in mind, we decided to replicate what had worked so well for me in the leadership race, and came up with what we called the "boonies strategy." We decided that Mila and I would spend most of our time on the road, four or five days out of each week, and cover the nonurban areas of the country. And travel we did. Between early April 1984 and the Liberal convention in June, we travelled 25,000 air miles, and were on the road for forty out of sixty-seven days, visiting fifty-four different cities and towns in eight provinces. To name just a few of the communities, there were trips to Newcastle, Bathurst, New Glasgow, Pictou, Surrey, Montague, Summerside, Val-Bélair, Shannon, Granby, Trois-Rivières, Ste-Foy, Timmins, Thorold, Chatham, Sturgeon Falls, Earlton, New Liskeard, Morden, Winnipeg, Calgary, Kamloops, Salmon Arm, Castlegar, Trail, and Cranbrook.

We met candidates and their organizers privately, and spent time building organizations and relationships, and developing our links and strengths, within these areas. Local mayors, teachers, and other community leaders joined our team. While there were few headlines in the national press, the regional media covered our trips extensively, and the local people noted and appreciated our visits. I was at Stornoway the day after the Liberal convention ended and I was startled as I watched myself lead the national news. It had been the first time in months I'd led any story in the media.

With the Liberal leadership hopefuls dominating the headlines, it came as no surprise to me that our numbers began to drop. Just over a month after Trudeau's announcement, Gallup had the Liberals ahead of us by five points. By the time John Turner had been elected leader, Gallup had them at 49 per cent and us at 38 per cent. Remembering that a month after our own convention we had shot up to 55 per cent with the Liberals at 27 per cent, I felt there was no need to panic.

Unfortunately, not all of the members of our caucus shared my view. As the Grit leadership race continued that spring, many of my MPs were close to panic. As I made my notes in caucus on April 30, preparing for my summation, which closed all our meetings, I heard yet another member take to his feet and express his fears. "[The voters are] going to change," I wrote and later said, "because we're going to persuade them to change. Because I'm going to knock the bejesus out of Turner/Chrétien. . . . Their support is two inches wide, ours is two feet deep. Hold our 80 seats, win 40 more? Liberal theory of leadership: no matter what you do, all will be forgiven if you change leaders prior to an election. 1) Doesn't say much for Canadian people. 2) Doesn't say much for us as politicians." I made a similar note during a caucus meeting on June 6 as yet another MP said he was anxious about losing his seat. "You sound just like a goddamned Tory," I wrote, "panicking at the first sight of bad news. If you don't like the numbers you can get the hell out." That was the end of that.

During the same period, MP Patrick Nowlan took to his feet in caucus and said that the tours Mila and I were taking were having a negative effect and that our numbers would drop in areas we visited. When I was about to respond, Alberta MP Steve Paproski beat me to it. "Pat, I joined this caucus in 1968," he said, to cheers and laughter. "You were an asshole then and you're an asshole today." There was nothing I could add.

During our few trips into major metropolitan areas, Mila, fluent in Serbo-Croatian as well as in French and English, helped me to reach out to ethnic groups that had never been courted by our party before. Like all Canadians, they wanted to hear our plans, and we found the Italians of Toronto and Montreal, the Asian communities in the West, and many other multicultural groups and leaders as eager as we were for a change in Ottawa.

I also made a special point of highlighting women's issues as we prepared our platform. Our caucus again retreated to Mont Ste-Marie in April, and in my summation I singled out the work of Kingston and the Islands MP Flora MacDonald. Also I had a warning for those Tories who were disparaging our efforts in this crucial segment of the Canadian electorate:

> No one in this country has done more to promote genuine equality than Flora. But she cannot do it alone. She needs our understanding and enthusiastic support. She needs us all speaking out in a major way on women's issues and social issues. By helping Flora, we are simply helping ourselves. Mila says she has never seen anyone induce more affection from an audience than Flora. Mila's no slouch herself so I think it's a great compliment. Fifty-two per cent of the population will be watching our actions in this sensitive area . . . Yesterday, another leading columnist wrote that the Conservative Party has never in its history made firmer and more realistic commitments to equality for women. A number of people, including a few in this party, seem to take unusual pleasure in talking about gender gaps and saying that, under my leadership, this party is backsliding from its commitments to women's equality. To say these statements have been unhelpful to our cause is to seriously understate the case.

During this period, there was continued unrest in Manitoba over language rights. Once again, there was a chance Conservatives would divide over the issue. Some of the statements coming from provincial Tories there were – in a word – atrocious. Another parliamentary resolution in Ottawa was proposed, and Trudeau and I spoke about it on the telephone shortly before his resignation announcement. Later, Broadbent, Trudeau, and I agreed on another resolution in support of francophone rights, which was debated in the House on February 24. I spoke to the resolution as follows:

> Mr. Speaker, today my thoughts are with that small group of people in Manitoba, isolated from Quebec and New Brunswick and Ontario where millions of their fellow French Canadians live in increasingly beneficial cultural, linguistic, and economic surroundings. I think of them and I salute them for their dignity and courage. On behalf of my party today, I feel genuinely honoured to assist in a process that begins to repair a grievance and historic wrong. I think as well of the other Manitobans whose vision of Canada, formed and shaped in circumstances different than mine, might make it difficult for them to understand or accept what I have said. I say to them now how deeply I regret the unsettling events of the past few months. Although we have disagreed on this fundamental issue, I know that Manitobans have been motivated by a different historical perspective of our nation and not by a sense of malice.
>
> I invite Manitobans, as Canadians, to bind up the wounds and to deal properly with the question of minority language rights. There can be no doubt where I stand. There can be no question as to where the obligation of a national political party lies. It lies today, as it shall tomorrow, in ensuring that our minorities in Canada are treated at all times with dignity and with justice.

While I spoke, Pierre Trudeau sat with his head bowed, nodding in agreement. While *Globe and Mail* columnist Jeffrey Simpson was to label my speech as "superb," I was more touched by the comments I received from my fellow members of Parliament. Franco-Ontarian Liberal MP Gib Parent sent a note across the floor. "Brian: As a Canadian I salute you," it said. One of my own MPs wrote, "I cannot recall another moment in my life when I have been so moved emotionally, and when I was so proud of being a Canadian, as when you addressed the House of Commons today on French rights in Manitoba. Surely, 99 per cent of our caucus can now walk with heads held high."

In March I made a decision that would prove to be a major turning point in my political life. I agreed to attend a public meeting in Winnipeg, where I resolved to make a pitch for national unity and minority protection the way Sir John A. would have. To say the atmosphere was tense is to understate the situation. "Mulroney set for Manitoba event," a *Toronto Sun* column was headlined the day of my speech. "Will he get French fried?"

Within the party in Manitoba, the anti-French anger was palpable – and very public. One federal Tory riding association, Portage-Marquette, put their fundraising on hold because of my stance, attempting to force me to change my position. "Thursday night is going to make him or break him in Manitoba," riding president Doug Edmondson told the press. "He would slice off five seats [in Manitoba] to get five in Quebec."

In an eerie precursor of what was to come during the Meech Lake debate, the provincial Tory leader, Gary Filmon, chose to put local politics ahead of the national interest. To avoid the controversy, he refused to cut short a vacation to meet his party's federal leader and to hear my case, in person.

There were upwards of two thousand people in the hall when I took the stage in Winnipeg on March 29. I have addressed hostile audiences in the years since, but nothing to match the anger from the crowd I faced that night. I was booed when I spoke a sentence in French. One man bellowed, "You're a lousy Frenchman," while another shouted out that my name was "Brian Trudeau." A placard that read "Brian, it's our way or the doorway" was hoisted in the air as I spoke.

The first few rows were occupied by former premier Sterling Lyon and other Tory MLAs who had led the delaying tactics against the moderate bill restoring some francophone rights. Their actions had caused the NDP government of Howard Pawley to allow the bill to die on the order paper. I stared at each and every one of them in turn as I spoke. "I stand before you tonight where the founder of this party Sir John A. Macdonald and his Conservative government stood in 1870 when the *Manitoba Act* was passed, ensuring linguistic equality in the new province of Manitoba," I shouted above the rising boos.

"It is my fundamental belief, as it was his, that real national unity will never be achieved until French-speaking Canadians living outside Quebec enjoy no less rights than English-speaking Canadians in my native province. That was Macdonald's message one hundred and fourteen years ago . . . It is my message tonight . . . The goal of language guarantees is not to make all Canadians bilingual – to force people to become something they are not. The purpose of language guarantees is to ensure that English- and

French-speaking Canadians can be themselves, that they can live their lives, communicate with their governments and with each other in one or the other of Canada's two official languages."

I tried to extend the hand of understanding to the group, agreeing that bilingualism had to be implemented in western Canada in a manner that took into account the distinct multicultural makeup of those provinces. I also assured the group that I had no intention of telling them from Ottawa how to run their provinces. I only asked them to reflect upon their actions in the pan-Canadian context. "You may disagree with me, my friends, for having come down on one side of the issue," I said. "But you would have had no respect for me if I had tried to come down on both sides."

Most people in the country saw my Winnipeg speech as an expression of leadership. Not only would the new Tory leader defend minority rights in the House of Commons, he'd march right into the lion's den and take on opponents of his vision. The message was clear. I wasn't going to be intimidated by anybody when it came to protecting minority rights in Canada.

"Mulroney sticks to his guns on language," the *Winnipeg Free Press* reported the next day. "Mulroney doesn't back down on stand for Manitoba French," another story in the *Toronto Star* was headlined. I had made my point. Politics isn't always about polls. Leadership is what truly counts. Offer it to citizens and they'll vote for you every time.

Three weeks before that speech, John Turner had entered the Liberal leadership race – and promptly landed on the wrong side of this important national issue. Rusty from his years on Bay Street, John handed me just the opportunity I was looking for, on his very first day back in the political arena.

"On the Manitoba question," he said, "I support the spirit of the parliamentary resolution, but I think we have to recognize that what is at issue here is a provincial initiative, and that a solution will have to be provincial. And I would hope that it would be solved by the political process and not by the judicial process."

It should be no surprise to anyone that I pounced on the remarks, particularly when dealing with Quebec journalists and audiences. "When Mr. Turner announced his candidacy he was asked what set him apart from Mr. Mulroney and he said, 'Why, my experience,'" I said in one interview. "And if by experience you mean declaring your candidacy on Friday, disavowing positions in regard to protection of minority rights on Saturday, repudiating decades of Liberal policy by Monday, reversing yourself by

Tuesday, and swallowing yourself whole by Thursday – if that's experience, I'll have none of it."

As June got closer, I began to make preparations for a two-day trip to Washington to visit President Reagan, American cabinet secretaries, and various members of the House of Representatives and Senate. My advisors were nervous. "There is too much danger in being associated with Reagan – Reaganomics north. . . . The maximum benefit for you and the party comes from activities in Canada," members of the party's tour scheduling group, chaired by Harry Near, wrote to me in March.

While I was sensitive to their concerns, the group didn't fully comprehend what I hoped my visit to Washington would accomplish. After months of my absence from the national news and headlines, my trip would serve to knock the new Liberal prime minister, whoever that would be, off the front pages for three or four days right after the leadership convention. It would also enable me to press directly to President Reagan the concerns I had heard time and time again during my "boonies" tours. One such concern, especially in Ontario, was the need for Canada and the United States to come together to curb acid rain emissions. Conservative MP Stan Darling, from Muskoka, wrote to me just before I left for Washington: "I am hoping you will have the opportunity to bring up the acid rain problem which is facing our two countries. It is hoped you will receive some form of a commitment from Reagan and in return a commitment from the next government – a Conservative administration headed by you . . . This is a high-priority problem facing Canada, and we will be on the side of the angels if we get onside rather than letting the present government be seen as the saviours of the environment. To date they have done bugger all as far as legislation is concerned."

Stan continued to battle forcefully on behalf of his lake-filled constituency for action on acid rain throughout our two terms in office. When President George H.W. Bush and I signed the acid rain agreement in the early 1990s, I made sure I gave Stan the pen the American president had used to affix his signature to the treaty. All Canadians owe a debt of gratitude to Stan Darling, one of the party's most effective MPs, for his tireless efforts over almost a decade to have our governments come to an agreement to combat this scourge that has done so much to harm our lakes, rivers, and streams. He was an excellent example of a hard-working local MP whose contributions on Parliament Hill in the end produce a great benefit to the country as a whole.

I met with President Reagan in the Oval Office on June 21, 1984. When we came into the historic room – built in 1909 for William Howard Taft, but moved to its present location for FDR in 1934 – I was immediately struck by how much smaller it was than I'd expected. I recognized Reagan's desk immediately. It was the same desk – the *Resolute* Desk, built from timbers from HMS *Resolute*, and presented to Rutherford B. Hayes by Queen Victoria as a mark of Anglo-American friendship – used by President John F. Kennedy twenty years earlier and often present in official photographs.

While Reagan and I traded jokes standing in the Oval Office, I happened to look down at the floor. If truth be known, I was looking for damage from Dwight Eisenhower's famous golf shoe spikes. I later found out that the floor had become so full of holes thanks to Ike that President Lyndon B. Johnson had replaced it with wood-grained linoleum! Reagan had become tired of the linoleum and hired the same contractors who had put in the flooring at his ranch home in California to install a white pine and oak floor in a wagon-wheel pattern. It definitely caught a visitor's attention. During a 2003 unofficial visit to the Oval Office to see President George W. Bush, I noticed that Bush had replaced this flooring once again, using almost the exact same pattern that Reagan had chosen.

During our forty-five-minute meeting, I pressed Reagan hard on acid rain, telling him that he could "capture the imaginations of all Canadians and Americans" if his country agreed, as ours had, to reduce acid rain emissions by 50 per cent over the next decade. With visits to Sault Ste. Marie, Ontario fresh on my mind, I then told Reagan, Vice-President Bush, and Secretary of State George Shultz that the bill currently before their Congress that would limit the amount of Canadian steel sold in the U.S. could kill five thousand Ontario jobs. This conversation about U.S. protectionism was one that I was destined to continue as prime minister.

Before I entered the Oval Office, Reagan and I posed for pictures in the Rose Garden. "What this continent needs is another Irishman," I quipped during the session. To my surprise, the president replied, "I agree" – thus running the danger of being accused by our ultrasensitive nationalists of interfering in Canadian affairs.

I took the case for Ontario's steel makers and workers directly to Secretary of Commerce Malcolm Baldridge by referring to the strength and durability of the relationship between our two countries. "I told the secretary that if I were president of the United States, I'd wake up in the morning and look at the disruptions around the world and I'd say, 'Thank God for

Canada,'" I reported to the press afterwards, when asked to describe our session. Baldridge had agreed, and he pledged that the steel legislation would not become law.

—

PERSONAL JOURNAL: JUNE 22, 1984

During the meeting yesterday I was struck by the president's remarkably youthful manner, his sense of humour, and strange to say, feeling of serenity. He seemed calm and composed, solicitous of others but very much in command. We discussed arms control negotiations, acid rain, steel imports, and methods of better managing our relationship. I had been told to expect that after a few comments others would take over the discussions on his behalf. The meeting lasted 40–45 minutes and he was the vigorous and lone American participant throughout. He was humorous and courteous throughout. He listened carefully and politely as I made pretty vigorous pleas on behalf of the Canadian position on issues. My impression was that if this were not an election year, responses to our views might be more prompt and accommodating. I dwelled at some length on the peace issue and said that Canadians would regard it as an indication of strength, not weakness, if he took further initiatives to induce and persuade the Soviets back to the bargaining table. He said that he had no response at all from the Soviets, however, and referred to a handwritten letter he had sent General Secretary Andropov from the hospital to which there had been no response. "I don't even know if they got it," he said. At the end of the meeting he said, "Brian, let me know if there is anything we can do. Don't go to Ireland again without me."

—

In a city where appearances are everything, Canadian Ambassador Allan Gotlieb pulled out all the stops and organized a glittering dinner party in my honour at the embassy. The American defense secretary, CIA director, and many other heavyweights attended. As Gotlieb later wrote in his memoirs, *The Washington Diaries*, "A night to be remembered. There was a sense of expectancy, a sense of excitement, a sense of being present at a special moment." Earlier in the book, he noted, "As the guests walked into the garden, Mulroney and I stood astride the garden door, and as I introduced them, Mulroney greeted each and every one with a few specially chosen words. He seemed to recognize virtually all of the guests, although they were, of course, strangers to him. He was carrying a mental file on everyone. It's as if he needed no introductions at all (another Lyndon Johnson in the making?). He and Mila made a brilliant impression. They dazzled the crowd." In a diary entry two days later, Gotlieb said it all, "The Mulroney visit was by any standard a remarkable success."

At home, the press ensured that Canadians were aware of the opposition leader's visit to the most important capital city in the world. Now my advisors could see why I had accepted President Reagan's invitation for a visit as they saw headline after headline. In the *Vancouver Sun*, writer Jamie Lamb summed up well what I was trying to accomplish on the eve of an election:

> The very fact he was here, talking to the figures that matter, will prove to make a difference, perhaps even the winning difference, in the coming electoral battle between Brian "Marty" Mulroney and John "Chick" Turner. The difference is a sense of occasion . . . the difference in personality between Mr. Turner and Mr. Mulroney will have a major effect on the electorate simply because there is little to choose between them on policy matters.
>
> There was a glimpse of one such character difference here when Mr. Mulroney visited the White House. Beneath the professional gloss of the successful politician, a gloss Mr. Mulroney wears like a fashion model, there was a sense of occasion. Mr. Mulroney seemed to think that a visit to the White House was pretty swell stuff, a heady moment for a boy from Baie-Comeau . . . That's a nice thing to see in a politician. By contrast, Mr. Trudeau always gave the appearance of accepting such meetings as nothing more than his due. Mr. Turner treats every such occasion as just another corporate meeting, but Mr. Mulroney actually seems to get a kick out of them. That enthusiasm, if transmitted to the electorate, may prove to make the difference in the election campaign.

The leader of Canada's Progressive Conservative Party, his fellow candidates, and the party at large would indeed rise to the occasion in the summer of 1984. Before the campaign we were as ready, I believe, as a party could ever be. (I had also already put a fox in the Liberal chicken coop by telephoning defeated leadership candidate Jean Chrétien to let him know I had been more scared of him as an opponent than I was of John Turner. Chrétien later recounted the call in his own book, *Straight from the Heart*, fanning the flames of mischief I'd lit after he left Turner's caucus.)

Prime Minister Turner, on the other hand, just wasn't ready. He was clearly exhausted from the leadership campaign, and was awkwardly readjusting to public life. His sense of political timing had gone. I was stunned when he flew off to Windsor Castle in England to ask Her Majesty to delay her visit to Canada, so that he could call an election. I was out west when I heard the news, and I simply could not believe my good fortune. If I had taken power in those circumstances, I would have spent the summer escorting the Queen throughout Canada, begun the internal healing process in the party, and then proudly escorted His Holiness Pope John Paul II across Canada on his tour of the country, scheduled to begin in mid-September.

I had been so certain that Turner would follow this course that I had in fact earlier told my senior staff and strategists to take some time off and Mila and I looked at the possibility of renting a cottage for the summer. At a gathering at Stornoway after the Grit convention, I wrote down six reasons why Prime Minister Turner would *never* call a summer election:

1) He had all summer to travel the country to reunite his party following the divisive race with Jean Chrétien.
2) He would look prime ministerial during the scheduled visit of the Queen.
3) He could shore up support among Roman Catholics during the September pilgrimage of the Pope to Canada.
4) He could distance himself from Trudeau by introducing a Throne Speech and budget in the fall session of Parliament.
5) He could use the time to distance himself from the Trudeau patronage appointments he agreed to make.
6) He could use the time to recruit star candidates that would now be attracted to a Liberal Party revitalized by a new leader.

But I was delighted to be wrong, when on July 9 Turner announced that an election would be held on September 4.

At the end of a successful meeting of western caucus members in Prince Albert, Joe Clark stayed behind and we had drinks together in my hotel suite. After a lengthy conversation in which Clark gave me helpful pointers on the running of a national campaign, he stood and gazed out the window at the setting prairie sun and said, "Brian, remember this. When the writ is issued, the responsibility is entirely on your shoulders. That is the ultimate test of leadership."

His sober analysis underlined the need for me to deliver a superb campaign performance and the perilous future that awaited me if I failed to meet expectations.

3. A Summer Election

As I WENT INTO the 1984 campaign, my philosophy within the party was simple: it didn't matter to me if you had supported me in the leadership or not. I wanted everybody inside the PC tent. It didn't matter if a candidate or strategist or poll worker hated me or loved me. That was irrelevant. I was the leader and I was going to be prime minister if I could energize the entire party and then the country.

With only a couple of missteps, we ran a flawless campaign.

—

PERSONAL JOURNAL: JUNE 14, 1993

At the governor general's final dinner for Mila and me that night Charest sat next to me. When he spoke quite bitterly of Pierre Blais not supporting him, a fellow Québécois, I reminded him that when I, a Québécois, had run in 1983, he had not supported me – but had chosen an Albertan, Joe Clark, over me! I urged his strong support for Kim, and urged him to set aside feelings about who stood where during the campaign, pointing out to him that, at the head table alone, the governor general, Mazankowski, Lowell, Clark, and Charest had all supported Clark for the leadership, and that I was the only one who voted for me! He laughed heartily and said, "Yeah, but look at the fun you've had making everyone work for you."

—

In his book *Fights of Our Lives: Elections, Leadership, and the Making of Canada*, Liberal insider John Duffy neatly summarized our effort: "The seven-week 1984 campaign saw Mulroney pull off three winning plays, any one of which would probably have given him victory. He successfully executed Joe Clark's western-based populist rush from '79 among English Canadians by lambasting the corrupt, arrogant Liberals. He flawlessly pulled off the Quebec Bridge as he had ordained, by offering Quebec a new constitutional settlement on more favourable terms than Trudeau's. Above all, he managed to replicate Trudeau's devastating leadership advantage of 1980 by nailing Turner in the first back-to-back French and English televised leaders' debates."

When Prime Minister Turner launched his campaign on July 9, Gallup had him leading us by eleven points. Without my doing anything, John managed to reduce his lead by trying to defend his deal with Trudeau that saw seventeen former Liberal MPs given patronage positions. Incredibly, Trudeau even made Turner agree to the appointments in writing before he could assume the prime ministership. Charley McMillan crunched the numbers for us and quickly figured that these appointments would cost Canadians $84 million in salaries and perks.

No one should be surprised that I exploited this fact shamelessly when my turn at the National Press Theatre's podium came. "One of the moral dilemmas of Mr. Turner is having agreed in writing, in advance, to this kind of situation," I said. "It's something right out of an Edward G. Robinson movie – the boys cutting up the cash. A little holdup, and then you're dividing the cash at night. I think that this is absolutely scandalous. Here is a new prime minister with his new minister of finance and his new minister of labour and the new morality. There's not a Grit left in this town; they're all gone to Grit heaven."

I challenged the prime minister to meet Ed Broadbent and me for a series of debates, stealing a bit of thunder from Ed, who was waiting to make his own opening statement.

Though I was pressed repeatedly that day about what constituency I would be running in, I told reporters that I believed my Central Nova constituents were owed the basic courtesy of a face-to-face discussion before I answered that question in public. "I shall go back to my voters, to my constituents, to speak with them," I told *La Presse*. "In due course, if a change is going to be made, I shall inform you as soon as possible."

What I didn't tell the reporters was that my decision to seek election in the riding of Manicouagan, where my hometown of Baie-Comeau is located, had been made weeks before. My friend Jean Bazin made a critical intervention during a meeting that spring at Stornoway when we were discussing where I should run. I can still remember his words: "Look, you sought and won the leadership of this party by holding out the hope that you could lead it to a breakthrough in the French-speaking areas of this country, and principally in Quebec. You can only do this if you run in Quebec. I know you have this wonderfully safe seat in Nova Scotia, but you didn't run for this job to be safe. You came here to take risks. You have to get rid of the idea that running again in Central Nova is even a possibility." It was at that exact moment that my decision was made: I'd be heading home to Baie-Comeau and the North Shore.

First, however, I flew to Nova Scotia to thank the people of Central Nova personally. Elmer MacKay would be back again as the PC candidate, and the people of the riding were well aware he'd play a prominent role in a Mulroney government. On July 13, I made my decision public. "I have just met with my riding executive and advised them of my decision not to seek re-election in the constituency of Central Nova," I explained, saying that it had been an extremely difficult decision, because the people of Central Nova had been kind, generous, and supportive from the beginning. "I have decided to seek election in the constituency of Manicouagan which contains my hometown of Baie-Comeau, where I was born and raised, and Sept-Îles, where I worked for many years for the Progressive Conservative Party. As leader of the party, I feel it is my duty to seek to extend our support in Quebec, and in the process, duly enhance our position as a national party, with substantial support in all regions of Canada. This election is about change – beneficial change for Canada. It involves changing old attitudes and old ways of doing things. It is in this spirit of constructive change that I undertake this challenge on behalf of my party. It is deeply satisfying to know that I do so with the good wishes and warm support of the people of Central Nova."

So confident were the Liberals of defeating me that the sitting Manicouagan MP, the easygoing André Maltais, greeted me at the airport on my first visit to the riding as a candidate! His bravado didn't faze me. Back home on the North Shore, I knew the friends and neighbours I had grown up with would do all they could to send one of their own to the highest office in the land. My campaign plane was proudly named *Manicouagan I* in their honour, and I flew in it to every corner of Canada that summer.

Only three days later, while flying back to Montreal from Baie-Comeau, I foolishly ceded the high ground to the Liberals and handed them a gift. It was dumb, and there was nobody to blame but myself. Just as Turner discovered on the bus during his own leadership campaign, I found out the hard way that journalists had changed the rules of engagement when covering politicians – but had neglected to tell any of us. With some small exceptions, I had enjoyed good personal relations with reporters since I was a university student. If truth be known, I tend to like people and I generally liked journalists in person. So I went for a stroll on that flight, and entered the section of the plane where the members of the press sat. Relaxed after some successful appearances on my home turf, I opened up when I was asked questions in what I assumed was an informal off-the-record discussion. While most of the reporters adhered to the past practice of not repeating this type of talk, Neil Macdonald of the *Ottawa Citizen* was making mental notes of everything I said. Forgetting what had happened to John Turner only weeks before when he confided in reporters with his version of leaving Trudeau's cabinet in 1975, I kept talking, just shooting the breeze with travelling companions at the end of a long day.

Macdonald's article was published on July 16, and it was devastating.

"Conservative leader Brian Mulroney has admitted that he tells Tories 'what they want to hear' and the rest of Canada something else," the report began, and it got worse from there.

> Questioned by reporters on his campaign plane about the apparent contradictions between his pro-patronage statements during his bid for the PC leadership and his now unrelenting criticism of the recent Trudeau–Turner appointments, Mulroney replied, "I was talking to Tories then, and that's what they want to hear. Talking to the Canadian public during an election campaign is something else." Mulroney also conceded he'd have done exactly what former Liberal MP Bryce Mackasey did when offered the ambassadorship to Portugal as a golden handshake. "Let's face it: there's no whore like an old whore. If I'd been in Bryce's position, I'd have been right in there with my nose in the trough like the rest of them." Asked how he can justify his castigation of Trudeau's appointments when he made patronage a virtual plank in his leadership speeches, Mulroney asked, "What speeches?"
>
> Toward the end of the conversation, Mulroney looked around and said, "I hope this is all off the record. I'm taking the high road now." He did not, however, impose any such stipulations at the beginning of the conversation.

After a good first week on the campaign trail, my remarks cost us much-needed momentum at a crucial time. Looking back on it now, I can see that I compounded my error in trusting the press by not immediately apologizing and moving on. My delay allowed the Liberals and the media to keep the story alive. Under strong pressure from my campaign team, I finally apologized to the Canadian people, in Sault Ste. Marie on July 18. My prepared statement read: "During the course of an informal conversation with certain members of the media last Saturday night while flying to Montreal from Baie-Comeau, certain casual and bantering remarks on the subject of political patronage were attributed to me. I do not deny having made these remarks, but I say simply they were made without any serious intent since they clearly did not represent either my attitudes or my position with respect to this important matter of public policy. I was mistaken to treat so important a matter in a way which might be misunderstood, and I very much regret having done so. As I have said since the outset of the campaign, I am committed to the attainment of new standards of quality in making public appointments, and that remains my commitment to the people of Canada."

That wasn't my only mistake during the campaign. More than a month into the race, at a stop in Kingston, I attacked the Liberals for excessive secrecy in government, especially in their handling of Crown corporations. "Not only is the door closed and not only are the files hidden from the scrutiny by the auditor general at the office of Petro-Canada; the doors are also closed at CN Marine, VIA Rail, Canada Post, and the Canada Development Corporation," I told an enthusiastic audience in Sir John A. Macdonald's hometown.

Later, once in office I backed away from my pledge to open up these files. Conscious of needing public servants and senior managers in Crown corporations to work with my new government, I didn't proceed as boldly as I should have. In retrospect, I know I made a mistake in not shining the light of public scrutiny on the salaries, perks, and benefits that a generation of Liberals had enjoyed, and augmented, on their appointment to various Crown corporations.

I prepared for the nationally televised debates more thoroughly than anything I had prepared for before. While I won the French-language debate on points on July 25, there were no knockout blows. But afterwards, my position as "one of the tribe" definitely took hold in Quebec. The door had swung wide open for us in the province, and now we had to prove we were worthy of Quebecers' trust. "Mulroney's advantage," a front-page headline in *Le Soleil* trumpeted. "Mulroney scores some points," *Le Droit* chimed in, while *La Presse* declared, "Mulroney emerges the winner." The French television network TVA said that I was the "big winner."

For the most part, the English-Canadian media missed what was going on in French Canada. One observer who didn't make this mistake was Jeffrey Simpson. "Academic studies of U.S. presidential debates uncovered a curious phenomenon – the immediate reaction of viewers to the debate often changed later on," he wrote in the *Globe and Mail*. "The phenomenon played itself out this way. Viewers formed tentative conclusions during and immediately following the debate. Then they listened to the interpretations of the media and their friends. Quite often, they changed their minds. If this phenomenon repeats itself in Quebec in 1984, Tory leader Brian Mulroney won Tuesday night's French-language debate hands down. Whereas some English-language journalists, including this one, called the debate a draw and English-Canadian headline writers favoured neutral headlines, the French-language press saw the debate differently."

The English debate was held on July 26. On that day, the patronage issue went nuclear for the Liberal leader. While many Canadians remember the debate's most dramatic moment, few recall that John and I were each holding our own for the first hundred minutes of the broadcast. Then he gave me my golden opportunity (why, I'll never know) and I seized it.

Turner: "I would say, Mr. Mulroney, that on the basis of what you have talked about – getting your nose in the public trough – that you wouldn't offer Canadians any newness in the style of government. The style that you have been preaching to your own party reminds me of the old Union Nationale. It reminds me of patronage at its best. Frankly, on the basis of your performance I cannot see freshness coming out of your choice."

Mulroney: "Mr. Turner, the only person who has ever appointed anyone around here for the last twenty-odd years has been your party. And 99 per cent of [the appointees] have been Liberals – and you ought not to be proud of that, nor should you repeat something that I think you know to be inaccurate. You know full well that [nose at the trough] was a figure of speech, and I do not deny it. In fact, I have gone so far, because I believe that what you did was so bad, I have gone so far, sir, as to apologize for even kidding about it. I have apologized to the Canadian people for kidding about it. The least you should do is apologize for having made these horrible appointments. The cost of that $84.4 million is enough to pay every senior citizen in this country an extra $70 at Christmas rather than pay for those Liberal appointments. I say to you, sir, you should produce that letter because you keep coming back to the situation. Please produce the secret letter [to Trudeau] that you signed when you undertook to make these appointments."

I was thunderstruck at what came next. If our debate had been a boxing match, John would have lowered his gloves, closed his eyes, and stuck out his chin.

Turner: "Well, I have told you and told the Canadian people, Mr. Mulroney, that I had no option."

I reacted swiftly and viscerally.

Mulroney: "You had an option, sir. You could have said, 'I'm not going to do it. This is wrong for Canada, and I am not going to ask Canadians to pay the price.' You had an option sir, to say no, and you chose to say yes to the old attitudes and the old stories of the Liberal Party. That, sir, if I may say respectfully, that is not good enough for Canadians."

Turner: "I had no option –"

Mulroney: "That is an avowal of failure. That is confession of non-leadership and this country needs leadership. You had an option, sir. You could have done better."

During the drive home from the television studio Mila and I sat in silence. "What do you think just happened?" I asked my top advisor as soon as we left the parking lot. "The earth just moved," she replied. At Stornoway I listened to a call-in radio show well into the wee hours of the morning. It was easy listening. By the time I finally got to sleep, I was leading among callers by a margin of eight to one.

The next morning we helicoptered to Sherbrooke, Quebec, for a meeting with our Quebec candidates. The transformation was extraordinary. They were all bubbling with enthusiasm, and ready to charge out of the room and take our case to every doorstep in Quebec. I knew the Liberals couldn't stop us now.

Michael Doyle of the *Winnipeg Free Press* sensed what was happening on the ground in Quebec. "It is difficult to put a finger on what is happening here," he wrote in August. "An electric feeling is in the air such as a person gets when he enters a bar and knows immediately that a brawl is going to break out. Political veterans watch for the mix of the crowd rather than its size or its decibel level. The Progressive Conservatives are now attracting the lively, the ambitious, the mirthful, the good-looking, and sometimes the irreverent. Even in Quebec."

Even the Liberal-friendly *Toronto Star* picked up on my theme from the debate's final exchange. "[Prime Minister Turner] may have judged that this risk was too high a personal and political price to pay for opposing these appointments; that judgment is a subject for legitimate political debate," the paper wrote in an editorial published the day after the English debate. "But Turner clearly had a choice. And he made it."

After our trip to Quebec, Mila and I flew to Hamilton, Ontario to begin another swing through that province. It was after midnight when we arrived at the Royal Connaught Hotel, but to our amazement we were met by hundreds of cheering supporters. Upstairs in our suite, our pollster Allan Gregg, a bright, irreverent, long-haired fellow, was waiting for us with long-time Tory organizer Paul Curley. For privacy, we took Allan into the bedroom and Mila and I sat on the bed to hear his report on the latest tracking numbers. Allan closed the door and then stood next to the bureau with his elbow on it. He pulled out a piece of paper and gave us the numbers: "Mr. Leader, you have been responsible for the greatest single change in the numbers since polling began in Canada," he said. "It is extraordinary what has happened. We are going to win this one big time. The election is now ours to lose."

By August 3, the polling numbers were public and all Canadians knew what we had learned privately that glorious night in Hamilton. In one poll, broadcast on CTV, we were at 45 per cent, to the Liberals' 36; weeks earlier, right after the Grit convention, the same polling company had the Liberals leading us at 49–39. We were also at close to 40 per cent support in Quebec, and climbing. The party faithful, its candidates, and its leader were fired up with enthusiasm, and it was showing.

"Brian Mulroney is on a roll," the *Ottawa Citizen* reported on July 31.

> Even if last week's debates didn't sway a single voter, the Tory leader's impressive performance has injected a powerful dose of adrenalin into his campaign . . . In a swing through southwestern Ontario over the past few days, Mulroney delivered one barnburner after another. Most observers agree his fiery address to a partisan gathering in Hamilton was one of the strongest of his political career . . . Mulroney had his Hamilton audience eating out of his hand with a series of lighthearted but biting attacks on Turner, the man he sarcastically calls "Mr. New." Moving in for the kill, the Tory leader notes that Turner's first act as prime minister was "not

> to help the unemployed or the elderly. It was to announce the patronage appointments of 19 Liberals." Sweat streaming from his face, Mulroney's voice begins to rise as he recalls: "Worst of all, the prime minister in the debate stood there helpless like a baby and said, 'I had no option.'" With clenched fist, Mulroney shifts into a shouting rage. "I say he had an option. The option of honour was to say no. I will not do it. It is wrong."

Our campaign in Ontario was also on a roll because of the active participation of Premier William Davis. I had asked Norman Atkins to be the national campaign chairman for the simple reason that I wanted Davis personally onside in the election. The premier didn't let us down. In fact, Bill joined for almost a week of campaigning at my side in the province he understood so instinctively and had governed for fourteen years like the pro he is. During one appearance in Simcoe, the worthy successor to premiers Robarts, Frost, and Drew told the crowd that I shared the "good old-fashioned values that you and I share." While I took anything I could from the Big Blue Machine to win that election, nothing mattered more than the personal support of a man I like and admire to this very day: the modest and generous William Grenville Davis of Brampton, Ontario.

I'll never forget one conversation I had with Bill aboard a campaign bus. I told him during a quiet moment just how pleased I was that the members of his famous Big Blue Machine were playing a major role in our campaign. Davis looked at me and calmly motioned with his pipe. "Brian, the Big Blue Machine is the best at getting the buses to meet your plane, taking you to a room overflowing with supporters, arranging the technology for the reporters to file their stories, and then getting everyone back safely on board the plane," he said. "But the leadership, strategy, and message for the campaign, that's what I do. The real Big Blue Machine." He sucked at his pipe. "You're looking at it right now."

John Turner's campaign, meanwhile, was in total disarray. It was a wreck. His buses got lost on one occasion, ending up in a forest near Granby, Quebec. The media travelling with him were not impressed. He spilled wine on his trousers at an event, and nobody had thought to ensure that the leader had a change of clothes available. Each morning I would examine the news clippings with eager anticipation, and craft my daily hammering of what Turner had said the night before.

In late August, all three party leaders gathered in Toronto for a debate on women's issues. Broadbent and I arrived on the stage first and had to wait a few moments for the prime minister to join us. Friendly as always, John came over and whispered, "Jesus Christ, it's tough out there," to Ed and me as we all shook hands. Ed and I exchanged glances and muttered polite agreement. But he wasn't done yet. "It's goddamned brutal," Turner continued, emphatically. Ed and I found the prime minister's anxiety encouraging.

But I had a great deal of sympathy that campaign summer for John Turner, who is an intelligent, thoughtful and principled man. He was raised in the old parliamentary school where people treated each other with respect and courtesy. John inherited a bad situation from Trudeau and paid the price; by that point, all I had to do was mention Trudeau's name in a speech and the crowd would explode with anger. But that's the way life goes in politics. You exhaust yourself in a great cause, and your successor pays the price after you have used up your party's credibility and goodwill. The same process later happened to me, as it had to Macdonald, Borden, and so many others.

—

PERSONAL JOURNAL: April 17, 1989

While the Liberals won't chance it, I believe their best [new leader] would be . . . John Turner! In fact, I believe he is more accomplished, more bilingual, and more attractive as a candidate than any of his challengers or than he's been given credit for. There are great flaws in his interpersonal skills that have scarred his leadership and induced the caucus revolts, but leading an opposition party in Canada is never easy, and many Liberals may want to think again before retiring him.

—

At every campaign stop outside the big towns I made sure to remind my audiences that Canada was a country of "small towns and big dreams." During one swing through New Brunswick I made a habit of pointing at CTV reporter Jim Munson, who was from New Brunswick, as I used the phrase. Then Munson turned the tables, once laughingly shouting that

Canada is really a country of "small towns and big tits." For the rest of the campaign Munson would stand there red-faced as the press corps and the travelling staff would face him and chant his version in unison when I got to that part of my speeches. Munson was later appointed by Jean Chrétien to the Senate, where his good nature makes it difficult, though not impossible, for Conservatives to hold his politics against him.

In Sept-Îles, Quebec, I delivered a speech on August 6 that provided a seminal moment in my career. In my speech, I carefully defined for Quebecers the new path of federalism I was proposing they follow along with me. For all the myths that have grown up around my address in Sept-Îles, it was in fact basically conservative. I announced to Quebecers that we had no interest in constitutional reform, Trudeau-style. Instead, we would accomplish change through the laboratory that is the economy. And when conditions were ripe, and economic conditions improved, Quebec, as I said that day, would want to sign the Constitution of Canada with "honour and enthusiasm."

Lucien Bouchard, who was working on my campaign, had submitted a draft of the address to me and Jean Bazin. Jean and I went through it as the two of us sat around a Sept-Îles motel swimming pool, excising a number of passages and rephrasing others. It was Jean who suggested that I use the phrase "honour and enthusiasm," as I spoke from the heart to my fellow citizens in my home province. My speech said, in part:

> We are on the threshold of a true national renewal. Let us end the bias of confrontation with the bias of agreement. Let us open avenues to solutions instead of putting up obstacles. Let us listen in order to understand, rather than condemn without hearing . . . To me, the Canadian federation is not a test of strength between different governments. Federal power is more than that of a policeman whose nightstick happens to be bigger than those of the others . . .
>
> One thing is certain: Not one person in Quebec authorized the federal Liberals to take advantage of the confusion that prevailed in Quebec following the referendum in order to ostracize the province constitutionally. My party takes no pleasure in the politically weak position in which these deplorable events have placed Quebec. If Quebec is strong, then Canada is strong. There is room in Canada for all identities to be affirmed, for all aspirations to be respected, and for all ideals to be pursued.

I know that many men and women in Quebec will not be satisfied with mere words. We will have to make commitments and take concrete steps to reach the objective that I have set for myself and that I repeat here: to convince the Quebec National Assembly to give its consent to the new Canadian Constitution with honour and enthusiasm. I am prepared to study possible changes to the amending formula . . . But our first task is to breathe a new spirit into federalism . . . There is no denying that the course we are embarking upon is full of pitfalls. It is also strewn with the rubble of repeated Liberal failures. There will be in Ottawa a spokesman who is willing to tackle all obstacles, undaunted by protocol or visibility, and determined that all his actions will serve the sole interests of the taxpayers.

—

PERSONAL JOURNAL: May 31, 1987

President Mitterrand arrived Monday morning and began a hectic and productive four-day Canadian tour. It was the first by a French president in 20 years. Charles de Gaulle's thoughtless – though I expect well-planned – cry from a balcony in Montreal had effectively derailed Franco-Canadian relations and for two decades had rendered them either meaningless or turgid. Mitterrand's ending comment in the House, "Vive le Canada," was a fitting tribute to a refurbished relationship I happen to view as extremely significant for Canada. Mitterrand has been the principal architect of this revitalized relationship from the French side and I am most grateful to him for the sensitivity and cooperation. I had made this initiative a key part of our constitutional reform process – normalizing relations with France; setting the terms for Quebec's participation, with New Brunswick, in the Francophonie Summit; new emphasis on the constitutional file, hopefully resulting in the reintegration of Quebec with the Canadian Constitution with honour and enthusiasm as I had said in my Sept-Îles speech in August of 1984.

—

It was clear that Quebecers were responding to my call as the summer came to a close. Like Canadians in all regions and provinces, they were tired of the confrontations that had defined so much of the Trudeau era. While Trudeau kept a low profile during the campaign, he did raise his head briefly, and graciously took the time to accuse me of leading "an unholy alliance of malcontents" during a speech at a Montreal church. Quebecers, I knew, realized by now that Trudeau was really gone. It was time to look forward.

When asked to respond to Trudeau's attack, I shrugged it off. "It's a free country," I told the press. "Mr. Trudeau is a fine gentleman who can say what he wants."

In Montreal, in what had been solidly Liberal seats, places where the Grits had won by 20,000-vote margins in 1980, I could feel the momentum shifting as I made three campaign stops there with only days to go. A huge and enthusiastic crowd packed Place Ville-Marie in the heart of the city that had become my home. This was where Claude Ryan and I had been dismayed to see the Trudeau rally in 1968. Now I was moved by this tremendous show of support as I looked out over the crowd and saw countless friends and colleagues from my past, there to cheer us on, in our final swing through my home province.

"For most of the week the Conservative campaign tour rolled through Quebec like a juggernaut, greeted at practically every stop by crowds whose size and enthusiasm astounded even the local party organizers," the Montreal *Gazette* reported in their election-day edition. "They turned out by the hundreds – in the Eastern Townships, in Montreal, both east and west ends. In Trois-Rivières more than 300 showed up to mob him at the airport at 9 p.m. on a night when there was a hockey game on TV. An hour later about 500 were at the airport in Quebec City . . . Again there was pandemonium at the airport in Sept-Îles when Mulroney arrived Sunday night to spend the final two days of the campaign in his home riding."

Later, my critics would trumpet their theory that I had made some sort of Faustian pact with Quebec separatists in order to obtain their support that summer. Their argument was stunningly ignorant and naïve. Premier René Lévesque of the PQ and Robert Bourassa, the leader of the Quebec Liberals, were no fools. They saw what was happening on the ground in their province and knew that they might end up dealing with me as prime minister. Why would they send their people out to fight me tooth and nail?

The critics missed another vital point. In the 1980 election the Progressive Conservative Party had received 12.6 per cent of the vote in

Quebec. This meant that roughly 87 per cent of the electorate voted for the other parties, principally Pierre Trudeau's Liberals. Now where do you think that 87 per cent came from? There were many Liberals and many separatists in Quebec, and in 1980 they voted overwhelmingly for Trudeau. And then in 1984 they voted for me. They did so because Trudeau and I were both part of Quebec society and, in their minds, strong leaders. And we were happy to have every vote.

A member of my staff panicked after Turner announced that two of our candidates in Quebec had voted "Oui" in the 1980 referendum; he worried that we would have to respond to the prime minister's accusations. I told him to calm down. "Turner should get his facts straight," I said. "We have at least a dozen candidates that voted 'Oui.' They're all federalists now, and we're going to win all their ridings."

With only days to go in the election my sister Olive sent me a letter about the campaign on the ground in Baie-Comeau. She also described the sorry economic situation I'd be inheriting, and did so more effectively than most national reporters. As a child of Baie-Comeau, Olive could see and feel the economic damage caused by more than a decade of Liberal mismanagement. While excited by the success of our campaign, as I read my sister's note I was humbled by the awesome responsibilities I'd soon be assuming.

"The election is only a week away now and I can't believe how well things are going," she said. "The PC radio and television commercials are terrific; our group has the French song on tape and now has a loudspeaker outside the door of the curling club so as to entertain the locals and our workers from time to time, to the vast amusement of all . . . This town is waiting your coming – as a saviour I'm afraid. Many people who were laid off years ago . . . are still waiting for the phone to ring; they can't sell their houses and so they can't move to look for work elsewhere. Most of the PC team are unemployed . . . Older retired people can't sell their houses and move away and the streets are often empty and an enormous number of people are living on change. One man suggested the PCs should allow mortgage costs on houses to be deductible . . . The whole town is awaiting a miracle. I've never seen anything like it."

On the Sunday night before election day, I flew into Wabush, Labrador, and was greeted at the airport by some union protesters and extreme left-wing troublemakers intent on using the presence of the national media to help them continue their battles with the Iron Ore Company of Canada.

Some of them chanted, "Go home, Brian; go home, Brian," as I got off the plane. That fired me up.

"I'll tell you this," I shouted, "it'll take more than a couple of malcontents to shout me down. You go home, because I *am* home. I'm home in Labrador. I'm home everywhere in the country."

My local supporters hustled me into a school bus, but a few of the protesters managed to follow. Jean Bazin and I were alone in the bus, and I sat there eyeing the protesters marching with their placards outside. Nothing, I should add, gets my competitive juices flowing more than a good heckler or a group of protesters. In a cocky mood, I slid open one of the windows and motioned to one of the fellows carrying an anti-Mulroney sign to come toward the bus. The man looked surprised and walked over. "Hi, Mr. Mulroney, how are you?" he said.

I smiled back with a show of molars that would have made Jimmy Carter proud. "Why don't you go fuck yourself," I said, and closed the window. The man was stunned, then furious, and he bellowed for his colleagues to join him for support.

Bazin just about had a heart attack. "Brian, what the hell are you doing?" he yelled. "What have you done? You're going to blow the whole goddam thing at the last minute."

Fortunately, the incident subsided, but I admitted sheepishly that he was right. "Jean, it was just too delicious, I couldn't resist," I said, reminding him that it had been the only time in the whole campaign I had cut loose.

Even in Sept-Îles I remained in the doghouse. "Mila," Bazin urged, when we arrived on September 3, "I want you to lock him in his room and don't let him out until the votes are counted."

And when they were counted the next night, my party had won 211 seats and received 50 per cent of the popular vote. And in Quebec, the province's voters were sending 58 PC MPs to Ottawa. I had kept my promise.

4. Transition to Power

THE DAY AFTER THE election Mila and I left the Mill Manager's House (now called the Annex) at De Manoir Comeau hotel and flew up to Sept-Îles for a celebratory lunch with local organizers. Mila had somehow found the time to purchase a teddy bear for the kids and she named it Victory. The children called it "Vic" for short.

With "Mr. Tory" in tow, we found that my new constituents were just as enthusiastic about the PC win as my childhood friends and neighbours in Baie-Comeau. They, too, were pleased with the verdict the Canadian people had delivered the night before. After a celebration that included the humbling experience of being effusively congratulated by lifelong friends, I took time out to speak to the press. As a Quebecer, I was still moved by the historic opportunity for reconciliation and renewal that our victory in the province represented. Perhaps, as a leading writer said, Louis Riel had indeed been given a proper burial at last.

"I have felt for a long time it was indispensable for Canada that Quebecers be given another federalist option to which they could turn, and against which they could measure the evolution of our collective society," I said. "There is no doubt in my mind that, in the heart of every Quebecer, there beats a love for Canada, an understanding of the greatness of what this country can be together."

Then it was on to Ottawa – signing autographs and posing for pictures with members of the travelling press gallery on our final flight aboard *Manicouagan I* – for a joyous reunion with the children at Stornoway. Mark was perhaps the most excited member of the family. Did he care that his father was now prime minister-designate? Not in the least. Mark was more inspired by the fact that a large detail of Mounties were now on hand to "play" with him. He also proved to be popular with the press – especially when he laughed uproariously the time I managed to lock myself out of

Stornoway while waiting for the arrival of the Clerk of the Privy Council, to begin briefing the nation's next prime minister.

The first of my postelection responsibilities was to turn my attention urgently to government transition matters, and to the selection of my first cabinet. Prime Minister Turner and I agreed on September 17 as the date for the transfer of power. Ever gracious, John invited me to greet Pope John Paul II at his side on September 9, when His Holiness was set to arrive in Quebec City to begin his historic visit to Canada. I declined with thanks, touched by the gesture but of the firm belief there could only be one prime minister at a time. I then plunged into meetings with Privy Council Clerk Gordon Osbaldeston and my advisors, where we discussed both an early parliamentary agenda and candidates for cabinet, parliamentary secretaries, and House and Senate officials.

As another Conservative government was preparing to take office in 2006, Osbaldeston reflected on our early days together during an interview with the *London Free Press*. "He [Osbaldeston] remembers dreading the arrival of Mulroney, who said in one public speech 'all he was really going to give public servants was pink slips and running shoes,'" the paper reported. "But upon meeting Mulroney and offering his resignation to the new prime minister, Osbaldeston was surprised. 'When he saw me, he put out his hand and said, "Gordon, it's nice to see you again, and I want you to know I trust you completely." That's what I call street smarts. He immediately dispelled any other thought I might have about our relationship and immediately allowed both of us to get to work without sparring back and forth. Trust is the name of the game.'"

As I stayed up late each evening to read the sobering briefing binders Osbaldeston had left for me at Stornoway, a simple truth became more apparent with each passing page: Canada was broke. There were many nights during that transition period when I couldn't sleep; the numbers I was about to inherit were that bleak.

Jean Chrétien was later to admit that his party left the "cupboard bare" when the Liberals turned the government over to us in 1984. Net public debt stood at approximately $18 billion in 1968. By the time Trudeau left office that number had ballooned to $206 billion, 46 per cent of Canada's GDP. "Trudeau and his ministers had demonstrated a continuing inclination to ignore the warning signs, concentrating instead on politically persuasive short-term nostrums," Michael Hart and Bill Dymond wrote in an article published in *Policy Options* in 2003, damning the government by saying, "Its focus on constitutional, social, distributional, and similar issues had come at the expense of sound economic stewardship."

The news in the briefing binders was all bad. "An economic projection for Canada . . . would most likely have a short-term profile of output growth which was lower than that of the [Lalonde] Budget projection, and interest-rate and unemployment-rate profiles which were higher," the Clerk wrote in one of his lighter passages. "In the corresponding revised fiscal projection, expenditures would be higher, most importantly because of the higher public debt charges attributable to the higher interest rates. Projected revenues would probably be somewhat lower, because of the negative impact of slower real growth on revenue bases. The projected deficit levels would be higher."

I shuddered when Osbaldeston provided more detail on his projections for the debt and deficit. "In 1982–83, expenditures grew by nearly 18 per cent, while revenues increased by only two per cent," he said, also noting that the only areas where government revenues increased between 1979–80 and 1984–85 (projected) were personal income tax and energy taxes. "In 1977–78, net public debt charges accounted for only $3 billion of the over $10 billion deficit. The growth of the public debt associated with large deficits year after year, and the major increases in interest rates which have occurred in the early 1980s, have resulted in steady growth in both the level of net public debt charges and their relative importance in the total budgetary deficit. By 1981–82, net public debt charges accounted for over $10 billion of the total deficit of $13.6 billion, and were projected at the time of the February Budget to grow to nearly $20 billion by 1987–88."

Seven years before the Progressive Conservative government forged ahead with the GST, Osbaldeston was looking to the future. To deal realistically and rationally with the dire economic situation we were inheriting would require a huge amount of political will. And only a determined prime minister, cabinet, caucus, and party could supply that. I marked the following passage one September night in 1984 after Mila and the children had gone to bed. "A major reduction in the deficit could require, for example, that the Government alter the tax systems in a fundamental way," the Clerk wrote, "or radically reshape the system of federal transfer payments to individuals and provinces. As well, the greater the desired shift in fiscal policy, the greater would be the number of individuals, businesses, and other institutions which would be perceived to be adversely affected by the associated changes." To put it another way: the more we did to avert the coming financial disaster, the more enemies we would make.

Things were not much better on the international front. The Cold War was still on, so all political action was played out against the all-too-real backdrop of Soviet nuclear missiles pointed toward western Europe and North America. This was brought home to me by a note in my first briefing book: "The Secretary of Cabinet will be available to brief you on emergency procedures that have been developed in case of nuclear attack, including your role in authorizing a NORAD response to such an attack."

Since deficit fighting was to be a number one priority, I had to chuckle at the example of restraint set by the Clerk. Many of the briefing binders I was working through were the same ones John Turner had been presented with a few months earlier, as he prepared to succeed Pierre Trudeau. Some of John's notations were even on the documents.

The need for discretion and secrecy in all of my dealings was highlighted by a page-one story attributed to "a top Mulroney aide" in the Montreal *Gazette* on September 7. The headline read: "Tories Might Fire 400 in Civil Service: Aide." I was learning fast about the great damage leaks can cause any PM. I sent all my senior and transition advisors a stern note: "The story is false in its entirety and does a great disservice to the party and to me. I need not remind you that I shall immediately sever all relations with anyone who needlessly and vexatiously leaks this kind of information to anyone."

There was much to be done during those first days in office, but there was also time for reflection. In less than fifteen months I had captured the leadership of a major party and led it to victory, becoming in the process the first person in Canadian history to achieve this without ever having held elective office. We had won 211 seats, the largest number in Canadian history. I personally had been overwhelmingly elected in French-speaking Manicouagan, having previously achieved a similar vote a year ago in Central Nova, which is almost exclusively English speaking. Moreover, we had elected a majority of members in every province, including the historic breakthrough of 58 seats in Quebec.

I was confident, but I was concerned about my own lack of experience, and that of most of my colleagues. Events in Ottawa have their own cycles and rhythms, from Throne Speeches to budgets to state visits, first ministers' conferences, and UN presentations. I had been opposition leader for less than a year, had never served in government, and had little feel for those movements and how they constrained time and options. Then there was what I might call the culture of Ottawa. The Liberals (who had had a lock on government for the previous twenty-one years) had over time acquired an ease with the leading bureaucrats and their governance. Many of them had taken up permanent residence in Ottawa and had become intimates – through friendships, intermarriage, or professional association – with decision makers in the senior public service and in the media, who routinely shared advice, impressions, and information with them.

Mila and I were new at the game, and we felt that if we treated folks fairly they would reciprocate. That was naïve. I had not fully understood the hostility that the sheer size of our majority would engender, to say nothing of the contempt that many in other ideological camps and interest groups would soon display for our agenda, and for me as its principal proponent. Our relationship with the Parliamentary Press Gallery, for example, did not seem very promising when a University of Western Ontario poll revealed that some 91 per cent of press gallery members had voted for our opponents in the election, with less than 9 per cent supporting us.

In the middle of one of my first meetings I got word that my Quebec campaign manager, Rodrigue Pageau, had died in Montreal. Apart from the personal and family dimensions of the tragedy, it also represented a huge political loss. I immediately made plans to travel to Montreal for the funeral, as I reflected on how skilfully Rodrigue had pulled the party organization together in Quebec after the leadership wars, only to learn in midsummer that he had incurable cancer. Despite his condition, and in considerable pain, he had flown in a small plane to be with us in Baie-Comeau on victory night. When we embraced, I had realized it would probably be the last time I would see him alive.

Because of the party's extreme weakness in Quebec over so many years, Rodrigue had initially faced an uphill battle in attracting candidates. The polls showed the Turner Liberals in a wide lead and to many ambitious Québécois, running under the PC banner looked like another trip to the abattoir. Even after the campaign was under way, we had been unable to find any candidates at all in many constituencies.

And then came the debates. By the time I had finished with Turner the lead had shifted dramatically in our favour, and the stampede was on. Previously reluctant candidates now fought openly for nominations at huge meetings of instant Tories. In a few cases, this led to future embarrassment, because some newly elected MPs came with a personal agenda that included cupidity, as we sadly learned, rather than a sincere wish to serve the interests of their constituents. It was one of the prices the party paid for the disintegration of its Quebec wing in 1934, when it was absorbed into the Union Nationale.

It is amusing to read the revisionists still going on about how the "separatists" or "nationalists" elected Mulroney. There is absolutely no doubt that the 1984 election was won by the debates. In Quebec my victory in the French debate reminded Quebecers that I was one of them, and they chose our party, not for ideological or partisan reasons, but for the personal reassurance I gave them. We bled away votes from all the other parties, but principally from the Liberals because of the strong support I was quietly receiving from Robert Bourassa and his provincial team.

Quebec's premier columnist, Lysiane Gagnon, spelled out the situation succinctly some years later: "Brian Mulroney won 'le Québec profond' [the heart of Quebec] because he was, in spite of his name, 'un petit gars de Baie-Comeau,' and a Université Laval graduate who had the accent, style, and sense of humour of a French Canadian."

Our Quebec victory should not have been surprising. A year before the election, on August 4, 1983, the Montreal *Gazette* had carried a front-page story headlined "Poll Gives Mulroney-Led PCs 55%" with the subheadline "Tory Support Hits 40% in Quebec." The support was there all along. All it required was a leader and an event to galvanize it, and the debates did precisely that.

Cabinet-making is a great challenge for any Canadian prime minister, and I was no exception. I moved fast on this, knowing that many factors had to be considered: individual competence, experience and probity, and regional, linguistic, and gender factors. I had Chief of Staff Fred Doucet book two suites on different floors of the Château Laurier where he and my two excellent executive assistants, Bill Pristanski and Hubert Pichet, met individually with each prospective choice. In forming my cabinet, there was no way I wanted to end up with serious regrets, as my Commonwealth colleague David Lange, New Zealand's prime minister, did after he left office. "Dear God! What a terrible lot of people they were," he wrote of his cabinet colleagues in his memoirs. "It is hard to believe I used to think so much of them."

The process went surprisingly smoothly. It was clear to me from the outset that Michael Wilson was the pick for Finance. I knew Mike, a former rugby player with loads of experience on Bay Street, was smart, tough, and energetic. What I didn't know is what a superb advisor and friend he would turn out to be. John Crosbie, a skilled lawyer and parliamentarian, was a natural for Justice, and I was to develop a deep respect for him and a genuine friendship with Jane and his family over the years. Bob Coates went to Defence on the advice of Bill Neville, although I had originally been thinking of a portfolio more in keeping with his strong organizational skills, developed as party president and after a quarter-century in the House. But I thought Bob would be a good Nova Scotia complement to Elmer MacKay, a great friend, a brilliant grassroots politician, and one of nature's gentlemen. As Solicitor General, Elmer would be responsible for the federal police and national security, and throughout our entire time in government he was a valued and trusted advisor. Otto Jelinek, a loyal friend and effective MP was named Minister of State for Fitness and Amateur Sport.

And so it went: B.C.'s John Fraser to Fisheries and Oceans, Alberta's Don Mazankowski to Transport, Saskatchewan's Ray Hnatyshyn as Government House Leader, Manitoba's Jake Epp to Health and Welfare, where he gave heft and reassurance to the Department, Sinc Stevens from Ontario in the powerful Regional Industrial Expansion portfolio, where he performed admirably, and the able Flora MacDonald to handle the sensitive Employment and Immigration job. That first cabinet included a total of six women ministers, a Canadian record at the time.

All told there were twenty-nine ministers and eleven ministers of state – a large cabinet, but necessary, given the size of our majority and the new reality of strong Quebec representation.

Only one member of our Quebec team, Roch La Salle had been a member of the House at the time of the 1984 election, and I gave him Public Works. Bob de Cotret had served briefly in the House and then in the Senate in the Clark government, and I appointed him President of the Treasury Board. Marcel Masse had experience in the Quebec government and a good knowledge of cultural affairs, so he was handed Communications, where his performance was highly rated. Lucien Bouchard had declined to run for us in 1984, but fortunately Bernard Roy had recruited another Bouchard, Benoît, a CEGEP director who was to provide valuable and loyal service to Canada and to me over many years. Benoît could barely speak English, so I appointed him Minister of State for Transport, assigning him to work with Mazankowski, who could barely speak French, figuring they would make a tremendous team together. And they did.

Joe Clark represented a challenge, although I had decided to give him External Affairs, if he wanted it. I had thought of naming him Senior Minister (in the style of Singapore's Lee Kuan Yew) and Ambassador to the United Nations, believing these responsibilities would appeal to Joe's interests and give him political clout, while at the same time allowing him whatever distance he might need to accommodate himself to the new realities of my leadership. I firmly rejected the strong and repeated advice of those who told me to exclude him from cabinet (as Mrs. Thatcher had done with Ted Heath, her predecessor). I was determined to work closely with the former prime minister and his key supporters to ensure that any leadership-race bitterness was banished and forgotten. My overriding goal was to build a strong, united government that could win elections and face challenges at home and abroad in times of crisis.

My approach was controversial. One senior advisor argued that having Joe in the cabinet would "sustain latent divisions and tensions." "Issues will emerge," he wrote on September 12, "where these latent feelings will come out, and the press – which is now the real opposition – will pounce on it. You have the option of either exercising your once, and only once, available option of giving Joe a position not to his liking on a take-it-or-leave-it basis – say Paris or London with disarmament responsibilities thrown in – or give Joe a cabinet role where it will be next to impossible to use your levers later, at great cost and embarrassment to you. Better to use that trump card now. In the event that you feel there is truly no option, Joe must go in cabinet, better a role like Secretary of State where you can contain him."

Despite this advice I was determined to treat Joe well and courteously. As Clark later wrote, our common success came not only because he was a "gracious loser but also because Brian Mulroney was a gracious winner." So when I asked him his preference as an appointment, he immediately indicated External Affairs, to which I readily assented, and where he served effectively for seven years with achievements that make him the most accomplished foreign minister since Lester B. Pearson.

When I had first been introduced to Benoît Bouchard in a Sheraton Hotel suite in Laval a year earlier, he was dressed in a tailored navy blue suit, smart silk tie and, as I noticed when he sat down, white socks! I detailed Bernard Roy to make sure he showed up for the swearing-in with another colour of socks. Meanwhile Fred Doucet advised all male nominees that dark blue business suits were de rigueur for the swearing-in and for photos of the new cabinet with the governor general. On the day of the event, Benoît showed up without the white socks but Joe Clark, in an obvious sartorial declaration of independence, was sworn in (and appears in the official cabinet photos) in a light brown suit.

The necessary security screenings of the men and women I was considering appointing to Canada's highest council led to at least one unexpected incident. James Kelleher of Sault Ste. Marie was one of the names I had submitted to the PCO for clearance in the run-up to the cabinet announcement on September 17. Since there were no RCMP agents available in the Sault, two officers from Sudbury were dispatched to do Jim's background check. While knocking on doors on the street where he grew up, the agents found few people who admitted to knowing Jim as a young man. Finally, one kindly lady said she knew the man they were asking about, and invited them in for tea. She regaled them with stories of a young Jim Kelleher and assured them of his loyalty to Canada.

The policemen, having enjoyed their tea and cookies, were curious to learn how she knew so much about the prospective minister. "Why," she said, "I should know all these things. I'm his mother, after all."

Jim was duly cleared and sworn in as Minister of International Trade and a member of the Queen's Canadian Privy Council.

While it was humbling and inspiring to have been elected by my fellow citizens as their prime minister, I was learning quickly that holding the job meant that I wouldn't be winning many popularity contests. Summoning MPs to cabinet and being responsible in part for taking them to the pinnacle of success was a joy, but a prime minister also has to deal with those many talented caucus members who don't make it into the Privy Council chamber. On September 16, I telephoned Jim McGrath, Al Lawrence, Steve Paproski, Allan McKinnon, Gordon Towers, Paul Dick, Lloyd Crouse, John Bosley, and Gabrielle Bertrand – all of whom were very able – to inform them that they would not be in my cabinet. I made notes to myself beforehand. "Calling you to tell you personally that I was unable to include you in the cabinet," I wrote. "New realities such as Quebec, women, regional observances mean reflection must be found. Regret I was unable to include you at this time. Other options we can examine together."

Unbeknownst to her husband, one MP's spouse wrote to me after her partner was left out of cabinet. "As God is my witness, I pray never to allow myself to condemn or hold bitterness toward you for what I can only describe as the death of a distinguished political career. Yesterday had to be the most exciting day for you and your family, especially your mother. For us, it was the saddest day of our lives . . . Perhaps the greatest toll is on our children – they are shattered. It all seemed so final. Please tell me I am wrong, and that yes, [my husband] can still hold his head high at home, in the House of Commons, and in his riding, where perhaps he will face the greatest humiliation . . . Believe me, I am very uncomfortable in having to put these words on paper." I felt, I suspect, even more uncomfortable reading the words, but becoming prime minister and leading a team in governing a vast and complicated land like Canada is about making hard choices. I had made mine and I couldn't look back.

The new cabinet was sworn in at Rideau Hall on that glorious September day in 1984. Multiculturalism Minister Jack Murta generated some of our government's first headlines when he announced we would be proceeding toward apologizing to the Japanese Canadians who had been mistreated by Canada's government during the Second World War.

"One could scarcely have asked for a more satisfying start for the new Conservative Government than a sign of willingness to try to clean up an old stain on the national character," the *Globe and Mail* said in an editorial. "It is not easy to understand why the Government of Pierre Trudeau made heavy weather of so obvious an obligation. The demands of common decency are at last being met."

It was a fittingly progressive beginning and I enjoyed those first reviews, knowing full well they wouldn't last. No prime minister who had read the briefing books I'd digested in the previous days could be under any illusion about the path ahead – the Trudeau legacy was devastating – nor believe that those positive editorials could continue for long.

PART V

The First Mandate

1984–1988

1984

The New Prime Minister

1985

1. The Shamrock Summit and Beyond

2. Budget Troubles and Steps Toward Free Trade

3. A Bad Month

4. Fighting Apartheid

1986

1. Vive la Francophonie – et l'Égalité

2. Washington, Tokyo, and Beijing

3. Toward a Cabinet Shuffle

1987

1988

1984

The New Prime Minister

THE RUSH OF EVENTS from that September to Christmas is a blur in my mind today. Right after the reception for family and friends at Government House, I convened our first cabinet meeting, where I set out the general tone of our policies and our approach to the task at hand. One of my first decisions was to place a portrait of Sir John A. Macdonald across from me on the wall of the cabinet chamber. While I had been on the job only a few hours, I already sensed that each of his successors must have sought the Old Chieftain's advice and understanding across the pages of history during the period they held the job he had perfected. I knew I would be no different and I wanted him nearby.

—

PERSONAL JOURNAL: FEBRUARY 23, 1987

Sometimes in cabinet, when I'm having a particularly difficult time of it, I glance at the painting of Sir John A. that faces me and wonder what that wise old head would suggest I do. Sir John A. and all his successors as prime minister have known moments of great sadness and personal defeat.

—

Going into my first cabinet meeting, I carried a briefing note from my senior policy advisor, Charley McMillan, who had summarized our strategy well: "The management of expectations will be the key element in the public's perception of your behaviour. The public wants change, but too much will scare people, too little will worry them."

Later, in a very tiny change that already seems part of ancient history, I told the cabinet ministers who were still addicted to the demon weed that they would all be banished to one side of the table. Nicorette gum was the order of the day for myself and the other recovering smokers. In those days we somehow believed that cigarette smoke wouldn't spread across a table!

Mila and I had to prepare for and take part in the celebrations surrounding the Pope's visit to Canada. For an Irish Catholic boy from Baie-Comeau, my role in greeting the pontiff in the nation's capital was the experience of a lifetime. Though awed at meeting the head of the Church and Saint Peter's successor, I also couldn't resist injecting a little humour into the occasion. As the Pope preceded me into a sparkling private reception at Rideau Hall to which the leaders of the other parties had been invited, I leaned down to Ed Broadbent and his wife, Lucille, in the receiving line after the Pope had passed by. "How do you like my new advance man?" I asked in a conspiratorial whisper, leaving Broadbent in stitches and supplying him with an anecdote he still relates today.

—

PERSONAL JOURNAL: SEPTEMBER 21, 1984

Late yesterday afternoon at the Old Mill in Hull we attended a private reception for the Pope who was departing Canada after a remarkably successful 12-day tour of the country. While conversing with some Vatican officials, Mila, Ben, Caroline, and I were asked into a private reception with His Holiness. He was clearly tired as the GG [Jeanne Sauvé] and I tried to explain the vast social infrastructure of Canada and answer any questions about it he might have. Although he had just come from a four-and-a-half-hour event at LeBreton Flats he was relaxed and upbeat as he warmly welcomed us, particularly Mila and the kids.

I asked what he thought I should say to President Reagan, with whom I would be meeting Tuesday, prior to his meeting with Gromyko. He began a lengthy discussion on the historic proclivities of the Russians to want to dominate, but concluded by saying that such a sense was now embedded in the Soviet psyche, via the ideology. When the GG remarked that in a recent meeting in Moscow she told a high-ranking official that Canada, being a middle power, might be helpful in the disarmament process provided that the USSR undertook not to export its revolution, the Pope intervened. "But they also have imports," he said. When we all looked perplexed, a smile came on his strong features and he said, "The Russians have imported many Eastern European nations to their revolution but none wanted to do so. So the Russians became more persuasive." The GG looked shocked, but given my own pro-Allied views I was delighted. He is clearly somebody pro-West and anti-Soviet, but recognizes nonetheless that "realpolitik" requires dialogue.

When we saw him off at the airport, he blessed the kids again. (Mila says that will keep them out of trouble for decades – I'm not so sure.) He said goodbye to Mila in Serbo-Croatian and told me he'd be back to Canada.

—

We also met the Queen and Prince Philip in Moncton on September 22. I reflected on the experience in my private journal that night.

—

PERSONAL JOURNAL: SEPTEMBER 22, 1984

My first private meeting with the Queen took place in her suite at the hotel in Moncton. We were alone, and she struck me as being composed, resolute, and quite sympathetic. We chatted about her day. I had heard a good CBC Radio program, Man on the Street, *earlier, and told her about it. Pursuant to a meeting with Premier Hatfield, and at his strong suggestion, I told Her Majesty of the strong monarchical traditions in the PC Party, and my intention to ensure they were respected.*

We chatted amicably about John Turner's decision to call an election in the first place. He had apparently conveyed to Her Majesty, at Windsor, that he had no mandate, that things could get worse, and he felt an early call was advantageous to his case. At this point, Philip entered, poured himself and the Queen a strong Beefeater martini, and offered me one. When I declined in favour of a soda, he laughed and said, "Thank God those charged with running the government stay away from the evil booze." I assured him it was rather a universal and widely advanced trait in Canadian politicians, and he chuckled, and joined in the conversation about John Turner, why he called the election, etc. I said that I had a high regard for John Turner as a person, but that someone had persuaded him to accept horrible political advice since attaining the leadership.

After drinks, we three descended to a private dining room, where Her Majesty offered a private, intimate meal in honour of the new prime minister and his wife. I think about twenty attended, all told. At dinner, the Queen told me of her affection for John F. Kennedy's mother, Rose, because, when she and Margaret were young, a relative died, and the two girls were banished to a small room when important guests called. Only Rose Kennedy came into the room and chatted with them. They were ignored by the other guests – and she remembered it, some forty years later! One shouldn't really cross the Queen, I concluded.

I was to develop an excellent relationship over the years with the Queen and other members of the royal family. Her Majesty proved to be among the wisest persons I was destined to encounter in public life. Considering that she began her reign with Sir Winston Churchill as her prime minister, this should surprise no one. I was able to draw upon this experience when I sought her advice in the years that lay ahead, and I remain grateful to this day for the thoughtful counsel she provided.

Canada's attachment to the monarchy is one that many in Canada – my Irish-Canadian compatriots, for example – and in the United States and overseas simply do not understand, and probably never will. "Canada is a land of small contradictions and larger contrasts," I wrote in a private moment in 1991. "A Roman Catholic prime minister swears allegiance to a sovereign who is also head of the Church of England and almost no one notices the irony. Fewer still would challenge it, and absolutely no one would consider changing it."

Later that night, Mila and I flew to Washington to meet President Reagan. While I knew critics at home would fan the flames of anti-Americanism, I felt that the visit was important, given the strained nature of Canada's relations with our most important ally. Rejecting the Trudeau approach to our neighbour and friend, I preferred that taken by Trudeau's predecessor, Mr.

Pearson, who travelled south for meetings with John F. Kennedy at Hyannis Port shortly after becoming prime minister in 1963.

Ambassador Allan Gotlieb's diaries mention the pressure I felt against going to Washington. "I have had several reports," he wrote, "of the department advising against this visit . . . Bravo to Mulroney for following his own instincts. A leader in command."

Entering the White House, now as prime minister, I met an American president on the cusp of re-election, a leader who had single-handedly restored American confidence after the malaise that had gripped his country during the previous years. With graceful good humour and steely resolve, he was well on his way to making history.

In the Oval Office and later over lunch, the president and I renewed the acquaintance we'd established the previous June. I emphasized my government's steadfast support of NATO and American leadership in dealing with the USSR. "Canada is not a neutral nation," I emphasized to the President and his senior advisors.

I again impressed upon him the need for urgent joint Canadian–American action on acid rain. Repeating themes from the election, I assured America's leader that Canada would give its neighbour the benefit of the doubt, and expected the same in return. We planned, I said, to maintain our independent stand in our foreign policy – and President Reagan and I were indeed destined to have sharp disagreements on the U.S. approach to Cuba, aid to the Contras in Nicaragua, apartheid in South Africa, and future arms controls negotiations with the Soviets. But I promised that we would reciprocate in his administration's wish for a return to the days of a special relationship between Canada and the United States.

"A healthy, strong relationship with the United States of America in no way presupposes any degree of subservience on our part," I later told Canadian reporters before my departure from Andrews Air Force Base.

I had also told President Reagan that my new government would encourage private investment from the U.S. in Canada for the simple reason that there wasn't the capital in our country necessary to create the millions of jobs we needed. I added in my remarks to the press the words, "I am concerned about the 1.6 million Canadians out of jobs who are not concerned about nationalism – who are concerned about providing for their families."

Beyond firming up our already good personal relations – a key part of the job of any Canadian prime minister wishing to advance the nation's cause in the world's most important capital city – the president and I also agreed to hold annual summits, and to continue to have our respective foreign ministers meet quarterly. "These two Irishmen are going to get along like blazes," Gotlieb confided to his diary after our White House lunch meeting.

In the course of my visit, I asked Gotlieb to remain as our ambassador, a post he had held with distinction since 1981.

A few days later, on September 29, following a dinner in our honour given by the Queen and Prince Philip aboard the Royal Yacht Britannia in Toronto, I was back at StFX for the twenty-fifth anniversary of our graduating class. I was accompanied on the flight east by Sam and Marty Wakim, Terry and Mary McCann, and Fred Doucet. We received a rapturous reception and were greeted with thunderous applause everywhere we went, leading me to conclude that the best way to go home to your university is to arrange for your election as prime minister some twenty days earlier!

With thoughts of some of my talks with President Reagan and the Pope still fresh in my mind, I spoke to my alma mater about the most pressing issue any political leader during the Cold War was forced to confront: the preservation of peace. "No matter how much we may accomplish here in Canada," I said, "I will have failed in my most cherished ambition if under my leadership Canada has not helped reduce the threat of war and enhanced the promise of peace . . . We have historic, commercial, cultural, and political ties with many countries around the world, including our potential adversaries. While we have many joint problems that can only be resolved in bilateral dealings with the United States, the Canadian interest in this world lies as well in sound multilateral institutions: economic and political forums where we can exert a positive and constructive influence."

While the class of '59 was there to reminisce, and to renew and share old friendships, the class of '87 had different things on their mind. StFX had won a football game that day, and the campus was definitely in a celebratory mood. A number of lively students, including a young woman who wore a pair of "Brian Mulroney shorts," surrounded this aging X-Man. "Twenty-five years ago last week I arrived at St. Francis Xavier as a student, and I got exactly the same kind of welcome," I joked to the press and students.

Back in Ottawa, my Prime Minister's Office (PMO) staff was headed by principal secretary Bernard Roy, my old friend and roommate, who took up his new responsibilities and challenges with his usual resolve, integrity, and commitment. He, too, was inexperienced in the ways of Ottawa, and this sometimes hobbled his effectiveness in dealing with a frequently reluctant bureaucracy, but I trusted him implicitly. He also had to assume special responsibilities for Quebec, given the embryonic nature of our organization there, the fact that almost all of our Quebec MPs were rookies, and the importance of the federal agenda to that province. I knew that Rodrigue Pageau's death meant that Bernard would have to do double duty most of the time.

Also in the PMO, Peter White and Tom Long assumed responsibility for appointments, Ian Anderson was made director of communications, while Bill Fox (a successful *Toronto Star* bureau chief and a witty raconteur from Timmins, Ontario) and Michel Gratton (a talented and hard-living Franco-Ontarian) were appointed press secretary and assistant press secretary, respectively. Fred Doucet became my senior advisor.

My old friend Pat MacAdam became special assistant for caucus and was joined by Tom Van Dusen and Camille Guilbault in helping me to build a relationship with caucus that was sensitive, effective, and durable. I was determined to learn from the Clark experience, which was summarized in a note sent to me by Bill Neville during the transition: "In retrospect, I think it is fair to say we took over the government the last time without anyone having given any serious thoughts to what caucus's role and relationship should be in a governing situation. As a result, we really didn't have one."

As far as I was concerned, my caucus was to be treated as family – a group to be trusted. Our meetings were to be a place for frankness, and for honest and open debate without fear of recrimination; and a place where all MPs – from the prime minister on down – would receive support and understanding.

Our caucus met on November 2 just before the House opened, and I addressed the group with pride:

> I've dreamed many times of this room being filled with Tories. And I'm sure everyone in this room is delighted Serge Joyal is back selling antiques! The role of caucus is teamwork and unity . . . We are friends, a family, and we will always leave this room as a united family. For new members, it is time to learn your roles and the system. Protocol and decorum must be followed in the House. Start with civility and respect. I will always listen to you and learn

> from you. I'm at your disposal. We are a family and there must be openness and frankness at all times. I will not make the Liberal mistake and keep the party in the Prime Minister's Office. We'll strengthen the party.
>
> The mood in the country is good and we lead all over . . . Almost 76 per cent of Canadians believe we are meeting expectations. The priorities mentioned by people? Selling off unprofitable Crown corporations is not a high priority. The public is saying they don't want us to be Bill Bennetts [premier of B.C.]. The immediate objective of our government is to take control and solidify our electoral support . . .
>
> There must be total secrecy in caucus. If we don't behave with dignity, [our positive image] could be lost. We have written a new page in Canadian history.

I also had a deadly serious message to deliver to caucus. "The 1988 election campaign begins now," I said.

Earlier, I had stunned the bureaucracy – and many Conservatives – by appointing Stephen Lewis, the former Ontario NDP leader, as Ambassador to the United Nations. I knew Stephen slightly, and Bill Davis recommended him highly. At the time of his appointment, Lewis had written a column in *Maclean's* magazine where he had suggested that I, his new boss, had just "acted with indecent haste, grovelling reverentially to the White House." Questioned by the press on his change of heart concerning the prime minister, Stephen responded, "For the first time in my life I'll have to learn the art of self-discipline," adding that he'd have to become "a little more eloquent" in the months ahead. His intentions suited me very well; I wanted a strong voice and a presence at the UN that would emphasize my views on apartheid and Third World development issues (particularly in Africa), while emphasizing the vital nature of the UN and its agencies to Canada's outreach and foreign policies.

—

PERSONAL JOURNAL: JANUARY 1, 1987

Impressive performance by Canada in foreign affairs, highlighted principally by stellar performances by Joe Clark and Perrin Beatty, with notable assists from outstanding ambassadors such as Stephen Lewis at the UN and Lucien Bouchard in Paris. If ever a case were required for the inclusion of "non-career officers" in the foreign service, these two make it with a vengeance. Lewis has been extremely effective and pleasant throughout, including some very tough issues, and has substantially enhanced Canada's standing at the UN and throughout its agencies.

—

During my years in office, Canada participated in every single peacekeeping mission, responded to every request for added assistance from the secretary general of the UN. According to a *Globe and Mail* report of February 28, 2007: "By 1991 Canada was providing 10% of the UN peacekeeping force. Today it is 0.1%." We also made a policy of prepaying our dues on January 1 each year as a signal to laggards like the United States, which was in serious arrears to the UN. "I don't want the secretary general of the UN to become a mendicant," I said at the time, "going around with a tin cup."

The new government was soon confronted by its first crisis, when the tragedy of vast starvation and death in Ethiopia exploded into the consciousness of Canadians, largely as a result of powerful film and commentary by Brian Stewart of the CBC. Like every Canadian viewer, I was shocked by what I saw coming through my television. A calamity was unfolding before our very eyes, children were dying in the ravaged country and nothing was happening to stop it. I contacted Ambassador Lewis to find out if he was hearing of any international initiatives being developed to combat the crisis. His answer was no. "I hope, Prime Minister," he then said, "that you're thinking of doing what I think you're thinking of doing."

I had a quick answer: "I am."

Joe Clark provided decisive leadership and recommended the appointment of David MacDonald as Canadian famine coordinator, empowered to cut through red tape to get food to the starving. This was a brilliant move. If we hadn't made this appointment, we'd still be working on the famine today. Joe was eloquent – "It is our duty as a people to respond" – and astutely saw to it that ordinary members of caucus, and through them the public, became part of Canada's response. "We will treat Ethiopia as an all-party matter," he told a caucus meeting on November 7. "We want support from all Canadians . . . MPs should contact service clubs and local mayors and ask them to lend their efforts to provide aid . . . There is a need for trucks as well as food. Perhaps service club names, for example, could go on the trucks they donate. Tents, bulldozers, and water drilling equipment are also needed. One of the faults in past Canadian foreign policy was that the Canadian people were shut out."

Joe and I bypassed normal bureaucratic channels to get the job done. He would call me and ask, for example, if I would call President Reagan or another world leader with a request to assist Canada. I authorized an initial $50 million in aid to Ethiopia, and the country responded overwhelmingly to our matching contribution program, swelling the total Canadian contribution to some $200 million. I recall a single mother sending in a cheque for $125 that would normally have been used to buy Christmas presents for her family; she told her kids that the family's donation was their joint Christmas present, and they all agreed. There were bake sales and garage sales, student councils became involved, and the money kept coming in. I was proud of this impressive response by our nation.

In a later 2004 documentary, Brian Stewart looked back on the crisis. "Lewis was surprised to find Mulroney shared a keen interest in Africa," he said. "And this unsuspected passion drove Canada into a leadership role in the crisis. Lewis himself later commented, 'It was clear that [Mulroney] had a particular feeling about the continent, and particularly that underdog feeling of Mulroney's where you come to the defence of the beleaguered. It was quite a fascinating dimension of the man, which is not widely appreciated by Canadians.'"

Stewart, obviously still angered and shaken by what he had witnessed two decades before, looked at the big picture in ending his piece. "The crisis saw a leadership and involvement in Africa that no other Canadian government has approached. Yet, it is now scarcely mentioned in our history. Other rich nations also lost focus on Africa, squandering a decade of possible development and leaving Ethiopia seemingly always on the verge of another catastrophe, like the one we once could not imagine in 1984."

French Prime Minister Laurent Fabius arrived in Ottawa for an official visit on November 7, 1984. He was young (only thirty-seven), brilliant, and very close to President François Mitterrand, who wanted stronger ties with Canada and, if possible, a resolution of the thorny triangular question involving Paris, Quebec, and Ottawa.

I had never met Mitterrand, but had a positive impression of this long-time socialist leader because of his denunciation, at a Paris press conference, of General de Gaulle's offensive "Vive le Québec libre" statement in Montreal in the summer of 1967. Fabius himself brought hearty rounds of applause from a crowd that gathered at a state dinner the night of his arrival when he ended his remarks by saying, "Vive le Canada." President Mitterrand had told Fabius, with whom I continue a very friendly relationship to this day, that I proposed to break the deadlock and lay the groundwork for a productive Canadian–French economic and political partnership. Pierre Trudeau's confrontational approach to federal-provincial relations – and Canada–Quebec–France relations in particular – had held up the creation of a French-speaking commonwealth of nations (what was later to become La Francophonie) for too long. That evening I made my views known.

"Six million of us," I said, "are immensely privileged to share with you the treasures of your language, and to live in the French culture. No one can fail to be aware of the tenacity and courage those French-speaking ancestors demonstrated in not only maintaining their heritage but seeing it flourish. We are not talking about simple nostalgia and folklore. Rather, we are talking about vital commitment and collective roots."

I then got to the heart of the matter: "Diplomacy, like candour, must reflect reality. So I cannot talk about Franco-Canadian relations without mentioning the parallel relations that exist between Quebec and Paris . . . The Canadian government intends to exercise all of its constitutional responsibilities in the field of international relations. Nevertheless, it considers it completely normal and desirable that the Quebec government maintain with France those relations justified by the cultural identity of the province of Quebec. Thus we recognize the legitimacy of privileged, direct relations between Paris and Quebec, as long as these relations respect federal institutions and involve subjects that do not conflict with federal jurisdiction. Quebec is an integral part of Canada, and she enriches Canada with her French culture. It is natural that Quebecers perceive your country as a partner in preserving and fostering their special character. We will follow these guiding principles, and we want to leave the rest to the common sense, loyalty, and maturity of the parties involved."

I also invited the visiting prime minister and his government to undertake initiatives with French-language groups and organizations throughout Canada. "That speech," journalist Graham Fraser (who has since been made Canada's commissioner of official languages) later wrote, "began the process of compromise and conciliation that made the first Francophone Summit possible."

During the visit a reporter asked Fabius to compare relations between Canada and France that fall with what they were like under the previous Canadian government. I found it hard to suppress a grin when I heard his answer. "Upon the visit of a French prime minister or a French minister, there were always problems with red carpets of etiquette," he said. "There haven't been difficulties of that nature this time. You will say this is a bit superficial, and I will answer, 'No,' because these problems are simply the surface, and on the political level these indicate other difficulties."

The very next day Michael Wilson delivered his first economic statement, entitled "A New Direction for Canada," to the House of Commons. Speaking on behalf of the government, the finance minister described the economic situation Canada was in. He held nothing back. "Our economic legacy," he said, "is one of high unemployment, inadequate investment, eroded confidence, and personal hardship . . . We are talking here not just of economic failure, but of human tragedy: of real economic hardship suffered by thousands of families; of the social and emotional suffering caused by the loss of a job; and of the loss of hope and self-esteem of young people who find themselves unable to make a productive contribution to society after spending so many years at school . . . No less serious or troublesome than the economic legacy is the deficit and accumulated debt situation which we have inherited."

Without fanfare the minister calmly and clearly told Canadians that the deficit in 1985 would stand at $37.1 billion – $9 billion higher than predicted by the Liberals – if nothing were to be done. And that was just the deficit. "In our centennial year the net federal debt was $18 billion," Michael added. "By the end of this fiscal year it will be $190 billion. If we reach the point where we must start borrowing money just to pay the interest on our debts, we know we have a problem. But this is the situation in which the Government of Canada finds itself today. This year almost 50 per cent of government borrowing is required just to cover interest costs and, if we do not take action, this will rise to more than 76 per cent by 1990. We believe we must act now to avoid a future crisis."

Michael then announced $4.2 billion in expenditure cuts and tax increases; a review of programs including unemployment insurance, housing, and transfer payments to individuals and provinces; changes to the Foreign Investment Review Act and the hated National Energy Program; an extension of the Spouse's Allowance Program to all widows and widowers between ages sixty to sixty-four; increases in pensions for veterans; and a job-creation program. He made it clear that we were serious about revolutionizing the way Canada's federal government did business.

"It has been a long time since a Canadian government had the nerve to confront its electorate (with only 58 months left in its mandate) and announce that all political bets were off, and everything entrenched and sacred was now debatable and negotiable," the *Financial Post*'s Hyman Soloman wrote later. "When did we ever hear that 77 per cent of federal spending can now be regarded as 'discretionary,' which is to say open to reduction and redirection?"

Politically, of course, our government had entered dangerous waters, and the opposition questioned our commitment to universality in social programs, quoting the "sacred trust" that I had used about our devotion to protecting medicare. All we had called for was a national dialogue on how best to ensure that our social programs targeted those most in need. "Why should bank presidents who make $500,000 annually avail themselves fully of the social system?" I was to ask repeatedly. Unfortunately, we left an opening in our lines, and the opposition and media were able to charge through it waving a battle flag called "universality." That issue was to follow us into 1985.

After Michael's first full budget the following May, in which he announced the government's plan to partially de-index Old Age Security from inflation protection, our opponents were able to refer to our earlier confusion, and thus create a situation where much of the Canadian public actually believed we were ending pensions for vulnerable seniors. Nothing could have been further from the truth, but once again Liberal Senator Keith Davey's famous maxim that in politics perception is reality was proved beyond a reasonable doubt.

We tried to swim against this tide. "Universality doesn't exist now," I told my caucus on November 14. "There will be no return to the means test. We have not tampered with one social program except to enhance it. We've raised some issues for discussion in order to help those who need it most." My old boss Alvin Hamilton got to his feet that fall and reminded our frightened caucus that even Saskatchewan's Tommy Douglas, the CCF–NDP father of medicare, had pointed out as recently as 1979 that universality didn't, in fact, exist in the application of many Canadian social programs.

Michael himself addressed caucus less than a week after delivering his economic statement. "On universality – we did not mention it," he said, "but we want to open the subject up for discussion to help ensure that people who need help the most will get it. Spousal allowance [for pensioners] and increases for veterans are established. Please let me know your views." Despite such measures the media delighted in portraying Michael Wilson as a heartless right winger.

In February 1993, I recalled these early rocky days of my prime ministership during a free-ranging discussion in Washington with the new American president, Bill Clinton. Official Canadian note-taker Jim Judd later wrote a report on that day's discussion in the Oval Office between a now battle-scarred Canadian prime minister and an American chief executive only days on the job:

> The prime minister noted that his own experience with controlling government expenditures had been very rough at times, so much so that he had "almost been run out of town on a rail." On one particular issue [Old Age Security] "all hell broke loose" and he had to backtrack on it. Compromise was an honourable solution to many problems in business or law, but in this business [politics] it was seen as a sign of weakness. The judgments that had to be brought to bear on fiscal questions such as these had to be political, first and foremost: "Don't listen to officials." In addition, timing was of the essence – it was very important to move early in the mandate . . . Referring to his 1985 approach to Old Age Security the prime minister characterized this as a "mother of a mistake" made because he was new in office, naïve, and just politically stupid. He had, on the advice of officials, gone for a "double bite," which then provoked demonstrations [by people] who portrayed him as a "black-hearted" millionaire. In fact, he came from a . . . family of six children whose father was an electrician.

Luckily, that November I was still unaware of the political trial by fire that would loom the following spring. Ten days after the economic statement was delivered, however, an event with huge long-term implications for Canada occurred. The Chairman of the Royal Commission on the Economic Union and Development Prospects for Canada, Donald Macdonald, gave us a clear hint about his forthcoming report. He called for a "leap of faith" and recommended the embrace of free trade with the United States. "If we do get down to a point where it's going to be a leap of faith, then I think at some point some Canadians are going to have to be bold and say, yes, we will do it," Macdonald, an experienced and highly regarded former Liberal cabinet minister, said that day. "It's another step in our evolution and we've got enough confidence in ourselves to do it."

In February of 1985, Macdonald spoke with characteristic honesty to the fears of those who came proudly from the Tory tradition and who, like Sir John A. Macdonald, Robert Borden, and John Diefenbaker, viewed the idea of free trade with the Americans with automatic, visceral suspicion. "If I had been asked two and a half years ago if I favoured free trade with the United States, I would have instinctively said no," Macdonald told an interviewer. "But now I realize that we need a global agreement with the United States to control non-tariff barriers." At that point, Michael Wilson, John Crosbie, Sinclair Stevens, James Kelleher (minister of trade), and I, together with a dynamic senior official at External Affairs named Derek Burney, began to anticipate the report and its implications with even greater interest.

While a royal commission was coming close to recommending free trade with the United States and was keeping the pundits busy that fall, Ambassador Lewis delivered an eloquent and passionate blockbuster of a speech to the UN General Assembly, calling South Africa's leaders "a beleaguered oligarchy," and speaking of outside opposition that would be "tenacious and unrelenting." This speech marked the first full Canadian statement in the UN Assembly plenary debate on South Africa in five years.

A few days later, on December 10, at the request of club president Ross Johnson, by now chairman and CEO of Nabisco, I made a major speech to the Economic Club of New York in the grand ballroom of the Waldorf-Astoria Hotel. Like Michael Wilson in the Commons, I spoke clearly of our economic problems and prospects while articulating the philosophy and policies the new government proposed to introduce to encourage investment, improve productivity, and enhance trade while creating jobs and wealth for Canadians: "To all who seek a definition of peaceful association between nations, I say look no further; it is unlikely you shall find a better illustration than the simple story of friendship and prosperity that has marked the evolution of our two countries over the years . . . These are the main reasons that my new government is so committed to rebuilding Canada's image in the world as a free, tolerant, and independent nation, as a reliable trading partner, as a good place to invest and do business, as a people committed to the entrepreneurial spirit, and as a nation that honours its commitments to its allies."

A proud, confident Canada was indeed open for business again.

On December 19, I wrote President Reagan about the upcoming "Shamrock Summit" to be held in Quebec City on March 17: "My hope is that our Governments can accomplish together something of lasting significance . . . I want to manage our bilateral relationship with the civility and priority that befit our respective roles as each other's greatest economic partner and ally . . . Quebec is where our predecessors [FDR and Mackenzie King] and Mr. Churchill carried out the first spadework on the foundations of the Atlantic Alliance. Our joint economic security and prosperity rest upon Western security. There is also the defence of our common environment in front of us. I have spoken to you of the public expectations in Canada that we can make some concrete progress in the very near future in cutting back the causes of acid rain. I urge you to give this matter your generous attention."

That same day, I fired up our troops at the last caucus meeting of the year. "Turner is worse [as opposition leader] than we thought," I said to cheers from the assembled Tory MPs and senators. "We're over 60 per cent in the polls in Quebec. I met with the PC Party headquarters staff this morning and the party is in good shape as well. Still, we have to always be careful. Journalists will try to weaken us, so you must remain cautious and careful. Remember there is no guaranteed employment for members of Parliament. We have to keep working to stay here. 1984 has been a great year. When the election was called, the Grits were 12 per cent ahead. Then, we beat them. We have to become the natural, national majority party." I then sent them home to their constituencies for Christmas with the words, "I salute you all."

The following day, I had my first meeting with South African bishop and apartheid opponent Desmond Tutu. Tutu is a small, athletic man with intelligent, lively eyes, elaborate manners, and a delightful sense of humour, and our friendship now stretches over twenty years of meetings from Ottawa and Montreal to London and Cape Town. That day, however, was all business, as I sought his advice on what role Canada might play in the seemingly stalled efforts to free Nelson Mandela, legalize his African National Congress (ANC), and end apartheid in South Africa.

"Do you think a middle power like Canada could have an effective impact on the situation?" I asked him.

Tutu was vigorous in his response. "I think Canada can have an important, even a lead, role in translating morality into political action," he said as our conversation flowed, until we had taken up twice the allotted time marked in our schedules.

As we concluded our meeting, Tutu told me he feared that because of so many other causes and demands on the world's attention, the fight for justice in South Africa would be forgotten. I told him that wouldn't be the case as long as I served as prime minister of Canada. "Desmond," I pledged as he left, "tell your colleagues and friends that they can count on Canada."

As Christmas approached, there were signs of difficulty. The size of our majority, it seemed, had turned many in the press gallery into active opponents determined to punish us at every turn. And "us," I found, included Mila. She and the three kids were enjoying life in Ottawa. With the children in the Lycée Claudel, Mila was fully occupied, accompanying me on visits abroad and across the country, and attending a large number of Cystic Fibrosis Association events as honorary chairperson, as well as events for literacy, another cause she supported. She was also busy organizing official formal dinners and arranging and completing our move from Stornoway to 24 Sussex. To handle all of this she took a small office in the PMO that had formerly been used for storage. This was an entirely proper decision, given the tremendous demands on a young professional woman who was barely thirty years old. To put it mildly, I was surprised when some in the media began to criticize her for having an office and a small staff, including Bonnie Brownlee, her highly effective executive assistant, to help her in her many and sensitive responsibilities.

At that point, I had already handed critics the ammunition that they would delightedly use for years to come. When I was sworn in I had inherited my predecessor's car, plane, and residences, for my use while I held office. The cars were a used Cadillac and a used Buick. The plane was an aging 707, some twenty-nine years old – so old, in fact, that it violated environmental sound rules, and could not land at major international airports unless the PM was aboard. For domestic travel, the government had acquired a small fleet of Challengers some years before to transport the governor general, prime minister, cabinet ministers, and visiting dignitaries. For some reason, this qualified me for description by the media as "the imperial prime minister."

And then there was 24 Sussex Drive. Built in 1866 by lumberman-politician Joseph Merrill Currier, 24 Sussex Drive was originally called Gorffwysfa, Welsh for "place of rest." But for me and those who preceded and followed me, the official residence was anything but restful. Lacking central air, the home was cooled during stifling Ottawa summers by noisy air conditioning units placed in windows. In the winter, family and guests often found themselves shivering in the 34-room limestone home. Prime Minister Paul Martin summed it up neatly during his own period as a tenant: "Too cold in the winter and too hot in the summer."

In his final term, Mr. Trudeau had been divorced, so for five years very little maintenance had been done at 24 Sussex, as he did little if any entertaining there. In fact John Turner was so concerned by the state of disrepair at the residence when he moved in that he commissioned a study on the costs of redoing much of the electrical wiring, which was considered unsafe. I was given the report that fall. It urged major expenditures, in the hundreds of thousands of dollars just in that one area alone. I made the decision to avoid or defer any major structural repairs. "I did not accept the report, notwithstanding its unquestioned value, because of the prohibitive costs," I told reporters. "I felt because of the kinds of criticism that it might engender, we just couldn't go along with it. So repairs have been kept to an absolute minimum."

I explained that the cost of renovations would be shared by the government, the party, and myself. And any renovations of a personal nature – we had added a satellite antenna at the Harrington Lake cottage, mainly so that I could remain on top of international news and events that affected Canada – would come out of my own pocket. I also announced that I would pay personally for the costs of our family's food while in office – the first and only prime minister to do this. In Michael Wilson's economic statement, I advised the country I would take a 15 per cent pay cut, and my ministers 10 per cent. We were setting an example.

When I met with the governor general to brief her on the economic statement, I shared these intentions with her. Jeanne Sauvé emphatically urged me against them. "Prime Minister," she said, "this is a mistake. None of what you propose to do will be appreciated. In this town, no good deed goes unpunished. You are needlessly penalizing your family, and any expenditure you or the party make at 24 Sussex will be turned against you." In a more personal tone, as warranted by our long friendship, she advised, "Brian, don't do these things."

By 1984 Jeanne Sauvé had been around Ottawa for a generation, first as a parliamentary spouse during Mr. Pearson's time, then as an MP, minister, Speaker of the House, and now, as governor general. Much better than I did, she knew the mindset of the nation's capital and could smell the attacks coming a mile away. My mistake, for which I paid heavily, was not listening to her that day and reversing course immediately. Instead Mila and I issued a cheque for $211,000 from our savings account to pay for furniture purchased for 24 Sussex. When I left office, we were accused in the media of trying to "remove" furniture from 24 Sussex. Yet it was ours, we'd paid for it, *and* in fact we left most of it behind.

When Brian Tobin became Jean Chrétien's minister of fisheries, it was revealed that he spent more on redecorating his suite of ministerial offices than Mila and I had on preparing the two prime ministerial residences for occupancy. This story, issued by Canadian Press, made the bottom of a page in *La Presse*. The double standard was obvious. Journalist Lysiane Gagnon wrote about that same double standard years later: "And Mr. Chrétien never goes anywhere without a huge retinue. For the Team Canada junket to Mexico and Latin America, he brought along forty-seven staffers; a simple overnight trip to Washington called for an entourage of twenty-three aides. In 1994, at a time when his government was shovelling its deficit to the provinces, which ended up cutting crucial hospital care, Mr. Chrétien and his entourage flew to St. Kitts–Nevis, in the Caribbean, for a ten-day holiday; he used a government plane which was stationed on the island for the whole duration of the holiday. Where are our self-righteous pundits when we need them? In the late eighties, when it was revealed that then prime minister Brian Mulroney owned a few pairs of Gucci loafers (which he had paid for from his own pocket) and that his wife used to shop at Holt Renfrew and order Chablis wine from hotels' room service, the highly principled English-Canadian chattering class went berserk. But Mr. Chrétien still is seen as the modest, endearing petit gars de Shawinigan."

By Christmas of that event-filled year it was becoming clear that the House of Commons was out of control. I had been limited in my choice for Speaker because so few Conservative MPs with some parliamentary experience spoke French. I considered Tory MP David Kilgour, John Turner's brother-in-law, but rejected him following a conversation with John, who expressed discomfort with the idea. I had settled on John Bosley, a pleasant, extremely intelligent MP from Toronto who had impressed me as a good debater in the House, with a working knowledge of French.

The House of Commons establishes how the nation regards its politics and its politicians. It has its own personality, which can run from noble to vicious, depending on the occasion, with all the stops along the way. Proceedings in the Commons had been televised since the late 1970s, and this had changed how parliamentarians performed their duties. Question period became almost the only time the press covered proceedings, and "acting" on camera was the order of the day. Like all of us, I learned how to handle the role.

In 1989 I was to draw upon my own experiences under the television lights in the Commons as Margaret Thatcher sadly contemplated the introduction of television into the mother of parliaments at Westminster. "She does not have to win every round in question period," I told her principal secretary for foreign policy, Charles Powell, during a transatlantic telephone conversation. "Debating points [with the Labour leader] are entirely secondary to creating a perception of calm and confidence . . . Decibel levels in the chamber are deceptive. They make great theatre but are lousy clips at night. The temptation will be overwhelming to recover lost popularity, and answer scathing articles. She will regain that by being above the fray and showing to the British public a side they don't often see – the human side. There should be some hesitation before responding and some acknowledgement of error, along with some good humour and an engaging smile."

Some months later, Margaret sent a note to Mila and added the following postscript. "Please tell Brian that the House of Commons gets noisier and noisier at question time – record decibels yesterday," the British prime minister wrote. "But, thanks to Brian's advice, I have not raised my voice once."

Any parliament functions effectively only in the presence of a strong, respected, and accepted leader, namely the Speaker. For some reason, Bosley was not able to fill that role. For all his fine personal qualities, he tended to be irritable and combative under pressure, whereas the great Speakers like Lucien Lamoureux were quiet and thoughtful, acquiring their moral authority from the members as opposed to trying to impose themselves as figures of authority upon the House.

A small group of Liberal MPs, dubbed the "Rat Pack," deliberately contributed to the uproar in the House by specializing in the politics of personal destruction. They wallowed in allegations of scandal without proof, vicious personal attacks on individuals deemed to hold "patronage" appointments, the ruthless use of innuendo and half-truths to smear ministers and their families, and abusive treatment of the rules of the House. Their tactics caused great pain to many, and Bosley did little to contain the damage.

One of the chief offenders was Don Boudria, who took special pride and delight in attacking the children and families of ministers. Years later, when he was fired from Chrétien's cabinet over a conflict of interest violation, it was interesting to see him in tears on the floor of the Commons, deploring the fact that his adult children had been drawn into the matter. As Mr. Diefenbaker used to say, "It's a long road that has no ashcans."

Though we are friends today, Brian Tobin was another yelling, gesticulating, shameless member of the Rat Pack. In his memoirs, *All in Good Time*, he explained the media's contribution to this new style of attack in the Commons. "During those years," Brian wrote, "which included the most notorious episodes of the Rat Pack, I was mentioned in dozens of media stories detailing the activities of Question Period, but only once in reference to my committee work . . . So 13 years of committee work yielded one mention in a *Globe and Mail* column written by Hugh Winsor, while 13 minutes of give-and-take in Question Period could earn headlines and evening TV news coverage day after day. That kind of sums it up."

Was the Rat Pack – Don Boudria, Brian Tobin, John Nunziata, Sheila Copps, Jean Lapierre, and Jean-Claude Malépart – simply an aberration and an embarrassment to the rest of the Liberal Party? Not according to a document from a Liberal caucus planning group that came into our hands. It coolly recommended that because I had led the party to a great victory and was its principal asset, much of the attack should be directed at me personally, the theory being that if you can denigrate and smear the leader, the rest of the party will suffer.

And so the frontal attack on me became unrelenting. Nothing was sacred as this campaign of denigration and smear (which the respected veteran journalist George Bain, in his book *Gotcha! How the Media Distort the News*, described as unprecedented in modern Canadian history) went on unabated for a decade. Many in the media became complicit in the opposition strategy. *Ottawa Citizen* editor Keith Spicer even announced on Radio-Canada's *Le Point* that since we had such a majority in the Commons, his paper would oppose us, to fill what he saw as a gap in the parliamentary opposition. The Liberals and the media worked together hand in glove, exchanging documents, political advice, and tactics in an attempt to bloody the government so badly it would have difficulty recovering. It was clear to me as I joined the family for our first Christmas at Harrington Lake that my caucus, my family, and I were in for one very rough ride.

These storm clouds aside, I'd also met the provincial premiers in November at Meech Lake and we had agreed to hold a full-fledged First Minister's Meeting early in the new year – the first of many, though I didn't know it at the time. Even René Lévesque, destined to be remembered as one of Quebec's greatest premiers, seemed willing to give the new government a chance, and he began to speak more openly about the "good risk" for his people to be found in Canadian federalism. In the new atmosphere he was even able to make jokes about comments from the English-speaking premiers that previously would have angered him. "Now you see why – vous voyez pourquoi je suis – separatist?" he scrawled, in both official languages, on a private note he sent to me, which brought grins to our faces as the meeting continued that day. In my dealings with him, Lévesque was always well prepared, polite, and respectful. I admired him as a genuine democrat, and so – in our brief time together as first ministers – our relationship was cordial and productive.

Ontario's Bill Davis, Alberta's Peter Lougheed, and Nova Scotia's John Buchanan, all veterans of Canada's constitutional repatriation wars, were also on hand that November day, and I could sense from them as well the desire to move forward in partnership. I assured the premiers that my government would be taking immediate steps to review and eliminate irritants that had impeded harmonious federal-provincial relations in the past.

Before the month ended, I contacted each premier outlining our progress. "This review turned up many such issues," I wrote. "A number affected all the provinces equally, and typically involved such apparently simple matters as a refusal to discuss issues of concern to them, or a failure to take minor administrative action to remove a problem. . . . I want to assure you that my government places great emphasis on constructive and civil federal-provincial relations, over the whole range of activities in which we have a common interest."

At Harrington Lake, the country residence nestled in the Gatineau Hills about thirty minutes from Ottawa, my family and I had the chance to rest briefly before a new year began.

—

PERSONAL JOURNAL: JUNE 27, 1993

And so I jot down these final thoughts in my little den at Harrington, a place that has brought us such sanctuary in the storms and joy and freedom as a family. Here the kids were happy, Mila was relaxed, and I accordingly, for a while, was able to shuck some of the responsibilities and genuinely enjoy myself with family and friends.

—

John Diefenbaker had been the first prime minister to use Harrington Lake as a summer residence. Supporters prevailed upon him to use it as a place where he could leave the burdens of office behind and enjoy the quiet and restorative solitude of fishing on the lake. I think I can speak on behalf of all the prime ministers who followed the Chief and say without hesitation that he made a wise choice. Despite our differences late in his life, I would like to think that Dief looked down on Harrington Lake approvingly during the many times the Mulroney family visited there. Mark and Nicolas, in particular, were quite the fishermen, and that would definitely have pleased the Chief.

Mila and I enjoyed Harrington Lake so much that we made the decision to move the family there each spring and to remain until September. Our loyal canine companions, Clover and Oscar, roamed freely, although Oscar became the only member of the family who didn't fully enjoy his time at the lake. None of us has forgotten the summer night he escaped into the darkness of a Gatineau evening only to meet up with a porcupine. It was a short encounter, and Oscar was soon at the door, his snout and face full of quills that were painful even to look at. We whisked the dog inside, and that night the prime minister of Canada, his wife, and their children spent many hours on the floor of the kitchen removing the quills from poor Oscar.

That Christmas of 1984 the family skated on the lake and spent hours walking through the woods. It was an idyllic time, much needed before we faced the new year that lay ahead.

1985

1. The Shamrock Summit and Beyond

By November of 1984 my principal secretary, Bernard Roy, was already receiving recommendations – mainly unsolicited – concerning appointments to the bench. While people meant well, and while it had been a long time since Tories had appointed anybody to anything in Ottawa, judgeships were of the highest importance, far beyond partisan considerations. I wanted the best judges possible on the bench, and I didn't give a hoot about their political background. An independent, competent, and respected judiciary is the backbone of Canada's very existence, and must be maintained by all federal governments because it is essential to the flourishing of our admired democracy. After reading one memo from Bernard to me about the lobbying that was going on concerning an upcoming vacancy to the Supreme Court, I cracked down, scrawling a note on the bottom of his memo: "BAR: I want . . . views on the very best judges/lawyers (men and women) from Atlantic Canada. Can I have this on an urgent basis? Partisan considerations are very secondary in this process."

In January 1985, I made my first appointment to the Supreme Court of Canada. After examining résumés, gauging opinions, and consulting as widely as possible, I decided that Mr. Justice Gerald La Forest of the New Brunswick Court of Appeal was the best candidate available for the position recently opened by a retirement. Acting on my instructions, Fred Doucet sounded him out, successfully, on the appointment. I then placed a call to speak personally with the judge during a break in a cabinet meeting at Meech Lake, keenly aware of the solemnity of the occasion. After his acceptance and expressions of gratitude, I was surprised to learn La Forest's main concern: "Who is going to pay for my moving expenses?" the future learned justice of the Supreme Court of Canada wondered.

I was able to smooth that one over, but discovered that La Forest carried this fear with him all the way into the Supreme Court chamber in Ottawa, even after his swearing-in. Chief Justice Brian Dickson soon informed me by letter that his new colleague's concerns about expenses stood a real chance of getting in the way of the justice's work on the most important bench in Canada. "You will appreciate," Chief Justice Dickson wrote, "that these personal concerns will necessarily distract him . . . and I would, therefore, very much appreciate it if this matter could be dealt with expeditiously." Another letter from Dickson informed me that Justice La Forest had more than moving expenses on his mind. "I wonder if it would be possible to assure Mr. Justice La Forest now that if any problem occurred [in selling his Fredericton home] whether his . . . residence would be picked up by the government," the chief justice wrote.

This was my introduction to the all-too-human side of the judiciary in Canada. Eventually, Mr. Justice La Forest was satisfied with all the arrangements, and went on to serve with distinction on the Supreme Court until his recent retirement. Over time, I appointed eight justices to the court and elevated another, Antonio Lamer, to the position of chief justice. I believe there is general agreement that these appointments were of the highest quality, and that there definitely was no partisan litmus test when I appointed a member of Canada's highest court.

Canada has a moderate, centrist Supreme Court composed of the most talented and thoughtful jurists the nation can produce. This high standard was maintained before my service as prime minister and continued afterwards under Jean Chrétien, Paul Martin, and Stephen Harper, who made their own appointments. Generally speaking, all of Canada's superior courts are a model of excellence, and it is vital that they remain so. If our courts were to become politicized, it would be a dark and dangerous day for Canada.

—

PERSONAL JOURNAL: JANUARY 16, 1985

John Crosbie and I yesterday resolved the question of our first appointment to the Supreme Court of Canada. I rejected John's legitimate wish to appoint a fellow Newfoundlander, because the leading candidate is clearly Justice La Forest of the New Brunswick Court of Appeal. Criticism of La Forest is extremely polarized – "too close to Trudeau, Liberal persuasion, etc." I've overruled such observations because of my view, backed by others such as Yves Fortier, Julien

Chouinard, the chief justice, etc., that there can be no partisanship in the appointments to the Supreme Court.

—

In early 1985 I turned to another distinguished judge, Mr. Justice Jules Deschênes, on a different legal matter. I asked him to examine the whole issue of Nazi war criminals who had escaped from Europe after the Second World War to slip into Canada and who could still be living here. I received a huge amount of abuse for this decision, much of it coming from traditional Tory constituencies of ethnic Canadians who originated in eastern Europe. Fiercely anti-communist, these communities were concerned about the Deschênes Commission accepting evidence from Soviet sources. While I was sympathetic, I allowed the commission to continue for one important reason: to me the idea of people who had participated in the extermination of Jews living in my country was odious and unacceptable. They had to be exposed, and then they had to be expelled from Canada.

—

PERSONAL JOURNAL: JANUARY 1, 1988

The decision by Pierre Trudeau to leave, untroubled, Nazi war criminals living in Canada surely must rank with the greatest sins of omission in the history of this nation. After serving as justice minister and 16 years as PM, Pierre Trudeau was – or should have been – aware of the fact that people guilty of the most heinous of crimes involving the slaughter of Jews were living in Canada. They lived here under false pretences and were never charged because it appears that Mr. Trudeau did not want "to trouble" the social fabric of Canada. I appointed the Deschênes Commission specifically because I believed that Mr. Trudeau had opted for "social tranquillity" rather than simple justice. It is repugnant to me in the extreme to think that criminals and murderers were allowed to enter Canada and prosper here, thereby sullying our citizenship, without challenge or accountability. For all those years criminals of the worst sort found sanctuary in Canada, when evidence of their guilt or their complicity was available for the minister of justice or PM if he was interested in finding out.

—

As 1985 began, plans by the American administration to counter the Soviet nuclear threat proved a major political challenge for my government. Before I became prime minister, Ronald Reagan had announced his dream of making nuclear weapons obsolete through the Strategic Defense Initiative (SDI), better known by its nickname, Star Wars. Utilizing the best diplomatic-speak, I announced that my enthusiasm for SDI was, shall we say, guarded. While determined that Canada assume her full responsibilities as a member of the Western Alliance after years of Liberal neglect, I found the thought of the weaponization of space and the creation of another costly arms race extremely disconcerting.

Joe Clark at External Affairs had similar misgivings. Still, he and I agreed that we at least owed the Americans the benefit of the doubt. Some in cabinet, Minister of Defence Bob Coates in particular, took a more hawkish view of Star Wars, and I believed those views should be fully aired. I firmly rejected the knee-jerk hostility to SDI, rooted in anti-Americanism, that came from Liberal MP Lloyd Axworthy and others. Axworthy's attitude was ironic, considering he had sat in a cabinet that decided to approve the testing of the U.S. cruise missile over Canadian soil with no public input or debate, both of which I planned as part of our SDI deliberations.

In January, Joe was blunt and realistic when he spoke about SDI in the Commons. "In the light of Soviet advances in ballistic missile defence research in recent years and deployment of an actual ballistic missile defence system, it is only prudent that the West keep abreast of the feasibility of such projects," he said, adding that the American plan was "highly hypothetical."

Joe's speech was brought to Ronald Reagan's attention, and the president called to talk to me about it. I made a note to file after his call. "He had read Mr. Clark's statement to the House of Commons concerning the support the Canadian government had offered the U.S. in regards to SDI research," I wrote. "He called to thank me and the government for their support at a critical time. I told him that while there would be differences between Canada and the United States in the future, we propose to resolve these differences in a friendly manner. I told him I would convey to Mr. Clark his message as well, because it was our intention to support our allies at critical moments."

As the weeks went by, SDI remained high on the agenda. In the spring, I made two decisions. First, following the advice of Privy Council Clerk Gordon Osbaldeston, I asked Arthur Kroeger, a respected veteran public servant, to study our possible participation in the program. We charged Kroeger with examining the economic, strategic, and scientific implications for Canada if we participated in the program. He travelled to Washington and learned that Canada could expect contracts worth only $30 million a year for SDI research if we took part. He also found out that senior Pentagon officials were suggesting that SDI was not really a high priority of the administration – an opinion that would surely have come as a surprise to President Reagan.

Second, I also thought it wise to have a parliamentary committee gauge public opinion, as only politicians can; while polling is helpful to any government, there are certain issues politicians instinctively get a feel for when they consult their constituents and the wider public. At the height of the Cold War, SDI was definitely in that category. I asked rookie London-area Conservative MP, the very able Tom Hockin, to co-chair an all-party committee that would hold public hearings and study the subject from all angles. While even the parliamentarians split in the end, Tom's committee recommended that in the interim the Canadian government not participate directly in SDI.

From Washington, the Canadian ambassador, Allan Gotlieb, sent me his own view of Canada's choices. A former undersecretary of state for external affairs, Allan had the necessary experience to examine the issue in the full contexts of Canadian–American relations and the wider geopolitical considerations that Canada, as a member of NATO and a G-7 country, had to consider. In his report to me, Gotlieb wrote:

> There remains the possibility, at least some day, that deployment will be up for negotiation in Geneva. Despite what the President says, SDI's use is eventually likely to be most pertinent as a bargaining chip, in some form or other. We can't say that. It is a concept too close to the President's heart, and a negotiating possibility too potentially precious to dilute by breaking Western ranks at this stage. But we can continue to make very clear our support only for

> research, as well as our continued expectations for the Geneva strategic negotiations. In doing this we should also make clear that there must be a clear distinction between research and deployment of any defensive system . . . We should also continue to emphasize our expectations for a successful Reagan–Gorbachev Summit in November, and improving USA–USSR relations. Whatever the actual prospects, it is important to maintain expectations, as these in turn influence the political climate and help to add pressures of some modest sort.
>
> All of this argues against saying no on SDI research. Although there is no formal U.S. invitation to sign on, we should not be deceived by formalities. I personally believe that nothing would astound both the Administration and the Congress more than if the Mulroney government would enunciate a negative policy on SDI. It would affect the way the U.S. Government sees Canada – more than any other decision would do. The impact of such a decision would, I believe, infuse virtually every aspect of the Canada–U.S. relationship. I won't dwell on its impact on the defence relationship. Anyway, we can't (and shouldn't) forbid Canadian private participation.

Another group whose advice I sought was a collection of senior party members from the Red Tory spectrum who reported solely to me. The fact that this committee – dubbed the Special Consultants – even existed was kept secret from my advisors and cabinet. Among those who sat on it were Robert Stanfield, Lowell Murray, David MacDonald, Hugh Segal, and Douglas Roche (a former MP whom I had appointed Canada's disarmament ambassador). After meeting four times between March and June of 1985, they sent in their first report. "Public opinion," they wrote, "the uncertainty of the SDI project, and the risk of a large financial obligation in the future all suggest that the government should refrain from endorsing the SDI program. This does not mean that Canadian firms would be denied the right to bid on research contracts. On the contrary, they could continue operating under existing arrangements. However, no special arrangements should be made to encourage them to bid on SDI projects."

With all this conflicting advice considered, and after cabinet consultation, I made Canada's decision: the Canadian government would not participate in SDI, but private companies and institutions such as universities could undertake research for the program. It was an honourable compromise. On September 7, after meeting with caucus, I telephoned President Reagan at Camp David before announcing my decision, which was later described as a "polite no" to SDI. Fred Doucet sat in my office as I spoke to President Reagan and later dictated a note to file capturing the discussion:

> The PM told the President of his great pleasure at seeing him recovering well from his recent illness – he had seen him [on TV] with short-sleeve shirt on at Independence and also riding his horse. The President thanked him and complimented the PM on his becoming a new father in recent days. The PM told the President that he was in the final stages of coming to a decision on [Secretary of Defense Caspar] Weinberger's invitation to have Canada participate in SDI research. The PM reviewed with him that on January 21, 1985, Canada had been the first country from the allies to express endorsement of the SDI concept. He went on to say that on numerous occasions he had had the opportunity to justify and emphasize Canada's decision, which decision would never be put in question. The PM explained to the President that in view of Weinberger's invitation to participate in the research in March, 1985, two Canadian initiatives had been undertaken to assess Canada's mood on this question: a) an all-party parliamentary committee held hearings across the country, and b) a government envoy was sent to Washington to determine specifics of the invitation. In view of this action, the government would have to make a yes-or-no decision. The PM then relayed to the President the decision contemplated to be taken later today: a) SDI is consistent with the ABM Treaty; b) SDI is a prudent action on the part of the U.S. in view of Soviet initiatives of a similar kind; . . . c) That there would be no participation on a government-to-government basis in SDI research, but that private industry and universities were free to participate as they wished . . .
>
> The President expressed serious disappointment at our non-participation but expressed his appreciation for the Canadian government's past and continuing support of U.S. initiatives . . . The President and PM agreed with each other that they should be in close touch informally as the Geneva Summit approaches and as other issues emerge.

I then spoke with the press: "After careful and detailed consideration the Government of Canada has concluded that Canada's policies and priorities do not warrant a government-to-government effort in support of SDI research. Although Canada does not intend to participate on a government-to-government basis on the SDI research program, private companies and institutions interested in participating in the program will continue to be free to do so . . . This government believes that SDI research by the United States is both consistent with the ABM Treaty and prudent in light of significant advances in Soviet research and deployment of the world's only existing ballistic missile defence system."

When questioned by reporters, I added the following: "We have supported the concept of research. Only a naïve six-year-old would fail to understand that the Americans are involved in this research because the Soviets have been doing it for a long period of time, expended billions of dollars, and committed thousands of personnel to it. And so the government felt that it was appropriate as an ally and a member of NATO that we convey that support [through Joe Clark in January]."

Soviet leader Mikhail Gorbachev and I exchanged letters on strategic questions late in September of 1985. There I was able to reiterate privately what I had said publicly concerning Canada's stance on SDI. "Canada's geographic location naturally requires us to take a particular interest in strategic issues and their associated arms control dimensions," I wrote. "My government attaches great importance to maintaining the integrity of the ABM Treaty, one of the key elements in the strategic balance. Strict adherence by both parties to its provisions is one of fundamental importance to the arms control process . . . It is Canada's view that research into strategic defences does not, in and of itself, violate the ABM Treaty. As President Reagan and I had occasion to agree at our meeting in Quebec . . . any steps beyond research would, in view of treaty obligations, be a matter for discussion and negotiation."

While working with President Reagan and other allies across the globe, I learned that true friends must look their counterparts in the eye and feel no hesitation in offering up the unvarnished truth. To tweak the American Eagle just for the sake of doing so – to earn nothing but easy and cheap applause from Canada's anti-American lobby – is an abdication of leadership and a dereliction of Canada's duty as a trusted friend and ally. The president of the United States (like any leader) has many friends, advisors, and others who tell him what they think he wants to hear. The three presidents

I dealt with – Ronald Reagan, George H.W. Bush, and Bill Clinton – didn't want friends like that. They wanted openness and honesty, and they always responded in kind.

In February of 1985, my government had to make a decision that wasn't nearly as difficult as Star Wars. Two weeks into the month, I travelled to Newfoundland to sign the Atlantic Accord with Premier Brian Peckford. In doing so, I fulfilled a pledge I'd made eight months before as opposition leader when I told the people of that province that I believed that both the federal government and provincial governments should play equal roles in the management of offshore resources. I also said that our party would recognize the legitimate desire of Newfoundland and Labrador to ensure that the development of Hibernia would maximize the social and economic benefits to the province. Our Liberal predecessors had resisted any such agreement. To me, the accord showed that two governments acting in unison and with common objectives could work in both the national and provincial interest.

"We have agreed to the creation of a joint agency to manage the offshore, which will report directly to both governments," I told the crowd in St. John's on February 11. "And, we have adopted the principle that revenue sharing between the two governments should be identical for all oil- and gas-producing regions without discrimination. Newfoundland will be entitled to establish and collect revenues from offshore resources as if these resources were on land." I went on to stress the main point. "Most of all, this agreement is about dignity. For Newfoundland and Labrador, long a have-not province, today marks the beginning of a new era – one that will enhance economic well-being and collective accomplishment. This agreement reflects important Newfoundland values and accommodates legitimate provincial aspirations in a generous Canadian perspective. This new attitude, a cornerstone of national reconciliation, will be instrumental in the development of policies designed to foster economic renewal."

I'd be less than truthful if I didn't admit I was very happy with the government's progress as I boarded the plane and flew back to Ottawa from Newfoundland. We had promised national reconciliation and now we were delivering.

Still, politics is not the gentlest of professions, and this was all too apparent as I headed home. I knew full well we were heading into rough waters, thanks to the actions of Defence Minister Bob Coates on a trip to

West Germany only weeks before. In January, I had learned from the Clerk of the Privy Council that Bob had visited a West German strip joint while staying at a nearby Canadian Forces Base. Gordon Osbaldeston and others outlined the possible security breaches inherent in such nocturnal activities, particularly at the height of the Cold War, and I asked them to investigate further. I myself am neither a prude nor a shrinking violet, but I found Bob's actions mystifying. I planned to give him a dressing-down and nothing more. He knew that what he'd done was plain stupid.

Then the *Ottawa Citizen* published a breathless account of Bob's visit to the club. The moralizing from the paper's editorial offices (where I suspect more than a few staffers might conceivably have visited an adult club in the course of a working day) rose to a fever pitch. This was becoming a big scandal – a "sex scandal" (although in fact it featured no sex).

I reacted poorly. Worried about the government's agenda being completely waylaid by this "sex scandal," I asked Bob to leave cabinet, an approach to ministerial responsibility that was to cost my government and me dearly during our first mandate. As it turned out, it was also unfair to Coates and, in later years, to others. In 1985 I believed that ministers should be held to the highest standards of professional and personal behaviour. Intellectually, I still believe that, and I have the political scars from lost ministers to prove it. Practically, however, I realize now that I handed the opposition and media yet another weapon to use against us later.

I thought that letting Coates go was the honourable way to proceed in a parliamentary democracy. This was one of my first serious mistakes as prime minister, and it came directly from inexperience in Ottawa. In those days I truly believed that any variance from the strict interpretation of ministerial responsibility and of proper personal conduct should be dealt with by a resignation, and over the years I followed this route with a number of ministers.

I was wrong. My errors were political, and I was later to watch Prime Minister Chrétien handle similar issues in a much shrewder and less demanding manner. Unlike Chrétien, who had spent almost two decades in the federal cabinet, I failed to understand that I was going to be pilloried for accepting ministerial resignations and not respected for demanding them. Chrétien was the better politician in this regard.

Bob announced his resignation at the end of question period on February 12, 1985. While I knew I was offering up visuals to press photographers and TV crews that would haunt the government for weeks, I felt I owed it to Bob to walk him to his car to show him my personal support. We shook hands, parted, and I slowly returned to my office. The whole episode took just a few minutes.

After I sat down I noticed that my secretary had left a handwritten note on my desk that had been delivered while I was outside with the now former defence minister. I shook my head as I read it, not sure if I should laugh or cry. It was from a backbench member of caucus. "Prime Minister," the MP wrote, "as I said months ago, I am here to help you. If you need someone in Defence who has grey hair, experience in administration, and some knowledge of defence, please let me know. You know I'll do whatever you wish."

The month was to end on a brighter note when Indian Affairs Minister David Crombie introduced legislation whereby Indian women would no longer lose their status and associated rights when they married non-Indians. This legislation, and Crombie's excellent work on the file, showed Canadians the concern our government had for minority rights in Canada, a concern shown throughout our two mandates.

With the Coates non-scandal behind me, it was my duty to represent Canada at the funeral of Soviet leader Konstantin Chernenko. Little did I know as I flew into a drab and dreary Moscow, made greyer still by the March weather, the oppressive Stalinist architecture, and the even more oppressive system Lenin and Stalin had imposed on their people, just how dramatically history would change in the coming six years.

In 1991, speaking behind closed doors with the other G-7 leaders in London, I recalled that 1985 funeral, noting that since then we had seen "1) Freedom of countries in eastern Europe. 2) Dismantling of the Warsaw Pact. 3) Unification of Germany with NATO membership. 4) Support [by the Soviets] of the UN Security Council on the Persian Gulf and Middle East overall. 5) Conclusion of START [Strategic Arms Reduction Treaty] and CFE [Treaty on Conventional Armed Forces in Europe] agreements with the U.S. 6) Elections and democratization of USSR. 7) The genuine desire of the USSR to enter the international community." I summarized with the words, "If Gorbachev had said in 1985 he proposed to do all these things, and would we help him if he did, I believe all of us would have hurried to write a cheque for our own contributions."

Besides the opportunity to take the measure of the new Soviet leader, the funeral allowed me, a rookie prime minister on the international political scene, the chance to meet with my G-7 partners ahead of our summit scheduled for Bonn that May. Those meetings served as a crash course in international relations and high-power summitry, bringing to life the personalities and the issues in a way that the dry briefing papers written by bureaucrats never could.

—

PERSONAL JOURNAL: MARCH 14, 1985

This morning we went to the German embassy for a meeting with Chancellor Kohl. He is big, hearty, and, as I found out, surprisingly perceptive in his analysis of people and events. Kohl, who spoke German throughout, began with words of gratitude for our decision to deploy 1,200 more troops in Germany. His reasoning was interesting: Canada, as a middle power, is held in high regard in Germany. That Canada, with no record of territorial design or ambition, would – in difficult financial times – take such a decision, made a profound impression upon Germans called upon to shoulder a major share of alliance costs.

—

Kohl, who privately had a delicious sense of humour, then turned serious, outlining a G-7 reality that continues to this day: the inability of the French and the Americans to understand each other. "The Chancellor allowed as to how there had always been problems with the French regarding their concerns about the Summit group being seen to discuss issues for which it had no formal mandate," the note-taker wrote. "At Williamsburg [in 1983], Kohl said he had to physically prevent Mitterrand from leaving the room when Reagan had circulated his draft on international security. In terms of applied psychology, the Chancellor suggested the Americans had much to learn. On a number of occasions he had tried to teach the Americans how to deal with the French. He had explained to them that while, as far as he was concerned, one nod to the [German] flag was clearly sufficient, the French required everyone to salute their flag at least five times a day. If Prime Minister Mulroney were to get this message across to President Reagan, he would be doing the Summit group an enormous favour . . . Mulroney might contribute, Kohl suggested, by helping make Mitterrand feel part of the gang and by helping the Americans to understand him."

I thought back to that advice from Helmut often in the years ahead. In April of 1990, for example, President George H.W. Bush and I met at the SkyDome in Toronto. Once again, French–American tensions were in the air and I was asked by the president's chief of staff, John Sununu, for my views. "In answer to a question from Sununu, the PM said that Mitterrand was feeling better now about the way he was treated," the note-taker wrote, "but that he could never forget the experience of having to move aside to 'make way for the President,' i.e., Reagan. The PM further explained that Mitterrand saw himself as the incarnation of the French language and culture around the world. He could not, therefore, afford to compromise on the level of respect shown to him by other leaders. Bush remarked that it should be possible to give it to him. Baker agreed but insisted that the USA could not compromise on the question of a political role for the USA in Europe. Sununu noted that what the French really wanted was to have the USA 'on call.'"

During my very first meeting with François Mitterrand in Moscow in 1985, I learned how the president of the French Republic and his officials viewed G-7 summits. Helmut, I discovered, had been accurate. "Mitterrand suggested that Chancellor Kohl was annoyed because France had refused to accept a further declaration on terrorism," the notes of this meeting report. "Mitterrand said he was not opposed to discussing this subject, but, he said, he was simply not prepared 'to entertain everybody's phobias.' While he accepted that some issues were very current in California, this did not, he stressed, suggest that the same views necessarily applied elsewhere."

Mitterrand also outlined his concerns about how bureaucratic and stale the summits had become. He complained that the Western Summit, which began as an informal get-together of the industrialized nations, had been transformed by the Americans into a policy-making body whose results had an impact on the entire world. While I hadn't yet attended a meeting, I'd seen enough of the preparation already in Ottawa to realize he had a point. "The Prime Minister agreed that the Summit machinery had become cumbersome. The day after he had assumed responsibility for the government, he had been informed that a group of officials were working on the agenda for a Summit meeting to take place in nine months' time. He agreed that on occasion the Americans could be insensitive to concerns they did not share."

The president and I also discussed domestic issues. While I wanted Canada and Quebec to participate in the inaugural meeting of La

Francophonie, Premier Lévesque was still pursuing an agreement with the federal government over his province's participation in this crucial international forum, and his terms were unacceptable to me. "The Prime Minister said he had rejected outright Quebec's proposals and had used the occasion to remind the Premier that, as Prime Minister of Canada, he had a larger and more recent mandate from Québécois than did Lévesque," the notes from that meeting record.

Adding a surprising social note, Mitterrand took the time to tell me that he had family members who had lived in Calgary.

—

PERSONAL JOURNAL: MARCH 14, 1985

Off to the British embassy for a meeting with Mrs. Thatcher, whom I had earlier met in Ottawa while in opposition. She is a delight. Clear-headed, well-spoken, resolute – and very supportive of Canada. She spoke favourably of changes in domestic policy under the new government and expressed great satisfaction at Canada's announcement yesterday to enhance our NATO complement by 1,200 personnel. "What a change – what a tremendous change to be dealing with you and a new government in Canada!" she stated.

—

When I met Margaret Thatcher in the safe-room in the basement of the British embassy, designed so that conversations could take place out of earshot of the ever-present KGB recording devices, she had already met with Mikhail Gorbachev, both in Moscow and previously in London. I was anxious to hear this veteran prime minister's impressions of the relatively young and vigorous Soviet general secretary. Considering the debate in Canada over Star Wars, I asked her if the Soviets had discussed SDI with her. Our conversation was summarized as follows by the Canadian note-taker:

> Mrs. Thatcher said that indeed the matter [SDI] had arisen early in their meeting and that, as had been the case during Gorbachev's recent visit to the UK, she had forcefully insisted that the Soviets could not separate the UK from the USA on this issue and that any

> such thought or plan ought to be put firmly from the Soviet mind. On the matter of Gorbachev himself, Mrs. Thatcher ventured he was the "standard Russian"; that is, he was simply incapable of understanding or accepting that a powerful country such as the USA would not use its power to get more. She said that she had insisted in her meeting with Gorbachev that President Reagan was a sincere and honest individual who was genuinely interested in reducing and controlling nuclear weapons. She added, however, that she believed that the Soviets genuinely considered themselves to be threatened by the Americans.

British Foreign Secretary Geoffrey Howe also had a question for me. "By the way," he said, "what has happened to Pierre Trudeau?"

"He's back practising law in Montreal and he was just awarded a peace prize in Washington," I replied.

Margaret took off her glasses and looked at no one in particular.

"It must have been the Lenin Peace Prize," she said with a steely grin.

I glanced over at Bob Fowler from External Affairs and realized that he'd gone white. Margaret couldn't have known – or did she? – that Bob had worked for Trudeau as a foreign policy advisor and that I, following Canadian tradition, had kept him on.

Margaret was no admirer of Trudeau, whom she called a "liberal leftist." According to Ronald Reagan's *Diaries*, at one G-7 meeting the Iron Lady made this clear. "I thought at one point Margaret was going to order Pierre to go stand in a corner."

—

PERSONAL JOURNAL: MARCH 14, 1985

> *I met at the Japanese embassy with PM Nakasone for an hour. Our meeting was excellent, held in a suspended Plexiglas room/cage, free from Soviet informers or bugs! Only the Japanese would be sensitive enough to devise a room that would clearly be devoid of hearing or listening devices. Our conversation dealt with the upcoming Bonn Summit and important bilateral issues. Nakasone is a handsome, dapper man with a warm smile and ready wit. He appreciated my reference to the Japanese presence in the PMO – namely, Charley*

*McMillan and his latest tome on Japan (*The Japanese Industrial System*), which, I assured the PM, was available in the best shops for* $24.95 *U.S.!*

Following a very cordial and productive meeting – trade positions, new investment possibilities in Canada, automobile quotas, emerging U.S. protectionism, etc. Nakasone handed me what appeared to be a large tea bag, which he said would keep my hands warm at the funeral, which it did. When I showed it to George Shultz, he remarked that only the Japanese would dream it up and make it replaceable! After a quick lunch at the hotel – and a pit stop to don my newly acquired underwear (Stanfields! Bob would be proud of me) – I was driven with our ambassador to Red Square.

—

When I met Mikhail Gorbachev for a forty-five-minute discussion, he was accompanied by President Gromyko, his chief of staff and an excellent translator, Victor Sukhodrev. I was flanked by Bill Fox, Peter Roberts, and Bob Fowler. We sat across from each other in the Catherine Hall at the Great Kremlin Palace. I was indeed a long way from Baie-Comeau.

—

PERSONAL JOURNAL: MARCH 14, 1985

Gorbachev is indeed an impressive individual. He speaks slowly and carefully. He is at home in this room in the Kremlin and his confidence shows. He began by thanking me for coming all this way, speaking about his regard for Canada, his trip to our country, commercial relations, etc. I thanked him and pointed out that while Canada was not a superpower, we were not without influence, and were deeply hopeful that genuine progress would be made at Geneva. On two occasions he deferred to Gromyko but maintained the dialogue himself. USSR would make every effort but there must be an adequate response from the other side.

—

Gorbachev started with a quick overview of the commercial relations between the Soviet Union and Canada. His opinions were obviously formed during his visit to Canada in 1983 while he was a rising member of the politburo in charge of Soviet agriculture. "During my visit to Canada," Gorbachev told me, "many Canadians said that the main difficulty in our economic relations flowed from the similarities between our two countries – geography, climate, resources. This made it difficult to identify goods for exchange. I did not agree. There are possibilities, if we act to deepen our relations and find them, such as cooperative ventures."

It was then my turn to address the new leader of the Soviet Union. "Thank you for your kind words of welcome," I said. "Our Canadian situation is unique. We are neighbours both of the United States and of your country. We genuinely seek friendlier and more productive relations with both our neighbours. As a new prime minister, I sense a feeling of new hope for East–West relations with your leadership and with the prospects for arms control talks at Geneva. I cannot remember wider support for any issue than now exists for Canada to contribute to the peace process at Geneva."

The general secretary, his face hardening, delivered his message. He was aware I'd be hosting President Reagan in Quebec City in just over a week's time, and I knew I wasn't his intended target. "But how do you evaluate the fact that, despite the Geneva talks, the United States continues to expand its military program?" he asked. "Congress is approving the largest military budget in history; the MX missile is to be deployed and deployment of American missiles continues in western Europe. How does that activity square with statements that the United States wants to halt the arms race and eliminate nuclear arms? How should this be understood in your view? Perhaps on the political side the talks will go on – but the military-industrial complex also goes on producing and holding everyone in its grasp." Gorbachev made a fist.

Remembering the old adage "Only Nixon can go to China," I explained the realities of American politics to the skeptical Soviet leader. "I believe two things about the United States," I said, looking him in the eye. "First, President Reagan believed that when he came to power he had inherited a situation of inferiority, in terms of weaponry, from President Carter. Second, I believe that he genuinely wants and will work with you to obtain arms control and eventual limitation of nuclear weapons. President Reagan, however, must speak from a position of strength within his country based on military parity with the U.S.S.R. On that basis, he can make the kind of moves that President Nixon made, for example, in recognizing China. President Carter just could not deliver such initiatives."

"We will act seriously and responsibly [at Geneva]," Gorbachev replied. "The other side will not be required to make one-sided concessions."

I went on to dispel some myths about Canada–Soviet relations that I had detected among some communist officials while in Moscow. "I want to tell you about the debate in our House of Commons, our Parliament," I said. "There is a record of the debates every day and I think reading it would surprise you. There is no assumption in the House that the United States is always right and your country is always wrong. There is a sense of fairness and objectivity. I know – I'm there answering questions from members of Parliament. Probably because of our proximity to the Americans, there is a fair and careful examination of Soviet positions. This influences our views and we certainly take it into account in our national judgment."

Gorbachev listened carefully to all I'd had to say. We both liked what we saw, and we knew immediately we could work with one another. Peter Hancock of External Affairs later summed up how we parted:

> During the farewell exchange, the PM said that he, like Gorbachev, was a relatively new leader and that he looked forward to working with him for some time. Gorbachev grinned, very much as a fellow politician, and said he looked forward to that too. What this record does not convey is the immediate glow of good chemistry between the two leaders; the calm, reflective, and conversational tone, remarkably devoid of cant and polemic; the interaction of both to each other's points – which suggests that an authentic dialogue may be possible with Gorbachev; the courtesy and cordiality with which the PM was received; including a rare conversation with the shadowy Alexandrov; Gorbachev's vibrant alertness and vigorous eye-contact, despite a gruelling schedule of calls; the fact that neither spoke from notes . . . and that Gromyko seemed not only comfortable in his subordinate role, but showed every sign of a man utterly relaxed and at ease with the prospect of Gorbachev taking care of business.

Summarizing our meeting, I wrote to Gorbachev before the month ended: "Our discussions strengthened my conviction that there is a basis for achieving better relations between East and West, although I do not underestimate the difficulties that lie ahead."

In 1991 at the G-7 Summit in London, François Mitterrand recalled Gorbachev's attitude to the Soviet policy that he had inherited of forced collectivization of farms. Chuckling, Mitterrand remembered a 1984 conversation between General Secretary Chernenko and Gorbachev that he witnessed at a French embassy luncheon while on a visit to Moscow. "How's the harvest?" the general secretary asked. "Bad," Gorbachev replied. "Why?" "The system is bad," Gorbachev continued. "When did that start?" his boss asked. "1917," said Gorbachev.

—

PERSONAL JOURNAL: MAY 29, 1990

(Written after lunch with President and Mrs. Gorbachev at 24 Sussex Drive)

On March 10, 1985, he said, they went for a walk at 3 a.m. The next morning the Politburo would meet to select a successor to Chernenko. He said he had had no ambition to lead but he'd told Raisa that if he were to be chosen, "This cannot be allowed to continue." That was the birth of glasnost *and* perestroika, *he said.*

—

At a reception inside the Kremlin for all the foreign dignitaries who had arrived for the funeral, I was approached by Imelda Marcos of the Philippines. She asked if I would be interested in visiting her country. As I tried to conjure up a diplomatic way of declining, I noticed another controversial figure coming my way: Yasser Arafat of the Palestine Liberation Organization. I had no desire to meet the terrorist leader, although a meeting was clearly what he intended. As Arafat got closer, it dawned on me that Imelda Marcos was the key to my escape. I gallantly put my arm under hers and swept her into another room. Arafat soon gave up the chase. I never did meet the Palestinian leader while I was prime minister. I was sensitive to his people's rights, and to the need for justice and fairness in all my dealings on the Middle East, but to me he was still a terrorist.

—

PERSONAL JOURNAL: JANUARY 1, 1988

Just prior to dinner Shimon Peres called me from Tel Aviv to thank me for the strong statement of support I had provided to the Israeli government in regard to disturbances over the holidays in the Gaza and on the West Bank. His response was to the fact that I was the first head of an important industrialized country to support Israel at a critical moment. Even Ronald Reagan, one of the strongest friends Israel has ever had, conveyed his displeasure with the actions of the Israeli government. My attitude is based on the belief that the Jews, having suffered so horribly over generations, have found a permanent home in a tangible, defined Israel, and that they alone must make value judgments in respect of their national security.

—

Back in Ottawa, and ahead of my summit with President Reagan, we announced that we would spend $300 million over the next decade to help cut Canada's acid rain emissions in half. The announcement featured tough new emission standards for automobiles, as well as funds to clean up air pollution from five smelters in Manitoba, Ontario, and Quebec.

Acid rain was at the top of my agenda as I waited for Air Force One, carrying President Reagan and his wife Nancy, to arrive in Quebec City on the afternoon of March 17. The president had once famously declared that trees caused acid rain. (This remark had made its way across the Atlantic, as my Moscow talks with Helmut Kohl had shown; when I mentioned the theory that acid rain came from trees, Kohl had added sympathetically, "Or from heaven.") I knew I had my work cut out for me on this subject. Well aware that I was taking a big risk, I rejected advice to lower my expectations about changing Reagan's position. As prime minister, and as the father of Canadian children who would join their generation in inheriting Canada's potentially tainted natural wonders, I felt I had little choice.

In our correspondence before meeting in Quebec City, Reagan had made it clear to me that our talks about acid rain wouldn't be simple. "Many key questions remain unanswered," he wrote in January, "and until they are, we are not prepared to undertake the very heavy expense of percentage reductions in sulphur dioxide emissions. But this decision remains open to future review and does not rule out greater cooperation in the area."

The day before Reagan's departure for Quebec City, he devoted his weekly radio address to the American people to his upcoming trip to Canada. "The United States is a pioneer in environmental protection, and we share with Canada a special responsibility for protecting our shared North American environment," he said, more encouragingly. "The problem of acid rain concerns both our countries, and I'm anxious to hear the prime minister's views on that subject." (And he was indeed to learn my views on acid rain, in Quebec City in 1985 and at each of our meetings until he left office in January of 1989. "We are poisoning our own lakes too, you know," he snapped at me in irritation during a behind-closed-doors meeting in Ottawa a few years later.)

On March 17, 1985 the Shamrock Summit got under way. I ended my speech at the airport with the closing words, "Mr. President, welcome to Quebec City, and welcome to Canada. You are here among friends." It was then President Reagan's turn to speak to Canadians. I could tell he was in good humour, and this became obvious to all when the Californian bravely spoke his opening sentence in a French that was on a par with John Diefenbaker's. When he was done speaking, President Reagan and I entered the same car and began the trip into Quebec City and to the historic Château Frontenac, which overlooks both the St. Lawrence River and the Plains of Abraham. (Ever the politician, Reagan kept reminding me to wave to the crowds along the route, telling me that his predecessor, Jimmy Carter had needlessly angered ordinary Americans by failing to do so.) On the ride in I told him my impressions of Mikhail Gorbachev. With the Cold War still in full swing, and although he was now into his second term, Reagan had yet to meet any of his Soviet counterparts. He listened as I described the new-style Soviet leader, and he asked me later to read to his delegation my private notes from my recent meeting with Gorbachev in Moscow. "He's no altar boy," I said, summing up my thoughts on his Soviet rival.

Reagan and I also talked about Central America and I urged prudence and moderation by the Americans in their dealings with Nicaragua and other countries in the region. Reagan was not convinced: "We believe we have to do what we are doing or we will have another Cuba," he replied. (While he didn't know it at the time, NDP Leader Ed Broadbent was very much a presence in the room. Ed had recently visited Fidel Castro in Cuba and had briefed me on his impressions of the Cuban leader, which I shared with the skeptical American president. Broadbent told me that Castro had said he regarded Reagan as the smartest president in fifty years in his approach to the Soviets.)

I told Reagan frankly that I believed Central America could become a quagmire for any American president who forcefully interfered in the region; this was long before the Iran Contras scandal hit the headlines and embroiled his presidency in controversy.

Our first round of private talks ended with Reagan telling one of his famous jokes. Chuckling throughout, he regaled his listeners with the story of the time men from separate American and British units found themselves in the same pub one day in England during the Second World War. As the British soldiers hoisted ales in honour of the king, the brash Americans returned a toast of their own. "Screw the king," the Americans said. Surprised, the Brits again held up their beers. "Screw the president," they answered. At that point the American soldiers chimed in, saying in unison, "We'll drink to that!"

That wasn't the only occasion Reagan had me laughing during his visit. In his memoirs, *Ronald Reagan in Private*, the president's executive assistant, Jim Kuhn, later described another Shamrock Summit Reaganism that helps to explain why Reagan was such a beloved leader. "Both leaders were scheduled to speak at an event . . . which required Mulroney and Reagan to walk into the event together," Kuhn wrote. "But, I earnestly explained to them, protocol dictated that they wait until the others in the U.S. and Canadian delegations had taken their places in the room first, which seemed to be taking a long time. Reagan looked at Mulroney and grinned. 'Brian, it's protocol – spelled bullshit.'"

In private again, we also discussed trade. I took this as an opportunity to make it clear to the Americans that the overall Canada–U.S. relationship was a matter of the highest priority for the new PM. "It's my baby," I said, "and I watch it like a hawk."

When we discussed Reagan's approach to taxation and deficits, I was able to glimpse the brilliant politician that lay behind Reagan's sunny smile. The president said he planned to take his deficit-fighting plans directly to the American people. "What about Congress?" I asked. "It is not necessary," Reagan replied, "to make Congress see the light – just to feel the heat." I made a mental note to remember this story whenever I had to face the Liberal-dominated Senate. I suspected there would be battles ahead with this group of unelected partisans, and I was right.

In public, Reagan and I issued a declaration on trade, charging our trade ministers with exploring ways of lowering trade barriers between our two countries. We announced that we'd agreed to upgrade the continent's northern defences. On acid rain, we appointed envoys to study the problem and report back. Reagan's choice was Drew Lewis, a former secretary of transportation. I called upon recently retired Ontario premier Bill Davis. A few days after the summit, I signed an official mandate letter for Davis, outlining his duties. I expressed my belief that it was in the realm of politics, not science, where he was likely to find the words and solutions that would bring President Reagan onside.

Although we made real progress there, the Quebec City summit wasn't without controversy – for some. After a private dinner at the Château on the first night, Ron and Nancy and Mila and I attended a gala in the president's honour. The evening concluded on a literal high note with both couples accepting the invitation of the great Maureen Forrester (a Montrealer of Irish descent) to join her on stage for the final chorus of "When Irish Eyes Are Smiling." It brought down the house, and was a joyous end to a glittering evening and special event.

And an appropriate one. Thousands of the Irish immigrants who came to Canada during the potato famine were landed on Grosse-Île, an island in the middle of the St. Lawrence River, a skip and a jump from Quebec City. The gala event was on St. Patrick's Day, the national feast day of the Irish everywhere, and both President Reagan and I were of Irish heritage. At that moment, in that place, what could have been more natural than for both leaders – at the end of the evening of celebration – to sing along with the cast a few bars of a great Irish song, in tribute to millions of our forebears who had contributed so much to both our countries?

But Canada's loony left and self-professed intelligentsia expressed strong disapproval, denouncing our Irish duet as "disgraceful" and as an example of "subordination." One Canadian historian went so far as to write that it was the most "demeaning" moment in the long history of U.S.–Canada relations. Not, mind you, the moment when President Kennedy called Prime Minister Diefenbaker an SOB. Not the moment when President Johnson seized Prime Minister Pearson by one of his lapels and told him, "You pissed on my rug," or when President Nixon called Prime Minister Pierre Elliott Trudeau "an asshole" on tape. And perhaps not even when Prime Minister Chrétien's communications director later referred to President George W. Bush as a "moron"; or when his energy minister called the president "a failed statesman"; or when a well-known Liberal MP referred to Americans as "a bunch of bastards." These last three incidents resulted in the cancellation by the Americans of a state visit to Canada, the greatest such debacle in history. Were these events "demeaning"? No, not at all; not like the sight of two Irish leaders happily warbling a few bars of a popular Irish anthem on St. Patrick's Day. How insecure can you get?

The anti-American lobby in Canada is not insignificant. It is located largely but not exclusively on the left, among left-wing political parties and unions, a wing of the Liberal Party, the CBC, the *Toronto Star*, assorted media types, and among some central Canadian academics. It is Pavlovian and unforgiving: any expression of support for America, its government, policies, or people (particularly from a Conservative government) is "capitulation" or "kowtowing," a "surrender" of our pure and exalted values to the squalid interests of a larger but unworthy neighbour and partner. These people are essentially peripheral to Canada's major political parties; they're mainly fringe players who ludicrously view themselves and their anti-American vitriol as indispensable to our national well-being.

This extremist crowd is separate from the much larger group of Canadians who are quite properly concerned about American incursions into our cultural and economic sovereignty and other expressions of our national life. They are constantly skeptical and wary of American intentions, but they remain open-minded and fair in their assessment of our powerful neighbour. These are the legitimate and thoughtful Canadian nationalists whom I have always respected; I paid attention to their concerns when I was in office.

Canadians in general loved the Irish duet, but the CBC replayed the clip constantly with commentary that it was symbolic of a humiliating example of "toadyism" and a subordination of Canada's interests. "I must say, these people really have a serious inferiority complex," said Margaret Thatcher after she saw a replay of such commentary during a visit to Toronto. "I certainly hope they don't go off their medication."

—

PERSONAL JOURNAL: APRIL 6, 1985

After some ten hours in his presence, Reagan gives me this impression: he is a kindly man, possessed of a warm good humour, generous instincts, and what appears to be a total absence of malice. He speaks ill of no one. While he clearly does not hold Pierre Elliott Trudeau in high regard, he made no disparaging remarks about him. He thought perhaps there was a flaw in President Richard Nixon's character that accounted for Watergate, but then he immediately went on to offer the highest praise for Pat Nixon. "An exceptional woman," he said. His feelings for the Soviets are visceral. "Strength is the only thing they understand, but I hope they understand I want peace."

Nancy's influence is remarkable. It is pretty clear to me that she has enormous sway over people and policy. Over dinner she asked interesting questions and I could feel her pride in Ron and her determination to protect him from those whose instinct is to harm. Reagan told me that he and Nancy write memos each night on important events. These will make fabulous reading because they are a completely united couple who, I suspect, see people and events in quite different lights.

At meetings Reagan starts off and speaks to the main issues. He is clearly in command but defers easily to subordinates for details. They do not intrude on the discussions unless he asks them to. He is ready with a friendly quip or allusion. When I read him my notes of my meeting with Gorbachev, where I said that Reagan had the strength at home to make peace, his eyes welled up. He seems deeply appreciative of small acts of friendship and truly grateful for kind words in defence of the U.S. He recognizes this may cause me difficulty with the NDP around and is clearly moved by straightforward declaration that I intend to give our friends, the U.S. included, the benefit of the doubt.

All told the meetings were productive and extremely helpful. I told him there will be differences – perhaps some serious ones between us – but I hoped to resolve them in private without recriminations and public posturing. For my part, the president strikes me, as he has for some years, as one who has been persistently underestimated by the trendy commentators and analysts. He is a shrewd judge of people and character. A deeply religious man, he appears free from theories. His views are simplistic but sound, rooted in proven results and not uncompromising virtue. RR may, 100 years from now, be revered as a truly great president because he made America feel good about itself again – made it throw off its self-doubt, accrued from Vietnam to Watergate, and become a more proud and unsullied nation, capable of providing strong leadership. He grasps the big picture.

—

An External Affairs report put the Shamrock Summit in proper perspective: "The [Canadian] embassy [in Washington] reports that the attention being devoted to Canada in official Washington and the U.S. media is unprecedented and uniformly positive," it stated. "Every U.S. cabinet secretary participating in the visit characterized it as a success, and most commented in superlative terms. White House Chief of Staff Don Regan added that the President was deeply touched by the spirit of the visit – that the sense of North American solidarity was a moving experience for Reagan . . . In summary, Quebec was a powerful summit in which the top leadership of both North American nations drew inspiration from a new vision of partnership. There has been a genuine change. The rhetoric is backed up by action in what may have been the busiest twenty-four hours ever spent on the Canada/U.S. relationship."

I was to see President Reagan, and the other G-7 leaders, in early May in West Germany. The Bonn meeting would be my first G-7 summit – the pinnacle of world politics – and I won't deny that I was more than a little nervous. Thanks, however, to my personal representative (or "sherpa," in summit-speak) Sylvia Ostry, I was well prepared as I landed in Bonn.

The French and Americans were in the midst of a major dispute whereby France would not agree to the next round of GATT talks beginning early in 1986 in Uruguay. Sylvia advised that I could work toward resolving this while around the table. I did attempt to bring the Americans and French together on international trade and other issues, and the key word is "attempt." Michael Wilson ended up christening President Mitterrand the "Sphinx" after watching me try to convince the summit veteran to come around to the Canadian and American position on the GATT during a break in the closed sessions. Mitterrand stared straight ahead, saying nothing, as I spoke with him in French.

Afterwards, President Reagan and Treasury Secretary James Baker were anxious to learn how our conversation had gone. "Has it led to a resolution?" Reagan asked. I confessed that my conversation with the president of France was very difficult to report on, for the simple reason that no conversation had taken place! Mitterrand was indeed the Sphinx that day, saying nothing, not a word, in reply to my arguments. The next day, however, he was ready to talk, and act.

Two very different characters – one, the sitting prime minister of the United Kingdom and the other a fallen American baseball star – came together and taught this rookie a lesson about summit communications while at Bonn. It happened this way. On the flight over to Europe I had read the sports pages, which were full of stories about former Detroit Tigers pitching star Denny McLain, the American League's last thirty-game winner, who had been found guilty of a string of racketeering and drug charges. During our first working dinner I discussed the news with a fellow baseball fan, a former sports announcer by the name of Ronald Reagan. "Brian, I couldn't believe what I read," Ron told me with sadness in his voice. Like me, he remembered the days when McLain had been one of Detroit's truly great pitchers. This led us into a discussion about the rise of drugs in professional sports, and our talk soon attracted the attention of the others, none of whom, I might add, had heard of Denny McLain.

Ronald Reagan then raised the "Just Say No" anti-drug program that Nancy had developed.

"Illegal drugs affect all our countries," our host, Helmut Kohl, suggested. "Why don't we put it on tomorrow's agenda for a brief discussion?"

At this point Margaret Thatcher joined in to announce that she agreed with Helmut's suggestion. With that decided, we went on with our talks. End of story.

Except that later, after I'd returned to the Canadian embassy to sleep, I happened to tune in to the *BBC World News* before bed: they were announcing that their prime minister had made a daring play while at the G-7 Summit. It seems Margaret Thatcher, worried about drug abuse, had convinced her fellow leaders to place the problem on the agenda for discussion the following day!

I never forgot the lesson that Margaret, who was by then attending her fourth G-7 summit, had taught this neophyte: stake out your position and execute.

By the time I arrived in Bonn in 1985, I had been prime minister for less than a year. But since I had won the leadership of my party in 1983, my life had been a constant campaign, and I knew it had been a busy and disruptive time for our children. While there are many trials and tribulations visited upon the kids of those who enter public life, there are some perks as well. For a brief few minutes at the summit, I cast aside my duties as prime minister and concentrated on being a father. Caroline's birthday was on the horizon, and I knew that my job gave me the chance to get her a unique birthday present. We were at a luncheon when I glanced down at the impressively embossed menu each leader had been given and had an idea. I sprang into action. "Ron," I said turning to President Reagan, "it will be my daughter Caroline's birthday on June 11, and I wonder if you'd sign this menu for her and I'll have it framed."

"Sure, Brian, I'd love to," he said, his face breaking into a smile.

I watched as he then handed it to Thatcher, and Margaret signed it immediately, then gave it to Nakasone, and so on around the table. Other menus started to go around and soon everyone was in on the act. I was to attend seven more economic summits and the tradition I started in Bonn continued at each one. Over the years I was able to get a signed menu for each of my children and a few special friends. Caroline's adorns the wall of her home today.

When I returned from Bonn, I began an important practice; I would write to each provincial premier after a G-7 summit to report on the gathering. I also wrote to a selection of my Commonwealth colleagues from the Caribbean, whom I'd met earlier in the year, and who appreciated Canada's efforts to keep them informed about high-level developments. "In many respects," I wrote, "Bonn was one of the most difficult economic summit meetings in recent years; indeed it came close to a breakdown without an agreed final declaration."

> The differences among leaders centred mainly on trade issues, although French President Mitterrand was also concerned about what he called the increasing institutionalization of summitry, and the tendency to give summits a decision-making role . . . The debt problems of developing countries did not receive as much attention at Bonn as they did in London [the year before]. However, we argued the need to address the special problems faced by the group of countries which are neither among the poorest nor among the major debtors, but which are in serious financial difficulties . . . I was concerned that the Bonn summit give appropriate emphasis to the problems of the environment, and that there should be specific reference to acid rain, air pollution, protection of the ozone

> layer, and the management of toxic chemicals and hazardous wastes. It is, in my view, especially significant that a consensus emerged on the idea that governments and private industry have a joint responsibility in preserving the environment and on the proposal that the "polluter pays" principle should be developed and applied more widely.

Newfoundland's Brian Peckford wrote back in late July. "I take this as another progressive step in closer federal-provincial consultation of matters that are of importance to both orders of government in Canada."

Japan's Yasuhiro Nakasone also wrote to me in the summit's aftermath. "In Bonn, I was strongly impressed by your active contribution to the discussions," he said. "Given the different positions taken by the United States and France, I was especially impressed by your mediating efforts which contributed in no small way toward arriving at an acceptable position for the group. Your bilingual ability, together with your sense of humour and persuasive argument, was a major asset for the group to arrive at common grounds."

1985

2. Budget Troubles and Steps Toward Free Trade

As the year continued, the high-decibel noise and confusion over the universality of Canadian social programs continued unabated. Even some of our more conservative-minded MPs were rattled. Toronto-area MP Don Blenkarn, who was definitely on the right wing of the party, spoke out strongly on the topic at a caucus meeting that winter. I was forced to reply. "Blenkarn raised hell about any changes to universality in regards to old age pensions," I said in my summation speech to caucus on January 30. "Now, it's unemployment insurance collections. Anyone who calls him a right winger again should be forced to spend an evening with [NDP MP] Dan Heap!" A few weeks later I used different words to calm PC members. "Anybody who attacks the concept of universality as it applies to the baby bonus will have serious problems with me!" I said, with baby Nicolas well on the way.

Privately, Finance Minister Michael Wilson and his officials were in the midst of planning our first full budget for May. They believed the Government of Canada had to partially deindex Old Age Security payments from full inflation protection to help us regain control of the nation's finances. I was under no illusions about the political difficulties the decision would create, but I figured, incorrectly as it turned out, that things couldn't get much worse in this area.

A week before budget day, I had a special message for members of our caucus. "There are 211 key salespersons for this budget," I said. "We must have the same message, the same themes, the same defence. There can be no divergent views. The budget will attempt to deal with a miserable fiscal heritage, but it will be tough, realistic, and fair. A budget is a fifteen-day election campaign. Every step by every player is indispensable. It's the most important day of the year, and vital for a new government. It will showcase our competence, credibility, and determination. It is vital for the minister of finance but we all must carry the burden. It's not Wilson's budget. It's our budget."

On May 23 Wilson took to his feet in the Commons and presented the first Progressive Conservative budget that was destined to be approved by the House, since the days of John Diefenbaker. It featured spending cuts of $1.8 billion and a surtax on incomes above $30,000 to ensure that Canadians who could afford it did their part in deficit reduction. It also contained the good news that next year's deficit would be reduced to $32.7 billion, $1.1 billion less than he had predicted in November. We increased contribution limits to RRSPs and to the child tax credit, and we cut grants and subsidies to industry and agriculture.

As part of our vision of rewarding Canadian risk-takers, we announced – to cheers from our backbenchers – that taxpayers would from now on be permitted a lifetime tax exemption on the first $500,000 in capital gains. And we announced that the OAS's inflation protection would be partially removed.

"The actions of this budget reflect our faith in people, in the ingenuity and the drive of individual Canadians to seize opportunities and to invest in their own future," the minister of finance said that day in the Commons. "We have brought forward measures which encourage Canadians to invest, on their own initiative, in the building of new and existing enterprises. This budget is far-reaching in its impact. It is a clear break from the past. We Canadians understand more and more the limits of what governments can do. It is now time to show what we can do – individually and together – when the opportunity is there."

Though he disagreed with the capital gains exemption, Jeffrey Simpson examined the budget fairly in a *Globe and Mail* column published two days after Wilson's address. "The Conservatives insisted [in the 1984 campaign] that 'jobs, jobs, jobs' would be their abiding priority," Simpson wrote. "But they never promised what the opposition parties are now demanding – more government spending. The Tories always viewed deficit reduction as their highest priority, the first step toward a sounder economy, business confidence, and lasting jobs . . . The Tories have done what the logic of their own goals impelled them to do – raise taxes and reduce expenditures. It is a testament to the immaturity of our politics that neither we nor they were prepared to confront the obvious during the campaign."

Faint praise, but I was willing to accept it. A week later I was happy to hear each provincial caucus announce at our national meeting that the budget had been well received in ridings from coast to coast to coast.

Within a few weeks, however, the unrelenting attacks from the media and opposition over the OAS changes began to hit home. Some of our MPs began to face fierce opposition to the move in their ridings. Many seniors started to believe their pensions were in danger, and naturally passed these fears on to their MPs. I scheduled a special weekend caucus meeting for June 15, knowing I'd hear an earful. Things were so bad it was already clear we'd have to change our approach to the Old Age Security payments. The question now was, how?

Michael and I agreed privately that there were four possible solutions: 1) Move immediately to superindex the Guaranteed Income Supplement. 2) Have him and Health Minister Jake Epp hold consultations for a month and then report to cabinet and caucus. 3) Retract totally. 4) Hang tough for the summer and begin the fall with a new proposal. We presented these options to caucus and invited comments from our MPs.

Michael addressed the group first. "We have to deal with the problems inherent with an aging population," he said. "There are now two people working for each person retired, but this won't last in an aging population. As a result, the GIS and OAS will become an increasing burden on expenses. We are very strong supporters of senior citizens, but this is a national effort to reduce the deficit."

Our party pollster, Allan Gregg, gave us an overview of our standing with the public, as revealed by his surveys and focus group sessions. "In June 1982," he told caucus, "the lowest percentage of the population satisfied with their government in the Western world was under the government of Pierre Elliott Trudeau. This new government shares the priorities of the Canadian population. The population is staying with this government because they want change. The attitude vis-à-vis our budget is favourable. Citizens know this budget is designed to encourage prosperity. Canadians expect their government to be fair."

Almost thirty MPs took to their feet and gave me their views on how they thought we should face the OAS issue in light of the growing controversy. The discussions were full and frank but no definite consensus emerged. Nevertheless, as prime minister and national leader, I was pleased to see Canadians from all walks of life, from both official language groups, and from all parts of the country discussing the matter honestly and openly.

"This kind of meeting makes for a stronger caucus," I said in my summation. "There is a new style of management in Canada as outlined in the

November statement and the budget. We have the lowest government expenses in seventeen years; the highest job creation figures in April and May since 1953. Confidence is coming back in the country and money is coming back in the country . . . If we are doing well in the country, it is good for your image. The population in Canada and in Quebec as well want anglophones and francophones to work together. I know we can do it. I am very proud of each and every one of you and I'm humbled by your support."

As part of my own efforts I spoke on June 5 to the Israel Bonds dinner in Montreal. There I assured – and not for the first or last time – the mainly Jewish audience that the prime minister and government would forever be "unshakeably committed to the preservation of the State of Israel." I also raised the pension de-indexing issue. "I would have loved to stand before you tonight and announce that the Government of Canada had reduced taxes and increased pension levels for our elderly citizens," I said. "Perhaps one day, that shall be my honour and privilege. But we are, for the first time in living memory, paying more – over $25 billion a year – on all interest payments than we are paying for all federal spending on health care and old age security."

June 19, 1985 was the day I had my famous encounter with Solange Denis of Ottawa on Parliament Hill. I had walked over to a small group of seniors who had gathered outside the Centre Block to shake hands, pose for pictures with tourists from across Canada, and hear any concerns that were raised. This was a common practice of mine. With the media in tow, Ms. Denis had her own plans. "You lied to us," she told me loudly, in an exchange eagerly covered by the waiting media. "You made us vote for you, and then goodbye Charlie Brown." (I later learned that Solange Denis was an active Liberal, who consulted with Finance Minister Paul Martin after I left office.)

Reporters asked me to comment after her outburst. "We're trying as best we can to deal with pension de-indexing in a fair way and, if the notion of fairness is offended, we're going to try to take a serious look at that, because it's important," I said. "Seniors deserve to be listened to with respect."

In cabinet the next day I discussed the incident, which was being played over and over again on TV and radio, and was the stuff of newspaper stories, all depicting Canada's frail pensioners rising up against the evil, heartless government. I told them the de-indexation controversy showed what reaction our government could expect as it tried to adjust Canadians' expectations of government largesse. "Ingrained in the Canadian psyche from years of benefits from the previous government was a desire to have everything yesterday paid with tomorrow's funds," I said. "It is virtually impossible to conduct a rational discussion on an issue like universality, and it is clear the government will have to engage in a much longer timetable to change existing Canadian attitudes . . . CBC Television presented the message they wished to project, as demonstrated by their representation of the sixty-seven elderly citizens protesting de-indexation on the Hill on Wednesday in a fashion that made it appear there were sixty-seven thousand present."

I met Michael Wilson for a private lunch at 24 Sussex. After even the reliably right-wing Business Council on National Issues, supposedly in favour of prudent fiscal management, withdrew its support, we knew we had to act. A week later, I spoke at a caucus meeting. Because of the well-organized opposition we faced on the issue, I knew we had no choice but to change our position, accept defeat, and live to fight another day. The challenge I faced was how to backtrack and still keep morale up before our MPs returned to their ridings for the summer. I spent many hours preparing my remarks, writing them out in longhand. I include them here, at length, because they explain so much about how I approached tough problems in caucus.

> After we won, the first prediction of the press was the caucus is too large and will split apart. Well, after a period of some newness and getting acclimatized to new surroundings, the caucus found its bearings and a great sense of togetherness and unity – and I applaud all of you for this . . . Reforms resulting from the McGrath Commission will make Parliament an even more rewarding and productive place for all members. Changes in caucus procedures this summer will hopefully make this institution more flexible and effective for you – and responsive to your needs.
>
> In an otherwise effective and well-accepted budget, we have opened an area of weakness. What began as a trickle of criticism one month ago has become a torrent. The matter is rendered more difficult by the systematic refusal of the media/networks to put forward our valid position on deficit control. We are being painted as uncaring reactionaries, heartless people who have selected the most defenceless groups in society for unfair treatment, a duplicitous group who promised to restore full indexation in the campaign and did the opposite.

No issue has troubled me more since I entered politics. As a part of a package designed to constrain expenditures and restore financial health to Canada, the [de-indexing] measure had considerable merit. As an isolated variable attracting the rage of a growing part of our constituency, it is . . . indefensible. We are now alone in our support of this item. We have been abandoned by everyone, ranging from Conservative premiers to the leaders of business groups, the timing of whose opposition dealt us a significant blow and left us – perceptually at least – bereft of allies. It is clear that we cannot resolve our fiscal problems in four years. We need at least another mandate to effect substantial change.

I have reluctantly come to the conclusion that we shall imperil future prospects if we persist in supporting this measure now . . . Michael Wilson is a valued friend and a tremendous colleague. He and I and others have been grappling with this matter for weeks. We have the following dilemma: an outstanding budget is being overshadowed by one provision that is perceived as being unfair. . . .

To change invites criticism. The same people who wrote yesterday that we were obtuse for including it will now write we are spineless for changing it. The headlines will read, "Mulroney Wavers"; "Mulroney Undermines Wilson"; "Government Capitulates." The alternative is even less appealing: a growing anger of the elderly who are being shamelessly exploited by the opposition and the press . . . Either way we are going to hurt. Either way the ministry and I are going to look indecisive for a while. But my obligation is to ensure that we are not . . . tarnished as an insensitive, right-wing, uncaring group. That perception, were it to stick, could cause us grave damage in the next election . . .

We are now three and a half years away from the next vote. We can recover and regroup, regain control of the agenda and return in the fall, renewed, ready to provide strong leadership. To ensure this, I believe we must act to relieve the pressure and rid us of this burden before the House rises . . . I didn't come here to be a hero. I came as a pragmatic individual seeking to do good, who takes life and people as they are and tries to help make the country a little better . . . I want the spotlight back on that record and back on you because you are what the community thinks of when it thinks of

> the government. You are why we were elected in the first place and why we shall be again. I am handing the Liberals and NDP a gun with which to shoot me. I would rather apologize, retrieve the gun, and proceed to shoot them.

Michael Wilson announced our decision in the Commons the next day. He reminded the House that our government had proposed similar changes to the pensions received by MPs and public servants, imposed a minimum tax on high-income Canadians, and taken many other measures to ensure fairness. Still, he said, it had become clear that a "great deal of confusion and anxiety has arisen over our proposals" to change the OAS. In order to offset the costs of changing our budget, Michael announced that the surtax on large corporations would be extended from twelve months to eighteen months, and that we would increase the federal excise tax on gasoline by one cent per litre, effective January 1, 1987.

It was then my turn to face the media, and I held a press conference on June 28. Reminding the press gallery that my party didn't believe itself to be a group of infallible emperors, I said it was our duty to listen to Canadians. "We are in Parliament as commoners, servants of the people," I said. "We never contended we were perfect, but we always said we would try to be fair. I think we violated that rule of fairness and we had to correct it. We acknowledged our error and we corrected it."

Pressure was also on me – and it would continue unabated into 1986 – to reverse another government decision I had personally announced in my riding on June 18. I had said that a new federal prison for hard-core offenders would be built in Port-Cartier. At the time unemployment there stood at about 40 per cent. As an MP and as prime minister, I knew it was my duty to help Canadians who lived in disadvantaged regions of the country. This was an approach I took very seriously and one I won't apologize for, even today. Hundreds of people have good jobs at that prison and are able to support their families and remain on the North Shore as a result. I was sensitive to arguments against placing a prison so far from Montreal and Quebec City, where most of the prisoners would come from, but felt I had to put the residents of Port-Cartier first.

The day after I made the announcement, caucus met in Ottawa, and Miramichi MP Bud Jardine criticized the prison decision. "The prison was going to Quebec," I told him, "the only question was where. Port-Cartier has

35 to 40 per cent unemployment. We saved the air base in your riding at Chatham. . . . There was a lot of politics and heart in this."

A year later Simcoe North MP Doug Lewis, who also represented a rural riding, wrote to Geoff Norquay, my stellar social policy advisor, to pass along his thoughts on the Port-Cartier prison issue. I knew after I read his letter that people outside Canada's large metropolitan areas would understand what I had done. I suspect they still do. "The Huronia Regional Centre is a hospital for the mentally retarded which has been in existence in the Orillia area for over one hundred years," he wrote.

> At the present time, it has a workforce of about a thousand people. The Penetanguishene Mental Health Centre has been located on the outskirts of Penetanguishene for most of the century. I believe that it employs about four hundred people. Both institutions are an important part of the economic base of this area. In discussing the issue of the location of the prison in Port-Cartier, I have been drawing a parallel between the prison and these institutions by painting the following scenario.
>
> Suppose the province was to produce a report saying that the [hospitals] were outmoded, dangerous [to staff and patients] and should be completely torn down and eliminated. Suppose further that the province decided to rebuild on the outskirts of Toronto so that the patients would be near their families and the institutions would have a ready supply of [medical staff]. The reaction of the listener is interesting. It sinks in that this would be a devastating economic blow to the area to have these two institutions removed.
>
> I go on to explain that the location of the prison in Port-Cartier is nothing more than a decision made by the government of the day in the same manner as the original decision to locate the "lunatic asylum," as it was then called, in Orillia in the last century. I then point out that, if we want a country where everything is located in Ottawa, Toronto, and Montreal, we can easily do that, but it will not result in any economic and regional balance in this country.

As June came to a close, the Special Consultants behind-the-scenes group submitted a report on free trade with the United States. They urged caution in approaching the issue. I was increasingly convinced, however, that this option was no longer available. Privately, I was beginning to conclude that Donald Macdonald had it right. Canada would have to take a "leap of faith" into free trade. In the ever-changing, ever-shrinking globalized world, I was becoming convinced that we would have to face the issue.

As the summer began, the party unleashed its secret political weapon on the unsuspecting residents of the lower St. Lawrence River area of Quebec: Irene Mulroney. My sister Olive later described my mother's appearance on the hustings in a chatty letter. "Doris [Recoski] had contacted her Canada Day people to say we were coming and there were receptions organized up and down the line," she said. "Doris presented 'the prime minister's mother,' and I took Polaroid pictures, *à la* Gary, which we presented then and there and people loved it."

Olive added that my mother received flowers from the captain and crew of the ferry that took them across the river. Apparently the Mulroney gang did their bit for federalism while in Harrington Harbour. According to Olive, "We were quite a hit and drove a couple of separatists on board the boat crazy – especially when we walked back to the boat accompanied by the whole town."

With the release of the Macdonald Commission report fast approaching, a decision on our government's approach to free trade with the United States was near. By now I had some inkling of the inherent conservatism and dislike of any new approaches automatically displayed by some senior bureaucrats at External Affairs. But Derek Burney was one official who didn't fall into that category. He had impressed me with his tough-mindedness and strong work ethic when I was preparing for my first meeting with President Reagan in September 1984. I was so impressed, in fact, that I had used back channels to arrange for him, along with Fred Doucet, to be in charge of planning for the Shamrock Summit as well, contacting Derek at home instead of approaching him at work.

Bolstered by my own impressions and by Derek's long-time experience serving Canada since the 1960s and his impressive record of accomplishment, I read with extra attention a paper on free trade he sent that summer.

"Who are the winners and losers?" Burney asked in his August 8 memo.

> Winners: all who can compete efficiently on a more level North American playing field, e.g., steel, high-tech, machinery equipment

> and parts, petrochemicals, fish and some agricultural sectors, some clothing and textile, most forest products, minerals, all Canadian consumers. Losers: those who cannot compete efficiently on a more level North American playing field (i.e., those [who are] losing now), e.g., clothing and textiles, furniture manufacturers, some brewers, some agriculture. Even weak sectors, however, have strong firms . . .
>
> What are the public's principal concerns? Erosion of sovereignty. Once you start, you can't go back: all of our financial, social, cultural, etc., programs and policies will be on the table and subject to decisions in Washington. Canadian industry is not able to make the adjustment. They need more, rather than less protection. It will lead to massive disinvestment.
>
> What is the price if we don't proceed? Continue to battle protectionist pressures in an ad hoc manner; avoid necessary adjustment (i.e., more competitive economy); no new incentive for growth, expansion, jobs; miss opportunity to forge better foundation for predominant trade relationship; rely exclusively on low common denominator; long-term potential of new MTN [multilateral trade negotiations]. Nothing ventured, nothing gained.

Two Albertans were destined to play a major role in shaping my final decision on free trade, Joe Clark and Premier Peter Lougheed. Only weeks after we formed the government in 1984, Joe sent me a letter that starkly laid out our position vis-à-vis the United States, whether we liked it or not: "Recent global economic developments – the challenges to free trade, the pace of technological change, the restructuring of Western economies, the emergence of the new Japans – point to a future in which the importance of the U.S. relationship for Canada will increase, not decline. We are being driven still closer to our neighbour by factors we have difficulty controlling. Protectionist sentiment in the United States today is strong and is unlikely to abate for the foreseeable future. This is the single most immediate threat to Canadian prosperity, whether we are the intended target or not. Canada is dependent on continued access to the U.S. market for its economic, even social, well-being. Securing this access is an overriding priority for Canada's economic development."

Joe attached a discussion paper for cabinet that we had reviewed by the time September 1985 arrived. It too laid out Canada's choices in the current climate. "Despite the tremendous reservoir of goodwill toward us that exists in the United States, there are no free lunches," it said. "The intimate and extensive links between us, as much as the state of our economy, no longer contribute toward our room to manoeuvre; rather, they make us more vulnerable. The clichés about the self-centred, hard-headed character of America contain more than a grain of truth. It is unrealistic to expect, in a competitive international climate where U.S. economic hegemony no longer applies, as it once did, any special favours unless these are seen to be in the U.S. national interest – either because Canada's position tips the balance on a complex issue, or because Canadian goodwill is calculated to be more valuable than some concession in question."

Joe also kept his eye on issues and initiatives that would ensure that our government continued to play a distinct Canadian role on the world stage, despite his belief in the necessity of our negotiating a free trade deal with the United States. "Over the next few months," he wrote to me in March 1985, "we need to find some areas where our actions can define a difference between Canada and the United States. We cannot create artificial differences, but we should not miss the opportunity to assert genuine differences of approach, particularly when that assertion involves no direct conflict with U.S. policy."

I heartily agreed with Joe on a plan to support UNESCO, from which the U.S. was withdrawing. "I think it's an excellent initiative," I wrote on my copy of the memo I returned to the foreign affairs minister. Two days later I had Joe's memo on my mind when I introduced UN Secretary-General Javier Pérez de Cuéllar to the House of Commons. "Mr. Secretary-General," I said, "if the multilateral system is, at worst, under siege or, at best, in a weakened state, then we pledge to strengthen the system."

As for Peter Lougheed, he had visited Washington over three days in May 1985 and held extensive meetings with cabinet secretaries and leaders in Congress. The veteran premier sent me a lengthy letter reporting on his impressions. The status quo, he wrote, was simply no longer an option. Canada, in his view, was on the verge of being severely damaged by the waves of protectionism that were about to be unleashed by forces out of control south of the border.

"The sectoral approach is not in the cards," he argued. "One individual described this approach as like 'trying to take the strawberries out of the jam.' It is clearly a non-starter. My reading of the Washington scene is that if Canada, through you, does not signal the desire for a new and freer trading relationship on a comprehensive basis, the United States will interpret your government's position as preferring a continuation of the status quo. The problem, Prime Minister, with the status quo is that it will not, in my view, remain as it is without a Canada/U.S. agreement. We cannot capture the status quo. It will be redefined in a patchwork of new protectionist and administrative measures. It is my assessment that if Canada does not initiate a new and comprehensive bilateral free trade arrangement with the United States by the end of 1985, the opportunity will probably be lost for many years."

Senior members of Canada's Privy Council Office were echoing the views of seasoned politicians like Joe Clark and Peter Lougheed. Ian Clark (Deputy Clerk of the Privy Council) described the mood in Washington in a paper he sent me in July 1985.

"There are no signs that evolving protectionist trends in Congress will in any way abate," he advised. "On the contrary, on matters such as steel and softwood lumber, there are signs of increasingly protectionist sentiment, fuelled by the record trade surplus. It is unclear whether the administration will be in a position to continue to resist the protectionist legislation expected to surface next fall. The 'window of opportunity' during which Canada can negotiate an agreement providing shelter from U.S. protectionism is not wide."

As I weighed this and other issues that summer, I also made two crucial appointments. Gordon Osbaldeston retired as Clerk of the Privy Council, and I turned to Paul Tellier to replace him. I had known Paul slightly from his days in the Trudeau government and his work on the unity file. When I became prime minister, Paul was deputy minister of energy, and I had been impressed with his work on the dismantling of the National Energy Program and the creation of the Atlantic Accord.

Paul was to stay with me as Canada's top civil servant for seven years. I later appointed him CEO of the CNR, where he proceeded to do a marvellous job in cleaning up and privatizing the railway. Tellier was highly competent, tough, demanding, and honest. He made the trains run on time, in Ottawa and Montreal, and always gave me his unvarnished opinion, whether I asked for it or not. My family and I enjoyed a close relationship with Paul, his wife Andrée, and their family. He was a major part of all the big decisions my government made, decisions that directly affected the future of Canada.

I also appointed Stanley Hartt to be deputy minister of finance. I had known Stanley for decades as one of the most successful lawyers in Montreal, and considered him to be one of the smartest young men of our generation. Earlier in 1985 he had accepted my invitation to run the National Economic Summit and I had been impressed with his efforts. At the Department of Finance he and Michael Wilson played indispensable roles in the major policy achievements of free trade and the GST. Stanley later returned for another tour of duty, this time as my chief of staff, where he again performed in his usual effective and successful manner.

It was a very busy August as my government, through Industry Minister Sinclair Stevens, announced the sale of Teleglobe Canada. This was our first privatization, and it marked the beginning of a series that would eventually take nearly one hundred thousand people off the public payroll. In time we privatized De Havilland, Air Canada, a portion of Petro-Canada, and a number of other public corporations.

But matters of state had to be put aside as the summer came to an end, and Mila and I anxiously awaited the arrival of our fourth child. Nicolas was born on September 4. "I don't know if it will be a boy or a girl, but I suspect it will be Conservative," I told the press outside the hospital before Mila gave birth.

And that's what has happened. Nicolas, who is now in university studying history, has become the most partisan of my children – and there's nothing wrong with that, in this dad's view. He was a delight as a child – and remains so today, of course. The media used to joke that he was the child who didn't walk, because it appeared we carried him everywhere! I loved the time I spent with my youngest son as he was growing up. He particularly enjoyed taking me to the movies. It was there, for example, that I spent a fun afternoon the day John Turner announced he would instruct the Senate to stall free trade. I was so worried about John's announcement that Nicolas and I decided to take in a showing of *Bambi*! As the rest of Ottawa consumed itself with that day's political news, we munched popcorn and enjoyed the cartoon movie, truly a world away.

—

PERSONAL JOURNAL: JULY 6, 1989

Mila has gone to Montreal where her friends are arranging an early birthday party for her, and Caroline and Ben are in France. So, I am batching it with Nicolas and Mark and enjoying the experience enormously. They are wonderful young children, a source of great pride to Mila and me. No legacy of mine as prime minister will ever come close to the magnificence of the children. I am greatly proud of all of them and most grateful for their presence and good health.

1985

3. A Bad Month

SEPTEMBER 4, 1985, the day Nicolas was born, was also the day I appointed Ontario's first black lieutenant-governor, Lincoln Alexander. When I telephoned to ask him to serve as the Queen's representative to Ottawa, Linc, whose sense of humour is famous and infectious, said, "Prime Minister, this will be the best appointment you'll ever make." I was proud to use the prime ministerial power of appointment to bring Linc and members of other visible minority communities into positions that had previously been denied them. David Lam, a fine Chinese Canadian, and Yvon Dumont, a proud Métis, also served in British Columbia and Manitoba, respectively. Like Lincoln Alexander they represented their Queen and provinces with distinction in their viceregal roles.

The next day, September 5, was the day the Report of the Macdonald Commission on the Economic Union and Development Prospects for Canada was released. As expected, the former Liberal finance minister recommended that Canada enter into free trade talks with the United States. Macdonald revealed the precarious state of the Canadian economy and government finances for all to see. "We've been trying to tell you for some time – this country is bankrupt," I told reporters afterwards. "I think maybe hearing it from perhaps a more independent source might inject a note of realism into the appreciation of some Canadians about the gravity of the economic situation we've been left with."

The rest of the month demonstrated all too well the strengths and weaknesses the PC Party displayed during our first full year in government. On the policy side, we officially began the process of free trade negotiations with the Americans. In the midst of this historic initiative, our lack of experience in the "discipline of power" – to borrow Jeffrey Simpson's famous phrase – meant that this crucial and far-reaching policy objective, like others that year, was obscured by missteps and ill-advised public comments. Some Tories later christened September 1985 "Black September."

First, there was the matter of some cans of tuna and John Fraser. Like me, John had contested the leadership of the party in 1976, and he had gone on to serve as environment minister under Prime Minister Clark. In opposition and government, John had proved a steady hand. It was no surprise to anyone when I brought him into my own cabinet as minister of fisheries. I was pleased with his progress in this crucial department until CBC Television's *the fifth estate* broadcast a disturbing episode, alleging that John had overruled his officials and ordered tuna that was unfit for human consumption be released for sale. The show made it sound as if John's actions had sparked one of the century's greatest public health disasters, and that Canadians should be terrified of the tuna they ate. I had not yet learned of *the fifth estate*'s remarkable capacity for distortion and deception, which was strongly denounced from the bench years later in an important libel case.

I knew the opposition would pound us without mercy, and suspected that once again we would lose control of the public policy agenda. Faced with the choice of writing or broadcasting stories about negotiating free trade or dismantling apartheid, or about possible scandal and missteps, the media would opt for the latter every time.

After doing my best to defend John in question period, I soon concluded this tactic was hopeless and that I was likely to lose my second minister. Still, I felt I owed it to John to review and reflect upon all the options. I spoke with him by telephone on September 22, to tell him that clearly we had a serious problem. Given the ferocity of the opposition and the media's "tainted tuna" attack on his ministerial judgment, the political fallout was very damaging. I spoke of his capacity to survive and to come back.

John replied. "I've done nothing wrong," he said. "The threat of closure of the plant was key." He argued that given the information he had received about the minor problems at the StarKist tuna-canning plant in New Brunswick, he would have been remiss in closing the plant. He said he was prepared to fight hard, but that if he couldn't be effective as a minister he'd resign.

The next day, I summoned him to 24 Sussex Drive; I made notes during and after the meeting. "I've concluded: Government hit," I wrote, "and you're hit. Both will be best served by your resignation. a) Ease situation. b) Bring you back. Lord Carrington Principle: Unfair but must be done. Must come from you – staff, no leaks, no press conference." I also made a note to file after John left: "John was forthcoming and courageous. Had a friendly and sympathetic meeting. Asked to speak to Cate. Agreed it was proper course and departed to prepare resignation in a cordial leave-taking."

Months later, before the Christmas break, John wrote me a note that testified to his honesty and integrity: "Dear PM: I'm leaving tomorrow with Joe Clark for India and Pakistan. Before going I just wanted to let you know that we are well and Cate and the girls have been brave and cheerful. We wish you and Mila and the children a very happy Christmas and God's blessing in the coming year. I am so very sorry that my actions caused you and the party and government so much distress. In time, I hope I can make it up to all of you."

The following year I was able to help John Fraser be elected Speaker of the House, a responsibility he fulfilled in a superb fashion.

Unfortunately, John's resignation didn't end the matter. You would have thought that ten thousand people died because of rancid tuna. No one even got sick. The media and opposition were able to keep hammering us over the issue because of ill-advised comments by Tory MP Fred McCain, who said the tuna issue had been discussed in caucus while I was present, which was not true. (That I, who had been involved in and followed politics since I was a teenager, would have not immediately sensed the political ramifications of a government allowing citizens to buy tainted tuna was something few considered when McCain's story was reported over and over.) Based on all the available information given to me, I had said publicly that nobody in the PMO knew about problems with the StarKist tuna until July 1985, and that I hadn't personally known until *the fifth estate* broadcast. Once these words were out of my mouth I had reason to regret them. Stories emerged alleging that some staff in the PMO had learned of the problems before the summer. Nobody had briefed me, but I continued to take the heat. Thanks to McCain's embrace of an outstretched microphone, the story had legs.

It got worse. John Fraser decided to tell the media that he had informed my office of the StarKist situation, contradicting me in the middle of a political crisis. The decibel level inside and outside the House rose even higher. And as if this weren't enough, a few fringe members of Ontario's Big Blue Machine put out their view – anonymously, of course – that my chief of staff, Bernard Roy, should take the blame and fall on his sword. *Pour combler le malheur*, Marcel Masse, our communications minister, came under investigation by the RCMP, who were looking into his campaign spending in the 1984 election. I asked for and received his resignation. The party's national director, Jerry Lampert, then told the press that the PMO had been informed two months previously of the investigation. A dangerous pattern was developing.

It was an angry prime minister who entered a caucus meeting on October 2. My notes tell the rest of the story:

> Have just come through an extremely bad week. 1) The resignations of two senior and valued cabinet ministers. 2) Direct contradiction of my statements by a member of caucus and the national director of the party. 3) Alleged attempt by the remnants of the Big Blue Machine to oust my chief of staff and replace him with one of their intimates. 4) The decisions regarding Northland Bank and the appointment of the Estey Inquiry. All of these isolated events, coming as they did in one bunch, combined to convey the impression of a government on the ropes and a prime minister under attack – being seriously undermined, not by the opposition but by his own troops.
>
> Let me deal separately with these incidents. 1) Resignations: They were painful but proper. 2) McCain [says], "I was wrong." Profuse apology, which I have accepted. Lampert's statements constitute a serious error of judgment [but they're] free from malice. I will advise steering committee to decline to accept his resignation. 3) Big Blue Machine versus Bernard Roy: Written by a senior journalist with known and demonstrated ties to some Ontario Conservatives. In the absence of conclusive evidence I cannot proceed further, except to note two things: a) how unhelpful the incident was to all of us. b) how it appeared to French Canadians, who having finally responded to the Conservative Party after seventy-five years, see a distinguished French Canadian as the apparent object of anonymous attack by a group of Toronto advance men, lobbyists, and hangers-on.
>
> Lessons from week: 1) Microphones and TV cameras should be avoided like the plague. 2) Any critical comment made about me or my staff will be magnified and seized upon to embarrass the government. 3) The great coalition we put together on Sept. 4 is still fragile. We have a unique chance at nation building and unity. There will be enough attacks upon us. Let us not attack each other. 4) Bad times

> in politics, as in life, must be handled with dignity and proper conduct. Long after the time is forgotten, people will remember how the PM and government acted during a difficult time.

Many months later, I was still answering letters about the tuna crisis – a crisis where *no one got sick*! During this time frame, a number of elderly people died of possible neglect in a nursing home in southwestern Ontario and little was said about it in the media – and nothing by *the fifth estate*. "I must point out, as I did in the House of Commons, that no threat was posed at any time to the public's safety," I wrote in reply to a letter from the Consumers' Association of Canada the following year. "The tuna did not meet accepted standards for texture and appearance, but was in no way unhygienic or contaminated. As you know, the tuna was recalled."

Sadly, StarKist was never to can tuna in Canada again, and hundreds of jobs were lost in Charlotte County, New Brunswick. In September 2005, the Saint John *Telegraph-Journal* looked back at the sad incident. "Former plant procurement manager Hubert McFee says Charlotte County never fully recovered from the loss of StarKist, a plant that had been operating since the mid-1960s," the paper reported. "Attempts to reopen the plant as a processing centre for other New Brunswick fish flopped . . . Mr. McFee says the employees couldn't believe the same tuna they ate right off the conveyor belt, bought by the case and even snuck out in their jackets, could be called 'tainted' and 'rancid' and cause such hysteria. 'Everybody was up in arms, they couldn't figure out where it came from. There was never anything wrong with that tuna, the employees used to eat it as it came off the line,' [McFee] says. 'This was mainly a media circus. If it wasn't so sad, you could laugh your head off.' Mr. McFee says the main inspector who was rejecting the tuna based on questionable standards was about as popular as a 'ham sandwich at a kosher picnic' among the workers at StarKist."

September 1985 was a rough month and ordinary Canadians took note. "I have never written to a prime minister before but I believe in you," a Saskatoon man wrote on September 24. "I saw a film clip of you in Parliament last night. You look run down. Please take a vacation and rest up. Canada needs you to be strong . . . Please take my advice."

September 1985 was also the month the government introduced new conflict-of-interest guidelines and I confirmed our plan to register lobbyists for the first time in Canadian history.

—

PERSONAL JOURNAL: JANUARY 1, 1987

This will be a trying and critical year. I admit that the constant media attack sometimes gets me down – but never out. My principal concern is always for our troops and supporters. How will they put up with this constant battering? How will they respond to the unrelenting media line of attack against the leader and the party? For my part, I remain confident and secure. I believe that we have done a very good job for Canada and shall be given the opportunity to do much more.

Somebody recently wrote that BM had a good year in 1986 but that he is still paying for a bad September in 1985. I think that is at least partly true. It is hard to blame a journalist for attacking my credibility when three of our own people – John Fraser, Jerry Lampert, Fred McCain – did precisely that in September 1985. While all later apologized for having been in error, the damage had been done.

—

Of course free trade was still our main policy objective that fall. By September 17, cabinet had reviewed the report of hard-driving International Trade Minister James Kelleher that I had commissioned at the Shamrock Summit. Jim prepared his report after extensive cross-Canada consultations with various interest groups. Our government established the ITAC (International Trade Advisory Committee) and SAGITs (Sectoral Advisory Groups on International Trade), and these both proved to be indispensable in the years ahead as we worked on what became the FTA, NAFTA, and Multilateral Trade Negotiations (MTN).

"I have now concluded that the time has come to explore more directly with the United States administration the scope and prospects for a new trade agreement," Jim wrote. "I am convinced that a process of complementary bilateral and multilateral trade negotiations will strengthen our economy, our capacity to compete in global markets, and our bilateral economic relations with Europe, Japan, and the developing world. It would contribute significantly to our government's program of economic renewal. I am convinced further that this vigorous approach to a new multilateral trade negotiation will reinforce our ability to act independently and credibly in foreign policy . . . Our discussions [with Canadians and Americans] have reflected the growing awareness in the country that we have reached the point of decision."

In cabinet on that historic day, we made the difficult decision to proceed with a request to the Americans for negotiations. As officials on both sides of the border worked at crafting language in the planned exchange of letters between President Reagan and myself that would satisfy both bureaucracies, I wrote Canada's concluding paragraph personally. "The negotiation of a new trade agreement will, of course, be extremely arduous," I wrote. "The challenge to succeed, however, and the fruits of success are well worth the enormous effort and good faith required for this initiative."

On September 26 – after changing Nicolas's diapers at 24 Sussex – I telephoned President Reagan.

"Before making the announcement," I wrote in my private notes of my side of the call, "and it will be a major statement, I hope I can be confident you will be ready to go to Congress soon thereafter, and support publicly this initiative. Any delay would leave me in a difficult position." I was delighted to hear that he would be able to respond favourably. I explained that I was going to describe our approach as "exploratory." My notes record that I said, "It is important to keep our agenda clear for U.S./Canada – to examine everything with an open mind. Commercial transactions will enhance our sovereignty. Canada is a partner, a smaller partner. This initiative does not jeopardize our cultural sovereignty – nothing inconsistent – fair trade package, national sovereignty, access to markets."

After the call, I filled my staff in on what President Reagan had said. "He has had discussions with many leaders of Congress, and he will begin immediately the process to secure the authorization necessary to proceed," I wrote. "He views this as a very major step forward in the liberalization of trade. He is fully cooperative and supports our initiative."

I later spoke in the Commons.

> I rise to inform the House and the country that I have today spoken to the President of the United States to express Canada's interest in pursuing a new trade agreement between our two countries . . .
>
> Throughout our history trade has been critical to Canada's livelihood. Now, almost one-third of what we produce is exported. Few countries in the world are so dependent upon trade. Trade simply means jobs. Yet our share of world trade has been declining.

> This trend ultimately threatens the jobs of many Canadians and the living standards of the nation as a whole. We must confront this threat. We must, as a nation, reverse this trend. To do so we need a better, a fairer, and more predictable trade relationship with the United States. At stake are more than two million jobs which depend directly on Canadian access to the U.S. market . . .
>
> No responsible person anywhere today advocates protectionism as a national economic strategy. Yet, sector by sector, region by region, country by country, Canada included, there persists the impulse to protectionism, whenever the going gets tough. Protectionist measures are always advocated as exceptional cases. But the barriers grow more numerous, more ingenious, and more insidious all the time . . .
>
> There is a general consensus that we must seek to secure and improve our trade with the United States. To shrink from this challenge and opportunity would be an act of timidity unworthy of Canada. It would be contrary to our national interest. Our political sovereignty, our system of social programs, our commitment to fight regional disparities, our unique cultural identity, our special linguistic character – these are the essence of Canada. They are *not* at issue in these negotiations. They will be stronger at all times in a Canada made more confident and prosperous from a secure and dynamic trading relationship with our biggest customer, our close friend and with all the world.

The die was cast.

Though he was to make the fight against free trade the centrepiece of his campaign against us in 1988, John Turner led off in question period that day with a question on, you guessed it, scandal. As I was later to tell my caucus, John (who was a dedicated parliamentarian) had forfeited the leadership of a once great national party the moment he donned a Rat Pack T-shirt one day in 1985.

To be fair, in posing his question about a now long-forgotten "scandal" John was only scoring a political point. Questions in the House and media stories about the supposed scandals continued to dominate both question period and the news. Exasperated – after all, we'd just momentously announced we wanted to negotiate free trade with the United States – I turned to a member of our caucus for advice. Richard Doyle, the respected former editor of the *Globe and Mail*, had earlier accepted my invitation to join the Senate. I asked him to draw upon his decades of media experience and advise me on the government's mounting image problems. Here is what he wrote:

> 1) The Government would seem to lack counsel in public relations in which senior advisors are consulted in the process of decision making and then absent when the government acts. 2) If there is to be a change in media access to government, it should be in the direction of more availability rather than less. 3) Ministers and members should have more advice on the relationship between their departments and the media. 4) Ministers and members should make more intelligent use of letters to the editor – a vastly underrated forum. If a newspaper declines to use a letter of reasonable content, the letter should be dispatched forthwith with the note, "This is the letter *The Bugle* didn't print." 5) The prime minister should, more frequently, share press conferences and similar forums with colleagues from the cabinet whose departmental efforts are in the news. 6) Ministers and officials should be reminded that if they make speeches or statements on the issues of the day, transcripts of what they said should be available the next day and not two weeks later when a reporter's version may well have become the accepted version. 7) Caucus is a confidential forum. If members do not accept that, it should become public. If its confidences are to be traded for media advantage, the great victory could be in jeopardy.

I was determined to avoid that.

1985

4. Fighting Apartheid

THE VERY NOTION of South Africa's apartheid was anathema to me, and while I was under no illusions about Canada's economic strength in the world, I also knew that Canada's role was not unimportant. I viewed apartheid with the same degree of disgust that I attached to the Nazis – the authors of the most odious offence in modern history. My strong and unswerving support of Israel and the Jewish community in Canada was based on this view. In both these areas, I was resolved from the moment I became prime minister that any government I headed would speak and act in the finest traditions of Canada.

Before our inner cabinet meeting in July in Baie-Comeau, I had asked Joe Clark to prepare a package of proposed sanctions against South Africa. I wasn't pleased when he recommended a cautious approach. Now, Joe and I may have had our early differences on the best way that Canada could assist in dismantling apartheid, but I never questioned his commitment to the cause. Upon reflection, I believe some of his early positions were influenced by the department he presided over. For many years the members of the Department of External Affairs had considered themselves an elite amongst federal public servants. Unfortunately, this led many to subscribe to an official culture and view of the world that only they understood. Above all, they didn't want a pesky politician – particularly a newly elected prime minister they hadn't yet "trained" – poking around in their files, election or no election.

Before the Baie-Comeau meeting, UN Ambassador Stephen Lewis had privately revealed what he had found at External Affairs to Charley McMillan. "He's shocked at what he sees in the Department," Charley wrote. "In-fighting, woefully weak analysis, no information exchange across departmental boundaries . . . On several political issues – Nicaragua, South Africa, SDI, UNESCO . . . he feels analytical work is weak and indeed misleading. He said that his experience has left him 'shocked' at what he's seen."

After discussions with me, and after inner cabinet review of the proposals, Joe announced on July 6 what came to be known as the Baie-Comeau round of sanctions. These included strengthening the voluntary code of conduct concerning the employment practices of Canadian companies operating in South Africa, and tightening the Canadian application of the UN's arms embargo on South Africa to include imports of South African arms. We also abrogated the Canada–South Africa Double Taxation Agreement; terminated the Export Market Development program for the South African market, as well as insurance provided to Canadian exporters by the Export Development Corporation; announced the end of toll-processing of Namibian uranium; and brought in a voluntary ban on the sale of krugerrands and other South African gold coins. In addition, we began to monitor and severely restrict official contacts between our two countries.

"Let us look to a brighter and better day, when such measures may be abandoned," Joe said in the Baie-Comeau Declaration. "When tolerance and understanding may grow out of the sad ashes of conquest, colonialism, and racial separation; when the people of South Africa may join in a common effort and build a common society . . . We look to the resumption of old ties and the creation of new ones when all South Africans are treated on the same basis under their law and constitution. The steps I have announced are signs of Canada's commitment to the goal."

Did we go far enough? No, but we had made a start, of which Canadians could be proud. Even the editorial writers at the *Toronto Star* – no friends of my government – took note: "This action by Prime Minister Brian Mulroney and his government is in the honourable Tory tradition established by John Diefenbaker, who helped forge a Commonwealth consensus to oust South Africa because of its inhuman policies. The new measures will help breathe some fire into Ottawa's increasingly limp approach to South Africa . . . The Mulroney government deserves credit for hewing closely to policies aimed at promoting peaceful, not violent change."

In early September Joe announced another round of sanctions that included a voluntary ban on further bank loans to South Africa, except those helping the majority black population; an embargo on air transportation between the two countries; and the allocation of $1 million in humanitarian aid to the families of political prisoners and detainees jailed by the South African government.

With my first Commonwealth Heads of Government Meeting (CHOGM) scheduled for Nassau later in the month, Margaret Thatcher and I began sparring in our correspondence over the issue of how best to fight apartheid. While disagreeing with Canada's approach, Margaret left room, barely, for compromise within the Commonwealth. "Like you, I loathe apartheid and want to see it abolished at the earliest possible moment," she wrote.

> I have made this quite plain to [South African] President Botha. I have tried to avoid prescribing what system of government should take its place: that must be for the South African people themselves to decide. But whatever system is chosen will have to command the support of the people as a whole. We thus agree as to the right objective: there must be urgent and fundamental reform. The question is how in practical terms this goal is to be achieved . . .
>
> I am firmly opposed to additional economic sanctions. I believe that such an approach is fundamentally mistaken and will not lead the South African government to make the changes which we all want to see. Indeed, it is likely to be counterproductive with the white community, playing into the hands of the right wing and thus putting a stop to further significant reform.
>
> I see no point in creating unemployment in Britain in order to increase black unemployment in South Africa. We would only worsen the cycle of frustration, violence, and repression there. Market forces are already exerting much more effective pressures than government-imposed sanctions ever will. Unlike such sanctions they cannot be dismissed as "foreign bullying" since they are seen to have been caused directly by the actions of the South African government itself. The question of subscribing to some "minimum additional measures" at Nassau, as you suggest, would depend entirely on what these measures might be. For the reasons given above, I would not be prepared to agree to additional economic sanctions, though it is obviously open to others to do so if they wish. But there might be measures in the sense of new practical political initiatives which Britain and the Commonwealth countries could take.

Despite our differences, I believe that Margaret was a remarkable leader. I was impressed with her from the first time we met, when I was leader of the opposition. Our meeting was in September 1983 at Earnscliffe, the Ottawa home of Sir John A. Macdonald, now the official residence of Britain's High Commissioner to Canada. We spent most of the time talking politics, and she had a great deal of funny, pithy, and valuable advice as to how I could get rid of a left-wing government at the polls. Just before our meeting ended, as we were rising from our chairs, she said, "Brian, the Middle East, nuclear weapons, international trade – for the media, we discussed all these." Sure enough, when I left Earnscliffe I was able, by following Margaret's advice, to convey to questioning journalists the impression of a lofty meeting held behind the gates of Sir John A.'s house.

As the years went on, I was to witness the British prime minister's wicked sense of humour on more than one occasion. "Margaret," Dutch Prime Minister Ruud Lubbers said at a 1989 NATO luncheon in Brussels, "my only disagreement with you is that you always think you're right." She paused for only a moment, a sparkle in her eye, before replying. "Well," she retorted, "that's because I am."

But whether Margaret liked it or not, my discussions with other Commonwealth leaders leading up to Nassau alerted me to the very dangerous possibility that the Commonwealth might split over the sanctions issue. Britain might go one way, with the rest of the group going the other and demanding sanctions.

I was well aware that Australian Prime Minister Bob Hawke would be a pillar of strength in this matter. I knew Bob, because he had graciously agreed to speak at my government's earlier National Economic Summit, where he performed brilliantly. During his visit to Ottawa we spent a long time together privately, and Bob and I hit it off, professionally and personally. A former president of Australia's trade union umbrella group, the Australian Council of Trade Unions, he was also a Rhodes scholar. His main claim to fame before he entered politics was his entry in the *Guinness Book of World Records* for his ability to consume massive quantities of ale: two and a half pints in eleven seconds, in fact, a feat likely to impress many of his fellow countrymen. While I probably could have challenged him in an earlier day, we were both now on our best behaviour. He was a typical Australian: brash, flamboyant, forthright, and brutally honest. I knew right away that I would love working with him.

With my first Commonwealth Heads of the Government Meeting coming up soon, I carefully reviewed a frank letter Bob had sent after our earlier talks in Ottawa. "As for the Commonwealth, I merely emphasize what I said to you in some detail in our private talks," he wrote in March.

"There is a great need for sane, moderate, and relevant voices between some of the more extreme positions, to which I referred, that are sometimes advanced at our Commonwealth meetings. We tried to provide this voice at [the last CHOGM]. I look forward now to being able to work together to this end. I am sure that you and I, speaking with the authority that attaches to our two countries, will be able to establish a strong and appropriate influence at the Bahamas meeting and beyond."

Before the summit, I asked Bernard Wood, director of the North-South Institute, to serve as my personal representative and to undertake a special fact-finding mission to southern Africa. I asked him to consult with leaders in the region and report back to me before I went to Nassau. "I have in mind that you would visit Zambia, Botswana, Zimbabwe, and Tanzania to obtain their views on the present situation . . . and on what concerted action the Commonwealth could undertake to bring further pressure on South Africa to begin the process of dismantling apartheid," I wrote. "I should like to underline that you may let it be known to your interlocutors that you enjoy my full confidence and that they should feel free to speak openly and frankly, confident that their views will be reported solely and privately to me. For your part, you will be bearing the message of Canada's concern over the situation in South Africa, and our determination to act in company with like-minded partners to bring an end to apartheid."

On my arrival in Nassau, in a gesture that spoke volumes about Canada's stature in the Commonwealth, the Queen personally asked me to work with other leaders to prevent a major split within the group. I assured Her Majesty that Canada would do everything in its power to prevent that from happening. But there was a sense in the air that we were facing a crisis. In my opening remarks I warned that "we must be aware that the effectiveness of the Commonwealth will be judged against the challenges of major current issues. An urgent case in point is, of course, South Africa."

> Racism and political oppression in Southern Africa have been central issues for the Commonwealth for a long time. Consideration of these issues has shaped the evolution and orientation of the Commonwealth over that period. At the 1961 heads of government meeting, Canadian Prime Minister John Diefenbaker declared apartheid to be incompatible with the values of this Commonwealth. A consensus was formed around this position, and the result was South Africa's departure from the Commonwealth . . .

> Now we are witnessing in South Africa a protracted crisis of unprecedented seriousness. The confrontation between oppressors and oppressed is intense and growing, as is the international reaction to the abhorrent practice of apartheid. The Commonwealth has been in the forefront of the international community on South African issues in the past. Its leadership remains crucial, and it is our responsibility to exercise that leadership thoughtfully, firmly, and well. The Commonwealth must respond to the quickening pressure for change in South Africa. All of our governments have taken steps to counter apartheid. In the present crisis it is imperative that we all signal together that there will be common, worldwide, and sustained pressure against apartheid – until apartheid is ended.

An important feature of Commonwealth meetings is the leaders' retreat, where the delegates, minus most of their delegations, go off alone and debate the issues of the day, leader to leader. In Nassau, these private talks had a definite sense of urgency because of Margaret's intransigence. The night before the retreat, in the suite of India's Rajiv Gandhi, I met with Gandhi, Bob Hawke, Kenneth Kaunda of Zambia, Sonny Ramphal (the Commonwealth secretary-general), and Robert Mugabe of Zimbabwe. I suggested that our various officials, under the leadership of Canada's Bob Fowler, begin to prepare a working document to present to the U.K. prime minister.

Rajiv and I met privately late the next night to plot strategy. The next morning, we met again for three hours with the larger group, and with our common policy agreed, I called Margaret. She agreed to see Rajiv and me at two o'clock. A marathon three-hour argument ensued. Before the three of us got down to business, she pointed out that we were meeting in the very room where John F. Kennedy and Harold Macmillan had met in 1962. As a Canadian, I chuckled quietly to myself because I knew that the British–American summit had been interrupted by John Diefenbaker, who'd invited himself along. JFK, who was definitely not one of the Chief's admirers, later described the trio's lunch. "There we sat like three whores at a christening," he told *Washington Post* editor Ben Bradlee, expressing his distaste at having to break bread with Diefenbaker.

Later that night, I wrote a note to file about Margaret's intransigence at this meeting: "She was, in regards to sanctions, completely adamant that

P.W. Botha would go the other way if Britain agreed to any further punitive measures. Gandhi and I vigorously disagreed and made strong arguments in favour of a more flexible British position. She was unmoved, and we returned to Gandhi's room for a full debriefing for the general group. People were pretty despondent with our report but we agreed, along with Hawke, to try once more at 9:30 p.m. at the Gandhi residence." I had a quiet dinner with Mila, then returned for our night meeting. "Prospects of a common position are extremely thin," I noted. "Margaret is obstinate but not unpleasant. I wish she were one or the other! It would make our position easier!"

During one of Margaret's outbursts in the Bahamas, I passed a note to our undersecretary of state for external affairs, Si Taylor. "What is really quite offensive is the implication that the rest of us are incapable of evaluating the impact of value judgments on our own societies," I wrote. "The truth is she came here knowing she would do nothing," he replied.

In his memoirs, Bob Hawke describes a tense moment between Margaret and me during those private talks. She reacted vehemently after I used the phrase "the fat was really in the fire" in my discussion with her. "At that her eyes blazed and she pulled herself erect in the chair," Hawke wrote. "'What do you mean the fat was really in the fire? What fat? What fire?' she asked imperiously. 'Brian, I was brought up to mean what I say, and to say what I mean. What do you mean, the fat was really in the fire?'"

Bob then interjected. "Margaret! For Christ's sake!" he shouted. "Forget the bloody fat and the bloody fire, it's got nothing to do with anything. Just listen to what Brian is saying, will you?"

"Brian, get on with it," he then added, "and leave the fat out of the fire."

I did just that, and we were eventually able to compromise. The Commonwealth's Nassau Accord, signed by all, including Margaret, featured a denunciation of apartheid, a ban on government bank loans to South Africa, and a halt on funding to trade missions in South Africa. Margaret agreed to consider limiting British imports of gold coins from South Africa. We also established a three-member Eminent Persons Group to promote dialogue on our behalf with the South African government, in order to bring an end to apartheid. I suggested appointing Pierre Trudeau to the group, but when I reached him at home and extended the Commonwealth's offer, he declined, saying, "Brian, thank you so much for thinking of me, but I am busy setting up my boys at home and school in Montreal."

The Nassau Accord also ensured that there would be further action on apartheid. We agreed that if the Commonwealth did not see true progress in the dismantling of this racist system within six months, then the leaders of Zambia, Zimbabwe, India, the United Kingdom, Canada, Bahamas, and Australia would meet again to reassess our position.

After Nassau I led the Canadian delegation in New York City at the events marking the fortieth anniversary of the founding of the United Nations. I met with various world leaders including President Reagan. He was on the eve of his first meeting with Soviet leader Mikhail Gorbachev, and I advised him that he should take the man at face value and give him the benefit of the doubt.

Once again, I lobbied the president on acid rain. Afterwards, I used a thank-you note to the White House chief of staff to continue to register my concerns to the U.S. administration. "[The discussion] was most helpful," I told Don Regan. "I was especially pleased to see the President's appreciation of the importance I attach to the acid rain question – positive action on this front has become, in the minds of many Canadians, the litmus test of the new relationship between our countries. I sensed at the meeting your full understanding of this and am most grateful to you for your support." Message delivered.

Reagan hosted a lunch for G-7 leaders at the American UN mission, where I struck up a conversation with Helmut Kohl. I had long been fascinated and sickened by the fact that the Berlin Wall cut through the two Germanys. On one side was the successful, democratic nation that Helmut led. On the other side was East Germany, drab, forbidding, and unfree, although it was considered by many to be the jewel of the Warsaw Pact nations.

"Will the wall ever come down?" I asked the man who would later lead German reunification.

"Yes it will," he replied without hesitation.

"When?"

"I don't know exactly."

"What's going to bring that Wall down?"

"Television."

Helmut's answer drew Margaret Thatcher's attention.

"Helmut," she said, "what's so marvellous about West German television that it could bring the Berlin Wall down?"

"The commercials," he answered. "West German television is broadcast to almost all of East Germany, and after they see enough of all these consumer products available to West Germans, they are going to say to themselves that they want this for themselves. At that point, when East Germans have had their fill of this stultifying system called communism, the Wall is going to come down."

And, of course, he was right.

I decided to pull no punches in addressing the UN General Assembly for the first time, during that 1985 trip to New York City. I'm happy to say that I shocked many observers when I made it clear to the South African government and others that Canada meant business.

> My government has said to Canadians that if there are not fundamental changes in South Africa, we are prepared to invoke total sanctions against that country and its repressive regime. If there is no progress in the dismantling of apartheid, our relations with South Africa may have to be severed completely. Our purpose is not to punish or penalize, but to hasten peaceful change. We do not aim at conflict but at reconciliation – within South Africa and between South Africa and its neighbours. The way of dialogue starts with the repudiation of apartheid. It ends with the full and equal participation of all South Africans in the governing of their country. It leads toward peace. If it is not accepted, the course of sanctions will surely be further pursued. Canada is ready, if there are no fundamental changes in South Africa, to invoke total sanctions against that country and its repressive regime. More than that, if there is no progress in the dismantling of apartheid, relations with South Africa may have to be severed absolutely.

Toronto Star editorial writers weighed in favourably the next day: "Prime Minister Brian Mulroney deserves credit for emphasizing peace and disarmament, condemning apartheid and terrorism, in his speech Wednesday to the United Nations' 40th anniversary General Assembly. The warm reception UN delegates gave Mulroney afterwards is but one indication that he was expressing the yearning of many of the world's people for international peace and human rights."

Editorial writers at the *Calgary Herald* concluded that I had hit a "UN homer." "Prime Minister Brian Mulroney was in the right spot at the right time with his anti-apartheid speech at the United Nations this week . . . His speech was one-up on his Commonwealth showing earlier this week when he was instrumental in winning crucial British support for renewed pressure on South Africa to speed its passage into a post-apartheid society . . . It was a big hit and delegates, rushing to congratulate him, had to be asked twice to clear the floor for the following speaker. After such a rare reception, especially for a Western leader, the PM might be forgiven for sensing that the UN, with all its squabbling, remains a peaceful haven compared to the House of Commons where rarely, if ever, is such enthusiasm shown for the prime minister's pronouncements."

One of the many opposition MPs who were able to put partisanship aside when it came to apartheid was none other than Rat Pack member Brian Tobin. After reporting on my activities to the Commons on October 28, I was gratified to receive the following note from Brian: "As a Canadian, I am proud of the efforts you made on this nation's behalf to preserve the Commonwealth and to combat institutionalized racism in South Africa. Your UN speech was superb."

My speech to the House deliberately stressed the common ground Commonwealth leaders had arrived at in Nassau. Unlike some, I genuinely believed Margaret Thatcher was as offended by apartheid as anyone else. While I had hoped she would go further in her formal opposition to the regime, I knew that isolating the British prime minister by hurling rhetoric at her would do little to help those imprisoned by apartheid. "But no matter how challenging the negotiations, all participants readily agreed on the urgency of the situation in South Africa, the rightness of the struggle against apartheid, and the need for a common and united front," I said in the Commons. "The accord articulates a unanimous call for the authorities in Pretoria to: 1) Declare that the system of apartheid will be dismantled and specific and meaningful action taken in the fulfillment of that intent. 2) Terminate the existing state of emergency. 3) Release immediately and unconditionally Nelson Mandela and all others imprisoned and detained for their opposition to apartheid. 4) Establish political freedom and unconditionally lift the existing ban on the ANC and other political parties. 5) Initiate, in the context of a suspension of violence on all sides, a process of dialogue across lines of colour, politics, and religion, with a view to establishing a nonracial and representative government."

Before leaving for Nassau, I had asked Canada's former deputy minister of finance, the earthy and brilliant Simon Reisman, the man who had negotiated the Auto Pact with Lyndon Johnson's administration, to provide me with his views on the organization needed to conduct free trade negotiations. I had known Simon for years, dating back to our salmon-fishing days (he was an expert and I was not) on Anticosti Island with Pierre Trudeau and John Rae years earlier, and I was well aware of his expertise in the field. While many knew he had served as John Turner's deputy in Finance, few realized he'd also served as an occasional economics advisor to my own 1983 leadership campaign. His long career in the public service included stints as a Canadian negotiator at the founding meeting of the General Agreement on Tariffs and Trade (GATT), and he had risen to the post of deputy minister of finance before moving into the private sector.

I suspect Simon knew I was already considering appointing him Canada's chief negotiator for the talks. "Reporting to Mr. Clark and the [cabinet] committee would be a negotiating team led by a chief negotiator," Simon wrote in a memo to me.

> This person should be nonpartisan, professional, a proven negotiator with an established track record, knowledgeable in trade and international economics. He should be highly sensitive to where the role of the professional ends and the political responsibility takes over. Above all, the chief negotiator should be tough-minded and should know the object is to get a good agreement for Canada, not an agreement for its own sake . . . Alarmists in Canada who are seeking reasons for obstructing your trade initiative have raised the red herring [of culture]. I am certain that the United States will not seek to intervene in our social programs during these negotiations or at any other time. (I am aware that special interests in the U.S. sponsoring protectionist actions have cited some of our social programs as giving Canadian enterprises a special advantage. The United States government will treat these arguments with the contempt they deserve.) You are perfectly safe in stating publicly, as you have, that Canadian social programs are a matter for Canada alone to determine . . .
>
> In adopting the goal of a comprehensive trade agreement with the United States you have launched Canada on the most important economic initiative of the century. With good management and a little luck you will be creating the framework that will lead to high and growing levels of production, income, and employment for Canadians in all regions of the country, and for generations to

> come. There are few areas of economic policy which command a greater degree of support from knowledgeable people in business and in the economic profession. Numerous serious studies in the past decade or two carried out by highly respected institutions and individuals have given this concept strong support. The opposing forces, while noisy, are for the most part ill informed, backward-looking, doctrinaire, chauvinistic, promoters of special interests, and devoid of any practical alternative. This is a concept whose time has come, and all good Canadians should work for its success.

Derek Burney later labelled this report an "unparalleled" fifteen-page job application.

On November 8, I placed Simon in the top job. The negotiations simply would not have been successful without him; throughout he showed himself to be knowledgeable, tough, honest, and funny. He chose as his deputy Gordon Ritchie, a young yet highly capable veteran of Canada's public service, and together they were to perform brilliantly, bringing the negotiations to a successful conclusion in 1987. Much later on, Ritchie proved particularly able when appearing before parliamentary committees to explain the completed FTA. "Gordon speaks in paragraphs!" I said on more than one occasion, with great admiration. Sylvia Ostry was the second deputy at the Trade Negotiations Office headed by Simon, and she too performed in an exemplary manner as deputy in charge of multilateral trade negotiations.

—

PERSONAL JOURNAL: JANUARY 1, 1988

Reisman was the best person for negotiating with the Americans. Moreover, in my judgment, he would make a very credible and effective spokesman whether the talks succeeded or failed. Clearly, if we succeeded, the opposition parties were going to oppose the deal as a "bad one for Canada." If we failed, the opposition strategy would be to state their support for free trade while deploring the "incompetence" of the government that prevented it from happening! Simon would be my hedge against failure and my spokesman in victory. I reasoned that if we failed – and we almost did – Simon would be an extremely persuasive advocate for the Canadian government that had dared to try but was prevented from success by inscrutable and unacceptable demands. If we did achieve an acceptable agreement, Simon would be no less effective, giving it his benediction in light of his 40 years' experience.

—

A memo to me from Charley McMillan, written the very day of Simon's appointment, gives an illustration of why I knew an experienced hand like Simon had to be in charge. "My own perception, shared with Bernard [Roy] and Paul Tellier, is that intergovernmental rivalry and suspicion are strong and getting worse," Charley wrote. "The sooner Reisman can get his act together the better. On the political side, there is a suspicion, acknowledged by Clark and his staff, that the structures have been loose and ill defined. He is taking steps to correct this problem. The vacuum has created pressures for a group of political staff to take over or at least support Clark's political committee and run it out of the PMO. Within the cabinet, there is a view that there has been too much talk about progress and not enough on real issues, hence the ambiguities on cultural issues and the lack of political strategy."

On December 4 I was scheduled to make an important speech to *Time* magazine's Speakers Forum at the University of Chicago. It was my intention to send a clear signal to the Americans that Canada's cultural sovereignty was as important to Canadians as our political sovereignty. There was no way any government led by me was going to put it at risk in the coming trade talks. "Should be a zinger on cultural safeguards and less beseeching in regards to U.S. attitudes to trade negotiations," I wrote on an early draft of the speech submitted to me by L. Ian MacDonald, whose elegant pen and deep knowledge of public policy made him a valuable member of my senior staff. "If they don't realize how important this is to their interests, we shouldn't have to implore them in any way to reflect upon it."

In the end, I spoke in a language all Americans could understand. "Canada and the United States are different, sovereign democracies," I told them. "In the United States, you cast the net of national security over more areas than we; in Canada, we cast the net of cultural sovereignty more widely than you . . . When it comes to discussing better trade rules for cultural industries, you will have to understand that what we call cultural sovereignty is as vital to our national life as political sovereignty. And how could it be otherwise living, as we do, next to a country ten times our size in population . . . If we and our American partners cannot strike a deal that will achieve these goals, a deal will not be struck."

Today, my government's success in fostering and protecting Canadian culture is an acknowledged fact. "The last time Conservatives did take the reins, under Brian Mulroney, cultural nationalists recall it as a golden age," the *Globe and Mail* reported shortly after Prime Minister Stephen Harper's victory in 2006. "Ministers Marcel Masse and Flora MacDonald brought in ownership restrictions, tax protection, and funding."

As Christmas arrived, I reflected on what had been a roller coaster of a year. I can't deny that I was frustrated. We were advancing our agenda on many fronts, laying the groundwork for free trade and for economic reform, and we were pursuing national reconciliation and beginning to make a positive impact internationally. But we had stumbled repeatedly on the political front. Our very real accomplishments were now obscured by the smoke of scandal and the noise of the opposition and the hostile media.

As I sat in front of the fireplace at Harrington Lake, I thought back to the first meeting of the Priorities and Planning Committee of cabinet the preceding January. That day we had anticipated many of the distractions the government might encounter in 1985. But we had let them happen just the same. "We must remember that the opposition can't hurt us by themselves," I had told my senior ministers then, "they need our assistance, and we've been giving it to them too often. We all need to improve our anticipation of troublesome issues within our respective mandates, of upcoming issues that are inevitable or have a date by which decisions are required . . . The initial period of grace for ministers 'learning their departments' is now over and increasingly we will be expected to demonstrate that we know what we are doing." After asking the civil servants present to leave the meeting, I emphasized this point even more strongly: "The transition is over: You *are* the government. Competence and caring are the issues – don't undermine them . . . That's why you are ministers!"

I had made my own share of mistakes in 1985. Still, I had many reasons to feel optimistic. One of them was encapsulated in a letter I received that holiday season from Canada's new ambassador to France, my old friend Lucien Bouchard. I had put some External Affairs department noses out of joint to advance this "outsider" because I believed he would do a fine job on Canada's behalf. From Paris, Lucien made it clear that he felt our cause was worth the flak we were taking and that the winds of change were at our backs:

> My concern and my thoughts are with you in the carrying out of the difficult but exciting mandate that the trust of the population, as well as your talent and your destiny, have earned you. No one knows better than you the weight of this burden on your shoulders, and no one better than you can measure the difficulty of the obstacles that block the road to the high goals that you have set yourself. But I have faith in your qualities of mind and heart, in your courage, and in the enthusiasm that radiates from you.
>
> I know that you are particularly pleased by the gestures that you have begun to make for Quebec. Among others, I am thinking, obviously, of the Francophonie Summit, which was made possible by the scope of your views on the blossoming of Quebec and on the crucial importance of its contribution to the Canadian identity. I see in this a catalyst for the global process that could lead to the formal adhesion of Quebec to a renewed Canada. At the end of the efforts that you have undertaken, there would thus be the recognition that the Québécois people have their own destiny, a destiny that they themselves would fully and freely assume in the heart of the Canadian confederation. This would be the ultimate reconciliation, the one that is closest to your heart – and that would mark out your place in history. I hope for this for all of us.

1986

1. Vive la Francophonie – et l'Égalité

As the new year began, I must admit to a definite political glow when I considered the situation in my home province. My fellow Quebecers had given me reason to believe that 1986 would be a year of promise, and possibly even of historic change. In December they had returned my federalist friend, former Liberal premier Robert Bourassa, to office with a strong majority. After almost a decade of rule by the Parti Québécois, the citizens of the province had sent a clear signal of their desire for renewed federalism, and of their profound attachment to Canada. To telegraph this change in mindset, on the day of his swearing-in, Robert returned the Canadian flag to the National Assembly, to the pleasure of the crowd that had gathered to wish him well.

Then there was the Francophonie Summit agreement referred to in Lucien Bouchard's letter. Although some members of Robert's party hadn't been impressed – fearing we would be assisting the PQ's electoral chances if we came to an agreement – I'd also spent part of the fall of 1985 negotiating a formula by which Quebec, New Brunswick, and Canada could participate in the first Sommet de la francophonie in Paris. In November, Premier Pierre Marc Johnson had agreed to our proposals, and the stage was now set for the historic gathering of francophone nations scheduled for February.

Even Parti Québécois stalwart Claude Morin, who had been Lévesque's minister of intergovernmental affairs, praised the deal, calling it "honourable, practical, and respectful," and noting that it "confirms that the federal government accepts that on the international scene Quebec can talk about its areas of jurisdiction." The *Ottawa Citizen* agreed: "For Canada, its birth represents a triumph of good sense and cooperation between Ottawa, Quebec, and New Brunswick."

The Trudeauites, of course, were opposed, but they were not the only critics of the deal. Tory MP John Oostrom, for one, forwarded an angry letter he'd received about the issue from a constituent. I was happy to respond to this person's concern: "For over fifteen years, efforts have been under way to organize an international meeting between leaders of these countries in which the French language is used," I wrote. "Last fall, the federal government reached understandings, with Quebec and New Brunswick . . . which clearly protect the sovereignty of Canada. The provincial premiers will contribute most particularly in those areas of provincial jurisdiction, while on matters of federal jurisdiction, such as international, political, and economic matters I, as the representative of the federal government, shall speak for Canada. One of the main goals of my government since assuming office has been to establish a climate of national reconciliation. It is, I believe, through cooperation and working together on matters of importance to francophones across Canada, such as the Francophonie Summit, that we will achieve the goal of greater national unity."

I stressed to caucus the importance of the gathering before I left for Paris. "Discussions . . . will place the summit in a larger perspective for us," I said. "1) Canada and la Francophonie. 2) A bilingual Canada. 3) Quebec's unique place in Canada. 4) Canada as the guardian of French culture outside of Quebec . . . Canada and Canada alone will speak on behalf of the country at the opening ceremonies. There will be a formula for Quebec to play its own, vital role." I stressed that I had kept the number of bureaucrats and assistants low to ensure the presence of ten MPs – eight of them Conservative – in Paris.

I spoke at the summit's opening, truly a moving moment for a son of Quebec's North Shore. Arrayed in front of me in the magnificent Palais de Versailles were the leaders of forty-one countries and governments. It was there, after the First World War, that my Conservative predecessor, Nova Scotia's Sir Robert Borden, had fought for the right of Canada and the other Dominions – nations that had shed a generation's blood on the fields of Europe – to sign the Treaty of Versailles independently. It was a significant moment in our nation's history; some say that Sir Robert was the true father of Canadian autonomy. Sixty-seven years later I made the following remarks (delivered originally in French):

> We cannot fail to recognize that we are, at this moment, participating in a historic event. There are very few examples in the history of international relations, or indeed anywhere in history, of an occasion on which so many heads of state and government have come

together in order to knit between their peoples the bonds of friendship which are already symbolized by today's meeting . . .

Canada comes before you, knowing that it can contribute a youthful, modern approach to la Francophonie, but one which is also imbued with pragmatism and tolerance. It is also proud of the reconciliation which it is achieving within its own borders. The presence of the premier of Quebec here beside me is a striking illustration of this. For Quebecers it is a great day when, because of an understanding we were willing to establish in a spirit of fairness and generosity, they can be represented as a participating government in this distinguished assembly. . . .

The poets and the village bards in all the regions and the epochs of la Francophonie are speaking to us and calling upon us to preserve and celebrate what we owe to them, that is to say, our own being and way of life.

Afterwards, in that splendid room at Versailles, President François Mitterrand leaned across and whispered to me, with great emotion, "You see, Bree-an, what we have done. La Francophonie is now the equivalent of the British Commonwealth."

—

PERSONAL JOURNAL: FEBRUARY 18, 1986

(Written in Paris)

At dinner last night I sat between the prime minister of Luxembourg and the PM of the Central African Republic. The latter, a former ambassador to Canada, deposed his predecessor in a coup; "I did it reluctantly," he said, "because military coups are unconstitutional." And he appears to be very happy in the saddle. Little wonder; he has a wife, three mistresses, 14 children, and an evident purse string – required presidential accoutrements in his country. The PM of Luxembourg, whom I had met on other occasions, couldn't have been more different – pragmatic and resolutely democratic. We both acknowledged the great benefits of a constitutional monarchy, but we were no doubt in the minority at the Élysée.

—

PERSONAL JOURNAL: FEBRUARY 25, 1986

(Written in Paris)

Prior to that dinner, President and Mrs. Mitterrand had received privately a relatively small group of people (Mobutu, Diouf, Fabius, the president of Lebanon, etc.) in an elegant little room. Mila and I got into an extended conversation with Léopold Sédar Senghor of Senegal, former president, and membre de l'Académie Française, *who informed us 1) that his son was a jazz musician in Boston, and 2) that one of his own favourite tasks has been translating Irish poets Butler, Yeats, etc. into Senegalese dialects and French. If the Irish only knew what had happened to their words!*

Haiti was represented by the minister of education, who told me he was educated by the Methodists and became a leader of that community. It was ironic to chat with this soft-spoken teacher, named just days earlier to his post, in France with Baby Doc [Duvalier] in exile on French soil – and us discussing culture and language. I suppose it is an indication that life goes on – always.

PM Fabius, for whom I have a high regard and respect, told me that the French would soon send Duvalier to some tiny dependency off the coast, together with the $800 million that Fabius estimated he had removed from Haiti. It struck me that the inevitable immorality of politics was illustrated by the fact that, had a revolution not intervened days earlier, I could have wound up discussing culture with Duvalier himself – rather than human rights and internal reform as we should have! It's a sad commentary on international relations that one is largely precluded from commenting publicly on internal abuses of a fellow head of government, though I'll be damned if I know why.

At the conclusion of the luncheon [the next day], the president gathered me, Paul Desmarais, Ambassador Bouchard and wife Jocelyne and led us through the Élysée to a small private room where, he announced, Napoleon had abdicated. The room was unchanged since June 22, 1815. Present on the desk was a copy (leather-bound) of the instrument of abdication. Mitterrand picked it up and began to read the entire, moving statement. The effect was dramatic. Paul (a great student of Napoleon's life) was clearly touched by this unusual spectacle of Canadians from Sudbury, Chicoutimi, and Baie-Comeau listening to the president of France in such remarkable circumstances. This vignette sums up the flavour of our entire visit – spontaneous, warm, fraternal. After 25 years of progressively deteriorating relationships, a fundamental change has taken place.

—

François Mitterrand had asked me to give an overview of the world economic situation in my speech, and so I highlighted Africa, one of my foreign affairs priorities. I reminded my fellow leaders that the very credibility of La Francophonie was at stake if we did not strengthen international cooperation through this new forum. Substance, as commentators had said, was crucial.

I recall with pride that Canada was able to focus the summit's attention on battling apartheid in South Africa, as well. Participants passed a resolution calling on the racist government there to dismantle apartheid laws and free all political prisoners, to lift the ban on the ANC and the state of emergency imposed in certain areas of the country, and to start negotiations with authentic representatives of the black population. We also called for the enforcement of UN resolutions on Namibia.

Not everything went smoothly at the francophone summit. Quebec Premier Robert Bourassa, trying to be cute, broke our clear-cut agreement. He announced to the press that he had made a proposal and led discussions behind closed doors regarding an area of foreign affairs, which is a clearly delineated federal responsibility. As a result I gave him the cold shoulder during the rest of the summit. "This is the kind of thing Trudeau predicted you would do," I told him later in a frosty telephone conversation, when he called to apologize. "This is why he wouldn't agree to a summit, because he was afraid of people like you. There will never be another Francophonie Summit unless you give me ironclad guarantees."

As I told the press, "You can only blindside me once."

A contrite Bourassa assured me there had been an "error in communications," and that no such lapse would ever happen again. In the twenty years since, it's been smooth sailing for Canada's involvement in the organization.

—

PERSONAL JOURNAL: FEBRUARY 25, 1986

(Written in Paris)

I had in fact taken considerable political risks to ensure Quebec's participation. The one thing I was fearful of was that Bourassa would be unwilling to resist being a prankster in Paris and that some untoward incident could jeopardize future cooperation in this area because of Anglo-Canadian reaction. And that is what happened. As Marc Laurendeau wrote in yesterday's La Presse, *Bourassa's vandalism was both inaccurate and unhelpful, and I deliberately played it down. But from now on I will deal with Premier Bourassa with extreme care in any matter involving sensitive issues.*

I had thought our relationship was sufficiently mature and responsible to preclude any such tomfoolery, but I was in error. No lasting damage was done, but concerns have been raised by his action, and we shall have to be very careful in the future. Indeed, one reason why it had absolutely no impact in Paris at the conference and interested only Canadian journalists, and why it was deemed peripheral, was that France and the other major leaders were enjoying both La Francophonie and their new relationships with Ottawa, so that they were not to be diverted by Canadian trivia imported to Paris for the conference.

—

After the summit, where France and Canada had worked to create TV5, the first transatlantic French-language television network, I stayed for two further days in Paris as part of an official visit to France. President Mitterrand spared no effort in hosting the Canadian delegation and in giving us a very enjoyable time. He understood that France, as the mother country of French language and culture, had a special responsibility in the world, and he took this role very seriously. He greatly appreciated the moves I had made with Quebec and New Brunswick that allowed the first Francophonie Summit to take place, knowing that it could hardly have occurred without the physical and financial participation of the second most important French-speaking country in the world, Canada.

As I've mentioned, François called me "Bree-an" and we were to develop a particularly close relationship. In 1989 he hosted the G-7 Summit in Paris as part of the celebrations marking the two hundredth anniversary of the French Revolution. One day during that visit, while we were waiting outside the Louvre, he suddenly turned to me, and without warning started to speak of the French presidential summer residence. "Why haven't you accepted my invitation to Fort de Brégançon?" he asked. (Actually, he had previously made this invitation to Mila at a dinner in Senegal.) Now, as any student of French history knows, a fortress has been in place on the tiny island of Brégançon since before the birth of Christ. The islet is separated from the Mediterranean coast by only a few feet of water but it towers over a hundred feet above the sea. No less a personage than General Charles de Gaulle was the first President of the Republic to stay there. Georges Pompidou spent his summers there, as did Valéry Giscard d'Estaing and other presidents, on through to Jacques Chirac.

Eventually, Mila and I and the children were able to accept his invitation. It was the most marvellous vacation of our lives. To this day I keep a picture of Fort de Brégançon in my study at home in Montreal and often look at it with fond memories – especially on cold winter days. I remember that protective French naval vessels kept a respectful distance from the island, but their officers and crew made sure they were available to ferry the Mulroney family to picnics and swimming outings in warm blue-green Mediterranean waters so breathtaking they seemed to come from a dream. The personal chef to the president was also sent to look after us, and we dined each night on different terraces commanding views that were dream-like as well.

The fortress was also the site of a near-tragedy involving my youngest son, Nicolas, which we were able to keep out of the news at the time. On our second trip to Brégançon, in 1993, Nicolas stroked a previously injured black Labrador that lived at the fortress, and the animal leaped up and bit our baby on the face. Mila reacted immediately, throwing herself between Nicolas and the dog, and instantly bandaging the wound. It turned out that the dog had punctured Nicolas's face only a half-inch or so from his eye. We rushed him to the local hospital, where President Mitterrand himself ensured that our son had the best of care, and all ended well.

On that 1986 Paris visit, Mitterrand asked me, "What can I do to show my appreciation for all you've done?"

"François," I replied, "there's a story in Canada that when General Georges Vanier was governor general, he wanted to make a state visit to

France. General Vanier had lost a leg on a French battlefield during the First World War and later served as ambassador to France. While he was governor general his old friend Charles de Gaulle held the office you do today. Do you know what de Gaulle is alleged to have said when told that Governor General Vanier would like to make a state visit?"

"I have no idea," François answered.

I did not hold back. "'Tell Governor General Vanier that if I want a visit from the Canadian head of state I will invite the Queen of England!' de Gaulle replied."

"Look," I continued, pressing my point: "Today our governor general is Jeanne Sauvé, a francophone from Saskatchewan who has lived in Quebec most of her life, and she has told me that her greatest desire is to make a state visit to Paris."

François cut me off. "Bree-an," he said, "when do you want her to come? When you find out, you let me know, and that's the day it will take place."

That night, I called Jeanne Sauvé from Paris. "Excellency," I said, "I've just spoken to President François Mitterrand, and he has told me that you are most welcome to make a state visit to his country and capital, and that he will personally coordinate all aspects of the visit."

Jeanne Sauvé's voice broke and I could hear the tears as she responded, "This is the highlight of my career."

In due course Governor General Sauvé was happy to be royally received by Mitterrand and the entire French elite in a long-anticipated formal state visit.

Another reason for the new mood in Paris was the fine work of Lucien Bouchard as our ambassador to France. He was extremely successful, probably the ablest ambassador Canada has sent there in modern times. Lucien was cultured, well educated, and extremely eloquent. He knew intimately what I wanted to accomplish in Canada–France relations, and worked tirelessly to that end.

—

PERSONAL JOURNAL: JANUARY 1, 1987

Both Mitterrand and Chirac have commented to me personally about the remarkable job Bouchard has been doing in Paris. He has aided substantially in rebuilding Franco–Canadian relations, which had

> *gravely deteriorated during the previous two decades.* As La Presse *recently reported in a major analysis of the relationship, Bouchard has also restored the Canadian embassy to its proper role vis-à-vis the Maison du Québec. All political leaders in France now know and accept that while Quebec's presence is important, and indeed supported by the government of Canada, the federal role and presence are paramount at all times, and in all circumstances.*

—

As we left France, I found myself in a car along with Undersecretary of State for External Affairs Si Taylor. Si told me of the days he'd been stationed at our embassy in Paris as a young foreign service officer. "You know, Prime Minister," he said, "Paris used to be Siberia for Canada – you have made it a second home."

On February 24, 1986, Tommy Douglas, the fearless yet gentle former premier of Saskatchewan and leader of the NDP, passed into history. Members of Parliament paused to pay tribute to Tommy that day. When it was my turn, I gave a heartfelt eulogy of gratitude on behalf of all Canadians:

> Canada has lost the voice and the vision of one of our great humanitarians and one of our truly outstanding parliamentarians. I knew of his reputation and his legend and, like many others here, was privileged to know the man himself. I knew of his personal qualities, his devotion to his church and to Canada and his love of his wife, his daughters, and his grandchildren. Tommy Douglas was an outstanding Canadian beloved by all members despite political differences. Perhaps the old Saskatchewan proverb said it best of all: "Tommy Douglas doesn't have to kiss babies, babies kiss him" . . .
>
> I could not help but remember something which I heard him say once at a political rally . . . He told of meeting an elderly farmer in Saskatchewan, and in searching for a compliment he said, "Well, I suppose there have been worse premiers than me." In the absence of any response at all, and thinking the farmer was hard of hearing, he elevated the decibel level and said, "I suppose there have been worse premiers than me." The farmer said, "I heard you the first time, I was just trying to remember" . . .

> His passing is not only a loss to all Canadians but, I think, a gentle reminder that no honour was greater to Tommy Douglas than the respect of his peers and the affection of common people.

I also spoke about the relationship between Tommy and my close friend Robert Cliche, which I had witnessed, first-hand, in Quebec so many years earlier. "I saw the courage and dignity with which they tried to establish their political party on Quebec soil," I said. "Subsequently Mr. Cliche spoke to me at great length about his relationship with [Tommy], his affection for Quebec, his respect for the French fact, his desire to set up a truly national political movement, and the courage he showed in the many positions he took in a spirit of understanding and solidarity."

One of my great pleasures as prime minister was the opportunity it gave me to honour Tommy, by making him a privy councillor in November of 1984 – a long-overdue honour for his contributions to Canada.

During my time in office, I developed a certain affinity with many NDP members. Ed Broadbent, Lorne Nystrom, Bill Blaikie, Ian Waddell, Svend Robinson, and others I faced off against in the Commons fought hard for their beliefs, concerns, and constituents, and they also fought fairly. That winter I even helped New Democrat MP Les Benjamin mark his wife's birthday. I soon heard back from her. "That likeable MP from Regina West – who happens to be my husband – is continuously coming up with new ideas each year to surprise me on my birthday," Connie wrote. "Receiving a personal call from the prime minister was certainly the culmination of all his previous efforts. Thank you for taking the time out of your very busy schedule to wish me a happy birthday. Now one must wonder what he's going to do to top this next year!"

A particular favourite of mine was Svend Robinson. Canada's first openly gay MP, Svend was no favourite of the less progressive wing of my caucus. Sometimes when that group had caused me grief, I'd invite Svend over to sit next to me as the House continued, and I enjoyed the angry stares from my backbench as I did so. Svend was committed to justice for Canada's native peoples, and he would sometimes send me notes that tipped me off about a question he was planning to ask in the Commons. This practice ensured that both he and aboriginal groups received a more complete answer from the prime minister. "Brian: A very hopeful answer," he wrote in a note he sent across the floor of the Commons during a 1987 question period, when there were major problems in the Queen Charlotte Islands. "Thank you for keeping the pressure on this vital question. I don't want the Haida, or myself, to be blocking loggers ever again!"

I recall that Svend questioned me in the fall of 1985 after a Commons subcommittee tabled a unanimous report, "Toward Equality," calling for the federal government to end discrimination (in the federal sphere) on the basis of sexual orientation. While we didn't move as fast as some would have liked, I am proud to say that we ended discrimination, for example, against homosexuals and lesbians in the Canadian Armed Forces.

On February 26, 1986, I discussed human rights with my caucus. "I am a strong supporter of the family, conventional values, conservative attitudes, and established religious convention," I said. "I am also a strong opponent of discrimination of any kind. I don't know how or why one becomes a homosexual, but all of us, including homosexuals, are children of God and entitled to understanding and tolerance."

Justice Minister Ray Hnatyshyn and I traded letters on the "Toward Equality" report early the following year. In reading Ray's letter, I was pleased to note he approached the issue the same way I did. "At that time, largely as a result of your positive intervention, the government made a commitment to take whatever measures were necessary to ensure that sexual orientation is a prohibited ground of discrimination in relation to all areas of federal jurisdiction," he wrote. "In the discussions following the tabling . . . the government indicated that it would examine the means to fulfill this commitment, including the necessity of an amendment to the Canadian *Human Rights Act*. I have examined the alternatives and believe the most meaningful way to meet this commitment is an amendment to the Canadian *Human Rights Act*, even though this may cause some controversy in caucus and cabinet."

I knew that "some controversy" was likely to be an understatement, but in my reply a few days later, I told Ray to go ahead. "With regards to sexual orientation, you noted in your letter that the government had indicated in 'Toward Equality' its intention to take whatever measures were necessary to ensure that sexual orientation is a prohibited ground of discrimination," I wrote. "I understand that the most meaningful and practical way of fulfilling our commitment is to amend the Canadian *Human Rights Act* to add sexual orientation to the prohibited grounds of discrimination. I would therefore support your recommendation to do so."

The government I had the privilege of leading never wavered when it came to placing the cause of human rights and social justice at the top of the agenda in both domestic and foreign policy. I am proud of this legacy, and look back on our accomplishments with a great deal of satisfaction.

One opposition MP who wasn't very effective in this period was Jean Chrétien. Jean had never come to terms with the fact that John Turner had beaten him in 1984, and he made no secret of his dislike of his party's duly elected leader. "John Turner is just like Doug Wickenheiser – he looks good until you put him on the ice," Chrétien had whispered to me the previous winter when we were at a funeral home, paying our respects to Claude Ryan and his family after his wife, Madeleine, died. Although the setting seemed inappropriate, I had to smile: Chretien had an earthy charm that served him well during his long career. But more than once I was shocked by how open Jean was in expressing his discontent. Few were surprised when he announced he was resigning his seat at the end of February 1986 and leaving politics. His campaign to undermine Turner was to continue unabated, directed from his office at an Ottawa law firm.

I joined in the tributes to Jean Chrétien on his last day in the Commons, and in my speech I recalled his finest hour: "As a Quebecer, I remember more specifically his steadfast and courageous leadership during the [1980] referendum campaign, since I worked for him at the time. He showed great leadership and generosity toward all his collaborators, and he showed understanding for the position of his opponents."

—

PERSONAL JOURNAL: APRIL 17, 1989

Chrétien, whom I know well, remains, nonetheless, an unknown in many ways. The darling of the English-language media, he has enjoyed good success in national politics and clearly has done quite well as a lawyer and lobbyist these past few years. I was struck, however, during our brief time together in the House, by his general unpreparedness, the vapid responses, and a speaking style that I thought had gone out with [Duplessis minister] Jos. D. Bégin. When I recently saw him on English TV, he was still making his "I love the Rockies" speech, with the same old jokes and in the same old style.

It will be interesting to see how this wears in 1989 or 1993, or whether he will make changes to his style and develop some content to his speeches.

—

Unlike the divided and gloomy Liberals, as personified by the brooding shadow that was Jean Chrétien that year, members of my own caucus entered 1986 enthusiastic and keen for the battles ahead. We gathered together for two days of talks on January 18–19, ready to roll up our sleeves and get down to work.

In my kickoff address, I said that members of Parliament "must feel and be a genuine part of the decision-making process." So I asked a number of key questions: "1) What structures ensure this will happen? 2) Does an MP feel encouraged to speak out and to make a difference in caucus? 3) Does the system itself inhibit this possibility? 4) Should there be changes in cabinet structure or committees to ensure full participation? 5) How is support secured from caucus before decisions are made?" I also asked for comments on my own role. "How can the PM make better use of his time? 1) To be more available to MPs. 2) To be more frequently in ridings. 3) To participate in regional caucuses. 4) To ensure follow-through on important matters raised in national caucus."

And then Tory MPs and senators had their chance. In the free-for-all that followed, I heard – and definitely took note of – complaints that some cabinet ministers, senior bureaucrats, and PMO staffers were not paying proper attention to MPs. That was soon fixed. In my view, members of Parliament are any government's front-line troops. They carry the message throughout their ridings in both good and bad political times. MPs of all parties bravely put their names forward and earn the votes and support of their friends and neighbours in communities and cities across this far-flung land. No actions by unelected advisors or civil servants angered me more than not giving elected members the respect they had earned.

That weekend Flora MacDonald sent me a quick note during the discussions, which I was later able to use effectively in caucus, the Commons, and on the hustings. She pointed out that under the last Liberal government of 1980 to 1984, approximately 400,000 jobs were created in Canada for a daily average of 250 jobs. Since our swearing-in in September 1984 up to January 1986, 450,000 new jobs had been created – about 1,000 each day.

We ended the weekend on a high note. I was moved by the excitement, energy, and unity I'd witnessed throughout those two days.

"With all the challenges and disappointments that come from leading a national party, it should be noted that there are often moments of pleasure," I said in conclusion. "One memory I shall always cherish – till the day they put me down – is of caucus, men and women who love Canada and admire each other, struggling to find a common approach to building a better country."

I also met early that year with Canada's top bureaucrats, the deputy ministers. This was the third time since becoming prime minister that I met privately with this crucial body of public servants, so key to any government's success. "I recognize you have been through a couple of disruptive years with elections, new ministers, new political staffs, new priorities, new cuts, and senior personnel changes," I told them. "This was inevitable during the transition year, but the transition is now over. If anybody in this country knows how tough it is to govern Canada, it is this group." I thanked them and told them I would continue to rely on them.

Canada has an excellent public service, and my government was well served by them at all times.

With caucus members loyally cheering him on, Finance Minister Michael Wilson introduced his budget in February. If Canadians doubted we were intent on repairing the nation's finances, this budget showed how serious we were. We announced a further $800 million in cuts to government spending, and raised taxes by $1.5 billion in our efforts to bring the deficit below $30 billion. Our government's expenditure plan marked the first absolute decline in total program spending in more than twenty years.

"My message today is a serious one, and in many ways not pleasant," Michael said with frankness. "But it must be said. And it must be understood."

When he was crafting his budgets, I always instructed Michael to ensure that the interests of disabled Canadians were not forgotten, whatever the economic situation. He never let me down. Every year there was action for the disabled. Our 1985 and 1986 budgets both included provisions to broaden and increase the definition and deductions for disability for income tax purposes. We increased, fivefold, our support for disabled persons' consumer organizations through the Disabled Persons Participation

Program. My government also established a permanent Status of Disabled Persons Secretariat, and I designated the secretary of state as Canada's Minister Responsible for Disabled Persons.

Our economic reforms were proceeding well. We'd built upon our first privatizations of 1985 with the sale of Teleglobe, and of De Havilland to Boeing in January, and unemployment was continuing to drop – to 9.8 per cent in February, for example. By March, the Bank of Canada's prime lending rate dropped from 11.74 per cent to 10.69 per cent, with the chartered banks soon following the central bank.

Nevertheless, we were suffering politically. On the heels of the previous Black September, the media were circling in search of further problems, and we were taking hits from all sides. On New Year's Eve of 1985, Minister of State for Transport Suzanne Blais-Grenier – a pedestrian junior member of cabinet who had acquired a reputation for high-flying, expensive travel habits – resigned after secret information about the proposed closure of an oil refinery was leaked.

There were bright spots, however, and I could take solace from the most unlikely sources every now and then. "Prime Minister Brian Mulroney has every justification for being underwhelmed by the objectivity of the nation's media," Toronto author and commentator Tom Harpur wrote in a *Toronto Star* column published in February.

> In a word, they have been, to date, unfair in the overall coverage of both the man and his government . . . Certainly Mulroney and his team have made plenty of mistakes. Certainly they deserve prompt and frequent criticism. But I have the uneasy feeling that he has broken the 11th Commandment, the one that is uniquely and superbly Canadian. It reads: "Thou shalt not look too good or be too successful." Mulroney has had the unforgivable arrogance to express full confidence in himself and the country. He has, it seems, done worse. He has tried to create a mood of reconciliation between Ottawa and the provinces, between Quebec and the rest of Canada, between east and west. Shockingly, he has been well mannered to our Queen and friendly to our neighbours. He has tried to get the economy moving again . . .
>
> Disagreement with [Mulroney] on this or that policy shouldn't cloud the fact that his government has many solid accomplishments

> already to its credit. In the words of the old song, it might be fairer if the media were to "accentuate the positive" – from time to time.

I reconsidered my plans to cancel my *Star* subscription and moved forward with my plans for Canada. I was encouraged when the Bourassa government again made a gesture demonstrating its commitment to renewed federalism: Intergovernmental Affairs Minister Gil Rémillard announced that his province would finally embrace the Canadian Charter of Rights and Freedoms. "We have absolutely nothing against the Charter . . . in Quebec," he said. "On the contrary, we want Quebecers to have the same protection of their fundamental rights as other Canadians . . . We do not have the right to take Quebecers hostage for the purposes of constitutional talks." Rémillard added that the gesture was a signal that Quebecers felt they belonged "to the Canadian federation" and that the Quebec government would remain "faithful to our federalist commitment."

As constitutional scholar Patrick Monahan later wrote: "It was a sign of good faith, a promise of a new era in Quebec–Canada relations."

1986

2. Washington, Tokyo, and Beijing

In advance of my second annual summit with President Reagan, Bill Davis and U.S. special envoy Drew Lewis released their acid rain report. They called on the Americans to spend $5 billion, split between government and industry, to investigate technologies for reducing acid rain emissions. While I felt that the report didn't go far enough, it at least marked the first time a top figure in the Reagan administration admitted that acid rain existed. Bill Davis, who had by then spent a lifetime in politics, asked critics of the report to try to understand certain political realities, especially those south of the border. "I don't think you have to be totally knowledgeable in this subject area to sense that if Mr. Lewis had come in with a report that said we will have a 50 per cent reduction across the board in the United States by 1994 no matter what the cost, that the administration might have found that less than acceptable," he said in his understated way.

Though I recognized the report was a positive step, I still kept my eye on the larger picture. "Its recommendations constitute a significant departure from positions taken in previous discussions with the U.S. administration," I said in a statement. "The report and its recommendations constitute an important step forward in this process, although our goal has to be a bilateral accord that deals once and for all with this issue."

Despite his reluctance to act on acid rain, President Reagan had been devoting a great deal of attention to relations with his country's northern neighbour before our get-together. "Since our March [1985 Shamrock Summit] meeting, the prime minister and I have worked to improve our relations still further," he said during his weekly radio address to Americans on January 4, 1986. "Already, we've committed ourselves to joint efforts in defence, the environment, and space. With regard to trade, I've informed the Congress that I want to begin negotiations with Canada on an agreement of historic significance to both countries. Our goal is to promote free and open economic competition and to reduce those few barriers to our trade that still remain. When Prime Minister Mulroney visits Washington this March, I believe the mid-1980s will already have taken shape as the most productive period in the long history of Canadian–American friendship."

My summit with President Reagan began with both of us speaking at a ceremony on the White House lawn on March 18, 1986, before going into a private meeting. Our conversation was free-ranging and we discussed both world affairs and bilateral concerns. I started with the former and I once again worked at the tricky but important task of explaining the French to the Americans. I had recently spoken with François Mitterrand, and I told President Reagan what his French counterpart had said. "He is reflective and philosophical toward you and the United States," I said. "He sees that Americans now feel good about themselves."

Ron made no comment, and I moved on to Canadian–American relations. "There is some political downside to my pro-American stance," I explained. "I don't equate stridency with effectiveness, and I start from the premise that Canada is independent but that we are friends. Any deals we make have to be good for both sides. I think Canadians share that view."

In replying, Ron said that he appreciated Canada's support, again thanking us for speaking up for the United States in their actions against Libya. He then brought up our acid rain announcement, slated for the following day.

I interrupted and looked him straight in the eye. "Acid rain is extremely important to Canada," I said. "It's the litmus test [of our relationship]." I also pressed the president on Canadian sovereignty in Arctic waters. The voyage of the U.S. Coast Guard's *Polar Sea* through the Northwest Passage the previous summer was still a major political issue for my government. "If the Canadian position on sovereignty is right, we can manage any traffic through the area," I said. "If not, then the Northwest Passage is opened up to others."

By "others" I meant the Soviet Union, and Ronald Reagan knew it.

"We won't challenge your sovereignty," the president replied. "We should work toward an arrangement."

One much more serious fault line that quickly showed itself was the issue of culture in the free trade talks between our two nations. Treasury Secretary Jim Baker said he believed Canadian concerns about culture could derail the negotiations. I tried to teach the brilliant Texan a thing or two about Canada. Americans take the influence of Hollywood, the record industry, the giant TV networks, and so on for granted; to them, the entertainment business is just another business. I explained that our culture was much more than just a business to Canadians; it was a means of expressing ourselves in our own voices. "Your influence is so great in the English-speaking market," I stated. "Our numbers make us fragile. We have some justified sensitivities and we hope you'll understand."

The state dinner that night was an impressive affair. Though I knew I still had a great deal of work to do, I was pleased by Ronald Reagan's toast. "We can work together to resolve the issue of acid rain, as we've worked together to resolve so many environmental issues before," he said, encouragingly. "We can ensure that our joint defence remains so strong that no aggressor will ever attack us. And we can reach a new agreement on trade that would help us achieve unparalleled prosperity for our citizens. I strongly endorse a prompt start to formal negotiations in the fullest possible scope to those talks. Before I leave the White House, Mr. Prime Minister, I hope that we can bring these negotiations to a successful conclusion. We can lead our people into the light of prosperity, freedom, and goodwill. Nothing less, of course, should be expected of two free peoples who live so close. Freedom is the fountainhead from which mutual respect and amicability flow. And freedom is what America – Canada and the United States – is all about."

My message when I spoke concerned free trade: "Are we in Canada confident enough in our ability to maintain our political sovereignty in a process that will lead to closer relations? And the answer is yes. Have we in Canada a cultural identity strong enough to live and grow in this process? And the answer is yes. And have we in Canada developed the economic and commercial enterprises necessary to prosper under greater competition? And the answer, again, is emphatically yes."

The next day, President Reagan publicly announced he was endorsing the report of our envoys on acid rain. "I wish I could say that our action today takes the acid rain issue off our bilateral agenda; unfortunately, this cannot be," he said. "Serious scientific and economic problems remain to be solved. But in the spirit of cooperation and goodwill which has come to characterize the way Canadians and Americans approach their common problems, I am confident that we have begun a process which will benefit future generations in both our great countries."

During a private luncheon in the president's personal dining room, the president showed he'd gone to bed the night before thinking about the Arctic. "Let the sovereignty issue lie where it is," he said. "Anything we do [in Canadian Arctic waters] will be with your permission."

Canada hosted a special dinner at the Canadian embassy during the visit, with Vice-President George Bush the senior American present. (In Washington, the American president rarely visits another nation's embassy – a tradition President George Bush later broke, when he attended our adieu dinner for him at the Canadian embassy on Pennsylvania Avenue.) In a city where appearances at power dinners and cocktail parties measure diplomatic success, the vice-president led a delegation composed of the most senior members of the administration. Never before had the Canadian embassy hosted such an affair.

"Of course, sir, Canada and Canadians are well known to you," I told Bush during my toast. "At Kennebunkport, in July and August, it must seem as if you are surrounded by Canadians who flock to the Maine coast, to take the sun, to stroll on your magnificent beaches. And to sample the superior Maine lobster – which in some places, I am told, is imported from New Brunswick. So you see, there is virtue in a liberalized trading relationship."

Little did I know my toast was the last laugh that I or my delegation would have for a while out of that embassy dinner. Though I was completely unaware of events taking place outside the dining room, I soon heard about them. Our ambassador's wife, Sondra Gotlieb, was working under a great deal of stress. The most senior members of the U.S. administration were coming to her home for dinner and the pressure was on. When she learned that one important guest was a last minute no-show, she snapped. In full view of the press, she slapped her social secretary.

I was informed of the incident when I entered the car to return to my hotel, and I realized instantly that the slap would overshadow my visit's success, both at the White House and on Capitol Hill, where I met with the Senate Foreign Relations Committee. Ambassador Allan Gotlieb was in my suite early the next morning, to offer his resignation.

I didn't hesitate. "Allan, you have been an outstanding ambassador," I said. "I don't know how significant this event was – and it very well might be – but I'm not going to accept your resignation. If I did, you would be ending your career in disgrace, and that would be deeply unfair to you and your family, considering your tremendous contributions to Canada. You can withdraw it."

And with that, the matter was closed. The slap was indeed one helluva story, but I never regretted rejecting Allan's resignation, despite the headlines. As Mila always says, "Brian, don't sweat the small stuff." While I won't deny that Sondra's act caused a bit of sweat, I had to put it aside and move on. In truth, Gotlieb was a superb ambassador and Sondra – whom he adored, and on whom he clearly relied – played an important role in his success.

—

PERSONAL JOURNAL: MARCH 31, 1986

Much of my time and energy has been devoted to restoring confidence in the party, caucus, and cabinet. I was extremely pleased to hear [CBC reporter] David Halton refer over the last fortnight to "the PM's outstanding confidence and enthusiasm" or to the "PM's tremendous self-confidence permeating the convention," because that is what I have been trying to convey – confidence and leadership – to the party and the country.

Although Canada is a parliamentary democracy, the PM's role is pivotal. He cannot delegate (although I would often dearly love to) party or government responsibilities, so he finds himself playing the role of leader, conceptualizer, cheerleader, fundraiser, etc., both in Ottawa and across the country. Since January, I have been to Montreal, Halifax, St. Catharines, Kitchener-Waterloo, Regina, Vancouver, Penticton, etc., to show the flag, rally the troops, sell the budget, meet the folks, entertain the boys, inspire some hope, articulate some vision, show understanding, and demonstrate compassion – without losing my temper or too many friends! Such are the demands of party and government leadership in Canada. Our geography is so colossal that the requirement of physical presence in each province/region at regular times adds a bruising dimension to one's responsibilities and one's working day. Stamina is the one quality that a Canadian PM requires in abundance.

—

In April, President Reagan proved true to his word when on our behalf he took on angry members of the U.S. Senate's Finance Committee. Led by Senator Robert Packwood, they were threatening to derail his request for "fast-track authority" to enter into free trade talks with Canada. Without such authority, Congress would be able to attach amendments to any treaty that was negotiated, and free trade between Canada and the United States would die the death of a thousand cuts.

By April 11, these senators were using the free trade issue as leverage to attack the president's overall handling of foreign policy. In addition, they had a litany of complaints about such things as the importation of Canadian hogs, potatoes, and softwood lumber, not to mention other long-standing disputes between our two countries. All politics is indeed local for many in the U.S. Senate. The committee illustrated all too well what I, as the leader of America's most important trading partner, had feared most: protectionism and partisanship. "We're dealing with the administration as a whole," I told the press after Packwood's announcement. "It might do something for Canadian nationalists, some of whom believe that the United States has been down there on bended knee just waiting for Canadians to negotiate a deal with them."

As matters came to a head on April 23, with the vote apparently going to be lost, Canadians unfamiliar with political life in Washington could see clearly from the comments of Hawaii Senator Spark Matsunaga, for example, why allies and their diplomats, going back to the days of Woodrow Wilson and the failed Treaty of Versailles, have often felt hostage to the parochialism of American domestic politics. Ronald Reagan had to get on the telephone personally and strong-arm wayward senators like Matsunaga who were threatening to vote against him. "I told the president that my position was based on a view that the president was neglecting Congress and its views on trade issues," Senator Matsunaga announced to the media. "We are not consulted at all. I told him that the Finance Committee wants to teach him that lesson and that I can't switch unless you can tell them that you have learned. To that, he said, 'Yes, I have.' And on that basis I have reconsidered."

That tipped the balance. Senator Matsunaga – whom we supplied with statistics about the number of Canadians who visited Hawaii each year – then voted to grant President Reagan fast-track authority. The U.S. Senate committee offered up a tied vote (10–10), but under the rules that meant victory for the president. The talks were on.

Reagan placed a call to Ottawa after the votes were tallied. "We started out this morning one vote behind," he recalled. "I was very concerned about the direction this thing was going. We had a meeting this morning – I was determined to make sure this thing would work. I really put on the full court press."

"Thank you for your work to ensure this historic initiative," I replied. "As we go to [the G-7 Summit in] Tokyo, the United States and Canada will demonstrate great leadership to the world on trade liberalization."

I then spoke to the press: "Although it was a close verdict, it represents in the United States system a go-ahead signal for the administration. The president has just confirmed this to me. He has also reiterated that he intends to start negotiations without preconditions. This has always been Canada's position. Events of today offered dramatic proof of the reality of the protectionist threat and of the immense challenge that lies ahead. Nonetheless, we interpret today's vote as evidence of the will of the president, his administration, and the Congress to overcome these pressures."

I sent a message to Alberta Premier Don Getty, chairman of the annual premiers' conference, and asked him to inform his colleagues of the news. I also wanted to reiterate that I believed a provincial role in the free trade talks was crucial. I concluded with the words: "I want to assure you of my strong desire to achieve a national consensus on this historic endeavour, and I look forward to working with you and your provincial colleagues to that end."

Only weeks later I met again with President Reagan, and with the other G-7 leaders who had assembled in Tokyo for the annual Economic Summit. My sherpa, Sylvia Ostry, along with other officials and Finance Minister Michael Wilson, had been highlighting the alarming importance of the G-5, a group from which Canada and Italy had been excluded. Just before Christmas, I had reviewed Sylvia's briefing note on the Tokyo Summit preparations. "The G-5 agenda has expanded to include a broader range of international financial and economic problems, including developing-country indebtedness, an area where there are real Canadian government and commercial bank interests," she wrote. "The G-5 has become a directoire for international economic policy. The implications of the growing influence of the G-5 for the future of the Economic Summit and some of the other international economic institutions are clear. If the work of economic policy coordination is done by the G-5, then the summit may become an empty shell on international economic issues, and Canada will lose an important opportunity to make a meaningful contribution to the debate on these matters."

I had also spoken with the American president about the issue before the summit. "I'm concerned that there may be a tendency toward G-5 activity actively replacing the summit as the locus for economic discussion," I told Reagan in a telephone conversation on January 7. "This would leave us and Italy as 'odd men out,' and would be particularly unwelcome for those of us who face a barrage of parliamentary questions. In my view there is little the G-5 can do or coordinate which would be less effective under the G-7 umbrella. In fact, there is an obvious downside to excluding two summit partners, both in terms of better economic coordination and the credibility of the summit as an effective instrument for the West as a whole."

At the G-7 Economic Summit in Tokyo in May, I made an impassioned case to the full session for the inclusion of Canada and Italy. When European Community President Jacques Delors said that if we were admitted, the EC would have to seek membership, I reminded him, not gently, that Canada was a sovereign nation, and that the EC was merely a political creation. "This is an outrage," I said. "I have never heard anything so offensive in my life." When Delors began to respond, Ronald Reagan leaned over to me and whispered, "Ah, shit, Brian, let's get out of here."

I kept up the fight. "Canada is not here asking for any favours," I said. "We're here as a major powerful nation that should be in the G-7 as a matter of course, on our merits."

I was not pleased to find Margaret Thatcher, our traditional ally, fighting the expansion of the G-5. After I had spoken, Ronald Reagan saved the day when he suddenly took to his feet, closed his leather folder, and announced, "I don't want to be part of any club that doesn't include Canada." Canada had prevailed, and the G-5 was folded into the G-7.

Pierre Trudeau's former principal secretary, Tom Axworthy, discussed this accomplishment in a column published in the *Toronto Star*. "Last week at the Tokyo summit, Canada won an important economic victory," he wrote. "Along with Italy, we were invited to join one of the most exclusive clubs in the world . . . Prime Minister Brian Mulroney deserves our congratulations for obtaining this concession over the objections of our European allies . . . There is no foreign or economic policy objective more important than working with our allies to make the new G-7 into a body capable of managing the modern realities of interdependence."

After the summit, I stayed in Japan for an official visit, including a further two days of talks with Japanese Prime Minister Yasuhiro Nakasone, who honoured Canada by requesting that I speak to the Japanese Diet. On May 7, I became the first Canadian prime minister to do so.

Terrorists had tried to disrupt the summit, and I chose to highlight this unfortunate reality of life in the late twentieth century in my address. None of us could have imagined then the horrors of 9/11 and the several other attacks destined to come in between. 1986 was also to be the year I overruled both our intelligence services and my own solicitor general, who had advised me not to host the 1987 Commonwealth Summit in Vancouver for fear that Sikh extremists there would make an attempt on the life of India's Rajiv Gandhi. There is no way a prime minister should ever give in to terrorist threats, even though the tragedy of the Air India bombing had already proved that murderous terrorists were on the loose in British Columbia.

"Terrorists and their backers wreak havoc among free citizens, savagely threatening the principles of freedom and justice in pursuit of their evil deeds," I told the Diet. "In their indiscriminate slaughter of the innocent, terrorists demonstrate their disdain for common decency; violence and anarchy are their only accomplishments. They murder the innocent to terrorize the living. They make a mockery of the institutions and conventions so carefully nurtured to promote and protect individual liberty. The struggle against terrorism is a battle in the defence of our most fundamental values; a struggle to preserve world order and civilized conduct among peoples – a battle where there can be no neutrals."

My trip to Asia included stops in South Korea. I also, very briefly, took an extremely tentative look from the demilitarized zone into dark and mysterious North Korea, a blight on freedom that divides the Korean peninsula to this day.

I also visited China. Before leaving for the East, I had met in Ottawa with the Chinese ambassador to Canada, Yu Chan. A note-taker recorded: "The PM noted that his government accorded a high priority to the continuation of Canada's excellent relations with the People's Republic. Noting that former prime minister Trudeau had recently visited Beijing as leader of a trade mission, the PM commented that at the time of his forthcoming visit that sense of continuity would be exemplified by the presence of several Canadians with strong ties to the People's Republic, including the Honourable Alvin Hamilton, who, as minister responsible for the Wheat Board, had signed the first Canada/China wheat agreement in the early 1960s."

Trudeau later sent a note, thanking me for the kind words I had delivered to senior Chinese officials about him.

—

PERSONAL JOURNAL: JUNE 15, 1986

I had an interesting chat Tuesday night with Pierre Trudeau at the Governor General's Dinner. He was very grateful for the Tom Forrestall portrait the govt. had commissioned of his three children, which I had presented to him as a gift from the people. He is deeply attached to his children, and for this reason, truly appreciated the gesture. In any case, he appeared in good form and good humour. In regard to the press he said, "I think I had a bit of an advantage. I came to Ottawa holding the media in absolute contempt and left years later having had no reason to change my opinion." He cited examples of absolute fabrications and falsehoods that had been printed about him and Margaret, and referred to a conversation when he confronted Richard Gwyn about an item that he felt fell into this category. "Prime Minister, I was merely taking some poetic licence," said Gwyn. "Poetic licence, it's a complete and utter fabrication!" said Trudeau. "We do not have a mature or well-educated or skilful press gallery. Most people recognize the mediocrity that exists in Ottawa. It is simply not up to par with other capitals. What they lack in talent and knowledge they make up for in nastiness and vindictiveness. Always remember, Brian, that their influence is as limited as their talent. Forget about them. Do your job and you'll be okay."

—

Inside Beijing's Forbidden City I met privately with Deng Xiaoping, the de facto leader of China. As we sat in oversized armchairs, in the Chinese style, I had the feeling I was truly in the presence of history. A veteran of Mao Zedong's Long March (100,000 set out and only 10,000 survived), Deng, the Great Reformer, had joined the Communist Party in 1925. A survivor's survivor, he had been purged from China's ruling party more than once, and always came back. He was famously flexible, and was willing to borrow ideas from Western capitalists. "It doesn't matter if a cat is black or white," he often said, "as long as it catches mice."

While he smoked and took aim at his spittoon during our discussion (a habit that I found distracting, as I was near the line of fire), the wily communist leader discussed the reforms then under way in the Soviet Union. "Gorbachev is not going to last as leader," he said matter-of-factly. "He may be popular, but you and I know that popularity doesn't mean a thing. His mistake has been to begin his political reforms before the economic reforms, so there is nothing to sustain them. There will be nothing to keep him in office as a result, and he will have no strength. His ambitions for political reform are going to overtake any possibility of the economy sustaining the Soviet people, and they will throw him out. What we have done is the reverse. We've tried to build the economic reforms into a system that precedes any democratic initiatives so that people were able to absorb the expectations as they occurred."

The Chinese leader turned out to be absolutely correct. Five years later Gorbachev was gone, and the Chinese communists keep chugging along, even today. Deng also confided that the major challenge the Chinese government faced was envy. Those Chinese who could afford and acquire consumer goods were happy, while those still waiting for them were envious and discontented. He added that life for a Chinese leader had been easier when he had nothing to offer his citizens!

—

PERSONAL JOURNAL: MAY 11, 1986

Deng is a remarkable individual – short, wiry, engaging, and very, very sharp. At 82, he is in quasi-retirement. "They rarely let me see foreign leaders," he said, "but I wanted, for one so old, to meet a leader who is so young." He does not engage in any matter of day-to-day administration.

Premier Zhao Ziyang had told me earlier, "We respect Deng for his great wisdom and experience, which is far greater than ours," but conveyed the clear impression that, while spiritual leadership and inspiration rested with the chairman, effective political, executive action was under his [Zhao's] and others' direct control. There was no mistaking the reverence with which the premier spoke of Deng at dinner, telling me he had known him since the early 1940s, and had been a subaltern through many years. Sometimes the life of a protegé has a happy ending.

Listening to Deng, with his large, luminous eyes, wistful chuckle, and appreciative asides, was like listening to a recording of history. I could not resist thinking of the wonderfully tumultuous career he had had, with at least three major reversals resulting in grave hardships and humiliations, all of which he appears to have endured with dignity, and without malice. That is what struck me most: his praise of opposition and good friends. Nor was his sense of realism far behind. "We must be prudent," he said, "so as not to provide expectations. We did so in '48 and it was an absolute disaster. Our future plans must be realizable, achievable, and we must not repeat the unfortunate experiences of the past."

He gave commitments about the security of foreign investments. "It will not change," he said. "This is a permanent policy." Through a haze of cigarette smoke, and the occasional blast into a spittoon (nicely avoiding the new tasselled loafers Mila had recently given me) Deng held forth on his view of China's future, the urgent development problems of the next 25 years, how to mesh socialism and modernism, and the problems posed by such a vast population. "Imagine," he said, "every year we have between six and seven million young people entering the job market. Work must be found for them, or social problems develop." In our terms, that is equivalent to finding employment for the entire population of Quebec every year – and one can only imagine how hopeless that prospect would be. Placed in that perspective, Chinese problems appear overwhelming, and they deserve all the help we can provide.

Deng wore his wristwatch upside down, which is how I was able to keep an eye on the progress of our meeting. As we approached the 45-minute point, aides began to appear, yet he kept speaking animatedly, much to their dismay. When we went past the hour mark, they became increasingly serious, in deference to his great age, but he still showed no sign of abating. The words came in a torrent, but a well-articulated, coherent, and cogent one. This is a man in full command of his faculties, and his only concession to age is a piece in his right ear, which caused him to sit uncomfortably on my right, so that he could hear me with his good ear.

—

I spent many hours in talks with Premier Zhao Ziyang as well. He was China's leading reformer and when I landed in his country in 1986, I had no idea that he would become its future general secretary. In this latter position he would serve only two years before being purged from power because of his support for the student demonstrators at Tiananmen Square in 1989. Who will ever forget the images of Zhao addressing the students with a bullhorn during that horrible period? "I have come too late," he said to the crowd. "You cannot go on like this. We were once young too, and we had such bursts of energy. We also staged demonstrations, and I remember the situation then. We also did not think of the consequences." A day later, over his objections, martial law was invoked. We all know what came next.

Zhao spent the last fifteen years of his life under house arrest. As we flew home to Canada, I took the time to write about him in my journal. Like many world leaders over the years, the premier obviously wanted me to pass on certain views to the administration in Washington.

—

PERSONAL JOURNAL: MAY 11, 1986

The boys from Taverne Aux Amies, in Baie-Comeau, would not be displeased to learn that Zhao sips beer all day, from morning 'til night, with no obvious adverse affects. In fact, he said it makes him more effective! I had four separate meetings with the premier, totalling some seven and a half hours. Two of our meetings took place at dinner, and, given the Chinese tradition of placing the leaders side by side at the table, we were able (through an interpreter) to engage in personal and entertaining conversation throughout, without the need of polite small talk with a third party in between.

The premier is of average height, handsome features, and pleasant demeanour. I had a good but largely ceremonial meeting with him in Ottawa, when I was leader of the opposition. He struck me as able then, and persuaded me – not that this is a requirement of anything – of it now.

He came alone to both dinners, no spouse in evidence. He asks questions politely, listens carefully to the response, and chortles in appreciation at some of my asides – which is more than I can say about some of my colleagues.

He dresses in Western clothes, elegantly tailored and properly matched. His clothes would be quite expensive by any standards, right down to the discreet monogram on his silk socks. He was clearly at ease with himself, and fully comfortable with his job, and his role in the hierarchy.

We spoke of others in China – the president, chairman, party general secretary. He spoke without a trace of envy. He described, at my request, the role and responsibilities of the party vis-à-vis the government, cabinet vis-à-vis the chairman, and so on. The ultimate power is exercised by a five-man presidium, of which he is a member. It meets once a week and appears to resolve party/government issues of great substance.

For one month a year he moves the entire apparatus to a resort area, where they work in the morning, rest in the afternoon, and socialize in the evening. This would be an interesting concept in Canada, but I'm not certain our cabinet could stand that much togetherness. This initiative requires the displacement of several hundred people, but, given the Beijing climate, is no doubt a valuable investment in the health of the leadership.

Two months a year, he tours the provinces, to meet with governors, party leaders, and workers, and he makes two foreign trips a year – which, all told, make a full schedule for someone who is 67 (albeit a most youthful-looking one). He told me of his trip to New Zealand, where his beer-drinking skills received both public prominence and admiration. He delighted in telling me that the New Zealanders had presented him with a splendid beer stein to mark his great skills in this area – a fact that similarly disposed Western politicians would go out of their way to bury!

He was fascinated by my views on the U.S., and asked countless questions about the functions of the Congress, the White House, the White House staff, etc. He was scheduled to receive Jim Baker, of Treasury, the next day, and I assured him that Baker had both clout and access to the president. I told him that it's my view George Shultz had established "clear hegemony," to coin a phrase, in the area of foreign policy, having fought and won the public battles in Washington. He chuckled at that one, thank God. That has been my view since my election, and I had the opportunity of viewing things first-hand.

His principal concern and dislike is clearly the Soviet Union. China hopes to improve commercial relationships, but he is personally suspicious, with excellent reason, of Soviet intentions. His principal message, in regards to the U.S., was twofold. a) The U.S. must become more even-handed in the Middle East, because failure to do so would eliminate PLO moderates, he said, like Arafat. There can be no solution, he said, and therefore no peace, in this most sensitive area, without greater U.S. "fairness and respect" for the Arab position. I explained that the U.S., like Canada, was fully committed to the integrity and independence of Israel, and that once the PLO recognized this fact and eliminated terrorism, there could be substantial negotiations and progress. We both wish for the creation of a Palestinian homeland and peace in the area.

I explained to him that the U.S. would never maintain an effective role in the Middle East if the cost were to abandon Israel, or diminish its support. This neither the U.S. nor Canada would ever do, I told him – implying that, as a result, perhaps the Middle East situation would be energized by leadership by other moderates, such as China. He looked pleased . . . or persuaded and thoughtful for a moment, before saying that China's credibility with Israel was low and that, therefore, he doubted the impact or acceptability any Chinese intervention might have.

b) The U.S. will jeopardize its new relationship with the mainland if there is any American "footsie" with Taiwan. He strongly stated he hoped the U.S. would eventually support the Chinese proposal of legal incorporation of the island into the mainland, while allowing it to maintain its government and customs.

I told him not to read so much into individual statements by congressmen, many of whom actively support Taiwan. "No," he said. "But how can the Americans justify selling sophisticated armaments to Taiwan, compromising our relationship?" I told him that that was not the administration's intention – that the administration was supportive of the Chinese link, and that he ought to dismiss as fabrications any suggestions to the contrary.

He was clearly concerned, however, by the nonchalance with which American leaders constantly make flattering statements about Taiwan, and I got the disturbing feeling that, if ever the Chinese needed a reason to sever or interrupt the American relationship, the Taiwan issue would provide ample justification. This would be a great tragedy, inasmuch as he carefully asked me, twice, to convey his views to President Reagan. I shall do so, immediately upon my return, including the full flavour of his apprehensions.

Few Westerners know much about the inner workings of the Chinese political apparatus. This is clearly a man of considerable substance, great dignity, and good humour. At 67, in a country that reveres age and reason, he is a relative youngster and someone who may well exercise influence in China for an extended period.

—

Hu Yaobang, the twelfth general secretary of the Chinese Communist Party, was another leader I met on that same visit. I also wrote about him in my journal.

I became the first Canadian prime minister to meet with the general secretary. The meeting lasted over an hour, the substance recorded by officials. I was struck by Hu's vigour, and the clarity with which he states his case. He's tiny, with a winning smile and easy, casual manner. The banter masks a firmness and, I suspect, uncommon political skill. Climbing to the top job in a political party of 42 million members is no small accomplishment. Even Canadian Conservatives – no slouches in political infighting and Byzantine behaviour – must view such talents with special respect.

He departs for western Europe next month – his first such trip abroad, at age 71. He said, "I will be like a country boy in a big city," and I resisted the impulse to say that it was such statements that caused me to keep my hand on my wallet! He gesticulates greatly when he speaks, which is made more intriguing by his dentures, which are a size too large and threaten to fall into his lap in mid-sentence. It is said he shall succeed Deng Xiaoping. Obviously, either he or the premier would be worthy successors.

Finally, I used my journal to reflect on the China trip overall.

We had a very successful visit in China. Much remains to be done in expanding the relationship, but persistent work by successive Canadian prime ministers, principally Pierre Trudeau, is clearly paying off. I

> *think the extent and the ability and the quality of my meetings with Chairman Deng, the premier, president, and general secretary, clearly indicate the value of this highly advantageous relationship.*

The trip featured other accomplishments; I announced an increase in Canadian aid to China, and increases in Export Development Corporation loans. Also, China and Canada inked an agreement ending double taxation.

1986

3. Toward a Cabinet Shuffle

Events in China were overshadowed in Ottawa by the growing conflict-of-interest controversy involving Industry Minister Sinclair Stevens. He resigned on May 12, 1986, and I set up the Parker Commission to examine his behaviour.

On April 29, 1986 a story in the *Globe and Mail* showed that Sinc's wife, Noreen, had negotiated a $2.6 million loan to his holding company. Unfortunately, this loan came from a firm associated with Magna, the car parts giant controlled by the prominent Austrian-Canadian entrepreneur Frank Stronach, which received large grants from Sinc's department. The concept of conflict of interest had existed before in embryonic form, but it was newly popular with the media, and they and the opposition had a field day. The public reaction was such that it became "another scandal," and Sinc didn't help by keeping his cards too close to his chest. Erik Nielsen was Acting PM during my absence, and he reported that the House was paralyzed by the accusations and the media were "going wild." He recommended a commission of inquiry, which was duly appointed and which subsequently found that Sinc had violated a number of provisions of the Conflict of Interest Code. It became clear that he had to resign.

I viewed Sinc Stevens as one of my best ministers. He was tough, smart, and shrewd. But looking ahead, I knew that the Liberals and NDP were going to make conflict-of-interest allegations a major plank of the election campaign in two years' time, and that I had to keep Sinc out of that election. Painful as it was, I had to call him in 1988 and tell him that I would not sign his PC nomination forms. It cut my heart out, but politically I had little choice.

Sinc never gave up, and to his great credit he fought the findings of the Parker Commission for nineteen years and was ultimately vindicated by a decision of the Federal Court of Canada, which ruled that Judge Parker had erred in finding him guilty of conflict of interest. What happened to Sinc

Stevens was a travesty, and I have to shoulder some of the blame for the sorrow inflicted unfairly on Sinc and his wife, Noreen.

On May 21, back in Canada, I addressed a nervous caucus. My private notes from that day reflect the gravity of the political situation. "Travelling with over fifty members of the Ottawa media looking for the slightest error is no easy task. That there were no mistakes of substance/style is a great tribute to the PMO and senior public servants," I wrote about our Asian trip. Then I turned to the Stevens affair:

> Judgment of commentators is severe: "Government is venal, MBM is incompetent." And what do the people think? Last week, at the height of this problem which has so clearly unnerved caucus, the Angus Reid [poll of Southam News] reports PCs 38 per cent, Liberals 36 per cent, and NDP 24 per cent. Liberals with 15-point lead in Quebec (over PQ)! This simply points out again the enormous separation between media-driven Ottawa and our own hometowns. It does not relieve me and the government of responsibility for either avoiding such problems or handling them better. It is said we acted too slowly in Sinc's case. Perhaps. Must be careful of new standards. [They are:] Accusation is made. Immediately the opposition and media play it. Minister must resign pending investigation. Government is accused of stonewalling. If you are PM, damned if you do act too quickly. Damned by others if you wait to allow for an explanation. So what do we do? MBM: Make changes. Said I would tighten up guidelines, exercise greater freedom, ministers clean up acts . . .
>
> It takes little to promote depression and criticism in this caucus. (Read anonymous criticism from caucus about Sinc, Erik, PMO, me.) Under the Liberals, in similar circumstances, you would search newspapers in vain for such criticisms . . . But on Friday, May 9, there were only 50 MPs in the House – 161 absent. What if there had been a vote and the government defeated? The Stevens affair would have been quickly forgotten. Then, who would be criticized/blamed? The PM, as all other prime ministers. If I became morose every time we were in difficulty or every time I was blindsided by members of our own party, I would have no time for anything else. But [being morose] is for followers – not for us. We

> are here because we are leaders. And leaders don't flinch in times of trial. Leaders lead.

The atmosphere in Parliament became even more heated when the United States announced it would be levelling punitive duties on imported Canadian shakes and shingles. Considering that free trade talks were set to begin, I publicly labelled the Americans' action "bizarre" and said it was "unjustified, unacceptable, and will not be accepted by the Government of Canada."

In question period, I called the action "pure protectionism." Ed Broadbent rose to denounce the U.S. tariffs, saying they would cost four thousand jobs in British Columbia. He also wondered whether President Reagan was actually announcing to the world that in areas where the Americans couldn't compete, they would be denying access to their markets to anyone who showed them up.

"I wouldn't disagree with that," I told the NDP leader, to his great surprise.

I sent a strongly worded protest letter to President Reagan. "I want to convey to you the profound disappointment of my government at the action you announced yesterday regarding softwood shingles and shakes," I wrote. "The imposition of a 35 per cent tariff is a punitive measure against Canadian products. This unjustifiable action is all the more appalling in the context of freer trade negotiations between our two countries that have been officially initiated this week. This American initiative is pure protectionism, the precise thing you and I pledged, in Quebec and Washington, we would seek to avoid. Canada is now placed in the position of being forced to consider an appropriate response. I deeply regret this action by the U.S. administration."

Ronald Reagan took note, sending a very frank letter to Ottawa, written very much in the style of one politician to another:

> Dear Brian, I want to apologize for the mix-up that resulted in word of the softwood shingles and shakes matter getting out without your being informed in advance. It was a bureaucratic foul-up, with two departments each thinking the other had taken care of it. Brian, I hope and pray this has not altered our personal relationship. I'm aware of your political problems but must point out I have some, too. The tidal wave toward protectionism here is not limited

> to the opposition. There is increasing support among Republicans as well. I intend to veto the trade legislation now before the Congress if it reaches my desk, but in this election year the override of such a veto is not an impossibility . . . I hope this clears the air a little and, again, my apology for the breakdown in communications. We must continue the progress we've made and, above all, maintain the friendship – both personal and between our two nations – which is so important to all of us. P.S. Vice-Pres. Bush is coming your way around the 12th of June. I hope you can find time for a meeting with him to discuss this problem.

I replied with an acceptance of his apology, but I still let him know how angry I was. Whether he knew it or not, his administration's actions had threatened the historic free trade talks we had announced. The stakes were that high. "I very much appreciate the powerful protectionist pressures with which you must grapple in your country," I wrote, "and I welcome the determination expressed in your letter to resist them. I too face such pressures, and it is precisely because we share this problem in common that we developed the approach at our meetings in Quebec and Washington . . . Actions such as the one respecting shingles and shakes make it very difficult for me to maintain in Canada a climate in which the negotiations can proceed."

It pained me to read letters like the one I received from the mayor of Mission, B.C., John Agnew. "The entire region is absolutely in tatters, devastated – one stroke of a pen and our main economic reason for being has been removed," Mayor Agnew wrote on May 26. "Overnight a living, vibrant area has been decimated – an entire industry has gone, or will within days be gone, unless you can help quickly. The cruel arbitrary U.S. action means that thousands and thousands of hard-working people will lose their jobs very very soon. Never before have I seen such fear, frustration, and anger on such a massive scale."

On June 2, I held a crucial meeting with the premiers where I undertook to keep them informed as the free trade talks got under way, especially on subjects like beer and wine, which were in their jurisdiction. I made it clear at the same time that trade negotiations with a foreign power were an area where the constitutional prerogative of the federal government was very clear. Joe Clark had sent me a memo on this topic shortly before the First Ministers' Meeting. "I have met or talked with premiers or designated ministers from all provinces," he wrote.

> This process has been useful as the more difficult positions taken by some premiers around the time of the Halifax First Ministers' [Meeting in 1985] have been significantly modified. There is now little talk of provincial vetoes or eleven negotiators. Mr. Reisman has had time to develop an effective mechanism at the officials level. Ontario and Quebec have moved a long way from their initial positions on the substance of the negotiations and can now be considered "on board" with the other provinces and the federal government on this matter. It is now time for the federal government to conclude the ongoing discussion of the role of the provinces by articulating a framework for cooperation. The distance between the provincial governments and the federal government on issues of process is narrowing but, if left unresolved, could shortly become a major problem for the substantive negotiations with the Americans. It is important that Canadians draw together as we embark on this negotiation.

Joe then outlined what he thought the framework should be: "1) The federal government must retain its right to set the mandate, negotiate the agreement, and ratify the agreement. However, the provinces should be consulted continuously at the level of officials and the political level must have a direct involvement. 2) The Federal-Provincial Committee on Trade Negotiations is working effectively and all provinces support its continuation. It should be the principal instrument for cooperation at the officials' level. 3) First ministers should meet in private about every six months during the negotiations. 4) Designated ministers should meet as required."

At the June 2 meeting, the premiers agreed to a scenario similar to the one Joe had recommended. They were now fully on board.

A few months earlier Bill Fox, my able director of communications, had made a recommendation I now accepted. "In eighteen months in office," he wrote one day in February, "you have yet to ask the CBC to provide television time for a major policy statement. I believe that the time has come for you to entertain such a request, and I believe the Canada/United States trade initiative is the issue on which to base the request. I would strongly recommend that we make the request on your behalf as soon as Congress has responded to the invitation. Once negotiations are well and truly joined, it will be most important to explain the initiative carefully to Canadians."

As I began working on my televised address, I also prepared to greet a special visitor: U.S. Vice-President George H.W. Bush. He arrived in Ottawa on June 13 to find that he was meeting with an angry Canadian prime minister. I told the number-two man in Washington frankly that the American decision to impose a tariff on our exports of cedar shakes and shingles was unacceptable, and that my patience with their protectionism was wearing thin.

Bush handed me a top-secret letter from President Reagan offering to assist Canada's efforts in smuggling to freedom five Soviet soldiers who had defected in Afghanistan. These sorts of communications between the Canadian and American governments were common during the Cold War. For example, I had been on the job as prime minister for only a few weeks when a senior Eastern Bloc foreign minister gave us inside information on Soviet arms control intentions vis-à-vis the United States during a stop in Canada. He met in cloak-and-dagger fashion with one of our diplomats while his plane was on a stopover in Canada. I approved passing his message on to the Americans.

Much later, when George Bush Sr. was president, he and I had a frank and top-secret discussion about another allied leader and government during a meeting at SkyDome in Toronto. A senior Canadian bureaucrat foolishly took a report of this top-secret conversation with him during a trip overseas soon afterwards and left it in a European hotel room while he went out. Unbeknownst to him and to my government, the report was subsequently stolen from his hotel room, copied, and returned by persons unknown. A year later at a NATO summit in London, President Bush said, "Brian, Brent Scowcroft would like to see you before the meeting."

Brent, then in his second stint as national security advisor, having served in the same post under President Gerald R. Ford in the 1970s, drew me into a corner where he said, "The minutes of our Toronto meeting were stolen by agents of a foreign government. Our agents inside their government stole them back." He smiled. "Here they are," he said, as he handed me the file.

Most of my discussions in Ottawa that June with Vice-President Bush were on topics of bilateral interest, including, once again, acid rain. "You agreed to aggressively seek $5 billion," I reminded Bush over lunch at 24 Sussex Drive, "and I'm concerned about recent noises. There has to be money on the table on the U.S. side. This is a bellwether issue for me among Canadians. They're saying that if I can't deliver on this, what can I deliver on? If there's no action before [the next Canada–U.S. summit], I'm in trouble."

I also raised the issue of Arctic sovereignty. For the life of me I couldn't understand why the power brokers in the State Department and American military couldn't see how their insistence that the Northwest Passage was in international waters would be harmful to U.S. military interests in the midst of the Cold War. If the Americans could traverse the passage using this argument, the Soviets could as well. "I want to tell you what I told the president," I said to Bush. "If we don't reach an agreement, then the Soviets will have an equal claim to use of the Northwest Passage. We take the view that we own it. We want to give you exclusive use. The *Polar Sea* incident was a great embarrassment to us, and we hope you'll take the longer view."

"The prime minister pulled no punches – he made very, very clear his concerns," Bush told the media afterwards. "He was very, very frank in not agreeing with what had happened . . . The message I brought to him from Washington is that our friendship is too important to let these matters disrupt it, and that we should put this tiff behind us and focus on the road ahead."

In a kind gesture I would soon find was typical, Bush wrote me a short note as he flew home to Maine aboard Air Force Two. "As I wing it to Maine after our swing from B.C. to Ottawa, I want to whip out this note to you – and Mila too – to say thanks . . . I am glad we had that direct and frank talk. We don't want to bruise a friend – ever. Your friend, our President, feels that way, too."

The American vice-president also heard Canada's concerns on acid rain from another source, when he met for an unprecedented session with seven of my cabinet ministers. The joint chairmen of the Fourteenth Annual Conference of New England Governors and Eastern Canadian Premiers also agreed with our position.

"We are gratified you have accepted the findings and conclusions of the [Special Envoys' Report]," Michael Dukakis of Massachusetts and Richard Hatfield of New Brunswick wrote to me the day I met Vice-President Bush in Ottawa. "It is significant that [both leaders] have affirmed that acid rain is a serious environmental and transboundary problem that needs to be addressed . . . Your acceptance of the Joint Report is an important first step, Mr. Prime Minister. We stand ready to work with you on follow-through and effective implementation in any way you feel appropriate."

On June 16 I spoke to Canadians from the Prime Minister's Office in the Parliament Buildings. The televised address was one of the most important of my career thus far, and as I waited for the taping to begin I had thoughts of both Sir Wilfrid Laurier, who was defeated over the issue of free trade in 1911, and Mackenzie King, who backed down after negotiating a deal on free trade with the United States in the late 1940s. I remembered reading Sir Robert Borden's memoirs as a student and I never forgot a passage that contained Laurier's address to the House after his government fell: "I have simply to say to the people in Canada who feared annexation and to the people in the United States who hoped for it, that they alike fail to take into consideration the manhood of a proud people who would equally disdain to be cajoled or to be coerced into a course inconsistent with their dignity."

But my student days were long behind me as I began speaking to millions of Canadians that day. In part, I said:

> I want to speak with you tonight about your government's trade initiative with the United States. Tomorrow in Washington, a historic process begins in earnest as Canadian and American negotiators start work on the trade talks between our two countries. These discussions represent an important turning point in the life of our country. The road ahead will not be easy, nor without risks. The path to great accomplishment never is. This is not for the faint-hearted, but then our country was not built by the faint of heart. Canadians in the past have never failed to respond to the call of their country. Tonight, I ask for your support as we embark on this difficult mission. I'm asking for your support in every region of Canada, in every corner of the land.
>
> Why are these talks so important, and what do they mean for all of us? Well, we are a trading nation. Since the beginning of our history, since the time of the voyageurs we have been a trading people. Our survival depends on our ability to trade. To illustrate this point, the livelihood of one in three of our fellow Canadians depends directly on trade. Almost 80 per cent of our foreign trade, $95 billion last year, was with the United States. We are one another's best customers in the most important two-way relationship in the world . . .
>
> History tells us that these talks are in the interest of both sides. History tells us that whenever barriers to trade come down, new

> prosperity follows. Take the example of the 1964 Auto Pact. It has worked well for both our countries and has meant jobs and growth and economic expansion for Canada. Today, everyone agrees it's been good for the country. Not everyone thought so at the time it was negotiated. The federal government of the day was roundly criticized by some prominent politicians and union leaders. They predicted that this new liberalized trading arrangement . . . would be a disaster. They were wrong. It's been a bonanza.
>
> We have not given up or lost any of our national sovereignty or cultural distinctiveness, any more than member states of the European Community have seen their sovereignty eroded by their historic free trade arrangements. Are France and England less sovereign or independent today because they joined the European Common Market? Any such suggestion is clearly preposterous.

Canadians appeared to welcome hearing about this historic issue directly from their prime minister, and I was glad to have the opportunity to speak to them without the filter of the press gallery.

Instilling discipline in both caucus and cabinet is a key role of the prime minister. I had dealt with the jittery caucus after the Sinc Stevens affair. Now I turned to my cabinet with some harsh words of warning. One day during the spring of 1986 I learned that no fewer than twenty-one ministers had missed the daily question period strategy meeting. With this sort of attendance record, the team was asking for trouble. "I can assure you that a very effective mechanism exists to ensure willing compliance with agreed-upon political objectives by cabinet ministers," I told the group. "I will go no further at this time, nor do I ever again propose to raise with any one of you the issue of dereliction of responsibility. I shall deal with it in another manner."

And a cabinet shuffle was indeed on the horizon. I met with the cabinet on June 26 and urged them to stay focused, despite the rumours flying around about who would be in or out. I also spent a great deal of time with my ministers after my televised address. Communication, I knew, would be key in selling free trade to the Canadian people.

"The government has presented this initiative as the pillar of our economic strategy," I told the ministers. "The government will be judged on the success or failure of the negotiations. I am personally and publicly committed to the success of this initiative. I expect 100 per cent from everyone . . . I have taken great pains to explain to the average Canadian where we are going and why. I expect this to be a continuing feature of this exercise. An ill-informed public will be a hostile public. We must bring the Canadian public along. There will be no success at the negotiating table if we fail to hold favour with our constituency; we can expect the U.S. negotiating team to exploit any daylight they see between ourselves and our constituency on this issue. However, the success of negotiations will largely be determined by how U.S.-based interests react. Therefore, a well-coordinated and well-resourced lobby, acting in a way which is fully consistent with our communications strategy, is absolutely essential. Communication has not been as effective as it could be. It has been reactive and driven by crisis and events. It must become more strategic and better coordinated."

In considering the coming cabinet changes, I carefully reviewed the second round of confidential letters I'd asked caucus to send me. In his letter Senator Lowell Murray highlighted the Constitution. "I have no idea what the state of play is on the question of Quebec and the constitutional accord," he wrote on June 20. "The Ouellet flip-flop and the new attitude of Turner should be welcomed and encouraged, not denigrated: If Quebec joins the accord, you will get most of the credit anyway . . . Am I right in suggesting that a major stumbling block might be the attempts of some provinces to bargain their support for the 'Quebec' amendment in return for their own favourite causes – Senate or Court reform, etc., etc.? [Ontario Premier David] Peterson has the opportunity to put on the Robarts mantle, and he should be encouraged to do so – to go public with a declaration that the historic importance of Quebec's adherence is such that achieving it should not be mixed up with other issues. It is absolutely unique in its importance. Furthermore the opportunity may not come again. It should be grasped in the national interest."

As I digested Lowell's memo I knew I was reading the words of Canada's next minister of federal-provincial relations. He was absolutely right about Liberal leader John Turner, who had announced his support of Quebec's five conditions for signing the Constitution during a June interview with *Le Devoir*. "I believe it would be useful for Canada [if an agreement] were reached before the next election," John told the newspaper's editorial board. "Quebec has decided in favour of being a part of the Canadian federation, during the 1980 referendum and during the election [of Robert Bourassa]. Now Canada has to respond."

NDP Leader Ed Broadbent was very sympathetic as well. I must say that for all our differences, both he and John Turner treated me and my government very fairly on the constitutional issue. Even today I have nothing but the highest praise for the leadership they showed on this vital national question.

The Constitution aside, Lowell's letter had me chuckling to myself as I read it in the privacy of my study at 24 Sussex Drive. He suggested – not knowing perhaps that Erik Nielsen was on the way out – that the government needed a new House Leader. Look back to the Diefenbaker era, he advised. "It used to be said of Howard Green that he prowled the corridors with a Bible in one hand and a stiletto in the other," Lowell wrote. "That is what you need as House Leader." He then suggested Jake Epp for this role.

Lowell was personally to play a crucial role in the events that followed. In the cabinet shuffle of June 30, four ministers, including Deputy Prime Minister Erik Nielsen, left cabinet. I added eight new ministers, including a young Quebec MP who'd impressed me since the day he'd arrived in Ottawa, Jean Charest. Jean was appointed Minister of State for Youth. Another francophone I'd been keeping my eye on was New Brunswick's Bernard Valcourt and he was appointed to cabinet as Minister of State for Small Business and Tourism.

Erik Nielsen simply had to go. Although he had some fine qualities, and had made significant contributions to the party and the government, the caucus had not responded well to his domineering style, and I had already decided to replace him with Don Mazankowski. I had known Maz for years, and he had functioned well as minister of transport. He was also very good with people, and he had the genius of follow-through. He never made careless or reckless promises, and this reliability is vital to the successful operation of a government. The fact that Maz was from Alberta suited me just fine. Alberta had been loyal to our party for decades, and I wanted to ensure it was properly represented in government. So Don Mazankowski became Deputy Prime Minister, President of the Privy Council, and Government House Leader.

As for Nielsen, he soon left politics – but not before demanding just about every patronage position possible from the federal government. First, he wanted to be chief justice of British Columbia and the Yukon. Justice Minister Ray Hnatyshyn advised me that the Canadian Bar Association, to which we had earlier granted important new vetting authority, had raised very strong objections to the idea, and had flatly refused to consider Nielsen for the bench. Erik, who had recently married a House of Commons security guard, then asked to be appointed ambassador to Washington, replacing Allan Gotlieb. This was clearly not on. Finally, he settled on being chairman of the Canadian Transportation Commission – the highest-paid patronage appointment there was, with a chauffeur and a limousine, and a gilt-edged pension. Even then he demanded special offices in downtown Ottawa, and much more. It went on and on. Soon afterwards he published his memoirs, where he bitterly attacked me and his former colleagues in the government over the issue of patronage. When you read his book you get the impression that his most cherished life ambition was to rid Canada of the evils of patronage!

"After a period of two years in September, it's time for a change," I told reporters the day of the shuffle. "We do the big things well; we do some of the small things poorly. I want better communication, I want better management, and we want to carry the message more effectively. And that requires from time to time changes and new people."

I met the same day with my new cabinet. "The appointments today represent the very best our party has to offer the Canadian people," I told them. "You are representative of all regions and political groups . . . We are strongest when we act as a team. We succeed when we have a game plan. We communicate best when we do our homework. As a government we have succeeded on the big issues – and lost badly on the small items. We need to tighten up our planning, to have all ministers working on the same game plan."

I spoke specifically about Maz, telling them, "He has my full confidence and absolute trust. When he speaks or intervenes, you may assume his word should be final . . . I see Maz's role as chief operating officer of the government while I stand back and focus on the larger picture – to do what I do best." Then I stressed our new approach. "What this cabinet change does is put politics at the top of the agenda. We have all spent too much time being bureaucrats and statesmen, and not enough time being salesmen and constituency workers . . . I am not depressed in any way by the polls or by the press. The election is more than two and a half years away. What we have to do is get out to the people, to sell our message, and to deal with what the people want: economic renewal and national reconciliation."

Lowell Murray became minister for federal-provincial relations and Government Leader in the Senate. I felt it important that someone from the

Senate assume this ministry. The coming constitutional talks were sure to be contentious, and I wanted our point man on the file to be someone who wasn't exposed to the daily partisan crossfire that is the Commons. I wanted the issue to be depoliticized, and in this case the Senate served me well. In addition, Lowell had courageously stood in the Red Chamber only a few years before and voted against Trudeau's repatriation of the Constitution over Quebec's objections. I knew he had a certain currency among Quebecers as a result. It helped that Lowell had also made himself more than functionally bilingual over the years. He could read, write, and speak excellent French – and he didn't learn all this in New Waterford. Lowell had worked in Quebec and he'd begun to understand, as few English Canadians do, its cultural patterns. He knew where its people stood and could interpret the signs and symbols that make up the political vocabulary of Quebecers.

Norman Spector, who was recommended to me by Fred Doucet, was brought in as cabinet secretary for federal-provincial relations. Spector came to Ottawa from the government of British Columbia, and I felt that Lowell from Nova Scotia and his deputy from B.C. – combined with a prime minister from Quebec – would constitute a team that would bring together the best in Canada.

In his book *Meech Lake: The Inside Story*, constitutional law professor Patrick Monahan accurately described the approach to constitutional talks that Lowell devised: "1) Limit the agenda. 2) Do not commence formal negotiations until success could be assured. 3) The principle of the equality of the provinces had to be maintained. Thus Quebec's demands would be met by generalizing the proposals so as to include the other provinces. 4) The federal government would act as a broker between Quebec and the other provinces, waiting until the end of the process before advancing its own proposals."

Early in the spring, speaking through provincial minister of intergovernmental affairs Gil Rémillard, Premier Bourassa had set out Quebec's five conditions for signing the Constitution. They were: recognition of Quebec as a distinct society, more power for Quebec over immigration, limitations on federal spending power, recognition of Quebec's right to veto constitutional change, and the right to participate in the nomination of Supreme Court justices.

"Quebec's future is within Canada," Rémillard said that day at Mont-Gabriel. "We believe in Canadian federalism because, within the federal system, Quebec can be faithful to its history and its unique identity while enjoying favourable conditions for its full economic, social, and cultural development."

Together my team and I created a special cabinet committee to examine Quebec's conditions. Its chairman, Lowell Murray, said later that he was surprised at the attitude some ministers brought to this table. "John Crosbie's instant reaction was to say, 'Never give the provinces an inch.' He could have been in Trudeau's cabinet. Marcel Masse expressed his disdain for the whole exercise. 'It's all plumbing,' he told me. And Benoît Bouchard came to the committee very much as a federal minister intent on protecting his department's turf." (Benoît was definitely evolving as his time in Ottawa and as secretary of state continued. One of the more nationalist members of my Quebec team, he nevertheless wrote to me in 1986 to ask whether the Queen could be invited to visit Quebec!)

In discussions with Lowell Murray and his officials I rejected the view of Jean Chrétien, who urged immediate action to bring Quebec into the Constitution, and advised my team that we had to proceed with caution and prudence. ("We were as cautious as Mackenzie King," Lowell said years later.) I shared this view with the premiers before their meeting in Edmonton that summer. "If we undertake to 'repatriate' Quebec, we must be determined to proceed," I wrote to each of them. "The consequences of failure would be very serious for the future of Canada . . . It seems to me that the only realistic way to proceed is first to bring Quebec back into the fold, and to undertake a more extensive revision of the Constitution at a later stage . . . Finally, it seems to me essential that, prior to any formal negotiations, we secure sufficient assurance that Quebec, the other provinces, and the federal government could reach mutually acceptable positions on each of the points." Clearly, it was vital to work hard to get an agreement behind the scenes, and thus avoid any public standoffs.

Premier Bourassa and I had met in Quebec City in early June and agreed that his government should explain its proposals to the other provinces. Bourassa then had an emissary visit the other provincial capitals, while I directed that exploratory discussions between federal officials and their counterparts in Quebec City could begin. We had to determine all around whether the basic conditions for successful formal negotiations existed.

In August, the Edmonton Declaration was the premiers' very public way of saying they agreed with me. It stated: "The premiers unanimously agreed their top constitutional priority is to embark immediately upon a federal-provincial process, using Quebec's five proposals as a basis of discussion, to bring about Quebec's full and active participation in the Canadian federation." Alberta Premier Don Getty, the host of the annual Premiers' Conference, was blunt as usual. "I think it reflects a moment in time when we have said this is our top priority to have Quebec fully into the Canadian federation," he said. "Let's get it done."

I agreed with Bourassa, who said that August 13, 1986 was indeed "a good day for Canada."

1986

4. The Apartheid Wars Continue

WHILE CANADA'S CONSTITUTIONAL talks were destined to move ahead, the situation in South Africa was static. Joe Clark had announced a further round of sanctions against the racist South African regime in June, and I was preparing to face Margaret Thatcher over the issue of sanctions once again. "What is more important is that we have a significant and coordinated Commonwealth response to South Africa in August," I had written her in late June. "Recognizing that South Africa plays a lesser part in our external trade than in yours, I can see that we may need to proceed with a broader range of measures than you might adopt. That would be consistent with the principle of equitable burden-sharing within the Commonwealth . . . It will be important to keep in touch during the coming weeks. I have recently spoken to Kenneth Kaunda, Robert Hawke, and Rajiv Gandhi and look forward to going over the ground with you when we meet on July 13. We shall want to see what we can do to achieve an agreed Commonwealth position at the London meeting."

In advance of that scheduled meeting of six Commonwealth countries in London set for August 1 (as agreed to at Nassau in 1985), I sat down with Margaret for seventy-five minutes at Mirabel Airport in Montreal. She was on her way back from Expo '86 in Vancouver, and had obviously not enjoyed her flight. What followed was one of the stormiest meetings I've ever been party to. And I am someone who had spent the better part of a decade negotiating with some of the toughest union leaders in North America during the 1960s and 1970s. Inside Margaret Thatcher that day there beat the heart of a Welsh union leader. The note-taker's account (including lines like "a theme to which she reverted several times during the conversation") was very restrained, and did not reflect the many moments when voices were raised: My own journal gives more than a hint of the tenor of the discussion.

—

PERSONAL JOURNAL: JULY 23, 1986

Margaret advanced again her view that sanctions were "immoral." I strongly objected, saying the U.K. already applied sanctions against South Africa and that she was in "up to her knees." Margaret tried to equate her position with leadership as opposed to followership (presumably the position of those who disagreed with her). I indicated that if she persisted in her view she could well jeopardize the success of the London meeting and could forfeit the position of moral leadership that Great Britain exercises in the Commonwealth. She appeared shaken by the firmness of the Canadian position (I almost had to raise my voice strongly at one point to interrupt her constant stream of argument), but indicated no change in her position whatsoever. She places great (I think, undue) stock in the position that President Reagan is to announce, and appears unconcerned about what might happen to the Commonwealth in the event of a substantial schism at the London meeting.

Margaret is firm, determined, and never impolite. I do not think she would be an easy person to work with or for, but one cannot deny her single-minded commitment to what she believes to be right. She is Ronald Reagan's greatest fan, and makes no bones about it. At the Mirabel meeting, she chuckled disapprovingly at the insensitive American position on shakes and shingles and the embarrassment it has caused a friendly government, but quickly recovered to suggest how much worse it could be if RR were not there! In fact, the only strong statement she made re the Americans was: "The four-hour notice they gave me about [the invasion of] Grenada and how upsetting that was." I didn't tell her that the Trudeau government got no notice at all!

—

With that, Margaret and I parted, knowing that we would meet again just a few weeks later. Despite the harsh words between us over sanctions –

and you can imagine what lies behind polite note-taker's reports of such statements as: "Sanctions are immoral because they would lead to the loss of thousands of black jobs and the consequent starvation of thousands of black children (this theme was reiterated a number of times during the conversation)" – she still wrote me a gracious letter two days after our meeting. "Thank you very much for your kindness in coming to the airport in Montreal for our talks," she said. "It was useful to establish where we both stand on the South Africa problem before what bodes to be a difficult meeting . . . in August."

Before heading overseas to what I knew would be the inevitable showdown between the rest of the Commonwealth and Britain's prime minister, I contacted Ronald Reagan. First I wrote to him in Washington. "No one wishes to see Mrs. Thatcher isolated," I said. "That would create a difficult political situation for us all. Should she, however, block all proposals for moderate action against South Africa, the pressure for Canada to act unilaterally, or with some Commonwealth countries, would become irresistible . . . The idea is to bring South Africa to its senses, not to its knees. I feel we could build a consensus around this with Kenneth Kaunda, Rajiv Gandhi, Bob Hawke, and the others if Margaret shows some flexibility. If we fail, the Commonwealth would lose much of its credibility."

I ended by asking the West's leading Cold Warrior to intercede with his British ally and friend, and to consider the gift we in the West might be handing the Soviets if apartheid were allowed to continue to enslave millions of black South Africans. "A delayed transition of power will be more violent and will offer more opportunities for Soviet interference," I concluded. "Consequently, anything you can do on your side to convince Margaret Thatcher that a pragmatic and flexible stance on her part will serve Britain's (and our common) interest would be welcome."

When we spoke on the telephone the night before I left for London, however, it became clear that Ronald Reagan saw the whole South African issue strictly in East–West Cold War terms. Over the years he and Margaret continually raised with me their fears that Nelson Mandela and other anti-apartheid leaders were communists. My answer was always the same. "How can you or anyone else know that?" I'd ask again and again. "He's been in prison for twenty years and nobody knows that, for the simple reason no one has talked to him – including you. Besides, if I and my people were being oppressed by a racist state whose actions were killing my brethren, I'd take help from anyone if the West wouldn't give it to me. And that includes communists."

I tried once again to move Reagan from his position, but I failed. "I'm on my way to London and I'll give your best to Margaret Thatcher tomorrow," I told him. "What we're attempting to do is what we have done in the past with our communication with Sir Geoffrey Howe [U.K. foreign minister] and Margaret Thatcher. We want to keep the Commonwealth together but not be a bunch of crazies about it. Then it's chaos for everyone. Canada has played a moderating role. We're going to be preaching moderation and sanity. I hope we can achieve our result without in any way humiliating Margaret Thatcher or the U.K. government."

"I wonder if the United States and the Commonwealth could set up a small group to go to Botha and Buthelezi [Zulu leader of the Inkatha Freedom Party]," Reagan replied. "Can we help in bringing about meetings or negotiations?"

"I'll mention your suggestion to Margaret tomorrow afternoon," I promised. "Perhaps such a small group can get something started. In the Commonwealth and in Europe, some groups are on a collision course. In fact, I notice that your Senate today has taken some action. As I told Margaret privately at our own last meeting, my concern about the development of public opinion is that Margaret or the U.K. would lose their leadership role in the Commonwealth. Canada very much wants the U.K. onside in all these things. Ron, if the Commonwealth on Tuesday took a few more moderate steps, not unlike the ones you have been considering, could that meet with general approval of the United States?"

Reagan's reply was measured. "I would not reject out of hand such movement; however, I hope that such measures would not include punitive sanctions that would put all the black miners out of work the next morning. As I was saying, I had a very interesting letter from Buthelezi – I'm very impressed with a twenty-eight-page speech he sent me. He outlines amazing figures against sanctions. He believes the ANC has been taken over by communists."

—

PERSONAL JOURNAL: July 23, 1986

There was no indication whatsoever from Reagan of support for the EPG–Commonwealth position. He absolutely supports Margaret and denounces the effectiveness of "prime-time sanctions" – a position quite at variance with the one he put forward when requesting Canada to support a policy of sanctions against Libya. He was, as usual, friendly and easy but spoke from notes, and I suspect, from conviction. He disagrees with the one man, one vote concept and sees the ANC as incapable of anything but violence and chaos. I had not called to argue and debate; I called to ascertain his position prior to London, and I concluded that the only thing that will change it is American opinion. If a firestorm erupts in Congress, he will change; otherwise, no.

—

At the Commonwealth Meeting in London, the other leaders and I dined at Buckingham Palace with Her Majesty the Queen. As only politicians can, we discussed among ourselves the role of media in our home countries and agreed how difficult the press could be. In a demonstration of how closely she keeps her eye on things throughout the Commonwealth, the Queen contributed this comment: "Any objective observer would say that Prime Minister Mulroney has the most difficult time of all," she said quietly. I still savour that Buckingham Palace moment.

—

PERSONAL JOURNAL: August 4, 1986

Last night's private dinner for heads [of government], hosted by the Queen, was interesting. She arrived in excellent cheer, and entertained Bob Hawke, Gandhi, and me with anecdotes about the Edinburgh Commonwealth Games, which she had just closed.

Right out of left field, Hawke asked her about the origin of a large mantel clock. When she said she had no idea, Hawke explained that his treasurer, Paul Keating, was an expert on clocks, owned the largest collection in the world, and would be unforgiving if Hawke returned home without an appropriate description of this one. Because Hawke had cornered the market on clock conversation, Her Majesty told him about Dickie Mountbatten eviscerating a series of vintage, collector-item clocks, and inserting electric mechanisms, so that the "antiques" could be plugged in and maintained with a minimum of bother! She said his grandson was now reversing the process, and restoring the timepieces to their erstwhile grandeur.

Her Majesty entered the small sitting room where drinks were served, shook all hands, received a curtsy from Mrs. T., and chatted easily with all. After dinner, she discussed her upcoming Vancouver and Quebec visits with me, and we left, all except Mrs. T. and Sir Geoffrey [Howe], whom I spotted in confidential conversation with Her Majesty as the rest of us were escorted out. Earlier, the Queen said to Gandhi, "How is the emotional one today?" referring to Kenneth Kaunda.

Kenneth Kaunda, who adores the royal family, and who interrupted proceedings after dinner to propose a birthday toast to the Queen Mum – 86 today – would be even more emotional if he had witnessed that scene. So, I refrained from telling him; I talked enough, as it is.

—

I spoke at the official opening of the London mini-summit, writing out my speaking notes in my own hand:

> In the Nassau Accord we expressed our views and intentions on apartheid. Conveyed our determination to meet again, and, in the absence of substantial improvement, to consider further measures. We appointed the Eminent Persons Group . . . Canada sees no substantial changes. Our challenge will be unity for Commonwealth. Strong leadership on one of the greatest moral issues to have confronted any group. Further measures we would consider are set out in this accord. We must now agree on which will be most effective. These measures do not preclude negotiations. They do signal that

any such negotiations must be undertaken swiftly and in good faith. An important question arises: Do sanctions/economic measures work? I don't know. The question has arisen before. When Canada was asked by the U.S. to apply sanctions against Libya, we did. When Canada was asked to apply sanctions against South Africa, we did. Ready to do more.

We must decide here to take initiatives/measures that will be helpful to achieving the ultimate objective: dismantling apartheid, securing freedom and justice for some twenty-five million ordinary people who are, like us all, simple children of God. Measures can cost some countries more or less, depending on investment and economic involvement. No one should be asked to assume a completely undue burden – it should be shared with relative fairness.

Canada in North America is far away. Our involvement while important is much less so than that of others . . . We do not seek to avoid our share of the load. Whatever costs are engendered by whatever decisions made here shall affect us all – and Canada will pay her way and carry her share of the burden. The leadership demonstrated by the Commonwealth at Nassau was noble. Other countries – the U.S., Europe – are following that lead. We cannot forfeit that leadership now. It has little to do with balance sheets. It has all to do with human dignity.

Were I a young black what signal will I receive from the Commonwealth? Must be on side of freedom. Twenty-five years ago Prime Minister Diefenbaker took the stand (with others) against South Africa that resulted in South Africa leaving the Commonwealth. After that London meeting, he flew to Ottawa, to speak to a PC convention. I was there. I still remember his speech about keeping a "light in the window for South Africa." In twenty-five years, SA has not fundamentally changed. Still based on belief that people are unequal. Twenty-five years from now . . .

—

PERSONAL JOURNAL: August 4, 1986

. . . I made the speech prior to adjournment. The Guardian *is giving it high marks, this morning, though even more pleasant were the words of congratulation from Kaunda, Gandhi, Mugabe, and Ramphal. Margaret was not pleased with my remarks. She said I exceeded the focus of the agenda items, but I suspect she was alone in that view. The conference continues today, and I think there should be some agreement on fundamental questions, though the U.K. remains adamant in its position, which is beginning to look worse – more like posturing and less like principle.*

—

The leaders also gathered at 10 Downing Street for further private meetings. I watched as Kenneth Kaunda launched a series of personal attacks on Margaret and on Britain's approach to apartheid. Eventually, Margaret got up and walked over to Kenneth and reached for his arm. "We must have some lunch because I want to be certain you're fed so we can have a vigorous afternoon," she told the African leader. That was Margaret Thatcher in action: completely unafraid of heated debate, but very conscious of the niceties that help ensure that discussions always continue. With that, we enjoyed a hearty British lunch and continued our talks. Eventually it was clear that Margaret Thatcher was alone in her resistance to sanctions.

Professor Linda Freeman captured Canada's efforts at that summit in her study entitled *The Ambiguous Champion: Canada and South Africa in the Trudeau and Mulroney Years*:

> During the London meeting, Mulroney pulled absolutely no punches, challenging Thatcher head on, but also employing his legendary negotiating skills and personal charm to bring her around . . . He offered to match British action – "You tell me, how much

> do you want. I'm prepared to put it on the table." He appealed to Thatcher to use her power to lead the way for other major Western leaders, particularly Ronald Reagan. All to no avail . . .
>
> While Mulroney tried to insist that Thatcher was against apartheid as much as he and that "she endorsed sanctions very emphatically," he was using Irish blarney to prevent a deeper split. Mugabe was closer to the mark in expressing his "utter dissatisfaction" with Thatcher's position, which, in his view, made Britain "an ally of apartheid." Rajiv Gandhi summed it up very clearly, "Britain is not the leader anymore – not in the Commonwealth – because it is compromising its basic principles for commercial ends." In leading this initiative, Mulroney, Hawke, and Gandhi moved into the vacuum created by Thatcher's abdication of leadership in the Commonwealth. Mulroney distinguished himself by confronting Margaret Thatcher in front of the other members and arguing their cause with great passion.
>
> Later in 1986 . . . Sonny Ramphal paid full tribute when he said, "It will be forever to the credit of Australia and Canada – of Bob Hawke and Brian Mulroney – that when the Commonwealth was on the crossroads of apartheid, they stood shoulder to shoulder with their non-white colleagues."

It is legitimate to ask why Margaret fought sanctions as fiercely as she did. I believe the answer is threefold. First, her Conservative caucus was very pro-South Africa, and I think they felt it was unfair to those people who had made South Africa the economic powerhouse it was to cripple them with sanctions. Second, I think the historic British investment in South Africa – investment that dwarfed that of any other Commonwealth country – made it easy for Margaret to view calls for sanctions from others with a certain amount of cynicism and contempt. Third, I believe to this day that Margaret simply didn't think that sanctions would work. She had followed the Rhodesian situation in the 1970s and believed that sanctions had not been effective there.

At the end of the mini-summit, Canada, joined by Australia, the Bahamas, India, Zambia, and Zimbabwe, agreed to adopt a program of eleven punitive measures against South Africa, which they recommended to the entire forty-nine-nation Commonwealth. They included a ban on new air links, a ban on new investment or reinvestment of profits earned in South Africa, a termination of any double-taxation agreements with South Africa, a termination of any remaining government assistance to investment or trade with Pretoria and of government procurement inside South Africa, a ban on any government contracts with majority-owned South African countries, and a ban on the promotion of tourism to the country.

—

PERSONAL JOURNAL: AUGUST 10, 1986

"Even after seven years as PM the public criticism hurts," Margaret told me. "It hurts me and my family but they never let it show." She also made a variety of other comments. "[Former prime minister] Ted Heath has become old and bitter. He never speaks to me, he never says hello. I am always polite, which he will grudgingly acknowledge, but no more. When my time is up, whether I agree with the choice or not, I will give the new leader every support. The last thing I want to become is another Heath – perceived by friend and foe as never having accepted my leadership and having done everything to undermine his successor. This parliamentary system is demanding and unforgiving for the leader. You need special skills to survive when you lead the party, the House, and the country. Ronald Reagan could not survive in this climate. His talents are in another direction.

"My most serious problem is with leaks. I must be very careful or any given matter will wind up in the papers. As a result I never discuss, if I can avoid it, a sensitive matter in cabinet. [Michael] Heseltine is merely looking for an occasion to become a hero. I'm still angry with myself. I should have fired him long ago.

"Foreign Secretary Joe Clark is doing a fine job. He and Geoffrey get on very well. What has happened is that you have given him confidence and it has greatly improved since [his defeat in the House in]

1979. He will never, however, be a leader of a govt. or a party with any success."

I reproduce her comments faithfully without characterization of any kind. She spoke candidly, without malice. For example, I think she genuinely likes Joe; she simply said the above statement out loud, as she did others, because she believes them. I merely listened to her entertaining views, delivered in a most pungent style.

—

Shortly after I arrived back in Ottawa, I saw again how the fight against apartheid crossed all partisan lines in Canada. From his office in Toronto Robin Sears, principal secretary to Ontario NDP Leader Bob Rae, wrote to share his views on my stance against apartheid:

> I thought it would be a frosty Friday that I would write a congratulatory note to a Tory PM on South Africa, but here it is. I first waved a placard against apartheid more than twenty years ago in front of a Loblaws store, and watched in agony the travesties of that regime at closer quarters during my work in the past five years. As an official of . . . Socialist International, apartheid was one of my briefs . . .
>
> Walking along the beach on Vancouver Island, while on holiday with my family, listening to news reports in my ear as I followed your progress at the mini-summit, I felt like whistling, and beamed with pride as a Canadian. Having suffered the arrogant intransigence that is British certitude when they are wrong and know and don't care, I have some inkling of what you endured in those tough hours of bargaining . . .
>
> Don't give up the leadership role you have established in this area, and don't allow your appropriate concerns about Canada–U.S. relations in other fields to dampen your efforts to encourage the U.S. administration to see the inevitable and democratic passage of events in Southern Africa. Some years ago, when someone close to him told me that Bishop Tutu was thrilled by your first conversation with him, I raised my eyebrows. Having

followed your efforts in conversation with members of your staff and friends in the NGO community more closely since then, my reaction to this news from London was not surprise, but simply delight.

1986

5. Tough Decisions Abroad and at Home

Foreign affairs continued to dominate the government's agenda in the fall of 1986. While our trade negotiators had had their first rounds of meetings, we were beginning to pick up disturbing signals from the Americans that caused us to question, in private, their true commitment to the talks.

Finance Minister Michael Wilson took these concerns directly to U.S. Treasury Secretary Jim Baker during a face-to-face meeting in September. He learned that the United States had fears as well. Mike sent an eyes-only memo to me reporting on his discussion with the powerful Texan. "I asked whether the U.S. administration was serious about a deal and whether he thought a deal could be done with Congress," Mike wrote.

> He's worried about Congress and said that any new Congress regardless of the party balance would be protectionist. However, he expressed his concern that if the discussions were not successful, they would not be reopened for "fifty years." He said we must and will have a deal. When the chips are down, the President will come through and win over Congress on this matter. He expressed some surprise about my comments on their negotiating team. He speculated that [Peter] Murphy was probably preoccupied with Congress and was spending his time helping formulate strategies to deal with Congress in order to forestall passage of the Trade Bill. He said that no one in the Administration was dragging their feet on this matter so that Murphy should feel he had good support for the negotiations . . . During the course of our meeting I got the clear sense that the two key people in the Administration were Shultz and Baker. Baker indicated that they were very close, agreed on most things, and essentially controlled matters in the government with Shultz covering off the external matters and Baker covering the domestic policy.

George Shultz was an effective secretary of state and an influential advisor to President Reagan. Few people in American history had his remarkable life of public service. Shultz liked Canada and knew a lot about us. I recall one evening in 1988 when I arrived for a state visit. In the helicopter from Andrews Air Force Base to Washington, Shultz heatedly raised concerns about an interview that appeared to be critical of Reagan which I had given to a *Washington Post* journalist. Because I had been tipped off by Ambassador Gotlieb, I waited until George finished his diatribe then calmly produced the entire transcript of the interview, which clearly indicated the journalist had distorted the meaning of my words. George was dumbfounded. After reading the transcript carefully, he put it in his pocket and apologized. The next morning he charged over to the White House and berated the senior staff for having raised such a flimsy matter with him, which in turn had caused him serious embarrassment with the prime minister of Canada. Of such things are diplomatic incidents made! This one, of course, confirmed George Shultz's great loyalty to Reagan and his personal integrity as secretary of state.

On September 17, foreign policy was again at the top of the agenda as Prime Minister Shimon Peres of Israel visited Ottawa. During our private talks I praised his calls for moderation in the Middle East, telling Peres that Canadians heartily approved of his approach. "Both courage and determination are needed to take risks," I said.

Peres thanked me for stopping an anti-Israeli motion from being passed at the Francophonie Summit, and I assured him I would do so again. Then I returned to the theme of moderation, noting that it was always easier to fend off critics of Israel in any Western country when Israel was reaching out to moderates in the Middle East. "Canadian policy," I told him, "is based on the recognition of Israel behind secure borders, together with a just solution for the Palestinians."

Superpower tensions were increasing that fall as well. As President Reagan and General Secretary Gorbachev prepared for their second face-to-face meeting at their (ultimately unsuccessful) summit in Iceland, I had an important visitor in Ottawa. After meetings with Joe Clark, the Soviet foreign minister, Eduard Shevardnadze, dropped by my office on October 2, only a few days before the talks in Iceland. I spoke for ninety minutes with the man who was to become Georgia's president after the breakup of the Soviet Union. The official note-taker's record of this meeting reads as follows:

On the basis of his short meeting with Mr. Gorbachev at the Chernenko funeral, the PM had made it known in Canada and in the U.S. that Gorbachev was a strong, disciplined, and capable person with whom transactions of substance could be made and honoured. His view had not changed. The leadership of the Soviet Union had made a strong impact in Canada and elsewhere. The PM was very, very encouraged by agreement to hold the Reagan–Gorbachev meeting in Iceland. He was confident that it would lead to further progress. He offered some personal views on the U.S., Canada's closest neighbour. That relationship had ups and downs. It must be seen in that perspective. Canada was much smaller but in 175 years there had never been a shot fired in anger and no soldier patrolled the 5000-km undefended border. This meant one of two things. Either Canada was a colony of the U.S. or it was a sovereign nation with excellent relations with a non-imperialist power. The latter was the case.

Canada and the U.S. were both friends and allies but Canada did not hesitate to differ on policy with the U.S. In this context, the PM cited three instances (SDI, the U.S./Nicaragua embargo, South Africa) where such disagreement had been made openly known to the U.S. and a separate course pursued. He had raised these instances because Canadian opinion, to be of value, must be seen against an understanding of the relationship between Canada and the U.S. . . .

If the Soviet Union were to put the question to him as to whether the USSR should take a chance on peace with President Reagan, his answer would be an unequivocal yes, with the assurance that the Soviet Union would not be betrayed or rejected. The Prime Minister was satisfied that President Reagan wanted peace and would work with the USSR to secure it. This was in contrast to the Carter era, where it was demonstrated that one could negotiate peace but it was difficult to bring it home and have it accepted in the U.S. itself. U.S. politicians must have the capacity to convince the U.S. people of a given course of action, otherwise it became valueless. President Reagan, who had started slowly with not a lot of favourable opinion, will now possibly go down as one of the most powerful and effective Presidents of this century.

After the Reagan–Gorbachev summit, I was miffed with President Reagan when he announced that his government would no longer adhere to the SALT II agreement on limiting nuclear weapons. Just as I had told the Soviet foreign minister, Canada was an ally and friend of the United States but not one afraid to disagree with our superpower neighbour. I wrote to Reagan about my concerns over his plans, and Privy Council Clerk Paul Tellier soon advised me that my letter had caused a stir in Washington.

"Your letter obviously made an impression on the president, as this is the first time he has sent you a letter on arms control which is not a general letter sent to all Allied leaders," Tellier wrote in a memo. "Given the unique, personal nature of Mr. Reagan's letter and the importance of the issue it addresses, we believe that a short reply is desirable."

"Thank you for your letter of Nov. 27, which I have studied carefully," President Reagan had written.

> I understand your concern about my decision to exceed the SALT II numerical sub-limits. In the same spirit of candor and closeness you cite, I would like to explain why I believe my decision is in the interests of the United States, our Allies, including Canada, and the cause of peace . . .
>
> I do not believe we are giving the Soviets an excuse for further buildup; SALT II is so favourable to them that they have little need for more strategic systems or warheads. As you know, under SALT II they have about doubled the number of their strategic ballistic missile warheads . . .
>
> In preparing for my meeting in Reykjavik and in instructing our negotiators since that meeting, I have been especially conscious of the views of key Allied leaders. Your personal counsel has been particularly valuable to me. Deep and stabilizing reductions in offensive nuclear forces is one of our common goals. As you and others have urged, I continue to attempt to move the Soviets away from reliance on their massive ICBM forces, which are the most threatening in terms of a first strike. My proposal to shift to a deterrent based on slow-flying retaliatory weapons – bombers and cruise missiles – was made to reduce the threat to both our countries, as well as our other allies . . .
>
> I know cruise missile testing is a contentious question in Canada and that my SALT II decision may, for a while, make it

> more so. Please be assured that your steadfastness on this important matter plays a key role in achieving progress toward the safer and more stable form of deterrence you and I have both long advocated. The Western Alliance needs your continued support and I am confident we can count on it.

I accepted the advice of the Clerk of the Privy Council and responded to Reagan's letter. "Dear Ron," I wrote.

> Thank you for your letter of December 8 in which you respond so candidly to the concerns I raised with regard to your decision to step outside of SALT II. Ron, I'm afraid that on this particular issue we must agree to disagree. Frankly, I am unable to see how exceeding SALT II limits will improve the negotiating climate in Geneva. As we in the West excoriate Soviet acts of non-compliance to arms control measures, so are they unlikely to be more forthcoming at Geneva if U.S. policy is seen to be drifting away from existing arms control agreements. Additionally, broad sections of our publics will not understand how we in the West can be seeking deep reductions in offensive forces while at the same time exceeding the already high ceilings on arms currently in place. All this being said, we in Canada remain ready to do our part to support the U.S. deterrent, and will, as I stated to you before, continue to test the air-launched cruise missile over Canada. There is no more compelling duty than for the Alliance to continue to demonstrate its solidarity, and to thereby deprive Moscow of easily won propaganda points.

As it happened, I gained some friends from an unlikely source as a result of my stance on strategic arms limitations. "We have noted the strong stand that you have taken in response to statements that the United States would no longer abide by the limitations on strategic nuclear weapons established by SALT II," David McTaggart, chairman of Greenpeace International, wrote to me in 1986. "We commend you for your leadership in asserting that the Government of Canada will not endorse breaking this or any other existing arms control agreement . . . We want you to know that your leadership on this matter is sincerely appreciated by our organization and our two million supporters worldwide."

On the domestic front, the fall of 1986 was explosive by any standard. By September I'd had enough of Speaker John Bosley. For all his many fine qualities, he was failing in his role.

—

PERSONAL JOURNAL: OCTOBER 13, 1986

Veterans such as Erik Nielsen, Harvie Andre, and Jim McGrath were strongly of the view that Bosley had lost control of the House and had to be replaced. Harvie told caucus that Bosley was one of the least effective Speakers in Canadian history . . . I consulted the Priorities and Planning Committee of cabinet in regard to the Speaker, and without exception they were of the view that he had been a failure and must leave. The strongest criticism of Bosley came from his old friends such as Crombie, Beatty, and Clark, who indicated that his removal was absolutely indispensable to restoring civility to the House and authority to the government.

—

When I instituted my practice of having each member of caucus send me each year a personal and confidential letter outlining his or her criticisms and concerns, Bosley's name came up in these letters over and over again. "Bosley's problem is the inconsistency of his rulings," one MP wrote. "It seems that from one day to the next the rules change." "I have increasing concern about John Bosley's ability to cope with his position," Chief Government Whip Chuck Cook wrote to me on one occasion. "Coast-to-coast television broadcasts make his job the most conspicuous one in Parliament. While Bosley shows some administrative weakness, the major weakness is his continually deteriorating control of the House and the respect of Members of the House. This can only result in a correspondingly poor perception by the public of our behaviour and by a super-critical press corps. The uproar constantly in the House must be shut down."

The government was suffering, and the Speaker had to go. On September 5, I instructed Joe Clark to speak to John Bosley.

As I would have in their place, John Turner and Ed Broadbent raised hell in the media. "It could produce a parliamentary crisis," Ed told the press, stressing that the Speaker technically worked for the entire House, not just the prime minister. I knew removing Bosley was a risk, but it was one I was willing to take. I felt I had the right to remove him for the simple reason that I had appointed him. Had he been elected by MPs themselves, I would have lacked that authority. For now, I would use it because I knew that once a more skilled MP was in the Speaker's chair, the opposition parties would benefit, along with the government, muting the criticism we would face for a short time. With that decision taken, I decided to ride out the controversy over the firing for a few weeks until the opening of the House, slated for the end of September.

Not all the commentary was negative, though I was still seen as having created a new problem. "The appointment might well have been a mistake," the *Ottawa Citizen* said in an editorial on September 6. "For whatever cause – Bosley's temperament, partisan hostilities – he has had a very hard ride in the Speaker's chair. Controlling MPs' conduct proved beyond his power, and he cannot have enjoyed the sniping he heard from both sides of the aisle . . . 'The House of Commons,' said Bosley, 'is in a crisis of its own making.' The prime minister, with the Speaker, must share blame for that crisis."

Although I headed a government of 211 MPs, I was conscious of my wider responsibilities to the institution of Parliament. MPs were not going to be "nobodies" (Trudeau's description) as long as I was prime minister of Canada. In our first Speech from the Throne back in 1984, I had promised to set up a special committee to recommend concrete steps to reform the Commons. I placed veteran Newfoundland MP Jim McGrath in charge, and eagerly awaited his committee's recommendations.

Jim wasted little time, and by June of 1985 we'd accepted his recommendations that we create a new Board of Internal Economy featuring representation from all sides of the House, allow parliamentary committees to review nonjudicial Order in Council appointments, and revamp committees so they more closely paralleled government departments. I'd also accepted the McGrath Committee's principal recommendation that MPs themselves should elect their Speaker.

On September 30, 1986, we laid the foundation for the "New House" Jim and his colleagues had called for, when MPs elected British Columbia's John Fraser as their Speaker, after eleven hours of voting. His election, a first in Canadian history, was a very important step in my government's regaining control of the agenda. John Fraser turned out to be a natural, and was destined to become a great Speaker, serving MPs of all parties and Canada brilliantly until he left politics in 1993.

—

PERSONAL JOURNAL: OCTOBER 13, 1986

I believe we are making progress in the House as a result of the election of John Fraser as Speaker. This historic initiative was part of the McGrath Committee on reform of the House, and appears to be having beneficial effects. Because all parties were required to cast ballots, they appear to have a proprietary interest in ensuring that John succeeds. For his part, Fraser has been cool, consistent, and good humoured in establishing both his authority and some degree of order upon the House. It is too early to tell, but I think his election might constitute a turning point for the government; we have been doing well on the big things but getting hurt in the House for the smaller matters that excite a rather indolent gallery. As the Globe *stated in a major editorial, Mr. Bosley was a disaster as Speaker and the Liberals played a major role in his demise. Their lack of respect for him and their guerrilla tactics ultimately proved so unnerving that, rather than respond with authority, he replied with petulance, thus earning the contempt of the opposition along with their disrespect. Jeffrey Simpson strongly attacked the "crocodile tears" of John Turner, whose tactics were largely responsible for savaging the hapless Bosley. In fairness, it is doubtful in retrospect that anyone could have done any better, given the horrendous Liberal loss and the bitterness it engendered, together with the emergence of the Rat Pack mentality, which celebrated character assassination, innuendo, vile misstatements, and outright falsehoods.*

—

"Parliament, Mr. Speaker, has made history today, and you, sir, are here as its principal witness," I told the Commons after the vote. "Parliamentary reform has begun slowly to envelop this institution, making it and its members stronger and more independent. In some measure, all of us have failed Parliament these last few years. A democratic instrument requires respect to renew itself and to grow."

I had to laugh when John Turner began his own remarks.

"For some of us," he joked, "it was an extremely difficult experience. It was the first time in my life that I ever voted for a Tory."

For all MPs it was the first time any of us had voted for a Speaker and the Canadian House of Commons, to this day, is better for it.

From Macdonald through to Mulroney, Martin, and Stephen Harper, every prime minister of Canada makes mistakes. In late October of 1986, I made a memorable one: the CF-18 maintenance contract controversy. While I believe we made the right decision for the right reasons, our communications and our strategic planning were, in a word, lousy, and I take full responsibility for what went wrong.

The dilemma facing us was this: that fall, the federal government had two aircraft procurement contracts percolating through the system, the CF-18 and the CF-5. My government had earlier privatized Canadair, selling it to Canadian-owned Bombardier company in Montreal, where they continued the strong national tradition of manufacturing aircraft. The CF-18 contract involved a transfer of technology that could significantly enhance Bombardier's scientific and technical know-how in the design and building of new aircraft. The value of this contract was approximately $80 million per year over twenty years. The successful low bidder for the contract, however, was Bristol Aircraft of Winnipeg.

It was at this point – October of 1986 – that my inexperience as prime minister led me to commit a major mistake. The Department of National Defence was pushing hard for a decision on the CF-18. I should have pushed right back and insisted that cabinet decide the fate of both the CF-18 and the CF-5 contracts on the same day, awarding the CF-18 to Montreal's Bombardier and the CF-5 to Bristol in Winnipeg.

As it played out, on October 31, 1986, the government decided that the CF-18 contract should go to Bombardier, provoking an enormous outcry in Winnipeg. Three months later, in January 1987, we decided to award the CF-5 contract to the Winnipeg company. But the damage was done. We had created a full-blown communications firestorm for ourselves in the West, where our opponents, especially Preston Manning and the Reform Party – which, for its own purposes, had been peddling the idea that the West was being discriminated against, in the teeth of contrary evidence – happily used this against us for months.

Despite the myths that have grown up about our CF-18 decision, the fact is I was driven by the belief that what we were doing was in the national interest. Federalist Quebecers who had watched helplessly as moving vans filled with head office staff and equipment from dozens of companies took to the 401 bound for Ontario, in the wake of the Parti Québécois victory in the 1976 election, couldn't help but remember those dark days. We knew that if we found ourselves in another referendum situation – facing the challenge of trying to show Quebecers that Canada does indeed work for them – then cementing the aerospace industry in Montreal, and in francophone communities outside the city, would play a positive role.

But this issue went far beyond Quebec. As prime minister, it was my duty to look to the future of the whole country, and in the CF-18 contract that is what I did. As we considered the bids, it soon became clear that the main issue concerned the transfer of the most advanced technology in the world, for these high-tech fighter planes, to a Canadian manufacturer *that actually built aircraft*, like Canadair, now Bombardier. Bristol (whose parent firms included Litton Industries) was foreign-owned, and I believed it crucial for the future of this vital sector of the Canadian economy that this technology remain in Canadian-owned hands – especially in 1986, with the Cold War still on. Above all, Bristol merely serviced jets, they did not build them.

Today, the numbers speak for themselves. By 2005, the Canadian aerospace industry's sales numbers had skyrocketed – from $8.7 billion in 1983 to $21.5 billion, including exports of $18.5 billion. By awarding the contract as we did, my government helped put in place the critical mass necessary to create this vibrant economic success story. Bombardier became Canada's premier *manufacturer* of aircraft. Montreal is one of three cities in the world – Seattle and Toulouse being the others – where an entire aircraft can be conceptualized, designed, built, and maintained. And Bombardier, enhanced in its manufacturing capacity by the new contract, has become an important Canadian firm headquartered in Montreal and controlled by a respected French-Canadian family; it is a symbol of achievement and pride both for Quebecers and all Canadians.

At the same time, Bristol has continued to prosper and grow, making a significant economic contribution to Manitoba and Canada. In fact, according to Daniel Hambly, a rising young historian at the University of Western

Ontario who, in 2006, wrote his master's thesis on the CF-18 contract controversy, the Winnipeg firm got the better end of the deal in a most important regard. "The maintenance contract for that particular aircraft was valued at $350 million," he wrote. "This contract was better suited to Bristol because it guaranteed more jobs (about 500) than the (approximately) 300 that the CF-18 contract would have created . . . By awarding the CF-5 contract to the Winnipeg firm, Mulroney kept true to his promise that 'all regions of the country would get their turn.'"

Hambly went on to note, "If the West was sending a message to the Tories about their 'rage' regarding the CF-18 contract, it certainly was not a clear message. In fact, contrary to accepted wisdom, the only clear message was that the CF-18 affair barely affected Tory fortunes at all. The impact of the issue was clearly exaggerated . . . Angry westerners had been told only parts of the CF-18 story." He was referring to the fact that one year later my party swept western Canada, including Manitoba, in the general election.

Even Howard Pawley, then the NDP premier of Manitoba, who used the CF-18 contract to attack me strongly, has since had a change of heart. "It does seem as though we were a bit unfair to Mulroney in retrospect," he said in a 2006 interview. "After all, he did support me with the French-language issue, and we did have a lower unemployment level than Quebec at the time."

NDP Leader Ed Broadbent was generous in his assessment at the time. "Any politician who has an ounce of brains and two ounces of responsibility knows that in a country like this you are going to make decisions like this that are going to be difficult, and one region or another is going to be disappointed," he said the day of our announcement.

Our timing of the announcement was way off. In retrospect, we might have considered, for example, announcing the CF-5 contract for Bristol on a Monday, and the CF-18 contract on a Friday. Instead, we waited three months, until January of 1987, and allowed the opposition and later myth-makers to convince many Canadians that the CF-5 contract was somehow grudgingly awarded to the Winnipeg-based company. Even in 2007, I have to admit that I can't really blame people who believe this – they've heard nothing to the contrary for years. As I said earlier, I blew it on communications, making a good decision look bad, and should have known better.

To govern is to choose. Being prime minister requires a capacity to decide and move on. Was this situation unique in recent times? Well, a few years later when Quebec shipyards pushed hard for us to split the upcoming $6 billion contract for Canada's naval frigate program – the largest such procurement contract in history until that time – I led the cabinet to reject that recommendation, and awarded the entire contract to Saint John Shipbuilding in New Brunswick. Many Quebecers complained quite bitterly, alleging unfairness. But we did this not to punish Quebec, but to help create a critical mass in this sector in the Maritimes.

Another case of a prime minister making a controversial choice comes to mind. Under the previous government of Mr. Trudeau, the choice of the architect for the vitally important new Canadian Embassy on Pennsylvania Avenue in Washington was made by an independent jury. Bob Fowler, who worked for us both, later described how Trudeau made his final decision on the awarding of the contract. At the appropriate time, the ten or eleven maquettes from the architectural finalists were lined up in room 311S on Parliament Hill for the prime minister to review. Fowler accompanied Trudeau into the room.

"Which one is Arthur's?" Trudeau asked.

"Mr. Erickson didn't make the final cut," Bob diplomatically told his boss.

"That's unfortunate," Trudeau answered, "because he won."

And so this historic commission was awarded to Trudeau's friend, Arthur Erickson. This anecdote is one striking example of a prime minister exercising his judgment, doing his job. And which Canadian who has toured this dramatically assertive architectural presence in the American capital can honestly say that Trudeau was wrong?

Before 1986 ended, I was looking ahead to my next annual summit with the American president. I wrote to Ronald Reagan in the fall and again pressed him over acid rain. There was no way he would be arriving in Ottawa in April of 1987 without knowing exactly how I felt.

"I wish to re-emphasize that the acid rain issue is a matter of the utmost importance to me," I wrote. "I am concerned that there appears to have been very little real progress since we last met. Your budgetary cycle is well advanced with, as yet, no indication that any funds are being sought to implement the Envoys' principal recommendation for the commercialization of clean coal technology. The characterization of programs already in existence at the time of our endorsement of the Envoys' report last March as somehow meeting the Envoys' criteria will not, in my considered opinion, fulfill the commitment."

My letter to President Reagan came only a few days after a high-level "think-in" on Canada–U.S. relations held under the leadership of Joe Clark and International Trade Minister Pat Carney. This gathering featured Ambassador Allan Gotlieb, Derek Burney (then associate undersecretary of external affairs), Don Campbell, assistant deputy minister with responsibility for relations with the United States, and various other experts. As Gotlieb records in his *Washington Diaries*, it was "the first such meeting that has taken place in a long time."

They reported their conclusions to me in a memo signed by Carney. They said they believed there was no need to change current Canadian policy toward the United States. Still, there was no doubt the trade environment was continuing to deteriorate, and the Reagan administration was also failing to deal with acid rain. "While recognizing these factors, Canada should maintain a moderate, confident tone, as well as a sense of realism vis-à-vis the USA's agenda and the Executive's ability to control that agenda, particularly in the last two years of President Reagan's mandate." They recommended that I press Reagan to include a strong endorsement of Canada–U.S. free trade negotiations during his upcoming State of the Union address. The group also suggested I sign a strong letter to the president on acid rain.

Another American I had dealings with in December of 1986 was the hugely influential Democratic senator from Texas, Lloyd Bentsen, who was to run as his party's number two man on the 1988 ticket then go on to serve in President Bill Clinton's cabinet as secretary of the Treasury. He told me that Congress wanted a free trade deal with Canada, and wanted it quickly. I cautioned him, warning that there would be a deal only if it was good for Canada, and reminding him that cultural issues were important to Canadians.

During both my mandates as prime minister I made it a point to meet – both in Washington and in Ottawa – with key members of Congress. Over the years I also pressed Canada's case with key interest groups and with the American media. While a good personal relationship with the president is crucial, developing the same with other American leaders is key as well.

The fall of 1986 brought good news our way. In late October, the respected Economic Council of Canada released their study of free trade between Canada and the United States. After careful examination of the prospect, they predicted that more than 370,000 new jobs would be created by 1995. The council also examined what they expected would happen to

Canada if the United States withdrew behind its border and sought the false comfort of full-blown protectionism. Faced with the Americans slapping a 20 per cent surtax on most of their manufactured imports, the council estimated that Canada would lose more than 500,000 jobs by 1995, unemployment would rise by 2.4 per cent, and our GNP would drop by 5 per cent.

We also put in place another brick in the foundation of economic renewal when Consumer and Corporate Affairs Minister Harvie Andre introduced our drug patent legislation. Under our plan, multinational drug companies would see their patents protected for ten years. In return for this extended protection, we projected billions of dollars in new investment by these companies in Canada. We rejected advice from the Privy Council Office not to take this route, but, as with my government's efforts to foster the Canadian aerospace industry any way we could, we saw in the future thousands of new, largely high-paying jobs for Canadians in the pharmaceutical sector.

Like so many of our reforms, that's what the drug patent legislation was all about – the future. I knew there would be screaming headlines about massive increases in drug prices for Canadians, and the threat of obstruction by the Liberal-dominated Senate posing as the consumer's friend, but I never for a minute suspected our course wasn't right. And today? Thousands of Canadians still work in that sector, following billions in new investment in the Canadian pharmaceutical industry, and Americans are lining up at the border to buy our cheaper drugs.

John Crow, whom I appointed as Governor of the Bank of Canada in the fall of 1986, was also to play a key role. My instructions to him were clear: wring inflation out of the Canadian economy. While I knew this would cost us politically, I also knew that governing wasn't a popularity contest.

—

PERSONAL JOURNAL: October 13, 1986

I suppose that, reading these notes, one could conclude that I have been troubled and upset by recent events. In fact, since July (the cabinet shuffle) I have had a good feeling, the strong impression that things have been improving. Mila and the children are in marvellous form and are a constant source of joy and delight to me. The baby is turning out to be a real winner, and I thoroughly enjoy my long walks (and talks) with him and the other kids. Mila herself has become a very significant and successful person in her own right. I think the way she organized the Cystic Fibrosis fundraising event in Ottawa so tremendously well has given her new confidence, and has provoked even greater affection for her in the country, where she is already so greatly admired.

Maz is performing well as DPM and his firm hand on House affairs and communications is beginning to be felt. Other key ministers are doing extremely well, though it will be some time before we begin getting some substantial measure of credit. The PMO is improving, and the addition of Dalton Camp (and others) will prove very helpful.

I suppose that we must proceed with our agenda, undeterred by the criticism, firm in the knowledge that we have brought good results for Canadians and growing prosperity across the country. If we can resolve the nettlesome problem of uneven distribution of wealth (boom days in Southern Ontario, and 24 per cent unemployment in Newfoundland), reform the tax system, negotiate some appropriate arrangement with the U.S., and agree upon a formula that will allow Quebec to sign the Constitution, we will have done a good job for the country.

—

1987

1. Strong Words with President Reagan

PERSONAL JOURNAL: JANUARY 1, 1987

Some reasons for confidence? . . . Si Taylor and Derek Burney, whom I named to the top DM jobs in External, have been tremendous – supportive of Clark, ingenious in policy option development, and very professional in their analysis of events.

The decision to replace John Bosley with John Fraser has been particularly helpful, in both the Commons and the country. He has reasserted the Speaker's control over the House and, in the process, made Parliament more effective and the Govt. less hamstrung.

Our agenda will indeed be full in 1987. If Maz can continue to make progress in the House, our legislative record should continue to be impressive. Our problem remains the deficit. It must be reduced. Wilson must – and shall – be supported in that process, but it means no money whatsoever for new spending on worthwhile programs and in needy areas.

I am progressively troubled by this fact. Politically, we get no credit for good economic management. If so, say some, why not say to hell with it and spend some money where it is needed, thereby earning at least the gratitude of beneficiaries! We must stay the course and try to bring to fruition some of the following: constitutional negotiations, tax reform, trade negotiations, capital punishment debate, family reinforcement measures, and aboriginal negotiations.

—

BY JANUARY OF 1987 I had had it up to the gills with the Reagan administration in Washington. Since coming to office in 1984, I had made it a priority to repair relations between Canada and the United States and, on a personal level, I had accomplished this goal. President Reagan and I got along famously, as did Joe Clark and his American counterpart George Shultz. This was a definite improvement over the Trudeau years, and I was proud that personal tensions had eased.

On the policy side of the world's most important bilateral relationship, however, the picture was very different. Whether it was the carelessness of the American free trade negotiator, or the distinct lack of progress on acid rain, or the failure by the administration to meet us halfway on Canadian sovereignty in Arctic waters, Canada's concerns were not being met. As a result, because of my pro-American stance, my government was taking more political hits than the *Bismarck* and I was getting very little in return.

By mid-January, Gallup had us behind both the Liberals and the NDP, and I knew it was time I lit a fire in the American capital. Like any Canadian prime minister, I faced two choices in confronting American inactivity on Canadian files. The safest method – and one that would have probably brought us up five points in the polls – was to call the media and launch into flights of fiery anti-American rhetoric. Liberals, up to the present day (as we saw in the 2006 federal election), have fine-tuned this tactic over the years.

There was only one problem with choosing that route: it was doomed to failure. The audience I needed to reach was in Washington. While I could have picked up the telephone and talked to President Reagan personally, I also had to reject that option. Immersed in the Iran-Contra scandal as he was, Reagan's grip on power was in peril. We had reports that his workday had been whittled down to almost nothing, and there was even talk of impeachment proceedings swirling in the halls of the U.S. Capitol building.

I also rejected a radical approach pitched by Ambassador Gotlieb from Washington. By telegram, he advised me to cancel the April Ottawa summit. "Even before the Iran crisis, it had become apparent that the president was becoming progressively less in control of the management of U.S.A. affairs and his interests more quixotic," he wrote.

> Most of his domestic agenda had been accomplished. The president's foreign policy agenda, largely unaccomplished, was dominated by arms control, Nicaragua, and the hostage issues. Even of those, as the record now shows, his approach was an explosive mixture of detachment, sentimentality, and subterfuge. It is not clear where Canada, and Canadian interests in general and

> Canadian expectations on acid rain in particular, ranked on the president's personal agenda. But it is clear that their management was delegated to a bureaucracy that was divided on their importance but united in the conviction that there was no money to spend . . .
>
> All this adds up to a poor prognosis for Canada's agenda here in general and for our aspirations on acid rain in particular. We face the prospect of a klieg-light summit in Ottawa for which we have only the slimmest chance of success on the most important issues, especially in terms understood by ordinary Canadians. No amount of creativity will turn this sow's ear into a silk purse. In these circumstances, I regretfully come to the conclusion that the government should not hold the summit as planned without great damage to its credibility. My recommendation is that the summit be deferred and an announcement to this effect be made at the opening of Parliament. Deferring the summit would be a political bombshell here. It would be seen as out of character. It would be a diplomatic move rarely employed. For just those reasons it would be effective in registering Canadian dissatisfaction on the U.S.A. political radar and showing Canadians, too, that the Canadian government means business. I do not believe merely threatening to defer would be effective. Some here would see it as just more whining; others would see it as not a very muscular power play. All would dismiss it.

Cool under pressure as always, Joe Clark strongly disagreed with our ambassador's recommendation. Joe fired me a memo shortly after he received a copy of Gotlieb's telegram:

> While I agree such action would be a bombshell and a dramatic signal of Canadian dissatisfaction, I suspect that it would open us to derision at home – the ultimate flip-flop – and would prove more damaging than effective in the short and medium term on matters of substance with the U.S. Telling the president not to come because his administration has failed to live up to a key commitment would be a crude, if not rude, message and at a time when the president is hurting domestically. I believe we could register our dismay in person with greater effect and in a spirit which will

> respond more tellingly to public expectations of our ability to manage this relationship. There may well be a perception that we have been "conned" on acid rain, or that we have obtained little in return for our actions on energy and investment but much remains at stake in our relations with the U.S. – not least the prospect, however difficult, of a trade deal. I believe we would be better to assert our concerns, our differences, and our expectations with neither bombshells nor excessive fanfare. We should in effect stand up – not down.

I decided to approach Vice-President George Bush instead. The previous year he had told me privately of his willingness to serve as a back-channel conduit to his president. On January 15, I took him up on his offer, ordering Allan Gotlieb to visit the vice-president first. While Gotlieb had faced some tough assignments in Washington over the years, nothing could have prepared him for the instructions Joe Clark and I had for him. We ordered him to visit Bush (as his published diary records, "at once, repeat, at once") and deliver a warning. Before I got on the telephone with Bush, I wanted him to be perfectly aware how seriously I viewed the situation. Whether the Americans realized it or not, our relations were on the brink of rupture.

Gotlieb saw Bush, and I soon had a report in front of me in Ottawa. "The ambassador told him that the prime minister had delivered on many matters respecting American demands but this had been met with nothing in return," it read. "He told the vice-president that warm friendship had been met with cold hands. The ambassador concluded his remarks by saying that were it not for the personal esteem in which the prime minister holds the president, he would have changed our foreign policy some time ago, since Canadians are increasingly pressing for a more aggressive stance by the government."

After letting Bush consider Gotlieb's words for a few hours, I spoke with him that evening. "(I know) the president has not been well," I offered. "I don't believe in blindsiding my friends. How do I get my message through? I remembered our discussions in Ottawa and decided to take advantage of your hospitality."

One by one, I forcefully walked the vice-president through our concerns. "Acid rain: I don't think the president understands it's the litmus test. Free trade: [U.S. negotiator Peter] Murphy has displayed persistent insensitivity. Arctic sovereignty: I'd like to remind you we have *two* neighbours and I'm talking to one of them. We've got to have movement. These are grave issues that are getting worse. Unless the United States comes through, you'll never have a more friendly prime minister for decades – and beyond."

Shocked at my tough tone, Bush pledged he would examine the files I'd raised and take my concerns in person to the president. While the VP was loyally keeping his cards close to his chest I sensed he already had a great deal of sympathy for Canada's positions, particularly on acid rain. I knew he'd do what he promised.

Later that week, U.S. Ambassador Thomas Niles said the call had worked. "You have certainly aroused Washington's attention," he told a Canadian official.

By January 21, Vice-President Bush and Treasury Secretary Jim Baker were in Ottawa for urgent discussions. We met at the official Government of Canada guest house at Rideau Gate. I carried into the meeting a stark briefing note that had been prepared at my direction. I referred to it occasionally as Bush and I spoke, and I reproduce it here in full as an interesting example of a hard-hitting, direct briefing note:

> 1) Reinforce telephone call: drifting towards rupture. 2) Register government's concerns re: U.S. failure to honour commitments primarily on acid rain, also on trade; negligence, insensitivity, actions, and public remarks; impasse on Arctic and other issues. 3) Effective follow-up. Visit itself not an accomplishment. Tone: Firm, cool, and confident, realistic during and after, tailor expectations to results. Problem in Canada: Commitments made by U.S. not met (acid rain, trade, Arctic); no real dividends on our priority items; perception is Canada is doing all the "giving" and is being compelled to sacrifice national interests; credibility of our approach to U.S. undermined. Problem in U.S.: highest levels are unaware, insensitive, or inattentive; issues significant to us seem peripheral to them; preoccupied by internal events, paralysis; delivery capacity is suspect. Remedy: On acid rain: 1) The Emperor needs clothes. This is the priority for us. 2) A real commitment by U.S., new funds targeted at transboundary emissions. 3) A commitment to medium-term targets, similar to our 50 per cent by 1994. On trade: 1) Assurance of no more restrictive action, for example, on steel, gas – cannot be bullied; 2) Clear priority, more sensitivity

re negotiations (State of the Union); 3) Baker role pivotal. Arctic: 1) Our sovereignty must be respected.

I had instructed Bill Pristanski to prepare a video of extracts from question period in the House of Commons. After lunch at 24 Sussex, I invited Bush and Baker up to the Freedom Room on the second floor and turned on the TV. They were then treated to twenty minutes of the opposition's vicious personal attacks on me for my pro-American stance, together with insulting anti-American statements, ridicule of President Reagan, and scorn for his country.

The two Americans watched this onslaught in stunned silence. Accustomed to a much less confrontational system, they were horrified by the insults I endured on a regular basis in the cauldron of the House. When it was over, I said quietly, "That's what I have to put up with every day."

Bush asked, "Can I have a copy for the president?"

"George, you can have the original," I said.

Later, at the press scrum, Bush reported on our discussions, "Boy, did I get an earful."

A few days after Bush's visit, I embarked on a trip to the front-line states in southern Africa – becoming the first Western leader to do so – as the war against apartheid continued. In Zimbabwe, my staff advised me that I had to have a meeting with the president, the ceremonial head of state. When I protested, they said the commitment was made, and that in any case the Canadian media were really enthusiastic about it. When I glanced at the program, I quickly figured out why: the head of state was President Canaan Banana. When I emerged from the meeting the next day, the first question was predictable, and it came from the hard-nosed and irrepressible Robert Fife: "Prime Minister," he intoned gravely, "how would you describe your meeting with President Banana?" With matching gravity I replied, "Fruitful."

While in Africa I learned that Vice-President Bush had kept his word. Ronald Reagan called me in Zimbabwe before he delivered his State of the Union address to say, "Brian, I've watched the tape and I got the message." He said he would give the free trade talks special emphasis in his speech that night, which would be seen by hundreds of millions of Americans.

"Now, today, we also find ourselves engaged in expanding peaceful commerce across the world," Reagan told his audience in the United States and throughout the world. "We will work to expand our opportunities in international markets through the Uruguay round of trade negotiations and to complete a historic free trade arrangement between the world's two largest trading partners, Canada and the United States. Our basic trade policy remains the same: we remain opposed as ever to protectionism, because America's growth and future depend on trade. But we would insist on trade that is fair and free. We are always willing to be trade partners but never trade patsies."

By March, President Reagan and his administration were also showing some small movement on acid rain. He released a statement pledging to seek $2.5 billion from Congress to invest in clean coal technologies. While I described this gesture publicly as "significant movement," I knew we still had a long way to go.

Reagan wrote to me privately before his arrival in Ottawa for our annual summit. I shook my head as I read his three-page letter, which soon made it clear that his visit wouldn't be easy, despite the missive's soothing rhetoric. He started off softly, showing me where he had moved on certain issues:

> I wanted to offer you my own thoughts on the substantive agenda for our April 5–6 meetings. In doing so, let me say that I have received a full report from George Bush about his January meeting with you and that we have taken a fresh look at the key bilateral issues in light of the concerns you expressed. The further steps I have directed on acid rain ensure that the United States will continue to work closely with Canada in the context of the Envoys' report . . . You will recall that I underscored our commitment to our free trade negotiations in my State of the Union address . . . Jim Baker and other cabinet members will be giving special attention to these talks in the months ahead. Our negotiators have both stated that the negotiations are on track. Although we must recognize that very difficult issues are yet to be resolved, there is no doubt in my mind that a mutually beneficial agreement will enhance the competitive position of our two countries.

I read on, steeling myself for the bad news.

"We will also want to discuss a number of bilateral economic irritants," he wrote. "In this regard, I am very concerned by your recently announced policy to restrict U.S.-owned film distribution companies. This policy seems discriminatory and would impede their long-standing business in Canada."

Once again our American neighbours were showing a startling ignorance of Canada's cultural concerns. In this I saw the hand of one of Washington's most accomplished lobbyists, Jack Valenti, a former presidential aide to Lyndon Johnson who now headed the Motion Picture Association of America, in ensuring that Reagan, himself formerly a Hollywood actor, was fully briefed on the film industry's worries about our attempts to preserve English-language cinema in Canada.

President Reagan raised the issue of Arctic sovereignty even though he had assured me in person at the White House the year before that his country wouldn't do anything in the North without Canada's agreement. "Brian," his letter continued, "this vexing issue has proven to be more difficult for us to resolve than I thought when we discussed it . . . While our negotiators should continue their search for a solution to this complex problem, I have to say in all candor that we cannot agree to an arrangement that obliges us to seek permission for our vessels to navigate through the Northwest Passage. To do so would adversely affect our legitimate right to freely transit other important areas globally."

With that position on the record, the third annual summit between the prime minister of Canada and the president of the United States began. Governor General Jeanne Sauvé and I met Reagan at Uplands and officially welcomed him to Canada. After the appropriate remarks from Her Excellency and the president, we travelled into downtown Ottawa by motorcade, arriving at Rideau Hall, where Reagan and I then went into a private meeting. We began by discussing the Iran-Contra controversy that had engulfed his administration. Ron told me that the details of arms sales to Iran and the subsequent illegal diversion of funds to the Nicaraguan Contras had not been fully reported to him. "I didn't know until the shit hit the fan," he said.

I then sat back and awaited his expected attack on Flora MacDonald's film policy; it soon arrived. "That film decision your government has taken must not happen," he said. He told me that a much higher percentage of American films would be affected by the policy than Canadian officials acknowledged. He reiterated that this file was a matter he followed personally, and he noted that many Hollywood producers were now filming their movies in Canada. "This must be very helpful to your economy," he said.

Once again, I had to remind an American audience of Canadian cultural sensitivities and the reality we lived in. "Only 3 per cent of feature films shown in English Canada are Canadian made," I told him. Three per cent.

With a twinkle in his eye, Reagan said he didn't believe there was anything inherently cultural about the films now being made in Hollywood. It had been decades since he'd starred in a movie, and his eyes had a faraway look. "In my day," he added, focusing once again on his brief, "90 per cent of the films made worldwide were American."

I saw this as my opening and made my move on acid rain. If Ronald Reagan thought that his restatement of his commitment to the Envoys' report was enough, he was about to find out how wrong he was. The report was only part of the solution, I said, and it was time the United States joined with Canada and negotiated a full acid rain accord, which, I said, "would confound our critics."

Reagan was surprised at my proposal and responded with some of his usual answers. "You really need to study the problem," he said and provided me with his own theory about the causes of acid rain; according to some experts, he said, it was caused by trees! Accumulations of humus, the result of forest fires, was the problem, he believed. He advocated deacidifying North American lakes by adding lime to them. He even suggested that industrial emissions were less harmful than those that occurred as a result of natural processes.

This angered me, and I countered by saying that if I had a magic wand and could clean up all of Canada's industrial emissions myself, the remaining 50 per cent of sulphur dioxide in Canada's air came from his country. I reminded him that clouds moved northward from the manufacturing hub of the Ohio Valley into Canada each and every day.

"I know that," Reagan conceded. "We are poisoning our own lakes too, you know," he added, as we wrapped up our discussions in a standoff.

That evening Jeanne Sauvé hosted a state dinner for President and Mrs. Reagan. Guests from across the spectrum of Canadian society attended, including a rising pop star who was beginning to make waves in Canada and the United States, a young francophone named Céline Dion.

The next day Reagan and I met again. I had let my visitor begin the previous day and now it was my turn. Having already hit the president pretty hard on acid rain, I now switched topics, raising Canadian sovereignty in the Arctic. Well aware by now of American fears of setting a precedent for other waterways around the globe, I reminded Reagan of the uniqueness of the Northwest Passage. The islands on both sides of the passage were Canadian, I said, and the region was "very unlike the straits and passages in the rest of the world you keep referring to."

I also raised his presummit letter. "Your views," I said in a steely tone, "are not acceptable and hardly form a basis for me to keep talking to you about these issues. You've gone backward since we met at the White House, and it's time to reconsider. If you are prepared to do so, we are prepared to search for a solution. But if this is your position, and there is a direct bloody challenge to our sovereignty, I'll be obliged to take all kinds of action to ensure that my government is not blown out of the water. This is a grave, grave matter."

—

PERSONAL JOURNAL: APRIL 7, 1987

I hit hard – very hard – on Arctic sovereignty, acid rain, and trade. [Defence Minister] Perrin Beatty, who was attending his first such meeting – and did very well – said to [Energy Minister Marcel] Masse, Joe, Gotlieb, etc., afterward: "I had no idea the PM was so direct and tough in these meetings. The CBC should televise any one of those sessions and Mulroney would be elected forever."

Trudeau, of course, used to snipe away in public but was always ineffective in private with the Americans. But Canadians got the impression he was tough with them when the reverse was true. I suffer from the problem of friendship. Because I favour civilized relations and do not go in for knee-capping friends, the Canadian press assume I am no less cordial in private. They would be astonished at what I actually say and do. My only interest is the advancement of Canada's interests.

—

My tone and argument must have registered. Later that morning, after returning from the cabinet chamber to my Parliament Hill office, Reagan got up from his chair and walked across to a nineteenth-century globe Paul Desmarais had given me. I asked Derek Burney to show the president the Northwest Passage. After Derek explained (not for the first time) the uniqueness of our claims, I pointed to the Northwest Passage and said, "Ron, that's ours. We own it lock, stock, and icebergs."

Reagan looked toward his own delegation and remarked that the Northwest Passage did appear to be situated in Canada's internal waters, saying, "That's not the same as the map they showed me on Air Force One."

Speaking almost to himself, he added, "All the islands are Canadian."

At this point Joe Clark spoke up, pointing out that Canadian Inuit lived on the islands surrounding the passage, and routinely walked across it on the winter ice. "That is what makes it different," Joe said.

The president and I departed shortly thereafter for a luncheon at 24 Sussex Drive. As we discussed East–West relations and the Middle East over lunch, I wondered if the incident in my office had fully registered. I soon had evidence of a change of position, and I can now say that all Canadians should be thankful to Paul Desmarais for giving me that globe!

In an interview some years later, Frank Carlucci, President Reagan's national security advisor, described how testy Reagan became that day when his officials continued to stall and stymie my government on the issues I had raised. According to a recent account published by Professor Jeffrey L. Chidester, research director for presidential and special projects at the University of Virginia, Reagan took Carlucci aside before entering 24 Sussex, and said, "I think we should do something for Brian."

Carlucci replied, "Mr. President, we're doing well holding our positions on acid rain, the free trade agreement, and the Northwest Passage," but Reagan restated his desire to make some concessions, saying, "Oh, no, no, no, we ought to do something." According to Chidester, Carlucci continued to push for the American positions and to resist the president's desire to "do something" for me: "'It was the only time [said Carlucci] I saw Ronald Reagan lose his temper. He turned to me and said, "You do it."' Carlucci went right from the meeting and grabbed Derek Burney, Mulroney's chief of staff, and asked, 'Derek, would you reiterate your positions [on acid rain, trade, and the Northwest Passage]?' When Burney asked why, Carlucci said, 'Because they're our positions now.'"

—

PERSONAL JOURNAL: April 7, 1987

When RR arrived for lunch at 24 he immediately asked to see me in private. We went to my den where he said, "You convinced me this morning that I must take further involvement on acid rain and Arctic sovereignty." Thinking he was referring to action taken some weeks ago, and very pleased that my vigorous work of the previous two meetings had paid off, I replied, "That's good, let's have lunch." "No," he said, "I want to move now and I need time with Cap and George." I said, "Okay, let's go right in, have a bite, and I'll cut lunch short so that you can huddle together in the living room in private."

So at 1:15, just as George was preparing to report on his upcoming summit mission, Reagan said, "Let's go to Brian's living room." I replied, "You can use it for free, and it's not bugged – but I can't vouch for my neighbours, the French and South African embassies." Thereupon began what I am sure was one of the most remarkable meetings that was ever held at 24 Sussex. Reagan, Weinberger, Shultz, Carlucci, etc., gathered in the living room for 45 minutes to hammer out the language required to accommodate Reagan's new instructions. Every once in a while Carlucci would emerge, seek Burney's approval on language, and return. Finally, at 2 p.m., Reagan strode out and said that he hoped that his new language, which represented a significant departure from his previous positions, would meet with my approval. I said it would, and he indicated that he would give the news at the tail end of his speech to the Commons. He said, "Brian, we've had excellent meetings, but I felt that the U.S. should do more. We're making progress. I don't want the press talking about another Reykjavik [scene of a recent disappointing meeting with Gorbachev]."

This was an impressive performance. He listened carefully to issues; he judged their relative importance to him and to me, and decided on instinct that movement by him was required, and he moved immediately. Less than an hour later he was announcing these initiatives to the House of Commons. Among the surprised listeners would have been Lee Thomas, EPA administrator, who had said to me the night before at the GG's dinner, "Prime Minister, the president has already moved ahead on acid rain. Politically, he can move no farther."

—

Once back on Parliament Hill, I decided to use my introduction of President Reagan to a joint session of Parliament to push the envelope even further.

"Canadians view with increasing concern the effects of acid rain upon our environment," I said. "But this is more than a Canadian problem. It is a transboundary problem which requires a transboundary response. I urgently invite the U.S. administration and the American Congress to join with this

Parliament and the Government of Canada in concluding a firm bilateral accord which will provide a North American solution to acid rain. In this matter, time is not our ally but our enemy. The longer we delay, the greater the cost. For what would be said of a generation that sought the stars but permitted its lakes and streams to languish and die?"

MPs and senators greeted my words with sustained applause.

During his speech, the president surveyed the world scene and also praised our free trade initiative, but what I was really waiting for came at the end.

"May I add a word about our discussions today on two issues of critical interest to our two countries," Reagan said. "The prime minister and I agreed to consider the prime minister's proposal for a bilateral accord on acid rain, building on the tradition of agreements to control pollution in our shared international waters. The prime minister and I also had a full discussion of the Arctic waters issue, and he and I agreed to inject new impetus to the discussions already under way. We are determined to find a solution based on mutual respect for sovereignty and our common security and other interests."

On Arctic sovereignty, Reagan was as good as his word. Canada and the United States signed the Canada–U.S. Arctic Cooperation Agreement in early 1988. As a result the United States agreed to ask Canada's permission to transit the Northwest Passage, and we agreed to give them a positive answer. "Eventually, we settled on a solution that reflected more or less what neighbours might do," Derek Burney, who negotiated the deal for Canada, later wrote. "I don't mind you cutting across my lawn to go to the corner store, provided you ask first."

Many years later, Colin Powell, who had been Reagan's national security advisor, spoke at a tribute luncheon for Derek Burney. "He chided me for the 'Rube Goldberg globe' that Mulroney had used to get the president's attention on the Northwest Passage," Burney remembered. "Powell added . . . he was always afraid of calls from two world leaders, Margaret Thatcher and Brian Mulroney, because, he said, they 'could get the president to do anything they wanted.'"

After the president's speech we headed for Uplands and the departure ceremonies before Reagan left for Washington. We were alone in a hangar – except for the ever-present Secret Service agents and RCMP officers – as we waited for Nancy Reagan and Mila to arrive. When their car drove up and our wives stepped out, both looking like a million bucks, Ron beamed and threw his arm around my shoulder. "You know, Brian, for two Irish guys we sure married up," he joked. I repeated that line seventeen years later, during my eulogy at Ronald Reagan's funeral, and as laughter rippled through the cathedral, a knowing smile crossed Nancy's face.

Back in Washington, Reagan reported on his trip to Ottawa in another radio address. "We spoke seriously about the environmental challenge of acid rain, for example, and we're going to do something about it," he said. "We also discussed our current efforts to tear down barriers to commerce and establish free trade between our peoples and countries. The enthusiastic reception I received from the Canadian Parliament suggests that a free trade agreement between Canada and the United States is an idea whose time has come. I pledged to Prime Minister Mulroney and the people in Canada that we're going all out to make this visionary proposal of the prime minister a reality. We'll do it for the prosperity and jobs it will create in both our countries; but, just as important, it will be an example to all the world that free and fair trade, and not protectionism, is the way to progress and economic advancement."

The day after Reagan's visit one of my senior ministers, Elmer MacKay, with whom I had developed an especially close friendship, slipped me a handwritten note. "My dear old mother told me this morning that I should tell you on her behalf how well you are doing and how great you looked and [that you] sounded better yesterday – better, she said, by far, than Reagan. PM, you sure have a way with mothers!"

President Reagan and I were to meet later at the 1987 G-7 Summit in Venice in June – though I didn't share the observations of Elmer MacKay's mother with him. At the summit's conclusion we had a full session on Canadian–American relations. With the deadline for the free trade talks only three and a half months away, I didn't waste time with opening pleasantries. I had told Ron many times that a binding dispute resolution system was key to Canada's demands. In repeating this in Venice I bluntly warned him that Canada needed to know if he couldn't deliver, as we'd then prepare to leave the negotiating table. "If you can't deal with your largest trading partner and best friend, who can you negotiate with?" I asked.

I also reminded him that the West Germans and the Japanese claimed that the U.S. deficit was the root cause of many world economic problems. A successful deal with Canada would help answer such criticisms, I argued. "The free trade deal could ultimately become a commercial SDI," I added in language I knew would strike a chord with him, "and be used as a model or shield elsewhere." While I knew his administration was worried about congressional reaction if Canada was successful in negotiating a unique and binding dispute resolution system, I told Reagan that Congress had to hear from him about this aspect of our case. What message would Congress be sending to the world, I asked, if talks with Canada ended in failure?

Reagan assured me again how much he personally wanted an agreement with Canada, and he stressed that he had recently made this point strongly with his shrewd and canny Treasury Secretary Jim Baker. After hearing this I left the meeting satisfied; I knew full well we'd have a deal the moment Baker was fully engaged in the talks. Baker had already sent signals to Michael Wilson that the talks would go down to the wire, and I felt we had his silent agreement that he'd ensure that the administration came through in the end. As we were to see in October of 1987 and on in later years when he served President George Bush as secretary of state, Jim Baker was a man of his word.

1987

2. Clearing the Decks

With our new approach to Canadian–American relations showing some results in 1987, I turned my attention to improving the situation in my own office. While I was proud of the work of my closest advisors, I felt that it was time the PMO focused its energy more effectively. There was a lack of cohesion and discipline in my office and this was reflected across the government.

Our government's own mistakes aside, our message also wasn't getting out because the PMO itself was under bitter attack. Members of caucus and the cabinet were grumbling, and their discontent was being picked up by the media. In fairness, this situation often prevails in our system, a result of the Canadian prime minister having more power concentrated in his or her office than any other leader in the Western world.

I tried to counter these attacks during our caucus meeting on February 18, facing the internal critics head on. "Any minister who says he was 'ordered around' by the PMO should resign," I told my MPs. "Individuals in the PMO do not have authority over caucus, ministers, or me."

But the sniping continued unabated. Clearly, it was time for me to act. It was simply too much to ask Bernard Roy to do all I was calling on him to do, day after day. He was my Quebec lieutenant and we had a Quebec caucus made up mostly of rookies, many of whom had never even been to Ottawa before their election. Many spoke little English and didn't know the rest of the country. They were in many ways brand new to Canada. Looking after them was too big a job for Bernard to juggle along with all his other responsibilities. I wanted Bernard to remain as principal secretary and to concentrate his energies fully on Quebec matters, including the upcoming constitutional negotiations, but I knew this meant I needed a chief of staff to free him up. I thought a great deal about making changes in my office during the summer of 1986 and again over the Christmas break, and I sought advice from respected Tories like former Ontario premier Bill Davis. Bill had won a majority in 1971 and watched as scandals and inexperience caused his government to be reduced to a minority just a few years later. He and I had many discussions in 1986 and 1987, and he recommended I bring Ed Stewart, who had served him as deputy minister for many years at Queen's Park, to the Langevin Block as my chief of staff.

I authorized Bill to make the necessary overture to Stewart, who declined. Bill also drew up a revised organizational chart for the PMO, which I was to rely upon when I made my final decisions in March of 1987. His confidential memo to me read in part:

> While only those who have experienced the situation you find yourself in really sense how difficult a time this is for you and Mila, there exists in my view a lot of goodwill out there and any number of people who wish to help.
>
> I have always had difficulty in expressing my personal feelings to people but I want you and Mila to know that you have Kathy's and my friendship, support, respect, and affection during this difficult period. I also believe, Brian, that with some luck and the tough decisions you are in the process of making that you'll be our prime minister for many years to come. I have the only other copy of this memo, which I shall have at my home in Brampton if you wish to call while you are away. I'd be quite prepared to visit you in Florida for a few hours if that would be any help. I apologize for the writing but I didn't feel comfortable in sharing these feelings with anyone. Take some time to have a rest and a little bit of fun while you are away. It's too bad the football season isn't with us so I could suggest a diversion to you. P.S.: Mila is still our best asset!

Bill agreed with the changes I was proposing – moving Fred Doucet over so he could devote all his energies to the organization of international summits, finding a press secretary to replace Michel Gratton, and a few other measures.

But I still needed a chief of staff, someone who was both a fixer and a player. Like all prime ministers, I had a close working relationship with senior officials in the Department of External Affairs. At a cabinet meeting one day in January, I sent Joe Clark a note, asking him to rate Under-secretary of State Si Taylor and his colleague Derek Burney. "Both are extraordinarily respected by EA officers," Joe replied. "Taylor's strength – his judgment; you could call it wisdom. He's consistently strong. His weakness – he is not a natural at administration (although that is not a problem in External). He is perhaps too traditionally deferential. I have to ask him for his suggestions. He doesn't always volunteer. Burney is much more hands-on and aggressive. Not as thoughtful, though seldom wrong. His weakness is probably best described as 'immaturity.' He is excellent now, will be superb in a couple of years."

I didn't have a couple of years. So early one morning in February I picked up the telephone and asked the PMO switchboard to connect me with Derek Burney. They found him in Los Angeles.

"Derek," I said, "how would you like to be my chief of staff?"

Hearing the shock in Derek's voice, I asked for his impressions of how he thought my PMO was operating.

"How candid do you want me to be?" he shot back. "Your office seems to me to be a bit like a wagon wheel without a rim. We all know you're the hub, but there are several people representing your views to the bureaucracy, and the messages do not get out."

"How do you think I feel," I replied, "going home at night and finding three memos from my staff on the same subject but each with different recommendations? I need someone to organize the place."

"But I'm not a political strategist, prime minister. I'm a public servant and have worked for governments of all political stripes."

"I don't need a strategist," I continued. "I am the strategist, but I need someone to organize my office. I want to focus my time on major issues like free trade and tax reform, not tainted tuna. You know those major issues and you can help."

Derek accepted my offer and became my chief of staff. For the next two years, especially as we were coming down to the wire on the Meech Lake Accord and the FTA negotiations, and were preparing for the 1988 election, it was vital for me to have someone of Derek's strength running the PMO. Determined and focused, he was absolutely crucial during the period that lay ahead. He knew my objectives, knew the bureaucracy, and helped us mightily to achieve both results and re-election.

As I was leaving office in 1993, I met with my successor, Kim Campbell, to discuss transition issues. "Get a Derek Burney to run your PMO," I told the woman who would shortly become Canada's nineteenth prime minister. "It will be the best appointment you'll ever make."

Marjory LeBreton, who had been working for the party for decades, came on board as deputy chief of staff, bringing with her the wisdom and good judgment acquired over decades in the service of every Conservative leader beginning with Diefenbaker, another decision I never regretted. She remained a close and trusted advisor until 1993, and I took a great deal of pleasure in appointing her to the Senate just before I left office. Senator LeBreton has served since then with distinction, making important contributions to the healthcare debate and other national issues. Prime Minister Stephen Harper made an excellent decision when he placed her in his cabinet as government leader in the Senate.

Marc Lortie, a bright and personable young man from External Affairs, also came aboard in March of 1987, replacing Michel Gratton as press secretary. Bruce Phillips left our embassy in Washington to take over the director of communications position, while Bill Fox, an experienced former newspaperman and political strategist, was promoted to special advisor.

I entered 1987 more convinced than ever that Canadians always respond to leadership when they see it exercised. Our policy agenda was my way of demonstrating leadership to Canadians. Two crucial policy issues on the government's radar were the overhaul of Canada's antiquated tax system – then in the planning stages, and ably led by Michael Wilson and Stanley Hartt – and constitutional renewal. Bernard Roy highlighted both initiatives in a strategy memo he sent me in January. "For the moment," he wrote, "[the Constitution] is 'beneath the surface' and we recommend you follow Senator Murray's strategy for keeping it low-key for as long as possible . . . Tax Reform. Again, this is a 'backroom' issue until the White Paper is released . . . However, you should be intimately aware of policy decisions going into the development of this extremely volatile dossier. Some ministers are increasingly anxious about the implications of this reform. However, the game plan for the next several months involves detailed planning, not salesmanship . . . We do not recommend that you, personally, highlight tax reform until such time as we understand the Wilson proposals in their entirety. Bluntly, there are obvious pitfalls in the path of a government which puts tax on food."

Such understatements heralded the discussion of a new consumption tax known as the GST. I was well aware of the "obvious pitfalls." MP Lawrence O'Neil put it best at a 1987 caucus meeting when he said, "Jesus, PM, if we tax food even my wife won't vote for me!"

Following Bernard's advice, I plunged into many hours of briefings on tax reform with Wilson and Hartt over the months that followed. As with so many of the issues we faced from 1984 until 1993, doing nothing wasn't an option, even if the politician in me sometimes longed for that choice.

"Failure to deliver on public commitment to comprehensive tax reform, broken promise," Wilson advised me in a memo that listed all the dangers we were facing. He concluded, "We could be looking at $2–3 billion shortfall in anticipated revenue by end of 1987–88."

There were no easy decisions. I decided that it was time to tackle the toughest of all – healing the country by making Quebec part of our Constitution.

1987

3. The Road to Meech Lake

Because the Meech Lake Accord was a central event of my time in office, and because I plan to deal with it in detail, some historical background may be needed to assist younger readers to understand this complex issue.

On May 20, 1980, a referendum was held in Quebec on "sovereignty-association," and the people of Quebec rejected this proposed relationship with Canada by a vote of 59.6 per cent to 40.4 per cent. Prime Minister Trudeau had an impact on that vote when, six days earlier, he told a federalist rally in Montreal's Paul Sauvé Arena: "The Government of Canada and all the provincial governments have made themselves perfectly clear. We have all said that a No will be interpreted as a mandate to change the Constitution to renew federalism . . . And because I spoke to these [Quebec] MPs this morning, I know that I can make a most solemn commitment that following a No vote, we will immediately take action to renew the Constitution, and we will not stop until we have done that."

I had arrived late in Montreal from Sept-Îles and so watched the rally on Radio-Canada with Mila, and did so approvingly. That night, few of us federalists in Quebec thought that the change and renewal promised by the federal government and English Canada would turn out to be a constitutional amendment imposed on Quebec against the will of its National Assembly, as expressed by both the Parti Québécois and the Quebec Liberal Party. We had failed to take into account the personality of Pierre Trudeau.

Gordon Robertson is an icon in Canada, a wise and judicious man who rose to head Canada's civil service. Clerk of the Privy Council and secretary to the cabinet for federal-provincial relations, he was widely admired and respected as a moderate leader of constitutional reform. As senior advisor to Prime Minister Trudeau, he knew the man well, over many years. This is how he described his boss in his memoirs, *Memoirs of a Very Civil Servant: Mackenzie King to Pierre Trudeau*: "Trudeau began as prime minister with a shyness that is hard to believe of the leader who would later contemplate and then carry out a 'coup de force' against the provinces or would so obviously mislead the voters of Quebec in his address at the Paul Sauvé Arena in May 1980 during the referendum campaign and then charge them with 'misunderstanding' what he had said. They should have known that he did not mean what he obviously intended them to think he meant."

Trudeau's old ally Jean Chrétien put it more bluntly fifteen years later. He clearly remembered the misleading nature of the Trudeau speech as he prepared for his own role in the 1995 Quebec referendum. "I will go on national television next week," he told his long-time assistant, Eddie Goldenberg [who recorded the incident in his 2006 book, *The Way It Works*]. "But I won't make promises that I can't keep after the referendum. I don't want to create the expectations that Trudeau, rightly or wrongly, created in 1980 at the Paul Sauvé Arena, and then find I'm not able to deliver. In the long run, that would be disastrous for the unity of the country."

The day after the referendum, Trudeau made a formal statement to the House of Commons. He reflected on the results of the referendum and announced the launching of a new constitutional process. He said that by voting for Canada in the referendum, "the people of Quebec have recognized that their fellow Canadians are prepared . . . to meet their legitimate aspirations." Quebecers, he said, had expressed "massive support for change within the federal framework," and the federal government had only two prerequisites for change: "First that Canada continue to be a real federation . . . Second, that a charter of fundamental rights and freedoms be entrenched in the new constitution and that it extend to the collective aspects of these rights, such as language rights."

Mr. Trudeau carefully kept secret his real ambitions and the means he was prepared to use to succeed. Years later he let the cat out of the bag in a remarkable statement that explains much of what subsequently happened: "Let's just say that in this last stage I felt one needed almost a putsch, a coup de force, and Gordon was too much of a gentleman for that. It was clearly going to be rough, and Gordon [Robertson] wasn't the man: a mandarin, concerned with the common weal, afraid of irreparable damage to the fabric of society. So I made a different choice." Trudeau appointed Michael Kirby, a former senior advisor to former Nova Scotia premier Gerald Regan, as secretary to the cabinet for federal-provincial relations.

In fact, the intense activity launched by the prime minister's post-referendum speech culminated in patriation with an amending formula, a

Charter of Rights, and a "notwithstanding clause" some eighteen months later, on November 5, 1981. Although the new constitutional arrangement was strongly opposed by both the government and the official opposition in Quebec, the federal government and the other nine provincial governments proceeded, regardless. In other words, Quebec – whose needs and challenges had started all this – was left out of the final product.

The 1982 Trudeau amendment was to Americanize the country as never before, transferring to the judiciary from Parliament the ultimate decision-making power in sensitive questions of public policy. As columnist Jeffrey Simpson later wrote: "Yet it remains the supreme irony that [Trudeau's] enduring constitutional legacy to Canada – one that will remain long after the Third Option, the CDC, the public ownership of Petro-Canada, etc. – will be the Charter, that most Americanizing of changes" (*Globe and Mail*, April 17, 1990).

The 1982 package also empowered provincial legislatures as never before because the new amending formula formalized their vital role in all future constitutional arrangements. (Had Trudeau himself subjected the 1982 Constitution to the 1982 amending formula, it would never have passed.) Much more ominously, in the Trudeau deal Ottawa agreed to a notwithstanding clause that allowed any province to override decisions of the Supreme Court of Canada in some specific but vital areas of national life. This constituted the most abject surrender of federal authority in our history.

I understood why the provinces demanded this clause as the price of a deal and I would have understood such a massive concession being made by Trudeau in order to secure a comprehensive deal. But he made the concession without getting such a deal. Quebecers – federalists and separatists – almost unanimously voted it down in the National Assembly.

That decision marked a defining and ominous moment in the evolution of the Canadian federation. As Marcel Adam, a leading Quebec editorialist well known for his support of many of Trudeau's initiatives, wrote: "It is indisputable that [Trudeau] did to Quebec what Ottawa had never done to any province since 1867: diminish its legislative powers through a reform rejected by its government and the majority of the opposition."

Defenders of the 1982 strategy now argue that they never expected to get agreement with a separatist government anyway, which raises a question about their not knowing this before they began, or on the night of May 14, 1980, when the formal undertaking was given to Quebecers. It also raises the question of why they did not simply wait for a federalist government to be elected in Quebec – after waiting for more than 100 years, surely another few wouldn't have hurt. The secondary argument advanced by many supporters of the 1982 decision – that patriation was acceptable to Quebec because it had been approved by over seventy federal Quebec MPs (in the Liberal caucus) – is ludicrous when one considers that the package introduced an amending formula that required, for the first time, the consent of provincial legislatures.

Former Conservative leader Robert Stanfield commented on the events of 1982 as follows: "No premier of Quebec within living memory would have agreed to the Constitution of 1982. English-speaking Canada forgot its history in 1982. We had abandoned our tradition of not changing the rules governing Quebec without Quebec's consent. I believed and I still believe that the exercise of 1982 endangers Canada as a country. We gave the separatists a stick to beat us with . . . Ottawa had not only missed an opportunity for constitutional renewal following the favourable vote in the referendum, Ottawa had betrayed the French-speaking Quebecers who had voted for constitutional renewal."

For my part, I fully supported the right of a duly elected prime minister as head of a majority government to proceed with a complete package of constitutional reforms. I agreed with both the notion of patriation of the Constitution and the concept of a charter of rights. My support was given, however, long before the final days of negotiation that produced a deal with a notwithstanding clause and without Quebec. I had been reassured by the prime minister's own words on the question only three years earlier: "No substantive changes in the *BNA Act*," he said in 1977, "will be contemplated without agreement in principle from the provinces." That position was fully consistent with the views and actions of all Canadian prime ministers and was perhaps best articulated by Canada's longest-serving prime minister, Mackenzie King: "There should never be suggestion of amendment affecting other parties to the contract save after reference and consent of those other parties."

In 1981, the country was given ample warning of what lay ahead. Senator Ernest Manning, a former premier of Alberta, pointed to the serious consequences of Ottawa and nine provinces imposing the 1982 Constitution on Quebec. "Where does Quebec stand on this matter today?" he asked on December 3, 1981. "She stands . . . more isolated than ever from the rest of Canada, more polarized, more angry, and more resentful because she feels she was betrayed . . . There is no real profit in gaining a new constitution if in the process you lose a nation . . . If adopted, it will pose the dangerous, unnecessary, and unacceptable risk of precipitating Quebec's separation from Canada. It is a ticking constitutional time bomb with the potential to blow Confederation apart." Mr. Manning foresaw the catastrophic possibility of the 1995 referendum, fourteen years later.

When the Queen came to Parliament Hill on a blustery April day in 1982 to sign the amended Constitution, Quebec was absent and the mood was sullen. Jeanne Sauvé, then Speaker of the House, told me of rising that morning in her apartment on Parliament Hill. Gazing out the window over the river to Quebec as a cold rain fell in early morning darkness, she whispered sadly to her husband, "My God, what have we done?"

Ottawa lawyer Guy Pratte, a Liberal who has acted as counsel for his party in the area of constitutional reform, confirms Sauvé's worst fears. Writing in 1998 in the book *Trudeau's Shadow*, he states:

> As a strategy for keeping this country together, it was a failure. Fifteen years after the Charter of Rights and Freedoms was enshrined in the law, Canada is more divided than ever, as demonstrated by the result of the recent [1997] federal election. Moreover, virtually every Canadian is resigned to the inevitability of another Quebec referendum sometime soon . . .
>
> Faithful Trudeau followers will blame Brian Mulroney and Robert Bourassa for reopening the constitutional debate with the Meech Lake Accord of 1987. But if the Charter really was the miracle cure to constitutional woes, why did the malady resurface with increased virulence just a few years after the prescription had been administered? As [historian Kenneth] McRoberts observes: "It is ironic that the national unity strategy, although conceived primarily in relation to Quebec, has had its main impact, not in Quebec, but in the rest of the country and has transformed the way many English Canadians think of Canada. As such elements of the Trudeau strategy as a charter of rights, multiculturalism, or the equality of the provinces have become central to English Canadians' view of Canada, so they have destroyed any willingness to recognize Quebec as a distinct society. Indeed, within the Trudeau strategy these principles were intended to negate Quebec's claim to recognition."

My own view is that Pierre Trudeau, following his defeat and announced retirement in 1979, read his political obituaries with dismay. The almost universal verdict was "eleven wasted years." When, a few months later, he was almost miraculously restored to office, I believe he resolved to create a substantive legacy that involved the National Energy Program and a major constitutional amendment so that he would ultimately be viewed as a prime minister who made a significant mark on history.

Nevertheless, there were many benefits to Canada in Trudeau's constitutional package, and these would only be enhanced if my government succeeded in securing unanimity, in bringing Quebec inside the constitutional fold. Quebec's inclusion would make the Constitution a symbol of unity rather than exclusion, and wash away forever the bitter aftertaste of the 1981–82 negotiations.

By 1983, as the country began to recover from a deep and painful recession, thoughtful people had started to reflect on recent events and to recommend future action. In September, Trudeau's closest advisor, former Privy Council Clerk and newly appointed senator Michael Pitfield, made the following observation, "We won the referendum, we said we would give Quebec a new deal, and we have not delivered a new deal. If we don't move soon, [Quebecers] are going to reconsolidate into a nationalist vein."

Senator Pitfield was both incisive and accurate. His statement disposes of a persistent myth: namely, that I sought a rapid arrangement for partisan purposes with Quebec "nationalists," who in the minds of revisionists are indistinguishable from "separatists." In fact – and this is key to understanding the issue – most French-speaking Quebecers are "nationalists" to some significant degree; some are federalist nationalists, some are separatist nationalists.

Most of the great Quebec leaders who served in the federal Parliament and in government during the first 135 years of Confederation – from Georges-Étienne Cartier to Wilfrid Laurier to Ernest Lapointe to Léon Balcer to Jean Marchand to Guy Favreau to Benoît Bouchard to Pierre Pettigrew to Jean Charest – were Quebec nationalists as well as Canadian federalists. They were Quebec nationalists in their sensitivity to Quebec's exposed position in English-speaking North America; in their understanding of Quebec's place as the heart and soul of the French language and culture on this continent; in their vigilant respect for Quebec's rights and for provincial autonomy, as provided for in the Constitution of 1867. They were loyal

Quebecers and proud Canadians because they also understood that Canada, the federal state conceived by our political forebears, offered greater security for Quebec society and hope for the cultural survival of francophones in other provinces. "Nationalism is not bad in itself and can perhaps be a positive factor in social solidarity," Liberal Stéphane Dion observed in 1996.

Mr. Pitfield's argument was that someone should take the initiative to bring Quebec to sign an amended constitution – and soon, lest those Quebec nationalists who supported federalism and who felt betrayed by the events that followed the referendum become separatists and be lost to Canada forever.

In the 1984 election I offered a vision of federalism that was quite different from that of the previous government, by seeking a mandate, from Quebecers and from all Canadians, for national reconciliation.

Why? Because we were entering challenging times and needed a fully united nation in support of our policies. A myth has emerged – championed by some Liberals and their media and academic acolytes – that we inherited from our predecessors a tranquil nation, free from separatists, and that only reckless actions by the new federal government seeking to make "Faustian bargains" with separatists kicked the sleeping dog awake and provoked all the difficulties that Canada subsequently endured. This myth – a bald-faced lie – has been carefully nurtured by Trudeau's disciples. In fact, the separatist government first elected in 1976 while Pierre Trudeau was prime minister had been re-elected in 1981 while he was in office, and was still in power when we formed the new government on September 17, 1984. So well established had the Parti Québécois become during this period (1976–85) that, even in defeat one year later, they managed to garner 39 per cent of the popular vote and keep solid control of the official opposition in the National Assembly.

In Sept-Îles in August 1984, in a discussion of the Constitution, I insisted that my new government would give first priority to economic renewal. Only then – and after careful preparation – would we turn to the objective of obtaining Quebec's assent to the Constitution: "One thing is certain," I said. "Not one person in Quebec authorized the federal Liberals to take advantage of the confusion that prevailed in Quebec following the referendum in order to ostracize the province constitutionally. My party takes no pleasure in the politically weak position in which these deplorable events have placed Quebec. If Quebec is strong, then Canada is strong.

There is room in Canada for all identities to be affirmed, for all aspirations to be respected, and for all ideals to be pursued. I know that many men and women in Quebec will not be satisfied with mere words. We will have to make commitments and take concrete steps to reach the objective that I have set for myself and that I repeat here: to convince the Quebec National Assembly to give its consent to the new Canadian Constitution with honour and enthusiasm."

I stressed the necessity of establishing precise ground rules and meeting minimal conditions of success in order to avoid another constitutional impasse. Looking back, I believe my caution would have done honour to Mackenzie King.

Indeed, following the election, I had to resist advice that I act precipitously from people such as Jean Chrétien. Recently, Chrétien has said that I "created the whole mess and suddenly, for reasons that were very marginal, reopened the wound" by initiating constitutional negotiations. But in late 1984, less than three months after I was sworn in as prime minister, Chrétien was singing an entirely different tune. At that point, he complained that I was missing a golden opportunity to commence constitutional negotiations, right then, immediately – not a moment should be lost, he argued, in getting Quebec back to the table. On December 18, 1984, *Le Soleil* reported that "Mr. Chrétien believes the new Conservative Prime Minister has a unique chance to succeed where Mr. Trudeau failed. The former minister spoke of a historic occasion presently offered to Mr. Mulroney to correct grievances for which Quebec will always blame Ottawa, if they are not resolved."

I convened the first ministers at Meech Lake on November 14, 1984, and then in Regina in February 1985, not to consider the Constitution but to discuss the economy, trade, energy, and other outstanding issues in federal-provincial relations.

In May 1985, Premier René Lévesque published a proposal for ending Quebec's constitutional isolation. Unfortunately, it would have removed the application of almost all of the Canadian Charter of Rights and Freedoms to Quebec. The rights of Quebecers would derive from a provincial statute, symbolizing a perpetual isolation of Quebecers from the broader Canadian community. From my point of view, the proposal was a nonstarter and I told Lévesque so, and treated it as such. The election in December 1985 of a federalist Liberal government under Robert Bourassa offered much more promise for the future. He had made it part of his election platform to seek constitutional reconciliation with the rest of Canada, and he had put forward conditions for Quebec's adherence to the Constitution. It was not lost on anyone when the new premier announced to tumultuous applause the day of his swearing-in that the Canadian flag was returning to the National Assembly after almost a decade's absence.

Before the ten provincial premiers met in Edmonton in August 1986, with the constitutional position of the new Quebec government high on the agenda, I wrote to the premiers on July 14, 1986, urging, as I had done for more than two years, caution and prudence on this matter. I told them that if first ministers were to take up Premier Bourassa's conditions for reconciliation, we should concentrate on that single objective, leaving more extensive constitutional revision for later. We should adhere to a realistic time frame; we should avoid linkages between the Quebec constitutional issue and other problems that inevitably arise in the management of the federation. Finally, I insisted on sufficient assurances of success on each of Quebec's conditions before undertaking formal negotiations.

When Intergovernmental Affairs Minister Gil Rémillard outlined Quebec's conditions, he added, "Quebec's future is within Canada. We believe in Canadian federalism because, within the federal system, Quebec can be faithful to its history and its unique identity while enjoying conditions favourable to its history and its unique social and cultural development."

I stress this careful approach on my part because it was the exact opposite of the gung-ho, politically motivated, rushed process that Liberal revisionists later ascribed to me. The point is important, because while I was concerned about the 1982 isolation of Quebec, I was also very wary of any initiative likely to produce a new impasse, a new failure that could be construed as a rejection of Quebec. I knew as well that complete indifference or failure to respond to a reasonable federalist proposal from a newly elected Liberal government in Quebec would provide ammunition to the PQ and put Quebec federalists on the defensive.

In any event, on August 12, 1986, the premiers decided to place top priority on the Quebec constitutional issue and on the province's conditions, and requested the start of discussions with Ottawa. They decided to put other constitutional matters such as Senate reform and the fishery on hold until Quebec's proposals could be addressed. Three months later, at a First Ministers' Conference in Vancouver, we reviewed the matter, reaffirmed this decision, and called for intensive discussions to evaluate fully the chances of success of formal negotiations based on Quebec's proposals.

As leader of the opposition, receiving congratulations in the House for my speech on Manitoba language rights

The '84 campaign is off and running

On the campaign trail with Ontario premier Bill Davis behind me

Watching the victory results in Baie-Comeau

On the day my government was sworn in, Mark was worried by all the pomp and ceremony. "Daddy, what's happening to us?"

With Governor General Jeanne Sauvé on the day of a Throne Speech

In the Prime Minister's Office with NDP Leader Ed Broadbent (left) and Liberal Leader John Turner

Meeting three world leaders in 1986. Ronald Reagan in Washington

Deng Xiaoping in Beijing, complete with spittoon

Margaret Thatcher at Mirabel, resistant to my plans for fighting apartheid

At the Commonwealth Meeting in London, 1986, with me, Bob Hawke, Margaret Thatcher, Sir Lynden Pindling, Her Majesty, Kenneth Kaunda, Sonny Ramphal, Rajiv Gandhi, and Robert Mugabe

At the first meeting of La Francophonie in 1986, sitting between François Mitterrand and Robert Bourassa

Two years later, hosting the G-7 Summit in Toronto at Hart House at the University of Toronto

A later G-7 Summit, French-style, at the Louvre

Always a warm welcome on my return home

Speaking to a joint session of the Senate and House in Washington

Ronald Reagan in my parliamentary office with the famous globe Paul Desmarais gave to me

Outside 24 Sussex with François Mitterrand

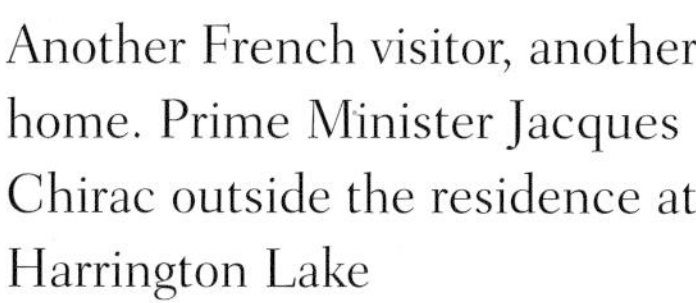

Another French visitor, another home. Prime Minister Jacques Chirac outside the residence at Harrington Lake

With two distinguished visitors to Ottawa

Such discussions at the ministerial and senior-official level went on for around six months, as Lowell Murray criss-crossed the country, tirelessly discussing proposals and procedures that might enable the first ministers to arrive at an acceptable agreement.

In March 1987 federal and provincial deputy ministers met in Ottawa to review Quebec's five conditions and to identify the principles that might form the basis of an agreement. After Senator Lowell Murray and Norman Spector, who was cabinet secretary for federal-provincial relations, briefed me on the officials' meeting, I made the decision: it was time for the politicians to re-engage in the process.

Spector sent me a memo on April 3, advising me that I should view the upcoming First Ministers' Meeting – slated for April 30 at Willson House at Meech Lake – as a full-fledged negotiating session. It was time to "actively pursue an agreement in principle on Quebec's five conditions," he wrote.

A few days later I sent a lengthy telegram to all the premiers. I identified where we already had agreement in principle. It was an impressive list: recognition of Quebec as a distinct society, its involvement in immigration, and the entrenchment of three justices from Quebec on the Supreme Court. In two areas – the amending formula and spending power – there were still questions. I knew, however, that a deal could be reached, as the obstacles were not insurmountable.

"This will be an important meeting," I wrote to the premiers. "It will be the first time since the patriation of the Constitution on April 17, 1982 that all first ministers meet to turn their undivided attention to the constitutional concerns that have led Quebec to abstain from full participation in Canada's constitutional evolution. The task at hand is a Canadian priority: Quebec's abstention is a matter fraught with consequences not only for Quebecers, but for all Canadians . . . On April 30, I would hope that, with the required level of political will, and with flexibility and understanding on all sides, we shall establish the basis for a successful resolution of this issue. Such an outcome could lead to an early and definite action by Parliament and the legislative assemblies so that Canadians might turn their attention to other important constitutional questions."

The weekend before we met at Willson House, I spoke with each current premier and some former premiers as well. I wanted to gauge the situation one more time. Alberta's Peter Lougheed summed up the sentiment of those who had participated in the patriation decisions five years earlier: "We couldn't get an agreement with René [Lévesque] because he, as head of a separatist government, took positions incompatible with a smoothly functioning federal state. We all hoped for the day that we could complete the process, and with the election of Bourassa's federalist government in Quebec, that day has now arrived." Robert Bourassa was quietly confident. I heard some not unexpected concerns from certain premiers, but I knew they could be handled. I was particularly happy after my conversation with David Peterson of Ontario, who was to play a principled and impressive leadership role in constitutional negotiations over the next three years. David was optimistic and blunt. "I'm onside and that was a very skilful federal presentation," he said. "I will be there and be on time. I will call any one of the first ministers if it is required, and I'm going to make a public statement that says most Quebec premiers in recent years haven't wanted to sign the Constitution. Here we have one who does, so let's do a deal with him, because the opportunity may never come again."

1987

4. Inside the Talks at Meech Lake

I DECIDED TO HOLD the meetings some twenty miles out of Ottawa at beautiful Willson House, a recently refurbished government facility on a promontory overlooking Meech Lake. Built in 1907, it is a perfect example of the summer retreats created by members of the upper class during the nineteenth and early twentieth centuries. The federal government had purchased the estate in 1979 with the idea that it could be used as a government retreat in the manner of Camp David, where, for example, Jimmy Carter brought Anwar Sadat of Egypt and Menachem Begin of Israel together to negotiate toward peace in the Middle East.

In 2006, Prime Minister Stephen Harper held an orientation session at Willson House for the new members of his cabinet and their senior advisors. Among those speaking to the group were my former chief of staff Derek Burney and my former Quebec minister Benoît Bouchard. "The last time I was here at Willson House," an emotional Bouchard remarked, "I watched on television, from here, as Meech Lake was killed. I thought my country was finished." There was dead silence around the room.

One of Harper's new ministers, Newfoundland's Loyola Hearn, spoke up. He too had memories. "I was in the Newfoundland House of Assembly that day," Hearn told the hushed audience. "When Clyde Wells learned that three Liberals would be voting for Meech Lake, he cancelled the vote."

"It was incredibly emotional for all present, especially the statement from Bouchard," said Burney, in particular the moment when Bouchard added, "because it was Mulroney, and Meech, that had made me a Canadian."

But that day was almost twenty years in the future as we made our way to Willson House in 1987. Gathering there were Canada's first ministers, representing four different political parties from all of Canada's ten provinces. I assumed the chairmanship, guiding the premiers through a series of six initiatives that came to be known as the Meech Lake Accord. The mood was good, the premiers well informed (thanks to Lowell and his team's superb preparatory work). It soon emerged that a clear desire existed to resolve this question in a reasonable way.

I specifically restricted the room to first ministers only, with officials and advisors thronging the floor below. Only Norman Spector and Oryssia Lennie, assistant deputy minister of intergovernmental affairs in Alberta, were admitted (the latter because Alberta Premier Don Getty was chair of the premiers). According to Spector, there were twin dynamics at work during the meeting: "One, everyone was looking for a deal; two, there were Mulroney's interpersonal and negotiation skills, which were among the finest I've ever seen."

Whether or not that view is accurate, I recall that I began with a brief opening statement that this was a continuation of a mission that had captivated me for most of my life, beginning with the Congrès des affaires canadiennes at Laval twenty-six years earlier. I wanted to know if a consensus could be reached around the table on Quebec's proposals and I proposed discussing the issues one by one, with the easier stuff first.

The meeting moved along crisply. Old hands like Richard Hatfield, John Buchanan, Brian Peckford, and Robert Bourassa – all veterans of earlier constitutional battles – kept their colleagues firmly fixed on an objective that had escaped them in earlier years: the desirability of a unanimous agreement and the powerful signal of unity and stability it would send to the nation and the world.

We began with the Supreme Court and immigration, and quickly reached agreement. As L. Ian MacDonald has recorded in *From Bourassa to Bourassa*: "Ottawa would agree to constitutionalize the Cullen–Couture agreement [on immigration]. On the Supreme Court, which would also entrench Quebec's three members, there was an awkward moment when Bill Vander Zalm amiably suggested that if Quebec could have three seats on the court, all provinces should. Mulroney called for a break, got Vander Zalm off to one side, and explained that a thirty-member Supreme Court was a non-starter, whereupon the premier of British Columbia withdrew his suggestion in the same genial spirit in which he had offered it."

Then came much harder issues – limitations to the federal spending power in areas of exclusive provincial jurisdiction, with an opting-out clause and compensation for dissenting provinces. By the end of the afternoon, however, agreement in principle was reached on this issue, as well as on one that I had brought forward: provincial involvement in Senate appointments. I felt this concept would particularly appeal to western Canada, and it was a definite concession. While Ottawa would still make the ultimate decision, the proposal would dilute the PMO's unilateral authority by inviting the provinces to submit for consideration lists of prominent citizens for appointments rather than the traditional and highly partisan patronage system that has long been deplored by Canadian taxpayers. The proposal was conceived and agreed to as a temporary measure until a complete Senate reform could be negotiated; meanwhile, it was to be a demonstration of Ottawa's good faith, since it meant giving up the patronage instrument as the prime minister's personal prerogative.

We were gaining momentum, but it all nearly came off the rails when Bourassa was advised that there had been a leak of his budget in Quebec City and that a crisis was developing in the National Assembly. Gil Rémillard has written about how coolly Bourassa handled the crisis. The premier stepped out of our meeting to find that Gérard D. Lévesque, his minister of finance, was on the phone preparing to resign because his budget was about to be leaked on the CTV evening news. "There's only one thing you can do," Bourassa responded. "Have the legislature convened and present your budget tonight at 8 p.m."

With that crisis averted, Bourassa did not rush back to join our session. He paused to talk to Rémillard, saying, "Gérard's call came at a good time. Brian and David are doing a good job, but it's really difficult. I'd rather not go back in there for a few minutes. They'll feel more comfortable talking without me. You and I can chat for a bit."

Eventually, Bourassa rejoined us, returning with a smile to proclaim, "All in a day's work!"

That was a seminal moment, because Bourassa's attitude and his decision to remain rather than to rush home sent a message of reassurance and authority to the other premiers. While Bourassa was out of the room, the conversation – but not the negotiations – continued: "For me," I said, "the issue isn't 'What does Quebec want?' I have always found that offensive. The issue is 'What does Quebec need?' so that it can sign the Constitution honourably and we can put all this behind us." I then decided to call a break for a quick dinner.

On the staircase, Richard Hatfield, the dean of the premiers and a seventeen-year veteran of constitutional wrangling, took one look at the beehive of provincial advisors and officials swarming about below and said, "Get them the fuck out of here. We'll never get a unanimous agreement on anything because they'll be picking flyshit out of pepper till Kingdom Come."

After dinner we resumed our deliberations. Western premiers Don Getty, Grant Devine, and Bill Vander Zalm (apart from the Supreme Court incident) performed strongly. Getty in particular, as chair, was balanced, fair, and effective in all his interventions. Howard Pawley of Manitoba was somewhat more hesitant because his province had insisted on a special provision requiring parliamentary hearings into the amended Constitution.

David Peterson from Ontario, Canada's largest province, and Joe Ghiz from P.E.I., Canada's smallest, both shone throughout the day. Peterson quickly assumed the avuncular role formerly played so well by his predecessors John Robarts and Bill Davis, providing thoughtful, generous commentary and leadership. Ghiz spoke eloquently about the benefits of a fully united Canada, saying, "I want my grandchildren to say of me that today I contributed to cementing the great Canadian adventure that began in Charlottetown. Until Quebec has signed on, this Constitution and this country are incomplete."

By ten o'clock at night, following many hours of debate, we had reached agreement. As I walked back into the room after conferring with my staff, the ten premiers began to applaud. It was one of the most touching gestures I was to receive in nine years as prime minister. I was deeply moved, and remain so until this day.

Then it was time to face the media. With the premiers standing behind me, I read a statement that said, in part: "What you have now is a whole country as opposed to a part of a country. I am profoundly convinced that, as a result of today's discussions, the bonds of Confederation will be strengthened and the unity of our people will be enhanced."

The premiers were generous in their assessment, both of the final product and of the careful manner in which the federal government had helped bring it about. "I think it's a superb time for Canada," Don Getty said. "The prime minister really was a supreme chairman." "It was a very positive meeting and a very important breakthrough," exulted Howard Pawley. "We want to bring Quebec into the fold and get on with other issues that confront the nation," said Joe Ghiz, echoing a comment heard from all the other leaders. "That was one of the rare times I saw Robert Bourassa deeply moved," Gil Rémillard recalled later. "He had tears in his eyes."

Bourassa was emotional when he spoke to the press as well. "It is a historic breakthrough for Quebec as a Canadian partner," he said. Richard Hatfield, who had been at the table in 1981–82, graciously praised my role. "He kept insisting that we think of Canada as a whole and it worked."

As I looked up at the media I could see tears welling up in the eyes of Normand Girard from *Le Journal de Montréal*, a veteran of decades of constitutional argument whom I had first known at Laval. "Bravo, Brian," he whispered as I walked by. "Enfin. Enfin!" (At last!)

I drove back to 24 Sussex with Bernard Roy, who had played a vital role in managing the Quebec relationship during the leadup to the formal meeting. As we rolled through the Gatineau Hills in the darkness, he said, "Congratulations, Brian, this is truly a historic night." Then speaking as a son of Quebec City who had lived with the sharp divisions and bitterness of the referendum debates, he quietly added, "Now perhaps we can put the malice behind us and build a new Canada."

"Maybe, Bernard," I responded, by now bone-tired. "Maybe."

From the residence I called Governor General Sauvé and explained the highlights of the agreement. She was thrilled and said, "Trudeau pushed all of those ideas in varying forms and I believe they are in the mainstream of modern political thought in Canada today."

Soon after, some of her dinner guests, including our close friends Jackie and Paul Desmarais, arrived at 24 Sussex for a celebratory glass of champagne. I was excited and happy but not exultant. As the guests sipped Dom Perignon, I stuck to soda water. Maybe it was over. Maybe. I knew that every provincial parliament still had to approve the deal.

As the media of the day have recorded, Meech was greeted with joy and relief across the country, and saluted as an act of nation building, endorsed by all eleven governments and by the three parties in the House of Commons. "Prime Minister Brian Mulroney and Quebec Premier Robert Bourassa deserve particular credit for this week's achievement, but all the first ministers acted creatively and wisely in the Canadian interest," a *Globe and Mail* editorial on May 2, 1987 read. "If their political will survives the next several weeks of local review, we may say that Canada has left yesterday's agenda behind and can move more united to meet the future."

When I entered the House of Commons the next day, members applauded as they never had before. John Turner crossed the floor to shake my hand. The galleries were full as I took to my feet. I was to have no greater moment in the Commons during my years as prime minister.

"I am honoured to inform the House that at about 10 p.m. last night the premiers and I reached unanimous agreement in principle on a constitutional package which will allow Quebec to rejoin the Canadian constitutional family," I said. "This agreement enhances the Confederation bargain and strengthens, I believe, the federal nature of Canada. Although it remains to be formalized, it represents in the judgment of first ministers of all political stripes, from all areas of the country, a historic accomplishment . . . Mr. Speaker, Sir Wilfrid Laurier once said, 'The governing motive of my life has been to harmonize the diverse elements which compose our country.' Surely that is the wish of every member, on all sides of this House. This is our policy. That is our purpose – building a stronger Canada for all Canadians."

Both Opposition Leader John Turner and NDP Leader Broadbent spoke eloquently, putting, as they always did on issues of national unity, country above party.

Over the next few days the response was extremely positive. One of Canada's most distinguished public servants and Liberal politicians, the Honourable J.W. Pickersgill, spoke of "the miracle of Meech Lake," and said, "On the eve of that meeting, I would not have given the first ministers one chance in ten of success. I was excited and delighted when they reached accord . . . once I read the document, I was satisfied it met the requirements of Quebec without in any way reducing the jurisdiction of the Parliament of Canada."

Roger Tassé, the principal author of the Charter of Rights and Freedoms, and a former deputy minister of justice and senior advisor on constitutional affairs to both Prime Minister Trudeau and Justice Minister Jean Chrétien, has said of the Meech Lake Accord, "The text has stood up to analysis. It is undoubtedly not perfect but its quality is certainly equal to that of the 1982 amendments . . . in this case, the product is a major constitutional accord that is decisive for the country's future, that completes the unfinished business of 1982, and that brings Quebec back into the constitutional fold; an accord that was signed by eleven Canadian first ministers – an unprecedented accomplishment."

The next day I received a letter from Senator Eugene Forsey, one of Canada's most celebrated constitutional scholars, appointed to the Upper Chamber by his friend Pierre Trudeau. "The accord is an immense achievement," he wrote.

> Frankly, I did not think it possible to get an agreement, except perhaps at a price which would be too heavy to pay. You got it, and, though there are some things I'd have preferred otherwise, and

> though the final form of the agreement may raise difficulties, I think the price is reasonable. I must add, as I have already said to a TV interviewer, a very great part of the success is due to your special gifts and long experience as a negotiator. I doubt if anyone else now in public life could have brought off this fact. The undertaking to appoint senators from lists submitted by the provinces is, in my opinion, a stroke of genius. Most of the proposals for Senate reform are, in my opinion, totally impractical. Here's one that is perfectly practicable, not even requiring legislation; and it will give us a Senate more representative, less partisan, less burdened by overwhelming majorities one way or the other, and likely to be more effective in promoting regional interests. It is a real and important Senate reform.

I continued to be cautious in my optimism. Lowell Murray and I agreed that we still had a long way to go. "I won't break out the champagne until the royal proclamation, but I think it's a go," Murray told the press that week.

On May 11, I spoke again in the Commons about the accord. All three parties united and passed a motion supporting the accord in the House that day. While preparing my speech I reviewed my senior-year thesis, "*The Politics of Quebec*," which I had written nearly thirty years earlier while studying at StFX. I ended my speech with a metaphor I'd also used back then. "Succeeding generations of Canadians have sought a more harmonious accommodation between our two principal language communities," I told the House. "Quebec's first premier after Confederation, Pierre Chauveau, compared Canada to the double staircase of the Château de Chambord. 'English and French,' he said, 'we climb by a double flight of stairs toward the destinies reserved for us on this continent, without knowing one another, without meeting each other, without even seeing each other except on the landing of politics.'"

Through Meech Lake, I hoped to help end this sad reality in our own time. The destiny of French and English, more than one hundred years after Chauveau, was now more fully bound together thanks in part to the compromises inherent in the Meech Lake Accord.

NDP MP Lorne Nystrom had a parliamentary page drop a note on my desk at the conclusion of my speech. "Just a note of congratulations," he wrote. "There is certainly a different atmosphere here on the Constitution than in 1981."

While the country was responding with generosity and goodwill, a former prime minister was secretly planning an attack designed to sabotage Meech Lake. And why? "Simple," said Francis Fox, one of Trudeau's former ministers, later. "He couldn't stand to see Brian Mulroney succeed where he had failed."

Astonishingly, most of the provisions that Pierre Trudeau later found so objectionable had been proposed (and some in even more radical versions) by himself and earlier federal governments in previous constitutional negotiations. You will find these proposals, in one form or another, in the Fulton–Favreau formula of the 1960s, in the federal-provincial constitutional discussions of 1968–71 and 1978–79, in the Victoria formula of 1971, in the federal government's Bill C-60 of 1978, or in the federal proposals during the negotiations of September 1980.

So, what did Meech actually involve? Well, it was a pretty straightforward constitutional agreement. Most of it had been under discussion for twenty-five years. The accord proposed to incorporate six provisions into the Constitution. Here they are, with Trudeau's previous position on them duly recorded:

1. Quebec would be viewed as a "distinct society within Canada," and linguistic duality across the country would be affirmed as a "fundamental characteristic" of Confederation. (At a First Ministers' Conference in September 1980, Trudeau was willing to accept these wordings: "Recognizing the distinct French-speaking society centred in though not confined to Quebec" or "Recognizing the distinctive character of Quebec society with its French-speaking majority." And in 1979 he said, as reported by the *Globe and Mail*, "I see a Quebec coming out of its referendum to continue building, within Canada, its own secure and distinct society, the equal of any in the world.")
2. The use of the federal spending power would be limited in areas of future shared-cost programs, and in areas of exclusive provincial jurisdiction. (In 1969, Trudeau offered to subject Parliament's capacity to make conditional grants to the provinces to a "national consensus" consent mechanism involving regional vetoes along the lines of what became the Victoria amending formula. He was also willing to provide unconditional compensation to non-participating provinces without the requirement

[agreed upon in the Meech Lake Accord] for the province to carry on a program compatible with the national objectives. In 1978, he was again willing to subject the spending power to a consent mechanism, but would have gone beyond shared-cost programs to include direct payments to institutions and individuals, including tax credits.)

3. The concept of unanimity, already established in article S.41 of the Constitution, would be extended to several other areas in regard to the amending formula. (Trudeau generally favoured the Victoria formula of 1971, which would have given a veto to Parliament, Quebec, and Ontario – but not to other provinces. In his letter of March 31, 1976 to the premiers, Trudeau suggested unilateral patriation of the Constitution and, in such circumstances, indicated a willingness to live with unanimity as the amending formula for all major constitutional amendments. In 1981, he accepted the "Gang of Eight" amending formula: obligatory compensation to provinces that opted out of an amendment related to education or other cultural matters that transferred provincial legislative jurisdiction to Parliament. At the same time, unanimity was recognized as the formula to amend provisions regarding certain matters such as the monarchy, the amending formula, the use of French and English, and the composition of the Supreme Court.)
4. The federal government would alone choose senators from lists of candidates submitted by provinces. (In 1969, the Trudeau government offered to allow the provinces to choose a proportion of the nominated senators. In Bill C-60 in 1978, the Trudeau government proposed the "House of the Federation." Half of the members would have been indirectly elected by the parties represented in the provincial legislatures and the other half by the parties represented in the House of Commons.)
5. The federal government would alone choose Supreme Court justices from lists of candidates submitted by the provinces. (At Victoria in 1971, Trudeau supported a very complex entrenchment of the Supreme Court in the Victoria Charter. In 1978, in Bill C-60, the Trudeau government again agreed to provincial participation in the nomination of Supreme Court justices. A concurrent veto could be exercised, but if there was a deadlock,

it would be broken by a nominating council set up along the lines agreed to in Victoria in 1971. In 1980, the Trudeau government was willing to support a proposal requiring provincial consent to federal nominations to the Supreme Court. All proposals by the Trudeau government would have provided for a guaranteed proportion of judges from Quebec.)

6. Immigration agreements between Ottawa and the provinces would be constitutionalized. (Trudeau's government negotiated and signed the Cullen–Couture agreement with Quebec.)

In the foregoing, I have condensed Trudeau's previous agreements with the terms of the Meech Lake Accord, but the pattern is absolutely clear.

1987

5. The Trudeau Factor

IT IS TIME TO talk about my relations, as prime minister, with my predecessor and constitutional adversary, Pierre Trudeau. Soon after my election, Trudeau came by to visit and said I could count on his advice on matters like the Constitution. I had long been impressed by the elaborate courtesies extended to former American presidents by their successors, "out of respect for the office," even when their earlier relations were not warm. I was determined to act in the same fashion toward my predecessor.

During the 1984 campaign I had promised a commission of inquiry into the Petro-Canada financial transactions. I was aware of substantive allegations about prominent Liberals – including some close to the former prime minister – making millions on the deal when Petro-Canada was set up. Upon reflection, I declined to proceed when it became clear that Trudeau would be forced to testify, thereby becoming caught up in a media circus that could badly hurt him and his family. Because I believed it would be wrong to drag a former prime minister through the mud, I cancelled plans for the inquiry. This decision infuriated Auditor-General Kenneth Dye, who initiated legal action to try to force my hand in this matter.

In 1985, at the Nassau Commonwealth Heads of Government meeting, I proposed Pierre Trudeau for membership in the three-member Eminent Persons Group on Apartheid in South Africa.

I also commissioned a portrait of Trudeau's three beautiful children by Atlantic Canadian artist Tom Forrestall, as a parting gift from the government. For this, Trudeau wrote me a lovely letter of thanks in 1986, which I received following an official visit to Asia. "When I returned from China at the end of April – where I preceded you by a few days and where, I am told, you put in a good word for me – I had the great pleasure of finding your letter of April 29 and Forrestall's wonderful painting of my sons," Trudeau wrote. "No doubt I should be thanking the Canadian public for this great show of generosity, and I am happy to do so through you.

"But I am certain that you, and quite likely Mrs. Mulroney, are responsible for selecting the type of gift, the artist, and the subjects that he has rendered so beautifully. I am deeply grateful, and I wish only that your children bring you as much joy as mine have brought me. Which goes to show that even life at 24 Sussex leads to happy tomorrows."

When Trudeau joined the Montreal law firm of Heenan Blaikie, I called him on his first day at work to wish him and his new partners well, and to jokingly comment that in light of his presence they were all personae gratae with the new government.

When Trudeau was named Companion of the Order of Canada in 1985, Mila and I offered to host a dinner for him, his family, and his friends at 24 Sussex. He politely chose to make other arrangements at Rideau Hall. When his good friend, Swedish Prime Minister Olaf Palme, was assassinated, I called to invite Trudeau to head the Canadian delegation to the state funeral. And when he was named a "Grand Montréalais," Mila and I made the trip to Montreal for an evening in his honour, to underline his contribution to Quebec and Canada.

It was against this background that I called Trudeau a few days after the Meech Lake Accord had been reached, to offer him a full briefing. I said, "Pierre, we've got a month or so in which we can modify this. I'd like to have the benefit of your counsel. I'm going to ask Norman Spector and André Burelle [Trudeau's former speechwriter and advisor] to brief you, and after you've had a chance to take a look at it, I'd like to have your views."

"I look forward to seeing them," Trudeau said, to which I replied, "Let me hear from you."

The briefing lasted three hours. Trudeau was courteous, although he expressed some reservations to my two emissaries.

I never heard from him again.

On May 26, 1987, Mila and I attended a gala dinner in Toronto honouring Cardinal Emmett Carter on the fiftieth anniversary of his ordination. Every dignitary in town was there, including Opposition Leader John Turner and Premier David Peterson. At the predinner reception I spotted Trudeau off in a corner. Mila and I went over and greeted our fellow Montrealer prior to entering the hall. He was uneasy and somewhat reticent in his response, but had every chance to speak privately with us, had he chosen to do so. As it was, we merely exchanged courtesies before lining up to file in with the head table guests.

The next morning, on May 27, the thunderbolt struck: a vitriolic front-page story in the *Toronto Star* (always a faithful Trudeau supporter) and *La Presse*. As a splenetic personal attack by a former prime minister against a governing prime minister, replete with vicious insults and specious argument, it was unrivalled in Canadian history.

After telling readers that the Constitution he had left behind was so perfect that it should last a thousand years, he struck:

> Alas, only one eventuality hadn't been foreseen: that one day the Government of Canada might fall into the hands of a weakling. It has now happened. And the Right Honourable Brian Mulroney, PC, MP, with the complicity of 10 provincial premiers, has already entered into history as the author of a constitutional document which – if it is accepted by the people and their legislators – will render the Canadian state totally impotent. That would destine it, given the dynamics of power, to eventually be governed by eunuchs. . . .
>
> That is why they are once again making common cause with the nationalists to demand special status for Quebec. That bunch of snivellers should simply have been sent packing and been told to stop having tantrums like spoiled adolescents. But our current political leaders lack courage. By rushing to the rescue of the unhappy losers, they hope to gain votes in Quebec; in reality, they are only flaunting their political stupidity and their ignorance of the demographic data regarding nationalism. It would be difficult to imagine a more total bungle.

The implications were clear. Trudeau was strong and courageous; the premiers and I were not. Captain Canada had arrived to save the country, reporting for duty.

One of the great joys of being prime minister was my association with Canada's military men and women, whose heroic conduct over decades has inspired much admiration at home and around the world. In my mind's eye I can still see a seventy-five-year-old George Hees, war hero and former minister of veterans affairs, standing ramrod straight beside Canada's Silver Star mother on November 11 at the cenotaph, the freezing rain dripping down his face as he took the salute on behalf of all the courageous Canadians who had fought and died for freedom.

I have also always regarded those who fought against the Nazis in the Second World War as particularly noble, because in my judgment the Holocaust was the ultimate desecration of humanity. With the Nazis openly persecuting and then slaughtering 6 million Jews, thank God so many young men and women summoned the courage to fight and overcome this evil force that had infected an entire nation, and that was threatening to exterminate an entire people and to enslave so many other nations. From British Columbia all the way east, out of a population of 11 million, one million young Canadians and Newfoundlanders, sensing the danger to our fundamental human values, signed up and shipped off to do battle with a vile and powerful enemy.

Pierre Trudeau was not among them. Although in his mid twenties, well educated, well informed, and in excellent health, he declined to serve. While compatriots like Pierre Sévigny, Guy Charbonneau, and Paul Sauvé were fighting off Nazis on the battlefields of Europe in the summer of 1943, Trudeau and his friends were fighting off black flies in Outremont. (It is false to suggest, as some bigots have, that all young French Canadians did likewise. In fact, thousands served bravely throughout the war, in all of its most dangerous theatres, and many were among the 45,000 Canadians who gave their lives.)

I was shocked and disappointed – but not altogether surprised – to learn in a book published in June 2006 by two of his close friends that during this same period young Trudeau wrote and acted in an anti-Semitic play, spoke strongly in favour of fascism, stated that England and Germany were equally responsible for the war, and urged Quebecers to resist conscription and to prepare to ethnically cleanse the province if need be, to ensure the creation of a pure French Catholic state.

"I am a French Canadian and I am not in favour of conscription," he wrote in 1941, as quoted in Max and Monique Nemni's prize-winning book, *Young Trudeau*. "I am not only against conscription, but I am also against mobilization, against participation, against rearming, against aid to the belligerents. I am against the war. Is that quite clear now, or are you again going to play on words?" At that time, Nazi jackboots occupied almost all of Europe.

Speaking of Canadians in favour of conscription to fight the Nazis, he was vitriolic. "The traitors should be impaled alive: we'll say no more about it, but let's not forget," Trudeau said at a campaign rally during an Outremont by-election in November 1942. "If Outremont is so infamous that it elects [the federalist candidate], and if because of Outremont conscription for overseas service comes into effect . . . I beg of you to eviscerate all the damned bourgeois of Outremont who voted [for the candidate who believed in Canada's participation in the war] just to serve their own interests."

Apparently as much in sorrow as in anger, the authors also wrote the following: "Neither in his published articles nor in his private notes did Trudeau give the slightest sign of opposition to the hateful prejudices so prevalent in his world. All told, in comparison to what others were saying and writing, we find that Trudeau could be criticized less for his anti-Jewish writing than for his silence, for his lack of any critical reaction to all the anti-Jewish tirades made by his peers, his teachers, and by the authors and the 'heroes' for whom he expressed so much admiration."

Trudeau carefully kept secret from Canadians this part of his past (not least from the voters in Mount Royal, a riding with a large Jewish presence, which elected him six times). His official biographer, former Liberal MP and respected historian John English, also published his first volume – *Citizen of the World: The Life of Pierre Trudeau* – in 2006. He too examined Trudeau's activities during the 1942 by-election, writing the following: "He minimized the German threat, ridiculed the King government, and, according to *Le Devoir*, said that 'he feared the peaceful invasion of immigrants more than the armed invasion by the enemy.' The French of North America would fight when threatened, just as they had fought against the Iroquois; 'today,' he scorned, 'it is against other savages.' Then Trudeau stated dramatically: the government had irresponsibly declared war even though North America faced no direct threat of an invasion, 'at the moment when Hitler had not yet had his lightning victories.' The newspaper quoted his dramatic conclusion in full: 'Citizens of Quebec, don't be content to whine. Long live the flag of liberty. Enough of band-aids; bring on the revolution.'"

Professor English called the speech "demagogic," and said it "seemed to equate the King government with savages, minimized the Nazi threat, and attacked immigrants (who, in Montreal, were mainly Jewish)."

Although much of the free world, including Canada, recognized the destructive and criminal nature of the Nazi war machine, Trudeau did not. In fact, as the Nemnis have shown, he was indifferent to its ravages and opposed to enlightened policies designed to wipe out the curse of Nazism.

Pierre Trudeau, Captain Canada? I think not.

Trudeau had his own impressive virtues and significant accomplishments, but none qualified him to moralize and insist that his vision of Canada – and his alone – deserved to prevail. The man who had surrendered to the provinces the most sweeping concession in history – the notwithstanding clause, for which he still didn't get a unanimous agreement – was reproaching others for the exercise of honourable compromise of the sort on which the nation was built. "Bunglers," "cowards," "snivellers" – Trudeau knew whereof he spoke.

In a later essay, "Hedgehog or Fox," Bob Rae got right to the point:

> What Trudeau was never prepared to admit was that it was the concession on the notwithstanding clause that gave more powers to Quebec than anything proposed in either the Meech or Charlottetown accords . . . Trudeau's lack of generosity to his successors reflects a churlishness that hardly does him proud.

People abroad noticed this, too. A few years later, when Mila and I were strolling with President Mitterrand through a small forest near Vimy Ridge prior to a ceremony to honour Canadian bravery during the First World War, we discussed Meech. I had a question: "François, what is the proper French meaning of the word *pleutre* (an archaic word Trudeau had used to attack me in the French version of his article)?"

"Well, Brian, it is a very insulting and demeaning word implying deep cowardice," Mitterrand replied. "But Trudeau would be very familiar with it," he said with a sad smile, "because it was frequently used in wartime France to describe those who lacked the courage to join the Resistance and fight the Nazis."

Following his receipt of the copy of Trudeau's letter, *La Presse* editor Michel Roy called the former PM and urged him to soften his personal attacks, warning him that they were "needlessly insulting and mean spirited." Trudeau refused. "That's what I intended them to be," he said.

Some thirteen years later I sat with Mila in Notre-Dame Basilica in Montreal at Trudeau's state funeral, listening to Trudeau's son, Justin, eulogize his father. Justin, a fine young man who is now a politician and a public figure, stated that his father once said, "Justin, never attack the individual.

We can be in total disagreement with someone without denigrating them as a consequence." Clearly, Justin had not read his father's response to my invitation to review Meech and call me back.

Opposition Leader John Turner reacted swiftly to the attack: "The article speaks to a different perception of Canada, a Canada of the past that has been dealt with and in many ways rejected by the people of Canada." Lowell Murray responded in print for the government. Trudeau, he wrote, is like a general "who longs for war during peacetime," and he reminded Canadians that "the quiet strength of those who foster peace is no less necessary for a country than the panache of the warriors."

But Trudeau had strong constitutional credentials and still had a constituency, especially among English Canadians, many of whom were attracted by the idea that Quebec – Canada's only majority French-speaking province – in spite of its severe minority status in Canada and North America, needed no further constitutional underpinnings to ensure its cultural and linguistic security and survival in Canada.

His admirers in the media – and he had many – were not silent either. Back in 1987, before the 500-channel universe, there were really only two English and French TV networks in Canada. The Ottawa bureau of the CBC was the most dominant player on the Hill, with the largest budget, number of correspondents, and influence. It was headed by an expatriate English-speaking Montrealer, Elly Alboim who, as national political editor and Ottawa bureau chief, set the agenda for political coverage there and, by extension, for many others in the press gallery. He was also deeply infatuated with Pierre Trudeau.

At a conference at the University of Calgary in 1987, Alboim delivered his view of Meech Lake. His astonishingly frank comments were later published in the book *Meech Lake and Canada: Perspectives from the West*. Alboim's comments did not go unnoticed. Professor John Meisel of Queen's University, a former chairman of the Canadian Radio-television and Telecommunications Commission and a veteran political scientist, examined them after Meech Lake had been sabotaged. Professor Meisel noted that Alboim shed some startling light on how he and his colleagues saw the Meech Lake Accord and how they approached the task of reporting it during its early phase in 1987. "Mr. Alboim, apparently knowing a great deal more than anyone else, was dead certain that the constitutional exercise was merely a personal ploy by Mulroney to make himself look better than Trudeau," Meisel wrote in his searing essay "Mirror? Searchlight? Interloper?: The Media and Meech," in the book *After Meech Lake: Lessons for the Future* (1991):

> The welfare of the country, in this view, was irrelevant and absent from the governments' minds. According to Alboim: "This was a highly political and highly cynical exercise that had very, very little to do with the re-constitutionalizing of Canada. It had very, very little to do with the final content of the document. The motivations were clear from the outset. Brian Mulroney needed, for his own purposes, to establish that he could do in Québec what Pierre Trudeau could not. *That was, to my mind, the sole motivation for the federal initiative*. I have no illusion that there was any vision of Canada, or any deeply felt sense of loss about Québec not signing the constitutional agreement in 1982. I think we were engaged in a highly political and partisan exercise by the Prime Minister. I think the motivations of many of the Anglo premiers were equally clear. They were dragged into a process that they did not want to participate in. They were blackmailed into a process they had difficulty staying out of and they were determined to capture as much as they could in exchange for their acceptance. There was no selflessness, the premiers walked in with an agenda, a very clear one and they knew that they could get and they got it. This wasn't a nation-building exercise."

According to Alboim himself, he believed there was something inherently wrong if the federal government and all ten provinces agreed, as they did at Willson House. He said he then sprang into action, utilizing the resources of Canada's public broadcaster: "When confronted with that sort of reality plus a clear understanding of the fragility of the deal and the rush to text and passage, we began a search for dissent . . . you look for someone who will question the deal. We went to Chrétien, we went to Romanow. We looked for constitutional experts. I looked around the country, searching for people who were going to say in that first week or two, boy, there's something wrong here."

Elly Alboim delivered this objective and fair-minded speech about the prime minister of Canada and his government, and his own role in reporting on their actions, in 1987, and returned to Ottawa into the welcoming arms of the CBC without, as far as we know, any reprimand. When the Liberals returned to office in 1993, few were surprised when Alboim left the CBC for a lucrative career as a lobbyist whose company prospered mightily under the Chrétien and Martin regimes – sometimes on the basis of untendered contracts from the Department of Finance – and who was last seen providing public relations counsel to the hapless Allan Rock.

I will leave the last word on Alboim to Professor Meisel. "Two features of Mr. Alboim's account are, no doubt, responsible for my reaction being so very negative: I find it frightening that anyone would feel so sure of himself in his reading of a government's and prime minister's motives – never mind that I find the reading to be ludicrous – that he would feel confident enough to plunge the medium for which he is responsible into the political process with the aim of offsetting the perceived cynicism and irresponsibility of the government. Second, I am deeply troubled by any journalist in possession, so to speak, of an immensely powerful instrument of opinion formation arrogating so critical a role to himself or herself, without being in any way accountable to anyone. My anxiety is all the more acute when the instrument is the public broadcaster."

Pierre Trudeau's splenetic attack on the Meech Lake Accord split the Liberal Party, particularly in Ontario, and put severe pressure on John Turner and David Peterson. As a Quebecer attacking Meech, he made it acceptable to denigrate and oppose the agreement in English Canada. Bob Rae put it well: "Trudeau made anti-French bigotry respectable."

The fact that Trudeau had approved of or personally offered provisions similar to Meech in the past seemed not to matter. The fact that many of his arguments were specious, while others were demonstrably false, seemed irrelevant. The master had spoken. It was going to be his way or no way at all. The "snivellers" could not be allowed to succeed where he had failed. He was going to make perfection the enemy of the good.

Trudeau was relentless in promoting his views of Meech, however hyperbolic and bizarre. He was later to tell a Montreal audience that the distinct society clause "would give the government of this society the power to say: 'Well, let's deport a couple of hundred thousand of non-French-speaking Quebecers . . . We have a right to expel people, certainly to shut their traps up if they think they can speak English in public.'" This, of course, was a completely false statement. It was also quite a remarkable one, coming from the architect of the notwithstanding clause, which was used to override the Supreme Court on the English signage issue, and from the man who imposed the *War Measures Act* during Quebec's 1970 October Crisis.

But it soon became clear that, as a result of this attack and the fallout from his many television appearances, Trudeau, who remained a revered figure among many members of his own party, had had a major impact upon the national debate. To be fair, Trudeau was not alone in his opposition to Meech. As most of the country celebrated this major step toward constitutional unity, Pierre-Marc Johnson, now Parti Québécois leader, denounced me and ridiculed the agreement, calling it the "Meech Lake monster" and adding, incongruously, that I "would sell the Yukon for twenty-five dollars."

Outside Quebec, Trudeau was fanning the flames, saying that the province had been given too much. Inside Quebec, his new allies the sovereigntists were denouncing the agreement because, they said, Quebec didn't get enough. In fact, the separatists knew only too well that Bourassa, by signing the Constitution, as he now proposed to do, would deprive the Parti Québécois of its main emotional assault weapon, to be used in any future referendum: namely, that the 1982 constitutional agreement was illegitimate and illegal because it did not bear Quebec's signature or the ratification of the National Assembly.

They knew that a ratified Meech Lake Accord would be lethal to the separatist cause because it would mean that Quebec had voluntarily affirmed its constitutional adherence to Canada. It therefore had to be destroyed, and the separatists happily joined forces with Trudeau to do whatever they could to sabotage it. Of course, when they eventually succeeded, they cried crocodile tears for Meech, saying that its death in the legislatures of Newfoundland and Manitoba proved that the English provinces were hostile to Quebec, which could never get justice in Canada, and that separation was the only remaining option.

Later, the absence of this agreement hurt us all badly in the referendum campaign of 1995. After assuming the leadership of the campaign from Jacques Parizeau, Lucien Bouchard jettisoned the existing campaign strategy and zeroed in on the "illegitimate Trudeau–Chrétien Constitution of '82" that, within days, as Quebecers absorbed the argument, became the constitution that "Quebec neither signed nor wanted." Support for separatism soared, and we came within an eyelash of losing the country.

Gordon Robertson, former Clerk of the Privy Council, was stinging: "Nothing, I think, in Canadian history rivals the irresponsibility Trudeau, a former prime minster, displayed in coming out of retirement to destroy the only prospect of an agreement that would bring Quebec into willing acceptance of the constitution that he himself had admitted was the calculated result of a 'coup de force.'"

Stéphane Dion, who at the time was an influential professor at the Université de Montréal (he later became an effective minister of intergovernmental affairs in the Chrétien government, and the Liberal leader after Paul Martin), had the final word: "After Meech we would have had stability for a very long time. And the worst constitutional error in the history of Canada is probably Mr. Trudeau's campaign against Meech." In June 2007, in an interview printed in the journal *Policy Options*, Dion took this argument one step further when he said, "Mr. Trudeau was wrong in saying that Meech would destroy Canada . . . We'll never know for sure on this issue, but I'm confident . . . that if Meech had passed, I would be a university professor today and we would not have had the second referendum."

1987

6. Showdown at the Langevin Block

As planned, the first ministers met for a followup meeting on June 2–3, 1987. I specify the two dates because we met for almost twenty consecutive hours, from mid-morning of one day to dawn of the next, sitting around a great oval table in the fourth floor boardroom of the Langevin Block.

"Room 414 North of the Langevin Block is a cheerless conference room, with narrow shafts of light filtered through fortress-style windows below the high ceiling," wrote L. Ian MacDonald in *From Bourassa to Bourassa*.

> During the later Trudeau years, it had served as a cabinet room while the formal cabinet chamber in the Centre Block was undergoing renovation. The building has at least a distant constitutional connection, in the sense that it is named for a Father of Confederation, Hector Langevin, a Quebec journalist who would serve as Public Works minister in Sir John A. Macdonald's cabinet, but was later forced to resign in disgrace over a patronage scandal. The Langevin is by no means one of the capital's more splendid buildings, but it is perhaps the most important. The first two floors house the Prime Minister's Office, the third and fourth floors the Privy Council Office. The two most powerful central agencies of the federal government are located under one roof, the real seat of power in the capital. The prime minister's second-floor office was directly below the conference room on the northwest corner of the building.

All of us at the table knew that finalizing a new deal for Canada was not going to be easy. Premier Peterson of Ontario in particular was under severe pressure from the Trudeauite wing of the party in Toronto, and his usual urbane demeanour and blithe manner had been replaced by deep concentration.

We began work on hammering out the precise wording of a legal text, something quite different and more exacting than the agreement in principle signed at Meech. The mindset of the key players seemed to be the following:

- Premier Pawley had been facing (and perhaps also inviting) pressure against the recognition of Quebec's distinct society as well as pressure from aboriginal groups. He also had concerns on the spending power clause, but was pulling in the opposite direction there from Premier Bourassa.
- Premier Peterson had publicly discouraged any renegotiation of the Meech Lake agreement, which he repeatedly referred to as a "fragile construction." Privately, he had tried to discourage Premier Bourassa from calling it into question. He was feeling pressure from certain middle-class and ethnic segments of Ontario, and had agreed to hold legislative hearings when he got around to tabling the resolution; he would be, I knew, a potential bridge builder between premiers Pawley and Bourassa.
- Brian Peckford of Newfoundland was a strong enthusiast for the accord, and a constant, vigorous voice in the debate.
- Premiers Getty, Vander Zalm, and Devine were solid supporters: their support had actually been strengthened by Trudeau's intervention, but they would have reacted negatively if Premier Bourassa were to attempt to reopen the Meech Lake Accord.
- Premiers Hatfield, Buchanan, and Ghiz were ready to support me fully at the meeting.

I began the meeting at ten o'clock by thanking the premiers for their public support of the Meech Lake agreement. I reflected on public discussion of the agreement and invited comment on reaction in the provinces. I noted that I was aware that all first ministers had faced pressures since April 30, but said that this, in my opinion, did not justify reopening the agreement. I outlined my view that two issues had to be dealt with on a priority basis – namely, the distinct society and spending power clauses – since my understanding of the situation was that in the other areas the texts were largely acceptable.

As we moved on, the mood was tense. Because I like cold rooms, the air conditioning was going full blast. Bourassa, however, hated cold rooms, and, knowing me well, had made his own preparations. At one point he placed his briefcase on the table, opened it solemnly, and ostentatiously hauled out a sweater, which he put on with a wide smile and wore for the rest of the long session.

I could see the pressure building on David Peterson. I felt badly for him, with the *Toronto Star* and the Trudeauites on his back. What was especially difficult for him was Trudeau's statement that all these premiers were "weaklings" who had made "concessions" to Quebec. Peterson had his own price for agreement that night, and for hours that put him at odds with Bourassa. He asserted that Ontario needed clarification on distinct society and on the Charter. Bourassa was unyielding.

Shortly after midnight, with the mood deteriorating, I called a break and went down to my office with its sweeping view of Parliament Hill. I sat alone facing my officials and said glumly, "There ain't going to be no deal." It was that bad.

Bourassa would not give an inch. I instructed my advisors to quickly make it clear to Quebec officials that, without some movement on their part, the deal would founder within hours, and that I was ready to pull the plug on the entire exercise.

By now Ontario and Manitoba clearly had an understanding that they would either stay put or leave together so that neither would be blamed for killing the deal. Peterson, his buttoned-down white shirt loosened and his flaming-red tie askew, was irate when he returned after the break, announcing heatedly, "I've got five experts who say this [distinct society] will create new powers." There had been a shouting match outside between federal Deputy Minister of Justice Frank Iacobucci and Ontario Attorney General Ian Scott, and I called in some of the Ontario experts to make their case. After that I called a break and returned to my office, where I asked Iacobucci and Roger Tassé to meet me. These were two outstanding jurists: Iacobucci, former dean of law at the University of Toronto, was deputy minister of justice, and was later to be chief justice of the Federal Court and a justice of the Supreme Court of Canada. Tassé had been deputy minister of justice and chief constitutional advisor to Trudeau during the patriation exercise. He was also widely acclaimed as a brilliant legal scholar, and the real architect and author of the Charter of Rights.

I said to them, "We are here to protect and enhance Canadians' rights. Premier Peterson is still concerned about the distinct society clause impacting minority language rights. Does it?"

"No, sir," Iacobucci said.

"No, Prime Minister," said Tassé. Then he added, "You know, Prime Minister, I wrote most of the Charter myself. Trudeau and Ian Scott are wrong. Nothing here dilutes minority language rights."

"Then," I said, "I want you to come back into the meeting and tell them what you just told me, in precisely those words."

That helped. Peterson grew more comfortable when Bourassa relented, and the inclusion of a non-derogation clause was agreed upon. But when the Ontario premier demanded an additional clause affirming the superiority of the Charter, Bourassa blew up. "It will be Meech Lake or nothing," he said flatly.

When Peterson said, "Robert, I'm going to have a tough time selling this. I don't want this power in the hands of a Lévesque or Johnson," Bourassa leaned over and said softly, "David, I don't blame you. I blame that bastard [Trudeau] last week for fucking up the whole thing."

Bourassa, who never used profanity (unlike most politicians, including me), startled us all with his statement and the emotion with which it was delivered. This phlegmatic, unruffled man was committing his province forever to Canada by helping to push this accord through, and here he was at two-thirty in the morning being nickeled and dimed, on advice that had been persuasively countered by Canada's leading experts on the Charter.

In fact, nine years later, Brian Dickson, chief justice of the Supreme Court at the time of Meech, said, "Let me say directly that I have no difficulty with the concept [of distinct society]. In fact, the courts are already interpreting the Charter of Rights and the Constitution in a manner that takes into account Quebec's distinctive role in protecting and promoting its francophone character. As a practical matter, therefore, entrenching formal recognition of Quebec's distinctive character in the Constitution would not involve a significant departure from the existing practice in our court."

I called another break, during which Ed Broadbent helped his fellow NDPer Howard Pawley resolve an issue on the spending power clause. ("Howard," he said, "take the goddamn deal.") I told federal officials at 3:45 a.m., "I'm going to call a vote. We'd better get ready to shut this thing down." By that time amendments had been put forward dealing with and clarifying the most sensitive issues.

At 4:45, as a new day began to break over Parliament Hill, I canvassed the premiers. Normally, I would have begun with Peterson on my immediate right. But this time I turned left and said to Bourassa, "Robert, are you in agreement with the amended accord?" and he replied, "Yes, Prime Minister, I am." And so it went around the table. Yes, yes. Pawley was still hesitant and stressed the parliamentary hearings he must hold, but then said, "I'm with you, Prime Minister."

The others – Ghiz, Peckford, Buchanan, Vander Zalm, Hatfield, Getty, solid contributors all – agreed.

Finally, I looked at Peterson. I knew that he was deeply worried by the fissures created in the Liberal Party by the Trudeau attack, but I also knew he would do the right thing for Canada. "Well, David," I asked, "do we have a deal?"

Peterson looked slowly down at the desk and finally said, "I'm in, Prime Minister."

Unlike at our meeting a month earlier, there was no sense of jubilation or great achievement. We were all exhausted, our emotions laid bare. In the brutal world of *realpolitik*, leadership had carried the day. These people loved their country and had risen to the occasion. They also knew they would continue to pay a price for that leadership well into the future.

At 6:00 a.m., I met the media outside the east door of the Langevin Building. Six hours later we reconvened in the Government Conference Centre for a signing ceremony. At the end of a sustained standing ovation after he signed, Bourassa said simply, "It is with great pride as a Quebecer and as a Canadian that I am here today to express my deep satisfaction with the reintegration of Quebec within the Canadian Constitution."

It had all been worth it. The countless hours, the sleepless nights, the bitter disappointments, even the reckless ad hominem attacks.

A constitutional proposal that results in agreement between the federal government and the English-speaking provinces is one thing. But that is not Canada. Canada comes into being only when the federal government, the English-speaking provinces, *and* Quebec sign on together. And that is what we achieved that day: the first major unanimous constitutional agreement since 1867 and the signing of the *British North America Act* itself.

A few weeks later, Gordon Robertson said, "The constitutional arrangement of 1981 was a rejection of virtually every change every government of Quebec has sought over the previous twenty years. But not one of the changes [in Meech] touches the basic distribution of government powers. Canada is not going to be fundamentally changed by Meech Lake. It is, however, going to be secure against the risk that a new wave of nationalism could rally support with the cry that the Constitution of Canada is built on a lie, the lie of renewal in 1980. A constitution that does not have the willing acceptance of the provincial leaders and people of Quebec could fatally weaken Canada. We cannot leave that shadow on the Canadian future. The price is not too high."

He spoke these prescient words eight years before the 1995 Quebec referendum. It is not as if Canada had not been warned.

1987

7. Foreign Affairs and the Death Penalty

IT MAY SEEM HARD to believe now, but the spring of 1987 was busy on other fronts besides Meech. In May President François Mitterrand made a historic visit to Canada. He travelled to the West, spoke to Parliament, and visited with Acadians in New Brunswick. Memories of Charles de Gaulle's divisive comments in 1967 were finally put to rest. "Today we turn a new page in the history of the relationship between France and Canada," I said in introducing the president to Parliament on May 26. "We cannot change the past, but we can shape our future. What matters is the chapter we write together. It holds great promise for political rapprochement, industrial cooperation, and increased trade. Mr. President, on behalf of all Canadians may I tell you that your presence here today will contribute enormously to the renewal of that relationship."

It was an obviously moved François Mitterrand who spoke in Ottawa that day. "I am not forgetting the special duties of my country . . . to that part of Canada which once belonged to France and which, to this day, continues to reflect its culture, language, and tastes," he said. "I send very warm greetings to all the men and women who are listening to me and who lived and are still living that great experience, but I fully realize that a country as great as yours needs to collect all its varied components to stand up and act . . . A country like France, an older country, which has suffered a lot and will suffer again, has also unlimited potential and opportunities, because everything remains to be done for the coming century. That is why I often ask my fellow citizens to unite, not to ignore their own differences . . . but to unite every time it is necessary to stand for the country or for mankind . . . Vive le Canada! Vive la France!" he concluded. A page had been turned.

—

PERSONAL JOURNAL: MAY 31, 1987

A few thoughts on a most hectic week. President Mitterrand arrived Monday morning and began a hectic and productive four-day Canadian tour. It was the first by a French president in 20 years. De Gaulle's thoughtless – though I expect well-planned – cry from a balcony in Montreal had effectively derailed Franco-Canadian relations, and for two decades had rendered them either meaningless or turgid. Mitterrand's ending comment in the House – "Vive le Canada" – was a fitting tribute to a refurbished relationship I happen to view as extremely significant for Canada. Mitterrand has been the principal architect of this revitalized relationship from the French side and I am most grateful to him and for the sensitivity and cooperation. I had made this initiative a key part of our constitutional reform process – normalizing relations with France, setting the terms for Quebec's participation, with New Brunswick, in the francophone summit, new emphasis on the constitutional file, hopefully resulting in the reintegration of Quebec to the Canadian constitution with honour and enthusiasm, as I had said in my Sept-Îles speech in August of 1984.

His trip was designed to be pan-Canadian as part of our initiative to convey to the French that the country does not end at the Ottawa River. For the first time, a French president visited Regina, Toronto, and Moncton – apart from his official duties in Ottawa, Quebec, Montreal, and Gaspé. His reception everywhere was very warm and impressive. His reception in the Commons was tremendous – he must have been very pleased. Which made the bitter denunciation by Pierre Elliott Trudeau of me, all premiers, and the Meech Lake Accord on Wednesday morning almost predictable, even to its timing. The visit must have annoyed Trudeau – his dislike of the French is well known. What better way to make known his disapproval of the Meech Lake Accord than to release a denunciation so breathtaking in its bitterness and invective that, if nothing else, it would consign the Mitterrand visit to the inside pages. In this Trudeau was successful. Only the future will tell whether his attempt to panic Canadians and scuttle the accord will be successful. For my part, I have been relatively untroubled by his assault and subsequent campaign. I may well be wrong but I think he mitigated whatever value his arguments might otherwise command by such a violent and vicious diatribe and against so many people – living and dead – that he appears unhinged.

One thing is certain that if the accord fails to win acceptance I genuinely doubt if fair and honourable grounds will ever be formed that will enable Quebec to join the constitution. It is doubtful that future prime ministers will want to run the risk I have for national unity, for fear of being blindsided by unprincipled attacks such as that launched with such poison by Trudeau.

—

Just before Mitterrand's visit, Mila and I celebrated our fourteenth wedding anniversary. While prime ministers receive impressive gifts when they travel abroad representing their country, no gift could ever come close to meaning as much as the one I found on my desk on May 26, 1987.

"I am so proud of you and the work that you are doing," Mila wrote. "Your day is coming, slowly but surely. For my part I cannot find the words to express how I truly feel, the pride and the joy and the respect. You have my love and friendship and support always."

Earlier in 1987 Mila and I both had to summon up all the strength we could as a couple when Ben was injured in an accident on a slide at Lycée Claudel just before our departure for Africa. I bared my soul in the pages of my private journal.

—

PERSONAL JOURNAL: FEBRUARY 23, 1987

On Friday afternoon Mila and I were devastated by the closest brush we've ever had with great tragedy involving our own immediate family. After a week of Oerlikon [a political controversy that led to André Bissonnette's resignation from cabinet] in the House, we were en route to Toronto to speak to a PC Canada Fund event in Toronto when a message came to the crew from Ottawa that Ben had sustained serious injury at Claudel, that it was to his back, and that he'd been taken to the hospital on a stretcher in an ambulance. With that peremptory notice the phone system went dead, and Mila and I were suspended with the worst thoughts of tragedy and pain for our beautiful son running through our heads. I immediately ordered the crew to return to Ottawa but for 30 minutes Mila and I sat transfixed with apprehension as we contemplated every possible scenario, including the most bleak and debilitating. We dashed from the aircraft to the Billy Bishop Lounge, where the doctor (God bless her) told us that he could move all his limbs, and that while it had been a close call he would be all right, and his recovery would be complete.

We were soon informed that our oldest son would be fine and that no permanent damage had been done.

These words ended the most dismal moments of my life. In my life I've never felt such sadness since Peggy told me on the phone 22 years earlier that Dad, in the hospital for a routine examination, was found to be terminally ill and would die within weeks. When the doctor's words were clear to me, I ran to the bathroom and broke down for the first time in decades. I was overcome by grief, and then relief, and this event – with its absolutely overwhelming serious, serious possibilities for Ben, a wonderful, generous little boy – was just too much. Having just come through a bruising, difficult week in the House, this may indeed have been God's way of putting life in proper perspective; of calling my attention away from the trivia to the overriding importance of the family, and the well-being of a great little boy, not yet 11 years old.

Mila and I rushed to the hospital and Ben was concerned about us – that we had had to cancel events and rush back. Neither of us could conceal the relief and gratitude we felt as we held and chatted with Ben – a handsome and generous boy who appears to have captured the best of both his parents and who will make an important and beneficial mark in life simply by being what he is and what he wants to be.

—

South Africa remained a priority. I had started 1987 by undertaking a trip to the front-line states in southern Africa. At Victoria Falls I met with Zimbabwe's Robert Mugabe, Zambia's Kenneth Kaunda, and Quett Masire of Botswana. Some were surprised when I said I understood – but didn't condone – the use of violence to battle apartheid: "I cannot speak for Robert

Mugabe, whose life has been entirely different, who was raised in an entirely different society and who has known repression and the lack of freedom and liberty. So we do not advocate the use of violence. Canada seeks to create a climate where differences are resolved. I recognize, however, that the sources of violence in South Africa are unique . . . We are children of our environment. We are what we are."

—

PERSONAL JOURNAL: FEBRUARY 23, 1987

There is a cast about Robert Mugabe and a sense of discipline throughout the party and country that I suspect would make unpromising any political career initiated in opposition to him. Mila and I had excellent private meetings at home with him and his wife Sally. He asked about Ronald Reagan and the U.S., and Mila and I both spoke supportively of the president and Nancy, and expressed the view and hope that they would like them as well if they were able to meet and come to know each other. He was fascinated to learn that RR had in fact called me the night before in Harare to inform me of his reaction to the Bush visit. But as we sat in the twilight of his home I could sense the gulf between him and the West, perhaps accentuated by the decade he spent in jail, by the arrest of his wife, by the death of his own child while in prison, by the lack of American–U.K. support of his long struggle.

—

I believed my visit to southern Africa was an important symbolic step. Here was a Western leader – the prime minister of a G-7 nation – on the ground, showing the people of the region they were not alone in their fight for justice. And a fight it was, as those front-line states were often attacked by the South African military. Pious talk about the effect sanctions might have on Western economies meant little to the people there.

The *Globe and Mail*'s Michael Valpy spent years stationed in Zimbabwe covering the fall of apartheid. While he could be a tough critic, he was always fair in his assessment of me. He even had some gentle fun at my expense, pointing out that when we appeared together in public, Mugabe, true to his African traditions, as a mark of friendship liked to hold my hand; Valpy took delight in my visible discomfort with this gesture. Long after my trip to southern Africa, Valpy's was the only journalistic voice raised to condemn a scurrilous invitation to deflower my sixteen-year-old daughter that appeared in *Frank* magazine, a vile scandal sheet published in Ottawa. At the time I called Valpy to thank him and to say that his defence of Caroline, in my view as her father, gave him a free pass to attack me for the rest of my career!

In 1987 Valpy wrote about my visit to Africa, saying I had broken through the West's "Cold War mental block on South Africa by rejecting the argument Pretoria has used so persuasively with the Americans: that it alone stands as a bulwark in the southern continent against the designs and advances of communism . . . What the prime minister has encountered – what perhaps he could only come to fully understand here, enveloped in the fabric of Africa – is the deep disappointment with the West and its South African policies."

While I pressed Robert Mugabe on human rights issues both on that trip and in the years that followed, I didn't go far enough. "I do not think that Robert Mugabe, who was unfairly jailed himself for ten years, is likely to capriciously incarcerate others," I wrote in a letter to Amnesty International in March of 1987. How wrong I was. Years later Mugabe turned into a dictator, visiting oppression on those who had already been oppressed. After my retirement from politics I watched, more in sadness than in anger, as Canada under Jean Chrétien abdicated its leadership role in the Zimbabwean situation. When Britain's Tony Blair fought at the 2002 Commonwealth Meeting in Australia to suspend Zimbabwe's membership in the Commonwealth because of Mugabe's indefensible human rights abuses, Canada remained silent, refusing to join with Blair.

Michael Valpy's report in the *Globe and Mail* speaks for itself: "Jean Chrétien undermined him [Blair] and Canadian officials boasted of his success. 'This was Canada's day,' said one. The Canadian delegation made clear that the government's prime objective was the maintenance of unanimity, the bureaucratic niceness of keeping everyone at the table, the objective of avoiding a black-white divide." To this Valpy reacted with scorn. "And Canada could have been in the forefront. During the struggle against apartheid [Canada under Mulroney] built an enormous reserve of goodwill for Canada in black Africa. Indeed, if any so-called white Commonwealth government does not have to defend its bona fides, it is Canada."

I left Africa firmly resolved to raise the temperature even higher in the councils of the world where Canada had a seat. My first opportunity came in June at the annual G-7 Summit in Venice. Though I knew the chances for success were slim at best, I instructed my sherpa, Sylvia Ostry, to place South Africa on Canada's summit agenda. I hoped the G-7 would establish a summit group, composed of foreign ministers, to tackle apartheid once and for all. This announcement, I hoped, would be part of the official G-7 Summit declaration issued at the end of our talks. I knew, however, that I'd be facing off against Ronald Reagan, Margaret Thatcher, and Helmut Kohl. Before we met, I wrote to my colleagues who opposed my plan.

"From my talks with African leaders," I told Helmut, "especially during my visit to Africa earlier this year, I have become more convinced than ever of the need for summit action. Silence would be conspicuous and would send quite the wrong signal. In the immediate aftermath of a whites-only election, silence would be read as indifference at best. It would certainly encourage complacency on the party of the government and lead to doubts among blacks about the seriousness of Western opposition to apartheid . . . All summit members are providing aid to some or all of South Africa's neighbours and to the victims of apartheid in South Africa. We have all substantially increased that aid recently. I believe we should be able to endorse what we are already doing in this area."

I tried a different tactic with Reagan. He had written to me on June 5 to provide Canada with an update on the situation in the Persian Gulf, where we supported American actions. In my response I linked the two situations.

"The bloody slaughter which has characterized this conflict, brought home most recently by the tragic loss of young lives on the USS *Stark*, convinces me that regional conflicts, once started, are extraordinarily difficult to bring to an end," I wrote. "As we act together in Venice to try to end a current conflict, let us also unite in demonstrating leadership in preventing another, this time in southern Africa. I fear that conflict there is almost certain if we in the West do not do what we can – and must – to influence the South African government to move in positive directions. Like the Persian Gulf, southern Africa is vital to the West. And like the current war between Iran and Iraq, a conflict in southern Africa will drift rapidly toward a bloodbath of unimaginable horror."

Ron and I also spoke on the telephone, and I made sure he knew the South African situation was important. It was time to call in some chips.

"South Africa is very important to us and to me personally, particularly in light of my hosting the Commonwealth and francophone summits this fall," I told him on June 8. "As I said in my letter, I want the summit to give a strong message condemning the apartheid government. It is important for summit leaders to be seen as addressing issues of real injustice. I recognize Margaret's position on this, but I would welcome your support for some specific reference to South Africa in the communiqué or statement emerging from Venice. No statement would be a statement."

Once in Venice, I wasn't surprised to meet general resistance to my hopes that South Africa would be placed in the final summit communiqué. Still, I fought as hard as I could, and I believe to this day that Ronald Reagan met me halfway. West German Foreign Minister Hans-Dietrich Genscher was another ally. We had breakfast on the terrace of my Venice hotel one morning and discussed the issue. Genscher, a member of the Free Democratic Party in Kohl's coalition government who served his nation as foreign minister for an incredible eighteen years, was closer to me on apartheid than his boss was. "Leave Kohl to me," he said, later delivering as best he could.

While the denunciation of apartheid that I had hoped for didn't make it into the communiqué, at least it was placed in the chairman's summary of political issues. Italian Prime Minister Amintore Fanfani said on behalf of all seven leaders, "A peaceful and lasting solution can only be found to the present crisis if the apartheid regime is dismantled and replaced by a new form of democratic, nonracial government."

Persistence, as I told the press in Venice, pays off.

"Some more sophisticated leaders, such as Britain's Margaret Thatcher, may think him naïve, but in the absence of Mulroney, there would be no Western leader talking about apartheid at all," the *Toronto Star* said in an editorial. "Certainly not Thatcher, who reportedly gave Mulroney a cold stare for presuming to raise the subject at a summit dinner. And not U.S. President Ronald Reagan, who remains opposed to increasing sanctions against South Africa's white government. And if no Western leader were addressing apartheid, what message would that send to Black Africa? That the West doesn't care. We have Mulroney to thank for making sure that message wasn't sent."

It should be noted that the *Toronto Star* consistently battled apartheid on its editorial and news pages during those years, and Venice was an important moral victory. With the world's most powerful nations now officially engaged, I knew that young Africans – some of whom I had met in January – would know now, at least, that someone in the world was listening.

I contacted the African leaders I'd met earlier in the year at Victoria Falls, telling them my actions in Venice had been influenced by our discussions in Africa. I didn't hide the fact I had helped achieve only a partial victory. "I regret that consensus was not achieved on the need for a separate, fuller declaration on South Africa which would have seized Summit foreign ministers of the issue through to the Toronto Summit (in 1988)," I wrote. "The Venice statement was, however, the most significant one on South Africa to have emerged to date from an Economic Summit and is one from which we can all take some satisfaction."

By the time the Venice Summit took place, President Reagan and Mikhail Gorbachev of the Soviet Union had begun talks aimed at reducing intermediate-range missiles in Europe. This led to one of the most spirited discussions I was ever to see around a G-7 Summit table. Italy's Fanfani, Nakasone of Japan, and I – leaders of three nations that didn't possess nuclear weapons – hung back and watched the others heatedly discuss the issue.

"There will be no denuclearization of Europe because you will destroy NATO," Margaret thundered.

"It's my skin," Kohl replied before she cut him off.

"No, our soldiers are there."

She then turned to President Reagan.

"If you don't have [intermediate-range missiles] in Germany, you're inviting Soviet attack. I hope we're not going wet around this table . . . You must say no [to Gorbachev]! They want all U.S. nuclear weapons removed from Europe, and I desperately want them in."

"He [Gorbachev] is our chance," Helmut replied.

"Considerably," Reagan added, but then Margaret jumped in again.

"I have 66,000 troops and Ronald Reagan has 358,000 in Germany," she said fiercely. "The short-range tactical nuclear weapons are part of our conventional defences."

Listening to that conversation – and so many others between leaders during that period – none of us around the table imagined the speed with which historic geopolitical changes would soon emerge, especially in the Soviet Union, making these concerns irrelevant. For now, the Cold War raged and I was witness to its intensity, time and time again.

There were lighter moments as well. During one lengthy session Joe Clark and I continued our finely tuned practice of passing notes back and forth. "If we arrived late for an event of this kind, the crucifixion would be swift," I scribbled to him when one participant was tardy arriving.

"For the Toronto meeting, there must be a way in which an abbreviated document is read by the chairman," I noted a little later as seventy-nine-year-old Prime Minister Fanfani spoke at length. "Who said advancing age induces brevity?" Joe nearly broke out laughing, but he kept his composure in the higher interests of Canadian diplomacy. I stared ahead stoically as he read my note, never cracking a smile, and refusing to make eye contact with my foreign minister.

International summitry, as I was to learn, raised note-writing to a new level. By the time I left office I had concluded that President George H.W. Bush was the absolute master, though I gave him a good run. I was again in Italy for a NATO meeting when a fellow leader's speech seemed to be going on forever. "George," I wrote on a piece of paper, before sliding it over to the American president, "given the time taken by the prime minister of Iceland, I have calculated that, on a per capita basis, you are now entitled to take the floor for approximately 180 hours!"

President Bush read my note, looked my way, and nodded gravely. Observers would have concluded that Canada's prime minister had presented a new trade proposal to the president, so serious was his manner.

George returned the favour at a later conference. His own national security advisor, Brent Scowcroft, was famous within the administration for falling asleep during lengthy meetings. As a result, George created the Scowcroft Award, awarded annually. In Brussels I discovered that Canada was in the running. As I sat focused on the discussions I noted that Secretary of State for External Affairs Barbara McDougall, who had just flown in from the Far East, was having some difficulties with the interminable debates. Soon a U.S. Secret Service agent arrived and handed me a "confidential message from President Bush." "Brian," he wrote, "please protect and do not show to your foreign minister under pain of death. You have heard of the prestigious Scowcroft Award awarded annually for that person who falls asleep during meetings and does it with the most style. Recovery counts, duration counts, and style counts . . . Last year Iceland and Japan waged a shootout at CSCE [Commission on Security and Cooperation in Europe]. Iceland won it. Their PM and foreign minister both zonked out – totally – during the Italian speech. It might interest you to know that Barbara McDougall has challenged today, but – too bad – it was but a modest effort. 'Style' OK, but 'duration' spotty. On 'recovery' she did very well, smiling, a good show. PS: It is unlikely she will win because her challenge was sporadic."

As I turned, laughing, toward Barbara, I noted that fatigue had indeed gotten the better of her, and she was struggling mightily to stay awake.

Barbara, I should note, had soon emerged as an extremely valuable member of cabinet, showing a blend of toughness and skill in her portfolio assignments, culminating in Foreign Affairs. Her ready sense of humour and her unyielding loyalty also contributed to the admiration in which she was held by her colleagues, including me.

Shortly after I returned from Venice, Simon Reisman put me on notice that we would have to begin planning a scenario whereby he would tell his American counterpart to go back to the drawing board or witness Canada walking away from the free trade negotiating table. The media would soon learn of his ultimatum, so proper management of the communications would be crucial, Simon warned.

"It is highly unlikely that the Americans will put on the table on Monday afternoon [June 22] a set of proposals on subsidies and dispute settlement that will fully accommodate Canadian concerns," he wrote. "Assuming, instead, that the American proposal, while short of the mark, is judged by the Canadian chief negotiator to offer a basis for further negotiation, the challenge will be to get things moving much more rapidly to meet the deadline of October 4."

Simon's memo highlighted a problem we struggled with throughout the negotiations. While every nugget of news from the talks ended up on the front pages of Canadian newspapers, the U.S. negotiator, Peter Murphy, operated in a comparative vacuum. He could lob bombs at Simon through the Canadian media, but wasn't constrained by any coverage by his own nation's press.

I had to put free trade aside as June wore on so that I could honour a commitment I had made during both the 1984 election and the 1983 PC leadership race. I had personally opposed the death penalty since I was in university. But I recognized that not all Canadians – or Progressive Conservatives – shared this view. My approach to this delicate topic was shaped at both StFX and at Laval. In the late 1950s a man I believed innocent, Wilbert Coffin, had been put to death in Quebec after an investigation and trial heavy with political overtones. I also looked on in horror when

Canada shocked the world by sentencing fourteen-year-old Steven Truscott to death by hanging, a sentence fortunately never carried out. As a young man I had been friendly with Arthur Maloney, who became a leading Toronto criminal lawyer, and Roy McMurtry, who went on to become Ontario's attorney general. Both men opposed the death penalty with a passion I admired. In that atmosphere, and with the friends I had, it was impossible to attend university without taking part in many spirited arguments over the state's ultimate sentence.

When I announced in Parliament that the government intended to hold a free vote on capital punishment, my seatmates in the Commons were Finance Minister Michael Wilson and Deputy Prime Minister Don Mazankowski, my closest associates. When I entered the chamber for the vote I can honestly say I had no idea how either of them would vote. (In the end, they disagreed with me, voting to restore the death penalty. Unlike Pierre Trudeau in 1976, I did not demand that my cabinet ministers vote the way I did on capital punishment.)

When I spoke to the House, I made no secret of where I stood.

"I will be voting against capital punishment on moral and logical grounds," I said. "I believe that it is wrong . . . There must be law and there must, in a civilized society, be respect at all times for that law. But for those who would change the law in such a fundamental manner, the onus is upon them to make a compelling case. For myself, I am not persuaded. I am not persuaded the death penalty works as a deterrent. Nor am I persuaded it is appropriate as punishment. On the contrary, I believe it is repugnant, and I believe it is profoundly unacceptable to take a life. It is wrong to take life and I can think of no circumstance excepting self-defence to justify it. I have held these views since I was a young student and I still hold them today."

I quoted Arthur Maloney and John Diefenbaker, two men who had fought capital punishment many years before.

"From my experience at the Bar I say that anyone who says an innocent man cannot go to the gallows is wrong, because I know differently," Diefenbaker said on April 4, 1966. "It is a frightful thing when a man you believe to be innocent and whose attitude is, 'Don't worry about me, God will not allow it,' walks to the gallows and months later the truth comes out."

When the votes were tallied, members of the Canadian House of Commons had said no to the death penalty by a vote of 148–127. Reflecting the progressive approach to social issues that defines the province to this day, Quebec MPs by a margin of 49 to 8 stood and voted against the return of the noose. Barry Moore, who represented Pontiac–Gatineau–Labelle, even left his hospital bed to register his nay.

"It was Parliament at its best," an observer in the public gallery told the media afterwards.

Parliament wasn't at its best later in the summer, and I can't blame anyone but myself. Almost two hundred illegal Asian migrants, mostly of Sikh background, had landed on the coast of Nova Scotia and announced they were seeking refugee status. This followed an incident the year before when a boatload of illegal Tamil immigrants had to be rescued from the waters off Newfoundland.

Canadians were angry, and my government responded in kind. Immigration Minister Benoît Bouchard brought forth a package that included stiffer fines for human smugglers and changes that would allow us to deport illegal immigrants much more swiftly.

"These, by and large, are illegal aliens," I told the media in late July. "People jumping the queue unfairly take other people's rights and other people's legitimate claims. This breeds unfairness, and unfairness will destroy the system."

Minister of Fisheries Tom Siddon, a sound, reliable colleague whose advice I always respected, brought along to a cabinet meeting a report from his constituency office in Richmond, B.C. During a two-and-a-half-week period that summer his staff had recorded seven hundred calls on the issue. Only one was critical of the government for detaining the migrants without counsel. "All other calls have indicated an opposition to them being allowed to stay for any other reason," the report to Tom stated. The typical comment was simply, "Ship 'em back." We gave in to this public pressure, and the House was called back quickly to pass the tougher rules and regulations.

I now think that I made a mistake. As a Quebecer of Irish origins, married to a woman whose family had come to Canada from eastern Europe, I knew better than most the special challenges faced by those who choose a new life here, far from their ancestral homes. Canada is a nation of immigrants, and I should have appealed to our better side instead of choosing the easy course. I remain uncomfortable with myself over this incident to this day.

Despite the government's and my heavy agenda, I spent as much time as possible that summer with Mila and the children. Earlier, Elmer MacKay had written me a note in cabinet reminding me what happens to those in public life who don't ensure time for their family. "It is very important for you to take some good time for yourself and family this summer. From my own experience I can attest how sad it is when kids grow up and others in the family grow old – you are not part of it – as would normally be the case."

In early September I served as host of the second Francophonie Summit. While I've long thought Quebec City to be one of the most beautiful cities in the world, it outdid itself as it prepared to host the leaders of more than forty French-speaking nations. The residents of Quebec City seemed to have a special bounce in their collective step as they prepared to greet the rest of the francophone world.

There had been some of the usual bickering between federal and Quebec organizers over the placement of flags and so on in the months leading up to the summit, but I can't say I was able to summon very much anger at Quebec officials over this. Quebec City was the site of the Plains of Abraham, after all, the place of a great defeat for a people and culture in 1759. Quebecers were now going to proudly show the world their vibrant, modern society, which had become a model for all.

Quebec Premier Robert Bourassa and I enjoyed better relations than any Canadian prime minister and his Quebec counterpart had for decades. The Meech Lake Accord, designed to reintegrate Quebec into the Canadian constitutional family, had been signed by all of Canada's first ministers, and the accord had by now been officially approved by Quebec's National Assembly. Quebec MPs were key to the success of the new federal government, and Quebecers – including the prime minister – were directing policy at the very heart of a G-7 nation's federal government, joining colleagues from each and every province as they did so. Quebecers were also responding to our call for free trade negotiations with the Americans with the sort of enthusiasm that was lacking in some other parts of the country.

Before the summit started, Robert Bourassa and I met for a celebratory lunch at Quebec City's Garrison Club. It was for me a great personal moment to return to the city I knew so well from my days at Laval, this time as prime minister on the eve of a historic summit. Two of my closest friends and former Laval classmates, Bernard Roy, now my principal secretary and senior Quebec advisor, and Lucien Bouchard, my summit sherpa and Canada's ambassador to France, walked with me across the picturesque grounds of the National Assembly as we made our way to the club to meet Robert. The three of us had first met in this very city almost thirty years earlier, and I was gripped by emotion when I thought of all we'd accomplished along the way.

Robert Bourassa met us on the street and we entered the club together. He brought along his own senior advisors, and our group had a luncheon like no other I was ever to experience in public life, so marked was it by friendship, a common sense of purpose, and an exciting vision of the future. Afterwards Robert and I spoke to the press and he made a comment I will never forget. "We are experiencing a moment of unprecedented national unity," he said. (It has been seventeen years since Newfoundland premier Clyde Wells and others sabotaged the Meech Lake Accord, and succeeding Quebec premiers haven't uttered such words during all that time.)

I was deeply honoured to begin the summit with a speech to the delegates who gathered in the National Assembly's Salon Rouge. Above us hung a portrait of the seventeenth-century Sovereign Council of New France, and I felt history's whisper as I began my remarks.

"More than two centuries ago, like a branch separated from its trunk, 60,000 French-speaking people were left to face their North American destiny alone," I said. "What fate awaited this small band of settlers so abruptly exposed to collective uncertainty and the need to question their own identity? Would the wide open spaces, so appropriate to their disproportionate dreams, imprison them in their isolation and cut them off from the rest of the world? . . . The answer, silent and persistent, could only stretch out in time and space . . . Today, it speaks out vigorously; the French language and the values it represents have survived and will always be alive in North America . . . Those 60,000 settlers are now 6 million people."

During the sessions I announced that Canada would forgive $325 million in Third World debt. In turn I pressed the group on human rights and the necessity of developing democratic institutions and freedoms in their countries. Canada and Quebec joined together, thanks in large part to Lucien Bouchard's inspired efforts as Ottawa's sherpa, and we laid the foundations of institutions that were necessary if La Francophonie were to succeed in the years ahead. We also helped launch TV5, a French-language television network that was soon showcasing Québécois cinema and television shows to a worldwide audience.

Caught up in the excitement, Robert Bourassa attempted to push the envelope of Quebec's autonomy on the international stage. In his book *From Bourassa to Bourassa*, L. Ian MacDonald described how I poured cold water on the premier's excessive enthusiasm: "The fact that Ottawa and Quebec were close partners . . . did not prevent Bourassa from manoeuvring for every advantage for Quebec at the table. When he intervened at a closed session on the international economy, President Haj Omar Bongo of Gabon said that he agreed 'with the proposal of Mr. Bourassa.' Mulroney, a cold fury in his voice, interrupted from the chair. 'Mr. Bourassa did not make a proposal,' he said icily. 'He made a suggestion,' clarifying that it was outside the agreement circumscribing Quebec's role at the summit. Then Mulroney pulled Bourassa aside and walked him down the corridor behind the Salon Rouge, pointing out that such interventions were 'very bad for Canada.' Bourassa nodded his agreement and his comments were never made public."

1987

8. The Free Trade Roller Coaster

WITH THE CLOSE OF the Francophonie Summit I had to face the alarming fact that the end point for a successful conclusion to the free trade talks was only a month away, with a deadline of October 3, at midnight. U.S. negotiator Peter Murphy still hadn't revealed anything worth Canada's while in regard to our key demand: a binding dispute resolution system. President Reagan had already heard about this issue directly from me, so I directed Derek Burney to approach his American counterpart at the White House.

Derek did so, sending a letter to Reagan's chief of staff, Howard Baker, on September 8. "We do not see a binational dispute settlement mechanism as a concession either side makes for the other," Derek wrote. "Rather, we see it as the sine qua non, politically and objectively, to make the agreement whole, i.e., to preserve the rules and disciplines against all other political considerations. It is that basic and it is that important. I want to stress that there is no possibility of our concluding a deal which does not include a genuine and objective basis for settling disputes arising from the agreement's rules. If it is your judgment that the administration cannot meet our requirements on the issue which I believe goes to the heart of the negotiations, it would be prudent to know soon so that we may take appropriate action. (I would note here that the prime minister will meet all ten Canadian premiers to review these negotiations on September 14.)"

Howard Baker replied three days later, saying that the administration wouldn't admit the talks could fail. "Our negotiators are meeting today and through the weekend, and we fully expect progress from those sessions. We ought to be talking instead about how to construct this historic arrangement and thereafter present it to the Congress, Parliament, and people of both countries. Derek, these talks will succeed or fail on the merits of proposals. But, however, should these talks reach a stalemate, I can assure you that it will not be due to a lack of attention of the president or his senior advisors."

The October 3, 1987 deadline for the president's use of "fast-track" negotiating authority – meaning approval or rejection but no amendments – eventually focused political minds in both capitals. The run-up to that deadline during September was the most hectic and emotionally charged roller coaster of any month during my nine years in office.

A series of special committee and full cabinet sessions in early September had revealed clearly to us all that the negotiations were at a standstill, in large part over Canada's demand for relief from arbitrary American trade remedy decisions. Equally, our negotiators had refused to budge on the bottom-line concern of the U.S. team: some easing of Canada's investment review decisions. Concerns around the cabinet table about the prospect of a failed negotiation were tempered somewhat by those with lingering apprehension about the political implications of a positive outcome. In other words, quite a few members of my cabinet would have been pleased to see the talks fail – Minister of Agriculture John Wise had strong reservations about any moves away from traditional Canadian support mechanisms for parts of our agricultural sector (especially dairy and poultry), although these concerns were more than matched by those of his American counterpart. Some have suggested that "agricultural trade" is the ultimate oxymoron in trade negotiations; reluctance to give ground on agriculture policy bedevils multilateral trade negotiations to this day.

Flora MacDonald often exemplified the historical reservations about free trade within Conservative ranks. She showed me a cartoon from the 1911 campaign to underscore how long-standing Tory sentiment against free trade had been. "No truck or trade with the Yankees!" had been Borden's rallying cry in the 1911 election. Her responsibilities as minister of communications, which included culture, gave her more immediate concern. Our negotiators had addressed this issue up front by eliminating culture from the negotiations and yet, to the Americans, what Canada saw as manifestations of culture – magazine, film and publishing policy, postal rates, and so on – the United States saw as business. That ambiguity, and the fact that the U.S. had GATT rights that prevailed in any event, served a useful purpose. We knew that even a complete exemption would not assuage the cultural lobby. Ironically, even many Canadian artists who performed south of the border insisted on being exempted from travel provisions that would have eased their entry to perform in the U.S. market.

Around the cabinet table Mike Wilson, John Crosbie, and Don Mazankowski were steadfast supporters of the negotiating process. By contrast, even though she was the minister of international trade, Pat Carney wavered from time to time, depending on her mood of the moment. In his memoirs, *No Holds Barred*, Crosbie refers to "Carney's difficult personality," and her discomfort with Simon Reisman's prominent public role seemed, on occasion, to undermine her judgment.

I had chosen Simon as our chief negotiator because of his extensive experience in trade negotiations, most notably with the Auto Pact, and because I knew he was more than capable of standing firm on Canada's behalf. Lester B. Pearson had described a constant problem facing any Canadian in Simon's position. "The picture of weak and timid Canadian negotiators being pushed around and brow-beaten by American representatives into settlements that were 'sell-outs' is a false and distorted one. It is often painted, however, by Canadians who think that a sure way to get applause and support at home is to exploit our anxieties and exaggerate our suspicions over U.S. power and policies."

Fortunately, the adjectives "weak" and "timid" do not apply to Simon Reisman, as anyone who has encountered him will attest. My instructions to him and the negotiating team had been explicit from the beginning. We needed an agreement that would provide conditions that were significantly better for Canada in the American market than the status quo. Equally, no deal was better than a bad deal.

In 1986 a severe protectionist chill had swept through Congress like a bitter November wind, threatening our access to our most important markets. A high percentage of our exports to the United States were subject to quotas, "voluntary" restraints, and other restrictions. As I had told the Commons, the Ottinger Bill, passed in three successive years by the House of Representatives, sought to destroy the Auto Pact, which lay at the heart of Ontario's economic power. There was a crisis a month for Canadian exporters as trade barriers were erected against their products. The Americans also demanded preventive action against Canadian steel, uranium, cement, subway cars, fish – in fact, virtually all of our exports south of the border.

In one well-known specific case, Canada had been hit with restrictions on sales of cedar shakes and shingles and, faced with similar action against our even more substantial softwood lumber exports, had concluded a "managed trade" truce whereby a 15 per cent export sales tax was attached to our sales to the United States for a five-year period. This had the advantage of at least keeping the extra revenue in Canadian, not U.S. Treasury, hands. Other sectors of our export economy faced similar pressures, either directly or indirectly. Even when Canadian products were not specifically targeted by American trade remedy measures, they risked, as in the case of steel, being side-swiped by actions aimed at others.

That is why the defensive aim of securing existing access to the U.S. market became as vital an objective for our negotiators as the benefits to be derived from more liberalized, tariff-free access. It was ironic that Ontario, the province with the most at risk on the former objective and the most to gain from the latter, was represented by a premier, David Peterson, who was, at best, ambivalent over the negotiations. Nationalist, anti-American sentiments provided a more basic inclination to oppose this major policy initiative of my government, and those sentiments flourished, particularly in Toronto, under the persistent drumbeat of the *Toronto Star* and the CBC, implying that if we successfully signed the deal, it would make Canada the fifty-first state. The coverage from the *Globe and Mail* was balanced, and the editorial view supportive of our initiative.

As the negotiations progressed, I arranged several briefing sessions with first ministers. While I was careful not to confer veto rights to any or all premiers and to preserve the federal constitutional authority for trade negotiations, I recognized that some elements of the negotiations (such as procurement, liquor boards) involved provincial jurisdiction. I also recognized that there was more general support than opposition from the premiers for the initiative, and knew that this would be helpful politically down the road. The strongest supporters were Bourassa, Getty, Vander Zalm, Devine, Hatfield, and, to a lesser extent, Peckford and Buchanan. Pawley and Ghiz were opposed, while Peterson, as mentioned, was ambivalent at best.

From September 2 to October 3, 1987 there were twenty-two meetings of the Trade Executive Committee (TEC), the Priorities and Planning Committee, and the full cabinet (and those are only the ones for which records exist). There were also many ad hoc meetings, regular preparations for question period, and discussions with the Americans (formal and informal) about the negotiations that added to the drama and tension. It was, as far as I was concerned, all free trade, all the time.

I had announced in March 1987 that the government was committed to protecting Canada's social programs, capacity to promote regional development, auto industry, agricultural marketing systems, and cultural identity. Concerns about each of these, and frustration over the uncertain pace of the negotiations, dominated cabinet discussions.

That frustration came to a head in mid-September when, after eighteen months of negotiation, it became evident that the United States was neither sensitive to the political risks facing my government nor committed to act on what I had characterized as the sine qua non for success: relief from capricious U.S. trade remedies. Despite assurances from President Reagan about the importance of the negotiations, there was little evidence of political commitment in Washington. The 10–10 vote by the Senate Finance Committee in April of 1986 to launch negotiations had almost derailed the initiative before it began and had served as an omen for the negotiating process as a whole.

Peter Murphy was an able enough negotiator but, without a political champion above him in the administration, he concentrated on "irritants" identified by officials from various U.S. agencies or key congressmen, and gave lowest common denominator replies to Canadian overtures. On more than one occasion, I observed to cabinet that "if the U.S. administration spent one-tenth of the time on Canada that they do on Nicaragua, we'd have a deal." The problem was that no one was in charge in Washington. Clayton Yeutter, the U.S. trade representative, was preoccupied with other issues, fending off pressures from Congress in implementing the 1986 Omnibus Trade Bill. Joe Clark tried persistently to engage George Shultz, but he, too, had other priorities.

Ambassador Allan Gotlieb was in the midst of this, and his *Washington Diaries* catch the sense of impending failure that had taken hold by mid-September. On September 15, with only eighteen days to the deadline, he wrote about an Ottawa meeting in the PMO boardroom with Don Mazankowski, Joe Clark, Michael Wilson, Pat Carney, Paul Tellier, Stanley Hartt, Gerry Shannon, Gordon Ritchie, Simon Reisman, and myself. The meeting was chaired by Derek Burney. "The atmosphere was grim," recalled Gotlieb. "Reisman gave a gloomy report on the negotiations, and I gave a gloomy report on the Washington political atmosphere. Apparently, what I said to the prime minister last week about the need to create a crisis is what prompted him to call this meeting. I repeated my advice: Reisman, on instructions, should break off the negotiations. To use my term, we should apply 'electric shock treatment.'" In an earlier private meeting with me in my office in September, Gotlieb had seen how angry I was with the American negotiators. In his diary he wrote: "Mulroney is bitter about this. If the United States turns their back on us, they'll feel our wrath, he said . . . The prime minister was talking more loudly than I can remember him doing before, although we were the only two in the room. He stood up, so I did too, and we remained standing throughout our discussion. I could feel the intensity of his wrath. He stood more and more closely to me as he spoke."

Clearly, we had to attract Washington's attention.

Secretary of Treasury Jim Baker was known widely as Washington's "go-to" guy. I sent Derek Burney and Mike Wilson to meet with Baker informally on September 19, during the annual International Monetary Fund meeting in Washington, to urge movement on the issue of relief from trade remedies. I had asked Derek to express to Baker my concern that the United States seemed more able to conclude an arms agreement with the Soviet Union (SALT II) than a trade agreement with its closest neighbour and ally. This seemed perverse to me. To the customary lament that "Congress would never buy" an agreement giving Canada relief from their trade remedy actions, my attitude was that the administration should "take a chance" with Congress, nonetheless. If Congress voted it down, so be it. After all, our negotiation was with the administration.

Although our message may have registered, Baker suggested only that the negotiators "deal with the underbrush," in other words, clear up the noncontentious issues as a way to maintain momentum. He may have been reluctant to upstage his cabinet colleague, Yeutter (Pat Carney's counterpart). In any event, Baker did not get involved at that time.

It was increasingly evident that the United States was assuming that Canada was prepared to accept any deal, however bad, in order to claim success. We had to disabuse them of that notion before we could expect any movement on the issues of greatest importance to us.

Throughout September the prospect of failure loomed ever larger. While for some around the cabinet table that spelled relief, the overall mood in the room was sombre. While walking away from a deal that failed to meet our twin objectives had short-term appeal, there was a definite political, as well as an economic, downside to a failed negotiation. As I explained angrily to cabinet, we were "being killed by indifference," with no one in Washington paying much attention to the negotiations. But if we were to pin the failure on a lack of focus or priority in the U.S. administration, that would simply underscore to our critics that the Americans were indifferent to a Canadian government committed to improving relations.

I knew we needed something to break the stalemate. At the September 22 TEC meeting, with the deadline only eleven days away, we set the stage for Simon Reisman to walk away or to suspend negotiations should there be no movement on trade remedies. Until then, negotiations had concentrated on possible definitions of allowable or nonallowable subsidies and some form of dispute settlement as a means to temper American actions against Canada. Most of the ideas came from the Canadian team. To that point, reactions from the U.S. had been both uncompromising and unpromising.

I indicated to the TEC, and later that week to full cabinet, that "barring a miracle, the enterprise has collapsed." While I had not given up, I wanted everyone to be ready for the worst.

At one o'clock in the afternoon on September 23, Reisman walked away from the table.

The pace quickened dramatically after that, and the focus shifted to the highest political level in both capitals. The Americans suspected initially that our action was simply a bluff or ploy. On September 24, Gotlieb's diary records: "[Senator] Chafee told me that our walkout was being interpreted by his colleagues on the Hill as a sign that Mulroney is weak – frightened of an agreement. How wrong can they get?" To kill that idea, Derek Burney was instructed to discourage Howard Baker from arranging a president-to-prime-minister telephone call, unless the Americans had something tangible to propose on trade remedies.

The minutes of the cabinet trade executive meeting for September 24, at 8:30 a.m., catch the emotions of that time: "[Pat Carney] noted that the current impasse would not be unwelcome to a number of cabinet ministers. She said that relief seemed to be the dominant feeling among her colleagues, and that there was not much will to continue. The prime minister responded that he was aware of this, and that he knew who the relieved colleagues were."

Jim Baker called Derek on September 24 and hinted that something along the lines of Sam Gibbons's proposal on dispute settlement might be the basis for a solution on trade remedies. The next day, however, presumably after some soundings with Congress, Baker backed away from any reference to Gibbons.

Gibbons, a Democrat from Florida, was the chair of the House Ways and Means Subcommittee on Trade. He had proposed that the application of the two countries' existing trade remedy instruments (antidumping, countervail, and so on) be subjected to binding dispute settlement by binational panels. His concept had not been fleshed out either in detail or actual practice. Nonetheless, it had the beauty of simplicity and, most importantly, would involve no onerous adjustment or new restrictions on Canada. All attempts at common definitions or "safe harbours" for subsidies had foundered, primarily because the implications for Canada would have been more severe than those for the United States. Because so much of what Canada produces has a trade dimension, unlike the U.S. with its massive internal market, any measure to modify subsidies or other supports to industry would have been much more restrictive for Canada. Gibbons's formula would, in effect, substitute binational panels for the more costly recourse to the U.S. courts, where decisions were not necessarily less arbitrary than those of their trade tribunals. The advantage of Gibbons's idea was that Canadians would be directly involved.

Gotlieb's diary entry for September 25, 1987 begins, "Everyone is scrambling to put Humpty Dumpty back together again." There were eight days to go.

On Saturday, September 26, the U.S. administration sent a two-page proposal attempting, once again, to define subsidies that would be permissible ("safe harbours") along with imprecise dispute settlement procedures. This proposal also featured the customary American wish list of higher thresholds for investment reviews and a series of irritants (such as beer, wine, pharmaceuticals) that Simon Reisman characterized as "scalps" intended to placate individual Congress representatives. Our team reacted coolly to this overture but sent a neutral response in order to avoid being blamed for failure. We were acutely sensitive to the record of events at this stage, wanting to be sure that the reasons for failure were defensible, especially to those who were counting on success from the initiative. I personally drafted the last paragraph, stressing to Baker the importance of his own role if a deal was to be achieved.

Despite a flurry of messages back and forth with Washington, and heroic individual efforts by Gotlieb, the prospects seemed dimmer as the month drew to a close. In Ottawa our emphasis moved to securing an honourable disengagement as opposed to producing new ideas to keep the initiative alive.

At the TEC meeting September 29, the consensus was that we should "play out the game" (assuming failure), and this set the stage for a discussion at the Priorities and Planning Committee later the same day. At this meeting, I asked Derek to give a balance sheet account of where matters stood. Derek was not only involved in frequent briefings from our negotiating team, he was also in regular, direct contact with the U.S. administration.

After recounting the pluses and minuses for each side, and assuming a breakthrough of some kind on dispute settlement, bearing in mind that we sought "better access" and "a shield against U.S. protectionism," Derek stated that the net result would be a decided plus economically and politically for Canada, but not an easy sell. He rated the prospects of a successful negotiation as "3 or 4 out of 10."

Pat Carney immediately challenged Derek's assessment. As "devil's advocate," she said that Canada risked "losing control of our economy, over regional development (like Hibernia), and would fall into U.S. line on films, videos, and so on." She added that what she saw would be "an exceptionally marginal deal in political terms." I invited other ministers to speak, and then summed matters up, saying I would rely on Derek to negotiate in good faith and determine whether the U.S. would meet our bottom-line objectives.

On that basis, I dispatched Derek Burney, Michael Wilson, Stanley Hartt, and Pat Carney to Washington on October 1 to signal clearly and firmly to Secretary Baker and Ambassador Yeutter that Canada was not prepared to accept any deal, and that "the deal we want, we do not see; the deal we see, we do not want."

Essentially, the Americans had proposed that we conclude a deal on the removal of tariffs – the key element of any free trade agreement – and leave the thorny issues like trade remedies and investment for a later date. We had concluded that this would not be good enough because our tariffs, on average, were slightly higher than theirs, so we had more to give than to get. That would not fly politically in Canada, even though, in economic terms, it would give a strong competitive impetus to our manufacturing sector. In fact, as I knew too well, *any* agreement between Canada and the United States risked being seen in Canada as more advantageous to the Americans. Before leaving for Washington, Derek received an intensive briefing from the Trade Negotiations Office (TNO) team and, on my instructions, had individual sessions with ministers like John Wise (Agriculture), Flora MacDonald (Communications), and Tom Siddon (Fisheries), whose concerns about the negotiation were the most acute.

On hearing Burney's crisp response, Jim Baker and others in the administration realized that they were staring failure in the face. And that, not surprisingly, is when Baker really decided to take charge. We assumed from the outset that relief from Canadian investment review provisions would be a major U.S. objective in the negotiations and, as secretary of treasury, Baker was responsible for investment policy. Investment and trade remedy instruments became the ultimate trade-offs we could offer to the negotiation, but the prospects for success were elusive up until the very last moment.

Pessimism was in the air everywhere. Gotlieb's diary entry for October 1 reads: "It is . . . two years since Mulroney first proposed a free trade agreement with the United States. But we've reached the end of the road . . . I know Mulroney does not want this agreement to fail. But he has been let down by the Americans and to a large extent his own cabinet." Writing in the *Globe and Mail*, Hugh Winsor summarized the mood, saying, "A quiet but honourable death of the Free Trade negotiations may not be all bad." I told Parliament that "the bottom line remained the same. This deal shall be in the national interest or there shall be no deal." In Quebec City on September 30, I had said, "If the U.S. persists in its refusal [to deal with trade remedies], it looks bad. But I think we had to try because it is in the best interests of Canada and Quebec."

Our group returned to Ottawa shortly after delivering our message. All were now thinking of damage control.

Later that evening (October 1), Baker called Derek Burney and asked explicitly whether the Gibbons formula on dispute settlement would be a basis to restart negotiations. I subsequently learned that, after our delegation had left Washington, Baker had taken several soundings with key senators on the Finance Committee and, while he had been skeptical initially, had concluded that the Gibbons formula just might fly.

Burney and Wilson asked to meet urgently with me that evening at 24 Sussex. They explained what they thought that the Gibbons formula meant and counselled that it was at least worth a further negotiating effort. I agreed and instructed them to resume full negotiations the next day in Washington. In effect, I charged Derek with the responsibility of securing a good deal if such were possible. If not, he was to try to bring the talks to an honourable conclusion.

As soon as they returned to Washington the next day (October 2), our delegation team – this time, Wilson, Burney, Carney, Reisman, and Gotlieb – discovered that they were not out of the woods yet. The devil, as they say, can be in the details, and we had few details at this point on the Gibbons formula, or anything else in the agreement.

Apart from confusion about the manner in which the formula would work, the second hurdle to overcome in the negotiation of Gibbons was how best to guard against unilateral changes being made to existing trade remedy rules by either party. On that, the best that could be obtained, over and above the application of prevailing GATT rights, was that Canada had to be specifically named in any new trade remedy legislation. What this did, in effect, was prevent Canada from being side-swiped by measures directed primarily at others. The Gibbons formula was to be in effect for seven years, while efforts to define subsidies continued. (In the absence of agreement on definitions, the formula actually became permanent in NAFTA, and was essentially emulated in the World Trade Organization Uruguay Round Agreement on Dispute Settlement.)

October 2 was a very long day for our team as they worked through the massive agenda from more than two years of negotiations, attempting to isolate areas of agreement and disagreement, and discussing with their U.S. counterparts how best to handle the latter. Gaps in perceptions about the Gibbons formula were very obvious. It was an equally long day for those of us standing by in Ottawa, receiving regular briefings from our team.

Midnight, October 3 was the real deadline for the U.S. administration to signal its readiness to enter negotiations under the fast-track authority and it proved to be a day of highs and lows like no other. The "Elements of Agreement" were beginning to take shape and, in an early evening call, Burney reported by telephone good progress on many fronts. An agreement on dispute settlement, however, was still much less certain. I urged Derek to impress on Baker again that the administration should "take a risk for Canada with Congress." What was unacceptable was an administration that would not fight for a good agreement, which was counter to the basic approach that my government and I had adopted in dealing with Washington. I reserved the right to call the president in the event the negotiations foundered on the key dispute settlement element.

At 9 p.m. the Canadian negotiators in Washington took a poll: they were unanimous. The deal was off. Derek phoned to tell me so.

I made arrangements to leave Harrington Lake and proceed to the Langevin Block to brief key ministers and later the media. When Derek called at about 9:30 to warn that a comprehensive deal appeared unlikely, I told him to advise Baker that I would be calling President Reagan at Camp David to put the following question: "Ron, how come the Americans can do a nuclear arms limitation deal with their worst enemies, the USSR, but can't do a trade deal with their best friends, the Canadians?"

Derek immediately met with Baker. According to Gotlieb, "Burney went back to see Baker alone to convey the news that the grand game was terminated and that we had failed. Our decision seemed to come as a thunderbolt to Baker. He pulled back and asked to be given more time. Burney agreed."

Burney's own memoirs record what happened next, an astonishing scene with Baker bursting into the Canadians' room and flinging a piece of paper on the table and saying, "All right, you can have your goddamn dispute settlement mechanism. Now we can send the report to Congress."

Shortly after 10 p.m. Burney called me again. "I think we have a deal after all," he reported, "including a dispute settlement understanding that meets your bottom line." He quickly summarized the key gains for Canada. I then polled the other seven members of his team – Michael Wilson, Pat Carney, Simon Reisman, Allan Gotlieb, Gordon Ritchie, Stanley Hartt, and Don Campbell. Their verdict was unanimous. They were exhausted but relieved, and very slowly the scale of the achievement swept through their office and my mind. I thanked them individually.

It had been an arduous struggle, a "near-run thing." After frantic final efforts, which Gotlieb describes as "a wild atmosphere, everyone running up and down corridors," a (possibly mythical) motorcycle courier dashed along Pennsylvania Avenue to deliver the notice to Congress just one minute before the midnight deadline. But our tactics, our firmness in the crunch, and our perseverance had paid off. In retrospect, it is apparent to me that Baker was ultimately as determined to deliver for his president as I knew Derek Burney and my cabinet colleagues had been for me.

The bilateral negotiating battle over free trade was essentially over. The battle for support in Canada was really just beginning.

At about 1:30 a.m. on October 3, I briefed the media outside the Langevin Block, saying, "A hundred years from now what will be remembered is that it was done. The naysayers will be forgotten."

The verdict of history is already evident. The Free Trade Agreement, and its successor, NAFTA, have increased trade threefold between Canada and the United States. Despite the vicissitudes of the economic downturn in 1990–91 and the peso crisis of 1995, these agreements served as a catalyst for productivity improvements, as well as for global trade liberalization. Together with the Uruguay Round and the creation of the WTO, they were fundamental to Canada's economic growth in the decades that followed. The proof of our success is the fact that even the bitterest opponents of the initiative in the Liberal opposition became champions of the FTA–NAFTA when they assumed power.

—

PERSONAL JOURNAL: JANUARY 1, 1988

The appointment of Derek Burney as chief of staff was a major and beneficial one. In truth he was, at the critical moments, my key agent in the free trade negotiations. He played an absolutely vital role in their successful conclusion.

By August it was abundantly obvious that I would either have to fire Carney as trade minister or assume responsibility for it myself. Pat Carney is a fine, principled, and able person, but she had not had an easy life.

By the late summer she was still locked into a venomous feud with Simon Reisman. She had implored me countless times to fire him, and Simon had not helped the situation with his peremptory treatment of cabinet ministers, senior aides, officials, etc. I had refused. Reisman was the best person for negotiating with the Americans.

At a meeting at Meech Lake in late August I constituted an executive cabinet committee on trade with myself in the chair. This had the practical – if less than evident effect – of removing Pat Carney from a position of control in the free trade negotiations. Derek Burney became my personal representative in this area, and it was soon obvious to ministers that I was going to personally call the shots from there on in.

What had particularly troubled me – apart from the constant demands from Carney that Reisman be fired and the growing petulance she exhibited in dealing with cabinet and officials – was the unnecessary enthusiasm for the prospects of an impossible conclusion to the negotiations. She had developed a theory that such a failure would propel Canada to a new position of leadership at the GATT, where we would emphasize multilateralism, etc.! I often pointed out to her that the two were not mutually exclusive and that our principal market was the U.S., that a FTA with the U.S. would, at this time in our development, be an act of uncommon vision and leadership that would benefit Canada for decades to come.

In any case, notwithstanding a heavy load – Chirac visit, Francophonie Summit, Royal Visit, Commonwealth in Vancouver – I began to exercise daily control, either directly or through Maz or Burney, on the trade file. Through this time frame we made some crucial decisions, including the one to order Reisman home. While we had encountered frustrations, and progress was unencouraging, my real reason for interrupting the process was to force President Reagan to place Jim Baker in charge of the American team – the only man in the administration with the clout, knowledge, and desire to make this happen.

Jim Baker was perhaps the only person in the administration at the moment who understood the importance of this initiative to the United States and who, because of his personal relationship with me, Wilson, and others, understood its vital political realities for us.

Moments after the removal of Reisman from the talks, White House Chief of Staff Howard Baker called Derek Burney to say that President Reagan wanted to speak to me urgently. I told Burney to advise Baker that I had nothing to say to Reagan and that there was little he could say to me – the problem was one of political clout on the American side, and that in my view Jim Baker was the only one who could do the deal. Soon thereafter Jim Baker took over and I designated Wilson and Burney and Carney as our reps, and the negotiations resumed at the political level, where it was crunched and the matters resolved.

On two occasions after Jim Baker became involved, the talks came within a flash of failing. In both cases the Americans, at the last moment, changed position and accommodated the Canadian view, particularly on the dispute settlement mechanism, which some Americans viewed as a "surrender of sovereignty."

Baker's involvement came during the IMF–World Bank week of meetings in Washington, and it was a measure of the importance Baker attached to his responsibilities that he devoted himself almost exclusively to the trade file and hardly set foot elsewhere during the period. I spoke to him personally about midnight on the night we had the deal, and I know his sense of accomplishment was real. He had, in my view, rescued the talks from certain failure on the American side

> *and contributed significantly to the realization of an important policy of President Reagan.*
>
> *It is interesting to note that after we concluded the agreement in principle on Oct. 4, the political rehabilitation of Pat Carney began in earnest. She had suffered badly because of her absence in Hawaii during the softwood lumber dispute and had irritated many important players – including Premier Peterson, whom she drove to distraction. Her political demise was widely talked about, but the same journalists inadvertently resurrected her with their predictions that the deal would never take place – that the American Congress would never agree to a dispute settlement mechanism, etc., etc.*
>
> *When the deal did occur, Carney was in Washington and was given all the credit – by Wilson and Burney, who in truth played more significant roles – and the Canadian press corps was so busy wiping the egg off its face that it forgot about Carney and began playing up – or attacking – the agreement itself. Meanwhile Carney has handled herself well in the House, has looked good doing it, and – in the ultimate reversal – has now claimed Simon Reisman as a bosom buddy with whom she wants to go into business in the future.*

—

I got home to Harrington Lake at about 2:30 in the morning. I had spoken again to Derek on the way up and was aware that our team was immersed in richly deserved celebrations in Washington. After going over the highlights of the agreement with Mila, who had waited up, I placed my last call, to Allan Gotlieb to thank him personally for his vital role in the successful conclusion of the FTA: "One day, I believe, history will record this as one of Canada's great achievements," I told him. "And the record will show that you played an exceptionally important role throughout."

The minutes of the full cabinet meeting of October 4 at 7 p.m. speak for themselves:

> The prime minister said that Canadian figures would have to be careful about their public rhetoric. He decried the boastful comment . . . about not leaving a nickel on the table. He was also amused by, if somewhat wary about, the comment by Premier Vander Zalm, which he reported as "fantastic, Canada got it all!"

> Ministers had to be careful, he said. The ministers of international trade and finance and the chief of staff had done a wonderful deal, but he was not going to be unduly jubilant in public. He thought there was a real possibility that we had indeed outsmarted the United States. In this room only, he said, he would say that Canada had come out a lot better than the U.S. Since every U.S. protectionist will say it is a U.S. sellout, circumspection would be required.

In 2006, Jim Baker described the deal from his point of view: "The catalyst for the agreement with Canada was the election of a conservative government headed by Brian Mulroney in 1984. Like President Reagan, he passionately believed in free trade and had the political courage in the face of significant domestic opposition to try to erase tariffs and other barriers to the movement of goods between Canada and the United States. The ultimate agreement was a testament to the vision, courage, and political will of these two great leaders."

1987

9. The End of an Interesting Year

SEPTEMBER 17, 1987 marked the third anniversary of my government's swearing-in. I was in a melancholy mood as the date approached. As I surveyed the scene from Harrington Lake one crisp fall morning, I imagined what I'd say were I to speak to Canadians in a special anniversary address. Taking out a pen, I wrote a twenty-one-page outline for a fireside chat, realizing all too well it was a talk I would never give.

"I'd like to talk to you tonight about what I've learned and what I've lost," I wrote. "About why we have failed and where we have succeeded. About where Canada is and what it can become. Three years ago today I became prime minister of Canada. By and large, we were new and untried. It had been twenty-six years since my party had formed a majority government. In fact, the Conservatives had been in office less than nine months in a quarter-century. That's a long time to be outside the government process, outside the group of people that had decided issues and shaped policy for much of our lives . . . I knew then there would be moments of severe disappointment and heartache for me, my family, and my party. And indeed there have been both."

I wrote about our accomplishments: a historic breakthrough for another federalist party in Quebec; the fact we'd promised "jobs, jobs, jobs" and delivered, as Canada's unemployment rate was now the lowest it had been in six years; the beginnings of tax reform; the removal of hundreds of thousands of low-income Canadians from the tax rolls; Meech Lake; an unprecedented role for Canada in the world and more. I also examined our failures:

> All of these important questions and challenges we have handled fairly, and I think, well. If that is the case, then I think the question is obvious: Why is the government not doing better with the voters? I think I am a large part of the problem. All political changes give rise to expectations. Our victory three years ago was the biggest in

> Canadian history, and as a result expectations were sky-high. Simply put, the government in general, and I in particular, have failed to live up to your expectations . . .
>
> As I reflect on my three years as prime minister, I can see serious mistakes, instances where I have let you down. The issue of patronage and ethics probably goes to the heart of it. The issue dominated the election campaign and you have been clearly very troubled by the manner and way my government has dealt with it. In truth, I seriously misunderstood the message you were delivering three years ago. I thought you were telling me to bring about greater fairness and better representation from all parties to the appointments process. What you really meant was the following: Clean the bloody mess up, once and for all.
>
> In this area we have doubled the number of women and ethnocultural representatives appointed to boards, agencies, and commissions. We have dramatically increased the number of women and minorities to federal judicial appointments. We have appointed more known partisans from other political parties than any other government in our history . . . Notwithstanding our efforts, you are clearly unimpressed by our objectives and our actions. I fear that this patronage issue has become a symbol, a test of integrity by which you judge the moral value of our accomplishments. Clearly we have failed you in this important area of ethics and propriety. I see this failure as very serious and accept full responsibility for it.

My notes continued as I wrote about creating an ethics commissioner whose office would be modelled on that of the auditor general, and about open tenders for government contracts, and I also highlighted a new appointments process. Of course, not all of these plans came to fruition. The creation of an ethics commissioner was fiercely resisted by the Privy Council Office. I mistakenly accepted their view that one of my duties was to hand over intact, to future prime ministers, the rights and prerogatives of the prime minister I had found upon arriving in office.

The *Globe and Mail* had recently published a description of the closets at 24 Sussex Drive that made it sound like I was living the life of a Russian czar, and my notes touched on these false impressions as well. "The image of a vain, high-living leader given to exaggeration has been conveyed to you so often that I can't blame you for accepting it," I wrote. "The truth is quite at odds with this impression. I am a prime minister who cares nothing about cars and diplomatic parties, but who cares a great deal about tolerance, prosperity, and unity – the very reasons I entered public life in the first place."

I read the speech to my cabinet, looking for their advice as to whether I should make it public. Led by John Crosbie, the cabinet objected, considering it "demeaning" and "inadvisable" for the prime minister to speak to Canadians in this fashion. I wonder today if I should have delivered that speech. While my critics would have panned it – accusing me of feeling sorry for myself – I've often thought that ordinary Canadians would have listened carefully and made considered judgments that would have likely gone my way. To reveal myself so publicly went against the natural instincts that had guided me since my Baie-Comeau days. But by not fighting back, I ceded the ground to my opponents, and continued to pay the price long after I left office.

While my government continued that fall to make reforms in ethics and appointments, we went forward with our trademark initiatives as well. On September 20, the joint Senate–House committee I'd established to study the Meech Lake Accord submitted its report, recommending that the federal government ratify the accord unchanged. "No one should expect absolute perfection in a compromise," the report read, "[and] nothing has been said to lead us to believe that the basic principles of the Canadian federation would be compromised." Four of the five Liberals on the committee, however, refused to sign the report.

A few days later Saskatchewan became the first English-speaking province to ratify the Meech Lake Accord.

With the Free Trade Agreement now a reality – and with Canadian and American lawyers fine-tuning the legal text in a process that would take many months – I continued Canada's efforts to help end apartheid in South Africa. In August I became the first leader from the West to meet with Oliver Tambo, the head of the African National Congress while Nelson Mandela remained in prison. When he sat down with me and Joe Clark in Ottawa, he got an earful.

While Joe and I were taking on the opponents of sanctions – powerful people like Ronald Reagan and Margaret Thatcher – Tambo was keeping silent as ANC supporters in Soweto placed gas-filled tires around the necks of their political enemies and set them alight in front of the world's media.

This was called "necklacing." "Our job is tough enough," I told Tambo, "without you making it even more difficult. Thatcher and Reagan already think you and the ANC are communists, and now you hand them this."

That year's Commonwealth Meeting in Vancouver was again a challenge as Margaret hadn't modified her anti-sanctions views: the lady, as she proudly put it in another context, was "not for turning." She arrived in Canada repeating her view that further sanctions against South Africa wouldn't work and were definitely not part of her agenda, regardless of the views of every other Commonwealth country. Every single one.

"We see no purpose in having an argument about sanctions," a British official arrogantly told the press. "We will concentrate on what's practical and constructive, not emotional and destructive."

As conference chairman, I took Margaret on in my opening address. "If we are to be effective, we must speak with a strong voice," I said. "Each member nation may take such action as it deems necessary . . . but as a community of nations, the Commonwealth should agree on fundamental and increasingly effective measures to deal with the situation."

In Vancouver I witnessed an unsavoury side to British diplomacy when, out of the blue, Margaret accused Canada of rank hypocrisy. Using statistics that she knew full well were already out of date, she released to the press figures purporting to show that Canada's trade with South Africa had increased by 25 per cent over 1985–86, while Britain's trade with the racist nation was declining. In fact, the sanctions my government supported had only been finalized at the Commonwealth mini-summit in London in 1986 because we had spent so much time trying to reach an accommodation with the British prime minister. The statistics reflecting Canada's actions hadn't started to show movement until January of 1987, and the truth was that our trade with South Africa had declined 52 per cent during the first six months of 1987.

With every Commonwealth country lined up on the side of sanctions, Margaret was the single holdout, again abdicating her nation's leadership role in the organization the United Kingdom had founded. Backed into a corner, she struck out and made Canada her scapegoat. Bob Hawke, Robert Mugabe, Kenneth Kaunda, and Rajiv Gandhi held a press conference to publicly criticize Margaret's desperate tactics, not to mention her rudeness.

In my closing remarks, I asked my fellow leaders, "Imagine a situation where Canada's 20 million whites were ruled by 5 million blacks, with the latter group establishing a racist system of government that denied the white majority even basic democratic rights and freedoms. Would the West – and the United States specifically – intervene then? You'd better believe it."

This comparison infuriated Margaret, and she glared repeatedly at me during the public and private sessions in Vancouver. Stephen Lewis later called my confrontation with Thatcher an "electric moment." I made no attempt to glaze over Margaret's self-imposed isolation.

"One of the central issues of this conference has been South Africa," I said in the same closing remarks, "and one of the central questions has been sanctions. Almost unanimously, we came to the conclusion that sanctions do work, that they shall continue to be applied, that they must be applied more intensively. That is the message which, with the exception of Great Britain, we send out from Vancouver."

The rancour aside, the Commonwealth did agree with Canada's idea for the creation of the Commonwealth Committee of Foreign Ministers to continue to keep the pressure on South Africa. Joe Clark became chairman of the committee group and was to serve effectively in that role in the years ahead.

Canada also successfully convinced the Commonwealth to issue the Vancouver Declaration on World Trade. It helped showcase the uniqueness of the Commonwealth, a voluntary gathering of nations from the First and Third Worlds, from North and South, nonaligned and Western. "[The Declaration] reflects the aspirations of peoples from all continents, and of all levels of development," I continued in my closing remarks. "The world trading system must be strengthened. Protectionism must be fought. The war of agricultural subsidies must stop in the interest of developed and developing nations alike."

Just as we had at the Francophonie Summit in Quebec City, Canada wrote off more than $300 million in Third World debt for the most hard-pressed African states represented in Vancouver.

"If the six other [G-7] countries applied similar measures on an equivalent basis, we would wipe out 15 per cent of the debt of these nations, which would be a significant step in assisting the poorest of the poor," I said. "They are making painful sacrifices. They deserve our help."

Leaders also ordered the Commonwealth Secretariat to commission a study of the impact of structural adjustment measures on women. The environment was on the agenda, as well, and we discussed stresses to the natural environment caused by poverty and rapid population growth. Canada was one of the countries that raised these early concerns about the implications of human-created climate change.

It had been a heavy agenda, but I was proud of Canada and the Commonwealth as the Vancouver meeting came to an end. I was able to reflect on the unique value of this world forum on the way back to Ottawa.

Any Commonwealth leader who has dealt with Her Majesty the Queen learns quickly that she holds strong convictions about the institution she heads. Her radiant smile said it all to her Canadian first minister when she attended a state dinner in her honour in Quebec City following the Vancouver meeting, in October 1987.

"In the Commonwealth, the heart of the institution is the idea itself," I had said in my opening speech in Vancouver, "this splendid voluntary association among member states . . . The Commonwealth brings to the problems of today a common heritage, a heritage which can create a community of values, and galvanize us to address our common problems in a particularly productive way. If it is the Crown which has given the Commonwealth its continuity, it is its citizens who give it a continuing purpose."

I wouldn't change a word today. I know Her Majesty would agree. As for Margaret Thatcher, she mellowed somewhat upon her return to London. A pleasant handwritten note from her soon landed on my desk in Ottawa.

"I cannot thank you enough for your superb organization of the conference and for the excellent arrangements you made for our security and comfort," she wrote. "Your own drive, the coordination of a friendly atmosphere, and spirited discussion – all contributed greatly to the success of the occasion. And may I add, your own questions and sensitive chairmanship were a model of how to run a large and divisive meeting. We all felt we had an opportunity to express our views."

Not long after the Vancouver Commonwealth Meeting, Canada lost one of its greatest democrats. Former Quebec Premier René Lévesque died on November 1, and I immediately ordered Canadian flags flying over federal buildings in Quebec lowered as a sign of respect. I was at home with the flu when I received the news. It was the first time I'd missed work since I took office. But ill or not, I resolved to attend Lévesque's state funeral in Quebec City, and was able to do so, joining Robert Bourassa in mourning a Quebec legend.

Later that month, MP Pat Nowlan made one of his trademark negative comments during a caucus meeting in Ottawa. I wasn't going to let his persistent negativity infect us all after such a productive year.

"Pat Nowlan says half the caucus is new and half of them won't be back [after the upcoming election]," I said during my summation. "Well, I think each and every one of you, in his or her own way, has made a significant contribution to Canada. I am not conceding a single seat. I will fight with all my heart to make sure that every one of you is back. What we have going on in the House is war – a political war of the toughest kind."

I stared directly at Nowlan as I finished my remarks.

"There are no shades of grey," I said. "You are on one side or the other."

As 1987 came to an end, it was plain that 1988 would be a crucial year for all Progressive Conservatives in Ottawa. I rallied our team at the last caucus meeting of the year. It was December 16 and we were all in fighting form.

"1988 is an election year," I said, "and unity is indispensable. This caucus has done great things and Canada is united and prosperous. The mood is good and the polls are up. I have worked too hard and we all have fought too long and done too much for Canada. I am not going to throw it away. I am not going to allow anyone else to throw it away. Let me tell you this: I do not want Serge Joyal back in charge of language policy in Canada. I don't want Marc Lalonde back to impose a new National Energy Policy on the West. I don't want the FTA torn up and with it the hopes it offered. In Canada the game of politics has one fundamental rule: unity. If you are united, you win. If you are not, you lose. This requires understanding and mutual respect. The other day Serge Joyal announced he was running again for the Liberals and he was asked how he thought he could win with everyone in Quebec supporting free trade. Listen to what he said: 'I am counting on the Tories to destroy themselves again on a sensitive national issue.'"

With that, our Progressive Conservative MPs left Ottawa both united and spoiling for a chance to fight the Liberals and NDP. But as I watched them leave the caucus room I knew one thing for sure: no Conservative had been returned with a consecutive majority government since 1891, under Sir John A. Macdonald himself.

It would be an enormous challenge in the new year to defy history and change all that.

1988

1. An Auspicious Start

PERSONAL JOURNAL: JANUARY 1, 1988

(Written at Harrington Lake)

It has been a long and difficult time (but a new poll has the government improving), and I am genuinely grateful to all those cabinet, caucus, and party colleagues who hung in there with us through the dark days. There will be tough times for us in the future, no doubt, but it is unlikely that anything can be as demanding and sustained as the period just ended. If adversity forms character, I want to formally state that mine is completely and permanently formed.

—

I SPENT MOST OF the trip from Harrington Lake to my office in the Parliament Buildings on January 2, 1988 in silence. The driver and the RCMP security staff seemed to sense the importance of the occasion and went about their duties with an added measure of solemnity. Coming onto Parliament Hill, I noted the statue of Laurier that faces out toward the landmark Château Laurier Hotel named in his honour. I recalled that Laurier himself had been defeated in 1911 when an election was fought over the issue of free trade with the United States. And here I was, travelling to my office to sign the Free Trade Agreement with that same United States, at the beginning of what was almost certain to be an election year.

I also took a peek at old Mackenzie King as my car drove by his statue at the other end of the East Block. King had started negotiations with the United States and then backed away, fearing the political consequences if he succeeded. Despite these warnings from history, I was confident that I could and would carry the country when I made the decision to go to the polls. Above all else, I was confident that Canadians would see that negotiating a comprehensive free trade agreement was about leadership. And, most importantly, about Canada's future.

President Reagan, home at his ranch in California, signed the FTA on his nation's behalf. In my office I took out my pen and did so for Canada. Later I briefly addressed the nation. "We have negotiated this agreement on terms that uphold the national interest and strengthen the unique fabric of Canadian society," I said. "I sign, on behalf of the Government of Canada, with pride in our country, faith in our people, and confidence in our future."

I caught up on some paperwork and then left my office and was taken back to the Gatineaus. I made a pit stop for an elegant meal after crossing over into Hull. When I arrived at Harrington Lake, the kids insisted we go skating. Only the next day was I able to reflect on the important event in the life of the nation that had just taken place.

—

PERSONAL JOURNAL: JANUARY 3, 1988

Yesterday at 4 p.m., following a conversation with President Reagan, I signed the Free Trade Agreement in my parliamentary office. It had been a long brutal road to secure the agreement and I felt both a sense of pride and a measure of accomplishment as I signed the documents and read a brief statement in French and English. No one can foresee the future. Therefore no one can accurately predict either the complete outcome of the trade debate or its ultimate impact on the country. I believe, however, that a number of points can be made with some assurance:

1. *The agreement is historic in both sweep and objectives.*
2. *It marks the creation of a free trade zone between the world's largest bilateral trading partners.*
3. *At a time when protectionism began to find great favour in the U.S. Congress and elsewhere, it turns the tide toward liberalized trade and against inward-looking pernicious protectionism.*
4. *The agreement will have a significant impact on the GATT, covering as it does trade in goods and services and agriculture.*
5. *It will polarize debate in Canada for the next year and impact considerably the general election, representing as it does a choice between honing our skills for the 21st century and attempting to*

arrest change by creating a sedate, unhurried, and progressively economically lifeless society in Canada.

When it was over, I worked for a few hours with Derek Burney, and, because Mila was in Montreal, had a quick chicken dinner in Hull at St. Hubert Bar-B-Q. This will surprise my detractors, who constantly imagine me spending my life in expensive restaurants. If only they knew!

Our agenda is, I think, a good one for this year: budget in early February, Olympics in Calgary, official visit to the USSR, industrialized G-7 Summit in Toronto, Washington Summit. Prospects for economic growth remain very good. The provinces will continue to ratify the Meech Lake documents. Tax reform will proceed. There will be serious legislative problems (because of opposition obstructionism) with the FTA-enabling legislation, but it will, I believe, all pass the House.

After the economic summit in late spring in Toronto, we will have to zero in on an election timetable. The question will be whether to go in early or late fall or the winter of 1989? If the present encouraging trends continue, the decision will no doubt become easier. But I do not for a moment underestimate the difficulties. Ranged against us will be, of course, the two opposition parties, the "cultural nationalists," trade union leaders, much of the press gallery, and all of the left-wing media and commentators. At the best of times, it is not easy for a Conservative leader to either win a general election or win a majority. History provides ample evidence of this. And so we are going to need all the strength of which we are capable and all the unity we can summon (plus a little good luck on the side!) if we are to emerge from this particular battle victorious – and victorious we shall be!

I plan, with Mila's invaluable assistance, to wage a campaign across Canada of uncommon intensity and directness and effectiveness. I do not fear the electorate in any way – indeed I look forward to their judgment – confident that in the end accomplishment will be rewarded and progress will be maintained. Serving as prime minister of Canada is a great honour given to few men and women. The greatest satisfaction comes from knowing from within your heart that you have done your very best to strengthen the unity and prosperity of Canada, that you have worked as hard and diligently as a human can, and that the large and small issues that affect the nation were handled effectively and well. History will record that this I have done, with the support of family and colleagues.

—

I knew my government had to convey an impression of competence in the months ahead. There had been some bumpy moments in the previous three years and further bumps simply had to be avoided.

The Meech Lake Accord was one definite bright spot. We had promised national reconciliation and we had delivered. Alberta had by now ratified the accord and Premier Don Getty was caught up in the new spirit as 1988 began.

"The Government of Alberta responded to Quebec's constitutional aspirations because we firmly believed that it was in the national interest to achieve a reconciliation," he wrote me on January 8. "As all governments worked toward a consensus on Quebec's five constitutional proposals, Alberta sought at the same time an express recognition that other dimensions of Canada's constitutional framework were equally important and equally in need of reform. We sought to achieve a package that would be acceptable to the people of Quebec, yet that would be respectful of the aspirations and needs of the other regions and provinces of Canada. I believe we achieved that delicate balance on June 3."

Little did Getty or I know what lay ahead. Ironically, it was only a few weeks later that members of Preston Manning's western-based Reform movement announced their decision to become an official federal party. Unlike his fellow Albertan Don Getty, Manning showed no signs of demonstrating either generosity or compromise in dealing with Quebec, or any other province or region.

Albertans like Deputy Prime Minister Don Mazankowski, Foreign Affairs Minister Joe Clark, and Minister of Consumer and Corporate Affairs Harvie Andre were providing their province with perhaps the strongest cabinet representation in history. My government abolished the National Energy Policy and the *Foreign Investment Review Act*, moved the head office of the National Energy Board to Calgary, and created a cabinet-level Western Diversification Agency in Edmonton. Western farmers had received record financial assistance from our government. Nevertheless, Manning launched his Reform Party with the argument that we had "ignored Alberta."

But with the FTA now signed and with Meech well on the way to ratification, my trusted colleague Finance Minister Michael Wilson, as always, was key to our projecting competence. After he brought down another budget in early February, he spoke to a joint meeting of the Empire and Canadian clubs in Toronto. "We live in a fast-changing, volatile world," he said. "It is difficult to predict the future and even more difficult to make specific plans to anticipate future conditions. The key to our success, whether as individuals, as companies, or as governments, is to be able to respond quickly and flexibly to change when it happens. The policy of our government is designed for just that."

Foreign affairs was another area where I demanded that my government shine. The annual G-7 Summit was scheduled for Toronto, and the pressure was on me as chairman. My sherpa, Sylvia Ostry, made it clear in one memo just how important the Toronto Summit was from the vantage point of foreign capitals. "In my association with summitry since 1979, never have I witnessed such intensive, widespread preparation for a summit as for Toronto," she wrote. "For example, the White House has established a senior cabinet-level task force involving secretaries Shultz and Baker as well as Howard Baker, which has met repeatedly to brief Mr. Reagan. As well, all sherpas (at a recent meeting) had met with their leaders to receive instructions prior to this second sherpa meeting. Another, more substantive, indication of the increased attention the summit is receiving this year is a concerted Japanese campaign of media leaks to get across, domestically, to Asian NICs [nonindustrialized countries] and internationally, Tokyo's views on, and priorities for, Toronto."

Planning for the summit was becoming a full-time job in itself for me. Environment Minister Tom McMillan wrote me during that planning period, asking me to ensure that the protection of the environment was placed on the G-7 agenda. As I reflect on these years I am struck by the priority my government continued to give to the environment, Third World development, and human rights – areas of concern not always readily associated with conservative governments.

"Canada is recognized as a world leader in environmental matters," Tom wrote. "We took the report of the World Commission on Environment and Development [the Brundtland Commission] to heart and issued the first response. Canada has been a key player in the development of the international protocols on sulphur dioxide, ozone, and nitrogen oxides, which are the building blocks of a potential international law of the air, and we will host the World Conference on the Changing Atmosphere the week after the summit. Moreover, by moving on acid rain, the *Canadian Environmental Protection Act*, and environment-economy integration, we have put the Canadian house in order." I agreed wholeheartedly with Tom's suggestion for the agenda.

As the chair I wanted to ensure that the format of our meetings in Canada's largest city featured the best of what I'd seen at Bonn, Tokyo, and Venice, and left out all of the worst features. When I contacted all my summit partners with my proposals early in the year, President Reagan was one of the first to reply. "Your desire to reduce the formality of the meetings, thus creating an environment more conducive to spontaneous discussion of key economic and political issues, is very much in line with my own thoughts," he wrote. "On the matter of the communiqué, I commend to you our experience at Williamsburg, where the topics actually discussed were included in the final statement."

While I was pleased with Reagan's thoughts on the summit, I was – yet again – frustrated by his administration's approach to acid rain. Joe Clark and his counterpart in Washington, George Shultz, had already met that year. The American secretary of state made it clear to Joe that an accord between Canada and the United States that featured specific targets for emission reductions, and a timetable to accomplish them, wasn't going to happen. Shultz (who couldn't have known that his country would in fact sign the Acid Rain Treaty with Canada, which contained both specific targets and a timetable in only three years' time) told Joe, "Canada is asking for the impossible. If an accord with anything less than targets and a timetable is a disaster, then we have a disaster."

Things were so bad that Tom McMillan and others were advising me to break off talks with Washington and embark on a public relations campaign in the United States to deliver Canada's message. Joe was more cautious. "[Clark] and his officials are aware that one of the main disadvantages of the 'break-off' option would be the adverse implications it would have on the government's approach to Canada–USA relations and its management of the relationship," Paul Tellier wrote in a confidential memo on January 15.

I chose a middle course and wrote to Reagan after I received a letter from him on the topic in late January. I threw his own words back at him:

> I must tell you that I was deeply disappointed and troubled by the American position expressed at the January 25 meeting. I detected no

> sense of urgency or of commitment to tackling the transboundary aspect of the acid rain problem as we are both obliged to do under international law. Above all, I was disappointed by the rejection by the American side of the very concept of agreeing to transborder reduction targets and timetables within which they could be achieved. This is the only way we can, in my view, achieve a meaningful and effective bilateral accord . . .
>
> Ron, I was struck by a phrase in your recent State of the Union address in which you noted that no agreement is better than a bad agreement. I agree. I believe that an acid rain accord which does not contain a commitment to reduction targets and timetables would be a bad agreement for Canada. I think such an accord would call into question our seriousness and credibility in tackling this problem . . . I would urge you to authorize your officials to adopt a position leading to firm and clear commitments by both of us to reduce the transborder flow of sulphur dioxide. We should, as you suggest, seize this opportunity, but it must be for an effective and credible accord.

Unlike his decisive actions in East–West relations and other important international issues, when it came to acid rain, Ronald Reagan, as I was to find out in April in Washington, was unable to fully seize the moment.

In March I attended another NATO Summit in Brussels. Western Europe and many of its leaders were caught up in the throes of what could be called "Gorbymania." While I liked and admired Soviet President Mikhail Gorbachev and believed he was the West's best hope for an end to the Cold War, I was growing concerned at the proclivities of many in the West to demand that we, and the Americans in particular, give away even more in our negotiations with him.

In 1983 and 1984, I had paid lip service to Pierre Trudeau's peace initiative. While I wanted peace as much as anyone, I never shared Trudeau's underlying belief that the United States and the Soviet Union were morally equivalent in terms of the Cold War. (In November 1985 I was given a briefing by a KGB defector, who told me that Trudeau's peace plan had been a great comfort to the Kremlin because it demonstrated Canada's lack of solidarity with the Western alliance.) To my mind, the issue was clear. The Soviet Union was a corrupt, totalitarian state in an advanced state of decay. I believed that the best way of dealing with it was to provide strong support to President Reagan's view that the ultimate objective had to be the dissolution of the Soviet Union – not a negotiation for equal coexistence.

Going into the NATO Summit I was fully in agreement with calls for cuts in the West's nuclear arms and conventional forces – but only if the Warsaw Pact cut even further. As I sat around the table in Brussels and listened to leader after leader tell the American president to trust Gorbachev and negotiate deeper cuts to the West's nuclear umbrella, I knew it was time for action by Canada. Taking my pen out, I rewrote my remarks to provide a ringing defence of American leadership in this vital area.

Reagan's National Security Advisor Colin Powell was at that meeting. He later described my speech: "[Mulroney] began by saying he knew a little about living next door to a superpower too," he wrote. "Mulroney then compared the three-thousand-mile undefended border between his country and ours to the bristling border between the Eastern bloc and the West. That armed frontier represented the past, he said. The U.S.–Canadian model must represent the future. Mulroney was eloquent, and he helped steer the day away from the Gorbymania that had dominated [the meeting] so far."

I was later to have occasion to point out to leaders from China, the Soviet Union, and other nations the view from my office on Parliament Hill. On a clear day, I would say, were it not for the office towers in Ottawa, you could probably see as far as the Canada–U.S. border at Messina, New York. "And what *don't* you see? Soldiers and fortifications," I said to Gorbachev, among others. "This is the way two advanced democracies function. Compare that with the Soviet–Chinese border and count the number of divisions on both sides."

Reagan was touched by my remarks in Brussels and wrote to tell me so soon after he arrived back in Washington:

> I just wanted to send you a short note to reiterate how impressed I was with your moving intervention on the second day of the NATO Summit. Your remarks effectively countered a disturbing tendency we see in some countries toward seeing the U.S. and Soviet Union as "morally equivalent," or in seeking "equidistance from the superpowers." Too often we take for granted the excellent relationship Canada and the United States enjoy – the undefended border, our extensive trade ties, unhindered travel across our borders, and the cooperative basis of our defense relations. Attention all too often is directed toward those few areas where we have differences.

> Your remarks in Brussels put the stress where it belongs – on the positive aspects not just of our bilateral ties but of the NATO Alliance as a whole. Again, Brian, many thanks for your thoughtful and effective intervention. Let us hope that we can continue to impress on our Allies that the relationship we enjoy is the model the Alliance should seek to emulate.

Domestic political matters were on my mind as well in Brussels, and I asked Ambassador Lucien Bouchard to come from Paris to Brussels for dinner in my suite. In a way it was just like old times at Laval: exhausted from a transatlantic flight followed by an all-day session, I met my friend in my pyjamas and bathrobe. Lucien had been a very effective ambassador for Canada – so much so that Jacques Parizeau had publicly complained about how Lucien had marginalized the Quebec delegation in Paris – and I thought he'd be a first-rate cabinet minister in my government.

"How do you feel about Canada now?" I asked my former classmate.

He told me he had acquired a brand-new appreciation of the country because of his experience representing Canada's interests internationally. "Canada is a magnificent country and I have been honoured to represent it in France," he said. "Canada has an important role to play in the world, and I have learned to love Canada. I would be pleased to come home and do what you wish."

And so Lucien Bouchard became a politician. He was sworn into cabinet as secretary of state as part of a crucial shuffle on March 31. Only a few days later, he spoke publicly after he met with representatives of the Association culturelle franco-canadienne de la Saskatchewan. "It is important that Quebec adhere to the Constitution," he said. "When it has done so, there will be an important distinct society in Canada . . . a part of the federation which makes a formal and honourable act of joining, which will be creative and productive for the federation . . . Canada can then move to the next stage, entrenching minority rights of francophones in the Constitution."

We began immediately to plan for a by-election so I could get Lucien into the House of Commons. While he wanted to run in a Montreal-area riding, I disagreed. I persuaded a good MP, Clément Côté, to step aside, and on April 29, Bouchard announced he'd be the PC candidate in a by-election I had called for June 20 in Lac-Saint-Jean.

And then the problems began. In short, Lucien's campaign was a disaster. Lysiane Gagnon, writing in *La Presse*, was soon describing him as one of the worst candidates she had ever seen. I began hearing other disturbing reports about a failing campaign. My friend L. Ian MacDonald came to my suite at the Château Frontenac to report that his fiancée, Lisa Van Dusen, covering the by-election for *Maclean's*, said Bouchard was faltering and that the campaign was staggering to a near-certain defeat. Polls showed Bouchard running behind the Liberal candidate Pierre Gimaïel, although I continued to run three to one ahead of John Turner in voter preference for prime minister.

I called Luc Lavoie, a shrewd and talented young journalist from Rimouski, by now a senior member of my staff, to my suite and instructed him to get up to Alma immediately and report back by Sunday. When Luc arrived at Lucien's campaign headquarters the next day, the candidate was gloomily making himself some toast and peanut butter in a deserted committee room. Lucien greeted him by saying, "Luc, I want you to package me an honourable defeat. I am beaten, and the biggest mistake of my life is to have agreed to enter politics. The campaign is lost, and I will call Brian and apologize and advise him of my impending defeat."

"Bullshit," Luc snapped, "that's the talk of a loser and I don't associate with losers." He called me at 24 Sussex and together, with Bernard Roy and Pierre-Claude Nolin, we began to devise a strategy that would turn a faltering campaign around.

First we deployed our best organizers to the area. As I told Graham Fraser in a later interview, I had shared some advice with Luc before his arrival in the riding. "Listen carefully, mon Luc, I'll explain how politics works," I said. "You take them [campaign volunteers] and name them everywhere. Give every one of them a job. Chairman of this committee, chairman of that committee, special consultative committee of legal advisors. Make sure each of them can go home to his wife and say, 'I'm really important to this campaign.'" And Luc did just that. Then Mila, Caroline, and I made two major swings throughout the riding. And I worked hard to persuade Robert Bourassa's provincial Liberals to swing away from Gimaïel to Bouchard, to ensure ongoing influence in the federal government.

Still there was no drastic change in Lucien's attitude. Like all of us, he prefers to put his best foot forward and to be seen in the most favourable light. Like many of us, however, there is a darker side to his personality, one that comes out in moments of stress and challenge. Within days I was receiving reports of disturbing temper tantrums and explosive outbursts that worried some and amused others. On one occasion, Bernard Roy and Luc Lavoie were in Luc's room at a motel in Alma as Lucien stomped about saying, "You are all a bunch of bastards. You just want to see me defeated. Brian is part of the cabal to bring me down, sending me to seek election by the polar bears at the goddamn North Pole!" Lavoie and Roy had trouble containing their laughter as they watched the strange scene unfold.

Lucien's paranoia was starting to show. His mood changed, however, as the new campaign strategy started to take hold.

On June 8 I went to Quebec City to meet with Premier Robert Bourassa. We had lunch at the Garrison Club and were greeted by a waiter who said, "Oh, it's my two favourite prime ministers. What will you have to drink?"

Robert ordered milk and I ordered a soda water; we both paused when the waiter left the room. "You know, Robert," I said, "we both have great jobs, but we've sure become dull as dishwater!"

Later that day we were able to announce $1 billion in economic aid for the province over five years. Of that figure about $120 million would be allocated in the north-central region of Saguenay–Lac-Saint-Jean, where Lucien's riding was located. Naturally, the media then began to report that I wanted my old friend elected so badly that I was attempting to bribe voters with $1 billion for a single by-election.

Mila and I campaigned intensively for Lucien Bouchard during that by-election, and Mila wasn't the only member of the Mulroney family to assist him. Caroline agreed to forego our family tradition of having a birthday celebration for her on June 11 so that she could help her father's friend get elected to the House of Commons.

On 24 June, she was to receive the following note, on the letterhead of the Secretary of State of Canada:

> Dear Caroline,
> I would like to thank you for your outstanding contribution to my election campaign and especially your touching tribute to the people of Saguenay–Lac-Saint-Jean. What a wonderful and symbolic coincidence that June 11th marked a double event: the region's 150th anniversary and a young girl's 14th birthday! Your presence at your dad's side during the festivities at La Baie was

most appreciated, all the more that my fellow citizens regard your father with such great esteem and affection. You brought a breath of fresh air and youthfulness to us all. And everyone present saw in you your mother's grace and kindness.

I can imagine how hard it must be for your family to reconcile the demands of political life with the joys and expectations of family life. But, believe me, it really is worth it. All of your parents' sacrifices and efforts have an impact on the entire country. And you can be assured that it will earn the gratitude and esteem of all Canadians.

I would like to express again my most sincere gratitude, and to you and all the members of your family my warmest wishes for continued health and happiness.

A friend and admirer,
Lucien Bouchard

Caroline kept the letter to herself. Less than two years later, shortly after I had fired Bouchard from cabinet, she walked into my study at 24 Sussex, dropped the letter on my desk, and left without saying a word.

While the ballots were being counted in Alma and across the riding of Lac-Saint-Jean, I was hosting the leaders of the G-7 at a dinner at the University of Toronto's historic Hart House. Derek Burney occasionally slipped into the room to keep me updated on Lucien's progress. These goings-on caught the attention of Margaret Thatcher.

"Are we winning?" she asked, her eyes twinkling.

I assured her that "we" were. And later, I had her and the other leaders sign the menu to present to my Laval classmate Lucien Bouchard, as a memento of the night he was elected to the House of Commons and became a full-fledged member of my government.

During this time I moved Pat Carney out of International Trade and replaced her with John Crosbie. I wanted John – with his eloquence and wit – in that crucial portfolio to aid us in the upcoming election campaign, which of course he did, to great effect.

"This puts us in fighting trim for an election," I told the press, "when it comes."

Meech Lake was another file that I kept a close eye on as we moved through 1988. Frank McKenna was by now the new premier of New Brunswick, having crushed Richard Hatfield and his Tories the previous October, taking every seat. I was chairing the Commonwealth Summit in Vancouver at the time of this Liberal landslide in the Maritimes, which caught the attention of Australian Prime Minister Bob Hawke. "Perhaps we should intervene in New Brunswick," he wrote in a note he slipped to me during the discussions about apartheid. "We can't have one group having all the seats!"

During the summer of 1987 I had urged Richard Hatfield to move forward with the ratification of Meech Lake, but to no avail. And now a new premier was in place, one who was opposed to the accord. "We have very profound concerns about Meech Lake and our concerns are just as legitimate as anybody else's," McKenna told the Canadian Club in Toronto on April 25.

Robert Bourassa never forgot McKenna's early opposition to Meech. In fact, he raised this subject during the final conversation I had with him before he died in 1996. "No one has ever helped us [Quebecers] try to get fairness and justice in Ottawa like you have, Brian," he told me. "And I will go to my grave always regretting clearly what Clyde Wells did to us all, to Canada, but also, in a very important way, what Frank McKenna did. He started the obstructionism that allowed the time to flow that eventually brought Wells to power."

I had a different view. While everything Robert said was true, I knew that McKenna came to deeply regret his earlier attitude. At a Francophonie Summit he later attended as premier of New Brunswick he became very emotional while discussing the defeat of Meech with Mila. "What a mistake I made," he said, his eyes full of tears. "I thought I was doing the right thing, but it turned out I made a great mistake by acting the way I did."

Other seeds that were to grow into weeds that strangled Meech were also planted that spring. In Manitoba Gary Filmon won a minority victory and became his province's premier. "Meech Lake is dead," Manitoba Liberal Leader Sharon Carstairs told the press on election night, taking consolation for her own loss in the difficulties the new House posed for passing the accord.

April was also the month the Liberal-dominated Senate sent the accord back to the Commons (where all parties had voted for it) with a series of sweeping amendments that would have gutted it. "The amendments that are being proposed are killer amendments and they have one purpose – to kill the accord," Lowell Murray quite accurately responded. "There are two visions warring within the bosom of one party [the Liberals]. This is the gang of '81 reunited in the Senate."

1988

2. Personal Diplomacy

I LEFT THESE worrying storm signals behind toward the end of April and travelled to Washington for my final bilateral meeting with President Reagan. While I planned to lobby Reagan once again for an acid rain treaty, I was also looking to the future, and had Congress and the future president of the United States in my sights.

—

PERSONAL JOURNAL: APRIL 28, 1988

I told Reagan that clearly there would one day be an acid rain treaty between Canada and the U.S. – the only question was when and whether it would be with me, a friend, or my successor, who would no doubt be less friendly. He went from no movement at all to agreeing on Friday at lunch that George Shultz and Joe Clark should meet urgently, but after the Toronto Summit, to see if a treaty could be negotiated from the eight-point plan I had left with him.

—

I made sure that a private breakfast with Vice-President George Bush was on my Washington agenda. We met at his official residence, the former Naval Observatory, in a residential area of the American capital. While quiet outside, it was anything but inside. George and Barbara Bush always had their homes filled by grandchildren who liked nothing more than dropping in on Grampy during meetings. George and Barbara were at the head of one of the closest families I have ever had the privilege to know, and seeing them with their grandchildren was always a joy. Barbara Bush is a strong-willed, intelligent woman who has made a major contribution to Bush's success.

She is also a warm, considerate, and loyal friend who has always been supportive of Mila and me.

At the breakfast I lobbied him hard on acid rain and, as I always hoped, George Bush the environmentalist then said publicly what he had been telling me privately for a number of years. "I hope this acid rain question, which is a problem for both countries, will be solved," he told the press who had gathered outside his residence. "I have that determination." The likely Republican nominee in that year's American election also said that battling acid rain "will be a priority" if he won.

—

PERSONAL JOURNAL: April 7, 1987

Reagan said to me that "George Bush is the most loyal, devoted vice-president there ever was and the best prepared to become president. He is also a man of great courage – he was shot down when he was just 19. But now they call him a wimp. Imagine! The problem with George on the campaign trail is that he doesn't seem able to generate gut enthusiasm for his cause." I should note that Ron said that with sadness and a wistful expression.

—

Next on my list was Congress. On April 27, I became only the second prime minister of Canada to address this body. Though I had been making speeches since I was a teenager, I have to admit I was nervous. Never having used a teleprompter, I was speaking from notes and had to wear my glasses. I shouldn't have done that; instead I should simply have had the font on my pages bumped up, as is commonplace today.

L. Ian MacDonald, who had held the pen on this speech, had done a magnificent job. It was not my intention to seek out headlines back home by being strident or unduly aggressive. This event was much too important for that. In part, my speech went as follows:

> You are aware of Canada's grave concerns on acid rain. In Canada, acid rain has already killed nearly 15,000 lakes . . . another 150,000

> are being damaged, and a further 150,000 are threatened. Many salmon-bearing rivers in Nova Scotia no longer support the species. Prime agricultural land and important sections of our majestic forests are receiving excessive amounts of acid rain. We're doing everything we can to clean up our own act. We have concluded agreements with our provinces to reduce acid rain emissions in eastern Canada to half their 1980 levels by the year 1994.
>
> But you know, that's only half the solution. Because the other half of our acid rain comes across the border directly from the United States, falling upon forests and killing our lakes and soiling our cities. The one thing that acid rain doesn't do is discriminate. It is despoiling your environment as inexorably as it is ours. It is damaging your environment from Michigan to Maine and threatens marine life on the eastern seaboard. It's a rapidly escalating ecological tragedy in this country as well as ours. Just imagine . . . for a second the damage to your tourism and recreation, to the timber stands and to fishing streams . . . to your precious heritage, if this is not stopped. We acknowledge responsibility for some of the acid rain that falls in the United States, and by the time our programs reach projected targets, our export of acid rain to the U.S. will have been cut by an amount in excess of 50 per cent. We ask nothing more than this from you.

New York Senator Daniel Patrick Moynihan began applauding with great vigour at this last remark, and was soon joined by the entire chamber.

Later I hammered home my main point: "I'll admit, without hesitation, that the cost of reducing acid rain is substantial. But the cost of inaction is greater still. Canada will continue to press fully its case to rid our common environment of this blight, and we shall persevere until our skies regain their purity and our rains recover their gentleness that gives life to our forests and streams, and we hope that the United States Congress and the American people will respond in exactly the same way."

In his published diaries, Allan Gotlieb recalls, "Mulroney was in superb form before a packed Congress. He delivered his speech in a brilliant manner, filling the chamber with his huge personality. Senator Wirth told me it was the best speech he had heard in the chamber given by a foreigner in the last ten years. Moynihan went even further."

I also met again with Senate Majority Leader Robert Byrd of West Virginia. I had visited with him when I was Opposition leader; he represented a state where coal is king, so I knew I had my work cut out for me. As reporters were being escorted out of his office to allow our private discussions to begin, I asked them to stay. I then began a tribute to the senator's leadership and called him, quite truthfully, a "remarkable" politician. "A beaming Byrd seemed to lap it up, basking in the glow of Mulroney's flattery," a Canadian journalist wrote. Another senator, I hoped, would now mark his ballot in Canada's favour – or at least not offer spirited resistance – when the acid rain treaty I envisioned became a reality.

There was an official dinner in our honour at the White House, with the Reagans as perfect hosts. I was never to truly get over the experience of visiting the Queen at Buckingham Place, and a state dinner at the White House left me with the same feeling of awe. On the big day you are taken to the second floor of the White House, to the president's residence, where you are received for drinks. At the appointed time you are brought down the stairs in a procession that includes a U.S. Marine Honour Guard escort complete with flags. I once again had that feeling I was indeed a long way from Baie-Comeau.

It was a grand evening. In an exchange of toasts, I spoke admiringly about Reagan, and brought tears to his wife's eyes. I spoke with Nancy during the dinner. "Apart from everything else that we all know you do, did you feel you had your own special responsibility these past eight years in the White House?" I asked the First Lady.

I'll never forget her answer.

"Brian," she replied, "I'm here to protect Ronnie from himself. He has such a big, warm Irish heart, he hates saying no to people. And a lot of people come into his office who have an agenda different from his; some of them are self-serving, and some of them want him to meet people and do things I would look askance at. So, I intervene when I have to do, to protect Ronnie from himself."

I believe Ronald Reagan would not have made it to the White House without Nancy. They were very much a perfect political team whose talents complemented each other perfectly.

We also had a private lunch with the Reagans during my visit, which I later wrote about in my journal back in Ottawa. It wasn't until six years later that the world understood the signals I picked up about Reagan's health, although I failed to grasp their significance at the time.

—

PERSONAL JOURNAL: JUNE 5, 1988

On Friday, Mila and I were invited back to the White House solarium for a private lunch, and while we had a most pleasurable time, I noticed that the president appeared down and somewhat uncertain, responding firmly only when Nancy had signalled her approval or enthusiasm. Of all the visits I've had with him this was the first time I noticed a withdrawal and a lack of curiosity on his part, the first and only concession I have seen to his advancing age. I can only hope that I am in half that good shape when I am that age – which in itself would be a tremendous accomplishment. Ronald Reagan has been for me a good ally and a trusted associate in international affairs. He is a deeply honourable man, unfailingly courteous and sensitive, with strongly held, simple, straightforward views. And he has been a remarkable success and a powerful friend of Canada. My guess is that we shall wait some time before the White House is occupied by someone with feelings as good and as strong for Canada.

—

I was in Florida on a day in November 1994 when Nancy called to tell me that Ron was about to release a statement announcing he had Alzheimer's disease. I was never able to speak to him again.

The personal diplomacy I had engaged in on my Washington trip was noticed in the capital. With the acid rain treaty and the FTA still not finalized by American lawmakers, I had little choice but to keep a high profile.

"This is to thank you for directing specific accolades at Jim Baker and me in your White House statement upon arrival in Washington," United States Trade Representative Clayton Yeutter wrote to me. "Vice-President Bush told me that it was the first time that any [head of government or state] had provided such a courteous gesture during the entire tenure of the Reagan administration . . . It was a thoughtful gesture very much noticed and appreciated. Your visit went very well indeed, and your journey to Capitol Hill was a particularly valuable investment of time. I watched members of Congress as they listened to your address . . . They liked you as a person and as a representative of the Canadian government, and they also responded positively to your message. Your individual meetings also hit a responsive chord, and that will help us as we move the FTA implementing legislation in the coming weeks."

As I said in Ottawa in 2006 at a ceremony where I was honoured as Canada's Greenest Prime Minister – in large part, I believe, because I was able to negotiate an acid rain treaty with the Americans – anyone who thinks that personal relations have little role in diplomacy knows nothing about either.

Back in Ottawa, I appointed outstanding lawyer John Sopinka to the Supreme Court of Canada. I appointed Sopinka to the court without his having any prior experience on the bench. While this was unusual, his brilliant record easily qualified him for the appointment. Justice Sopinka became the first Canadian of Ukrainian origin to serve on Canada's highest court.

Toward the end of May I went to Europe for a final round of consultations with G-7 leaders before I would bring down the gavel at the Toronto Summit. I held a meeting with French President François Mitterrand, and the following is a summary written by an official note-taker:

> This meeting focused on the Toronto Summit and followed a tête-à-tête between the two leaders which had dealt with other issues. PM Mulroney began by stressing that Toronto was to be an economic summit . . . President Mitterrand was very agreeable on all aspects of the PM's presentation. He said that normally the communiqués are too long and that the leaders come to summits to get to know one another better. He said the format would cause the leaders to work hard and noted in passing that it would be the last such event for President Reagan.
>
> President Mitterrand returned to the summit and asked specifically what PM Mulroney wanted from Toronto. The PM mentioned the need for positive messages on international debt and the multilateral trade negotiations including the Montreal mid-term review. He also noted that structural adjustment was important. He added that it was important to give a signal of confidence to markets.
>
> President Mitterrand said that in communist countries, when leaders meet, the communiqués are drafted in advance and bear

> little relation to actual discussion. He said that economic summits have suffered from the same fault and we should avoid this. He said that leaders have been too timid on international monetary reform . . .
>
> At lunch President Mitterrand said that he wants to avoid a directoire and wants a return to informality at the summit . . . He said the world cannot be run by the seven countries: there are other players – the Third World, the other Europeans, and the communist countries.

Margaret Thatcher and I had a similar discussion in London. We did, however, find a little time to talk politics. After the meeting and lunch at Number 10, I got into the back of my car with a question for my chief of staff.

"Derek," I asked, "who is John Major?"

"He's a junior minister in Mrs. Thatcher's government," Burney replied. "Why do you ask?"

"Because Mrs. Thatcher just told me that he's going to be her successor."

Derek and I both chuckled and agreed that, on this one, Margaret Thatcher had to be dead wrong. But she turned out to be right again.

Before the Toronto Summit, I marked the fifth anniversary of my election as Tory leader by granting Graham Fraser of the *Globe and Mail* an interview. "The caucus is the heart of the machine," I said. "It's the heart of our movement, because the caucus is the genuine microcosm of the country."

Fraser went on to ask if I thought the party had changed since June 11, 1983. "Yeah, I think it [has], but I think it is in the stream of progressive, modern thought that Bob Stanfield and Joe Clark pursued in general measure," I replied. "I think that what we have done is make a number of significant changes. The most obvious is our breakthrough in French Canada . . . Secondly, a breakthrough in the cities. We became more urban. We also became more ethnic, if you will, and I think we became more representative, strongly more representative of women."

Caucus was on my mind that day because we had held a particularly exciting meeting before the interview. I had fired up the troops by asking them to imagine who would be sitting on the government benches if the PC Party was not in power.

"We are not perfect," I told caucus. "We represent a different Canada, a different set of values, a different approach to regions and people. Just consider a coalition government from the NDP and Liberals," I said. "Herb Gray in Finance; Lloyd Axworthy in Trade; Sheila Copps in Health and Welfare; Svend Robinson in Justice; John Nunziata as Solicitor General; Sergio Marchi in Immigration."

With the election nearing, I made sure I involved each and every member of caucus in our planning. As one of my MPs said in caucus earlier that year, "The issuance of the writ focuses the mind!" On June 14 I signed individual letters to all Tory MPs asking them to report back to me by the end of the month. "I would like to have your views as to what matters should have priority in our platform and in planning for our second mandate," I wrote. "When I receive these recommendations from you and other caucus members, I will want to put a caucus process in place to develop and discuss these in greater detail. For the present I need to know what items you regard as of highest priority in a platform."

Thus began one of the busiest periods I was to experience in all of my years as prime minister. West German Chancellor Helmut Kohl arrived in Canada on June 15. Helmut, the most political of all the G-7 leaders, gave a rousing address to a joint session of Parliament. In introducing him to MPs and senators, I reminded him of another Canadian prime minister's connections to Germany. "The Right Honourable John Diefenbaker . . . an illustrious leader of my party in the House of Commons, traced his ancestral roots to Germany," I said. "He would be very proud, sir, of your presence here today."

Kohl then stood up and moved his massive bulk behind the podium for his remarks. All of six feet four inches and weighing in at about three hundred pounds, it was for good reason that he was sometimes called the "colossus with a human touch."

"You, Prime Minister, since the days you participated in your first summit have played a most helpful role in bridging differences of approach among the partners participating in the economic summit," he said. "You have made an essential contribution toward enlarging the G-5, which today includes Canada as well, for the development of international economies. This was certainly an essential step. In many of our meetings I have been struck again and again by your effort to contribute toward progress and to produce acts of solidarity, and in this way bring about solidarity among the participants in these meetings."

While I certainly wasn't going to shy away from praise from anyone in an election year, Kohl's remarks did remind me of Lyndon Johnson's line after he once received similar comments. "My father would have been pleased. My mother would have believed it," the big Texan once said.

Then came the passage in Helmut's speech that I had really hoped for.

"I congratulate you . . . for concluding the FTA with the United States of America," he said. "This is a forward-looking step."

During our private meetings, Kohl and I discussed my arrangements for the G-7 Summit. Note-takers captured our discussion: "On political topics, Chancellor Kohl expressed the hope that the dinner conversation in Toronto would concentrate virtually exclusively on East–West issues and that the political declaration would reflect only what was actually discussed by leaders. He did not see the Middle East or the Philippines or any other topic being of the same significance. He urged the PM to stick to his guns on this one, adding that he would support him completely."

Then it was on to Toronto – a city in the grip of what I can only describe as summit fever. Torontonians had begun to shuck off some of their inward-looking tendencies and were realizing that their city was becoming, in the phrase of the day, "world class." I like to think our decision to hold the summit in Toronto helped those feelings along.

As host, one of my duties was to greet the arriving participants at the airport. In the case of Japanese Prime Minister Noboru Takeshita, this led to one of my most entertaining experiences involving interpreters.

"Noboru," I asked my guest carefully as we rode downtown in a limousine, "did you have a career outside of politics before you entered into the profession?"

My question was patiently repeated by the translator in Japanese as I waited for an answer. He then answered in Japanese, which was in turn translated into English.

"Yes, I did," he said.

"What did you do?"

Again, I sat back and patiently awaited the translation from English into Japanese and vice versa.

"I was a teacher for a number of years," he said.

"What did you teach?"

The translator did his job and I soon had my answer.

"English," Noboru said with a smile.

The weather in Toronto was gorgeous, and Fred Doucet had made flawless arrangements indoors, too. I knew my desire for a more informal summit had been realized when President Reagan arrived for a dinner wearing a blazer and slacks. President Mitterrand even went for a stroll one day, meeting, greeting, and bringing smiles to the faces of the many delighted Torontonians on sunny restaurant patios.

I was pleased that the G-7 leaders agreed with me that the environment was crucial, endorsing the concept of sustainable development. As a group, we encouraged the nations of the world to sign and ratify the Montreal Protocol on protection of the ozone layer. The G-7 also sent from Toronto the message that further action was needed on climate change, acid rain, water pollution, and other ecological issues.

Canada's goals were achieved, for the most part. Thanks to hard work by Derek Burney and other officials behind the scenes, the leaders endorsed the FTA. It had been left out of earlier drafts of the communiqué, and we soon got it back in. The G-7 agreed to cooperate to maintain noninflationary growth while reducing global imbalance. We also achieved movement on trade liberalization, including agriculture, and on our proposals to ease debt burdens faced by developing countries.

To my personal pleasure, I was able, as chairman, to salute Ronald Reagan on behalf of all the leaders. Toronto was his final G-7 Summit. "His place in history is secure," I said. "Ronald Reagan has been for all of us at this table a gracious friend and a trusted ally. We shall all miss his warmth and his wisdom. He leaves Toronto today with our respect and our affection and our best wishes for good health and every happiness for Nancy and himself."

Helmut Kohl sent me a letter after his return to West Germany.

"You as host, having already put so much effort into the preparations, deserve special credit for this success," he said. "For this I wish to express my special appreciation. Thank you once again for the excellent organization."

Any prime minister tries to do a good job for the country on the international stage – and it is an added bonus when this benefits you politically. Success at Toronto was very much part of our re-election efforts, and in this we succeeded. A Gallup poll released on July 1 said that 55 per cent of Canadians had been impressed with my performance as chairman of the G-7 Summit. Another plank in our election platform was in place.

But not all the leaders had headed home. Margaret Thatcher had earlier accepted my invitation to address Parliament, and she did so on June 22. As usual, she didn't pull any punches, wading directly into the free trade debate.

"I understand that it may be a controversial matter in this chamber," she said. "I will only say that I do not underestimate Canada's courage in taking this step in partnership with its giant neighbour. On the basis of Britain's experience of joining the European Community, you need have no fear that Canada's national personality will be in any way diminished. Fifteen years of European Community membership have left our people no less British and no less proud of their history and independence. Moreover, protectionism is not a lifebelt which keeps an economy afloat. It is a millstone that drags you down and penalizes consumers and workforce alike. Subsidize the inefficient and soon that is all you have; you lose the competitive edge to export abroad and keep prices down at home."

Liberal faces were glum and their applause muted as the prime minister of the United Kingdom marched right through Canada's emerging national debate with all guns blazing.

That very same day the House of Commons again ratified the Meech Lake Accord. To the chagrin of the Liberal senators who had rejected it, the vote was 200 to 7. "The House of Commons has spoken for a second time in very persuasive terms," I said afterwards. "We have done what we had to do; we've fulfilled our leadership responsibilities to the nation. There is no doubt in my mind that this will be ratified and become part of the Constitution of Canada."

1988

3. Preparing for the Vote

Meanwhile, in caucus, a minor revolt was brewing, which could – if left unchecked – have rocked the foundations of the French–English coalition I had worked so hard to put together. That coalition was what had brought us to power, and I intended to stay there.

As mandated by legislation, we had updated Canada's official languages laws. These changes had allowed some members of the less than progressive wing of my party – "lemmings" in the words of Tom Van Dusen – to once again start fear-mongering over the issue of French-language rights. At a caucus meeting in June, for example, I watched sadly as MP Ron Stewart got to his feet and talked about the "funeral of the English language in Ontario."

I had thought we had learned our lesson during the Manitoba Crisis in 1983, but it was obvious that some in the party hadn't yet caught on. In a proposed amendment to the bill, one Tory MP even called for English to be made the official language of the Canadian Armed Forces!

I came back from Harrington Lake one day in early July for the sole purpose of speaking to my caucus on this sensitive matter. The notes I made for my speech read as follows:

> I was 49 on my last birthday. Liberals in power for 40 of those years, PCs nine. Of that, I have supplied over three and a half years myself, with your help. There is no mystery as to why this happened. We couldn't win before because we couldn't win in French Canada. We couldn't win in French Canada because we were portrayed to be anti-Quebec. So it became a chicken-and-egg thing – with us as the losers. How to illustrate consequences? How to understand the damage this party will inflict upon itself if some of you insist on proceeding this way? . . .

I set out my position clearly when I sought the leadership. I spoke to the issue directly when I addressed the convention. I believe in fairness and equality, and I believe that official bilingualism in Canada can bring greater equality and fairness to this nation, Canada . . .

C-72 is not perfect. No product of human endeavour and political compromise ever is. Under the British parliamentary system, political parties can only exist if all members ensure that a sense of reasonable accommodation prevails. That means fighting the good fight but, at the end of the day, coming together to provide a unified profile of leadership. For five years, on all the great issues, we have had tremendous and ongoing and vigorous debates, long and powerful caucuses, but we emerged united.

That unity has enabled us to make history together: FTA, Meech Lake Accord, record prosperity, low unemployment, childcare, broadcasting policy . . . Think of all you have accomplished. Think of how much will be . . . jeopardized by the election of the Lib/NDP alliance . . . You know how little would be left for everyone from western farmers to Ontario small businessmen if they got their hands on the throttle.

Official languages [law] is a symbol of the nation. If we diminish its value and strike out against its strengths, the country will deal with us effectively and permanently in the next election. How do I explain an amendment that says bilingualism should be recognized by the government for its potential for divisiveness when I have always said it should be an instrument of unity? How do I explain a proposal that English should be the language of combat in the armed forces when members of this party and caucus distinguished themselves in battle – men like Pierre Sévigny, Paul Sauvé, and Guy Charbonneau.

I have come here to fight Grits, not Tories. For five years I have been your leader and your ally. Now I need your help. Sir John A. said, "I need you with me, not when you think I'm right – but when you think I'm wrong." I need your support. I think I've earned it . . . The bill on official languages is the policy of this government. It is the policy of this party. It is the policy of this leader. I ask for your unanimous support, which will stymie our enemies,

> honour our commitment, and ensure the re-election of a PC majority government.

I was exhausted as I left the caucus room. There had been complete silence as I spoke and rousing applause when I finished. I had carried the day.

Unfortunately, my influence didn't reach to the opposition side of Newfoundland's House of Assembly. On July 7 that province ratified the Meech Lake Accord – but every Liberal save one voted against it. That party's new leader had a lot to say after the vote. "It would be open to Newfoundland to rescind this resolution, so long as it is done before proclamation," Clyde Wells declared. "I would take steps to see that is done."

At the time I privately dismissed as irresponsible the musings of this obscure Corner Brook lawyer. While we had both been at Dalhousie at the same time, I had no recollection of ever meeting him. This would soon change.

Don Mazankowski and I met for a private lunch at 24 Sussex, as we frequently did, one day during this period. Maz, as he was affectionately known throughout the party, House, and country, had made a powerful difference since replacing the abrasive Erik Nielsen as deputy prime minister. His friendly, down-to-earth style made him accessible to MPs and supporters, and his focused approach and indefatigable work habits combined to make him a valuable chief operating officer of the government. I had come to have enormous confidence in him and his good judgment. So intimate was our association that Maz was later to remark, "I knew precisely what the PM was going to say before he said it – and I could finish off his sentences almost all of the time." He was also tough-minded and unafraid – along with Paul Tellier, Bernard Roy, and Derek Burney – to give me the unvarnished truth, no matter how painful, at all times.

But on this day we disagreed. I wanted to keep the House in session throughout the summer and Maz demurred, arguing that the rules and traditions would not accommodate such an approach.

"Maz," I said, "I don't give a good goddamn. This election is going to be about leadership and, after the G-7 in Toronto, I want to use the summer to showcase leadership on vital national issues so that it can be contrasted with Liberal inertia and negativism. So find a way to get it done."

Which is precisely what Maz did, thereby opening up great new electoral opportunities.

—

PERSONAL JOURNAL: JULY 24, 1988

The stunning victory by Lucien Bouchard in the Lac-Saint-Jean by-election energized our troops across Canada and constituted a major setback for the NDP and Liberals in Quebec – to say nothing of the so-called national media, which had been openly predicting our defeat! The decision to keep the House sitting through the summer has enabled us to compile our legislative agenda on everything from privatization of Air Canada, to childcare, to broadcasting, to official languages. We have been able to announce a number of significant and high-profile items we have been working on for a long time and which have reached fruition – Hibernia, cleanup of the St. Lawrence River, Teleglobe, environmental initiatives, etc. – all of these events have contributed to the view that ours is a competent govt. with a strong agenda that is now producing visible benefits for Canadians. People are now beginning to identify us as the reason for their improved circumstances, and their new mood is being translated into higher approval ratings for the govt. and me in all the public opinion surveys. And this, in a word, translates into joy for Mila and me and our supporters who have worked so hard and waited so long to see the turnaround happen.

—

In 1987 I put together a private group composed of political veterans from across the country who had themselves won many elections – Bill Davis, Peter Lougheed, Frank Moores, and Bob Coates were among the members. We would meet from time to time for dinner, or I would call them for their views. At one such dinner at the Château Laurier, during a spirited discussion on what to do tactically with the Free Trade Agreement, Lougheed made a point that I immediately sensed was of capital importance.

"I know everyone feels we should run on the FTA as a fait accompli," he said, "but I disagree. I think we should pass it through the House but not the Senate, thereby keeping open the question of ultimate passage. This enables us to run on the promise of free trade and the tremendous benefits it will bring Canadians, without having locked them into a done deal. That way we leave the negative, destructive role to the Liberals who will attack a promising future, vow to kill it, while putting nothing hopeful or visionary in the window."

As soon as the words came out of Peter's mouth I knew this was the strategy we were going to follow, and during the second week of July we got powerful assistance from an unexpected source: the Liberals.

—

PERSONAL JOURNAL: JULY 24, 1988

Last week, Wednesday, John Turner announced that he had told the Liberal senators to hold the free trade bill hostage and ensure its non-passage once it has left the Commons. This is a most unusual move and, to date, the reviews have not been favourable. Most commentators and editorialists have zeroed in on the profoundly antidemocratic nature of the ploy. It raises again the vulgar and crass demeanour of Liberal arrogance – their divine right to rule whether the people agree or not. In fact, I had intended to call an election after the FTA had cleared the House. Where the Liberals could have clearly caused me great difficulty would have been to do the opposite of what Turner has now announced – namely, indicate their intentions to hold proper hearings in the Senate and then at a time of their choosing, return it to the Commons with one or perhaps two amendments – such as the water provisions – of such a compelling nature that we would be forced to acquiesce or face serious hostility. That way they could have displayed both reasonableness and opposition. Now they have surrendered some serious options and made Turner look weak and unprincipled in the process. Their action is predicated on their view that the FTA must be passed by January 1. In fact, the governing documents say January 1 or later. There is nothing magic about the date, and nothing will complicate it if that target date is not adhered to. So they have not affected my capacity to delay if I thought it desirable.

Moreover, the second part of their argument is also flawed. The Constitution gives me the authority in these circumstances to appoint senators to break a deadlock. With eight vacancies now, that I will soon fill, the Independents already there, and with the Liberals such as Leo Kolber, George Van Roggen, and Ian Sinclair, who actively support the FTA, there are more than enough senators to defeat Turner's holdup.

But for me to proceed this way would be to repeat Turner's error. I am not going to proceed along those lines when the political landscape is changing steadily and in a manner that helps us. The question then is, why did Turner agree to such a reckless and undemocratic suggestion? I believe the answer has nothing to do with Canada, the opposition or the Liberal Party. I believe the answer is the disintegration of Turner's leadership is now so substantial and the damage from the imminent publication of the Weston book is so great that he decided to throw caution and good judgment to the winds in an attempt to stampede me into an election.

At roughly the same time I was visited at Harrington by Bernard Roy, Derek Burney, Norm Atkins, Allan Gregg, and John Tory – a remarkable young man who will play a very important role in the future of our party – who provided me with our latest numbers. In a survey that ended July 10, Decima reports that we have made dramatic improvements across Canada and that we have returned to first place with the NDP in second and the Liberals in third. I have kept these numbers deliberately secret, not even sharing them with P&P Friday and Saturday. I did not want them to be influenced by them, if the numbers are right – or subsequently disheartened, if the numbers are wrong. I instructed Gregg to go back into the field twice to ascertain the solidity and accuracy of the numbers and report to me in mid-August.

The most startling and rewarding dimension of this major poll is the extent of the increase in voter satisfaction with our personal conduct. There has been a modest cooling off of support for Ed Broadbent – though he remains very high in some personal attributes – and a substantial increase in all categories of leadership, to the point where I now substantially lead the others on the key questions: Who do you trust to lead Canada into the next decade? With regard to Mr. Turner, the voters' response can only be described as calamitous. In all 17 areas of leadership examined he is now in dead last and declining rapidly. I've been most encouraged to note not only the steady improvement in all areas but the significant jump in polling data from April to July 10. It is almost as if voters, for the first time, have paid close attention to me on the fundamentals of what we are starting to achieve compared with the alternatives in the Liberals and NDP, and gave us good marks.

These figures, of course, give us a major advantage strategically as well. Because large segments of the Ottawa press gallery dislike me personally, they automatically assume that most Canadians feel the same way. In fact, the reverse is true. This data indicates we can plan our moves with the media none the wiser. I've always felt that it was a great advantage for the leader to be underestimated by the media and his opponents. I have benefited from this for some time and do not want anything to change this reality.

In any event, it is very gratifying to see the tide turning. When I gave Mila the Decima polling results last week, she literally jumped into my arms with joy. She has been through a lot, and we have worked extremely hard through almost unrelenting attack to bring this kind of change about. It has been a long time coming, and it would be gratifying to see these trends compared to any other sources in the future.

—

John Turner had a terrible summer as opposition leader. The Chrétien forces were actively doing everything they could to destabilize his leadership, riding presidents were calling for him to step down, and he continually trailed both Broadbent and me in any poll that examined the issue of leadership. For him the fall would be worse – due in large part to a book scheduled to be published in September. Greg Weston's *Reign of Error* presented a portrait of a leader in crisis. What neither Turner nor Weston knew was that I, thanks to a friend, had got my hands on an advance draft of the book. I read it as I flew to Newfoundland to make the announcement that Hibernia would go ahead.

I felt sorry for Turner on a personal level as I read page after page of anonymous quotes from so-called "party insiders" lacking the courage to let Weston use their names, but I knew the book would help me politically. It would generate a lot of press and lead to more questions in the public's mind about Turner's leadership. Could a man who couldn't run his own party be trusted to run the country? When faced with this question I was sure that Canadians would answer clearly with a resounding "No."

I wasn't the only politician preparing for an election in August of 1988. South of the border, Jim Baker stepped down as secretary of the treasury in order to become George Bush's campaign manager. He sent me a thank-you note before vacating his cabinet office. "I really enjoyed working with you," he wrote, "and appreciate your thoughtfulness of me. Now let's win these two elections and we can do it again." Some months later I spoke with a victorious George Bush as he celebrated his victory on election night in Houston. I was pleased to learn from the president-elect that he was going to announce his decision to appoint Baker secretary of state the next day.

I also received some subtle pressure from a royal source. A committed environmentalist, Prince Philip approached me on August 20 and asked me to do what I could to advance plans for another national park in Canada. "Your government has already established a record of five new national parks and I understand that an agreement has now been reached . . . to do with the establishment of a Grasslands National Park," he wrote from London. "I am writing to ask you to do your best to see that the Grasslands National Park is formally dedicated with the least possible delay."

Only a month later my government and the Government of Saskatchewan were able to sign a formal agreement to create Grasslands National Park. When completed, the park – which includes the Frenchman River Valley, the only place in Canada [I learned] where the black-tailed prairie dog can be found in its natural habitat – will encompass nine hundred square kilometres as further lands become available. As a history buff, I was also happy to play a role in the establishment of Grasslands because it is the area where Chief Sitting Bull and his Sioux people sought refuge after the Battle of the Little Bighorn south of the medicine line.

It was a distinct pleasure to write to Prince Philip later that year to officially inform him that we had acted on his suggestion. In the nineteenth century, British essayist Walter Bagehot wrote that the role of the Crown is "to be consulted, to encourage, and occasionally to warn." In this case, I was more than happy to receive the prince's encouragement.

In 1988 we also created the South Moresby National Park Reserve in British Columbia. In all, eight national parks were established while I held office. Under my government's Green Plan, Canada was on a path to create five more by 1996 and another thirteen by 2000. This would have significantly expanded the national parks system, begun by Sir John A. Macdonald with the creation of Banff National Park in 1885.

As the summer came to a close, a major piece of legislation still needed to pass the Commons – the Free Trade Agreement. I spoke in the course of the debate on August 30 summing up in the following words: "When you dispel all the myths, when you analyze all the alternatives, you find that this FTA meets the most fundamental test of all: it serves the national interest. We have the ability to manage change."

Our bill was approved by the Commons the next evening. Once the passage of the bill became clear, demonstrators disgraced the chamber that has represented Canadian democracy since the days of Sir John A. Macdonald. I was shaken by what I witnessed that evening.

—

PERSONAL JOURNAL: SEPTEMBER 1, 1988

The FTA easily passed the House last night. The opposition continued their best nationalistic stance – including flags, the singing of "O Canada," etc. – but all proceeded normally with relatively little attention given to the vote itself on the TV news later. One incident causes me to write this note. The NDP had given their gallery passes in the House to supporters who, during the vote, began to shout slogans, interrupting the historic proceedings and refusing to respect the admonishments of Speaker Fraser – always a figure of great courtesy. For one brief moment, with shouts drowning out the Speaker, and opposition members not sure whether to applaud the rowdy demonstrators or avert their eyes in embarrassment, I got the sinking feeling one must have when a mob has taken over a civilized institution.

The House of Commons can be a rude, abrasive, and bruising place. It often lacks in decorum and self-respect. But it is a genuine and unique expression of liberty and freedom. For a duly elected MP to be able to rise daily and attack the PM directly and the government is, while lacking in pleasure for the prime minister, an important daily affirmation of raw democracy. It is the way the Fathers of Confederation envisioned the House, without perhaps the TV. With the vote suspended by a group of self-proclaimed patriots, a chill went up my spine as I witnessed the Speaker – a symbol of authority and respect – unable to control a group that had chosen to disrupt rather than adhere to legitimate processes.

For a fleeting moment I got a tiny glimpse of anarchy and what a disgusting and awful thing it is – a mob exercising hegemony and control over democratic institutions. Mila and I have been in many brutal and raucous meetings, from Pembroke to Moncton. But they were demonstrations organized by interest groups to make their case in an aggressive adversarial way, with pandemonium and violence sometimes being the result. This incident took place in the House of Commons, and I was deeply struck by the fragility of civilized conduct and its tie-in to democracy – and how very much we can lose if such behaviour were ever countenanced in Canada.

The magnificence and splendour of Parliament was briefly suspended – held hostage by a small and, I suppose, basically harmless group of citizens who had decided that their views, and only their views, were right, proper, and legitimate, thereby requiring precedence over all others – including those of elected members of Parliament – at variance with their own. I am not one to go on and on about the House. My appointment of the McGrath Commission is an indication of how I truly feel about its importance and the independence of members. I have often sat in the House and reflected on its simple beauty, its noble role, and my great good fortune in playing a modest role in its evolution.

—

On September 22, I fulfilled a promise I'd made while I was leader of the opposition: I stood in the Commons as prime minister and apologized for the internment of Japanese Canadians during the Second World War. As I spoke I noticed that Ed Broadbent, whose first wife had been of Japanese origin, was crying.

I looked to the galleries, overflowing with elderly Japanese Canadians and their families, and saw the same outpouring of raw emotion from a group of loyal Canadians whose reputations and honour had been tarnished and besmirched by a government that led Canada from this very chamber almost fifty years earlier.

After the apology and the announcement of the $300 million compensation package we'd negotiated with the Canadian Association of Japanese Canadians, I received a moving letter from Cardinal Carter in Toronto, which read:

> At this moment I wish to address you, not to offer advice nor to point out an obligation but to commend you most highly as a

> humble citizen of this country for your historical gesture to our Japanese fellow countrymen. For better or for worse, I was old enough at the time of the events to be very conscious of them, and while I understood the distress and the war hysteria under which we all laboured, even at that juncture I felt a great hurt and a deep sadness. If ever there was a collective miscarriage of justice and a condemning of persons as guilty without proof this was it . . . I love my country. I have seldom been ashamed of her, and this one exception is now expunged by your gracious and timely intervention. I speak for no one but myself, but I am convinced that my sentiments reflect a consensus particularly of those of us who were alive and grown up at the time of this unfortunate lapse from grace and judgment.

Art Miki also wrote to me: "On behalf of the National Association of Japanese Canadians [of which he was president], I wish to express our deepest appreciation and congratulations on acknowledging the wartime injustices of the 1940s inflicted upon Canadians of Japanese ancestry and the symbolic redress that was announced . . . I was personally moved by your sincere expression of apology and the supportive comments by your colleagues in the House of Commons."

On one of my final days in the House of Commons in 1993, Bill Blaikie, a courtly and effective NDP MP, sent me a short handwritten note from across the floor. "Did you know, that speaking of Japanese-Canadian redress, Art Miki is now a Liberal candidate," he wrote. "The NDP befriended them over the years, the Tories, as government, delivered the redress, and now he runs as a Liberal. Any explanation?" I had none.

Before calling the election I went to New York and addressed the United Nations General Assembly. While it was no secret I was planning a federal election, I was directing another important election campaign as well. In reviewing my files for this book, I was surprised at how much time I spent campaigning – with letters, phone calls, and during meetings with foreign leaders – for Canada's election to the UN Security Council. We mounted a serious effort, and Joe Clark and his team at External – including our new UN Ambassador Yves Fortier – did excellent work on our successful campaign. In just two years' time, when Saddam Hussein invaded Kuwait, we'd all learn just how important that Security Council seat was.

During my address I called the UN the "crucible of human hope for peace in a troubled world." It's a belief I still hold today. I also kept up the pressure on the racist government in South Africa. "The movement in favour of human dignity is now irreversible," I said, adding that it was only a question of time before apartheid was dismantled. "Only then will the children of Mandela know the gifts that freedom brings."

I had a message for the Americans, too, at a time when their politicians were fully engaged in a presidential election. "In a world where rivers and winds cannot be contained by laws or borders, it is clear that domestic initiatives by themselves are inadequate," I said. "Canadians know all about this. Our economy, as well as our environment, is being damaged daily by acid rain. We have taken important internal measures to address the problem. We have urgently pressed our neighbour to follow suit and to conclude a treaty with us that will reduce the environmental damage from this blight by stated amounts within specific time frames. But acid rain is not limited to one nation or one continent. It is an international problem and it demands, I believe, a viable international solution. The greenhouse effect, the deterioration of the ozone layer, and the disposal of toxic wastes are cause for legitimate concern both here and around the world . . . Canada strongly supports the call for a UN conference on sustainable development in 1992. The global challenges we face are great, but we are proving they can be met and they can be resolved. Mankind is not destined to destroy itself."

I was satisfied that I had done my best as I left that podium in New York City. It was now time for the Canadian people to decide.

1988

4. Campaign '88

On October 1, 1988 I went across to Rideau Hall and officially asked Governor General Jeanne Sauvé to dissolve Parliament to make way for an election. We chatted for a few minutes before I had to go out and face the cameras.

"Prime Minister," she said, "I've been around here a long time and to have concluded the Free Trade Agreement with the Americans, and to have completed our constitutional adventure that we began in 1980 and 1981 with the Meech Lake Accord, that's truly a historic mandate you've just finished. I wish you well as you seek ratification of both of these from Canadian voters."

I then left Ottawa to attend the wedding of Mila's brother John to Manuela Soares in Montreal. Even prime ministers have to arrive before the bride, and I made sure I wasn't late; Mila would never have forgiven me. At the church I was met by a large gathering of reporters and further RCMP security staff. I entered and waited for the service to begin. And waited. Only later did I learn why the event was delayed. John had arranged for his bride-to-be to arrive in a large white convertible. As the car pulled up with Manuela sitting alone in the back seat, the RCMP ordered it to keep moving. With the prime minister just entering the church, they weren't allowing anyone to stop! After going around the block Manuela was finally able to convince the officers that she had important business to attend to inside the church, whether they and the prime minister they were guarding liked it or not. The story still draws a laugh – an embarrassed one from me – at family gatherings.

Shortly after the election, and after a rest at Harrington Lake over Christmas, I wrote the story of Campaign '88 in the pages of my journal. I can add very little to this account today.

—

PERSONAL JOURNAL: JANUARY 1989

By causing such delay in the House on all major issues, the opposition parties had unknowingly become our allies. They ensured overload of the system, but they had not anticipated the effects of a summer session.

The session allowed us to demonstrate to Canadians that, indeed, we had an agenda – obscured by all the sound bites over the last four years – and that the opposition parties had little to offer in this area that was different or appealing. It allowed us to justify certain initiatives that ensured the modest momentum that began with my address to Congress, the Lac-Saint-Jean by-election, and the economic summit, and was sustained all summer and into the early autumn. And it allowed me, as prime minister, to stake out an unchallenged national leadership role, in areas ranging from C-72, to Hibernia, to childcare, to literacy . . . to the settlement of Dene–Métis land claims in the Northwest Territories, all in a nonpartisan manner.

During the period from April to October, we planned and executed one of the most audacious comebacks in history – from 27% in April to 43% in October. We built a head of steam and enthusiasm that enabled us to launch our campaign with momentum and strength. We turned to deal with, and overcome, the setbacks that we were sure to encounter.

In fact, my chief concern was John Turner. I told my cabinet his standing was so low with the public that he would have no difficulty, at all, exceeding these expectations, and when he did, the press would declare him a "new Turner," and attempt to elect him.

On the day before the debates began, I was given a CHRC poll by Pierre Blais that indicated only 8% of respondents in eastern Quebec thought Turner competent to be prime minister! Blais was somewhat perplexed when I indicated to him and others how displeased I was with such numbers, because they would make it so easy for him to rebound, later – which is precisely what happened.

I believe John Turner, following his humiliating defeat in '84, was fully and genuinely resolved to reform the Liberal Party, and prepare for battle in '88. But the job never got done. The Liberal Party, which had been in first place for the better part of three years, entered the election in third place, with no money, no candidates, no platform, and a leader who commanded neither respect nor confidence.

How did this happen? How did John Turner, whom I believed to be much more capable than his reviews, allow this to happen?

The principal responsibility of a political leader is to ready his troops for battle – particularly a leader unburdened by the responsibilities of office. I watched John Turner carefully, every day, for four years, and I think his good intentions got hijacked by an unusual combination of institutions: the press gallery and the Rat Pack.

The Rat Pack, a small group of shrill but essentially unimpressive backbenchers, emerged to national prominence in the fall of '84. Their specialty was calumny, smear, and character assassination. They were unrelenting in their attacks on government members, and unrestrained by any notion of fairness.

While Turner could not get a headline with a major speech on agriculture, Don Boudria and Sheila Copps got one every day, with a new accusation, charge, falsehood, or fabrication. I watched Turner change from being clearly embarrassed by such misconduct, to countenancing it, to encouraging it, to embracing it. One day he put on a Rat Pack T-shirt – thereby, as leader of the opposition, publicly condoning such grave misbehaviour. The next day, I told my caucus John Turner had just forfeited any chance of ever again becoming PM – that eventually Canadians would scorn such grotesque unparliamentary behaviour, and all those associated with it.

Because of the overt conspiracy between the Rat Pack and much of the press gallery, every conceivable personal charge, alleged scandal, conflict of interest allegation, et cetera, was given incredible publicity – and with it, our popularity began to decline, with a corresponding rise for the Liberals.

Suddenly, in '85, on the basis of this, they were in first place! I suppose that Turner, grateful for any blessing, and heedful of the maxim that governments defeat themselves, began believing that this line of attack alone could win him the election. Hence, very little was done by his party to correct a grave financial problem, attract new candidates, hold vigorous and stimulating policy conferences – such as Kingston, as they did in Pearson's day – or develop an international profile for their leader. (In fact, I don't think that Turner made a single trip outside Canada, with a view to having him meet foreign leaders, discuss Canada's role in the world, et cetera.)

I concluded that Turner thought we were inevitably doomed, as a government, that he was going to win by default, and that he could therefore contemplate returning in 1988 with such a bankrupt outfit and, remarkably, expect to win.

I thought, from the beginning, that the Rat Pack was the "kiss of death" for the Liberals – that Copps, Nunziata, Boudria, et al., had become firmly embedded in the public mind as representatives of the Liberal Party, and that Canadians would never entrust their government to people of that stature . . .

In politics, you should never, ever underestimate your opponent. When Turner was at his lowest, I never took my eye off him, and I never tolerated dismissive comments about him. I always stated, privately, that he was more gifted than anyone in his caucus, and could be difficult.

It was the Liberals' error to underestimate me. To them it was the joyful and inexorable consequence that, if the press gallery held me in low esteem, so did the people of Canada! So persuaded were the Liberals of this new truth, that they said the campaign would be between "Honest John" and "Lyin' Brian." That is where the fatal blunder was made.

The 1988 campaign was about leadership: competence, vision, integrity, strength, and accomplishment. And in every single one of these attributes of leadership, by the summer of '88, John Turner ran dead last. Unfortunately, as the Liberals were to learn too late, the dislike of me by the Ottawa gallery was not widely shared by the average Canadian voter, who, when asked who would make the best PM, invariably answered: 1) Mulroney, 2) Broadbent, and 3) Turner.

Broadbent, too, had fallen for this line, and began to believe the clippings that were constantly adoring and fawning! To be fair to him, his treatment by the Ottawa gallery was so outstandingly supportive that it would have been extremely difficult for him to resist the romance in the air. When one is constantly described in the most glowing terms, I suppose it is natural to begin the fatal process of believing them. (I would like to enjoy that opportunity!)

He was busy calling everyone a liar – me, Joe Clark, Pat Carney, Jake Epp, et cetera – in the House, so busy, in fact, that he struck out badly in the Lac-Saint-Jean by-election after predicting victory, and began to fade in the stretch, as we geared up, through the summer and early autumn, to wage a historic election campaign.

Our pre-writ strategy had worked remarkably, and by October 1, we had climbed to first place and 43% of the vote – which is precisely the number we achieved on election day, seven weeks later. Our campaign strategy earned us an entry into the debate weekend with little change, except for a sharp decline in Liberal and Turner leadership numbers.

They were deeply mired in third place when Broadbent opined that the election would probably eliminate the Liberals, and give rise to a PC/NDP two-party nation! I was astounded that he would make such a statement. I knew it would scare the hell out of undecided Liberals, and drive them right back to Turner.

I quickly told the press that Broadbent's prediction was quite premature – that one should never be so cavalier in dismissing a once-great political party, and I had learned that just when you thought the Grits were dead, they had a nasty habit of rising and biting you!

The comment was typical of the growing arrogance of the NDP. The day the writ was issued, Broadbent said that not only was he going to do well, but also that he was going to win at least 25 seats in Quebec – this from a party that had just been clobbered in Lac-Saint-Jean!

—

The Debates:
Fearing that any moderately good day for Turner would be turned into a great victory, before the writ was issued I made two decisions: 1) the debate must be held early, to give me the time to recover the momentum, if required; and 2) only two debates on successive nights would take place – effectively ruling out a separate-night encounter on women's issues, which, if the first debates did not go as well as hoped, would again interrupt our campaign momentum, and allow the media to predict that the new Turner was on the rampage and heading to victory. In fact, I wanted the debates held the previous week, and only the problem of a possible conflict with the World Series ruled it out. I anticipated that any serious problems in the campaign could result from the debates, and I wanted the running room, after, to regain the lead, if that proved necessary.

With me at the studio the first night were Derek Burney (who was also present on the second night), Lucien Bouchard, Marc Lortie; and Bruce Phillips and Lowell Murray on the second night. Mila was, of course, with me throughout. She was, as usual, a remarkable figure of strength and wisdom during the campaign. Her judgment is unfailingly good, and her knowledge of people tremendous. She has a splendid effect upon Canadians, generally, invigorating our campaign across the nation, and stimulating our workers to greater accomplishment.

When the debates were over, analysts ranging from Jeffrey Simpson (*Globe and Mail*), ("Mr. Mulroney needed only to escape from the two debates without a serious blunder," Simpson wrote. "This he did. He left no new hostages to political fortune, nothing new that the opposition parties could use during the campaign. Mr. Mulroney's advisors will clearly be pleased that he escaped. He drew no blood from the others, but only a little bit was drawn from him.") to Keith Spicer (*Ottawa Citizen*), Lysiane Gagnon (*La Presse*), and Joe O'Donnell (*Toronto Sun*), concluded that I had won handily, or had come out completely unscathed, denying Turner and Broadbent any blood, thereby achieving my principal objective. Quite frankly, that was my own opinion, as well.

After the debates, I spoke with many intelligent and tough-minded people – Norm Atkins, Lowell Murray, Derek Burney, Dalton Camp, Bruce Phillips, Peter White, Sam Wakim, Paul and Jackie Desmarais, Arthur Campeau, Terry McCann, Fred Doucet, Jean Charest, Lucien Bouchard, Benoît Bouchard, Marj LeBreton, and Allan Gregg. Every single one of them – except Jean Charest – was of the same view: we had done extremely well, and had come out on top, or had held our own. Not a single one suggested, directly or indirectly, that I had done badly, that Turner had done especially well, or that our campaign was in any way affected by the debate. In fact, Marj LeBreton reported an enthusiastic response from the party across the country. (She was in early phone contact with party leaders, as part of her campaign responsibilities.) Norm Atkins and John Tory, usually quite reserved in their assessments, were absolutely jubilant in their verdicts.

What happened? Because very intelligent and shrewd people cannot all be wrong. I think, in retrospect, Premier Bourassa put it best of all. There were two debates, he said: Mulroney against Turner, and Mulroney won; number two, Turner against Turner, and Turner won. I do not want to make excuses, or diminish anyone else's accomplishments, but I think Bourassa had hit the nail right on the head.

Not only had the Liberals and Turner slipped badly since the by-election, but the opening week of their campaign was a historic disaster. In fact, on Wednesday, prior to the debates, Peter Mansbridge of the CBC announced the existence of a plot (another) by the Liberals to replace Turner in mid-campaign. Apart from the campaign fiasco of childcare, and the aborted Quebec campaign, and the forty campaign promises, Turner's back was clearly hurting him, and his lifeless, unimpressive debut gave further credence to the rumours of a putsch, and the arrival of electoral disaster. When John Turner entered the TV studios, therefore, expectations were not low, they were subterranean. Just getting to the studio was for him a great accomplishment, that day.

When I look back on that night I remember it being obvious to me that Turner had improved. He had spent a great deal of time in debate preparation, and it showed. He looked right into the cameras and his once-famous blue eyes blazed in a way they hadn't in 1984. I remember reflecting on his courage as the cameras were about to go on. To have taken the abuse and disloyalty from his own party – after so many years of service – was a profoundly unfair thing for John Turner and his wife and family to have to endure. And there he was in front of me in the studio, in great pain, but still soldiering on in spite of it all. He struck me as a gallant warrior and a very worthy opponent. Four years earlier, in a different studio, Turner had been rusty. He was anything but rusty in Campaign '88.

As Turner went on the attack over the FTA, I wasn't worried. I had heard his criticisms on the floor of the House of Commons hundreds of times. When your opponent is trying to sow false fears among the electorate for political gain, you get to a point where you stop listening. And that's what I did during the debates. What I should have realized is that most Canadians – well intentioned, honest, and hard-working – don't have time to follow the to-and-fro of politics on a day-by-day basis. In the midst of an election, however, they were doing their democratic duty and watching the campaign. As a result many heard in the debates for the first time the charges that they were going to lose their medicare, their pensions, and even their country because of free trade.

Today, almost twenty years after the campaign, I note that every single one of Turner's charges has turned out to be completely false. But on the night of the English debate in 1988 those charges, in the minds of many people, rang true.

—

PERSONAL JOURNAL: JANUARY 1989

Allan Gregg reported that the perception of Turner as a possible PM was the lowest any leader had attained since polling began in Canada.

And John Turner proceeded to do precisely what he had to do: he exceeded expectations. By performing well, he was seen by his supporters and others to have performed "brilliantly." By performing "brilliantly," he knocked Broadbent out of the box completely, assumed leadership of the anti-free-trade forces in the country, and rescued his party from an almost-certain third-place finish. He also succeeded in placing us on the defensive, and forcing a change in strategy. His message, at the tail end of the English debate, was direct, clear-cut, effective – and false. As Joan Cohen, the Ottawa editor of the Winnipeg Free Press, *reported later, "Everything that John Turner said about the Free Trade Agreement is demonstrably false. His message is a lie."*

It also found favour with many Canadians.

He accused me, quite simply, of selling out my country – of promoting an agreement that would end medicare for the sick, pensions for the elderly, regional development for the poor provinces, and destroy the sovereignty of Canada.

The effect of his charges meant that I was a disloyal Canadian, resolved to deliver the nation which I served into the clutches of the United States, in exchange for the honour, as he said, of becoming governor of the 51st state. After the campaign, Turner expressed anger at the subsequent attacks I, in my campaign, mounted upon him, and his "integrity." That indicates how little he knew me – to think for a moment that he could indulge in such vile and demeaning slurs and falsehoods about me, without getting a response that would blow him right off the campaign trail. Ironically, for Turner and Michael Kirby to cry foul is particularly delicious – their first advertising on French TV was a scurrilous attack on the honour of my Quebec colleagues and myself. They openly announced that former cabinet colleagues were bums and bandits. The attack was so offensive that I denounced Turner for using it during the French debate.

Apart from their reversal of expectations, Turner received tremendous assistance from English-language journalists, in particular the anti-free-trade hard-liners – Carol Goar, Don McGillivray, Pamela Wallin, Marjorie Nichols, et cetera – all of whom prepared glowing tributes to the "new Turner" and his spellbinding performance, which quickly turned into a "crusade for Canada." They also went on TV as commentators, and within days had contributed significantly to the perception that Turner had won, that his crusade was launched, that he had courageously and single-handedly resurrected a faltering campaign, and was on his way to defeating free trade and becoming prime minister.

Within days, the perception that Turner had won the debates began affecting the polls. His crowds were bigger; his fundraising improved. He began getting favourable press, along with political capital. His MPs, who wanted to throw him out the previous Wednesday, were now jostling one another to be seen with Turner on TV. (Regardless of partisanship, I enjoyed the spectacle and knew, of course, that Turner enjoyed it infinitely more! After all he had been through, it must have felt very good!)

—

Any doubts I had I shared with only two people: Mila and Derek Burney. "I believe strongly we are going to win and we are on the way back," I told Burney in my den at 24 Sussex a week or so after the debates. "We're starting to come back, but for the first time I don't exclude the possibility of losing." Neither Mila nor Derek ever passed on these private thoughts to anyone.

My journal entry continued:

—

The day after the debates, we had a crowd of some fifteen hundred, two thousand people in Verdun, Quebec. The remainder of the week we spent in Ontario, at excellent meetings, with good, responsive crowds. We did five public meetings on Saturday, October 29, from Pickering to Kingston, all of them enthusiastic.

But the fallout from the debates was beginning to tell. Prior to my speech in Kingston, Flora told me she was going to lose her seat – which she did. (Flora, who had formerly worked in the political studies department at Queen's University and was a long-time stalwart of Conservative backrooms, had first been elected in 1972.) Flora has been an excellent member and minister. She was captured by her officials in Communications, however, and began to see the department's priorities as much more important than those of the government. Early last summer, she came to me to indicate that she should resign, because of delays in introducing the broadcasting bill and other problems with the Americans in regard to film policy. She was concerned that her credibility had been affected, and said that she wanted to step aside.

I was able to persuade her to remain without great difficulty, but was struck by the fact that, while this was not a question of principle, and when the government was going through an enormously difficult time, and needed all hands on deck, Flora, of all people – a genuine PC partisan – would persist in moving her own agenda forward at the expense of that of the ministry. Lowell had been concerned – as had Joe – at her sulking, in Priorities and Planning, in recent months, and as one of them said, "If Flora keeps talking about resigning, maybe the people of Kingston will hear it, and take her at her word!"

Flora's despair was no doubt caused by legitimate concerns, because the public service unions had targeted her for defeat, and free trade was not popular in eastern Ontario, but also because the public mood had begun to shift substantially across the country. Polls, influenced by the commentary post-debate, began to boost Liberal fortunes, and place us in an extremely precarious and challenging position.

—

Flora wasn't the only member of my team who panicked. I'm surprised today that I didn't write about the actions of Norm Atkins in that post-debate period in my journal. After all, my campaign manager had taken it upon himself to visit my chief of staff to advise him I should announce that I would hold a referendum on the FTA if re-elected. Burney exploded and tore a strip off Atkins, saying, "I've never heard of anything so goddamn stupid in my life. Can you imagine what Turner would do to the PM? He would accuse him of abdicating leadership – in the midst of a campaign that is all about leadership."

Derek kept the news away from me for a few days, but he finally told me about it during a conversation at 24 Sussex. "I hope you kicked his ass right out of your office," I said.

I had no time for such games. Harry Near later told journalist and author Graham Fraser, who wrote *Playing for Keeps: The Making of the Prime Minister* (1988), that I had held our campaign together. "After the debate the prime minister literally carried the campaign on his back for four or five days." And that's what it felt like, as my journal recounts.

The experience firmed up for me a belief I'd had for years about election debates. I've never cared too much who wins them, because they are only important if they help you win the election.

By this point, Broadbent and Turner were targeting seniors, telling the most vulnerable members of our society that I was going to take their pensions and medicare away. While politics is a contact sport, I still feel they went too far by trying to frighten Canada's seniors. I faced the issue on November 2 in Victoria.

"Let me tell you this – my mother is a senior citizen who receives medicare and a pension," I said. "If Mr. Broadbent did what he did in Edmonton, and walked into her senior citizens' home and said that her pension and medicare were being challenged, or were being affected, I want to tell you, quite properly, she'd be on the phone to me right away saying, 'Hey, Brian – son, I love you dearly, but I love my pension too.'"

Organized hecklers kept trying to interrupt me that day in Victoria. They did not know it, but they were about to play a crucial role in ensuring a PC victory. I agreed to meet with three of them in front of the cameras so they could discuss details of the FTA with me face to face. Recalling all the trouble that John Crosbie got himself into when he admitted he hadn't read each page and clause of the FTA, L. Ian MacDonald turned to Marc Lortie when he heard of our plan. "Has he studied all the details of the agreement?" he asked.

"We're about to find out," Marc answered.

In fact, I had made it my business to analyze each clause of the eventual deal as Simon was negotiating it. By the time the FTA talks were over, I had pretty full knowledge of all the agreement's intricate details. But today I am still amazed that I was willing to debate with professional protesters, with cameras there to record every moment. One misstep on my part and the whole campaign – and my prime ministership – could have been lost.

That didn't happen.

With the challenge issued, I was soon heading to the upstairs lounge of St. Michael's University Racquet Club, where I found myself debating with John Wilcox, Dave Szollosy, and John Lewis Orr, my three hecklers from earlier that day. We began by discussing clause 1807, section 9. These men had shouted out that number during my speech, saying it was the smoking-gun clause that would lead to the end of medicare and pensions.

"1807 deals with the dispute panel procedures, right?" I said to them. I read the clause out loud. "This, sir, if I may say so respectfully, hasn't the slightest thing, directly or indirectly, to do with medicare, old age security of any kind," I said.

We kept debating and I never backed down.

"Medical care, social programs, regional development are not part of the agreement," I continued forcefully.

"They can be made part of the agreement," Wilcox replied.

"They cannot, neither under the GATT, nor under international law," I answered. "What you are saying is that your interpretation of what might happen is that. That's your interpretation. It's not in the agreement, agreed?"

While I didn't convince my three new friends, I was reaching my true audience – millions of Canadians – who would be tuning in to the exchange on television that night. They saw a prime minister who knew the FTA from cover to cover and embraced it fully.

"May I ask you this," I said to the trio at the end. "When is the last time a prime minister has sat down and listened to you?"

It was a major turning point in the campaign, and I'll always be indebted to Messrs. Wilcox, Szollosy, and Orr for their help in bringing the FTA to fruition.

The Canadian business community, led by Tom D'Aquino and the Business Council on National Issues, rallied vigorously in support of free trade. During the election campaign, business leaders spoke out bluntly and purchased ads in favour of the trade agreement. Their support was unprecedented and effective.

Two important messages were sent from outside the country as well. Both Margaret Thatcher and Ronald Reagan spoke out in favour of the FTA. Margaret in particular gave her opinion on what might take place, internationally, if we reneged on the FTA. It would be "very difficult for any prime minister of Canada to negotiate another international agreement with another country," she told the *Washington Post*. "When a country has gone in good faith to negotiate a major agreement with another country, it would be a body blow if that agreement were not ratified. A great blow. . . . If you've done a prolonged negotiation and you're not prepared to do everything you can to see that it goes into legislative form with all the working systems, et cetera, then how can you ever negotiate again?"

She repeated much of that when she telephoned me in Baie-Comeau on November 22 to congratulate me on my victory. She told me she had met with a group of Canadians in London only a few days before. "You better get back home to vote for Brian," she said. "If ever a Canadian prime minister repudiates an international treaty, it would be the end of any influence for Canadians in the international sphere."

In his own call to Baie-Comeau, President Reagan was more philosophical. "Brian," he said, "it must be the Irish in us!"

My journal entry on the campaign continued:

> *The days between October 31 and November 11 were absolutely crucial. In a telephone call to me, on October 30, Allan Gregg advised we were down almost, as I remember, in a tie with the Liberals, and they were coming on strong. He also made a statement that I considered one of the most important of the campaign. His analysis of the data indicated that, as a result of his unexpectedly good showing during the debates, Turner had become a bridge for people intending to cross over and join the anti-free-trade side. His advice was that we should use our tour team and advertising shells to "blow up the bridge" – in other words, examine carefully the record of the new crusader, and see what Canadians thought of him when their memories were jogged.*
>
> *Mila and I undertook, the next day, the most punishing two-week schedule that we have ever been on – and few Canadians have been through leadership and election campaigns as we have. Our objective was clear: to expose, one after another, the lies that Turner had insinuated into the debates; to allay the fears of the elderly and the sick, who were terrified as a result of the falsehoods; to zero in on the discordant Liberal caucus over four years, the gutter tactics of the Rat Pack, the collapse of Turner's leadership, and the absence of a credible team of candidates or programs – and to bluntly ask, "Do you want this man and this party to guide Canada's future?"*
>
> *Michael Wilson, John Crosbie, and others were on the attack, but it was very much a leader's campaign. The TV reporters had little*

interest in covering anything else, no matter how good, but there were exceptions, and important ones. Turner was in effect called a liar by Emmett Hall, the father of Canadian medicare, and by Claude Castonguay, the principal architect of the Quebec plan. Distinguished business leaders got into the fray, and they carried a lot of weight – particularly in Quebec, where the entire leadership group has become entrepreneurial. Third-party endorsements of free trade, and denunciations of Turner's statements during the debate as falsehoods, were very effective during this crucial period.

The pressure was on, but, as the press reported, Mila and I never wavered or faltered. Doug Small, of Global Television, who was with us for most of that period, described it as the "most impressive display of campaigning under fire" that he had ever seen. Meeting after meeting, day after day, I bore in on Turner and his falsehoods, his bankrupt party, his divided caucus, and his own record of failure as minister of finance. The press were searching for any sign of anxiety or concern, but all they saw was a national campaign running like clockwork, and a leader who spoke confidently to boisterous meetings.

That period took all the strength and commitment and leadership of which Mila and I were capable. The media were searching for a sign of weakness, or a hint of failure, so that they could write confirmatory stories that would send our campaign into a tailspin. In fact, I was very concerned about the evolution of events, but convinced that, if I held firm and showed no hesitation, our troops would retain their confidence, and we could then go on to victory, despite the fact that some columnists like Roy MacGregor were predicting my imminent defeat.

That belief got two body blows. On Sunday, November 6, I remember vividly that I was in my den at 24 Sussex, after returning from a brutal but successful tour, which we thought had arrested any decline. That day, however, I was advised by Harry Near that Gallup would publish a poll the next morning, showing the Liberals 12 or 14 points ahead. I knew that this could have a devastating effect on morale. But I firmly believed the poll to be false, and Allan Gregg confirmed that judgment. In fact, he said, "You can take it to the bank, and be one hundred per cent sure it's wrong." So, we advised all party leaders, that night, to hang tough – and to get the word out, nationwide, that our numbers completely contradicted Gallup.

If that were not bad enough news, Bob Coates, an old friend and excellent grassroots politician, who had been an MP for thirty years, called to say, "The election is lost. We can't recover from the fear-mongering campaign that the Liberals have been conducting."

I discussed the call with Mila, who was dismissive. We felt that, while we had gone through some extremely difficult moments in the previous ten days, we had bottomed out, and had begun to rise again. The numbers in the Gallup may have been right, fleetingly, but if so, they were completely out of date.

In that ten-day period, the Liberal campaign faltered badly. They had no second wind, and no counterpunch. Post-debate, Turner began to float – avoiding press conferences, policy discussions, and issues. He began to talk of how the momentum had shifted, how he could feel a win coming on. He stuck with his litany of accusations against me and the free trade deal, and began to coast. The old Liberal arrogance, and the belief in the divine right to rule, were surely and effectively strangling whatever life Turner had managed to infuse into his campaign.

My attack on Turner was unrelenting. Not only were we blowing up the bridge, but we were forcing him to defend his leadership, his record, and his plan for the future. Because he had none, he apparently declined his advisors' counsel to switch to the sales tax question, or other matters. He stood transfixed in the headlights of the assault, repeating his invitation to Canadians to join his crusade against free trade, with fewer and fewer takers.

I remember speaking to Allan Gregg again early on the morning of November 11. "You've made up all the ground and moved ahead," he told me by telephone. I then took part in Remembrance Day ceremonies at the National War Memorial in Ottawa. The governor general was there as well.

"I'm worried," Jeanne Sauvé whispered to me. "How are you doing?"

I shared Gregg's news with her. "You don't have to worry any more," I said. "The election is over."

The best rally of the campaign was organized by Luc Lavoie and took place in Quebec City on November 11. Four or five thousand people were there, flags flying, bands playing, emotions flowing freely. The national campaign was originally designed to be structured around the team, but in Quebec the entire campaign was based on my leadership, and my ability to ensure a strong role for Quebec in the government of Canada. Clearly, my success in bringing about the Meech Lake Accord and the Free Trade Agreement, together with excellent relations with Robert Bourassa and his government, had created a positive and productive atmosphere for the Conservative Party throughout the province.

The previous night, in Mississauga, I had felt the tremendous intensity of a huge crowd in a special way. I got the impression they were saying, "We are not going to be browbeaten by the media or anybody else; we think this government has done great things for the prosperity of Ontario, and we are going to bloody well ensure that government's re-election!"

We generally knew a little in advance about impending publication of public opinion surveys in various Canadian news outlets. I had no such advance knowledge in Quebec City and woke to a glorious headline in Le Soleil *that we would sweep every seat in eastern Quebec, an excellent beginning to what turned out to be the happiest and most enjoyable day I have ever had on the campaign trail. Our bus left Quebec City and headed out for Baie-Comeau along the old Route 15 that my father used to drive. The day was sparkling as we passed Baie St-Paul – crisp and sunny – and that splendid stretch – one of the most beautiful in Canada – from La Malbaie to Tadoussac. The mood was joyful and confident. The campaign had been brutal and challenging but we were going to win. Here and across the country. It became a growing love-in at each of our eight stops that day. I was to get 80 per cent of the vote in Charlevoix, a remarkable and humbling experience, a gift from ordinary, hard-working people along the North Shore, who perhaps identified with me and my candidacy, because I was really one of them – from the same roots, same home, same place.*

We poured on the effort across the country, particularly in Quebec, where we had worked so hard, through so many setbacks, to try and build a genuine democratic party, with a base, an identity, and a future. I knew that if we could win big in Quebec, we could not only reverse decades of political despair but that we could do something remarkable, because of a strong, national majority government, and implement the FTA.

The final sprint, from Vancouver back to Baie-Comeau in seven days, was exciting, and powerful political theatre. The polls showed our comeback, and still the Liberals showed no counterattack. And so

I continued to pound them, and the hecklers would delight us, at large, large rallies in Vancouver, Calgary, Winnipeg, Fredericton, Scarborough, and Yarmouth.

I had instructed our campaign planners, some weeks earlier, that I wanted to spend time in Quebec, so four days of the final week were devoted to a tremendous blitz of ridings in Montreal, the West Island, the North Shore, and South Shore. We ended, on day fifty of the campaign, at a huge rally in Trois-Rivières organized by Pierre Vincent, our outstanding young MP, after which Mila and I had a great lunch together before heading for the airport for our flight to Baie-Comeau, to await the results the next day.

Four days earlier, Allan Gregg had come to see us in our hotel in Toronto, just prior to my appearance on "The Journal," with Barbara Frum. He told Mila and me that, give or take a few, we would win 183 seats. As Mila and I had a bite to eat, Mila said she thought we'd win 170. On election night, we had won 171, a figure later reduced to 169 by recounts. She was pretty close.

It was snowing in Trois-Rivières that Sunday afternoon, and for the first time since my election as prime minister, I felt genuinely relaxed over lunch. Mila and I relived some high and low points of the campaign, and I felt a quiet but deep sense of accomplishment. We had persevered, we had taken the criticism, but had not taken our eyes off the principal objective – the re-election of a majority PC government on a platform of proven competence and prosperity, and a plan for Canada's future that was daring, as represented by the FTA abroad, and national reconciliation with the Meech Lake Accord, at home.

No one knows, for sure, how history will judge either of these initiatives, or any other element of the campaign, or my entire stewardship. That afternoon, I knew I had done my best for my country, and for my party, and I experienced the joy that comes from achievements in the face of long odds and great challenge.

The next evening in Baie-Comeau, the emotion I felt when our victory was proclaimed was relief and gratitude. The joy was what I felt with Mila, over lunch, in Trois-Rivières.

On election night I was once again in a room at Hotel Le Manoir Comeau. I had no feelings of triumph, instead I felt awed and very humble. I also remember being overcome by a sense of history. You had to hearken back to the memory of the founding leader of our party, Macdonald of Kingston, to find another Tory PM who won back-to-back majorities.

"Sir John A. would be proud of his pony tonight," I told a friend.

Mila and I soon left the hotel and were driven to the recreation centre in Baie-Comeau. Just as on September 4, 1984, it was jammed with thousands of friends and neighbours. I greeted as many as I could and finally made my way to the stage to address the nation.

"Because the issues were historic, the campaign was especially challenging," I said. "But, however impassioned the debate, this campaign has shown that Canadians agree on what it is that we most cherish in our national life. Our sovereignty, the protection of minority rights, our unique social programs, our concern for the environment, our commitment to regional development – these have their source in a Canadian tradition of tolerance and sharing. It is something we expect of each other and our governments. The election, then, has not been about those values, but about the means to give them greater effect. So now is a time for healing in this land. For in the end, irrespective of party preference, we are all Canadians, we all love our country, and we all put the national interest first."

Campaign '88 was over.

The first hint that I wasn't going to enjoy the brief honeymoon period usually afforded re-elected prime ministers came during the press conference I held in Baie-Comeau on November 22. Les Whittington of Southam News got up and asked me when I was going to resign! Some honeymoon. On the same day Premier Frank McKenna announced that he believed I had a mandate to proceed with free trade – which he supported – but that I lacked one to proceed with Meech Lake – which he didn't.

While I had hoped for a quieter time as Christmas approached, this was not to be. I gathered my cabinet together on December 7. "The election was about trade," I told the group, "but in a subliminal way it became one about competence. Canadians had to choose which group of men and women they wanted to lead them and they chose you. And at the basis of this success has been unity – unity of caucus, cabinet, and party." Lucien Bouchard appeared to listen intently as I spoke those words. I would soon find out the hard way that while he might have heard my words, he didn't understand their meaning.

On December 15 the Supreme Court of Canada released a decision that threw two governments into crisis – mine and Robert Bourassa's. The court struck down sections of Quebec's Bill 101, ruling that the Quebec law's provisions restricting the use of English signage were unconstitutional.

As prime minister and as a Quebecer, I thought the Supreme Court's compromise decision – French signs outside and bilingual signs, with a predominance of French, inside – was the solution. Above all else, I didn't believe that any government should ever use the notwithstanding clause. (I should note here that I was surprised to find that Pierre Trudeau, always apparently opposed to the clause, forced on him by the provinces as the price of their agreement, once assured Cardinal Carter in a private letter that he would, without hesitation, invoke the clause to countermand any law permitting abortion on demand.)

Right away I began a series of telephone conversations with Robert Bourassa. We both knew that Meech Lake hung in the balance. If he chose to use the notwithstanding clause to protect Bill 101, the opponents of Meech would pounce.

"You could kill Meech," I warned Robert. "Don't do this. Trudeau and his friends will use that."

"I know, Brian, but what choice do I have?" he replied. "Claude Ryan says he will resign if I don't."

"I don't believe you," I snapped back, not for a moment thinking that Ryan, the distinguished Quebecer who had led the No forces in 1980, would ever pour that sort of gasoline onto a crisis in Quebec.

Later I came to believe that Robert was telling me the truth. Ryan was indeed responding to the crisis-like atmosphere in Quebec over the ruling. On December 18, for example, ten thousand people jammed the Paul Sauvé Arena in Montreal for a rally, where they demanded that Bourassa use the notwithstanding clause.

I also believe that Bourassa's decision to invoke the notwithstanding clause was profoundly affected by his own memories of the October Crisis of 1970, which took place while he was a rookie premier. Speaking to his fellow first ministers at Harrington Lake in 1992, he was to remind them of that dark time. "I have faced political violence," he gravely told those premiers who doubted the seriousness of language matters in Quebec. "One of my ministers was assassinated. I took action to keep control of the situation."

Writing in the journal *Policy Options* years later, Gil Rémillard gave us a glimpse of what was going on behind the scenes in Bourassa's government in December 1988. He recalled a conversation that took place in Quebec City in the midst of the crisis.

"I have a lot of difficulty using the notwithstanding clause," Rémillard told Bourassa.

"I understand you, me too," Bourassa replied, "but our first responsibility is to keep social peace. If you have sixty thousand people in the streets in December and bombs, what is it going to be in the spring?"

"You know, Mr. Bourassa," Rémillard cautioned, "we're risking scuttling Meech Lake."

"Yes, I know," Bourassa answered. "That's what Brian told me yesterday. We are lucky to have him. He is doing an extraordinary job for Quebec."

That conversation took place on the evening of December 16 on the roof of Premier Bourassa's office (known as "the Bunker"), where he liked to walk in the open air admiring the Quebec City skyline. That troubling conversation, Rémillard recalls, took place on a cold night, against a backdrop of the Quebec flag snapping in the wind outside the National Assembly.

The next afternoon a crisis meeting took place in one of the sombre rooms inside the Bunker. There it was spelled out to Bourassa that if he really wanted to protect the language law from legal challenge, he would have to bite the bullet and use the notwithstanding clause. Rémillard recalls that Bourassa's trusted advisor, Jean-Claude Rivest, said, "That's it, Robert. If you want this damn law, you have to say that you are setting the Charter aside. And, Robert, I'll tell you exactly what that means." At this, Rémillard writes, "Jean-Claude got up and went to the blackboard. He took a piece of chalk and drew a tombstone with a big cross and, in capital letters, the word MEECH. Then he sat down. Premier Bourassa got up without saying a word and left the room. No one had anything left to say."

Further west, Premier Gary Filmon of Manitoba had earlier shut down debate on Meech in his legislature, after he'd spoken eloquently in favour of the accord during Manitoba's debate on ratification. "Were we to change or amend this resolution, it would be undoubtedly lost. Let there be no pretending or posturing," he said. "If this House changes the Meech Lake Accord, we have abandoned and lost the accord and the new beginnings it stands for . . . The significance of Meech Lake goes beyond the specific constitutional changes that it will achieve. The real significance of Meech Lake goes to the heart of the idea of cooperative federalism. After fifteen years of conflict, confrontation, and mistrust, Meech Lake marks a new beginning for federalism."

I telephoned Filmon and congratulated him on the leadership he had shown. To this day, it remains one of the best speeches in defence of

Meech Lake. Filmon then abruptly changed his mind. More worried about his own political future than that of the country, Filmon linked Meech Lake to Bourassa's decision to invoke the notwithstanding clause. This was a disaster.

"The accord made it a fundamental obligation of all governments to protect minority language rights," he told his legislature. "I believe the decision made yesterday by the Government of Quebec to restrict minority language rights in that province violates the spirit of the Meech Lake Accord . . . I have concluded that the debate on the resolution now before us and the public hearings would not serve a useful purpose and may invite a very negative anti-Quebec backlash."

I wrote to Filmon right after, barely able to control my anger. I reminded him of a few facts about the notwithstanding clause. "I reject the linkage which is drawn between the Meech Lake Accord and the action of the Quebec government," I wrote. "As you know, I personally view the notwithstanding clause as inconsistent with a Charter of Rights. However, you will recall that a number of provinces, including Manitoba but not Quebec, insisted on including the notwithstanding clause in the Canadian Charter of Rights and Freedoms and the federal government agreed as the price of patriation."

I held meetings at 24 Sussex, and it was agreed that I should write Bourassa with as firm a protest as I had registered earlier in Saskatchewan on similar, but not identical, language problems. The letter used harsh language, but less harsh than the words I had used in private conversations with Bourassa earlier – but to no avail, as he had proceeded with Bill 101.

Internally, my own government was facing a crisis. Lucien Bouchard was again acting in an unstable manner. Unable – unwilling? – to look beyond the borders of his own province in the midst of a crisis, or unable to understand the need for discretion when directing a party, government, and country, he told me he wanted to announce his personal support for Bourassa's use of the notwithstanding clause, although such a statement was contrary to the government's policy, as laid down by me as prime minister.

In the Commons, the Opposition were taunting Lucien, and he began to buckle under the pressure. I learned that he was threatening to quit the party. We had an emotional private meeting in my office, at the end of which he undertook to say nothing that was at variance with our position to the press. We shook hands and he left my office. Shortly afterwards, acting against our specific agreement, he contacted a reporter. "The notwithstanding clause is a mechanism essential to the protection of certain values in Quebec," he told La Presse Canadienne. Because he was secretary of state, the statement was doubly embarrassing, and the Opposition exploited it fully over the next few days.

I was furious, and the next morning began to make plans to fire my former classmate for his disloyalty and insubordination. Paul Tellier and Derek Burney advised against this move, arguing that we were all exhausted and that after the Christmas holidays – rested and more thoughtful – we could regroup and resume our activities with ample time to ensure that such a misstep never happened again. They also wanted to avoid a public split on an issue involving one of the most sensitive areas of any federal government's responsibilities. A year and a half later, I reflected on my decision in the pages of my journal.

—

PERSONAL JOURNAL: MAY 1990

Tellier and Burney are outstanding public servants of excellent judgment and I agreed with their views. I believe now that I made a serious mistake. I should have asked for Lucien's resignation in December of 1988, in his interest and mine. Clearly Lucien is not capable or interested in shucking off the tribal instinct to sovereignty for Quebec. He is a good and honest man but one who fails to see the beauty of a great pluralistic nation, preferring instead the comfort and security of a small, more cohesive, and unitarian nation-state, with whose language and traditions he is familiar and proud.

—

I could have spared the government, the country, and myself an enormous amount of difficulty had I done what I wanted to do and fired Lucien Bouchard, on the spot, that day.

The House of Commons was in an uproar as well. The Rat Pack's Sheila Copps sank to the lowest point of her political career in question period on December 22. As I was speaking to the members in French, attempting to calm the waters as we dealt with the language-on-signs issue, she revealed a lot about herself. "You are a slimebag," she shouted across the floor, as recorded in Hansard. "Speak in English."

Despite my party's recent victory, many MPs from across the aisle were intent on continuing to fight the election campaign. On the night of the vote ratifying the Free Trade Agreement, December 22, there were noisy demonstrations in the House, flags were waved, and my government and party were once again accused of selling the country out. This slur came mainly from the Liberals, who in five short years would embrace the FTA as if it were their own.

It was a disgusting spectacle.

In the middle of the ruckus, Brian Tobin came over to my seat and asked me privately whether the government would, as usual, be providing and organizing planes to take all the members home for the holidays. I was stunned at his request, considering the abuse we were taking from his side of the Commons, and was momentarily speechless. I quickly recovered.

"Get your own fucking plane," I told him.

And Merry Christmas to you, too.

1988 was over.

PART VI

The Second Mandate

1989–1993

1989

1. The Start of the Last Good Year
2. Tiananmen Square and Beyond
3. Behind the Scenes with Reagan, Thatcher, and Others
4. After the Fall of the Berlin Wall

1990

1. Nation of Discontent
2. The Bouchard Bombshell
3. Distractions Along the Way
4. The Shadows of Ghosts
5. Oka, Iraq, and Thatcher's Fall
6. The Home Front

1991

1. Two Wars: the GST and the Gulf
2. The Battle for Canada's Soul
3. Ireland, Europe, Bob Rae, and Sir John A.
4. A Coup in Moscow

1992

1. A Bleak Start to the Year
2. Plain Talk with George, Dick, and Boris
3. Joe Clark's Instincts
4. The Guns of August
5. Charlottetown

1993

1. Bill Clinton and Others
2. Resignation

1989

1. The Start of the Last Good Year

BEFORE CHRISTMAS 1988, officials in the Department of Finance advised me that the country appeared to be heading into a mild recession. Still, they said, Canada would have a "soft landing" because the nation's main economic indicators were strong. Only three days into the new year, however, the Clerk of the Privy Council warned me in writing that the picture was now anything but reassuring. "The fiscal forecast is currently being updated," Paul Tellier wrote. "It seems clear at this point that reducing the deficit next year will require a combination of revenue increases and spending cuts as high as $7 billion. Any large fiscal restraint package will have to include expenditure cuts. There are, however, no easy expenditure cuts left – these were made in your first mandate."

Had I known then just how damaging the coming recession would be, I might have reconsidered my quest for re-election the year before. I had definitely learned by now that few easy matters land on the prime minister's desk for resolution.

As always, Canadian–American relations were a firm priority. Canada's veteran ambassador to the United States, Allan Gotlieb, officially stepped down in January of 1989, and I replaced him with my former chief of staff, Derek Burney. (I had already convinced the talented Stanley Hartt to leave the private sector and return as my new chief of staff. In choosing to serve Canada, he gave up hundreds of thousands of dollars a year in compensation, and I will forever be grateful.) I wanted the incoming Bush administration as well as congressional leaders to understand that Ambassador Burney, like Gotlieb, had my full and absolute confidence and that they could speak as freely to him as they spoke with me.

In Derek, I knew I had found my man. There was also a new man about to take up residence in the White House, and in my journal I wrote about my contact with him early in the year.

—

PERSONAL JOURNAL: April 17, 1989

President-Elect Bush called me the day before his inauguration, without warning, at about 5 p.m., to say he wanted his first visit to be Canada, and that he would like to come by in early February. He was casual in conversation, friendly and open. I was struck immediately by the fact that, unlike President Reagan, he clearly was not consulting notes, and was speaking extemporaneously. Ronald Reagan always followed a script, even in these conversations. (I will never figure out why, because, after he moved home to California, he and I had had a number of telephone conversations – all spontaneous, all informative, and all entertaining.)

—

President Bush and I agreed upon February 10 as the date for his visit to Ottawa.

Before that conversation I had once again reminded the incoming president that our two countries had to show real progress on acid rain. "Acid rain is an anomaly in our relationship," I wrote to Bush on January 11. "I sincerely hope that this will soon cease to be the case."

On January 30, I shuffled the cabinet in a major way. The shuffle was designed both to replace veterans who had been defeated in the election and to inject some new blood into the government's front benches. Among others, I brought Jean Corbeil in as Minister of Labour, and Gilles Loiselle as Minister of State for Finance, Alan Redway from Toronto became Minister of State for Housing, and Bill Weingard was made Minister of State for Science and Technology. Two new women entered the cabinet: Kim Campbell, as Minister of State for Indian Affairs and Northern Development, and her fellow British Columbian, Mary Collins, as Associate Minister for National Defence. Doug Lewis, an able and sensible lawyer from Orillia, became Minister of Justice and Attorney General, and the scrappy Bill McKnight from Saskatchewan became Minister of National Defence. Jake Epp was switched to Energy, Mines and Resources, Marcel Masse returned to Communications, where he excelled, while

Robert de Cotret went to the Treasury Board; Harvie Andre was the new Minister of Regional Economic Expansion, and Bernard Valcourt became Minister of Consumer and Corporate Affairs, with Gerry Weiner moving to Secretary of State. Tom Hockin was moved from Minister of State for Finance to Minister of State for Small Businesses and Tourism. And I appointed Lucien Bouchard to Environment, and to both the Priorities and Planning Committee and the new Operations Committee of cabinet.

Emphasizing the importance that I attached to the environment, I told the media gathered outside Rideau Hall that, "this places the environment at the forefront of all our initiatives. We have created as well a ministerial committee on the environment whose evolution will ensure that the environment not only receives priority treatment, but is not subject to override by other committees of cabinet."

I had strong words for my new team at our first cabinet meeting. "I want to remind you that we sit at this table in tough times," I told them. "There is no money for many of the new programs that you thought you came here to promote. There will be new money to spend on programs eventually if we continue to act responsibly in fiscal matters. But first we must make inroads in the mountain of debt . . . Don't forget your constituents. Often ministers get too busy to remember who sent them here. I want you to retain a sense of perspective. It is far too easy for a cabinet minister to become an advocate for the constituency that the department oversees. I want you to focus on the government's overall agenda and not only on your ministerial responsibilities."

The day before President Bush arrived in Ottawa, Paul Tellier reported to me that our staunch opposition to apartheid was having the desired effect on the racist government of South Africa. "In the last six months the South African media has clearly focused on Canada as being public enemy number one internationally," Tellier wrote. "It regularly comments on the 'irrationality' of the Canadian government's behaviour on the apartheid issue and in particular on sanctions. This propaganda is lapped up by a very insecure white population that chooses to look elsewhere to lay the blame for its increasingly isolated position. The RSA government, in focusing on Canada, is clearly readying the white population for further action on our part at which time it will reinforce its view that we are out of step and isolated from other more significant players, such as the U.K."

I had further good news when I heard President Bush's speech to Congress on February 9. I had waited almost five years for an American president to speak the words he did that night. "If we're to protect our future, we need a new attitude about the environment," he told Congress. "I will send to you shortly legislation for a new, more effective *Clean Air Act*. It will include a plan to reduce by a certain date the emissions which cause acid rain, because the time for study alone has passed, and the time for action is now. We must make use of clean coal. My budget contains full funding, on schedule, for the clean-coal technology agreement that we've made with Canada. We've made that agreement with Canada and we intend to honour that agreement."

The next day, the forty-first president of the United States arrived in Ottawa. It wasn't lost on observers that the first foreign visit that the new president made was for talks with Canada. There's nothing followed more closely in foreign capitals – then and today – than the movements and the statements of the president of the United States. I was to receive telephone calls in the coming four years, for example, from other world leaders asking me to speak with Bush on their behalf. One day I got a call from Abdou Diouf, the president of Senegal, asking me if I would intervene with the president in regard to a certain matter.

"I'll be happy to, Abdou, but why would you call me about it in these circumstances?" I asked.

"Oh," he said, "I just saw the president on the television here in my office and he told CNN that as soon as the press conference was finished, he was going to call you. So, I figured, if he's going to call you, I might as well tell you so I can get the matter resolved in the same telephone call."

Diouf, I recorded at the time, "is an exceptional individual. Almost seven feet tall, lean and angular, he speaks impeccable French in a soft, mellow tone that does not conceal a strong sense of authority. His country is very much a democracy. With some sixteen opposition parties squabbling for attention, a pretty vigorous press, and more than its share of economic problems, Senegal holds promise, but for the moment little else."

While he was in Ottawa, President Bush reiterated his commitment to fight acid rain. This wasn't surprising, given his love of the Maine coast, where he has spent every summer, with the exception of his war service, for the last seventy-five years. When you're with him, you can see his love of the land and his enjoyment of the sea. President Bush later told me that he had gone to Camp David the weekend just before his speech and studied the various reports that he'd received from his officials on the subject of my long years of negotiations with President Reagan. At the presidential retreat, Bush decided to overrule the hard-liners on his side, including Vice-President Dan Quayle and Chief of Staff John Sununu, and to announce that he would press Congress for an accord with Canada to cut the emissions that cause acid rain.

I was very pleased by this development, and said to the press, "This, I think, is real progress."

During that first Bush visit, East–West issues were also on the Ottawa agenda. The new president was still feeling his way around American–Soviet relations after spending eight years as vice-president with someone else in overall command. I felt he should seize the moment and told him so. "They sit in Moscow and go right to the heart of our weaknesses, like you did to [Democratic nominee Michael] Dukakis with the Boston Harbor speech," I said. "On the other hand, we're great on policy but lousy on politics. You have to take the initiative – maybe with a trip to eastern Europe."

"You're right," Bush replied. "We must take the offensive. We cannot just be seen as reacting to yet another Gorbachev move. We need to do it to keep public opinion behind the alliance. Maybe eastern Europe is it – to get in there in his end zone. Not to stir up revolution, but we're right on human rights, democracy, and freedom."

James Baker's memoirs, *The Politics of Diplomacy*, record more details of that visit. "In Ottawa . . . in a meeting with the President and me, [the Canadians] pointed out in their typical straight-talking manner just what the problem was," he wrote. "At Treasury I had spent a great amount of time negotiating the US–Canada FTA, so I knew our Canadian interlocutors well. The United States was fortunate to have them as solid and supportive friends. The President agreed. It was the first of many meetings where Mulroney would play a critical role in shaping our thinking."

I reported on Bush's visit in my private journal as well.

—

PERSONAL JOURNAL: APRIL 17, 1989

President Bush made a very favourable impression on his first trip here. I had come to know him well during the previous four years and had visited with him on three or four occasions at his residence, while he had come to 24 Sussex twice. He was well informed, considerate, and thorough – but he displayed a glimmer of steel that I believe characterizes a firm and independent man. For someone who, until recently, had a fuzzy and "wimpish" portrayal – perceptions are invariably inaccurate and unfair – my guess is that George will prove to be perhaps more resolute than his predecessors. He was certainly more aware of all aspects of his brief and spoke knowledgeably for some hours on a variety of intricate matters ranging from NATO negotiations to Japanese trade, without reference to a single note.

—

In March, I travelled to The Hague for a crucial environmental summit where I was proud to sign, on Canada's behalf, an agreement calling for tougher international action to fight atmospheric pollution. It was sad, however, to note that the United States, the USSR, Britain, and China – all major polluters – were not part of the conference. French Prime Minister Michel Rocard, a highly competent and well-organized leader, had not invited the superpowers, except for a last-minute invitation to President Bush (after American protests) and to Mrs. Thatcher, neither of whom attended. Rocard, however, had personally persuaded me to be there, hoping that Canada's participation would put further pressure on the Americans. "If we don't begin immediately, life on this planet will be impossible in three centuries," Rocard said that day.

There was a great deal of participation by Arab leaders at this conference, and links were established that would prove crucial in 1990 and 1991. I had meetings with several leaders from the Middle East, notably King Hussein of Jordan and President Hosni Mubarak of Egypt. I later invited Hussein to speak to the House of Commons – the first time in history that an Arab leader had done so. I worked with him, even though he went "off the reservation" offering back-channel support to Saddam Hussein during the 1990 Gulf War. Despite this, I still did my best to ensure that Bush at least understood his position, and encouraged the president to see the king in the summer of 1990, at Kennebunkport.

During our first meeting, the king mentioned quietly that he'd piloted the plane that had brought him to the conference at The Hague, filing a false flight plan to lessen the chances of being shot down by his enemies. "You must do everything you can to help make peace between Israel and the

Palestinians right now," he told me. "Just look who comes after; if you think Arafat is an extremist, look at who are his likely successors. And look who might come after me!"

Mubarak and I also hit it off particularly well. He had a dry sense of humour, something I learned in the run-up to the Gulf War. We had lunch together during the 1990 UN Children's Summit in New York City, and we discussed what sorts of military involvement our respective nations might be asked to contribute. His advice was that as prime minister of Canada I shouldn't be too concerned about the safety of Canadian pilots if our warplanes were committed. "Don't worry about the Iraqi air force," he said reassuringly, "they're useless. I know, because we trained them."

I then went off to London for extensive discussions with Margaret Thatcher. While she hadn't participated in the conference at The Hague, she told me that Britain might soon sign on to the deal. We spoke for two hours inside 10 Downing Street. We again discussed the situation in South Africa, and note-takers recorded the substance of our talks.

> Mrs. Thatcher stated that President Botha's days were numbered. He had suffered two strokes and Mr. de Klerk is a genie who will not go back in the bottle. The purpose is to get rid of discrimination. Namibia's independence was an enormous plus. Mrs. Thatcher anticipated that South Africa's commercial banks will have financial problems within a year caused by sanctions. De Klerk, however, would negotiate with Buthelezi and Mandela would be released if violence was renounced. This is because de Klerk is realistic and realizes that there will be violence if Mandela dies in prison. She concluded that there was no point in sanctions; what was important were the free elections in Namibia . . .
>
> Prime Minister Mulroney stated that, while he was a supporter of sanctions, he could never and would never support violence. Sanctions are working . . . Canada has done everything it can. PM Mulroney reported a conversation at The Hague with the president of the Ivory Coast. The president had said, "Leave South Africa alone, things are going fine. Don't interrupt trade." The point was that the French-African leaders differ in view from Mugabe and Kaunda. PM Mulroney said that Canada would have to fish or cut bait on South Africa. Sanctions would be dropped if there is progress, but if there is not, we might be pushed to break relations.

> Mrs. Thatcher said Canada will not have to do that. What with Angola and Namibia, and with Botha on the way out, there is progress to be found. Relations with South Africa should not be measured by trade. Africans from other countries go to South Africa to work. The economic success of South Africa is essential to their progress. Don't hit them when they are going the right way.

Margaret also hosted a dinner party for us at 10 Downing Street. She brought together an eclectic gathering that included industrialists, senior British politicians, and a few others. I wrote to her when I returned to Ottawa: "I had an especially enjoyable and instructive trip to London – and I want to thank you sincerely for your generous hospitality and good counsel. Our private meeting was particularly helpful to me, and I am carefully weighing your views in a number of important areas. Your thoughtfulness in arranging such a glittering dinner party at Number 10 gave a special dimension to our visit – although Mila still talks about Roger Moore and Michael Caine!"

While I was away, Pierre Trudeau issued one of his irritating, yet increasingly effective, polemics in opposition to the Meech Lake Accord. In a letter to *La Presse*, he wrote that the accord was a "monster" that never should have raised its "hideous head." He announced again that there "has never been any need of a Meech Lake agreement to bring Quebec into the Constitution," an opinion shared by very few Québécois.

I knew there would be major changes on the political front as well, as I expected that John Turner would soon announce his retirement plans. Ed Broadbent had already done so and was vacating the leadership of the NDP. I reflected on the changing situation in the pages of my journal.

—

PERSONAL JOURNAL: APRIL 17, 1989

Turner is nursing a lot of bruises from the election campaign and a lot of displeasure with many of his caucus members whose disloyalty and disruptive behaviour he appropriately feels cost him either the election or an enormous amount of credibility. In any case he is quite bitter and will be taking his frustrations out on me and the government in stinging fashion. Although Turner is most unhappy about it, the verdict from his party is that his leadership is at an end. Less than five years ago he was declaring his candidacy and the media were canonizing him as a certain winner. In the quite brief period since, he has led the Liberal Party to two of its most stunning defeats in its history, and will surely be removed as leader at a review vote, unless he signals by the early autumn his intentions to step down.

Broadbent has announced his retirement, and the only candidate I can see generating some excitement and substantial improvement for the NDP – Stephen Lewis – has clearly stated he will not run. Whoever emerges will not be a match for Broadbent's legacy and may suffer in comparison.

I had some individual meetings with premiers Peterson and McKenna prior to the First Ministers' Conference that dealt with the economy and Meech Lake. My impression is that while McKenna may be agile enough to find a way in the end to support Meech Lake, Filmon has, by his statements, placed himself beyond the pale. In any case, because of his minority status he couldn't deliver in his legislature if he wanted to.

In many ways, the Trudeau offensive against Meech Lake has borne fruit. Meech Lake, in the minds of some, has become synonymous with "giving in to Quebec" and "giving up too much" to bring Quebec onside, a sign of weakness toward the provinces in general and Quebec in particular. Although no French Canadian of stature has endorsed the Trudeau position, it is ironic in the extreme to note that the Manitoba Conservative Party provincial caucus – which fought any extension of French language rights tooth and nail – is now a fierce ally of Mr. Trudeau, whose positions are so strongly supported by groups distinguished principally for their open hostility to Quebec or to the extension of minority language rights. There are, of course, those who oppose Meech Lake for good reasons, but the Trudeau message in code really means "putting Quebec in its place" – with all of the dangerous consequences for Canada should that view ultimately prevail.

—

Turner did in fact announce his resignation in May. I authorized his close friend Conrad Black to approach the former prime minister on my behalf with an offer.

—

PERSONAL JOURNAL: JULY 6–7, 1989

I thought it important that a former prime minister, if even for a brief period, should be given the option of considering an attractive appointment – ambassador to the Vatican – upon his retirement. I moreover thought that, given the tumult in the Liberal Party during his leadership, Turner might be glad of the opportunity to take himself "out of the traffic" politically for a while in elegant and comfortable surroundings in Rome. I was also influenced by the fact that Turner had always been a devout, practising Catholic with a genuine affection for ecclesiastical leaders.

Conrad had him in and called to tell me that, while he was genuinely appreciative of the offer, he felt he had 10–15 years left in the business community and could not accept. Conrad, who is a friend of both Turner and me – unusual but true – strongly urged him to accept what he said was a thoughtful and generous gesture. He declined, although Conrad subsequently told me at the Hollinger dinner that John has an unrealistic appreciation of his market value after all he's been through. I think Conrad's assessment is quite accurate. People throng around powerful officials, especially the prime minister. The unspoken implication is always how exceptionally well one will do after politics and how attractive one will be to business, universities, law firms, etc. In fact, anyone who believes that is seriously deluding himself. Canadians have not yet developed the delight that Americans experience in seeing their former leaders looked after.

In Canada, prior to age 65, there is no pension, no staff, no security for a former prime minister, simply the overwhelming gratitude of the nation! I expect to leave Ottawa with the same friends I arrived with, and a substantially reduced net worth. Mila and I have been using our savings on an annual basis to supplement my present income, drastically reduced from its level ten years ago. At this moment it is not my intention to run again in '92–'93 but Mila and I have agreed that no formal decision will be made until early 1992. Whatever happens, I expect no soft landings. I have always worked hard for a living; I do so now, and must do precisely that whenever I leave. I also know that some who find the family so irresistible today will somehow find others with that same quality when I leave 24 Sussex. That is simply one of the facts of political life, and anyone in this business forgets this at their peril.

—

In early May I visited Boston and Washington. I met with Massachusetts Governor Michael Dukakis and was pleased to hear his thoughts on acid rain. In front of the press the defeated Democratic nominee predicted that the United States could pass a law before 1989 ended that would help curb transboundary air pollution.

My trip to Boston also allowed me to speak at the John F. Kennedy Presidential Library and enjoy a tour with Ted Kennedy and JFK intimate Dave Powers as my guides. After breakfast, I delivered a speech before a roomful of Kennedys and their supporters, as we enjoyed the glorious view of the sparkling waters off the Massachusetts shore. "I am here today as prime minister of Canada, a nation whose relationship with the United States of America was described by Winston Churchill a half century ago as 'an example to every country and a pattern for the future of the world,'" I said. "But I am here today as an individual as well, whose life was touched and whose career was influenced by President Kennedy, a happy, human man who exemplified not perfection, but purpose, and who brought to the notion of public service a sense of excitement, and a degree of nobility, rarely equalled in the records of time. All who knew President Kennedy – and those of us who did not – celebrate today his genuine achievements, as we salute his special talents that made it all possible."

Ted Kennedy presented me with an impressive bust of his slain brother, and it remains in my study at home today. I often look at it while I'm working at my desk and reflect on the tragedy – for Americans and for the whole world – that happened that sunny day in Dallas.

In Washington, I took part in the opening ceremonies for the new Canadian Embassy building on Pennsylvania Avenue. I've reflected before in this book on the importance of appearance in Washington and I'm proud Canada was able to lobby successfully and become the only nation to have its embassy located on the most important street in Washington – a home-court advantage for Canada if ever there was one. The building is 250,000 square feet, and it contains the sculpture "Spirit of Haida Gwaii" by famed artist Bill Reid, its own art gallery, an auditorium, and a library showcasing the very best of Canada. Secretary of State Jim Baker personally took part in the opening ceremonies. Another signal sent.

Mila and I had lunch with George and Barbara Bush at the White House, and the president and I had lengthy private talks in the Oval Office. I looked around at the changes since I had last visited; a replica model of the USS *Constitution* was now in place, and I also noticed a picture of a little girl on the president's desk. It was a snapshot of Robin Bush, his daughter who had died of leukemia in 1953. To this day, mention of her name brings tears to the former president's eyes.

President Bush was still seeking ways of building on the positive relationship with Mikhail Gorbachev established by his predecessor. In private I argued that he could do this by going back to the days of the Eisenhower administration and introducing a modern-day Open Skies system, which would allow unarmed aircraft from each of the superpowers to be sent over the other's airspace to verify each nation's word when it came to arms control agreements and weaponry. (Bush in fact proposed an Open Skies plan during a speech in Texas only a few days after my visit.)

After our discussions, reporters pressed the president on acid rain. "If there's anything that the prime minister of Canada has been clear with me about – and he's been clear with me on everything – it is this subject," Bush said.

As for me, I took a surprising question on Canada's medicare system. "It's an integral part of our citizenship," I answered. "We strengthen it every opportunity we can, and we don't see it under any challenge or attack."

Then came the followup question. "Could you explain that to Mr. Bush, so we can get that same health system in the United States?"

I chuckled to myself as I gave a careful diplomatic answer. The irony was striking. Only a few months earlier I had been accused of threatening the very existence of medicare because of the FTA, and now here I was in Washington, at the White House, being lobbied to promote medicare with George Bush himself!

Another important event in the Canada–U.S. file was the visit to Ottawa that year of Democratic Senate Majority Leader George Mitchell of Maine. He proved to be a key ally in Canada's battles to convince his nation of the need for a proper acid rain treaty.

Ambassador Derek Burney sent me a detailed memo that I reviewed before Mitchell arrived in Ottawa:

> Your meeting with Senator George Mitchell next week is a historic event. It is the first time a Senate majority leader has paid an official visit to Ottawa in living memory, and it testifies to the importance which Congress accords Canada – and which Mitchell attaches to relations with Canada. Of the 40 invitations Mitchell has received to travel abroad, this is the first he has accepted . . . Mitchell welcomed the president's clean air proposal and promised to work with the administration in achieving the objective of reducing sulphur dioxide emissions by ten million tons by the year 2000. He said the proposal was the result of a decade of work by many concerned individuals, and cited your work in particular . . . But Mitchell has not disguised the fact that "further work" will be required before he can sign on to implementing legislation. While personally in favour of controls which will benefit Maine and the Northeast, he also has to be cognizant of the concerns of his colleagues from West Virginia and the Midwest, who are worried about the adverse impact on employment of controls on local electricity-generating plants fired by high-sulphur coal.

Once in Ottawa, Mitchell said in private what he later told the press: Canada's work was far from over. He asked me to ensure that we kept up the fight for a full-fledged acid rain treaty. "There is a dangerous illusion this problem has been solved," he told reporters, "that it has been taken care of, merely by virtue of the president's statement . . . An accord would ensure continued progress in this area. We don't just want to achieve reductions in emissions on a one-time basis and have them increase over time."

In my own remarks I assured the visiting American senator that I had no intention of letting the Bush administration off the hook with only a domestic clean air bill. I admitted that some "hard bargaining" still remained, and reiterated that a full bilateral accord on acid rain was the only result Canada would be satisfied with.

Out of the blue, my government faced a serious domestic crisis after a copy of Michael Wilson's "Budget in Brief" was stolen from the printers and leaked to Doug Small, a Global TV journalist. I was furious when I spoke at an emergency cabinet meeting called to address the crisis on April 27. "This is a case of theft," I said, emphatically. "Thousands of Canadians have the opportunity to do this every day, and the system functions because they do not."

I wasn't the only one to deplore these actions. Barbara McDougall slipped me a handwritten note during that meeting. "My mother, who will be eighty years old this weekend, phoned Global TV last night to tell them their news show had been her favourite for ten years but she would never watch it again because of their use of stolen property. She did this without talking to me or my sisters first!"

After consultations with constitutional experts like Eugene Forsey and Roger Tassé, I decided that Wilson would read his budget to the media shortly after Global had broadcast budget details. To my disgust, the opposition had earlier denied our request for unanimous consent for Wilson to deliver his budget that evening in the Commons.

In July, at Harrington Lake, I reflected on the budget leak and the overall political situation in the private pages of my journal. Questions about the leak and Wilson's future had followed me overseas to Africa and Europe, and I was quite disturbed even months later.

—

PERSONAL JOURNAL: JULY 6, 1989

The spring session did not go as well as hoped. Two leaks of secret budget information forced us to release it to the media prior to introduction in the House – a most exceptional but necessary procedure made inevitable by the refusal by both opposition leaders to allow extended hours for the House to be apprised of the document. We survived the first part of the problem. In fact, Wilson looked good and the opposition churlish. In regard to the second leak I fear we did less well, and the cost to Michael's reputation was considerable. The facts are simple. After we became aware of the stolen document given to Doug Small, the budget was released. It appears that a second document found its way to an insurance company in Toronto, again prior to publication of the budget, and that Wilson's office was informed. Indeed, we were informed of this fact (which I assumed was directly tied in to the first theft, then under investigation by the RCMP) after question period, and after Wilson had made his initial morning presentation to the House but before the official tabling of the ways and means motion at 5 p.m. The opposition went into a frenzy and stated that Wilson, having failed to divulge this information to the House, had been guilty of misleading and lying to the House – the most serious charges that can be made in our parliamentary system.

John Turner is still fighting the last election and he was badly stung by Wilson's charge during the campaign that he was a liar. So this spring he returned the compliment – with a vengeance. Turner and the Liberals mounted a ferocious, unremitting attack on Wilson's credibility and did great damage to Michael in the process. I was in Dakar and Brussels for the most intense period but returned to announce my full support for Wilson and turned the tables on the Liberals by denouncing Turner for his "historic duplicity" and "betrayal of Parliament" by having introduced the War Measures Act *in 1970 (which threw hundreds of Canadians, including journalists, in jail without trial) on a promise to Parliament that all justification and evidence would be promptly conveyed to them. In fact it never was – and to this day, the true reasons and the firm evidence for the invocation of such a draconian measure have never been shared with Parliament or the nation. (My guess is that the information is flimsy and unpersuasive and sustains the view that Trudeau and his government panicked and responded excessively to what was a serious but not nation-threatening series of events.)*

In any case, the counterattack blunted Turner's attack and his claim that Wilson had "misled" Parliament, and that an innocent journalist, Doug Small, was abused by a capricious government! In quite typical Turner fashion, he damaged Wilson but left the substance of the budget completely untouched! The entire debate on Budget '89 – one of the most brutal and challenging since the war – was conducted in high moral fashion about Wilson's "integrity," while issues of great substance went unchallenged. In a word, there was John Turner's problem: he had no sense of political strategy, no capacity to resist the temptation to go for the easy headline. A political leader must know when to sustain abuse in silence in the interest of pursuing a larger goal. He must know what his longer-term objectives are and not be driven from their pursuit by seductive side issues or temporarily gratifying eight-column headlines. He must also treat Ottawa-driven issues with considerable skepticism, because they are unlikely to have any resonance with ordinary voters. In fact, when the entire Ottawa press gallery is recommending a particular course of action, it is generally both prudent and wise to do the precise opposite.

The extent to which the Ottawa gallery has become disconnected from Canada's realities (especially the older and sedentary types like Don McGillivray and Hugh Winsor, driven more now by personal animus than professional pride) is of course widely known and lamented. Their consequent lack of influence with Canadians is an important new factor in national politics, one that a political leader should be aware of, and one that should be carefully weighed in any significant political/strategic consideration or decision.

Wilson had never had his credibility challenged before this. He tried to discuss the proprieties of resignation with me at 7:30 the evening of the Global broadcast – but I cut him off and would not hear of it. After my return from Europe and my subsequent rousing defence of him in the House, he again told me he thought he had been badly damaged and wanted me to reflect upon the appropriateness of his remaining in the portfolio. I again refused to entertain such a discussion because I firmly believed that he had done nothing wrong, and that if a finance minister is in fact to be considered responsible and forced to resign from office because of criminal acts committed by people over whom he had no control, that would be a profound distortion of the genuine sense of parliamentary responsibility and would undermine all future ministers of finance whose careers could be terminated by an unknown felon who stole his papers and leaked them to third parties.

Last week I read that Michael was booed at a CHIN picnic in Toronto. That must have been a deeply humiliating experience for Michael, because he is a proud and principled man. But the fact is, with TV in the Commons, the opposition can mount a sustained personal attack on any minister, and the mere fact of denying his guilt day after day undermines his innocence. Having gone through the experience themselves, I have noticed a much greater sympathy by these ministers for the position I frequently find myself in – of being on the receiving end of many such opposition campaigns designed merely to smear and diminish. I have also found that re-election by the people of Canada with a commanding majority and personal re-election to the Commons with the highest margin of any candidate in Canada (80 per cent) are compelling replies to anyone who challenges my honesty or integrity.

Wilson has been shaken in his self-confidence, and has become unusually abrasive and petulant in dealing with his cabinet colleagues. We are going through a difficult time, trying to prepare for the release of the outlines of the GST this July, and I have urged Michael to take a long vacation with his family so that he can take on what will be the biggest challenge of this second mandate – the sales tax [GST].

We have dropped in public favour these last six months, though not as much as I had anticipated, given the tough nature of many of our budgetary provisions. I expect we will decline even further, with the upcoming NDP and Liberal leadership conventions. Although no one of substance has yet announced his/her candidacy in either party, my guess is that Nelson Riis will emerge to lead the NDP and Jean Chrétien the Grits. Both will be extremely tough adversaries and I take absolutely nothing for granted. The battle will be long and difficult, though if Chrétien continues the drift to the left that began under Trudeau and strongly continued under Turner, our task might be made a little easier because the differences will be clearer.

—

1989

2. Tiananmen Square and Beyond

THE SPRING AND summer of 1989 continued at a fast pace. This was a year dominated by foreign policy and would feature the Francophonie Summit in Dakar, Senegal, a NATO Summit in Brussels, and the annual G-7 gathering, slated for Paris to coincide with France's celebrations marking the two-hundredth anniversary of the French Revolution.

In Dakar, President Mitterrand surprised us all by taking a page out of Canada's book and announcing that his country would be forgiving $3 billion in debt owed by the mainly Third World nations making up La Francophonie. I was also pleased that the forty-two nations unanimously adopted a Canadian-sponsored resolution on human rights. In addition, we worked hard on an environmental resolution aimed at bringing more Third World countries into the battle, with assistance from richer northern nations like Canada and France.

"And for Canada there was the added benefit of Quebec, the petty flag wars with Ottawa behind it, feeling a sense of strength and pride which makes it a more comfortable member of Confederation," journalist Patrick Doyle wrote at the conclusion of the summit.

I then moved on to the NATO Summit in Brussels, where leaders were once again attempting to reconcile our different approaches to the changes taking place in the Soviet Union under Mikhail Gorbachev. President Bush wanted NATO leaders to endorse his call for sweeping conventional arms reductions between NATO and the Warsaw Pact in Europe. He was offering the Soviet Union a 20 per cent cut to American forces and parity in troops stationed in Europe. Under his plan, such a deal could be concluded with the Soviets at talks in Geneva within a year.

The sticking point for Bush – and for Margaret Thatcher – was the fact that the West Germans were calling for a link to be made in these conventional force reduction talks with the short-range missiles in Europe. Both the United States and Britain argued such linkage could lead to the elimination of these important missiles, which they saw as key to the West's nuclear deterrence shield. This was such a huge issue that the whole Alliance was in danger of splitting over it, and the talks behind closed doors among leaders, and their foreign ministers, were tense. I will never forget one of Helmut Kohl's interventions. "There will be free elections in [East Germany], perhaps in one or two years' time," he said forcefully. His remarks were greeted by stunned silence. Who among us knew the Berlin Wall would fall in only a few months' time?

Margaret Thatcher also spoke out strongly, as my notes reveal. Interestingly, she had put up quite an argument against the American proposal in private, but had come around by the time the meetings in Brussels closed. "NATO is a winning concept," she snapped. "NATO has kept the peace for forty years and American and Canadian forces are indispensable to Europe. These countries [in the Eastern Block] have no idea what freedom is and no idea how to build a market economy."

In the end, the leaders approved Bush's sweeping proposals. And the foreign ministers – thanks in large part to Canada's Joe Clark – reached a compromise agreement to hold talks with the Soviet bloc on the reduction of short-range nuclear forces. Joe suggested the wording that committed NATO to a "partial" reduction in these nuclear forces.

"I know that Mr. Clark's role last night was absolutely key," I told the press afterwards, adding that the compromise "came from Mr. Clark's deft pen."

Joe was to play a key role once we were home as well. Like everyone who saw the images of student protesters bravely facing off against tanks in Beijing's Tiananmen Square, he and I were shocked and sickened when the Chinese government massacred hundreds, perhaps thousands, of their own young people on June 4. Joe spoke for the government in a special emergency debate in the Commons after that terrible weekend.

"What is transpiring in China is a tragedy of global proportions," he told a hushed chamber. "I know that all members of the House of Commons and, indeed, all Canadians, share a deeply felt sense of horror and of outrage at the events that have unfolded over the last few days in China."

I thought back sadly to my visit to China and my talks with the Chinese leadership in 1986 before I braced myself to speak to the press in the aftermath of the massacre. What do you say in such circumstances? I tried my best. "We are appalled by the tragedy that has been visited upon young people in China seeking greater democratic freedoms within the system,"

I said. "It's a calamity for them and it's a calamity for the breath of fresh air that was a democratic impulse running through China."

I also spoke in Vancouver just a few days after the Chinese attack on the students. "I say to those young heroes: 'Do not despair, victory must eventually be yours because liberty can never be denied.' Canada abhors the great tragedy that has been inflicted on those brave young leaders in Tiananmen Square. Indiscriminate shootings have snuffed out the precious human lives but they can never snuff out the fundamental urge of human beings for freedom and democracy."

We recalled our ambassador, and Joe hauled in the Chinese ambassador to Canada to register our disgust. While Joe ably handled the day-to-day details of Canada's overall response, I decided to concentrate on convincing my fellow G-7 leaders to condemn the Chinese at our upcoming summit in Paris in July. Working closely together, François Mitterrand and I were able to overcome the reluctance of Japan and the United States, and impose real sanctions against China. These included the suspension of arms trade and World Bank loans to China, as well as a ban on high-level ministerial contacts between the Summit countries and the Chinese.

Zambia's Kenneth Kaunda happened to be in Ottawa shortly after the events in China, and we spent an hour in private discussing the battle against apartheid, another stain on world affairs. "What you are doing in Canada is very important," he told the press afterwards.

As we prepared to depart again for Europe, I plunged into extensive consultations with my Summit partners ahead of our gathering in Paris. I wrote in my journal about one discussion in early July.

—

PERSONAL JOURNAL: JULY 6, 1989

President Bush called for a twenty-minute chat about the upcoming Paris Summit. He asked for my views about what President Mitterrand might do and what others might expect from the U.S. I told him we shouldn't expect great surprises from the French (although Mitterrand in Dakar, without warning, sprung his plan for Third World debt relief upon La Francophonie) because they are fearful the rest of us, particularly the U.S., would resent being upstaged at such an event. I told Bush the French will focus principally on the debt question and seek broader support on the declaration of the environment of The Hague.

George is en route to Poland and Hungary prior to the summit and is concerned about expectations there of the seriousness of U.S. support. He said, "Solidarity [the Polish democratic movement] is talking about $10 billion in support and we aren't even in that league."

I told him that the G-7 had in the last five years provided record economic growth and prosperity, even if it was unevenly shared, and that we should do nothing to inhibit that growth. "Sometimes," I said, "the smartest thing to do is to do nothing, and this is one of those times – except for the debt and environment problems, where progress is imperative." He was in full agreement. I filled him in on my most recent meeting with President Reagan in Toronto. He said Barbara and he would be extending an invitation to visit with them in Maine in August and we made plans to chat, possibly in Paris.

—

Before arriving in Paris, I stopped in London on July 11 for talks with Margaret Thatcher. Almost immediately, she told me she hoped we wouldn't be discussing South Africa at the summit. She didn't get her wish, and the G-7, at Canada's insistence, later issued a declaration that once again condemned the racist regime there and called for the release of Nelson Mandela.

On that visit she seemed surprisingly vulnerable. "When things go wrong, everything goes wrong," she complained at one point, referring with obvious frustration to her struggles with high inflation, the resistance to her hated poll tax, and a host of other political problems. She also complained about the press, something I rarely heard her do, but which did not offend my ears.

Because Britain was slated to relinquish control of Hong Kong to China in 1997, she was badly shaken by the events in Tiananmen Square. The official notes of our meeting summed up her chilling remarks: "Mrs. Thatcher commented that the first task was to reassure the Hong Kong population, and secondly to have international cooperation in case 'Armageddon' should occur. The Summit countries should be thinking about Armageddon, but they could not speak about it in public because of the fear that would create. Regarding eastern Europe, PM Mulroney pointed out that the kind of money that President Bush had offered is the kind of money which Canada could offer. Mrs. Thatcher agreed, saying that Walesa [in Poland] had an expectation of billions, not millions, and that was an expectation which simply could not be met."

Her comments about Hong Kong were on my mind throughout my short stay in Britain. "The problem of Hong Kong is not only a problem for the United Kingdom," I told the press. "The problem is a problem for the world." My government felt a strong kinship with Hong Kong, and it wasn't difficult to see why. In 1988, over half of the 45,000 people who emigrated from the colony came to Canada.

Margaret displayed her mischievous side that week. Ahead of the summit she sat for an interview with *Le Monde*. In that prominent French newspaper, on the eve of the two-hundredth anniversary of the French Revolution, she took it upon herself to tell French readers that the concept of human rights was enshrined in Britain through the Magna Carta back in 1215, making the French celebrations of their fairly recent event somewhat frivolous to her Anglo-Saxon mind.

I sat with her at the main event in Paris and couldn't help but notice that she wore the controversy she'd created – leading to her being booed along the Champs-Elysées – as a badge of honour! Mitterrand had assembled leaders from around the world, and protocol dictated that heads of state sit with the president of the French Republic. As a result, mere heads of government like myself, Thatcher, and Helmut Kohl didn't rate. This slight didn't go unnoticed by the Iron Lady. "Brian, look at this," she whispered to me. "Who is that, down in the front row with Mitterrand? It's somebody we don't even know, and all of us, leaders of G-7 countries, we're up here." She was clearly implying that we were stuck in the peanut gallery!

Margaret and I also discussed a G-7 newcomer, Sosuke Uno of Japan. He had come to office only the month before and was already embroiled in a sex scandal involving a geisha. "Have you met the new prime minister of Japan?" I asked her.

"Brian, isn't he the one who visits bordellos?" she replied. "Now, why would I spend time with him?"

At the G-7 meetings themselves, I continued to push Canada's main goal that the leaders ask the OECD to develop a system of environmental standards and monitoring. I was struck during the discussions by how high the environment had moved on the agenda of the world's most exclusive club since my first summit in 1985. In the end, we succeeded, and the leaders issued the following declaration: "There is growing awareness throughout the world of the necessity to preserve better the global ecological balance. This includes serious threats to the atmosphere, which could lead to future climate changes. We note with great concern the growing pollution of air, lakes, rivers, oceans, and seas; acid rain; dangerous substances; and the rapid desertification and deforestation. Such environmental degradation endangers species and undermines the well-being of individuals and societies," it read in part. "Decisive action is urgently needed to understand and protect the earth's ecological balance. We will work together to achieve the common goals of preserving a healthy and balanced global environment in order to meet shared economic and social objectives and to carry out obligations to future generations." At least the words were in place.

With George Bush having replaced Ronald Reagan, I noticed how the tone of the G-7 meetings had changed.

—

PERSONAL JOURNAL: September 4, 1989

At the Paris Summit Bush had done an excellent job – in much the same way as he handled the NATO summit in Brussels a few months earlier. He had gone out of his way to develop a relationship with Mitterrand that changed the dynamics of the summit because it altered the alliance anglo-saxonne, *as Mitterrand described it, between Ronald Reagan and Margaret Thatcher, which traditionally had placed the U.K. in a position of privilege vis-à-vis the U.S. when compared with the other European summit participants. Mitterrand as chairman promptly embraced Bush and was especially supportive of most American positions, including many to which he had previously expressed considerable hostility when they had been espoused by Ronald Reagan!*

The fundamental difference between Bush and his predecessor is that Bush has intimate personal knowledge of most important international dossiers, and it shows. Ronald Reagan always spoke at summits on matters of substance from cards. Bush is entirely different. He has a vast knowledge of the personalities and the policies of governments and international agencies, accumulated during lengthy

> *service at the UN, CIA, in China, and as vice-president, and he carries that information and knowledge well.*

—

While in Paris, President Bush and I firmed up plans to meet informally at Bush's summer residence in Kennebunkport on the Labour Day weekend. He had first suggested such a meeting after my trip to Washington in May. "I really enjoyed our visit and chat," he had written. "The next time we meet there will be too much pomp, so let's plan another chance for a private, easy talk – grandkids, dogs, your kids."

But there was still a full summer ahead before I'd take in the salty breezes of the Maine coast. Mila and I continued our practice of moving ourselves and the kids to Harrington Lake for the summer months that year. Prince Andrew had married Sarah Ferguson in 1986, and my family was honoured to host the young royal couple for a luncheon at Harrington on July 19, 1989. (Nicolas was particularly thrilled at the manner in which our royal guests arrived – they swooped in by helicopter.) That lunch was the start of a firm friendship between the four of us that continues to this day. Sarah often sought Mila's advice over the years. It is no secret that she had a great deal of difficulty adjusting to the demands of life as a member of the royal family, but it is less widely known that she often turned to Mila for comfort in the years before the couple divorced.

In 1992, for example, she wrote Mila after a photographer had caught her in a compromising private moment. "I am so sorry for the problems I have caused you and our friendship – I was so looking forward to coming to see you – especially when I was desperately in need of peace. All the work and organizing you did – and I am so sorry. Thank you for being such a great support and friend."

Then she reflected on how the prying photograph came about:

> I was in total private in seven acres of undergrowth . . . with the road some two and a half miles away. The "snake" crawled on his tummy for two and a half miles and sat in a tree three days – only moving for some hours in darkness. OK . . . so no excuses, but, more to the point, it was a definite tipoff from "The System" who are, and were, trying to discredit and embarrass me before my stay

> at Balmoral with the Queen. Very clever, the timing of the photos coming out was too accurate: they didn't print for eight days – waiting until I got there . . .
>
> Ooh, Mila, when will I ever learn? I just love life, I love laughing, working hard, playing hard, and just living, and if I see an opportunity to travel and it hurts no one and nobody minds – what is wrong? Well, anyway, low-profile time – Andrew has been fantastic and a total support so maybe all this horror will sort itself out . . . The children are really happy and secure and seem to be better than they have ever been, although "The System" is trying to say I'm an unfit mother. Well, that is the only ounce of confidence I have – the house is one big nursery.

I remember Mila's sadness as she prepared her response to the young duchess. "Life can be terribly demanding when you are serving the public," Mila told her. "I often wonder if the general public, left to their own devices, and uninfluenced by the media, would not be more generous, more human. I think they would."

But those trying times for Sarah were in the future as we enjoyed a summer's day together. "Harrington Lake looked on the horizon like an oasis of paradise, especially with the noise and heat of our 'green bird' that delivered us to the kindness and delicious hospitality of yourselves," Sarah wrote to us upon her return to Britain.

In the summer of 1989, American Vice-President Dan Quayle was under fire. I had learned by this point just how mistaken FDR's first vice-president, John Nance Garner, had been when he said that the vice-presidency is about as valuable as a "bucket of warm spit." When he was vice-president, George Bush had demonstrated to me the importance of this office. Those foreign leaders who dismiss the vice-president do so at their peril, as it was always my experience that the person who holds the job has one thing most people in Washington can only dream of: regular access to the president. As a result, I made it my business to keep in touch with vice-presidents George Bush, Dan Quayle, and Al Gore. Anyone who could help advance Canada's cause in the most important capital in the world was on my radar screen.

One day in July I asked the PMO telephone operators to put me in touch with the vice-president of the United States. (Those operators were wonderful; they could seemingly reach anyone, anywhere, at any time. Just before I left office I signed personal thank-you notes to each member of that team of unsung heroes, who worked long hours with no complaint and no public acclaim.) Dan Quayle was soon on the line and I gave him a pep talk. I told him that Mila and I had read press reports that he was under attack in a new book for his performance in the 1988 campaign. As always in such situations, the harshest criticism of the embattled vice-president came from anonymous "insiders." "I became prime minister when I was forty-five, with young children," I told him. "I have been the target of the worst press, and the most unflattering books by 'insiders' of any prime minister in memory. In retrospect, what the books did for me was: 1) Strengthen my hold over the party. 2) Increase my popularity with ordinary voters because of the obvious unfairness. 3) Help me win a strong Conservative majority, the first Conservative leader to win back-to-back majorities since 1891. Tell your wife and your children, from a family that has lived through worse: Don't worry about it. Don't be distracted by it. Don't acknowledge it. If you don't pay any attention to it, it will melt like a snowbank in May."

Quayle soon followed up with a handwritten letter: "Brian, Your phone call was very special and one of the nicest gestures I've seen in my thirteen years of politics," he wrote. "Marilyn and I are eager to meet you and Mila and get to know your wonderful country better. The president feels he had a great trip to Europe and from back home things seemed to go well for all. Again, thank you for a very special call. Be of good cheer, Dan Quayle."

While public life has its definite rewards, they often come with a price. Just ask Sarah Ferguson or Dan Quayle, two people who tried to serve their respective countries the best way they could.

Closer to home, that summer of 1989 also saw another impressive young person go through his own trial by fire. My consumer affairs minister, Bernard Valcourt, a young Brayon from Edmundston, had been involved in a serious motorcycle accident. While dismayed to learn that he'd been drinking before getting on his motorcycle, I resolved to give him another chance. I accepted his resignation from cabinet but invited him to recover at Harrington Lake. Bernard lost an eye in the accident, and we spent many hours in conversation as I walked with him through his valley of pain and humiliation.

—

PERSONAL JOURNAL: JULY 6–7, 1989

I spoke again this p.m. with Jacqueline Valcourt, Bernard's estranged wife who is at his bedside in Quebec City. His accident was severe, although the doctor told me a few days ago he expected him to make a full recovery, following reconstructive surgery. I was dismayed to learn from Jacqueline that Bernard is in danger of perhaps losing an eye as a result of the impact. This is a great tragedy, although it is really quite miraculous that he survived at all. Valcourt is one of the most able and promising young politicians I know. With any luck, he will surpass this and he may go on to be premier of New Brunswick or prime minister of Canada one day. To have been a senior cabinet minister and a Priorities and Planning member at age 36 is already a remarkable achievement.

—

As the summer came to a close, Mila and I prepared the children for our trip to Kennebunkport to visit with George and Barbara Bush. The boys and I loaded up on fishing gear, and Caroline was busy reading up on foreign policy. While still a teenager, she had already developed a keen interest in foreign affairs and wasn't going to pass up on the chance to pepper the president of the United States with questions in such an intimate setting.

Mila and I laughed as our helicopter whirred closer to the presidential compound at Walker's Point. Forget the Marines, the honour guard was made up of Bush grandchildren, who were everywhere. I made extensive notes after our visit was over.

—

PERSONAL JOURNAL: SEPTEMBER 4, 1989

The substantive discussions with President Bush took place over breakfast – bacon, eggs, and coffee – on the outdoor terrace beginning about 7:30 a.m. They broke up some four hours later, interrupted only by appearances by National Security Advisor Brent Scowcroft and

Chief of Staff John Sununu. We covered the waterfront: bilateral matters – acid rain, trade irritants, FTA application problems, etc. – and international affairs, where the president was eager to review events in Colombia; how Canada would cooperate in certain aspects of the national strategy to be announced a few days later; our recent rebuff of Panamanian President Noriega; Canada's intention to seek membership in the Organization of American States (which I had not mentioned publicly in Canada); and a followup of his major issues flowing from the Paris Summit. The president was especially interested in my analysis of the personalities and policy mixes of the summit leaders based on my five years of attendance at these events. It says something about the vicissitudes of public life that five years' service almost qualifies me for veteran status, and with it an aura of wisdom!

Bush is more personally engaged and more forceful than Ronald Reagan. He is very much a family man and appears to never sit still. Once he went off with Caroline and Ben to fix the ball machines at the tennis courts, and the next thing I found him standing on a boulder with Mark, alone and in deep and apparently enjoyable conversation. Anyone who cares that much for children has a streak of genuineness and decency that will see him through any amount of political adversity.

—

(My journal reminds me that the four of us also spent part of dinnertime talking politics. My telephone call to Vice-President Quayle earlier that summer was still on my mind, and we discussed how political reputations could often be unfair.)

—

Barbara said, "That's exactly what I mean" when I was alluding to the fact that some leaders are historically underestimated and then acquire great authority and stature in office, to the consternation of former critics and commentators. She was clearly referring to the satisfaction she felt at seeing the truth slowly but certainly emerge about her husband! The Bushes don't appear to make much time for recriminations, but George took a swipe at a conservative political consultant in

Washington, whom he described as "an awful hypocrite." This came up in his denunciation of Joe Calzone and other Republican advisors who had worked for Dan Quayle and had then undermined him by blabbing to Jules Witcover and Jack Germond who published a devastating book on the campaign. George said that this was the "worst goddamn abuse of confidence" he had ever seen in his life, and expressed support for Quayle when I asked how he was getting along.

—

On September 8, President Bush sent me a brief telegram following our visit. In it, he combined thoughts of business and of pleasure: "I just wanted to report to you that I followed up on our conversation at Kennebunkport relating to the involvement of our summit partners in the Colombian drug issue. I did call Helmut Kohl, as you suggested, and he said he would be pleased to propose to Mitterrand a Summit 7 initiative. I also called Margaret to explain to her what we are doing. She was pleased and very supportive of the notion. Now we must hope that the results are up to the brilliance of our idea. Barbara and I enjoyed the Mulroney family visit to Kennebunkport more than I can say. We look back on it with great nostalgia."

September 4 was the fifth anniversary of our initial victory in 1984. In my journal, I reflected on our first election, the political situation, and my best friend.

—

PERSONAL JOURNAL: SEPTEMBER 3–5, 1989

(Written at Harrington Lake)

September 3

Tomorrow is an important day – the fifth anniversary of our first election to government – and Nicolas's fourth birthday. All the family is ready for a major celebration of the more important event – the birthday. But I'd argue there will be a few good words said about the election. On the 17th I will have been prime minister for five years. It has been a considerable accomplishment to have come from the outside, having never held a seat, to win the leadership, unite the party, make a major breakthrough in Quebec, and in the process win the largest number of seats in Canadian history in 1984, following up with another majority in 1988 – the first such back-to-back majorities in Canada in 35 years.

While sitting outside in the sun today, with a strong breeze blowing off the lake, I felt a measure of real achievement and pleasure. Mila and the children are in wonderful shape and an absolute joy to behold. The party, if one can judge from our just completed national convention – which brought some 4,000 delegates to Ottawa – is united and confident. And the government is strong and positive as we approach the opening of Parliament on September 25 and await the dramatic changes and challenges the GST, Meech Lake, and new leadership in both the Liberal and NDP parties will provide. The smart money says McLaughlin and Chrétien will emerge. If so, Chrétien and his populist approach (refreshing in one who became so wealthy as a bank director and corporate PR man!) will certainly cause Liberal fortunes to rise very, very substantially in the months following their convention in June 1990. My expectation is that that popularity will be maintained at least until the summer or early autumn of 1992 – and then, hopefully, a consideration of alternatives will introduce some realism into the equation.

Chrétien is a man of some considerable charm and certain political advantages. His disadvantages include intellectual insolence and a very considerable measure of vanity. These, combined with habitual Liberal arrogance, could cause him serious difficulties. He already has a tendency to underestimate his political adversaries, and this is never a prudent or helpful quality in seeking high office.

My only concern with the NDP is that whoever is chosen will be able to retain the bulk of NDP support next time around, because any erosion in the support has usually benefited the Liberals. Moreover, the perception of Chrétien as a left-winger will attract substantial NDP support to the Liberals if it is not quickly *fastened down by a good and effective national leader. However, all of this is speculation about events months and perhaps years off, much of which can and perhaps will be changed by events and people unknown and unidentified today.*

Just had a chat with Sam Wakim. Few people played a more important role in our victory in 1983 than Sam. He single-handedly put together the Ontario organization when nobody else would, and he has received very little in return. The double standard of the press is revealing even in regard to party organizers. Because Norman Atkins was part of the Big Blue Machine and a good source for many in the Toronto media, there was little criticism when my government, in 1984, awarded Atkins (through Camp and Associates) the largest advertising contract we award. There was also hardly any criticism when I put Norman in the Senate – the greatest patronage gift a PM can make, in Norman's case, given his age, worth some $5 million over his lifetime!

And yet, if I were to do something similar for Sam, who has been with me through everything for 30 years, the denunciation would be overwhelming. The difference is that Sam is not a favourite of the press, he is not part of any trendy in-group and, worse, he is entirely devoid of any self-serving gossip and "anonymous" background stories about how he "made" Mulroney, how he "advised" the PM to do this or that at a critical juncture, etc. Sam is simply a decent, loyal, and devoted friend of mine who played a major role in my success in winning and retaining the prime ministership – and hence, he is uninteresting and unworthy, clearly a "crony" and a "hack" who seeks only "patronage" and is not as "selfless and honourable" as many with an authentic Albany Club background!

September 4
9:45 p.m.
At this hour five years ago the election was over and we were on our way to a record landslide. I remember my sentiment that night as being similar to the one I experienced immediately following my election to the leadership of the party; it was as if I had become detached from events and able to watch events unfold as if in a film. I was both a spectator and a participant, but I remember it best from the perspective of a spectator! There was joy, apprehension, and resolve – an odd mixture.

And in both of these historic moments I had a sense, after the result was announced, of having succumbed to the tug of fatigue, and I found myself floating through the rest of the night, enjoying it fully, but being somehow removed from the reality of events. In fact, following the leadership convention, a special caucus was called for Monday morning at which all members, premiers, and leadership contenders spoke. Again my recollection of this particular event, which remains quite vivid, is that of watching a newsreel unfold, evaluating my own performance and that of others with no sense of having participated in it myself! Whether this was induced by loss of weight, loss of sleep, or genuine shock at the result, I do not know. Perhaps that is why Dr. Pivnicki [Mila's psychiatrist father] comes in handy for so many people.

September 5
Ed Broadbent called this afternoon to indicate he is disposed (though not yet decided) to accept the job I offered him. It is the presidency of a new federal government human rights institute based in Montreal at a salary in excess of $100,000 per annum. His hesitation was based on a lack of information, and I undertook to secure it for him. I gather it is his intention to announce Friday that he will resign his seat early in the new year and yet be able to advise the press that he has not yet decided upon his future. I was happy to offer Broadbent the job, and I think he will do an excellent job in filling it. I wonder, however, if Ed – who had denounced government patronage eloquently – felt a slight twinge of remorse as he discussed with me ("the architect of political patronage") so elegant a reward for himself. Because indeed it is a reward – for service rendered to Canada – and I see nothing deplorable in that. My guess is if this comes to pass, the media will be chuckling approvingly, just as they would have attacked vigorously had I chosen to appoint an equally impressive person of Conservative persuasion to the post! I have long since gotten used to the double standard of the Ottawa gallery, as have most Canadians who think about it for a moment. The only people totally oblivious to their own duplicity are certain members of the gallery themselves, but their lack of professionalism has so diminished their credibility that, in reality, they have ceased to be much of a factor anymore.

Tomorrow I begin a two-day series of meetings with the new Japanese Prime Minister, following which I will be chairing a two-day P&P, then on to La Malbaie for a visit with the Desmarais family, a speech in Montreal on the 17th (the fifth anniversary of my swearing-in as PM), and will be back to Ottawa to resume parliamentary obligations on September 25.

We have a full plate, not including extensive and difficult foreign travel during the next three months. Tax reform, Meech Lake, UI reform, interest rates, control of the deficit, etc., will make for a challenging time with certain inbred possibilities of further declines in political popularity. But I have a very good feeling about the country, where we're going and where we'll likely wind up. Despite all the criticism and political rhetoric, Canadians know they have a very good thing going for them, beginning with an irreplaceable nation and a magnificent quality of life. So they're not about to do anything dramatic that could fundamentally alter these realities.

For my part, after five years as PM, I feel more confident in the job, more sensitive to the country's deepest aspirations, and more aware of the realities of daily political life, with the scars to prove it. What matters is that I continue to provide good leadership to the country and party, do my very best, ignore the guerrilla attacks from the opposition and media, and not be diverted from our agenda. Only by consistent, strong leadership and firm adherence to our basic beliefs will the country continue to grow and prosper – enabling us to be judged properly and reasonably by the electorate in 1992 or 1993.

—

I was very happy as September came to a close when Robert Bourassa and his Quebec Liberals were returned with another majority mandate. I was pleased for him as a friend, but I also knew his victory was good for the country. This confirmed federalist had signed on to Canada with his signature on the Meech Lake Accord and I was confident it would be ratified in the coming months.

My caucus gathered on September 27. In my closing remarks I once again reminded the group of my rules for caucus. While many had heard a version of this speech before, I felt a reminder was in order. Michael Wilson had earlier announced details of what would become known as the GST, and I knew some of our MPs would be tempted, in the words of Lyndon Johnson, to "piss outside the tent" in search of headlines back home. (When it came to members like Pat Nowlan and Alex Kindy, I occasionally found myself [to borrow a phrase from Bob Rae] with MPs who were inside the tent, pissing in.)

"Caucus membership in good times and bad, is like being in a family," I said, according to my notes. "They come together. You can't walk away from the kids when times are tough . . . Major initiatives must be sustained and supported by caucus, otherwise the whole system cannot go forward. Members cannot get the party benefit of my leadership, our national campaign, and the great issues we defend, and then snipe at us from the sidelines. Caucus members must know their deliberations shall remain confidential and shall not be reported . . . Once caucus has decided, solidarity and mutual support are required."

Before the month was out, I invited Ray Hnatyshyn out to Harrington Lake for a heart-to-heart discussion. He had been defeated in the election, and while this was a great loss to the party, government, and me personally, I knew the country as a whole would benefit if he accepted the offer I had in mind.

Governor General Jeanne Sauvé had served as the Queen's representative in Canada since 1984. While I had extended her mandate by a year, she had by now told me that she and her husband, Maurice, wanted to return to Montreal and enjoy their retirement near their only child, Jean-François. Mme Sauvé had performed extremely well as governor general, and her flawless bilingualism and high degree of elegance had added prestige to the office. Replacing her would not be easy.

The office of Governor General of Canada is very important in our national life. In our parliamentary system, debates in the Commons and in committee often become extremely personal and sometimes even brutal. It is important for Canadians that we have a depoliticized place, as personified by the governor general and his or her office, where people get together and seek out the common national interest. And the governors general I have known have fulfilled that role admirably, benefiting all Canadians in the end.

In seeking out a replacement for Mme Sauvé I decided, in today's terminology, to think outside the box. I was attracted to Ray because he was of Ukrainian descent, was a westerner from Saskatoon, and combined a joyous attitude with a great personality and sense of humour. While his French was fairly weak, I expected that his other great qualities would more than compensate for it. I discussed my idea with Don Mazankowski and no one else, and then invited Ray to come out to the lake. To ensure even further secrecy, I dismissed the staff so that Ray and I could speak in total privacy. We chatted for about half an hour as we sat outside the residence overlooking the lake and the trees in their full colours before I made my move.

"Ray," I said, "I have decided to recommend to Her Majesty that you become the next governor general of Canada."

He looked at me as if he were about to have a heart attack and then began to cry. I got up and went inside the house to get him a glass of water.

"Prime Minister," he said when I returned, "I apologize for my reaction but, as you spoke, I was thinking how astonished my late father would have been, to find out that I would be accepting the position of Governor General of Canada."

"Ray," I replied, "not as astonished as my late father would be to find out I was offering it!"

We chuckled happily together for a few more minutes and then it was time for Ray to return to Ottawa.

"I have not discussed this with cabinet and I still have to advise Her Majesty, so this has to remain an absolute secret, Ray," I told my nominee as he stood up to go. "You cannot discuss it with anybody."

"Can I talk to Gerda about it?" he asked.

"Of course you can talk to your wife, but no one else."

I walked him out to his car and we shook hands as he got in. I wished him well and remained in place as he began to back the car out. Ray pulled up right next to me, stopped, and put the window down.

"Prime Minister," he said, "will you do me one final favour?"

"Sure, Ray," I replied, "what do you have in mind?"

He grinned before answering.

"If anything happens to me on the way back to Ottawa, would you leak this one to the media?"

As Canada's twenty-fourth governor general, Ray Hnatyshyn and Her Excellency Gerda Hnatyshyn placed their own endearing stamp on the office. One of their most lasting contributions was the establishment of the Governor General's Performing Arts Awards. Ray also highlighted the contributions made by members of Canada's multicultural communities, and he worked hard on his French-language skills throughout his term of office, never becoming so self-important that he couldn't poke fun at himself over the issue.

"Hnatyshyn and his wife Gerda discharged their duties at Rideau Hall with dignity and grace, the likes of which had not been seen since the time of Roland Michener," wrote historian Dr. Christopher McCreery, Canada's foremost expert on the office of governor general.

After Ray returned to Ottawa – with no incident en route – I had an important dinner guest at Harrington, as my journal records.

—

PERSONAL JOURNAL: October 1, 1989

After Ray's departure, Premier David Peterson arrived at the lake for dinner. He has had a rough summer with the Patti Starr fundraising scandal and is now somewhat more tolerant of others than he was when his honeymoon with the Toronto and Queen's Park media was raging, and he could do no wrong. Having been badly assaulted by the media for the first time, he has emerged chastened and more sympathetic. He told me that for the first time since entering politics his motives were impugned, and his integrity so assaulted on a daily basis, that last summer he was unable to sleep nights for an extended time. I genuinely commiserated with him but told him that my treatment by the Ottawa press gallery had been so brutal that I had long since put them out of my mind and had learned to conduct my affairs as far away from them as humanly possible. Indeed, the last election confirmed that their opposition and daily onslaughts were not necessarily unhelpful in getting re-elected!

He is concerned with Meech Lake. We agreed that he would see Bourassa this week and convey to him the need for a more direct and persuasive federalist approach from him prior to and during the First Ministers' Conference. We agreed that I would speak with McKenna, Wells, and Ghiz on bilateral matters to improve the mood of the upcoming FMC and seek to lay the groundwork for an approach to New Brunswick to break the Meech impasse, followed by – if possible – an approach to Manitoba (although he is not hopeful about that because, as he said, "Sharon Carstairs is even more hypocritical than Sheila Copps!")

Peterson said he would be willing to make Ontario officially bilingual if Bourassa would reciprocate. This is a courageous step by Peterson, but I doubt if Bourassa could respond in a helpful way.

Trudeau should never have patriated the Constitution without securing reciprocal protection for language minorities, but he was so obsessed with patriation that he threw everything, including caution, out the window and gave the provinces a new lethal weapon called the notwithstanding clause. The clause crippled individual rights and undermined the authority of the Supreme Court of Canada. Moreover, having proceeded without Quebec, he ensured that any attempt to bring Quebec in on honourable terms could be scuttled by denouncing it as a "sellout" to Quebec, thereby ensuring its repudiation by English-speaking Canada. Having failed miserably to unite Canada through constitutional reform, Trudeau is resolved that none of his successors should succeed, lest his failure be exposed for the horrendous one it is.

I have had some difficult moments with Peterson. His opposition to the FTA was negative and short-sighted. But on other matters – Meech Lake being one – he has been open-minded and generous in his view of Canada. I construed his offer to meet as a sincere one, and the three hours we spent together tonight were very productive and, I believe, helpful to the well-being of the federation.

—

On October 10–11, King Hussein and Queen Noor of Jordan visited Ottawa, in response to my invitation. Just as Chaim Herzog became the first-ever Israeli leader to address Parliament in 1989, King Hussein became the first Arab leader, as I noted earlier, to speak to Canada's parliamentarians during his visit.

"We believe that peace will only come on the basis of respect for security, well-being, and legitimacy of all states in the region, and of respect for the rights of the Palestinian people," I said in my introduction of the king. "And those rights include their participation in the determination of their own future."

Hussein provided MPs and senators with a brilliant overview of the situation in the Middle East. I was pleased that he chose to quote the words of a former Canadian prime minister. "Aggression, in any part of the world, constitutes in the long run, a threat to every other part," the king said, using the words of Lester B. Pearson to make his point. "If it is true that we cannot tolerate a city of residential suburbs surrounding slums and degradation, it is equally true that we cannot be safe in a world community which condones lawless aggression in any part of it."

The king and queen's visit that year to Ottawa cemented a friendship that continued throughout my service as prime minister and beyond. King Hussein was soft-spoken, respectful, knowledgeable, elaborately polite, and always seeking a positive solution for the Middle East. The world lost a great statesman when he died in 1999.

1989

3. Behind the Scenes with Reagan, Thatcher, and Others

It was once again time to head overseas. The Commonwealth Heads of Government Meeting was to take place that year in Kuala Lumpur, and I knew that apartheid would once again top the agenda. I had decided to embark upon a trade promotion tour of Pacific Rim countries in the leadup to the summit and was poised to deliver the annual Singapore Lecture speech. Before leaving the continent, however, I stopped in Los Angeles, where I addressed the World Affairs Council. I used my speech to continue to prod the Americans to ante up when it came to providing aid to countries like Poland and Hungary that were breaking away from the Soviet bloc. I announced a Canadian aid package of $42 million – the Americans would have to offer up $500 million to match Canada's aid in real per capita terms – that was designed to provide both immediate food assistance and economic development funds.

One of the Canadians in the audience that day was none other than NHL superstar Wayne Gretzky. Pointing out his presence in the crowd, I recalled for everyone the words I'd heard as a youth: "I can remember my father telling me one day, 'Brian, I've got something important to tell you. You go out and get yourself a good education, son, because there is no money in sports.' Thanks, Pops." Wayne, thinking, no doubt, of his multi-million dollar contract with the L.A. Kings, laughed as hard as everyone else.

During my short stay in Los Angeles, I was able to spend a few hours with former president Ronald Reagan. With sadness I noticed an accentuation of what I'd seen during our meetings in Washington in 1988 – his growing detachment from life. On the drive to the council meeting where he was introducing me, I attempted to engage him in a discussion of President Bush's recent overtures to the Soviets.

"Ron," I asked, "have you heard from George on it?"

"No," he answered, looking out the limousine's window.

"Has Jim Baker called you about it?" I continued.

"No."

I found what he *didn't* say telling. He didn't add that his former colleagues should have called him; he just said nothing. That wasn't the Ronald Reagan I knew.

That evening, however, my concerns dissipated somewhat. He and Nancy hosted a small dinner party in our honour and as we all chatted over drinks he was as funny and engaged as always. He spoke about the importance of the Canadian North, and how he and I had resolved, to some extent, issues of sovereignty in Canada's Arctic waters. It almost seemed as if he were president once more. Again, I chalked up my fears about his health simply to his advancing age.

—

PERSONAL JOURNAL: NOVEMBER 5–6, 1989

We spent the evening at their Bel Air home with Charlie and Mary Jane Wick and Jimmy Stewart, the actor, and his wife Gloria. It was a delightful dinner, with Nancy and Ron in great good humour. They were on their way to Japan a few days later where Ron was to pick up $2 million for speeches and endorsements – which may have somewhat explained the good humour. At dinner Nancy unloaded on her favourite target – Raisa Gorbachev – while after dinner both Charlie and Ron told jokes.

—

I was to return to Los Angeles shortly before I left office in 1993. After a special ceremony in my honour at the Reagan Library, Ron and Nancy had us to dinner at their beloved Rancho del Cielo. Located in the mountains north of Santa Barbara, it was the one place Reagan truly felt at home. After our arrival by helicopter, he took Mila and me on a tour of the ranch, telling us proudly that he chopped and stacked wood there every day as a hobby. I was reminded of my first visit with him in June of 1984. As he escorted me out of the office, he put his arm on my back and urged me to go first. Out of respect I declined, but before speaking I put my hand on his arm. That arm was like absolute steel; the only person I'd met previously with a similar arm was Elmer MacKay. Like Reagan, Elmer cut and stacked wood in his spare time.

The Reagans' home was a small and modest Mexican-style house. We had an early dinner that day, just the four of us sitting around a tiny table. That was when it became obvious that things had gotten worse. Ron, whose term of endearment for his wife was "Mummy," was relying heavily on Nancy that night.

In the middle of a story, he stopped and said, "Mummy, where was I?"

Nancy, without missing a beat, said, "Oh, Ronnie, you were telling Brian about your trip to Berlin." He smiled and continued. He halted again a few minutes later, however, and Nancy again had to steer him back in the right direction. Mila and I found ourselves looking down sadly at the table.

A few years later, after the public announcement that the former president had Alzheimer's, Nancy described to me a dinner that she and Ron had had in a Beverly Hills restaurant in the 1990s. When they entered the restaurant, accompanied by the Secret Service, there were hardly any other patrons. By the time they'd finished their meal, however, the place had filled up. When the Reagans rose to leave, everyone in the restaurant burst into a round of spontaneous applause.

"What that's about?" Reagan asked.

"Ronnie, that's for you," she replied.

"Why?"

"Because you were president of the United States."

"Is that so?" he said with a soft smile, and he turned slightly and waved to the crowd.

After California, we were soon on our way to the Far East. The highlight of the trip was, of course, the Commonwealth Heads of Government Meeting (CHOGM) in Kuala Lumpur, Malaysia. I will never forget the beautiful resort where the leaders' retreat was held. There are so many positive memories – despite what was to come with Margaret Thatcher. The twenty-one-year-old king of Swaziland, King Mswati III, came by my room to speak with me privately about Canada's stance on South Africa, and brought along both of his wives. (The second of his father's sixty-seven sons, King Mswati had, in late 2006, thirteen wives and twenty-seven children.) While I was speaking to His Majesty, I remember looking out the window and seeing Benazir Bhutto, the prime minister of Pakistan, walking along the beach in her flowing sari.

I got to know Benazir very well in those years. She was a courageous young woman who was the first female to serve as prime minister of her country. She was later deposed in a coup and threatened with arrest. Manfred G. von Nostitz, who served as Canada's ambassador to Pakistan from 1988 to 1991, wrote to me in 2005 about how I handled this tricky diplomatic situation:

> In August 1991 Benazir was ousted by the more traditional military/feudal establishment and was threatened with arrest. You were concerned about her welfare, and asked your staff through informal private channels (not conventionally through the Department of External Affairs) to ascertain from me, the Head of Mission on the ground, what could be done practically and meaningfully to help Bhutto. After consulting with Bhutto, I replied that you might wish to consider appointing a distinguished Canadian legal expert to come to Pakistan and do an impartial public legal report on the constitutional and juridical issues revolving around the dismissal and status of Bhutto. This would have to be a clinically objective report no matter how the chips fell. If on balance there were a legal case against Bhutto, we would also be obligated to publish it. This was an unorthodox proposal leaving Canada open to criticism for interfering in the domestic politics of a sovereign and Islamic state. It was also risky because the legal situation was not clear-cut. It was therefore not favoured by the External Affairs bureaucracy. To my pleasant surprise, however, you immediately agreed to this proposal and appointed Ron Atkey, a Toronto lawyer, to come to Pakistan and draft such a report. Atkey produced an excellent concise document which over all was supportive of Bhutto's constitutional and legal rights.
>
> I presented this report first to the Pakistani government and then made it public. I was beaten up over this overt Canadian interference in Pakistani affairs, including a raking over the coals by the very president, Ghulam Ishaq Khan, who had been instrumental in ousting Bhutto in the first place. However, there was prevalent in Pakistan a grudging respect for what Canada had done because the document was not at all polemic and just stuck to the dry constitutional and legal issues. I survived diplomatically because I had a very good personal relationship with the president and because

> Canada was one of Pakistan's major donors and supporters of the Afghanistan cause. There was thus no real negative fallout for Canadian/Pakistani relations in spite of rhetorical threats made in some quarters. Most important, the Atkey report was a godsend to the beleaguered Bhutto and her political party. It no doubt helped her at that time to stay out of jail, and to eventually be re-elected for a second term in 1993.

I remain in contact with Benazir to this day. Upon our first meeting in Kuala Lumpur, she took it upon herself to tell this Tory that she read the *Toronto Star*! "I'll make sure I cancel that," I quipped, later telling reporters that Benazir was a great example of a democrat. "The only dismaying thing I heard was that she indicated at one time or another she had read the *Toronto Star*. That didn't throw me completely but we will have to review our aid programs," I laughingly said.

Toronto Star publisher John Honderich and I later had a friendly joust by letter concerning the incident. "I'm sure it's a very reassuring thought to realize that wherever you go in the world, you can't escape the *Star*," he wrote, enclosing a copy of the *Star*'s coverage of the exchange.

I soon fired back. "I noted that Prime Minister Bhutto, following her intemperate remarks about reading the *Toronto Star*, returned to Pakistan to be confronted by a nonconfidence motion in her government," I wrote. "I hope it is not contagious."

I covered the main events of the CHOGM in a lengthy entry in my journal in which I expressed my anger and dismay at the actions of Margaret Thatcher.

—

PERSONAL JOURNAL: NOVEMBER 5–6, 1989

> *The principal event at the CHOGM was a clash between Margaret Thatcher on one side and Bob Hawke and I on the other. After 17 hours of meetings, the foreign ministers committee, skilfully chaired by Joe Clark, agreed on a common position on South Africa. At the retreat when this report was to be considered by the heads of government, Margaret Thatcher jumped up and said, "While there are a few things I could disagree with in this, I won't, and I propose its adoption."*

Rather than allow this to unravel I promptly jumped up and seconded the motion, which was then made unanimous. The triumph was short-lived. Without any forewarning, the U.K. government shortly thereafter issued another document that took issue with much of the guts of the document Mrs. Thatcher had just approved! When I heard the news on the BBC World Service sometime later that night I immediately called our office in Kuala Lumpur – the significance of the document had gone over most of their heads – and told them all hell would break loose the next day. And it did.

Margaret always believes in a good attack and, knowing what her position was, she attacked. When I walked in with Hawke and Clark and Raymond Chrétien, and took my place next to Margaret – separated only by the mild-mannered Sultan of Brunei – she leaned over and in the tone of voice she saves for wayward ministers she immediately said, "And what, Brian, have you been up to?"

To which I responded, "The issue, Margaret, is what have you *been up to, and I mean to find out!" After the chairman asked for comments, Hawke began by denouncing her actions as "a strange way to do business." (Mugabe, who was absent, would a few hours later denounce it as despicable.) I reviewed what had taken place and said, "In Canada you do not sign a deal at five and repudiate it at six. The Commonwealth can only function on a basis of trust and confidence among leaders. I do not quarrel with Mrs. Thatcher's right to speak her mind. I quarrel with the right to tell us one thing and then without warning do another – that sends to Pretoria a signal of discord on sanctions when unity had already been achieved." I told her – and she was sitting about three feet away – that her conduct was unacceptable and violated the fundamental concept of British fair play that governed our conduct at these meetings – and as far as the Government of Canada was concerned, this was something we would never do and for which the Commonwealth was owed an explanation!*

In a brief intervention, Margaret blustered on about "free speech" and how "astounded" she was that anyone would find anything untoward about what she had done, only "getting our story out." And therein is the crux of her problem. And so it turned out when she returned to London. Margaret feels she has to win every round, best every opponent, and defend every British interest – always with the adoring British press lapping up every morsel, carefully fed by Bernard Ingham, her press secretary and a man of enormous influence with her and the people of the U.K. The Ingham technique has, until recently, worked brilliantly in Mrs. Thatcher's favour. It consists of trading access for favourable treatment – always placing Mrs. Thatcher's interventions favourably, no matter the manner in which they were actually received; excluding the non-U.K. reporters from closed briefing sessions when inside information is provided about another of Margaret's "brilliant" and "historic" stands; and disparaging openly, if off the record, any leader or delegation that dares disagree with Mrs. Thatcher's position or view of the world on that given day. The technique is most profitable for Mrs. Thatcher. No other leader of a free society commands such uncritical and unwavering support from his/her national media.

I like Margaret Thatcher and admire a great many of her achievements that are truly substantial, and in some ways, historic. She is tough, speaks clearly, prepares thoroughly, sits patiently through long meetings, is often very courteous with others, and has shown many kindnesses to Mila and me. I am therefore at a loss to understand why she would allow Ingham to undermine Sir Geoffrey Howe after the most recent cabinet shuffle and be so scornful of most of her other senior ministers and advisors.

Two days following the Commonwealth meeting she had to weather the greatest crisis of her stewardship, the resignation of Chancellor of the Exchequer Nigel Lawson. (In her memoirs, Margaret later criticized Lawson's lack of gravitas*: "At first, I could hardly take him seriously. I told him not to be ridiculous. He was holder of a great office of state. He was demeaning himself . . .") Suddenly, all of the chickens were coming home to roost. The British, civilized people that they are, have taken great offence at her attitude, which they once considered to be tough, determined, principled, and resolute – and the opinion polls now show her at the lowest ebb of popularity of any PM since polling began 50 years ago.*

Margaret got off-balance with the international media in her conflict with the Commonwealth and then again because of Nigel's resignation. If she learns to be more considerate, fair-minded, and generous to people and colleagues, she will survive and win again. I doubt, however, if she can survive at all unless she brings some discipline and sensitivity to Mr. Ingham's propaganda service, which has clearly run amok.

—

We left Kuala Lumpur for the trip back across the Pacific so that I could attend the Organization of American States (OAS) Summit in San José, Costa Rica. This was an important event for Canada as we had just announced our intentions finally to join this crucial body in our hemisphere. I reflected in private on my reasons for taking this step, a move I'd argued for strongly during my leadership bid in 1983.

—

PERSONAL JOURNAL: November 5–6, 1989

After a long flight to San José the Organization of American States meeting was a pleasant and fascinating two days. I had decided in February that it was time for Canada to join. Our agenda of environment, debt, drugs, etc., was largely influenced by developments in our own hemisphere from which we were removed because of our persistent refusal to join the only regional instrument of multilateral dialogue – the OAS. I did not discuss it with External because the old boys' network would have sought to kill the idea. Clark, however, was receptive and we decided to proceed at the earliest possible moment. It was ironic that Canada, a country providing leadership in forums as diverse and challenging as the Commonwealth and La Francophonie, rejected opportunities to play a constructive role in our own backyard. Fear of conflict with the Americans was the principal reason in the past for the decision. The insecurities of the left, visceral anti-Americanism, and a fear of change do not make for a sound foreign policy. I expect many difficulties in the years ahead with our decision to join but I am satisfied it is a proper and imaginative thing to do for Canada. The meetings were excellent – a wind of democratic change has swept across Latin America. Almost all governments are democratically elected today, compared with only a handful a decade ago. It was important that Canada encourage this movement to democracy by working itself directly into the great debates in the region. Which, with 500 million plus people, also presents great economic opportunities for Canada.

—

This Conservative, a friend of Ronald Reagan to boot, also struck up an unlikely friendship with Daniel Ortega, the Sandinista leader of Nicaragua. I wrote about him in my journal as well.

—

I had productive bilaterals with Menem (Argentina), Arias (Costa Rica), Barco (Colombia), Perez (Venezuela), and lengthy chats with Bush – all expressed delight at Canada's decision. The most fascinating conversations took place with Daniel Ortega of Nicaragua with whom I had lunch and dinner the same day and hence some two or three hours of discussions. I returned to Ottawa and told P&P on Tuesday morning that my conclusion was that Ortega would try and sabotage the February elections precisely because he thinks they are going to lose. He sees his party as the only one "that can bring stability" to his country. I told him that that was exactly what I said about my party, but that at least two other parties in Canada had different ideas on the subject!

He told me that Perez in Venezuela had been democratically elected, but that when he sought to introduce austerity measures, there had been looting and loss of life – his point clearly being that democratic elections do not guarantee stability. I agreed but told him only democratic elections grant moral legitimacy to a government, and that prosperity could never come to a people deprived of fundamental freedoms, as evidenced by the upheaval in Eastern Europe and even the Soviet Union. I told him of the abuse a democratic leader takes in the House, in the media, and from the people – but that once the people have spoken in a free election, no one quarrels with their choice until the next election is called pursuant to constitutional customs or requirements.

He appeared somewhat astounded by my ready acknowledgments of all the drawbacks and deficiencies inherent in a democracy and was, I suspect, unconvinced by my fervent assertion they all paled into insignificance when compared to the majesty of a free people exercising its democratic rights. He is a doctrinaire Marxist, not without a certain disarming good nature and funny laugh, but I don't know if I persuaded him of the beauties and values of a democratic political system and a free market economy. In any event he seemed ill at ease in the presence of so many people celebrating democracy. He looked especially out of place when President Menem of Argentina, in a moving statement, said, "No one fully appreciates freedom until it has been taken away once." I was not surprised when he chose to skip the major Arias celebration of democracy before a huge crowd in Democracy Plaza. It would not have been an appropriate setting for a man in a military uniform who had just announced his intention to suspend the peace process and resume a military offensive in Nicaragua against his "enemies."

—

Ortega was famous for wearing his battle fatigues wherever he went. We – accidentally, mind you – proved to be quite a contrast the night all the leaders gathered for dinner. My lead advance man, Jean-Maurice Duplessis, told me that the dinner was "black tie." We were in Central America and I have to admit that this information surprised me. I shared my puzzlement with George Bush. "Are you sure?" he asked.

I assured the American president I was correct. "I've spoken to my guy Duplessis, and in Quebec a Duplessis is never wrong." This Quebec-insider joke was probably lost on President Bush.

I showed up that night in black tie. As I walked onto the stage I noticed that Ortega was, as usual, wearing his battle fatigues. Figuring he was making a political statement, I didn't pay it any mind as I took my seat. But as I looked around I noticed, to my horror, that I was the only person on the stage in black tie. I looked for Duplessis in the crowd, but he was nowhere to be found.

In April of 2006, I met up with Duplessis once again when I was in Ottawa to accept the honour of being the Greenest Prime Minister in Canadian history. Jean-Maurice appeared in his new incarnation as head advance man for Prime Minister Stephen Harper.

"Tonight, sir," he whispered to me as he ushered the prime minister into the room, "no black tie." He then disappeared just as quickly as he had that night in Costa Rica.

Back in Canada I was pleased to welcome Poland's Lech Walesa to Ottawa. Polish Canadians in particular were proud that the famous Solidarity leader, who had dared to stare down their homeland's Communist dictators, was being formally received in Canada. In private, I explained to him the details of our $42 million aid package for his country and Hungary. I also told him that Canada was Poland's fourth-largest creditor and that we would be supporting a further rescheduling of his country's debt to the tune of $2.6 billion. Per capita, Canada's planned contribution was perhaps the largest in the G-7.

Walesa looked at me over his bristling moustache and said it wasn't enough. "I don't want a beautiful tie to put on a corpse," he said dismissively.

I was stunned. When he repeated this comment in public I was more than stunned, I was mad as hell. I had Joe Clark call in the Polish ambassador and tell him that my government was going to cancel the whole program unless and until I received an apology from Walesa. It came that afternoon. Walesa, a former worker in the Gdańsk shipyards, had many good qualities, but experience in international diplomacy was not one of them.

I took time out and examined our overall political situation once again as I confided in my journal. Not all the news was good.

—

PERSONAL JOURNAL: NOVEMBER 5–6, 1989

It's hard to believe that just about one year ago today, we had begun to turn the corner and were making one of the great political comebacks on record. Gallup had us down by some 10–15 points and yet I can remember doing the Remembrance ceremonies on November 11, having earlier received our overnight reports that showed an ongoing deterioration of Turner and the Liberals on the leadership issue and dramatic improvement by us – so great, in fact, that Gregg was predicting a majority government!

The autumn has been very eventful – opening of House, state visitors, foreign travel, etc., and yet there is a degree of tranquility that *doesn't match the turmoil in some parts of the country. Our agenda has been powerful – and widely disliked, because it seeks to deal with some of the deep-seated weaknesses in our economy. We have slashed Via Rail and the incredible annual subsidy ($641 million for a service patronized by 3 per cent of the Canadian people!), introduced a GST, proceeded with abortion legislation – in short, we are taking on just about every difficult issue around and paying a great price in popularity. These are issues, however, that must be tackled, and hopefully, if they are properly handled, the country will acknowledge gutsy decisions in time for the next election – though I'm not holding my breath!*

In any case, both Turner and Broadbent are out of the House for extended periods – as am I – so reality will not fully reappear there until after both leadership campaigns. Peter Connolly, Turner's chief of staff, called me last night at the lake to ask if I could ensure a senior job for him in the public service after Turner's resignation in mid-January. Peter is divorced with young children in Ottawa, and it is important for them that their dad is around so I will look for a very good opportunity for him in the public service on an agency, board, or commission. [I did, in fact, later appoint Peter vice-president of the Canada Mortgage and Housing Corporation.] *Although Peter is a partisan Liberal, he is not mean-spirited in the sense that Bob Kaplan is. Kaplan is possibly the most disliked member of the House. Perhaps one day he will have significant cause to regret the indiscriminate manner in which he sullied reputations and besmirched character. Connolly is the norm – tough, partisan, but a gregarious guy – and fortunately in politics Kaplan is the exception.*

Last week, the media reported that GCI had received hundreds of thousands of dollars for their representation on behalf of the successful bidders on the Pearson Airport complex. Although these lobbyists function quite legally (and we have forced them by statute to register as such), I find their billings excessive and, possibly, improper. Many of our friends and former staff people set up business as lobbyists and most do a very good job. Some, however, have become both greedy and visible and this combination has been odious to me and hurtful to the government. The Liberals, of course, did it in spades for years but they never attracted the attention the Tories do. I have been troubled and saddened by the objectionable appearance of some of our supporters who came from backgrounds so modest that a bus ride was a treat but now tool around town in BMWs and Caddies. Who was it who said, "God save me from my friends"? So true.

—

Meech Lake heated up again as we moved through November. Ahead of a First Ministers' Conference, Newfoundland's Clyde Wells announced his plans to rescind his province's approval of the accord. While I had tried to reason with him in a lengthy letter, it was hopeless.

Lowell Murray also wrote to me ahead of the conference. While worried about Wells, he pointed out that some of our cabinet members and MPs were not doing all they could to bring Manitoba onside. "But I must say in all candour that some of our cabinet colleagues have to understand that they have to help bring Filmon gently around by making judicious use of the carrots and sticks at their disposal and by playing a part in our federal strategy," Lowell wrote. "Filmon's political staff think they have a live-and-let-live agreement with [Manitoba MP] Charlie Mayer and Maz in which we understand their need to dissociate themselves from us on Meech Lake, and some other federal issues, but it's business as usual when it comes to satisfying Manitoba's agenda."

He also argued that the time wasn't right for us to force the issue. "I do not question David Peterson's good faith in that he wants Meech Lake to succeed and is giving it his best efforts," he wrote. "Nevertheless I am convinced that his goal is to crunch the issue now, and put Meech Lake behind us, one way or another, so that it does not dominate the Liberal leadership campaign and possibly cripple their federal party for a generation to come. I believe that this is also Clyde Wells's motivation in trying to precipitate a confrontation at the FMC so that he will be free to move quickly to rescind the resolution passed last year by the Newfoundland House of Assembly. Our strategic interest is the opposite of Peterson and Wells. Trying to crunch Meech now would probably not succeed. We need to have the June deadline draw closer in order to increase the pressures for a successful outcome – pressures now starting to gather in the English-Canadian business community, in the editorial rooms, and in the other political parties."

During our meetings on November 9 and 10, Gary Filmon, Frank McKenna, and Clyde Wells all said that the accord as it then stood was unacceptable to them. I announced that Lowell Murray would travel the country as my special emissary all the same and that I would bring the group together if Lowell determined there was any room for compromise in the coming weeks and months. For good measure, the premiers also lined up unanimously against the GST. It was not a happy time.

Lowell sent me another crucial memo outlining our Meech strategy before the month was out:

> What I want to emphasize in this note is my sense that we are going to come under intense . . . pressure on Meech over the next couple of months and that we will have to implore our cabinet and caucus colleagues to stick to the "approved line" and to trust us to make the judgment calls on timing and strategy. The fact is that our public position the next little while is to emphasize the need for the holdout provinces to come together and to encourage them to do so, to try and narrow the agenda, seek common ground, etc., to see whether there are one or more ideas that would achieve unanimity of all eleven governments within the time limit. As you will recognize, the chances of this happening are slim. Which will bring us back to Meech Lake, the only package that *has* substantial support. Can we achieve agreement of the three holdouts to ratify Meech on the basis of some progress on various future constitutional reforms? At that point you can take the leadership and try to crunch the issue . . . We need time to let the pressure mount and we will have to keep our own sang-froid until the time is ripe for us to show our hand.

1989

4. After the Fall of the Berlin Wall

DURING THE FIRST Ministers' Meeting that November the Berlin Wall fell, and the world was forever changed. A few days later President Bush called me. Well aware I was about to visit with Mikhail Gorbachev in Moscow before the month was out, he asked me to pass on a private message to his Soviet counterpart. "Tell him, Brian, that I will not posture on the Wall," Bush said. And he kept his word. While Bush could have taken his own domestic polling numbers into the stratosphere with only a single boastful, victorious, tub-thumping speech to an American audience, he instead did what was right. Mindful of the dangers of instability in the Soviet Union and respectful of Russian pride, he kept his counsel, and the world is better for it today. It was perhaps one of his finest moments as president.

As preparations for my departure for Moscow continued, one day Privy Council Clerk Paul Tellier walked into my office sporting a wide grin. In his hand was a letter he wanted me to sign. As I read it, I understood why he was smiling. "Excellency," my letter to Gorbachev began. "May I extend my personal congratulations and those of the Canadian government to you and the people of the Union of Soviet Socialist Republics on the anniversary of the Great October Socialist Revolution." Taking out a pen, I signed my name with a flourish.

Mila and I arrived in Moscow on November 20. As we sped from the airport in our motorcade, we could see with our own eyes the deterioration in the infrastructure that had been masked on our visit only five years earlier. Now we witnessed Muscovites lined up for food, staring blankly with forlorn looks on their faces. There was no hiding the fact that the Soviet Union in late 1989 was a once proud power in rapid decline. Joe Clark's translator, who had assisted him on previous visits to the Soviet Union, summed it up best: "The political situation is better now," he said, "but there was more meat then."

I had faced some criticism because I hadn't already joined the parade of world leaders travelling to Moscow in those days for private meetings with this new-style Soviet leader. "After welcoming you, let me immediately criticize your government," Gorbachev said to me at the beginning of the public portion of our first meeting. "If we meet as rarely as it is now, with that much time between visits of Canadian prime ministers to the Soviet Union, I'd think this is inconsistent with the dynamics of the world and with the dynamics of our relationship." It had been almost twenty years since the last Canadian prime minister, Pierre Trudeau, had undertaken a complete state visit to the Soviet Union.

Gorbachev then asked me if I agreed with his assessment. I said that I did, and "that's why I fully expect the president to accept our invitation to Canada to speak to the Canadian Parliament next year."

Privately, Gorbachev, himself a rookie leader in 1985, knew full well why I hadn't come for an extensive visit until then. He knew that I believed that Western solidarity, combined with increased economic pressure on the USSR, was the best way to ensure reform. I had been on a learning curve and felt that in the interests of NATO and Canada's position in the G-7, I would hold off on a visit to Moscow until after we'd been re-elected.

Gorbachev and I had our first discussions while sitting across from one another at the twenty-five-metre-long birch table that adorns the Catherine Hall inside the Kremlin. It is a room that takes your breath away, and I couldn't help but steal glances at the eighteen modelled bas-reliefs that show Catherine the Great's achievements as absolute ruler of the Russian Empire so long ago.

We spoke privately for more than four hours.

"The world debates how much time Gorbachev has," he told me, speaking of himself objectively. "What really matters is that the country won't go back. The leadership team can affect the approach and the pace, but the country itself has begun to change and will go on doing so. So I'd say of Gorbachev, 'He's done his part.' But of course I intend to go on."

"I have more confidence in your political longevity than my own, and I plan to be around for some time yet," I replied.

He then said something I will never forget. "My greatest challenge is to change attitudes at every level of Soviet society and throughout the Soviet economy." He added that time was the one tool he lacked to accomplish his ambitious agenda.

Gorbachev was aware that I'd be seeing President Bush in the coming days. With the Berlin Wall now down, he was obviously preoccupied by the prospect of a united Germany.

"The West should act prudently," he said. "Kohl is sometimes not prudent enough – maybe because he is facing elections. But it's dangerous to appeal for votes among the revanchists. Bush and Baker went through a difficult process in adjusting their thinking, but the results are realistic enough over the wide range of U.S. foreign policy. So I'm confident there will be useful discussions in Malta. The West should be less arrogant. Sometimes you talk as if only the East has to change. As we say, 'as if you had God by the beard' – that you had a hotline to God. But the West has to change, too. The whole world has to."

I agreed with him, and during a gala state dinner hosted by Soviet Prime Minister Nikolai Ryzhkov on the first night of our visit, I told the Soviets that even the G-7 had to change. I promised that I would approach my G-7 Summit partners in Houston in 1990 and propose that the leader of the USSR be personally briefed by the G-7 chairman each year. I also said the USSR could count on Canada's support as the Soviets tried to participate more fully in the world's trading system.

"Sharing strategies and insights at the highest level could be of substantial economic benefit to the Soviet Union and the West," I said. "In this age of interdependence, there need not be more East–West divide or North–South gap."

Gorbachev read a copy of my remarks, which led him to say, "I decided that relations will be better."

On the personal side, Gorbachev and I, along with our wives, cemented our positive feelings during a private lunch inside the Kremlin. In the guest-house I wrote about the experience in a private note-to-file that night:

> At private Kremlin luncheon with Gorbachev, Raisa, and Mila – in an ambiance of considerable warmth and good humour – following points were made. 1) His ambitions for Malta revolve around getting to know Bush better, getting to understand intimately his priorities, and using the opportunity to convey his objectives and rationales for various initiatives. 2) He expects neither miracles nor definitive solutions at Malta and has no surprises or grand designs up his sleeve. 3) He found "entirely normal" that GB, having been

> VP for eight years, would want to take an appropriate amount of time to come up with his own policies and approaches for his own administration. 4) He spoke warmly of Ronald Reagan and said he had invited him to visit Moscow as a private citizen in the spring. Raisa offered no comments. 5) Mila mentioned Barbara's very successful visit to Canada and expressed the hope Barbara's letter had been received – which R[aisa] acknowledged it was. She also expressed the view that she was looking forward to working closely and "in friendly fashion" with Barbara. 6) They clearly have an affectionate and mutually supportive relationship. They discussed both their courtship and early days together – much like a successful North American couple might do on the *Tonight Show*.
>
> 7) He said Raisa would confirm that he never entertained, years ago, any serious thoughts of one day running the shop, and that his ideas for reform began to emerge when he was first transferred to Moscow some years ago and was brought into the decision-making process at a lower level. (In fact when he first became leader he called for a critical memo he himself had sent the Kremlin years earlier, which had never been acted on!) 8) He felt GB was "quite conservative" in his view of the world. I explained he was simply reviewing all options while he prepared carefully, and reminded him of the realities of political and philosophical swings within the Republican Party. I told him again that GB had resisted calls by some congressional leaders to grandstand at the Wall and he said, "Yeah, [George] Mitchell." 9) This is a man calmer, more soft-spoken and reassured than I remember him, clearly transformed by the burdens of governing. 10) When Raisa said both their mothers thought, given the criticism he was subjected to, the Soviet Union didn't deserve him, he chuckled good-naturedly but clearly did not disagree with the assessment! When I asked whether his mother might influence timing, Raisa said firmly, "He will serve two full terms."

I also held extensive discussions with Soviet Prime Minister Nikolai Ryzhkov and made notes on those talks as well.

> 1) Completely against German reunification. I told him Kohl was advocating it principally for his party and national interest. 2) Aid to Cuba, Mongolia, and Vietnam is substantial and must be

> allowed to "run down." 3) Aid to Eastern Europe is misunderstood and in fact USSR owes, due to five-year pricing system, some of its partners – only Poland owes USSR – about $1 billion (U.S.). 4) Advised him there could be no reform of agriculture (his biggest problem) until they allowed the farmers to own property. They are considering the concept of fifty-year leases, but I told them only ownership and the capacity to hand down "father to son" would ensure a productive agricultural sector. 5) Asked for Canada to come in, take a section or substantial parcel of land and develop it for agricultural purposes as a pilot project, in wheat, beef, pork, etc. I will ask Maz to review possibilities and be in touch with him. 6) The previous evening, PM Carlsson of Sweden told me he thought the Soviet "bottom line" was not reality for Poland and Hungary, outside the Warsaw Pact . . . 7) I told him story of 175-year peace with U.S. as evidence that . . . the Americans had never had imperialistic yearnings – otherwise they would have taken over one of their neighbours. I told him that the U.S. sometimes acted in that way due to bad advice given to or accepted by the president of the U.S. but that the entire history of the U.S., as it involved the national character, showed an inclination toward peace, unless betrayed or attacked. I concluded on this point by telling him that President Gorbachev was fortunate in having an interlocutor like President Bush because, with him, he would always know where he stood – and unless provoked, [Bush] would always be on the side of peace. (Minister Shevardnadze, who was seated in front of me, asked if I could comment on his gut instinct that Secretary Baker was "a man of his word." I said that he could put that one "right in the bank"; for example, that Baker had set aside an entire week, though he was supposed to be chairing the IMF–World Bank meetings in Sept.–Oct., 1987, to personally conclude the FTA – because he recognized its importance and because he had given us his word – as had George Bush – that, in the crunch, if required, they would work to attempt to make it happen.) Shevardnadze said he was genuinely impressed by this illustration and that no one understood the American psyche better than Canadians.

Ryzhkov had noted the independent stands my government had taken on many issues that put us at odds with our American neighbours. "Canada's voice in international affairs was greater and stronger than ever," he said, as recorded by Anne Marie Doyle of the Privy Council Office, who sat in on the meeting. "The USSR had noted Canada's position on SDI and Mr. Ryzhkov suggested that Canada and others who had taken this position had been proven right. He was gratified moreover that the Canadian and USSR position coincided in many ways."

My five days in the USSR also took us to the Ukraine. In Kiev, I announced that Canada would soon open a consulate there. Two years later, in 1991, I ensured that Canada became the first Western nation to recognize the independent Republic of Ukraine.

Freedom was definitely stirring as I went about my business in Kiev. As reluctant members of the Soviet empire, local Ukrainian officials were accustomed to conducting their business with foreigners in Russian. In this way Soviet officials could always keep track of what was being said.

In one meeting in Kiev, our discussions did indeed begin in Russian, with a translator on hand for me. Then, all of a sudden, the Ukrainians began speaking to me in their native tongue. The Soviet foreign affairs official in charge looked shocked, but there was nothing he could do. I had planned for this possibility, and at the exact moment the Ukrainians began speaking their own language, Roman Waschuk, a young Ukrainian-Canadian translator from our embassy in Moscow, moved up to the table and began translating for me. The whole time, tears were streaming down his face at the thought that the language of his ancestors was now finally being recognized.

Roman (now minister-counsellor [political/economic] at the Canadian Embassy in Berlin), wrote to me during the summer of 2006 to share his memories of that incident. "It was in the meeting with Communist Party of Ukraine First Secretary Volodymyr Ivashko that the shift took place," Roman recalled.

> I was standing in the second row as Prime Minister Mulroney sat down at the meeting table, flanked by Nikita Kiriloff, the (brilliant and professional) chief interpreter for Russian. Ivashko started his greeting in Ukrainian, rather than Russian, and kept going. Nikita looked up at me quizzically, gave me an "over to you" nod, and started to get up from his chair. Though I'd thought about the language issue in policy terms, I hadn't at all counted on suddenly branching out into a new career in interpreting, starting at the very top, with the

> PM. The emotion I showed outwardly came from a combination of nervousness, professional vindication (I'd told Ottawa this might happen), and, yes, the realization that years of Saturday school and university study of a language and heritage that my grandparents and parents had cherished were helping to make a difference at a crucial time for Ukraine. Mr. Mulroney, I think, understood the pressure that this sudden role reversal put on an amateur interpreter, paced his delivery accordingly, and, through his reassuring manner, helped build up my confidence in between events.

Roman also played a crucial role in an event that followed. He continued:

> Driving with Mr. Mulroney to the Taras Shevchenko monument, his major outside appearance, I reviewed his prepared remarks (with a view to interpreting), and wondered what the opposition demonstrators would be up to: would they show enough restraint to avoid provoking an ugly incident? Looking at the end of the PM's text, I noticed that a well-intentioned community advisor had slipped in a final exclamation ["Glory to Ukraine!"] that was common enough in the diaspora, but would have been highly inflammatory in Kyiv at that time (less so now). The PM agreed to drop this line; simultaneously, the demonstrators stuck to our suggestion about postering only positive messages about the Canada–Ukraine connection. The Shevchenko event turned out to be a win-win for all involved, with Mr. Mulroney taking time before leaving to talk to the unofficial side of the assembled crowd.

As Roman recalls, I did indeed lay a wreath at the statue of nineteenth-century Ukrainian poet and nationalist Taras Shevchenko. As I walked away from the statue and followed my KGB bodyguards back to my limousine, I heard shouts from a large crowd that had gathered across the street to watch the ceremony. I asked Chief of Staff Stanley Hartt why we were being moved away from an obviously friendly gathering of ordinary Ukrainians.

"The KGB has ordered me to get you in the car," he said.

"Well, Stanley, you can get in the car if you want, but I'm going to greet the crowd," I replied.

With that, I brushed off my bodyguards and walked over and shook as many hands as I could. Even the KGB could not stamp out the fires of

Ukrainian nationalism that had burned across so many decades of Soviet occupation, and I felt it was my duty to offer any encouragement I could.

It was nearly midnight when Mila and I returned to the guesthouse in Kiev. I stayed up in the early morning hours and wrote a note-to-file about my talks that day:

> I have just returned from dinner given for us by the Chairman of the Council of Ministers of the Ukraine. I was seated between Prime Minister Vitaliy Masol and Communist Party Secretary Volodymyr Ivashko, both of whom I had lengthy meetings with earlier in the day. Secretary Ivashko is clearly the superior, a fact mentioned to me during a conversation with Deputy Premier Gusev whom Ryzhkov delegated to accompany me to Kiev and Leningrad – although no such mention was necessary.
>
> Secretary Ivashko had been on holidays (and was to return tomorrow morning upon our departure) when he got a call from Gorbachev asking him to ensure his presence during our visit. Shevardnadze also, and quite independently, told Clark this was going to happen. He does not appear to be an immodest man but he made it quite clear to our delegation that he had again spoken with Gorbachev this morning, a call he initiated. I can only assume that Moscow was somehow responsible for the elaborate courtesies provided us in the Ukraine.
>
> At dinner he made the following points:
>
> 1) Gorbachev is completely supported by the Central Committee, both personally and for what his policies have come to represent.
>
> 2) Following the initial euphoria, Gorbachev went into a period of decline due to unrealizable expectations from which he is now slowly recovering.
>
> 3) Gorbachev will still be in "absolute command" five years from tonight. On a scale of 1 to 10, as a political certainty, this would rate "over 9."
>
> 4) Gorbachev does not have an identified or hidden enemy of substance to cause him any difficulty or concern.
>
> 5) Yeltsin is a joke – a nonstarter. He was especially dismissive of him, though not in any fearful way as one might seek to diminish the perception of a strong adversary.

> 6) The Ukrainian Party has 3.4 million members of a total of 18 million nationwide. They are solidly behind Gorbachev.
>
> 7) A durable peace that would eventually free up resources to concentrate on consumer goods is the driving force behind Gorbachev and his policies.

I was tired but pleased as we headed home to Ottawa. While I was unsure exactly how the next few months and years would turn out, I was sure of one thing: there was no turning back for the people of the Soviet Union and the courageous Mikhail Gorbachev.

On November 29, I flew from Ottawa to Washington in response to President Bush's request to brief him in person on my impressions of Gorbachev. I met with Bush, Secretary of State James Baker, National Security Advisor Brent Scowcroft, and a few others over dinner in the White House. Bush was only days away from his first summit with Gorbachev, and the stakes were high.

"I am under no illusions, but Gorbachev would have to be one hell of an actor if he was taking me in," I told Bush. "He is for real, is there for the long haul, and thinks you are, too. He is not looking for a handout but he is looking for a hand up."

I kept my word to Gorbachev and lobbied hard for the USSR to be granted observer status at the GATT, as well as for the progressive integration of the Soviets into the International Monetary Fund, the World Bank, and other international financial institutions. I told Bush that starting with him at our G-7 Summit in 1990, the chairman should brief the Soviet leader each year after our summits. I then suggested that Bush might send out signals to our NATO partners that American forces need not forever be in Europe.

"George," I said, "your Malta meetings with Gorbachev are a historic opportunity for you to take some chances for a genuine peace."

I read the president the private notes I had made while in the USSR and he asked me about every detail. Thoughtful and contemplative, he wanted as much information as possible before he extended his hand to the Soviet leader. I told Bush that I had detected an overwhelming hatred among the Soviets for the thought of German reunification, and how Gorbachev had likened it to eating "unripened fruit."

Jim Baker and others kept trying to return the conversation to the continuing aid the USSR was providing Fidel Castro's Cuba. "We have real problems with what they are doing in Cuba," Baker said. "Can you imagine the reaction in Congress if we try to get economic funds for the USSR while they pump $6 billion annually into Cuba?"

I reminded Baker of what Ryzhkov had told me: that Soviet aid to Cuba must be allowed to "run down." The Americans had little sympathy for this viewpoint, so I switched to a family analogy. "Castro is, for the Russians, what an embarrassing Uncle Harry can be for many families – the relative you wish would never show up to family events but, when he does, you have to manage him as best you can," I said.

I had noted in Moscow that questions about Castro tended not to get straight answers. This, I told Bush, was evidence of their profound embarrassment over their declining empire's own Uncle Harry.

Our embassy later filed an official report on the meeting. "The president, Secretary Baker, and the others were extraordinarily attentive throughout, genuinely curious about several assessments, and most emphatic about Soviet actions with Cuba," it read. "The meeting was exceptional for several reasons: It was the fifth bilateral between the PM and the president this year; it had been requested by the president on the eve of his Malta meeting with President Gorbachev; and the prime minister's impressions, assessments, and recommendations dominated the discussion, i.e., for the most part, the Americans listened . . . The prime minister appealed strongly to the president, as leader of the Alliance, to be guided by his own gut instinct but to seize the historic moment and extend a hand to President Gorbachev, especially on arms control. It was evident from President Bush's statement on leaving Washington the next day that the prime minister's message, even his exact words, had registered. In short, the White House dinner was a classic example of the exercise of influence at the most senior level."

On December 4 I travelled to Brussels for another meeting of NATO leaders. Bush, Italian Prime Minister Giulio Andreotti, and I were asked to brief the group on our recent talks with Gorbachev. "The timing of these discussions could hardly have been more fortuitous or more dramatic," I said in my remarks behind closed doors. "The Berlin Wall had just been opened, a non-Communist prime minister had come to office in Poland, the Hungarian Communist Party had voted to transform itself, Zhivkov had been pushed out of office in Bulgaria, and Dubček was, again, addressing vast crowds in Wenceslaus Square."

I reviewed my private talks with Gorbachev, step by step, and left my colleagues with the following to ponder. "He is a politician who desperately needs help but can't afford to openly ask for it," I said. The ball was in our court. Margaret Thatcher sent a note my way when my presentation was over. "A marvellous exposition," she wrote. "All the things we really wanted to know. You must have had a fascinating meeting."

Of all my nearly nine years as prime minister, those two months – November and December 1989 – were among the most exhilarating I was to experience. The world was literally changing in front of our eyes, and Canada and Canadians were being asked to play a significant role on history's stage at a vital moment. As I look back on 1989 today, I think that it will stand out in history like 1919, another pivotal year that we are only beginning to fully understand.

But there wasn't time for this sort of reflection as December of 1989 came to a close. In her farewell address to the nation, outgoing Governor General Jeanne Sauvé made a thinly disguised plea for the ratification of the Meech Lake Accord as the clock ticked down. "As a francophone, I have walked the slow road of patience long enough to appreciate the victories that were necessary to fulfill the legitimate ambitions of those men and women who had to protect and win recognition for their cultural heritage," she said. "[Canadian] unity is an illusion if it is not based on defined foundations that promise to be durable, and whose durability is not beyond testing of the building's material and organization. Such testing cannot be undertaken unless we accept, once and for all, the inevitable compromises, and unless the parties involved ratify their pact and do not let Canada drift into an unforeseeable future."

As 1990 dawned, our political support, as gauged by Gallup, had dropped to 26 per cent from 43 per cent a year earlier. Joe Clark sent me an excellent memorandum in December that articulated his concerns about where we were going as a party and country:

> I am very worried about the future of our country and government, and want to set out my concerns to you directly, before we begin a meeting on Saturday that could lock us dangerously into a narrow course. In summary my views are:
>
> 1. The deficit is a major priority, but not the only one. Far more important is the authority of the government to govern, and the capacity of the nation to hold and mobilize the loyalty of its people. We both know that national unity is always the central

issue in Canada. Our fixation on the deficit is steadily eroding our ability to lead and unite Canadians. The accusation is that we care about the deficit, but we do not care about the country. Our great accomplishments – respecting Quebec, the environment, international relations – are all overshadowed by the desire to cut back. Our most imaginative people, who should be finding ways to inspire and lead Canadians, are instead captured by the negative discipline of restraint.

2. I do not believe Michael [Wilson's] argument that restraint now will leave us free to reassert our leadership and popularity later. For one, the Finance projections have been wrong, and the GST now deepens the deficit rather than relieving it. More fundamentally, if the reputation takes hold that we don't care about the elderly, or sovereignty, or the regions, we can never buy that back.
3. The real threat today is not our Gallup standing, which is transitory. It is, instead, the quiet separation of people (at least in my region and I think in yours) who are becoming steadily less committed to Canada. That is happening for various reasons, but we aggravate it by giving them nothing to dream about, no unifying sense of Canadian pride. There has never been a greater need for a national government to lead our people. We have the talent to do that, and in Meech Lake . . . the tools to do that. But our signals are not about leadership and pride; they are exclusively about cuts and taxes. That is a serious self-inflicted wound.
4. We are being driven by an artificial timetable . . .
5. We must consider how to bring balance to this exercise. You can't do it alone, and frankly too many of our colleagues who could help are losing heart . . . You waged a spectacular comeback campaign in 1988. But we won't have free trade and Turner next time. What we will need is a broad program of accomplishment and a clear vision of this unique country. Spending control must be part of that, but so must a commitment to the broader purposes of government, and that is what we are in danger of destroying now.

Joe's concerns were mine as well. But what could we do? We had to deal with the deficit and had to implement the FTA. We had to bring in the GST.

I was torn between the logic of his arguments, most of which I could not disagree with, and what I believed to be my larger obligations as prime minister to ensure the future well-being of Canada.

And so the last good year ended on a bittersweet note. My government and the Conservative Party were about to enter into extraordinarily difficult times, and I knew I would pay a significant price. That turned out to be a considerable understatement.

1990

1. Nation of Discontent

If I had to use a single word to describe the mood in Canada in 1990, it would be sour. There were tensions between English and French, and between aboriginal Canadians and non-aboriginals. There was dissension even within my own cabinet, and Joe Clark began the year tottering on the brink of resigning as minister of external affairs. In the midst of it all, a recession hit most of the industrial world very hard, Canada not least. In fact, the sorry state of the economy left me with only two choices. I could spend money wildly, as Pierre Trudeau had, in an attempt to curry public favour, or I could proceed quietly and deliberately with the deep structural changes we were already making – free trade, lower interest rates, the GST, privatization, and deregulation – that I knew would provide long-term benefits to Canada. I was all too aware, however, that they would provide us, politically, with no relief in the short term.

By now I was under no illusion that there would be much sympathy for the government, and I didn't seek any. It was my belief that we would be vindicated by history, but there was little comfort in this as 1990 played out day to day.

The year began with a litany of warnings. In Edmonton on January 3, former Alberta premier Peter Lougheed spoke out. "The high dollar is clearly hurting our exports," he said in a message aimed more at Bank of Canada Governor John Crow than myself. "We've lost some of the benefits of the FTA that we envisioned in the short term." Only a few days after Lougheed's remarks the dollar climbed to 86.5 cents, its highest level since 1980.

Next, Royal Bank Chairman Allan Taylor told his bank's annual shareholders' meeting that uncertainty over national unity was threatening Canada's economic and financial stability.

In a more welcome move, members of the nonpartisan group Friends of Meech Lake also stepped forward in January. Robert Stanfield, Stephen Lewis, and Senator Solange Chaput-Rolland went public with their deep concerns about the state of the federation. They strongly urged Canadians to rally around the Meech Lake Accord. While I was pleased with their efforts, I knew by now that Clyde Wells was unlikely to listen.

Just before the two-day meeting of the Priorities and Planning Committee at Meech Lake, I discovered that I faced serious internal difficulties, primarily in the brooding presence of Joe Clark. He sent me a lengthy memo on January 3 that I digested carefully and quietly as I prepared to meet with P&P to craft our strategy for the new year. "I start with three related opinions: first, that the country faces an unparalleled crisis of will, and could begin to come apart quickly," Joe wrote.

> Second, that the national government is the only agency with the inherent authority to reverse that disintegration; and third, that our current priorities prevent us from exercising that leadership, because our general policy is focused too narrowly on the deficit, and our constitutional policy focused too narrowly on Quebec.
>
> You know my view that another round of major cuts will both divert us from the more urgent priority of national unity, and lock us into a sterile self-definition that deprives us of the legitimacy to lead. At the end of the December 21 P&P, you referred to the financial consequences of departing from the Finance track. No one has done the calculus of the costs of adhering to that track and, so long as you appear personally committed to that course, few will try to. Generally, I agree with trying to do different things simultaneously, [but] I don't think that will work now. If we don't choose to devote all our energies to reviving the federation, the government will slip back to the only priority it knows, which is the Finance agenda.
>
> It is not the Constitution that has gone wrong in Canada. It is that many Canadians no longer feel a compelling need to stay together – options that were unthinkable in 1980 are attractive now, outside Quebec and inside Quebec. Part of that is our doing. Not only did the Free Trade Agreement strip away bad myths about economic insularity; the debate also rejected the artists and intellectuals who had defined "English Canada," and *nothing has replaced them*. Quebec has a sense of identity. Canada does not, in any way that matters. In asking "What does Canada want?" Bourassa might have thought he was posing a constitutional question. It is much more than that, and if a legitimate sense of Canadian identity does

> not emerge, two certain consequences will flow. First, Quebec will feel no reason to be part of a larger community that has no sense of itself. Second, Canadians elsewhere will have nothing to rally around, no dream, no purpose, no reason to make the extraordinary efforts that will be required to rebuild a whole Canada . . . So I believe we must give much more deliberate thought and priority to how we inspire a sense of pride and purpose in Canada, particularly Canada outside Quebec. Of necessity, that will require the kind of intelligent activism by the national government to which, as a practical matter, another round of deep cuts is antithetical.

Joe was clearly in a funk, a dangerous one for the overall health of my government. When P&P gathered later that January, the measured tones of Joe's memo were a distant memory. I wrote about his behaviour in my private journal.

—

PERSONAL JOURNAL: JANUARY 20, 1990

They were unusual meetings in a number of ways and somewhat troubling. Contrary to his usual reasoned and useful contributions, Joe Clark made, over two days, a series of interventions that were bizarre and somewhat unsettling. He began by accusing Allan Gregg and John Tory of having "cooked the books" with their polling data, with having written the conclusions of their polling update before receiving the data, presumably to mislead the cabinet. Tory was shocked and livid and strongly denied any such thing.

Next, he said that most ministers didn't believe in what they were doing, that they wouldn't run again, that the government had lost its legitimacy, and that he no longer found we represented the principles he had come to defend! He has been increasingly erratic since the late fall, but I thought a Christmas holiday would do him some good. It didn't. Whatever the reasons, it appeared that he was searching for a reason to resign and was seeking to involve or encourage others along the road. If so, there will be no takers in this cabinet. All are onside and will weather the storm, although I expect a number will not seek re-election in 1992. Many will have been in the House for 20 years by that time and will be quite normally intending to do more agreeable things with the rest of their lives.

The problem really is that Joe and some others are concerned by the emergence of an apparently one-dimensional agenda of the government, one seemingly focused on the economy to the exclusion of all other important socially progressive matters. They believe Finance is driving the agenda, forgetting of course that we are merely following an economic policy announced last year and to which all subscribed, given the brutal new fiscal realities due to unexpectedly high interest rates which developed in late 1988 and early 1989. In this time we have had a bad news budget and a bad news year (we are in third place in the polls, but that too we had anticipated, and I had forewarned caucus). But unless we persevere we shall lose all credibility. Interest rates are too high and the dollar rose to 86 cents making both new investment and FTA opportunities difficult to achieve. It may be that Joe, who does not have a viable alternative to offer, will in the end refuse to back Wilson and the government's economic strategy. In which case I shall have no choice but to accept or demand his resignation.

This is not something I would look forward to, but I could not make an exception to a general expenditure cut for Overseas Development Assistance or External simply to mollify Joe. In fact, to be fair, I believe that Michael Wilson did assure Joe that, if he went along with a cut last year, there would be no repetition this year. Even with that, Wilson agrees that our forecasts were not met. Interest costs are substantially in excess of those contemplated, and a new tough across-the-board reduction in all expenditures is required urgently now. So be it. I am not happy about rates or expenditures but Wilson has been a first-class minister of finance and he must – and shall – be sustained, irrespective of the challenge. I offered Joe, as a courtesy, the governor general's job and would be happy to appoint him to London, Paris, or the UN if he wished. I have difficulty, however, in believing that even in his own best interests he could be persuaded to leave the House of Commons. I believe he genuinely loves the place and, by and large, performs well, so he will labour on for years.

For my part, I intend to announce my retirement as party leader in the early autumn of 1992 to ensure that a new and, I hope, younger leader will be chosen with ample time prior to the next election, likely for the spring of 1993. During the Central Nova by-election I told Gilbert Lavoie of La Presse *– who is now my press secretary! – that I felt two terms would be just about all one should serve, that renewal is very important in a political party, and that the leader must be alert to new blood and new ideas and keep an open mind about the ultimate decision. Indeed for understandable reasons I send out absolutely contrary signals to ensure that I never become a lame duck or that any jockeying begins in the party or the government. I plan to be freely ready at the appropriate time.*

By 1992 I will have been party leader for more than nine years and prime minister for more than eight – with the Lord's blessing – longer service in office than any Conservative in Canadian history with the exception of Sir John A. himself. We have already achieved a great deal, and I suspect that in the next three years we can do much more. I hope at that point we will have a heritage of achievements that will serve the country and the party well for decades to come. Although Mila and the children and I have enjoyed our time here, we are not in any way captivated by the office nor intoxicated by the allures of office. Mila and I in fact chatted over the holidays about what I might do, where we might live, where the children would go to school, etc., when I step down. I would like to leave the country/government in good shape and, if the good Lord willed it, a party in office and stimulated by the dialogue of change. I would like to turn the office over to another Conservative, ensuring continuity and appropriate change. Obviously I have shared this with nobody but Mila.

—

In the pages of my journal I also admitted privately to myself what I could not say publicly: our constitutional accord was in serious trouble. While I knew I would fight until the last minute on June 23 to secure its ratification, I feared that nothing we did would succeed in the end. I felt helpless – but I couldn't let anyone know my true feelings.

—

The outlook for Meech Lake is not good. Trudeau and other adversaries have succeeded in portraying Meech Lake as a sop to Quebec –

as a favour to that province that others don't get. The success of Meech Lake would, as Bourassa said in a telephone conversation tonight, highlight his failure of 1981–82, which PET is determined to avoid. He and his allies – ironically many of them strongly anti-French and anti-Quebec – are determined to throw out the baby with the bathwater. I do not know what the future would then hold for Canada. I personally view Trudeau's vindictive and vicious attacks as completely unpalatable, because the failure of Meech could produce damage to Canada that might be irreversible. My guess is that if Meech fails, Quebec will withdraw from all constitutional consultations, thereby rendering any reform impossible. There will then begin to emerge de facto two Canadas that could, over time, cross the important psychological divide to reality. My view is that French-speaking Quebec regards Meech as a most important symbol of their devotion to Canada. They support Meech because it gives them an honourable vehicle to affirm their belief in and support for Canada.

To reject Meech would deal that commitment to Canada a grave blow. There would be a serious view of betrayal as there was following 1981–82. Or, will there develop a resolve, a sense of dignity that might cause people to say, "If Meech was an excessive burden for English-speaking Canada to have for durable unity, let us release you of that burden now so that we can go our own separate ways." Many people in Canada, abetted by the arrogance of the 1981–82 Trudeau failure, are saying, "Okay, let them go." What a tragedy, what disunity will then be visited upon the nation because of the stubborn, obtuse position of the opponents of Meech. If there is another referendum on Quebec's commitment to Canada, that night, as the returns come in, I fear that Canadians will be saying to themselves: "My god, to think we could have avoided all this." The terms and conditions of Meech Lake will look very reasonable that night. Those who described it as a sellout will be nowhere to be seen.

—

Toward the end of January, I had to face a sad duty and accept Jean Charest's resignation from cabinet. While in New Zealand for the Commonwealth Games, Jean, as minister of fitness and amateur sport, became involved in the case of a young Québécois athlete named Michel Brodeur. In pre-Games trials, Brodeur had met the international standards for his sport but hadn't met the more demanding Canadian standards.

Jean was working to ensure that young francophone athletes were fairly represented on Canadian teams. When a coach named Daniel St-Hilaire went to court in Montreal to attempt to reverse the Canadian team's decision over Brodeur, Jean lobbied on Brodeur's behalf with Team Canada officials. He was able to get assurances from them that Brodeur would be allowed to represent Canada if the court ruled in his favour. Jean put this commitment on paper and faxed it off to St-Hilaire's lawyer back in Montreal.

When Jean's letter was tendered in court, a great deal of confusion ensued. The minister's staff mistakenly concluded that the judge wanted to speak with Jean to clarify the letter. So Jean then did what a cabinet minister can never do: he telephoned the judge. As soon as he discovered he had been misled, Jean terminated the conversation. But it was too late. Jean knew he had to resign, and I knew I had to accept it. "The simple fact that I had placed the call carried the supreme sanction," he later wrote. "I gave my resignation to the prime minister thinking I had just ended my political career."

Before he decided to resign, I spoke with Jean by telephone. "I have very good relations with my Liberal critic, Don Boudria," he told me, "and I think he would tend to view this indiscretion with a good heart."

"Bullshit," I replied. "The only way that you're going to survive in politics is if I'm able to let you resign and then bring you back later. People like Boudria will crucify you on the floor of the House of Commons if you don't leave cabinet. They will tell you one thing but they're going to do another." In fact, before I even knew of Jean's problem, Liberals Jean Lapierre and Stan Keyes had staged a press conference to demand Jean's resignation.

It was no great secret that I believed Jean Charest to be one of the government's great assets and the party's rising star. I quickly resolved to put him on the back benches for a few months and then return him to his rightful spot at the cabinet table. I called his father, Red, in Sherbrooke, knowing how worried he would be, and reassured him that, at an appropriate time, Jean would re-enter cabinet *par la grande porte*, which is precisely what happened when he was sworn in as environment minister in 1991. Before then, as Canadians would soon find out, I had some additional plans for him.

Speaker John Fraser, who had had his own problems in 1985, sent me a short note about the Charest incident on January 24, which I appreciated.

"My dear Prime Minister," he wrote. "A very painful decision but you are absolutely right."

I spoke to caucus that day as well. "In 1984 this party was fortunate in electing some outstanding young people from across the country," I told my troops. "One of these was Jean Charest. I've always said that I view him as an extremely promising young man. Nothing that has happened recently has changed my mind."

The signal I sent was clear: Jean Charest would be coming back. In due course, he would go on to become the premier of Quebec.

Overseas, the new president of South Africa, F.W. de Klerk, dropped a bombshell on February 2. During a historic speech at the opening of his nation's Parliament, he promised to free Nelson Mandela "without delay." He also legalized the African National Congress and other organizations that had battled apartheid for so long. "The season of violence is over," he said. "The time for reconstruction and reconciliation has arrived . . . The alternative is growing violence, tension, and conflict. No one can escape the simple truth."

Joe Clark and I decided to keep Canada's sanctions in place until all the apartheid laws were officially off the books in Pretoria, although we sent encouraging words to the South African government as well.

And then the impossible took place. On Sunday February 11, Nelson Mandela left his prison cell as a free man. I sat transfixed in my second-floor dressing room at 24 Sussex with the television on as Mandela and his wife Winnie walked through the gates that had hidden him from the world for almost thirty years. Nicolas, who was then four years old, dropped by to see what his dad was doing. "I want you to watch everything that goes on," I told him as I picked him up and placed him on my lap. "This is a powerful moment in history. A great man is leaving prison, and I want you to watch it and I want you to remember it."

Mandela looked thinner than I expected – my perception of his strength perhaps shaped by the power of his message – and I was struck as well by the words he aimed at countries like Canada, telling us to maintain the pressure on Pretoria. Our first instincts had been correct.

The next day I had my first telephone discussion with the ANC leader. The Privy Council warned me ahead of time to expect that South African security forces would be bugging the call, but I didn't care. In fact, I hoped the spies heard what both of us had to say.

"I am honoured by your call, as the attitude of Canada is well known," Mandela told me. "We regard you as one of our great friends because of the solid support we have received from you and Canada over the years. When I was in jail, having friends like you in Canada gave me more joy and support than I can say. There could have been no greater tangible evidence of friendship than your concern for me and my family and the strong action you and the Government of Canada took while I was in jail to help us defend the interests of the new South Africa we want to build."

Mandela concluded the call by telling me something that was truly touching: "Because of this support I would be honoured to make my first speech before any Parliament to the Parliament of Canada."

"Mr. Mandela," I replied, "you can count on me getting a plane over there real fast."

Mandela had not even left the prison when a letter from Margaret Thatcher arrived on my desk. True to form, she was already suggesting that the Commonwealth should relax its sanctions, and she informed me that the United Kingdom would be proposing lifting the ban on new investment in South Africa. I was having none of it at this early stage, and fired back a letter to 10 Downing Street as quickly as I could.

"The Canadian government continues to adhere to the position adopted at the Heads of Government Meeting in Kuala Lumpur that the sanctions which we have imposed on South Africa should remain in place until such time as there is clear evidence of irreversible change toward the dismantling of apartheid," I wrote. "There is still much ground to cover before all conditions are met for the lifting of sanctions. At this time, Canada would actively discourage the international community from the relaxation of measures whose effectiveness largely depends on a coordinated, common approach." I suspect that she did not enjoy reading my letter.

During the jubilation over Mandela's release, Canada hosted the first joint meeting of the twenty-three foreign ministers from NATO and the Warsaw Pact since the Berlin Wall fell the previous November. I had lobbied hard for a new Open Skies treaty and was proud that this first discussion of the concept was being held in Ottawa.

History, however, had its own way of seizing agendas in that historic season, and the conference was dominated by discussions over German reunification. With memories of the Second World War forever seared into the collective consciousness of many European leaders – from both the

East and the West – there was great unease at the thought of German reunification. The Soviets, who had lost more than 20 million citizens during the fight against Hitler, were particularly opposed.

These understandable fears, however, had to be balanced against cold hard facts. Germany was heading toward reunification whether the crumbling USSR liked it or not. The question we really had to face was how to manage these countercurrents. Politically, it would have been impossible for Helmut Kohl to allow the four Allied powers from a generation ago to dictate what the new Germany should look like. At the same time, these four powers had to have a role because of Europe's recent past.

It was in Ottawa that U.S. Secretary of State Jim Baker and Soviet Foreign Minister Eduard Shevardnadze, along with West German Foreign Minister Hans-Dietrich Genscher, came up with the Two-plus-Four Formula. The two Germanys could negotiate their own *internal* reunification issues while the four would discuss *external* issues with the two. The invitation to start the discussions would come from the Germans.

Keeping the other European countries out of the talks – many of which had experienced Nazi tanks and storm troopers on their streets just a generation before – while still keeping them supportive of a new Germany would prove a difficult diplomatic challenge if there ever was one.

Joe Clark and I met with Baker and Shevardnadze over breakfast at 24 Sussex on February 12. We discussed the German issue at great length. "We are trying to think things out," Shevardnadze told us frankly, "to find variants and solutions. I just don't know. It is only natural for the Germans to want to unite. On the other hand, no one knows what might be the consequences."

Shortly after the two foreign ministers left 24 Sussex, I summed up the discussions in my journal.

—

PERSONAL JOURNAL: FEBRUARY 12, 1990

Shevardnadze a courtly thoughtful gentleman – who greeted Nicolas and Mark with a big kiss as they went off to school – was quite direct and candid. He said that at their just concluded plenary of the party both he and Gorbachev had come under attack by the old conservatives for allowing the "disintegration of the empire." One bluntly told them that they had surrendered their eastern buffer, diminished influence throughout Eastern Europe, destabilized the Soviet Union internally, and got nothing in return. "All you get," said one critic, "are compliments from the Western media and Western leaders, and we are becoming extremely wary of you for that."

He appeared to be somewhat morose, though not depressed, clearly troubled by the implications of the enormous change that had continued to sweep the USSR, even since our last meeting in November. He is greatly troubled by German reunification though resigned to it. He urgently wants tangible, meaningful progress and improvements in agreements on nuclear weaponry, conventional forces, and reforms of an economic nature, because the need is so urgent within the USSR. He sounded somewhat plaintive, almost like a union negotiator who is pleading for something visible and honourable to take back to the members because the pressure on him is so great.

—

I met the next day with Hans-Dietrich Genscher in my office on Parliament Hill.

"How will reunification work on a practical level?" I asked the West German foreign affairs minister. "For example in your department, foreign affairs. If you unify the East German and the West German foreign ministries, then how will you divide up responsibility in terms of representation? Who goes to Washington and who goes to Moscow and who goes to Ottawa?"

His response was confident.

"Nobody will be going from their side; it is all going to be us, from the West."

"You're not talking about unification then, you're talking about a takeover."

"Precisely," he said.

Genscher thanked me for telling the press that Canada and Canadians supported reunification.

"[Your statement] is important for the dignity of Germans," he said. "Those who would criticize unification don't know what they are saying. If Germans thought others, particularly their allies, were against unification, it would give power to the extreme right and left elements in the two Germanys."

By then I had had enough discussions with Helmut Kohl on the issue to completely understand the German position. A pan-European leader of vision and substance, Kohl was already looking ahead to a unified Germany within NATO, and toward the creation of the euro and the enhancement of the concept of European values and citizenship in a manner that would forever eliminate the possibility of war in Europe. As I watched Kohl and François Mitterrand advance this plan together, I felt, as always, that Kohl had provided his French colleague with a moral proxy to speak on Germany's behalf. Owing to Germany's past, Kohl believed that it was often easier for German opinions to be put forward through Mitterrand. Their brilliant alliance was destined to change the face of Europe forever.

Most people are unaware that it was in Ottawa where many of the foundations of the successful reunification of Germany were laid. But it wasn't easy, as the following memo sent to me by Joe Clark after the conference demonstrates:

> For background, you should know about a bitter and divisive exchange which erupted near the end of Open Skies, in a special NATO caucus I chaired. It concerned Germany, specifically, the Two-plus-Four arrangement. The six affected countries consulted no one else before issuing their brief statement. That offended the dignity of every other country, but it outraged Germany's immediate Western neighbours, because of the implication that the security interest of (e.g.,) Holland would be considered by the six. Hurd and Baker immediately recognized their error and made it clear that a) this was one consultation, involving other nations with specific treaty obligations, and there will be other consultations; and b) NATO would be fully and regularly briefed.
>
> Genscher arrived later at the meeting and was intransigent, claiming unification is principally an "internal" question to Germany. As chairman, I took the heat out of the debate and reached agreement on explanatory language I would use at the evening press conference. The Italian minister agreed, but warned Genscher not to underestimate the concern of allies, to which Genscher replied, "You are out of the game." I quickly ended the meeting. Genscher and Kohl believe that "outside interference" by allies would hand a "nationalist" issue to the extreme right. The Soviets, in particular, are nervous about unification, and need to be seen to be involved. Before

> Ottawa, there was no structure formalizing the involvement of anyone outside Germany. Ottawa changed that – that could become the most important accomplishment of this conference.
>
> Naturally, other countries want into the consultation. Canada does. Some argue that we should protest the Ottawa arrangement because it leaves us out. That would be extremely short-sighted and could undo a very important accomplishment, and undermine Canada's claim to be involved in negotiations respecting Germany. Our standing is high after the conference. Nations around the table appreciated how we defused an ugly atmosphere. To a country, they agree that Two-plus-Four is better than the void that existed before Ottawa.
>
> Our challenge is to build on the Ottawa agreement – always bearing in mind the extreme sensitivity of the German question. A last comment: we were fortunate to be in the chair. The issues in Europe are so compelling that geographic Europeans are inclined to leave us out. That makes the constancy of our troop commitment all the more important. Chairing puts us at the centre of the action, and gives us an unusual opportunity to influence next steps. As we discussed, the CSCE [Confederation for Security and Cooperation in Europe] holds the best prospects for us. My strong advice is that, if asked, you speak positively about Two-plus-Four (the Ottawa Agreement) as an important step toward the kind of consultation required respecting German unification.

Jim Baker wrote me shortly after his return to Washington. "Thanks, Brian, for the breakfast," he said. "As it turned out, what happened at Ottawa could have real historical significance."

Kohl was set to meet with President Bush at Camp David toward the end of February. I hearkened back to Clark's memo when I spoke with Bush shortly before Kohl's arrival there on February 24. "I'm concerned personally that unification for Germany appears to be fuelled not just by the legitimate desire of the two states to come together," I told him, "but by the total collapse of the economy of one state and the economic strength of another. I told Genscher you're not really talking about a merger here; this is a takeover."

Bush then told me it had been suggested to him that NATO allow Soviet troops to remain in East Germany all the same. That idea angered me.

"I don't see how, in fairness, we can accept that," I said. "The minimum price for German unity should be full German membership in NATO and full support in all the Western organizations and full support for American leadership of the Alliance. I indicated to Genscher and I will tell you: we are not renting our seat in Europe. We paid for it. If people want to know how Canada paid for its seat in Europe they should check out the graves in Belgium and France. NATO got us this far. Solidarity in the Alliance will get us further."

"Brian," Bush was later to write, "was right on target."

As we all now know, Germany was successfully reunited, and stability was maintained in Europe. I was deeply honoured when Chancellor Kohl told a committee of the German Reichstag in late 1993 that Germans will always remember three foreign leaders for their work in assisting their nation's successful quest for unity. "Looking back, I must name three people who really helped us," Kohl said on November 4, 1993. "I am referring only to heads of state and government . . . There was George Bush, who did not hesitate for one minute when it came to German unity . . . There was Brian Mulroney. And there was Mikhail Gorbachev."

"The success of German unity is a triumph of liberty manifesting itself," I was to write Kohl on October 2, 1990, when his nation officially came together as one. "I want you to know that you can count on Canada's continued support and our own active engagement in the shaping of a 'New Europe.' This applies to the reform of existing institutions and the creation of new ones. This also applies to our support for reforms in the Soviet Union and in central and eastern Europe."

In the midst of all these important foreign policy events, there was an incident involving Lucien Bouchard that I learned about much later. He met on February 14 with my speechwriter Paul Terrien, to discuss Bouchard's upcoming speech in Toronto. Terrien warned him that portions of his draft could embarrass the government, due to their overtly Quebec nationalist tone; he was shocked by Bouchard's response. "In any event, Paul, you know that my objective is to embark on politics at the Quebec provincial level," the federal minister said.

Luckily, I was unaware of these discussions as the month continued. The next day I took part in ceremonies on Parliament Hill marking the twenty-fifth anniversary of the Canadian flag. More than thirty years had passed since the PC youth platform at StFX that I helped craft had called for the adoption of a distinctive flag for Canada. I had also had the temerity to lobby Diefenbaker himself for a new flag. Not surprisingly, the Old Chief ignored the advice of a young student from Baie-Comeau.

After the ceremony – as Dief surely glared down at us from above – I walked back to my office, through a snowstorm, with Hilary Pearson, Mike Pearson's granddaughter whom I had named as a confidential note-taker for our cabinet meetings. (Pearson later married one of my smartest young associates from the Privy Council Office, Michael Sabia. The couple eventually landed in Montreal, and we remain friends to this day.)

February was also the month Michael Wilson brought in his budget. It featured no new taxes and he promised to hold the deficit at $28.5 billion. While spending was forecast to increase 3.4 per cent, Wilson countered this by trimming $2.5 billion over the next two years in transfer payments to the provinces. Spending in defence, foreign affairs, and Indian affairs would be allowed to increase to 5 per cent. Michael also cancelled the Polar 8 icebreaker we had announced in 1985 and froze the budget of the CBC for two years. He also announced plans to privatize Petro-Canada and Telesat Canada as a tradeoff.

One day after the budget, I shuffled the cabinet again. Kim Campbell had impressed me and I promoted her to the position of Minister of Justice, the first time a woman had held the post. Bernard Valcourt was returned to cabinet as Fisheries Minister. Tom Siddon went to Indian and Northern Affairs, and Marcel Danis, who emerged over time as a smooth operator and effective parliamentarian, was named Minister of State for Youth and Amateur Sport. Another significant change was the elevation of Lucien Bouchard, whom I named as my political minister for Quebec.

I also sat for a full-fledged press conference and later described the experience in my journal. I was at Harrington Lake for the weekend when I got out my pen once again and reviewed recent events, with time for personal-family reflection as well.

—

PERSONAL JOURNAL: FEBRUARY 24, 1990

The kids are growing by leaps and bounds and doing extremely well, thank God. Ben's marks have improved substantially, presumably in keeping with his size, which, for a boy of thirteen, continues to astound me. The other day he borrowed a pair of loafers from me and, to my astonishment, they fit him perfectly! Nicolas has just turned the corner from infancy into childhood and he is a true delight – although both Mila and I are privately pained to see his growing independence. This week he announced his intention to henceforth go alone *to his piano lessons and then asked me if I thought "Mommy should take a skiing lesson or should I just show her how?" All this and not yet five!*

Mark, Mr. Energy, returned from the ski hills and immediately joined Mila and me for a skate on the lake. His enthusiasm and good nature are becoming legendary in our family, at least, and while I often wonder what the future has in store for him, I never doubt that it will be somewhat different and probably very exciting.

In any case, I am listening to my favourite Yves Montand tapes and cleaning up some paperwork to clear the decks for a great deal of focus and attention that now, after the budget, must be spent on Meech Lake.

The budget appears to have gone down reasonably well, though it was tough and its consequences pervasive. The provinces especially have been complaining because of some reductions in transfer payments but the downward deficit track must be maintained if we are to contain some strong inflationary pressures and reignite the job creation instincts in Canada. Our economic record these past five and a half years has been impressive, but we have a long way to go to repair an economy that Margaret Thatcher described at the Paris G-7 Summit as having been "enormously wounded by Pierre Trudeau." I don't think Margaret realized how much of an understatement she had made, because Trudeau placed the economy on a trail of industrial and productivity decline which, combined with his almost incredible overspending for 15 years, has been the source of most of the agony and difficulty my government has had to endure.

Both the cabinet shuffle and press conference yesterday appear to have been quite well accepted. Kim Campbell in Justice was the star of the show and will no doubt be an important player in this party (perhaps one day as leader) and government for an extended period of time. I brought Valcourt back and hope he will do well in Fisheries and I am expecting a good deal from Harvie Andre as new Government House leader, given the enormous challenges we will face in Parliament in getting the GST and other contentious pieces of legislation through. I would expect to make more substantial changes in the summer of 1991 – probably involving all major portfolios because people like Clark and Wilson will, for example, both have been in their portfolios for almost seven years; clearly by any standards, time for a change. Wilson, Maz, de Cotret, and Loiselle have done outstanding jobs preparing the budget, and Tellier has emerged as perhaps the most influential Clerk of the Privy Council in decades. Stanley Hartt is getting a very good handle on the PMO just in time, I fear, to resign sometime next summer. Stanley is a brilliant, impressive, if somewhat disorganized chief of staff who made a very considerable financial sacrifice to rejoin me in Ottawa. It has been difficult for him as Derek Burney's successor because of Derek's tremendous reputation for tough, effective management of people, policy, and systems throughout the Government of Canada. But Stanley has improved markedly these last six months and I shall miss him in the fall.

My meeting with the press was a bit of a nonevent. I had not returned to their "press theatre" since January 1987 – over three years. For a while, the gallery thought I would return on bended knee and sent me summary resolutions reminding me of my obligation to "openness" and "respect for freedom of the press," all of which I discarded. After a year, they began to sound more reasonable and after another year, during which we won another commanding majority, they actually sounded somewhat contrite. What eventually got to them, however, was their realization that they had deprived themselves of regular exposure to the head of government, thereby doing a substantial disservice to their readers/viewers and serious damage to their own reputations, because of their progressively limited access to real decision makers in town.

I had always accepted the notion of an adversarial relationship with the media. Indeed, while I found it personally disagreeable, I even tolerated a period of great personal hostility and quite evident unfairness and bias without any response, believing somewhat naively that eventually they would find their professional moorings and rediscover the basic tenets of journalism that they had so demonstrably abandoned. Where I drew the line, however, was at the deep disrespect and malice showed by some gallery members, without the slightest repudiation by its executive members – indeed, when silence and qualified grins suggested nothing less than complicity and approval. So I withdrew from the offensive farce they staged and refused to attend a press conference, in the certain knowledge that whatever obligation I had to meet regularly with the press did not extend to condoning juvenile delinquency by its members. Moreover, I knew that whatever contempt they had for me was completely irrelevant, if the Canadian people granted me their confidence, which they did in impressive and historic fashion on November 21, 1988. Somehow that night in Baie-Comeau, the unrelenting attacks by the media over the previous four years were dealt with by the voters as I watched another strong majority government being formed under my leadership. The Canadian people were telling me and many others that they had paid little attention to the members of the Ottawa gallery.

In fact, press conferences with the gallery, now that they've been re-established on what appears to be a reasonable basis, are neither very challenging nor stimulating. Broken-down one-trick ponies like William Johnson will get his biased question on language in; David Halton usually asks a sensible question on foreign affairs; Daniel Lessard and Pierre April do likewise on domestic issues. All told, back to business in the same old stall.

This morning, Saturday, I was awakened by an impromptu half-hour phone call from George Bush, who was at Camp David preparing for a meeting with Helmut Kohl on the issue of German reunification. On Thursday Helmut had called from Bonn and reviewed with me the options and steps he was considering in light of the Ottawa Two-plus-Four agreement and the GDR general elections. On Tuesday, while I was at Harrington, PM-elect Kaifu of Japan called to thank me for the encouragement and support he had received here last summer on his first foray as PM of an extremely fragile, delicate government. The previous Saturday, Ted Kennedy called from Palm Beach where he was on a brief holiday, to discuss his upcoming Moscow trip and to get my views on my most recent exchange with Gorbachev. And on the previous Tuesday, Nelson Mandela, freed from prison two days earlier, called to thank me and the government for our unwavering support during their difficult hours. All told, fascinating moments and rewarding experiences, all of which make for Mila and me a sense of accomplishment and contribution that I believe historians will acknowledge and that Canadians will enjoy.

—

On February 25, I had an unusual telephone conversation with former president Ronald Reagan. Nicaraguans had democratically removed the Sandinistas – and my military fatigues–wearing acquaintance Daniel Ortega – from power in free elections, and I was calling him with my congratulations. Ron had taken a lot of flak on this file over the years, but now in 1990 the citizens of that tiny Central American country had chosen freedom.

The PMO switchboard soon had Reagan on the line. The first words out his mouth startled me. It was a very emotional former president who picked up his phone.

"Brian," he said, "Kelly is dead. Kelly was so wonderful."

I hadn't a clue what he was talking about.

"That's too bad," I said carefully.

There was a long silence, so finally I said, "Ron, who is Kelly?" I had assumed he was referring to a mutual Irish friend.

"Brian, don't you remember?" Ron replied. "Kelly was the horse from the RCMP Musical Ride you gave me when I retired. The other day I got a call from the ranch because Kelly couldn't be found. They located her in a little valley on my property. She had fallen into a ravine and sustained a neck injury. The vet said she was in critical pain and put her out of her misery." I made sympathetic and consoling noises, and the conversation soon ended.

Ambassador Derek Burney telephoned me the same day with some important intelligence from the U.S. capital. He had recently had a discussion with Jim Baker, and the secretary of state had said that the Mexicans had told the Americans that they wanted to explore a free trade deal with Washington. Baker said that the administration felt the Mexicans were going "too fast," but added that "the Mexicans asked how Canada would react."

"Canada would be influenced by how our own FTA was developing," Derek had shrewdly replied.

Derek went on to report that the U.S. was trying to slow the Mexicans down, out of concern that the opening of such bilateral negotiations with Mexico might have a negative effect on the Uruguay Round of GATT talks.

I told Derek that we would have none of it. Baker was envisaging a situation where North American trade would be governed through a hub-and-spoke system. Washington would be the hub, with Canada and Mexico just spokes. This was a complete nonstarter for me. If there was to be a North American trade deal (one that did indeed come about later through

NAFTA), all three countries would have to have the same benefits and the same access.

And that is how Canada, in the view of some, hijacked the U.S.–Mexico free trade talks. I was soon on the phone with President Bush. It turned out he was being told by U.S. Trade Representative Carla Hills, a tough and effective negotiator for her country, that a bilateral deal between the United States and Mexico was the route to take. "The United States would take care of Canada," Bush told me, using Hills's words.

"Carla Hills is magnificent," I told Bush, "but on this one, I don't give a good goddamn what Carla thinks. I'm telling you, as the head of a sovereign government that's already signed the FTA with the United States, that we are going to be part of the hub. We are not going to be on the periphery of anybody's economic activity in this area."

I strongly registered these concerns with Mexican President Carlos Salinas during a three-day visit I made to Mexico in March. Today, as I look back on the success of both the FTA and NAFTA, I chuckle to myself when I consider the arguments thrown at us during those days. With both agreements Canada's loony left argued that I was sending Canada into the swirling vortex of American self-interest. This couldn't have been farther from the truth. With both deals it was the Americans, at the beginning, who didn't want us in, so intent were they on protecting their own sovereignty. I had to fight to get us to both negotiating tables, and we were winners in the end.

By 2005, Canada and Mexico were exchanging $17.8 billion worth of trade – an 876 per cent increase over pre-NAFTA levels. In the same year, total trade between Canada and the United States had grown to $610 billion – a 227 per cent increase over pre-FTA levels. A report prepared by the Library of Parliament in 2006 says that exports account for 40 per cent of Canada's GDP, and that "close to 2.3 million jobs have been created in Canada since 1994, representing an increase of 17.5 per cent over pre-NAFTA employment levels."

After my Mexican visit on March 16 and 17, I headed to a Commonwealth Caribbean Conference on March 19 in Barbados, where I said that Canada would forgive $182 million in debt owed by Caribbean countries. The chief beneficiary was Jamaica, which owed more than $93 million. I also promised $10 million for the University of the West Indies and $2.5 million for airport improvements in the region, and undertook to set aside $1 million to help create a Caribbean trade office in Ottawa. While these moves were anything but popular at home as the recession deepened, I knew they would be of great value to the struggling nations of the Caribbean.

I later made a lengthy journal entry encompassing the events of March.

—

PERSONAL JOURNAL: MARCH 25, 1990

After a busy week travelling to Mexico and Barbados on state visits, I returned to celebrate my 51st birthday with the kids at 24 Sussex and put in train our strategy to get Meech Lake moving forward. After secret meetings with Bourassa and Peterson at Harrington I had instructed Lowell to meet with McKenna, who had been the first to object to Meech but now sees the enormous difficulties Canada may face if it is turned down. He is hence resolved to be helpful, to seek to avoid that, and to avoid as well the opprobrium attached to him personally by French Canadians if he were seen to be the villain in the piece. (Bourassa holds him personally responsible for many of the problems today.) The deal was that he would agree to present a companion resolution for which "indications of reasonable support from elsewhere," namely the feds and a few other provinces, would persuade McKenna to approve Meech as is – without amendments prior to June 23 – with action on his resolution to follow later. Had McKenna declined to present the resolution, Lowell told him, "I'd do it myself."

The advantage of proceeding with McKenna is obvious. Thorough support for his resolution will bring him onside, thereby bringing the number to nine of ten provinces that will have signed Meech Lake. That will then leave only Manitoba offside with, of course, Wells threatening to rescind. McKenna did well in introducing and defending his resolution and I followed through with a nationwide TV address Thursday, which appears to have been well received and which had the merit of indicating flexibility and putting the ball squarely in the dissident provinces' court. As Lowell put it, "The burden of proof has now shifted to those provinces who had been demanding that Ottawa show at least a glimmer of flexibility to now show some themselves."

Just took a call from John Buchanan, who is in Corner Brook with Joe Ghiz, Frank McKenna, and Clyde Wells. John is deeply disappointed with Clyde Wells. He says he is absolutely obstinate and has been persuaded by Trudeau that he can sabotage Meech Lake with no consequences. (What a tragedy if Trudeau turns out to be wrong, as he usually is on matters of great substance.)

—

1990

2. The Bouchard Bombshell

THE YEARS 1989 AND 1990 produced such a mountain of problems – the beginnings of a major worldwide recession, the implementation of the FTA, decisions on the GST and its introduction in such perilous economic times, serious international problems from South Africa all the way to changes in eastern Europe – that I was effectively working seven days a week, twelve to fourteen hours a day, trying to keep my caucus and the government focused on the most important policy questions confronting us. The progress of the Meech Lake Accord was just one file, although a vital one.

The June 23 deadline for passing Meech was on my mind as I watched a helicopter bank its way over Harrington Lake on March 3. I later made a note about what happened after it landed.

> Premier Bourassa arrived by helicopter for a private luncheon at Harrington Lake. He was alone except for his EA . . . a young man from Baie-Comeau! . . . We chatted about the Liberal leadership and the pending publication of Trudeau's new pamphlet later this month. He sees Trudeau as being thoroughly discredited throughout Quebec and entirely "without influence" among French-speaking Canadians. Our meeting over lunch lasted some two and a half hours . . . I began by indicating that Meech Lake was clearly destined to fail unless certain changes were [made] now. I said as well that I would not bring forward any resolutions that conveyed the appearance that Quebec was being isolated. In other words, while I was seeking, by presenting a companion resolution, to break the deadlock, I would not do so unless it met with his tacit approval. After lengthy discussions he seemed, in general, in cautious agreement and said that he would meet secretly with his [senior advisors] and report back by Tuesday next. Mila and the

> kids came by during lunch to say hello and Nicolas gave him a drawing of his helicopter!
>
> He was positive about his own political situation, being clearly in control, and was unworried about federal budgetary policies, saying his own would be at least as tough. When I told him that I had recently called Claude Ryan to wish him a happy sixty-fifth birthday he was surprised that such an event had taken place . . . though happy I had called. He also told me he had not spoken since the last election to Raymond Garneau, whose nose was still out of joint because Bourassa had failed to support the federal Liberals on the trail.

I kept my caucus as fully informed as I could. We met on March 7 and I told them, "We're having serious, ongoing discussions with the premiers, designed to save Meech, to move it off dead centre. We could make a deal tomorrow with New Brunswick and Manitoba but lose Quebec! . . . Why does Pierre Trudeau oppose it? Because during his lifetime, he does not want anyone else to succeed, because such a success points out the enormity of his own failure in 1981."

In Washington that spring, Lucien Bouchard, as I later learned from Derek Burney, refused the suggestion that he visit Banff National Park and declare his pride at being the minister in charge of such a beautiful place. "I could not do that," he said. And at a dinner at the Canadian embassy, Bouchard also took it upon himself to tell Vermont Senator Jim Jeffords that "we Québécois feel closer to you Americans than we do to English Canadians."

For the first time ever, I am now going to tell the whole story about Lucien Bouchard and his betrayal of Meech Lake and of our friendship.

Much of what follows in the narrative of this crucial period was not brought to my attention until much later. As Marcel Danis, an excellent cabinet minister and MP, sadly told me in June of 1990, "When I heard stories of Bouchard's disloyalty, I couldn't bring myself to repeat them to you. After all, you were like brothers." But a volatile mix of events was brewing all the same, behind my back. They would not explode for another four months, and it would be years before the real truth about Bouchard's activities would become known.

In a cabinet shuffle after the 1988 election, I had elevated my old friend Lucien to the politically sensitive environment portfolio and appointed him to the vital position of Quebec lieutenant. I believed that he would be adept at handling these responsibilities – including protecting me from unfair attack and unpleasant surprises – which was the reason I had provided him with such an easy entry into high office. I placed him in positions of responsibility and trust because I knew after thirty years of seeing his talent and skills that he could do the job. I viewed him with the affection and trust a man usually has for a brother.

Things had not gone easily for Bouchard in Ottawa. After an inept by-election campaign in 1988, he was initially unsteady in the House and largely unfamiliar with the country outside Quebec, which placed him at a significant disadvantage. But I saw him frequently, encouraged his initiatives, and gave him solid support in his roles as minister and as Quebec leader. I trusted him completely, so I did not interfere in any way in what he tried to do, except to provide guidance and counsel when he sought these from me. His mood and personal situation had improved enormously with his remarriage to an enchanting young American named Audrey Best. I hosted a champagne reception for them at 24 Sussex, and when Alexandre, their first son, was born in a small hospital in Hull, Mila in typical fashion arrived with gifts and a TV to make sure the new mother was comfortable.

On January 13, 1990, Bouchard instructed his riding staff to commence preparations for a brunch on May 17 – one week after the tenth anniversary of the Quebec referendum – at the Alma arena. Denise Falardeau, Bouchard's riding president, began to suspect he would use the occasion to resign. According to Marie Therrien, his scheduling assistant, he was already aware of the PQ general meeting that would be taking place in Alma to mark the referendum's anniversary. Lucien Bouchard also informed her of an invitation he had received to address the Montreal Chamber of Commerce on May 23. He went on to tell her that date was important because it was exactly one month prior to the June 23 deadline for the ratification of Meech.

More straws in the wind. According to Camille Guilbault, my Quebec caucus liaison officer in the PMO, beginning in February Lucien Bouchard was frequently heard to say, "Meech is dead." A few days later, he told my speechwriter, L. Ian MacDonald, that "Brian is screwed with Meech. It's not going to pass."

On January 16, 1990, Jean Chrétien had waded into the Meech debate, as part of the formal launch of his leadership campaign to replace the retiring John Turner. He later admitted publicly that he consulted with Pierre Trudeau as he was preparing his remarks. "In my opinion, the current text of the accord does not help to promote the fundamental values shared by Canadians," Chrétien announced. "Today's Quebec does not need this accord to assert itself and to thrive within the Canadian federation . . . If the accord is not ratified before this date, the world will not stop turning, and the country will not break up."

The reaction to Chrétien's message was caught in the next day's headlines: "Chrétien est plus que jamais opposé au lac Meech" (*Le Soleil*); "Chrétien urges scrapping Meech Lake Accord" (*Winnipeg Free Press*); "Chrétien issues anti-Meech Lake manifesto" (*Globe and Mail*).

On March 13, my government's Quebec caucus held a private evening session at Meech Lake. My Quebec leader, Lucien Bouchard, stood and urged the group to remain united in their support of the government and Meech. MP Marcel Tremblay made notes of Bouchard's comments and gave them to me later. It was an impressive address. "One day we will no longer be in politics, but we will remember this evening," Bouchard had said. "What brought us to Ottawa is Meech. I think that Meech is not dead because it is necessary for the future of the country. Reason will surely prevail . . . We must support all initiatives favourable to Meech."

Jean Charest wrote to me afterwards about the events of the evening. "The meeting was a long one with several interventions, some of them very emotional, on the issue of what we would and would not do if Meech was not ratified," he wrote. "I did not intervene during the meeting. At the end of the meeting Lucien Bouchard, as Quebec lieutenant, rose to sum up. He made a short, precise speech to emphasize the need for the Quebec caucus to offer its full support to the PM and the PM's initiatives to save the accord (the McKenna companion resolution had not yet been put forward). The second point that Lucien Bouchard made was that caucus should support all efforts to implement the accord until 23 June 1990 and, if not approved, the caucus could then weigh its options at the summer caucus meeting to be held in August in Gaspé. Bouchard also stressed the importance of members of caucus refraining from making public statements that could be harmful to the efforts put forward to save Meech."

I had told the cabinet and caucus that there would be no dilution of Meech, but that with Frank McKenna and Clyde Wells still offside, we had to look for a vehicle that would give them some "running room" and bring them back into the fold.

Lowell Murray proposed and worked out the idea of a companion resolution that would be put forward by McKenna on March 21. Jean Charest later described this approach as "a parallel accord to preserve their initial agreement while addressing the concerns of those who had objections," in his book *My Road to Quebec*. "This was a good way to respond to the many legitimate concerns of those who wanted to correct what they saw as serious oversights in the Meech Lake Accord and still ensure the Accord's survival."

I kept in close personal touch with Lucien Bouchard during this period. Although fully occupied by the state visit to Mexico on March 16 and 17, followed by the Commonwealth Caribbean Heads of Government conference in Barbados on March 18 and 19, I had phoned Bouchard in Vancouver from Barbados for lengthy discussions on our strategy and our work behind the scenes to ensure final ratification of Meech. He publicly endorsed the strategy of the companion resolution and was the one who proposed Jean Charest as chairman of the parliamentary committee struck to study the McKenna idea. Bouchard knew there would be no changes to Meech come June 23 and, as an experienced labour negotiator himself, he understood the need for an instrument that would bring McKenna in from the cold and perhaps persuade Wells to endorse Meech.

As I said in a major televised address to the nation the next day, "First, however, Meech must be passed, because I am convinced, more than ever, that Meech Lake represents our best hope for unity. Meech Lake would become part of the Canadian Constitution by the June 23 deadline. And a companion resolution would follow. Premier McKenna has not closed any doors on the timing of the second resolution, nor on the range of amendments it would contain. [In this way] it is possible to extend a hand to Canadians who feel they were overlooked by the Meech Lake Accord – aboriginal Canadians, northern Canadians, certain women's groups – without undermining the accord and the consensus it represents."

After I had made clear to the nation that Meech had to pass *unchanged* but that the McKenna resolution could be the basis for subsequent renewal discussions, I received a call from Paul Desmarais. He asked if I would agree to appoint a trusted representative to review future suggested amendments if Jean Chrétien – whose daughter France was married to Paul's son André – did the same. Paul informed me that Chrétien's nominee was Eric

Maldoff, a Montreal lawyer, and I promptly told Paul to have him contact my chief of staff, Stanley Hartt.

Extensive consultations took place between Hartt and Maldoff, who were assisted by outstanding constitutional counsels, Roger Tassé for the government and John Laskin for the official opposition. Whenever an accommodation was reached on an issue, the text was sent to Mary Dawson, associate deputy minister of justice, to be drafted into proper constitutional language. She in turn made certain that her drafts were available to members of the Charest Committee, which was now up and running.

Maldoff had told Stanley Hartt he was "absolutely sure" that Chrétien would endorse the result of their labours at the June 1990 First Ministers' Meeting, which did not affect the integrity of Meech but could serve as a road map for future reform. Immediately after the June 9 signing ceremony, Maldoff invited Stanley to a Château Laurier suite – the pair took a tunnel connecting the Government Conference Centre and the hotel to avoid the press seeing them together – where John Rae and Eddie Goldenberg, Chrétien's closest allies and advisors, were waiting. They had drafted a short endorsement for Chrétien to release to the media. They described to Hartt the reasoning behind their recommending to Chrétien why he should offer this eleventh-hour support of Meech Lake: if Chrétien eventually became prime minister, the national unity issue would now be solved and behind him, instead of "darkening the horizon" for the entirety of his tenure.

Though shown the statement and given a chance to read it, Stanley was not given a copy of the endorsement to take with him, nor did he ask for one. Advisors are advisors, after all, and no draft would have been final until their boss gave his final approval; I would have expected no less from my staff. Stanley left the suite confident that Chrétien's three top aides, at least, realized the consequences for Canada of the death of Meech, and that they would carry their views to Chrétien in person. The reason? At a dinner at the elegant Westmount residence of Senator Leo Kolber the previous summer, which was attended also by Marc Lalonde and Tom Axworthy, Trudeau told Chrétien point-blank that he would publicly oppose him at the Liberal leadership convention if Chrétien supported Meech in any way. More recently, with the convention only weeks away and with Chrétien's opponents Sheila Copps and Paul Martin both strongly in the Meech camp, I suspect that Trudeau repeated his threat. I assume that it was in response to such a move by Trudeau that Chrétien made a choice that would "darken the horizon" and almost cost Canada its unity five years later.

On March 23, Bouchard offered public comments on the McKenna resolution: "I am not at all distraught because I have confidence in Mr. Mulroney, I have confidence in the strength and solidarity of the Quebec caucus, and I know that nothing will jeopardize Quebec's interests. Meech Lake must pass as is and never will Quebec be isolated as long as we are going to be there . . . If you read carefully the speech delivered by Mr. Mulroney on television the other night, you will see that no endorsement has been given to the substance of Mr. McKenna's resolution; the process has been adopted. This is McKenna's resolution; it has been introduced here to see if it can rally some people, what kind of modifications can be brought to it, and this will be a positive exercise."

He expanded on this view in the *Globe and Mail* four days later: "The Meech Lake Accord must pass as is, and that is the point of the exercise. It is to convince people that there are things that can be examined after the accord, so that they can sign the accord. If the public hearing process enables the government to convince the recalcitrant provinces to pass Meech, it will have worked well. If not, we have nothing to lose."

There it was: a tidy statement of reality from a man who had been closely involved in the strategy designed to save Meech and was fully supportive of the Charest Committee. He knew that Charest would bring in "recommendations" for consideration, but that these could be considered only after Meech had been proclaimed.

I believed that the federal government and its agencies should reflect all Canadians and a range of political views, not simply those of the governing party. That's why I had appointed record members of people of other parties to high office, ranging from Stan Waters of the Reform Party to the Senate, to the NDP's Stephen Lewis as Ambassador to the UN, and Liberal Donald Macdonald as High Commissioner to London. I tried to do the same by recruiting to federal institutions, including our party, caucus, and government, people who had supported the Oui side in the 1980 Quebec referendum. Most, but not all, of these people became, and remain, federalists. Those critics who pour scorn on my efforts in this regard should reflect on the alternative, which was to excommunicate and isolate the 40 per cent (in 1980) or 49 per cent (in 1995) of Quebecers who voted Oui. Reconciliation was the only rational course.

We all knew that the Parti Québécois remained unalterably opposed to Meech because the accord's ratification would mean that Quebec fully accepted its place in Canada. But Bouchard knew something very important that I did not: Parizeau and the PQ leadership had determined that Meech could sound the death knell for their sovereigntist ambitions, and they were desperately trying to undermine it. They had secretly decided to try to destabilize the government by luring Quebec MPs away to form a new federal separatist party. They would argue later that this was necessary because Meech had been sabotaged by "les Anglais"!

Parizeau's attitude was simply that Meech was too great a threat to the ongoing mission of the sovereigntists. How to stop it? Undermine the government that created and defended the accord by persuading enough MPs to leave, thereby creating a minority government that could easily be defeated on any one of a series of nonconfidence motions. In the wake of that upheaval, and with the clock running out on June 23, Meech would become a dead letter – and no longer a deadly threat to the PQ. As former PQ minister Louise Beaudoin later put it: "The failure of Meech – to me it was unbelievable that English Canada would reject as minimal a deal as that, but a deal that nevertheless would have put an end to sovereigntist hopes for many years. Completely unbelievable! But when it happened I knew this was our chance."

Bernard Landry, deputy to Jacques Parizeau, was chosen to lead this remarkable effort of stealth and duplicity. Through intermediaries he contacted Conservative MPs François Gérin, Nic Leblanc, and others, encouraging them to leave my caucus and form a new party. There was fever in the air, and accusations were flying about those who were "true Quebecers" and those who were not. Some of our members succumbed to the pressure.

We now know that Jacques Bouchard (no relation), a senior assistant in Lucien Bouchard's office, was the principal coordinator of much of the clandestine activity. Let me spell that out: the PQ campaign was, in part, directed from Lucien Bouchard's own office while he was a cabinet minister and the Quebec lieutenant responsible for loyalty and discipline among our caucus members. Another secret agent was Marc-André Bédard, a former PQ justice minister who was a close ally and friend of Lucien Bouchard from their home region of Lac-Saint-Jean.

On March 25, Camille Guilbault hosted a dinner at her home for some leading Quebec ministers and their wives; Lucien Bouchard, Jean Charest, and Pierre Blais were in attendance. Over dinner and wine, Bouchard (following a decision reached in an earlier conversation with me) asked Charest to assume the chairmanship of the committee to examine the McKenna resolution. Charest got to work the following day. Bouchard also told the dinner guests that the previous Saturday his assistant, Jacques Bouchard, had met with François Gérin, an erratic and unpredictable MP, and had reported to his boss "alarming things" about Gérin. Small wonder: at that time Gérin was in direct touch with Bernard Landry, who was urging him to cross the floor and form a separatist party. And Jacques Bouchard was privy to all these activities – as was his boss, Lucien Bouchard.

On April 1, Newfoundland, Finance Minister Hubert Kitchen said, "Quebec got us by the short hairs on Upper Churchill. We've got them in the same place on Meech Lake." With that questionable justification, Premier Clyde Wells proceeded five days later to rescind the approval of Meech Lake given two years earlier by the elected members of the provincial assembly.

At that point, I made a very serious mistake. The argument about the meanings of the "distinct society" and "spending power" clauses in the accord had become poisonous. We countered the Trudeau–Wells interpretation and charges with strong, learned legal opinions, but to little avail. Since the Quebec language-on-signs decision and the use of the notwithstanding clause to bring in Bill 178, public support for Meech had declined significantly in English Canada. I was being personally battered by the Reform Party and some hardline commentators as a prime minister who would "sell out" Canada's national interest to buy favour in Quebec. While this calumny made its way across the country, a fascinating situation arose: Pierre ("Why should I sell your wheat?") Trudeau, whom western Canadians had reviled for fifteen years, suddenly regained their favour when he joined forces with the Reform Party and the Parti Québécois in attacking the accord and speciously promised that there would be no consequences in Quebec if Canadians rejected Meech.

In retrospect, at some earlier point I should have made a reference to the Supreme Court of Canada, inviting our country's top jurists to declare which version was right, the government's or Trudeau's. A subsequent speech by Chief Justice Brian Dickson made it clear that our interpretation had powerful support at the highest court. At the very least, the imprimatur of a Supreme Court decision would have taken the argument out of the political arena. I profoundly regret to this day not having taken this step to depoliticize the issue, which would have dramatically altered the debate and contributed greatly to the unity of Canada.

On April 6, Lucien Bouchard and Gil Rémillard met the media in Tadoussac, in my riding, for an important environmental announcement. Bouchard's significant statement about the realities of the evolving situation demonstrated the extent to which he was involved in and supported the Meech process:

> The process undertaken by the parliamentary committee is not a process to change Meech, but to pass Meech as is, and not amend it a few days later. It is not feasible to amend the Meech Lake Accord afterward – not before, not during, not after – without the agreement of Quebec and without the agreement of the Quebec caucus in Ottawa.
>
> You are looking at someone who is a member of the Quebec caucus, who has political responsibilities within the Quebec caucus, and who has attended two meetings of the Quebec caucus over the past two weeks, including the last one where it formally asked us to express its full support for the position to pass the Meech Lake Accord and never to amend it or to allow Quebec to be isolated.
>
> There is another difference, sir. This prime minister is not Pierre Elliott Trudeau. It's Brian Mulroney, and he would not allow Quebec to be isolated. Brian Mulroney is working to bring Quebec back into the Constitution.

On May 3, Marcel Danis got wind of secret meetings occurring at the behest of Bernard Landry and attended by Jacques Bouchard, François Gérin, Louis Plamondon, and Nic Leblanc. Danis had declined an invitation to attend, and a few days later, in the Government Lobby, he confronted Lucien Bouchard, telling him he found his conduct "completely unacceptable," especially since these meetings involved one of the minister's senior staff members, Jacques Bouchard. Bouchard replied that he was aware of the meetings, but that they were "innocuous," and that the attendees did nothing more than talk. At no time did Bouchard inform me in any way of this treachery among members of my Quebec caucus, of which – as we now know – he had personal knowledge and in which he was now playing a personal role.

On May 4, a copy of the draft Charest Committee's report was given to Lucien Bouchard and Patricia Dumas, his chief of staff.

I had arranged for the PC national caucus to meet in Mont-Tremblant. We had been through a lot together, and they had been marvellously supportive through brutally difficult times. The recession was on, free trade had not yet produced beneficial results, the GST was as unloved as any measure possibly could be, and we were continuing to lose support as Preston Manning and his supporters spread venom about us and ate into our base in western Canada.

Because of our demanding schedules, Mila and I arrived by helicopter, and I recall the sense of relief I felt as I saw the lodge and met and mingled with our caucus members. I remember a sense of sanctuary – of finding refuge among friends – as the storms swirled outside and pounded against the walls of our hotel. Little did I know that my closest friend had other plans for the weekend, and for me.

On Saturday May 5, Mila and I awoke to a massive front-page story in *Le Devoir*, in which Bernard Landry was smugly predicting wholesale defections from our Quebec caucus and the creation of a new separatist party in the Commons.

"Landry Confirms His Party Wants to Form Sovereigntist Wing in Ottawa," the banner headline shouted. "I would like them to stay until the end of their mandate rather than leave Ottawa," Bernard Landry said in the story, "and to form a distinct, partisan movement within the Conservative Party while continuing to support it. This sovereigntist movement would endeavour to show that sovereignty is the best solution for Quebec and Canada."

The story went on to report:

> Landry gained the impression and indeed the belief that Conservative MPs were keenly interested in the meetings that he and other key PQ figures held over the past few months. "As a starting point for discussions, the idea was well received. The next step is for them to make a decision in all conscience and honesty. This is no small thing; it is a major and momentous decision. They will have the enormous task of ensuring a harmonious transition from the federal system to sovereignty. I hope they have the necessary courage and magnanimity."
>
> Most of the Conservative MPs approached are excited by plans to form a sovereigntist wing in Ottawa, while others are torn by the idea, says Landry, noting that they have great respect for the leader who got them elected. "Mr. Mulroney deserves their respect if only for having promised in Sept-Îles to bring Quebec back into

> the constitutional fold with honour and enthusiasm. They are wondering how they can be faithful to Quebec and still show some measure of loyalty to their leader. It's an agonizing situation for some of them."

I was thunderstruck by the story and called Camille Guilbault, who brought Bouchard to my suite at once. As Mila, Camille, and I listened, a contrite Bouchard sat there and assured me that he knew "absolutely nothing" about the story, or any of the twisted arrangements and secret meetings and communications behind it. I said, "Lucien, I certainly hope so. I have placed my full trust and confidence in you." As we stood at the door he said to Mila and me, "There is nothing to worry about."

A few hours later, I met again with Lucien Bouchard and with André Harvey, Quebec caucus chairman, and Bouchard assured both of us, "There is nothing to worry about and I will deal personally with anyone out of line on the constitutional question." (This moment of infamy was captured by my PMO photographer.) Although the rest of the caucus event was a success, the newspaper article had thrown a pall over my mood and raised questions for the first time about whether I was being told the truth. But Camille Guilbault called right after the caucus to say that our meeting seemed to have smoothed over any problems with Lucien Bouchard, although, she added perceptively, "he has become like a yo-yo, constantly changing his mood and his mind."

That night, in my final address to the caucus, I discussed Meech. "Meech Lake will mean a strong federal government working with strong provincial governments to achieve national objectives for the benefit of all Canadians," I said. "Here, among the splendours of the Laurentians awakening to the spring, it's not easy to imagine how any of us could explain to our children and their children how and why we let this magnificent country slip away. That we gave up on our country, and the country of our ancestors, through lassitude or complacency, or intransigence." Or treachery, I might have added.

On May 7, Charest met with Bouchard to discuss the draft committee report that had been given to the minister on May 4, and was told that Bouchard was in strong agreement. On May 8, Bouchard attended the regular breakfast meeting of Quebec ministers and gave a favourable review of the draft report. That night he joined me and a dozen others for a convivial and well-lubricated reunion dinner of the key members of the Cliche

Commission at the Ritz-Carlton Hotel in Montreal. For three hours we – commissioners, lawyers, investigators, and members of the press who had covered the hearings – relived the harrowing and hilarious moments of a royal commission that had jolted Quebec and marked our lives. Fernand Roberge, the talented and affable general manager of the Ritz, had put his best foot forward and, as we dined in his private boardroom and drank some of his best wines, I took in the atmosphere of laughter, friendship, accomplishment, and solidarity that brought us together that night to celebrate the fifteenth anniversary of the commission. Robert Cliche – the key player – had died some years earlier, and as I finished the final toast in his honour, I turned to Lucien and invited him to join Mila, Nicolas, and me for the flight back to Ottawa.

On my government Challenger, we continued the warm discussions of the evening, chatted about his young son, Alexandre, and our kids, and discussed the next morning's caucus meeting and the future steps in the Meech process. Then we talked briefly about his upcoming trip to Norway for an environmental conference, after which he planned to take a brief holiday in Paris. As Mila embraced him on the tarmac, I told him I would see him the next morning at caucus and said a warm good night.

I did see him in caucus, after which we had a brief friendly chat about his trip to Europe. I was soon off on a series of intense economic, constitutional, and foreign affairs meetings that dominated my schedule and left me with little time for exercise and family. Thank God for Mila's sense of priorities and organizational skills, because she invariably managed to ensure that time was found for the important things in life.

Later the next day, Bouchard met with Privy Council Clerk Paul Tellier for a thorough discussion of what Charest's report might recommend, and then he had a pleasant dinner at the Mirabel Hotel with Bernard Roy, where they reviewed political and constitutional matters. Bernard subsequently reported to me that "all is well."

On or about May 10, Marcel Danis arrived at École sécondaire St-Paul de Varennes in his riding for a discussion with the students. There he encountered Bernard Landry, who asked him if he intended to become a PQ candidate in the next election. When Danis said no, Landry said, "We'll make you an ambassador for Quebec after the next election." He then asked Marcel to convey to me the following message: "The action undertaken [to destabilize my government] is not against you personally. I recognize the vast work you have done for Quebec via free trade and Meech Lake but, for the independence of Quebec, it was the only solution." Marcel chose not to convey this insulting message.

On May 11, Bouchard arrived in London, and there was an obvious and abrupt change in mood. He told his executive assistant, Martin Green, of the PQ meeting in Alma scheduled for May 18–19 and of his desire to send a telegram commemorating the tenth anniversary of the referendum, an intention he had carefully concealed from Bernard Roy, Paul Tellier, and me.

The next day he met Pierre Marc Johnson in Bergen, Norway, for dinner. Johnson was appalled by his conduct, which he described as that of "*un chien enragé*" (a mad dog).

On May 13, Green accompanied Bouchard on a six-hour walk around the city of Bergen, during which Bouchard presented his theory that Quebec and Canada could not coexist. He claimed that Parizeau, whom he disliked intensely, was not a real Quebecer. He spoke of the memory of René Lévesque and again told Green he was going to send a telegram to Alma.

On May 14, Bouchard began the day by telling his staff to hold all calls from Ottawa, an extraordinary move for a cabinet minister. He described to Pierre Marc Johnson his frustrations with the report of the Charest Committee (with whose conclusions he had fully agreed all along). Green and Arthur Campeau had seen Bouchard drafting his Alma message from written and typed notes, and Johnson asked Bouchard if he thought it was appropriate for a federal minister to send such a telegram. Bouchard said he had discussed it with Marc-André Bédard, a former PQ justice minister, who told him it was incumbent on him to send the telegram. Johnson concluded that Bouchard, in his emotional state, was definitely going to resign his cabinet post and leave the federal Conservative Party.

On May 15, the Charest Committee reached a tentative agreement on a draft report. Charest's many attempts to reach Bouchard were unsuccessful, since he was not taking calls from his colleagues in Ottawa, although he remained in close contact with the PQ.

On May 16, Camille Guilbault managed to reach Lucien Bouchard in Paris and faxed him a copy of the report, which would be tabled the next day. He continued to refuse calls from Charest, whom he had strongly supported for committee chair only weeks earlier.

On May 18, Martin Green arrived at Marc Lortie's apartment in Paris to find Bouchard and Micheline Fortin working on the telegram. When Green saw it he said, "This is a letter of resignation."

As Fortin made arrangements to send the telegram to Alma via the Canadian embassy, Bouchard again refused to take calls from Paul Tellier, Jean Charest, and others. The telegram went off. Among other things, it said, "Your meeting will also celebrate the tenth anniversary of one of the high points of Quebec's history. The referendum concerns us all as Québécois. Its commemoration offers another opportunity to recall the sincerity, the pride, and the generosity of the Yes we defended at the time, around René Lévesque and his team. René Lévesque's memory will unite us all this weekend. He was the one who led Québécois to realize they had the inalienable right to decide their own destiny."

—

PERSONAL JOURNAL: MAY 19, 1990

Imagine my horror when Paul Tellier called me this p.m. to advise that Lucien Bouchard, on government business in Paris, had sent a telegram of friendship and what appears to be solidarity to Jacques Parizeau and the entire PQ national executive meeting in Alma to celebrate the 10th anniversary of the referendum!

At this most sensitive moment of the entire Meech negotiations, when symbolism is often as important as substance, with 35 days to go before the expiry of the June 23 deadline, one of my most senior ministers, with no advice to me or anyone in the government, conveys greetings and good wishes in the most fulsome and supportive tones to the leader of a political party determined to take Quebec out of Canada. When Tellier called him in Paris a few hours ago, he was truculent and haughty, unconcerned with the damage he may have done to our most sensitive negotiations to finally unify Canada, and quite oblivious to the embarrassment he had caused the federal government and its leader.

—

In Ottawa, MP François Gérin began to execute Bernard Landry's grand design by resigning as a member of the government caucus and announcing that he would sit as an independent.

When Bouchard returned to Canada and a flood of screaming headlines, I dispatched two trusted lieutenants, Bernard Roy and Luc Lavoie, to meet with him to ascertain what precisely had gone off the tracks. They were as much in the dark as I was, because his conduct in Europe bore no relationship to his friendly, supportive demeanour in Canada. Not once during his absence did he call me, his friend and leader, to discuss the horrendous act he was contemplating.

I instructed him to appear in my den at 24 Sussex, which he reluctantly did at 9:45 p.m. on Monday, May 21, 1990. He was surly, clearly disturbed, and a far cry from the relaxed old friend who had travelled with us from Montreal one week earlier and on whose behalf Mila, Caroline, and I had campaigned less than two years before. I had jotted down some notes in French, which I consulted as I spoke to him as soon as he sat down: "I won't comment on the content of the telegram you sent to the PQ," I said. "Given our constitutional objectives, its timing was of little use and worrisome. The opposition will ask for appropriate explanations tomorrow. I will need your cooperation to explain a gesture so highly unusual and inappropriate. Paul Tellier informs me that you are not disposed to do this, in which case I will require your resignation immediately. Having negotiated the Meech Lake Accord myself, it is obvious that I will never allow its substance to be diluted. The strategy developed via the Charest Committee permits us to conserve totally the integrity of the Meech Lake Accord. Otherwise it will become a dead letter on June 23, because I will never allow its benefits to be diminished or Quebec to be isolated at the constitutional table."

Bouchard mumbled some regrets. I stood up, walked him to the door, briefly discussed the logistics and timing of his departure, wished his family well, said good night, and closed the door on him – and on a thirty-year friendship.

That night I thought about our times together. After law school I had secured for him his first major assignment as counsel to the Cliche Commission. I had defended him publicly when he was strongly attacked by the public sector unions while he was Quebec's negotiator in 1980. Then, although he had no diplomatic experience, I had appointed him as Canada's ambassador to Paris. A few years later, I had made him secretary of state, secured the resignation of Clément Coté, a good MP, to open up a by-election, and campaigned vigorously to ensure his election to the Commons. Soon thereafter, I promoted him to the strategically vital environment portfolio, and elevated him to the position of Quebec leader. Throughout, I had provided him with unshakable friendship and support. And yet, in less than two years, he had abandoned the government with no forewarning, not even the courtesy of a phone call to me.

Jean Charest was among those most betrayed by Bouchard. In his 1998 memoir, *My Road to Québec*, Charest described how he personally briefed Bouchard on the content of the report that was being drafted on May 8:

> He then announced in response to a question from me, that he was going to be out of the country on the day the report would be made public – a date only ten days away! I was dumbfounded. My brother Robert, who was a member of Bouchard's political staff, and who informed him daily of all developments regarding the drafting of the report, had not even been told.
>
> I made repeated attempts to reach him in Paris, to no avail. He was, for all intents and purposes, incommunicado. After he insisted that I chair the committee, and without ever letting on that he harboured any serious reservations about the report we were preparing, he was now laying low, far from the heat of battle and impossible to reach. It was then that I realized there could no longer be any doubt about his true intentions. His absence had been carefully planned.
>
> The rest is history. . . . When I read his letter of resignation, I could not believe the lengths to which he was prepared to go in distorting the facts to suit his own purpose.

In the weeks that followed, I grieved for the loss of my friend and colleague. I was tormented by the possibility that this rupture came as a result of something I had done, or neglected to do. I tended to view these events as part of a failure by the country to develop what Gilles Loiselle used to call a "grander vision of Canada."

I carefully read and reread Bouchard's letter of resignation and had the same shocked reaction as Charest. His farewell speech to the Commons also contained gross distortions and misstatements of fact, and was constructed to generate support for him in the PQ and with broader public opinion in Quebec. The message struck me as contrived. It simply didn't ring true, but I couldn't put my finger on the fatal flaw in his argument.

By midsummer my staff had gathered much information that suggested well-planned deceit and betrayal, but there was no conclusive evidence, no smoking gun. I chose to remain silent, and as the years went by and Bouchard wrote and spoke of this historic matter, his version of events gained credence and acceptability: according to his version, he had resigned from cabinet because the federal government, led by me and assisted by Jean Charest, had conspired to so dilute Meech as to make it unrecognizable and completely unacceptable to Quebecers. The fact that the Meech Lake Accord signed on June 9, 1990 was identical to the original document signed on June 1, 1987, and that not an ounce of dilution had occurred, was never mentioned. How lucky it was, he implied, that Quebec had him on its side – a man of honesty and loyalty who had blown the whistle on these scoundrels and had saved Quebec's dignity in the process.

Fourteen years later, on Friday, April 24, 2004 in Montreal, I sat in the spartan premier's office at the corner of Sherbrooke Street and McGill College Avenue waiting for Jean Charest, who had been meeting with the heads of Crown corporations in the Eastern Townships. When the premier swept in through a private entrance a few seconds later, trailed by his bodyguards and assistants, he greeted me by waving a book, saying, "Have you seen this? They've finally found the showstopper!" When I asked to look at it, he said, "I'll have a copy made right away of the relevant pages. Take a moment to read them. They deal with our friend Bouchard and what he really did to both of us."

Charest re-emerged a few minutes later and handed me the photocopied pages that had caused him such consternation. It was the third volume of a biography of Jacques Parizeau by Pierre Duchesne, and the excerpts dealt with the PQ effort directed by Parizeau and led by Landry and Bouchard's closest hometown friend, former justice minister Marc-André Bédard, to destabilize and overturn my government by persuading MPs to resign and form a new separatist party. According to Bédard, the campaign went well. When two ministers, Gilles Loiselle and Monique Vézina, and seven or eight Conservative MPs heeded the call, Bédard became confident that we were heading toward a minority government in Ottawa. "Parizeau, highly excited, said to me then, 'Mr. Bédard, we're going straight ahead! I want you to overthrow this government for me!'" Duchesne also wrote that "Bernard Landry confirmed as well that 'he already had 10 MPs that he himself had recruited. Canada was close to catastrophe.'"

Then the author dropped the atom bomb: "With regard to Lucien Bouchard," he wrote, "no Péquistes had to persuade him. Approximately two weeks before he resigned, he entered into communication with the office of Jacques Parizeau to prepare meticulously his exit from the government of Brian Mulroney. Nothing was improvised."

I was thunderstruck, unable to believe my eyes. The author continued to provide more evidence. "At the beginning of May Bouchard met former PQ Minister David Cliche privately and said, 'David, I can't stand it any longer. Meech is collapsing and Mulroney has betrayed me by giving Jean Charest a mandate to weaken the Accord. . . . I've got to find a way to get close to the PQ.'" According to Duchesne, Cliche suggested Bouchard should visit Alma when the PQ held its tenth anniversary tribute to the 1980 referendum. "'Great idea,'" said the minister, "but on being informed he will be in Sweden that day, Bouchard says, 'I have another idea, the good old telegram . . . I could write one to welcome the militants [to Alma].'" The two men then agreed to work on a draft text that would be submitted to PQ Leader Jacques Parizeau.

On Monday, May 14, Cliche arrived at Parizeau's office on the fifteenth floor of Place Ville-Marie and told Jean Royer, chief of staff, that he wanted to see Parizeau on behalf of Lucien Bouchard. The PQ leader was extremely wary and received Bouchard's emissary and his offer to send the telegram with gravity and apprehension.

"I want to be clear, Mr. Cliche," Duchesne reports Parizeau saying. "If Mr. Bouchard sends me a telegram, it's to be read aloud." (In other words, check with Bouchard again to be sure that he fully understands the enormity of what he is doing.) Cliche responded that Bouchard was fully conscious of the impact of his offer.

Parizeau told his biographer that his prudence was motivated by Bouchard's untrustworthiness: "I don't trust him as far as I can throw him," he said. (I am reluctantly forced to admire his wisdom in this matter.)

Royer asked Cliche if Bouchard would accept a suggested text. "Of course," replied the emissary. Claude Beaulieu, who worked in Parizeau's office, prepared a draft that Bouchard would put in final form and to which Parizeau himself contributed six minor corrections. Duchesne writes:

> Contrary to what Lucien Bouchard affirms in his memoirs, it is therefore well before the tabling of the report drafted by Jean

> Charest that he decided to send a most compromising message to the national council of the Parti Québécois. As he knew the Péquistes were going to profit from this event to underline the tenth anniversary of the 1980 referendum, his text had to invoke this episode and have a clear political objective. The tabling of the Charest report on May 17 constituted nothing more than a further pretext designed to allow Lucien Bouchard to break with Brian Mulroney . . .
>
> Once again, contrary to what Lucien Bouchard led people to believe in his autobiography, he didn't prepare his message on the invitation of the PQ. The testimony of David Cliche is sufficiently precise and eloquent to affirm that the initiative came from Lucien Bouchard.

Bouchard's loyal servant David Cliche then drove the more than four hundred kilometres from Montreal to Alma and hand-delivered the precious missive to Parizeau the night before the meeting. The telegram sent so "emotionally and spontaneously" from Paris (according to Bouchard) took a decidedly circuitous route to its destination.

"In the entourage of Jacques Parizeau," Duchesne states, "the Bouchard initiative appeared so improbable that they were surprised to see Cliche appear in Alma stating triumphantly 'I have the text.'"

David Cliche played a minor role in this tawdry event, bringing together the seducer Parizeau and the less-than-reluctant virgin, Bouchard. As a defeated member of the PQ government, the unemployed Cliche was hired as a consultant by the federal environment department – with my approval. His appalling behaviour would have shocked his late father, Judge Robert Cliche, who valued loyalty and integrity above all.

Parizeau, to his credit, was still deeply suspicious of Bouchard and his motives, and insisted that Cliche reassure him personally that Bouchard would stand behind the deal, and that he fully appreciated the impact of what he had done. "It's not necessary, Mr. Parizeau," Cliche replied. "We have discussed all this, him and me."

The next morning in Alma, Parizeau read Bouchard's "spontaneous" message to two hundred cheering sovereigntists, and the Canadian political world changed.

As I put down the pages in the premier's reception room, I felt ill. For a few fleeting seconds I had trouble breathing. For fourteen years I had suspected the version of events that Bouchard had provided to the world was untrue. It had never occurred to me, however, that the entire episode had been a complete hoax. He had fabricated every word of his story. He had conspired secretly with Parizeau at least two weeks beforehand to betray me, all the while pretending to be my friend and a loyal minister of the Government of Canada. He had let down his country, his government, his Quebec caucus colleagues, and me, his prime minister, trusted ally, and old friend.

Had Bouchard left openly on a question of principle, I would have been dismayed, but I would have understood. No one is perfect in politics – certainly not me, as this book confirms – and nothing is forever. But this "resignation" was a complete contrivance. Not only was no principle involved, but he had ascribed his actions to noble motives, when the truth revealed the exact opposite.

Quebec's leading columnist, Lysiane Gagnon, made an astute analysis of this squalid event: "The biography by Pierre Duchesne on Jacques Parizeau contains an explosive revelation . . . The book places an unforgiving and devastating spotlight on the conduct of Lucien Bouchard when he decided to break with the Mulroney government. This revelation will have the effect of seriously undermining the credibility of Mr. Bouchard because it establishes a flagrant and rigorously documented denial of a myth that he has propagated for 14 years."

The final irony is this: Lucien Bouchard had had *nothing* to do with Meech. He was in Paris, as Canada's ambassador to France, during the entire period. He played no role in its conception, negotiation, explanation, or defence. He was not involved in the tough, complex, and draining discussions that produced unanimous agreement on two occasions. And then, right out of the blue, he announced that he was going to defend Meech against the imagined depredations of its architects. The people who had given birth to Meech and nurtured it through its difficult infancy could no longer be trusted with its well-being, he implied. Only Lucien Bouchard had the credentials for this sensitive task.

When as a federal cabinet minister he said to David Cliche, another federal employee, "I must get closer to the Parti Québécois," he was speaking of a political party that stood in complete and ferocious opposition to Meech. The success of Meech, as Louise Beaudoin said, could have resulted in the complete undoing of the separatist movement. And so to "save" Meech

Lake, Bouchard in stealth and secrecy abandoned the people who had created it, and joined those whose primary mission was to destroy it.

That April day in Premier Charest's office, I was overcome with sadness and regret. With the benefit of hindsight, I could clearly see for the first time how foolish I had been in placing such loyalty, trust and friendship in a man incapable of reciprocating such feelings. It was my mistake. I paid heavily for it. Unfortunately – and this is why I will never forgive myself – so did the country.

1990

3. Distractions Along the Way

On April 10, I was scheduled to travel to Toronto's SkyDome to watch the Blue Jays play the Texas Rangers. President Bush and I planned a few hours of discussions on the margins of the game. We were also scheduled to throw out ceremonial first pitches. In what would be any advance person's worst nightmare, April 10 also happened to be the day the House of Commons approved the GST! And here I, the leader of the majority party that had pushed the new tax through the House, would be walking out in front of thousands of full-throated Canadians in a baseball stadium, with television cameras on hand as well.

As expected, I was given a terrible raspberry by the crowd. Afterwards, members of the American media covering the event asked me how I felt at hearing all the boos with George Bush by my side. With a smile I told them that I felt as ashamed as any other Canadian to see the visiting president of the United States treated in such a manner!

Memo to all future prime ministers: don't attend a Blue Jays game after you bring forth a new tax. Bob Rae, who also found himself booed at SkyDome during those years, later produced a perfect strategy. In front of thousands gathered to congratulate the Blue Jays on a World Series win, when his name was called he held up a sign: "No speech today, Hooray for the Jays." This earned the less than popular premier of Ontario the respect of the crowd and allowed him to avoid the boos that I knew only too well.

On the serious side, President Bush and I were able to announce that negotiations between our two countries on an acid rain treaty could begin as early as that summer. We'd come a long way since I first broached the subject with Ronald Reagan.

Back in Ottawa my caucus had voted to expel Alex Kindy and David Kilgour after they voted against the GST in the Commons. I wholeheartedly supported the decision because it was unacceptable to me that members of caucus would vote against the most important tax change brought about by a federal government in many decades. I also found it amusing that Kilgour would later join the Chrétien Liberal caucus and cabinet and sit quietly by as that party warmly embraced and profited from the GST he once so despised.

Senator Bob Dole and his wife, Elizabeth, a member of the Bush cabinet, also visited Ottawa in April. I followed my usual practice with senior members of the U.S. Congress when they came to Canada and treated them like visiting heads of state. That strategy often paid off when matters of crucial importance for Canada – the acid rain treaty, for one – came before American legislators.

Some of the most interesting conversations with the Doles, however, involved a domestic issue. They asked me to explain why the Meech Lake Accord appeared to be in danger of not being ratified.

"Forget Canada," I told them over lunch at 24 Sussex. "Let's assume that the United States decided they had to have a new constitution and all the states met with the federal administration for an extended period of time. Finally, they came up with a new document. But it was not endorsed by New York, California, Florida, and Texas. That's approximately the equivalent of Quebec's population in this country."

"Well, that couldn't happen," Bob Dole replied.

The Doles were shocked when Trudeau's deal from 1981–82 was explained to them in American terms.

"It gets better," I continued. "In those negotiations, the governors of the fifty states wound up with the power to override important provisions of the American Bill of Rights and decisions of the U.S. Supreme Court."

Elizabeth Dole cut me off right there.

"Are you telling me that the governor of Mississippi would have been given the right to overrule Supreme Court decisions on issues like *Brown versus Board of Education* [a decision that desegregated American schools]?" she asked.

"That's exactly what I'm telling you," I answered.

"Who did this?" she continued.

"Pierre Trudeau, the same fellow who is demanding perfection in the Meech Lake Accord."

P.E.I. Premier Joe Ghiz spoke before the Charest Committee on April 30. He was blunt, telling the committee that Clyde Wells was standing in the way of constitutional reform on a whole series of critical areas. If Meech Lake dies, he said, Canada will face political instability.

At the end of the special Quebec caucus meeting at Mont-Tremblant (where, as I have noted, in Mila's presence Bouchard had said that he knew "absolutely nothing" about the PQ trying to suborn our MPs), I spoke to the press. I admitted that our party would take hits for two years because of the important structural changes we had initiated, but I was able to point to a recent International Monetary Fund report that complimented us on the FTA, GST, and reforms to Unemployment Insurance. "We're going to take a shellacking for an extended period of time, not because we enjoy it, not because we're masochists, but because we're going the right way," I said.

I also had a warning for any MPs who were thinking of bolting caucus to lobby for separatism. I demanded support for our efforts at securing the passage of Meech Lake.

"We're a federalist party, we stand for Canada . . . a united Canada," I said. "That's what we're fighting for. If a member decides that this view is incompatible with his own aspirations he can pack it in."

A few days later I met privately with a group of distinguished Canadians including Robert Stanfield, former Trudeau minister Francis Fox, Ed Broadbent, Jack Pickersgill, and others. It was a brainstorming session, and we were hoping this group, some of whom had been working on constitutional issues for a generation and more, might have some ideas for breaking the impasse. I took notes as each person spoke.

"Trudeau and Chrétien are totally out of touch with modern Quebec," Fox, who knew both men well, said. "They are totally misleading people with their 'don't worry, be happy' attitude."

Eric Kierans, who had served in the cabinets of both Trudeau and Robert Bourassa, was also passionate. "Bourassa cannot move and shouldn't be asked," he thundered. "I supported Meech because Canada is not and can never be a unitary, centralized state. If you sell it, do so as a decentralizing instrument as contrasted with a highly centralized instrument."

The veteran Pickersgill, who had worked (while an assistant to Mackenzie King and Louis St. Laurent) at bringing Newfoundland into Confederation, was angry and sarcastic: "Trudeau was a wonderful 'One Canada' man, but he gave more away to the provinces than any prime minister in my seventy-five years of observing prime ministers. Clyde Wells is so far removed from any kind of reality."

I discussed the seriousness of the situation in the private pages of my journal – long before I learned about Bouchard's betrayal. It makes for painful reading today.

—

PERSONAL JOURNAL: MAY 19, 1990

The Meech Lake negotiations have reached a critical point and unforeseen events are beginning to impact negatively our hopes of salvaging an honourable deal, through the Charest Committee process. The Charest Committee reported Thursday, a unanimous report that generated good support in English Canada but tepid support, if not hostility, in Quebec. I dispatched Lowell Murray on a cross-country tour to meet with premiers, having spoken with all of them personally and maintained good and frequent communication with Premier Bourassa. In fact, we have met secretly at his Hydro-Québec office on Sunday nights at two-week intervals, in anticipation of the publication of the report. I had explained to him what I thought would be in the report, and how we might accommodate the requests of other provinces without violating the integrity of the Meech Lake Accord as negotiated.

The problem in Quebec, we agreed, would be one of optics: having negotiated an acceptable deal in '87, Quebec would now be told by the dissident provinces that they would not honour it; that new demands would have to be accepted by Quebec, dealing with new subject matter, even though the Quebec Round that resulted in Meech Lake was brought about at the request of the premiers themselves in Edmonton in 1986! I quite understand the impression of "humiliation" this new list of add-ons in Charest might convey in Quebec, even though much, if not all, of the list could perhaps be refined and accommodated without the least adverse impact upon Quebec. The fact is that the perception would be entirely different if not carefully explained or if whipped up into something it is not by a resolved adversary of Meech, such as Jacques Parizeau.

My hope was that the waters could be kept calm until Murray reported back, and we ascertained if a deal might be possible, using the same time frame to meet privately with Bourassa's emissaries in Montreal to explain how each item might be dealt with, without damage to Quebec's interests. (At this moment, Stanley Hartt, Roger Tassé, and Mary Dawson are meeting in the Ritz with Bourassa advisors Jean-Claude Rivest and Diane Wilhelmy, their second such meeting in three days.)

I have known since our national caucus at Mont-Tremblant last month that François Gérin would be impossible to keep onside, even though he along with other Quebec members had agreed at an earlier caucus meeting at Meech Lake (!) that they would remain serene until June 23, to see if our attempts to save Meech might work out.

And, in fact, on Thursday François announced that he was going to sit as an independent because the Charest Report constituted a significant change in approach by the government and by the PM and that therefore he would sit in the House solely to promote the cause of sovereignty, independence, or "sovereignty-association" – no one was quite certain of his real objective. His departure was neither a great surprise nor a serious loss. I always liked François but found him to be progressively unreliable and unstable as events unfolded and the pressure mounted. But he was never a bad MP, nor in any way wilfully hurtful to me or the family.

My frustration with the arrogant approach of Wells and Carstairs grew daily, and over the last few months it spread rapidly to many other "nationalist" members of the Quebec caucus. When Wells, who by age 30 could not speak a word of French, lectured the nation on how Meech Lake could "damage our bilingual Canada," most Quebec members could barely contain their rage. When former PC Party president Peter Blaikie announced he would prefer living in an independent Quebec to a united Canada with Meech Lake, French-speaking backbenchers who were acquiring both an understanding and love of Canada shook their heads in bewilderment and spoke in terms of great sadness when discussing what they referred to in caucus as "the monumental stupidity of Mr. Blaikie."

Despite such provocations, along with the venom and hatred served up almost daily by columnists such as William Johnson of the Montreal Gazette*, the caucus resolved to keep its cool and see if the premiers and I could work things out.*

To me, the solidarity of the Quebec caucus was key for another reason: any undue criticism of Charest or the process we were following would put greater pressure on Bourassa publicly to dig his heels in, to avoid "embarrassment" or "humiliation" or the "isolation" of Quebec. Inasmuch as I would never be party to any action that would so treat Quebec (or for that matter any other province), such fears were groundless. But because Quebec had been isolated before [in 1981], it is difficult to blame anyone for having reasonable apprehensions a decade later.

And so I was very pleased with the solidarity and tranquility of the Quebec caucus these last few weeks. Not that I wanted to deprive anyone of his/her freedom of speech, but the strategy we were pursuing was the only one that would allow us to keep Meech whole and, while sensible, it was also fragile, and a thoughtless statement or untoward act could easily derail the entire process. I believe the case for Canadian unity is so vital that I am inclined to take any reasonable initiative to ensure its durability. The Meech Lake Accord, which binds Quebec to Canada, is indispensable to Canada's unity and Quebec's dignity. As J.W. Pickersgill said, "Meech is a miracle – it unites Canada on terms so reasonable, they may never come again."

—

Then my journal turns to the horrifying news of Bouchard's telegram to the PQ, and the events that followed. "Lucien is one of my oldest friends," one paragraph begins.

The journal resumes:

—

I think I have lost my wager with myself, my dream for a new and durable dimension of Canada unity – that we can build a country big enough, and flexible enough, that all Canadians would find for themselves self-fulfillment, pride, identity and dignity within its borders, that would make hopeless any appeal to separation that would result in a small, lesser citizenship. The joy – spontaneous and real – felt throughout Quebec and Canada in the weeks following the signing of Meech Lake filled me with great hope. The love of Canada was strong and it was articulated as eloquently in English as it was in French.

And then came the assaults on Meech. For a month Stanley Hartt has been holding secret meetings with Eric Maldoff, a representative of some key Jean Chrétien advisors. These meetings, initiated by them, have served to narrow disagreement on text that, we are assured, will be acceptable to Chrétien and Wells and Carstairs. Obviously, Chrétien is searching for ways to avoid blame if Meech fails. I think, however, his early and unrelenting attacks on Meech Lake, which he now acknowledges were excessive and needless, will never be forgotten in Quebec. I am profoundly worried and saddened by the failure of many Canadians to realize that Meech is not a giveaway to Quebec, that it is a symbol of the revival of the nation. I am also deeply troubled by the misconceptions of (many) English-speaking commentators who think that Quebec is bluffing, that there is not substantial anger and humiliation that flows from '82 and that the rejection of Meech by Newfoundland, New Brunswick, and Manitoba, merely means that nothing happens, that we start again as one big happy family.

I wish they were right, but my gut tells me they are wrong. One day, the terms of the Meech Lake Accord will look reasonable to all Canadians, but that day may come too late. It is almost inconceivable to me that three premiers representing a small percentage of the population can be so short-sighted as to place in jeopardy the very future of one of the world's great nations. And yet, by refusing to ratify a deal their duly elected predecessors had signed, premiers McKenna, Filmon, and Wells are doing precisely that. May God bless us all and give us the wisdom and generosity to guide Canada through the shoals of a great and – I fear – national challenge.

—

In spite of the tremendous demands as June 23 drew closer, I had to fulfill my other responsibilities as prime minister. UN Secretary-General Javier Pérez de Cuéllar would be arriving for a four-day visit to Canada in late May; Soviet leader Mikhail Gorbachev would be in Ottawa for two days of talks ahead of his crucial meetings with President Bush in Washington; and seventy-one-year-old Nelson Mandela would be making a triumphant visit to Canada in mid-June that would include a historic speech to Parliament. On July 1, Her Majesty the Queen would be speaking to Canadians on Canada Day – and these were just some of the scheduled events as the Meech Lake deadline approached.

I held extensive discussions with Secretary-General Pérez de Cuéllar. We signed the UN Convention on the Rights of the Child on May 28, and the distinguished visitor publicly thanked Canada for its "unflagging support for the organization" during his stay.

When Mikhail Gorbachev arrived in Ottawa on May 29, his trip marked the first time since 1971, when Aleksei Kosygin held high office in Moscow, that a Soviet leader had come to Ottawa for talks. The crowds that gathered to see the USSR's final leader obviously sensed the new spirit that Gorbachev's visit embodied. Afterwards, we decided to walk back to my Parliament Hill office from the National War Memorial, where we had laid wreaths, and to greet as many Canadians as possible along the way. Like most Western politicians, Gorbachev seemed energized by the chance to mainstreet through our capital and by the rapturous applause he was given. He also took an impromptu stroll down Sparks Street on the first night of his stay. "I'm glad the Cold War is over," an excited youngster shouted at him. Others carried copies of one of his books, hoping for a signature.

In public, Gorbachev said that Ottawa seemed so clean to him that Canada must be taxing oxygen, which led me to interject, "I want all Canadians to know that the idea for a new tax in Canada came from President Gorbachev and not me. I've got enough troubles right now!"

Gorbachev, en route to Washington for talks with President Bush, was increasingly fearful of German reunification. During our private talks he told me that he believed that the intention of NATO, and of the United States in particular, was to turn the organization into "the basic instrument of Western politics in Europe," and to have it be controlled by the Americans.

In my debriefing for Canadian officials afterwards I described his "extraordinary visceral fear of Germany, which was exacerbated by the speed with which changes were occurring." Gorbachev told the Ottawa press that the pressure he faced from the West to accept a united Germany as part of NATO risked a return to the old days of heightened East–West tensions. "You must give thought to the other side," he said. "This is not a basketball match and maybe we should declare a time out."

When Gorbachev and I met in my office for intensive private discussions, I told him he'd have to accept a united Germany within NATO. "I urge you not to pronounce your opposition to this view in Washington because Bush cannot and will not relent on this question, and you will wind up humiliated."

He looked at me sadly and I could see a hint of resignation in his eyes, which I later that day conveyed to Bush in one of our many telephone conversations. Perhaps to let me know that the USSR's spying apparatus had not collapsed along with its economy, Gorbachev smiled as he began next day's meeting, "You look well, Brian. And how is our friend George?"

I gave him what support I could, knowing full well that the genie wasn't going back into the bottle. "The unpredictable velocity of change has created a degree of insensitivity about the legitimate security apprehensions of the Soviet Union," I said, proposing that NATO now begin a reorientation of its thinking based on Article 2 of the NATO Charter. This article had been drafted by Lester Pearson and defined the institution as a political *and* military one. Gorbachev said he hadn't considered that idea, and promised to begin thinking it over on his way to Washington.

Mila and I hosted him and his wife, Raisa, at lunch at 24 Sussex and I later wrote about the event.

—

PERSONAL JOURNAL: MAY 29, 1990

He said that he and I were the same, "men of action," whereas Mitterrand, whom he likes and admires, was nevertheless a "windy intellectual." Mitterrand had lectured him on making better use of his time by not going to Parliament so often. "I never go to the National Assembly," said Mitterrand, "it would be a waste of time." In fact, said Gorbachev, he only found out later from Margaret Thatcher that since Napoleon the President of the Republic was prevented from ever going to Parliament. Gorbachev laughed uproariously at his own anecdote.

Raisa, in commenting on the profiteers who emerge at times of economic difficulties, spoke of "thugs" and "bastards" who were poisoning the atmosphere. Both Mila and I were startled to hear such a comment from a petite, elegant lady, but he just smiled, nodded, and went on with his own point.

—

Mila and Raisa visited the Canadian Museum of Nature in Ottawa and the Museum of Civilization in Hull, thrilling legions of schoolchildren on day trips. "What is the most interesting thing here?" Raisa asked kids at the Canadian Museum of Nature. "The dinosaurs," they shouted back in unison. My own kids would have agreed.

Despite the hectic schedule I, of course, made time for the kids. One day in late May they convinced me to play hooky from the office, and we all went to an Ottawa theatre to see *Teenage Mutant Ninja Turtles*. Finding ourselves facing a huge lineup, a quick family vote had us heading to see Canadian Michael J. Fox's *Back to the Future III*.

During this period Mila joined thousands of members of Toronto's Chinese community in the frantic search for a suitable bone marrow donor to help save the life of six-year-old Elizabeth Lue of Scarborough. The little girl had aplastic anemia and would die unless a match were found. Mila joined other prominent Canadians in giving blood, and taped a special message that was played at the SkyDome urging Toronto residents to get tested. Mila also visited Elizabeth at Toronto's Hospital for Sick Children. More than ten thousand people from across Canada's Asian communities came out for testing in the end. While Elizabeth eventually lost her valiant battle, passing away tragically on August 31, 1990, she lives on today through a foundation in her name that funds research into bone marrow disease. "Elizabeth has left a legacy of hope," her equally brave mother, Philippa Lue, said on the first anniversary of her daughter's death.

On June 17, Nelson Mandela arrived in Canada for a two-day visit. Large crowds greeted him everywhere he went and this living legend quickly stole the hearts of Canadians. His speech to Parliament on June 18 is one of my greatest memories of my time as prime minister. MPs and senators of all parties sensed the historic importance of what they were about to witness, and the atmosphere was electric with anticipation. The Commons exploded with cheers and applause from all sides when I led Mandela into the chamber.

"Canada's involvement in the struggle against apartheid has deep roots, extending far beyond the efforts of this government and this Parliament and encompasses a multitude of Canadians who have assisted the people of South Africa, individually or through churches, trade unions, educational institutions, and non-government organizations," I said in my introduction. "I remember, Mr. Mandela, with pride, the stand taken by Canada's prime minister, John Diefenbaker, at the Commonwealth Conference of 1961, which resulted in South Africa's withdrawal from that body. Prime Minister Diefenbaker brought the Commonwealth to declare unequivocally that racial discrimination was totally contrary to its fundamental principles and that, if South Africa did not change, Mr. Diefenbaker said then South Africa must leave. He did so against some considerable opposition, but with the strong conviction and the certain knowledge that it was right. Mr.

Diefenbaker's action marked the beginning of international pressure on the apartheid regime."

I also chose this moment to pay a special tribute to Joe Clark.

"If I may be allowed a strictly Canadian note," I said. "Outside South Africa itself there are few international leaders, in my judgment, who have made a more sustained and a more effective commitment to fundamental and beneficial change in that country in recent years than the present Secretary of State for External Affairs of the Government of Canada, the Right Honourable Joe Clark."

Mandela, imprisoned for so many years, then made his way to the podium as the House erupted into roaring cheers, waves, and shouts of greeting. Mandela urged Canada to keep its sanctions in place. He also praised the actions my government had taken, and I was secretly proud to hear the words that followed.

"In this context, I would also like to pay special tribute to the prime minister of this country, Brian Mulroney, who has continued along the path charted by Prime Minister Diefenbaker, who acted against apartheid because he knew that no person of conscience could stand aside as a crime against humanity was being committed," he said. "Mr. Prime Minister, our people and organization respect you and admire you as a friend. We have been greatly strengthened by your personal involvement in the struggle against apartheid with the UN, the Commonwealth, the Group of Seven, and the Francophonie summits. We are certain that you will, together with the rest of the Canadian people, stay the course with us, not only as we battle on to end the apartheid system, but also as we work to build a happy, peaceful, and prosperous future for all the people of South and southern Africa."

During our private talks I asked Mandela what he thought South Africa would look like in five years. He told me that he couldn't be sure. There was one thing, however, he was definite about: South Africa would never again have a whites-only election. "Future elections will be nonracial," he said firmly. "In the meantime, the maintenance of sanctions is essential. The South African government is feeling the pinch."

At a state dinner in his honour in Toronto, I was able to announce that Canada would be contributing $5 million to help with the repatriation and resettlement of South African exiles and the reintegration of political prisoners into their communities.

1990

4. The Shadows of Ghosts

Despite the distractions of these important foreign visits, that spring getting Meech Lake through was my main challenge. The Quebec National Assembly had ratified the version arrived at in the Langevin Block meeting on June 23, 1987. By law that set the clock ticking, since all provinces were required to agree to a constitutional change within three years, or the amendment would fail.

It was very clear to me that getting a new unanimous agreement from the premiers on Meech – in the wake of the Charest Report, the McKenna resolution, and the Bouchard betrayal, and in a deeply antagonistic political environment – was going to take every ounce of talent, energy, and leadership that I possessed.

Although the 1988 general election was principally about free trade, I campaigned extensively on Meech as well, despite the opposition of Trudeau and the PQ, so the national mood was good as the bill slowly made its way through the House of Commons and the provincial legislatures, one by one. On July 7, 1988, Newfoundland became the eighth province to ratify the accord.

In 1989, however, Liberal Clyde Wells had been elected the new premier of Newfoundland, and on October 18 he wrote me a ten-page letter in opposition to Meech, saying that he had campaigned on a promise to rescind his province's approval of the accord if certain changes were not made. Of this letter constitutional law expert and Osgoode Law School dean Patrick Monahan has said, "Reading the letter, one is struck by the one-sided nature of his analysis . . . one searches in vain for any sense of balance or proportion."

Wells was impressively uninformed about the evolution of French Quebec and had received most of his opinions in this regard from Pierre Trudeau, whom he admired greatly and whose rigid, almost messianic, views he worshipped. Trudeau now had his camel's nose inside the tent. All that was required to sabotage Meech would be for Wells to refuse to honour his province's commitment. Mr. Trudeau's influence was personified by Deborah Coyne, who became Wells's constitutional advisor, and was later acknowledged to have been Trudeau's lover and the mother of their daughter.

Soon thereafter, however, I received a different view from the west coast. Bruce Hutchison, the grand old man of Canadian journalism, pointed out that Wells had failed to mention that Newfoundland itself was granted "distinct status" in the Constitution when it entered Confederation in 1949. Among other examples, Hutchison pointed to the recognition of Newfoundland's distinct education system, the fact that a distinct regime for the fisheries was maintained, the fact that the new province was to receive subsidies and tax rentals not received by other provinces and, in addition, transitional grants from the federal treasury to enable it to provide adequate public services. Mr. Hutchison concluded in his letter to me, "But these variations from the Constitution of the existing provinces did not give Newfoundland any claim to powers additional to those in the Terms of Union . . . After a layman's long observation of public affairs I judge that the accord is vital to future national unity and that the failure of the provinces to reach agreement on a necessary process would be a catastrophe for all their citizens. With respect and regret, it seems to me that the Newfoundland government, fearing the accord, sees only the shadows of ghosts."

In a stunning move, on April 5, 1990, Clyde Wells rescinded the Newfoundland Assembly's previous approval of the accord. John C. Crosbie, a proud Newfoundlander, in his book *No Holds Barred*, makes no secret of his opinion of Clyde Wells, "As a foe, he was one of the most miserable people I've ever encountered. Clyde was one of the most stubborn beings alive . . . When it comes time to hang somebody because of how we're going to suffer as a result of Quebec's leaving Confederation, Newfoundlanders will hang the poor soul who happens to be in office when it happens. The one they should hang is Clyde Wells!"

From May 24 to 28, I held lengthy, intensive, individual meetings with all the premiers in the second-floor Freedom Room (so designated by Margaret Trudeau) at 24 Sussex. The room provided a commanding view of the Ottawa River and the rolling Gatineau Hills sloping gently off in the distance, but we didn't get to enjoy it. The meetings were exhausting, lasting in some cases for more than four hours as I carefully reviewed each premier's proposals and assessments, and probed for areas of commonality that might produce an agreement. The final meeting was a breakfast with Robert Bourassa.

—

PERSONAL JOURNAL: JULY 22–26, 1990

It was clear when the premiers visited with me at 24 Sussex that Filmon and Wells were absolutely hostile to Meech. Filmon's opposition was entirely political and tactical because he had earlier introduced Meech into the Manitoba legislature and made one of the most eloquent speeches ever in its support! He withdrew that support after Bourassa invoked the notwithstanding clause on Bill 178 (which had nothing to do with Meech!). And, as his popularity rose because of his anti-Quebec stand, Filmon proceeded to dig himself in more deeply in opposition with each passing day. By the time he arrived at 24 for our preliminary meetings he was smug, haughty, and careless in his opinions and of the possible consequences for the nation if Meech were to fail.

Wells arrived absolutely certain of his position and astonished that anyone would ever question the rectitude of his views. Simply put, Wells believed that there should be one government in Canada, the federal government, in a unitary state! In fact, he said as much, to the horror of his colleagues, during the meetings. He believed that Meech weakened the federal government and that all Quebec had to do was sign on the dotted line of 1982 and that all would be well.

He repeatedly told me that people like Pierre Trudeau, Don Johnston, Eugene Forsey, and Deborah Coyne had assured him he could turn down Meech with no consequences in Quebec.

I spent four hours and 20 minutes with him at 24 on Sunday. Monday morning Robert Bourassa arrived at 24 for his (the last) meeting and told me Wells had awakened him at 1 a.m. to tell him, "The PM has really shaken me up about Meech" and began discussing matters with him.

In fact, the report from Bourassa was encouraging because I had been tough, even brutal, with Wells. I told him that if Meech passed, two things would happen: first, he would get the important beginnings of Senate reform and, second, that we would get to keep a united Canada. If, however, Meech failed, two things would also happen: first, Senate reform was dead and, second, the probability that Quebec would dramatically alter its relationship or sever its relationship with Canada increased immeasurably.

I was pleased that, at least, I had shaken him out of his arrogance that Meech could be set aside without consequence – even though, as subsequent events established, my achievement was quite superficial when compared with his extraordinary vanity that his view and his view alone of Canada should persist and prevail.

—

On May 28, after hosting President Gorbachev for two days of important discussions, I announced that I had invited the premiers to dinner in Ottawa for one last try at saving Meech Lake.

I told the Commons that some "crucial differences" remained after my one-on-one meetings with the premiers the week before. "While I do not want to underestimate the divergences on the remaining issues – they are there and they are serious – in point of fact what is in dispute is modest, extremely modest when compared with what is really at stake. What is really at stake is Canada."

On June 3, I hosted a working dinner for the first ministers at the Museum of Civilization in Hull, exactly three years after Canada's first ministers had worked until dawn at the Langevin Block, across the river in Ottawa, to forge the deal we were now working to save. A lot had taken place during that three-year period. In New Brunswick in 1987, Richard Hatfield had been defeated by Liberal Frank McKenna, an opponent of Meech Lake, before the accord could be ratified in that province. In April of 1988, the government of Meech signatory Howard Pawley of Manitoba was defeated and Tory Gary Filmon had been elected head of a minority government. Filmon withdrew Meech from his legislature after Quebec's Bill 178 was introduced, and an all-party committee of his provincial legislature reported in October of 1989. All three parties signed on to the report, which featured a demand for the insertion of a so-called Canada clause before Manitoba would pass Meech. This clause would have, in effect, completely changed Meech's distinct society clause regarding Quebec. Constitutional scholar Patrick Monahan later dismissed the whole exercise as "the constitutional equivalent of digging a hole and then refilling it with dirt so as to disguise its existence." But Manitoba, rightly or wrongly, had never voted to approve Meech, which darkened my prospects.

This was the reality I faced as I headed into the museum's fifth-floor dining room, which faced the Ottawa River, and from which we could see the Parliament Buildings, bathed in splendid light.

We dined on roast tenderloin of beef with grilled shrimp, fiddleheads, and roasted potatoes. While I sipped my customary soda water and ever-present coffees, waiters brought the premiers Ontario wines. British Columbia's Bill Vander Zalm was incensed at this slight to his province. His "vintage" concern provided the only humorous moment in what was about to come. I simply pushed my food around my plate; I hadn't come that night to eat.

I set the stage in my opening remarks, which launched the most challenging week of my public life.

Senator Lowell Murray, government leader in the Senate and minister of federal-provincial relations, who had worked tirelessly and innovatively to make the negotiations successful, was the only other person in the room with the premiers. He held the pen that night and took detailed notes through the tumultuous week, excerpts of which are reproduced here. His notes form part of my collection in Library and Archives Canada and have never been revealed until now. I make no apologies for setting them down in detail and at length. This is, as far as it can be reconstructed, history in the raw, and you are at the table.

At 8:30 that night I began with a little familiar history, starting with Trudeau's speech in May 1980 at the Paul Sauvé Arena in Montreal. I took us quickly up to 1987, when we "reached unanimity at Meech Lake on a series of amendments to the Constitution which would bring Quebec back into the constitutional family. The 1982 amending formula provided for a three-year period for ratification and proclamation of an amendment. Those three years have seen Meech Lake nickeled and dimed almost to death. Quebecers want to be part of the constitutional family but they do not want to be frisked at the door in somebody's test of constitutional purity. Think of the consequences of success. The immediate consequence is that we get to keep this country together, this awkward, difficult, magnificent country."

I then referred to the view across the river in the setting sun.

"From this room we can see Earnscliffe, the residence of Canada's first prime minister. In correspondence, Sir John A. Macdonald repeatedly expresses his conviction that if he and his contemporaries could keep the country together from day to day and month to month, the growing strength of the new country would ensure its unity. We face a similar challenge today. Jean Chrétien himself is quoted in yesterday's *Le Devoir* as saying that a referendum on sovereignty-association today would be lost by the federalist forces. *La Presse* carries a poll indicating growing support for sovereignty-association even among Quebec's business people, the Conseil du Patronat. This federation can only survive if there is trust among us. Trust is the element that is helping to thaw superpower relationships in the world. A *New York Times* editorial this weekend, dealing with arms control and verification, points out that the U.S. and USSR have finally decided to trust each other even if they can't verify the commitments on both sides. We aren't the Soviets and the U.S. We're fellow Canadians, brothers around the table. I am not trying to build a superpower. I want to build a super country."

I then turned the floor over to Robert Bourassa. He gave what was one of his finest speeches. "I was elected in 1985 on an economic platform," he said. "I said, Let's look for a face-saver to reintegrate Quebec in the Constitution . . . I was very happy three years ago when we signed the Meech Lake Accord. A constitutional settlement would let Canada get on with the job of integrating into the international economy, of tackling environmental problems, and so forth. What a surprise and disappointment the past three years have brought with the opposition to Meech Lake. Imagine dismantling a country because of a constitutional theory! I have a great sadness tonight – what a waste of energy! One of the most privileged countries in the world, meeting in such a dramatic atmosphere. Four hundred journalists outside, speculating on the breakup of the country. I am worried about the pressures for a referendum in Quebec. We would lose a referendum on sovereignty-association today. The federal system will be difficult enough to defend in the next few years, with fiscal pressures, the GST, etc. As a Canadian, I am worried about what happens if Meech Lake fails."

The premier of Nova Scotia then cut in. "I was there," said John Buchanan, "when the commitments were made at the Paul Sauvé Arena in 1980. I was at the First Ministers' Conference in 1981 when Lévesque and Parizeau walked out. I said we must never let it happen again. We must have a commitment to bring Quebec back to the table."

With premiers like Gary Filmon and Clyde Wells in mind – men who in their public and private remarks had demonstrated a remarkable ignorance of the realities of Quebec history and of developments in that province since the Quiet Revolution – I spoke again of what was at stake for the Quebec premier. "Bourassa is in a unique situation among first ministers," I said. "I know that the opposition leaders, whatever our differences, are loyal Canadians as I am. The same holds true for the political situation in nine provinces. But Bourassa is the only first minister whose opposition leader is dedicated to the breakup of Canada."

That provided fertile ground for the next speaker, a dynamic and impressive farmer – with a Ph.D. – from Saskatchewan. Though much maligned by some today, Grant Devine was a man whose instincts were right on Meech and on Canadian unity. He never spoke better than he did that night.

"What the hell is the prize when we end up a broken country?" he said, with raw emotion in his voice. "Who gives a shit about the Senate then? My opposition leader, Roy Romanow, believes in the 'triple-A' – Abolish, Abolish, Abolish. Why should you wreck a country for something like that? If Manitoba is the only province in Canada that has a veto, I don't care. I'll sell it in Saskatchewan. The future of our economy is linked to western diversification. I'm a Ph.D. in economics. I'm a farmer. I'm a politician. But all our efforts are not worth a damn if some Reform guy on horseback or in a jeep takes control. And for what, the Senate! Do you want a sunset clause after fifty years, then abolish it! Ten years? I'll go along with that. They have an equal Senate in the United States, but it's not the prize some Canadians make it out to be. Has the 'three-E' Senate made North Dakota relatively more prosperous than Saskatchewan? No."

And on it went, around the table, with every province having its say.

"We have to look at the realm of the possible rather than seek perfection," Alberta's Don Getty said. "Without Meech Lake, globally we look like jerks. Our economy will be in trouble, there will be no Senate reform. With Meech Lake, we save the country, we reinforce economic stability and prosperity, and we'll reform the Senate."

P.E.I.'s Joe Ghiz took direct aim at the holdout premiers – McKenna, Filmon, and Wells. He had particularly tough words for Wells. "If we leave here without resolving the constitutional issue, Canadians will be very angry," he said. "Politicians are held in low enough esteem now, and the future of the country is in the hands of the eleven politicians around this table. I know we need to address the concerns of New Brunswick, Manitoba, and Newfoundland. But I say to those three premiers, you are wrong collectively in saying that it is Robert Bourassa and the rest of us who have to compromise. If that's your bottom line, let's go home tomorrow morning! Bourassa can't compromise, I agree with him one hundred per cent.

"Clyde, you didn't win Newfoundland because of opposition to Meech Lake. You won because of the Newfoundland Tories. I knew at the Langevin Block in 1987 when I signed Meech Lake I wasn't articulating the popular mood in Prince Edward Island or Atlantic Canada. I have opposition within my own caucus, and pressures on my caucus from outside. But Meech Lake was right for the future of our country, and now we have to solve this problem. Clyde, you want certainty on the distinct society? The reality is you're not going to get it. We're not going back to the legislature by June 23 to pass amendments to legitimize Meech Lake for Newfoundland. I can do it but can Peterson? Can Don Getty, who is down twenty points because of Meech Lake?

"We made Senate reform subject to the unanimity formula at Meech Lake because other provinces would not accept a veto for Quebec alone. Should P.E.I. have a veto? We have fifty times the power of Quebec and seventy times the power of Ontario, given our respective populations. God bless Canada, but we have it. Bourassa cannot possibly agree to remove the unanimity rule and his own veto. We are looking principally to you, Clyde Wells, for compromise. The prospect of failure makes me weep. I will feel that I have let my small province down, and my country, if I pay heed to polls in English Canada suggesting that we should let Quebec go, and all that."

When Ghiz finished, there was silence in the room. His eloquence and passion had stunned his colleagues.

Manitoba's Gary Filmon, in his reply, gave us all a hint of what was to come. "It seems we have learned nothing from the past three years and the building up of pressures and animosities between Quebec and the rest," he said. "I don't doubt the prime minister's economic analysis is right, but the reality is that unless you commit yourself to the process started by Frank, and continued correctly and courageously by the Charest Committee, we will not have a solution . . . Meech Lake is a body blow to aspirations for Senate reform, to women's rights because the 1982 achievement is weakened, and to aboriginal constitutional reform. Reasonable changes can be made in a companion resolution with some certainty of passage. I don't even have to consult the opposition on this. But if I come back with nothing, if I capitulate to Ghiz, it's impossible. We have to talk about certainty. We have to get it done before June 23."

Clyde Wells then spoke for the first time. "My position is that the nation comes first, Newfoundland second," he said. "I am dedicated to the preservation of Canada as a federal state and to the fundamental principles of federalism. These are the equality of citizens and the equality of provinces. There is a further Canadian commitment to the personal well-being and economic equality of opportunity for its citizens. Newfoundland has the highest unemployment rate in the country. We have a per capita earned income 58 per cent of the national average. This is the fault of the present structure. Forty-eight per cent of our provincial revenues come from federal transfers. For the national good, we have to stop this trend. Your federal deficit is primarily because of equalization payments in the range of $30 billion annually. Our economy is inadequate to produce the necessary revenues for our provincial treasury. This must change, but it never will so long as the federal government is responsible to a House of Commons 60 per cent of whose members come from two provinces. There is no balance in the exercise of national legislative power in this country. This is normally the role of a Senate. We must balance the principle of the majority of the population with the principle of the majority of the constituent parts of the federation. Senate reform will allow smaller provinces to fully participate in national legislative power. This is the *magic* of a federal system exemplified by a 'three-E' Senate. I support the concept of Quebec as a distinct society but cannot allow it to impair fundamental principles of a federal system."

Ontario premier David Peterson's opening remarks were powerful. "I want you all to know that I accept the seriousness of the situation that confronts us," he said. "I believe that we are facing the possible breakup of this country. If Meech Lake goes down, this country will be transfixed on constitutional issues for the indefinite future. Aboriginal reform is put off, Senate reform becomes impossible. Without Meech Lake, we'll be considering how to negotiate the breakup of the country. I have some familiarity with Quebec. I've seen crisis situations in the relationship in the past. But I believe this one is more terminal, more serious, more focused. There is no easy way out, as there was in the past. I see a solution if we gather up threads that we see in four pressure points, those on Wells, Filmon, McKenna, and Bourassa.

"The operating premise is that Meech Lake has to pass. Then what? There are a number of things in Frank's resolution we can agree to. That

Robert can agree to. Frank stuck his finger in the dike. Then we had the Charest Committee. At least we are moving. When we meet tomorrow, it should be as informally as possible. We want to search for a vehicle. Let's look at the list of relatively uncontroversial matters that we can agree to constitutionalize. Then let's look for an accord for some other questions. Or some combination of amendments and a political accord. Gary has problems, but he has jockeyed pretty well in his minority situation. Clyde has different objectives . . . We have to understand that these are the most important three days in our lives. The issues are bullshit by comparison with the stakes. History will come down hard on our shoulders if we blow it. Let's give ourselves the time we need."

I then wound things down, well aware that Monday would be a long day.

"One of the reasons for wanting to put this unfinished constitutional business behind us is that it will let us get on with addressing other important national and regional concerns," I said, facing Wells directly. "I want to begin the process of meeting legitimate concerns of Newfoundlanders. I understand something of the alienation on the Rock. Years ago, I took the position that the Quebec–Newfoundland hydro contract was wrong for Newfoundland, and that the wrong should be redressed. I took that position ten years ago, not before a Newfoundland audience but in Quebec, and Robert knows that my position on this has not changed. I want to use my office and the influence of the federal government to help arrive at a solution to this. But we have to solve the threat to us as a nation posed by Quebec's isolation in 1982. If not, who is going to go to the Paul Sauvé Arena next time there is a referendum in Quebec? What will the prime minister of Canada say? What do we do for an encore?" I ended on a high note: "I am very encouraged by what I hear tonight. Tomorrow I want us to pick up where David left off. We will try to work from a piece of paper that will express some concepts and some thoughts that we can pull together."

The blow-by-blow account of the next four days of negotiations in a windowless room at the Government Conference Centre – the old railway station, and, ironically, the place where Trudeau and nine premiers had negotiated a constitutional deal over patriation that excluded Quebec – is given in detail in Appendix A. It is based on the careful notes taken by Lowell Murray, the only notes of that event. These details appear in this book as an important contribution to the historical record, and I recommend that interested readers consult the Appendix.

A summary of these days of exhausting debate – involving eloquence, idealism, raised voices, anger, and despair – is hard to produce. Perhaps it is simplest to say that while Frank McKenna, Gary Filmon, and Clyde Wells started the debate as holdouts opposed to Meech Lake, McKenna came to accept the majority view in favour of the accord. By the time we came to the last day – with the crowds of media outside seeming to grow with every passing hour as the entire nation speculated on what was happening in these sessions – Filmon's Manitoba (with the two Opposition leaders, Sharon Carstairs and Gary Doer, offstage but playing a role) and Clyde Wells's Newfoundland were the only two provinces still uneasy about the accord, despite a generous gesture sacrificing some of Ontario's Senate seats, by David Peterson the previous day.

That final day's proceedings catch the overall tone of the meeting.

We gathered the next day in a state of near exhaustion. I started the session by paying tribute to David Peterson. He had earned it. "It is not every day that I think of David Peterson when I get up in the morning, but, David, what you and John and Frank did – in giving up Senate seats – is a tremendous act of generosity for the country," I said.

But I soon realized we weren't fully out of the woods. "The legal opinion is completely unacceptable to our lawyers," Gary Filmon announced. "There is a 'but' and an 'and' that change the sense. My lawyers were specifically excluded from the discussions."

We then did a clause-by-clause review of the document to ease Filmon's concerns. Finally, we were agreed – the Meech Lake Accord had been saved.

"From my point of view, this is the last time constitutional change will have to be negotiated by the famous 'eleven men in a room,'" I said. "We were stuck with this process as a result of 1982, but this is the last time. This is a bridge to walk across into the next century. I will sign the final communiqué on behalf of the Government of Canada. Robert, where do you stand?"

"I am very pleased to sign the document," Robert Bourassa answered. "This will be crushing for the enemies of Canada in Quebec. A lot of people argue in Quebec that, in terms of power politics, it will be better to stay out of the Constitution to increase our bargaining power and our leverage. In terms of Canada, however, it is better to move ahead together. Reintegration is better. This gives us the chance to move from the Constitution to other matters, and it will make a better future for Canada."

I then called on Peterson.

"I'm on," he said. "This is a hell of a lot tougher than Meech Lake. The country has changed. Much of the symbolism has changed. But this is our only chance to make the country whole. Some people in Ontario say Bourassa is a closet separatist. This is not so. There is no short-term political incentive for the premier of Quebec to sign on. There are political pressures on everyone here, but I see no other solution than the one that we have before us. Everybody has spilled some blood. If we handle it right, the healing process starts right away. Without this agreement, it's disaster time. With this agreement, we have a commitment to new institutions, to better reflect the reality of the country. Clyde speaks for the less powerful regions. There is a cry from them. I hear it."

"You've responded to it," Wells said generously.

"Never in history have there been so many political parties juxtaposed to kill the other parts of the country," Peterson continued. "We have the Confederation of Regions party in Ontario, the PQ in Quebec, the Reform Party in the West, and all the rest of them."

"David," I said to Ontario's premier, "I thank you for your remarkable leadership on behalf of Ontario in the interest of the nation."

On to New Brunswick. "I was against Meech Lake when it was popular to be in favour of it," McKenna said frankly. "Now I have become increasingly in favour of it as it has become popular to oppose it. I have matured, as the country has, over a three-year period. In some things I was wrong. I'm a lot humbler than I was. I understand the country better. Canadians are hurting. Our love for the country has to be unconditional. I could not have lived with the failure to reintegrate Quebec. I would have carried the scar to my grave."

"I'm going to sign it with more pride than I signed the document in 1981 and in 1987," John Buchanan said on behalf of Nova Scotia. "In the 1981/82 patriation, seven million Canadians weren't there. I'm happy for Robert Bourassa, who is a statesman and a true Canadian. From 1980 to 1982 there was animosity around the table. In 1987 and again at this conference, there was none. This is a learning experience for me. I have learned more about this country this week than I could ever have learned in any other forum. Nova Scotia is the better for this. We are fervent Nova Scotians and ardent Canadians, and we have wanted this agreement. I have a daughter-in-law whose brother is a sergeant on the Montreal police force. They have communicated to me the personal anguish that so many Quebecers feel about the discussion in this country over the past three years. We want this document, they say, we want to stay in Canada. It is with great pride that I will sign for Nova Scotians regardless of political party."

"There has been some stubbornness in the delegations, but in the end we have succeeded," Bill Vander Zalm observed. "This is incomplete, it is imperfect and some will take potshots at it. But it meets in good part the concerns of many Canadians, and I will sign." British Columbia was on board.

"I can't say I have appreciated the process," Gary Filmon said when his turn came. "It has been long and arduous and I have never been so exhausted. There is blood on the table, but it has come from our commitment to our provinces, our people, and the country. I have a great deal of respect for every one of you. You're good people, you're great people, and you do credit to the country. But the latest advice from my lawyers has taken the wind out of my sails. I know the lawyers are meeting, and I hope there will be a resolution of the problem. I am concerned about the possibility that this document will not be signed by everyone. I hope each of us can sign, subject to the knowledge that we have a difficult process back home and that we not prejudice the rights of people to appear in public hearings. I hope the problem can be resolved shortly."

"This is a good document," Grant Devine declared. "I came here with a liability – people think I'm loyal to the prime minister! I know the political risks we face. I'm going into an election. We all have problems. I am compassionate but I'm also competitive. We must have integrity and loyalty. I passed the original Meech Lake resolution right after Quebec did. I got the support of Blakeney, who had signed in 1981. It became unpopular, but we will never get a chance to get Quebec in on such reasonable terms. If we do this unanimously, we will succeed. If we don't, and we have to answer the question 'Why didn't you?' and the answer came down to *and*s and *but*s and legal drafts, how can we explain it?

"I think we have a good chance to reunify the country. What we sign will be subject to passing by all our legislatures. I acknowledge the contribution that Ontario, Nova Scotia, and New Brunswick brought to this table. My ranchers will never believe that these three old provinces led Senate reform! Quebec wants to come in. If we turn it down over an *and* or a *but*, people will never forgive us. On one side, we would be fooling around at the margin of the margins. We have history in our hands. People are praying for us. It's the right thing to do. I'm going to sign."

"It's a pleasure to sign," Joe Ghiz said. "I have been a strong supporter of Meech Lake since 1987. This has been a historic and emotional week for the country. We've all given it our best shot. We've achieved the only compromise that was achievable. We are dealing with the heart and soul of the nation. And it is always hard to deal with emotion in a rational way."

Don Getty was passionate, and even spoke of his private difficulties. He moved us all very deeply that day. "This is the conclusion of a journey we set out on in August of 1986," he began. "I chaired my first Premiers' Conference in Edmonton when we agreed to make Quebec's return the top constitutional priority, and to negotiate on the basis of Quebec's five conditions. The meeting was not without trouble. Even then we could see that because Quebec was out, the impression would always be created that we were all trying to entice Quebec back in. I always knew that if you could unlock the door to Senate reform, you could move people. We moved Senate reform from number 200 to the number-one constitutional priority. What is in Meech Lake for Alberta? There is a new passing of responsibility and influence on national decisions back from the centre. A really strong country can't be just strong at the centre but strong at the parts. If people don't feel part of the country, the country cannot be strong. For Alberta and smaller provinces, the Meech Lake provisions on the spending power give us a better opportunity to influence national programs that are in exclusive provincial jurisdiction anyway. We get a chance to nominate senators and we open the door to real Senate reform. We get a chance to nominate judges for the Supreme Court of Canada. We get a chance to negotiate new immigration agreements and we get the same right to a veto over national institutions as the big guys have.

"I felt that Meech Lake itself, in unlocking Senate reform, was an achievement of great significance. We took our time with Meech Lake. We had public meetings. It sat six months on the order paper. But Alberta never breaks a commitment we make. At my party convention, in the spring, I was told I could kill the Reform Party by telling people that we're going to kill Meech Lake. Instead I made a speech on Canada, and the meeting exploded in my favour. I came to this conference with the objective of pulling three provinces in without hardening attitudes. I have never done things for Alberta at the expense of the country, and I never will. For me it has been a lonely journey on Senate reform. Some say that Senate reform would take place 'some day.' But now it is the number-one item on the constitutional agenda . . . What we now have on Senate reform that we didn't have at Meech Lake is agreement on the objectives – an elected, effective, and more equitable Senate. We're moving forward. The pressure is kept on with the provision for reports on progress at six-month intervals. So there is now added pressure for Senate reform. And there will be a dramatic opportunity for moving ahead with Senate reform at the First Ministers' Conference coming up. The lawyers are still out there working on their draft. But if a great act of statesmanship gets lost as a footnote to a failure, it would be a tremendous tragedy.

"We achieved so much with the help of Clyde and Frank and Gary. I don't look at those meetings as pressure. I look at them as a chance to do something higher and finer for the country. These meetings have reinforced my admiration and respect for all of you, and my affection for Clyde and Gary and Frank.

"The people of the country are watching us. I speak to my wife on the telephone every day. She and her friends have been doing nothing all week but watching this drama unfold in Ottawa. My one son goes back to jail every night. He's a breath away from addiction. And he's worried about the country. I'm very proud to sign."

I told Getty on behalf of all of the premiers: "Everybody here and many Canadians have known of the tough times that you and Margaret and your family have been going through, and we all admire your dignity under such trying circumstances."

The eyes of ten first ministers then turned toward the premier of Newfoundland.

"This has been an exhausting process," Clyde Wells said. "You know my position. I appreciate the commitment of everyone. There is no lack of commitment. There are strong views here. The process is awful. I know we're all committed to replace it. I know what's at stake here. I came to put the interests of the nation first and to subordinate Newfoundland's interests to those of the nation. I must have the freedom, without undue pressure or fear of having my dedication questioned, to hold and express my views conscientiously.

"I regret that I cannot, for the reasons I have indicated, sign the document as it is. I will honour the commitment to take the proposal back to Newfoundland to place it before the cabinet and to ask for legislative approval in a free vote, or to put it to a referendum. I must say that a referendum now is almost out of the question. I'll invite every one of you to appear before the legislature to make the wonderful arguments you've made in this room. I'll do everything I possibly can to facilitate this. I will express honest and frank views, but I will not campaign against this agreement. In constitutional terms, the document is not right for a federal country. However, I will put it forward in a way that I hope will receive legislative approval. I will give you the opportunity to make your appeals to the legislature and people of Newfoundland."

"Thank you for your assistance, you and Frank and Gary," I replied. "Am I right in concluding that while you want some time, and your inclination is to consult with your cabinet, you would recommend this position to cabinet?"

"No," Wells answered. "You know my personal intellectual concern. I've been deeply moved, but I'm too involved. I'll take it to cabinet and have cabinet make the decision whether to take it to the legislature for approval or to a referendum."

I tried again. "Can you endorse it in principle?"

"I'll put an endorsement that will leave the decision to the legislature or to a referendum," Wells said. "I'll make the strongest argument I can consistent with my intellectual convictions, to get its approval. I will do nothing to impede ratification."

Later, at about ten-thirty that night, we gathered for a final celebratory meeting open to the public and media in the Government Conference Centre, where all the leaders spoke and signed the official document committing the country to constitutional renewal.

My remarks were deeply felt and optimistic about our future: "History will record that premiers Peterson, Bourassa, and others . . . remained true to their vision of Canada and stood by their original endorsement of the Meech Lake Accord. History will also record that premiers McKenna, Filmon, and Wells have found it possible to expand the consensus. And history will record that Canada's first ministers persevered for seven days to find a way for Quebecers to feel truly part of a united Canada. No one loses in the agreement before us. And Canada wins . . . We should soon be able to turn the page on this chapter of constitutional reform, but we should not forget some of the lessons we have learned from it. One crystal-clear lesson is that a way must be found to ensure public involvement in the constitutional amendment process. None of us wants to put the country through this wrenching process again, and I think I can say without fear of contradiction, none of us wants to go through it, ourselves, again . . .

"After 123 years of Confederation, many English Canadians either do not understand or do not accept that the francophone–anglophone duality remains at the core of our nationhood. And, in Quebec, the regional and cultural complexities of English-speaking Canadians and the profound dissatisfaction with the status quo evident in the West and East have not been fully understood . . .

"With this agreement, we reject the small view of Canada's future. We keep faith with the Fathers of Confederation. We validate the sacrifices of successive generations of Canadians. With the agreement before us, we preserve for our children a united and promising land. Let's work together in a spirit of harmony and trust to complete this chapter of constitutional reform by June 23. Then let's have the biggest, noisiest, happiest, most joyful Canada Day celebration of our lives. And then, united again, let's get on with building the best, most competitive, most compassionate, most tolerant country in the world."

Bourassa was as eloquent and passionate about Canada that night as I was ever to hear. His remarks truly moved me. "For the first time in its history, Quebec sees its distinct character recognized in the Constitution," he stated. "English Canada has understood and accepted that we are recognized for who we are . . . For many Quebecers, since 1981, on the occasion of the exclusion of Quebec from the Canadian Constitution, Canada was a legal country. Now, with the ratification of the Meech Lake Accord, for all Quebecers, Canada is a real country."

We also agreed to the establishment of a national commission to examine the triple-E Senate. Even if nothing came of it in five years – by July 1, 1990 – Peterson's deal-breaker would kick in. We would begin discussing territorial representation on the highest court in the land and agreed to strengthen the rights of women and minorities. Parliament would strike a committee to examine a Canada clause, starting in July of 1990, to report by year's end. We also agreed to study the overall issue of constitutional reform and agreed to acknowledge public discussion on the issue of distinct society.

I covered extensively what came next in my handwritten journal.

—

PERSONAL JOURNAL: JULY 22–24, 1990

July 22:

When we left the conference centre at about 2 a.m. June 9, after the signatures and speeches, Mila said to me, "I don't think you should trust Clyde Wells in any way. I think he has no intention of honouring his signature!"

We were in the car heading for 24 Sussex and I asked why. She replied, "Instinct or intuition, call it what you like, but I watched Wells's face when you and the other first ministers spoke, and he looked like a man who can hardly wait to get out there so that he can break his word!"

I told Mila that he had signed a constitutional instrument on television, undertaking to deploy his best efforts to ensure that the matter came for a vote before June 23, and there was no way for him to avoid holding one. Mila simply replied she had become concerned over the months that Clyde Wells was merely an agent for Pierre Trudeau and his philosophy and that, in the crunch, Wells would be loyal to Pierre Trudeau and would dishonour his signature on a formal document rather than follow through on some undertakings of which his mentor disapproved, even though the eventual costs to Canada might prove to be catastrophic.

I have come to value and rely on Mila's judgment and instincts a great deal. On most important examples, she has turned out to be right. I don't know whether it was the fatigue, the satisfaction, or the serenity that comes from having completed a most challenging task, but I do remember dismissing Mila's concerns by the time we arrived at 24 Sussex, perhaps because I could not conceive of a betrayal so coarse and unprecedented – although in the previous week there had been ample evidence that Wells was a stubborn, vain, and erratic individual.

Filmon had half-heartedly (at best) accepted Meech, even though he had eventually wound up with support from Gary Doer and Sharon Carstairs. In any case, the three Manitobans all endorsed Meech as amended and resolved to bring it to a vote before the 23rd. Filmon had frequently warned me of Elijah Harper of the NDP – that he would oppose Meech, and that this procedural opposition would cost the legislature 48 hours, after which full consideration and debate could begin.

After returning home, the three Manitobans (through their House leaders) prepared a resolution for consideration by the House. It was promptly attacked by Elijah Harper as being fundamentally flawed for procedural reasons. This view was upheld by the Speaker, thereby allowing Harper to exhaust the legislature's time (and relieve Filmon's responsibility) to debate and pass an amended resolution prior to the 23rd.

Had Filmon's government brought in a proper resolution on June 11, would it have passed by the 23rd? And what effect would passage have had on a clearly recalcitrant premier of Newfoundland and Labrador? Historians will decide what effect that procedural flaw in Manitoba had on the subsequent history of Canada, but clearly, in my judgment at least, the effect will have been substantial, and all of it damaging.

On Monday after the signing, Wells called me to say that a referendum was out, but that he would be holding a free vote in the legislature to that end, and to ensure that all MHAs received the best views of the first ministers, he proposed to invite me, along with a number of other premiers, to St. John's to speak to the House prior to the vote. I accepted in principle, but left the detailed discussions to Lowell.

July 24:

Some days later, Wells called again to repeat his invitation. I was disinclined, because he had already seriously violated the "even-handed approach" he had assured his fellow first ministers he would adopt, and was now actually campaigning to subvert the agreement he had just signed! He said he wanted MHAs to hear some of the serious economic and political forecasts I had made privately. When I indicated that would be impossible (a PM forecasting possible economic damage for his own nation was certain to be a self-fulfilling prophecy), he asked whether I would speak privately to the party caucuses, a proposal I did not reject. A few days later he told Lowell that the idea was no longer acceptable – and that if I refused his original offer, I would be blamed if Meech were rejected by the Nfld. legislature!

At about this time, Mose Morgan, former president of Memorial University and a great supporter of Wells, contacted Paul Desmarais, former chancellor of Memorial, and urged me strongly to attend and speak. (Paul Desmarais played an absolutely key and constructive role throughout, attempting to get both Wells and Chrétien to give support to Meech.)

In a final call to me, Wells reiterated his original invitation, but hinted he might invite people on the other side such as Don Johnston and Pierre Trudeau. I immediately told him he had invited the prime minister and premiers, and that I would not participate in any debating society he chose to put together for the occasion. Finally, it was agreed that Peterson, McKenna, Devine, and I would speak to the legislators, after which they would exercise their rights and vote it up or down.

—

I was later to learn that Wells and his team were planning not to allow the vote to proceed at all. A disturbing incident occurred at the Conference of Eastern Canadian Premiers and New England Governors in Mystic, Connecticut. Dr. Charles MacMillan, economic advisor to the Maritime provinces, was approached by Premier Wells. "He told me he wasn't going to hold a vote," a shocked MacMillan wrote later.

The Ottawa *Citizen* of Monday June 18 reported: "Premier Clyde Wells said today the Saturday deadline for ratifying the Meech Lake Accord should be ditched. He also suggested he might cancel a planned vote on the constitutional package in Newfoundland. Wells said his final decision on a vote will depend on what happens in Manitoba, where the accord is bogged down in procedural wrangling and opposition by native groups. 'If Manitoba can't have a vote before June 23, then whether Newfoundland does it or does not is academic,' Wells told reporters as he entered a conference with New England governors."

After this conference, premiers Peterson, McKenna, and Ghiz all called Lowell Murray and advised him that they did not believe Clyde Wells intended to hold a vote. They also told Murray that I should not go to Newfoundland, as it was a trap. And on June 20, Bill McNamara, an accomplished young lawyer who had become a strong Meech supporter, called his classmate and friend Deborah Coyne to suggest that, given the unanimous agreement, they bury the hatchet and join forces in supporting the initiative prior to the vote. "There is not going to be a vote," Wells's constitutional advisor told McNamara firmly.

I must take some of the blame for the hostile political environment around this time. After we had finally reached an agreement on June 9 in the Langevin Block, in a relaxed encounter with journalists from the *Globe and Mail*, I remarked that, because of the unique circumstances, I had had to "roll the dice" to get a deal. By this I meant simply that I had had to try everything humanly possible in that limited time frame to achieve success, otherwise the initiative would have failed. My intention was benign and the phrase was one I had frequently used in the past. (Another similar colourful phrase was used by the negotiators trying to bring peace to Northern Ireland about this time. When it seemed that the deadline would pass before all of the details were agreed, they commented that they might have to "shoot out all the clocks!" It was a fine, memorable phrase, and nobody objected.)

Publication of my words, however, created a furor and caused me serious embarrassment, as they conveyed the impression of a prime minister prepared to act like a riverboat gambler with the future of the country. A colourful turn of phrase, innocently intended, became a club that was used by my many opponents to beat me mercilessly for a number of days. The statement is still referred to by some of Meech's fiercest opponents as evidence of skullduggery on my part.

In politics, when you do or say something that your opponents can enthusiastically transform into an attack on you or your motives – however innocent your intentions – it's your fault. And this damaging blunder was mine, no one else's.

My journal continues:

—

PERSONAL JOURNAL: JULY 26, 1990

On the basis of that understanding, we all went to St. John's and spoke. I was not present the first day but learned that the premiers, particularly Peterson, spoke extremely well. Just prior to Peterson's speech, Wells's attorney-general, Paul Dicks, spoke of Meech as a surrender to Quebec, suggesting that I was Neville Chamberlain (and presumably Quebecers were Nazis, although he didn't go quite that far). He clearly conveyed his contempt for Meech, the federal government, Ottawa, Quebec, and me, in no particular order.

Peterson was shaken by this appalling display of tastelessness by a senior minister of Wells's government, and called me right after to advise me to stay away. He thought Meech was going to pass, but he said Wells was "a crazy bastard" and would look for someone to blame right up to the final moment.

Lowell immediately called Wells and excoriated Dicks, saying that had the roles been reversed, "Mulroney would have fired on the spot a minister who made such pejorative allusions to the premier of Newfoundland." Wells immediately called me to say that I shouldn't pay any attention to "an idiot who ran off at the mouth," and said he thought my appearance, scheduled for the next day, could have "a significant and beneficial impact" on the vote!

I went to Newfoundland the next day for two reasons: first, because I wanted to help get the four or five Liberal votes required to pass it; and, secondly, I wanted to prevent what Lowell and I were convinced Wells sought to do: defeat Meech Lake and then blame my failure to show up as evidence of callous disregard from Ottawa, typical of the entire perfidious manner Meech was put together in the first place!

I spoke for about an hour without a text. When it was over Wells told Murray, "The PM made a superb speech – I expect it will have a significant impact."

I then went off to have dinner with Wells and his wife, Eleanor, a very nice woman who received me very graciously and began by saying, "I just told Clyde that, having watched your speech very carefully, I am persuaded you scored points, because the tone and the approach were right and will impress Newfoundlanders."

Throughout a delightful seafood dinner we chatted about mutual friends (Frank and Janis Moores, Rick and Roseann Cashin), our families, and Canada. From time to time I sought to elicit Wells's view on how the vote would go the next day, but with modest success. He did say that Meech was in no way comparable to Trudeau's surrender of the notwithstanding clause because the clause "destroyed at least half the impact and effectiveness of the Charter." I was struck by that statement, because it was the first and only time in our association that I had heard him criticize Trudeau directly. He told me that every Liberal attending the Calgary leadership convention from Newfoundland would support Chrétien, and was obviously skeptical of any suggestion I made that Chrétien's anti-Meech stand would eventually damage him and perhaps doom his party. Wells was clearly of the view that he could shoot down Meech Lake without consequences of significance to the future of the nation.

Just prior to leaving his home to head for the airport (I had thanked Eleanor warmly and signed her guestbook "With gratitude for a delightful evening," I recall), I said directly, "Clyde, this vote tomorrow is of great significance to Canada. On a scale of 1 to 10, can you indicate to me now how the vote will go?" He replied, "That it will pass? A 5!" With that I stepped out into a very rainy St. John's night, went to the airport, and flew home, where I convened a meeting for approximately midnight.

On the plane, Lowell and others told me of the glowing media reports and private compliments that had been made about my speech during the two-hour dinner. I spoke to Mila, my toughest critic, and she thought it had been one of my best. Interestingly enough, what she liked most was the tone, which echoed the comments made by Eleanor Wells! I was pleased with my effort and gratified by the analysis because of the symbolism of such a speech. Had I bombed, one would have heard the comments instantaneously across the nation, all of it critical and predicting that, as a result, the vote would probably fail tomorrow!

As it was, I shared David Peterson's optimism that the vote would probably pass – not by much, but that Wells would find a way to free up a few Liberals who would support the Tories (courageous souls they were, to a man and a woman). I was pleased as well by Wells's assessment of 5 out of 10 for passage, given his ferocious opposition to the accord itself. It was in my judgment a positive signal, one among others (however faint) that had been discerned earlier by premiers Peterson, McKenna, and Devine, and conveyed directly to me.

When I met at 24 Sussex with Murray, Tellier, Spector and Hartt, I believed the mood was confident. They had all heard from their own sources and were strong in their praise of my speech and the fact that it would appreciably help tomorrow's vote. And then, more good news: John Crosbie called to say that their overnight polling revealed an 11 per cent jump among Newfoundlanders, who now said they thought Meech should be passed. John Crosbie, Rick Cashin, Craig Dobbin, etc., were extremely pleased both with the speech, its impact upon individual MHAs, and the prospects for the vote the next afternoon. When the group left and I finally got to bed I was confident, satisfied that I had done my very best. I looked forward to a close but positive vote.

—

(Right after the Liberal convention, in fact, Frank McKenna told Lowell Murray that Newfoundland MP Brian Tobin had told him he was sure Meech would have passed – if a vote had been held.)

—

At about 10 a.m. the next day I was advised by Paul Tellier that Wells had just informed Lowell Murray that he might cancel the vote scheduled for the afternoon. A lengthy meeting began soon after at 24 with Maz, Stanley, Tellier, Spector, and Murray. I made and received many calls from Paul Desmarais, who was in close contact with Chrétien's campaign chairman, John Rae, in Calgary, and Mose Morgan in St. John's, who was growing more exasperated by the minute with his "star student," who now was hours away from betraying his signature, his commitment to me and the first ministers, and his understanding of the nation – which included Mose!

It was decided that, given the formal undertaking by the three Manitoba party leaders that Meech would already have passed had it not been for the procedural flaw and that, in any case, it would pass within a brief period of time, the Government of Canada could address the Supreme Court for a ruling on time-frame extensions if the Newfoundland legislature passed Meech that day. Such passage would have meant that nine provinces representing well over 90 per cent of the population had voted to approve, with the one remaining province having been temporarily prevented from acting, having previously conveyed its intentions to pass it through public undertakings by the three leaders. Based on this clear demonstration of intent and good faith, we intended to ask the court to declare the Saskatchewan passage in 1987 as the trigger date, thereby giving Manitoba time to act, following which Quebec would vote the resolution one more time, becoming the last (rather than the first) province to ratify Meech.

I discussed this with Bourassa, and Spector did likewise with officials in Quebec. They were apprehensive but supportive. Maz had tried to persuade Filmon to keep his legislature going and at least had persuaded him not to adjourn/prorogue. In Manitoba, when they rose at noon, they did so in a manner where recall was a simple task.

Lowell went before the TV cameras to announce our strategy and to indicate it was predicated entirely on passage of Meech through a vote that afternoon in the Newfoundland legislature.

Notwithstanding the best efforts of Tom Rideout, John Crosbie, Mose Morgan, etc., Wells decided to cancel the vote. He would move to adjourn the legislature, thereby depriving MHAs of their right to vote on a matter of historic national import.

Wells had been in touch regularly with Filmon ever since the Ottawa meetings and has since admitted he called him at 1:30 a.m. Nfld. time, which would have been precisely when we were meeting at 24. Filmon never shared any of this information with us. He had made his bed with a Trudeau Liberal and was going to stick with him. Even Filmon's predecessor, Sterling Lyon (no friend of mine, even though I appointed him to the highest court in Manitoba), would have been uncomfortable with this remarkable irony.

Mose Morgan made one last effort to convince Wells to hold the vote and was rebuffed. John Crosbie, Rick Cashin, and Frank Moores believe that the vote would have succeeded. In retrospect I am not sure.

It is obvious now (and confirmed by the spectacle of Wells being hugged by Trudeau and Chrétien at the Calgary convention) that Mila's gut feeling was right, the night we all signed the agreement in Ottawa at the Conference Centre. Wells had signed the document – with the greatest of reluctance – and had sought since then every conceivable opportunity to undermine it at home and to ensure its eventual defeat. Wells is an intelligent man with, no doubt, many fine personal qualities. But his misleading the nation, the first ministers who were invited down to speak, and the members of the House of Assembly was the work of a vain, egocentric, and consumed man. It was to be his vision of Canada – or perhaps no Canada at all. The lawyer from Corner Brook who fancied himself somewhat of a constitutional scholar confirmed, in the crunch, the adage that "a little learning is a dangerous thing." Not for him the admission of error of a Frank McKenna or "The country must come first" attitude of a David Peterson or the "It's not perfect but it means greater unity and achievement" approach of a Don Getty. Clyde Wells had come from complete obscurity to centre stage in less than a year and, if nothing else, he would ensure the nation remembered him, no matter the cost. And so Clyde Wells, in a fit of petulance and rage, stomped his foot and

> *decided the duly elected members of the House of Assembly would never have the opportunity of voting on a matter that might well affect the ongoing existence of Canada, because he decided to cancel their vote. He extinguished the most fundamental right a parliamentarian has, simply because he did not want to run the risk that it might pass.*
>
> *In a most illuminating exchange, Bill Cameron of* The Journal *in a CBC TV interview three times says to Wells, "But, Mr. Premier, you had the prime minister down to speak to your legislature and then you invited him to your home for dinner. Did you, Mr. Wells, at any time tell the prime minister of Canada during these hours you were together that you intended to cancel a historic vote the very next day?"*
>
> *And three times Premier Wells replies, "Honestly, Bill, I just don't remember."*

—

And that is exactly what Wells did. He walked into the Newfoundland Assembly and adjourned the House, thereby depriving the elected members of their right to vote on a major constitutional change that he himself had signed and sworn he would put to a vote.

Robert Stanfield commented on this episode in a letter he wrote to me when I announced my retirement three years later: "As prime minister, you have had your disappointments, notably Meech Lake . . . but I doubt if God Almighty could have changed the mind of Wells and stiffened the back of the premier of Manitoba."

With that Meech Lake was killed off; it didn't fail. I had three times succeeded in securing unanimous agreement. Yet Meech was suffocated in a cruel act of political infanticide by the premier of Newfoundland. With that accomplished, Wells flew off to the Liberal leadership convention in Calgary, where he was greeted by Jean Chrétien with the memorable words, "*Merci, Clyde, pour ton beau travail.*" (Thank you, Clyde, for your good work.)

In my extemporaneous remarks to the legislature in St. John's, I had said, "Nobody can predict the future, but I know this: that if Mr. Parizeau gets a chance to have a referendum, on referendum night, as you, every one of the members of this House of Assembly right here and all the rest of us too, on that night when you're sitting there with your families and your children, one thought is going to go through your mind. And that thought, when you're looking at your kids, is: Do you mean to tell me that we could have avoided all of this through Meech Lake? And I can also tell you that night, if that night were ever to come, the terms of Meech Lake are going to look very, very reasonable indeed to every member of this House of Assembly, and every House of Assembly across Canada."

Five years later, Mr. Parizeau got his referendum. As Canadians watched transfixed in horror, all night the television screens flashed numbers indicating a likely separatist win. At the very end and by an eyelash, the cause of a united Canada prevailed, by a mere 54,288 votes out of 4,757,509 cast. And we know, because he has openly admitted it, that if the vote had gone the other way, even by one vote, Parizeau would have taken Quebec out of Canada in a heartbeat.

When the media sought the next day to question Mr. Trudeau and his acolytes about this devastating result – so contrary to what they had so often predicted – the answer was "no comment."

For me, the end of Meech was like a death in the family. I carry with me to this very day a throbbing sense of loss for one of the greatest might-have-beens in Canada's 140-year history. I carry with me as well the scars from those battles – some self-inflicted, others not – that I wear as a badge of honour secured in an honourable attempt to strengthen our nation.

That fateful night – June 23, 1990 – while others celebrated in Calgary, I spoke with a broken heart to a shaken country, "I do not hide from you my great disappointment at the setback Canadians have suffered today. But there is no dishonour in having tried to overcome a serious threat to our unity. No achievement is possible without great effort. Such effort always carries with it the risk of failure. But I would rather have failed trying to advance the cause of Canada's unity than to have simply played it safe, done nothing or criticized from the sidelines. To govern is to choose. To lead is to run the risk of failure."

But in fact Meech was not a "failure" – it was a success. The process proved to be its undoing: three times I secured unanimous agreement, along with signed undertakings by the provinces to hold a vote in their legislatures. But what can be done when a premier dishonours that undertaking and cancels the scheduled vote, thereby destroying the agreement?

I leave it to others to argue whether the partial agreement of 1982 – a Constitution assented to by nine provinces – justifies the fundamental compromises accepted by the federal government. But I must confess that twenty years after the Meech Lake debate began, I am still intrigued by the logic of those who earnestly defend the 1982 compromises, which led to an incomplete constitutional agreement, yet condemn the relatively modest compromises of Meech Lake, which produced unanimity and would have obtained the belated consent of Quebec to the 1982 Constitution, thereby strengthening the cause of Canada's unity.

1990

5. Oka, Iraq, and Thatcher's Fall

ONLY A WEEK AFTER the death of the Meech Lake Accord, Her Majesty the Queen came to Ottawa to participate in Canada Day celebrations. She addressed a crowd of seventy thousand on Parliament Hill and made a heartfelt plea for Canadian unity. Her address that day was the most emotional I'd ever seen her give, and I was touched by her genuine affection for Canada.

"Canada is a country that has been blessed beyond most countries in the world," she said. "It is a country worth working for. There is in Canada, and about Canadians, a constant search for fairness, a receptiveness to honourable accommodation, enabling the two principal language communities to flourish within the Canadian family. Those values are needed now, more than ever. Beyond the celebration of today lies the challenge of tomorrow. The unity of the Canadian people and their will to live together will be tested in the months ahead. It is my fondest wish for this Canada Day that Canadians come together and remain together, rather than dwelling on differences which might further divide them. I am not just a fair-weather friend, and I am glad to be here at this sensitive time. I hope my presence may call to mind those many years of shared experience, and raise new hopes for the future. The unity of the Canadian people was the paramount issue in 1867, as it is today. There is no force, except the force of will, to keep Canadians together."

Three days later I left Canada to attend a crucial two-day summit of NATO leaders in London. The Alliance eventually decided to extend the hand of friendship to its former adversaries in the East Bloc by inviting Gorbachev himself to meet with the group at a later date. I discovered that I couldn't leave Meech Lake behind. "I saw you on television, Brian, looking so tired," a concerned Margaret Thatcher told me. She then gave me a good pep talk, reminding me that it is in a crisis that a leader is truly tested.

She was right, I was exhausted, but there was no time to rest. After the NATO meeting I flew back across the Atlantic to attend the annual G-7 Summit in Houston, Texas, where George Bush and I met privately at Manor House before the official group discussions. I found that he was still bristling at suggestions that his country should hand over billions of dollars in economic aid to the USSR while that country was still pointing ICBMs at the United States and was giving billions in aid to Cuba.

Still, I told the president, we had to do everything we could to keep encouraging Gorbachev's reforms. Michael Wilson and I described to him Canada's idea that the G-7 countries commit to undertake a joint study of the best way to offer economic aid to the Soviets. I hoped this suggestion would bridge the division within the group. Helmut Kohl, for example, wanted as smooth as possible a transition to a united Germany and hoped that billions could be found to mollify the USSR.

"I note that you link the short-term credits issue to the need for a constructive approach by the Soviet Union on the question of German reunification," I had told Kohl in an exchange of letters before the summit. "I agree that the Economic Summit in Houston must address these questions and would suggest that they be considered, at the same time, in the context of an assessment of the progress which is actually being made toward a market-based economy in the Soviet Union."

In the end, the G-7 reached a political agreement to remove barriers to free trade in agricultural products, agreed to send experts to the USSR to report back on the best way for the West to offer aid, and announced a renewed commitment to battle greenhouse gases. We also fought off a move by Japan to drop the sanctions against China that the G-7 had announced the previous year in Paris. Canada's sherpa, Derek Burney, wrote the compromise paragraph that saved the day, which read: "We acknowledge some of the recent developments in China, but believe that the prospects for closer cooperation will be enhanced by renewed political and economic reform, particularly in the field of human rights."

I wrote to President Gorbachev shortly after I arrived home from Texas. "In your letter to President Bush, you asked us as Western leaders to support your effort to change things. When we discussed your letter, I advised my summit colleagues that we should say yes. I am gratified they all shared that view. We say yes to the sustained dialogue that you have proposed. We know that your reform policies, if effective, will not only benefit your nation. They will advance the interests of all of us."

On the social side, George Bush had planned the summit with a Texas flair. One event found the leaders in a barn, wearing Stetsons and cowboy boots, and I'll never forget watching Prime Minister Thatcher delicately step around cattle droppings. A stroll down Whitehall it wasn't.

To my surprise, François Mitterrand seemed to enjoy the wailing country and western music, and I remember him tapping his booted foot and humming along. "François," I said, "vraiment, aimes-tu la musique du Far West?"

"Oui, Brian," he replied. "Je suis Hopalong Cassidy!"

While I was in Houston, word reached me that Canada had been hit by another crisis. In March, natives at Oka, Quebec had erected a barricade to block the expansion of a golf course on disputed land. On July 11, one hundred Quebec police officers had stormed the barricade. In the melee that followed, a thirty-one-year-old officer, Marcel Lemay, was killed. An extremely tense standoff became worse, and the army was called in.

Members of the Mohawk Warriors Society then blockaded the Mercier Bridge, cutting off thousands of South Shore residents from their commute into downtown Montreal. Non-aboriginals now got into the act, holding protests and even burning effigies of natives to express their rage.

—

PERSONAL JOURNAL: JULY 22–24, 1990

I had hoped that following the collapse of Meech, the royal visit, the NATO Summit in London, and the Houston meetings, I could recharge my batteries for a while and then begin rebuilding the cabinet, PMO, our agenda, and, eventually, our credibility across the country. But the day the summit ended, a police officer was killed in a shootout at Oka and since then the Mercier Bridge has been barricaded by Mohawk warriors, and a sense of unease and dissatisfaction (and racism) has been building (pro and anti) in some quarters across Canada. As a consequence, I have been preoccupied and troubled as we have tried to wrestle with the great emotional issues of land and law and order, both of which predominate in this dispute.

As usual, the natives have a valid position, but it has been despoiled first by the warriors, who took the law into their own hands and also by the outsiders who seek publicity at the long-term expense of the fundamental interests of native peoples. I am not happy, either, with Canada's achievement vis-à-vis natives or my own government's – even though we tried mightily on constitutional amendments, public expenditures, etc. The fact is that Canada's native peoples have been abused and mistreated for generations and that Canada has never been ready to finally come to grips with their historical claims on land and self-government. It is one of the great ironies of my life that the Meech Lake Accord, which brought Quebec back to the constitutional table, thereby strengthening immeasurably the possibility of obtaining justice for Canada's natives, should have been defeated, in some measure, by the efforts of Elijah Harper in the Manitoba legislature, with the enthusiastic support of native communities across Canada!

—

Not wanting to pour gas on an already flaring situation, I kept out of the public eye after I flew home to deal with the crisis. Chief of the Defence Staff General John de Chastelain briefed cabinet. I asked him how long it would take to remove the warriors from the bridge. He didn't smile as he answered my question. "About twenty minutes," he said, "but people will be killed."

Law-abiding citizens were outraged at the sight of masked natives with guns controlling a federal bridge, forcing commuters to waste hours in a circuitous drive twice a day to get to and from work. A dramatic assault on the bridge would have satisfied some understandable frustrations, but it would have exacerbated tensions for decades.

I decided on a carrot-and-stick approach. As a carrot, I announced on August 8 that the highly respected Alan Gold, chief justice of the Quebec Superior Court, would serve as mediator to seek agreement on preconditions to full negotiations. The stick? I also said that the Canadian Armed Forces would be available to the Quebec government, which ultimately did call on them. Bernard Roy agreed to serve as federal negotiator. All parties in the dispute knew he had my full and complete trust.

There were still scuffles to come, and photos of Canadian soldiers and Mohawk warriors rifle-butting each other haunt me to this day. In late September, the remaining Mohawks, who had holed up in Kanesatake's detox centre, finally left, ending the seventy-eight-day standoff.

"Firmness, patience, and concern for human life have carried the day," I said at the end of the crisis. I also pledged to place native concerns at the top of my government's agenda. While I didn't like the tactics used by the Mohawks, centuries of ignoring native issues, by governments of all parties both federally and provincially, were now being felt.

"The agenda I have outlined is very far-reaching," I told the Commons. "Its goal is to create a new relationship between aboriginal and non-aboriginal Canadians. It will take courage to see things as they are, honesty to acknowledge them for what they have become and the common resolve to correct them for future generations. Most of all, it will take sustained and firm leadership on the part both of governments and aboriginal peoples. And I give Canadians the assurance of the Government of Canada that every effort will be deployed to ensure that it will be done."

On August 2, 1990, Iraqi dictator Saddam Hussein upped tensions throughout the world, and especially in the volatile Middle East, when he invaded and occupied neighbouring Kuwait. As the world would soon see, anyone who still harboured foolish illusions that George Bush was a wimp was in for a big surprise.

Bush called and asked me to travel to Washington for an off-the-record discussion and briefing over dinner at the White House. As soon as Stanley Hartt and I arrived, the president handed me his government's latest intelligence reports on the situation in the Middle East and told me I could take them back to Ottawa – an important gesture of trust on his part. He then had National Security Advisor Brent Scowcroft update me on immediate American plans to place forces on the ground in Saudi Arabia. As we spoke, Scowcroft said, two squadrons of American F-15s, as well as a brigade from the famed 82nd Airborne Division, were under orders for deployment.

I asked how long it would be before a truly significant American military presence would be available in Saudi Arabia. "By Sunday," Scowcroft replied.

I also asked Bush and Scowcroft about the safety of Americans and other nationals who were still in Iraq. "Have you thought this through fully?" I asked, well aware that a hostage crisis could weaken Americans' support for military intervention and limit the administration's options.

Scowcroft had a chilling response. He said that President Jimmy Carter's decision to view the release of American hostages in 1979–80 in Iran as paramount had been a grave error. "The containment of Saddam Hussein is the objective, and while potential hostages found in a theatre of war would be a major concern, they could not be allowed to become the focal point of the American strategic effort," he calmly responded. George Bush and his team meant business.

I repeatedly urged Bush to work at building a broad consensus among his international allies before taking any American action. I told him to look to the UN, NATO, and the USSR for support. "You must have consensus and you, a former U.S. ambassador to the United Nations, are perfectly situated to achieve just that," I stressed.

We discussed possible reactions among allies and the need for their support. When Bush mentioned Thatcher, I said, "George, the one you need first is Mitterrand. He's sensitive to slights, but will respond strongly if he feels America is consulting with him first. He's a strong ally but wants France to be treated with respect at all times. You should call Mitterrand at three tomorrow morning, your time, so yours is the first call he receives in Paris tomorrow when he gets to his office at nine. He will be well aware what time you are placing the call from Washington. Tell him what your early response and plans are. He will want to help only if he thinks he is receiving fair treatment from the United States."

On the spot, Bush picked up a phone by his chair and asked the White House operator to wake him at three so he could place the call. Sure enough, the president of France was immediately responsive, and remained onside throughout the crisis.

Before arriving in Washington I had spoken on the telephone with our NATO partner, President Turgut Özal of Turkey. He had met with an emissary of Saddam Hussein, who had told him, "The West is bluffing." The Turkish leader, whose country shares a border with Iraq, said to me that he was willing to blockade all oil coming out of Iraq. He warned, however, that Hussein could still get his oil out and raise the much-needed cash to fuel his military objectives, by sending it through Aqaba in Jordan. I shared all of this information with President Bush.

I also conveyed to Bush the shocking story Egypt's Hosni Mubarak had told me after he met with an emissary from Baghdad. "Mubarak said the Iraqi came in and announced that Kuwait has five hundred billion dollars they can put their hands on," I told Bush. "The first thing they would do with that money would be to help Egypt. They were trying to tell Mubarak that there would be $20 billion for Egypt if Egypt supported Iraq. Mubarak said, 'We won't sell our principles.' He told the Iraqi he thought they would be driven out of Kuwait. The Iraqi response was that they would never accept that. What has clearly happened is that the Iraqis have just robbed the bank and will split it up with whoever will support them."

On August 24 Canada dispatched two destroyers and a supply ship to the region to assist in enforcing the UN economic embargo against Iraq. In mid-September I also announced that a squadron of CF-18 fighters from Europe would be deployed to the Persian Gulf to support the UN mission. On September 15 the governor general signed the cabinet order placing the Canadian Task Force on active duty.

Margaret Thatcher soon wrote to me: "I just wanted to let you know how very much we appreciated your decision to send aircraft to the Gulf, to join Canada's ships there. That is very welcome indeed. It is so important that we should all be seen to be present alongside the United States. That is the best hope of convincing Saddam Hussein that there is no way out except withdrawal from Kuwait."

I kept up my efforts to promote a diplomatic solution to the crisis. During an earlier visit by my family to the Bush retreat in Kennebunkport, the president had expressed his anger at King Hussein, who he thought was attempting to play the two sides in the conflict off against each other. I felt that the king was being squeezed into these positions by Saddam Hussein, and urged the president to meet with the Jordanian king in person. That channel of communication, I argued, would be crucial in the coming weeks and months. Bush did later bring King Hussein to Kennebunkport, and tensions eased somewhat.

I also told the president that it was vital he seek a UN resolution authorizing the coalition's actions. "Without that," I said, "Canada cannot support this initiative."

I travelled to Kennebunkport a few weeks later for further discussions with Bush as the crisis evolved. At the time, the president was receiving military advice, some of which called for the United States on its own to undertake a surgical strike into Iraq. Using an apt sports analogy, I advised the president to reject such advice. The coalition was coming into being, Bush was up "70–0," I said. There was no need for a "long bomb," I told him. An apt comparison.

After our meeting, Bush and I spoke to the press. "Certainly one of the most important days of the United Nations since its foundation," I said, "have been the series of resolutions in respect of Iraq, where the United

Nations . . . dealt effectively and well with a rogue leader who sought to annex another nation and believed that he could conduct himself with impunity, both vis-à-vis his Arab neighbours and the world."

A few weeks later Bush met with Mikhail Gorbachev in Helsinki. "Saddam is a bad guy who has gone off the deep end," the latter told the American president. While the USSR had some concerns about the use of force in the Middle East, Gorbachev said he wouldn't stand in the way. His country was now playing a positive and constructive role on the world stage. History was again moving quickly.

"I was very pleased and impressed with your success earlier today in Helsinki. Both the message and the signals sent a powerful signal to Iraq that its options dwindle daily," I wrote to Bush the day his meetings with his Soviet counterpart concluded. "I believe your strong and thoughtful discussions over the last few months have energized the Security Council, inspired our allies, and thrown the fear of God into Saddam Hussein! If presidencies are defined by specific events, it seems to me that your careful and effective handling of this major crisis will impact heavily and beneficially on the manner in which the Bush administration is judged by history."

Shortly after making the announcement that we were enlarging the Senate to ensure passage of the GST – a definite unpopularity generator, if there ever was one – I departed for New York City and the UN World Summit for Children. I had been asked to co-chair the event, along with President Moussa Traoré of Mali, and more than seventy world leaders had agreed to attend, the largest such number in history to that date. It was among the most challenging assignments I had ever faced. All the leaders wanted to speak, and keeping order for addresses by leaders of the stature of Margaret Thatcher, Helmut Kohl, and others was, shall we say, challenging. We warned them ahead of time. "We must all be succinct and make our statements within the time allotted," Traoré and I wrote each participant beforehand. "We will be obliged without exception to tap the gavel at time plus fifteen seconds and bring down the gavel to end interventions at time plus thirty seconds." Despite the written warning, some leaders tried to get around our gavels. Kohl even gently reprimanded me when I let Margaret, in his view at least, speak too long.

While all the goals of that summit have not yet been achieved, we were able to make progress in helping to make a better world for children. "That meeting produced a declaration and plan of action that are among the most rigorously monitored and implemented international commitments of the last decade," a UNICEF press statement said in 2002. "Annual national and periodic reviews of the 1990 goals have produced the most extensive set of data ever compiled on the status of children . . . One area of notable improvement [since 1990] is child health. Over the last decade, low-cost, high-impact programs have helped drop global under-five mortality rates by more than 10 per cent, with 63 countries achieving the summit goal of one-third reduction . . . But the overall picture shows how much work remains unfinished. Nearly 11 million children still die each year, often from readily preventable causes. An estimated 150 million children are malnourished. Over 120 million are still out of school. Tens of millions work, often in abusive conditions. Millions more are exposed to conflict and other forms of violence."

With figures like those we can't claim the summit was a complete success. Much work, here in Canada and around the globe, remains. We gave it a start and it is to a whole new generation of world leaders that the torch has been passed. Let them learn from our failures in the years since 1990 and move forward.

The Children's Summit was a place where the world gathered, and several leaders held bilateral meetings where the Gulf War was discussed. During one of my meetings with President Bush, for example, I filled him in on a luncheon conversation I had had with Queen Noor of Jordan. Note-takers recorded the conversation I had with the president:

> The PM had emphasized to the queen that Saddam Hussein must leave Kuwait quickly. The PM knew the American mood and knew that the American people would get tired of a limbo situation, especially one involving enormous costs. They will act swiftly, especially if challenged. They would destroy Saddam Hussein "in 15 minutes." . . . The queen then asked about a face-saver for Saddam Hussein. The PM said that, if Saddam Hussein sent a direct signal of his intention to withdraw, many things might be possible. Saddam Hussein could have his territorial and financial claims arbitrated at the World Court. The Arab states themselves could pick up the tab for the costs of his invasion . . .
>
> The queen had listened very carefully. She asked whether there was any difference between the president and Secretary Baker on this issue. The PM had demonstrated graphically that

> there was no daylight between the two. The queen stated that she wanted to give these impressions immediately to her husband, who was about to meet Iraq's foreign minister. The PM reiterated that time was running out but that a clear signal of withdrawal might lead to a face-saving meeting with the secretary-general and others. "My husband must know this," repeated the queen . . .
>
> The president stated the PM's report was interesting. He had put the U.S. position "exactly right." The president recognized that, as an American, the queen was under immense pressure. Nevertheless, he and the administration generally were infuriated by Jordan's most recent calls for a political conference. He reiterated to the PM that, according to Mubarak, King Hussein "had been bought" by Saddam Hussein prior to the Kuwait invasion.

My dealings with President Bush during this time were not restricted to the troubling events in the Middle East. On November 15, to my great relief, Bush ended a decade of frustration and formally signed his government's *Clean Air Act*, paving the way for the long-awaited acid rain treaty between Canada and the United States. He made a special point of inviting Ambassador Derek Burney to the ceremony and of praising Canada's role in forcing the United States finally to take this step. "I would first like to welcome the ambassador from Canada, our friend, Derek Burney, who represents, I think, by being here, his countrymen's concern for our common environment," Bush said, before signing the bill.

I headed to Paris in November to participate in the meetings of the Conference for Security and Cooperation in Europe, where leaders were attempting to craft what became known as the Charter of Paris for a New Europe. The meeting marked the successful attempt by western Europe – and Canada and the United States – to bring the former East Bloc countries into what had become known as the "new world order." Some later called it the "peace conference" of the Cold War.

Before leaving for Paris I met at the Ritz in Montreal with British press baron and Labour MP Robert Maxwell, who was accompanied by his Canadian advisor André Bisson. As he left, Maxwell said, "Prime Minister, I regret to tell you that your friend Mrs. Thatcher will soon be overthrown by her own party." When I expressed my disbelief, Maxwell showed me a *Times* editorial appearing the next morning that described such a challenge

August 1992. I and Joe Clark and a new group of premiers – including Mike Harcourt, Roy Romanow, Bob Rae, and Donald Cameron – assemble at Harrington Lake to hammer out what will become the Charlottetown Accord

Inside the room at Harrington Lake

Working to persuade Clyde Wells at Charlottetown

June 23, 1990. The day the Meech dream died

June 9, a general view of the table

June 9, and even Clyde Wells and Gary Filmon are laughing, with Bill Vander Zalm in the background

June 1990. In St. John's to address the Newfoundland legislature, prior to their holding the vote promised by Clyde Wells

June 4, 1990. Now things are tense, as I meet with Ghiz and Peterson

Roger Tassé, Lowell Murray, Paul Tellier, and I fear that the deal may be falling apart

June 8, and things are looking up, as Grant Devine, Frank McKenna, Don Getty, I, and John Buchanan relax

A post-wedding reception for Lucien Bouchard and his new wife, Audrey Best, that I gave at 24 Sussex in February 1989

At the fateful Quebec caucus meeting in Mont-Tremblant, May 1990, Bouchard tells me and André Harvey (standing) not to worry about stories of possible defections, that all is well

June 1987. At the Langevin Block, with Bourassa and Vander Zalm

David Peterson is at the centre of a group of advisors discussing "distinct society"

Success, as everyone applauds the agreement

April 1987. The conclusion of the first Meech Lake negotiations with all the premiers. From the left: Richard Hatfield, Robert Bourassa, David Peterson, John Buchanan, Howard Pawley, Bill Vander Zalm, Joe Ghiz, Grant Devine, Brian Peckford, and Don Getty

At the negotiating table

Pawley, Bourassa, me, Devine, and Hatfield

With three members of the free trade negotiating team – Gordon Ritchie, Derek Burney, and Simon Reisman

The night we won "the free trade election." November 1988 in the arena in Baie-Comeau

Greeted by Marjory LeBreton after winning

Moving the Free Trade Agreement in the House, December 1988, with Mike Wilson (on my left), Marcel Masse, Joe Clark, and (half hidden) John Crosbie

and said, "This is only the beginning. She is through" – a comment he repeated to me for effect, and clearly with some pleasure.

With this information in mind, I watched Mrs. Thatcher closely throughout my time in Paris and made journal entries about her performance under stress, with her leadership being decided – and possibly ended – by a vote of her caucus back in Westminster.

—

PERSONAL JOURNAL: NOVEMBER 18–21, 1990

Nov 18:
As I listen to Javier Pérez de Cuéllar speak to the opening session of the CSCE I am struck by the serenity of Margaret Thatcher, who is seated immediately across the table from me. During my conversation with her earlier this morning she was good natured and fatalistic about tomorrow's vote on her leadership. [Her assistants] Charles Powell and Bernard Ingham are also both encouraged. In any event, her cabinet colleague Douglas Hurd appeared slightly more ominous in his observations, though not in any way disloyal. We merely agreed on the dangers inherent in the secret ballot [of caucus].

As I write, Margaret is, as usual, extremely attentive to the speaker, making the occasional note, paying no attention to Hurd or Ricard, who bookend her. In Canada, political leaders have their leadership review votes when they lose elections. Although I believe and hope she was sincere, it remains astonishing that her leadership is challenged after she won three majority victories for the Conservatives.

Nov 19:
At lunch today Margaret, in thanking me for messages of support, acknowledged for the first time, at least to me, that much of the criticism directed at her style was due to the fact she was a woman. I quite frankly agree with her view. It is extremely difficult to govern today, and doubly so if you are a non-male. She was quite free from rancour or bitterness and made no criticism of Geoffrey Howe or Michael Heseltine. She expressed astonishment that she should be challenged after three majorities. I told her that in Canada one normally got a

statue for an achievement of that nature! She said she had challenged Ted Heath because he had lost.

It is now 5 p.m. and Vaclav Havel has just finished speaking. Margaret, however, remains in her seat. She hasn't moved, attentive to the speaker and courteous to all. She looks good, and unhurried and unconcerned, but I can only surmise that deep down she is in a state of great turmoil. She is one of the historic figures of the modern period. Despite our differences on South Africa and sanctions, often acerbic and blunt, I have viewed her with a genuine respect, and hope sincerely she passes the test tomorrow.

Nov 20:
Mrs. Thatcher arrived at the conference this morning about an hour late. This never happens. She is normally the most punctual of leaders. Clearly on this historic day she has been in telephone conversation with MPs, etc. In any case, we shall know early tonight whether this remarkable woman will continue in office or whether she will be unceremoniously dumped while attending a very important international conference. (If it went that way, she would no doubt enjoy the parallel with Churchill, whom she affectionately refers to as Winston.) In any case, she is sitting across from me, some 20 feet away, carefully listening to the oratory of the president of Yugoslavia. She looks striking in an attractive purple suit, resplendent with a beautiful and expensive charm brooch on her right lapel. During all of her public appearances, she has maintained a jaunty, confident air, very much a leader – under attack, perhaps, but not one whose dignity has been impaired by the process. I am confident that she will win tonight, although Robert Maxwell predicted to me Friday night in Montreal that "your friend is finished." But, should she be dislodged, both the U.K. and the world stage will quickly miss her leadership and panache.

Nov 21, 1:45 a.m.:
I have just returned from Versailles, where Mitterrand hosted an impressive formal dinner. Mrs. Thatcher turned up, alone, in spite of the very disappointing vote results broadcast a few hours earlier. She looked very sad when Mila and I chatted with her, while waiting to be called into the salon. The best I could think of saying was, "Margaret,

for what it's worth, we'd vote for you any time." She squeezed my arm, hugged Mila, and said nothing.

Prior to dinner all heads of government were required to get together for drinks. I had seen Margaret in a conversation with a group but I stayed off, almost in a corner, with Mila. We were both tired and despite the splendour of the evening wanted only to get back to the hotel for some sleep. At that point Margaret came up and said simply: "Brian, I need a friend to talk to." I was overwhelmed by the sadness in her eyes and her loneliness at that special moment. She seemed to be reeling from the news and said softly, "I won't leave. If they want me to go, they will have to force me out." From this I concluded, perhaps erroneously, that she didn't believe the ballot next week was inevitable. She said, "What concerns me is the party, the divisions in the party."

I said, "But Margaret, you were challenged, you didn't cause the divisions." She looked at me forlornly, and I asked myself what the prime minister of the United Kingdom, with three majority victories to her credit, was doing at Versailles on the night of her greatest political defeat.

I told her about Diefenbaker, who refused to be driven out and insisted on facing a convention. She looked at me and responded simply, "You know, Brian, I don't want any harm to come to the government or party." Mrs. Thatcher's character and absence of malice were again revealed when she said, "You know that Heseltine has millions. Obviously all those dinner parties with MPs have paid off for him." When I interjected, "It possibly helped as well that he picked up some bills" (referring to dinner) she, thinking I was alluding perhaps to other bills by MPs, said, "No, I have no evidence at all of that." Even at this low point, and in private, she rejected an occasion to denigrate her adversary because it would not have been the truth. I have often noticed that quality in her, her great personal honesty and her almost brutal instinct in defending her own views, but a capacity to turn the page, holding no grudge, after the battle was over. Our own ferocious battles over sanctions against South Africa provided ample evidence of that. Over the years she developed, with Mila and me, a very warm and enjoyable relationship – although I am certain that, to the end, she will consider me a "wet"!

Her searching me out tonight was also exceptional. During such receptions she invariably toured the room chatting with everyone and saved private chats for private moments. She must have been truly bleeding inside to have sought me out for such a sad exchange, because it was not in her character to do so, at least not with me.

We chatted about the vagaries of political life, and Mila and I escorted her to dinner. Dinner was long and she looked stricken throughout, and only martinis and unusually animated conversation kept her attention. She may indeed rebound and win next Tuesday. But I write this note because I fear the end may have come for a most remarkable leader.

—

While I received many shocking letters over the years, the one dated November 19, 1990 and signed by the thirty-ninth president of the United States, Jimmy Carter was simply astounding:

> Iraqi troops must withdraw from Kuwait and President Saddam Hussein must also comply with the basic UN Security Council resolutions. These decisions were well considered and justified. It is of great concern, however, that reliance on international condemnation and economic sanctions to implement the UN resolutions is dissipating . . . Although a military invasion may ultimately become necessary to force Iraq to withdraw from Kuwait, at least one prerequisite should be mandated in a Security Council resolution: the failure of good-faith negotiation with the Iraqi leaders. It violates all principles of dispute resolution to demand total capitulation by Iraqis before their concerns, justified or not, are adequately considered . . . I urge you to make this fateful decision only after assuring adequate opportunity for a peaceful alleviation of the crisis.

Jimmy Carter, a former president, was questioning American foreign policy on the eve of military action! The letter (which was sent to the leaders of all UN Security Council countries) proved once and for all the former nuclear submariner's aversion to war. I quickly let the U.S. administration know about the letter and resolved to stay out of this internal American dispute. I had had enough problems with a former prime minister in Canada, and couldn't concern myself with the actions of a former American president.

Before leaving Europe, I held talks in Rome with Italian President Francesco Cossiga, Prime Minister Giulio Andreotti, and His Holiness the Pope. As always, Pope John Paul II was concerned with the plight of Canada's native people and I filled him in on our plans, post-Oka, to deal with this important file in the months ahead, of which he expressed his approval. The Pope also told me that the same principles that had brought Western forces to Saudi Arabia to effect the removal of Iraqi forces from Kuwait should be applied to the case of Lebanon and the situation faced by the Palestinians.

With that, it was time to leave Europe for high drama in Canada.

1990

6. The Home Front

The aftershocks from the sabotage of Meech Lake continued to rock the domestic scene. Robert Bourassa had by now appointed the Bélanger-Campeau Commission to study the political and constitutional status of Quebec in light of this new reality. Support for sovereignty now reached a record high, and I'm confident in saying that Quebecers would have voted overwhelmingly for sovereignty had a referendum been held that awful summer.

I met with the PC Quebec caucus in Gaspé on August 25. The stakes for the country, my party, and myself were very high going into that meeting, and I knew that a number of our disillusioned MPs were thinking of defecting. "It was very tense," a cabinet minister told the press at the time. "It was clear that some people were prepared to leave caucus if they weren't satisfied with what the prime minister had to tell them."

Lucien Bouchard had by now set up the Bloc Québécois. He was the most popular politician in the province, and the Bloc was cutting into our support in Quebec. On St-Jean-Baptiste Day, following the parade in Montreal, I answered the phone in the bedroom at 24 Sussex. Two Quebec MPs, Louis Plamondon and Benoît Tremblay, were calling to inform me of their intention to cross the floor and join Lucien Bouchard. When I suggested that they meet with me first, there was hesitation. When I told Plamondon that he owed me, a party leader who had led him to two victories in a row, at least this courtesy, he demurred, saying he would call me back after consulting with others. Sometime later he called to say his decision was final. I learned later that the person he consulted was Lucien Bouchard.

A month earlier, Bouchard had said, publicly and in the House, that he would never do anything to destabilize the Conservative caucus, that he would never consider setting up a separate party, and that he strongly urged everyone to support Prime Minister Mulroney, who had defended "the superior interests of Quebec."

With Preston Manning building support for the Reform Party in the West, we were bleeding from both sides. (John Crosbie gave me his own characteristically blunt views on Reform in his annual letter to me in December 1990. "Generally speaking, in Western Canada our problem is the Reform Party," he wrote. "The problem in the West is not western alienation so much as it is western hallucination. Our progress in deficit reduction and in other areas that appeal to those of a conservative nature has to be gotten across and the Reform Party has to be confronted.")

I also watched as Ontario's David Peterson called an election and ended up being the first politician sacrificed to the electorate's angry mood. He had played a vital leadership role in Meech Lake – even offering to give up Ontario Senate seats to help the smaller provinces – in the best traditions of Ontario's leaders, and voters repaid him with a crushing defeat on September 6 that brought in the province's first NDP government, under Bob Rae.

In September I told my full caucus that the time had come for us to ask ourselves some tough questions in light of all that had gone wrong. "We must redefine ourselves as a political party," I said in my opening remarks. "What does the Conservative Party become? What do we stand for? What makes us different from the Liberals and NDP? Have we lost our philosophical moorings? Are we trying to be all things to too many people and coming out looking like nothing of substance? What are our common values that we seek to articulate and defend? Why should Canadians give us their confidence? What do we want to do for Canada now and through the next half of our mandate? These are fundamental questions only caucus can answer."

Members of caucus and cabinet were also up in arms because I was seeking to provide $2.7 billion for the Hibernia project in Newfoundland. Clyde Wells, who had often denigrated the project in the past as not being worth "two fish plants," had changed his mind and was now asking for federal support. My initial reaction was to listen to caucus and cabinet and kill Ottawa's contribution in light of Wells's role in killing Meech, but I never really believed in that sort of retribution, and John Crosbie convinced me to take the high road.

Newfoundland owed a lot to Crosbie, as did Canada. I accepted his advice and began to work to secure support for Hibernia. "Clyde Wells is not Newfoundland," I told caucus. "He wilfully sabotaged a great Canadian initiative [Meech Lake], but he is not Newfoundland. Had he allowed that vote, it would have passed and Newfoundlanders today would be thrilled. But he didn't allow the vote, and he didn't hold the referendum he promised.

Therefore, Newfoundlanders cannot be held responsible for his mean-spiritedness and short-sightedness. I need your help to put forward this huge package of assistance, which will trigger the development of Hibernia."

Caucus and cabinet eventually came around, though some members begrudged the decision. In the bleak economic climate of the early nineties, this outlay of cash to Hibernia was a tremendous drain on the resources of the federal government, but the results now speak for themselves. Thanks in large part to Hibernia, Newfoundland's economy has taken off. I still marvel at the statesmanlike attitudes expressed, especially by the Quebec members of my caucus and cabinet. They stand in stark contrast to the lack of generosity and vision Newfoundland's premier displayed during that dark period.

"Let me say to you on behalf on my constituents in Ferryland District and indeed on behalf of many of your silent supporters, thank you," Newfoundland Tory MHA Charlie Power wrote to me afterwards. "What you have done is a noble deed! It shows your true leadership skills to be able to rise above the pettiness and do what is right. Newfoundland is grateful."

At the same time, the federal Liberals, now led by Jean Chrétien, had begun to play with the very legitimacy of government in Canada itself. They threatened to scuttle legislation on the Goods and Services Tax in the Senate, thereby denying a duly elected government the right to govern. They soon turned the Red Chamber into a circus – blowing kazoos, singing bawdy songs, encircling the Speaker like portly members of a middle-aged gang, and generally casting a dark shadow over Canadian democracy. Journalist Jonathan Ferguson wrote on October 13: "Pounding their desks, slamming Senate rule books on the floor, blowing horns and whistles, and yelling in chorus, Liberal senators set a new low for parliamentary decorum . . . 'Our behaviour was outrageous,' Royce Frith, deputy Liberal leader in the Senate, said sheepishly."

—

PERSONAL JOURNAL: OCTOBER 13, 1990

So far Jean Chrétien's tenure as new Liberal leader has been undistinguished. He has been unimpressive in press encounters and equally so with the voters. His impact in Laurier-Sainte-Marie, the Ontario election, and the Manitoba vote was not immediately viewed as beneficial. He told Michel Vastel in a prominent interview that the 52 Liberal senators will do "exactly what I tell them to do." He then met with the Senate Liberal caucus and announced that "the GST will not pass. It is dead. We will kill it in the Senate." That statement for me was the trigger for the appointment of eight more senators. I had begun filling all the vacancies that had accumulated during the Meech hiatus, but I had strongly resisted advice all summer from the cabinet that I move then to invoke the clause [to create new senators]. In my judgment the deadlock emerging in the Senate on a number of important legislative measures was cast in stone by the injudicious statement of Mr. Chrétien.

I immediately instructed Paul Tellier – I called him at home as soon as I had seen Chrétien on the 10 p.m. news – to follow through on a plan that had been initiated over the summer months by the PCO and other government agencies. We contacted Balmoral Castle, where the Queen was in residence, to get her approval, and Marj LeBreton began calling the new senators across the country to ensure their presence the following day for their swearing-in.

Keith Boag was saying last week on CBC's Midday *that he was informed by the Liberals that we caught them completely off guard. They never thought I would act so quickly to invoke the clause because they were unaware of all the preparatory work that had taken place during the summer. The swiftness of our decision confronted them with a fait accompli.*

For the first time in 45 years the Liberals lost a vote in the Senate because there were more Tories than there were Grits. I was not surprised by the vehemence of the Liberal reaction, but nobody could have anticipated the vile display of stupidity and the unrelenting campaign of character assassination they directed at Conservatives – new ones like Dr. Wilbert Keon and old ones like Guy Charbonneau. No one was spared as the Liberals saw a Conservative in 24 Sussex in 1984 and 1988, saw him install his former justice minister and House leader as governor general, and now contemplated the loss of their final Senate bastion.

During the ferocious assault upon Senate Speaker Guy Charbonneau, the Liberals' shameless spear-carrier, Jacques Hébert, called him a Nazi and a Hitler. In fact, when 23-year-old Guy Charbonneau was fighting Nazis on the battlefields of France, 22-year-old Jacques Hébert was fighting off boredom in Outremont.

On Thanksgiving eve, Senator Royce Frith made an agreement with Lowell Murray that would allow the resumption of normal business, an agreement that was promptly violated. All parties have their difficulties and we have ours. All parties have had moments of shame and we have had ours. But never since this nation was formed has their been a spectacle more degrading or an atmosphere more venomous than that engendered by the Senate Liberals who will surrender everything – including their honour – before they will surrender political power.

—

The sour atmosphere in the Red Chamber began to affect even happy warriors like Senator Heath Macquarrie. "I used to love the Senate," he wrote to me in sadness that fall. "But that sentiment seems fanciful after the last terrible three months."

The silly season continued unabated. In early October, I announced that my party, as a courtesy, would not field a candidate against Jean Chrétien, who was seeking a return to the Commons in a by-election in the New Brunswick riding of Beausejour. He repaid this gesture a few days later with typical elegance, telling an audience in Moncton that I had lost touch with reality and that I was suffering from a "kind of madness." He said that Canada was drifting into dictatorship and that my popularity had sunk so low I felt I no longer had anything to lose. When I heard about his speech I knew that, with Chrétien back on the scene, the level of civil political discourse in Canada was not headed for any rebound.

In my own attempts to improve political and historical discourse in Canada, I apologized on behalf of the Government of Canada to Italian Canadians who had been interned during the Second World War. It was an overdue gesture that meant a great deal to many Canadians of Italian origin who had suffered needlessly so long ago.

"The Canadian Jewish Congress welcomes the apology that you made to Italian Canadians for their unjust treatment during World War II," Alan Rose, executive vice-president of the CJC wrote to say. "Your act was a courageous response and will be welcomed by the ethnocultural community and indeed by all Canadians. The Canadian Jewish Congress believes that injustices should be admitted and put to right, thus your action is particularly welcomed."

Ontario developer Elvio DelZotto, a prominent Liberal but good friend of mine, also wrote to me. After a heartfelt thank-you on behalf of Italian Canadians, he added a postscript that speaks to the multicultural reality of Canada – one of our greatest strengths: "You might be interested to know that my secretary Marisa Francescut's uncle fought for Canada and died in Holland, while her father served in the Italian army and is now a Canadian citizen."

On December 11, my government, I'm proud to say, made history by announcing its Green Plan. The environment was a vital part of our vision and national policy as we approached the end of the twentieth century. While we received few positive headlines at the time, I knew we had done the right thing.

"You know, I interviewed him about [the environment] once and I think he just got it . . . I don't know how else to describe it," former *Globe and Mail* reporter and environmentalist Alanna Mitchell told a CBC Radio panel in April of 2006 when I was named the Greenest Prime Minister in Canadian history. "It's as if the penny somehow dropped in his head and he understood that this is not a social issue, it's not a soft issue. This is at the core. This issue lies at the core of our economy – and he somehow was able to understand that."

Bob Slater, a former Environment Canada official, spoke on the same CBC panel that day, zeroing right in on the Green Plan. "They actually created a special environment committee of cabinet," he said. "This was the first attempt certainly in Canada, only one of two countries in the world that were actually trying to do this, to join all the dots together across government, across the country in terms of the environmental performance of Canada . . . And so that Green Plan was a couple of years in the making, a huge amount of effort, a huge amount of political capital expended in getting agreement and a large sum of money, three billion dollars. But at the end of it you had a policy framework for all of the federal government and you had a plan of action that took you out in the next ten years."

In a nutshell, the Green Plan promised more than one hundred measures to protect Canada's land, water, soil, forests, and wildlife over the next five years. I can't claim today that we met all of the ambitious goals we set out for ourselves. But of one thing I am certain: we spent our political capital and placed the environment at the forefront of the federal agenda, right across the government. We meant business, and the results are there for all to see. Sadly, this commitment didn't continue after I left office. As Alanna Mitchell told CBC listeners, "What happened during the Chrétien years was that we lost some of that traction on it, and I think it happened without Canadians really realizing that they needed to really agitate, that they needed to really let politicians know."

As Christmas approached, I remained worried as I watched the nation's mood worsen. I wore my heart on my sleeve when I spoke in Buckingham, Quebec – where my parents had once lived and my sister Olive was born – shortly before Christmas as I talked about Canada "the country we risk losing."

> Europeans are working hard to achieve what some in Canada would have us throw overboard. In 1992, 340 million Europeans will form a common market; in 1994, Europe will have one central bank; and by 1999, they plan to have a common currency . . .
>
> How would Europeans who are in the process of developing a new kind of federalism, react if we were to tell them, "In Canada, we've decided to embark on a long, complex, and costly process of tearing our federation to pieces. And then, we'll start the long, complex, costly, and very uncertain attempt to put it all back together again"?
>
> What can Canadians possibly gain by diminishing our size and influence in the world, while elsewhere new political and economic blocks are being formed? While others are uniting to prosper amid fierce global competition, certain people suggest that Canada should fragment and weaken in the face of those same forces . . .
>
> In Buckingham, as in Baie-Comeau, and from Newfoundland to British Columbia, men and women have preserved in their hearts the country they inherited from their parents, in order that they could pass it on proudly to their children. This country, this Canada, already existed thousands of years ago, when aboriginal people displayed to their children the splendour and grandeur of our wilderness. It also exists for the child who arrived this week at Mirabel in the arms of immigrant parents. As long as someone can

look at the Atlantic, the Lièvre, and the Pacific, and proudly say, "This is my country. This is where I want to live," there will always be a great and beautiful country called Canada.

To my friends in Buckingham I extend my best wishes on your town's centennial. Long live Buckingham! Long live Quebec! Long live Canada!

Canadians were so unsettled that I reached out for advice to my old ally, our ambassador to the United States, Derek Burney. I wanted to get a frank opinion, from the outside, about whether the party and I could recover from this national malaise. After taking some soundings from his Washington base, he sent me a memo in which he held nothing back, and which I reproduce in edited form here:

The mood of the country is sour . . . The sense of "being Canadian" is shallow and there is little desire to pull together . . . The combination of a fractured consensus on the Constitution and a recession of yet unknown duration or depth is daunting. The debate within Quebec seems preordained and the rest of Canada does not seem to care . . . The prescriptions are few and, while no one relishes throwing in the towel, most see the country entering its most precarious period ever. Few have much confidence in the potential of any leader or any plan to pull us through. There is not much point assessing what went wrong or why. As prime minister you are, of course, the lightning rod for the blame and the negative personal sentiments are deeply ingrained, especially outside Quebec. By non-Quebecers, you are seen more as a Quebecer than as a Canadian, and the national perception is that fundamentally skewed. The one thing the government has consistently been given credit for previously – sound economic management – is fading under the downturn of the economy. Monetary policies, which earn plaudits from the gnomes in Switzerland, are biting hard at the core of our most successful entrepreneurs and even diluting the benefits anticipated from free trade . . . Most predict a profound fragmentation of the national political scene at the next election, i.e., Italian-style, with five or more parties in Parliament, none with more than 100 seats and, as evidence of the volatile mood,

> estimates for the PCs ranging everywhere from first to last place.
>
> The Prospects: Your fate and that of the country are seen as inextricably linked. Given the grim prospects for the country, it is not surprising that most judgments about political recovery are heavily hedged – "only with great difficulty"; "maybe, but it is a very deep hole"; "only with dramatic action on a whole host of things including himself" . . . Interestingly, those who have some confidence about the future of Canada per se also see you as the best one available to retrieve the situation . . .
>
> Conclusions: The constraints – constitutional, economic, fiscal, caucus – are formidable, and the prospects for success for any leader, or any plan, are not appealing. There are internal and external events well beyond your control but which, inevitably, may help or hinder whatever you try. You cannot lead by attacking enemies of the past or the present. You cannot win the next battle with tactics or strategies from the last campaign, or policies designed to fight the last recession. There is a chance, however slight, that you and the country can prevail under a bold, persistent vision for Canada, some fresh talent around you, and a bit of Irish luck. As always, your own instincts and your own judgment are better in assessing the likelihood of success than any poll or advisor.

Another blunt advisor that cold December was Parry Sound-Muskoka MP Stan Darling. Like Derek, he gave me a brutally honest assessment, this time of the government's standing amongst the citizens of small-town and rural Ontario. "The great number of letters I receive are negative and against the GST and yourself as PM, I am sorry to say," he wrote in his annual letter. "Canadians, as you are aware, have a pet hate against you and have sworn they will never vote for you again. I point out time and time again that you are being compared at the present time with the Lord himself or the Archangel Gabriel, and you come out a poor third, as would anyone . . . Canada Post has also been an albatross, especially for rural MPs. The closing of many rural post offices has made us as popular as a skunk at a garden party and, again, it is going to hurt us in the next federal election."

Stan did see one bright spot, sort of. "Your address to our last caucus for 1990 was inspirational and outstanding," he continued. "It is unfortunate that we cannot tape these and play them to our constituents. Admittedly, the odd word might have to be bleeped. However, both you and I, from time to time, express ourselves straight to the point and rather strongly, but more power to you! I know I speak for the caucus when we say that we are behind you 100 per cent, but 160 faithful voters isn't a hell of a lot when it comes to election day."

Canada was in crisis, my party and government under attack from all sides, and the poor economy was only worsening. The year ended as it began: with the future uncertain.

At Harrington Lake during the first few days of the new year, I officially closed out 1990 with a lengthy entry in my journal. I had already given the public a look at my thinking, saying the following at a year-end press conference, "I suspect what we're talking about here is substantial change. The alternative to a fundamentally reformed Canada is no Canada."

And that is what we faced, the end of Canada. I had been shaken to the core.

—

PERSONAL JOURNAL: JANUARY 2, 1991

The death of Meech leaves me with a great personal dilemma. Of all my colleagues, I am, I believe, the best equipped to deal with the historic challenges that will soon emerge from Quebec. That fact should militate in favour of my staying until the matter is resolved and leading the party once more into battle in 1993. But in the process of doing Meech, FTA, GST, etc., I have become very unpopular across the country. I will now have to see if this unpopularity is durable or if it is a cyclical demonstration of discontent we have seen before. Timing becomes crucial. If I am unable to reverse some of my own numbers by July 15, 1992, I will most probably resign the leadership and arrange for a convention in November or December. Traditionally, a new leader and an exciting convention generate new support for the party. Moreover, the winner would automatically become prime minister with all the authority she or he would need to make a powerful impact on the nation.

It may be that I have been too pro-Quebec to ever again be elected. That is certainly the view promulgated by the other parties in that part of the nation. Ironically, for one who is seen as being too pro-Quebec, I may have diminished my appeal in Quebec because of the failure of Meech. In other words, Quebecers might say, "Brian fought hard for us and did his best, but in the end Meech was rejected by others. We know it is not his fault, but we want to try something altogether new."

Had we not been betrayed by Lucien Bouchard, the caucus solidarity would have been total. It was he who conspired to bring about the defections of other Conservative members. Had he remained faithful, we could have withstood the consequences of Meech politically because of the instinctive ineffectiveness of the Bloc Québécois and its new appeal to Quebec nationalism. Moreover, it could have assisted us in keeping national unity on an even keel, diminishing the failure many Canadians felt at the repudiation of Meech – for which, in the eyes of many, the federal government was responsible, even though Wells was the agent of its demise. The country has entered a phase of poisonous cynicism.

Only if I can conclude objectively that my continued service as prime minister would be of benefit to Canada will I stay on. I have no other reason to stay in office than the unity of this great country. Canada's unity has frequently been placed in the balance. I am deeply saddened and profoundly worried that it is happening again on my watch when unity could so easily have been secured, and at such a modest cost, by the Meech Lake Accord. But I must now turn the page. Meech will never come again, and only history will say how right or wrong we all were.

—

1991

1. Two Wars: The GST and the Gulf

The new year was only a few days old when I had a sobering conversation with Quebec Premier Robert Bourassa. He had by now been diagnosed with melanoma and was undergoing painful treatments to battle his cancer. Both as prime minister and as a friend, I feared the consequences for the nation if he lost his fight.

—

personal journal: January 5, 1991

I spoke with Robert Bourassa in Florida a few hours ago. He told me that his health had improved and that he had added a few pounds and that he will be back on the job within 10 days. He sounds stronger on the phone but he has understandably been shaken by his brush with cancer. His former chief of staff, Mario Bertrand, told Paul Desmarais privately three weeks ago that it was terminal, that Robert Bourassa would not survive the spring. If this turns out to be true, an already dangerous political situation would perhaps explode in the absence of Bourassa's vast experience and great political skills.

Today he sounded pessimistic about the situation, wondering aloud if sovereignty could be contained and how and if he could avoid a referendum. I suggested he postpone his party convention due to his state of health but he said that, inasmuch as this will be the first in two and a half years, such a decision would not be acceptable to the party. Very sadly he reflected on how all this could have been avoided had it not been for Trudeau and Wells, and said that he was completely satisfied that history would view what we had done at Meech in a most favourable light. He told me that he would be having lunch [in Toronto] with Premier Rae on Thursday and then returning to Montreal.

His illness has greatly damaged the federalist cause at this crucial juncture in our history. The crowning irony is that Robert Bourassa, the man so derisively treated by arch-centralists like Trudeau and columnist William Johnson, has emerged as the most indispensable figure on the side of federalism in the province. Because of the abuse to which he has been subjected by these same people, and the impugning of his motives in English-speaking Canada, the larger question today is whether he is still inclined to fight the federalist battle to save a country so little disposed to salvation.

—

I too was pessimistic. The GST had gone into effect on January 1, adding to an already worsening recession. On the ground in their constituencies, our MPs were facing constant criticism. I did my best to keep them focused. "I understand the negative perception of the GST in your riding," I told Niagara Falls MP Rob Nicholson in a letter I signed on January 3. "Although the introduction of this tax was not expected to be a popular measure, it is an important element of our agenda for the continued prosperity of Canada. [We will soon] be able to dispel misconceptions about the tax more effectively, and to illustrate its significant benefits."

With the GST now a Canadian reality, I reflected on the long road we had travelled to get this modern, fair, and reliable tax in place. The way had been filled with obstacles, both managing the difficult politics of such a reform and withstanding the countless criticisms that had gone into its development and administration.

As far back as 1987, Michael Wilson had been sharing with me his various tax reform proposals. On one of those visits, he showed up with a bold, new idea. In addition to reducing income tax rates, both personal and corporate, by five or six points, and broadening the base by removing many deductions and incentives, he suggested replacing the manufacturers' sales tax with a value-added tax that would work and look much like the European VATs, or like New Zealand's "goods and services tax."

Michael was adamant that we had to do this. He argued that, with the huge tax reductions he envisaged in personal income taxes, the new value-added tax could be implemented in a way that was truly "revenue neutral," meaning that the federal government would not be extracting any more from taxpayers than it was giving up in rate concessions on the income tax side. He also felt strongly that we should implement the income tax cuts and the new consumption tax at the same time.

The manufacturers' sales tax, created in the 1920s and imposed on manufactured products at the point that ownership of the goods was transferred to a wholesaler, distributor, or retailer, was a hidden tax and as leaky as a sieve! When retail sales were rising in the late 1980s, revenues from the MST were unpredictable at best and falling at worst. Things were so bad that the tax had become sort of voluntary; a manufacturer collected it from his customer only if he couldn't figure out a way to avoid it. Techniques for avoidance included setting up a distribution company (to perform many advertising, marketing, transportation, warehousing, and other distribution functions) so that a "sale" was effected at a much lower price, even if it was to the manufacturer's own affiliate, and not to a third party. Many ingenious companies sought special exemption orders – there were eventually more than twenty-two thousand of them! – that set a customized rate of tax for a company's operations because only part of the price was for a manufactured good, and the rest was for sales and marketing. (The MST had been 9 per cent when the Conservatives came into office in 1984, and had risen, by fiscal necessity, to 13.5 per cent by the time we got rid of it.)

Michael told me that Stanley Hartt had threatened to toss the Finance officials who first presented him with this idea out of his office if they ever brought up a European-style VAT tax again, until he realized that falling sales tax revenues could cause the deficit to rise at a time when we were fighting so hard to reduce it. The proposed tax had other advantages. It was consistent with a free trade environment because it provided a mechanism to remove taxes on the inputs of exported goods and services, and did not put our exports at a competitive disadvantage. It also removed a subsidy we were unwittingly providing to imports by taxing them at the value for duty as they came across the border, thus catching them before all sorts of costs were added. Interestingly, a VAT tax of at least 15 per cent is a condition of admission of any country wishing to join the European Union, because it is a tax structure that is suitable for a free trade environment and that can't be manipulated to hide government subsidies the way the income tax system can be.

I knew enough about politics to predict that this innovation, however neat in its design and conception, was going to cause one helluva big political row. Voters would never accept that this was just a simple replacement for the MST, a tax that they had never even heard of. Here was a tax on everything that moved, from your laundry bill to the doughnut you bought at the coffee shop, and we were going to tell people that it replaced, in Michael Wilson's phrase, "a silent killer of jobs"! (It didn't help the perceptions about the tax that when we finally implemented the GST, John Crow, the governor of the Bank of Canada, believed that manufacturers would take advantage of the implementation of this tax by *not* removing the MST but would simply heap the value-added tax on top of the existing, hidden tax, thus creating a serious risk of inflation. As a result, the central bank managed interest rates up into the high double digits, which raised the dollar to a level of 89 cents U.S., thereby fuelling one-day shopping excursions to the border states, and hurting the reputations of not only the GST, but of the Free Trade Agreement itself.)

I envisaged a bitter political battle over what became known as the GST. (To his great credit, the ingenious Marcel Côté later came up with the French name "la taxe sur les produits et services," or TPS, in order to avoid a previously suggested French acronym resembling that for "sexually transmitted diseases.") But I must confess I did not foresee the kind of childish antics that were employed when the bill got to the Senate, when noisemakers better suited to a New Year's party were used by those senior practitioners of sober second thought to obstruct legislation adopted by the elected House of Commons.

I knew immediately that I had a significant choice to make between the easy political way out and a policy that was good for the country, and consistent with our fundamental goals of developing our trading relations with our neighbours and maximizing our opportunity to gain from selling our wares and our skills to our partners. The business community would support our efforts, maybe even muttering to themselves how brave and stalwart we were to replace an outdated consumption tax with a new and modern one. But virtually everyone else, from small merchants to millions of consumers, would absolutely hate it.

It didn't take long to figure out that the issue was tactics and timing. Michael still wanted the income tax and sales tax reforms to go together as one revenue-neutral package. I knew that a government, even one soaring in the polls (which we were not), could not take on two major battles at once. Back then we still had the Free Trade Agreement to win, and it was too important to risk by clouding the election with another controversial item. I asked Michael Wilson to publish his tax proposals as a single tax reform initiative, but to leave the sales tax reform as an issue for debate and discussion while we proceeded to put in place the income tax changes. The latter would cleanse the system of a hodgepodge of deductions and incentives that distorted the economy more than they encouraged economic activity.

That strategy would leave us clear to go to the voters with significant tax reductions flowing to businesses and individuals while we fought for our cornerstone achievement, the Canada–U.S. Free Trade Agreement. But no one could accuse us of hiding our intention of modernizing the sales tax system. Our intention would be clearly stated in an unambiguous policy document.

There was still the little matter of what would be in and what would be out of the tax base. A value-added tax requires a different way of thinking. Manufacturers' sales taxes (and provincial retail sales taxes as well, for that matter) are imposed *on* something or removed *from* something. For example, you can take a retail sales tax off books to show your commitment to literacy. But a value-added tax is on consumption and it should be applied on the widest base possible, to allow the rate to be the lowest possible. Only savings and investment, and certain types of financial transactions, are typically not in the base.

The bitterest debate was over imposing the GST on food! Taxing the necessities of life such as food, clothing, and shelter evoked a vision of the widow on welfare forced to cut back on even her meagre diet. The image was too painful for most elected members to contemplate, and the caucus reported back, after the Christmas break in 1987, that taxing food was where they would draw the line.

We had to find a way around this serious problem, but it wasn't simply a matter of saying, "Okay, we won't tax food." Trying to define what was a taxable restaurant meal and what constituted a grocery item produced ludicrous results that exposed the proposed tax to ridicule in the court of common sense. If you bought a single doughnut at the local coffee shop, it was a restaurant snack, and therefore taxable. But if you bought six doughnuts to take home to serve to your family, they became "groceries" and therefore not taxable. While this rule was in force, cooperative people in line at the doughnut shop learned to combine their orders until they reached six to save the tax.

Ultimately, a compromise was worked out that made the administration of the tax more difficult, but the tax itself much more politically palatable.

Instead of 5 per cent, the rate would be 7 per cent, but food and resale housing would be exempted. A generous low-income sales tax credit was included, and we were able to say truthfully that the GST, as ultimately proposed, legislated, and implemented, was progressive because Canadians below a certain income level were effectively spared the tax and were in fact better off.

At the federal-provincial finance ministers' meeting just before Christmas in 1987, Michael Wilson decided that he had better tell his provincial counterparts about his decision not to include food in the base before he made a public announcement to that effect. Ideally, we had wanted the provinces to harmonize their retail sales taxes with the new GST. This would have eased administration costs (starting with reprogramming or replacing cash registers throughout the country), and allowed the combined federal-provincial rate to be much lower, by broadening the base on which the provincial taxes were applied. It would also have allowed the provinces, which have constitutional authority over the contract of sale, to require that the sticker price on an item in a store be inclusive of all taxes, something that the federal government alone could not do.

The provinces all resisted joining in a single, harmonized tax, because they understood, as I did, the politically risky nature of such a decision. So when Michael imparted his news to his provincial colleagues, there was dead silence, for almost a full minute. Then Mel Couvelier, minister of finance of British Columbia and chair of the provincial ministers' group, spoke up. "We really should have nothing to say about this, Michael, because none of us have had the courage to join you in this exercise, but you can tell from our reaction that we think it that is the wrong thing to do," he said. He meant "wrong," not from the point of view of tax design, enforcement, administration, and revenue stability, but from a political point of view.

For sixty years, royal commissions and expert panels had strongly recommended some variation of this change. Governments had all backed off when the final dimensions and political costs became clear. We were told this resistance would dissipate because Canadians – a hardy and honest folk – would prefer knowing up front what their taxes really were, over the deceit of hiding the tax in the product. Of course, this turned out to be balderdash. We brought in the GST because we believed it was right for Canada – principally aiding exports and eliminating the deficit – and to do so we had to fight a ferocious battle with the opposition parties and interest groups, while enduring the unrelenting hostility of hardy and honest Canadian taxpayers themselves.

Michael Wilson had all along been championing a fully disclosed, visible tax. He objected strenuously to any argument that we should, even if we could, attempt to include the GST in prices. Unfortunately, the visible tax, when it was ultimately legislated, provoked consumer outrage. It also led the Canadian Federation of Independent Business, which represents owners of small and medium-size enterprises, to start their "Don't Blame Me for the GST" campaign, little realizing that a merchant who rails against a tax his customers dislike hardly stimulates sales.

Today there is general agreement that sales tax reform was a historic piece of the framework our Conservative government put in place to update our tax system and create a business-friendly environment. As a tax imposed successively on each stage of production, but credited when the good or service is passed on to the next level of trade, it enables producers to eliminate tax on their inputs. This is particularly helpful to farmers and fishermen and other small-business operators. It creates an incentive to declare income, because people who sell for cash turn themselves into the ultimate consumer and bear the tax rather than being able to claim credits. It has stemmed the huge hole in consumption tax revenues and enabled subsequent governments to put Canada's fiscal house in order. Four provinces have now harmonized their taxes with the GST, and the Harper government is working on an initiative to persuade the others to do the same, probably in conjunction with a further planned reduction in the rate to 5 per cent.

I suppose he who laughs last laughs best. When Prime Minister Harper's government initiated the first reduction in the rate from 7 per cent to 6 per cent, the cries of outrage from the Liberal benches were amusing to me, if not embarrassing to them. The people who originally opposed the GST for purely political reasons were now demanding that other taxes be reduced instead. "The GST is a fair and progressive tax and should not be touched," the Liberals said.

Compounding the political problem caused by the GST was the high interest rate policy zealously practised by Bank of Canada Governor John Crow. As instructed, Crow was trying to wring inflation out of the economy, and his crusade was succeeding, but in the short term at least it led to a high Canadian dollar, which resulted in diminishing exports and deepened the recession. Former deputy FTA negotiator Gordon Ritchie went on the offensive in January 1991, calling Crow's monetary policy "highly perverse." Unless it was reversed, Ritchie argued, "the benefits of free trade will be at best substantially postponed." Ritchie was right.

(After my retirement from politics, I was to learn how Crow's stringent approach even attracted the attention of foreign bankers. William McDonough, president of the Federal Reserve Bank of New York, told me he thought the Bank of Canada had gone overboard. "Your government was not given much running room by the Bank of Canada," he said.)

As much as my government was wounded by Crow's policies, I felt at the time that the Bank of Canada was pursuing policies that would benefit the country down the road. While we didn't know how long the recession would last, we were well aware that if we left Canada with a free trade agreement with the United States, a reformed tax system that featured a consumption tax (the GST), and a low inflation rate relative to where it had been, we would be leaving a positive economic legacy.

In November 2006, the Bank of Canada published their *Renewal of the Inflation-Control Target*. Looking back, the report's authors wrote: "Since Canada adopted an inflation-targeting regime in 1991, the record shows that inflation has been low and stable and, as a result, Canadians have benefited in a number of important ways. An improved inflation environment has allowed consumers and businesses to manage their finances with greater certainty about the future purchasing power of their savings and income. Low, stable, and predictable inflation has helped encourage more stable economic growth in Canada and lower and less variable unemployment."

Vindication came late for John Crow, Mike Wilson, and me.

In cabinet and caucus I struggled with members of my team at figuring out the best way to demonstrate fully to Canadians the economic mess we had been left to deal with in 1984. Perhaps a direct, brutally frank speech to the nation was in order, I suggested at a Priorities and Planning Committee meeting in January. Canadians are reasonable people, I argued, and if given the truth in a nonpartisan fashion by their prime minister, they'd have a greater understanding of the challenges we faced as a government.

Joe Clark disagreed in a note written the day I made my suggestion. "Admitting fiscal weakness dilutes our authority for dealing with other urgent issues, including particularly the question of national unity," he wrote. "I will never forget Jimmy Carter's grave mistake, in July of 1979, in delivering an address to the nation, which he believed to be an honest description of the nation's psychology, and which the public interpreted as an indication that the leader thought the nation was weak. He never recovered his authority, in part, I believe, because countries expect their leaders to be free of doubt about basic questions. Whatever our critics say now, no one doubts your belief in the strength and future of Canada, and that assessment is a great asset to us in the debates and decisions of the next several months."

Clark was right – a "malaise" speech by me at the height of a recession, and at a time of constitutional uncertainty, and while Canadian troops were poised for battle was probably not one of my better ideas. I shelved it.

We demonstrated no hesitation in foreign affairs that winter. I recalled the House of Commons for an emergency debate as the United Nations deadline for Saddam Hussein's withdrawal from Kuwait on January 15 drew nearer. With Canadian Armed Forces personnel on the front lines in the Middle East, I wanted the representatives of the people to have a final say before a possible war began.

As I prepared my remarks, I thought back to the reception we had hosted for the diplomatic corps only a month before on Parliament Hill. I had made a special point of speaking directly with Iraq's ambassador to Canada, Hisham Ibrahim al-Shawi, who was leaving the next day for a trip to Baghdad. "Mr. Ambassador," I said, "I don't know how much influence you have with your president, but you will do your country, your president, and the world an enormous favour if you tell Saddam Hussein the following. And tell him you heard it directly from me. Unless he withdraws from Kuwait, there will be a war and he will lose. There is not the slightest doubt about that. You are aware of my relationship with President Bush, and I can assure you he means business. Unless Saddam Hussein backs out of Kuwait he will rue the day he allowed this to happen."

The ambassador nodded silently as I spoke, and hurried away. While I don't know if he delivered my message to his leader, he showed his true colours in the end. In 1994, only months away from retiring, al-Shawi took $250,000 in embassy funds, flew to London, and defected, joining the Iraqi National Congress in opposition to Hussein.

The Commons was tense as I got to my feet on January 15. As I began my remarks, protesters in the galleries began chanting, "No war. No war." With Canadian lives on the line, I understood and respected the emotion behind the voices shouting at me. If Hussein acted the way I suspected he would, I knew that in a few short hours I would become the first prime minister since Louis St. Laurent to commit Canadian soldiers, airmen, and sailors to battle. Hussein had made clear his threats to use weapons of mass destruction against coalition troops, making my government's decision all the more chilling.

"The question before Canadians now is a simple one," I told the House. "If Saddam Hussein does not withdraw peacefully from Kuwait and the use of force is required, where will Canada stand? On this simple question of right and wrong, will we continue to support the international coalition, or will we stand aside and hope that others will uphold the rule of international law? . . . Today, with the extraordinary unanimity that has accompanied the relaxation of East–West tensions, the authority vested in the UN by its architects – including prime ministers King, St. Laurent, and Pearson – can be exercised by our generation to preserve international law and order . . . I have heard it said that Canadian interests are not engaged. When the United Nations is discredited, when a member state is invaded, when human rights are abused, when people are being slaughtered, I say that Canada's rights and Canada's interests are very much engaged and must be defended."

Having mentioned Mackenzie King, I then made a special point of speaking to one group of Canadians who were quite rightly fearful over the question of their rights and civil liberties if Canada went to war: "I want to assure Iraqi Canadians that they will not be subject in any way to illegal surveillance or unwarranted detention, as was the case in regard to other citizens during World War II. That lesson fortunately has been learned in this country."

While Audrey McLaughlin of the NDP responded with a reasoned and measured speech – one that Conservative members considered carefully – in opposition to my government's actions, Liberal leader Jean Chrétien, now back in the Commons after an absence of almost four years, offered up one of the most bizarre suggestions and baffling statements I was to hear during my decade as a member of Parliament. "If faced with an act of war, we say on this side of the House that it is premature and that our troops should not be involved in a war at this moment and our troops should be called back if there is a war," he said.

Members of the Liberal Party hung their heads, while everyone else scratched theirs at this pathetic comment. Laurier, King, St. Laurent, and Pearson must have been rolling in their graves to hear their successor as

Liberal leader argue that if bullets started to fly, Canadian soldiers should cut and run. Fortunately, former prime minister John Turner was not about to stay mute. Although the party he had recently led attempted to muzzle him, he was given the opportunity to address the House on January 16. In many ways it was Turner's finest moment as a parliamentarian. With Chrétien glaring at him from his seat, Canada's seventeenth prime minister rose to speak.

"This Parliament and our country, Canada, are faced with a clear choice," he said. "We can continue to stand behind the United Nations and its resolutions for which we voted and which told Iraq what it must do to avoid war. We can remain an integral part of the most determined demonstration of collective political will ever marshalled by the United Nations to stand up against aggression. In my view it is the choice which all our history and the long tradition of Canada's support for the United Nations oblige us to make today. To do otherwise would repudiate the votes we have unfailingly cast in support of United Nations resolutions. It would also repudiate our commitment to internationalism and to the United Nations, the hallmarks of the Liberal Party and Canada's foreign policy for decades."

Turner then attacked the anti-Americanism that now infected his party. Although this sentiment had been fostered, in part, by him during his years as leader of the opposition, he was now on the right side of the issue.

"The United Nations, *not* the United States, set the January 15 deadline," he said. "Anyone who knows the United Nations . . . knows that it is very jealous in being master of its own destiny. Nobody pushes the United Nations around, not even the United States. No one nation, especially the United States, is able to impose marching orders on that institution . . . Canada has had a proud role in the United Nations right from the beginning. This country has stood by the United Nations even when other countries, including the United States, lost faith in that organization."

When John finished, I immediately got to my feet and led my caucus in a standing ovation for my former opponent. I also crossed the floor to shake hands with a valiant MP who had once again – as in the national unity battles – chosen country over party.

Predictably, the Chrétien Liberals exacted their revenge. They denied the former prime minister use of the Centre Block office that had formerly been made available to him, and attacked him in the press. John Nunziata, an original Rat Pack member, spewed at Turner some of the venom he usually reserved for me. "It's his [Turner's] revenge and he's trying to pave his way into certain boardrooms," he said.

I made extensive journal entries as the clock wound down, closer and closer to war.

—

PERSONAL JOURNAL: JANUARY 16, 1991

12:35 p.m.:
I have just arrived from national caucus. They are very supportive, although many have gone through the earlier period with as much anguish as me. No decision is as difficult as a declaration of war. I have been deeply troubled by this question and indeed in one recent 24-hour period, following a number of sleepless nights, found myself coming down on a side of the case opposite to the one that I had been privately supporting intellectually only 24 hours earlier. After countless hours of study, meetings, and reflection, I concluded that the course to follow was what I outlined in the House yesterday. The day before, in a confidential tête-à-tête with Jim Baker in this office, I conveyed to him my intention to recommend this course to the government. He in turn confirmed that GB had not yet made any decisions about the use of force. I believe, however, that the decision has been made – only the question of timing remains in doubt. Baker confirmed what Scowcroft told Burney on Saturday morning, namely that George Bush would be using a special code to communicate with me, to give me advance notice of their intentions.

In all my conversations with Major, Bush, Mitterrand, Kohl, etc., the mood has been sombre. No one wants this war. Everyone believed until the very last moment that Saddam Hussein would signal his intention to withdraw. His refusal to do so will mean certain destruction, because someone must now defend the UN and liberate Kuwait. I fear not that we shall be unsuccessful in this but that the ultimate consequences in that part of the world will be grave and long-standing. Will this make Saddam a hero? Will this trigger an attack on Israel? What will happen to supportive Arab leaders? These are vital questions. I do not know all the answers but I sincerely believe that Canada's national interest is linked inextricably to the maintenance of the United Nations and its ability to ensure world order. For this reason, Canada must endorse the UN and its resolutions by helping, if necessary, expel Hussein from Kuwait with force.

3:30 p.m.:
Paul Tellier has just advised that, as we anticipated, the strike will be launched tonight at 7 p.m. Ottawa time. The information came to top Department of Defence reps in the Gulf from their American counterparts. It will be aircraft missile attacks launched from battleships in the Gulf. I shall wait to hear from George Bush later today. Obviously there is a lot of speculation, but my instinct, following conversations a few days ago with George Bush, James Baker, and Brent Scowcroft, tells me this is probably an accurate report.

5:58 p.m.:
George Bush: "I'm calling you on a matter of great importance. I have ordered our aircraft to strike Iraq." Nicolas and Mark are with me in the den – Mark with his skates ready for tomorrow and Nicolas in his pyjamas, writing a note. If only Saddam had listened to any one of hundreds of visitors, he could have avoided all the sorrow he will cause to be visited upon the children of Iraq. God knows, we all worked tirelessly to avoid the conflict, but Saddam refused to listen to anybody. He was going to grab a neighbour, strip it of its sovereignty, murder its citizens, and then expect the world community to idly sit by and do nothing. Canada will fight to defend its interests, which lie clearly in upholding the integrity of the United Nations resolution. I have instructed Paul Tellier to gather cabinet tonight, after which I shall make a statement to the nation.

—

I brought the cabinet together and we gave formal authorization to the chief of the defence staff for Canadian forces for our brave pilots to undertake sweep-and-escort missions over Kuwait and Iraq. "The time has regrettably come . . . to act in the interests of preserving world order and in safeguarding the effectiveness of the UN," I told a hushed House of Commons that night.

Hussein responded to the UN action by firing Scud missiles into Israel, killing innocent civilians. I was disgusted and dismayed at these attacks and quickly let Israel know of Canada's support.

"We are very appreciative of your warm message of sympathy and support, which eloquently demonstrates the friendship and solidarity of the Canadian government and people for Israel," Prime Minister Yitzhak Shamir replied. "Of special concern to us is not only the unprovoked Iraqi attack on a civilian population, but the fact that this dastardly act was met with acclaim and approval throughout the Arab world . . . It is good to feel that across the oceans Israel has friends like you and the people of Canada."

I spoke to President Bush throughout the crisis. Hours before he announced the commencement of land operations on February 23, he telephoned me in Ottawa. I took notes as we spoke.

"'Just checking in,' he said. 'The deadline is past. Going to have statement at 10 p.m., and I see no way to avoid a ground war. I will authorize General Schwarzkopf to go ahead. Long talk with Gorbachev today . . . Asked me to stay in UN for 48 hours. I said no . . . Showing no compromise . . .' I have become convinced that it will be very, very fast with low casualties, certainly much less than predicted earlier. Rapid surrender predicted by coalition partners.' Bush sounded cool, relaxed and confident, no bragging – only resolve, though expressed in low-key manner."

By February 27, the Gulf War was over. After more than thirty days of aerial bombardment, coalition land forces entered Kuwait, and Hussein's forces were decimated in only one hundred hours. I spoke with President Bush at 9:20 that evening. He had just given a nationwide television address announcing the end of hostilities.

"I said that I had been with him in the White House when, in August, he had told me pointedly of his intention to deploy troops within 48 hours to Saudi Arabia, thereby putting in gear the chain of events that culminated in today's remarkable victory," I wrote in my notes as we talked. "I said that while the military diversion was outstanding, I thought the political leadership he had demonstrated in working through the UN, keeping the coalition intact, and making some key decisions was at least as impressive and historic. He was deeply gratified by the comments and most appreciative of Canada's support throughout, particularly, as he said, in light 'of the opposition to this policy in your cantankerous Parliament!' He said he was having a drink in the residence with Powell, Cheney, Sununu, Quayle, and Barbara. I said, 'Put your feet up and have one for me – You really deserve it!' He ended by sending love to Mila and the kids and 'See you soon.'"

Beyond the success of the Gulf War in cementing the role of the United Nations as the world's premier body in preventing aggression, there was a more important result for which I will be forever grateful. Although Canadian CF-18s made fifty-six air-to-ground attacks on Iraqi troops in Kuwait during the course of the Gulf War, no Canadian personnel were killed. Putting members of the Canadian Armed Forces in harm's way was one of the most difficult decisions I ever had to make as prime minister.

1991

2. The Battle for Canada's Soul

BEFORE THE GULF WAR was even over, the battle for Canada's soul reached a new level. The Quebec Liberal Party's Allaire Report was released, saying that Canada should be given eighteen months to either back the report's demand for exclusive Quebec jurisdiction over twenty-two areas, or face a referendum on Quebec sovereignty. These twenty-two areas included culture, health, labour, public security, communications, energy, environment, agriculture, and regional development. Ottawa would retain sole jurisdiction over defence, customs, and currency, while there would be shared powers in such fields as foreign and native affairs, taxation, justice, fisheries, and transport. Quebec and the rest of Canada would retain a common Parliament, but the Senate would be abolished and the Bank of Canada reorganized to add regional clout. Quebec would have a veto over future constitutional change.

Publicly, I called the report a "working document" and said I did not perceive it to be a threat. In my private journal, I revealed my true feelings – thoughts I couldn't share with the public or anyone within my government.

—

PERSONAL JOURNAL: JANUARY 30, 1991

Yesterday the Quebec Liberal Party tabled its constitutional proposals, and I fear they have placed us, perhaps intentionally, on the slope to national disintegration. The demands, coming as they do, from a supposedly federalist party, are preposterous and will reduce the federal government's powers to pulp, to zero. If such "demands" are not satisfactorily negotiated over the next 18 months, Robert Bourassa will propose to hold a referendum on sovereignty at that time, namely late 1992, ironically the 125th anniversary of the country's founding.

I am no longer sure that Canada can be saved, her unity maintained. Nor am I sure that I'm the leader to bring that about. I've taken a lot of hits in the last seven years, and many of them took a toll on my credibility and on the perception of me as a fair and even-handed prime minister. Many good Canadians have come to the view that I have always leaned over backwards to accommodate Quebec, and that in the process I have inflicted unfairness on other regions of the country. I have stepped in from time to time and resolved some important questions in Quebec's favour. But I have taken exactly the same position regarding other areas of Canada. Perhaps the most significant was in the wake of the sabotage of Meech Lake by Clyde Wells; I nevertheless persuaded cabinet and caucus to approve Hibernia simply because I felt it was fair for Newfoundland and Labrador. The perception of favouritism for Quebec is ultimately reduced to Meech.

As I sit writing these notes in my downstairs den at 24, I wonder if I can successfully complete the job that must be done to keep the nation whole. And if not me, who? Chrétien is unable to get even a hearing in Quebec, so overwhelming is the contempt in which he is held. Audrey McLaughlin is a nice person, but with only one Quebec member and an embryonic knowledge of French it is unlikely she can make the hard decisions this will require. Although both the government and I have recovered quite nicely in recent polls and in our own data because of our handling of the war in the Persian Gulf – the competence factor is receiving high marks when my own performance is compared with that of Chrétien and McLaughlin – I am far from being in an ideal position from which to handle such a burning issue. If I thought that a new leader from outside Quebec could better handle this I would step aside without hesitation. People like Clark, Maz, Wilson, Beatty, Campbell, and McDougall are very competent and have done well in government. Each one has been an excellent colleague, and I have great confidence in them and indeed in others in the cabinet. No one is irreplaceable; although some political leaders think differently, I do not. I have no doubt that any one of the above or some others would perform admirably as prime minister and that such a change would evoke approval in many parts of the country.

But how would it be received in Quebec? How would the Quebec caucus react? Could the new leader do anything different or in a manner that might arrest the growth of sovereignty in Quebec while engineering an acknowledgement of the need for fundamental constitutional reform elsewhere in Canada? These are all important questions that must be answered soon. Our time frames are all short and the challenge is colossal. I have never run away from a fight and I have no intention of doing it now. But having done my very best for Canada – from Meech to the GST, and from FTA to the war in the Gulf (some successes and at least one significant failure) – it may be that I can now best serve the country I love so deeply by turning over its leadership to a new person, better able to lead in these difficult circumstances than I.

If the heir were truly apparent I would do so soon. Because none is, I shall watch carefully, more so than in the past, for those special qualities that would allow somebody different to make a beneficial difference to the unity of Canada. Holding Canada together is, in the end, the prime minister's only duty, because without unity the future is lost. It is to ensure that future that I commit every effort, including the courage to remove myself from the scene should it become in any way evident that a new leader could achieve for Canada a degree of unity that I could not.

—

I decided to go on the offensive. On February 12, I spoke to a combined meeting of the Empire and Canadian clubs in Toronto. I assured the audience that my government was intent on restructuring Canada, not dismantling it. Now was not the time for Canadians to give up on each other, I said.

"We must deal with the sense of powerlessness in the West, and disparity in the Atlantic," I argued, in the heart of downtown Toronto. "We must listen to the concerns of the North and the voices of our aboriginal peoples. We must seek to understand the growing feeling of frustration of many Ontarians, whose contribution to Canada is rarely recognized. We must find a way to ensure that Quebecers, whose special character so enriches the distinctiveness of our national life, become enthusiastic and willing partners in Canada."

The next day, I spoke to the Quebec Chamber of Commerce in Quebec City. With the Allaire Report still fresh in my mind, I was frank. "I say to those who want to go in a different direction from the rest of the world . . . show us how your plan could improve the lot of Quebecers and Canadians,"

I urged. "Tell us how Quebec could benefit from a split with the other provinces when it is more dependent on interprovincial trade than it is on foreign trade."

I also told the crowd bluntly that Quebec's choice was clear. The province's citizens had to decide "between remaining citizens of Canada and becoming citizens of another country." Beware of the "dream merchants" who tell you separation will be easy, I warned; Ottawa won't be giving up all its powers anytime soon.

In March, I again laid out the facts during a visit home to Baie-Comeau. Sovereignty-association is off the table, I said, and the time has come for real questions to be answered: "It's going to be a straightforward proposition – do you want to be a Canadian, yes or no? If you don't want to be a Canadian, are you ready to tear up the Canadian flag and your Canadian passport and repudiate 125 years of history? I can tell you right now that if that question is put, the answer to that question is going to be no."

After the Quebec government endorsed the Allaire Report, my frustration and tough language increased. The National Assembly was also about to receive the report of the Bélanger–Campeau Commission, which would call for a referendum on Quebec sovereignty by 1992. Speaking privately to my cabinet, I questioned just how representative of the whole Quebec population the commission really was. Regardless, I told my ministers, the outlook for federalism in Quebec is very, very bleak. We could lose the country, and Quebec's supposed federalists (the governing Liberals) were not helping.

Benoît Bouchard wrote me a heartfelt letter during this period. He was torn between two loyalties – to Quebec and to Canada – and was finding life in Ottawa harder and harder:

> Prime Minister, I am not a separatist! I believe we must do everything humanly possible to save Canada. The Meech Lake Accord was rejected. So be it. Now we have to accept the consequences . . . I feel and continue to feel frustrated because, through your harsh criticism in front of my anglophone colleagues, you risk laying all the blame at Quebec's door . . . Brian, you must understand how hard it is to be a Quebecer in Ottawa, especially these days. I know that the rest of Canada sees our province as the spoiled child of the federation. It seems so much easier for them to accept giving $2 billion to Newfoundland or $1 billion to the West

> than $1 million to Quebec. I'm not being paranoid: this is the cruel, day-to-day reality. Why do they want to make Quebec feel that it must always go cap in hand? Is poverty easier to bear in Montreal than Newfoundland? Why is a 20 per cent unemployment rate in Summerside or Portage la Prairie more serious than in Roberval? I don't have the answer, but again, I can no longer live with the frustration.

I later met privately with Benoît and we worked together to help him remain part of the Quebec team in the federal capital. Little did Benoît know that his true test – and mine – would come during the summer of 1992.

President Bush came to Ottawa fresh on the heels of the coalition victory in the Gulf War, his first foreign trip after the war. Domestically, his approval ratings stood at 91 per cent and anything seemed possible. For me, March 13, 1991 marked one of the greatest days of my prime ministership. It was on that day, on Parliament Hill, that Bush and I signed the Canada–United States Air Quality Agreement on Acid Rain.

It had been quite a journey. As Bush and I prepared to affix our signatures to the document, I thought back seven years to when, as leader of the opposition, I had first raised the issue with President Reagan. Until he left office in January 1989, I pressed Reagan for action at every single one of our countless meetings, continually broaching the subject, even when members of his administration grew very tired of hearing it. (I always felt that if I had taken Reagan in person to an acid-rain-ravaged Canadian lake, I would have had greater success.) Once George Bush took office, I redoubled my efforts and quickly discovered I had a much better ally on environmental issues.

And now here we were, about to sign an agreement that would see the United States cut its acid-rain-causing emissions by 50 per cent of the 1980 level by the end of the 1990s. Canada agreed to reduce its emissions by half by 1994. The two countries also agreed to permanently cap sulphur dioxide emissions at 13.3 tonnes annually in the United States and 3.2 million tonnes in Canada.

"They [the Canadians] were on us like an ape," Bush said that day in Ottawa. "The fact that Canada and the U.S. were able so quickly to craft a wide raging and effective agreement on such a complex subject says a lot about the extraordinary relations of our two countries . . . And I think we're doing something good and sound and decent today."

What has happened in the sixteen years since? According to a study prepared by the nonpartisan Library of Parliament in August 2004, total Canadian sulphur dioxide emissions were 20 per cent lower than Canada's agreed-upon national cap and 45 per cent below the 1980 baseline level. In the United States, sulphur dioxide emissions had dropped by 32 per cent from the 1990 level and were down a total of 35 per cent from the 1980 level.

Our efforts received a major assist when the governments of Quebec and Ontario brought in tough new emission standards for their major industrial atmospheric polluters. The federal government assisted by giving the big smelters owned by Noranda and Inco funds to help them cut their emissions.

I'll leave the last word on acid rain to Elizabeth May, former executive director of the Sierra Club of Canada and the current leader of the Green Party. "Brian Mulroney did not let the ball drop on the importance of fighting acid rain," she told the CBC on April 20, 2006. That same day she told the *Ottawa Citizen*: "Mulroney placed acid rain as his top bilateral issue when dealing with the U.S. He insisted on real action at home, with agreements with the seven eastern provinces to cut acid-rain-causing emissions by 50 per cent. Ultimately, the U.S. agreed to the same binding target." She then added: "Someone clever once said: 'To leave a legacy, you have to know one big thing and stick with it.' Fortunately for Canadians, Mr. Mulroney was determined to leave a legacy and he stuck to it. He decided acid rain was a problem, and he cleverly combined charm with resolution and got former president George Bush Sr. to sign a treaty reducing acid-rain-causing emissions by 50 per cent."

Could my government have done more? No doubt. But I am still proud that the emissions that cause acid rain are down 40 to 50 per cent from the day Bush and I signed the treaty.

As we signed the agreement, a special member of my caucus sat beaming in the front row. I made a point of acknowledging him. "Stan Darling," I said, "was one of the often unmentioned guiding lights who fought the fight over many long and difficult years to make this possible. And while you and I get to sign it today, Mr. President, what we sign is a tribute to Stan Darling and so many members of Parliament and members of Congress and members of the administration on both sides who deserve this tribute today."

Afterwards, we presented the pen we used to sign the agreement to Stan as a tribute to his long fight to make politicians aware of the need to fight acid rain in Parliament, in the Conservative caucus, and in my government.

Had we had another pen, I would have given it to Fred Doucet, whose work on this file was unstinting.

Bush and I had extensive private discussions during his Canadian visit. The official note-takers wrote: "The PM observed that approval for the coalition conduct of the war rose to 75 per cent in Canada once the air attack began. Canadians were proud to have served with naval and air units . . . The PM noted the immense difficulty . . . in committing a country to war. The president said he was glad that, in the end, the issue had gone to Congress. Otherwise, the administration might be knee-deep today in law suits and constitutional squabbling . . . The PM wondered when we would stop being held hostage by all the Middle East players who, for 45 years, have spent $100s of billions on arms. (The President observed dryly that we would earn such respite either through energy self-sufficiency or immediately after an election!)"

We also held a working dinner at 24 Sussex and were joined by Joe Clark, who was just back from a trip to the Middle East, and U.S. National Security Advisor Brent Scowcroft. The Americans listened to Clark's briefing intently, after which Bush let us in on his thinking about the Iraqi dictator and how the American president would approach him in the days ahead. "It would be better to make Saddam Hussein's departure a precursor for normalization of relations with Iraq rather than an objective," he said.

National Security Advisor Brent Scowcroft explained, "The last thing we want is to try to hunt him down in Baghdad."

Bush, who was clearly a leader at the top of his game, then described the hard truth of the situation. "We have to straddle a careful line on this," he said. "If we push too hard, that would only mean the United States would have to keep forces in the region longer."

I told the group why Canada had acted as it had. "There were some who thought that the most effective foreign policy derives from independent and outspoken criticism of a major ally," I said. "This is not my government's approach. I am convinced that judgments of approval flow from actions, not postures, in crises like the Gulf. That lay behind our decision on the FTA as well as on the Gulf, and on trade negotiations with Mexico. You know, George, I may be more confident about the country's future than my own right now, but it is very important that leaders do what they believe is right. For Canada, it is never easy living next to the giant, and it was easy to rally emotion against positions such as Canada's during the Gulf War, but I'm undeterred.

"But if any of us live to 110, no one is likely to see a more skilled diplomatic and military effort than yours in the Gulf," I said, winding down the dinner. "There were times of deep worry and even uncertainty, but the president 'never flinched.' He made a couple of moves that Carmine De Sapio of Tammany Hall would have enjoyed."

I had called for a UN conference on arms control in the midst of the Gulf War and told Bush what I had feared most in committing Canadian personnel to an armed conflict in the region. "George," I said, "we had no fear at all of Saddam Hussein. What frightened us were the Chinese missiles, Russian tanks, French aircraft, American radar, and British bombs with which he had been armed. We had to avoid a repetition, in the Middle East or anywhere else, of the stupid situation where we supplied the weapons and then were surprised when somebody used them."

In public, Bush made a brief pleasing reference to Canadian unity: "We [Americans] are very, very happy with one united Canada that has been friendly . . . and when you have the unknown you've got to ask yourself questions," he said.

On March 16, former British prime minister Margaret Thatcher stopped by for a visit. By now out of power, deposed by her MPs and replaced by John Major, she was on a speaking tour of the United States. I arranged for a Canadian plane to pick her up in Vancouver and bring her to Ottawa. She was accompanied by her son, Mark, and we had dinner at Harrington Lake. I wrote about the visit in my journal after she retired for the night.

—

PERSONAL JOURNAL: MARCH 16, 1991

She will begin writing her memoirs – "Nothing gossipy but I plan on telling the truth" – in the next few months, and was struck by the fact that George Shultz told her that, apart from researchers and historians, she will need archivists. That threw her for a loop, but she is resolved to write two volumes, 800 pages each, of memoirs "of substance."

She belted down two double whiskey and sodas before dinner, followed by some excellent wines, before the long day took its toll. By 10:30 she was having trouble controlling her yawns, so I suggested she retire to bed, which she accepted immediately. On two occasions she

> *said, "Brian, you've accomplished a great deal. Don't leave defeated." Clearly she was trying to warn me against staying too long if the unpopularity continues. She also wants me to go out on top and not suffer the indignities to which she had been subjected. It was a delight to see her again in such good form. She might have a few scores yet to settle, but if so, it will be done with some considerable excitement.*

—

Sure enough, Margaret stirred up a little excitement in Canada upon the publication of her memoirs, *The Downing Street Years*, in 1993. "Brian Mulroney and I were to become good friends, though we were very different sorts of politician and were to have some serious disagreements," she wrote, accurately. "As Leader of the Progressive Conservatives I thought he put too much stress on the adjective as opposed to the noun." Also accurate.

In his 2006 book, *Morning in America: How Ronald Reagan Invented the 1980s*, McGill University historian Gil Troy wrote:

> Along with Margaret Thatcher's Great Britain, the three leading English-speaking nations were now led by conservative, market-oriented, capitalist revivalists. Controversial and confident, pragmatic but polarizing, the three leaders would help shift the ideological, political, social, and economic centres of gravity in their respective countries, as well as worldwide. [Thatcher and Mulroney joined Reagan] in a wide-ranging, plain-speaking, trend-setting assault on the Western elite's big-government, union-friendly, high-tax, collectivist conventional wisdom. All three believed that the debate was not simply about core values and common sense. None of them succeeded as dramatically as their supporters hoped or their opponents feared. Mulroney emerged as the most moderate, Thatcher the most strident. All three, however, helped reorient the collective conversation from focussing on government solutions to the practical and philosophical consequences of relying on government handouts. All three offered models of bold, symbolic, tone-setting leadership suited to the media realities of modern politics. At the same time the three unintentionally demonstrated the broad social consensus supporting the liberal

> democratic social welfare state in Western countries, as well as the structural and ideological forces fighting change but guaranteeing stability in their respective polities.

On March 27, the Bélanger–Campeau Commission in Quebec issued its report calling for a referendum on sovereignty to take place no later than October 1992 if the province did not receive acceptable offers to end the constitutional impasse from the rest of Canada. This threat was the genesis of what later became known as the Charlottetown Accord, which was submitted to a nationwide referendum on October 26, 1992.

From that moment forward, to borrow a phrase that Hugh Segal uttered at an Ottawa briefing a few months later, the object of the exercise from my point of view was trying to ensure that we in the federal government "took the bullet out of the chamber." We would do this by putting forward a proposal that we hoped all Canadians could live with. While Charlottetown was indeed to prove an awkward and ungainly agreement, it was definitely better than the alternative: another referendum in Quebec, minus a federal deal.

I also met with my nervous caucus on March 27 and shared a story Alberta MP Jim Edwards had told me. At a recent public meeting in his constituency, Jim had produced a document outlining a new split between federal and provincial powers. "Jim read out the document to people in Edmonton and asked, 'What do you think?' 'Pretty good' seemed to be the general response. 'That would be popular in Alberta.' He had read from the Allaire Report!" I used this example to warn caucus that we were being confronted with the greatest challenge in the nation's history. "Some see it as a great burden," I told them. "I prefer to see it as a great opportunity for our caucus. Dissatisfaction with the federal system, as Jim illustrates, is not limited to Quebec. We can restructure Canada to satisfy all regions."

I had to spend an increasing amount of time that spring steadying my caucus troops as they faced attacks from both flanks, from the forces of Preston Manning and Lucien Bouchard. "I'm very confident about Canada's future because the Bloc Québécois and Reform Party are cut from the same cloth," I said one Wednesday in April. "They're incapable of taking a broad, generous view of Canada. They both view language as an instrument of division rather than an instrument of unity. Yes, appearances are bleak. People are upset, crabby, self-centred, selfish. Of course they blame politicians and never themselves. It's now our job to get Canadians off the psychiatrist's couch and back to reality."

A cabinet shuffle would be key to my plan, and Joe Clark would play a pivotal role. On April 21 I announced that Michael Wilson would be moving from Finance to International Trade, with Deputy Prime Minister Don Mazankowski replacing him. I also moved Clark from External Affairs to Constitutional Affairs, making him the point man on the Constitution. I wrote extensively about my motivation behind this change in the pages of my journal.

—

PERSONAL JOURNAL: APRIL 27, 1991

For months I was resolved to proceed with a major shuffle, to turn the page on Meech, prepare for the new Speech from the Throne, and an autumn of historic consultations and negotiations. I had long since determined that Joe Clark should take over the new Constitutional Affairs department. He is a westerner, bilingual, with the prestige of a former prime minister and, most importantly, free from any direct association with Meech, GST, FTA, [armed forces] base closings, UIC reforms, etc., because he essentially spent most of the last six and a half years out of the country. As sec. state for external affairs, he was in the enviable position, and one he filled very well, of always being seen on the international stage defending Canada's interests, and hardly ever in the House being held responsible for any of the domestic crises and problems. He had made some public comments indicating his preference for External and indeed, during a telephone conversation when he was in New York prior to [Jacques] Delors's visit, he indicated he could handle both External and the Federal-Provincial Relations Office if he had a minister of state to help him on the unity file! I told him this was unacceptable and had Spector arrange for a luncheon meeting with him the following Monday at 24 Sussex.

During the luncheon, which was interrupted repeatedly by calls from the doctors in Florida [my mother had had a heart attack], I told him of my decision. I broadly set out the fundamental reasons for the shuffle and read him a seven-point outline of his new responsibilities that I had handwritten in anticipation of the changes. The stories of "bargaining" that subsequently surfaced are false. He was immediately taken by the extent of the changes I was contemplating and the expanded authority I envisioned for him in his new role. Lowell has played a more modest role and Joe's, of course, would be quite different. He asked for no changes at all and requested only, in a subsequent conversation from Florida, both an office and ongoing access to the Challenger fleet, to which he had become accustomed in his External Affairs days. I approved those requests, of course, and in P&P moved to strengthen the committee he will chair, to ensure that he will have all the authority he requires to do an effective job.

In any event, it went smoothly with Maz, Wilson, Crosbie, McDougall, [Benoît] Bouchard, etc. – all of whom are genuine team players and a delight to have on board.

I hope that by October–November 1992 we will have: 1) Prepared a constitutional position that is generally okay for Quebec and the other provinces, thereby obviating the need for the Quebec referendum on sovereignty; and/or 2) Agreed with the other premiers on the general thrust of a constitutional package of sufficient attractiveness and clarity to also achieve the above result; 3) Agreed with other parliamentarians in the House on the principles and thrust of a new deal to be negotiated with the provinces if the provinces' consent/approval is granted to the govt. by way of a national referendum. Any one of these would meet the fundamental needs of those who believe in Canada and would avoid the Quebec referendum on sovereignty, which at the moment, I believe, would secure majority approval. Ideally this would allow me to step down after two full terms, as I have publicly indicated I would, having brought the economy back to a strong growth position, reversed the course of deficit-debt spending, done the FTA, GST, Meech and, in the meantime, completed the preparation of sound proposals.

I believe I am personally paying the price for controversial leadership and change, which most Canadians know they require but refuse to thank me for. I also believe that I should have the foresight, detachment, and humility to examine the situation clearly and honour my commitments in a timetable order of precedence: 1) the country, 2) the government, 3) the party, 4) myself and my personal interests.

I believe the re-election of a new prime minister, perhaps a non-Québécois, will dramatically alter the political landscape, strengthening us in English Canada while allowing a small number, perhaps 15 or 20, to be elected in Quebec on their own merits because they will have established enviable reputations as MPs or ministers. This way the Conservatives, in the wake of a successful convention with a good budget in the late spring of 1993 and the excitement and approval the public traditionally accords a new and different leader, can recapture confidence in the West, Ontario, and the Atlantic; sustain substantial losses in Quebec; and still emerge with a minority – and perhaps a majority – government. Caucus support remains strong and encouraging throughout these difficult times, and I feel serene knowing I will continue to do my best for the country while working very confidently and privately to ensure the political well-being of the government and party by fulfilling another vital dimension of leadership – knowing when to step down and arranging the transition in a constructive and positive way at the most advantageous time for all.

—

Catherine Clark, Joe's bright and articulate teenage daughter, had a very funny take on her father's new responsibilities as constitutional affairs minister. When she heard the news she said, "Well, so long Paris; hello Moose Jaw."

On May 13, we fired our first salvo with the reading of the Speech from the Throne by Governor General Ray Hnatyshyn. In it we set out plans for a new joint Commons–Senate committee that would spend five months seeking public, provincial, and territorial reaction to a constitutional proposal Ottawa would unveil in September. We also announced the appointment of former chief justice Brian Dickson to set up the terms of reference for the Royal Commission on Aboriginal Affairs. We pledged we would seek a national consensus on education – a provincial matter – that would cut the illiteracy rate in half; double the number of post-secondary graduates in mathematics, the sciences, and engineering; and quadruple employee job training by the year 2000.

The next day I reflected on Joe's appointment. He would be key to the plans we'd announced in the Speech from the Throne and I was obviously pleased with what I had seen so far. The summer of 1992 and his controversial handling of the nation's most sensitive file were still far away.

In mid-May, I left the Constitution behind and headed off to the Far East for an eleven-day trade mission. Though we had entered into the FTA with the United States and were about to start official negotiations with the Mexicans and the Americans that would lead to the creation of the NAFTA, improving our trading relations with nations outside of North America was also a firm priority. I used the trip to announce the opening of five new trade offices in Japan and one in Hong Kong.

As we flew across the Pacific toward Hong Kong, I was summoned to the cockpit to receive a radio communication from Norman Spector. (The plane I flew on during my years in office had some humbling flaws. Condensation formed above my head on every flight, to drip on me during every takeoff and landing. Much worse, it had no telephone or communications system allowing me to be in direct contact with my office – or indeed with anyone else – in case of an emergency.) He informed me that my friend, Rajiv Gandhi of India, had been assassinated. I was stunned. Gandhi, with whom I had worked extensively at battling apartheid, was an outstanding young leader. While inexperienced, and certainly not as tough as his mother, Indira, Rajiv had a good heart and a tremendous vision for India on the world stage. He and his Italian-born wife, Sonia, were a fascinating political couple, and I knew at once that India and the world had lost a bright light.

My visit to Hong Kong was crucial. With China set to assume control in 1997, it was vital that Beijing be sent a signal that the course they would follow in the former British colony when it came to human rights was a real concern to the West. A five-day visit by the political leader of a G-7 country – one that still had not resumed high-level ministerial contacts after the Tiananmen Square massacre in 1989 – would play its own small role in relaying this message, which was duly sent. I knew, too, that Canada stood to benefit from nervous Hong Kong residents choosing to immigrate to or invest in our country, and so it proved. I like to think that this well-timed visit raised Canada's profile in Hong Kong at an important point in its history.

In Japan, I was honoured to have an audience with Emperor Akihito. During a 1986 visit to the country for that year's G-7 Summit, I had met and had dinner with Akihito's father, the elderly Emperor Hirohito. Given his role in the Second World War, I was ambivalent about meeting the wizened "sun-god." I couldn't, however, deny Emperor Hirohito's hold on his country, where his people treated him with dramatic reverence. In our conversations I found Hirohito polite and respectful, but with little to say about the wider world.

Akihito was much more modern and better informed than this father about the world outside the walls of the imperial palace. He took Mila and me on an unforgettable tour of his palace. Kokyo Palace is situated in a large park that is surrounded by moats and huge stone walls – in the middle of downtown Tokyo – and features numerous small ponds and rivers, all beautifully natural. The lands used to be the seat of the Tokugawa shogunate that ruled Japan for almost three hundred years before being overthrown. The new palace was completed in 1868, and the breathtaking grounds and structures Mila and I saw that day had been lovingly rebuilt after being destroyed by Allied bombs during the war. We were struck by how thoroughly modern the traditional palace seemed – very austere and minimalist, with its own special beauty.

Close to the palace lies Canada's splendid new embassy, which I had the privilege of officially opening in the course of my visit. Designed by the famed Toronto architect Raymond Moriyama, it remains an impressive reminder of Canada's place and role in one of the most important capitals in the world.

Some of my private talks with Prime Minister Toshiki Kaifu took place at the Akasaka Palace, the impressive Tokyo residence where the Japanese invite their visiting state dignitaries to stay. We discussed the past and the future as note-takers recorded.

> PM Mulroney said that, in Prime Minister Kaifu's excellent Singapore speech, he had referred to Japan's sensitivity to the sufferings caused by Japanese forces during the war. There was sensitivity in Canada on this subject, notably related to the Canadian role in the defence of Hong Kong and the deaths of 550 Canadians in defence of the colony as well as to the suffering of POWs afterwards. This issue was likely to be a subject of press questions. Prime Minister Kaifu had impressively turned the page in Singapore. Neither prime minister, PM Mulroney continued, had been old enough at the time to have had anything personally to do with the events of the war. It would be much appreciated, especially by the families of those who had suffered, if Mr. Kaifu could confirm that

> his remarks in Singapore were intended to apply as well to the Canadians who had fought and died in the Asia-Pacific theatre and in Hong Kong. Mr. Kaifu replied that he wished to take the opportunity to confirm that Japan's actions had brought unbearable suffering in Asia and the Pacific during the war on people in the region, including the Canadians who had served in the Asia-Pacific theatre.

Both publicly and privately, my visit to Japan also allowed me the chance to state Canada's support for Japan's inclusion as a permanent member of the United Nations Security Council. The time had come, I believed, for the world to leave the Second World War behind and to look toward the future.

Back home in Canada, I was confronted by an Angus Reid poll that illustrated the difficulties that had been created by the recent sabotage of the Meech Lake Accord. The poll reported that only 30 per cent of Quebecers felt profoundly attached to Canada as compared with 56 per cent in a similar poll taken one week before the 1980 referendum.

With that news in mind, I boarded a helicopter for the short trip to Kingston and the grave of Canada's leading Father of Confederation, Sir John A. Macdonald. On June 6, I joined Kingstonians and others in honouring Sir John A. on the occasion of the one-hundredth anniversary of his death. As we waited for the ceremony to begin, I marvelled at the simplicity and dignity of our first prime minister's family plot. My journal reveals that I took comfort in the example Sir John A. had left me and all the prime ministers who followed him.

—

PERSONAL JOURNAL: JUNE 10, 1991

As I reflected on Macdonald's extraordinary challenges and the unfailing criticism to which he was subjected, my own problems appeared somewhat more manageable, and I disembarked the helicopter from Kingston in a more confident mood than I had felt in some time.

—

That journal entry also allowed me to express some fatherly pride.

—

Tomorrow is Caroline's 17th birthday. I can hardly believe it. Yesterday it seems she was just a baby and now she is a beautiful young woman. On Saturday night we had a dinner in her honour, and she looked marvellous and acted the same way. She has turned out to be an intelligent and surprisingly mature young woman, completely unaffected by the trappings of high office – but very sensitive to the attacks to which I am regularly subjected (although she complains in private to her mother but never to me). Among our guests was Peter Ustinov, who all evening long gave us a virtuoso performance that no one could possibly match. I had worked with him at the Children's Summit at the UN – he is a pillar of UNICEF – but had not had the opportunity to appreciate fully his brilliance and humour. Caroline and Gerda Hnatyshyn, who sat at our table, laughed until the tears rolled down their cheeks. All in all, a memorable birthday dinner for a wonderful daughter.

—

1991

3. Ireland, Europe, Bob Rae, and Sir John A.

In 1991, Europe was often on the agenda, and I travelled there more than once. In June I flew to Germany for extensive talks with Chancellor Helmut Kohl. Recognizing the new realities of the post–Cold War world, I planned to announce while on the trip that we were scaling down the Canadian Armed Forces' presence in western Europe, although I knew this would be a controversial move in some quarters. Still, I felt Canada owed it to Mikhail Gorbachev to show him real, tangible gains arising out of his reforms.

I spent many, many hours in private and informal talks with Kohl, explaining my plan. Despite his growing domestic unpopularity, I found the chancellor in fine form. He wasn't even slightly worried about his nation's upcoming elections. "All things considered, I am looking forward to going through a great battle; I want it and it gives me satisfaction," he told me. "I have been through the worst now and I'm looking forward to winning. And I still have some work to do. I have been chairman of my party for eighteen years. I will have been chancellor for nine years in a few months which puts me in a league with Bismarck, Adenauer, and that other guy we don't mention anymore. What more could I want? To be sure, I have made mistakes, but the broad outline of what I have been trying to do is right, and I know that my policies are sound. In 1989, I presided over the breakdown of the Wall, and in 1990, the re-establishment of German unity. By 1994, a great many important European decisions will have been taken, and then I will be content."

I shifted the discussion to the upcoming G-7 Summit in London where we would be joined by Gorbachev – a historic first. I told Kohl that Japanese Prime Minister Kaifu had made clear his lack of enthusiasm for the Soviet leader during our talks the month before in Tokyo.

Kohl exploded. He shook his head vigorously, and roared that he simply could not understand the attitude of the Japanese. "The truth is that

Gorbachev has set about changing the world: NATO is changing, we have achieved German unity, and by 1996 the Baltics will be independent," he said fiercely. "I do not know whether Gorbachev will be there for a long time, but he is reliable – if he changes his position, he tells you. It is important for us that *perestroika* continue. Under his presidency, we have witnessed the amazing performance of the citizens of Leningrad deciding democratically to change their city's name back to St. Petersburg. No one would have believed this possible at the end of the Andropov/Chernenko era."

Kohl also discussed President Mitterrand of France and the always complex challenges of dealing with the French on the world stage. Having had many similar conversations with President Bush and other senior American leaders over the years, I could only chuckle as Kohl vented his frustration: "Mitterrand has the memory of an elephant – which is something that Reagan and Shultz never understood. The French are unique, and things will only work out if you accept this fact and get on with it."

Publicly, the German chancellor gave voice to what many around the world were thinking as they considered Canada's unity situation. "Nobody else in the world can understand what is happening in Canada," he said, bewildered that such a successful country was threatening to break up.

Kohl and his wife, Hannelore, took Mila and me to their favourite Sunday brunch restaurant near their home. We toasted our successful visit with a bottle of German white wine – Forster Ungeheuer Riesling Beerenauslese, bottled in 1953, the year Mila was born. It was a fine early birthday present for my wife. As I flew home to Ottawa from Frankfurt, I wrote extensively of my talks with Kohl in my journal.

—

PERSONAL JOURNAL: JUNE 16, 1991

Kohl is at the top of his form. Germany is reunited and prospering. European unity progressing well, détente across Europe, and his own emergence as a leader of great accomplishment and skill. He is looking toward the 1994 German elections, which he believes the Christian Democrats can win. His comments on François Mitterrand were especially revealing:

1. *In 1982, Kohl was sworn in as chancellor on a Friday, swore in his ministry on Monday morning at 11 a.m., and by 5 p.m. was in Paris,*

mounting the steps at the Élysée Palace. Thus was born the special relationship between the conservative German and the socialist Frenchman, one of the unlikeliest and most successful in history. Indeed it can be argued that it formed the basis for the latest impulse toward European integration, the successful response to Gorbachev, and European support of the Gulf War, and was a major contribution to NATO solidarity. At its basis was a very wise German observing the greatest courtesies toward the president of the French Republic, a much older individual susceptible to such attentions and concerns.

2. *Sometime later, Kohl received a call at 3 a.m. from Stauffenberg, his minister of finance. The French franc had weakened, was under severe attack, and the Bundesbank and the German finance group wanted approval for a course of action that would have been unhelpful to the franc. Kohl told Stauffenberg, "No matter what your experts are saying, Germany will support France. You are instructed to take appropriate action in this regard." Apparently this action was criticized by Helmut Schmidt and others, and Mitterrand never commented on it directly, but he knew that in the crunch, Kohl had not wavered and had stood firm. ("Chirac is close to me philosophically, but he is unreliable because he is too nationalistic," Kohl said.)*
3. *At the lowest point of his career, Kohl said he was accused of financial improprieties involving 30,000 Deutschmarks. "Imagine," he said, "me who had raised millions of DMs for [my party] . . . accused of improper activity for such an amount." In any case, the public parliamentary inquiry dragged on for three months, and it was "the most painful and humiliating period" of his career. At the same moment, he made one of his regularly scheduled visits to Paris to see Mitterrand – whom he affectionately described as "François le premier." Upon arriving in Paris, he was informed that after the meeting Mitterrand wanted to give a reception for him – to which he took mild exception because he wanted to return early to Bonn. Mitterrand, however, insisted and after the meeting Kohl was escorted into a hall at the Élysée Palace where Mitterrand had gathered 300 ministers, justices, academicians, diplomats, artists, etc. Mitterrand proceeded before the French and German media to deliver himself of a major speech on Europe and Kohl's role in it.*

"Then," said Kohl, "Mitterrand said something to the effect that France valued Kohl and had confidence in him." This was widely reported in Germany, Kohl said.

The most moving part of the story came as Kohl concluded it. His eyes welled up with tears, and as one trickled down his left cheek, he smiled and said simply, "That's François," as if to indicate that Mitterrand was genuine and that he, Kohl, would never forget the support. It was one of the most moving moments I have witnessed in almost seven years as prime minister. Here I was with Mila, having cake and coffee with Helmut and Mrs. Kohl in the dining room of their private home, only two interpreters present, and the tears of the chancellor of Germany wiped away generations of mistrust of France and spoke eloquently of his sincerity and decency as a person and of his almost childlike gratitude for the generous and thoughtful gesture from his friend François at a crucial moment in his life.

—

Planning for the G-7 Summit continued during that summer. At the suggestion of President George Bush, he and I agreed to meet at the seventy-fifth anniversary Major League All-Star Game taking place that year in Toronto at SkyDome. The president brought along baseball legends Joe DiMaggio and Ted Williams. Before the game, Bush and I spoke privately and at length. Only Derek Burney and Brent Scowcroft sat in on our discussions.

"I don't envision either a miracle or blank cheque for Gorbachev in London," I told Bush. "Our readiness to assist will be linked to fundamental commitments by him for real reform in the USSR."

Bush stressed that he wanted another bilateral summit with Gorbachev in the months ahead, whatever happened in London, then complained, "As long as the USSR continues to build missiles aimed at New York, and spend more than 20 per cent of their budget on military expenditures, it is very hard for me to contemplate any kind of bailout." Once again he raised Cuba: "In the grand scheme of things, Cuba is tiny but the Soviet support of Castro's regime is making it very difficult for the United States to respond more positively." Bush said he wanted to try to convince Gorbachev, in private, that he could relinquish his support of Fidel Castro without diminishing the USSR's global interests.

"Do you think Gorbachev can survive much longer?" I asked.

"His situation is better than it was last winter," Bush replied, saying that Gorbachev had "a good chance" because he had improved his power base, the Soviet military was now more quiescent, reformers were emerging, and he had a tactical arrangement in place with Boris Yeltsin.

According to Bush, the Central Intelligence Agency now saw less of a chance of a military coup, but the spy agency's analysts wondered whether Gorbachev could handle the KGB – an interesting prediction, given the later rise of Vladimir Putin, a former head of the KGB.

We then moved the discussion to the topic of the Middle East. I asked Bush what would happen if the United States called a peace conference to take place in two or three weeks and publicly issued invitations for the Mideast players to "come for lunch and the weekend." I wondered aloud if there was any advantage for Bush to now force the issue. The president told me he did not want to be in the position of having anyone say no to such an invitation. Scowcroft added frankly that he believed Israel might respond positively to an invitation but then refuse to negotiate, arguing they had made a sacrifice just by agreeing to come to Washington!

Derek Burney's notes sum up the rest of our conversation:

> The prime minister said his government stood firmly for the defence of the integrity of Israel. "We love Israel," he said, "but we must do everything we can to ensure there is no repeat of war in the region, which would be destructive beyond imagination." The prime minister insisted that the U.S. has "the moral right to insist on movement." U.S. taxpayers can't be expected to pay and pay and reap no benefits. "You set the agenda and the ground rules," he urged . . .
>
> The prime minister reiterated that the president had a moral right to act: "No one else has it and I genuinely believe you have earned it." [The PM said that] no one had the right to decline either; anyone who did would be the real loser. Given that the president had risked the full prospects of his presidency on a war which could have gone a different way, "You are fully entitled to act. The situation must not be allowed to unravel."

Shortly afterwards, I departed for Europe, starting with a very special visit to Ireland. Charles Haughey, the long-serving prime minister, had arranged a state visit to my ancestral homeland. Haughey had a great deal to show.

He had done much to modernize his nation, and had presided over its extraordinary transformation from the bleak country Mila and I had seen on our honeymoon in 1973 to the point where it was on its way to becoming a nation with the highest per capita income in Europe, with the exception of Luxembourg.

It was a very sentimental visit for me. Speaking amidst the grandeur of the great dining hall in Dublin Castle, I thought of home. "I remember as a boy returning to school in the winter to our small house on Champlain Street in Baie-Comeau," I told the banquet crowd. "It was dark by the end of the afternoon and the freezing winds whipped across the bay, making the snowbanks seem even more enormous and our isolation even more complete. And in my mind's eye, I can still see my mother ironing the children's clothes and softly humming 'The Mountains of Mourne' and 'Mucushla,' ballads of a land she had never seen but loved so dearly."

The trip also allowed me, Mila, and all four children the opportunity to visit Leighlinbridge, the little place in County Carlow where my ancestor Pierce Mulroney farmed and ran an inn in the eighteenth century. (With a population just under six hundred in 1991, the village boasted seven pubs! My ancestor had clearly picked the right business, although competition must have been an issue.) His grandson, also named Pierce, became the first Mulroney to make the journey to Canada, arriving in Quebec in the 1830s. (The name Pierce lives on: in 2006, I was moved when I walked into Caroline's hospital room and held her newborn twins in my arms. Caroline reached her arm around me at that moment and told me the boy would be named Pierce. I knew that my mother and father would have been so proud, and my tears flowed freely that day.)

As we passed Kelly's Pub in the heart of Leighlinbridge a local man who had obviously been celebrating the arrival of the Canadian Mulroney throughout the day presented me with a pint of Guinness. "Now *this* is Ireland," I said with a laugh, before handing the glass to Mila for a sip.

"Mr. Mulroney is a good family man who rose to great heights," Grainne Mulvey, a thirty-three-year-old seamstress, told the visiting Canadian reporters. "His wife and children are beautiful. Imagine that a man with his roots in this tiny village could have so much. His ancestors left here, made new lives in North America, and now he has done things never dreamed possible."

Before we left for London and the G-7 Summit that day, Prime Minister Haughey had one more elegant surprise. As we walked toward the plane in Dublin, the Irish band struck up a memorable rendition of "Happy Birthday." Mila turned thirty-eight that day, and she, our children, and I were touched at this very Irish gesture.

A part of us all still remains in Ireland.

In London, my wife and daughter quickly captivated the British capital. They were on the front pages of all the papers almost every day. Mila and Caroline met royalty, served as star ambassadors for Canada, and had the time of their lives, particularly Caroline. But suddenly it all went sour. British reporters phoned journalists in Canada and consulted members of the travelling Canadian press corps, who worked their usual magic. Soon the tabloids were printing negative items about our family. By the end of the summit, the pejorative references made by Canadian reporters and picked up by their British colleagues were so insulting that Barbara Bush called Mila and Caroline to express her support, and Danielle Mitterrand dropped by in person to tell us how disgusted she was by the treatment my wife and daughter received on that trip. I told our kind supporters not to fret – it was par for the course for many members of the Ottawa press gallery.

—

PERSONAL JOURNAL: JULY 18, 1991

I left No. 10 Downing St. last night at about 10:30, and Norman Spector joined me for the short ride to the Four Seasons, our hotel. My mood was excellent. Our trip to Ireland had been a success, the summit had gone extremely well, and Canada had been able to play a constructive role in some important areas. The Gorbachev meetings (and I will be seeing him at the Soviet embassy in an hour) had been almost flawless (in significant measure due to the announced START agreement on arms reduction with George Bush and to John Major's easy and effective management style of the conference). The final event had been an intimate dinner at No. 10 with serious discussion of the Middle East and China (Hong Kong) interspersed with laughter and singing (before dinner), and with some excellent jokes and good humour.

As I reached the hotel, a Canadian journalist yelled, "What do you think of the charges?" As I had no idea what she was talking about I entered the hotel, where Gilbert Lavoie handed me a CP wire story to the effect that an Ottawa justice of the peace had approved the laying of charges against some 13 people, from RCMP Commissioner Norman Inkster to Bernard Roy. My shock and dismay were total. I knew most of the people involved (some I have never met) to be honest and decent, but I feared greatly for their reputations, even though I am sure of their innocence and of the eventual restoration of their reputations. This was the culmination (for the moment, and at an extremely low and dubious judicial level) of a campaign against the government by one Glen Kealey, a man obsessed with the idea that the government was guilty of extensive wrongdoing after he failed to get a contract to provide the federal government with a building of some kind, back in '84/'85. After having been turned down by the Crown, and the police who claimed the "evidence" did not justify the laying of charges of any kind, he eventually found Ms. Coulter, a JP used to dealing with highway violations, and persuaded her to hear evidence in camera and recommend the laying of charges! When Bernard Roy left Ottawa after genuinely serving Canada and me, he was seriously out-of-pocket, having lived for four years on revenues of one-third of what he would have earned had he remained in the legal profession at Ogilvy! If Bernard ever did anything wrong, let alone "criminal," in his entire life, I'll jump tomorrow from the CN Tower. He is a completely honest and incorruptible person (along with the others charged) whose life has been seriously upset and professional advancement greatly damaged by charges that no doubt will either be dismissed or established to be groundless.

I immediately met with Maz and McDougall and spoke with Tellier. By the time I got to bed at about 2:30–3 a.m., I was exhausted and demoralized. Just as we were starting to come back, following a very successful summit and prior to a most crucial party convention in August, I was blindsided by an event that was a nightmare for any head of government, let alone one struggling to keep his country together. It seems that any time I have taken a major foreign trip, some event back home has arisen to cause us great damage and diminish the results we had been working so hard to achieve. Both Mila and I were deeply saddened by what had happened, for the families of those involved principally, but also for ourselves, who will have to carry on in a progressively difficult and frequently hostile climate.

Anyone seeking the leadership of a political party would be wise, with his spouse, to consider the new realities of Ottawa; the media and the opposition have taken the legitimate adversarial nature of Parliament and politics to extremes. There has emerged a climate of mistrust and suspicion, so imbedded in our daily lives that Mother Teresa herself would be hard pressed to succeed.

—

In my opening remarks at the G-7 Summit I hammered home two distinct themes: arms control and the United Nations. On our proposed arms control declaration, I said, "I find it extraordinary that we are having difficulty agreeing on the kind of message we want to give on such a key lesson of the Gulf War. If our publics could see us haggling over such a critical issue, what do you think their reaction would be?" I also made a strong pitch for the United Nations: "The end of the Cold War has given the UN the opportunity to bring about a more stable world order: we must use it and strengthen it. In Canada at least, the involvement of the UN in the Gulf War made the difference in public opinion: without it, we could not have sustained a military commitment."

But the real news from the summit would be the presence of Soviet leader Mikhail Gorbachev. He was scheduled to hold a bilateral meeting with each leader separately and then join us together for behind-closed-doors talks. History was again on the march. We spent many hours debating how to receive him and how much economic support we would be willing to offer. I laid it all on the line, as best I could, recalling the astonishing progress that had been made since Chernenko's funeral in 1985. "If Gorbachev had said in 1985 that he proposed to do all these things, and would we help him if he did," I said, "I believe all of us would have hurried to write a cheque for our own contributions."

As we wrapped up our discussions before Gorbachev's arrival the following day, I had one final point to make. I turned to Helmut Kohl. "If a month from now," I said, "Gorbachev is overthrown and people are complaining that we haven't done enough, is what we're proposing the kind of thing we should do?" Kohl said we were following the right course, reminding us he'd recently met with Gorbachev in Kiev and that the Soviet leader had told him our aid package was both needed and wanted by the USSR.

When the historic moment came and Gorbachev made his presentation to the summit leaders, I took notes as I looked around the table. Reviewing them today, I am reminded that Gorbachev, a very proud man who wore power comfortably, looked insecure and seemed to be pleading as he spoke to us. He stuck closely to his text. President Bush looked at Gorbachev directly throughout, and took copious notes, and John Major was an attentive, low-key presence in the chair. All of the other leaders were fully focused on the man from Moscow. While he asked for assistance, Gorbachev was by now fully aware he wouldn't be receiving the billions of dollars he had requested in the run-up to the summit.

I smiled to myself as Gorbachev addressed American concerns about Fidel Castro's Cuba – sort of. "I'm looking George in the eyes – we're not creating a new Guantanamo . . . Changes are coming there," he said. (Guantanamo in 1991 connoted nothing more than an American military base long established on the island of Cuba.)

He also addressed issues in eastern Europe as a whole. "The USSR is closely linked with eastern Europe," he said. "Perhaps they were tired of us and then we had a very clumsy divorce. Now, like husband and wife in these circumstances, we are getting signals from them about new cooperation."

Referring to the Baltic states, Gorbachev used an analogy that I knew I had to answer. In fact, I was furious, but knew that I had to control my temper. "France gave ten years for its colonies to deal with problems," he said. "Prime Minister Mulroney is tackling his own constitutional problem of Quebec." When my turn came, I set the record straight at once. There was no way I would allow a leader of the Soviet Union, even one that I admired, to get away with such a comparison. "You made a passing comment about Canada that was not aggressive or hostile but simply illustrative," I said. "I accept it in good faith. But here are the facts: 1) Canada was formed by the free and willing coming together of the founding provinces, French and English, 124 years ago. 2) Eleven years ago, a referendum was held by the duly elected separatist government of Quebec asking the population for the right to negotiate not separation, but sovereignty-association with the central government. It was strongly rejected. We have never used force to ensure the country was united or that any citizen would remain Canadian."

Canadian honour restored, I changed gears, saying, "President Gorbachev, you are in a unique situation that gives you an advantage over us. You already know that the verdict of history will be favourable on what you have done. Your problem is to keep alive politically and economically long enough to ensure that your achievements are not reversed by others during your own lifetime. What I have seen around this table is a genuine desire by all leaders to help you and . . . your objectives. What makes your achievements so remarkable is perspective. We inherited strong economies and we all work at making them stronger. You inherited an economy and political system in advanced disrepair. You must rebuild both from scratch. That is an enormous difference. That is why, as fellow leaders, we have such admiration for what you have been able to achieve."

To illustrate for Gorbachev why G-7 leaders would not be signing blank aid cheques before he implemented profound structural reforms to his country's economy, I told him a story about McDonald's of Canada and its problems setting up restaurants in the Soviet Union, as recounted by my friend George Cohon, the company's president. "George Cohon told me that securing rights to land in the USSR has been like dental surgery," I said. "And he is a persistent man! He worked for seventeen years to set up McDonald's Moscow operation. It employs eleven hundred young Muscovites." Gorbachev nodded resignedly as I spoke, knowing that what I said was true and was delivered with understanding.

A few minutes later, a handwritten note from George Bush was placed in front of me, which read, "Brian: Damned good. I worried that he might think, until your comments, that we were lecturing him, putting him on the carpet so to speak. GB."

Bush later described this meeting in his book, *A World Transformed*. "I did worry when some of the group put Gorbachev on the spot with a hail of detailed questions on his reform measures – delivered in lecturing tones," he wrote. "Jacques Delors, the head of the European Union, interrogated Gorbachev like a professor questioning a student. The implication was, if you don't pass, beware. Others, such as Brian Mulroney, made equally important points, but in a more collegial tone, without the lecture and the scolding."

A crucial sidebar to the meeting with Gorbachev was the joint Soviet–American START (Strategic Arms Reduction Treaty) talks. While previous arms control agreements between the two superpowers had limited the growth in weapons of mass destruction, the successful conclusion of the negotiations would mean that their respective arsenals would actually be reduced by thousands of nuclear weapons. "Here we were talking about peace and economic help to the Soviet Union, while it seemed to everyone that what the Soviets wanted to do was to deploy new weapons aimed at us," Bush later wrote.

My notes describe what came next: "Over coffee, GB said to Maz, Barbara [McDougall], and me: 'Forty per cent of my advisors are recommending that I go for the treaty with the present wording of the contested clause. But I won't do it, so it looks like no deal. No START.' Immediately after . . . GB got me aside and said: 'You won't believe it and I won't put it this way publicly but he collapsed over lunch. Gave us everything we wanted on START. We have a deal.'"

Less than two weeks later, the two former Cold War rivals signed the START agreement when Bush visited Moscow. In the words of the treaty, they each agreed to

> Reduce and limit ICBMs and ICBM launchers, SLBMs and SLBM launchers, heavy bombers, ICBM warheads, SLBM warheads, and heavy bomber armaments, so that seven years after entry into force of this Treaty and thereafter, the aggregate numbers, as counted in accordance with Article III of this Treaty, do not exceed: (a) 1,600, for deployed ICBMs and their associated launchers, deployed SLBMs and their associated launchers, and deployed heavy bombers, including 154 for deployed heavy ICBMs and their associated launchers; (b) 6,000, for warheads attributed to deployed ICBMs, deployed SLBMs, and deployed heavy bombers, including: (i) 4,900, for warheads attributed to deployed ICBMs and deployed SLBMs; (ii) 1,100, for warheads attributed to deployed ICBMs on mobile launchers of ICBMs; (iii) 1,540, for warheads attributed to deployed heavy ICBMs.

I have reproduced this actual wording from the agreement as an illustration for my younger readers of the success of the Bush–Gorbachev partnership during that era. As one who grew up in the 1940s and 1950s and came of age in the 1960s, acronyms like ICBM, and words like "heavy bombers" and "warheads" were part of daily life. Thanks in large part to the work of Gorbachev and Bush in London and throughout their years of leadership in their respective nations, today's youth encounter these words only in history class.

Gorbachev left London knowing his country would receive technical assistance for economic reforms from the International Monetary Fund and other world bodies. I also met with the Soviet leader privately and described to him Canada's three-year program of technical assistance, including $10 million to help with the cleanup of Chernobyl and with training in the environment, energy, and agriculture sectors. I told him that Canada's Export Development Corporation had approved a $72 million credit to assist in developing a hotel complex in the USSR. We also freed up $150 million in aid that I had frozen at the time of the Soviet crackdown in the Baltic states earlier in the year.

"Canada is a privileged partner of the Soviet Union," Gorbachev told me during our talks. Then, as now, I regarded the $222 million aid package as a wise investment in peace.

Back in Canada, I immediately plunged into talks with my cabinet as we worked to craft a set of constitutional proposals for release in the fall. Every single person around the table understood just how high the stakes had grown, and my ministers held nothing back. As a Quebecer, I found it instructive to watch the Ontarians struggle with the issues. During one meeting that summer, Constitutional Affairs Minister Joe Clark slipped me a note. "PM: Throughout these discussions, Ontario has been the most cautious, conservative voice," it read. "Perrin [Beatty] is reconciled to basic changes, including re the Distinct Society, but urges that we move very carefully. Barbara [McDougall] is worried that we will be seen to be giving away the country. Michael [Wilson] and Doug [Lewis] are both swallowing hard and believe we have to accommodate Quebec but worry we will be seen by ordinary Ontarians as having gone too far."

As I've noted earlier, Ontarians are the only ones in the country who firstly view themselves as Canadians and only secondly wear their provincial allegiance. Many members of Canada's media establishment are located in Toronto, and as staunch opponents of the Meech Lake Accord, they had been very successful at stoking public opinion against any accommodation of Quebec. I could see and hear this dynamic at work around the cabinet table throughout the summer of 1991.

One Ontarian whom I needed to engage fully in the process if I was to be successful was Premier Bob Rae. I had always liked Bob and other members of his family, especially his brother John, a leading Liberal strategist. I remember telephoning Bob at Queen's Park the day after his surprising and historic victory in September of 1990. It turned out that I was the premier-designate's first caller. He recounted our conversation in his book, *From Protest to Power*.

"Bob, I have one word for you," I said.

"What's that, Prime Minister?" he asked.

"Vindication, Bob, vindication. You don't have to take any crap anymore from all those people who said you could never get there. You're there. You've made it to the mountaintop, and nobody can take that away from you."

"Well, it was certainly a long struggle and a big surprise," he replied.

"Enjoy yourself today," I advised, speaking from experience, "because it won't get any better than it was last night and it is today. Those bastards in the civil service are going to start coming at you with paper and you'll be fighting just to get to Sunday."

Bob Rae's government, like mine, was soon caught up in the cruel recession that was especially hard on his province's manufacturing base. He suffered that first ten months in office – and continued to suffer right up through his unsuccessful run at the federal Liberal leadership in 2006 – from an economic situation and an eventual record that was mostly out of his control.

Joe Clark had met with Rae in the spring, and he sent me a helpful memo highlighting the discussion on constitutional matters. At that meeting, Rae was clearly troubled that he hadn't yet had a face-to-face meeting with me, and he raised my strong personal relationship with Quebec's Robert Bourassa as a contrast. He was surprised when Clark correctly informed him that I had seen Bourassa in person only once since the end of the Meech Lake process in June 1990. Joe told me that he felt Rae was a different kind of Ontario premier and that his view of his province's role in constitutional negotiations ran counter to those of the Ontarians in my cabinet.

"The NDP treats Ontario as a 'region.' . . . Earlier premiers would never do that," Joe wrote. "They equated Ontario's interest with the national interest. Rae obviously believes that Ontario is slipping relative to the rest of Canada. My own view is that, on the Constitution, we have to deal with three Ontarios: a) rural (threatened, anti-French, more rigid than western Canada); b) urban (generous on constitutional issues, in the Robarts tradition); and c) ethnic (which doesn't have much sense of historic or 'constitutional' Canada, sees its champion in the Charter, and could go either way re Quebec)."

Joe's memo then examined the NDP nationally as it faced the shared challenge of recrafting the Constitution. I sorely missed Ed Broadbent as I read on. "I believe the NDP . . . is strongly tempted to play politics with the Constitution," Joe wrote. "I told Rae that his party worried me more than any other national party on that issue and that I hoped any 'Gordon Churchill strategy' would be resisted by NDPers with a broader view of the country. He did not dispute my concern, and said that he thought that both [Saskatchewan Premier Roy] Romanow and [B.C. Premier Mike] Harcourt hoped the issue could be avoided in the provincial election. We should consider what advice we can give our friends in those provinces (and to what effect). Rae and his government will argue that the economy is key to getting Ontario onside on the Constitution. In fact, he is committed to making progress on the Constitution. His 'economy' position may be for public purposes, or to rally support within his own government."

Rae and I finally broke bread together at Harrington Lake on July 26. We sat alone for about an hour on the screened-in porch overlooking the lake. In economic matters, I urged restraint by his government. "We've learned from Mr. Trudeau that deficit spending simply doesn't work," I said. "All you do is weaken the economic superstructure. If deficit spending solved problems, after fifteen years of Trudeau, Canada would be problem free today! But not only do we have all of these problems in Ottawa still, we are left with an enormous fiscal overhang that prevents you and I from doing the things we'd like to do in this debilitating recession." His counter-argument, which was also true, went something like this: "Look, I'm caught up, as premier of Ontario, in a particularly difficult situation because of the erosion of my economic base, and I'm going to have to make decisions that attenuate the social impact upon people."

Rae did later embrace fiscal restraint, but by then it was too late for him politically. Still, I thought that his Social Contract (whereby he attempted to save jobs in Ontario's public sector by having workers take unpaid days off – "Rae Days" – and exempted the lowest-paid, mainly women workers) was particularly forward-looking. But his former allies in the public sector union movement – especially teachers and provincial government employees – saw only the short-term pain, and, choosing ideology over reality, they blindly went ahead and set up the conditions that later saw thousands of their members put out of work.

In our talks that day, Rae made it clear to me that he felt Ontario was changing, with regionalism on the rise there. He also assured me his government would play a positive role in the constitutional field. In his memoirs, *From Protest to Power*, Rae wrote about what came next:

> Mulroney made a point of driving me down to the scrum at the gates to Harrington and joining me in front of the cameras. This was symbolically important: he could just as well have had me go

> out alone . . . He made the point in front of the media that he had heard clearly about the impact of the recession on Ontario, and at the same time said that any constitutional solution had to be arrived at, and would be arrived at, with the cooperation of the government of Ontario. From my perspective, mission accomplished. When I returned to Toronto, my own troops were less happy. Where were the arguments about free trade? Why have your picture taken with the most unpopular leader in Canada? How could any self-respecting New Democrat possibly cooperate with the man partisan rhetoric had turned into the devil incarnate? Wasn't I making the same mistake as David Peterson in associating myself with this man in the appeasement of Quebec?

While I've never asked him in our many discussions in the years since, I suspect that the sobering realities of governing were already leading Rae to the conclusion that many in the NDP did indeed prefer "protest to power" and that he might someday consider finding a new political home. Ironically, some of my own MPs also made it clear that I had made an error in allowing myself to be photographed with Ontario's first-ever NDP premier. Every political party, it seems, has its own dinosaurs.

As we moved into August, I had a great many political chores to undertake. My new senior advisor, Hugh Segal, sat me down for a frank chat one afternoon at Harrington Lake. "You're on television too much," he warned, "and you are becoming personally identified with every tough issue the government has run with." In his memoirs, *No Surrender*, Hugh relates my response to this criticism:

> Do you think it was my first choice to be out front and centre on the GST? That was Finance's formulation. Do you think I want to be on TV every night dealing with the constitution? Don't you think I know how it helps the Mulroney-haters and the opponents of the government? But the truth is, there has to be absolute consistency between what I say in caucus on Wednesday mornings and what I'm seen to say in public in defence of our program and our ministers. Silence from me will let Lucien or Preston start picking away at our caucus one by one. We can't hold the government unless we hold the caucus. The caucus did in Diefenbaker, Stanfield, and it did in Clark. It's the Conservative virus and it's intergenerational. My

> own popularity is a small price to pay for caucus unity, holding the government, and pulling the federalist options together so we won't see a pro-sovereignty vote in Quebec. That's my first responsibility.

Our party had a five-day convention scheduled to take place in Toronto, and I spent many hours preparing for it, very much in line with the role I'd outlined for myself in my conversation with Segal. Our polling numbers were atrocious and it was my job to rally the grassroots party workers from each and every constituency in Canada. There were more than 2,500 of these hard-working volunteers on hand, and it was my job to ensure they left Canada's largest city energized and prepared for the battles to come.

For once, a hostile media played right into my hands. Protesters had constructed an anti-poverty shantytown of about ten tents outside the Metro Convention Centre to illustrate, so they thought, my government and party's lack of caring for the poor. Although only a handful of protesters were on hand, the media reported this gathering as if thousands had descended on our policy convention to attack the hated Tories. Hugh Segal described the impact on the delegates.

> The delegates saw the small gathering of tents and they saw the TV coverage. They had ample evidence, uninfluenced by Mulroney's rhetoric or their own bias, of how the media could hijack any event, amplify dissent to the point of absurdity, and magnify the anti-government, anti-party, and anti-Mulroney sentiment in the land. This produced, beyond the normal affection for a leader who had brought them to power twice with historic majorities, an outpouring of confidence and affection I had never seen before.

I made countless speeches to different delegations during the convention, in one instance making fifteen addresses on a single day. The professional protesters provided constant fodder for my speeches. "Six tents, twenty-one people, two guys selling hot dogs – after being prime minister for seven years I think I'm entitled to a better demonstration than this," I said, over and over, to rounds of applause and cheers.

During my opening address to the convention on August 7, I reminded delegates that the founder of our party, the great Sir John A. Macdonald himself, had been down and out in 1873 when he lost power to the Grits under Alexander Mackenzie:

A leading Toronto newspaper wrote "It can hardly be doubted that his role as a Canadian politician is played out, and that his career has come to a close in the midst of a disgrace." Well, Sir John A. survived both his unpopularity and a bad press – and eighteen years later he was still prime minister of Canada!

I'm not guaranteeing you eighteen more years but I am telling you this: if we maintain our own unity and resolve, we are going to win a third consecutive majority government. Why? Audrey McLaughlin knows one reason why. In a newspaper profile late last year she observed: "Whatever else you say about Mulroney, he's decisive. Pick the issue – free trade, deregulation, privatization, the GST, the Middle East, high interest rates – Canadians do not like the decisions, but they got decisions" . . .

I am not here as prime minister to speak for any special interest, I am here taking strong decisions in difficult times for a united Canada. I am before you, tonight – bloodied and sometimes bowed – but completely determined to fight another winning battle for a better Canada.

1991

4. A Coup in Moscow

On August 18 Canadians received a strong reminder of how tiny their internal problems were when compared with other nations in the world. That Sunday morning, news reached the world of an attempted coup in the Soviet Union and the apparent overthrow of Mikhail Gorbachev. Gorbachev and his family, on holiday in the Black Sea area, had apparently been kidnapped by troops acting for the hardline communists who had taken over, and nobody had heard from him. The Soviet news agency TASS suddenly announced that the president was sick and that he had asked to be relieved of his duties.

As soon as I heard about the coup I began, thanks to the switchboard operators at the PMO, to gather intelligence from fellow leaders around the planet. Among the first I reached were Chancellor Helmut Kohl and President George Bush.

"I don't know anything specific yet," a shocked Kohl told me. "This looks much like the Khrushchev takeover. But, I don't have the impression the Red Army is behind it. If you ask me, I'm worried about Poland and other countries. It will be a real problem if a large number of Soviet citizens try to enter the European Community via Poland." We agreed to keep each other updated as we gathered information from our respective sources.

George Bush was at his summer residence in Kennebunkport. "We've got to play it cool," he told me.

The Privy Council Office soon had a report with information supplied by our embassy in Moscow. It made for chilling reading. "Our embassy reports that Moscow is virtually under siege, with massive armoured troop movements inside the city. It is almost impossible to get around, except by metro. This morning, the crowd standing vigil outside the Russian Parliament has grown to more than 30,000. The adjacent bridge has been barricaded. The regime is already cracking down in the Baltic states. The commander of Soviet military forces in the region yesterday informed governments of Lithuania, Latvia, and Estonia that he had been ordered to take control in all the Baltic states. According to Canadian Baltic community representatives and media reports, the Soviet military is positioning itself for a takeover, abetted by hardline communists."

The next day, I had extensive discussions with French President François Mitterrand. Like me, he was concerned that no one had heard from Gorbachev, or even seen him. "He would never agree to this," I told Mitterrand, "regardless of what the coup leaders are saying. This is an illegal takeover, and we have to resist it, and we must defend Mikhail." I suggested to Mitterrand that he and Kohl fly suddenly and unannounced to Moscow and demand to see Gorbachev. The coup leaders would be hard pressed to deny such a request from Europe's foremost leaders.

I then discussed the idea with Bush. "Mitterrand is intrigued by the idea and ready to do it provided 'he is asked in the appropriate manner,'" I told the U.S. president, around nine o'clock the morning after the coup.

"It's the hard-liners," Bush told me, "Pugo, Kryuchkov, Yazov, Pavlov. We're not sure where Moiseyev is. The rumour is that he flew down to break the news to Gorbachev. We were surprised like everybody else."

"George," I replied, "one point where you may get some criticism on behalf of all of us, they may say, 'Well, if you people had been more generous in London, maybe this wouldn't have happened.'"

"I'll get hit for holding the country too close to Gorbachev," Bush said. "I'll point out it's a damn good thing, because look at the changes that have taken place. And if we had tried to pull the rug, it would have happened sooner."

"Any doubt in your mind that he was overthrown because he was too close to us?" I asked.

"I don't think there's any doubt," Bush answered. "It will be interesting to see what the new 'leaders' say. At first, they said he had health problems; maybe that means Gorbachev's fingernails wouldn't come out. Even more important is the economic chaos and disorder that goes with it, and the economic drift. And, I think, for these guys, the downgrading of the Communist Party. These are hard-liners and they see the party that was their life's blood – and the KGB, that has been the silent hand forever – undermined and threatened as well."

In his book *A World Transformed*, President Bush described the conclusion of our telephone call that day. "Brian asked if I felt there was any significance in the fact that the Union Treaty was to be signed in the next few days," he wrote. "He believed that Gorbachev coming back to sign it would be 'the kiss of death' to the traditionalists and that this may have precipitated the coup. I wasn't certain, but it was a good possibility. (Brent Scowcroft and I later agreed it was probably a contributing factor to the timing.) 'Yeltsin is out there on top of a tank saying this coup must be reversed,' I added. 'You have to give him credit for enormous guts.'"

Over dinner at 24 Sussex more than a year later, Boris Yeltsin explained to me his role in fighting off the coup. I wrote down this account shortly after he left.

> Re the coup: He had had no prior knowledge of it at all, he had found out about it from radio reports at 8 a.m. He immediately gathered his key advisors and decided to fight. Four attempts were made on his life during the period, he said. He said clearly the mastermind was KGB Chief Vladimir Kryuchkov and that it would take "very long" for the criminal charges to be heard and resolved in court. He also said that, if [any of the coup leaders were] found guilty of treason and sentenced to death, he would commute the death sentences to 15 years in prison! He . . . [had] called Kryuchkov and told him he was doomed, that the people would sweep him away, and that the only way to legitimize the coup was for them to fly to Crimea and have Gorbachev sign the document surrendering power. Then, with a chuckle, he said, "An hour after they took off on this goose chase, I sent another plane to Crimea to arrest them all!"

While I instructed External Affairs officials that Canada's main priority was the safety and return of Gorbachev and his family, this message was not clearly transmitted to the department's minister, Barbara McDougall. Her first public comments concerning the crisis reflected the cautious and conservative thinking prevalent among the bureaucrats in the Lester B. Pearson Building. In this case, Barbara, a superb political performer, was poorly served by her officials.

The following day I announced publicly that Canada was immediately suspending all aid to the Soviet Union. I dispensed with the advice from the ever-cautious bureaucracy who had warned me that Canada should be prepared to work with whoever was in power in Moscow. I would have none of it. "[Mulroney] demanded that Soviet authorities divulge his whereabouts, dared them to put him on television, and insisted they guarantee his, and his family's, safety," Carol Goar wrote in the *Toronto Star.* "When the junta proclaimed . . . that Gorbachev was too ill to govern, Mulroney was openly skeptical. The President had seemed 'in great shape' a month ago in London, he observed. He railed at the usurpers. He made it clear Canada wanted nothing to do with them. Indeed, he went a good deal further than some of the bureaucrats at the department of external affairs would have liked . . . By associating himself as strongly as he did with Gorbachev, he might have jeopardized relations with the new regime. Canada's $1.3 billion trade with the Soviet Union might have suffered. Its influence in the post-Gorbachev world order might have waned. As it turned out, his approach was entirely right."

I chose the course I did because the USSR was clearly at a crossroads. We were heading toward either the evolution of a more democratic, more free-market Soviet Union under Gorbachev or Yeltsin, or toward a return to Stalinism under the plotters of the coup, in which the military would dominate and hostility toward the West would be the order of the day. The stakes for the USSR – a country with nuclear missiles still pointed at the West – were frighteningly high.

In the end, Gorbachev was returned to power, unharmed. Boris Yeltsin, Gorbachev's successor, who had stared the plotters down defiantly from the Russian Parliament, also chose democracy and reform, refusing to give in to those in his country who wanted a return to the former oppressive regime.

On August 22, Gorbachev and I spoke on the telephone. "I thank you for calling as a friend," he said. "I thank you for your support and for the very strong stand you have taken, Brian, for me and my family. Now is the time to move on to new challenges. Thank you for your great support."

After the coup had failed, Hugh Segal and I discussed the role of personal diplomacy on the world stage in a wide-ranging conversation at 24 Sussex Drive. I recap this conversation here, as he describes it in his book, *No Surrender*.

"You know, one of the things the most extreme Canadian nationalists fail to realize is that while we may believe Canada is the most important place in the world, as it is for us and our children, there's an entire world out there that doesn't share that view," I said. "Oh, they like us well enough. They think we're decent and helpful, by and large, and we're listened to on occasion. But I'll tell you, Hugh, that's not because of who we are or where we stand or the geopolitical framework. That's because of how hard we work to make sure we get noticed. That's what few people understand about the job a Canadian prime minister has."

"But isn't that what our involvement in the UN and NATO and La Francophonie, and all those institutions is all about?" Segal asked. "I mean, we only establish our credibility because of our presence in those organizations, so we find a way to get consulted in the process."

"That's actually 100 per cent wrong," I answered. "There are all kinds of countries in La Francophonie and the Commonwealth and the UN and NATO that don't get consulted by the United States on policy in the Mideast or Central America. There are all kinds of countries in NATO and the UN that the Russians don't call on when they're trying to shape a Western response to their situation. Our membership gets us no leverage and no particular place at the table. Our membership has to be personified in a way where other countries with the economic power to have an impact on our quality of life want to deal with Canada, because they believe the country and its leadership can make a contribution."

"In other words," Segal said, "it comes down to interpersonal relations."

"Absolutely," I answered. "Without that, we just don't count, certainly not in terms we would like to count."

A few days later, Mila and I travelled to Kennebunkport – in a tradition we still continue to follow at least once a year – to spend time with George and Barbara Bush at their summer home. President Bush had a surprising suggestion for my future as we talked in Maine that summer.

—

PERSONAL JOURNAL: AUGUST 27, 1991

I advised the president and Brent Scowcroft as soon as we arrived at Kennebunkport of my intention to announce, the next day, Canada's recognition of independence of the Baltic states and the re-establishment of full diplomatic relations. We had a full review of the remarkable developments ongoing in the USSR and then left for a boating trip with Barbara, Mila, and the kids. After dinner we went out on our ritual stroll down to the gate. But this time we examined a new medical clinic they've installed for George Bush – who says it costs $60,000 and that he's going to buy it after he leaves office. On the way back to the house, George was using his walking stick and said *that he had had secret conversations with Brent Scowcroft, Jim Baker, and U.S. Ambassador to the United Nations Tom Pickering about the upcoming replacement for Javier Pérez de Cuéllar as Sec.-Gen. of the United Nations. George said, "Brian, I don't know whether you plan to run again but if you decided to retire after your second term, I think you would make a first-rate Secretary-General. The U.S. and our allies will support you, and we can make this happen."*

I told him that I was genuinely flattered by his interest and support, that I had not thought of such a prospect, and that I was busy and engaged putting together constitutional proposals in Canada. Standing outside the main house, where it was quite cool and dark, he said, "You've got a proven track record as a leader, unafraid to tackle bruising, controversial issues. You understand the nuances and implications of foreign policy having operated as prime minister of a country at a G-7 level for seven years; you and Canada are known to be strong supporters of the UN and you have friends and supporters around the world. You have my total support and that of all G-7 leaders, I would bring Gorby and Yeltsin onside, and I'm telling you, Brian, it is a readily doable proposal."

I thanked him again for his interest and support and went to our cabin, where I discussed it with Mila. (In fact, just prior to my visit, Tellier called urgently to convey a conversation with Gotlieb. Allan had been invited to lunch by his old friend Tom Pickering at the UN who had explained this possibility and sought to ascertain my interest. Gotlieb said he had no idea but would find out – hence the call to Paul Tellier.)

The next morning I was up and began meeting with GB, Brent, and Derek on the ongoing crisis and our major bilateral issue – the Memorandum of Understanding on the softwood lumber issue. After some three hours of conversation and calls to Helmut Kohl, Toshiki Kaifu, Jacques Attali (Mitterrand's economic advisor), and Jim Baker in Wyoming, we went fishing for an hour. Prior to our joint press conference, I was free to speak privately with Derek Burney and told him of the conversation of the previous evening. He was stunned but very pleased at the thoughtfulness and courtesy. I told Derek I had no idea what might happen but it was most unlikely that I would accept even under the most favourable of circumstances because my primary duty lay in Canada, in trying to put together constitutional proposals that would help the country unite. There is no set of circumstances that would cause me to accept, but I readily agree with both Mila and Derek that it was a huge honour to have been asked, especially under such circumstances. As I said to Derek, "It would take quite a lame candidate to be unable to win a race for the UN job in 1992 with George Bush as his campaign manager."

—

As I look back today, perhaps it would have been better if I had moved on to the United Nations at that time. Hugh Segal told me he thought I should take the job. "If you accept that gratitude is the least likely emotion to be expressed at election time, especially after a grinding recession, and if you remember that the good voters of Britain shot down Winston Churchill in 1945, there are likely to be zero electoral benefits in '92 or '93 for free trade or the Gulf War. And you would be an outstanding secretary-general," he told me. But I felt the risks to Canadian unity were enormous and that I owed it to my country, my province, my caucus, and my family to remain on course until the constitutional bullet was indeed removed from the chamber. Lowell Murray was blunt: "If you leave, the disintegration of caucus is weeks, not months, away."

Once my decision was final, I explained my reasons to Hugh Segal. "How the hell could I have done that, Hugh, when most of the cabinet, including Maz and Benoît, said it would be next to impossible to keep the caucus together or get any kind of agreement on the Constitution were I to leave?" I said. "Besides, look at Bourassa. The man had life-threatening cancer and had every reason to leave, but he hung in. He put off treatment because he didn't want to leave the province during Oka, then he stayed on after and between treatments to bring some closure to the Meech process. My taking a UN appointment would be perceived as disloyal to the caucus and cabinet, and especially to people like Bourassa, who are staying to find a way to keep the country together."

Step one in our constitutional renewal process came in late September of 1991, when my government released our fifty-nine-page constitutional proposal *Shaping Canada's Future Together*. "Renewal is what Canadians everywhere seek for our country – not confrontation, not division, not rupture," I told the Commons when the document was unveiled.

I had invited retired chief justice Brian Dickson to lunch at Harrington Lake one day in August. I shared with him a draft of our proposals and asked him to write me a private response. While I was confident of handling the political side of the question, I wanted the legal opinion of a man who'd spent a lifetime serving Canada as a distinguished lawyer and jurist. Former Chief Justice Dickson didn't disappoint. On October 25, he sent me a fourteen-page personal letter after he'd carefully examined *Shaping Canada's Future Together*. "The proposals which your government had advanced are far-reaching, bold, and complex," he wrote. "The proposals constitute a comprehensive constitutional package which will no doubt undergo change, refining, and fine tuning as the open process, which is mandated, proceeds."

Dickson took the same hard line concerning the Quebec "dream merchants" that I had taken earlier in the year. "Some of the reports from Quebec suggest that, following separation, it will be 'business as usual' on the economic front, that Quebec can become a separate state yet integral to Canada's economy," he wrote. "In my view, those expressing that sentiment are either painfully naïve or merely deceptive . . . I cannot but believe that secession by Quebec would lead to outright disaster, to Quebec and to Canada . . . I am at a loss to know how, under the present Constitution, to which Quebec is subject, that province could legally secede from the rest of the country. Our Constitution makes no mention of the right of a province to withdraw from the federation. The patriation of our Constitution was delayed for some 50 years because the federal authority and the provinces were unable to agree on the language of an amending formula. That is a small change compared with the suggestion that a province can unilaterally, and perhaps against the will of the rest of the country, leave the federation and become an independent state."

Dickson also reviewed what had brought Canada to its present impasse. "I think that among the contributing factors the following are dominant: a) the patriation of the Constitution in 1982 with the inclusion therein of the Canadian Charter of Rights and Freedoms, the whole without the concurrence of Quebec; b) the defeat of the Meech Lake Accord an event, in my view, to be deplored and with potentially tragic consequences for our country. The Meech Lake debacle was mistakenly regarded by many in Quebec as a rejection of that province and its people by the rest of Canada and other Canadians; c) the exercise by the Bourassa government of the 'notwithstanding clause.' . . . These factors and a resurgent sentiment of nationalism, separatism, and sovereignty in Quebec have led to the present critical state in our national life."

Dickson then concluded. "I sense a new willingness on the part of most Canadians to find a solution which will maintain Canada as one of the world's great nations; a desire to understand and to communicate their concerns and aspirations to other Canadians. I hope the proposals now advanced will help to heal the wounds from Meech Lake and will lead to a new and unified country, and a more prosperous future for all Canadians. Sir John A. Macdonald's wording delivered 130 years ago is relevant today: 'Whatever you do, adhere to the Union. We are a great country and we shall become one of the greatest if we preserve it; we shall sink into insignificance and adversity if we suffer it to be broken.' Prime Minister, this letter is written in response to your request and in the hope that it may be helpful to you and your immediate advisors in the ongoing constitutional discussions. The proposals are a giant step toward national reconciliation."

The former chief justice's conclusions were reassuring, but they went only so far in allaying my worries. As we launched our proposals to general approval from many quarters, I was already detecting a dangerous division over the Constitution at the highest levels of my government. Paul Tellier, Norman Spector, and Joe Clark were obviously not singing from the same hymn book. Joe, in particular, resented the long-range planning and strategic thinking advocated by my Clerk of the Privy Council and chief of staff.

"But what worries me more is the possibility that Norman and others might be leaping ahead to speculate on what we might need six months from now," Joe wrote to me on September 30. He also expressed concern about the proposal to supersede Quebec's referendum with a nationwide referendum of our own. "That is fruitless. It will be late October, at the earliest, before we have any reliable reading of public or provincial opinion . . . There are several ways to doom this project. One is being too clever and changing a strategy before we know whether it works."

The situation came to a head before the year was out. Suddenly, in December, Norman Spector resigned. While I was sleeping in my hotel room in Vancouver on December 4, my chief of staff slipped a strange resignation letter under my door. It was a bombshell, and scathing in its criticism of Joe Clark. "The middle of the night is not a good time to write a letter like this," Norman began. "But there is probably never a good time, and it must be written. This is not an easy letter to write and I imagine it will not be easy to read. It is handwritten to ensure you have total control over its contents."

As I read on, it became clear that Norman was profoundly depressed over the handling of constitutional reform:

> I have grave misgivings and profound disagreements on the constitutional file. These have been growing over time, and have now reached the breaking point. The minister responsible is mismanaging Canada toward disaster. Openness is a vice when coupled with chaos. And prejudice is simply a testament to inadequacy in the face of complexity. The bureaucracy is an organizational mess, defying its only purpose. Inflating the number of people and decision-making nodes adds only confusion and not value. And freshness is no virtue when accompanied by inexperience. Everyone is involved and no one is accountable. And PMO exacerbates and does not mitigate the resulting dysfunctions. My name will never be what it once was, but I hope it will never be associated with incompetence, improvisation, and clumsiness. My health will never be the same but it is time to have the checkup I have been avoiding so as to not learn the truth . . . I will always value having had the opportunity to serve you . . . Now I will have an opportunity to write history, and to comment on the making of history as I saw it and see it. I don't think either of us will suffer in the telling.

I did not want to admit it, but Spector's criticisms were becoming more widely shared across the upper reaches of my government. Questions were being asked (in a whisper, mind you) about Clark's suitability for the job I had entrusted to him.

I soon had a meeting with Spector at 24 Sussex and asked him directly what he wanted to do with his future. He said he intended to return to British Columbia and perhaps teach at a university.

"Well, Norman," I said, "that's what you *plan* to do. What would you *like* to do?"

"Well, I'd love to be Canada's ambassador to Israel, but that will never happen because I'm Jewish," he replied.

Up until then, there had been an unwritten policy in the Government of Canada that implied that Jews had dual loyalties and thus could not be appointed ambassadors to Israel. After Norman left, I called the deputy minister of external affairs and asked if the current list of proposed ambassadors was complete. Specifically, I asked, "Do you have someone for Israel?"

"Yes," came the response.

"I think you now have a new candidate. I want you to put forward the name of Norman Spector for Israel," I said. "This question of dual loyalties that I've heard about, that's never prevented us from appointing French Canadians to Paris, or English Canadians to England. So let's just toss that aside as a silly part of our past, and I will sign the order appointing Spector to Tel Aviv."

And that was the end of it. Norman Spector went on to serve his country with distinction as Canadian ambassador to Israel.

When I travelled to Harare, Zimbabwe, in October (where I gave the assembled Commonwealth leaders a stern lecture on the need for many to improve the human rights situation in their own countries, now that South African apartheid was clearly on the way out) I saw again how Canadians weren't the only ones following our constitutional squabbles. During a lengthy dinner and conversation with Australian Prime Minister Bob Hawke, I discovered he had definite opinions on Canadian ideas to reform their upper house!

"If there's any possibility of avoiding the idea of an elected senate, you should seize it," Hawke told me. "I've always thought Canada had the ideal situation – an appointed senate with no power. Once you set up a second house you get plenty of problems. Senators are only human and will try to justify their existence. An elected senate with effective powers is inimical to good government. In Australia, there has never been a senate that has functioned as a 'state' house. Why would Canada be any different?"

I resolved not to share Hawke's views with Don Getty in the months ahead.

I also had a frank exchange with Zimbabwe's Robert Mugabe. "Your idea of getting rid of political parties and making Zimbabwe a one-party state will be the kiss of death," I warned. "Canada and other countries will have serious problems with it. We have no tolerance for giving foreign aid money to tyrants." As we are fully aware today, Mugabe – an international pariah now – did not heed my warning.

Nelson Mandela stood in stark contrast to the despot that Mugabe was to become. In Harare I saw how this brilliant leader was becoming an increasingly effective diplomat. Mandela pressed me hard for a contribution of about $10 million to assist in the political struggle that lay ahead. When I reminded him of our earlier contributions, he politely dismissed my concerns and kept arguing. Finally, I gave in, assuring him we would make another significant contribution. At this, Mandela rose and said, "Canada has been a tremendous friend of our cause and Prime Minister Mulroney has supported us for years, worldwide. We are extremely grateful." Then he shook hands, turned, and headed for the door where he stopped and looked at me with a big smile wreathing his face.

"Oh, by the way, Brian," he said, "could you make that contribution in American dollars?" Even I burst out laughing.

This was my last face-to-face meeting as prime minister with Mandela, though we remained in frequent contact by telephone as the situation in South Africa evolved. When he was sworn in as president of South Africa in 1994, all the world celebrated. In Australia, Prime Minister Paul Keating asked his rival and predecessor as prime minister, Bob Hawke, to represent that country at Mandela's swearing-in, in recognition of Hawke's remarkable work within the Commonwealth at ending apartheid. Prime Minister Chrétien made no such decision, and I watched the ceremonies from afar.

Mandela, whom I continue to see during my yearly business trips to South Africa, has not forgotten our work during the 1980s and early 1990s. "On the tenth anniversary of our democracy, one recalls the momentous time of our transition and remembers the people involved both within and outside South Africa," he wrote to me in April 2004. "As prime minister of Canada [and within the] Commonwealth, you provided strong and principled leadership in the battle against apartheid. This was not a popular position in all quarters, but South Africans today acknowledge the importance of your contribution to our eventual liberation and success. On a personal basis, I have greatly enjoyed your friendship and support over many years and look forward to your regular visits with Mila to Cape Town to review and reminisce."

Sadly, the anti-Mulroney mentality that gripped the upper reaches of the Chrétien government affected one of these later visits. Just before we arrived in South Africa, Canada's high commissioner in Pretoria was astonished to receive instructions from Ottawa that he was to provide Mila and me with no assistance as we went about arranging a meeting with our friend Nelson Mandela. That instruction came from James Bartleman, foreign policy advisor to Jean Chrétien. We met with Mandela anyway.

In all areas of diplomatic activity, the fall of 1991 continued at a hurried pace. After responding positively to an invitation from former U.S. secretary of state George Shultz, I gave the commencement address at Stanford University in California on its one-hundredth anniversary. I used my speech that day to help prod the Bush administration and our other allies into taking the necessary next step in the continuing evolution of East–West relations.

"The North Atlantic Treaty remains an indispensable insurance policy against a return to the autarchy of the 1930s," I told the crowd of ten thousand. "Association in NATO could be extended eventually to former adversaries, were they to want it, once they had fully and irreversibly embraced the transatlantic democratic values that we share. In any case, the fledgling democracies would succeed in economic and political reconstruction much more quickly if they were spared the wasteful cost of useless military expenditures. Can you tell me why a country on the verge of bankruptcy would commit 25 per cent of its GDP to military weaponry? There is no good value in that at all. The 25 per cent of the GDP should be devoted to the children and to the well-being of their citizens and to consumer goods and to hope and aspiration for people in those countries. Only in that way will there be a secure and durable peace."

Inviting former members of the Warsaw Pact to join NATO? Senior members of the governments of some of our closest allies were shocked and angered by my suggestion, particularly the British. Even at External Affairs in Ottawa, my idea of bringing in former enemies like Poland, Hungary, and Czechoslovakia ruffled a few bureaucratic feathers, shall we say. To them, this suggestion smacked of heresy after almost fifty years of a very bitter Cold War.

My chief foreign policy advisor, Paul Heinbecker, had contributed a great deal to that speech, as he did to many others. A professional foreign service officer, he was meticulous, effective, and loyal in every way. Because his daughters, Yasemin and Céline, went to school with our children, Mila and I had a warm relationship with Paul and his wife, Ayşe Köymen, outside of the office as well. I was later to appoint him Canada's ambassador to Germany, and was pleased when he later was named to the post of ambassador to the United Nations. More than a year after my Stanford speech, Paul wrote to me from Germany and enclosed a clipping from the *International Herald Tribune*. "You will remember the grief that some people in External Affairs and others, including the British, gave us over your Stanford University speech in which you advocated expansion of NATO," he wrote. "In the interim, as the quotation from Dick Cheney indicates, the idea has almost become conventional wisdom."

NATO leaders gathered in November of 1991 as we continued to grapple with the ever-changing face of Europe. The former Yugoslavia was by now in flames, and I called on these Balkan countries to sit down and negotiate a settlement to their conflict. Little could I, or anyone, have imagined the horror and atrocities that would soon follow in Bosnia and Serbia.

NATO had some internal tensions as well. François Mitterrand had refused to sign an American-drafted document urging the Soviet Union to move toward democracy, create a free-market economy, and put its nuclear weapons under the control of a central body. He called the declaration "patronizing." This was a typical response by Mitterrand to anything suggesting to him a dilution of his authority as president of the French Republic. Quite frankly, I always admired him for his refusal to compromise the grandeur of his office.

As December approached, the West once again had to wrestle with changes in eastern Europe. A referendum on Ukrainian independence was slated for December 1, and Ukrainian Canadians – like their compatriots in all Western countries – were lobbying hard for our governments to recognize an independent Ukraine, if that's what voters chose. Mikhail Gorbachev disagreed, hoping against all odds that Ukraine would opt for membership in the federation he was now proposing.

President Bush and I discussed the situation and our respective positions over the telephone on November 30. Bush had already spoken that day with both Gorbachev and Russian President Boris Yeltsin. "Canada has a large ethnic Ukrainian population in the western provinces and Brian was already under pressure to recognize Ukraine," Bush later wrote in his account of our discussion that day.

"I'd like to do nothing harmful to Gorbachev," I said, "even though we all sense it's a lost cause regarding holding the Union together."

"It seems so," Bush agreed.

"It's almost a personal thing – to help Gorbachev," I went on. "I feel almost the same way as I did when we had to deal with the Baltics. We don't want to do anything disruptive. It's a matter of semantics, of wording, but our approach is not far off from yours. We'll recognize or acknowledge the independence of Ukraine, then we'll negotiate the establishment of diplomatic relations."

"That's what we're going to do," Bush replied.

On December 2, to the great joy of Ukraine's democrats and the Ukrainian diaspora around the world, Canada became the first G-7 nation to recognize Ukraine. Though it pained me to go against Gorbachev's hopes, we could all clearly see by now where the USSR was heading – into the dustbin of history.

Early in December I had lunch with Jean-Bertrand Aristide of Haiti. He had recently been overthrown in a coup, and I used the luncheon to re-engage our government in the cause of democracy in Haiti. I worked closely with François Mitterrand and President Carlos Andrés Pérez Rodríguez of Venezuela in promoting this cause. The Bush administration, on the other hand, was very suspicious of Aristide. They felt he was a communist, not a true democrat. Bush used to say, "Here comes Mulroney. I'm sure he'll talk to us about his friend *Aristidey*."

I was later to remark to President Bill Clinton that America's apparent indifference to the Haitian situation made little sense to me. North Americans were concerned with issues of peace halfway around the world, but often seemed to care little about what was going on in their own hemisphere. After I left office, and with Clinton fully engaged and willing to back democracy in Haiti with troops, Aristide and democracy were restored to that troubled Caribbean country – for a short while. After my retirement, I was honoured when Haiti awarded me the Grande Croix de l'Ordre honneur et mérite national for my work on that nation's behalf.

Happily for the world, the final days of the Soviet Union played out peacefully. On December 21, eleven former Soviet republics agreed to form the Commonwealth of Independent States. The USSR would be no more. President Gorbachev of the USSR would resign his post on Christmas Day and the Soviet flag would be lowered from the Kremlin ramparts it had flown above since 1917.

On Christmas Eve, Gorbachev called me from his office inside the Kremlin. With a strong sense of being witnesses to history, Mila and the children sat with me in my second-floor study at Harrington Lake as I took the call. "Your contributions to the destiny of your country and the whole world have been unique," I told Mikhail. "The world will never be the same after your reforms, arms reductions, and your other international policy initiatives. Politics can be very cruel, but your contributions, I assure you, will be recognized and appreciated when you leave office and when they are compared with those of your successors."

Mikhail assured me that the USSR's command and control systems for nuclear weapons would be transferred the next day, quickly and safely. "I'm not worried and neither should you be," he said.

As the call wound down he asked me to convey my best wishes and thoughts to Mila. I expressed the same about his wife and family. And then the call ended.

A letter – one of the final ones Mikhail Gorbachev signed as the USSR's president – was delivered to me at Harrington Lake on Christmas Day. It had been roughly translated at what was now the Russian embassy in Ottawa. "Dear Brian: The calm and respectful attitude of the Canadians, their support and solidarity in these hard years, have been held here in high esteem," he wrote. "We see that the people of your country wish success to the reforms and democratic transformations which not only we but the entire world need. All that are the signs of the new times for the sake of which we have done a good share of work. And that inspires me. I believe in the eventual success. I thank you and Mila for your friendship. Goodbye."

I thought about Gorbachev and his family all through that very emotional Christmas Day. I imagined the anguish they would be going through at what normally is a festive time of the year. My sadness was tempered, however, by the knowledge that he – and we in the West, his former enemies – had done the right thing by history. When I was growing up, the hostility of the Soviet Union – the unforgiving, implacable hatred of its Communist rulers for the West – was the defining issue of our time. I thought of the countless billions of dollars that the West had spent in the defence of a free Europe, and what the Soviets had wasted through the Warsaw Pact. Generations had grown up in the shadow of a mushroom cloud. I remember the airport at Mont-Joli, right across the river from us in Baie-Comeau, where American and Canadian forces flew in while they were constructing a radar site north of us. I also remembered reading as a young boy an article from one of the magazines my parents had around the house. One line, "We will remember your lies, Mr. Molotov" – referring to a Soviet foreign minister's appearance at the United Nations – stayed with me for years.

I recall how shaken we all were at Laval University in October 1962, when we became aware that the Soviet Union had installed in Cuba strategic missiles aimed at North America. We anxiously read newspapers as the

Cuban Missile Crisis unfolded, all of us wondering if nuclear war was at hand. Such anxieties were in the marrow of the bones of anyone raised during the Cold War.

For me to have been personally involved with the key player in ending this insanity – speaking with Gorbachev and receiving a written communication from him in the USSR's last moments – was deeply moving. I ended 1991 deeply gratified that Canadians had allowed me to play a role in this unfolding drama, which I was sure would be ultimately beneficial for us all. I felt a very lucky man.

1992

1. A Bleak Start to the Year

PERSONAL JOURNAL: JANUARY 4, 1992

My own schedule and agenda in '92 will be the three Cs: Constitution, caucus, and communications. If we can focus on the substance of the Constitution, spend time holding the parliamentary caucus together – and that can be almost a permanent job in itself – and communicate to the country we may just be able to put together a package that will fly. There has not been great improvement in the national mood these past six months. If a referendum were held on sovereignty today in Quebec I think it would pass. Likewise, if a referendum were held across the country calling for the endorsement of any proposal that seemed conciliatory to Quebec, it would be rejected. It is almost as if Canadians – whose entire existence has required honourable compromise – have come to eschew the notion as being weak willed, unprincipled, and lacking in leadership.

—

THAT IS HOW MY journal began as the new year dawned. With a sombre mood hanging over Canada like a darkening cloud, I didn't find my usual comfort at Harrington Lake over the holidays. While my family kept me grounded, I couldn't shake the knowledge that the summer residence of the prime minister of Canada was located in Quebec. By the end of the year it was very possible that Quebec would have voted to leave Canada. This thought haunted me as I stared out across the lake, writing in my journal.

I knew we were heading into an extraordinarily difficult period, with each day a "make or break" one for me as prime minister. The situation was bleak, and becoming bleaker still because of the actions of members of my own government.

—

When we met in the Langevin Block, Joe Clark said, in response to a statement by Segal that Chrétien might, as opposition leader, attack his credibility, "My reputation is such that there is nothing Mr. Chrétien can do or say that would damage it in any way."

I thought Spector and Tellier were going to choke on the spot. I was simply amused, as I'm the one who is always portrayed in the media as being ego-driven . . .

It became very clear in August that whatever his qualities – and Joe Clark unquestionably has many fine ones – he is essentially process-oriented. Rather than sit down, develop a coherent strategy, devise objectives and the means of achieving them, he is all over the lot, writing endless memos to increase the confusion for staff, contradicting himself on government policy, reversing course after meeting the Quebec caucus.

In August I had to get involved in the national unity committee because it had broken down almost completely, with the bitterness between Quebec and non-Quebec ministers almost palpable. At one meeting in the summer, the Quebec ministers suddenly got up, left the meeting, and went for a walk, triggering the story in the press that the whole exercise might collapse. That would have been the end, so I quietly spoke with Joe Clark, outlined some ideas to him, worked privately and quietly with recalcitrant Quebec and Ontario ministers, and used P&P meetings in Kelowna and Sherbrooke to reassure the chair of the national unity deliberations, thereby producing a compromise report we tabled for Sept. 23 that was endorsed by all members of cabinet.

Thus, we avoided an open crisis among government members about whether we had gone too far or not far enough in seeking to accommodate legitimate regional, linguistic, and cultural realities. The proposals were well received in English Canada and indifferently received in Quebec, where they came under immediate and blistering attack from separatists and the political class and the so-called elite, and received little direct support except for La Presse *and other Power Corp. papers where Paul Desmarais made certain a fair and reasonable assessment was available.*

Joe Clark continued, in the month following, to do an excellent job on process – he was out selling across the country, meeting with natives, premiers, etc., seeking to advance the cause. Let me not misstate the case: Joe Clark has, in my mind, many fine abilities. He is good in the House, has an excellent understanding of the country, a quiet but genuine sense of humour, and a set of principles that he seeks to live his life by, and to a degree, succeeds. He has been for me a loyal and helpful cabinet colleague. And I, in return, have treated him with unfailing respect and courtesy as befits a former prime minister and national party leader – indeed, my open and constant support of him, both at External and now at FPRO, and my confidence in him, as illustrated by these assignments, indicate the regard I have for him and is responsible, in some considerable degree, for his political rehabilitation in the party and the country. In eight years he has gone from being attacked as a klutz destined for the trivia notes of history to an accomplished politician who, if I were to step aside, would become a leading candidate to succeed me as prime minister. And, as I've already written in these notes early last year, he has many of the qualities and has worked on some of the skills required to become now an effective party leader and prime minister. If indeed he were ever to emerge as my successor, I would be pleased and would work closely with and for him because I think a government he would lead would be head and shoulders above anything Jean Chrétien and Audrey McLaughlin could put together.

In fact, on the leadership question, Joe Clark, McDougall, Campbell, Beatty, et al., have emerged as the likely prospects, and each one has much to commend him/her. In the last six months, Kim Campbell has shucked off the sadness that had enveloped her following her marital problems – a second divorce – and has been the most effective legislator and spokesperson on the government side . . . Beatty is good, honest, and ambitious, but whether his "me first" attitude will generate much support or loyalty remains to be seen. Charest remains the greatest potential star in the party, Valcourt is the finest natural street politician, but both are young, have made mistakes in judgment that warranted their removal from the cabinet earlier, and both are French Canadians at a time when the party and country might, quite properly, be seeking an English-speaking leader from outside Quebec or Acadia.

I continue to envision the strong likelihood of finishing the year . . . depending on developments in the unity file, Quebec referendum, etc., then arranging for a leadership convention in the first quarter of 1993 that would allow a new leader from English Canada some six to eight months as prime minister in a strong economic growth period, giving him/her the chance to make his/her mark on the national consciousness before issuing the writ. I would wager that in such circumstances a new prime minister from the West or Ontario could cripple the Reform Party, damage the Chrétien Liberals badly, and hold the Bloc to a reasonable number in Quebec, thereby almost guaranteeing a PC minority, and perhaps majority, government.

Now, I have my failings but I am no fool. Our numbers have been so low for so long that it is normal for caucus members to begin to worry about their own fates in any upcoming election. In spite of this legitimate concern, plus the inclination to say, "Well, we might do a lot better with a new leader who is not carrying all the scars and luggage the PM bears," I can say that I have had no difficulties at all with rumblings of discontent about the leadership in the media or the slightest suggestion that any problem exists anywhere. I must say in my public statements that I have every intention to lead the party and win a third majority. If ever I blink the slightest and indicate I will not, the entire bureaucracy would freeze, the leadership races would be on, discipline would be impossible, and I would be incapable of carrying on over the next crucial 12 months.

—

As I headed back to work early that January, the first items on my agenda involved a major change in personnel. Yves Fortier, who had served Canada with such distinction and value as ambassador to the United Nations – particularly when Canada took a seat on the Security Council and remained there throughout the Gulf War – was returning to private life, with my deep gratitude. To replace him I appointed Louise Fréchette, who became the first woman to serve as Canada's UN ambassador.

In my own office Gilbert Lavoie, who had performed great service for me as press secretary, resigned, and I replaced him with Mark Entwistle. Hugh Segal then officially took over as my chief of staff. He was, in a word, superb, the Canadian version of Al Smith, Franklin Roosevelt's legendary "happy warrior." He was bright, genial, entertaining, witty, and he came with a profound knowledge of the history and players in the Progressive

Conservative Party. Hugh had served Bill Davis in a similar capacity and soon began to perform minor miracles on a daily basis. I was blessed to have chiefs of staffs of the stature, ability, and integrity of, for example, Bernard Roy, Derek Burney, Stanley Hartt, and Hugh Segal. I will always be grateful to them for their sacrifices, their devotion, and their loyalty.

On January 27, Finance Minister Don Mazankowski announced that the federal deficit would be $1 billion higher – at $31.5 billion all told – than forecast. Maz pointed out accurately that the recession had robbed us of revenues. We were not yet fully aware of the length and breadth of this downturn and the damage it would eventually do to the public finances we had worked so hard to restore.

An announcement the following day by Communications Minister Perrin Beatty showed our balanced approach to deficit reduction. He outlined a five-year $140 million plan to strengthen Canada's book publishing industry while tightening rules against takeovers by foreign companies. My government strove to maintain and enhance areas of vital national importance, such as culture, communications, health and welfare, which sometimes meant having to starve other areas. Today, our success in fostering and protecting Canadian culture is an acknowledged fact. "The last time Conservatives did take the reins, under Brian Mulroney, cultural nationalists recall it as a golden age," the *Globe and Mail* reported shortly after Prime Minister Stephen Harper's victory in 2006.

At the same time, the Reform Party's Preston Manning was soothingly telling Canadians he and his party would cut government spending 15 per cent across the board. My caucus went silent when I described to them just what Manning's proposals would mean. "It would lead to the closure of CFB Borden in Ontario, hasten the end of medicare, see the closing of veterans' hospitals, and the reduction of veterans' payments and old-age pensions," I said. "Beware of any politician who says his solutions are easy," I warned. The advice still holds.

On Saturday, February 1, I had my first encounter with newly elected Russian President Boris Yeltsin, who arrived in Ottawa after talks with President Bush at Camp David. I had planned a dinner party for him at 24 Sussex, and I knew it was going to be an interesting evening from the moment we first shook hands. Yeltsin, as we used to say in Baie-Comeau, had arrived "in pretty good shape." And his happy mood was not diminished by the servings of the best French champagne Mila provided for him. He became more and more gregarious as the evening progressed and – like *les gars* in the Taverne aux Amis back home – it was simply impossible not to like him.

Don Mazankowski engaged Yeltsin in discussion. "Mr. President," Don asked, "when you first took office you had an approval rating of 93 per cent. Having governed for a few months, you've indicated you now have an approval rating of 79.6 per cent. May I ask how you know that?"

Boris grinned the most Russian of grins. "I don't," he said. "But I've learned that, in this business, when you're going to bullshit you've got to sound precise."

That day happened to be the president's sixty-first birthday, and Mila arranged for a large cake to be brought into the dining room in his honour. Boris jumped up and immediately reached out with his mangled hand (the result of a childhood accident) and scooped a chunk of cake right off the top in, I suppose, a Russian tribute to the excellence of the product.

During our serious discussions, it was apparent that Yeltsin had arrived well briefed on Canada's aid contributions to the former Soviet Union and of my intention to continue in the same vein for the new Russia. Bureaucrats at External Affairs later gave a confidential report of my talks with President Yeltsin. "President Yeltsin and his team were clearly very pleased with the reception they got in Ottawa," they wrote. "President Yeltsin, at dinner and at the press conference later, contrasted the concrete offers on grains and on technical assistance from Ottawa with the more vague promises that they had received elsewhere . . . All in all, President Yeltsin expressed a good deal of satisfaction, saying, in effect, that when Canada said it would do something, it actually did it."

The next day I wrote private notes of Yeltsin's visit and our conversation. I had found Yeltsin to be one of the most fascinating and entertaining world leaders I had ever hosted, as the notes reproduced below make clear.

> President Yeltsin arrived last night for a working visit, following his Camp David meeting (GB called me while Y was en route to fill me in on their discussions). After some five hours of conversation I gained the following impressions:
>
> 1. He is direct, brusque, knowledgeable, and somewhat authoritarian. He is still basking in the glow of his electoral victory, and his role in thwarting the coup, replacing Gorbachev, and emerging as a leader. But he has a good sense of humour and an excellent

political touch, as evidenced by his meeting and photo session with our household staff to thank them for an excellent meal and the birthday cake and the "Happy Birthday" they sang – he was 61.

2. He is very realistic about his political situation; in other words, either he produces results or he's gone. That's why he spoke so glowingly about Canada's contributions (on a per-capita basis one of the highest in the world) and my role in the G-7 leaders. In our conversation I itemized exactly what we had done, what we could do, and how he could get greater contributions and assistance from other G-7 countries, except Japan, and from international organizations, IMF, and World Bank, prior to Munich Summit.
3. He does not like Gorbachev at all. He repeats in public that he has respect for the former president and that Russia provides him with offices, staff, etc., to run the Gorbachev Foundation. But in private he barely conceals his contempt. Apart from the hostile behaviour of two rivals, he clearly is still smarting both at his treatment by G in the late 1980s and G's "lack of nerve and fundamental principle" to carry through and make reforms. In fact, he says there were no reforms whatever achieved under G and that G is personally responsible for preventing a genuine reform movement from emerging for seven years. His view is that G, to the end, remained a committed communist trying to graft onto its ideology components of the market system. He [said] it was like trying to graft (ask Nick the translator for exact image, something like a snake to a porcupine!) two mutually repellent strands of human endeavour together in a single unit. He also told me that G had sworn to him that he would never under any circumstances return to politics. He would not say why such a commitment was given or requested.

He then talked, with great satisfaction, about his role in fighting the attempted coup, ending with – as I have reported earlier – his sending the coup leaders on "a goose chase," whereupon he "sent another plane to the Crimea to arrest them all!"

As for the Crimea, he said it had been given to the Ukraine "unconstitutionally" and that many MPs in Russia were demanding its restoration.

He did not appear too engaged or interested in the question but allowed as to how matters would change if there were a Crimean referendum that opted for a return to Russia: "Then we would have to negotiate immediately with the Ukraine," he stated, implying by his tone that the result ought to be favourable to Russia. The Georgian leader was nobody but "a dictator no republic in the commonwealth will ever take in," he said, suggesting that unrest in the republics will eventually dissipate.

I concluded by noting, "Understandably, he is a tough, intelligent politician who, I suspect, will continue to take the brutal decisions on the economy back home, while eventually acquiring more sophistication and skill and acceptance internationally. I told him that in a democracy the political adversary was always 'expectations,' an upwardly moving target that is extremely difficult for democratic leaders to meet. If he can begin to meet those expectations in the same degree in Russia relatively soon, he may indeed turn out to be a long-term survivor in the new Russia."

As February went on, my government continued to move forward on environmental issues. Ottawa and Canada's major carmakers signed an agreement to phase in tailpipe pollution controls that were as tough as those already in place south of the border. Environment Minister Jean Charest also announced we would be spending another $95 million to help Canadians start dealing with various industrial waste sites across the country. To give an idea of the magnitude of the problems, Charest's program would be aimed at putting together a list of the sites Canadians had to clean up. We were starting from scratch. In spite of the economic squeeze we were in, we still made our best efforts at continuing on with the Green Plan, but it wasn't easy.

Within a few weeks, Health Minister Benoît Bouchard and Fisheries Minister John Crosbie would also make important Green Plan announcements. Bouchard soon gave details of a $170 million action plan to help Canadians better understand how the environment affected their health. The program aimed to set quality standards for water, air, and food. It also would study the effects of pollutants on high-risk groups such as aboriginal Canadians, pregnant women, and children. As for Crosbie, he announced we'd be spending $44 million to assess the impact of toxic substances on fish and their habitats.

In February, the United Nations Security Council voted to approve sending a United Nations peacekeeping force to the former Yugoslavia. I immediately announced our willingness to contribute up to twelve hundred troops to the mission. As always with the United Nations, we held true to our belief that a strong UN enhanced Canada's position in the world and greatly benefited the world community. Our troop contribution also showed that while our manpower contributions to NATO forces in Europe were winding down, Canada's commitment to the European continent would never falter. Later in 1992, we also agreed to send up to 750 troops to Somalia to help that country deal with a brutal famine and civil war. The UN, then and now, is a key venue that allows Canada to participate in effective multilateral foreign policy initiatives.

Jordan's King Hussein arrived in Ottawa in March. He was on his way to Washington and wanted my advice before arriving in the American capital. As I had told his wife, Queen Noor, the year before during a luncheon in New York City, his stock was low in Washington, because it appeared to the Americans that he had tried to have it both ways during the Gulf War. Note-takers captured the seriousness of the hard line I had to take with him. While I knew George Bush was willing to put the past behind him, Hussein, I warned, still faced a challenge.

"The prime minister [said] that Saddam Hussein was 'the kiss of death' in North America," the note-takers recorded. "Everyone thought that he was an animal. Everyone was satisfied that the war was necessary and right. The only thing public opinion criticized the U.S. administration for was not getting rid of Saddam Hussein completely. The problem was that the UN embargo was leaky. Not everyone was fulfilling UN orders. All members of the United Nations had to respect United Nations decisions. Some people in Congress and the media would try to draw the king into a defence of Saddam Hussein. The PM advised the king to avoid being drawn into such a defence. The U.S. administration had come to the view that it was time to re-establish relations with Jordan but the media would want to relive the past."

King Hussein (short, trim, with a wide smile) was a man of great intelligence and equal courtesy. He was generous in his observations, fair-minded in his interpretations, and an extremely effective spokesperson for his country, his region, and his vision for the world. The king would soon return to favour in the United States, of that I was sure.

Mila and I kept in touch with him and Queen Noor – who attended Caroline's wedding in Montreal in 2000 – after I left office. We were privileged to attend a private dinner-dance at their Ascot estate outside London which Queen Noor gave in his honour. The effects of Hussein's cancer were plain to see, and the once-vibrant man appeared to be in terrible discomfort. Approximately one hundred of his friends, an eclectic group including Prince Charles, King Juan Carlos of Spain, and actor Harrison Ford, had been assembled that night, and Mila and I, along with our great friends Galen and Hilary Weston, still consider ourselves honoured to have been included.

As Joe Clark continued his cross-country consultations on constitutional reform, in February a CROP poll brought mixed blessings. It showed that support for sovereignty had dropped to 46 per cent from 64 per cent only fifteen months previously. Forty-two per cent of Quebecers were now opposed to sovereignty. Politically, however, my party stood at 11 per cent, with the Grits on top nationally at 39 per cent. Even the Reform Party, at 15 per cent, stood higher than we did. I put my best foot forward when answering questions from the media on Parliament Hill. "The steady erosion of support for sovereignty in Quebec," I said, "that's the poll that should interest Canadians today."

On March 12, 1992, Joe Clark and provincial representatives – minus Quebec, of course – agreed to try to achieve a new constitutional deal by the end of May. In an atmosphere dominated by the recommendations of the Bélanger-Campeau Commission Report in Quebec, it was entirely legitimate for us and the premiers to try to craft a constitutional package that would both enhance the federation and satisfy Quebec's demands.

As my journal makes clear, however, I had private misgivings.

—

PERSONAL JOURNAL: MARCH 14, 1992

Following a lengthy (private) dinner meeting 10 days ago at the Dorval Hilton with Premier Bourassa and Jean-Claude Rivest, where we explored all facets of the upcoming Beaudoin-Dobbie Report [issued by a parliamentary committee that consulted with Canadians about proposed constitutional changes], Paul Tellier and I returned to Ottawa and announced that RB would now view this as "an excellent base to negotiations." In short order Bourassa and his people panned the report [entitled A Renewed Canada*] and then, unbelievably,* *joined the PQ in a ringing denunciation of Beaudoin-Dobbie in the National Assembly. In fact, it is the most comprehensive and generous report ever submitted by an all-party Commons–Senate committee.*

The problem is that Quebec continues to move the goalposts. What found a reflection in Meech Lake has now come to symbolize a layer of Bélanger-Campeau. Though both are of a recent date, and in no way reflect the traditional demands of Lesage, Johnson, Duplessis, etc., they're in fact designed to accommodate the needs of a separatist Quebec rather than the needs of a strong Quebec within a federalist Canada. Coming as it did at the end of the constitutional affairs ministers' first meeting in Ottawa, the National Assembly vote was extremely damaging to my attempts to find a constitutional solution to the most challenging crisis this country has faced since its inception.

Nor was the case aided by a particularly careless Marcel Masse statement that Beaudoin-Dobbie was unacceptable to Quebec. Because it was a parliamentary report and not a government position, Masse was not bound by the rules of cabinet solidarity. His thoughtless statements, however, wounded his Quebec colleagues who had worked so hard on Beaudoin-Dobbie and conveyed the impression of disunity in government ranks.

Last night, Bob Rae called me pleased with his success at "opening up" the constitutional process in Canada. It has just begun to dawn on him that with this "achievement" goes some considerable responsibility. How do we make this expanded procedure work? More players, more problems. The clock ticks on inexorably toward October 26, 1992 and the moment of crisis in Quebec. Rae told me how flabbergasted he was to have had a private word with Clyde Wells, who told him "not to worry – nothing was going to happen in Quebec."

I like Rae personally, I think his heart is in the right place on this great issue . . . but Jeff Rose, from CUPE, his constitutional affairs advisor, is going across the country badmouthing us and blaming us, without realizing every word is being reported right back to us. Rae's cabinet has been objectively declared perhaps the most mediocre in modern Ontario history. Rae is clearly the strongman at Queen's Park. If he can rid himself of those who see conspiracies and secret deals around every corner, he will be able to play the traditional Ontario leadership role in national affairs – one so ably played by Robarts,

Davis, and Peterson. If not, and with Quebec absent from the table, I fear for the process, and the result.

I have rarely been as concerned and fearful for Canada's future as I am today. The PQ and the BQ will stop at nothing to destroy Canada. But if the Quebec Liberal Party has become a paler version of the PQ and will not stand up for Canada, we will have little chance to carry the day on behalf of federalism. In 1980, Claude Ryan and his party were devoted, passionate federalists. This made a key difference in the debate. No doubt Mr. Trudeau's excellent speech at the Paul Sauvé Arena contributed as well to the successful outcome. But the seeds of great danger had already been sown – 54% of French-speaking Quebecers had voted for sovereignty-association.

As October approaches, my sense of dismay grows. If Canada fails, the principal reason can be found by historians among the columns, editorials, and newscasts of this age that encourage Canadians to reject compromise, to celebrate regionalism, and to move away from the fundamental generosity of Macdonald and Cartier, without which Canada no longer has a raison d'être or the political capacity to sustain it.

—

That spring the Supreme Court unanimously ruled that David Milgaard, who had been in prison for twenty-three years since being convicted of the 1969 sex-slaying of Saskatoon nursing assistant Gail Miller, should have a new trial. Milgaard soon walked free, after the Saskatchewan government announced he wouldn't be retried. In subsequent years, another man, Larry Fisher, was tried and convicted of Miller's murder.

Milgaard's release was a testament to his mother's unshakeable belief in his innocence. On a visit to Winnipeg in September of 1991, I overruled advice from my staff and had a conversation with Joyce Milgaard. (I had been disturbed at the manner in which Justice Minister Kim Campbell had previously brushed off Mrs. Milgaard. "Madam, if you wish to have your son's case dealt with fairly, please do not approach me," she had said to the distressed mother. Joyce, like all of her son's supporters, was hoping that the Department of Justice would refer David's case to the Supreme Court. Kim Campbell had rejected Milgaard's appeal to her over his conviction, and I was privately furious with her about it.)

I thought of my own mother as I approached Mrs. Milgaard in Winnipeg that day. I knew that my own mother would have protested the innocence of any of her children and that she wouldn't have been out there twenty years later if she didn't completely believe it. I offer a condensed version of our conversation below.

"His mental situation is not good now, and anything that you can do to help toward getting him transferred would be appreciated," Mrs. Milgaard told me. "We just feel he needs to have some peace of mind, and I'm afraid that the case will not be reopened before David has lost his sanity. It's so important. And, of course, the other question is, anything you could do for a speedy review? Because now the Saskatoon police have apparently admitted they haven't given full information to the Justice Department, that really the minister was working with just half of the things she should have had, and I find that so . . . difficult."

"That was the most recent information?" I asked.

"Yes, yesterday."

"Yesterday, and I've just checked in Ottawa and I gather that information is either en route or has just been received down there so they'll be taking a close look at it very, very soon. What about – you mentioned his health?"

"He's been in the hospital."

"I know he's been hospitalized but –"

"You see," Mrs. Milgaard continued, "he's asked for a transfer to Rockwood or a transfer to Collins Bay. It's not that the other inmates are against him: it's just that they're constantly questioning him and saying, 'How are you doing, Dave?' It's friendly, but he needs some peace of mind."

"It's hard on him?" I asked.

"It's very difficult for all of us."

"How are you getting on?"

"Just the fact that you're talking to me makes me feel better."

"I'm happy to do it."

"And anything you can do to help, we would just be so appreciative."

"Well, Ms. Campbell is going to take a look at the new information that's come in."

"A speedy review?"

"Well," I continued, being extremely prudent in my answers, knowing that our dialogue was being recorded and every word would be parsed, "I can't speak for her, but I will be talking to her when I get back. I hope you're well."

"I'm trying my very best."

"I know you are. You're working very, very hard. You're very courageous."

"Thank you for that."

"And I've taken note of your other request and we'll do what we can."

"We are just asking for justice. But now. It would be terrible for me to have justice for David in Canada and not have him able to know he's got it. Okay?"

"Is he –?"

"It's that desperate."

"Is he that sick?"

"It is that desperate."

"I didn't realize," I said. "I knew he was ill. But I didn't realize he was that sick."

"It is exactly. I would never be coming to you otherwise."

"I'll look into it right away."

Joyce Milgaard later wrote in her memoirs, *A Mother's Story*: "Prime Minister Mulroney could have walked away at any point in the lengthy conversation, but he didn't. David had been right. Perhaps a chat with the prime minister was just what we needed . . . David had been depressed, but that meeting with Prime Minister Mulroney put a smile back on his face. It was his idea, and now there we were, Brian Mulroney and I, together, on the front pages of newspapers across the country."

When I got back to Ottawa, I arranged for a fast review of David Milgaard's medical condition. He was soon transferred to a minimum-security institution. In an exchange of letters with Mrs. Milgaard, I told her, "I, too, hope the matter will soon be resolved." I then had Hugh Segal summon Justice Minister Kim Campbell to my parliamentary office in Centre Block, where, because of the sensitivity of the matter, I met with her alone, although I debriefed Hugh Segal and Gilbert Lavoie immediately after.

"The matter has been reviewed by the department and I have conveyed our decision," she told me.

"Kim," I answered, "that is not acceptable to me. The law provides for a reference to the Supreme Court, and it is my intention to ensure that this case is in fact referred to the Supreme Court."

My tone was firm and my words unequivocal. She understood and changed her tack quickly.

"Prime Minister," she answered, "if this is the case, may I make the announcement myself?"

And with that, Campbell announced the reference to the Supreme Court of Canada. The political details are unimportant. What matters is that David Milgaard, wrongly convicted and imprisoned, is now free. That fact is a tribute to his mother, to her courage and her love for her son. Without her, and her tenacious Winnipeg lawyers, Hersh Wolch and David Asper, David Milgaard would still be wrongfully imprisoned.

On April 22 and 23, our efforts on behalf of Canada's aboriginal people bore fruit when the Gwich'in of the Mackenzie Delta in the Northwest Territories became the first members of the Dene Nation to officially sign a land claims deal with Ottawa. The agreement, signed in Fort McPherson, gave two thousand Gwich'in title to almost twenty-four thousand square kilometres of land – an area the size of Nova Scotia. They also received $75 million, over fifteen years, for education and culture and were now the co-managers, along with the federal and territorial governments, of a sixty thousand-square-kilometre settlement region. On the same trip to the Far North, Environment Minister Jean Charest announced that a twenty-two thousand-square-kilometre area of Baffin Island was being set aside to create a national park.

That month, a dark episode in Canada's past came back to haunt the present. Canadian Press uncovered documents from the 1950s and 1960s showing there had been a government-sponsored purge of homosexuals in the civil service. When the documents became public, I quickly denounced the purge, and said such actions were odious and an obvious violation of human rights. I wanted to make my views very clear, at a time when the rights of homosexuals were on the minds of many of our more conservative-minded MPs. I tried to put those prejudices to rest during a speech to caucus. "My question is, where do homosexuals come from?" I asked. "Well, they come from heterosexual parents like us. Would we want our children discriminated against, for employment or any other reasons, if they were homosexual? That's the real question we must reflect upon and decide. My mind is already made up. There should be no discrimination of any kind against members of the gay community."

1992

2. Plain Talk with George, Dick, and Boris

President Bush called me on May 1 while I was in Williams Lake, British Columbia. First, he sought my advice on the televised speech to the nation he planned to give that night concerning the race riots in Los Angeles. He was appalled by what was going on there, and we discussed what the tone of his message ought to be. On the world front, he was still struggling to decide whether the United States should participate in the upcoming Earth Summit in Rio on climate change. I told him that his own reputation as an environmentalist, plus the tremendous work he had done on the Canada–U.S. acid rain file, meant that he, as a world leader, simply had to show up in Rio to play a leading role on behalf of the environment.

On May 20, I arrived in Washington for what proved to be my last talks with President Bush in the Oval Office. He was in the throes of an election year, and things weren't going well. His re-election campaign had featured a great deal of empire building and ducking and covering by senior staff, unsettling him and angering Barbara. In private, I advised him to persuade Jim Baker to step aside immediately as secretary of state and return as his campaign manager. It seemed to me that Baker was the only Republican in Washington capable of pulling everything together to form an effective election campaign that would ensure Bush a second term. Bush, I felt, deserved better management help than what he was receiving.

"Brian," Bush replied, "when you get a chance, get Jim aside and mention that to him yourself."

I soon did, but Baker said he felt the nation's interests had to come first, meaning he couldn't contemplate such a move until after the Munich G-7 Summit in July.

Politics took up a large part of the journal entry I made after this American visit.

—

PERSONAL JOURNAL: MAY 22, 1992

*Mila and I returned last night from a busy and, I think, successful trip to Washington and Baltimore, where I gave the commencement address at Johns Hopkins University. Strange dichotomy: George Bush, way down in the polls and running behind independent candidate Ross Perot, was in good cheer. Bouncy, confident – at the top of his form. In spite of my fears expressed during our tête-à-tête, George seemed to think that Perot would collapse before the convention and be out of the way by Labour Day, opening up a direct race with Clinton that he fully expected to win. That night at dinner at the embassy, Barbara was more careful of her assessment and said to me, "I'm not worrying about anything. This will be my last campaign and I am going to give it my very best. Whatever happens will be OK." (*Washington Post *publisher Kay Graham, who was seated to my left, told me that before my arrival she had had a most unpleasant exchange with Ted Kennedy, another guest, who had apparently bawled her out over a* Newsweek *piece on him the previous summer. Kay was very upset by Ted's attack, and I tried to comfort her by saying that she would never have the problem with me in Canada, because the attacks were so numerous that I would never know which ones to respond to on a given day.)*

The next day after Johns Hopkins, a lunch with Speaker of the House Tom Foley, and being invited on to the Senate floor by George Mitchell and Bob Dole, I met privately with VP Dan Quayle. At the end of the meeting, he said, "Brian, I should tell you as a friend that we could lose this thing in November. Two years ago, one year ago, six months ago, this thought never crossed my mind, but now all the Republicans are saying, 'Tell the President to do something, anything – just lead!' We'll fight on, but I now recognize we could well lose." What a switch. George Bush with approval ratings in the 20s and Quayle being perceived in some quarters as the stronger half of the ticket after all the abuse he has taken.

—

I spoke with the president for forty-five minutes. On the official level, it was one of the darkest meetings I was ever to have with him. (Socially, things couldn't have been better. President Bush and Barbara attended a dinner at the Canadian embassy – a rare event for a sitting president – and they were joined by Chief Justice William Rehnquist, Speaker of the House Tom Foley, Secretary of State Baker, and others.) Despite the FTA, American actions on the trade file were hurting us in Canada.

Note-takers summed up our official discussions in the Oval Office that day.

> The PM led the discussion through the 45 minutes . . . and concentrated on bilateral trade and Uruguay Round concerns. He explained to the president that the political and economic implications of the bilateral trade disputes were very serious in Canada. Support for the FTA has fallen . . . The disputes over lumber and Honda undermined the confidence of investors and exporters alike and poisoned perceptions about the FTA in Canada. There were elements of unreality in Canada about the agreement, just as there were about politics in the U.S., but the negatives were there, nonetheless. The PM wanted to reverse the negative trend; he wanted to raise the commitment to resolve problems and reduce the stockpile of disputes . . . Actions of late – "stomping all over us" – were painful and embarrassing. They served only those who opposed his general approach to the U.S. ("Why has your great friend Bush behaved this way?") . . . Scowcroft observed that the beer negotiations illustrated to him just how foul the atmosphere was between officials in both countries.

At a White House luncheon afterwards, Jim Baker shocked me with his open skepticism about the value of G-7 summits. "An initiative that Canada and the U.S. should take would be to prevail upon the others to have a summit only every other year," he said.

Derek Burney jumped in. "Are you really saying we don't need summitry?" he asked.

"Yes, that's what I am saying," he answered. "I've been to the last eleven and I don't think they're advancing solutions to the issues. We could do without them."

Derek and I were firm in disagreeing with Baker's view. Just as the world was changing so radically, we knew it was key that the United States – the world's sole remaining superpower – remain committed and engaged.

I spoke out against a post–Cold War return to American isolationism during my speech at Johns Hopkins University. I didn't mince words and raised a few hackles at the State Department and White House in the process. "The process of change today is exhilarating and its direction encouraging," I said. "But the pace of change is wearying and its dimensions disorienting. It is not surprising that pockets of nostalgia remain for the certainties and predictabilities of the Cold War, despite the sterility at its core. Which industrialized nation could not rationalize turning inwards now, after decades of military expenditures and foreign aid contributions? And, yet, withdrawing from the world at this time would be an error of historic scale because neo-isolationism in the 1990s is even more dangerous than its progenitor in the 1920s . . . Without the active and constructive engagement of the United States . . . the world suffers from uncertainty, hesitation, and drift."

Regardless of the views of the American secretary of state, I spoke hopefully of the upcoming G-7 Summit in Munich as my speech continued. "We know what the problems are and we know what the solutions are," I said. "At the Munich Summit in July, seven nations representing almost 63 per cent of the world's GNP will meet. Let us resolve there to work with the people in the former Soviet Union and solve these problems through decisive leadership and a strong, helping hand. Helping the new republics will take compassion, patience, ingenuity, and a great deal of money . . . What would our reaction have been to Kerensky in 1917 if he had said the czar was dead and he needed our help to forestall the seventy-five years of blind-alley economics and dead-end government of communism? What do you think our reaction would have been if, say, twenty years ago or ten years ago, the Soviet leadership had said, 'The empire is over, communism has failed, the Warsaw Pact has disintegrated, our economy is bankrupt, and we are going to lay down our arms. We seek your friendship and your help'? And yet, we are now in danger of allowing our exhaustion from the pace of change to overwhelm the exhilaration we first felt when the Berlin Wall came down and to distort our judgment about our own longer-term interests. I believe the West's collective response so far has been hesitant and timid and out of scale with both the need and the opportunity.

"Leadership will cost money. But the Marshall Plan cost much more money than has been transferred to the former Soviet Union so far, and it repaid its investment a thousand times over . . . To the end of 1991, Canada, with a relatively small population approaching 28 million, had disbursed over $1.6 billion in credits and aid to the former Soviet Union, the second-highest per-capita assistance of the G-7, exceeded only by Germany. In 1992, we are providing an amount approaching a further billion dollars, for a total of almost $2.5 billion in Canadian assistance."

It was high time, in other words, that the Bush administration and Americans in general seize the moment. They could not allow Russia and all the former East Bloc nations to fail at this crucial point in history.

Former President Richard Nixon agreed with my attempts to prod the Bush administration toward a greater role in the rebuilding of the former Soviet Union and Russia in particular. I called Nixon on June 24 to explain Canada's efforts in this area. Though he'd been out of office for almost twenty years, Nixon still had analytical skills and influence, both at the White House and with an important element of the American foreign policy establishment. I was later to learn that President Nixon enjoyed our association. "Nixon treasured his relationship with Mulroney, to whom he spoke quite often about foreign affairs," Nixon's assistant, Monica Crowley, wrote in her memoirs of her years with the former president, *Nixon in Winter*. "Mulroney's contribution is very courageous," Nixon told Crowley. "Canada doesn't have a lot of money to throw around."

It was a measure of the tremendous impact Nixon had made on his country and the world that he still wielded such influence so many years after leaving office. I remember sharing a banquette with him at La Grenouille on the Upper East Side of Manhattan one day in the 1990s. Every person who entered the restaurant would rush over to shake his hand, wish him well, and ask for an autograph. After one well-wisher left his side, he looked up with a wry smile on his face. "Not so bad, Brian," he said, "for a guy who's supposed to be all washed up."

During our lunch he discovered that my daughter, Caroline, was studying at Harvard. He later sent a copy of one of his books to her, along with a handwritten note. "Whatever happens," it read, "don't let those Harvard people get you down."

After my retirement from the prime ministership, I spoke at the Richard Nixon Library and Birthplace in California. Afterwards, I visited Nixon's first home, which is located on the museum's property. Climbing the stairs to the second floor of that little house and seeing the tiny room, its ceiling less than six feet high, where Richard Nixon and his two brothers slept during the Depression, I got a true glimpse of the thirty-seventh president's background. I understood, for the first time, why Nixon had had such a chip on his shoulder. Some people respond to poverty and hardship with sunny optimism; others, like Nixon, respond with deep-seated ambition, nurtured by suspicion and distrust.

As prime minister, my last written communication with Nixon was to take place the following year. I sent him a note when I heard that his wife, Pat, was dying. Nixon wrote back in his own hand. "What a thoughtful man you are – handwritten notes to Mrs. Nixon and to me, a scarf for her and cufflinks for me, and a spectacular floral arrangement for her," he wrote. "As you probably surmise, she is in a very tough battle. But as I said in my Fund TV broadcast in 1952, the Irish never give up. I look forward to our meeting when her condition is resolved. In the meantime she joins me in expressing our deep appreciation and best wishes to you and your First Lady."

In June of 1992, I attended the Earth Summit in Rio. Environment Minister Jean Charest and Canada's ambassador to the Earth Summit, Arthur Campeau, had arrived in Brazil before me. They called me in Ottawa suddenly one night to warn that the conference was in danger of failing, but that Canada could help prevent this. With the Bush administration refusing to sign the UN Convention on Climate Change and the UN Convention on Biological Diversity, other G-7 countries, they said, might hide behind the American decision, thereby scuttling the conference. I authorized my envoys to announce that Canada would indeed affix its signature to both documents, becoming the first nation to do so.

"We don't subcontract our rights and obligations to the United States in any way, nor does anyone else," I said after I arrived in Rio. "This is our responsibility as a country to evaluate." The director-general of the United Nations Environment Programme told the press that Canada had helped break a logjam. "We are grateful to Canada and we are grateful to the prime minister," he said.

"Let's face it, Canada saved the biodiversity treaty," Elizabeth May of the Sierra Club of Canada added. "Let's not be modest just because we're Canadians. Brian Mulroney accomplished something really significant by being willing, within hours of Bush saying he wasn't going to sign it, by saying Canada was."

I had, of course, lobbied Bush repeatedly to at least attend the Rio conference. "Look, George," I said to him more than once, "there is a French expression 'Les absents ont toujours tort.' In other words, if you're not at the table, you're going to get blamed. So you're much better to be there, to defend your interests, and to speak about your record, and then to make your own mind up whether you're going to sign onto this or not."

The Rio Earth Summit laid the groundwork for the Kyoto Protocol, which the Americans have also refused to sign. Under Kyoto, Canada committed to reducing greenhouse gas emissions to 6 per cent below 1990 levels by 2008–12. However, under the Liberal governments of Chrétien and Martin, our emissions actually increased by 24 per cent, as opposed to the Americans' 13 per cent increase. Simply put, we are in no position to be giving advice to the United States or anyone else. Canadians no longer occupy the moral and environmental high ground.

From my own experience, I would offer two observations on addressing environmental issues. First, it doesn't really matter what the process is, so long as the problem is addressed by leadership; where political will prevails, solutions will follow. Second, there are few durable solutions on the environment, or on any other international issue, without the engagement of the United States and the leadership of its president. So whether the process proves to be Kyoto or something else, let's acknowledge the urgency of global warming. And then let's get the United States to the table. It isn't by lecturing the Americans on their record on emissions reduction that we'll succeed, especially when our own record is nearly twice as bad as theirs.

Another key point: before I got off the telephone with Jean Charest that fateful night fifteen years ago, I gave him another clear instruction. "Get [Environmental Protection Agency head] Bill Reilly on the phone and tell him beforehand that Canada is going to sign," I said. Taking your closest friend and ally by surprise is no winning formula, either.

In Rio I also pressed the cause of Third World aid and development. "The developing countries have to see an advantage in ecological preservation for themselves," I said. "If the only reason they have development is to pay off interest to [First World] financial institutions, then obviously they are going to do quite a job on their own environment," I argued, pointing out that $50 billion annually in interest payments alone was leaving poor nations and being sent to rich nations. "That really does not make a great deal of sense."

Cuban President Fidel Castro had praised Canada during the summit and I had taken the time to send him a letter of appreciation. After my speech to the Earth Summit I returned to my seat. Within minutes a rather menacing group of Cuban security guards approached. One was carrying a handwritten note from Castro. "I infinitely thank you for your note of yesterday," he wrote in Spanish. "It has been the greatest stimulus that I have received during these days, as I feel a great appreciation for you and your opinions. I take this opportunity to congratulate you on your speech to the conference. You spoke as more than a friend, you spoke as a member of the Third World family, which so appreciates the noble, generous, and disinterested cooperation of Canada. If I do not see you, I wish you a good trip and I remind you that Cuba awaits you. F.C."

I never did visit Cuba as prime minister. My reasoning was simple. Relations between Canada and Cuba functioned very well, and our trade was growing. With Reagan and Bush in the Oval Office for most of my tenure, I felt it would be a needless provocation on Canada's part if I were to take a page out of Trudeau's book and travel to Havana just to poke the Americans in the eye – although I had many times publicly disagreed with U.S. policy toward Cuba and the embargo, describing it as "self-destructive."

Coincidentally, Fisheries Minister John Crosbie had visited Cuba just before the Earth Summit. He came back to Ottawa with a delivery of Cuban lobsters from Castro to me. John also filed a report about his lengthy and informal talks with Castro while he was there.

> I inquired of President Castro whether he was considering retiring in view of the fact that he has been in power for 33 years. He was cool to this suggestion, replying that he would retire when the Cuban people thought that he should remove himself from the scene. The Cubans present assured him that this was not the position of the Cuban people! He referred to the length of the reign of Queen Victoria, Emperor Hirohito, and various other worthies to indicate that he had no intention of retiring at the moment . . . I asked President Castro if they did any polling in Cuba. He said they did but it wasn't necessary since they already knew what the Cuban people thought and wanted! . . . It is my own view that the U.S. blockade and general hostility toward Castro and Cuba [are] what keeps Mr. Castro firmly in power. I could not see any evidence of any desire to overthrow the regime.

> I believe so long as the Cubans are faced by this foreign enemy so close to them that they will continue to support Mr. Castro and the present system.

Only John Crosbie would have the nerve to ask Fidel Castro when he was stepping down!

Just after the Earth Summit ended, Clerk of the Privy Council Paul Tellier retired from the public service. He had come to see me after the 1988 election to say that he would be accepting an offer to work in the private sector in Montreal. I knew the company and urged him to stay in Ottawa. "I think there's something better for you that will come along," I said.

By then I knew full well that CN needed to be cleaned up before it was privatized. So I was later able to call Tellier and say, "Now we have the job that will interest you. If you wish, I will appoint you president and CEO of CN in Montreal." Tellier took the job and performed magnificently.

I was sad to lose Tellier, a superb Clerk and advisor who had been part of every major decision my government had taken. He was replaced by Glen Shortliffe, another highly competent public servant, who went on to serve me and my successors extremely well.

I soon had to prepare myself for another visit, on June 19, by Russian President Boris Yeltsin, to whose country Canada was committing a further $100 million in aid. Note-takers described his reaction: "President Yeltsin responded that he thanked the prime minister wholeheartedly. The five months which had elapsed since he had been in Ottawa had not been wasted. In contrast to the mainly talk that he had heard elsewhere, Canada provided very practical assistance. Canada talked specifics. Russia was going through an exceptionally hard time. People were living with clenched teeth. He and his government were working for liberty, democracy, and market-economic reforms."

In 2006, I was pleased when Russia's current president, Vladimir Putin, announced that Canada's assistance to his country during my time as prime minister had not been forgotten. "I would like to point out that the solid foundation of Russian-Canadian cooperation was laid in the early 1990s, mostly due to the efforts of Brian Mulroney," he told the press. "I hope that Canada will continue to support joint projects and plans that have been charted over the years."

Mila and I hosted another dinner for Yeltsin, accompanied this time by his wife, Naina. It was another unforgettable evening at 24 Sussex. Before dinner Yeltsin enjoyed several cocktails. Then he sat down on a large custom-made couch that we had brought with us to Ottawa in 1983. As he sank deep into its generous pillows, his face broke into a big smile, and he began to bounce around like a little kid. "Brian," he said, "*this* is a couch." He then announced his solemn refusal to get up from the couch because it was so comfortable! We were at an impasse, and one of us would have to blink. As host, it was me. Jokingly, I told him that if he would get up and come to dinner, Mila and I would send the couch to him in Moscow. He agreed.

A couple of weeks later the home phone rang and my wife answered. "Mila!" Yeltsin shouted from Moscow, "where's my sofa?" He hadn't forgotten. We quietly shipped the couch to Russia, where I hope Yeltsin took good care of it as a cherished Ottawa souvenir.

Note-takers recorded our discussions that evening:

> Of his family life and work schedule, [Yeltsin] said that he works 20 hours a day, including Saturday and Sunday mornings. He takes Sunday afternoons off and plays tennis on Tuesdays or Wednesdays. He lives in a four-room flat; his youngest daughter and her husband live with them. It is a very noisy, downtown flat with no air conditioning and the windows cannot be opened due to pollution. Therefore, he often sleeps at a residence in the suburbs, a thirty-minute drive from downtown . . . President Yeltsin said that he had two daughters but had always wanted a son. One of his grandchildren had been specially named "Boris Yeltsin." There was security for his grandchildren but not for his daughters.
>
> The PM asked for his impressions of Gorbachev. President Yeltsin accused Gorbachev of a lack of willpower and of being slow to move on reform. Gorbachev had been very much under Raisa's influence. Mrs. Yeltsin interjected that it had all been Raisa's fault. Continuing in that same vein, President Yeltsin noted that he had achieved greater reductions in nuclear missiles than Gorbachev had ever planned. He also noted that land could now be privately purchased, even by foreigners. Mrs. Yeltsin interjected that this was not so: she claimed that, so far, foreigners could only have ten-year leases on land. President Yeltsin countered that he had issued a decree to permit ownership of land by foreign investors, and that it

> had been enacted. President Yeltsin noted that the Communist Party's power had been destroyed; it no longer had any influence. Mrs. Yeltsin disagreed. She said that, on the contrary, especially in some of the republics the Communist Party remained powerful.

Yeltsin's expression showed that he was somewhat offended that his wife would contradict him in front of others. He was the president of Russia, after all. "Boris," I said, "don't be offended. In this house you'd better get used to it – I have."

1992

3. Joe Clark's Instincts

Before I recount the events of July–August 1992 in relation to the Constitution, I should review the situation we found ourselves in. I had appointed Joe Clark as head of the newly created Ministry of Constitutional Affairs in 1991 because I thought he had the credibility and the energy necessary to pull together a new proposal that we could submit either to the House of Commons or to the country for approval. The Bélanger-Campeau Commission, appointed by the Government of Quebec, had concluded with a recommendation to the provincial government that a referendum on the question of sovereignty be called before October 26, 1992 if no other offer was forthcoming from Ottawa and the nine other provinces. The clock was ticking.

In Quebec the political situation was clouded by the sabotage of Meech, the preposterous recommendations of the Allaire Commission, and the actual hearings of the Bélanger-Campeau Commission, which had tended to minimize the benefits of the federation and to enhance the attractiveness of the sovereignty option.

In English Canada, there was a growing weariness with the constitutional file, and with any further amendments to the Constitution to accommodate Quebec. Increasingly, the feeling was "To hell with them – if Quebecers aren't satisfied, let them go." This attitude had a degree of refreshing clarity about it, which masked the cataclysmic consequences for us all, were separation ever to come to pass. Moreover, with each passing day the situation was exacerbated by the Reform Party's Preston Manning saying that Quebec had already received too much. Meanwhile, Lucien Bouchard of the Bloc Québécois was saying over and over again that Quebec had been shafted by the failure of Meech Lake, and that the province had received nothing of significance from Confederation.

It was against this challenging background that Joe Clark began his work. Although Joe was a strong supporter of Meech, I think that he began to believe the propaganda from those in English Canada who criticized us for the manner in which the negotiations had been concluded – the "eleven men in suits," the closed doors, the take it or leave it attitude, the interminable meetings – all of which suggested improper, perhaps even extortionate, tactics by the federal government. To his credit, Joe was determined to bring a greater transparency to the constitutional amendment process, and to open it up to include the territories, aboriginal groups, and other stakeholders. His consultations in the previous fifteen or so months were vast and expansive, and he was tireless in the pursuit of relevant opinion across the country. Joe was a master of process, and he built a consultative mechanism of great complexity – and significant effectiveness – as he sought to align the interests of the provinces and the federal government in a new constitutional initiative that would find favour with Canadians.

He had done an enormous amount of work prior to my leaving for the Munich G-7 Summit. When I left, it had been agreed among us, and at cabinet, that the Government of Canada's position would include the equivalent of a double-E Senate – elected and effective. We were resolved that if we failed to get this at the negotiating table, the government would walk away and put together a complete package of reforms, which it would submit to Parliament for a debate and then place on the ballot – either for a national referendum and/or the Quebec referendum in October of 1992 – as an alternative to sovereignty.

You can imagine my surprise then, when I received an urgent telephone call at the G-7 Summit, advising me that Joe had agreed with the nine provinces on a triple-E Senate – elected, effective, and equitable. He had done so without consulting me or any of his cabinet colleagues. This news sent shock waves through the telephone lines between Ottawa and Munich and ignited perhaps the most explosive challenge of my nine-year term as prime minister.

Joe had placed the government in a no-win situation. On one side, Quebec had already indicated that it had no intention of accepting a triple-E Senate; on the other, some western provinces were now viewing it as a fait accompli. To proceed in these circumstances would be to repeat the 1982 scenario in which Quebec was left out of the final accord. Not to proceed, on the other hand, would be to place some of the western provinces – particularly Alberta – in a position where they could say, "Mr. Clark agreed with us on a triple-E Senate; now it's up to Mulroney to deliver. Otherwise, we'll take the position that he has sold out to Quebec." As a Quebecer, I had had this accusation made against me on other occasions, when our initiatives on behalf of Alberta were forgotten all too soon in the swirl of easy and misleading headlines and facile quotes.

Alone in Munich, I was thunderstruck by the news, and furious that Joe Clark would place the government and me in such a hopeless position; and that he would do so without the courtesy of calling me for prior approval or advice.

These selections from my journal capture some of the drama of the weeks following this shocking news.

—

PERSONAL JOURNAL: JULY 11, 1992

I fear that the constitutional arrangement agreed to by Joe Clark this week along with the premiers may have produced the worst of all worlds for the government and ensured the elimination of most if not all of our political options. During my meetings with the premiers and subsequent meetings with Clark, Tellier, et al., prior to the Friday Toronto meeting, the following points were agreed: 1) Breaking the Senate deadlock was critical to our plans. 2) With six premiers favouring an equitable Senate, three favouring a "triple-E" and one (Romanow) wavering, all of our pressure was to get Romanow onside so as to have the requisite 7/50 support (at least seven provinces, with more than 50% of the Canadian population was the required minimum) for Senate reform. 3) The aboriginal leadership was sensitized to our approach in direct conversations with me, Joe Clark, and Benoît Bouchard, and advised that unless there was an agreement on the Senate that was 7/50 and included Quebec, they ran the risk of losing all the considerable gains they had achieved. 4) The territorial leaders were so onside that Tony Penikett (Yukon) said to Nellie Cournoyea (N.W.T.) in the upstairs den at 24, "Nellie, has it ever occurred to you that the premiers most hostile to aboriginal rights are also the most supportive of triple-E? Get onside, Nellie, with a Senate that B.C., Ontario, and Quebec – representing 85% of the population – can support, namely the equitable model." Penikett was also very frank, and warned Joe, Benoît, and me that one of the greatest obstacles to any arrangement was Romanow and suggested that the feds should look for ways to "put him in the kitchen again," thereby increasing his visibility and sense of importance. 5) The discussions in Toronto were to bear directly on the Senate and unless a full agreement was struck, Clark was to terminate all discussions Friday night, cancel any Monday multilateral meeting, and prepare for a House sitting on July 15, at which the federal government would present Parliament with its version of constitutional reform.

This was the substance of the agreement reached with Clark, in the presence of Benoît Bouchard, Hugh Segal, Paul Tellier, Jim Judd, and Jocelyne Bourgon. To further drive home the absolute necessity of keeping the federal government's options open, I called Clark in Toronto early Friday morning before my departure for London.

As we got off the plane in London, Craig Oliver of CTV shouted out, "Prime Minister – what do you think of the deal Mr. Clark and the premiers put together in Toronto?" I put on a jaunty smile and gave him a harmless quip, entered the VIP lounge, and earnestly called my assistant, Mark McQueen, to find out what had happened. I was floored by his report of what had apparently taken place.

I called both Tellier and Clark when I arrived – it was about 6:30 p.m. Toronto time – and reviewed developments with Joe, who had gone to Toronto with a small delegation. Tellier remained in Ottawa to work on our federal proposals to Parliament for July 15. Tellier had, in Clark's presence the day before, Thursday, at 24 Sussex, posed the blunt question, "Prime Minister, when do we stop negotiating with the provinces?" and I had replied, "Tomorrow." Tellier was growing progressively concerned about Clark and his negotiating approach. He wanted a deal so badly, Tellier feared he would do anything to get one, including badly weakening our strategic position. This had given rise to many heated exchanges involving Tellier and Clark, and a growing apprehension in Tellier and his officials that Clark might do something foolish or damaging. Meanwhile, as Tellier consistently pointed out, the clock was ticking, and if offers/positions were to be presented to Parliament on July 15, the on again–off again discussions with premiers at the multilateral level must cease so that the government could draft coherent proposals that would attract opposition support, provincial support, be endorsed by cabinet and caucus and, if need be, form the basis of our position in Quebec if they were to hold a referendum, or if the decision was made to proceed with a national referendum. Hence the need to bring discussions to a close and to keep open the government's options to allow it to respect and achieve . . . primary political and Quebec policy objectives.

—

That was the arrangement the Government of Canada had with Mr. Clark, and that was the understanding I, as prime minister, had with him prior to my departure for Munich.

While I was in Europe I tried to keep in touch with developments in Canada, which was made more difficult by having to operate in different time zones. My journal continued to reconstruct these events from my Munich perspective:

—

On Friday night while I was at 35,000 feet flying to London for meetings with the PMs of the U.K. and Japan, Joe Clark (in Vancouver) called Tellier in Ottawa to say that a Senate deal might be achieved on an equal basis. Tellier's reaction was negative, pointing out that Quebec's representation would go from 24 senators to 8, and then both Bourassa and Rae would have serious problems. Joe Clark returns to meeting and reports to Premier Harcourt (the host of the premiers' meeting) who is headed to the airport; Harcourt announces to press that there is no agreement in principle, but there is enough to keep discussing next Tuesday. It was at this critical moment that Joe Clark ought to have announced, pursuant to my instructions, and our collective agreement the previous day, that federal participation had ended. That he was now returning to Ottawa to prepare proposals and would cause them to be tabled as agreed and formally announced on Wednesday night.

Instead, he was on the phone to me in London, reviewing the preceding information. I was worried by developments, but Clark, incredibly, construed this conversation as approval by me, and so advised Tellier. Tellier called me moments later and advised me of the construction Joe Clark put on our conversation. I became quite angry. I told Paul Tellier to call Robert Bourassa immediately to see where he stood on this development. Any movement to triple-E, which was evi-

dently unsupported by Quebec, could place us in a precarious position and undo much of our strategy. Moreover, I was deeply concerned about isolating Bob Rae, who had been a most constructive player throughout. Indeed, I had earlier told Romanow and Penikett that any attempt to force Rae to accept triple-E would be self-defeating because Rae would be "eviscerated" if he agreed to place Ontario's 10 million people on a status of equality with P.E.I.'s 120,000.

On Saturday, Tellier attacked Joe Clark very seriously, saying he had broken faith with me and with the entire federal government strategy. Tellier's concern was that Joe Clark was so concerned with making a deal, basically any deal, that he gave little attention to its long-term implications for the effective functioning of the federal government or the limitations it would place on the options available to the government if we had to go to the House or to a national referendum. Tellier said, "The problem, Mr. Clark, is that for you, long-term thinking is three hours."

On Sunday night, however, the situation began to change. Bourassa called Tellier at home and told him, "Le concept d'un sénat égale, c'est OK." This is significant because Paul Tellier worked for Robert Bourassa in the '70s, knows him very well, and is capable of reading his signals and codes.

Monday morning Tellier advised Joe Clark of Robert Bourassa's call and Rae, who had also heard from Bourassa, confirmed that Bourassa could in principle accept triple-E. On Tuesday at about 11 a.m., Harcourt resumed the meetings. Early on Jeff Rose advised Rae that Benoît Morin – the equivalent of Quebec's Clerk of the Privy Council – had just told him that Robert Bourassa could no longer live with a triple-E. Paul Tellier spoke with Morin to confirm that Bourassa had withdrawn his support for a triple-E because Quebec would be a loser in both houses of Parliament. During lunch at the Pearson Building, the tone was sombre and the mood worse. Unanimous verdict: there was no way we were going to get a deal. Harcourt then added a further cold shower to the proceedings by saying, "In any case, I have no intention of signing anything until I have a referendum in B.C." Filmon and Wells promptly added further opinions. McKenna made a passionate speech about how awful they all would look if they didn't get a deal, Canada deserved better, etc. And Ghiz chimed in with similar eloquent views. At 2:30 or 3:00, Rae called

Bourassa but did not state his opposition to triple-E. Rae told Bourassa that if opposed, he should have a formal conference and say so personally. Bourassa declined to do so.

After lunch they began looking at powers of the Senate and Rae at about 4 p.m. began to speak. Apparently to the stupefaction of his own delegation, he said, "Well, if I accept equal, I'll need more seats in the Commons." This of course was manna from heaven for the triple-E proponents. After all, Canada's largest province had just succumbed, could the federal government be far behind? As it turns out, no.

In subsequent hours, the conversation went on to produce, at about 10 p.m., the Constitutional Agreement of '92. It was by now about 4 a.m. in Munich and I had gotten to bed at about 2 a.m. after having concluded another long day doing business lunches, dinners, and bilaterals, with quick calls squeezed in to Tellier and Segal whenever possible. At about 7:30 a.m. I asked Paul Smith to give David McLaughlin, my deputy chief of staff, responsibility for co-ordination of Segal and Tellier while I was on the road. When McLaughlin gave me the outline of the deal, I exploded in anger because I thought instinctively this would cause enormous problems for the country, and us, down the road.

On Monday morning I had already begun to share my apprehensions with Maz and Barbara McDougall. When I met with them prior to the G-7 plenary session an hour or so later, I was even more outraged. I could not see how such an arrangement could find favour in Quebec or Ontario which, after all, accounted for some 70% of Canada's population, making a 7/50 arrangement absolutely unthinkable. Moreover, the arrangement constitutes such a departure from Beaudoin-Dobbie and our own government's position and is such a break with agreed-upon instructions that I was deeply troubled by the political consequences. I told both ministers under the seal of cabinet confidentiality that Clark may have boxed us into a deal that we couldn't deliver on, thereby reducing if not eliminating all of our options. I had time for a brief exploratory chat with Tellier prior to a meeting in Munich at noon – 5 or 6 p.m. Ottawa time.

Meanwhile the deal was being celebrated outright in all the English dailies in Canada. Joe did a lot of media that day and evening, plugging the deal, and so as not to be entirely out of step with my minister, I gave a second scrum later that day in which the press reported only that my level of enthusiasm had increased marginally.

On Wednesday night following the G-7 and the final meeting with President Yeltsin, the press conference, etc., Mila and I finally got home to the hotel for dinner with Mark and Nicolas at about 7:30 p.m. I spoke with Tellier, Segal, and at some length Bourassa. He was pleased with many of the positions in the deal, but expressed considerable concern about the Senate. His tone, however, was generally positive, and I had Paul Desmarais call La Presse *publisher Roger Landry to ascertain from his vantage point RB's true opinion. The word came back to me from Desmarais that Bourassa finds much that is favourable in the document. His concern is the Senate and aboriginals. Bourassa told me that his cabinet had reacted quite favourably, that his mutual party contacts were positive, and that his view of the Senate was that it was really a "debating society" with little power – although he remained concerned by the numerical drop and how this could marginalize "les francophones dans un pays officialement bilingue." By and large, I detected no alarm in Bourassa's comments. In fact, I believe that an impartial observer might have concluded that I was more worried about how it might fly in Quebec than Bourassa was!*

I proceeded home from Munich on Thursday and greeted Bourassa's press comments with the news that I was encouraged by his attitude and approach, and that the participants had built a base that was clearly useful and constructive. Friday morning I met with Clark, Tellier, Segal, Bourgon, and Judd in the boardroom. After a strategy review I told them privately that my gut reaction was that this would not fly in Quebec and that we were out on a dangerous limb. I then spoke with Bourassa, who declined to come to a first ministers' conference until all of Meech was there, not just the "substance," said that Rémillard was now upset and considering resigning . . . and asked for time to review his clarifications, which more and more look enormous and unsupportable to me.

After this, I went to a lengthy Priorities and Planning meeting, and then a press conference and in both I defended Clark's deal and offered as persuasive a defence as I could. And who knows? It may all turn out to work effectively, but I have doubts that have continued to grow from the moment I first heard of Clark's failure to shut down the process last Friday.

I now fear that he may have inadvertently stopped all of our important options. If Quebec turns against triple-E, can the government give a motion for support for a national referendum that includes the triple-E Senate? If Quebec repudiates triple-E, but it retains strong symbolic value in English-speaking Canada, what happens in the event the parliamentary motion does not endorse such a Senate? How can we regain the momentum in a national referendum if we cannot – without losing all our Quebec members or, say, all of our western members – define the substance of the constitutional changes we propose and the question to accompany it? When we meet the House, what do we say our position is: a triple-E Senate or an equitable-model Senate?

Joe has not done this with malice, but success at what cost? That is our dilemma today. In fact, I have been totally supportive of Joe. I have worked hard to ensure him caucus and cabinet support and would have enthusiastically celebrated constitutional achievement that strengthened the nation, enhanced its unity, and honed its competitiveness.

I have written here in the past (and he, of course, knows nothing of this) that I would be happy to have him as my successor, and there was much in him that would ensure he now could do a good and successful job as PM and party leader. I have often been warned, however, that at the end of the day, having said yes to every interest group, and having persuaded the media that we are "only inches away from a deal," Joe will turn over to me what in reality is an impossible and divisive situation to resolve. Unfortunately, I think that these warnings were right and within the next few weeks, I will have to come to grips with a problem as thorny as any I have encountered as prime minister to date. I can only hope that either I am wrong in my analysis or, if I am right, that my adversaries do not quickly discern what an awful mess I have just been handed by Joe Clark, and that with my colleagues we have time to devise alternative solutions that will see us through this remarkably difficult period.

I think such solutions are few and far between, and Joe's descriptive phrase about a solution being "inches away" is fundamentally wrong. "Miles away, further away than ever" might be more accurate ways of describing the distance now separating Quebec from the rest of Canada at a moment when, had the strategy been faithfully executed, we could have been closer than at any time in our recent history.

The final irony: the reviled Meech Lake Accord, described as so destructive of Canadian unity, has now been completely resurrected and rehabilitated, standing proudly in the latest constitutional package as "an essential building block of national unity." How can it be that Meech Lake opponents like Wells and Filmon now embrace Meech with open arms? Because Meech was never what it was described to be. It was merely a convenient whipping boy and lightning rod for all the anti-Quebec and anti-French passion that welled up in the land following the use of the notwithstanding clause to pass Bill 178. And now that others have been given what they want, forgetting that Meech was brought about by the premiers as a Quebec round in '86, to complete the work of '82, and secure Quebec's signature on the Constitution – Meech has lost its banality? and its odour? Come home, Meech, all is forgiven, where have you been all this time? We have been looking for you, we missed you.

—

As these events unfolded, confusion reigned across the country, and particularly in Ottawa. Quebec's mood was best summed up by an editorial in *Le Devoir* that simply said, "Non," the single word taking up the entire space. On my return from Europe, I cancelled a caucus meeting and immediately called a meeting of the full cabinet on July 15. I began by providing my colleagues with an overview of what had happened in the previous weeks. I asked them for their unvarnished views as to where we should go next.

Not since Mackenzie King met with his colleagues in the old cabinet room in the East Block during the conscription crisis of the Second World War had a government, party, and caucus been so close to splintering. The atmosphere was very tense and my ministers were visibly shaken. Many were furious at Joe Clark. The meeting was unlike any other I was to preside over while prime minister. I have distilled its essence in the following account.

"A lot has happened on the constitutional front over the last two weeks," I began by saying. "So, I want to review with you where I think we stand and where we're headed over the next few weeks. At the end of May the multilateral process looked like it was heading for failure. On June 21–22 I sent Paul Tellier across the country to assess whether there was the political will to do a deal. On June 23 Paul reported to me at 24 Sussex that a deal did not seem to be in sight. I then made a statement in Charlevoix, on Saint-Jean-Baptiste Day, indicating that while the government's first preference was still a negotiated agreement, in its absence, the government would table its own proposals before Parliament on July 15.

"The following Monday, I met with the premiers, listened to their disagreements, and decided to lob the ball right back in their court: 'If you want a deal,' I told them, 'then you go and see if you can sort out a compromise on the Senate.' That day, six premiers favoured an equitable Senate, three a triple-E, and Romanow was all over the lot. The following Friday, there was a meeting of the premiers. It resumed the next Tuesday, July 7, where an agreement was reached – but not on the equitable model but on a watered-down triple-E. That in itself is no mean feat.

"This agreement gives us a base to work from. It is not perfect. But nothing is. Joe is the first to admit it. I know that some of you have improvements to suggest: strengthening section 121; more precision on the inherent right of self-government; and many of you are not comfortable with a triple-E Senate. But let's remember that we are seeking a negotiated deal, not an imposed agreement, like the 1982 Constitution. That means we are in the world of the possible, the world of the good, not the perfect."

After a further summary, I concluded by saying, "The task we face is a difficult one. There are no guarantees. But I think we have to try to build on the agreement and bring Quebec in. If we don't succeed, we'll have to look at other options. But for now, colleagues, that is what I see lying ahead. What I would like to do today is hear your views on where we are. We can take all the time we need. I'd like your guidance on the political management of the file over the coming weeks. How do we avoid isolating Quebec while at the same time not alienating the rest of the country – who, after all, have agreed to the deal on the table?"

I was aware, in making those opening remarks, that the government had been placed in an extremely dangerous situation that could bring harm to the country. Yet for all my frustration and anger with the moves that Clark had made in my absence and without my approval, I had to recognize that, given Bourassa's oblique negotiating style, a signal might have been given to Clark that allowed him to conclude legitimately that Bourassa was onside, in principle, with the idea of a triple-E Senate. I never, of course, at any time placed in doubt Clark's commitment to Canada, his love of the country, and his desire to move ahead. Perhaps, I concluded, the fault for the imbroglio rested with Bourassa and not with Clark.

But this matter had to be resolved by cabinet, and after my opening remarks I asked each minister for his or her view of the situation. I believe this was the first time, in all my years in office, that I ever proceeded in this manner. But, given the extraordinary importance of the issue at hand, I had to ensure that each member of cabinet was consulted and had every opportunity to express himself or herself.

The meeting was tense and difficult because what the ministers were really being asked to do was to pass judgment on the results of Joe Clark's initiative, with him sitting to my left at the oval cabinet table. I turned to Bernard Valcourt to start, and I took notes as each minister spoke.

"I don't want Quebec blamed for killing this," Valcourt said. "Let it die as it is and then resurrect our own offer."

From Manitoba, Jake Epp, as shrewd an observer as existed in Ottawa, spoke next. "While we can't isolate Quebec, the triple-E Senate is seen as just as important, symbolically, in the West as the distinct society is in Quebec," he said. Pierre Cadieux said he had visited both the West Island and Lac-Saint-Jean in previous days and found people in both areas firmly opposed to the agreement as negotiated.

Michael Wilson outlined four main points. First, he said, people are completely fed up with the debate; second, Ontario MPs were concerned about the Senate proposals because the House of Commons would be bogged down with this kind of Senate; third, the aboriginal issues lacked definition and precision, which worried Ontario. Of course, he added, section 121 was the biggest concern, if the devolution of powers was to be balanced by strengthening the economic union, and this hadn't yet happened.

Jean Corbeil was straightforward. "This will never pass in Quebec," he said flatly.

"It is completely unacceptable for them and for me," Marcel Danis opined, adding that he had spoken with thirty-five members of Parliament about the deal. Danis' comments were interesting, because he had been Joe Clark's Quebec campaign manager during the 1983 leadership campaign.

The tension in the room grew as Joe listened in silence to this wave of denunciation. Now he intervened for the first time, blurting out to his startled colleagues, "Who cares about the rest of the country?"

"We do," Benoît Bouchard answered.

"Bullshit," Clark said.

Everyone looked at him.

And so it went on, around the table. Jean Charest made a series of excellent points, as did the reliable and thoughtful Charlie Mayer from Manitoba. He pointed out that his province needed a federal government that could act in the national interest.

Gilles Loiselle, a rising star from Quebec who had served in communications before moving into the diplomatic arena, said flatly, "This agreement has absolutely no chance of being accepted as is. Even the principles are not acceptable. Prime Minister, you personally must now assume the leadership and make a final exploration of the file, to see if it can be salvaged without squeezing Bourassa any more, because he is already in serious difficulty in Quebec."

Harvie Andre pointed out that the deal was being greeted as a huge victory in Alberta, although he added that a triple-E Senate was not worth sacrificing the country for. He suggested a possible ten-year trial, a referendum with regional majorities, and if it failed, we'd simply abolish the Senate or make it into a permanent constituent assembly.

Elmer MacKay, a man of solid judgment, provided a lucid position, as did Kim Campbell, who supported Andre's views. The able Tom Siddon pointed out that most of our twenty-eight-point package had been achieved, and that we were left with the enormous challenge of the triple-E Senate. "The country is looking for a federal proposal," he said. He then concluded, to smiles and chuckles around the table, "Prime Minister, I admired your defence of this crazy triple-E proposal in Munich – you almost had me believing it!"

John Crosbie denounced the contortions that we were going through, describing our discussion as a "constitutional barf fest." He was just warming up. He went on to describe the triple-E Senate as barbaric and ludicrous. "Walt Disney couldn't have dreamt up anything better than what we have on the table as a result of all these meetings. If the country is going to be dissolved, let it say so. If French and English can't live together, let them say so. Not one other province will leave Canada if there's no triple-E Senate, or anything else, except maybe Clyde Wells, who would leave – but who would be taking me with him!"

Doug Lewis, Gerry Weiner, Lowell Murray, Benoît Bouchard, and others all contributed usefully to the discussion. By the end of the meeting there was unanimity: no one supported the deal that Clark had brought home. I received strong instructions from the cabinet to take over the negotiations and, with Joe's help, to try to fashion a constitutional package that would find unanimous approval with all of the players and that would offer a viable proposition for a national referendum.

I was untroubled by the fact that a large package would be easy to attack, and that a national referendum on such an important and complex series of issues could fail. I had no problem contemplating such a result, because Canadians would have had the opportunity to speak to the issue themselves and to decide if they wished these types of reforms or not. With Meech Lake, what had so dismayed me was that Clyde Wells had deprived Newfoundland legislators of their right to vote on the proposal in the House of Assembly. A simple, autocratic move by one man had stood in the way of democracy. That wouldn't happen again.

After that long and exhausting cabinet session, I began a series of intensive consultations with the first ministers to find out if a deal was possible. I needed to ensure support of the Meech provisions in order to make the conditions right for Bourassa to return to the table. As I worked the phones, mainly from Harrington Lake, I was near despair.

Over the next few days, I involved Joe Clark closely in the process. In spite of our difficult past and recent events, Joe and I were sufficiently professional to be able to set these aside and work toward a common solution – if one could be found. On July 22 I met with Joe at Harrington Lake. My journal notes explain for the first time why Joe took the position he did.

—

PERSONAL JOURNAL: JULY 22, 1992

(Harrington Lake, 10:20 p.m., after meeting with Joe Clark)
I had a lengthy meeting with Joe Clark today to renew the constitutional file. The meeting was constructive and cordial, though a degree of wariness pervaded the discussions. Prior to lunch, we sat in the main room and after a discussion about his holiday in Nantucket, I said, "Joe, I do not believe in criticizing anyone if I was not in the room. But on June 23 we met. June 24, I spoke in my riding followed by meetings with aboriginals, territorial leaders, premiers and then a Thursday meeting at 24 Sussex. All of this activity was aimed at one of

two results: either get an agreement on the equitable Senate or break off discussions so as to present a resolution to the House that would constitute a federal offer. I spoke to you in this regard Friday morning prior to my departure for the airport. When I arrived in London seven hours later, you had the beginnings of a deal on a triple-E Senate, not the equitable model which I always believed the only one sellable in Quebec and the rest of Canada (though not of course the first choice of three premiers). What in the name of God happened to draw you off course in this way? What happened in the meeting?"

Clark began a detailed reply. He then told me something I did not know (or, if I had been told, I had completely forgotten it). He said that in the afternoon, as the discussion evolved toward some kind of triple-E, he suggested a break, during which he called Bourassa and spelled out to him clearly specifics of the proposed Senate changes under discussion. He said that Robert Bourassa was in no way hostile to the triple-E concept (though it was not his first choice) and discussed with him changes to modalities that could make it more workable. I was aware that Bourassa had conveyed directly to Tellier and Bob Rae his tacit acceptance that "en principe, je ne suis pas contre un sénat égal; j'appuis cela. [In principle, I am not against an equitable Senate; I support it.]" But this was the first I learned of a similar conveyance of views directly to Joe Clark. Had Bourassa been firmly opposed (as I was afterwards, because I thought ultimately it would be rejected in Quebec, Ont., and B.C.), he should have said so directly to Clark Friday night. That would have made it impossible for Clark to engage in further discussions at the coffee break, and he would have had to advise premiers that it was a no-go and not started. This time, Bourassa's reluctance to be direct and categorical in conversations, I think, persuaded Joe Clark a triple-E was doable when it was not, thereby encouraging Joe unfairly into a position which has caused enormous difficulties for the government, and no doubt great problems for the nation.

Joe Clark explained that he had been reflecting on how this whole situation had developed, and he said, "Your belief was that if negotiations failed, we could carry a resolution in the House and a referendum in the country. You have always had the kind of belief in our capacity to come from behind and win. My belief was that a negotiated settlement was indispensable – we needed the support of the parties to carry the day." And then he added the very significant and revealing words – and I jotted them down immediately after he uttered them, in the bathroom at Harrington Lake – "You and I had different instincts, and I was not prepared to defer to yours. Going into the meeting I was trying to get mine."

—

1992

4. The Guns of August

It was time to summon the premiers. I chose Harrington Lake as the site of our meeting on August 4 because I thought it would provide a relaxing atmosphere after such tumultuous events. And the Harrington Lake venue would allow Premier Bourassa to return to the first ministers' table without having to leave his own province.

On their arrival, I took all the premiers down to the dock, where we socialized and enjoyed the summer scenery before the meeting began. Once inside the house, Joe Clark and I sat at opposite ends of the table, and I started things off with a tone-setter, an action plan, which I had written out by hand in advance of the gathering.

"Welcome to Harrington, and a special welcome to Robert Bourassa after a two-year absence," I said. "It has been a difficult two years, and therefore today signals a step forward. The multilateral process that resulted in the understanding of July 7 has been important, and it allowed us to reach consensus on many significant issues. We now face the most difficult part of the process, confronted by two fundamental realities. The nine-province agreement is supported by many Canadians in English Canada. In Quebec and elsewhere, there has been significant public opposition to major parts of the agreement. The challenge is to find the flexibility needed to reconcile the differences among premiers, and between those who agreed with the July 7 undertaking and Quebec, because the decision in 1982 to proceed with the nine-province agreement – and without Quebec – is one that no one would want to repeat, so disruptive have been the consequences.

"Canadians want this divisive issue to be behind us. They want us to provide the political will and leadership required to turn the July 7 agreement into a statement of national unity that reflects broad pan-Canadian, English- and French-speaking approval. If we succeed, for Canada, the sky is the limit. If we fail, the consequences, both economic and political, will be direct and damaging for all around this table, both within Quebec and across the country. Failure would also result in increased division and recrimination in the country. Failure would also have a troubling but measurable impact, on the eve of a Quebec referendum – not something anyone would wish to see . . .

"So the purpose of today's meeting is to allow me, as prime minister, to assess whether there is sufficient flexibility on substance on all sides to justify the resumption of negotiations at the level of first minister – or to conclude that the parties have agreed to disagree; and that, given the tight time frames and impending referendum in Quebec, such a meeting – with a predictably unproductive outcome – would be most unhelpful to those federalists in Quebec who seek to defend the cause of a united Canada.

"I have indicated that today is not a negotiating session, nor have the territories or aboriginal leadership been invited, so as to allow us, as the only elected heads of government in the federation, to speak frankly and directly to one another about the next few challenging months in Canada's history. Accordingly, it would be inappropriate to begin negotiating the aboriginal package – though clearly we can discuss the concepts and the extent to which they may be acceptable to our respective legislatures or parliaments. It would be inappropriate to begin by dissecting the elements of Meech, inasmuch as, after Mr. Clark spoke with all of you, I gave Robert Bourassa the assurance that the substance of Meech had been generally agreed upon, so as to enable him to accept my invitation to be here, today, thereby fulfilling, at least in part, his undertaking to Québécois not to engage in multilateral discussions until the fundamentals had been retrieved.

"It is also important to underline the significance of the precept that guided your discussions – namely that, until all is agreed, nothing is agreed. Therefore, the notion that someone loses when another gains is both irrelevant and inapplicable because, only when you conclude that Canada gains most, do we have a truly national deal with an opportunity for success. Many of you will want to hear from Robert regarding the July 7 agreement. Just before we do, I would begin by asking Premier Ghiz, incoming chair of the annual Premiers' Conference, to outline for us his news concerning the process that led to the Pearson Building agreement."

The premiers then began to speak. They were helpful, the attitude was constructive, and the tone was brutally honest. Joe Clark and I each took extensive notes – he shared his with me after the meeting – and I have relied on both sources to reconstruct the discussion that day, which is reproduced in detail in Appendix B.

My journal summarizes that fateful first ministers' meeting.

—

PERSONAL JOURNAL: AUGUST 9, 1992

(Written at Harrington Lake)

The seven-hour meeting last Tuesday here at Harrington was constructive, though not particularly promising. It is clear that the "historic deal" proclaimed on July 7 is largely an illusion. It became very clear that many premiers are in disagreement with the aboriginal clause as negotiated and many, in some case others, will no longer support the triple-E Senate. Wells says he only supported a triple-E Senate and was formally opposed to the aboriginal clause, a key provision. Cameron says he left without shaking hands and agreeing on anything because the aboriginal agenda was driven by "guilt and intimidation" and that he never really supported the triple-E. Harcourt says the aboriginal clause as drafted cannot be sold in B.C. Ghiz asserts that he wanted the abolition of the Senate and only agreed to the triple-E to solve the issue – on the condition that it would bring Quebec back to the table. Because it has demonstrably done the opposite, Ghiz has withdrawn all support for the triple-E and also finds now that the aboriginal clause wording "went too far." So it went around the table – leaving any reasonable person to wonder what in God's name possessed Joe Clark to proclaim this disaster the greatest constitutional agreement since 1867!

—

The premiers and I gathered again at Harrington Lake on August 10. My opening remarks were a synthesis of earlier discussions and agreements and an enumeration of the outstanding challenges we would have to confront.

After setting the agenda, in some detail, I opened up discussion on aboriginal issues. Before long, I could see that an unlikely alliance was shaping up on the subject of self-government, as my handwritten notes reflect.

"I see clear potential to solve concerns of Newfoundland in what you've said," Clyde Wells told me. "The inherent right to self-government must be tied to a land base and there should be a new clause to define scope of inherent rights."

His eyes glittering mischievously, Robert Bourassa joined the discussion with his former nemesis. "We are ready to make proposals," he said. "The reference to the courts is major for us. If the inherent right is not well defined, it could include James Bay. I can't fail to agree to reassess. On that basis, Clyde is speaking on behalf of Quebec!"

After the chuckling at this statement had died down, Don Getty had a question for Quebec's premier. "How do you get to the table to make proposals?" he asked.

"I have no objection to going to a multilateral conference to give Quebec's position," Bourassa said, later mentioning the "ferocious public relations campaign" the Cree of northern Quebec had raised. Bourassa also reminded the group of the earlier conflict with the Mohawk warriors at Oka.

We then broke for lunch and a much-needed break. While we were moving forward, it was by inches, not miles. After our meal, I turned the discussion to the Senate.

"On Senate reform, two things became clear [on August 4]," I said. "We have points of commonality on election and, by and large, on powers; but there are significant differences on numbers and distribution of seats. A number of premiers made it clear that their support for the equal model was conditional on their understanding that this approach would lead to a successful resolution of Canada's constitutional difficulties. Since July 7, Joe and I have canvassed every possibility to see if the equal model could be adjusted to make it acceptable to all parts of the country."

I then ran the premiers through the various scenarios: extending the need for a double majority vote to areas like broadcasting, cultural institutions, immigration, and family policy; replacing the absolute veto over ordinary legislation with a suspensive veto and a vote in a joint sitting of both houses of Parliament; guaranteeing more francophone seats in the Senate to reflect Canada's linguistic duality; reserving a francophone seat in the new Senate from each of the nine English-speaking provinces; adding seats to be elected by all French Canadians; guaranteeing 25 per cent of the House of Commons seats for Quebec; adding Commons seats to Quebec's representation to compensate for its loss of Senate seats and more.

I then asked Joe Clark to review all of these options for us.

This produced a lengthy and serious discussion among the first ministers, on all the issues before us. Frank McKenna suggested that if Quebec accepted the concept of "equal," the province's Commons representation could be increased by sixteen seats as compensation.

"This destroys it," Clyde Wells said in response. "I'd never try to sell it in Newfoundland."

Bob Rae, always a strong and intelligent voice, also intervened strongly. "It would be absurd for me to renounce my July 7 decision," he said. "It would also be absurd to refuse to consider new ideas that will resolve the matter."

The premier of Canada's largest province then turned directly to Bourassa. "Is there any way this can be the basis of negotiation?" he asked. "I think this can be done in a way that's saleable in the rest of the country."

"Goodwill is vital and there is goodwill," Bourassa replied. "I am worried by the impact of this on the country in ten or fifteen years with such a reform adding a new Tower of Babel."

Two very different concepts of Confederation were laid out when Don Getty of Alberta spoke.

"We're trying to close a gap [on Senate reform] but we've been arguing something more fundamental – the equality of provinces," he said. "I don't understand why Robert Bourassa doesn't view triple-E as saleable. This is not about more senators for Alberta. This is about a new basis for Canada."

Joe Ghiz jumped to the defence of Quebec's premier. "I have respect for Robert Bourassa, and if he says he can't sell it (triple-E), I'm with him. We have an obligation to support him," he said.

McKenna agreed. "I don't have the sacred trust of preserving culture and language," he said. "We are giving separatists an issue to clobber him [Bourassa] to death."

We were heading toward a failed conference. I jumped in to outline the high costs of failure.

Bob Rae then gave a passionate address. "I'm not going to participate in a gangup on Quebec," he said. "Recrimination is useless here. I was in favour of patriation in 1981, but we now all have to live with its consequences."

"I agree with the prime minister on the gravity of the situation," Joe Ghiz said. "We should hear from Robert Bourassa about what happens to the country if we fail. People say this country is not going to break up. I don't believe that. Breakup is imminent."

"Ghiz is absolutely right," Donald Cameron of Nova Scotia said. "If this process fails, we lose the referendum in Quebec and the Canadian people won't be too happy. What's the use of having a Senate if you have no country?"

There was complete silence as Robert Bourassa spoke.

"You ask what are the chances of the separatists winning?" he said. "Forty per cent of Quebecers are strong federalists and 40 per cent are separatists. That leaves 20 per cent in the balance. If this round ends in failure, there is a serious risk you will have a vote for independence because Quebecers will feel rejected if they get the message they are not welcome in Canada. I will be in an extremely difficult position if I have nothing to offer Quebecers."

"Robert, if you need something, join us at the table and we'll have something for you by the end of the month," Bob Rae offered quietly, a little later.

As the day came to a close, I summed up the situation as I saw it. While we faced major areas of disagreement, no one wanted to walk away from the table or to see Canada fracture. It was clear to all that Quebecers had to have an offer from the rest of Canada for their consideration in October. It was also clear that all Canadians wanted a say in the matter. Our course was set.

"I agree with the prime minister's passionate statement," Roy Romanow said at the end of the session. "A referendum is required to consult all Canadians."

In public the next day I announced that I had called a full-fledged constitutional conference for August 18.

In the meantime, as they say, life goes on. On August 12 the United States, Mexico, and Canada agreed to the NAFTA. Michael Wilson, who was responsible for concluding the negotiations for Canada, stated the obvious when he said he believed it to be a good deal for all three countries – and especially for Canada. On the other hand, union leader Bob White promised an all-out fight against it, and my ally on the Constitution, Bob Rae, labelled NAFTA a sellout of Canada's economy. Ratcheting up the rhetoric for NDP consumption, Rae also said it was a blatant move on my part to assist in George Bush's re-election efforts. *Plus ça change; plus c'est la même chose.* It was like 1988 all over again.

The next day I faced a crucial caucus meeting. I spoke to my MPs and senators frankly about the constitutional negotiations and gave them an indication of where we were heading.

"Since July 7 [Canadian] unity has been challenged as never before," I said. "Never in my nine years as party leader and eight years as PM have

I gone through a more difficult thirty-day period. Because once the July 7 deal was announced, certain premiers seized upon it as a done deal, to be put to Quebec almost on a take-it-or-leave-it basis. 'We made compromises among the nine English-speaking premiers and the federal representative to arrive at this arrangement – so none of the fundamentals can be changed. Quebec will have to accept this,' they said. Or, 'We got the triple-E and now all Brian Mulroney has to do is sell it in Quebec. If he refuses to do so, it's because he and Robert Bourassa want to take it away from us.' This was not what Joe Clark intended – but this is the way it evolved. Joe Clark intended a framework for future negotiations. And the reaction in Quebec to the deal? Absolute incredulity. There was a major problem: nine provinces and feds, without Quebec – that's exactly what Trudeau did, and it's what we swore we would never do. There has been intense pressure from the Alberta and Quebec media, putting our members in extremely delicate positions. We have also faced hints of defections 'if we don't get our triple-E.' Remember, this is a concept rejected only weeks earlier by virtually every Alberta MP! It illustrates well the irrationality of politics."

A few days later I made a journal entry after I arrived home from Ottawa General Hospital. Mila had broken her ankle and I had gone to emergency to assist my wife. She had to spend a night in the hospital and I was lonely without her.

—

PERSONAL JOURNAL: AUGUST 16, 1992

If I were to die tomorrow I think I would go (not happily) but at peace because of the wondrous pleasure Mila has brought to my life and the truly impressive way she has raised the children. When I watched Caroline speak yesterday at 24 Sussex at the AIDS benefit, in flawless English and French, I was filled with pride and commitment. She is 18, intelligent, demure, and disciplined – a healthy combination for someone headed into the tough competition at Harvard – but most of all a wonderful child who, like her brothers, has brought Mila and me such tremendous joy.

—

Caroline had organized a volleyball tournament at 24 Sussex, as an AIDS fundraiser. Young people of all political persuasions who worked on the Hill and around Ottawa joined in for an afternoon of sports and entertainment to help fight this terrible disease.

After I announced my resignation plans less than a year later, Dr. Bruce Mills, executive director of the AIDS Housing Group of Ottawa, recalled that tournament in a letter to my family that I will always cherish.

> It is with much pride that all of us here at AIDS Housing Group of Ottawa and Bruce House convey our gratitude and our very fondest farewell to the Mulroney family as you leave Ottawa. . . . To Caroline, our deepest appreciation for raising nearly $15,000 last year at her volleyball tournament at 24 Sussex. The amount of work that you dedicated to putting the tournament together was remarkable, and the outcome was certainly worthwhile. Mila's broken ankle was most unfortunate, and we understand she scored her point before removing herself from the game. You became a heroine to our patients, who said that your broken ankle was certainly a sign of your commitment to an important cause. And to the prime minister, who took time out to visit with us when we met Caroline at 24 Sussex right in the middle of constitutional talks, our highest respect and thanks for taking time out of such a busy schedule. Please know that all of us here at AIDS Housing will miss the Mulroney family deeply, especially the feeling that the care, treatment, and support of our AIDS patients mattered very much to you.

Long after we had left Ottawa we stayed in helpful touch with Bruce House because I had been so moved by the enthusiasm Caroline and her siblings showed for such a worthy cause.

I sat in my study at Harrington, reflecting on my wife and children in silence and solitude. My mind was racing, making sleep difficult, and I also reviewed the constitutional situation as the summer night rolled by.

—

PERSONAL JOURNAL: AUGUST 16, 1992 (CONTINUED)

The meeting here at Harrington last Monday with the premiers has given rise to a full First Ministers' Conference along with aboriginal leaders and territorial leaders next Tuesday. The meeting itself was relatively productive, the mood reasonable, but I am filled with apprehension about both the anticipated results of next week and the future itself. The meeting this weekend of the youth federation of the Liberal Party of Quebec is very worrisome, and perhaps a harbinger of trouble to come. Their rejection of federalism as the preferred option of their party was unprecedented and, I think, unacceptable for the Liberals. Robert Bourassa should have long ago rid himself of the leadership of that group, starting with the president, Mario Dumont, for the simple reason they are sovereigntists and should be in the PQ, not the Liberals.

When Robert Bourassa answered a question Monday night and told the premiers he could lose a referendum, Filmon smiled and said, sotto voce, "They'd never separate." Whereupon McKenna exploded and said, "For Christ's sake, Gary, read the Quebec papers. It's staring you in the goddamn face every day." I was very troubled by the poisonous atmosphere in western Canada being fed by the Calgary Herald, *the* Edmonton Journal, *and the* Sun *newspapers, and the impact it might have on our own caucus members. The message from the western media was, "We have our triple-E. July 7 was a done deal. Now it's up to Mulroney to sell it to Quebec, otherwise he will have established that he is more a PM for Quebec than a PM for Canada." I had, of course, heard the reverse of this refrain over the years from hard-core separatists in Quebec, resolved to do and say anything that might contribute to the dismemberment of Canada. I have never before heard such provocative and reckless language from so-called mainline newspapers and commentators, with so little concern for its consequences. At the 24 Sussex FMC in late June Don Getty told me that "no PM in Canadian history had done more for Alberta and the west than Mulroney" – dismantling NEP, deregulation, FTA, NAFTA, abolishing FIRA, moving the NEB to Calgary, creating the*

WDO in Edmonton, etc. He was right. All of these actions my government took because I thought they were fair to Alberta, a province badly abused by the Liberals. The appointment of three powerful P&P ministers like Maz, Clark, and Andre from Alberta was also a signal of fairness I sought to send to the people of Alberta. But the July 7 deal has gone a long way to ensuring that I and the government once again never get credit from Albertans.

—

On August 18, the First Ministers' Conference took place at the Pearson Building. I had come down with the flu and wasn't sleeping; nor was Mila, due to the cast on her broken ankle. So it was understandable that Mike Harcourt later told a journalist that I seemed to be in a "savage mood" as our discussions got under way. I would prefer to remember myself as serious, contemplative, and weighed down by responsibilities as the first ministers – joined now by the leaders of Canada's native organizations and territorial premiers – met for five days of talks. Bob Rae later likened my negotiating style to that of Lyndon Johnson, a comparison I enjoyed. "I mean, this is a guy from the Lyndon Johnson school of persuasion," he told journalist Susan Delacourt, as recounted in her book *United We Fall*. "He's just somebody who gets you in the room and stares you right in the face." Delacourt made her own assessment: "Watching Mulroney negotiate is like watching Wayne Gretzky, swooping through the defence to score goals. In fact, the intensity of Mulroney's style, his frequent shots on net, can stun a novice, as many provincial politicians have found."

From LBJ to Gretzky, I can't really complain. There were other sources of encouragement in the heat of battle. "PM: Hang in there," Don Getty wrote in a note he slipped in front of me during a particularly difficult session. "The second eight years are easier."

When it was all said and done, we did arrive at a deal, despite my earlier doubts. I wrote an extensive passage in my journal covering these incredible events.

—

PERSONAL JOURNAL: AUGUST 24–25, 1992

(Written at Harrington Lake)

We did it! We actually did it! The first ministers in five incredible days in August '92 actually decided to put Canada's interests far above their regional or provincial interests, thereby allowing the evolution of a constitutional agreement that just may succeed in keeping this country together. It was the toughest five days of my life, because I knew that the absence of an agreement with the premiers probably would trigger a Quebec referendum on sovereignty, perhaps ending Canada as a united country. Certainly I could and would have presented a purely federal constitutional proposal to the House, to which supportive provinces could subsequently sign their assent, thereby constituting "an offer" (to Quebec, prior to the Quebec referendum), but given the constitutional requirements of provincial approval imposed by the 1982 amendment, such a step would be much less compelling than a negotiated settlement with the provinces. That we were able to conclude a unanimous agreement makes this for me all the more precious and valuable.

The unanimity lends an aura of moral strength to proposals that seek to bind a nation and people together. Canada could not again afford the hurt and the poison that flowed from Mr. Trudeau's decision to proceed against the wishes of the Quebec National Assembly in '82. This is a broadly based, well-balanced agreement that will fundamentally and, I think, beneficially alter the federation. It is much more than a Quebec round – it has evolved into a genuine Canada round with features from aboriginal self-government, to a restructured Senate, to a Canada clause, that should strengthen Canada and engender greater participation among her citizens.

When we ended, I spoke quietly about Canada and how I believed all participants had contributed to its betterment and perhaps salvation. For a moment I was overcome by emotion and relief. As I struggled to compose myself, Don Getty rose and led all participants in a thundering standing ovation. I felt true friendship with all who were there, from Bourassa to aboriginal leader Ovide Mercredi, because they all had participated in the achievement of pulling

Canada back from the brink of possible destruction. And I felt a great burden being lifted from my shoulders, that somehow persistence, discipline, and devotion to Canada had paid off – and that all the abuse and personal attacks and criticisms over the last two years, so demoralizing to my party and government, and so powerful for my family and friends, had been worth it. My primary and overwhelming objectives and concerns have been the unity of Canada. It is a cause to which I would unhesitatingly give my life, so great is Canada's potential, so profound is its capacity for good in the world – if only Canadians themselves could appreciate the splendour of their common heritage. Some days I despaired of ever getting through – over the bigots, the ill-informed, the biased, the unhappy, the angry, whose voices seemed to dominate our nightly newscasts – to the vast majority of ordinary, common Canadians whose wisdom alone has kept Canada united for so long.

But in the end we prevailed and the first ministers responded nobly and generously. Historians will no doubt write about turning points and crucial junctures in the talks. The truth is, there were none. I believe we succeeded for one simple reason: that the participants were persuaded that the national interests must dominate, and the failure to do so would bring damage to Canada and considerable opprobrium in history to each and every one of them. I believe that the Harrington Lake talks were the crucial ones, without which no success could have been achieved. It was Robert Bourassa's first meeting in two years. They could take the measure of him and contemplate the significance of the challenge, together with the cost of failure.

At Pearson, there were at least a dozen times the entire thing might have been blocked or perhaps gone off the rails – only to be rescued by a fresh approach suggested by a premier or federal representative, a willingness to try again or to re-examine previously intransigent positions. Each participant contributed significantly to the exercise that has become so successful. Including, I must recall in fairness, Premier Clyde Wells of Newfoundland.

What are the next steps? Tomorrow, I meet full cabinet and fly to Charlottetown for a meeting of first ministers Thursday. My hope is that we will there approve the legal version of the statement of principles to which we agreed at Pearson, and consider ratification. I think the decision to proceed with the passage of referendum legislation has proved to be important. It now appears that, given the unanimous nature of the document agreed to, provincial governments are concluding it would be in their interests that there be a national referendum and, as Bob Rae said last night, "as soon as possible." I told Robert Bourassa that if we ever got a good deal, he would have to cancel his proposed referendum on sovereignty either totally, or arrange to hold a referendum jointly with the next provincial election on the offer for renewed federalism. Since the deal, I have urged him strongly to 1) roll out the referendum at Saturday's provincial Liberal convention, 2) join in a national referendum, 3) if successful, proceed to ratify constitutional resolutions in National Assembly after all other provinces and the feds have done so. So far he seems to be doing well in Quebec, although the opposition will be both vindictive and personal, but I think that this will come to be seen by Quebecers as a good and balanced deal. As Claude Ryan said today, "Meech Lake plus, plus, plus."

My hope is that we will have a national referendum and that it will be strongly supported by Canadians, French- and English-speaking both. My expectation is that, if we get it all done early in the new year, I will announce what I had planned to announce in September '91 – had Meech gone through – and that Mila, the children, and I will get on with the rest of our lives.

In retrospect I must record that, while the July 7 accord made final agreement almost impossible, without the networking and good faith that went into that accord, the August 22 accord would not have been possible! Clark had done good work with the natives and provinces, and when I began the final push, I was clearly building on a lot of effort and accomplishment in a list of areas. It was crucial to my strategy that we solve the Senate first, then aboriginals (to put a human face on our efforts), then division of powers, Canada clause, etc. I was able to get through this because of earlier work, obviously, but also because of the enormous contribution of Paul Tellier, Jocelyne Bourgon, and Suzanne Hurtubise, three public servants as devoted and talented as this nation has ever seen. If we get this ratified in the next four months – and God knows how I have learned to take nothing for granted – we may be ushering in one of the greatest periods of unity and prosperity that this nation has ever seen.

A defeat in the referendum for the PQ and BQ would leave them and their cause gravely weakened, and imperilled at the next federal/provincial elections. The signature of Quebec on the Constitution would subsequently raise serious doubts about the capacity of any government to argue its illegitimacy and hence the case for future referenda and separation. A nation is entitled to address such fundamental questions as self-determination – but not every decade. If Quebecers support this (along with other Canadians), it will be my position that no further right will ensue to allow for the secession of any province. I believe this view will be sustained by the people and by history.

In my calls to the opposition leaders today, Audrey McLaughlin was congratulatory and warm, and Jean Chrétien was crisp and cold. He is clearly one unhappy man. Whatever the future brings, his willingness to proceed without Quebec in '82 and his opposition to Meech from '87 to '90 has given him a reputation that few would envy. He has not changed much, and is clearly morose in contemplating the beneficial electoral effects this may have on me. Canada's future looks more secure today than at any time since the fateful decision in '82, and God willing, will go on forever.

—

Bob Rae telephoned me when the Pearson round was over. "I wanted to say personally to you that you really did quite a marvellous job," he said. "Without your special skills there would have been no deal. I think you should have a national referendum. Do it quickly."

Bob's call was one of the small touches of class, typical of him, that make political life both bearable and memorable. I would not soon forget it.

1992

5. Charlottetown

Our final talks were held in the most appropriate Canadian city, Charlottetown, Prince Edward Island, site of Confederation in 1867.

—

personal journal: August 30, 1992

(Written at Harrington Lake)

I have difficulty believing it is almost done. In the upcoming referendum I certainly don't want to take anything for granted, but great hurdles and obstacles have been overcome, with the constitutional agreement achieved last Friday, some 48 hours ago. Charlottetown was a winding up session, a clearing up of language, a reconciliation of interests (in some cases), and an agreement on the manner in which ratification should most expeditiously be obtained. Again, all participants were constructive, although two were extremely difficult to deal with on important issues. Clyde Wells decided that after showing great flexibility (to the point of, in effect, endorsing all of Meech), he would not agree to make unanimous the process whereby judges are appointed to the Supreme Court of Canada. His insistence that all provinces submit names for all vacancies (i.e., Nfld. submitting names for Quebec vacancies) consumed hours of discussion late Thursday and early Friday and precluded unanimity on the point.

His determination on this obscure point was bizarre. (After hearing Clyde Wells rant on for long moments on whether he should be able to recommend Quebec and Saskatchewan justices, for example, Bob Rae whispered to me, "Jesus, PM, he is one scary guy.") And indeed he was, but fortunately less so than in Meech. When I asked him how he could feel comfortable recommending candidates to fill a Quebec vacancy when he was not familiar with its civil code or jurisprudence, pointing out that because he could neither speak nor read French, it would be impossible for him to appreciate and judge fairly the work of various judicial candidates in that jurisdiction, he just put his head down and said he wouldn't agree to anything and that "Newfoundlanders would never be satisfied with anything less."

To which Joe Ghiz responded, "For God's sake, Clyde, you may be the only person in Nfld. and Labrador who either knows or cares anything about this obscure matter in the first place."

Wells believes that the nominating provision allows the Government of Quebec to appoint the justices. Of course it does not, but despite the best efforts of everyone (especially Roy Romanow, who said specifically, "Clyde, when there is an opening on the Prairies and it is Saskatchewan's turn, I specifically want the government of my province to submit the names for consultation and choice by the prime minister, and I specifically do not *want the premiers of Nfld. or Quebec horning in on our concerns.") We were unable to persuade him, so Nfld. will probably have a second question on their ballot dealing with the procedure whereby future Supreme Court candidates are chosen – no doubt a subject that will dominate political debate in Nfld. among the fishermen and plant workers for months to come.*

The next sticking point was B.C. representation in the Commons. Mike Harcourt is new to this game and is a nice, good-natured guy. But he is less well informed and effective than others around the table, and so when the Pearson Building agreement was announced, the B.C. reaction was that Premier Harcourt had been "asleep at the switch," and B.C. had not obtained a fair number of MPs in a redistributed House of Commons. He became a figure of ridicule back home, with commentators out there describing him as "Premier Bonehead," no doubt to his embarrassment and anguish. It was clear that his proposal to extract himself from the dilemma (by adding B.C. seats) was not going down well with others, particularly as it would benefit few provinces and had the effect of ballooning the house by 19 seats in '96 – a quite unacceptable prospect in view of the size enhancement already achieved at Pearson in compensation for Senate seat losses by Ontario and Quebec. Accordingly, on Friday afternoon, toward the very end, I put forward a modified proposal that gave

Ontario, Alberta, and B.C. a few more seats and alluded to the 95% rule and said, "Colleagues, we have someone at this table who is wounded. It is irrelevant to me how the wound was inflicted, but I do not want the premier of B.C. to leave here in that shape. I want him and all of you to walk out of this room looking and sounding like winners. And so I ask for your concurrence and support in accepting this proposal and making it happen." They all agreed, and we all moved on to the next contentious matter.

At Pearson, Ovide Mercredi had agreed that "provincial and federal" laws would govern all areas seeking, and affected by, aboriginal self-government. Without such assurances, neither Bourassa nor Wells would have agreed, and there would have been no unanimous agreement. The problem was that OM does not want to spell this particular conception out clearly in the first place, and Wells and Romanow quite properly were adamant about its inclusion. (The night before, OM had directly attacked Clyde Wells as having been "an obstruction and thoroughly hostile" to native aspirations, to which I replied that, to the contrary, Clyde Wells has made many compromises and was trying to be constructive, and such attacks were unhelpful.) After considerable inconclusive debate, I said publicly to OM, "This matter must now be resolved, time has run out. This is one for the chair – so, Ovide, I am asking you to consult with your people and bring me a text that Robert Bourassa and Clyde Wells can live with." And then I adjourned the meeting for a half-hour.

Various texts began to emerge, because private bilaterals were going on between ministers and aboriginal representatives outside the room. When discussions resumed, Robert Bourassa was attracted to a text that was drafted by Ron George and others and was pushing for its acceptance, in spite of the fact that Ovide Mercredi had returned with a text that went a long way toward accommodating Bourassa and Wells. Rae told me OM would never agree to this. The temperature of the debate began to escalate and I began to worry about damage to the alternative settlement. Throughout, Bourassa had been extremely cautious, checking out each change in wording with a legal team in a nearby room (in fact, in his closing remarks, while thanking others for their openness toward Quebec, he apologized for his "prudence," which provoked gales of affectionate laughter from all around the table, and a remark from Bob Rae, who said, "Robert, check that with your advisors.") On the aboriginal text, he was very cautious, anticipating quite accurately a ferocious attack on that part of the agreement by Parizeau.

Given the stalemate, I adjourned for a few minutes and asked Clyde Wells to meet with OM, Ron George, and others, who agreed then to delete wording in Ovide Mercredi's draft about riots, etc. ("the pestilence clause," so Rae observed), and Clyde Wells returned to report this development to me. Meanwhile, Benoît Morin, lawyer, Clerk of the provincial cabinet and influential Bourassa advisor, had entered the room and was advising Bourassa to hold firm to the earlier text, saying that the OM text was insufficiently conclusive in respect to the applicability to Quebec's laws. At that point I asked Clyde Wells to come to my end of the table to discuss both his views and opinions with Robert Bourassa. With Morin looking over Bourassa's shoulder, CW leaning over between Benoît Bouchard and me, all of us in a small scrum at the chairman's section of the table, the conversation went something like this:

Wells: *Robert, I have examined this carefully and with the deletions I have secured from Ovide Mercredi, I am satisfied with this clause.*

Bourassa: *But, Morin tells me this is not entirely adequate.*

Wells: *Well, it's not perfect, but in my opinion the wording of this clause satisfies both our objections. It represents something both of us can live with and defend. In fact, Robert, I think it's an improvement over the earlier document you've been working on and would be happy to say that publicly.*

Mulroney: *In that case, Robert are you ready to move, because time is pressing and a deal is at hand?*

Bourassa: *Well, PM, you have heard the legal opinion from my new lawyer, Clyde Wells, so I am supposed to accept!*

Wells: *Robert, this is one of the best legal opinions you will ever get.*

Mulroney: *Clyde, on that basis, would you agree to provide expert testimony about the judicial intent of this clause before the Quebec National Assembly to counter the anticipated attack on it?*

Wells: *Only if it will help, PM, only if it will help!*

Thus ended negotiations of the '92 Charlottetown constitutional agreement, with Clyde Wells and Robert Bourassa pleasantly (perhaps even joyfully) cooperating on the drafting of an acceptable clause in respect of some important possible implications of native self-government. I gavelled the meeting back into session, quickly resolved other outstanding issues, and then moved to the final question: the manner of ratification. We had prepared a draft that would enable provinces with referendum legislation to conduct the referendum on their territory and pursuant to their legislation – provided there was an identical question put to all Canadians at the same time on the same day across Canada. This view was quickly accepted and I wound up the meeting with a press conference.

I flew back to Ottawa with Joe Clark, Benoît Bouchard, and some of my key staff members for a national caucus meeting late Friday afternoon. Joe, Benoît, and I received a triumphant welcome from caucus. I spoke first and introduced both Joe and Benoît and then wound it up with a summary of expectations for the future and our expression of gratitude for their marvellous support. The applause was powerful, sustained, and moving. To have had their support over nine long difficult years has made the difference between success and failure. Without their understanding, loyalty and support, all would have been lost earlier, particularly at the time of Bouchard's great betrayal. But they have proved all the doubters wrong. Honour and compromise live on in Canada.

I left the Hill in a rainstorm and drove to Harrington, where a royal welcome awaited me from Mila and the kids. What a wonderful wife and family I have. They have been my real inspiration, my shelter in the storm, my reason for persevering. Tonight, Nicolas was frightened by something he had seen on TV, and asked me to lie with him in bed until he got to sleep. As I hugged him to sleep, I thought of what we had accomplished, and what promise Canada holds for other children his age. I have done my best. The agreement is a fair, balanced, and intelligent approach to the enormous challenges we have faced. I am confident we will succeed in our public consultations across Canada in late October but, whatever the outcome, I know that every effort has been made, every possibility has been examined, and every constructive idea has been embraced by all participants to ensure that

Quebec remains within Canada, and that this country remains strongly united for decades and decades to come.

—

Hugh Segal has written about our conversation as we drove to the Charlottetown airport en route to Ottawa.

"Well, what do you think?" I asked.

"If it was this hard to get all the federalists together on an agreement, imagine the referendum," Segal said.

"We're going to have to try, Hugh."

"It's going to be like open-heart surgery without an anaesthetic."

"But at least we start with a patient very much alive," I said.

"Yes, sir," Segal said. "But will anyone ever thank you for that?"

"Look out the window when we're flying home," I answered. "Thanks are not what this is about."

On September 8, I officially informed the House of Commons of the Charlottetown Accord, and the campaign to ratify it through a national referendum was soon on.

Today, the rush of events as the campaign was waged that fall are a blur. But I remember the Wilhelmy–Tremblay affair all too well. Almost as soon as the campaign began, it was crippled, if not killed outright, in Quebec as a result of late-night intercepted telephone calls between Robert Bourassa's two chief constitutional advisors, Diane Wilhelmy and André Tremblay. The two described Charlottetown in the most withering terms, indicating that it contained no gains for Quebec. A few translated excerpts from their conversation convey the overall tone: "My knees are worn." "We're walking on our knees, as you know. I think they are full of holes . . ." "Oof, what madness . . . That's when I said, 'It's a national shame.' We should leave. Mr. Bourassa should take the plane right away and come back here . . . It's like humiliation . . ." ". . . It's terrible." "In any event, we caved in; that's all." In effect they were stating that Bourassa had collapsed and surrendered Quebec's traditional demands in exchange for a meaningless document.

I was thunderstruck as I listened to the tapes, which were broadcast and reprinted again and again by the Quebec media for a week. I knew the effect would be cataclysmic. Parizeau and his now familiar allies, Trudeau and

Lucien Bouchard, were gleeful, describing Charlottetown as a meaningless trifle. I knew Tremblay and Wilhelmy and had high regard for their skills. I was astonished by their indiscretion but even more by the nature of their criticism. If they really felt that way they should have told the premier so in Charlottetown and resigned then and there.

Clearly, it would be an enormous challenge for our side to recover from the lightning strike of this self-induced damage. In fact, in Quebec, we never did.

—

PERSONAL JOURNAL: SEPTEMBER 19, 1992

(Written at 24 Sussex Drive)

I filled Margaret Thatcher in (by phone) on the Canadian referendum situation and entered the house – I had been out by the pool getting some sun – to take calls in rapid succession from premiers (like Harcourt). The Yes side has had an awful week, so much so that people like Lysiane Gagnon are already predicting a victory for the No side in Quebec. It is difficult to imagine two events more damaging than the Wilhelmy affair followed by André Tremblay's alleged remarks to the Quebec Chamber of Commerce. For seven days these two events have dominated the news, caused us to drop precipitously in the polls, and have greatly eroded the Yes side's greatest assets in the campaign: Robert Bourassa's credibility in defending Quebec's interests compared with that of Jacques Parizeau. We have been unable in consequence to get our message out at all, as the perception grew about Bourassa's "weakness" as a bargainer and negotiator. All of a sudden the issue wasn't the substance of the agreement but whether anyone as "weak-kneed and unprincipled" as Bourassa could even be trusted to defend Quebec's "intérêts supérieurs," and the answer, of course, is a resounding no.

Support for the agreement has fallen, and Hugh Segal and I met secretly with Bourassa and [his chief of staff] John Parisella at the Dorval Hilton Thursday night to review our plan. As the leader of the Yes side, Bourassa is in control. In Quebec we all function under an umbrella group of which he is chair. Both Hugh Segal and I were unimpressed by the preparations for the referendum on October 26 and urged on them a tighter organization, a more carefully crafted message against the No, more direct informational advertising, and a tougher engagement against the adversary. Perhaps it was Robert Bourassa's general funk with the Wilhelmy tapes affair all last week, combined with polls showing us 15 points behind, but he was not in a good fighting mood. I tried to pep him up with a review of his achievements and a profile of the undecideds we have put together, but all to no avail. He was clearly dispirited when he left, although by no means predisposed to write off the referendum campaign. He knows now that it will be dirty and brutal, and he must engage energetically if we are to win.

I try to hide my concern with what is happening in Quebec. Since August 28 Bourassa seems to have wasted a great deal of time calming his ministers – Frulla, Hébert, and others – who thought, at first glance, that the Charlottetown Agreement did not give them enough for their respective interests. Then there was endless conversation about an exchange of letters, followed by the requirements of both governments to agree on a question, tabling in our respective houses, debate, vote, and finally, the issuance of writs. Meanwhile the opponents, soon to be joined by Trudeau, were shooting at the agreement before the ink was dry without a sustained or coherent response from the Yes side, for the above reasons.

Tomorrow, Sunday, I shall tape with Bernard Derome (of Radio-Canada) here at 11 a.m., fly to B.C., then Saskatoon, London, Sept-Îles, etc., and the campaign is on. I plan to progressively up the intensity of the campaign, the salience of the message, the consequences of a No, and the remarkable benefits of a Yes result. I think the campaign will do very well throughout English Canada, including B.C., where things appear to be very unpredictable for the moment. Quebec will be tremendously challenging. I think we can win, but it will require all our skills, cooperation, efforts, time, and a degree of good fortune to overcome the difficult situation in which we now find ourselves.

It is doubtful that the Yes campaign can stand much more of these Quebec City revelations and I, for one, am in no mood to tempt fate by seeking to find out.

—

PERSONAL JOURNAL: OCTOBER 10, 1992

(En route from Winnipeg to Ottawa)

5:30 *p.m.:*

I've just concluded another brutal week of campaigning in the referendum and the outlook remains grim. From the very beginning the Yes side, particularly in Quebec, has been hit with a number of extremely damaging broadsides, and has not run a very impressive or effective campaign – and as a consequence we are trailing badly in Quebec and are in a tough fight elsewhere, especially in B.C. First there was the Trudeau attack, in which the former prime minister called Robert Bourassa a political blackmailer interested in bleeding Canada of all of its powers, and described the Charlottetown Accord as a "deplorable mess," saying that separation was "preferable to its acceptance." This is happening at a time when support for federalism is waning because a) Trudeau misled the Québécois, as Pitfield has said, with his 1980 referendum promise, and betrayed them with patriation; and b) Meech was killed at the last moment in large measure because of the Trudeau–Coyne–Wells connection. It takes, as Gordon Robertson has written, great dishonesty for PET to mislead Canadians about the agreement, hence, playing directly into the hands of the separatists, who are delighted with the attack on Robert Bourassa from their new and helpful ally Pierre Trudeau; c) The Sihota comments: In an unguarded moment and without realizing the house camera was on him, B.C. MPP Moe Sihota told a B.C. audience that "Robert Bourassa has been stared down by the other nine premiers, that he had been given nothing at the table not already there on July 7." One can imagine the alacrity with which Parizeau jumped all over this cadeau *and again Bourassa took a terrible pummelling in the French media. (The French-language journalists, with few exceptions, are having an extremely difficult time concealing their pro-sovereignty bias. Their reporting has been, by and large, unprofessional and unfair but, in this climate, it is absolutely futile to spend any time complaining or seeking retractions.)*

I've been working my heart out – five to seven meetings of various kinds a day, six or seven days a week – and working up to 20 hours a day. I don't know how helpful I've been, although our crowds are large, friendly, and generally sympathetic. If I link Parizeau's real intention to a No vote on October 26, I am accused of fear-mongering. If I put forward uncontested views and opinions of institutions of substance like the Royal Bank, I am accused of economic terrorism. If I draw attention to the fact that Quebec would surely lose its 31 historic gains if the No wins by tearing up the paper on TV to convey the reality of what will happen, I am accused of hyperbole. And if I repeat, word for word, what Jacques Parizeau said he plans to do with a No vote, I am accused of predicting the end of Canada, inducing a run on the dollar, and being responsible for consequently higher interest rates!

What I have been doing in Quebec, ably assisted by Benoît Bouchard, Pierre Blais, etc., is to provide manpower, encouragement, enthusiasm, and backing for a poorly organized Oui *campaign and an understandably shell-shocked Robert Bourassa. Apart from the above three disasters, which have affected Québécois' perception of his reliability to always defend their interests, he has been put into situations where he encountered hostile crowds in St-Georges and an incredibly abusive group of law professors and students at the University of Sherbrooke. He is working hard and complains little, but he has not been well served by his advisors and organizers who, though they had two years to prepare for this, appear totally taken aback at how to run the campaign, deal with bad news, handle setbacks, reorient the campaign, or attack, attack, attack. There are some exceptions, most notably Marc-Yvan Côté who is a happy warrior and an effective, dynamic politician who delivers what he has committed to do.*

I try and phone Bourassa at least once a day to review strategy, pass on any encouraging news, give him our overnight poll results and latest analysis, and generally buck up his spirits. It is a shame to see his contribution to such a wonderful national achievement so trivialized and demeaned throughout Quebec.

Should this fail I don't believe that Quebec will ever again, certainly not in my lifetime, achieve such gains. And should, because of a No vote, Quebec in 1995–96 decide to follow a road to independence (for which the entire country shall pay most heavily), these careless and reckless people who egged the No side on will have much to reflect upon and much to answer for.

My meetings today in Manitoba were excellent. In Steinbach, to the Polish and Ukrainian congresses, I made good speeches explaining the agreement, the benefits, and consequences – and I think scored some points. Hugh Segal says the more people know about the agreement, the more inclined they are to support it. The distribution this week of the Charlottetown Agreement and the release today of the legal text themselves should go a considerable distance in allaying fears and countering falsehoods about what is in the accord. For seven weeks immediately following the agreement, our opponents had a field day as we were getting legislation through the House, deciding on legal interpretations, etc. The No side was hitting us with every falsehood in the book. They didn't have to come up with any alternatives – they only had to destroy. And they were helped along in this noble task by a media so far removed from objectivity as to be dangerous.

I will work flat out through to the end. I am counting on Robert Bourassa to do well in the TV debate – without a success there, I doubt we can turn it around fully in Quebec. And I am counting on the undecideds understanding the significance of the deal for them and their kids – and voting in English Canada in significant numbers to carry the day. Already the knives are out – not in the party and the government, but in the media.

If the referendum is defeated, there will be a loud and large cry for my resignation. Canadians will quickly forget that the deal was concluded by 13 governments – four Liberal, four PC, four NDP, and one independent, and four aboriginal associations; that it was endorsed by Jean Chrétien and the federal Liberal caucus, and by Audrey McLaughlin and the NDP caucus; that it was enthusiastically supported by the Canadian Labour Congress, the Business Council on National Issues, the Canadian Chamber of Commerce, and most interest groups across Canada. All of this will quickly be forgotten if we are unsuccessful and Canadians, led by the national press gallery, will be angrily demanding the prime minister's resignation. "After all," they will say, "it was his deal. He alone is responsible."

And in some ways, I suppose, they are right. My experience has been that when things go brilliantly, others get the glory. When things are tough and failure looms, the finger is pointed at the prime minister. That is probably the way it should be in any case – although I wouldn't be offended by a modest reversal of these realities every once in a while! In any case, I think we can still win. I believe we can pull it off, and because I love Canada so much I will expend every effort I can to help contribute to a victory for the Yes side on October 26, 1992.

—

After weeks of campaigning, October 26, referendum day, arrived. I worried privately about the effects of my own unpopularity on the vote. There was no denying that for many Canadians my endorsement made the proposal toxic. As my years in office wound down, my approval ratings eroded. Many voters across the country thought first of my mistakes and failings when they looked at the government, relegating our achievements to the back burner. The Yes side appeared to be headed to defeat, but I had done my best.

—

PERSONAL JOURNAL: OCTOBER 26–27, 1992

(Written at Harrington Lake)

Oct. 26, 9 a.m.:
Mila and I will soon be leaving to vote in the referendum. We will then be spending the day at the lake. I have invited Maz, Benoît, and Hugh for dinner, and a few others, and some time about midnight I'll go to the Reading Room at the House to speak briefly to the nation. The first call I received this morning was from Bernie Ostry [a distinguished public servant in both Ottawa and Toronto], who said, "Congratulations. You fought a tremendous fight irrespective of the outcome and, more importantly, you did the right thing for Canada. All one has to do is look at those who make up the No team to realize that the Yes camp is where Canada's future has to be." Bernie is pretty profane, so he had a few choice words for Trudeau, and his henchmen Keith Davey, Jim Coutts, and Jerry Grafstein, who, among other things, "spend all their fucking time either screwing Jean Chrétien or Canada – they want to make certain that no one succeeds where their guy failed."

The final conversation with Bourassa took place on Thursday evening in Montreal following another long day of campaigning and prior to my departure for the West. He told me his greatest regret, if the accord were defeated, was that never again could he contemplate a set of circumstances that would give rise to such gains for Quebec. He was serene and analytical, recognized the possibility of an upset victory, while acknowledging the likelihood of defeat. I told him he had waged a very effective campaign and that I was proud to have been associated with him in such a noble cause that would, if successful, unite Canada. He responded by speaking of his high regard for me personally, the fact that I had never let him or Quebec down.

It was one of the most poignant conversations I have ever had in public life – two Quebecers from different backgrounds, different interests, different parties, different governments, different priorities, coming together with others, seeking to make a beneficial difference for our province and our country. Should the referendum be defeated this evening in Quebec, I hope that one day the full story will emerge of Robert Bourassa's devotion to Quebec, combined with his determination and affection for Canada. There is no doubt his primary love is for Quebec, as mine is for Canada.

We see the emergence of the federation, then, according to different priorities. The question is, are they irreconcilable? Can they be accommodated to the mutual advantage of all? In different ways the Charlottetown Accord responds in the affirmative. We can love Canada in different ways and all still be loyal Canadians. Only the separatists, English- and French-speaking, generally eschew that position. It is perhaps because of that bond – gentle, diverse, and reassuring – that Pierre Berton described the Charlottetown Accord as a "miracle."

A few moments ago I spoke with Marc-Yvan Côté, minister of social affairs and chief organizer for the Oui *in Quebec. He is doubtful, in fact very doubtful, we can win tonight and said, "The publication of the Wilhelmy tapes screwed the* Oui*."*

4:10 p.m.:

I have just spoken with Allan Gregg, who says we should win the popular vote 51.5 per cent, but that it would take almost a miracle to pull through in Quebec, Manitoba, and B.C. I shared this info a few moments ago with Robert Bourassa, who was highly pleased at the prospect of a national win in popular vote together with the possibility that a win, while not impossible in Quebec, could be replaced by a loss of between 4 and 8 per cent – a far cry from the 20–25 per cent loss predicted by most polling organizations. In any case, it was now quite obvious that a complete victory is beyond our grasp tonight. I am in a good and relaxed mood, however.

My hope obviously was for a win in ten provinces. My objective was to pass the accord into law and then announce my resignation. This latter objective will not change. My expectation is that whatever happens I will be publicly announcing my intention to resign on or about Jan. 15, with a leadership convention by May 1 and a final transfer of power by no later than May 15. This would mean turning over the government to a new prime minister, who could then have three or four months in office to make new trends and favourably impress Canadians with a new face and style and ability before calling an election for early autumn.

On the referendum campaign, Mila and I have seen no expressions of hostility – which for me is exceptional – and much evidence of goodwill. The party itself is back into its second-place position – weak though it may be – in all the public opinion polls. In spite of these promising signs, I believe the combination of a poor economy (the recession has in fact been more painful than any of us anticipated), the lingering antipathy from the GST and FTA, and the bitterness fuelled by the non-ratification of Meech have combined to form a hurdle of formidable dimensions for any government I lead. I have no doubt we can significantly improve on our standings with the issuance of a writ – we're well organized, well financed with excellent new candidates joining many battle-hardened pros who are ready to do battle again, and who indeed could win. But I had intended to leave, if Meech had passed in June of 1990, in September 1991. I stayed because it was clear that the Quebec caucus would have disintegrated under other leadership and in the face of the destabilizing efforts of Jacques Parizeau and Lucien Bouchard. I was also forced to forgo any considerations whatsoever of the UN secretary-generalship for precisely the same reasons.

The government and party will, I believe, do better if the new leader and prime minister is not from Quebec. After Trudeau and me, Canadians are legitimately wondering about opportunities for others in the top job, especially with Jean Chrétien riding high in the polls as opposition leader. I believe that Jean's lead is an illusion and will vanish quickly if he is confronted with a new prime minister leading a renewed party and government. The ideal: probably a woman as PM and preferably one from western Canada. This would destabilize the Reform Party in the West, cripple the Liberals in Ontario and, if she were bilingual, allow for enough PCs to be elected in Quebec to form a strong government. This would seem to favour Kim Campbell. But perhaps Barbara McDougall could win, or Perrin Beatty or Jean Charest – and Bernard Valcourt would be a colourful addition to the race. A true generational change is required. Too many of us have been around too long. It's time for younger people with new approaches.

But will this reality discourage Joe Clark from trying again? And perhaps winning? I don't know. He is in good stead in the caucus and well regarded in the country because of his unity work, but that may be because he is number two, three, or four. If he were number one, would it again come crashing down around his ears within months? And if that happens, how damaging again would it have been to the party – to the country? I am always irked by the fact that his insistence on meeting the House on Dec. 13, 1979, when it could have been readily avoided, gave rise to the 1980 defeat and the return to power of Trudeau. I think this is his greatest problem in any campaign and his greatest handicap, should he win. But that's for democracy and another day.

I'm exhausted following the campaign and a brutal year and have put on too much weight with all the junk food and too little exercise. I look forward to tonight's verdict and then to getting on with the rest of my life. The kids are great and Mila has, as usual, been marvellous. They say there is life after politics. We are about to find out soon.

Oct. 27, 5:50 *p.m.:*
Well, we got clobbered [54 per cent of Canadians, six provinces, and both territories voted no]. I was surprised by the rejection in Nova Scotia and the tightness of the race in Ontario. The rest, while disappointing, was not entirely unpredictable – although even pollsters can be wrong. Mila and I spent a quiet evening at Harrington – Maz, Benoît, Lowell, Hugh, Marj, and John [Tory] – joined us for an informal supper, along with Peter C. Newman. We watched on two TVs, in English and French, set up in the dining room. After an indication of the Quebec and Ontario results, I went upstairs to the den with L.

Ian MacDonald and Paul Terrien to work on my remarks to the nation, which I delivered from the Reading Room of the House about midnight. Returning to the lake at about 1 a.m. with Mila, I felt a great sense of loss for the nation but a degree of equanimity in that I had tried my hardest, done my best. In a major essay on page one of today's Globe, *Thomas Courchene wrote: "Historians will eventually marvel at the incredible balancing act embodied in the Accord." I think he's right. History will judge our efforts very favourably and that, in itself, is an important dimension of governing. Policies rejected one year may in retrospect look brilliant a decade hence. Leadership is the capacity to envision that reality over years and to proceed irrespective of the criticism. That is what I have sought to do.*

Mila, Mark, and I had a relaxed brunch together and then we listened to Nicolas's piano recital. I took some calls from President Bush, Ted Kennedy, Bill Thorsell, Mayor Doré, Premier McKenna, etc., and then went for a long walk in the woods with Mark – Nicolas later joined us. Mark was only five, I think, when we first came to Harrington and I have difficulty now remembering our first days here in 1984. It seems so long ago, with the velocity of events blurring my memory. The children are growing up beautifully, untouched really by the brutality of politics and the cruelty of the media. How they have emerged is little short of miraculous. Both Caroline and Ben called again today, worried about me and the results. Isn't life amazing? Already, my children are beginning to worry about their Dad. Surely it must continue to be the other way around. As we walked home at dusk in the autumn cold, I nudged Mila and Nicolas and thought of the beauty of Harrington Lake. We shall never enjoy such privacy and family pleasure again. And how I shall miss the challenges and the job of prime minister in the most ennobling dimension: bringing and keeping Canadians together so that in their souls they come to appreciate the splendour of what we have if we remain united – and appreciate the enormity of their loss, should we ever drift apart.

Despite the referendum loss I was a contented man. While it is perhaps a cliché, I do believe that in a democracy the people are always right. Canadians had spoken, and I couldn't complain at the result. Regardless of what side citizens had ended up on in the Charlottetown debate, the constitutional battles would now be put aside – temporarily, mind you. But for now, the bullet had indeed been removed from the chamber by a democratic vote, and Canada remained whole. It was time for me to move on and leave those questions to a whole new generation of leaders. My time had passed.

—

PERSONAL JOURNAL: DECEMBER 30, 1992

Tomorrow night is New Year's Eve – our last at Harrington Lake and my last as prime minister of Canada. I wrote the first draft of my resignation letter on Christmas Eve and intend to send it to Senator Gerry St. Germain on Jan. 31 after I've spoken to caucus. It will call for a leadership convention at the earliest possible moment, and I expect to turn over responsibilities no later than May 15, 1993. It will have been a remarkable run, almost nine years as PM, making me, I believe, the sixth longest-serving prime minister in Canadian history. But the time has come to move on, to turn this over to a different and perhaps younger person – a decision I made a few years ago and propose now to execute.

Because the media speculation began on referendum night, I had to act with the cabinet, caucus, and government to shut it down by stating clearly that I was staying – when in fact it was a holding operation, because my decision to leave had long since been made. It was, however, vital that complete solidarity be maintained, so after a brief holiday in Florida and New York City I returned to the House and undertook a seven-city fundraising tour for the party. We raised over $2 million with the dinners, ending the year in the black, and with the party electoral machinery under John Tory and Pierre Blais as advanced as I've ever seen it this long before an election. Having met with the national executive and party leaders across the country, I can say how gratified I am by their support, which, like that of caucus, is generous, unstinting, and unfailing. Indeed, if there has been a single dimension of my responsibilities as party leader that has constantly pleased and encouraged me, it is my personal relationship with my caucus and my party. In a very real sense, Mila and I regard them as family and treat them accordingly. Tonight I had a call from an MP thanking me for intervening, via Hugh Segal, with the CIBC to save *his business and home from bankruptcy. He was with his wife and children when he called, and the delight and emotion in his voice were obvious. Such are the events that bind a leader to his caucus and produce outstanding solidarity in the face of hostile media opinion and great political adversity.*

—

1993

1. Bill Clinton and Others

PERSONAL JOURNAL: JANUARY 1, 1993

(Written at Harrington Lake)

I believe that I could win another government in 1993 – probably only a minority at this stage – but with a resurgent economy, a good campaign, a few mistakes by my opponents, who knows? The reason I will not run is the answer I must give to the following question: If you run again and win, either a majority or minority government, what do you want to achieve? And my answer simply is "more of the same." I do not believe that honest answer to be adequate, so I will step aside.

—

AS THE HOLIDAYS came to an end, I was much more confident about Quebec's rightful place in Canada than I had been a year earlier. I was in a very reflective mood as I contemplated the political prospects for myself and the government as my final few months began. Was it Irish bravado that had me believing that I could win another mandate in 1993? Perhaps – and I know what my critics would say. Still, I am confident in saying this: the PC Party would have been left with a hell of a lot more than two seats had it been me facing off against Jean Chrétien in October 1993. But that's for historians to decide.

Caroline was home for the holidays from Harvard, and Mila and I were realizing then just how much we missed our daughter, who was already embarking upon a new life of her own. She was filled with enthusiastic stories of life at Harvard, books she had to read, interesting classmates and professors she was meeting, and papers she was writing. While proud of her success, I had more than a few moments of a certain kind of happy sadness that all parents will understand as I realized she was all grown up.

Before Christmas we had visited with her at Harvard, where I gave a toughly worded speech at the John F. Kennedy School of Government, calling for military intervention in Bosnia-Herzegovina and a military blockade of Haiti. With my daughter in the audience I had also said what we all knew: that there had been no peace to keep in the former Yugoslavia and that the world had done shamefully little to end the Haitian dictatorship. I used the speech to warn the incoming president of the United States, Bill Clinton, against any drift toward isolationism in the coming four years. Caroline told me I'd gotten my speech "just right," and I enjoyed her critiques of both its substance and delivery.

As I watched Caroline and her brothers frolic outside the residence at Harrington Lake, I added to my New Year's Day journal entry.

—

In 1983 and 1984 I was like Bill Clinton – young, dynamic, and full of ideas and energy – sure I could conquer the world if given half a chance. Today, much of my personal agenda has been achieved, most of my ideas have become law – or were rejected because they were not as valuable as I originally thought! And I fear my vision for the nation might be obscured by fatigue, exhausted by the agenda and refighting old battles. It is wrong to stay too long, both for the party and the country. PET's final term in office – when he sought historical vindication after defeat at the hands of Joe Clark – was the most damaging for Canada. The fact is that such events often occur when a leader stays on too long and substitutes his personal obsessions for a nation's goals. The two are not necessarily congruent. The nation, as we are witnessing with Clinton and Gore in Washington, needs both renewal and reassurance. I think Canada needs new people with new ideas – the great enthusiasm with which they can either excite or inspire the nation. I feel that because I can no longer properly do this, the time has come for me to step aside for a new leader and prime minister.

—

The next day, I wrote about the steps I would be taking to ensure a proper transition for the party and the government.

—

PERSONAL JOURNAL: JANUARY 2, 1993

Tomorrow I will be seeing ten ministers re a cabinet shuffle that I have been working on in secrecy for some time. Five senior ministers will step down, reducing the size of the ministry to 35, including the PM. The key move Monday morning is that of Kim Campbell to DND and DVA, along with her appointment to the operations committee of cabinet, where she will replace Joe Clark. Kim is one of my favourites in cabinet – tough, disciplined, intelligent, combative, bilingual – and I think she could effectively replace me as party leader and prime minister. There are of course others, thankfully, of equally impressive skills – Wilson, Charest, Valcourt, Beatty, Bouchard, to name but a few.

After a swearing-in in mid-May, the new PM could bring in a new cabinet, a new Speech from the Throne, a new budget – all in a climate of rebounding consumer confidence and quite strong economic growth – attend meetings at the White House, then the G-7 Summit in Tokyo, tour the country in August and call an election on Sept. 1 for Oct. 15. One of the principal reasons for the selection of this date, Jan. 31, to make my announcement, is because it is after Jan. 21, the day 46-year-old Bill Clinton and 44-year-old Al Gore will become president and vice-president of the U.S. The impact of these young men taking over control of the most powerful country in the world will have in a short time an adverse impact on the hopes of 59-year-old Jean Chrétien, who was first elected to Parliament 30 years ago! It will also have a favourable impact upon the leadership aspirations of younger people such as Kim, Charest, Valcourt, Beatty, and others I have promoted and whose careers I have sought to advance.

Wilson, should he run, would command powerful support in Ontario and perhaps elsewhere because of the great respect he enjoys in the caucus and country. As a colleague he has been superb, and I have no doubt that Canada's interests would be well served with him as prime minister. He is slightly older than me and therefore could not benefit from the new wave of youthfulness that is about to engulf the continent. But he brings other qualities that the convention might find very persuasive, though the odds would appear to favour other contenders.

I've had many conversations with George Bush since the election, and I'm delighted to see him in Moscow tonight with Yeltsin for START II, after a successful visit to Somalia. It is an impressive foreign policy end to what I'm sure will be judged a successful foreign policy presidency. The recession did enormous damage to his domestic plan – as it did to mine and so many others – and I am delighted to see him exit on such a high and elegant note.

I have had two conversations with Clinton since his election. He comes across in private as he does in public – competent, earnest, friendly, unassuming – but he is also clearly ambitious, single-minded, and hard-nosed or he wouldn't have got the job in the first place. I regret that I will not be working with him for any extended period of time.

—

Once the cabinet had been shuffled in the way I outlined in my journal, I headed off to Florida for a brief holiday. Bill Clinton telephoned again to discuss NAFTA. I urged him to deal with his personal concerns about the deal without reopening the whole treaty.

Up until this point the only people I had talked with about my resignation (besides Mila) had been Don Mazankowski, Governor General Ray Hnatyshyn, and Michael Wilson. I had filled Maz in on my plans during a 1992 luncheon in Edmonton. A definite political pro, he knew it was indeed time for me to leave, but he grew quite emotional at the prospect of the end of our professional relationship, which had been so productive and successful. Tears interrupted our lunch that day at the Macdonald Hotel. As for Ray, we had talked quietly one night that fall over coffee at Rideau Hall.

At a lunch in December with Michael at 24 Sussex I had obliquely referred to my leaving office soon. Because of his tremendous friendship, support, and loyalty, I felt I owed him at least a hint of my intentions. I hadn't carefully considered the fact that Michael would inevitably have to share this information with others to ascertain what degree of party support there might be for him if he chose to run for leader. I later had to shut down the rumours that came from his camp, which were my own fault.

If anyone was demonstrating the way to leave office with dignity and class, it was George Bush. I had last seen him in October of 1992, when I travelled with Carlos Salinas of Mexico to San Antonio, Texas where we all signed the NAFTA. After his defeat by Bill Clinton in November, Bush had reached out to Mila and me, inviting us to make an informal visit to Camp David on the last weekend he would serve as president. It was unlike any other visit I made, both before and since.

—

PERSONAL JOURNAL: JANUARY 17, 1993

(After Camp David)
I found both George Bush and Barbara to be in good shape, mentally and physically. Clearly he has shucked off his post-election depression and is looking forward to going on with life. He will write a book, build a library at Texas A&M University, do some boards and consulting, make a few speeches but keep a very low profile. He expects that his son, Jeb, will run for governor of Florida and that George Jr. will run for governor of Texas against Ann Richards – so that contact is enough for him. Barbara has signed a contract for $2.5 million for her memoirs. "No dirt," she told me. And she looks forward to getting that done and getting down to a good life. She is building her dream house in Houston, where they will spend seven months of the year followed by five in Maine.

Both Barbara and George Bush spoke about James Baker III, and they clearly still hold him in the highest regard. They say he is deeply troubled by the investigation into the Clinton passport matter, and fears his reputation will be badly damaged. [It was alleged that a State Department official had pilfered Clinton's passport file, looking for a rumoured letter in which he had, as a young man, renounced his American citizenship.] Both say he is innocent of any wrongdoing but is devastated by what is happening. George Bush said he never expected to be defeated and never zeroed in on his own vulnerability on the economic side.

Two final vignettes –
Church service:
Toward the end, the community choir of spouses and military personnel sang the final hymn, which all understood would be the last George Bush would ever hear at the Camp as president of the United States.

As it neared the end, some of the women in the choir, standing perhaps six feet away from us and the Bushes, began to sob. As tears poured down their cheeks they sang on, while the president and Barbara stood transfixed by the special emotion in that tiny chapel. It was the passage of power as seen up close by some ordinary American citizens as they said goodbye to their beloved commander-in-chief on a quiet mountaintop in Maryland. The poignancy and simplicity of the moment were priceless.

Aspen Lodge:
As we started saying goodbye around noon, Barbara handed George Bush a copy of a subpoena her staff person had been given on Friday by a representative of the special prosecutor investigating the Clinton passport affair. As I finished sipping my coffee I looked at the president of the United States – who had just authorized a strike against a nuclear facility in Iraq in support of United Nations Security Council resolutions – preparing to leave office, after a lifetime of service to his nation, as he slowly and sadly read the legal document exhorting and instructing all to "keep records, notes, etc., etc." relating to the alleged incident. While the document and case in no way implicate him personally, I was struck by the melancholy of the situation inherent in a great modern democracy, namely that public service comes at enormous cost to those who have chosen to serve their country.

—

Only someone as gracious as George Bush would organize a final reception for his closest advisors at Camp David and invite the chairs of the Clinton transition team – Vernon Jordan and Warren Christopher – to join in along with the chief justice and members of the Supreme Court, and the Joint Chiefs of Staff. We shared drinks and reminiscences for a few hours prior to the church service. He was leaving the presidency in the manner in which he had always served: with class. It was an extraordinary weekend and a high honour to have been invited, as a Canadian prime minister, to spend those two historic days with President Bush and his fabulous Barbara.

Before he left the White House Bush sent me a letter. "I think it is fitting that you were my last guest as my presidency is drawing to a close," he wrote.

As you recall, my first presidential trip was to Ottawa in February 1989. I remember the contrast between the bitter cold outside, and the warm friendship we kindled in our conversation that day. Through good times and bad, I have been comforted by the fact you have been a wise counsel, a strong supporter, and a true friend. Our efforts to ensure smooth implementation of the FTA and to bring the dream of NAFTA to reality should be the envy of all. I want you to know, however, that I have never seen relations between our two countries as only the sum of trade issues. I have never wavered in my belief that when Canada remains engaged in world affairs, then democracy, peace, and freedom are advanced. I think back to Desert Storm and how leaders like yourself committed your countries without reservation to ensuring that Saddam's aggression would not stand.

I think back to those perilous hours in 1991 when the future of the Soviet revolution hung in the balance. Your strong opposition to the coup gave hope to democratic forces in Russia and silenced critics who said we had not done enough to help then-President Gorbachev. Your counsel in handling the transformation in the Soviet Union – from strengthening Yeltsin, to managing delicate relations between Ukraine and Russia – has been invaluable. Canadian soldiers keeping the peace in Latin America, Europe, Africa, and Asia are testimony to Canada's commitment to bring about a true and global collective security. I could go on and on – Bosnia, Haiti, the Middle East.

It's a record that should make every Canadian proud. It's a record that brings to life the true meaning of partnership between our two countries. Although my public life is coming to an end, Barbara and I will be cheering you on. Now, as always, our love to you, Mila, and the children. P.S. Brian, You're a true friend. It will ever be thus as far as I'm concerned. Good luck.

This may be an appropriate place to reflect on Canada's role in the world, especially a world dominated by the United States.

Immediately after the Second World War, with Japan and much of Europe flattened by war or captured by communism, Canada – its own territory untouched physically by the conflict – began punching above its weight in international relations. In those years, we played a powerful role in constructing the international security architecture that has kept the peace for over fifty years; in founding the United Nations, NATO, NORAD, and other institutions, Canada was always a constructive and admired contributor.

The cornerstone of Canada's remarkable influence was its special relationship with the president and the people of the United States. Winston Churchill had foreseen this in a brilliant speech in 1939, when he described our relationship and the promise it held: "That long frontier from the Atlantic to the Pacific oceans, guarded only by neighbourly respect and honourable obligations, is an example to every country and a pattern for the future of the world."

In the 1990s, with the collapse of the USSR, we witnessed the emergence of a unipolar world, led by our neighbour, a great democratic nation that possessed the most powerful economy and military the world had ever seen. All roads now led to Washington, and the leaders of some 194 nations jostled with each other to position their countries for access and influence there.

This, however, was not a great challenge for Canada. We were already there. Our unique relationship with the United States was carefully nurtured by most prime ministers and governments. We knew that the support of other nations for Canada and its initiatives was affected by the high regard in which Canada was held by the president of the United States, and the consequent influence we enjoyed throughout the administration and Congress.

This special relationship of two great nations was based on shared fundamental values, liberty and democracy, and we have not hesitated to defend them from attack. Of course, the handling of this relationship – so indispensable to our economic well-being and national security – requires skill, sensitivity, and an awareness of the nuances of opinion and power in the White House, the Congress, the media, and interest groups. In addition to knowing how things work in Washington, the prime minister must understand the special responsibility the United States bears in this new international order. This is not a matter that a prime minister can delegate to any member of cabinet.

No prime minister expressed this better than Lester B. Pearson, who wrote in his memoirs: "We should exhibit a sympathetic understanding of the heavy burden of international responsibility borne by the United States, not of her own imperial choosing but caused in part by the unavoidable withdrawal of other states from certain of these responsibilities, or, if you prefer, from imperial power and privilege. Above all, as American difficulties increase, we should resist any temptation to become smug and superior. 'You are bigger but we are better.'"

No prime minister of Canada – certainly not myself, or Mr. Pearson – always got this relationship right. And sometimes, when problems surface, they are generated by decisions or indifference south of the border, yet the Canadian prime minister, irrespective of party, will always get the blame.

I find it amusing that, in some Canadian quarters, friendly relations with the president of the United States are viewed with scorn and alarm. A relationship that leaders of other nations would treasure is derided by these same critics as a sort of subordination, unworthy of an independent nation.

Some contend that only leaders who agree with the United States gain influence in Washington. That was not my experience. The Americans know we are a different country and they respect that. I disagreed with President Reagan, as you have seen, over some of his most cherished initiatives and policies: we said no to President Reagan on SDI, we said no on Cuba, on Nicaragua, and on apartheid in South Africa. I also had to fight hard with him over acid rain and major trade issues, and President Bush and I also had our moments. But we made our point in the traditional Canadian manner, which was respectful of the president, the high position he held, and the great nation he led. This attitude was reciprocated and it produced impressive results for Canada.

A line from Shakespeare's *Measure for Measure* is instructive: "O, it is excellent to have a giant's strength, but it is tyrannous to use it like a giant."

When I was in office, I believed that it was in our relationship with the United States that the prime minister should play his or her most important and constructive international role, and I still believe this today. Having established a relationship of friendship, trust, and mutual respect with the president of the United States, Canada's leader is uniquely qualified, through ongoing private dialogue, to influence decisions that ensure that America does not use its power "like a giant."

My experience has been that when presidents listen carefully to Canadian prime ministers, they become more thoughtful and more respectful of the sensitivities and needs of the international community and of multilateral institutions.

As I reflect on my association with American presidents, I am struck by just how fortunate I was in the quality of the men whose term in office coincided with my period as prime minister. Ronald Reagan emerged as a global icon whose impact on American and world history will no doubt lead to his being considered one of the truly great presidents of our time.

George H.W. Bush's sophisticated appreciation of the nuances of foreign policy ensured that the world under U.S. leadership emerged stronger from the convulsive changes he helped to bring about, including the collapse of the USSR, the implosion of the Warsaw Pact, the reunification of Germany, and the Gulf War victory. His place in history will be a large one.

Bill Clinton, with whom I served for only a matter of months, is clearly the most gifted politician, by far, of his generation. We developed an excellent personal relationship, and I was not surprised to see him evolve into a highly effective world leader.

If in the business world today, cash is king, in the world of the Canada–U.S. relationship, access is worth its weight in gold. It is a privilege that Canada should never squander or surrender.

Back in Ottawa, rumours of my possible resignation had reached a fever pitch. With my visit to President Clinton coming up soon, I had to squelch them. The Cold War was over and the United States, now the world's only superpower, was under new leadership. I felt it was crucial for Canadian interests that we insist upon Canada being the first nation to enter into talks with the forty-second president. That would send a powerful signal to the United States and to the world of Canada's influence and importance. For this reason, I had to postpone my resignation announcement. With his administration focused almost completely on domestic policy, Clinton would have had little inclination to meet with a lame-duck prime minister.

On January 31, I spoke forcefully about the matter to the cabinet and caucus. "At the caucus after the October 26 referendum, I outlined my future intentions," I said. "Now, apparently these statements are inadequate for some people, particularly those known as 'unnamed ministerial allies,' 'influential party insiders,' 'a senior party member who wishes to remain anonymous' . . . Bill McKnight has accurately said, 'Prime ministers only announce their departures. They do not announce they are staying.' I have no such departure to announce.

"At the moment my principal concerns are the illness of Robert Bourassa, which may be extremely serious and could have untold consequences for the future of Canada; meeting with President Clinton; economic trade difficulties with the United States; structural cabinet changes and reorganization; and a new budget . . . I do not dance to tunes played by the Ottawa media. I owe them nothing. I have said everything I have to say on this matter. I have nothing to add except this: there will be an election in the fall of 1993. We shall win that election and this party will form the next government of Canada."

A few days before I spoke, an old friend from Laval University, Senator Pierre de Bané, had called. He told me that he had heard the rumours and noted that some ministers were cranking up their leadership organizations. "Your government could soon be paralyzed," he warned. "I want you to know that this has happened before, under Trudeau." As a former member of Trudeau's cabinet, de Bané was able to describe how Trudeau had dealt with the problem I was now facing. At a cabinet meeting, Trudeau simply announced that if he caught anyone campaigning he would personally ensure their defeat. This was one of the few lessons from Trudeau with which I was in full agreement, and I promptly told my own cabinet, in unmistakable terms, that I would do exactly the same thing. This threat had, I am told, a considerable impact.

On February 5, I arrived once again at the White House, this time to meet Bill Clinton. During our initial face-to-face talks in the Oval Office, the Canadian note-taker was assistant secretary to cabinet Jim Judd, who was later appointed head of CSIS. He recorded the meeting as follows:

> The PM said he had not come today seeking hard-and-fast decisions on issues, but instead wanted to treat the discussions as a sort of overview between friends. He thought it might be useful to take some time to talk about some of the policies, both in failures and successes, he had had to contend with in his "nine years of kicking around." Noting that the president had recently dealt with the issue of gays in the military, the PM observed that his government had to recently deal with the same question. He remarked that he headed a conservative government in Canada, not "a wild-eyed bunch of socialists," and that the rescinding of the Canadian policy of banning gays from the military had been carried out only last fall. "We have not had a peep out of our people since then," the PM noted . . . The whole debate over the question in Washington had just been "awful," added the president . . .

> The PM commented that the president would have to deal with debt-service costs, with entitlement programs, and with tax increases. On the revenue side, he continued, "You have room to move, especially with the wealthy, and you can tax the hell out of gasoline, alcohol, and tobacco." Noting that he was himself a reformed smoker, the PM said that there was a lot of revenue potential to be found in the American tobacco industry, given the low prices charged for tobacco products. The president asked how much cigarettes cost in Canada. The PM, in turn, asked me. I [Jim Judd] responded that a package of 20 cigarettes would cost about $5 to $6 in Canada as opposed to around $2 in the U.S. The president reacted with considerable surprise, observing that the U.S. Treasury takes only 25 cents per package in taxes.
>
> [The PM then told the president that Mrs. Clinton was welcome to examine Canada's medicare system] . . . The PM was not recommending wholesale adoption of the Canadian plan by the USA, but there might well be elements of it that could work in the USA. He added that while the Americans had the best technology, equipment, and hospitals, there were also 40 million Americans not covered by the health system. Perhaps, he went on, there was too much technology and equipment in the USA. At the end of the day, he concluded, it was, in some respects, very much a moral issue. The president agreed and said that attitudes in the USA on issues like this continue to surprise him. For example, he had just learned that there are 72 countries around the world which already have the kind of family-leave legislation that he had signed that morning.

Before the president and I headed off to lunch, we chatted informally. "I have appointed Hillary to head a panel to examine health care in the United States," Clinton said. "What do you think?"

"She's certainly the brightest and ablest, but in Canada, if you really didn't like your wife, you'd appoint her to head a committee to study health care," I answered, causing Clinton to burst out laughing. "Because there is no solution. She'll become the target of personal attacks from all the special interests. So if we were in Canada I'd say, 'Don't do it.'"

Jim Judd also took notes at our luncheon, which involved a number of others, including Vice-President Al Gore.

The PM said he hoped his comments had helped, as he assumed that the president was not offended by the prospect of being re-elected. The president said there was no way that he would find such an idea offensive. In fact, he added, since World War II this had been difficult, as only Reagan and Eisenhower had been elected to and served out two full terms . . . The other dimension of the [Canada–U.S.] relationship, the PM said, is the reality that when the U.S. coughs, we get pneumonia. What you do here almost inevitably has an impact on Canadian interests . . . The PM then referred to a quote by Dean Acheson about "those sanctimonious Canadians." This may be accurate at times but we have to be realistic too, recognizing that we live cheek by jowl.

Canada is, at the end of the day, the USA's best and most reliable partner. It was important, therefore, that the president send a strong signal that we are different and important and that the USA has to avoid side-swiping us.

The president then asked the prime minister, "What is your take on Haiti?" The prime minister said the situation is bizarre: we can reach halfway around the world to deal with issues like Somalia but we cannot seem to tend to our own backyard. Canada was very much on Aristide's side. While [Aristide] had "made a fool of himself" after coming to office, he had changed for the better since then . . . In the domain of foreign policy, he went on. "This is where you should focus in the next several weeks." A president can get away with a domestic failure but a foreign policy setback – an embarrassment of the country internationally – is much harder to handle . . .

The PM remarked that "if you want to deal in Europe, call François Mitterrand." While one would not look to the G-7 for popular political leaders these days, the institution of the G-7 is key in international affairs . . . There was, however, a real need for summits despite the fact they had become increasingly farcical with limited real conversations . . . There was a strange chemistry among the leaders at these meetings. Helmut Kohl was really a secular socialist who has never really gotten over the German role in World War II. In some respects, Mitterrand is a kind of moral proxy for Kohl. The latter thinks the world of Mitterrand, referring to him as "François le premier." If you want to get to Kohl, the PM commented, call Mitterrand.

Canada, the prime minister added, is in a very strange situation: we are members of the Commonwealth, second after the U.K.; and we are also a member of La Francophonie, where we are second after France. La Francophonie now has 49 countries in it and is very important for Mitterrand, as language and culture very much drive him . . . The vice-president asked if the Chancellor [Kohl] had an equal impact on Mitterrand. The PM responded affirmatively, "They are like Bobbsey twins." He explained that on his last visit to [Germany] he had spent some time with Kohl at his own home. Kohl had talked about his relations with Mitterrand then, noting that they had had [almost 100] bilateral meetings by that time . . .

The vice-president then remarked that before lunch there had been a brief discussion about how Americans took Canada for granted. The PM agreed that this was true. He mentioned that in the course of a visit to China, he had met with Li Peng, who in the course of their discussion had described the USA as an imperialistic nation. The PM had asked him how he had gotten such an idea, pointing out that Canada and the USA shared a 5000-mile border with no troops on it. If the Americans were such imperialists, he added, he should return home immediately to order troops to the border. Li Peng was so taken with that story that he had the PM repeat it later to Deng Xiaoping.

[The PM] went on to say that he had noticed that the president was planning to visit Detroit soon and said he had told a story about Detroit when he had been at Harvard, with Teddy Kennedy, late last year. The last time there had been any hostility between our two countries had been in the War of 1812, in the course of which, we had seized Detroit. But, the PM added, we had given it back. On reflection, he did not recommend the president using that story when he was there.

—

PERSONAL JOURNAL: FEBRUARY 7, 1993

After eight years of meeting with Republican presidents, with whom I had excellent personal relations, I stepped into the Roosevelt Room and, at the request of Secretary of State Warren Christopher, became the first head of government to sign the White House guest book of the Clinton administration. Immediately after I walked into the Oval Office and was greeted by the new president, who looked me carefully in the eye as if sizing me up, and welcomed me to the United States and the White House. He struck me as being somewhat taller and leaner than I had imagined. He is built somewhat like me, along Irish truck driver lines.

I was very impressed with him throughout our 40-minute tête-à-tête in the Oval Office, private luncheon, and press conference. He is a good listener and from time to time he would say, "Great, that's right, Brian. That's absolutely right," and jot down a note. Basically I told him that this was an informal get-together. He seemed delighted at our private talks, and before going to the family quarters for our private lunch, I got him to autograph Caroline's invitation to the inauguration. After lunch, and while we were getting ready to go to the press scrum, I entered the lobby to find the president proudly telling Vice-President Gore about Caroline, which pleased Al greatly because his daughter is also at Harvard. When we got to lunch, Gore was chatting with Maz and others. He told the president that in Rio, "on the day I got the call from Warren Christopher informing me about the vice-presidency and I said I would get back to him within 24 hours, the prime minister called me over to a conversation he was having with President Bush and said, 'George, have you read Al's book on the environment?' George said no. 'Well,' said Mulroney, 'you should. It's very good and has some very good policy recommendations in there!'"

I remembered the incident well and was quietly pleased that Gore took such pride in it, proof of course, if any is needed, that foreign policy is progressively the product of careful attention to both substance and personal relations. After the lunch we took questions from the media on the south lawn of the White House and said goodbye; I did a CNN interview and came home. I doubt I'll ever again meet Bill

Clinton as prime minister of Canada. [I was wrong.] It was vital, however, for Canada's ongoing interests that this first meeting be as successful and productive as it was. Without going into details, I hinted to him that I would soon, with Mila, make a decision on my future and would let him know. I will of course find it difficult to leave, and no doubt find it difficult to accommodate a significantly less stimulating environment. I will also miss not having gotten to know President Clinton better, because he is both a nice person and someone capable of becoming an impressive president. He has presence, the royal jelly, and with his ambition, grace, and charm he may just be able to do significant and durable things for his country. I wish him well.

—

I also confided to my journal about the leadership machinations going on in Ottawa.

—

Somewhat to my surprise, I have not yet announced my intentions, as I had planned to do in caucus on January 31. In fact, the private and confidential heads-up I gave to Michael Wilson – because of his vital role in 1983 and his unwavering loyalty since, when he declined my offer to make him ambassador to Washington – has caused more difficulties than I anticipated. Rather than keep my plans about the future to himself and Margie, Michael began campaigning to succeed me. A few days after our "extremely confidential" luncheon in late December, Michael met with Bill Davis for coffee and said, "Bill, I hope and expect the PM will stay and lead us into the next election, but if he doesn't I wanted you to know that I'll be a candidate to replace him." Davis just about fell off his chair and rushed to phone John Tory, who called me. I was unperturbed, but as it turns out I should have been more realistic. Word of Michael's campaign, however discreet he thought he was being, got around, and soon other aspirants, emboldened by Michael's activities, began to quite openly solicit support.

—

I continued to work hard at making caucus meetings – serious as they had to be – entertaining and enjoyable, despite the many tough issues we faced. On February 10 I entered the caucus room confident that my team would soon be laughing as hard as I had been that week, thanks to Scarborough East MP Bob Hicks, who had been in government since 1984. A firm advocate of NATO and defence issues generally, he had earlier given an electrifying address to caucus, defending parliamentary decorum. If you want to see a parliament out of control, look to New Zealand, Bob had said, reading out lively insults delivered by former New Zealand prime minister Robert Muldoon when he was in power.

I decided to play a trick on Hicks at our next meeting.

"I received a telegram from a Mrs. Grace Muldoon in New Zealand," I solemnly announced that day. "'I understand the memory of my late beloved husband has been disparaged by some Hicks in your caucus,' it said. 'I do not have my husband's elegance or command of English. But tell Hicks he is lower than a snake's belly, and if he ever comes to New Zealand he'd better protect his gonads.'"

The room filled with laughter and the member for Scarborough East turned bright red, a huge smile on his face.

Before February was over, Joe Clark dropped by to see me.

—

PERSONAL JOURNAL: FEBRUARY 18, 1993

Joe Clark has just left my office after an hour-long meeting. Our principal areas of difficulty over the years were few; I was pro-Israel and he tended to take a pro-Arab position while at External Affairs. And on the Constitution, his decision to proceed without consultation July 7, 1992 while I was in Munich was both provocative and unconstructive.

He has been reluctant to make his plans known since the referendum on the Charlottetown Accord. I have no doubt he hoped for another and successful run for the leadership if it became open. My info, however, is that he has been advised by most of his principal erstwhile supporters to banish any such thoughts. Accordingly, he came to see me today to tell me of his intention to publicly advise his Yellowhead constituency executive on February 20, Saturday, of his intention to stand down and his wish that they proceed with the selection of a new candidate.

He has been talking with universities and think tanks about a further association, and I told him I would follow through on his behalf with Boutros Boutros-Ghali at the UN in regard to the availability of a future special emissary role on behalf of the Security Council. He told me that would please him a great deal, and urged me to make contact and relay, confidentially, the news of his availability. I will do so and report back to him ASAP.

It will be strange but good I think for the PC Party to turn the page on both of us and reach out to a new generation for leadership. Now the time has come for others to improve on what we both sought to do, both to the best of our ability, honestly seeking to serve Canada.

—

1993

2. Resignation

ON FEBRUARY 24, I announced my plan to resign. After a breakfast at 24 Sussex with my closest friends and advisors, I travelled to Parliament Hill to make it official. After thanking my family, my party, and staff, I addressed those who matter the most.

"In a special way," I said, "my gratitude goes to all the people of Canada who have honoured me with the greatest privilege a citizen of this country can ever know. At all times, my effort was devoted to our common dream of a better, more united, and more prosperous Canada, for them and for their children. I did not always succeed, but I always tried to do what would be right for Canada in the long term – not what could be politically popular in the short term. And so I leave with thanks and good wishes to all I have encountered along the way. I wish you all well. Now history will make a final decision on what we did and what we are leaving our successors."

Less formally, I told reporters outside 24 Sussex Drive, "This is a beautiful view . . . but it ain't free."

A few days earlier, when I told my youngest son Nicolas, then seven years old, that his father would have to find a new job, he was greatly concerned. While in office, Mila and I took pains to remind the children that living at 24 Sussex and Harrington Lake was a temporary privilege, and that we'd some day return to Montreal. "The planes, the cars, none of it is ours," we'd say to the kids. When Nicolas was even younger, we'd had Ottawa artist Shirley Van Dusen paint a portrait of our baby that we hung proudly at 24 Sussex. One day he asked, "When we no longer be prime minister and the taxi comes to take us to Montreal, can you bring my picture with us?"

"Don't worry, Nicolas," I answered, "we'll be taking it with us."

That pleased him greatly, and the Van Dusen portrait now hangs in our winter home in Florida. And his dad's new job has worked out just fine.

In the following days, I was to receive many special letters. My mother was one of the first to write. "I am not going to say I am sorry you stepped down because I am not," she wrote. "I am absolutely delighted, and the timing was perfect. And Mila, you were always there for Brian, a model for future prime ministers' wives and a wonderful wife and mother and a gracious and caring daughter-in-law. I wish you the best in your new, calmer, lives." Then, with a mother's objectivity, she wrote about her brother's high opinion of me. "Brian, Uncle Jimmy said to tell you he was always proud of you – knew you would do well – and he does not see anyone able to fill your shoes."

Deputy Minister of Finance David Dodge, who later became the governor of the Bank of Canada, wrote to me the next day. "My colleagues at Finance and I watched your press conference yesterday both with great sadness and with great pride: great sadness that you were stepping down as prime minister but great pride that we had played a small part in helping you and your government achieve the economic reforms you noted in your remarks," he wrote. "When the history books are written a decade from now, I know they will indicate that your economic reforms were unparalleled by any Canadian government in the 20th century. My only regret is that the real fruits of your efforts will only become fully evident after you leave office . . . Thank you for giving me these opportunities to serve both you and my country."

Another generous letter came from one of my predecessors as PC leader. "I hope you are stepping down with as much peace of mind as I did," wrote Bob Stanfield.

> I cannot really say why I was at peace with myself, because I knew I ought to have defeated Pierre following the near-tie of 1972, and I knew I had made or at least permitted serious mistakes following 1972. I guess my peace of mind came from my success in Nova Scotia. I used to say that I had nothing further to prove to myself. You certainly have nothing further to prove to yourself.
>
> I am confident that future Canadians will thank you warmly for [the FTA] and for the courage you have shown in backing the policies of the Bank of Canada and in trying to get our fiscal house in order. You must be very tired. You ought to be. For what it is worth, I think you made the right decision in stepping down. You leave the party in a strong position, and you leave the country with inflation low and exports expanding . . .

> I apologize for inflicting my writing on you, but as a former leader of the party I feel the occasion justifies even my handwriting. I cannot close without thanking you for your kindness to Anne and to me. I apologize again for not feeling able to accept positions in which you have felt that I could have served the country. I am not only a modest person, but responsibility has bothered me increasingly as I have grown older. Every good wish to you, to Mila, and to your children. May the future be as rewarding as you deserve.

At a cabinet meeting on March 11, I did my best to ensure a vigorous leadership battle. Believing that my successor would be one of the men or women sitting around the table with me, I contrasted my situation with that faced by John Turner when he took over from Pierre Trudeau in 1984. "He had no staff, no organization, no money, no polling data, and no strategy," I said to my ministers. "Turner also got stuck with hundreds of Trudeau patronage appointments. If you're thinking of running, and the object of the exercise is to become prime minister for eighty days, we could follow the Trudeau–Turner example. But since the real object of the exercise is to be prime minister for ten years, the leadership campaign and the election campaign have to be viewed as one. I urge all of you to view it as such. The finances of the party must be sound. The party organization must function independently and must offer fresh, dispassionate advice to the new leader. Third, the convention must be fair, democratic, and exciting. If not, we will be deprived of four months of television coverage. In the absence of a good race, the press will line up against any front-runner. A CBC reporter just told Bill Fox, 'If there's no fight, we'll give them one.'

"All options will be open for the new leader. We'll have a draft Speech from the Throne ready, a budget, and government reorganization, which I have prepared but which I'll hold for the new leader. There will be up-to-the-minute polling and overnight tracking data available. All the preparations for the G-7 Summit in Tokyo in July will be made. The sherpas are already instructed. And I think [PC Canada's] David Angus will be telling you that we have, as a party, $6 million in the bank now. My role in the leadership race will be simple – none. While I will continue to exercise the full responsibilities of a prime minister, uppermost in my mind will be the well-being of my successor."

It soon became evident that few of my ministers were listening to my plea for a "good race." Perrin Beatty announced in mid-March that he would not be contesting the leadership and that he would be backing Kim Campbell. (At a subsequent cabinet meeting I watched with amusement when he stood as Kim Campbell entered the room and quickly moved to get her a coffee. This gesture brought home to me my new status as an outgoing prime minister.) Barbara McDougall, Bernard Valcourt, Michael Wilson, and Don Mazankowski had already arrived at the same conclusion as Beatty.

—

PERSONAL JOURNAL: JUNE 13, 1993

On March 16 I got a call from Pierre-Claude Nolin, urging me to stiffen Charest's spine, because Nolin feared Charest would drop out altogether, before he even got in. When Charest arrived, down in the mouth and quite desolate, I told him that almost ten years earlier to the day I had made a decision that the pundits and pollsters said was crazy – I decided to contest the leadership when the so-called experts said Clark had it won. I told Charest to pay as much attention to the media stars and pundits as I did – namely zero. An hour later Nolin called [to say Jean Charest was running].

—

Shortly after my resignation I was proud to supervise the progress of a bilateral constitutional amendment. This one – close to my heart – entrenched the equality of the two language groups in New Brunswick. Approved by the Commons on February 1, it became part of our Constitution upon its proclamation by the governor general on March 12, 1993.

Despite my retirement announcement, the job of prime minister continued. Bill Clinton had called to tell me that he wanted to meet with Russian President Boris Yeltsin. He confessed, however, that he was in a bind. He had promised during the recent campaign to focus like a laser beam on the economy, and because of this he didn't want to leave North America at this point. He was also aware that Yeltsin was in the midst of a national plebiscite on his leadership and he didn't want the Russian leader to have to travel to the United States at that sensitive time.

"Could Canada accommodate such a meeting?" Clinton asked.

"Yes," I answered, "we could do it in Vancouver."

We agreed that Canada would host the two presidents in early April at a summit meeting at the University of British Columbia. When this plan became public, I received a call from Richard Nixon, on March 19. He was obviously working hard behind the scenes at pushing Clinton toward a strong commitment to aid for Russia. By now it was clear to every Western observer that Russia could easily collapse if the G-7 countries did not provide a major infusion of cash. The conversation was vintage Nixon.

"I wanted to talk to you urgently," Nixon began. "It is vitally important that a G-7 meeting on Russia be held immediately after the Russian election. Canada has been in the forefront on the Russia file, and your influence is absolutely key because of your relations with Mitterrand and Kohl. Of course, Yeltsin has made mistakes. Who the hell hasn't? When I saw Mitterrand in Paris, he was negative on this because of Yeltsin. He said he preferred Gorbachev's 'manners.' Nothing has changed since. We also have to shut down the Japanese. They need a swift kick to make them stop talking about those four little Kuril Islands." At the end he made a direct appeal. "You could have an enormous influence on this. It will be such a tragedy if the Russian experiment fails. Democracy will not survive the defeat of Yeltsin."

Of all the conversations I had had with Nixon over the years, this was the one where I found him to be most passionate. While older and greyer, he was still very much the man who'd negotiated face to face with Leonid Brezhnev in Moscow, San Clemente, and Washington; earlier, while still vice-president, he'd taken on Nikita Khrushchev in the famous kitchen debate. Some would argue that the SALT I agreement he had hammered out as president had brought Russia and the West to where they stood in 1993. Clearly, he was determined to use every ounce of power that remained to him to help craft the post–Cold War world. It was an impressive performance.

When I arrived in Vancouver for the Yeltsin–Clinton summit, I announced a $200 million economic and technical aid package for Russia. This included $10 million in direct humanitarian assistance and a $30 million line of credit to help Russia's decaying health and education systems. "Russia is at a turning point and the democracies of the world must help," I told the press.

I hosted a luncheon for the two leaders at the official residence of UBC's principal, which offered breathtaking views of the Georgia Strait and the Coast Mountains – the perfect setting for the two presidents to get to know each other. Yeltsin, as always, put on quite a performance. Clinton and I peppered him with questions in light of the upcoming vote in Russia on his leadership. I took notes as he spoke.

"I'm able to contain the reactionaries," he told us, describing his survival of recent impeachment attempts. "Had it been anyone else in power they'd have crushed them! I learned my lessons at their school, so I know how to act. This is a plebiscite as opposed to a binding referendum on April 25. If I lose I will immediately retire. The major issue for voters is the first question: 'Do you have confidence in the president?' If the answer to that is okay, all the rest will follow: 'Do you approve of the socio-economic policies carried out by the president and government of the Russian Federation since 1992?'; 'Do you consider it necessary to hold early elections for the presidency of the Russian Federation?'; 'Do you consider it necessary to hold early elections for the people's deputies of the Russian Federation?' On the Congress of Deputies he had this to say, 'They were brought up in 1917, all of them. I'm not overconfident but I hope for 67 per cent in plebiscite.'"

As I already knew, Yeltsin was tough, and indeed he went on to win his plebiscite – but not with the overall average of 67 per cent he predicted.

While in Vancouver both he and Clinton praised Canada's Russian aid packages.

"I'm very grateful to the government and the prime minister of Canada, my friend Brian, for having on this occasion putting to us a very specific, a very concrete package of aids to reform," Yeltsin said.

"I want to thank the prime minister for his leadership role in the process of reform and democracy in Russia," Clinton told the press. "He deserves a good share of credit."

The truth is that only Germany, on a percentage basis, had provided more aid to the former Soviet Union and the new Russia than Canada. I was confident even then in predicting that history would judge that the course we followed was correct.

As host, besides kind words of praise, I received a special gift from Yeltsin. He presented me with a beautiful hunting rifle that had been hand-tooled by a Russian craftsman. Clinton eyed the rifle enviously.

"How do I get a gun like that?" he whispered to me.

"Bill," I said, "it's easy. Two hundred million bucks!"

In April 1993, my government introduced a piece of legislation that still gives me particular pride, thanks to an effective group of female lobbyists.

That month I was attending one of Nicolas's 6 a.m. hockey practices, as usual, when the mothers of his teammates approached me. I had noticed before that, apart from the boys on the ice and some of the members of my RCMP security detail, these early-morning practices were attended mainly by mothers. "Where are all the fathers?" I'd wondered on more than one occasion. That morning a few mothers at the rink began talking about how they all knew women who were being stalked by ex-boyfriends or husbands. Why isn't the federal government doing anything to protect such women, they asked? I didn't have a proper answer and brooded on the question as Nicolas and I were driven back to 24 Sussex Drive. While Nicolas was getting ready for school, I called Hugh Segal. I described my conversation with the women at the hockey arena and said that I agreed with them, that Canada needed anti-stalking legislation.

Hugh contacted Justice Minister Pierre Blais, telling him that the prime minister wanted such legislation brought forward on an urgent basis, and that is what we did. I mention this incident because it shows the speed with which a prime minister can get things done. I wouldn't have such authority much longer, and I was glad to be able to use it to such a worthwhile end.

Nicolas also played T-ball and I attended those games, too, as often as possible. The first time I went I noticed the same phenomenon as at the hockey arena – only the mothers were on hand. But then a funny thing began to happen at both games. Each time I went to the arena or the ball diamond, there were more and more fathers. At one T-ball game I quizzed one of the mothers. "What happened?" I asked. "Why are all the dads here now?"

She laughed. "We told them that if the prime minister isn't too busy to attend his child's game, you'd better start coming as well."

A fixed crossing from the Canadian mainland to Prince Edward Island had been dreamed of and talked about since before Confederation. In my lifetime both the Diefenbaker and Pearson governments had promised the construction of a link, which figured prominently as an issue in several federal and provincial elections in the 1960s.

By the 1980s, engineering and construction technology, environmental science, and new concepts of public-private partnerships had advanced to the point where this huge undertaking deserved another try. Two of my public works ministers, Stewart McInnes and his successor Elmer MacKay, were from Nova Scotia (on a clear day MacKay could see P.E.I. from his Pictou constituency), and both strongly pressed the issue on their departmental officials and on skeptical cabinet colleagues, who wondered aloud about our political priorities, especially after the Island elected four opposition Liberal MPs in 1988. But we pressed on because to me the long-term economic advantages to P.E.I. and Canada of a permanent crossing were obvious, and the opportunity to complete another chapter in the nation-building enterprise undertaken by Sir John A. Macdonald was simply irresistible.

Because the Terms of Union of Prince Edward Island's entry into Confederation in 1873 referred to a ferry service from the mainland, the termination of that service required a constitutional amendment by both the provincial legislature and the federal Parliament. Meanwhile, environmental concerns (especially those for the Island's famous fishing grounds) had to be resolved, the dislocation of ferry workers addressed, highway improvements in New Brunswick as well as PEI arranged, future toll increases controlled, and hundreds of other issues settled before we could proceed. Those issues were hotly debated at public meetings on the Island and in other parts of Atlantic Canada that would be affected by the project. Many of the Island's canny politicians, provincial and federal, Grit and Tory, kept their cards close to the vest until late in the process. Joe Ghiz had covered his bases by holding a plebiscite in January 1988, which produced a vote of 58 per cent in favour of the fixed link.

We entered into an agreement with a consortium of three Canadian enterprises that came together under the name Strait Crossing Inc. The private sector financed, built, and were to operate and maintain the link – thirteen kilometres spanning the channel and two seven-kilometre sections joining existing approach roads. The annual federal subsidy to be paid out over the first thirty-five years of the contract – $42 million in 1992 dollars – would be less than the projected cost of maintaining the ferry service. We concluded the agreements for this tremendous undertaking and got the legislation through during the final months of my premiership. It opened in June 1997 and today, ten years later, the bridge is a big tourist attraction in itself. The Confederation Bridge has been an economic boon to P.E.I. – the province's exports to the United States have jumped 600 per cent, and total exports as a share of provincial output have doubled – and to the

Atlantic region as a whole, an accomplishment that continues to give me real pride and satisfaction.

As we moved into May, I made my final overseas trip, visiting Great Britain, France, Germany, and Russia. With the G-7 meeting in Tokyo fast approaching, it was my job to nail down Canada's positions vis-à-vis our allies in advance. I also wanted to stress to them the importance we attached to the security of our peacekeeping forces in the former Yugoslavia.

In Moscow, Boris Yeltsin invited Mila and me to spend the night at the Kremlin – but not on our famous couch! As we lay in bed that night, we marvelled at how lucky we'd been to have been given such opportunities to serve our country. It's a conversation I'll never forget. Growing up on the North Shore, I would have never even dreamed of one day sleeping behind the walls of the Kremlin.

During a state dinner, Yeltsin continually pointed with pride to the musicians – "the presidential orchestra" is how he described them – who were entertaining the crowd. My ears perked up when the orchestra launched into a very Russian-sounding version of "Farewell to Nova Scotia"! This fine old Canadian folk song proved to be too much for one musician who collapsed during the performance and had to be carried out!

The next day Yeltsin and I, along with our wives, boarded his presidential helicopter for the trip to his dacha in Zavidovo. Unlike the Americans' *Marine I* – which was sleek and technologically advanced – Yeltsin's helicopter was noisy and uncomfortable, and Mila and I hung on for dear life. A hostess came by offering us a vodka, but I managed to politely decline! Once we were airborne, with great pride Yeltsin showed the big telephone that sat on his desk aboard the chopper.

"Brian," he said, "you can call anyone in the world from that phone. Who would you like to call?"

"I don't need to call anyone, Boris," I answered, but Yeltsin was insistent. "Anyone in the world." I finally gave in and said I'd like to speak with Canada's ambassador, Jeremy Kinsman, back in Moscow.

Yeltsin was pleased and grabbed the phone, barking orders into the receiver that I presume demanded that the ambassador be tracked down. He then slammed the phone down. But nothing happened. No one called back!

"Where the hell is the Canadian ambassador?" he shouted down the receiver, a few minutes later. The Russian official on the other end of the line was obviously telling the president he didn't know. I never got to make my call.

Yeltsin sat pouting for a few minutes, until I decided to improve his mood with a light comment. "Boris," I said, "Canada is a G-7 country with a lot of money and I don't have a helicopter. And if I did, it definitely wouldn't have a phone."

He seemed to feel a little better after that. We soon arrived at his dacha, where Mila and I had one of our most unforgettable dinners. A Canadian note-taker later came to my office, sporting a big grin, to hand me the written report of the evening. Delving into it, I understood why the official was smiling. It must have been an unforgettable dinner for the note-taker as well!

> President Yeltsin said he was very happy to see the prime minister and Mrs. Mulroney. (He raised his glass and said that he and his wife had developed a deep sense of affection for the prime minister and his spouse after all the times they had met and everything they had done together, and this is why he wanted to see them here.) . . . The PM wanted to know how far Zavidovo was from Moscow. President Yeltsin: "Two hours by car or 30 to 35 minutes by helicopter . . . I am not coming here every Friday or Saturday. It all depends on how the wild animals behave."
>
> The PM then wanted to know what animals are hunted in Zavidovo. "Boars all year round – you can shoot them at any time of the year and their population still grows. There is also deer, white-spotted deer, moose, fox, rabbit, and wolf." PM: "In abundance?" Yeltsin: "Hard to tell, but I know that you can find many boar, deer and white-spotted deer on the grounds . . . I don't know if they are easy to hunt or not; fox and hare are not easy, but to shoot a wolf is very difficult." PM: "Why?" Yeltsin: "I will tell you later, after you see the hide."
>
> "By the way, the woods are full of mushrooms and berries and the rivers and lakes full of fish like pike, trout, and perch. Mila will go fishing trout. They are that big!" MPM [Mila]: "I will try to catch one." . . . PM: "Boris, when you were younger, rearing your family, did it ever cross your mind that you would become the president of Russia?" Yeltsin: "Never. During the war my family and myself were

very often hungry. I was a small boy – 12 years, no 10 years old and I saw how our chiefs were eating, so I told myself one day I will eat like those chiefs." PM: "Seems sensible to me." [Yeltsin, I'll never forget, reached over and ate everything that was on Mila's plate after his own was emptied!]

(The couples are served Siberian meat dumplings, first stuffed with fish, then with meat.) Yeltsin, raising his glass: "To you, Brian, to your future." The PM said he spent nine years as PM and that sometimes an event predetermines your success. Did President Yeltsin, who was born in a small town and whose destiny had its ups and down, who became president of Russia, ever experience such an event which influenced his life and career? Yeltsin: "There is one. It is when my mother gave birth to a son." The PM then wanted to know if the image he had of Yeltsin leaving the party, when he got up on the podium, opened the door, went down the stairs, passed the delegates, walked through the corridor, opened the door, and was greeted by crowds of Moscow, was that image associated with instinctive decision?

Yeltsin: "Not an instinctive decision. I was disappointed by the CP. I no longer viewed the party as an ideal. I resented the injustice, the difficult life people had to face, while those party leaders were only thinking about their own well-being, were not interested in improving the standard of living of our people . . . I came to that decision once I reached the conclusion that a socialist system cannot exist. In seventy years, it did not give happiness to the people, neither will it ever give any. The theory of Marx is just a Utopia, nothing more."

The prime minister started to ask a question when President Yeltsin interrupted him and said: "What is this? Are we working on a biography of Yeltsin? Is this a public discussion devoted to Yeltsin? Let's talk about Mila or Somalia or Ethiopia." . . . Yeltsin: "Brian, you have been PM for nine years. To take upon yourself the responsibility of managing a country like yours for so long is astonishing. As far as I am concerned I have four years of presidency . . . which two are already behind me . . . To stay in power for nine years one must have exceptional abilities."

(The PM then explains the difficulties of a Conservative coming to power in Canada. He explains Louis Riel to Yeltsin and his execution's effect on Tory fortunes for generations. He also explained the 1984 election and the debate to the Russian.) Mrs. Mulroney drew attention to the fact that her husband not only knew how to lead in the debate but also managed to unite different people: right-wing-oriented people, some anti-French people, separatists who want to separate from the country, and with them formed a majority. The PM, she said, knew how to bring people together, and this was a contributing factor that led to victory at the elections . . . (The couples then went outside and returned at 11:00 p.m. and had tea before retiring.)

Yeltsin and I and our wives did go out that night – wild boar hunting. A Russian boar's hide is stored somewhere in a secure facility controlled by Library and Archives Canada. Despite the extensive use I have made of their records for this book, I must confess that I have not visited the boar's hide recently.

On May 9 Mila and I had a final meeting with Chancellor Kohl and his wife, Hannelore, after which they took us to Heidelberg.

—

PERSONAL JOURNAL: MAY 14, 1993

Helmut had been a student and professor here from 1951 to 1958 and took Mila and me on a walking tour – three hours – from philosopher's path through the old city, to the university, then to an old Catholic church where we sat for 20 minutes as he quietly dissected the Pope's problems in central Europe. He said Germans and others will refuse to follow on such matters as birth control, and that the Pope is turning out to be a philosophical reactionary of limited effectiveness for the Church. I was drenched by all the activity, but even with a light jacket on he never even broke into a sweat. We went to a restaurant where we were joined by his wife. He spoke of his respect for ex-chancellor Willy Brandt (who told him privately, "I'm glad you're in this job!"); his disgust for Helmut Schmidt: "a money-chaser who, like Trudeau, considered himself perfect, though few others shared the opinion!" [He also spoke about the USA]: "I went walking with my sons in Boston and saw homeless Vietnam vets on sidewalks – this is a disgrace. They let the infrastructure of the U.S. erode."

We choppered back to Bonn at 11 p.m. Next day at lunch, he said Churchill was most impressive leader of modern times.

—

We also visited London and Paris. Prime Minister John Major and I met for almost ninety minutes in the cabinet room at 10 Downing Street. As with all my talks on that trip, we spent most of the time discussing the UN mission and the dangerous situation in Bosnia. Major was concerned about Bill Clinton going out on a limb and not being backed properly by other nations on this critical issue. "We want a strong Clinton and strong United States," Major said.

Though only recently re-elected, Major told me he was under serious attack and had already become the most unpopular British prime minister in history. He confided that no fewer than seven of his ministers were "disloyal," and that he would be removing them in an upcoming cabinet shuffle. His cabinet, it seemed, represented only the beginning of his internal problems. "There are fifty dissidents in Parliament, twenty-five of whom are blind Thatcherites who will follow her to the death, even if it means the destruction of the government and party," Major said. "I am going to fight back, and hard."

John Major, who deserves more credit for his achievements than he has received, has a great sense of humour, which I enjoyed immensely. For example, he'd sent me a short note during a state dinner at the previous summer's G-7 Summit in Munich: "Brian, The last time I was in a room with so many mirrors, the police were called in."

In Paris, the situation in the former Yugoslavia also dominated my discussions with Prime Minister Jacques Chirac and President François Mitterrand. Mitterrand spent a great deal of time asking Mila about her personal impressions of events and personalities in the land of her birth. I also made clear Canada's positions for the upcoming G-7 Summit, which my successor would attend.

At lunch, Mitterrand joked about the realities of political unpopularity in the modern age. "Why did you quit?" he asked me. "You could have won again – we're all down now."

It is time to reflect on popularity – and its dangers. A few hours before his assassination on an Ottawa street in 1868, Thomas D'Arcy McGee told the House of Commons: "I hope that in this House mere temporary or local popularity will never be made the test by which to measure the worth or efficiency of a public servant. He who rests simply upon popularity builds upon shifting sand."

Almost 140 years later, the astute Washington columnist Maureen Dowd made the same point in a more modern context: "In a nation ruled by polls and ratings, where even newspapers have focus groups to see what kind of news readers want," she wrote, "we are losing sight of something we should have learned as teenagers: just because something is popular doesn't mean it's right."

I've done my share of polling, and I fully understand how useful it can be. But today I am wary of the media's addiction to public opinion polls. "Who's up?" and "Who's down?" seem to have replaced "What has he or she done?" and "Will his or her actions benefit the country in the long run?" as the litmus tests of political leadership. And in my experience – as an observer as well as a participant over many years – only a superhuman politician in any democracy (but perhaps especially in Canada) could maintain high approval ratings while making profound structural changes in the country.

We all enjoy being liked, and I was no exception. I knew, however, that if I made major changes that I saw as necessary for the country's long-term benefit, my disapproval numbers would rise sharply. And they did. My only consolation, then and now, was the hope of an approving verdict rendered by a more reflective nation in the fullness of time.

Of course, along the way I did encounter my share of popularity, and I was not offended by it. In my first election win in 1984, the largest in Canadian history, I won fifty-three more seats than the Liberals did in the so-called "Trudeaumania" election of 1968, and in 1988 I won thirteen more than that same supposed high-water mark of popularity. With that result I became the first Canadian prime minister to win back-to-back majorities in 35 years, and the first Conservative to do so in one hundred years. In the process, I became one of only three prime ministers in history to win both 50 per cent of the seats in the House and 50 per cent of the popular vote. And during this period I ran as a candidate in three different constituencies – one overwhelmingly English-speaking and Protestant, the others mainly French-speaking and Catholic – winning them all with over 70 per cent of the popular vote. By the time I left office, I was the sixth-longest-serving prime minister in Canada's history. In fact, in the seventy-three years since 1935 the Conservatives have had twelve leaders. As I write this, I have given the party more time in office than the other eleven combined.

Yet why, with this kind of record behind me, were so many English-language members of the Ottawa press gallery focusing not on the hard-won achievements of my government as I planned to retire, but on what they constantly described as my "deep unpopularity" and my "historic low ratings," even describing me as Canada's "most hated prime minister"?

The media's equation was simple: popularity means competence and accomplishment. Anyone whose popularity declines during their time in office is clearly a failure. I had lost popularity, so therefore I must have done something terribly wrong. Was it poor policy, or perhaps a serious character flaw, or both? They weren't sure, but they were certain of their theory.

In 2006, I watched the movie *The Queen*. At one point, Her Majesty, stunned by Britons' hostility toward her in the wake of Princess Diana's death, stares forlornly at her prime minister and says, "It was the first time I've known hatred." That scene hit me hard. I knew exactly what she was feeling.

The truth is, my party did lose popularity – large chunks of it – even before the worldwide recession hit. But for obvious reasons: when Preston Manning created a second conservative party, he cut into our base and our approval ratings tumbled. When Lucien Bouchard created the Bloc Québécois over his contrived grievance regarding Meech and made a direct appeal to Quebec's nationalists, the support level of all federalist parties – the Liberals, the NDP, and the PCs – fell sharply.

Both of them, however, turned out to be one-trick ponies: their common achievement was to eat into Conservative support to an extent that ensured the election of Jean Chrétien three times. Quite an achievement for Manning and Bouchard, defeating a Conservative government with policies friendly to Alberta and Quebec in order to elect as prime minister a man whose party had devastated both of those provinces – Alberta with the National Energy Program and Quebec with the unilateral patriation of the Constitution. You can't make this stuff up!

I realize that politicians should not complain about strong criticism from the media or elsewhere. It goes with the territory and is a necessary ingredient of a healthy democracy. Politics is not for the timid of spirit, the faint of heart, or the tender of soul. Nevertheless, it is hard to operate, year after year, in what columnist George Bain described as an atmosphere of unremitting antipathy, cynicism, and disrespect. In my experience, things became so bad that I felt the press was not just filtering our message (an appropriate function) but actively blocking it.

Nevertheless, my advice to any young person contemplating politics as a career is to reject the easy, popular route and to always do what you believe to be right for Canada. Keep your eye on the long-term prize. The attacks of the critics may be brutal, not to mention hurtful to both you and your family, but years later you will be rewarded for having done things for the greater benefit of your country. Personally, I was proud when McGill University's North American Studies Institute declared in 2000 that my government had the best economic record of any Canadian government in fifty years. Again, in 2003, the Institute for Research on Public Policy determined in a major analysis that I was the second most accomplished prime minister (after Pearson) of the last fifty years. Not to mention being named Canada's Greenest Prime Minister. In hindsight, I would say, not bad.

On May 25, I headed to Iqaluit for the final signing ceremonies leading to the creation of Nunavut. While plans had been in the works for years, my government had made the new territory a special priority. It was clearly unacceptable for the residents of the eastern Arctic to have to travel all the way to Yellowknife to secure necessary legislation and political support.

The final announcement was greeted with great joy by the Inuit and the other residents of the land that would become Nunavut in 1999. I was pleased to see Gordon Robertson, the former deputy minister to Alvin Hamilton in the Department of Northern Affairs, in the audience. Gordon's role in the north stretched back to the days in the 1950s, when from Ottawa he had helped James Houston in his self-appointed task of bringing the glories of Inuit sculpture and art to the outside world.

In my Iqaluit hotel room I pondered the challenges the Inuit faced in their struggle to foster and develop their culture and language. This reality was brought home to me when I turned on the television, only to be confronted by the supper-hour news from Detroit!

Today schoolchildren from across Canada continue to be excited by the Canadian North and Canada's third territory. John Diefenbaker's Northern Vision obviously lives on. I still receive letters from kids as they work on projects about Nunavut, which pleases me no end.

While my government had resolutely kept up the pressure on communist China since the 1989 massacre in Tiananmen Square, as I prepared to leave office I knew that another signal had to be sent. Paul Desmarais (founder of the Canada-China Business Council) was one of the leaders of the Canadian business community who saw that China would be the key economic player on the world stage in the coming quarter-century. At his suggestion, I hosted a dinner at 24 Sussex for Chinese Vice-Premier (and later Premier) Zhu Rongji. Attended by Paul and André Desmarais, the dinner was intended to demonstrate that Canada would be prepared to fully engage with China in the years ahead – cautiously, of course, in light of our appropriate human rights concerns. During a subsequent visit to China after leaving office, I was told that my family and I would forever be welcome in China because of the positive signal I had sent with that invitation.

In early June I visited Washington for the final time as prime minister, to hold a breakfast meeting with Bill Clinton. It had only been two months since I'd last seen the recently inaugurated president, and I was shocked at the change in his appearance. His face was blotchy and he had put on weight. He was tired and exasperated, because he was under relentless attack. Bill told me how down he felt and how unhappy he was about his own prospects. I could relate to his situation and proceeded to give him a pep talk.

"Stop campaigning and making speeches and working until midnight," I said. "It's time you started giving Congress some TLC. You should use Camp David and pose for pictures with the necessary congressmen and senators. You must wear your unpopularity as a badge of honour. Return to your campaign thrust by moving toward the centre. You shouldn't take any of this personally; it's much too early in your first term."

I also reminded him about the 1981 British poll in which a vast majority said that Margaret Thatcher would be remembered as the worst prime minister in the country's long history. Then along came the Falklands crisis, and she was re-elected twice before she left office.

While I knew Bill faced a tough battle in the three and a half years ahead, I could already sense he'd come out a winner. It was not for nothing that he'd been dubbed the "Comeback Kid."

And then I returned to Canada for the final stretch in my prime ministership. There were still some thank-yous to perform. I described one in my journal.

January 1991. Speaking to caucus before the vote in the House that takes us to war against Iraq over Kuwait

Representing Canada's environmental position at the Rio conference

Three events at 24 Sussex Drive. Breakfast

A family photo

Dinner with Boris Yeltsin delights Barbara McDougall, Benoît Bouchard, and Hugh Segal

With my valued friend Paul Desmarais

The last Mulroney family grave in Leighlinbridge, Ireland

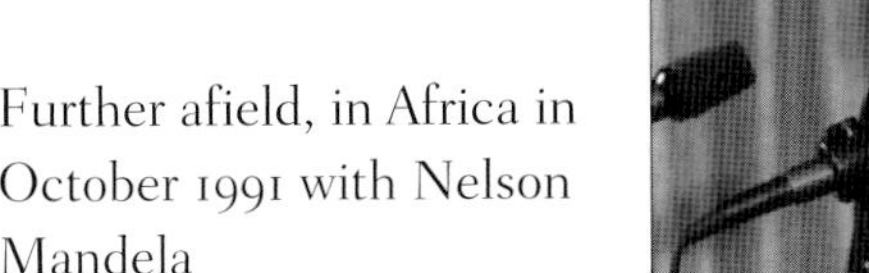

Further afield, in Africa in October 1991 with Nelson Mandela

With George Bush at Kennebunkport in 1990

Finally signing the Acid Rain Treaty in March 1991

January 1993. A visit with George Bush at Camp David on the last weekend of his presidency

Another forest scene – this time in Russia in May 1993 with Boris Yeltsin and his wife, Naina

With Helmut Kohl and his interpreter

February 1993. With Bill Clinton in the White House

April 1993. Introducing Clinton to Yeltsin in Vancouver

March 1993. A final visit from Mikhail Gorbachev

February 24, 1993. Announcing my resignation to caucus

April 1993. Chatting with leadership candidate Kim Campbell in the House

My last cabinet meeting, with Elmer MacKay, Don Mazankowski, and Joe Clark

With Mila, a last hug in the Prime Minister's Office

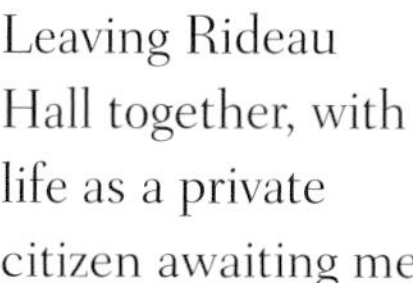

Leaving Rideau Hall together, with life as a private citizen awaiting me

—

PERSONAL JOURNAL: JUNE 4, 1993

(After meeting with Premier Bourassa)

Robert Bourassa has been my greatest and most reliable ally. He is also a good and reliable friend. He supported Meech, Charlottetown, GST, FTA, NAFTA, and never once took a cheap shot. We reminisced about our 1976 luncheon, when we were both recently defeated leadership candidates, and how I had forecast his successful return in a few years. Our meeting was warm, nostalgic, and enjoyable – typical of the man and an exemplification of our long association.

—

After nine years in office I knew that I'd have difficulty adjusting to a new life. The prime minister's day runs to a very definite, well-planned rhythm, and it may be worth setting it out in some detail here.

Of course, there is no such thing as a "typical day" in the life of the prime minister. On many days, I would be elsewhere in the country or the world on official business.

When I was at home at 24 Sussex, however, some degree of predictability was possible. I would rise at 6:30 and go to my dressing room beside the master bedroom on the second floor, where I would skim the headlines of the papers, shower, and get ready for the day. Already I would hear the chatter and laughter of the children from the floor above, as they dressed and prepared for another day at the school they all attended together, the Lycée Claudel. At about 7:15, I would join the kids in the kitchen nook where they all had breakfast and talked up a storm while they scrambled for school books and mittens before leaving at 7:50.

I would usually go to my downstairs den to place a quick call to the Clerk (of the Privy Council), my chief of staff, or Maz about whatever was important that morning, before receiving a guest for a working breakfast. These breakfasts took place frequently, and the guests could range from an important foreign visitor – though not a head of state – to cabinet ministers seeking advice for special problems, senior party officials, or friends who were currently in town.

At about 8:50, I would leave for my office on the third floor of the Centre Block. I was escorted to Parliament Hill in a convoy of three cars driven by RCMP officers assigned to the prime minister's official security detail, an elite group of men and women who looked after the family and me in a highly professional manner for my entire nine years in office. Upon our arrival in Ottawa in 1984, the RCMP assigned us code names: I was known to them as OAK 1, Mila as OAK 2, Caroline as OAK 3, and so on. We inherited most of the personnel, and the vehicles, from Pierre Trudeau. I suspect my schedule was not unlike his or those of my successors – although security is much greater today than it was back then.

My working day was tightly organized. It always began with a meeting with the Clerk and my chief of staff to preview the day; the decisions, communications with world leaders, domestic challenges, parliamentary activities, and, occasionally, important appointments or party matters that were on the agenda.

The day of the week was important. Tuesday was Policy and Priorities, the inner cabinet meeting that I chaired, which started at nine-thirty and usually ended around noon. On days when full cabinet met, the schedule was almost identical.

Wednesday was caucus day, the most important on my calendar. That morning I would have breakfast at the official residence with three or four backbench MPs, listening to their frank views on the world, on our achievements and our challenges, before attending national caucus, which sometimes lasted until one o'clock, as everyone had their say.

On other days, there would be quick, ad hoc get-togethers throughout the morning with ministers, senior public servants, and PMO advisors to deal with issues as they arose. The in-tray of a prime minister is never empty and the phones are never silent, and people tend not to want to contact you when they feel that everything is going just fine. Problems, usually unanticipated ones, can be anticipated. Visitors – either distinguished arrivals from abroad or important Canadian figures – have to be accommodated, usually with photographs taken in the Prime Minister's Office to commemorate the occasion. All prime ministers have official photographers who record history on a daily, even an hourly basis, and I frequently sent copies – duly autographed – to my visitors. I was extremely well served over the years in this demanding job by four talented photographers, Peter Bregg, Bill McCarthy, Andy Clark, and Ken Ginn.

Following a review of the matters before the House and the questions that were likely to arise that day, I would return to 24 Sussex at about 12:30 for lunch – often with the Clerk, my chief of staff, or close parliamentary colleagues – to discuss policy questions, political problems, or forthcoming travel plans. After lunch, I would quickly shave, change shirts, and head back to the office for further preparation for the main event of the day: question period. Canadians are sufficiently acquainted with these forty-five-minute daily theatrical performances, full of feigned outrage and unrequited indignation – in both official languages – and will not require a detailed description from me. There were moments, however, of genuine passion, real importance, even danger during these sessions, and these moments I treated with genuine concern. The rest was showtime.

After question period, the afternoon was a time for more meetings. The range was enormous. Frequently, there were groups of wide-eyed schoolchildren visiting the Commons for the first time, and I would often try to see them in my office. Similarly, there were often premiers in town for discussions with the government, as well as mayors, religious leaders, university presidents and the like, many of whom were advancing a case, and all of whom were glad to go back and report that they had given the prime minister a piece of their mind. There were many, many celebrities – Olympic athletes, Sir Edmund Hillary, Peter Ustinov, and Gordie Howe, to name but a few.

There were also regular "business" meetings with Gérard Guy and Keith Morgan, who looked after my constituency so effectively, and countless cups of coffee and informal discussions, ranging from caucus liaison with Tom Van Dusen and Camille Guilbault to administrative matters with the invaluable Marilyn Burke; appointments with my superb deputy chief of staff, Marjory LeBreton; domestic and international travel plans with the dynamic and highly effective Luc Lavoie, Stuart Murray, Bob Chant, and Stu Braddick; and general political reviews with Pat MacAdam.

For a Canadian prime minister, travel eats up many weeks each year. (Margaret Thatcher once remarked in reference to our vastness that "in an hour I can get to any spot in the United Kingdom, but in an hour Brian can't even get to the airport!") Travel inside our far-flung country is time-consuming but vital – both for the country, which sees that the prime minister takes the regions seriously, and for the PM, who avoids being stuck in an Ottawa bubble. And since Canada, as these memoirs show, is a member of so many important international organizations like the G-8, NATO, the UN, the Commonwealth, the Francophonie, the OAS, and so on, preparation for and attendance at regular events abroad, in addition to official bilateral visits, is equally time-consuming and constant.

Usually, I left the PMO at about 6:30, after placing a number of calls across the country, whether to the ailing spouse of a member of caucus, a medal-winning Canadian athlete, the bereaved family of a fallen police officer or, more informally, to MPs, supporters, and friends – just to stay in touch. On good days, I was able to attend my children's school or sports events, and to enjoy family life and a dinner at home, often joining the kids for a swim in the famous pool before dinner. Unless, of course, I had to deliver a speech in the National Capital Region and return home later with Mila to say goodnight to the kids. At the end of the day, I would repair to my study with briefing books, correspondence, and PCO documents on security or international matters. Typically, as I wound up this task, I would call Paul Tellier or Maz at home for a brief conversation, then join Mila on the second-floor Freedom Room for a private chat before turning in around midnight. While we were at Harrington Lake, I exercised on my stationary bicycle every day, swam, took long walks, and in winter skated and played hockey with the kids. At 24 Sussex, I regret to say, my exercise regimen was not followed so faithfully.

From morning to night, I was accompanied by at least one of my executive assistants. These young people worked long hours, dealt with sensitive matters, and coordinated multiple flows of information intended for the prime minister. They also became witnesses to my private and family life, which required discretion and good judgment. I am pleased to say that all the people who filled this responsible position for me – Bill Pristanski, Hubert Pichet, Rick Morgan, and Paul Smith – did so with great professionalism, dedication, loyalty, and skill, and I am deeply grateful to them all.

It was a very full day, every day, in Ottawa, especially on Parliament Hill, and every appearance on the street anywhere was likely to lead to a request for autographs or posed photographs. I always enjoyed these occasions, but they did take time. So did the necessity whenever I or my family went outside, to allow for my RCMP bodyguards to get into position and help us move from point to point. Mila and I appreciated everything they did, but we looked forward to returning to normal, unsupervised life.

As my days in office ran down, I thought a great deal about the economic challenges we had confronted so long ago, back in September 1984, when I was first presented with the PCO's briefing binder making it clear that Canada was in terrible shape.

Generally speaking, most new governments tend to follow the broad economic path of their predecessors, with only minor changes of direction. (This would prove to be what the Liberals under Chrétien did when they succeeded my government; although apparently determined to revoke our major economic policies, they in fact proceeded to accentuate and build upon what we had done.)

Confronted by the Trudeau legacy, however, I knew that we would have to change course. To put it frankly, the Trudeau government had almost succeeded in erecting a democratic socialist state in Canada. Over a fifteen-year period, its spending policies and its economic nationalism (not to mention its anti-Americanism and quixotic foreign policy) had produced a deeply worrisome national balance sheet. As Ontario Liberal leader David Peterson said when I was sworn in, "Brian Mulroney has inherited one helluva mess." Truer words were never spoken.

Even Jean Chrétien famously admitted that the Trudeau government "left the cupboard bare." Chrétien knew very well what he was talking about; as a senior cabinet minister – including time as minister of finance – for the entire Trudeau period, he was complicit in creating the economic and fiscal wreck that we inherited.

Adding to our challenge was the fact that the Liberals' disastrous economic and spending policies had many vocal supporters – in academia, the media, the unions, the public broadcasters, and the like. As I learned to my cost, every brick that we removed from that debt-creating edifice provoked howls of outrage from that constituency. Taking away a benefit – *un droit acquis* – was always unacceptable, even if the benefit was unaffordable.

It was all part of what was grandly called the Just Society. For the decade and a half that Trudeau was in power, the average increase in public spending was 14 per cent every year. When Trudeau came to power in 1968, he inherited a fiscal situation that was in rough balance. When he left office, the deficit had exploded to $38.4 billion, in 1984–85, and at 8.7 per cent of GDP was the highest in Canadian history. In 1993, when I left office, the deficit was at 5.8 per cent, down by one-third.

The national debt? When Trudeau arrived, it stood at $18 billion; when he left, it had risen to $206 billion, an increase of almost 1000 per cent. This meant that our new government had to confront the fact that 32 per cent of total government spending had to go to pay the interest on the debt. As a result, our administration was left with a series of brutal decisions to make in cutting program spending, which had reached $1.23 for every dollar of revenue. This in turn meant that overall spending exceeded revenues by $16 billion. In those days, Canada was borrowing just to pay for the groceries.

By 1991–92, however, our operating balance was $6.8 billion in surplus, a $22.8 billion swing since 1984. In effect, excluding debt-servicing costs, the government was being run in the black. All of the deficits and increases in the national debt since 1984 were attributable to the interest payments on the debt that existed before my team came to office. We did not add a nickel to that debt.

And the really good news? Exports grew enormously as a result of the Free Trade Agreement (which was responsible for four new jobs in five, and the lion's share of corporate profits) powering the Canadian recovery and enhancing Ottawa's revenue stream in personal and corporate income tax. The GST, which the Liberals swore they would abolish, now accounts for $33 billion of Ottawa's tax receipts. In the end, of course, they recognized the value of the GST and left it in place, knowing full well that it was right for the country and right for the times.

It can fairly be said that it took nine years of hard work by my government and another six by the Chrétien government to clean up the mess I inherited in 1984. For years to come, Jean Chrétien got partisan mileage from his claim that he had inherited a record deficit from my government. That statement is false. The truth is that Michael Wilson and Don Mazankowski planted the garden, and Paul Martin got to pick the flowers.

So what economic shape was Canada really in as my time in office came to an end? In spite of a serious global recession that hit Canada hard, employment was up 1.4 million jobs from the 1984 level. We had cut spending and the size of government more deeply than Ronald Reagan had, and we had privatized and deregulated more swiftly than Margaret Thatcher. The prime rate was 6 per cent, the lowest in twenty years. Our inflation rate was well below 2 per cent, the lowest in thirty years. The OECD and the IMF were both forecasting that Canada was about to beat all of the other G-7 countries in job creation.

McGill University economics professor William Watson later wrote in *Policy Options* magazine that "a really good case can be made that Brian Mulroney's administration provided the most far-sighted economic leadership in the last half century."

Another even more pleasing judgment of Canada's economic health was given in 1992, when the United Nations stated that Canada ranked number one in the world for its quality of life.

This was the country I was turning over to my successors.

—

PERSONAL JOURNAL: JUNE 13, 1993 (MORNING)

On the speeches to the convention last night, Jean Charest gave a barnburner and Kim Campbell sounded like an accountant before the Rotary. He clearly has the momentum and now could win today on the first ballot, and definitely if a second ballot is required. What a sea change. After my retirement announcement, the boomlet for Kim – sustained by polls – grew at an incredible rate. Within days pundits were declaring that the race was all over.

Without seeking to interfere in any way in the race, I told caucus and cabinet that this party would never ever deliver up its leadership uncontested, and certainly not to someone it hardly knew. Immediately after Feb. 24, I went to Toronto and predicted a wide-open aggressive race with many candidates offering themselves up. And then one by one they all began to drop out. Wilson, McDougall, Beatty, Valcourt, Maz, etc., almost all citing the almost insurmountable Campbell lead.

No matter how hard and strenuously I argued with them and urged them on – "How can you drop out of a race when not a single delegate has been chosen yet? This race will look completely different June 1 than it does on March 1" – no matter what I said, nothing mattered. They were all convinced the race was over before it began.

As people continued to drop out, I grew alarmed and offended. Alarmed at the vacuum that could develop in a three-month campaign with a paucity of candidates, and offended that people who in opposition would have jumped at the chance to run were now declining en masse because as ministers they clearly feared that their "reputations" would be sullied if they failed to win or do extremely well. (I exclude Mike Wilson and Maz from this. Mike did have a great deal to lose from a poor performance, and Maz properly decided his lack of French was an insurmountable barrier.) But for the rest of them – McDougall,

Beatty, Hockin, Valcourt, etc. – to have sat this out simply because the polls, which are completely worthless anyway, said they couldn't do well was to me an appalling admission.

The race didn't happen, in part because of a strategic blunder made by Senator Norman Atkins, who early on devised and promoted the "coronation strategy" and used every lever he could to either discourage other candidates from running or convince them that Kim had it in the bag. He went so far as to tell the media that Barbara McDougall should not run – imagine an articulate, accomplished, seasoned woman being urged to stay out of the race – because there was no support for her, that the convention was over, and that she would only wind up hurting herself! This from an unelected organizer who begged me for a Senate appointment and – at that juncture in early March – had not even declared his conflict of interest, namely that his nephew David Camp was Kim's Vancouver campaign chairman! Bizarre. Rather than encouraging others into the race, thereby making it more exciting and attractive for the party, Norman was ensuring that Kim was being set up for a fall. With everyone out of the race and her the overwhelming front-runner, the most inexperienced strategist could predict the result: excessive expectations would become Kim's greatest enemy, and in the absence of any serious opposition the media would quickly cut her down to size.

In fact, the pro-Kim boom became so excessive that my earlier pleasure at her success and at the prospect of the first woman PM being a Conservative began to erode. All these factors began to worry me greatly: David Camp's statement to CTV the day she announced in Vancouver that "soon the Mulroney years will all be forgotten"; a campaign staff loaded with lobbyists who in March were discussing transition and who could get such-and-such jobs in the PMO; a candidate I had made, but who had managed never once to mention my name or my contribution in her opening statement, or, I believe, in any of the five policy debates, and who, after the Calgary debate (where she had done well) described with contempt to Lowell Murray her opponents as "pygmies"; a growing sense that she was beginning to believe the glorious polls and treat them as her due. I was also personally offended that a party I had led to power and kept there for almost a decade would either back away from its leader or the government's accomplishments; although I was much more offended by the thought that the leadership of the party and post of prime minister of Canada could go to anybody almost by default.

Candidates should have been ready, if they believed strongly in themselves, to run the risk of personal humiliation in order to contest the position of prime minister. Sure there were great risks involved, but the chance to lead a great nation should have brought out the daring in them all so that they were able to offer Canada their brand of leadership. For two years Doug Lewis (whose skills and loyal support I valued greatly and who had been replaced by Kim in Justice) had been badmouthing her and her policies. He frequently voiced his misgivings about her to Michael Wilson. I was well aware of his views but put them down to the fact that he was simply offended by the portfolio change and the high profile it had given Kim. When Michael Wilson decided to size up support for his potential bid, he went immediately to his old friend Lewis, by now my Ontario organization co-chairman. To Mike's horror, Lewis indicated that he was leaning toward Kim! – and that he thought that Wilson shouldn't run because he couldn't win! Wilson was livid when he told me this and cited it as one of the reasons for abandoning his goal. The polls were driving the agenda completely, and my words to cabinet and caucus were immediately ignored – no matter how often and how persuasively I urged prudence in viewing public polling numbers in such a climate, and how confident I was that such numbers are always significantly altered by a leadership race itself. Here we were by the end of the first week in March with all the potential candidates (of the cabinet heavyweights) dropping out of the race before a single, solitary delegate had been chosen because, as they and the media repeated as a mantra: "It's all over, Campbell has this won."

And so, as mid-March approached, Kim was clearly going in – because of her extraordinary appeal – and everyone else was getting out. Except Jean Charest, and his prospects and resolve appeared to diminish with each passing day and with each new defection to the Campbell bandwagon, leading clearly to a crushing first-ballot victory on June 13. Or so the experts thought. Within a week of my announcement I was visited at 24 by Pierre Blais, my campaign chair in Quebec and a very close friend of Jean Charest. He came to tell me that he was thinking of supporting Kim Campbell. I told him not to get involved – I needed him as campaign co-chair and that, in any case, Charest was his friend. He said 80 per cent of Quebec would vote for Campbell and that the race was over. I said, "You're nuts, this race hasn't begun." But a few days later he called from Whistler to say he was supporting Kim. I said, "She's a wonderful person, and I wish you well, but be ready for a fight."

I thought they were both extremely impressive candidates. Either would make an excellent prime minister. But no race meant no exposure, no excitement, no interest, no testing – and probably a winner who couldn't win a general election.

—

On June 11, the tenth anniversary of my election as leader of the Progressive Conservative Party, I returned to the Ottawa Civic Centre as the convention got under way. In those ten years, I had spent one as leader of the opposition and almost nine as prime minister. I had promised the Conservatives I would lead them to power, and I had delivered – providing our party with the longest unbroken period in office since Sir John A. Macdonald.

Organizers had arranged a ninety-minute tribute in my honour that my family and I enjoyed immensely. There were videotaped messages from Bill Clinton, Boris Yeltsin, and François Mitterrand, among others, and performers like David Foster, Christopher Plummer, and Jean Lapointe – with an assist from Health Minister Benoît Bouchard – to entertain us all.

"We kept our word," I told the crowd of seven thousand in my closing remarks. "I say to my fellow Canadians, no government could have ever done what you have done. Look around you, look at the beauty of what you've achieved. Look at the splendour of your Canadian citizenship. The world admires what you've done for your families and your communities and your country, and I say, may God bless Canada and may God bless every one of you . . .

"I want to say to Mila and the children how much your love and laughter have meant to me, how indispensable you've been to everything we have been able to do . . . On the 24th of February, when I announced my resignation, Mila had to go to Montreal with the kids, and I stayed home with Nicolas, and we were watching a hockey game. And at the hockey game, the announcers continued to say Prime Minister Mulroney resigned his job today. At the commercial break I put the TV on mute, and Nicolas looked at me and said, 'Don't worry, Daddy, I'll help you find a job.' So, Nicolas, the time has come.

"And the time has also come to thank, to say good night and *au revoir*. To all of you, I say in the words of Yeats: 'Think where man's glory most begins and ends, and say my glory was I had such friends.'"

Mila and the children joined me on the stage and then we left, with the cheers and applause still ringing in our ears. Back at 24 Sussex we hosted a reception for some of our closest friends. I didn't want the night to end.

After Kim Campbell's victory two days later, on June 13, I returned to Harrington Lake and continued writing in my journal.

—

PERSONAL JOURNAL: JUNE 13–14, 1993

June 13, 11 p.m.:
Well, Kim did it. She won cleanly and well. Her delegate support was broadly based and held firm in the aftermath of a mediocre speech last night. I feel good tonight, now that doubt has been removed. I feel good that I will be succeeded by a woman as prime minister, the first in 126 years. (Following written at midnight after calls from the new PM, Maz, etc.) I was surprised that Charest's speech didn't carry him to victory, it was that good. He's a marvellous campaigner and could have inflicted enormous damage upon the Bloc Québécois. That is my only regret.

Can Kim do this now? I don't know. The office carries a certain majesty, and she is shrewd, ambitious, and intelligent, so she may be able to project a message of change and efficiency and competence that would make her a highly potent force, including in Quebec. We spoke for about 30 minutes. She spoke of her deep gratitude to me for having made her success possible, for all she has learned from me: "And how grateful I am to have experienced government at the feet of a leader like you and watched and learned how you handle caucus, government, crises, and political challenge." I told her that I was grateful for her kind words, that avoidance of error should be her principal objective. We agreed to meet tomorrow at 3:00 p.m. at 24 for our first informal meeting to plan the transfer of power. She wanted to know about the House tomorrow and I told her I would take counsel from Maz – who advised not to attend.

She told me she was much more serene in her life, having had to learn the hard way about the brutality of the Ottawa media and the gruelling realities of the major leagues. She was awed by her new responsibilities, determined to proceed carefully to build upon "your decade of tremendous success." I told her that she would have lots of opportunity to distinguish herself from me and her government from mine and she said she planned to respect the main thrust but build her own image – which I completely encouraged her to do. I don't know if she fully understands the enormity of the burden she is about to assume, but she is calm, resolute, and good humoured. Success has been achieved by others with a whole lot less!

June 14:

At 2:40 p.m. at 24 Sussex while I waited for Kim, Michel Cogger called in a panic. He was with L. Ian MacDonald and had met with Jean Charest and [his mentor] George MacLaren at the Château immediately following the Kim–Charest lunch. Charest said it was a disaster – that she spoke only of her great political skills, that she failed to define a role for him. MacLaren said, "To hell with her, Jean, we'll just go to the private sector." Both Michel Cogger and L. Ian were horrified at the prospect of a serious split and bad blood in Quebec.

When Kim arrived at 3:10 p.m., we discussed it before getting into other questions during a two-hour meeting. She said she had been generous but had declined to specify a role because of imminent government restructuring, that Jean would have a key role, etc., etc. I asked her if she had followed the advice I gave her before her luncheon with Jean: "I need you and I want your help and you're the rock upon which I'll build my church!" She said no, but that she had made her intentions clear. I advised her to call Jean and tell him she was tired and regretted they hadn't connected fully, but they would meet again tomorrow or the next day to begin to define his principal role in the new government, and she agreed.

At 7:15 p.m., she called me urgently at the lake. She had not called him because Jodi White had called with Jean's demands – ITC and International Trade. She was afraid the fact was she was being "set up," that he had "made up his mind to quit" and was trying to make her look like the fall guy to ruin her in Quebec, that he was being advised to leave for five years and then return to run for leader. I was concerned about this attitude, one that struck me as being paranoid.

I told her not to worry, that Jean would stay, that she should call him again and say she regretted the contretemps, but that he would play a major role in her cabinet – plus the political organization in Quebec. I then told her that Mila had called Charest's wife, Michèle, to congratulate and commiserate with her, and say that now we all had to pull strongly behind the new leader and that Kim should not be consumed by her fears about being blindsided by Jean. I'm frankly astonished at both her suspicions and the apparent bad blood. Unless this is stopped – and I have called a love-in caucus for 9 a.m. tomorrow to help her affirm and assert her leadership – our success in rebuilding the party and government could be compromised.

Call from Cogger, who told me that Charest would not attend unity caucus the next morning, bad blood and mixed signals contributing to a worsening situation. Joe Clark was egging him on (and subsequently told Kim that he took Charest's defeat harder than his own. She was astounded by this). I told Cogger to tell Charest that I would construe his absence as a personal insult and that I wanted him there cheering. The next morning I met Kim at 8:50 and we went to the caucus, which Charest attended, and which, to my astonishment, Joe Clark boycotted. The caucus was hugely successful, and I really laid it on in regard to healing wounds now.

Wednesday I arranged for a special Priorities and Planning meeting. Charest was not there, and I instructed David McLaughlin to order him to attend. He was brooding and came toward the end when I was again preaching unity and paying tribute to both of them. I arranged for a House of Commons tribute – on my last day in the House of Commons as prime minister, and Kim's first as new leader and PM-designate. To my horror, when I rose to speak and compliment Jean, he was not in his seat! I immediately said he was held up in an important meeting and would be there soon, knowing he was watching somewhere on TV. He clearly understood the gravity of the situation his continued absence might create and arrived in the House from somewhere and received a tremendous ovation. Kim spoke extremely well and I felt we were getting close to healing a very serious breach. At the final cabinet meeting Thursday, I complimented them both and said that unfortunately in leadership campaigns there can only be one winner, that is, Kim – and we all support her 1000 per cent.

The mood was good and clearly improving. At the GG's final dinner that night, Charest sat next to me. I left that evening thinking that everything was done, unity would be complete. A few days later, Kim called to consult me on Quebec cabinet appointees; she left out Jean Corbeil, a Charest supporter, saying he was "divisive" and "unhelpful." I pointed out that his exclusion would cause a powerful eruption of anti-Campbell sentiment in Montreal, which she would not be able to contain. Moreover, because he was Charest's most prominent ministerial supporter in Quebec, she would be seen as vindictive in excluding him, it would divide the organization into warring camps and, on the eve of an election, play right into Chrétien's and Bouchard's hands. I told her that whoever advised this course should be fired, because it was political lunacy. I told her that Quebec was her most pressing and worrisome area, and that Charest had to be DPM and whatever else he wanted, and that he had to be kept happy.

After an hour she called back to say she had changed her mind and that Corbeil would be staying in Transport. I admire her open-mindedness and her intellectual honesty. She appears to listen genuinely and is persuaded when the advice is sound, and acts upon it.

On Thursday night, we had a wonderful relaxed dinner together and she handed me the attached cabinet list. I thought it was fine except for one particular proposed appointment to External Relations which I suggested might not be totally appropriate. She had not realized the implications and said she would change it, which she did the next day.

I also gave her a short list of some appointments to be made – including that of her key Quebec supporter, Marcel Masse, to be Canada's representative to the Francophonie, and a more extensive list of lawyers deserving to be made QCs. I told her that I would make the appointments if she preferred. She indicated she would look after this matter at her first cabinet meeting. When that day arrived, however, all appointments were cancelled, without any warning.

—

On June 16 I walked to the floor of the House of Commons for the final time and for my final question period.

"This is my last day in the House of Commons as prime minister of Canada," I said. "I have been very privileged to have been accorded the opportunity of serving my fellow citizens and I am proud of what our government was able to achieve since 1984. And I want to thank and congratulate all the members from my party who stood by me and who worked tirelessly so that we could try to meet the commitments that we made to Canadians. I'm leaving my successor my briefing book, and page one has just one piece of advice: Duck! I also want to offer my best wishes to all members of both opposition parties. I know that the leader of the official opposition will miss me – he usually does." Even Jean Chrétien had to smile at that. I finished by saying that "I will always keep fond memories of this place and of all the friends that I have made here."

The next day was my last cabinet meeting. It was a very emotional group that gathered in Centre Block that day. I wasn't the only one who would never be back in this room, full of the echoes of so much history. Barbara McDougall began by thanking me for my efforts in promoting and encouraging women to serve in public life and cabinet. A little later, a gracious Joe Clark spoke about how generous I had been to my former opponents within the party. He then proposed that the 1983 leadership convention be officially declared over, with me the winner. An equally gracious John Crosbie seconded the motion.

Benoît Bouchard brought tears to my eyes when he described how Canada had not been a real country for him until I had brought him into politics. His experience as an MP and cabinet minister had made him a Canadian.

Staff at the Privy Council Office had prepared bound copies of a document called *The Achievements of the Government of Canada*, and each minister received one. We began passing them around the table and signing them for each other. There was also a more exciting gift that I knew my kids would enjoy. I was presented by Marcel Danis with a pair of season's tickets for the Montreal Canadiens.

For my final remarks to the cabinet as prime minister, I chose a quotation from Teddy Roosevelt I'd first come across while a student at StFX so long ago: "It is not the critic who counts: nor the man who points out how the strong man stumbles or where the doer of deeds could have done better. The credit belongs to the man who is actually in the arena, whose face is marred by dust and sweat and blood, who strives valiantly; who errs and comes short again and again; because there is no effort without error or shortcomings, but who does actually strives to do the deed; who knows the great enthusiasms, the great devotions, and spends himself for a worthy cause; who, at the best, knows, in the end the triumph of high achievement, and who, at the worst, if he fails, at least he fails while daring greatly, so that his place shall never be with those cold and timid souls who knew neither victory nor defeat."

Kim Campbell spoke last, praising my leadership skills and thanking me for the fine shape in which I'd left both the party and the government.

I pushed my chair back, with a final nod of farewell to the portrait of Macdonald of Kingston. I was first among equals in that room no longer. It was an emotional moment when I left the cabinet chamber in a flurry of handshakes and hugs.

—

PERSONAL JOURNAL: JUNE 25, 1993

(Final day as prime minister of Canada)

I will be leaving with Mila in five minutes to meet the GG to submit my resignation. My feeling is bittersweet, some sadness at leaving such a powerful and exciting job that I sought to get but serenity in the knowledge that it was time, and that I was leaving on the high road in the manner of my choosing and with a strongly united party and government taking over. Had the Charests and their children to dinner last night at the lake to encourage them to support Kim – and of course to enjoy their delightful company.

(Later that morning)

Well, I am now a private citizen again (almost); I'll keep my seat until an election is called. Mila and I drove down to Government House in a jeep listening to Yves Montand and Cage aux Folles *music on the stereo. I told her I felt sad but fortified. I had a feeling of emptiness as we drove, knowing I would be leaving the excitement and challenge of a powerful office for the private sector. But, as we drove almost in silence, listening to the music on a beautiful June morning, I also had a great sense of accomplishment for the government, party, and myself.*

Last night Lowell Murray called, expressing his thanks for everything I had done. He said that very few prime ministers get to do one great thing and that I had done many – FTA, NAFTA, tax reform, the GST, Gulf War, Meech, Charlottetown. Lowell Murray said that Macdonald, King, and Mulroney had made profound and durable changes to Canada and to benefit her future, and that I should take both pride and comfort in the fact that history should acknowledge this. Whatever, it was good to hear, and I very much appreciated both his call and his friendship.

Early this morning, George Bush called from his car en route to New York to say goodbye and to indicate how proud he was of our friendship; I spoke with Paul Tellier, David McLaughlin, and Glen Shortliffe, having spoken last night with Mother, Peggy, Doreen, Pat Mulroney, Doug Bassett, et al. to say thank you and goodbye.

The GG met me for the transfer of the great seal and then, over a cup of coffee, privately he said that no political leader he could recall had ever been able to unite the party, keep the troops together, and wage so many battles – many of them successful – as I. He spoke of his and Gerda's great debt to us for the appointments and the friendship over the years, and said he would always treasure his association with the Mulroneys.

At 24 Sussex we didn't enter, just met Ben there, who got in with Paul Smith [my devoted and effective executive assistant] and we drove Mila to Rinaldo's and drove Paul and Ben back toward the lake. While we were a few hundred yards from the entrance to Harrington, we listened to the noon radio coverage of the event (we were listening to Radio-Canada), and heard the first-ever reference to my new status when a reporter referred to "former prime minister Mulroney." I smiled and said to Ben, "Well, I guess now it really is over."

—

We spent two days at Harrington Lake as a family before our final departure. I had many calls – Bill Clinton called to wish me well – and my first Clerk of the Privy Council, Gordon Osbaldeston also telephoned. In 1984, when I took office, his account of Canada's bankrupt state had appalled me. Now, as I left office, his message was much more welcome. "Your achievements such as FTA, NAFTA, GST, privatizations, deficit reduction have been heroic – that is the only appropriate word – and they shall live on long after the critics have been silenced," he said. "I am only calling to tell you that you have done a magnificent job for Canada and we have admired you greatly." Those were just the words a retired prime minister needed to hear.

—

PERSONAL JOURNAL: JUNE 27, 1993

We will be leaving Harrington for good at 5 p.m. en route to the airport for a flight to London and Nice. We are now truly looking forward to leaving, getting an extended holiday in Europe with the children, returning to Canada in late July, and starting a new life. I will be accepting an offer to return to Ogilvy Renault as senior partner using that as my base of operations. And so I assume my new life will be challenging and interesting. I'm not trying to kid myself, however. I know there will be real problems of decompression, trying to adjust to new realities after nine years in the most powerful and stimulating job in Canada.

As I look out on beautiful Harrington Lake on this warm and very still June day, my feelings are mixed and somewhat confused. I wish my successor very well, but I feel a twinge when I hear references on the TV to the "prime minister" and I know they are not talking about me. Can she hold the caucus, party, government together over the next months and win an election? As for myself I took steps to provide Canada with tough medicine – a course I thought was both wise and very much required. Was I right on the major issues? No one can be sure, but I believe history, both in the shorter and longer term, will indicate our actions were beneficial for Canada. I actually did govern not for good headlines in ten days but for a better Canada in ten years. I paid the price in media hostility and public disapproval. But I did so knowingly and willingly. Leadership is about courage, strength, and resolve, often in the face of overwhelming criticism and adversity; it is about taking positions you believe to be in Canada's long-term interest and sticking to them.

I'll miss Harrington, I know. And I'll miss the job – caucus, the House, the problems, the achievements, the excitement. But I've achieved a degree of serenity. The time has come, the country needs a change, and in great democracies the people must be served. I leave with a happy heart and a sense of fulfillment at having done much and at all times having done my best for Canada.

—

Appendix A

Inside the Meech Lake Debates

(Government Conference Centre, June 4–8, 1990)

This account is based on the extensive notes taken by Senator Lowell Murray, the only person present besides the ten premiers and the prime minister. He kept the only notes of the final Meech Lake negotiations.

Those in attendance were:

Prime Minister:	Brian Mulroney
Premiers:	Robert Bourassa, Quebec
	John Buchanan, Nova Scotia
	Grant Devine, Saskatchewan
	Gary Filmon, Manitoba
	Don Getty, Alberta
	Joe Ghiz, Prince Edward Island
	Frank McKenna, New Brunswick
	David Peterson, Ontario
	Bill Vander Zalm, British Columbia
	Clyde Wells, Newfoundland
Also in attendance:	Senator Lowell Murray, for the Government of Canada

When we met the morning of June 4, 1990, I asked the first ministers to consider an approach based on four panels, the ultimate objective being a working document with which they could all agree. In brief: Panel I was the Meech Lake Accord. Panel II consisted of a number of constitutional amendments that the first ministers seemed to have agreed to in discussions prior to this conference. Panel III dealt with a further constitutional agenda in which certain parameters or objectives were spelled out quite precisely; for example, principles of Senate reform that would help make the unanimity formula more acceptable. Panel IV contained *des observations d'ordre général* or "clarifications" regarding, for example, clauses on the distinct society, the spending power, and the promotion of linguistic duality. In anticipation of the meeting I had consulted late into the previous night with Lowell and officials to prepare a work plan. The atmosphere on June 4, while friendly, was tense from the outset, as it became evident that Wells and Filmon had similar if not identical strategies and objectives that were at significant variance on some fundamental issues. I knew I had my work cut out for me if we were to get unanimity, as required.

"All this is of little value unless you [view the document] as a working hypothesis," I said to the premiers. "It would give us one piece of paper to begin our deliberations. I emphasize it is not cast in concrete. It provides for proclamation of the Meech Lake Accord. It provides for action on a number of questions of substance. It provides a future constitutional agenda where the objectives will be made more specific. Finally, it deals with other apprehensions in the category of clarifications. Except for proclamation of Meech Lake, which must be done by June 23, we have not put any dates or deadlines on this. That is for discussion. The questions are whether this is a constructive approach and whether you think it is doable. If you think so, I would bring back a working document in several hours' time."

The premiers responded in turn.

"We have to get this on paper," David Peterson said frankly. "I think it enormously constructive and maybe the only chance we have. I can argue with what should go in what panel, but these are enormously difficult questions and you have tried to be sensitive to everyone. Let's get it on paper and get down to the details."

"I agree," John Buchanan added. "This covers most of the concerns I've heard."

"You have put everything in there in a multi-dimensional matrix," Grant Devine said. "Clyde, Gary, and Frank would have to look at how it addresses their concerns. Is there to be one companion resolution or several? I would like to see as much certainty as possible on the Senate. An elected Senate, first of all. Then we can have discussions on 'effective.' There are maybe some magic words we can use to define a more equal Senate or one with fairer representation. There are various degrees of commitment or hardness."

"I want to hear from Gary, Clyde, and Frank," Don Getty said simply.

The premier of Manitoba spoke first. "Nothing you have put in panels II, III, or IV has to be actioned by June 23," Filmon objected. "If the implication is that all this will be done in the future, beyond June 23, we might as well not waste our time discussing it."

Clyde Wells chimed in. "I am apprehensive about the approach," he said. "Our ability to change Meech Lake is impaired. Some of the issues you have set down for the future or as clarifications must be dealt with as additions to Meech Lake. In the amending formula, for example, and the relationship of the Charter to the distinct society."

Robert Bourassa kept his cool. "Much will depend on the wording of these additions and understandings," he said. ". . . We cannot accept that the distinct society clause would have less substance than the clause on multiculturalism." . . .

"I believe the prime minister's outline is a sound basis for continuing the discussion," Frank McKenna replied. "We have a large menu."

"I agree with Frank," Getty said. "I don't have a better process to offer. Even if Clyde had one to offer, I think we must consider what is doable rather than what is perfect. Everybody has to put some water in his wine. I can't possibly look at reducing Meech Lake. I don't want any part of it."

Again, Wells threw down the gauntlet. "I don't feel comfortable discussing the amending formula in the future," he said. "It has to be dealt with now."

As the discussion began to deteriorate, I said, "We've got to get off the dime. Let's come back at five o'clock."

This didn't please the premier of British Columbia. "Why five hours' delay?" Bill Vander Zalm asked. "Wait until those turkeys in the media get a hold of this. You'll find out for yourself."

"The problem of a promotion clause for the federal government on linguistic duality has come up," I said, turning to Filmon. "It seems to be a nonstarter, not just in Quebec but in western Canada. Gary withdrew the Meech Lake resolution from his legislature because he thought the Anglos are an oppressed minority in Quebec. Now he would be in the difficult position of justifying his opposition to linguistic duality."

"It was Bill 178," the Manitoba premier sputtered. "It was the notwithstanding clause and the idea that the distinct society clause could be used instead of the notwithstanding clause."

"Let's get rid of the notwithstanding clause," Peterson, no fan of Filmon, replied. "That's Ontario's agenda."

"This is a complete and total rejection of Newfoundland's position," interjected Wells, his voice rising almost to a shout. "It meets none of our concerns, not the distinct society, not the spending power, not the immigration provisions of Meech Lake."

Frank McKenna had a much different impression. "I like the document," he said. "It addresses the concerns about substance that were expressed across the country. I like the commitment to an open, public consultative process."

"I could entertain some things by way of constitutional amendment right away, others by way of political accord," Grant Devine said. "We could pass an amendment to the Constitution for the election of senators and agree to a process for the other two Es."

Joe Ghiz was also positive: "The document addresses concerns Canadians have raised. It's a good attempt to allay those concerns. It's a good step. It should receive our support."

Bill Vander Zalm, although he was onside, observed that "this is far more difficult than what we agreed on at Meech Lake."

By this point, Gary Filmon was mad. I had to keep my own anger in check as he spoke. "All this is a rejection of your earlier efforts to put legal words on some of these concepts," he charged. ". . . You have given us half of the loaf. It is unacceptable to Manitoba."

Don Getty attempted to keep the discussion moving forward, despite his own valid concerns. "I know what you are trying to do, and I appreciate it," he said. "Much of this is the result of Senator Murray's trips around the country and your consultations with us. I congratulate you for reaching out to close the gulf . . . This document makes it appear as if a number of other items have jumped past Senate reform. This would be a significant change. The add-ons coming from the McKenna resolution and elsewhere appear to pre-empt Senate reform, in that they would be passed almost immediately. We don't want to tell Albertans 'Senate reform is number 1, but we want you to pass nine others first.'"

I spoke again, trying to encourage the recalcitrant premiers to keep their eye on the bigger picture. "We can't get the Senate reform unless we have the signature of New Brunswick, Newfoundland, and Manitoba on the document by June 23," I said. "I tried to pull together all the items on which we are ready to agree. I wish Clyde, Frank, and Gary had been at Meech Lake. I believe they'd have seized the opportunity as we did. We have to trust one another. If there is no trust, Clyde, Gary, and Frank, we won't get to Senate reform. We'll be knee-deep in the referendum that Mr. Chrétien now admits is inevitable if Meech Lake fails."

David Peterson was becoming exasperated – and I couldn't blame him. The possibility of Canada's dissolution was leading him to chain-smoke. "So I don't like this, but give me a better idea!" he shouted. "I agree with Frank. This is an accommodating document. Everybody's got problems, but where do you have the most problems? Do you want to walk out in fifteen minutes and say screw it? This is messy, but it is as good as anyone I know on earth can devise. I would give blood to get Meech Lake done. I represent 40 per cent of the country here. Grant, do you want to go back and say we couldn't put it together? Do I want to go back to Toronto and face the prospect of higher interest rates as a result of the failure of Meech Lake, and political instability? I sit here and I see that we're close to a goddamn disaster. Everybody who spoke is right. We're all going to get hell whether we pass it or not pass it. Let's go for the least amount of hell in the most noble cause. I would sit here for the next month to get an agreement . . . The judgment of history on all of us will be terrible if we let this opportunity pass."

"I think this document is at least a good basis of discussion," Bourassa said calmly after Peterson's justified outburst. "It is practical. It gives priority to ratifying Meech Lake. A second priority are the parameters to discuss Senate reform in the second round." . . .

"If Meech Lake passes, Quebec will have made a strong commitment to Canadian unity," I added. "This will have a unifying effect in the country. It will carry us through difficult times in the next decade. This document has laid out the process and some of the principles. If Meech Lake passes, we get to keep Canada; we get Senate reform and other constitutional reforms. If Meech Lake fails, we get no Senate reform and the future of this country is in danger."

Wells made it clear he hadn't listened to the others, save Filmon. He was digging in once again, building trenches that would be impossible for the other premiers – particularly Bourassa – to cross.

"I disagree with your logic," the lawyer from Corner Brook told us. "A sense of national crisis has been fuelled by the artificial June 23 deadline and by these apocalyptic scenarios. Your package not only does not reflect Newfoundland's concerns but specifically rejects them. Your document reflects the concerns of a small minority. The concerns of the majority are not addressed . . . We must have a three-E Senate with equal representation for each province and powers equal to those of the House of Commons. It is the only way that we can prevent such destructive measures as the creation of the Department of Industry, Science and Technology, which is supposed to have a national mandate, but at the same time has a mandate for regional development in Ontario and Quebec. ACOA [Atlantic Canada Opportunities Agency] is not accomplishing its objectives. A three-E Senate is the only answer to the imbalance of national legislative power among the regions."

I wasn't going to let his comments about ACOA stand; as I answered Wells, my anger showed for the first time. "The federal government is spending more per capita on research and development in the Atlantic region than anywhere else," I shot back. "I could quote you the statements of Premier McKenna and others about the progress that ACOA has made in the Atlantic provinces, and the progress the Western Diversification Office has made in the West . . . The best constitutional document in the world is not worth a damn if within three years a province reneges on its commitment. There has to be trust among us."

Wells snapped back. "Your government is spending more per capita on job creation elsewhere than in Newfoundland," he snarled. "We don't want handouts. We want a balance of economic opportunity and the dignity that we can achieve through a three-E Senate."

"I know you'd rather pay equalization than receive it," I replied. "I want to help you get it. You know my views on such matters as the Lower Churchill Falls and the Hibernia projects. But it is not the institution of a three-E Senate per se that is going to achieve these things for you. Look at Mississippi. Look at North Dakota. Are they better off because the United States has a three-E Senate? If the nation is not together, the damage to Newfoundland and Labrador and all the poor provinces will be the greater. Much of what we can do for the Atlantic provinces or the West is possible only if there is the strength that comes from unity."

Frank McKenna then showed that he, too, had a temper. The lectures from Wells were starting to get to us all. "Clyde, I resent your suggestion that millions of Canadians are concerned with your points but only a trivial number are concerned with mine," he said hotly. "I have had public hearings in New Brunswick on these matters. You have not had such hearings. All of us have to sublimate our pride to a greater cause, the best interest of Canada . . . But I'm sick at heart that we are allowing constitutional experts to take over our political responsibility for the interest of Canada. Clyde, I respect your vision of Senate reform, but there are not many who think Senate reform is the answer for Newfoundland. Have you the right to enforce your personal view of what's right on everybody else?"

The meeting began to wind down. While there had been tough words and even tougher lines drawn, at least we were all still talking. We agreed to meet again the next day. Outside the Conference Centre, Frank McKenna announced that his province would now move to ratify Meech Lake. While this announcement didn't give us the public support we had expected, it gave me and the other members of the federal team a much-needed boost.

Perhaps the strangest public comments at the end of that day came from Gary Filmon. "Filmon said the federal government was bargaining in bad faith; it was now an advocate of Meech Lake," Andrew Cohen later wrote in his book *A Deal Undone*. "Odd, that. At Meech Lake, Brian Mulroney was criticized for acting as a mediator. Now he was criticized for being an advocate."

We met again the next morning and the Senate was high on the agenda.

"With regard to the amending formula as it affects Senate reform," I said, attempting to lower the temperature in the room, "various more flexible formulae have been suggested." . . .

"We don't want the veto," Vander Zalm said.

"We do," Getty replied.

"Could we preserve the general amending formula for Senate reform but provide that any of up to three dissenting provinces could by referendum veto a proposed Senate reform?" David Peterson wondered aloud. "We could perhaps keep unanimity for seven years, then let it sunset and have my referendum formula kick in."

"You've still provided a veto for Quebec. I'm not concerned about Alberta or British Columbia's attitude," Wells interjected. "I'm concerned about Quebec. Robert said he would never agree to reduce Quebec's proportion of seats in the Senate."

"Either unanimity or Peterson's proposal would be fine with me," Getty said. "It gives Alberta the protection it needs."

"Unanimity would be easier to defend," Wells said. "It's not a veto for B.C. and Alberta that concerns me. It's the political pressures in Quebec to keep Quebec's share of the Senate."

"Quebec has a partial veto on a number of subjects dealing with Senate reform, by virtue of the 1982 Constitution," Bourassa calmly observed.

The lack of understanding of Canada as a whole and of Quebec's special role in Confederation that I was hearing from Wells was simply staggering.

"They're in a minority in North America facing real demographic pressures and conscious of the need to protect their position within Confederation," I tried to explain to Wells. "Can't we come up with a flexible amending formula on a regional basis? It's a mathematical and legal question."

"Anything we do that leaves a veto for Quebec is unacceptable," Wells answered flatly. "I'd be better able to sell unanimity. We'd have less trouble. The real problem is that no Quebec government could ever give up its 25 per cent of the Senate. That's what Bourassa told me."

"I never said that," Bourassa retorted. "Obviously I don't want to weaken our position in Canada. But everything depends on the powers in such a Senate."

"British Columbia with three million people has six senators," I said, poking another hole in Wells's case. "New Brunswick with fewer than a million people has ten senators. The unfairness jumps right out at you. But Clyde, you're prepared to see this situation perpetuated if you don't get everything you want."

Bourassa once again tried to demonstrate the political realities of modern Quebec to Wells, but the Newfoundland premier wasn't listening. "For most people in Quebec, there is not much in Meech Lake," Bourassa told Wells. "It is mostly symbolic. Now you want to subject our veto to a referendum. You know the tradition in Latin American countries. The referendum would not be on Senate reform but on the federal government versus the Quebec government. On grounds of principle you can defend a referendum, but in practice it would launch a major debate on our federation. Why in Newfoundland is it so difficult to convince people that Quebec needs a veto on Senate reform?"

Though obviously angry, Peterson attempted to interject the spirit of compromise into the discussion.

"Let us have a federal-provincial legislative committee on Senate reform – a National Select Committee," he proposed. "If we did it today, it would have an immediate high profile. It would start building a national consensus on Senate reform. It would create a massive public discussion according to the principles that we have set out in the prime minister's paper. We could provide for equality of representation for each province on the commission. This could be presented as a model for future constitutional change. One of the things that fucked us was trying to make the 1982 process work."

"Yes, but you'll still leave Quebec with a veto," Wells objected.

Joe Ghiz then made a crucial intervention.

"No other prime minister would sit around here for three days listening to this stuff," he said. "Quebec can't compromise on its veto. Let me convey to you an idea suggested to me by the Honourable J.W. Pickersgill. It is that we move immediately to give each of the western provinces and Newfoundland ten seats in the Senate. In the case of Newfoundland, this would automatically give that province ten MPs. It would increase your clout at the centre."

"Newfoundland has no right to hold up the constitutional development of the nation contrary to the majority of the people," Wells replied. "I didn't hear it first from you. You heard it first from me."

Bourassa once again tried to explain the realities of modern Quebec to Wells. "You must understand the nature of the political dynamics of any referendum in Quebec," he said calmly. "Nominally, it would be on Senate reform. But the federal government would have to intervene. This would be another source of confrontation. It would be very difficult to convince my colleagues that this is a good idea."

"What other proposal have you?" Peterson asked Bourassa.

"My proposal is to respect what was signed in 1987," Bourassa answered simply. "Senate reform would not be the issue in the referendum. People would vote for or against the government, for or against the federation on all sorts of extraneous issues."

Wells then aimed another shot at Bourassa. "The nine other provinces are prepared to put our trust in the people," he told the man, Bourassa, who had campaigned tirelessly for Canada in the 1980 Quebec referendum.

I intervened. "In the crunch you have to lead public opinion, even when public opinion wants to refuse to be led," I said. "Look at what Peterson has done with Bill 8 on French-language services in Ontario, despite its unpopularity, because of his commitment to the country and to national unity. Look at the GST. I knew it would rear back and bite me. I knew it would be a colossal blow. But look at the Public Accounts, look at the amount of revenues that will go to service that national debt. We have to stabilize the fiscal position of the country."

Soon after we broke for lunch and a much-needed break.

Shortly after we resumed, P.E.I.'s Joe Ghiz took the floor. I had come to genuinely like and admire him. His interventions were crucial that day.

"We could make the Pickersgill proposal an incentive for Senate reform by providing that if no Senate reform had been achieved under the unanimity formula within two years, the four western provinces and Newfoundland could go from six to ten senators each," he said.

"And that the Senate would be elected. It's the ass-kicker," Wells said, his doctrinaire approach dampening the mood in the room once again. "Without it, the proposal is not worth a damn. Forget it."

"With the same powers as the House of Commons?" Don Getty asked, facing Wells. "That's ridiculous."

A little while later, Wells appeared to show some flexibility. "That would be okay by me," he said, referring to my suggestion that the issue of public hearings be left to each individual legislature to decide. "I intend to emulate Manitoba and provide for obligatory public hearings where constitutional amendments are involved."

As the talks continued, I tried to keep the group moving forward.

"Remember, nothing is agreed unless everything is agreed," I said as the discussion around Senate reform continued. Listing some of the details of areas of concern, I said, "If we could agree on words, we could look for a vehicle that would not cause problems for Quebec. I'm looking for a comfort zone for Manitoba and Newfoundland that will not create political damage for Robert. I hope it can be done. We all know that symbolism is the killer in these matters. Frank has his linguistic promotion clause, which is a very sensitive matter in New Brunswick, and with linguistic minorities. Newfoundland has another problem with the spending power clause in Meech Lake. But, as David said, we have to prioritize. We have to deal with the issues of the greatest sensitivity."

We broke for dinner. During such breaks, officials were so busy fine-tuning drafts on the fly that if anything, I was often more tired after a break than I was before one.

A draft was circulated as soon as we all gathered again. "It is very important that I have a language promotion clause or I will come home with virtually nothing," McKenna announced as soon as he reviewed it. "This was the centrepiece of my objections to Meech Lake, the inadequate protection of linguistic minorities."

"Western premiers couldn't live with 'promote,'" Getty said simply, adding that he didn't like the idea of having the Senate looking into the activities of provincial legislatures. "Let the Senate stick to the federal jurisdiction."

"I'm not uncomfortable with the promotion clause," Peterson said. "But we have to prioritize and separate the essential from the marginal. I take Getty's point about stacking things against Bourassa."

"The promotion clause is important," McKenna answered. "You have to realize that we have the Confederation of Regions Party advocating English supremacy in New Brunswick; then we have separatists of various kinds, including some Acadians, who advocate duality in all our government structures and some form of political independence for their region."

"This text is even longer than Meech Lake," Bourassa observed worriedly. "Much of this could be put into a press communiqué. Further, I'm concerned about the commitment to consider reverting to unilateral federal action for the territories to accede to provincehood."

"I'm honour bound with regard to the territories," McKenna answered. "They want to be helpful on Meech Lake."

"Twenty-four thousand people!" Bourassa said, shaking his head.

I soon gavelled the meeting to a close. Thanks in large part to Joe Ghiz, we had at least kept talking. Don Getty put it best in his remarks to reporters that night. "I feel so much better about the future of my country," he said. "Meech Lake had a faint heartbeat, and that heart is beating away now and I love this battered country."

The next day, June 6, we began with a sobering assessment on the Senate proposals from Robert Bourassa. "The media reports in Quebec last night and this morning about the proposal to give western provinces and Newfoundland additional seats in the Senate if Senate reform has not been realized within a certain time are that I have compromised on the Senate," he said matter-of-factly.

Getty and Vander Zalm also told us they were being hit hard by the media and various interest groups in their respective provinces.

Peterson disagreed. "It has played remarkably well," he said.

"People are rooting for us now," McKenna agreed.

Wells argued it was time for us to face the public. "It is very difficult for me to explain what is going on from the point of view of Newfoundland's interests when I have to respect the confidentiality of private meetings," he said.

I tried to reassure him, reminding him that "until everything is agreed, you're not bound to anything."

Don Getty tried to keep the discussions moving. "How soon can we get on with the Senate-reform process?" he asked.

"Supposing we have a First Ministers' Conference on the economy in Calgary in early November, this could be followed by a First Ministers' Conference on Senate reform, say at Whistler, B.C. before the end of 1990," I replied.

Wells then went after Bourassa over the Senate, suggesting to the Quebec premier that his province had no right of veto on any aspect of Senate reform.

"Your right of veto is at this table," Filmon chimed in, aiming his remarks at Bourassa.

This angered Peterson. "Meech Lake is being used as a hostage to advance other agendas," he thundered, angrily stubbing out another cigarette. "I see serious problems about electing senators before there is comprehensive Senate reform," he observed a few minutes later.

"If this Senate proposal goes ahead, and we could work out something with you regarding the [Stan] Waters [elected senator] problem, could you commit to staying with the interim appointment process in Meech Lake?" I asked Don Getty, responding to Peterson's concern.

"I would be inclined to give you that commitment by the end of the day," Getty said. "I want to move this forward."

After a break for lunch we began our afternoon discussions, again reviewing a draft of a possible compromise deal. Wells didn't like it. In fact, it soon appeared there wasn't anything from our previous discussions he found appealing.

"Nothing on page two gives me any concern with regard to timing and certainty," he said. "However, I am concerned about the timing and certainty of Senate reform; also about the Canada clause, about the distinct society as it affects the Charter and the distribution of powers, and about the spending power."

"You have a high degree of trust in the rest of us for everything on page two, but a low degree of trust in us for page three," Peterson snapped at him.

"I have a lower degree of concern," Wells said matter-of-factly.

This proved too much for Frank McKenna.

"He is not interested in getting my items through," he said, his anger rising. "He wants to get his items through . . . At some point we will have to trust each other. If we don't have that bond, we are going nowhere as premiers or as a nation. We have to be sensitive to Robert and Gary, but we have to trust each other."

Though I agreed with Peterson and McKenna, it was my job as chair to lower the temperature.

"Clyde, Gary, and others have problems," I said a few minutes later. "But at the end of the day we have to do this before the nation and before history. The most important commitment comes when each of us has to speak to this publicly. People want a deal that we can all take out in the sunshine. Where do you – Robert, Clyde, Gary – think the federal Parliament can be most helpful? Wherever it is, I'll move. I know we need assurance and certainty, but there must also be trust."

My calming words didn't have the desired effect. As we moved into the evening session, the atmosphere remained tense and brittle. One bright spot was that Wells and his officials had met with staff and experts from Quebec and Manitoba, and with law professor and constitutional expert Peter Hogg, who was serving as an advisor to Ontario's delegation. The atmosphere among the assembled premiers was not positive, however.

"We need some chemistry here," Peterson almost shouted. "We're falling asleep while the whole thing is going down the fucking tubes and we're pretending nothing is happening."

"We're not pretending," Gary Filmon replied.

"I don't think the group will accomplish much in time for us to deal with it tonight," Wells chimed in.

In his usual calm, analytical manner, Bourassa spoke up. "It is clear in the jurisprudence of the Supreme Court of Canada that the distinct society is an aspect to be considered," he said. "But the Charter prevails clearly over the distinct society. My only problem in accepting changes, even in reaffirming the jurisprudence of the court, is that Quebec loses. The floor becomes the ceiling. You know how much of a face-saving presentation my five conditions of 1985 were. Look at the provisions of Meech Lake. We already have the immigration agreement. We have had three judges on the Supreme Court for a long time. The distinct society clause has no real impact. As for the restraints on the federal spending power, the feds are broke anyway. I can say some reassuring things about the Charter and the distinct society outside the meeting, but to put something in writing or to add it to the Constitution is impossible."

Wells then said he would like to meet further with Quebec officials. Again, this proved too much for Peterson. "We're close to the end of the line," he said. "We have to figure out how to solve this or go out and face the breakup of the country."

"The problem is one of theory rather than practice," McKenna said. "I would hate to tear the country apart because of fear of a possible Supreme Court of Canada judgment ten years from now. There is already jurisprudence on the Charter. It can be revisited down the road."

"I agree with McKenna and Peterson," Joe Ghiz added. "But the only way to solve this is through a process. There is no way that Bourassa can live with a single word of derogation on the distinct society clause as it is now contained in Meech Lake."

"Every time something comes up, we are told nothing can be done," Wells replied. ". . . Bourassa can do something if he has a mind to do it."

"Look at the way the interpretive clauses in Meech Lake are written," Bourassa said. "As it is, linguistic duality is described as a fundamental characteristic of the Canadian federation. The distinct society is not. It is quite possible that the courts will interpret the clause to mean that the protection of a fundamental characteristic is stronger than the promotion of distinct society."

"What is Clyde worried about?" Peterson asked aloud.

"I am concerned about the balance of the nation in the future," Wells replied. "In every federal state there are two equalities: the equality of citizens and the equality of the component parts of the federation. A constitutional provision which accords a special legislative status to one of the component parts of the federation, a status that the other component parts do not have, upsets the essential balance of the federation."

Once again, I tried to calm the waters.

"The meeting is in a temporary slump," I said as Wells's speech still echoed through the room. "We are looking for the kind of accommodation that will give Newfoundland and Manitoba as much comfort as possible with as little hurt as possible for Bourassa. Look what we have done so far. Look how far we have come at this meeting. There are obstacles but none of them is insuperable."

"Canadians think Meech Lake tilts the scales in favour of one part of the country," Wells answered.

"Do we have a package in writing that is almost final that we can consider?" Getty jumped in, his patience with Wells at its end. "I think this will be more useful than Clyde's speeches about that Canadians think."

When we met again on the morning of June 7, I had no idea that our session would be even more difficult. Lawyers and experts from various delegations

– including Newfoundland and Quebec – had met the night before to examine the relationship between the Charter and the distinct society clause. The group had hashed out a working draft and we began the day with Clyde Wells reporting on their progress. "We still have to find an ingenious way to provide these assurances regarding the relationship of the distinct society to the Charter and to legislative powers," he said, sounding positive.

Wells then got hit with opposition from a surprising quarter.

"Newfoundland described the draft to me," Gary Filmon announced. "I conveyed the intent to my legal advisors, who say that the text might be worse than nothing at all."

"Are you saying there is a draft that would satisfy Clyde and might satisfy Robert, but that your Manitoba lawyers might throw it out?" an incredulous Don Getty asked.

I quickly moved the meeting toward a break and had a heart-to-heart chat with Filmon over coffee. When we reconvened, I reported back to the larger group.

"I have been having some chats with Gary and Clyde," I said. "Gary has two problems right in town with him – his opposition leaders, Carstairs and Doer. With regard to the distinct society, we have language that essentially everybody accepts. I am devising a vehicle that I've shared with Gary. There are also some ideas about a Canada clause. Gary will chat with his opposition leaders and will make his determination then."

Filmon was having none of it. "I came saying I needed certainty for all our changes prior to June 23," he said. "I'll get nothing. I came saying I was against the Meech Lake amending formula, which is a straitjacket for Senate reform. I get no change. I came saying we had to have legal assurance that the Charter takes precedence over the distinct society. I came saying we need a Canada clause to adequately describe all the characteristics of Confederation. All I get is a committee to study it. My senior staff is dead against this package. My legal staff say it's a joke. I have no reason to carry on . . . If it is me holding up the rest of you, then I might as well leave. There is a hell of a lot of public opinion with me. The question is whether I could get anything through the legislature. I will see Carstairs and Doer. I want to take my lawyers. They think it's a crock."

After we broke again, Filmon, joined by Wells, went off to consult with Sharon Carstairs and Gary Doer. When they returned, all thoughts of compromise seemed to have left them. Wells began a full frontal assault on each of Quebec's major concerns when he described what he and Filmon now thought suitable as a draft agreement.

"If Quebec is not prepared to concede that its proportion of senators will change, we're finished," he said. "I will need a referendum. I may have to say what a terrible mistake it was to concede the Senate reform veto to Quebec. So far as the relationship of the distinct society clause to the Charter and to the question of legislative powers is concerned, I would think we could get unanimous acceptance by all first ministers to a political statement as to what the distinct society means. But the political statement would have to be done in such a manner that the court can and would have to be likely to take it into account. While this may not be worth much, still it is something. If we do it this way we will have eleven first ministers making a statement and a court would not refuse to consider it. I have sold it to Carstairs on that basis. With regard to the Canada clause we have made some adjustments and have some copies to distribute. This is an add-on in a companion resolution after Meech Lake is passed."

"I take it this is your final position," Bourassa asked, without any outward emotion.

"I don't see how anything less than this would be acceptable," Wells replied, standing up as if he now planned to leave the room.

Canada seemed to hang in the balance at that very moment. Bourassa turned to Wells.

"Could you sit down?" he said sharply to Newfoundland's premier, who was now heading to the door. "Since this could be the crucial moment of our meeting, I want to say a few things. Quebec was excluded in the 1982 patriation of the Constitution. In 1987, at Meech Lake, we had unanimous agreement to the Meech Lake Accord. Now you are coming back with conditions. You should understand the growing impatience of Quebec with this whole process. It was willing to discuss the question of Senate reform, but if the legal implications of the proposal indicated that we were losing seats, this is something I could not discuss. You are now bringing a Canada clause which dilutes the Meech Lake distinct society clause. Most jurists accept that the distinct society is already not very much. You want a declaration with a legal impact. This is totally unacceptable to Quebec. If this is your final position, I have to leave the room. It is sad for the country. I represent seven and a half million Canadians. It is sad if the Constitution does not recognize us for what we are."

I jumped in. "The Canada clause has escaped first ministers for years if not decades," I told Filmon and Wells. "You left with an acceptable draft on the distinct society relationship to the Charter and legislative powers. The Canada clause was to be referred to a future meeting. You've come back with something different. There was general recognition that the Canada clause is not on right now. There is no consensus at this table as to what it should contain. We've all been struggling for a way to get as much certainty as possible that Senate reform should go ahead. The discussion is a segregated one. But you've come back with a package. It would be destabilizing to accept this as a package deal. We've avoided package deals. Let's discuss this one by one. It would be unacceptable to put something on the table on a take-it-or-leave-it basis. We've operated successfully dealing with one issue at a time. I would look at some way of expressing the content of the text you have submitted. Clyde has put together language on the guts of the matter. We should be able to find a vehicle. Then we can deal with the Canada clause. Then we can talk about the future of Senate reform."

When I finished, Wells and Filmon chimed in again. Both said that Filmon would face a political problem at home without the Canada clause, drafted as they wanted.

Bourassa tried reasoning with them again but soon grew angry. I completely agreed with him at that moment.

"Almost all the experts say there is no danger to the Charter from the distinct society clause," he said. "Every day I attend this conference I'm discussing this simple, almost symbolic recognition of Quebec for what we are. What a situation when millions of Canadians are endangered by the few. I have had enough of fighting to be recognized for what we are. I have had enough of discussing legal niceties. My people discussed ten hours with you on these points."

David Peterson exploded with impatience. "We have just witnessed a decision that is irreversible," he shouted at the two holdout premiers. "Gary and Clyde, you two guys have sounded the fucking death knell of this country. Whether you have done it out of intellectual conviction or out of devotion to your law books doesn't much matter. Remember what was said. This is a fucking disgrace."

Then it was my turn.

"Everyone accepted the wording you had worked out on a very sensitive clause, Clyde, with regard to the distinct society," I said. "But so far as the Canada clause is concerned, this has bedevilled first ministers for a long time. We thought the way to handle it was to refer it to a parliamentary committee which would report to a First Ministers' Conference in the late autumn. I believed that you would take that brief to the Manitoba leaders on behalf of all first ministers. I shared your views on the wording of the distinct society/charter/powers clauses and I accepted your political judgment on the mechanisms for a Canada clause. I expected you to help Gary tell Carstairs and Doer to goddamn well get onside. If they signalled to Gary they could go along, it would be easier for him. Do you realize we're talking about Canada breaking up over a Canada clause? It was your substance, my mechanism. You and I were in agreement and we're still in agreement. Gary is the only one with a minority situation at home. Let's revisit all this. Let's assume we'll find something on Senate reform."

"I thought we had it resolved. David's outburst upsets me," Wells replied.

"We'll go back to where we were, and agreement on your language and my vehicle," I told him. "There are ten out of eleven who agree on the language."

"I don't want to see Gary isolated," Wells said.

"We're going to leave here with a deal, because if we don't they will remember us as a bunch of stubborn dolts," I told him. "Remember that *New York Times* editorial I quoted to you the other night? The need for trust? Gary Filmon is not going to bust up a country on the question where a Canada clause goes. God bless you, you went to the wall, Clyde. We've got problems not with Gary Filmon but with his two colleagues. If they had been here the last five days, they would understand what we are trying to achieve. I thank you, Clyde and Gary. You and Gary and I agree on the substance of the distinct society. I think we agree that a vehicle can be found.

"Do we resolve the question of the Canada clause by putting it atop the agenda for the next First Ministers' Conference?" I continued. "Canada has lived without a Canada clause for 123 years. Or do we break up on the question? We can't solve it tonight. Trudeau and the rest of them sat here for a day with their pens and pencils trying to draft a Canada clause during the 1982 exercise. No success. I believe we can be helpful to Gary, but I don't know how, just yet. I do know it would be preposterous for this country to break up on this. Imagine my four-year-old saying, 'Daddy, what happened to Canada?' and me replying, 'Well, Nicolas, we couldn't agree on the Canada clause.' I have no goddamn intention of saying that to my son." I was becoming heated. "This is a country in which I could come from an electrician's house in Baie-Comeau to 24 Sussex in one generation. We are a G-7 country. The prime minister of Canada sits at the same table with the U.S., the U.K., Germany, France, Japan, and Italy. We are not Libya. We are not Zimbabwe. Even the aboriginals don't want the Canada clause. Have you heard [native leader Georges] Erasmus's statement about this? You want a Canada clause to recognize multiculturalism. My wife came to this country as a child with her Yugoslav immigrant parents. As a result of the 1982 Constitution, Mila has more constitutional recognition than the people who belong to the French-speaking society of Quebec, which has been here for 350 years."

John Buchanan and Bill Vander Zalm shouted, "Hear, hear" in unison when I finished.

"Carstairs and Doer have put unfair pressure on Gary," I added. "The ten of us can find a solution that will keep you whole, that will keep you on top."

"I went to see them myself," Bourassa added. "I have had enough of trying to ask these people to recognize the status of the seven million people I represent. I won't be here to discuss the distinct society."

"Frank wants to speak," I said when Bourassa finished.

"No, you have said everything I could say and said it better," McKenna answered.

"I want to hear Gary," Bourassa announced.

"I went to meet the opposition leaders to put in the best light what we have been talking about here," Filmon replied. "Whatever we decide here has to go through my legislature. I put the case to them and asked for some latitude. The answer was that if there is no assurance on Charter protection, there is no deal. We went through the discussion with them and they're not prepared to agree."

"What was the flavour of the meeting?" I asked.

"Stubborn. Different degrees of stubbornness on different points," Filmon answered.

"This compromise was acceptable to me but Manitoba disagreed," Wells said. "I didn't insist."

"Why didn't you?" John Buchanan asked.

"The result of a failure will fall on Gary's head, not on Carstairs or Doer," Vander Zalm observed. "To have these two opposition leaders involved is ridiculous."

"If there is no support from them, the discussion is academic," Filmon replied.

"Then they'll wreck the country, not you," Peterson snapped.

"If this meeting adjourns and Quebec is not here when it reconvenes –" Joe Ghiz began before Robert Bourassa interjected.

"I cannot attend any more discussions on the distinct society," he said. "This is humiliating to my fellow citizens."

"If this conference breaks up, I'm walking out with Robert Bourassa," Ghiz continued.

"So am I," said McKenna.

"You talk about public opinion, Clyde," Ghiz said angrily. "Public opinion has been fuelled by anti-Meech statements, many of the most strident made by yourself. You have spoken all over the country. You're now of the view that there was an acceptable compromise between you and the prime minister. I give you full marks. I say you should stick with it. You'll do Gary Filmon a favour by isolating him. He'll come with his fellow first ministers because it's right for the country. Let Sharon Carstairs and Gary Doer defeat it. Let them take the responsibility. Gary Filmon will emerge as a great Canadian when he comes to the legislature with an agreement of eleven first ministers. Let those two bloody opposition leaders kill it. You talk about a Canada clause. A Canada clause is not worth the powder to blow it to hell. You talk about juridical equality, Clyde. I represent one hundred thousand people in Prince Edward Island and we are more equal than anyone and always will be. Don't tell me you need to put it in a Canada clause. Multiculturalism? I'm the son of an immigrant. He came in 1944 and peddled goddamn dry goods on his back, selling goddamn brushes from farm to farm, and his brother after him, and my grandfather before them. And you're telling me that I need protection? Here I am running for political office in the smallest 'c' conservative province in Canada. And I'm going to tell the people of Canada that someone wanted to break up a country for this stuff, for words, for legal and constitutional theories? Let's get on with it."

"I was here in 1981, now I'm astounded that the ghosts of the past are here with us, nine years later," an equally passionate John Buchanan said. "I signed a document in 1987 and I've never reneged on it. I will honour my signature. The people and legislature of Nova Scotia will honour it. If this meeting breaks up, I'm going out with Robert Bourassa and want the people of Quebec to know it."

"On Senate reform, I swallowed the veto for Quebec," Wells said as the tension in the room increased. "On the question of certainty of change to

Meech Lake, I swallowed it because the rest of you wanted to proceed on the basis of trust. I went to the meeting with Manitoba. My proposal was not acceptable to Manitoba. I come back here and always I run into a brick wall with Quebec. Nothing is possible. All I'm doing is accommodating and switching, yet David makes these accusations against me. And Joe, my friend of twenty years. I've tried honestly to find solutions. Yet I have to put up with these personal attacks. I've abandoned every damn principle I've every advocated. I still have my responsibility to Newfoundland, and I still have a greater responsibility to the nation. I've tried to accommodate. I've done it honestly. I have not done it in bad faith. I don't appreciate these accusations. I don't appreciate being shit upon in this way. Don't you ever have any doubt about my dedication to this country."

"People will say we created this thing, we couldn't fix it, we screwed it up," Don Getty replied. "We don't need to debate. Clyde doesn't need to answer Joe or Grant. We didn't answer you every time you made a speech."

"I didn't appreciate the personal attacks," Wells answered sulkily.

"Joe likes you. He is your friend," Getty continued. "But we're about to blow up this battered country. It will be unforgivable, it will be preposterous. The people of Canada will never forgive us. We have to focus on the ball, on how to win. There is a guy in Quebec, the separatist leader, hoping we'll unravel. I can't believe he can beat us."

"Ghiz is Clyde's best friend," I said. "I have developed a tremendous affection for all of you. Don Getty has shown such instinct and such sensitivity as I have never seen. We are the inheritors of a great nation. Yet there is a guy sitting in the Café de la Paix in Quebec with a cigarette in his mouth and a bottle of wine in front of him waiting for us to break up. I want to disappoint Parizeau."

At this point Wells appeared to be in danger of breaking down completely.

"I have no animosity to anyone," he sputtered. "My concerns are well known. I am concerned about the future of Canada as a federal state. I want a place for all of us and a very special place for Quebec especially. But I don't appreciate the comments of David and Joe. I have strong opinions but they are based on principles. I'm not rejecting Quebec. I *do* love Canada."

Grant Devine tried to appeal to Wells's considerable vanity. "Clyde, your influence is extremely significant," he said. "If the country learns you found a solution, the solution will sell. You have been very helpful. I've seen you bust your buns. I'm very grateful. You had a solution in your hands. How could we let it slip through our hands? You've brought us to the brink of solution. Now we're on the brink of breaking up."

I followed Devine's lead. "Did any of you see CBC-TV's *The Journal* last night?" I asked. "Bill Rowe from Newfoundland was saying that Wells has made a name here. His credibility in Newfoundland cuts across party lines. He has all the flexibility he'll ever want to come to an agreement here that will be supported in Newfoundland."

Don Getty poured it on. "Over four days I have developed a tremendous affection for Wells," he said. "I had watched him from a distance and thought him stubborn. I have seen him change, I have seen him working like hell. I didn't bring my lawyers with me. Most of what we are talking about has to do with the spirit of Canada. The country doesn't hold together by constitutions, courts, and government. It holds together because there is a national spirit. This is not a question of commas or legal theories. It is unbelievable, it is preposterous, it is unforgivable that this country that we love, for a couple of legal opinions and a couple of opposition leaders, we blow it. Our children would say you had a jewel of a country and you blew it. We sit around here because of a few Manitoba lawyers who say we're going to humiliate Quebec, we're going to force them to seriously consider separating from Canada. Bourassa will be finished, despite all the talent and devotion he brings to this country."

Mercifully we broke soon after. Bourassa, however, had had enough, and announced publicly that he would no longer allow his province to be humiliated.

This rattled Filmon. "Bourassa has put out a press statement saying he will not take part in any discussions on the distinct society," he said when we reconvened. "The meeting is falling apart. I have to decide whether there is any purpose in Manitoba participating. I'm tired. Again last night I didn't get my eight hours' sleep. I can't make the proper decision. I can't trust my judgment. I'm at the end of my rope. We're operating in an atmosphere of coercion. We're going nowhere. I can't go home with my head held high."

"I went to the maximum," Bourassa told him. "I met Sharon Carstairs and Gary Doer. Now in Quebec people are saying, 'Why does it take them so long to accept us?' I'm saying that when the distinct society is discussed I won't participate. We cannot contemplate any changes to the distinct society clause."

"I will try tomorrow to bring forward a piece of paper that could be ratified by everyone," I said. "We may not need a formal discussion on the distinct society. We will try to deal with it more simply. I had no more advice than any of you about Bourassa's press statement. We are all getting hit, but Bourassa has a particular problem. We've all tried. Today we didn't succeed."

"The Quebec media have it that I met Carstairs and Doer 'on my knees,'" Bourassa continued. "After four days, for Quebecers to hear we are discussing this is incredible. Now the country is at stake."

Peterson appealed for calm: "We have had a lot of tough discussion and there has been an awful letdown. Let's try to keep maximum flexibility tomorrow. Let's make sure we keep some level of civility and decency in the discussion."

"You're all on the wrong subjects," Getty added, shaking his head sadly. "The subject is Canada. It has been a bad day for Canada, a tough difficult day."

John Buchanan ended that day's formal talks where we – and the country – had begun. "I was here for the failure of 1982 and I don't want to be part of another failure," he said.

We agreed to meet again in the morning.

"This is not bargaining tactics," I told the group as we got under way on the morning of June 8. "I am trying to get back to where we were at three o'clock yesterday. The resolution of these two issues – the distinct society and the referral of the Canada clause – would allow a complete focus on one issue, the Senate."

Wells then spoke: "I share Gary's concern. I can't accept this process. I've swallowed one principle after another, but I don't want to be nickeled and dimed anymore. In my absence, part of the basis of our understanding – the Senate reform agreement – appears to be gone, or to have dissipated. I can't accept that. If the Senate proposal is watered down to any degree, I cannot go without a referendum, and depending on the content of the Senate proposal, I would have to recommend against the referendum. The process is wrong. If you have a package, let's look at it. I would sincerely attempt to persuade Sharon, if I can accept the proposal myself, and provided that Gary can accept it."

"There was no scuttling of the Senate proposal," Don Getty answered. "No one is stronger on Senate reform than I am. I have more riding on it than anyone. Clyde came back from his meeting saying he was faced not with two opposition leaders but with a united Manitoba. I thought we had a united group of first ministers."

"No, I never agreed to yesterday's proposal," Filmon objected. "I agreed to submit it to the opposition leaders."

"You'll get a 'yes' from Doer and a 'yes-but' from Carstairs," I said.

As the discussion continued, Filmon began to fall apart. Like a petulant teenager, he stood up and began packing his briefcase. "I'm leaving. I've had enough," he said.

"This is not a macho thing. Sit down!" Don Getty roared.

"Listen to what I'm saying," Filmon pleaded.

I simply couldn't believe what I was seeing and hearing. I looked Manitoba's premier directly in the eye. "If this craters, you're a dead man, Gary," I told him. "You're a hero for a time, but then you're dead. I recognize you have a burden none of us bears because of your minority position. I've put in language here what I'm told would be acceptable to Manitoba. Bring the other two leaders into this room. I'll leave, if you like. You can pin those two things on them."

"Put it all on the table," he replied. "The only thing that will get them to fish or cut bait is the total package. We've done it your way for six days, and it hasn't worked."

"Produce the total package and I'll do my best," Wells said.

"If this gets these two items off the table, we put them aside without prejudice," I interjected. "If we're talking about a total package, we will then have the question of the Senate to determine, and then we can judge the whole package. Meanwhile, nothing is agreed to until everything is agreed to. When you've moved to a final package, you can take the entire package to them before accepting it finally yourself."

"I object to them being part of any discussion," Bill Vander Zalm spoke up. "I object to the Constitution being decided by two opposition leaders. We've got to take the lead."

"I know what will fly on the distinct society," Filmon answered. "Clyde and I spoke to them."

"They'll endorse this," I said firmly.

"They won't," Filmon answered.

"Then they should say that to the premiers assembled," I continued.

David Peterson agreed: "This is an extremely critical moment. We agree on everything tentatively. Everyone has to have a proper comfort level.

Everyone has to go home with his dignity intact. Invite them in and tell them, 'Here is the deal we agreed on.'"

"Doer will say that in terms of vehicle he'll accept a joint legal opinion received by first ministers as a proper reflection of their understanding," I told Filmon. "Carstairs wanted something harder. But if Filmon and Doer were onside, Carstairs would join them."

"But *I'm* not onside," Clyde Wells announced. "I'm not going to facilitate approval of what I object to."

We then took a break. What I didn't know at the time, as I huddled with Lowell Murray and other senior members of my team, was that David Peterson was in a huddle of his own with some of the constitutional experts he had wisely assembled as part of his delegation; they would soon prove their worth.

When we reconvened I began by discussing Senate reform proposals.

"The Ghiz/Pickersgill 'kicker' was well received at this table," I said. "Bourassa took it under reserve. I know that Bourassa has had conversations in this room conveying his concerns to others."

"I've checked with our legal advisors," Bourassa said. "We have a legal opinion that Quebec has a right of veto on its proportion of senators. The proposal on the table would reduce our political weight. If we were a province like Ontario, we might be able to make that gesture to the smaller provinces, but as the only French-speaking province in Canada, we cannot agree to lessen our weight in a national institution like the Senate. Also, the Edmonton Declaration of 1986 made Senate reform a second-round issue. We could live with any formula that does not reduce our proportion. Vander Zalm came with a solution. People are fed up with the disgraceful Senate over the last two years. It is fraudulent, it is immoral, it has cost hundreds of millions of dollars to Quebec on Bill C-22. No province is more favourable to Senate reform. The Vander Zalm proposal would be acceptable to everyone. People are saying enough is enough."

"I thought the Vander Zalm proposal was dynamite," I observed.

"My proposal provides a kicker to vacate Senate seats where the incumbents had been appointed prior to 1987," the B.C. premier said. "This doesn't preclude us from achieving Senate reform prior to July 1993. Hopefully we would do so."

"Your proposal is not an ass-kicker. It's an ass-kisser," Wells objected. "There'd never be Senate reform. It's an inducement to keep things the way they are. There is no way in the world I'd ever accept it. I want an effective kicker to Senate reform."

"My proposal involved an undertaking on the part of all of us that Senate reform would become the key constitutional subject," Vander Zalm said. "No subject other than Senate reform could be discussed until Senate reform was achieved."

"But that would paralyze the process," Wells argued.

"We should consider Vander Zalm's proposal," I suggested.

"When I indicated a certain amount of approval for the Pickersgill/Ghiz proposal, I gave up the most sacred of my constitutional cows: my opposition to the Quebec veto or indeed to unanimity as elements in the amending formula for Senate reform," Wells replied. "I certainly could not accept anything less than the Pickersgill/Ghiz proposal. I'd have to put it to a referendum. I don't accept that Quebec has a right of veto now. I don't accept Robert's contention. If you're going to insist on maintaining Quebec's proportion of Senate seats, we might as well kiss Senate reform goodbye."

While it was almost a hopeless cause, Bourassa once again asked Wells to consider the unique position of Quebec in both North America and Canada.

"If we were an English province, I could go along with some of these ideas, but we are not," he said. "We are the only French-speaking society in North America."

"There are nine other provinces," Wells replied. "Some are on the receiving end of generosity from the rest of the country. They want the dignity and respect you want for the people of Quebec. There comes a time when I have to stand up for what is right. This is where I draw the line. Not only do I object, I could not recommend such a plan to the legislature and people of Newfoundland."

After another break, we resumed our discussions at three o'clock.

"We have had some creative proposals from Getty and Vander Zalm," I said. "We've reached agreement on some of the fundamentals. But we have come a cropper on the sweetener to ensure Senate reform will take place."

"I have talked about the double-majority proposal with six lawyers," Bourassa explained. "At first sight, it seems attractive, but how do you define culture? Most of the things that would come under this heading are provincial jurisdiction anyway. You are not suggesting that our double majority should extend to all legislation. I would be dropping our right of veto on the proportion of seats for a double-majority veto on legislation. That does not amount to very much."

"We came here worried about Meech Lake and its impact on the future of Senate reform," Wells replied. "I swallowed hard, and I would have to justify according that right of veto. That is why the Pickersgill/Ghiz kicker was put in. There is only so much to give."

"I have to live with the Edmonton Declaration," Bourassa said. "The Quebec round was to be completed, then we would move to Senate reform. I have used all kinds of words to try to explain that we are not working on Senate reform, we are working on an agenda, then we are working on parameters. But I can only go so far with this. With regard to our right of veto over our proportion of seats in the Senate, if you don't understand it, I can have one of our lawyers explain our position. If Meech Lake was as popular as it was three years ago in Quebec, I might be able to accept some of these suggestions. But Meech Lake is not popular. It's becoming a humiliation for Quebec."

"There is no magic in Senate reform," Grant Devine observed. "I'm willing to trash it. We're down to a political decision. I supported Meech Lake, I'll continue to support it. I have to give an edge to Clyde on this legal argument. Quebec will still have the veto under unanimity. We're that close. I appeal to Robert. If Clyde can sell this, we're out of here."

"I support Senate reform for the same reason I support Meech Lake," Peterson said. "I support Meech Lake because it gives substance to the cry from Quebec. I support Senate reform because it gives substance to the cry from the west. I'm diminishing my own power. But I want the guy in Saskatchewan or Newfoundland to have an equal place with dignity and self-respect. Our institutions have to shape and reflect that idea or federalism won't persevere."

"I'll stay there as long as necessary, but ultimately this comes down to trust," put in Frank McKenna. "We are scaring the bejesus out of people. They're down on their knees, praying."

"First ministers have done a tremendous job today under very difficult circumstances," I added by way of encouragement, a few minutes later. "We are not there yet, but we are getting there. It has been a very constructive day. I believe the future of Canada will be played out in Quebec in the next two and a half to three years. I don't believe Bourassa would call a referendum, which, as Chrétien said, would result in a vote in favour of sovereignty-association. You all deserve credit and patience for a good try. I am fifty-one years old, I was born in Quebec, my father is buried there, and I will probably be buried there." . . .

A short time later, Clyde Wells read aloud a letter from Eugene Forsey, the constitutional expert, who was now resigning from Newfoundland's delegation in opposition to Meech.

"I have heard your letter from Eugene Forsey and I've heard what he has been saying for many months now," I said. "But nobody knows that right after the Meech Lake conference, Forsey gave me advice contrary to what he is giving Clyde." I told the group that I had in my files a letter from Forsey celebrating the achievement of Meech. When Wells, who looked absolutely stunned by my statement, said he couldn't believe it, I told him to check with Forsey. (The next day Wells reported it was true and that Forsey asked him to thank me for not having made the letter public.)

Following a quick dinner, we assembled once again. I started by reading a draft communiqué that was based on previous arguments I'd heard around the table.

"I ask that you consider two questions: first, is there anything so offensive in this draft communiqué that it would be worth risking the breakup of the country?" I said. "Second, is there anything not in this communiqué that is so critical to achieve at this time that it is worth risking the breakup of the country?"

"I'm going to hold a press conference and inform the people where I stand," Wells replied stubbornly.

"I have asked you and I ask you again, you undertook that you would have no press conference this evening," I answered calmly but firmly.

"I agreed to put off an earlier press conference, but we have come to the time where I must report to the people," Wells announced.

"Newsworld said there was an agreement in principle," I continued. "I intend to tell them it's dicey. We cannot reach agreement tonight, so please put off your press conference. Please give Canada the benefit of a night's reflection. Don't take steps that might paint yourself into a corner."

"I made up my mind after that session yesterday," he replied. "I was going to call a press conference at 11 a.m. today. I deferred it at your request. I cannot mislead the people of Canada and Newfoundland any more. I have not been frank."

"I'm in exactly the same position," Filmon chimed in. "Here we have something labelled 'Final Communiqué.'"

"I will label it 'A Federal Proposal – Draft Communiqué,'" I said.

"I've been manipulated," Wells said, pouting. "I'm upset by this approach. I'll be here tomorrow morning; meanwhile I'll be letting the people know where I stand."

"Clyde and Gary, when are your press conferences?" I asked.

"I haven't scheduled it," Wells said.

"Then give Canada one night," I asked him. "We'll go public tomorrow and I'll call on you first to get your case out to the Canadian people."

"I've withheld it all day," he continued. "I'm having my press conference."

At that Joe Ghiz exploded in anger.

"The vengeance of the nation will be upon you," he told Wells, his voice rising. "You're wrecking this nation, sir."

"You will lose the nation, you will lose Senate reform, and you will save your vanity," Bourassa added, his eyes narrowing as he looked directly at Newfoundland's premier. "The prime minister is asking you for one single night for our country."

"What's wrong with that?" I asked Wells.

At this point David Peterson spoke up, making a gesture that will forever stand as an example of Canadian statesmanship and vision.

"So there are two matters of substance – the Senate and the distinct society," he said, facing Wells. "I will give you some Senate seats. Here is a proposal under which Newfoundland gets eight, P.E.I. four. New Brunswick, Nova Scotia, and Ontario give up Senate seats. Quebec keeps its twenty-four, Ontario goes down to eighteen, Manitoba, Saskatchewan, Alberta, and British Columbia go up to eight."

Wells was stunned by this generosity from the leader of Canada's largest province. "I can't help but be moved," he said. "I just think it's terrific. I can only be impressed with your devotion. What will that do for the Senate reform? Unanimity will still be there."

"This is not the biggest win for me," Peterson told us later in the meeting. "It's coming out of my hide. There is only one fucking thing I can say. I can't say it's in Ontario's interest. I can say it's in the nation's interest."

"I'll give up the seats for Nova Scotia," Buchanan added.

"I will do so for New Brunswick," McKenna said. "Give us five years with the present seat distribution to try to work out real Senate reform."

With that, we had the makings of a generous agreement that would benefit Canada in the long run. While a great deal of fine tuning had to be made overnight, I left the Conference Centre pleased at what we'd accomplished and much more confident of my nation's future.

(The subsequent train of events is picked up in the chapter entitled "The Shadows of Ghosts.")

Appendix B

Arriving at the Charlottetown Accord
(Notes of the Meeting at Harrington Lake, August 4, 1992)

This account is based on extensive notes of the discussions, taken by both Joe Clark and myself.

Those in attendance were:

Prime Minister:	Brian Mulroney
Minister for Constitutional Affairs	Joe Clark
Premiers:	Robert Bourassa, Quebec
	Donald Cameron, Nova Scotia
	Gary Filmon, Manitoba
	Don Getty, Alberta
	Joe Ghiz, Prince Edward Island
	Mike Harcourt, British Columbia
	Frank McKenna, New Brunswick
	Bob Rae, Ontario
	Roy Romanow, Saskatchewan
	Clyde Wells, Newfoundland

"Prime Minister, you're in a very difficult situation," Ghiz said, speaking out. "We have to be careful to avoid the mistake of isolating one province. When we reached the end of the process, on July 7, my impression was that Quebec was fully informed. I supported, on the basis that that package had substantial support from the government of Quebec. It was reported to us that Premier Bourassa could live with the Senate and the aboriginals. If elements of July 7 now turn out to be unacceptable, we should be able to review and revise them, to make them acceptable. It's not right to say that compromises are already made, and that no further compromises are permissible."

Ghiz said he felt the mistake at Meech had been treating the agreement as a "seamless web" and that this should not be repeated in 1992. "On the Senate," he continued, "I personally favoured its abolition, first; secondly, an equitable Senate. But I'm ready to go to a triple-E Senate if Bourassa can live with it. Otherwise, I will not be party to isolating Quebec again." (In my notes I underlined that sentence of Ghiz's, which he had delivered passionately.)

And then Bourassa began his presentation. The group hung on his every word.

"It's a moment of great joy to be here and to be back discussing important matters among ourselves," he said. "It was not an easy decision I faced two years ago, to avoid further conferences, but I had to do something. We had sung 'O Canada' with tears in our eyes – and then Meech wasn't ratified. I've known political violence before. One of my cabinet ministers was assassinated; I had to take action, to keep control of the situation in Quebec. From 1982 to 1990, Quebec was left aside and some are saying that this meeting (July 7) is a third strike."

Bob Rae angrily interjected at this point, telling Bourassa that July 7 had not been a rejection of Quebec.

"I don't agree with that," Bourassa said. "It is interesting to note that no one, five years later, has been able to come forward with a mistake in Meech Lake. Breaking up Canada would be, as Talleyrand said, 'more than a crime, it would be a mistake.'

"I have met, bilaterally, often, to compensate for my absence from the multilateral process," he continued. "Having an agreement was important for you, politically. I told Joe Clark that there is no way the aboriginal issue is acceptable to us, that courts could adjudicate on the territorial integrity of Quebec. We were for an equitable Senate. We could look at dimensions of 'equal'. . . On July 7, the Clerk of my council called a close advisor to Bob Rae to say, 'An equal Senate is unacceptable.' When Joe Clark called me, on Friday, I was quite clear that I couldn't accept anything because I hadn't consulted with my cabinet, caucus, et cetera. That's the past. The question is what do we do now? The reaction to the July 7 agreement in Quebec was aggressively negative (particularly due to the triple-E Senate) . . . Part of the reason why Canada is distinct from the U.S. is linguistic duality. This would no longer be applicable. With such a reduction in the Senate, the proportion of francophones would be extraordinarily reduced, bilingualism would be lost with only a handful of French-speaking senators, which goes against history and the very idea of a bilingual Canada."

As it had stood since 1867, there had at all times been a minimum of thirty French-speaking senators in the Red Chamber. What could happen under triple-E, he argued, would be that if Quebec respected its English-speaking minority – as the province would – there would probably only be eight French-speaking senators elected from Quebec, along with two English-speaking ones. There was also the chance that no French-speaking senators would be elected in the rest of the country. Bourassa expressed the view that this situation would run counter to the fundamental building blocks of Canada. "This is a gold mine for Parizeau," he said.

Bourassa then noted that Quebec had an existing right of veto on the basis of the twenty-four Senate seats that now existed. In making this point, he cited a legal opinion from former Ontario attorney general Ian Scott. This greatly annoyed Bob Rae, and he immediately cut in, wondering aloud how appropriate it was for an opposition MPP to be providing advice to another province's premier!

But Bourassa concluded this part of his remarks the following way: "I'm very conscious that it will be very difficult to change what was signed by the English-speaking provinces and Mr. Clark, and I am very concerned by this dilemma we must now confront."

Bourassa then turned to the aboriginal issue. "It is completely unacceptable because it challenges the territorial integrity of the province of Quebec, and it will never, ever fly. We must find something in the nature of a political accord because the amputation of our territory could begin under the July 7 agreement, and I, as premier of Quebec, will never sign it – nor would any other premier."

"Our concern is with the power of the courts?" I asked.

Bourassa said yes, adding he believed that "there would be an exceedingly high risk to social peace [in Quebec]" if aboriginals were told they had lost the provisions that had been agreed upon on July 7.

I persisted, asking Bourassa to say clearly where he believed Quebec's territory would be affected by changes to the Constitution involving aboriginal peoples. Bourassa replied that he was concerned about the James Bay hydro-electric project being reopened as a result. He argued the changes would be an "imputation of ownership" by aboriginals.

Bob Rae spoke next. "The critical point," he said, "is that there is no point in recriminations. We're here fundamentally because the Quebec referendum requires us to be here. That is why Ontario is here talking about the

Constitution and not NAFTA. We could make life difficult for one another, but it's much better that we come out of this meeting committed to meet again, and that there can be no national agreement without the Government of Quebec. This is impossible to do in the absence of Quebec. We must take what's been said into account, respect the spirit, tenor, and the framework of the July 7 agreement, but it is now in limbo, and will be, for some time. July 7 must be seen as a basis from which we move. It is not an ironclad agreement. I suggest that we meet one day a week for the next three weeks, because we can't do this without Quebec. They must be present."

Alberta's Don Getty was gentlemanly and even-handed, but tough. "Robert Bourassa mentioned the July 7 agreement," he said. "He understands the need for face-saving. What he has to consider is a huge welling up of anger in western Canada."

He then turned dramatically and addressed Quebec's premier directly.

"What do you think we were doing, for five months, Robert, as we negotiated, which led to the July 7 agreement with the English-speaking provinces and Mr. Clark?" he asked.

Bourassa joked and again raised the opinion he had received from Ian Scott. "I hide all the legal opinions I receive that say the distinct society constitutes special status," he said.

Getty wasn't laughing. He said that arguments that an equal Senate were unpopular were not impressive, "because I have never heard the damn thing being sold" in Bourassa's province. "We may want to change a transferable vote or something," he concluded, but not the "elements or principles" of the July 7 deal.

Bourassa got the point. He said seriously that he totally understood his Alberta colleague's point about anger and agreed that it involved the credibility of all politicians around the table. There was nobody, however, who could demonstrate a tangible change were the distinct society to be in the Constitution. The July 7 proposals for aboriginals and an equal Senate, in contrast, were very tangible. "They create another order of government; they create another House of Commons," he said. "Let's compare apples to apples."

Donald Cameron of Nova Scotia entered the discussion to note that Bourassa wasn't the only premier absent from the process until now. "Only Rae, Ghiz, and I were there, all along," he said forcefully. "At Meech, there was a signed deal. On July 7 I signed nothing and I didn't shake anyone's hand saying, 'We have a deal.' I have very serious concerns about the proper proposal for the Senate. My concern is what we're being asked to give up. Alberta is fine; it has no sales tax; it has the lowest personal income tax in Canada and is extraordinarily wealthy. In Ontario, Bob, you think you have an economic crisis? Let's talk about unemployment in Nova Scotia. We've had the equivalent of those recession numbers for almost ten years. I indicated that Nova Scotia would not agree to an amended Senate, nor accept less seats in the Senate. I don't like proportional representation. I pleaded that the provinces should decide the issue of gender equality. On the aboriginal question, Nova Scotia was concerned about the wording of this. The aboriginal file is being driven by guilt and intimidation and nothing more. Any time [Nova Scotia raised it, we were] attacked and told we were bigots. If federal and provincial powers are defined and limited in the Constitution, so too must aboriginal authority. I think Joe Clark did an exceptional job, in spite of all this – a sentiment, I must report, that was shared by other premiers."

A chipper Clyde Wells then addressed the group. "The table is complete again with Robert Bourassa back," he said. "It is impossible for us to deal with things without Quebec. With regard to the Senate, our objective is to put some balance into national decision making, as in the United States. I understand the concerns on proportional representation, the transferable vote, and I am ready to revisit that. On the aboriginals, I share Quebec's views and have held these views throughout. We've got ourselves into a bind because of a sense of guilt. We can make adjustments in this, so if the courts decide, six years from now and say, 'Here's what it should be on the aboriginals, the inherent right to self-government must be tied to a land area,' I don't have a closed mind on anything before us. I have strong views, but not a closed mind."

Gary Filmon followed. First he addressed Bourassa.

"We can only accomplish what must be accomplished with you here," he said. "Probably the only way to keep control of the agenda was to do the dramatic things that you did. We were shooting for the target – the subject of Meech-plus. The weaknesses of Meech were: it was too narrow in its definition of fundamental characteristics, and too narrow in what it sought to achieve in constitutional change. I'm committed to the [July 7] agreement, even though I didn't sign it."

"What about the agreement, Meech Lake, you did sign?" I wrote to myself, as Filmon spoke.

Filmon said he felt the deal addressed the weaknesses in Meech Lake, going on to note that 70 per cent of Manitobans were against distinct society, "but I keep it in there, because the package must satisfy everybody. We don't want to break the country apart."

I posed this question to Filmon: "If Robert Bourassa tells you, 'Gary, I can't sell this in Quebec, in a referendum, and the Canadian option will lose,' would you still resist change in the package?"

Filmon mumbled a non-answer, saying he didn't know what specific matters I had raised.

"Is the concept of equality sacrosanct?" I asked Filmon.

Bob Rae answered instead, arguing that if the principle of equality is triple-E, then it is not necessarily sacrosanct. "How do we work out the chemistry between equal and equitable?" Rae asked. "We have tried that before . . . Why not try again with Robert at the table?"

Wells said that there was no way his province could agree to unanimity on Senate reform in the future, unless there was an equal Senate.

Roy Romanow was very practical. "It's not easy to leave here, and simply say that we've agreed to meet again," he said. "To do what? The process followed outside Quebec has some credibility, an 'offer' has been made, and we were on television saying the offer was doable. And this now causes us difficulty. I see room for change and negotiation on the July 7 package . . . I'm prepared to look at the Senate and the method of selection. Do we consider a division of powers? If so, which ones? The time frame to do a lot of this is too tight, but we need some time, particularly today, to find out where our ongoing discussions will lead us. We reached a plateau on July 7 and we must use this for the future. I'm with Clyde Wells on this one. I have an open mind on the subject."

Frank McKenna weighed in. "No one could seriously say that July 7 was the end of the road and the end of our work. We should agree on a process, today, to find acceptable solutions so that we can go on living as Canadians."

Mike Harcourt pointed out there would soon be a referendum in British Columbia, as well. Both distinct society and aboriginal self-government had to be defined to get any package accepted by his electorate, he said. "Where do we go from here?" he asked. "We use July 7 as a framework to work from. The aboriginal matter must be more clearly defined, or it's not going to pass in British Columbia. Ovide Mercredi was told this by me, directly. A triple-E Senate? Our preference is for the third option. The options are: number one, abolition; number two, equitable; and number three, equal. In other words, that would be their least favourite option. We prefer abolition. We must find a way for you and Robert Bourassa to put your stamp on this."

I agreed with Harcourt's last point and noted that the separatist elite in Quebec was against everything we did. "You can't have a referendum in Quebec that is a smokescreen," I said, "because Canadians would insist on the question actually being about separation."

That said, I switched to the concept of an equal Senate. "The people against it include Jean Chrétien, Paul Martin Jr., Claude Castonguay, Lysiane Gagnon, Alain Dubuc, Solange Chaput-Rolland, Claude Ryan, Ghislain Dufour, all of them leading French-Canadian federalists," I said. I told the group about a recent meeting I had had with twenty-five people in Roberval, Quebec, all of whom wanted to keep Canada together. "'Even Chrétien is against the equal Senate,'" they told me. "It clearly is a tough sell, probably a fatal sell," I added.

Filmon cut in and said that selling an equal Senate in Quebec couldn't be any more difficult than selling the distinct society in Manitoba.

Before I could answer, Bob Rae, mercifully, brought that part of the meeting to a close. "We have to sell different things in different parts of the country," he said. "There are elements of any deal that are hard to swallow."

After a break, I restarted the discussions with some frank talk for Robert Bourassa. Many governments represented around this table, I said, believed Quebec had encouraged others to believe an equal Senate was doable in Quebec. "You are the one going to the abattoir," I said. "We need to know if it is a tough sell or no sell. If it is a tough sell, we can look at modalities."

"My challenge is more like war, not an abattoir," Bourassa replied.

I turned to him again.

"Robert, I'm going to ask you, in front of everybody, can you sell a triple-E Senate?" I asked.

"No," he said simply. "My people would consider me eligible for a mental institution if I tried to do that." He stressed that every member of his caucus and cabinet were federalists, and not one had told him they would fight for a triple-E Senate.

Joe Clark then spoke up, at my invitation. All eyes turned to the other end of the table where the former prime minister was sitting. "Unless we have a sufficiently broad agreement on the Senate, there's no need for a further meeting," he said.

Bourassa told us he needed any deal to expressly show confirmation of provincial jurisdiction in areas like health and education, in order for him to be able to sell it to Quebecers.

Don Getty exploded at this. If Quebec gets the powers it says it needs, as well as distinct society, he told Bourassa, "There is no bloody way we can turn around on the equal Senate. Can't you sell one damn thing for the rest of Canada? This is as big for us as the distinct society is for you."

Calmly and rationally, Bourassa explained that the Senate is a central institution. "The prime minister asked me if I could sell [an equal Senate] in a war? The answer is no." (He later called the ratification of the Charlottetown Accord a "war for Canada.")

As the discussion continued, Filmon pressed Bourassa. He asked that if Quebec's premier couldn't sell a triple-E Senate in the time remaining before Quebec's referendum, could he instead sell a reformed Senate that wasn't triple-E, without a veto?

I urged Bourassa to answer the question. Shrugging, he said it was probably easier for him to sell equitable than it would be to sell equal. Without a veto for Quebec, he continued, everything would depend on what powers were devolved to his province. Not having the veto, however, meant that the proposal was less than Meech, he added.

Getty warned that no first minister should misjudge the anger that would well up among Canadians if a triple-E Senate was no longer on the table.

"Where is that anger?" Frank McKenna responded, telling us he hadn't detected any in his own province over the issue.

Romanow warned that anger would arise because citizens of the nine English provinces would see Quebec as having rejected the July 7 agreement.

The atmosphere grew even more tense as the discussion moved into the evening. Bob Rae was frustrated. He asked all of us to consider the actual powers we were talking about. "Everyone is talking about the same kind of a Senate, but we are calling it different names," he said. "A constitution should not fail for that reason. We can't be seen to fail, but if we do, what is the alternative?"

I was equally frustrated but did my best not to show it. I then told the first ministers what I'd write if I were an objective journalist reporting on the meeting. "In a morning," I said, "we could tighten up the aboriginal package." On division of powers, the prime minister could, "by and large," live with what was proposed, as Premier Bourassa hadn't arrived at

Harrington Lake with outrageous demands. "He is not asking to run our foreign policy," I said.

This led to one of the very few humorous moments of the day. Upon hearing what I'd said about Quebec and foreign policy, Roy Romanow jumped in.

"No," he said, "Saskatchewan is."

Don Getty admitted the real challenge now was to protect linguistic duality in a possible package. "If there is a way to do that and keep the principle of equal, then do it," he said.

"I will think about that," I answered, before bringing us back to what we really faced. "If you are going to have a formal First Ministers' Conference, we would need to emerge with a federalist option that can be presented to Quebec, or with some basis that would allow Quebec to roll over the referendum . . . The only thing we know for sure is that only one premier here is going to war."

"Quebec is going to get what it needs," a passionate Bob Rae answered.

I then reminded the group that I had appointed Alberta's Stan Waters to the Senate – after he was elected by Alberta voters – after the Meech Lake Accord failed. "That indicates good faith," I said. "We are right up against it: without a solution, we lose; with a solution, we win. Can we get together and produce something saleable? I think we can. But if you think we can't, tell me now."

"I'm not optimistic," Don Getty said.

I had put to the premiers the following five points that I had jotted down in my notes during the marathon discussions. In order to have a formal First Ministers' Conference: 1) all premiers must be present; 2) all must agree, today, that there's enough flexibility for us to try to get a deal; 3) the substance of Meech Lake must not be reopened; 4) no new issues must be brought to the table at this time; and 5) a specific time frame for meetings must be agreed upon by Friday of this week.

With some grumbling, we all agreed. Battered and bruised as we were, we agreed to meet again on August 10, in formal session.

(The subsequent train of events is picked up in the chapter entitled "The Guns of August.")

Notes

Part I: Chapter 2: Growing Up in Baie-Comeau

page 17. *"It was a mad race over unpaved roads"*
In 1958 I wrote a letter to the editor of the Halifax *Chronicle-Herald* describing the state of the roads on the North Shore: "As a provincial government project, not a penny of federal funds has been expended on it. As for its pavement: dust rising from streets in Seven Islands, Baie-Comeau and even the twenty-year-old Quebec City–Baie-Comeau highway would gladden the heart of any producer of western films, so banish the thought that asphalt is soon to be laid on the new route . . . This very important sector of Quebec is paying its own way."

page 18. *"But most of our time was spent at the Mulroney family home"*
As a primary school student, I described my early farming experiences. "Last year I spent my vacation on my uncle's farm on the outskirts of the city of Quebec," I wrote for the school newsletter in grade 5. "There were many interesting things to see and to learn on the farm. Before the end of the summer I had learned how to milk a cow, which is something, and to do the chores too, but that was like doing nothing for me! Besides this, I had loads of fun swimming in the river that flows in back of the farmhouse. My uncle said that when he first took this farm it was all bush, but because it looked like good farming country, he got to work and cleared out a good deal of the brush and built his farm. He has ever since been improving the soil making it a very prosperous farm. I think life on the farm is very interesting. How about you?"

page 18. *"As part of a school project, I kept a daily diary"*
My childhood diary lasts only from September until December 1947, and I produced about 3,500 words. While I have kept notes throughout my life, it was not until 1984, when I was leader of the opposition and then prime minister, that I was to try my hand at sustained journal writing again.

Part I: Chapter 4: The Making of a Young Tory

page 40. *"Now, as the Secretary of State for Canada, the Honourable Mrs. Fairclough"*
I never forgot Ellen Fairclough and the trail-blazing example she set. As part of Canada 125 celebrations in 1992, I arranged for her to be granted the honorific "Right Honourable" to recognize her contributions to Canada.

page 41. *"On the 17th I will have been prime minister for five years . . . indifference in Pearson"*
Mr. Pearson officially left office on April 20, 1968, only two days before the fifth anniversary of his assuming the prime ministership. When the House assembled on April 23, MPs expected that the new prime minister, Mr. Trudeau, would allow Pearson's colleagues to pay tribute to the former prime minister that day. Trudeau had different plans, having received approval from the governor general to dissolve Parliament earlier in the day, thereby denying MPs the chance to praise Pearson. This didn't bother Pearson in the least. In his memoirs, Pearson wrote, "Stanley Knowles later complained that Trudeau had not allowed the House to pay me a deserved tribute. I noted in my last prime ministerial diary, 'Tough.'" One suspects the Chief might have had a different reaction.

page 44. *"Ace McCann (later mayor of Pembroke, Ontario)"*
Ace and I remain close friends. In fact, one of the first interviews I gave to a Canadian newspaper after I left 24 Sussex Drive was to the mighty *Pembroke Daily Observer*. The Pembroke paper was trying to get a reaction to the 1994 announcement by Mayor McCann that he wouldn't be seeking re-election as mayor in that fall's municipal race. A persistent reporter from the *Daily Observer* named Milnes kept leaving messages about Ace at Ogilvy Renault, until I finally gave in and called him back. Almost ten years later Arthur Milnes started working for me as my research assistant on these memoirs. "Mulroney Praises Pembroke Ace" was published in the paper on September 9, 1994.

page 44. *"In November of 1958 I attended . . . the McGill Council on World Affairs"*
Students never change. "Was in Montreal last week for the McGill World Affairs Conference," I told Pat MacAdam in a letter afterwards. "The conference, of course, was very 'educational' – that's usually a convenient adjective – but the nightlife was superb. Lowell and I went out to a few clubs and had one hell of a good time."

page 51. *"'For the record, of course I would be interested in taking her place, in case anyone asks you!'"*
A similar letter arrived after the death of Senator Richard Hatfield in 1991. Unlike Pat Carney, my correspondent wasn't a politician. "As a native New Brunswicker, I like all Canadians mourn the death of [Hatfield]," it read. "With his untimely death, a void has been created in the Senate of Canada. To fulfill this vacancy I would like to be considered for the appointment of Senator . . . Your thoughtfulness and consideration of this request would be greatly appreciated." Some people believe that it is always easy for a prime minister to get people to accept senior appointments. In fact, Bob Stanfield declined my offer to be our ambassador to the United Nations, and Douglas Bassett, a highly successful president of CTV, declined an equally important diplomatic assignment.

Part II: Chapter 1: Université Laval

page 61. *"In 1964 I definitely landed myself in the soup"*
I can't claim I hadn't been warned about appearing to criticize the monarchy or Canada's ties to Great Britain back then. "I regret to read of your hopes that Canada would one day be without 'this tremendous tie to England,'" Dalton Camp wrote to me in a March 1961 letter after I had appeared in *Maclean's*. "If you mean what I think you do, then I cannot possibly support your candidacy for the office of prime minister."

page 62. *"Her Majesty is always well briefed"*
The Queen's love for, and pride in, Canada and Canadians is something she never hid. "I was particularly struck by the words used by Premier Bourassa when he said he signed the [Meech Lake] Accord 'with great pride as a Canadian' and referred to Canada as 'one of the greatest countries of the world,'" she said in Quebec City in October 1987.

Part II: Chapter 2: Ottawa Interlude

page 72. *"With a personal library in excess of eight thousand volumes"*
Upon my election as PC leader in June 1983, Roy Faibish allowed me to become a member of a select club, those who could borrow books freely from his library. "Dief and P.E.T. occasionally used the library," he wrote to me on June 28. "You are most welcome."

Part II: Chapter 3: Legal Hurdles

page 88. *"Mila was privileged to be given a tour of the Diefenbaker Canada Centre"*
The Centre unfortunately had a shaky financial future, which came to my attention during my first mandate. In late 1987 I told John Turner, another fan of John Diefenbaker, that my government would be providing almost $800,000 over a two-and-a-half-year period. "I share your views on the importance of keeping the Diefenbaker Centre open," I wrote to Turner on November 23, 1987. "It is both a tribute to a great prime minister and a contribution to Canadian history." The Centre is still going strong today, and the efficient and courteous staff provided much assistance as I was researching these memoirs.

page 90. *"In any case, on a personal level he and President Kennedy did not enjoy one another's company"*
Knowlton Nash's *Kennedy and Diefenbaker; Fear and Loathing Across the Undefended Border* quotes Bobby Kennedy on his brother's relationship with Canada's thirteenth prime minister: "My brother really hated John Diefenbaker. In fact, my brother really hated only two men in all his presidency. One was Sukarno [dictator of Indonesia], and the other was Diefenbaker."

page 92. *"He also toyed with the idea of supporting the NDP . . . Trudeau in 1968"*
"At least two men were not surprised by the abrupt manner in which Mr. Bouchard broke with the PQ," Lysiane Gagnon wrote in March 2001. "One is Brian Mulroney . . . Another one is a former federal Liberal party executive, who recently told me a little-known story. In the weeks before the 1968 election, Mr. Bouchard, then a successful lawyer in Chicoutimi, agreed to run as the local Liberal candidate. Two days before the nomination period closed, he backed off, leaving the Liberals with no time to find a replacement. Mr. Bouchard had realized that the Social Credit candidate was stronger than expected, and he didn't want to risk losing the election. Another year [2001], same story."

Part II: Chapter 6: Politics and Strikes

page 113. *"Early on in the campaign, I was there as George Hees agreed to return to the party fold"*
Almost twenty years later, George, who had sat in caucus with every Tory leader from Drew to Clark before my arrival, gave me excellent advice on caucus relations in a memo sent directly after I was elected PC leader in

June 1983. "It will be obvious to the lower two-thirds of the caucus that you cannot promise anything to anyone, because there are simply not enough places to go around," he wrote. "However, I am firmly convinced that by following a certain plan, you can let the members in the lower two-thirds . . . know that you are aware of their work and appreciate it when it is good . . . The plan would be: 1) Pick out one of your very able assistants, and have him or her go over the Hansard Index each day to see which members in the lower two-thirds . . . asked a question or made a speech the day before. 2) Pick out a good point that was made, and dictate a short paragraph to the MP such as: 'Dear [first name] I thought the point you made in your question [speech] yesterday . . . was a good one. What you said about . . . was particularly effective. Keep it up. Brian.' . . . These notes will convince members of . . . caucus that what they do is noticed and appreciated, and that they have a chance of realizing whatever ambition they have . . . if they keep working effectively." George, who was well aware of what happened internally in the party to a generation of leaders who didn't make such small gestures, was right. I followed his advice faithfully.

page 114. *"On election day in 1965, the PCs were once again losers"*
In fact, Eddie Goodman, Flora MacDonald, and other strategists at party headquarters jokingly planned to link arms and jump from the roof of the Château Laurier as penance in the event of Diefenbaker's return to power. "They wrote some make-believe campaign slogans," the journalist Geoffrey Stevens later wrote. "Someone – MacDonald thought it was Brian Mulroney; Goodman said it was [James] Johnston – came up with the unanimous winner: 'Let's give the old bugger another chance.'" I can't honestly remember, but for what it's worth today, that slogan has Lowell Murray written all over it.

Part II: Chapter 7: Trudeau's October

page 131. *"My law practice continued to grow"*
It wasn't all work, as I was reminded when examining my files from the period in Library and Archives Canada. "Greetings," I wrote in a postcard I sent from Europe to my colleagues in the firm's labour department during that period. "It's been sheer drudgery. Visits to museums, churches, and other historic sites and nothing but work, work, work all the time. Regards. MBM."

Part II: Chapter 8: Mila

page 137. *"After some reticence, given my age, Dimitri and Boba welcomed me into their lives"*
I had one very direct conversation during those days with Boba, which she later recounted for Mila's biographer, Sally Armstrong. "One day Brian came to me and asked, 'What is it you don't like about me? I have a good profession. I come from a good family. I have a good job.' I said, 'It's your age. She's very young. I want her to finish school.' He raised his voice and said, 'Boba . . . I never met anyone like Mila. Whether you like it or not, I'll be around her for 40 years.' He won me over." Mila and I celebrated our thirty-fourth wedding anniversary last May.

Part II: Chapter 9: Tricksters, Crooks, and Scum

In this chapter I have relied heavily on a speech about the Cliche Commission that I gave to the Empire Club in Toronto in October 1975.

Part III: Chapter 1: "Politics Ain't Beanbag"

page 159. *"The media's idea that this was a band of wealthy Montrealers"*
In fact, a future chairman of Metro Toronto, Paul Godfrey, was one of my earliest supporters in 1976. I always valued his friendship and advice.

pages 167–68. *"I turned out to be his target and John Diefenbaker didn't miss"*
Sitting in the stands that night I understood the full meaning of CCF MP Colin Cameron's comments, made after witnessing Dief's famous evisceration of Mike Pearson in the Commons in early 1958, when the new Liberal leader, in his maiden speech, said John Diefenbaker should resign and turn the reins of office over to Pearson. "When I saw him bring whole batteries of rhetoric, whole arsenals of guided missiles of vitriol and invective in order to shoot one forlorn sitting duck – a sitting duck, indeed, already crippled with a self-inflicted wound – I wondered if the prime minister really believes in the humane slaughter of animals."

page 168. *"Years later, writing in his memoirs . . . Sean O'Sullivan discussed"*
Just to show that notions of forgiveness are never far from my soul, as prime minister I later took part in the opening ceremonies of the Father Sean O'Sullivan Room in the East Block on Parliament Hill, a small sanctuary where parliamentarians can meditate and reflect.

Part III: Chapter 2: Life at the Iron Ore Company of Canada

In writing this chapter I have relied heavily on Alexander "Sandy" Ross's September 1982 *Canadian Business* profile, "The Tories' Turnaround Artist: Could closet Tory candidate Brian Mulroney run the country like he runs Iron Ore Co.? The country should be so lucky."

page 189. *"After you caught your first salmon"*
John Rae is a student of political history himself: for example, he sent me a copy of Robert Caro's latest volume on the life and times of Lyndon Johnson when I was ill in 2005. John, therefore, was well aware of the proclivity many prime ministers have shown for fishing. The day after John Diefenbaker's historic victory over the Liberals in June 1957, he retreated for a day of fishing on a Saskatchewan lake. "Not much of a fish you caught there, eh?" one of his companions joked at the end of the day. "No," Dief answered, grinning, "I caught the big one yesterday." While I didn't go fishing on September 5, 1984, I knew exactly what Dief had meant on that afternoon nearly thirty years earlier.

Part III: Chapter 3: No Discipline, No Power

page 194. *"Laurier described as skills in the 'supreme art of governing men'"*
Sir Wilfrid Laurier, in what I consider one of the greatest speeches ever given in the House of Commons, used the phrase on June 8, 1891 while delivering his famous eulogy in honour of Sir John A. Macdonald, who had died at Earnscliffe two days previously. I first read this Laurier speech while researching my undergraduate thesis at StFX in 1958–59.

Part III: Chapter 5: The 1983 Leadership Campaign

page 225. *"Shouts of 'Where's Mila?' were aimed my way at each event"*
In 1987 I received a glowing fan letter from a student in Ontario. "From here on in, I will tailor my career to mirror yours," he said, adding that he wanted to become a labour lawyer, enter business, then lead the PC Party, and become prime minister. "All I need now to help me be more like you is a girlfriend as beautiful as Mila. I'll keep trying but I haven't had much luck."

page 227. *"While Mila was my key asset"*
Other key supporters included Fred Doucet and Stewart McInnes in Nova Scotia; Jacques Blanchard, Desmond Hallissey, and Gary Ouellett in Quebec; and Allan Scales and Leo Walsh in P.E.I.

Part IV: Chapter 2: Exit Trudeau, Enter Turner

page 285. *"Mila's no slouch herself"*
She became an expert stump speaker, displaying her wit and humour from the platform when the occasion called for it. "It never dawned on me when I accepted [a speaking invitation to the Gatineau Hills Gentlemen's Club] that there would be so many people in Ottawa interested in leadership review," Mila said to roars of laughter shortly before I announced my resignation plans in February 1993. "I don't know what *he's* doing, but I'm here tonight to tell you: I'm staying."

page 293. *"Chrétien later recounted the call in his own book"*
"Then I received a call from Brian Mulroney, offering sympathy and saying that he had a new poll in his hands," Chrétien wrote in *Straight from the Heart*, published in 1985. "'Jean, you lost,'" he said, 'but I know that I will be the next prime minister. According to my polls, if you had been leader, I would win six seats at best in Quebec, but with Turner, I'll win 26 seats at least.' 'You're bragging Brian,' I said. But it has since been established that he was not."

Part IV: Chapter 4: Transition to Power

page 313. *"The secretary of cabinet will be available to brief you"*
While a firm advocate for peace, I was well aware of Canada's responsibilities as a member of NATO and NORAD during the Cold War, terrifying as the possibilities were. "For better or worse, nuclear weapons are a fact of life," I wrote Liberal MP Warren Allmand in 1986 after he said Canada should follow New Zealand's lead and ban NATO ships with nuclear weapons on board from entering Canadian waters. "They cannot be dis-invented. Our partnership with our European and American allies is based on a recognition of this fundamental reality. As long as the Soviet Union continues to possess nuclear weapons, it would be irresponsible for the Alliance as a whole to renounce their own capability."

Part V, 1985 Chapter 1: The Shamrock Summit and Beyond

page 363. *"Summarizing our meeting, I wrote to Gorbachev before the month ended"* I shared my positive impressions with President Reagan in the days and months ahead, as he later noted in his memoirs: "As we shook hands for the first time, I had to admit – as Margaret Thatcher and Prime Minister Brian Mulroney predicted I would – that there was something in his face and his style, not the coldness bordering on hatred I'd seen in most senior Soviet officials I'd met until then."

page 365. *"as the father of Canadian children who would join their generation"* Two years later, a young student reminded me there were possibly future political considerations I had to take into account as well in fighting acid rain. "Mr. Prime Minister, my friends and I are very concerned about acid rain," the student wrote to me after visiting Parliament Hill in March 1987. "For example, what if we all grow up [brain damaged] and vote NDP?"

page 368. *"Thousands of the Irish immigrants who came to Canada during the potato famine were landed on Grosse-Île"* All buildings and other historical sites on Grosse-Île were officially transferred to Parks Canada from the Department of Agriculture in 1988. "I am fully committed to ensuring that the Government commemorates the past as it builds for the future," I told the chairperson of the General Assembly of Irish Organizations, Pádraig Breandán Ó Laughlin, in an April 1993 letter. "The site's significance for the Irish, as for the hundreds of thousands of other immigrants who passed through Quebec, will be symbolized fully and appropriately."

Part V, 1985 Chapter 4: Fighting Apartheid

page 404. *"'Brian, get on with it'"* Mrs. Thatcher later provided her own perspective on the discussions in her memoirs: "At 2 o'clock Brian Mulroney and Rajiv Gandhi arrived at the house to show me their best efforts. Alas, I could not give them high marks and spent the best part of two hours explaining why their proposals were unacceptable to me . . . After dinner I was invited to join a wider group and put under great pressure to agree to the line they wanted. Bob Hawke bitterly attacked me. I replied with vigour. In a steadily worsening atmosphere, the argument went on for some three hours. Fortunately, I can never be defeated by attrition."

Part V, 1986 Chapter 1: Vive la Francophonie – et l'Égalité

page 423. *"but all of us, including homosexuals, are children of God"*
I used a more bare-knuckles approach in caucus on another occasion. "All right," I told the group, "statistics tells us that 10 per cent of the population is homosexual, and since we in the Conservative Party are representative of the population, there are at least twenty gays in this room. Am I wrong? Is there a flaw in my logic? Are you ready to deprive these people of their rights?"

page 426. *"I always instructed Michael to ensure that the interests of disabled Canadians were not forgotten"*
Before I left office, Justin Dart, of the U.S. President's Committee on Employment of People with Disabilities, praised my government's record in this area, and in particular, the work of one of my caucus members, Dr. Bruce Halliday. "I recently returned from a meeting . . . dealing with a unique Canadian initiative on disability," he wrote to me on April 20, 1993. "Once again, I was reminded of Canada's progress in this field, particularly during the Conservative administration under your leadership."

Part V, 1986 Chapter 2: Washington, Tokyo, and Beijing

page 432. *"Our ambassador's wife, Sondra Gotlieb, was working under a great deal of stress"*
Sondra Gotlieb wrote to me within days of the slap incident. "I hope you can forgive me for marring your visit to Washington," she said. "I feel absolutely devastated and heartsick."

Part V, 1986 Chapter 3: Toward a Cabinet Shuffle

page 459. *"'We were as cautious as Mackenzie King,' Lowell said"*
A thorough man, Senator Murray reviewed our government's previous internal discussions on the Constitution when he took over the federal-provincial relations portfolio in 1986. Lowell later sent me a copy of a report about a discussion in my office between myself, the minister of justice, and senior officials concerning Quebec and the Constitution that took place on April 29, 1986. "The minister of justice asked the prime minister how high a priority he attached to this file and how high a price the federal government was ready to pay to reach an agreement with Quebec," the report stated. "In response, the prime minister asserted that

the government had to try to obtain a deal, that the government would be pilloried if it did not try, just as it would be pilloried if it tried and failed. He described the endeavour as 'perilous.'"

Part V, 1986 Chapter 4: The Apartheid Wars Continue

page 467. *"Prime Minister Diefenbaker took the stand . . . against South Africa"* Before I left for London, I had the Privy Council do some historical research. Diefenbaker, I was proud to read, wrote the following to Prime Minister Harold Macmillan before he attended the famous 1960 Commonwealth Conference: "In view of developments since May which give no indication of any change of attitude by the Government of South Africa, I feel obliged to let you know that unless significant changes occur in the Union Government's racial policies, Canada cannot be counted on to support South Africa's readmission to the Commonwealth." Macmillan attempted to moderate Canada's position but to no avail. With Canada standing with Third World members of the Commonwealth, South Africa withdrew its application for readmission in March 1961.

page 468. *"Eventually it was clear that Margaret Thatcher was alone"* "In fact," Mrs. Thatcher later wrote, "the formal discussions were every bit as unpleasant as at Lyford Cay, though at least they were shorter. My refusal to go along with the sanctions they wanted was attacked by Messrs. Kaunda, Mugabe, Mulroney, and Hawke. I found no support." I should note that Mrs. Thatcher was always greatly assisted throughout her time in office by Lord Charles Powell, her senior foreign policy advisor, who in my judgment ranked among the most outstanding public servants in the world.

Part V, 1986 Chapter 5: Tough Decisions Abroad and at Home

page 477. *"I am unable to see how exceeding SALT II limits will improve the negotiating climate in Geneva"*
My views couldn't have been of any surprise to President Reagan. I had written to him in June 1986 as well. "The prospect, implicit in your proposal, of abandoning the ABM Treaty in a more modest time frame than that proposed by the USSR, coming so soon on the heels of your recent statements on SALT II, could raise serious concerns among Canadians who believe deeply in the importance of maintaining and building the existing arms control regime . . . The Soviet Union has somehow been

perceived by our publics to be more forthcoming than the United States. It will be vital, therefore, in terms of Alliance cohesion, to maintain your willingness to move forward with reasonable and realistic proposals."

page 485. "*Another American I had dealings with*"
Allan Gotlieb's diary entry for December 9, 1986 deals with the visit by Bentsen and other senators. "After lunch I went to Question Period with the senators, who were introduced by the Speaker. We watched the proceedings from the gallery. Mulroney could not have paid the opposition parties enough to perform as they did. What a favour they did for Canada. Both displayed their deep anti-American sentiment. Lloyd Axworthy, in particular, attacked the United States over nuclear submarines in the Arctic, their issuing exploration permits in the Beaufort Sea within Canadian territory, and so on. Bentsen and his colleagues must have thought, God, we'd better deal with Mulroney, he's sane. Mulroney must have been very pleased." And indeed I was. (*The Washington Diaries*)

Part V, 1987 Chapter 1: Strong Words with President Reagan

page 489. "*I was proud that personal tensions had eased*"
While acknowledging that differences of opinion existed between Canada and the United States, former secretary of state George Shultz, in his memoirs *Turmoil and Triumph*, wrote that he found his quarterly meetings with his Canadian counterpart extremely valuable. "On the airplane heading home [from Ottawa in the early 1980s], virtually all the [press's] questions were about the Middle East. 'Why are you wasting time on Canada?' was the attitude. Still, in these quarterly meetings, which were especially productive after Brian Mulroney and Joe Clark came to power, I was determined to work through innumerable problems, large and small, dealing with them early and transmitting the message to the Canadians that the United States recognized the importance of our relationship and would spend time and effort on it. The policy would pay dividends to both countries, but it wasn't an easy sell [in Washington]."

page 497. "*Reagan . . . walked across to a nineteenth-century globe*"
I still have this globe, displayed on the landing of the main staircase of my home in Montreal, where it serves as a daily reminder of Canada's sovereignty in Arctic waters.

Part V, 1987 Chapter 6: Showdown at the Langevin Block

page 544. *"We were all exhausted"*
One of my Ontario MPs, Bill Weingard, had warned me around this time that I shouldn't allow myself to get too tired. "I know you are worried and I know you are tired," he wrote. "But, my friend, you looked *very* tired this morning. Remember, you are no use to us dead." "I'll try not to expire in the near future," I wrote back a few days later.

Part V, 1987 Chapter 7: Foreign Affairs and the Death Penalty

page 549. *"Some were surprised when I said I understood – but didn't condone"*
The previous June I had stated clearly in a letter to South African President P. W. Botha where I thought the roots of blame for the violence in the region truly lay. "I cannot, quite frankly, concur with the hypothesis . . . that South Africa's problems stem from international terrorism or that they can be solved by strikes against alleged ANC installations in neighbouring states," I wrote. "Violence and the threat of violence appear to me to be endemic to the internal political situation in South Africa – a situation in which the majority of South Africans are excluded from full political participation."

page 555. *"You are now entitled to take the floor"*
During an interview with President George H.W. Bush's daughter, Doro Bush Koch, in 2006 I shared with her what came next. "The Prime Minister [of Iceland] went on and on, and President Bush looked absolutely exhausted trying to keep up with this guy," Doro quoted me in her book, *My Father, My President*. "Finally, the secretary-general of NATO banged his gavel calling for a coffee break, and the president came staggering over to see me because we were sitting just opposite. He said, 'Brian, what the hell happened?' I said, 'Well, George, you just learned your first rule of modern diplomacy as President of the United States. The smaller the country, the longer the speech!'"

Part V, 1987 Chapter 8: The Free Trade Roller Coaster

In this chapter I have relied heavily on the excellent day-by-day descriptions of the dramatic events to be found in Allan Gotlieb's *The Washington Diaries: 1981-1989*.

page 565. *"It was ironic that Ontario"*
Just after my resignation announcement in February 1993, I couldn't help but refer to Ontario's opposition to the FTA in remarks behind closed doors on March 10, 1993. "It's time to retire [when] NDP premiers have come out strongly in favour of deficit reduction and David Peterson assumed chairmanship of a committee promoting free trade," I said, to laughter from caucus.

page 570. *"Baker really decided to take charge"*
Today, Baker says the FTA is one of the most significant accomplishments of the Reagan era. "The third major accomplishment of President Reagan's second term, after tax reform and international economic policy coordination to defeat protectionism and stabilize exchange rates, was the Canada–United States Free Trade Agreement," he wrote in his 2006 memoirs, *Work Hard, Study . . . and Keep Out of Politics*. "It went into effect in January of 1989, and removed many trade barriers between the United States and its largest trading partner. More important, perhaps, it served as a model for the North American Free Trade Agreement (NAFTA), which went into effect five years later and made Mexico, Canada, and the United States the world's largest trading bloc . . . The agreement was a huge success. Trade between Canada and the United States more than doubled in the decade after it went into effect. The result: higher economic growth, more jobs, and better wages in both countries."

Part V, 1988 Chapter 2: Personal Diplomacy

page 599. *"Seeing them with their grandchildren was always a joy"*
"One day my wife, Mila, and I were there, and we were sitting . . . having a glass of coke, and a couple of sandwiches," I told Bush's daughter Doro Bush Koch in an interview for her book *My Father, My President*. "All of a sudden, the doors open and the grandchildren came in. They were crawling all over him. He never missed a beat. He kept talking to me. He enjoyed every second of it. The dogs were running around and, I said to myself, this guy's got his values in the right place."

page 607. *"Lyndon Johnson's line after he once received similar praise"*
On June 27, 1989 I laughed along with other Canadian parliamentarians when Chaim Herzog, the president of Israel, himself used the Johnson phrase in acknowledging the introduction he had received before speaking!

Part VI, 1989 Chapter 3: Behind the Scenes with Reagan, Thatcher, and Others

page 692. *"I had decided in February that it was time for Canada to join"*
During the Ottawa convention week in 1983, my campaign published its own daily "newspaper" *Let's Win Together!* In it I made clear my view that Canada should fully engage throughout the Americas. "We should join the OAS [Organization of American States] and take a position of responsibility in our hemisphere," I wrote. "We should also remember that this is our hemisphere and the U.S. is our friend and represents many of the same values we stand for and Cuba does not."

Part VI, 1989 Chapter 4: After the Fall of the Berlin Wall

page 699. *"It was perhaps one of his finest moments as president"*
In a sometimes critical volume on the George H.W. Bush presidency – *The Rhetorical Presidency of George H.W. Bush* [Martin J. Medhurst, editor] – Professor William Forrest Harlow of Texas Tech University concludes his essay, *And the Wall Came Tumbling Down*, the following way: "While his choice to speak only ceremonially on the German question raised objections from some, Bush's lack of policy-making speech ultimately helped to make sure that Germany was not pulled from the path of democracy. This deliberate silence helped coordinate the efforts of U.S. allies and foes alike, and ultimately proved the correct choice in Bush's rhetorical management of the fall of the Berlin Wall and eventual German reunification. The Cold War ended without its last battle having to be fought."

Part VI, 1990 Chapter 1: Nation of Discontent

page 731. *"It turned out he was being told by U.S. Trade Representative Carla Hills"*
During talks with President Bush and President Salinas at the official signing ceremony for NAFTA in Texas in October 1992, a story involving Carla Hills and Canada's John Crosbie had us all laughing. "The three trade ministers [at the meeting with the leaders] then reviewed the course of the negotiations, paying tribute to the officials from the other countries," the Canadian note-taker wrote. "Mr. Wilson recalled his colleague John Crosbie's remark at a cabinet meeting that there was a lot of 'Bush and Hills between Canada and Mexico.'"

page 731. *"I strongly registered these concerns with Mexican President Carlos Salinas"* President-Elect Bill Clinton later asked for my opinion of his Mexican counterpart on January 7, 1993. "Salinas," I replied, "he's a dynamic piece of work. He's got his six-year term and he's going to change the world during his term. I'm impressed. He's an honest, straightforward dealer and always delivers on what he says."

Part VI, 1990 Chapter 2: The Bouchard Bombshell

page 739. *"Maldoff had told Stanley Hartt"*
Maldoff and Stanley Hartt worked effectively together. "Stanley, this 'thing' is working," Maldoff wrote to Hartt on May 1, 1990. "A deal is within reach which would allow everybody to claim victory . . . There is a great deal to do in very little time. It will require concerted and concentrated efforts, but I doubt there is anything more important or urgent at this time. So, let's get on with it."

Part VI, 1990 Chapter 3: Distractions Along the Way

page 756. *"This earned the less than popular premier"*
In his book *From Protest to Power*, former premier Bob Rae reminds all politicians who visit sporting events why it is sometimes wise to accept the advice of senior officials from the civil service. It was his deputy minister of education, Charles Pascal, who gave Rae the idea of holding up a sign, "No Speech Today. Hooray for the Blue Jays," instead of giving a speech at Toronto's SkyDome. "This was one of the best pieces of speech advice I ever got from a deputy minister, since as soon as I held up the sign, the boos turned to cheers," Rae wrote.

page 758. *"'Clyde Wells is so far removed from any kind of reality.'"*
Jack Pickersgill travelled to Newfoundland to meet the new premier shortly after Wells took office. "He's really not a good listener," Pickersgill said dryly, when asked by Senator Lowell Murray for his reaction.

Part VI, 1990 Chapter 4: The Shadows of Ghosts

page 771. *"I simply pushed my food around my plate"*
I noted that evening that Premier David Peterson of Ontario had no complaints as he sipped his Ontario wines. The last time wine was an issue at a First Ministers' Meeting had been in October 1987 after the successful conclusion of the Free Trade Agreement with the Americans. Vander

Zalm had expressed concern about the possible effects the FTA would have on the wine producers in his province. Peterson wasn't as worried. "We make junk," he said, a comment I was sure he wouldn't make in the Niagara region while on the hustings, but, in fairness, a remark that – pre FTA – wasn't uncommon among wine connoisseurs around the world. "Speak for yourself," Vander Zalm shot back!

page 783. *"When we left the conference centre"*
A few hours later, I received an emotional call from Paul Desmarais Jr. The Desmarais family had come to Canada hundreds of years earlier, eventually settling in northern Ontario, but had moved to Montreal where Paul Sr. developed his great fortune – all the while remaining strong French-Canadian federalists committed to a united Canada. I knew Paul Sr. intimately, as I have already written, and was present moments after the birth of Paul Desmarais III.

My friend's joy at the result we had achieved provoked such a profound reaction in me as I ended the call and sat, alone in my study at 24 Sussex Drive, that I was overcome by the moment.

Part VI, 1991 Chapter 1: Two Wars: The GST and the Gulf

page 831. *"Predictably, the Chrétien Liberals exacted their revenge"*
"Turner was ostracized [by the Liberals] to the point that he often found himself sitting alone in question period, with all of Chrétien's allies keeping their distance," Chrétien's biographer Lawrence Martin later wrote, adding that at least one Grit MP, Joe Comuzzi, respected Turner so much that he sat with Canada's seventeenth prime minister – his party's former leader – each time he could.

Part VI, 1991 Chapter 4: A Coup in Moscow

page 874. *"Boris Yeltsin . . . who had stared the plotters down . . . chose democracy"*
Up until my final G-7 Summit – at Munich in 1992 – and beyond, I'm proud I did all I could to support Yeltsin, and encourage other leaders from the West to do the same. "I strongly suspect that we will be judged by future generations on how we respond to the historic changes occurring in the former Soviet Union," I told my fellow leaders in closed session. "The consequences of failure of reform of democracy and economic reform are very grave for all of us. We need to send a message of hope and encouragement to the people of Russia and the other countries of the FSU [former Soviet Union]. They are bearing the brunt of change.

Yeltsin should be received very warmly, giving the world a clear signal that we support his commitment to reform."

Part VI, 1992 Chapter 1: A Bleak Start to the Year

page 899. *"That spring the Supreme Court unanimously ruled that David Milgaard"*
This section has greatly benefited from my reading of the book by Joyce Milgaard and Peter Edwards, *A Mother's Story*, a copy of which is in my home library.

Part VI, 1992 Chapter 2: Plain Talk with George, Dick, and Boris

page 903. *"Bush, I felt, deserved better management help"*
My notes from that meeting with President Bush remind me that we discussed Ross Perot as well. I had some advice for the president. "He's a one-trick pony with a lot of cash," I told Bush. "He's running a campaign on talk shows to avoid brutal one-on-one debate. He's vague on policy, mining discontent and offering simplistic solutions. But remember that telephone banks do not make campaign buses run on time – only a national political party can. Perot doesn't have one and he must be forced by you to run hard without one and before he can build one. This will lead to sound systems that fail at rallies, crowds that don't show up, deadlines missed by the press. His absence of policy, organization, and political expertise will result in the development of: irrationality, thin skin, outbursts, and unpredictability. Questions will then arise as to his fitness to govern; his finger on the nuclear button and his firmness under pressure."

page 905. *"Jim Baker shocked me with his open skepticism about the value of G-7 summits"*
Later that year Derek Burney, my G-7 sherpa, looked at the overall economic summit situation in a confidential memo he sent to me from Washington. "At the close of Munich," he wrote, "we discussed the problems facing summitry, a process I believe risks sclerotic decline . . . The elaborate nature of summit preparations and the grandeur of these annual events have become disproportionate to the results. Major issues are often blurred to avoid disharmony. Regular meetings of the G-7 finance and deputy finance ministers have, to a considerable extent, siphoned off what was originally the raison d'être of summitry – greater coordination of macro policy. Compounding these trends is the negative attitude of the current U.S. administration toward summitry, which is

genuine, pervasive, and troubling . . . Canada, along with Japan and Italy, has the most to lose from diluting the significance and frequency of summitry . . . What is needed most, however, is not another layer of coordination, rather a clear signal of leadership from summits." Derek's words should still be considered by the Canadian prime minister of the day.

Part VI, 1992 Chapter 3: Joe Clark's Instincts

page 916. *"and that he would do so without the courtesy of calling me"*
Mark McQueen, Hugh Segal's executive assistant, later wrote a memo to file about Clark's behaviour, arising out of the July 3, 1992 meeting he chaired. "At approximately 5:30 p.m., I fielded a telephone call from the prime minister regarding developments at the Royal York Hotel on the multilateral meeting of premiers, ministers, and Mr. Clark. The meeting came out of a luncheon held earlier in the week at 24 Sussex with the prime minister. Note that the flight departed Ottawa at 10 a.m., local time, and arrived in London, England at roughly 5 p.m. . . . I reported [to the PM] that there appeared to be 'no deal,' and any other analysis would be a rosy interpretation of the outcome . . . I also passed on that it appeared as though there had been agreement to a further meeting in Ottawa the following Monday with constitutional ministers to discuss various outstanding issues, with the premiers returning on Tuesday for further talks on the Senate. The prime minister indicated that 'there had been no permission given for any more meetings . . . Mr. Clark hasn't checked with me.' I reported that, nevertheless, it appeared that there would. I was told to get Mr. Clark or Mr. Judd on the phone and to get them to 'call the U.K. ASAP.' I then spoke with Jim Judd, who was sitting in a hotel room . . . with Minister Clark, and asked, almost pleaded with, him to have his minister call the U.K. He agreed. Ten minutes later Mr. Clark appeared at the news conference . . . The first or second question referenced whether he had spoken to the prime minister that day. Mr. Clark responded that he 'had a choice of talking to the prime minister or being here with you . . . naturally, I chose to be here' in an extremely tongue-in-cheek manner . . . Mr. Clark confirmed to the press that there would be meetings in Ottawa on Monday and Tuesday. I received a second call at about 6:05 p.m. from the prime minister seeking an update . . . I was given the telephone number in his hotel room, and undertook to have Mr. Clark phone immediately. I then called Jim Judd a second time, and he was calling the PM for the first time [to my knowledge] at that very moment, probably about 6:10 p.m. local time."

Part VI, 1993 Chapter 1: Bill Clinton and Others

page 965. *"Bill Clinton telephoned again to discuss NAFTA"*
The president-elect of the United States had tracked me down in Florida. "I'm a snowbird," I joked to Bill Clinton who laughed heartily. "I found out long ago that my popularity increases drastically the longer I'm out of the country. So, I'm here for a while." Then, we got serious. "Well, my main argument in the House of Commons," I told him, "my main opposition, from the socialists is that manufacturing jobs will disappear in Canada and flow to Mexico where wages are a fraction of what they are in Canada. I say that if that were the only criterion, Haiti would be the manufacturing capital of the world. The United States of America and Canada have the most sophisticated economies in the world and here you have Mexico willing to trade their way to prosperity. We should be encouraging this guy rather than have him line up waiting for an American or Canadian aid cheque."

page 972. *"On February 5, I arrived once again at the White House"*
Environment Minister Jean Charest pushed hard in reminding me to ensure that environmental concerns should be on the bilateral agenda for my visit. "You know better than anyone else that environmental issues have played, and will continue to play, an important role in shaping the [Canadian–American] relationship," Charest wrote. "From the Shamrock Summit of 1985 to the signing of the Air Quality Accord in 1991, you were unswerving in the priority you attached to this issue. You also instituted the practice of regular contact between your ministers and their counterparts. I have found the meetings with the administrator of the [U.S.] Environmental Protection Agency extremely productive and your expression of continued support for this approach would send an important signal."

page 978. *"I continued to work hard at making caucus meetings . . . entertaining and enjoyable"*
I also took time, whenever possible, to meet with the family members of my MPs and ministers. In fact, it was one of the more enjoyable parts of my job as prime minister. Members of my team were most appreciative, as this letter from Kim Campbell shows. "Thank you so much for the time you spent with my mother yesterday," she wrote to me on Sept. 17, 1991. "She was just thrilled to have a few moments alone with you. Her visit here is my last year's Christmas present. She has not been well enough to make the trip until recently. She is enjoying Ottawa enormously – her last visit was in 1944 as a young WREN. To have met and

talked with you is the highlight of the visit. I am pleased to be able to share my Ottawa life with her – so I am particularly delighted that she had a chance to see and meet the warm human being that I am so proud to serve. She also thinks you are even more handsome in real life than on television. Again, warm thanks, Kim."

Part VI, 1993 Chapter 2: Resignation

page 981. *"In the following days, I was to receive many special letters"*
Some of my Liberal opponents wished me well. "Best wishes in your new endeavours as you transfer the reins of power," Eglinton-Lawrence Liberal MP Joe Volpe wrote. "As a fellow politician (my philosophy and partisan differences aside) I empathize with the sacrifices that you and your family have made for Canadians and the principles that you believe in." A letter from Bob Hawke of Australia also meant a great deal to me. "As we have agreed before, we were as one [within the Commonwealth] on every major issue of importance that I can recall. Above all else, you were a magnificent pillar of support in the struggle we waged to bring to an end the evil system of apartheid in South Africa. This is something I will never forget . . . In the broader international sphere, we were so often able to communicate and get a common line of action between our two countries. This was particularly important for a sometimes delicate relationship with the U.S. In particular I remember the way you responded so positively and quickly when I talked with you about our responses to the Gulf War." By this point, Hawke had been pushed out of office by Paul Keating and ended his note with the following: "I can assure you that life after Parliament can be extremely interesting and rewarding!"

page 982. *"I did my best to ensure a vigorous leadership battle"*
I had discussed the race with cabinet at a meeting held the day after my resignation announcement as well. "The prime minister referred to the need to [elect] a new leader of the Conservative Party and observed that it was impossible for anyone not actually in the position of prime minister to understand the effort that was required for the position and the unbelievable time demands – but despite these cautions, being prime minister was a marvellous way to serve Canada," the report of that day's general discussions reads. "The prime minister addressed the issue of the leadership campaign and warned potential candidates of the degree of public scrutiny they could expect. He also stated that the government must have its rules to ensure that it manages effectively and in a way that serves to protect the transition process. Ministers have a duty to the public and to the government that supersedes their role as leadership

candidates." With Liberal ministers out on the leadership hustings in 1968, Mr. Pearson's government lost a vote in the Commons that could have seen the government fall before the new leader was in place. Only Bob Stanfield's decency, and his lifelong practice of putting the nation first, prevented an election. I had never forgotten this 1968 incident and resolved firmly that it would not happen on my watch.

page 984. "*'We could do it in Vancouver.'*"
I was well aware of the fondness the Clinton family had for Vancouver. "Hillary and I were in Vancouver two years ago and had the best time of our lives," he told me over the telephone before his inauguration. "Now, however, they've got me in a bubble so I don't know how much I'll see."

page 985. "*Yeltsin was tough, and indeed he went on to survive his plebiscite*"
"The Russian people have delivered a resounding vote of confidence in your leadership and have given you a clear mandate to push ahead with reform," I wrote President Yeltsin, in a congratulatory letter on April 26, 1993. "You can count on Canada's continuing support within the G-7 as you proceed with economic and political change." In a letter signed the day before I left office, I reiterated these views to Mart Laar, the prime minister of Estonia. "I fully share your view that President Yeltsin's decision to hold a vote was a bold display of democratic conviction. His impressive victory gave him a clear mandate to move ahead with political and economic reform. It is essential now to continue support for President Yeltsin and the Russian people in their efforts to establish democracy and a market economy."

page 995. "*On May 25, I headed to Iqaluit*"
This trip North of 60 to sign the Nunavut land claims agreement gave me the opportunity to try out my Inuktitut. "Quviassuktunga tikigama nunavumut [I'm happy that I arrived in Nunavut]" I said as the crowd at Inuksuk High School roared. I was able to take my audience back to December 1991 and a memorable telephone call I received from Indian and Northern Affairs Minister Tom Siddon during the land claims negotiations. Siddon was blunt, telling me there would be no deal unless my government agreed to create a third territory. On the spot, I gave my approval. "You really have no idea what an accomplishment it is to get this kind of agreement in this kind of economic climate through the Government of Canada," I said in my speech. "I was of course sympathetic to what was going on, and from time to time it is not unhelpful to have the prime minister on your side. But I can tell you that without Tom

Siddon's tenacious leadership we would not be celebrating this remarkable achievement today."

page 1000. *"From morning to night"*

This is an appropriate place to thank all of the household staff who helped us at 24 Sussex Drive over the years: Eileen Watkins, Esther Gammad, Tony and Adelina Punilhas, Kim Cross (the household coordinator), John Leblanc, Barry Gorr, Ljubica and Jo Kovacevic, Mina and Willy Narciso, Linda Narciso, and Cathy Auchinleck.

I would also like to recognize our RCMP security staff: Denis Gagnon, William Robbe, Bruno Lavoie, Pierre-Paul Périard, Al Cyr, Forest Dunsmore, Stan Menzies, Kelly Anderson, and Trevor Edwards.

page 1006. *"We kept our word"*

In a speech like that, or indeed a book like this, it is impossible to thank all of the fine people with whom I served in office. But now is a good time to recognize a few whose contributions in cabinet should not go unnoticed.

Duff Roblin was a highly successful former premier of Manitoba who performed with great distinction as government leader in the Senate.

Bob Layton was a true gentlemen who performed ably both in cabinet and as national chairman of caucus, a position to which he brought high energy, warmth, and good nature.

Frank Oberle and Paul Dick, two of my earliest supporters, turned out to be highly effective cabinet ministers: always well prepared, well spoken, and strongly supportive of the government and of me.

Shirley Martin was a delight to be with, and she defended her region's and Ontario's interests with charm and effectiveness.

Pierre Cadieux and Gerry Weiner were two representatives of the West Island of Montreal who turned out to be reliable and admired members of caucus and cabinet.

Mary Collins, from British Columbia, and Alan Redway, from Toronto, also served loyally and impressively, and I relied heavily on their good communication skills.

Pauline Browes was a diminutive powerhouse from Scarborough who worked extremely well with Jean Charest as minister of state for the environment, on our national projects in this vital area.

Andrée Champagne, a Quebec television star, performed well in cabinet and as deputy speaker of the House of Commons, as did her fellow Québécois, Michel Côté.

Gerald Merrithew was a strong advocate for New Brunswick and for Atlantic Canada as a whole.

Select Bibliography

Armstrong, Sally. *Mila*. Toronto: Macmillan, 1992.

Bain, George. *Gotcha! How the Media Distort the News*. Toronto: Key Porter Books, 1994.

Baker, James A., with Thomas M. DeFrank. *The Politics of Diplomacy*. New York: G.P. Putnam and Sons, 1995.

Baker, James A., with Steve Fiffer. *"Work Hard, Study...and Keep Out of Politics!" Adventures and Lessons from an Unexpected Public Life*. New York: G.P. Putnam and Sons, 2006.

Borden, Henry, ed. *Robert Laird Borden: His Memoirs, Volumes One and Two*. Toronto: Macmillan, 1938.

Bouchard, Lucien. *On the Record*. Translated by Dominique Clift. Toronto: Stoddart Publishing, 1994.

Bradlee, Benjamin C. *Conversations with Kennedy*. New York: Norton, 1975.

Brodsky, Alyn. *Grover Cleveland: A Study in Character*. New York: Truman Talley Books, 2000.

Brown, Patrick, Robert Chodos, and Rae Murphy. *Winners, Losers: The 1976 Tory Leadership Convention*. Toronto: James Lorimer and Co., 1976.

Burney, Derek H. *Getting It Done: A Memoir*. Montreal and Kingston: McGill-Queen's University Press, 2005.

Bush, Barbara. *A Memoir*. New York: Lisa Drew Books, 1994.

———. *Reflections: Life After the White House*. New York: Simon and Schuster, 2003.

Bush, George, and Brent Scowcroft. *A World Transformed*. New York: Alfred A. Knopf, 1998.

Cahill, Jack. *John Turner: The Long Run*. Toronto: McClelland and Stewart, 1984.

Campbell, Kim. *Time and Chance: The Political Memoirs of Canada's First Woman Prime Minister*. Toronto: Doubleday, 1996.

Cannon, Lou. *President Reagan: The Role of a Lifetime*. New York: Simon and Schuster, 1991.

Caplan, Gerald, Michael Kirby, and Hugh Segal. *Election: The Issues, the Strategies, the Aftermath*. Scarborough: Prentice-Hall, 1989.

Caro, Robert A. *Master of the Senate: The Years of Lyndon Johnson*. New York: Alfred A. Knopf, 2002.

Carter, Jimmy. *Keeping Faith: Memoirs of a President*. New York: Bantam Books, 1982.

Charest, Jean. *My Road to Québec*. St. Laurent, P.Q.: Editions Pierre Tisseyre, 1998.

Chrétien, Jean. *Straight from the Heart*. Toronto: Key Porter Books, 1985.

Christopher, Warren. *Chances of a Lifetime: A Memoir*. New York: Simon and Schuster, 2001.

Clarkson, Stephen, and Christina McCall. *Trudeau and Our Times*. Vol. 1, *The Magnificent Obsession*. Toronto: McClelland and Stewart, 1990.

Clinton, Bill. *My Life*. New York: Alfred A. Knopf, 2004.

Cohen, Andrew. *A Deal Undone: The Making and Breaking of the Meech Lake Accord*. Toronto: Douglas and McIntyre, 1991.

Cohen, Andrew, and J.L. Granatstein, eds. *Trudeau's Shadow: The Life and Legacy of Pierre Elliott Trudeau*. Toronto: Random House of Canada, 1998.

Cohoe, Margaret M., comp. *Sir John A. Macdonald: A Remembrance to Mark the Centennial of His Death, 6 June 1891*. Kingston: Kingston Historical Society, 1991.

Creighton, Donald. *John A. Macdonald: The Young Politician*. Toronto: Macmillan, 1952.

———. *John A. Macdonald: The Old Chieftain*. Toronto: Macmillan, 1955.

Crosbie, John C. *No Holds Barred: My Life in Politics*. Toronto: McClelland and Stewart, 1997.

Crowley, Monica. *Nixon Off the Record: His Candid Commentary on People and Politics*. New York: Random House, 1996.

———. *Nixon in Winter: His Final Revelations About Diplomacy, Watergate and Life out of the Arena*. New York: Random House, 1998.

Delacourt, Susan. *United We Fall: In Search of a New Canada*. Toronto: Penguin Books, 1994.

Diefenbaker, John G. *One Canada: The Crusading Years 1895–1956*. Toronto: Macmillan, 1975.

———. *One Canada: The Years of Achievement 1957–1962*. Toronto: Macmillan, 1976.

———. *One Canada: The Tumultuous Years 1962–1967*. Toronto: Macmillan, 1977.

Doern, G. Bruce, and Brian W. Tomlin. *Faith and Fear: The Free Trade Story*. Toronto: Stoddart Publishing, 1991.

Doyle, Richard J. *Hurly-Burly: A Time at the Globe*. Toronto: Macmillan, 1990.

Duchesne, Pierre. *Jacques Parizeau*. Tome 1, *Le Croisé*. Montréal: Québec-Amérique, 2001.

———. *Jacques Parizeau*. Tome 2, *Le Baron*. Montréal: Québec-Amérique, 2002.

———. *Jacques Parizeau*. Tome 3, *Le Régent*. Montréal: Québec-Amérique, 2004.

Duffy, John. *Fights of Our Lives: Elections, Leadership and the Making of Canada*. Toronto: HarperCollins, 2002.

Eden, Sir Anthony. *Full Circle: The Memoirs of Sir Anthony Eden*. London: Cassel and Company, 1960.

English, John. *Citizen of the World: The Life of Pierre Elliott Trudeau*. Vol. 1, *1919–1968*. Toronto: Alfred A. Knopf, 2006.

Ford, Gerald R. *A Time to Heal: The Autobiography of Gerald R. Ford*. New York: Harper and Row, 1979.

Fox, Bill. *Spinwars: Politics and New Media*. Toronto: Key Porter Books, 1999.

Franks, C.E.S. *The Parliament of Canada*. Toronto: University of Toronto Press, 1987.

Fraser, Graham. *Playing for Keeps: The Making of the Prime Minister, 1988*. Toronto: McClelland and Stewart, 1989.

Freeman, Linda. *The Ambiguous Champion: Canada and South Africa in the Trudeau and Mulroney Years*. Toronto: University of Toronto Press, 1997.

Goldenberg, Eddie. *The Way It Works: Inside Ottawa*. Toronto: Douglas Gibson Books, McClelland and Stewart, 2006.

Goodman, Eddie. *Life of the Party*. Toronto: Key Porter Books, 1988.

Gotlieb, Allan. *The Washington Diaries: 1981–1989*. Toronto: McClelland and Stewart, 2006.

Grant, Ulysses S. *Personal Memoirs*. New York: Modern Library, 1999.

Greene, John Robert. *The Presidency of George Bush*. Lawrence, Kans.: University Press of Kansas, 2000.

Gruending, Dennis, ed. *Great Canadian Speeches*. Markham, Ont.: Fitzhenry and Whiteside, 2004.

Hall, Trevor. *In Celebration of the Queen's Visit to Canada*. Don Mills, Ont.: Collins Royal, 1984.

Hambly, Daniel. *The 1986 CF-18 Maintenance Contract: A Legitimate Grievance or an Issue of Mis-information?* Master's Thesis, University of Western Ontario, 2006.

Hart, Michael, with Bill Dymond and Colin Robertson. *Decision at Midnight: Inside the Canada-US Free-Trade Negotiations*. Vancouver: University of British Columbia Press, 1994.

Hawke, Bob. *The Hawke Memoirs*. Port Melbourne: William Heinemann Australia, 1994.

Horne, Alistair. *Harold MacMillan*. Vol. 1, *1894–1956*. London: Macmillan, 1988.

———. *Harold MacMillan*. Vol. 2, *1957–1986*. London: Macmillan, 1989.

Hutchison, Bruce. *Mr. Prime Minister, 1867–1964*. Don Mills, Ont.: Longmans, 1964.

Johnston, Donald. *Up the Hill*. Montreal: Optimum Publishing International, 1986.

Karabell, Zachary. *The Last Campaign: How Harry Truman Won the 1948 Election*. New York: Vintage Books, 2000.

Koch, Doro Bush. *My Father, My President: A Personal Account of the Life of George H. W. Bush*. New York: Warner Books, 2006.

Kuhn, Jim. *Ronald Reagan in Private: A Memoir of My Years in the White House*. New York: Penguin Books, 2004.

MacDonald, L. Ian, ed. *Free Trade: Risks and Rewards*. Montreal and Kingston: McGill-Queen's University Press, 2000.

———. *From Bourassa to Bourassa: Wilderness to Restoration*. Montreal and Kingston: McGill-Queen's University Press, 2002.

———. *Mulroney: The Making of the Prime Minister*. Toronto: McClelland and Stewart, 1984.

MacGuigan, Mark. *An Inside Look at External Affairs During the Trudeau Years: The Memoirs of Mark MacGuigan*. Calgary: University of Calgary Press, 2002.

MacLaren, Roy. *Honourable Mentions: The Uncommon Diary of an M.P.* Toronto: Deneau, 1986.

Major, John. *John Major: The Autobiography*. New York: HarperCollins, 1999.

Martin, Lawrence. *The Antagonist: Lucien Bouchard and the Politics of Delusion*. Toronto: Penguin Books, 1998.

———. *Iron Man: The Defiant Reign of Jean Chrétien*. Toronto: Viking Books, 2003.

———. *The Presidents and the Prime Ministers: Washington and Ottawa Face to Face: The Myth of Bilateral Bliss, 1867–1982*. Toronto: Doubleday, 1982.

Martin, Patrick, Allan Gregg, and George Perlin. *Contenders: The Tory Quest for Power*. Scarborough: Prentice-Hall, 1983.

McCall, Christina, and Stephen Clarkson. *Trudeau and Our Times*. Vol. 2, *The Heroic Delusion*. Toronto: McClelland and Stewart, 1994.

McCreery, Christopher. *The Order of Canada: Its Origins, History, and Development*. Toronto: University of Toronto Press, 2005.

McGrath, Jim, ed. *Heartbeat: George Bush in His Own Words*. New York: Simon and Schuster, 2001.

McLaughlin, Audrey. *A Woman's Place: My Life and Politics*. Toronto: Macfarlane Walter & Ross, 1992.

McRoberts, Kenneth, and Patrick Monahan, eds. *The Charlottetown Accord, the Referendum and the Future of Canada*. Toronto: University of Toronto Press, 1993.

McTeer, Maureen. *In My Own Name: A Memoir*. Toronto: Random House of Canada, 2003.

Medhurst, Martin J., ed. *The Rhetorical Presidency of George H. W. Bush*. Texas: A&M University Press, 2006.

Meighen, Arthur. *Unrevised and Unrepented: Debating Speeches and Others*. Toronto: Clarke, Irwin and Company, 1949.

Michaud, Nelson, and Kim Richard Nossal, eds. *Diplomatic Departures: The Conservative Era in Canadian Foreign Policy, 1984–1993*. Vancouver: University of British Columbia Press, 2001.

Milgaard, Joyce, with Peter Edwards. *A Mother's Story: My Fight to Free My Son David*. Toronto: Doubleday, 1999.

Monahan, Patrick J. *Meech Lake: The Inside Story*. Toronto: University of Toronto Press, 1991.

Mulroney, Brian. *Where I Stand*. Toronto: McClelland and Stewart, 1983.

Murphy, Rae, Robert Chodos, and Nick auf der Maur. *Brian Mulroney: The Boy from Baie-Comeau*. Toronto: James Lorimer and Company, 1984.

Nash, Knowlton. *Kennedy and Diefenbaker: Fear and Loathing across the Undefended Border*. Toronto: McClelland and Stewart, 1990.

Nemni, Max and Monique Nemni. *Young Trudeau, 1919–1944: Son of Québec, Father of Canada*. Toronto: McClelland and Stewart, 2006.

Newman, Peter C. *Here Be Dragons: Telling Tales of People, Passion and Power*. Toronto: McClelland and Stewart, 2004.

———. *Renegade in Power: The Diefenbaker Years*. Toronto: McClelland and Stewart, 1963.

O'Sullivan, Sean, with Rod McQueen. *Both My Houses: From Politics to Priesthood*. Toronto: Seal Books, 1986.

Parmet, Herbert S. *George Bush: The Life of a Lone Star Yankee*. New York: Simon and Schuster, 1997.

Pearson, Lester B. *Mike: The Memoirs of the Right Honourable Lester B. Pearson*. 3 vols. Toronto: University of Toronto Press, 1972.

Penslar, Derek J., Michael R. Marrus, and Janice Gross Stein, eds. *Contemporary Antisemitism: Canada and the World*. Toronto: University of Toronto Press, 2005.

Pickersgill, J.W. *Seeing Canada Whole: A Memoir*. Markham, Ont.: Fitzhenry and Whiteside, 1994.

Poitras, Jacques. *The Right Fight: Bernard Lord and the Conservative Dilemma*. Fredericton, N.B.: Goose Lane Editions, 2004.

Pope, Sir Joseph. *Memoirs of the Right Honourable Sir John A. Macdonald*. Toronto: Musson Book Company, 1894.

Powell, Colin, with Joseph E. Persico. *My American Journey*. New York: Random House, 1995.

Rae, Bob. *From Protest to Power: Personal Reflections on a Life in Politics*. Toronto: Viking Books, 1996.

Reagan, Ronald. *An American Life*. New York: Simon and Schuster, 1990.

Ritchie, Gordon. *Wrestling with the Elephant: The Inside Story of the Canada-U.S. Trade Wars*. Toronto: Macfarlane Walter & Ross, 1997.

Robertson, Gordon. *Memoirs of a Very Civil Servant: Mackenzie King to Trudeau*. Toronto: University of Toronto Press, 2000.

Schull, Joseph. *Laurier: The First Canadian*. Toronto: Macmillan, 1966.

Segal, Hugh. *No Surrender: Reflections of a Happy Warrior in the Tory Crusade*. Toronto: HarperCollins, 1996.

Sheppard, Robert, and Michael Valpy. *The National Deal: The Fight for a Canadian Constitution*. Toronto: Fleet Books, 1982.

Shultz, George P. *Turmoil and Triumph: Diplomacy, Power and the Victory of the American Ideal*. New York: Charles Scribner's Sons, 1993.

Simpson, Jeffrey. *Discipline of Power: The Conservative Interlude and the Liberal Restoration*. Toronto: Macmillan, 1980.

Smith, Cynthia M., and Jack McLeod, eds. *Sir John: An Anecdotal Life of John A. Macdonald*. Toronto: Oxford University Press, 1989.

Smith, David E., Peter MacKinnon, and John C. Courtney, eds. *After Meech Lake: Lessons for the Future*. Saskatoon: Fifth House Publishers, 1991.

Smith, Denis. *Rogue Tory: The Life and Legend of John G. Diefenbaker*. Toronto: Macfarlane Walter & Ross, 1995.

Steed, Judy. *Ed Broadbent: The Pursuit of Power*. Toronto: Penguin Books, 1988.

Stevens, Geoffrey. *The Player: The Life and Times of Dalton Camp*. Toronto: Key Porter Books, 2003.

Thatcher, Margaret. *The Downing Street Years*. New York: HarperCollins, 1993.

Tobin, Brian, with John Lawrence Reynolds. *All in Good Time*. Toronto: Penguin Books, 2002.

Troy, Gil. *Morning in America: How Ronald Reagan Invented the 1980s*. Princeton, N.J.: Princeton University Press, 2005.

Trudeau, Pierre Elliott. *Against the Current: Selected Writings 1939–1996*. Edited by Gerard Pelletier. Toronto: McClelland and Stewart, 1996.

Tupper, Sir Charles. *Recollections of Sixty Years in Canada*. Toronto: Cassell and Company, 1914.

Turner, John N. *Politics of Purpose*. Toronto: McClelland and Stewart, 1968.

Valenti, Jack. *A Very Human President*. New York: Norton, 1975.

Van Dusen, Thomas. *The Chief*. Toronto: McGraw-Hill, 1968.

Van Dusen, Thomas, with Susan Code. *Inside the Tent: Forty-Five Years on Parliament Hill*. Burstown: General Store Publishing House, n.d.

Watts, Ronald L., and Douglas M. Brown, eds. *Options for a New Canada*. Toronto: University of Toronto Press, 1991.

Werth, Barry. *31 Days: The Crisis That Gave Us the Government We Have Today*. New York: Random House, 2006.

Weston, Greg. *Reign of Error: The Inside Story of John Turner's Troubled Leadership*. Toronto: McGraw-Hill Ryerson, 1988.

Wiegman, Carl. *Trees to News*. Toronto: McClelland and Stewart, 1953.

Acknowledgements

I have never been impressed by the tradition of leaving public office on a Friday only to begin working on memoirs by Monday. Important issues of public policy frequently need time – years, sometimes decades – before their value can be fully and fairly assessed by one's fellow citizens. And so I decided to wait a while before I wrote a memoir.

As I plunged into a new and busy life as a lawyer, corporate director, and speaker at conferences around the world, I had less and less time even to consider undertaking such a demanding task. Accordingly, my initial enthusiasm for "doing some writing and lecturing" or "setting the record straight some day" soon disappeared under the weight of the day-to-day requirements of earning a living and raising a family.

A few years after my resignation, I was confronted with the horror of false allegations being made about me by the Government of Canada. I sued, won an apology and a favourable financial settlement. After an interminable investigation, I received a complete exoneration from the RCMP Commissioner six years later. These years of great anguish for my family were not conducive to writing memoirs. I was much too involved with my own defence and ultimate vindication. I will deal with this extraordinary abuse of a citizen's rights and the attempt to destroy a former prime minister of Canada simply because he represented an opposing political party – an event unique in the long history of this country – in another book, at another time.

Some time ago my old friend and college roommate, Samuel Wakim, Q.C., suggested I lunch with his client Avie Bennett, then owner of McClelland & Stewart, to discuss this book. The lunch was delightful and Avie was persuasive; I agreed to begin thinking seriously about the process of writing my memoirs.

In early 2003, after repeated urgings from friends like Paul Desmarais, Peter Munk, Jean Bazin, Pierre Karl Péladeau, and Jonathan Deitcher, I sat down and wrote the first chapter of this book, pretty much as it reads today. Then I began the slow process of writing successive chapters on my childhood, my teenage years, and my boarding school and college years, while I continued to travel the world on business. The hundreds of handwritten pages are dotted with headings like "Paris to Singapore," "London to L.A.," "Seattle to Chicago," and "Palm Beach to Cape Town." Sometimes I thought that the growing pile of manuscript looked more like a travelogue than a serious memoir.

After I left office, a rookie reporter from the *Pembroke Daily Observer* interviewed me for a story he was doing on my old friend Terrence "Ace" McCann, the local mayor. Following that September 1994 encounter, Arthur Milnes would call from time to time asking for a comment or an introduction to a possible interview subject. He had moved to the *Kingston Whig-Standard* when I persuaded him, in July 2003, to join me as researcher and assistant in the preparation of these memoirs. He soon became the first person to be granted unrestricted access to my collection at Library and Archives Canada in Ottawa, which consists of more than three thousand boxes containing approximately four million pages of documents.

I needed to consult and draw on this collection, which I knew would, with Arthur's research skills in play, provide documentary support for my work. For over four years Arthur and I have worked together, and it is safe to say there would have been no final product without him. While I was sick with a life-threatening illness for nearly a year, Arthur continued his research in my archival collection, his work adding to the primary sources I was able to draw on after I had recovered and returned to writing. An accomplished student of history, particularly that concerning Canadian prime ministers and American presidents, Arthur combed all available research materials and provided me with the very best and most helpful items from the archives. He also prepared timelines and searched for "nuggets" that would give the book focus and allow me to bring to it some perspective and a sense of humour. He was diligent, devoted, and highly professional, and he contributed greatly – with the valued assistance of his wife, Alison Bogle – to the ultimate result. Any mistakes are mine, but much of the enthusiasm was his.

I did not keep a daily diary while I was prime minister. I wish I had. From time to time, however, I would sit down – after an important event or state visit, for example – and write an impressionistic view of what had happened, commenting on the venue, the participants, and the substance, and enlivening the text with anecdotes. When I reviewed them, I was surprised to discover that these handwritten private notes contained over one hundred separate entries totalling 1345 pages.

I decided to incorporate some of these entries from my private journals into this book. In doing so I was conscious – and I hope the reader will be as well – of the judgment of former British prime minister Harold Macmillan on his own private diaries. According to his official biographer, Sir Alistair Horne, "Macmillan himself always warned that his diaries should be treated with caution; that, written in the heat of the moment, they were not always factually accurate, nor fair, in that they gave vent to passing piques, which he would often modify or expunge the following day. But they did represent both the mood and the colour of the times, and what Macmillan himself was then thinking, without the influence of self-justifying hindsight." Macmillan's cautionary statement applies to me as well. (Some entries from these personal journals have been lightly edited for publication.)

Douglas Gibson has been my editor throughout, and I am very happy he was: careful, thoughtful, and persistent, Doug steered this enterprise away from trouble and toward the sanctuary of publication time and time again. Not for nothing is he widely known and admired as one of Canada's most outstanding literary leaders. His patience, encouragement, and unflagging support for the project got me through moments of lassitude and laxity, steering me back to the discipline and focus required to produce any work of substance.

Doug Pepper, president and chief executive officer of McClelland & Stewart, took over the company just as I was getting started and infused my efforts with the great energy, drive, and ambition that characterize him. Together with Luc Lavoie, he developed a sales promotion and merchandising plan that would inspire (and terrify) any first-time author. I also thank copy editors Anne Holloway and Ruth Peckover, and the team at McClelland & Stewart, who worked so diligently to produce this complex book.

At Library and Archives Canada, special thanks must be conveyed to Ian Wilson, Librarian and Archivist of Canada; to Peter DeLottinville, Director, Political and Social Heritage Division; to archivists Maureen Hoogenraad, John Bell, Brian Murphy, and George Bolotenko, Political Archives Section; and to Muguette Brady, archival support clerk. Alix McEwen, Reference Archivist, Vicky Dalrymple and Kirsten Jensen, Textual Records Consultation Unit, and Antonio Lechasseur, Director, Client Services Division, also deserve mention, as does Geoff Ott, who has been of particular assistance over the years. Sarah Stacy of Library and Archives Canada helped with photographs.

St. Francis Xavier University Archivist Kathleen MacKenzie, Nancy Marrelli, Archives Director at Concordia University, and Robert Paul, Archival Coordinator, Diefenbaker Canada Centre, merit my warm thanks. The courtesy extended to Arthur and me by the Queen's University Archives and all its staff was deeply appreciated. A general expression of gratitude is also due to Librarian William Young of the Parliamentary Library. Historian and Senate Assistant Dr. Christopher McCreery provided both welcome assistance and expertise in matters relating to the governor general.

Among those who read portions of the manuscript or contributed material are Derek Burney, Stanley Hartt, Lowell Murray, Mila, Caroline and Mark Mulroney, Sam Wakim, Bernard Roy, Luc Lavoie, and Marjory LeBreton, who, together with her able Chief of Staff, Sandy Melo, provided us with great help and good counsel from beginning to end. Former ministers who assisted with research are Michael Wilson, Barbara McDougall, Jake Epp, and Charlie Mayer. The latter two, both outstanding legislators from Manitoba, helped significantly with reconstructing events surrounding the CF-18 issue. In this regard, Daniel Hambly, a young historian, allowed me to peruse his master's thesis and to discuss it with him on a number of occasions. Kate Malloy, editor of *The Hill Times*, granted Arthur access to her electronic archives and provided timely and generous assistance. The Honourable Peter MacKay personally provided useful information, and his staff were very helpful on a number of occasions.

In the United States, we consulted with Trevor Armbrister, who had worked with President Gerald Ford on his autobiography; David A. Horrocks, Supervisory Archivist of the Gerald R. Ford Presidential Library and Museum in Michigan; Justin Cooper, who served as the researcher on President Clinton's memoirs; Joseph E. Persico, who worked with General Colin Powell on his autobiography; and Jim McGrath, spokesman for the Office of President George H. W. Bush. They were all extremely helpful, warm, and supportive as were the entire staffs at the Reagan and the Bush presidential libraries.

My sisters Olive (Mrs. Richard Elliott) and Peggy (Mrs. Joseph Fitzpatrick) provided vital insights and recollections and reviewed the chapters on my early years. Paul Desmarais, Jackie Desmarais, Bernard Roy, Michel Cogger, Peter White, Sam Wakim, Gerry Doucet, L. Yves Fortier, L. Ian MacDonald, Bill Fox, Bill Pristanski, Bonnie Brownlee, Hugh Segal,

Pierre Roque, and Paul Tellier discussed sections with me and provided words of correction, caution and, sometimes, approval throughout the exercise. Gérard Godbout, who served as my senior translator in the Prime Minister's Office, provided his usual impeccable translations, and Hélène Proulx of Senator Lowell Murray's office and Hélène Chalifoux, Mila's assistant, played an important supporting role throughout, as did Arthur's brother, William L. Milnes, a teacher and translator from Montreal. Clerk of the Privy Council Kevin Lynch and his excellent staff responded to requests with speed and efficiency. Bill Pristanski, Hubert Pichet, Rick Morgan, and Paul Smith, my executive assistants both when I was in opposition and when I was in government, continued their devoted and loyal support in varying ways throughout the entire exercise of producing this book.

Francine Collins and Marilyn Burke round out this list but, if the truth be known, they should well have been mentioned first. Marilyn performed superbly at a high level in the PMO while I served in government. Since then she has continued to provide me with services relating to archival relations and to sensitive research projects, and her quick recovery of items ranging from long-forgotten speeches to a favourite family photo has been most impressive. Marilyn has been invaluable.

When I returned to Ogilvy Renault fourteen years ago I was joined by a young assistant named Francine Collins. She has played a major role in my relaunch into the business world and my reintegration into the law firm. Francine is talented, knowledgeable, and disciplined. Given my great number of business and professional interests, which generate an enormous amount of international travel, I don't quite know how she is able to keep everything running so smoothly. Added to this is the fact that, after most of my trips, I would drop handwritten notes of thirty, forty, or fifty pages on her desk, leaving her the excruciating job of deciphering my handwriting and typing a legible first draft. Almost every word in this book was handwritten by me and typed by her. She clearly had the more difficult job, for which I thank her deeply.

Special thanks are due to Samuel Wakim, Q.C., and William Ross, Q.C., of the law firm Weir, Foulds of Toronto, who are responsible for negotiating the agreements required to publish this book. Their wise counsel has served me well. I also owe special thanks to Alain Paris, FCA, whose financial acumen and good judgment (including on this project), and friendship, have been so valuable to me and my family for over thirty years.

Ogilvy Renault has been my professional home for forty-three years – with time off for a few other careers in between. The loyalty and support the firm has shown to me over the years have been unstinting, and I conclude by thanking co-chairs L. Yves Fortier, Q.C., and Norman Steinberg, along with Managing Partner Pierre Bienvenu, and Managing/Operations Partner John Coleman.

Some years ago, I established scholarships at Canadian universities in honour of my late parents. The proceeds of this book will be dedicated to those scholarship funds, to salute the memory of two people whose love and sacrifice made it possible for me to be here to write this book.

M.B.M.
Montreal, June 2007

Permissions

Photograph Permissions

Each photograph is provided either by the Mulroney Family or by Library and Archives Canada, Brian Mulroney Collection.

Additional photograph permissions: "On the bench at the Commission alongside Robert Cliche," Michel Garneau. "Leading the St. Patrick's Day Parade in Montreal," J.J. Raudsepp. "Yes!" (Mila Mulroney at the 1983 convention), *Kingston Whig-Standard*, Ian MacAlpine.

Thanks are due for the assistance of Arthur Milnes, Marilyn Burke, Anton Koschany, and Sean Tai in creating the photograph sections.

Text Permissions

Excerpts from *The Ambiguous Champion* by Linda Freeman reproduced with permission of the author.

Excerpts from *Waterfront Blues* by Alex Pathy reproduced with permission of University of Toronto Press.

"Brian Mulroney and the Crisis at Loyola" by Donald C. Savage reproduced with permission of the Canadian Association of University Teachers.

Excerpts from "Let's accentuate the positive" by Tom Harpur reproduced with permission of the author.

"PM showed real concern for Gorbachev's fate" by Carol Goar reprinted with permission of Torstar Syndication Services.

Every effort has been made to reach the copyright holders of material reproduced in this book, and the publisher welcomes further information on the matter.

Index

Note: The initials BM have been used in subheadings to stand for Brian Mulroney